CW00867140

ALSO BY BRENT CASSAN

REFERENCE

Modern Communication Technology in a Changing Society:
a Bibliography (With Godwin Chien Chu)

Street and Interurban Railroads:
a North American Bibliography
(Second edition)

Heavy Metal: the Essential Bibliography
of American Railroading

American Railroading:
a Basic Research Bibliography

American Railroading:
a Basic Research Bibliography

Volume 1
A-N

Compiled by
Brent Cassan

CreateSpace Independent Publishing Platform

Charleston, S.C.

2014

Dedicated to Gregory P. Ames
and
the many other librarians
who provided assistance over the years.

Preface

A quick guide to the scope of this bibliography can be gained by scanning the *abbreviated* subject-heading outline listed below:

Abandonments:
Accidents, derailments:
Accounting:
American Railway Car Institute:
Atlases:
Automatic train control:
Baldwin Locomotive Works:
Bibliography:
Brakes:
Brotherhood of Railway Carmen of the United States and Canada:
Colorado:
Construction; maintenance:
Dieselization:
Economics:
Engineering:
Finance:
Firemen:
Freight cars:
  Tank cars:
       Puncture mechanisms:
       Specifications:
Freight rail:
Hazardous materials, transport of:
High-speed rail:
Hill, James J.:
Interstate Commerce Commission:
Labor:
Law:
Legislation:
Locomotives (Steam):
  Boilers:
       Inspection:
Management:
Medical and surgical:
Mergers :
Nashville, Chattanooga, and St. Louis Railway:
New York (City):
Pacific Northwest:
Pacific railroads:
Passenger rail.
  Discontinuances:

Photography:
Public policy:
Pullman porters:
Railroads and state
Rails:
Regulation:
Safety:
The Signalman's Journal:
Statistics:
Stories, anecdotes, narratives:
Strikes:
Structures:
Technology:
Terrorism:
Ties:
Track geometry:
Unemployment insurance:
United States. Congress. Senate. Committee on Science
  and Transportation:
Vulcan Iron Works:
Washington (State). Department of Transportation:
World War II:
Yards:

From this it can be seen that the bibliography covers items published on cities, states, regions and for America as a whole. It includes personal, corporate and government authors as well as university research centers, foundations and private institutes as publishers. Also included are publications from the many railway brotherhoods. The numerous periodicals published on railroads and railroading can be found here. Finally, it provides subject headings on the nuts and bolts of railroading: maintenance-of-way, track, switches, ties, turnouts, freight equipment and motive power, and so on. The employees who operate this complex machine are featured prominently: conductors, engineers, brakemen, telegraphers and porters and many more. Important events across the eras are here: the grand endeavor for a railroad to the Pacific, the writings of engineers and railroad builders, the narrow gauge phenomenon, the realities of bankruptcies, reorganizations, mergers and consolidations, dieselization, and the demise of the passenger train as it was known in the 1920s. Histories of individual railroads are numerous and there are entries as well for labor unrest, the robber barons, unemployment, and the long hours and low wages of early railroad work. The beauty of the railroad is to found in entries for art, prints, and photography. Dining car recipes, railroad china and flatware are not forgotten. And there is room for the humor and tall tales of railroad men and women, their deeply personal accounts of the trains that ran in every corner of America.

Items included in this bibliography fall into the following categories.

a. Business consultancy reports.
b. City, regional, state, and federal government publications.
c. Corporate publications.
d. Historical society reports.
e. Monographs from standard publishers
f. Pamphlets.
g. Periodicals and serials.
h. Professional associations and their publications.
i. Theses and dissertations.
j. University research center reports.

The occasional broadside (2560, 13511, 15152) and sound recording could not be resisted. (Maps, timetables, films and videos were excluded for the most part.)

The heart of this bibliography began with the listing of items in my own collection, primarily publications on steam locomotives and early freight-car design and construction. The next step was to visit the on-line catalogs of various university and public libraries. Personal visits to the University of Missouri-St. Louis, the University of Chicago, Columbia University, Northwestern University, Texas A & M University and the New York Public Library proved extremely valuable. To round this out, the on-line catalogs of the *Library of Congress* and *World Cat-OCLC* were checked in detail. This bibliography would have been impossible without the years of labor that have gone into the creation of library catalogs, their constant upkeep and expansion over the years. *OCLC* proved extremely valuable in the area of corporate and federal government publications, and in the difficult area of trade catalogs published in the 1800s and early 1900s, it proved to be a virtual treasure trove of extremely rare publications. It is *the* indispensable resource for material in monograph form for any researcher—in *any* field of endeavor.

A bibliography on such a broad topic as "Railroading" will have its limitations. By its very nature, it is certain that it could never be absolutely complete for any time period or for any one area of concern. Publications will always elude the net. I fear that some venerable classics may have been missed, and perhaps the best railroading book of all time came out the day after the file for Volume 1 was closed on April 12, 2013. In addition, personal bias may have acted as a censor from time to time. ("Those yellowed, flimsy tomes from Podunk Correspondence School on Coffin feedwater heaters are too lowly to be included here!") Again, there is the danger that the big-city bibliographer will turn his nose up at "little" publications from back-country publishers. In addition, complete statements on the publication history of a title through all of its various editions and reprints cannot be guaranteed. Furthermore, journals have a habit of changing their titles, ICC publications notoriously so, but I have tried to indicate information on such changes when available from my sources. (The symbol < has been used to indicate its preceding title, and > to show it is subsequent title.) Annoyingly, the initial year of publication for a large number of serials could not be established, and "Ceased publication" dates are available only infrequently. By intention, certain areas of railroading have been touched on only very briefly or not at all. Street and interurban railroads were not included as they were covered in this compiler's bibliography (Entry 12756). Literature promoting the agricultural and mineral lands as well as the scenic resources of a particular railway has not been included except to show a few examples that are typical of the genre, namely entries 2754, 2757, 2758, and 2763. (Entry 8934 could not be resisted as it shows a flare for what now seems as the truly bizarre.) *World Cat-OCLC* is an excellent source for all forms of promotional or advisory literature, and extensive examples can be found easily by searching its on-line files under the corporate name of the railway.

From the standpoint of actually being able to examine a desired publication, I regret to write that quite a large number of titles are exceedingly rare, and one can only weep for the many small press items and trade catalogs that may have never made it to any library at all. *World Cat-OCLC* is an excellent source to discover where cataloged items are held, and you may find that only one library in the land is listed as holding the particular item that you are so keenly interested in. Without this very valuable feature it would be impossible to predict where it might be: it could be on the shelves of a small local library, in a large state historical society, a labor research institute, a railway historical society, a university library or a professional engineering library. Library policies on access to rare publications vary. Many such items will no doubt be in rare book collections, perhaps under lock and key, quite possibly not even obtainable through interlibrary loan due to its rarity and/or fragile condition. A personal journey of a thousand miles and a fine display of good luck may place it gently in hand. Many libraries, notably the University of Chicago, are actively microfilming hard-to-find railroad publications and thus "doubling" the availability of the rarest of the rare. Google's digital book program also offers possibilities. Many fine out-of-print railroad publications can be found through *www.abebooks.com;* e-*bay* has also provided its surprises. Otherwise, the old tried and true libraries, like the Northwestern University Transportation Library, the John W. Barriger III National Railroad Library in St. Louis, the Smithsonian or Harvard's Baker Library may be our only hope.

Happy hunting!

B.C.
Victoria, Canada
18/4/2014
cassan1us@yahoo.com

Volume 1
A-N

A

1. *AAR railroad cost indexes.* Washington, DC: Association of American Railroads, Economics and Finance Department, 1986-   Quarterly. (*<AAR railroad cost recovery index.*)

2. *AAR railroad cost recovery index.* Washington, DC: Association of American Railroads, Economics and Finance Department, 1982-1986.. Quarterly. (*< Indexes of railroad material prices and wage rates. Railroad of Class I; > AAR railroad cost indexes.*)

3. Aaron, Benjamin. *The Railway Labor Act at fifty: collective bargaining in the railroad and airline industries.* Washington, DC: National Mediation Board, 1977. 301 p.

4. Aaron Galleries. *Dinah blow your horn: railroad imagery in American printmaking, with an essay by Kevin Sharp.* Chicago: The Galleries, 1999. 32 p. (*Catalogue, 5.*)

5. *AARS news.* Homewood, IL: American Association of Railroad Superintendents, 1996- Bimonthly.

6. Abbey, Wallace W. *The little jewel: Soo Line Railroad Company and the locomotives that make it go.* Pueblo, CO: Pinon Productions, 1984. 216 p.

7. Abbott, Dan. *Colorado Midland Railway: daylight through the Divide.* With photographic contributions from the collection of Richard A. Ronzio. Denver, CO: Sundance Books, 1989.376 p.

8. _____. *Stairway to the stars: Colorado's Argentine Central Railway.* Editorial consultant, Gary Morgan. Ft. Collins, CO: Centennial Publications, 1977. 160 p. (Also: Golden, CO: Colorado Railroad Museum, 2005. 224 p. *Colorado rail annual, no. 26.*)

9. _____, Dell A McCoy. *The Gilpin Railroad era: Black Hawk, Central City, Nevadaville, Russell Gulch.* Denver, CO: Sundance Books, 2009. 416 p.

10 Abbott, Morris W. *Cog railway to Pike's Peak.* San Marino, CA: Golden West Books, 1973. 48 p.

11. _____. *The Pike's Peak Cog Road.* San Marino, CA: Golden West Books, 1972. 176 p. (Centennial ed., 1990. 176 p.)

12. *ABC's of car and locomotive wheels.* Omaha, NE: Simmons-Boardman Books, 1986. 82 p.

13. Abdill, George B. *Civil War railroads: a pictorial story of the War between*

the States, 1861-1865. Bloomington, IN: Indiana University Press, 1999. 192 p.

14. _____. *A locomotive engineer's album: the saga of steam engines in America.* Seattle, WA: Superior Pub. Co., 1965. 190 p.

15. _____. *Pacific slope railroads, from 1854 to 1900.* Seattle, WA: Superior Pub. Co., 1959. 182 p.

16. _____. *This was railroading.* New York, N.Y., Bonanza Books, 1943. 192 p. (Reprint: 1958, Bonanza Books)

17. Abendschein, Frederic H., and Dan Cupper. *Career of a champion: the story of the first GG1.* Quarryville, PA: Lancaster Chapter, NRHS, 1984. 56 p.

18. Ablett, Harold A., and Vernard A. Keerbs. *Study of feasibility of trailer-on-flatcar railway transportation.* Washington, D.C., U. S. Dept of Commerce, Office of Technical Services, 1958. 81 p.

19. Abraham, David G. *Transportation rates and costs for selected virgin and secondary commodities/* [by] David G. Abraham, William B. Saunders, Thomas G. Woodall. Washington, DC: Moshman Associations, Inc., Springfield, VA: National Technical Information Service, 1974. 234 p. (*NTIS; PB-233871*)

20. Abram, Michael E. *The Railway Labor Act/* 2d ed. Washington, DC: Bureau of National Affairs, 2005. 781 p. (Railway and Airline Labor Law Committee. Section of Labor and Employment Law, American Bar Association.)

21. *Accident bulletin.* Washington, DC: G.P.O., 1901-1916. Quarterly. "Showing collisions and derailment of trains and causalities to persons." (> *Accident bulletin.* Interstate Commerce Commission. Bureau of Statistics.)

22. *Accident bulletin.* Washington, DC: G.P.O., 1917-1940. Annual. (< *Accident bulletin.* Interstate Commerce Commission, Bureau of Transport Economics and Statistics; > *Accident bulletin.* Interstate Commerce Commission. Bureau of Transport Economics and Statistics.)

23. *Accident bulletin.* Washington, DC: U.S. G.P.O., 1941-1962. Annual. (< *Accident bulletin.* Interstate Commerce Commission; > *Accident bulletin.* Interstate Commerce Commission. Bureau of Economics.)

24. *Accident bulletin.* Washington, DC: Interstate Commerce Commission. Bureau of Economics, 1963. Annual. 1 v. (> *Accident bulletin.* Interstate Commerce Commission. Bureau of Railroad Safety and Service.)

25. *Accident bulletin.* Washington, DC: Interstate Commerce Commission. Bureau of Railroad Safety and Service, 1964-1965. Annual. 2 v. (< *Accident bulletin.* Interstate Commerce Commission. Bureau of Economics.; > *Accident bulletin.* Federal Railroad Administration. Bureau of Railroad Safety.)

26. *Accident bulletin.* Washington, DC: U.S. Dept. of Transportation, Federal Railroad Administration. Bureau of Railroad Safety, 1966-1970. Annual. 5 v. (*< Accident bulletin.* Interstate Commerce Commission. Bureau of Safety and Service; . *> Accident bulletin.* Federal Railroad Administration. Office of Safety..)

27. *Accident bulletin.* Federal Railroad Administration. Office of Safety. Washington, DC: U.S. G.P.O., 1971-1970s. Annual. (*< Accident bulletin.* Federal Railroad Administration. Bureau of Railroad Safety; *> Accident/incident bulletin.* Federal Railroad Administration. Office of Safety.

28. *Accident/incident bulletin.* Washington, DC: Federal Railroad Administration. Office of Safety, 1975-1996. Annual. (*< Accident bulletin.* Federal Railroad Administration. Office of Safety; *> Highway-rail crossing accident/incident and inventory bulletin*; *Trespasser bulletin; Railroad safety statistics.*)

29. *A.C.F. news.* New York: American Car and Foundry, 1926-? irregular.

30. Ackerman, William K. *Historical sketch of the Illinois-Central Railroad, together with a brief biographical record of its incorporators and some of its early officers.* Chicago: Fergus Printing Company, 1890. 3, 5-153 p.

30a. _____. *History of the Illinois Central Railroad Company and representative employes/* Chicago; Railroad Historical Co., 1900. 802 p.

30b. _____, Stephen A. Douglas, Sidney Breese. *Early Illinois railroads.* Chicago: Fergus Printing Co., 1884. 174 p.

31. *Across the Sierras in winter.* San Francisco, CA: California Historical Society, 2001. 25 p.

32. *An act to aid in construction of a railroad and telegraph line from the Missouri River to the Pacific Ocean: approved July 1, 1862.* Chicago: Tribune Book and Job Steam Printing Office, 1862. 16 p.

32a. Adamiak, Andrew J. *Poughkeepsie railroad station /* 1993. 130 l. (Thesis, B. Arch., Roger Williams University.)

33. Adams and Westlake Company. *The Adams & Westlake Company, Elkhart, Indiana: 100 years of service to American industries.* S.l.: s.n. 1957. 27 p.

34. _____. *Adlake car lighting fixtures: electric-acetylene gas-oil-candle.* Chicago, Ill., Adams and Westlake Co., 1911. 1 v.

35. _____. *Adlake car lighting fixtures: oil and candle lamp section.* New York, N.Y., Adams & Westlake Co., 1900s. 1 v.

36. _____. *Adlake catalogue of engine signal lamps, coach and caboose marker or tail*

lamps, switch lamps, semaphore and train order signal lamps, bridge lamps, electric railway signal lamps, lanterns and locks. Chicago, Ill., Adams & Westlake Co., 1907. 199 p.

37. _____. *Adlake common standard trimmings: Harriman Lines.* Chicago, IL: The Company, 1800s-1900s. 40 p.

38. _____. *Adlake 1911 catalog reprint.* Don Stewart, editor. Phoenix, AZ: Key Collectors International, 1982, c1911. 19 p.

39. _____. *Adlake 1936 catalog reprint.* Don Stewart, editor. Phoenix, AZ: Key Collectors International, 1982, c1936. 24 p.

40. _____. *Adlake trimmings for railroad cars.* Chicago, Ill., Adams & Westlake Co 1936. 96 p. (*Catalog no. 134*)

41. _____. *Adlake trimmings for railway cars and steamships.* Chicago, Ill., Adams & Westlake Co., 1911. 1,421 p.

42. _____. *Electric headlights for street and inter-urban railways: made by the United States Headlight Co.* Chicago, IL: The Company, 1901. 64 p.

43. _____. *General catalogue of electric headlights ... made by the United States Headlight Co.* S.l.: s.n. Adams & Westlake Co., 1906. 76 p.

44. _____. *Makers of passenger, parlor and postal car lamps in brass, bronze, fire gilt, silver and nickel plate, locomotive head lights, lanterns, switch, signal and station lamps and general railroad specialties.* New York, N.Y., The Company, 1882. 106 p.

45. _____. *Postal car equipment catalogue, no. 131.* New York, N.Y., Adams & Westlake Co., 1916. 65 p.

46. _____. *Railroad car trimmings.* Chicago, Ill., The Company, 1891. 430 p.

47. Adams, Braman B. *The block system of signaling on American railroads: the methods and appliances used in manual and automatic block signaling, also descriptions of hand-operated and power operated interlocking machines.* New York, Railroad Gazette, 1901. 262 p.

48. Adams, Brooks. *Railways as public agents: a study in sovereignty* / Boston, s.n., 1910. 164 p. Railroad and state. Railroad law. Northern Pacific.

49. Adams, Charles Francis. *The case of the Union Pacific Railway Company : statements made by Charles Francis Adams, before the Committee on Pacific Railroads, February 11, 1888, and February 24, 1886.* Boston : R.A. Supply Co., 1888. 49 p. United States. Congress. Senate. Committee on Pacific Railroads.

50. _____. *Chapters on Erie: and other essays.* Boston, J.R. Osgood and Company,

1871. 429 p.

51. _____. *Notes on railroad accidents.* New York, N.Y., G.P. Putnam's Sons, 1879. 280 p.

52. _____. *Railroads: their origin and problems.* New York, G.P. Putnam's Sons, 1878. 230 p., (Reprint: New York, NY: Harper & Row, Rev. ed. with appendix, 1969, [*The Allan Nevins reprints in American economic history.*])

53. _____, William B. Williams, John H. Oberly. *Taxation of railroads and railroad securities.* New York: Railroad Gazette, 1880. 49 p.

54. Adams, Charles J., and David J. Seibold. *Great train wrecks of eastern Pennsylvania.* Reading, PA: Exeter House Books, 1992. 204 p.

55. Adams, D.E. *Cost/benefit analysis of thermal shield coatings applied to 112a/114A series tank cars.* Buffalo: Calspan Corporation, 1974. 24 p. (FRA/ORD&D-75-39.) Prepare for the Federal Railroad Administration.

56. Adams, Gerald H. *Railroad management and planning: a bibliography with abstracts/* Springfield VA: National Technical Information Service, 1976- (*NTIS/PS-76/0170.*) v. 1. 1964-1973.

57. Adams, Henry Carter. *Report on transportation business in the United States, at the Eleventh Census, 1890.* Washington, G.P.O., 1894-1895. 2 v. (Part 1-Transportation by land; Part 2-Transportation by water.)

58. Adams, John M. *The history and future of the banking industry's role in equipment financing with Conrail and its predecessor roads/* 1981. 186 l. (Thesis, Rutgers University, American Bankers Association, Stonier Graduate School of Banking.)

59. Adams, John Winthrop. *Great railroad photographs from the collection of the Smithsonian Institution.* Philadelphia, PA: Courage Books, 1994. 128 p.

60. Adams, Kramer A. *Logging railroads of the west.* Seattle, WA: Superior Publishing Co., 1961. 144 p.

61. Adams, Michael Jacob. *The Pullman porter: the dual strategy of the Brotherhood of Sleeping Car Porters and the civil rights movement.* St. Louis, MO: 1992. 130 l. (Honors thesis, Dept. of History)

62. Adams, Philip Tyler and Dana Story. *Daily except Sundays: the diaries of a nineteenth century locomotive engineer.* Roseville, MN: Edinborough Press, 2005. 135 p.

63. Adams, Ramon F. *The language of the railroader.* Norman, OK: University of Oklahoma Press, 1977. 180 p.

64. Adams, Richard D. *The Alley Popper: a history of the Pittsburgh & Susquehanna and its predecessor companies.* Victor, NY: Richard D. Adams, 1980. 76 p.

65. _____. *The Lancaster Locomotive Works.* Strasburg, PA: Friends of the Railroad Museum of Pennsylvania, 1990. 34 p.

66. Adams, S.T. *The evolution of the locomotive.* San Jose, Press of Eaton Company, 1912. 24 p.

67. Adams, Samuel Hopkins. *The Harvey Girls.* New York, Random House, 1942. 327 p.

68. Adams, Walter M. *Four-eight-fours on the Missouri Pacific* / Pencil sketches by Charlie Duckworth. St. Louis, MO: Missouri Pacific Historical Society, 1977. 16, 2 p.

69. _____. *The White River railway: being a history of the White River Division of the Missouri Pacific Railroad Company, 1901-1951.* North Little Rock, AR: W. M. Adams, 1991. 180 p.

69a. *Adaptive reuse of railroad stations : a bibliography.* Monticello, IL: Vance Bibliographies, 1986. 5 p.

70. Addison, Douglass D. *Great Northern Railway ore docks of Lake Superior photo archive.* Hudson, WI: Iconografix, 2002. 126 p.

71. Adelman, William J. *Touring Pullman: A study in company paternalism: a walking guide to Pullman community in Chicago.* 2d ed. Illinois. Chicago, IL: Illinois Labor History Society, 1977. 46 p.

72. Adler, Dorothy R. *British investment in American railways, 1834-1898.* Edited by Muriel E. Hidy. Charlottesville, VA: Published for the Eleutherian Mills-Hagley Foundation by the University Press of Virginia, 1970. 253 p. (Thesis, Cambridge University, 1958.)

73. Adler, Philip. *A historical study of management-labor relations pertaining to the dieselization of railroads in the United States.* Columbus, OH: 1966. 276 l. (Ph.D., Ohio State University)

74.. *The advance advocate.* St. Louis, MO: International Brotherhood of Maintenance - of-Way Employes, 1903-1918. Monthly. 16 v. (< *Trackmen's advance advocate*; > *Advance guide.*)

75 *The advance guide.* Detroit, MI: United Brotherhood of Maintenance of Way Employees & Railway Shop Laborers, 1918-1919. Monthly. 2 v. (< *Advance advocate*; > *Railway maintenance of way employes journal.*)

76. *Advanced train control systems, 1991: proceedings of a symposium, June 17-19, 1991, Denver, Colorado.* Washington, DC: Transportation Research Board, National Research Council, 1991. 161 p. (*Transportation research record, no. 1314.*)

76a. Advisory Committee on Way and Structures. *Rules governing the use of motor, hand, velocipede, push and trailer cars*/ Cleveland: Advisory Committee on Way and Structures, 1931. 6 p. (*Circular no. R.7*)

76b. _____. *Standard material specification, J-58. Specifications and instructions for ordering and inspecting lumber and timber for railway use.* Cleveland?. s.n., 1900s 64 p.

77. Aeronautical Research Foundation. *A pilot study of the impact of the St. Lawrence Seaway on the Eastern railroads.* Cambridge, MA: Aeronautical Research Foundation, 1958. 1 v. (Prepared for the Traffic Executive Association, Eastern Railroads.)

78. *Agent of change: the railroads in West Virginia.* Huntington, WV: Huntington Museum of Art, 1991. 20 p.

79 Ager, Arthur F. *Report on engineering survey of operations and facilities of Pacific Electric Railway Company.* Los Angeles, Calif., Public Utilities Commission; State of California, Transportation Department, Engineering Division, 1947. 167 p. 34 l. of plates.

80. Agou, Christophe. *Life below: the New York City subway.* New York, NY: Quantuck Lane Press, 2004. 112 p.

81. A'Hearn, Frank M. *Fundamentals of the locomotive machine shop.* New York, N.Y., Simmons-Boardman Publishing Company, 1926. 242 p. (*Railwaymen's handbook series*)

82. Ahlbeck, D.R. *Development of safety criteria for evaluating concrete tie track in the Northeast Corridor: volume 1, remedial projects assessment.* Washington, DC: Federal Railroad Administration, Office of Research and Development, 1986. 109 p. (*FRA/ORD-86/08.1*)

83. Ahlbeck, D.R. *Development of safety criteria for evaluating concrete tie track in the Northeast Corridor: volume II, track safety evaluation*/ Washington, DC: Federal Railroad Administration, Office of Research and Development, 1986. 78 p. (*FRA/ORD-86/08.2*)

83a. Ahmad, Aziz. *Analysis and design procedure for highway-railroad grade crossings*/ 1977. 148 l. (Thesis, Ph.D., Texas A & M University)

84. Ainsworth, Jeff. *Southern Pacific steam motive power pictorial, Los Angeles Division* / La Crescenta, CA: Monte Vista Publishing, 2002. 74 p.

84a. _____. *Steam through Tehachapi: Los Angeles to Woodford*/ Grand Junction, CO: Monte Vista Publishing, 2008. 148 p.

85. Air Brake Association. *Modern freight train handling.* Chicago, IL: The Association, 1967. 160 p.

86. _____. *The principles and design of foundation brake rigging.* New York, NY: The Air Brake Association, 1921. 121 p.

87. *Air brake hand book* .... Altoona, Pa., The Times Tribune, 1929. 262 p.

87a. *Air brake patents.* v. 1-15. 1842-. (Issued by United State Patent Office, 1924 ; compiled by Westinghouse Air Brake Co.)

88. *Air-brakes : references to books and magazine articles* / Pittsburgh, Carnegie Library of Pittsburgh, 1915. 55, 3 p. "Reprinted from the Monthly bulletin, July, 1915."

89. *The air conditioned train of the Baltimore and Ohio Railroad on the exhibition track outside of the travel and Transport Building at A Century of Progress.* Chicago : s.n., 1933. 11 p. (Century of Progress International Exposition, Chicago, 1933-1934.)

89a. *Airline and railroad labor and employment law: a comparative analysis: course of study materials.* Philadelphia, PA: American law Institute/American Bar Association/American law Institute/American bar Association Committee on Continuing Professional Education, 2011. 2 v. (2294 p.)

90. Akers, Dwight LaBrae. *Recapitalization of the Chicago and Alton Railroad Company.* 1909. 5, 65 l. (Thesis, M.A., University of Chicago.)

90a. Al-Nazer, Leith. *Track inspection time study.* Washington, D.C.: Federal Railroad Administration, Office of Railroad Policy and Development, 2011. 93 p. Internet resource: http://purl.fdlp.gov/GPO/gpo26599

91. Alanis Enciso, Fernando Saul, Carlos Alberto Roque Puente. *Nos vamos al traque: la contratación de braceros ferroviarios en el ámbito regional durante la Segunda Guerra Mundial: el caso de San Luis Potosí,* 1944/ San Luis Potosí, Colegio de San Luis, 2007. 111 p.

92. Alaska. Department of Transportation and Public Utilities; and Sverdrup & Parcel and Association. *Alaska Railroad condition assessment.* Anchorage, Alaska, Sverdrup & Parcel and Associates, 1984. 2 v.

93. *Alaska Canada rail link: rails to resources to ports: the Alaska Canada Rail Link Project, phase 1 feasibility study.* Whitehorse, Yukon, ALCAN RailLink, Inc., 2007. 2 v.

94. *The Alaska Railroad.* Washington, D.C.: U.S. Department of Transportation; Federal Railroad Administration, 1979-1984. (Annual) http://www.alaskacanadarail.org/documents/Executive%20Report.pdf

95. *Alaska's railroads.* Anchorage, AK: Alaska Geographical Society, 1992. 96 p.

96. Albert, David and George F. Melvin. *New England diesels.* Omaha, NE: G.R. Cockle and Associates, 1975. 232 p.

97. Albi, Charles. *Dreams, visions and visionaries.* Golden, CO: Colorado Railroad Museum, 1993. 237 p.

98. _____, Kenton Forrest. *Colorado Railroad Museum roster of equipment: data, photographs ....* Golden: CO: Lakewood Printing and Stationery Co., 1976. 20 p.

99. _____, _____ *The Moffat Tunnel.* Rev. ed. Golden, CO: Colorado Railroad Museum, 2002. 52 p.

100. Albrecht, Emil. *Emil Albrecht's Union Pacific small steam power.* Edited by James W. Watson and F. Hol Wagner, Jr. Denver, CO: Motive Power Services, 1985. 112 p.

101. Albrecht, Harry P. *Broad Street Station, Pennsylvania Railroad, Philadelphia, 1881-1952.* Clifton Heights, PA: s.n., 1972. 48 p.

102. _____. *Camelback locomotives.* Clifton Heights, PA, s.n. 1971. 28 p.

103. _____. *The Consolidation type 2-8-0.* New York, NY: Fox-Shulman, 1952. 47 p.

104. _____. *Pennsylvania Railroad K-4s; steam locomotives of yesteryear. Text by Motive Power Dept.* Philadelphia, PA: Printed by Larchwood Press, 1967. 38 p.

105. _____. *A picture study of the K-4, including specifications, text, tender data, drawings, roster and other information about the famous locomotive.* Rev. ed. Harry P. Albrecht; Pennsylvania Railroad, Motive Power Department. Clifton Heights, PA: H.P. Albrecht, 1976. 40 p.

106. _____. *Those amazing class "D" locomotives.* Clifton Heights, PA: Albrecht, 1981, 78 p.

107. _____. *World famous Horseshoe Curve . . .* Clifton Heights, PA: H.P.A., 1973. 64 p.

108. Albright, Chester Eben. *Review of Rockport Tunnel on the Lehigh Valley Rail Road near Rockport, Pa.* 1883. 60 l. (Thesis, Lafayette College, Easton, Pa., Department of Civil Engineering.)

109. Albright, George Leslie. *Official explorations for Pacific railroads.* Berkeley, Calif., University of California Press, 1921. 187 p. (*University of California, Berkeley, publications in history, v. 11*) Reprint: Mansfield Center, CT: Martino Pub., 2009.

110. Alcoa Aluminum. *New applications of aluminum in the electric railway field.* Pittsburgh: Aluminum Company of America, 1929. 29 p.

111. *ALCO historic photos.* Albany, NY: Fort Orange Press, 1975. 113 p. (National Railway Historical Society. Mohawk & Hudson Chapter; American Locomotive Company) (2d ed.: 1979. 115 p.; 3d ed.: 1984. 107 p.)

112. *ALCO historic photos: erecting cards; a catalog of ALCO locomotive erecting cards in the Library of the National Railway Historical Society at Schenectady, NY.* Schenectady, NY: National Railway Historical Society; Mohawk & Hudson Chapter, 1976. 19 p.

113. ALCO Power, Inc. *The Alco story, from 1837 into the future.* Auburn, NY: Alco Power, Inc., 1979. 1 v.

114. Alco Products, Inc. *Locomotive handbook.* New York, N.Y., J.C. & W.E. Powers, 1917. 196 p.

115. Aldrich, Mark. *Death rode the rails: American railroad accidents and safety, 1828-1965.* Baltimore, MD: John Hopkins University Press, 2006. 446 p.

116. Aldridge, M. Dayne, Thomas Campbell, Alfred Galli. *Coal as a rail fuel: an assessment of direct combustion.* Morgantown, WV: West Virginia University Energy Research Center, 1980. 34 p.

117. Alers, George A. *Railroad rail flaw detection system based on electromagnetic acoustic transducers.* Washington, DC: Federal Railroad Administration, Office of Research and Development, 1988. 53/54 p. (*DOT/FRA/ORD-88/09.*)

118. Alexander Car Replacer Manufacturing Company. *The Alexander engine & car replacer : the best wrecking frog in use.* Scranton, PA: Alexander Car Replacer Mfg. Co., 1900. 1 v. (unpaged).

119. Alexander, Edwin P. *American locomotives: a pictorial record of steam power, 1900-1950.* New York, NY: W.W. Norton, 1950. 254 p.

120. _____. *Civil War railroads and models.* New York, NY: C.N. Potter, 1977. 255 p.

121. _____. *The collector's book of the locomotive.* New York, NY: C.N. Potter, 1966. 197 p.

122. _____. *Down at the depot; American railroad stations from 1831 to 1920.* New York, NY: Bramhall House, 1970. 320 p.

123. _____. *Iron horses; American locomotives, 1829-1900.* New York, N.Y., W.W. Norton & Company, 1941. 239 p. (Reprint: Dover Publications, 2003. 239 p.)

124. _____. *On the main line; the Pennsylvania Railroad in the 19th century.* New York, NY: C.N. Potter, 1971. 310 p.

125. _____. *The Pennsylvania Railroad; a pictorial history.* New York, N.Y., W.W. Norton, 1947. 248 p.

126. Alexander, James R. Jaybird: *A.J. Moxham and the manufacture of the Johnson rail.*

Johnstown, PA: Johnstown Area Heritage Association, 1991. 83 p. (Johnson Company (Johnstown, PA)--History)

127. Alexander, S.A. *Broke down, what should I do: ready reference for locomotive engineers and firemen. 5th ed.* York, Penn., Gazette Printing House, 1884.

127a. Alft, E.C., William Briska. *Elgin time: a history of the Elgin National Watch Company, 1864-1968* / Elgin, IL: Elgin Area Historical Society, 2003. 120 p.

128. Alger, Horatio. *The Erie train boy.* New York, NY: Hurst & Company, 1900? 201 p.

128a. *All aboard.* Springfield, MO: Frisco Railroad Museum, 1986-   . Quarterly.

128b. *All aboard.* Springfield, MO: St. Louis-San Francisco Railway Company, 1948- . Monthly. Published every six weeks, Jan. 1967-   .

129. *All aboard for yesterday!: a nostalgic history of railroading in Maine.* Camden, ME: Down East, 1979. 168 p.

130. *All-time index : Railroad magazine, Model railroader, Trains magazine, Railroad model craftsman.* Rev. 2nd. ed. New York : Wayner Publications, 1978. 241 p.

131. *Allegheny Portage Railroad : its place in the main line of public works of Pennsylvania : forerunner of the Pennsylvania Railroad.* Philadelphia : Pennsylvania Railroad, 1930. 45 p. (*Pennsylvania railroad information, v. 2, February 1930.*)

132. Alleman, Norville James. *Progress report on the effect of the ratio of wheel diameter to wheel load on extent of rail damage* / Urbana, IL: The University of Illinois, 1945. 19 p. (*Illinois. University. Engineering experiment station. Reprint series, no. 33.*)

133. Allen, Benjamin Joseph. *The economic effects of rail abandonment on communities: a case study.* 1974. 193 l. (Thesis, Ph.D., University of Illinois, Urbana-Champaign.)

134. Allen, C. Frank. *Design for wrought iron railway bridge*/ 1872. 26 l. (Thesis, B.S., Massachusetts Institute of Technology, Department of Civil Engineering.)

135. _____. *Field and office tables, specially applicable to railroads.* New York, NY: McGraw-Hill, 1903. 293 p. (4th ed.: 1931.)

136. _____. *Notes on railroad engineering and economics of location.* Boston, Massachusetts Institute of Technology, Civil Engineering Department, 1893. 323 p. "Reproduced from handwritten copy."

137. _____. *Railroad signals.* S.l., s.,. 1914. 42 l. 92 leaves of plates. Typescript with printed plates. Corrected draft.

138. _____. *Railway curves and earthwork.* New York, NY: McGraw-Hill, 1903. 198 p. (7th ed. rev.: New York, McGraw-Hill, 1959.)

139. Allen, Charles F. *N.Y.C. & H.R.R.R. electric zone, New York District, Sept. 30th 1906.* S.l., s.n., 1906. 1 v. (unpaged)

140. Allen, G Freeman. *North American railroads today.* London : Brian Todd Publishing House, 1990. 123 p.

141. Allen, Gary G. *Nevada Northern; sagebrush short line.* Los Angeles, CA: Trans-Anglo Books, 1964. 49 p.

142. Allen, Horatio. *The railroad era: the first five years of its development.* New York, N.Y., H. Allen, 1884. 32 p.

143. Allen, Jeff, Tom Lurino, Mark Ackelson. *Acquiring rail corridors: a how to manual.* Washington, DC: Rails-to-Trails Conservancy, in cooperation with National Park Service and the Trust for Public Land, 1996. 136 p.

144. Allen, John Sinnickson. *Standard time in America: why and how it came about and the part taken by the railroads and William Frederick Allen.* New York, s.n., 1951. 20 p.

145. Allen, Lane & Scott. *System of steam railroads, street railways of Philadelphia; a complete guide, with maps, showing the streets of Philadelphia upon which there are passenger railways, and the streets crossed thereby; together with the routes of the steam roads with the city limits and all stations on these roads.* Philadelphia, Allen, Lane & Scott, 1887. 1887. (Reprint: Forty Fort, PA: H.E. Cox, 1971. 96 p.)

146. Allen Paper Car Wheel Company. *Railroad wheels and equipment.* New York, N.Y., Allen Paper Car Wheel Co., 1882? 1 v.

147. Allen, Richard Sanders. *Rails in the north woods.* Lakemont, NY: North Country Books, 1973. 194 p. (Rev. ed. 1978. 202 p.)

148. Allen, Ruth Alice. *The great Southwest strike.* Austin, TX: The University of Texas, 1942. 174 p. (*The University of Texas publication, no. 4214, April 8, 1942.*) Missouri Pacific railroad strike, 1885-1886. Knights of Labor.

149. Allen, Thomas B., Roger MacBride Allen. *Mr. Lincoln's high-tech war: how the North used the telegraph, railroads, surveillance balloons, ironclads, high-powered weapons, and more to win the Civil War.* Washington, D.C., National Geographic, 2009. 144 p.

150. Allen, W.F. *Map illustrating the proposed system of standard time as reported to the General and Southern Railway Time conventions: at their meetings United held on April 11th and 18th, 1883, and unanimously recommended by the conventions for adoption by the railway lines of the States and the Dominion of Canada.* New York, NY: National Railway Publication Company, 1883. 1 map, hand col., 90 x 122 cm

151. Allen, William Frederick. *Short history of standard time ... and its adoption in*

North American in 1883. Philadelphia: Stephen Green Print. Co., 1904. 76 p.

152. Allen, William L. *Rail traffic to and from Brooklyn, New York* / 1964. 25 l. (American Society of Traffic and Transportation.)

153. Allhands, James Lewellyn. *Boll Weevil; recollections of the Trinity & Brazos Valley Railway*. Houston, TX: The Anson Jones Press, 1946. 334 p.

154. _____. *Looking back over 98 years: the autobiography of James L. Allhands*. Malibu, CA: Pepperdine University, 1978. 382 p.

155. _____. *Railroads to the Rio*. Salado, TX: Anson Jones Press, 1960. 213 p.

156. _____. *Uriah Lott*. San Antonio, Tex., Naylor, 1949. 187 p.

157. Allman, William Parker. *A network-simulation approach to the railroad freight train scheduling and car sorting problem*. 1966. 227 l. (Thesis, Ph.D., Northwestern University.) Simulation methods. Scheduling.

157a. Alnes, Stephen. *The troubled Milwaukee Road*. Minneapolis: Upper Midwest Council, 1979. 45 p.

158. *Along the line*. Boston : New Haven System Employees, 1924-   . Monthly. "Published by and for the Employees of the New Haven System."

158a. Alpert, Steven M. *Assessing the level of service for shipments originating or terminating on short line railroads* / 2007. 78, 6 l. (Thesis, S.M., Massachusetts Institute of Technology, Department of Civil and Environmental Engineering.)

159. *Alternative ways to improve the visibility of railroad-highway crossing signals. Vol. 1, Research report*. Washington, DC: Federal Highway Administration, 1983. 113 p. (*FHWA/RD-83/051*.)

160. Alton, Ralph Henry. *The multiple control system for large electric motors*. 1908. (Thesis, Electrical Engineering, University of Maine.)

161. *Altoona and the railroad: an annotated bibliography of books about the PRR in the collection of the Altoona Area Public Library*. Altoona, PA: The Library, 1980. 36 p.

162. Aluminum Association. *Aluminum for more efficient railroad cars*. Washington, DC : Aluminum Association, 1980. 23 p.

163. Aluminum Company of America. *A report on Alcoa aluminum in the railroad industry* / Pittsburgh : Aluminum Company of America, 1955. 7 p.

164. Alva-Hurtado, Jorge Elias Domingo. *A methodology to predict the elastic and inelastic behavior of railroad ballast*/ 1980. 442 l. (Thesis, Ph.D., University

of Massachusetts.)

165. Alvarez, Eugene. *Travel on southern antebellum railroads, 1828-1860.* University, AL: University of Alabama Press, 1974. 221 p. (Thesis, Ph.D., University of Georgia, 1966. 227 l.)

166. Ambrose, Stephen E. *Nothing like it in the world: the men who built the transcontinental railroad, 1863-1869.* New York, NY: Simon & Schuster, 2000. 431 p.

166a. Ambrose, William M. *Coal railways: rivals for black gold: railroad development and operations in central and eastern Kentucky, and the north fork of the Kentucky River.* Lexington, KY: Limestone Press, 2010. 2 v.

166b. American and Mexican Railroad and Telegraph Company. *Pacific railroad and telegraph grants from the Mexican states, Chihuahua and Sonora, to General Angel Trias : as representatives of the American and Mexican Company, located in the City of New York.* New York : McSpedon & Baker, 1861. 18, 2 p.

167. American Arch Company. *Designs covering arrangement of security oil burning brick manufactured by American Arch Company as applied to locomotives of the Atchison, Topeka & Santa Fe Railway System.* New York? : American Arch Company, 1927.

168. _____. *Designs of security brick arches on the Ann Arbor Railroad.* New York? American Arch Company, 1921. 13 l.

169. American Association of Demurrage Officers. *Proceedings of the ... annual convention of the American Association of Demurrage Officers ...* Scranton, Pa? The Association, 1908-1915. Annual. 8 v. (< National Association of Car Service Managers (U.S.). *Proceedings of the annual convention of the National Association of Car Service Managers.*)

170. American Association of Dining Car Superintendents. *Proceedings of the American Association of Dining Car Superintendents ... annual convention.* S.l., s.n., 1902- Annual.

171. *American Association of Freight Agents ... annual meeting ...* / Chicago? American Association of Freight Agents, 1910-1920. 10 v. (< American Association of Local Freight Agents' Associations ... *annual meeting ...*; > American Railway Association. Freight Station Section. [1921]. *Proceedings of the ... annual session of the American Railway Association, Division 1, Operating, Freight Station Section.*)

172. American Association of General Passenger and Ticket Agents. *Proceedings.* Cleveland, OH., Short & Forman, 1889-1913. Annual. (< National Association of General Passenger and Ticket Agents. *Proceedings*; > American Association of Passenger Traffic Officers. *Proceedings.*)

173. American Association of Local Freight Agents' Associations ... *Annual meeting ...*

Chicago, IL:? American Association of Freight Agents, 1901-1910. Annual. 9 v. (*< National Association of Local Freight Agents' Association (U.S.) Proceedings of the ... annual meeting of the ... ; > American Association of Freight Agents ... 1910...annual meeting of the ...)*

174. American Association of Passenger Traffic Officers. *Proceedings.* Evanston, IL: The Association, ?

175. American Association of Private Railroad Car Owners. *AARPCO: a collection of classic private railroad cars.* Kettering, OH: Fleet Graphics, 2006. 113 p.

176. _____. *AAPRCO roster of private railroad cars.* Fort Worth, TX: American Association of Private Railroad Car Owners, 1981. 625 l.

177. _____. *Private varnish.* Mountainside, NJ: American Association of Private Railroad Car Owners, 1983?- (Bimonthly)

178. American Association of Railroad Superintendents. *Proceedings of the annual meeting.* St. Louis, American Association of Railroad Superintendents,   Annual (irregular) Published 1910-1972. Volume numbering begins with v. 26 in 1913.

179. _____. *Proceedings of the annual meeting and regional meeting.* Homewood IL: American Association of Railroad Superintendents, 1973-   Annual. Annual meeting and winter meeting 1984-   . Regional meetings are also called winter meetings. (*< Proceedings of the annual meeting; > AARS news.*)

180. American Association of State Highway and Transportation Officials. *Intercity passenger rail.* Washington, DC: American Association of State Highway and Transportation Officials, 2009. 24 p.
http://downloads.transportation.org/IPRT-2.pdf

180a. American Automatic Connector Company. *A performance record of the American automatic connector.* Cleveland: American Automatic Connector Co., 1920, 16 p.

181. American Bankers' Association. *Tours to the forty-second annual convention of the American Bankers' Association, Kansas City, Missouri, September 25 to 30, 1916. three special trains via the New York Central Lines.* New York : New York Central Lines, 1916. 28 p.

182. American Bar Association. Tort and Insurance Practice Section. *Issues in railway law: limiting carrier liability and litigating the railroad crossing case.* Chicago. IL: Tort and Insurance Practice Section, American Bar Association, 1990. 251 p.

182a. *American Bell Company, bell founders : office & salesroom, no. 32 Liberty Street, New York City : have always on hand, church, academy, factory, steamboat, railroad station, plantation, and farm bells : fire alarm bells, cast of any desired weight : proprietors of Harrison's Patent Rotary Apparatus.* New York : G.A. Whitehorne, Printer, 1863. 40 p.

183. American Brake Company. *Locomotive brake catalogue.* St. Louis, American Brake Company, 1898. 68 p.

184. _____. *Locomotive driver and truck brake.* St. Louis, The Company, 1900. 78 p. (*Catalog 1900.*)

185. American Brake Shoe Journal Bearing Research Laboratory. *Facilities for finding facts : a report on the American Brake Shoe Journal Bearing Research Laboratory.* St. Louis : American Brake Shoe Company, 1954. 22 p.

186. _____. *In action against the hot box : a progress report.* St. Louis : American Brake Shoe Co., 1955. 16 p.

187. American Bridge Company. *Album of designs of bridges, roofs, turntables, iron trestles, pneumatic and masonry structures* / Chicago: The Company, 1899. 10 l., 28 l. of plates.

187a. _____. *The American Bridge Co., Chicago, New York, Pittsburgh: centennial exhibit, Machinery Hall—section D, 4 column D, 33 and 34, 1876.* Chicago, IL: The Company, 1876. 25 p.

188. _____. *The following illustrations represent a few typical railway and highway bridges built by the American Bridge Company of New York.* New York, N.Y., American Bridge Co., 1908. 55 p.

189. _____. *General specifications for steel railroad bridges.* New York? American Bridge Company, 1900. 23 p.

189a. _____. *Illustrations represent*[ing] *a few typical railway bridges built by the American Company of New York.* New York, American bridge Co., 1908. 55 p.

189b. _____. *Standard railway turntables* / New York: American Bridge Co., 1923. 41 p.

190. _____. *Standard railway turntables continuous type.* New York, NY: American Bridge Company, 1923. 13 p.

191. American Car and Foundry Company. *A.C.F, American Car and Foundry Company.* New York, N.Y., A.C.F., nd. 18 p.

192. _____. *The American Car and Foundry Company presents the Talgo: built at the Berwick, Pennsylvania and Wilmington, Delaware plants.* S.l., American Car and Foundry Company, 1949. 3, 31, 3, 2, 2 l.

193. _____. *Annual report.* New York? ACF, 1900-   Annual

194. _____. *[Catalogue].* St. Louis, Mo., American Car and Foundry Co., 1901. 168 p.

195. _____. *Catalogue B.* New York: American Car and Foundry Co., 1903. 256 p.

196. _____. *Covered hopper cars/* New York, NY: A.C.F., 1900s 8 p.

197. _____. *Illustrated catalogue of street railway cars and suburban coaches, including ten popular colors for car body painting.* St. Louis, MO" American Car and Foundry Company, 1896. 131 p.

198. _____ *Press material for release May 12, 1955 on the new ACF Talgo: America's first lightweight, low-center-of-gravity streamliner.* New York: ACF Industries, 1955. 18, 6 l.

199. _____. *Steel postal cars and interior equipment describing 60-foot all steel full postal car exhibited at the M.C.B. convention, Atlantic City, N.J., June 1913; rex pouch racks, automatic pouch racks, folding lavatory, water cooler; approved by the Post Office Department.* New York, N.Y., Winthrop Press, 1913. 52 p. Plans, plates.

200. _____. *Tank car classifications for ladings.* New York: American Car and Foundry Co., 1947. 32 p.

201. _____. *Welded tank cars.* New York, NY: A.C.F., 1953. 20 p.

202. American Car Spring Company. *Circular of the American Car Spring Company to railway operators and managers.* New York : American Car Spring Co., 1865. 16 p.

203. American Chain & Cable Company. *Wreck master's manual.* Wilkes-Barre, PA: Hazard Wire Rope Division, American Chain & Cable Co., 1949. 3 v. in 1. (11, 23, 23, p.)

204. American Electric Railway Engineering Association. *The engineering manual of the American Electric Railway Engineering Association, covering its standards, recommendations and miscellaneous methods and practices.* New York: Published from the office of the Secretary, 1930. 1 v. in various pagings.

205. _____. *Proceedings.* New York, NY: American Electric Railway Engineering Association, 1911-1932. Annual. (< American Street & Interurban Railway Engineering Association. *Proceedings;*[1906-1910])

206. *The American engineer.* New York, Holley & Colburn, 1857-   (*<Holley's railroad advocate.*)

207. *American engineer.* New York, N.Y., Simmons-Boardman, 1912-1913.

208. *American engineer and railroad journal.* New York, N.Y., Forney, 1893-1911. (*<Railroad and engineering journal; >American engineer, the railway mechanical monthly.*)

209. American Engineering Works. *Cars—gable and hopper bottom : American*

Engineering Works, Chicago, Illinois. Chicago : American Engineering Works, 1902. 8 p. (*No. 2M-6-1-02.*)

210. American Federation of Labor. Railway Employees Department. *The outside repair of locomotives and freight cars; data concerning contracts and costs*/ Chicago: Railway Employees Department, American Federation of Labor, 1921. 82 p. Prepared for: Interstate Commerce Commission.

211. American Frog and Switch Company. *American railway track equipment.* Hamilton, OH: The Company, 1935. 24 p.

212. American Geographical Society of New York. *The golden spike; a centennial remembrance.* E. Roland Harriman and others. New York, NY: AGS of New York, 1969. 118 p. (*Occasional publication no. 3*)

213. American Heritage. *Railroads in the days of steam.* Narrative by Albert L. McCready in consultation with Lawrence W. Sagle. New York, NY: American Heritage Publishing Company, 1960. 152 p.

214. American Hoist & Derrick Company. *American snow plows and wings: truck mounted, manufactured by American Hoist & Derrick Co., Road Machinery Division.* S.l., American Hoist & Derrick Company, 1940? 8 p.

215. _____. *Building a railroad; a handbook devoted to a new, speedy and economical method of performing every operation from grading right-of-way to ballasting and maintaining track.* St. Paul, Minn., American Hoist & Derrick Company, 1914. 66 p.

216. _____. *Catalog no. 106.* St. Paul, Minn., American Hoist & Derrick, 1914. 160 p.

217. _____. *Catalog no. 110.* St. Paul, MN: American Hoist & Derrick Company, 1925. 142 p.

218. _____. *Ditcherology; the science of ditching and ditcher maintenance.* St. Paul, Minn., American Hoist & Derrick Company, 1919. 192 p.

219. _____. *Fourteen years on line: being a record of fourteen years' service by the American railroad ditcher.* St. Paul, Minn., American Hoist & Derrick, 1920. 71 p.

220. American Institute of Chemical Engineers. Center for Chemical Process Safety. *Guidelines for chemical transportation safety, security, and risk management.* 2d ed. Hoboken, NJ: Wiley, 2008. 166 p. + 1 CD-ROM.

221. American International Association of Railway Superintendents of Bridges and Buildings. *Proceedings of the ... annual meeting of the American International Association of Railway Superintendents of Bridges and Buildings.* S.l., s.n., 1891-1895. Annual. (>Association of Railway Superintendents of Bridges and Buildings. Convention. *Proceedings of the ... annual convention of the Association of Railway*

Superintendents of Bridges and Buildings.)

222. American Iron and Steel Association. *The duty on steel rails: authentic statistics which end all controversy.* Philadelphia: American iron and Steel Association, 1890. 4 p. *(Tariff tract, no. 5, 1890.)*

223. _____. *The wearing qualities of American steel rails.* Philadelphia, Pa., American Iron and Steel Association, 1879. 16 p.

224. American Iron and Steel Institute. *Railway track materials.* New York, N.Y., American Iron and Steel Institute, 1949. 121 p.

225. _____. *Steel products manual: wrought steel wheels.* New York, NY: American Iron and Steel Institute, 1955. 61 p.

226. _____. *Steel products manual: wrought steel wheels and forged railway axles.* New York, NY: American Iron and Steel Institute, 1973. 116 p.

227. *American journal of railway appliances.* New York, N.Y., American Railway Publ. Co., 1883-1892.

228. American Labor Party. *Tragedy unlimited; what to do about the Long Island R.R.* American Labor Party/Long Island Transit Committee, Hempstead, NY: The Committee, 1950. 22 p.

229. American Locomotive Company. *Alaska-Yukon-Pacific Exposition, Seattle, Washington, 1909: exhibit of American Locomotive Company and Atlantic Equipment Company.* New York? American Locomotive Company, Atlantic Equipment Company, 1909. 31 p.

230. _____. *Alco diesel locomotive instruction book.* New York, NY: American Locomotive Company, 19--? 1 v.

231. _____. *Alco-GE diesel electric locomotive, 1500 hp road switcher maintenance manual.* Schenectady, N.Y., American Locomotive Company; General Electric Company, 1947. 1 v.

232. _____. *ALCO-GE diesel-electric road locomotive: instruction book.* S.l., American Locomotive Company; General Electric Company, 1944? 208 p.

233. _____. *American Locomotive Company.* Omaha, NE: Kratville Publications, 1969, 1910. 241, 181 p. (Reprints of catalogs and bulletins, 1910-1918.)

234. _____. *American Locomotive motor car.* New York, N.Y., American Locomotive Company, 1907. 19 p.

235. _____. *American Locomotive went to war.* New York, N.Y., 1945. 28 p.

236. _____. *American locomotives.* New York, N.Y., J.C. and W.E. Powers Press, 1910. 1 v.

237. _____. *Annual report.* New York, N.Y., American Locomotive Company, 1902-

238. _____ *Atlantic type passenger locomotives, built by American Locomotive Company.* New York, N.Y., The Company, 19--? 64 p.

239. _____. *Bulletin.* New York, N.Y., The Company, 19--?-

240. _____. *Coal-burning steam locomotives on the New York Central System.* New York : American Locomotive Company, 1946. 8 p.

241. _____. *Cole four-cylinder compound locomotives, built by American Locomotive Company.* New York, N.Y., American Locomotive Company, 19--? 35 p.

242. _____. *Consolidation type freight locomotives weighing less* than *175,000 pounds, built by American locomotive Company.* New York, N.Y., The Company, 19--? 72 p.

243. _____ *Data and tables on the subject of train resistance and power of locomotives.* New York, N.Y., The Company, 19--? 31 p.

244. _____. *Description of the Mallet articulated compound locomotive built by American Locomotive Company.* New York, N.Y., The Company, 19--? 32 p.

245. _____. *Dynamic breaking: road locomotives.* Schenectady, NY: American Locomotive Company; General Electric Company, 195-? 26 p.

246. _____ *Eight-wheel type passenger locomotives built by American Locomotive Company.* New York, N.Y., The Company, 19--? 60 p. (*Code: CALLIMI*)

247. _____. *Electric motor and trailer trucks for all classes of service; built by American Locomotive Company.* New York, N.Y., The Company, 19--? 58 p. (*Code: CALDEREROS*)

248. _____. *Electric motor and trailer trucks : for all classes of service* / New York : The Company, 1907. 114 p. (*Code: Calacandam*)

249. _____. *Electrical maintenance manual.* Schenectady, NY: The Company, 1951. 1 v.

250. _____. *Exhibit of the American Locomotive Company at the Louisiana Purchase Exposition, St. Louis, Mo., U.S.A.* S.l., The Company, 1904. 45 p. (Reprint: NRHS, Mohawk & Hudson Chapter; Old Dorp Books, 1976. 43 p.)

251. _____. *Forty years of motive power progress on the New York Central.* New York, N.Y., American Locomotive Company, 1945. 19 p.

252. _____. *Fundamentals of diesel engines.* Schenectady, N.Y., American Locomotive Company; General Electric Company, 19--? 12 p. (*School instruction series, no. 899*)

253. _____. *Growing with Schenectady: the story of a century of locomotive building in Schenectady.* Schenectady, N.Y., American Locomotive Company, 1948. 46 p.

254. _____. *Illustrated catalogue of locomotives.* New York, Press of Unz & Company, 1901. 78 p.

255. _____. *Light locomotive details.* New York, N.Y., The Company, 1915. 177 p. (*Catalogue no. 10053*)

256. _____. *Light locomotive parts and general products catalog.* New York, N.Y., The Company, 1918? 172 p. (*Catalog no. 10057*)

257. _____. *Light locomotives.* New York, N.Y., The Company, 1900. 70 p. (*Catalog no. 10042*)

258. _____. *Light locomotives built by American Locomotive Company.* New York, NN.Y., The Company, 19--? 72 p. (*Pamphlet no. 10030; Code: CALEBIT*)

259. _____. *Light locomotives for domestic service built by American Locomotive Company.* New York, N.Y., The Company, 19--? 52 p. (*Catalog no 10051; Code: UCAHU*)

260. _____. *Locomotive handbook.* New York, American Locomotive Company, 1917. 195 p.

261. _____. *Locomotive maintenance manual: road locomotive with model 244 engines.* Schenectady, NY: American Locomotive Company, 1954. 1 v.

262. _____. *Locomotive tests: a compilation.* By W. F. M. Goss. New York, N.Y., American Locomotive Company, 1906. 55 p. (*Code: CALDERILLA*) (Pennsylvania Railroad)

263. _____. *Locomotives for export.* New York, N.Y., J.C and W.E. Powers, 1910. 104 p. (*Catalogue no. 10036*) (Spanish and English)

264. _____. _____. New York, N.Y., American Locomotive Sales Corporation, 1918. 181 p. (*Catalogue no. 10045*)

265. _____. *Manual for enginemen: 660-hp switcher, 1000-hp switcher, 1000-hp road switcher; Alco Diesel-Electric, GE.* Schenectady, N.Y., American Locomotive Company, 194-? 47 p.

266. _____. *Manual of the American articulated compound locomotive.* 2d ed. New York, N.Y., American Locomotive Company, 1920. 8 p.

267. _____ *Manual of the Walschaert valve gear for engineers, firemen and machinists.* 3rd ed. New York, N.Y., American Locomotive Company, 1895 30 p. (*Pamphlet no. 10033*)

268. _____. *The "Milwaukee" type: a high speed, high-powered, streamlined steam locomotive, the first of its kind to be build in this country; ordered by the Milwaukee Road for the "Hiawatha", the Milwaukee new de luxe, high-speed streamlined train which will operate between Chicago, Milwaukee, St. Paul and Minneapolis.* New York? American Locomotive Company, 1935. 11 p.

269. _____ *Mogul type freight locomotives: built by American Locomotive Company.* New York, N.Y., The Company, 19--? 60 p. (*Code: CALLIMAQUE*)

270. _____. *Operation and service manual.* Schenectady, N.Y., American Locomotive Company, 1949? 2 v.

271. _____. *Pacific type passenger locomotives built by American Locomotive Company.* New York, N.Y., American Locomotive Company, 1903. 48 p. (*Code: CALLEGENIE*)

272. _____. *Panama-Pacific International Exposition, San Francisco, 1915: exhibit of American Locomotive Company; builders of over 55,000 locomotives; locomotive builders since 1835.* New York, N.Y., s.n., 1915. 22 p.

273. _____. *Prairie type locomotives, built by American Locomotive Company.* New York, N.Y., The Company, 19--? 40 p. (*Code: CALLINICUS*)

274. _____. *Rotary snow plow.* New York, NY: The Company, 1905? 28 p. (Reprint: Ocean, NJ: Specialty Press, c1973. 28 p.)

275. _____. *Schenectady's nonagenarian industry, 1848-1938.* Schenectady, N.Y., The Company, 1938. 23 p.

276. _____. *Six wheel type switching locomotives, built by American Locomotive Company.* New York, N.Y., The Company, 19--? 62 p. (*Code: CALLIMORFA*)

277. _____. *Standardized locomotives built for the U.S. Railroad Administration by the American Locomotive Company.* New York, N.Y., The Company, 1919. 36 p. (*Pamphlet no. 10049*) (Reprint: Ocean City, NJ: Specialty Press, c1973. 36 p.)

277a. _____. *Switching locomotives : 0-10-0, 0-8-0, 0-6-0.* New York: American Locomotive Co., 1913. 11 p. (*Bulletin no. 1015.*)

278. _____. *Symposium on diesel locomotive engine maintenance.* Schenectady, N.Y., American Locomotive Company, 1953. 146 p.

279. _____ *Ten wheel type locomotives, weighing less than 150,000 pounds, built by American Locomotive Company.* New York, NN.Y.,: The Company, 19--? 54 p.

280. _____. *TP-401 for model RS-3 road switcher.* Schenectady, NY: American Locomotive Company; General Electric Company, 1950. 40 p.

280a. _____. *Tractive power tables of simple locomotives.* New York : American Locomotive Company, 1910. 5 p. (*Bulletin no. 1002.*)

281. _____. *Via Union Pacific ...: war challenges the railroads.* New York, N.Y., American Locomotive Company, 1943. 1 v.

282. _____. *Walschaert valve gear as applied to large American locomotives.* New York, N.Y., The Company, 19--? 44 p.

283. *American Locomotive Company: catalog to holdings of the ALCO collections* 2d ed. (American Locomotive Company Historical Society). Schenectady, N.Y. New York, NY: ALCO Historic Photos, 1987. 16 p. (*Record Group 3*)

284. *American locomotives, 1871-1881; a collection of locomotive drawings and plans with descriptions, specifications and details, originally published in 1883 under the title Recent locomotives, by Railroad Gazette Publishing., New York, and augmented with new material from various sources.* Edited by Grahame Hardy and Paul Darrell. Decorations by E.S. Hammack. Oakland, CA: G. Hardy, 1950. 1 v.

285. American Palace Car Company. *The American Palace Car Company, London, New York, Toronto. Parlor, sleeping and dining car combined in one ...Private demonstration car "Columbia" on the tracks of the Pennsylvania Railroad, Atlantic City, N.J., June 13, 14, 15, 16 ...* New York? M. King, 1906. 7, 1 p.

286. American Petroleum Institute. Measurement Coordination Department. *Measurement and calibration of tank cars.* Washington, DC: American Petroleum Institute, 1966. 41 p.

287. *American practice in block signaling, with descriptions and drawings of the different systems in use on railroads in the United States.* New York, Railroad Gazette, 1891. 72, 6 p. ("The pages which follow are a reprint of articles which appeared in the Railroad Gazette in 1890 and previous years.")

287a. American Public Transit Association. *The case for business investment in high-speed and intercity passenger rail.* Washington, D.C.: American Public Transit Association, 2011. 9 p.

288. American Public Transportation Association. *Manual of standards and recommended practices for rail passenger equipment.* Washington, DC: APTA, 1999. 682 p. Looseleaf. Passenger Rail Equipment Safety Standards Task Force.

289. American Railroad Association. *Proceedings of the Session of the American Railroad Association.* New York, NY: The Association, 1891-1933. Irregular.

(< *Proceedings of the General Time Convention*; > American Railway Association. Session. *Proceedings of the Session of the American Railway Association*)

290. _____.*Proceedings of the Session of the American Railroad Association*. New York, NY: The Association, 1919-1900s. Annual. (< American Railway Association. Session. *Proceedings of the Session of the American Railway Association held at ...* ; > The American Railway Association. Session. *Proceedings of the Session of the American Railway Association.*)

291. _____. Committee on Demurrage and Storage. *Report of the Committee on Demurrage and Storage*. S.l., American Railroad Association, Committee on Demurrage and Storage, ?-1919. (> American Railroad Association. Committee on Demurrage, Storage, Reconsignment and Diversion. *Report of the Committee on Demurrage, Storage, Reconsignment and Diversion.*)

292. _____. Committee on Demurrage, Storage, Reconsignment and Diversion. *Report of the Committee on Demurrage, Storage, Reconsignment and Diversion*. S.l., American Railroad Association, Committee on Demurrage, Storage, Reconsignment and Diversion, 1920-?

293. _____. Committee on Electricity. *Report of Committee on Electricity*. New York: American Railroad Association, Electrical Division, ?-1900s.

294. _____. Committee on Railroad Business Mail. *Report of the Committee on Railroad Business Mail*. New York: American Railroad Association, Committee on Railroad Business Mail, ?-1920s.

295. _____. Mechanical-Equipment Painting Division. *Proceedings of the sessions of the American Railroad Association. Section III-Mechanical Equipment Painting Division*. 1920.

296. _____. Section III, Mechanical. *Proceedings of the session of the American Railroad Association, Section III, Mechanical*. New York, The Association, 1919-1920. Annual.2 v. (> *Proceedings of the session of the American Railway Association, Division V, Mechanical.*)

297. _____. Section V. Transportation. *Proceedings of the session of the American Railroad Association, Section V, Transportation*. New York: The Association, 1900s-?

298. _____. Section VI, Purchases and Stores. *Proceedings of the session of the American Railroad Association. Section 6, Purchases and Stores*. New York, NY: The Association, 1900s-1920. Annual 1 v. (< Railway Storekeepers Association. *Annual meeting of the Railway Storekeepers' Association*; > American Railway Association. Purchases and Stores Division. *Proceedings of the annual meeting of the American Railway Association, Division 6, Purchases and Stores.*)

299. *American railroad journal*. New York, Simmons-Boardman Pub., 1832-1886. 60 v. (>*Railroad and engineering journal*, 1887-1892.) Merged with *Van Nostrand's*

engineering magazine, to form: *Railroad and engineering journal.*

300. *American railroad journal.* San Marino, CA: Golden West Books, 1966-

301. *American railroad journal, and advocate of internal improvements.* New York, D.K. Minor, 1832-1837. 6 v. Weekly. (>*American railroad journal and mechanics magazine.*)

302. *American railroad journal, and general advertiser for railroads, canals, steamboats, machinery, and mines.* New York, NY: D.K. Minor, 1840s. Weekly. (<*American railroad journal and mechanics' magazine*; >*American railroad journal, and iron manufacturer's and mining guide.*)

303. *American railroad journal, and iron manufacturer's and mining gazette.* Philadelphia, D.K. Minor, 1840s. Weekly. (< *American railroad journal, and general advertiser for railroads, canals, steamboats, machinery, and mines*; > *American railroad journal.*)

304. *American railroad journal and mechanics' magazine.* New York, D.K. Minor & G.C. Schaeffer, 1838-1840s. Semimonthly. (<*American railroad journal and advocate of internal improvements;* > *American railroad journal, and general advertiser for railroads, canals, steamboats, machinery, and mines.*)

305. *American railroad manual for the United States and the Dominion ... also, an epitome or brief history of the charter under which each road was originally constructed.../* Compiled and edited by Edward Vernon. New York, American Railroad Manual Company, 1873-

306. *American railroads.* Lawrence, KS: University of Kansas Press, 1970. 126 p.

307. *American railroads: an annotated guide to reference sources*, by Thomas F. Pappas. 1992. 144 l. (Thesis, M.A., Kent State University)

308. *American railway accounting: a bibliography.* Elizabeth Cullen, compiler. Washington, D.C., Railway Accounting Officers Association, 1926. pp. 789-885. (Reprint: from Railway accounting procedure, 1926.

309. *The American railway and supply directory of 1873: containing an official list of the officers and directors of the railroads in the United States and Canadas, together with their financial condition, amount of rolling stock, &c./* Boston, MA: Greenough, Jones & Co., 1873- 536, 58 p. ("Also, a railway supply directory of all the principal dealers in railway supplies in the United States, arranged under appropriate headings, lists of master car builders, master mechanics, railroad societies, &c.")

310. American Railway Association. *The American Railway Association rules and the Interstate Commerce Commission regulations for the transportation of explosives and the American Railway Association regulations for the transportation of inflammable articles and acids.* 1908. 1 v. (89 p.)

311. _____. *The American Railway Association rules and the Interstate Commerce Commission regulations for the transportation of explosives, effective April 13, 1909: the American Railway Association regulations for the transportation of inflammable articles and acids, effective July 1, 1909.* New York: American Railway Association, Interstate Commerce Commission, United States Army, Ordnance Department, 1909. 32 p. (June 1909. *Form No. 1720.*)

312. _____. *Automatic train control: Bulletins no. 1-9.* Washington, D.C., A.R.A., 1929-1931. 9 v. (Committee on Automatic Train Control)

313. _____. *Catechism on the standard code of train & telegraph rules.* New York, N.Y., H.A. Rost, 1894. 24 p.

314. _____. *Code of car service rules; Code of per diem rules, and Code of switching reclaim rules. National car demurrage rules.* New York: American Railway Association, 1911. 362 p. "Cases arbitrated". p. 99-362.

314a. _____. *Code of car service rules* / New York : The Association, 1913. 45 p. "Original and amended forms of car service rules."

315. _____. *Code of rules (M.C.B.) governing the condition of, and repairs to freight and passenger cars for the interchange of traffic.* Chicago, The Association, 1919. 240 p.

316. _____. *Fuel economy on locomotives.* Chicago, The Association, 1921. 51 p.

317. _____. *Manual of standard and recommended practice.* New York, American Railway Association, Mechanical Division, 1922. 12 pt. in 1 vol.

317a. _____. *Manual of standard and recommended practice.* New York : American Railway Association, Mechanical Division, 1931. 12 pt. in 1 v.

318. _____. *Manual of the electrical section/* New York, NY: American Railway Association, 1929. 1 v (various pagings).

319. _____. *Proceedings of the American Railway Association.* New York, N.Y., The Association, 1886-1912. 6 v.

320. _____. *Proceedings of the Meeting of the American Railway Association held at …* New York, The Association, 1891-1899. Semiannual. 17 v. (< General Time Convention. *Proceedings of the General Time Convention held at the …; >* American Railway Association. Session. *Proceedings of the Session of the American Railway Association held at …*)

321. _____. *Proceedings of the Session of the American Railway Association.* New York, NY: The Association, 1919-1934 11 v.. Annual. (< American Railroad Association. Session. *Proceedings of the Session of the American Railroad Association.*)

322. _____. *Proceedings of the Session of the American Railway Association held at ...*
New York, NY: The Association, 1900-1916. 34 v. Semiannual. (< American Railway
Association. Meeting. *Proceedings of the Meeting of the American Railway Association
held at ...* ;> American Railroad Association. Session. *Proceedings of the Session
of the American Railroad Association.*)

323. _____. *Program of the railroads to provide adequate transportation service in ...*
/ New York: The Association, 1923-1924. Annual. (> Association of American
Railroads. Car Service Division. *Report of the Car Service Division for the year ...*)

324. (Blank entry)

325. _____. *Roadway and ballast*/ Chicago, IL: The Association, 1973. 300 p.

326. _____. *Rule book of the American Railway Association.* New York,
The Association, 1916. 759 p. (Also: 1905. 237 p.) Handbooks, manuals

327. _____. *Rules governing the loading of lumber, logs, stone, etc., and loading
and carrying structural materials, plates, rails, girders, etc.* New York, N.Y., American
Railway Association, 1917. 176 p. Loading rules.

328. _____. *Rules governing the loading of lumber, logs, stone, etc.: and loading
and carrying structural materials, plates, rails, girders, etc.* / New York;
The Association, 1922. 251 p.

328a. _____. *The standard cipher code of the American Railway Association* / New York
: The American Railway Association, 1906. 75 l, 1 p.

329. _____. *The standard code of the American Railway Association.* New York, NY"
The Association, 1904. 129 p.

330. _____. *The standard code of the American Railway Association: block signal rules.*
New York: American Railway Association, 1909. 46 p.

331. _____. *The standard code of the American Railway Association: interlocking rules.*
New York, NY: American Railway Association, 1909. 15 p.

331a. _____. *The standard code of the American Railway Association : train rules
adopted April 14, 1887 ... and block signal rules ...* / 8th ed. New York? The Association,
1897. 206 p.

332. _____. *The standard code of the American Railway Association: train rules, block
signal rules, interlocking rules.* New York, N.Y., American Railway Association, 1920.
597 p.

333. _____. *The standard code of the American Railway Association: train rules,
block signal rules, interlocking rules.* New York, N.Y., The Association, 1928. 709 p.

334. _____ *The standard code of the American Railway Association; train rules for single track-adopted April 25, 1906; train rules for double track, adopted April 25, 1906; train rules for three and four tracks, adopted April 5, 1905. Rules governing the movement of trains.* New York, N.Y., The Association, 1906. 143 p. (Later ed. published in 1916. 131 p.)

335. _____. Car Service Division. *Annual bulletin* / Washington, DC: American Railway Association, 1900s- . Annual. Railroads. Statistics.

336. _____. _____. *Cars of revenue freight loaded* / Washington, DC: American Railway Association, Car Service Division, 1926-1988. Annual. (> Association of American Railroads. Car Service Division.)

337. _____. _____. *Information bulletin. Revenue freight loaded week ended Saturday October 8, 1921- Saturday, May 11, 1935.* Washington, DC: 1921-1935. Weekly. (> Association of American Railroads. Car Service Division. *Revenue freight loaded and received from connections.*)

338. _____. _____. *Monthly statement of revenue freight cars awaiting repairs, class one roads.* Washington, DC : 1927-1934. Monthly. (> Association of American Railroads. Car Service Division. *Monthly statement of revenue freight cars in unserviceable condition, class I railroads.*)

339. _____. _____. *Railroad car loading, 1918 to 1923; a study of the fluctuations in the movement of commodities during the various seasons of the year.* Washington, DC: American Railway Association, Car Service Division, 1923. 2 p.

340. _____. _____. *Summary of monthly revenue freight car ownership, class I roads.* Washington, DC: American Railway Association, Car Service Division, ?-1933. Monthly. (> *Summary of revenue freight car ownership, class I roads.*)

341. _____. _____. *Summary of revenue freight car ownership, class I roads.* Washington, DC: American Railway Association, Car Service Division, 1933- . Monthly. (< *Summary of monthly revenue freight car ownership, class I roads.*)

342. _____. Committee on Automatic Train Control. *General description of automatic train control installation on Chicago, Rock Island & Pacific Railway : Regan Safety Devices Company* / Chicago: American Railway Association, 1923. 1 v. (various pagings)

343. _____. _____. *General description of automatic train control installation, General Railway Signal Company on Delaware & Hudson Company* / Chicago : American Railroad Association, 1925. 1 v. (various pagings)

344. _____. _____. *General description of automatic train control installation, Miller Train Control Corporation on Chicago & Eastern Illinois Railway* / Chicago : American Railway Association, 1925. 22 l.

345. ____. ____. *General description of automatic train control installation :
National safety Appliance Company on St. Louis-San Francisco Railway.* S.l., s.n., 1925.
22, 3 l., 2 leaves of plates.

346. ____. ____. *General description of automatic train control installation,
Sprague Safety Control & Signal Corporation on Great Northern Railway* / Chicago:
American Railway Association, 1925. 12, 2, 4, l. 5 leaves of plates.

347. ____. ____. *General description of automatic train control installation,
Sprague Safety Control & Signal Corporation on New York Central Railroad.* Chicago:
American Railway Association, 1925. 19, 6, 2, 6 l, 3 leaves of plates.

348. ____. ____. *General description of automatic train control installation, Union
Switch & Signal Company, General Railway Signal Company on New York, New Haven
& Hartford Railroad* / S.l., The Committee? 1927. 1 v. (various pagings)

349. ____. ____. *General description of automatic train control installation, Union
Switch & Signal Company on Boston & Maine Railroad* / Chicago : American Railway
Association, 1927. 47 l., 6 leaves of plates.

350. ____. Committee on Car Service. *Report of the Committee on Car Service.*
New York: American Railway Association, Committee on Car Service, ?-1920s.
(> *Report of the Car Service Division for the year ...*)

351. ____. Committee on Freight Handling Service. *Report of the Committee
on Freight Handling Service.* New York: American Railway Association, Committee
on Freight Handling Service, /-1920s.

352. ____. Division I. Operating. *Proceedings of the ... annual session of the American
Railway Association. Division I, Operating.* New York, NY: American Railway
Association, 1921- Annual.

353. ____. Division II-Transportation. *Report of Division II-Transportation.* Chicago?
: American Railway Association, Transportation Division, 1900s. (*Circular.* American
Railway Association.) Freight cars. Freight.

354. ____. Division IV-Engineering. Electrical Section. *Proceedings ... annual
meeting.* Chicago: American Railway Association, 1929-1932. Annual (irregular)
(> Association of American Railroads. Division IV-Engineering. Electrical Section.
Proceedings ... annual meeting.)

355. ____. Division V. Mechanical. *Code of rules (M.C.B.) governing the condition
of and repairs to freight and passenger cars for the interchange of traffic.* New York :
American Railway Association, 1919-1933. Annual.

356. ____. ____. *Proceedings of the session of the American Railway Association,
Division V, Mechanical.* New York, NY: The Association, 1922-1932. Annual. 11 v.

(< American Railroad Association. *Proceedings of the session of the American Railroad Association, Section III, Mechanical;* > Association of American Railroads. *Proceedings of the session of the Association of American Railroad, Operations and Maintenance Department, Division V, Mechanical.*)

357. _____. _____. *Progress report on tests of trucks and truck springs designed to promote easier riding and reduce harmonic action* / New York ? American Railway Association, Mechanical Division, 1934. 2, 216 p.

358. _____. _____. _____. *Specifications for tank cars: standard: Revised 1920. Effective November 1, 1920.* New York: American Railway Association, 1920. 66 p.

359. _____. _____. _____. *Specifications for tank cars.* S.l., American Railway Association, 1922. 1 v.

360. _____. _____. _____. *Specifications for tank cars: standard; effective March 1, 1931. Revised 1930.* Chicago: American Railway Association, 1931. 81 p.

361. _____. _____. _____. *Wheel and axle manual : recommended practice : adopted 1928.* Washington, DC : American Railway Association, 1928. 220 p.

362. _____.Division V. Mechanical. Equipment Painting Section. *Proceedings of the session of the American Railway Association. Division V, Mechanical Equipment Painting Section.* New York, NY: The Association, 1920-   . No annual meetings in 1921 and 1922. (< Master Car and Locomotive Painters' Association of the United States and Canada. *Proceedings;* >

363. _____, Freight Claim Division. *Classification of freight loss and damage by commodities, effective January 1ˢᵗ, 1929.* Chicago: American Railway Association, Freight Claim Division, 1929. 8 p. (*Circular, no. FCD-338.*)

364. _____. _____. *Proceedings of annual session.* S.l., American Railway Association, 1892-1934. Annual. 43 v. (> Association of American Railroads. Freight Claim Division. *Proceedings of annual session.*)

365. _____. Freight Station Section. *Proceedings of the ... annual session of the American Railway Association, Division I—Operating, Freight Station Section.* Chicago, New York: The Association, 1920s-1930s. Annual. (< The American Association of Freight Agents ... *annual meeting* ...; >*Proceedings of the Association of American Railroads. Operations and Maintenance Department, Operating-Transportation Division. Freight Station Section.*)

366. _____. Medical and Surgical Section. *Proceedings of the ... Annual Meeting of the American Railway Association, Medical and Surgical Section held at* ... Bethlehem, PA: Times Pub. Co., 1920s-1934. Annual. Imprint varies. (< American Railway Association. Medical and Surgical Section. Session. *Proceedings of the Session of the American Railway Association, Medical and Surgical Section held at* ... ; > Association of American Railroads. Medical and Surgical Section. Meeting.

Proceedings of the ... Annual Meeting of the Association of American Railroads Medical and Surgical Section held at ...)

367. _____. _____. *Proceedings of the Session of the American Railway Association, Medical and Surgical Section held at ...* S.l., American Railway Association, 1921-1920s. Annual. (> American Railway Association. Medical and Surgical Section. Meeting. *Proceedings of the ... Annual Meeting of the American Railway Association Medical and Surgical Section held at ...*)

368. _____. _____. *Report of the Committee on Physical standards* / S.l., s.n., 1908. 12 p. (*Circular, no. 39. American Railway Association. Medical and Surgical Section.*)

369. _____. Purchases and Stores. Division VI. *Proceedings of the annual meeting of the American Railway Association: Division VI: Purchases and Stores.* New York, NY: The Association, 1920-   . Annual. (> Association of American Railroads. Purchases and Stores Division. *Proceedings.*)

370. _____. Safety Section. *Proceedings of the ... annual session of the American Railway Association Safety Section held at ...* Bethlehem, PA: Times Publishing Co., 1921-1934. Annual 14 v. (> Association of American Railroads. Safety Section. *Proceedings of the annual session of the Safety Section.*)

371. _____. Signal Division. *Proceedings.* Bethlehem, PA: Times Pub. Co., 1920-1921. Annual. 2 v. v. 16 (1919) – v. 17 (1920). (< Railway Signal Association. *Journal the Railway Signal Association*, v. 1-15; > American Railway Association. Signal Section. *Proceedings.*)

372. _____. Signal Section. *American railway signaling principles and practices. Chapter 23, Highway crossing protection.* New York, NY: American Railway Association, Signal Section, 1928. 21, 6 p.

373. _____. _____. *Direct current track circuits.* New York, The Section, 1928. 31, 10 p. (Chapter 7 of *American railway signaling principles and practices.*)

374. _____. _____. *Manual of recommended practice.* New York: The Association, 1900s-   . (< Railway Signal Association. *Manual of the Railway Signal Association.*

375. _____. _____. *The manual of the American Railway Association, Signal Section.* New York: American Railway Association, 1900s-1922. (< *Manual of the Railway Signal Association;* > Association of American Railroads. *Manual of recommended practice.*)

376. _____. _____. *Proceedings—Signal Section, American Railway Association.* New York, American Railway Association, 1919-1934. 11 v. Biennial. Numbered in continuation of Journal of the Railway Signal Association (Revised ed.) v. 1-15 which it supersedes.(< Railway Signal Association. *Journal of the Railway Signal Association. revised ed.;* American Railroad Association. Signal Division. *Proceedings*; > Association of American Railroads. Engineering Division. Signal Section. *Proceedings.*)

377. _____. Special Committee on National Defense. *Official public bulletin.* Washington, DC: Special Committee on National Defense of the American Railway Association, 1917. 1 v. At head of title: Railroads' War Board. (> American Railway Association. Special Committee on National Defense. *Official information.*)

378. _____. Telegraph and Telephone Section. *Proceedings of the session of the American Railway Association, Telegraph and Telephone Section.* S.l., The Association, 1919-1934. Annual 16 v. (< Association of Railway Telegraph Superintendents. *Proceedings of the annual meeting of the Association of Railway Telegraph Superintendents*; > Association of American Railroads. Telegraph and Telephone Section. *Proceedings of the ... session of the Association of American Railroads. Telegraph and Telephone Section*)

379. _____; Gibson, Pribble & Co., Richmond, VA. *United States safety appliances for all classes of cars and locomotives (A.R.A. edition).* 13th ed. New York, Published for the American Railway Association, 1928. 120 p.

380. American Railway Bridge and Building Association. *Bridge and building news.* Homewood, IL: American Railway Bridge and Building Association, 1939-   . Quarterly.

381._____. *Bulletin.* Chicago, Ill.,: American Railway Bridge and Building Association, 1910-   . Irregular.

382. _____. *Development of turntables to meet operating conditions for the modern locomotive showing the best improved practice.* S.l., American Railway Bridge and Building Association, 1927. 53 p.

383. _____. *Index. Proceedings of the American Railway Bridge and Building Association, 1891 to 1920 inclusive* [volumes 1 to 30] with no. 30. Elgin, Ill., American Railway Bridge and Building Association, 1921. 15 p.

384. _____. *Proceedings of the ... annual conference of the American Railway Bridge & Building Association.* Homewood, IL: The Association, 1979-   Annual. (<*Proceedings of the ... annual convention of the American Railway Bridge and Building Association.*)

385. _____. *Proceedings of the ... annual convention of the American Railway Bridge and Building Association.* Homewood, Ill.,: ARBBA, 1891-1978. Annual. 25th, 1915. Subject index. Vol. 1-30, 1891-1920 (with no. 30). Imprint varies.

386. _____. *Proceedings of the Twenty-fourth Annual Convention of the American Railway Bridge and building Association, successor to the Association of Railway Superintendents of Bridges and Buildings held at Los Angeles, Cal., October 20-22, 1914.* Elgin, IL: Brethren Publishing House, 1914. 308 p.

387. American Railway Car Institute. *Age of passenger train cars in commuter service : owned by Class I railroads, 1949.* S.l., American Railway Car Institute, 1949. 31 l.

388. _____. *Railroad car facts : statistics on car building & car repairing, 1961.* New York : American Railway Car Institute, 1962. 81, 13 p.

389. _____. *Railway passenger car standards.* S.l., American Railway Car Institute, 1951. 32 l.

390. American Railway Development Association. *Proceedings of the ... annual meeting.* Eden Prairie, MN: American Railway Development Association, 1920- . Annual. 100th (2006).

391. American Railway Engineering and Maintenance-of-Way Association. *A.R.E.A trackwork plans and specifications.* New York, The Association, 1934. 1 v.

392. _____. *Bulletin/* S.l., s.n., 1900-1911. (> American Railway Engineering Association. *Bulletin.*)

393. _____. *Communications & signals manual of recommended practices.* Landover, MD: American Railway Engineering and Maintenance-of-Way Association, 2005. 5 v.

394. _____ *Field handbook for concrete railway structures.* Landover, MD: AREMA, 2000. 134, 16 p.

395. _____ *General specifications for steel railway bridges, 1910.* Chicago, Ill., The Association, 1910. 30 p.

396. _____. *Manual for railway engineering.* Washington, DC: American Railway Engineering Association, 1996. 4 v. (Also: 1993, 2 v.)

397. _____. *Manual of recommended practice for railway engineering and maintenance-of-way.* Chicago, Ill., American Railway Engineering and Maintenance-of-Way Association, 1905-1907 2 v. (> American Railway Engineering Association: *Manual of the American Railway Engineering Association.*)

398. _____. *Manual of recommended practice; definitions of terms, designs and plans, specifications, economics of construction and maintenance, principles and practices for railway engineering.* Chicago, IL: The Association, 1969. 2 v. (loose-leaf)

399. _____. *Manual of the American Railway Engineering Association/* Chicago, IL: The Association, 1929. 1531, p. Editions also for the years including 1911,(477 p.), 1919 (680 p.), 1921 (1004 p.),

400. _____. *1999 manual for railway engineering.* Landover, MD: American Railway Engineering and Maintenance-of-Way Association, 1999. 4 v.

401. _____. *Proceedings/* Landover MD: American Railway Engineering and Maintenance of Way Association, Communications & Signals Functional Group, 1998. Annual. 1 v. (< American Railway Engineering Association. Communication

and Signal Division. Technical conference. *Proceedings*; > American Railway Engineering and Maintenance-of-Way Association. Communications & Signals Functional Group. Technical conference. *Proceedings* of the ... *annual conferences*.)

402. _____ *Proceedings of the ... annual conference*. Landover, MD: The Association, 2000- . Annual. Also issued on CD-ROM.
(< *Proceedings of the ... annual conferences.)*

403. _____. *Proceedings of the ... annual conferences: Communications & signals ... [and] Track & Structures*. Landover, MD: The Association, 1999. Annual. 1 v.
(< Track & Structures Conference. *Proceedings*; American Railway Engineering and Maintenance-of-Way Association. Communications & Signals Functional Group. Technical Conference. *Proceedings*. > American Railway Engineering and Maintenance-of-Way Association. Conference. *Proceedings of the ... annual conference*.)

404. _____. *Proceedings of the ... annual convention of the American Railway Engineering and Maintenance-of-Way Association*. Chicago, Ill., The Association, 1900-1911. 12 v. Annual. (> American Railway Engineering Association. *Proceedings of the ... annual convention of the American Railway Engineering Association.)*

405. _____. *Roadbed Stabilization and Ballast Symposium*/ Landover, MD: American Railway Engineering and Maintenance-of-Way Association, 2000. 365 p.

406. _____.*Supplement to Manual of Recommended Practice*. (Addenda to edition of 1907.) S.l., The Association, 1908. 41 p.

407. _____. *2007 manual for railway engineering*. Landover, MD: American Railway Engineering and Maintenance-of-Way Association, 2007. 5 v. (loose-leaf) +CD-ROM

407a. _____. *2012 manual for railway engineering*. Lanham, MD: American Railway Engineering and Maintenance-of Way Association, 2012. 4 v.

408. American Railway Engineering Association. *Bulletin*. Washington, D.C., American Railway Engineering Association, 1911-1997. Quarterly.

409. _____. *General index to the Proceedings, volume 1 to 16 inclusive (1900 to 1915)*. Chicago, Ill., American Railway Engineering Association, 1917. 271 p.

410. _____. *Handbook of instruction for care and operation of maintenance- of -way equipment*. Chicago, IL: American Railway Engineering Association, 1957. 2d ed. 149 p.

411. _____. *Maintenance of way cyclopedia: a reference book*. New York, N.Y., Simmons-Boardman Pub., 1921. 1 v.

412. _____. *Manual for railway engineering, 1995*. Washington, D.C.: American Railway Engineering Association, 1995. 2 v.

413. _____. *Manual for railway engineering. (Fixed properties)*. Washington, D.C.,

American Railway Engineering Association, 1971?-

414. _____. *Manual of the American Railway Engineering Association*. Chicago, Ill., American Railway Engineering Association, 1905-   (1911 ed., 477 p.; 1916 ed., 680 p.; 1921 ed., 1004 p.; 1929, ed., 1531 p.; 1938 ed., 1611 p.; 1946 ed., 2 v.< American Railway Engineering and Maintenance of Way Association: *Manual of recommended practice for railway engineering and maintenance of way* [1905-1907].)

415. _____. *Portfolio of trackwork plans*. Washington, D.C.: American Railway Engineering Association, 19--?-

416. _____. *Proceedings, technical conference*. Landover, MD: American Railway Engineering and Maintenance-of-Way Association, Communications & Signals Functional Group, 1998. 1 v. Merged with: Track & Structures Conference. Proceedings, to form American Railway Engineering and Maintenance-of-Way Association. Proceedings of the ... annual conferences. (< Association of American Railroads. Communications and Signal Division. *Technical Conference*; Association of American Railroads. Communications and Signal Division. *Annual Technical Conference*. [proceedings]; > Track & Structures Conference. *Proceedings*; American Railway Engineering and Maintenance-of-Way Association. *Proceedings of the ... annual conferences*.)

417. _____. *Proceedings of the ... annual convention of the American Railway Engineering Association*. Chicago, Ill., Committee on Publications of the Association, 1912-1973. 62 v. Annual. (< American Railway Engineering and Maintenance-of-Way Association. *Proceedings of the ... annual convention*; > American Railway Engineering Association. *Proceedings, technical conference.*)

418. _____. *Proceedings, technical conference*. American Railway Engineering Association. Washington, D.C.: American Railway Engineering Association, 1974-1982. Annual. 9 v. (< *Proceedings of the ... annual convention of the American Railway Engineering Association*; > *Proceedings of the American Railway Engineering Association.*)

419. _____. *Proceedings of the American Railway Engineering Association*. Washington, DC: The Association, 1983-1997. Annual. 15 v. (< *Proceedings, technical conference*. American Railway Engineering Association; > *Track & Structures Conference. Proceedings.*)

420. _____. *Railway track & structures cyclopedia*. New York, N.Y., Simmons-Boardman Pub. Co., 1921-

421. _____ *Specifications for movable railway bridges*. Chicago, IL: American Railway Engineering Association, 1953. 1 v.

422. _____ *Specifications for steel railway bridges: for fixed spans not exceeding 400 feet in length*. Chicago, Ill., American Railway Engineering Association, 1938. 1 v.

422a. _____. *War emergency yard improvements: abstract from report of Committee on yards and Terminals to the nineteenth annual convention : including a Catechism of yard design and operation* / Chicago : The Association, 1918. 8 p.

423. _____. Committee on Track. *Trackwork plans.* Chicago: American Railway Engineering Association, 1921. ii, 94 leaves of plates; plans.

423a. _____. Construction and Maintenance Section. *Wood bridges and trestles.* Chicago : American Railway Engineering Association, 1948. 127 p.

424. American Railway Master Mechanics' Association. *Annual report of the American Railway Master Mechanics' Association.* S.l., s.n., 1868-1880. 13 v. (> *Report of proceedings of the ... annual convention of the American Railway Master Mechanics' Association* [1881-1918.])

425. _____. *Attachments between engine and tender, foot-steps and hand-rails.* S.l., s.n., 1893. 5 p.

426. _____. *Constitution and by-laws of the American Railway Master Mechanics' Association and proceedings of the meeting, held in Cleveland, Ohio, Sept. 30th, and Oct. 1st, 1868. The second annual report of the American Railway Master Mechanics' Association, in convention at Pittsburgh, September 15th and 16th, 1869.* Cincinnati, OH: Wilstach, Baldwin & Co., 1869. 82, 1 p.

427. _____. *Locomotive dictionary.* New York, The Railroad Gazette, 190? 1 v.

428. _____. *Report of committee on compound locomotives.* J. Davis Barnett. S.l., s.n., 1890. 11 p.

429. _____. *Report of committee on locomotive headlights.* Chicago, American Railway Master Mechanics Association, Office of Secretary, 1914. 330 p.

430. _____. *Report of committee on piston valves.* S.l., n.p., 1905. 53, 1 p.

431. _____. *Report of committee on recent improvements in boiler design.* St. Paul. Minn., The Association, 1903. 27 p.

432. _____. *Report of the proceedings ...* Cincinnati, Ohio, American Railway Master Mechanics' Association, 1868-1918. 50 v. Annual. (< American Railway Master Mechanics' Assoc. *Annual report...; >* Master Car builders' Association. *Report of the proceedings*; American Railroad Association. Mechanical Division. *Proceedings.)*

433. _____. *Shop tests of locomotives.* S.l., American Railway Master Mechanics' Assn., 1941. 14 p.

434. *American railway review. Public works, patents, finance, engineering.* New York, American Railway Bureau, 1859-   Weekly.

435. *American railway signaling principles and practices.* New York, N.Y., American Railway Association; Association of American Railroads, 1927-1961. 26 v. "Chapters issued before 1935 by the American Railway Association, Signal Section; 1935-1960, by the Signal Section of the Association of American Railroads; 1961- by the Association's Communication and Signal Section."

436. *American railway times.* Boston, Mass., Robinson & Co., 1849-1859. Weekly. (>*Railway times*, 1860-1872.)

437. American School of Correspondence. *Electric railways.* Chicago, Ill., American School of Correspondence, 1913. 296 p.

438. American Short Line and Regional Railroad Association. *Short line and regional railroad facts and figures: freight in focus.* Washington, DC: American Short Line and Regional Railroad Association, 2007. 19 p.

439. American Society for Testing Materials. *Standard specifications for cast-iron car wheels, adopted September 1, 1905.* Philadelphia : s.n., 1905. 6 p.

439a. _____. Symposium on railroad materials [and] lubricating oils. Presented at the second Pacific Area National Meeting, Los Angeles, Calif., September 18-19, 1956. Philadelphia: American Society for Testing Materials, 1957. 169 p. (Special technical publication, no. 214.)

440. American Society of Civil Engineers. *New York tunnel extension, the Pennsylvania Railroad; description of the work and facilities.* New York: The Society, 1910. 2 v.

441. American Society of Mechanical Engineers. *Contribution of research to railway progress/* Ann Arbor, MI: Edward Bros., 1933. 154 p.

441a. _____. *Mobile and locomotive cranes: safety standards for cableways, derricks, hoists, hooks, jacks, and slings.* Santa Ana, CA: Global Engineering Documents, 2002. 46 p.

442. _____. *N&W 611—class J steam locomotive: national historic mechanical engineering landmark, May 1984.* New York? American Society of Mechanical Engineers, 1984. 18 p.

443. _____. *Railway mechanical engineering: a century of progress: car and locomotive design.* New York, American Society of Mechanical Engineers, 1979. 445 p.

444. _____. *Test code for steam locomotives.* New York: American Society of Mechanical Engineers, 1941. 27 p.

445. _____. *USRA steam locomotives: Atlantic Coast Line 1504 and Baltimore and Ohio 4500: a national mechanical engineering landmark.* New York? American Society of Mechanical Engineers, 1990. 15 p. (HH 02 90)

446. _____. Rail Transportation Division. *Rail transportation proceedings.* New York: The Society, 1970-1975. Annual. (> *Joint ASME/IEEE Railroad Conference)*

447. _____; American National Standards Institute. *Track bolts and nuts.* New York: The Society, 1983. 5 p.

448. _____; Institute of Electrical and Electronics Engineers. [Papers] New York: Institute of Electrical and Electronics Engineers, 1900s-1976. Annual. (> Joint ASME/IEEE/AAR Railroad Conference. *IEEE technical papers presented at the ... Joint ASME/IEEE/AAR Railroad Conference.*)

449. American Society of Railroad Superintendents. *Proceedings of the ... meeting of the American Society of Railroad Superintendents.* Boston, Rand Avery Supply Co., 1881-1900. 30 v.

450. American Standard, Inc.; WABCO. *Railroad freight car classification yards: installations ...* Swissvale, PA Union Switch & Signal Division, American Standard, Inc. 1980? 40 p.

451. American Standards Association; American Society of Mechanical Engineers; United States. Naval Facilities Engineering Command. *USA standard: safety code for cranes, derricks, hoists, jacks and slings; crawler, locomotive and truck cranes. New York, NY: American Society of Mechanical Engineers, 1969. 24 p.*

452. American Steel & Wire Co. *American fence posts for farm, railroad and city use.* Chicago : American Steel & Wire Co., 1900s. Serial publication.

453. _____. *American rail bonds and bonding appliances.* Chicago, Ill., The Company, 1926. 100 p.

454. _____. *Catalogue of railroad fence, steel fence posts and gates* / S.l., American Steel & Wire, 1932. 108 p.

455. _____. *Catalogue of railroad fences and gates* / Chicago, Milwaukee : Osgood Co., 1911. 88 p. (*Catalogue no. 7, July 1911.*)

456. _____. *Rail bonds and appliances.* Chicago : American Steel & Wire Co., 1911. 192 p. (*Catalogue no. 3.)* Includes manual.

457 _____. *Rail bonds for power and signal circuits.* New York, American Steel & Wire; United States Steel, 1941. 110 p.

458. _____. *Rail bonds : for power and signal circuits.* Cleveland ? American Steel & Wire Co; United States Steel Co., 1947. 77 p.

459. American Steel Foundries. *Early railroad days; prints from the collection of American Steel Foundries.* Chicago, Ill., 1943. 1 v.

460. _____. *The modern freight-car truck.* Chicago, Ill., American Steel Foundries, 194-? 12 p.

461. _____. *Road testing freight car trucks.* Chicago, Ill., American Steel Foundries, 1943. 28 p.

462. American Throttle Company. *The American multiple-valve throttle.* New York, American Throttle Company, 1938. 19 p.

463. American Train Dispatchers' Association. *Four tricks a day: the shorter work day for train dispatchers and how to get it.* Chicago, IL: American Train Dispatchers' Association, 1929. 16 p.

464. _____. *Proceedings of the ... annual convention.* Buffalo, NY: Webster Brothers, Printers, 1885. Annual. 1 v. (< American Train Dispatchers' Association. *Proceedings of the annual meeting;* > Train Dispatchers' Association of America. *Proceedings of the annual convention.*)

465. _____. *Proceedings of the ... annual meeting of the American Train Dispatchers' Association.* Buffalo, NY: Railroad Herald, 1884. Annual. 1 v. (> *American Train Dispatchers' Association. Proceedings of the ... annual convention ...*)

466. American Vanadium Company. *Vanadium rails.* Pittsburgh, Pa., The Company, 1914. 24 p.

467. American Welding Society. Committee on Railroad Welding. *Railroad welding specification : car and locomotives* / Miami, FL: American Welding Society, 1993. 318 p.

468. *America's first installation of system-wide railroad radio communication.* Chicago: Chicago South Shore and South Bend Railroad, 1949. 10 p.

469. *America's freight system in the 80's and 90's ... but how to get there? Conference proceedings.* Cambridge, MA: Transportation Systems Center, 1976. 175, A-14 p.

470. Ames, Charles Edgar. *Pioneering the Union Pacific; a reappraisal of the builders of the railroad.* New York, NY: Appleton-Century-Crofts, 1969. 591 p.

471. Ames, E.W. *Ignitron multiple-unit cars for the New Haven Railroad* / New York : American Institute of Electrical Engineers, 1954. 6, 4 p. (*Transactions paper, 55-202A.*)

472. Ames, Gregory P. *Old Maud – a life & times: America's pioneer mallet locomotive.* Warren, NJ: On Track Publishers, 2006. 142 p.

473. Amory, Jonathan. *Economy in the generation of steam, with some suggestions upon the proposed substitution of coal for wood upon railroads.* Boston, Bazin and Chandler, 1857. 45 p.

474. Amrine, Lowell. *Six-axle quartet: an essay of diesel portraiture*. Claremont, CA: Galliard Press, 1980. 96 p.

475. Amsden, Perham Littlefield. *A history of the Belfast and Moosehead Lake Railroad*. 1951. 106 l. (Thesis, M.A., University of Maine.)

475a. Amtrak. *Amtrak: an American story*. Washington, D.C.: National Railroad Passenger Corporation, 2011. 143 p.

476._____. *Amtrak's contractual relationship with the railroad industry and costing methodology*. Washington, DC: National Railroad Passenger Corporation, 1994. 33 l.

477. *Amtrak: background and bibliography*. Samuel P. Goodwin, editor. New York, Novinka Books, 2002. 73 p.

478. *Amtrak car and locomotive spotter*. Rev. 4th ed. New York, Wayner Publications, 1980. 117 p.

479. *Amtrak car diagrams of the 1970s*. New York, Wayner Publications, 1987, 1978. 89 p.

480. *The Amtrak railway system: a periodical bibliography of an inter-city transportation network*. Glenna Dunning, compiler. Monticello, IL: Vance Bibliographies, 1985. 41 p.

481. *Amtrak, ten years of controversy: a guide to the literature*. Ronald Dale Kerr, compiler. Evanston, IL: Transportation Center, Northwestern University, 1982. 68 p.

482. *Analysis of Class 1 railroads*. Washington, DC: Economics and Finance Department, Association of American Railroads,1900s-   Annual.
(< *Operating & traffic statistics*.)

483. *Analysis of community impacts resulting from the loss of rail service: final report (revised)*. Pittsburgh, CONSAD, 1975. 4 v. (*Planning project no. 7)*. Consad Research Corporation; United States Railway Association.

484. *Analysis of locomotive cabs: final report/* Washington, DC: National Space Technology Laboratories (U.S.); Federal Railroad Administration, Office of Research and Development, 1982. 170 p. (*DOT/FRA/ORD-81/84.)*

485. *Analysis of plan of reorganization of Norfolk Southern Railroad Company*. New York : Pflugfelder, Bampton & Rust, 1939. 4 p.

486. *Analysis of railroad operated ferry and lighterage operations*. Chicago, IL: A.T. Kearney; United States Railway Association, 1975. 220 l. (*United States Railway Association, planning project no. 6.)*

487. *Analysis of the impact of coal trains moving through Morehead City, North Carolina.* Raleigh, NC: Coastal Energy Impact Program, Office of Coastal Management, N.C. Department of Natural Resources and Community Development, 1981. 47 p. (*CEIP report, no. 25.*)

488. Anand, Pooja. *Cost-effectiveness of reducing environmental risk from railroad tank car transportation of hazardous materials/* 2006. 378 l. (Thesis, Ph.D., University of Illinois at Urbana-Champaign.)

489. Andersen, Espen and James L. McKenney. *Union Pacific Railroad: transition to client-server.* Boston, MA: Harvard Business School, 1994. 25 p.

490. Andersen, G.R. *Hot boxes and train operation* / New York : American Society of mechanical Engineers, 1953. 5 p. (*ASME. Paper no. 53-A-124.*)

491. Anderson, Arthur Marvin. *Louisiana and Arkansas Railway: its territory, industries and financial condition: with illustrations from photographs.* New York: Fisk & Robinson, 1904. 77 p.

491a. Anderson, Burt T. *Survey of railway highway grade crossing accident statistics.* New York: B.T. Anderson, 1936. 17 p. (*Bulletin #11.*)

492. Anderson, Carter S and Walbrook D. Swank. *Train running for the Confederacy, 1861-1865.* Mineral, VA: W.D. Swank, 1990. 74 p.

493. Anderson, Charles E. *Rationale for generic evaluation of tank car thermal protective systems* / San Antonio, TX : Southwest Research Institute, 1981. 78 p. (U.S. Army Ballistic Research laboratory.)

494. Anderson, Dale G., Floyd D. Gaibler, Mary Berglund. *Economic impact of rail branch-line abandonment: result of a south-central Nebraska case study.* Lincoln, NE: Agricultural Experiment Station, Institute of Agriculture and Natural Resources, University of Nebraska-Lincoln, 1976. 26 p.

495. _____, Marc A. Johnson, L. Orlo Sorenson. *Rail-line abandonment in the North Central region.* Manhattan, KS: Agricultural Experiment Station, Kansas State University,1979. 36 p. (*Kansas Agricultural Experiment Station, bulletin. 627*)

496. Anderson, Don. *Development of the Chicago, Milwaukee & St. Paul Railroad Company to 1875.* Milwaukee, WI: Don Anderson, 2002. 24 p. (*Anderson's 19th century railroading history pamphlet series, no. 2*)

497. _____. *Early 20th century railroading in Wisconsin: steam railroads & electric railways, circa 1905 thru 1915.* Milwaukee, WI: D. Anderson, 2002. 95 l.

498. _____. *The Milwaukee & Mississippi Railroad: the first railroad in Wisconsin, February 25, 1851.* Milwaukee, WI; Don Anderson, 2002. 13 p. (*Anderson's 19th century*

railroading history pamphlet series, no. 1)

499. Anderson, E. Ellery, John Henry Gear. *Statement of the indebtedness and liabilities of the Union Pacific Railway Company : January 13, 1897, referred to the Committee on Pacific Railroads and ordered to be printed* / Washington, DC: U.S. G.P.O., 1897. 62 p. (*54th Congress, 2nd session. Senate. doc. no. 62.*)

500. Anderson, Elaine, James Lee, Lance E. Metz. *The Central Railroad of New Jersey's first 100 years, 1849-1949: historical survey.* Easton, PA: Center for Canal History and Technology, 1984. 238 p.

501. Anderson, Eva Greenslit. *Rails across the Cascades.* Wenatchee, WA: World Pub. Co., 1952. 64 p. (2d ed.: 1977, 76 p.; 3d ed.: 1980, 76 p.)

502. Anderson, George B. *One hundred booming years: a history of Bucyrus-Erie Company, 1880-1980.* South Milwaukee, WI: Bucyrus-Erie Co., 1980. 303 p.

503. Anderson, George E., Richard E. Taylor. *Copper Country rail*/ Charleston, SC: Arcadia Publishing, 2008. 127 p. (Copper Range Railroad Co.)

504. Anderson, George LaVerne. *Four essays on railroads in Kansas and Colorado.* Lawrence, KS: Coronado Press, 1971. 80 p.

505. _____. *General William J. Palmer: a decade of Colorado railroad building, 1870-1880.* Colorado Springs, Colo., Colorado College, 1936. 172 p.

506. _____. *Kansas west.* San Marino, CA: Golden West Books, 1963. 168 p.

507. Anderson, Gerald B. *Acoustic detection of roller bearing defects. Phase I, laboratory test.* Washington, DC : Federal Railroad Administration, Office of Research and Development, 2003. Computer file 1 v.; digital, PDF file with ill. Bearing Test Facility, Transportation Technology Center, Inc (TTCI), Pueblo, Colorado.

508. _____. *Acoustic detection of rail car roller bearing defects : Phase II, field test report* / Washington, DC: Federal Railroad Administration, Office of Research and Development, 2003. 1 v. (*DOT/FRA/ORD-00/06.II*)

509. _____. *Acoustic detection of rail car roller bearing defects. Phase III, system evaluation test.* Washington, DC: Federal Railroad Administration, Office of Research and Development, 2003. http://purl.access.gpo.gov/GPO/LPS55011 (*DOT/FRA/ORD-00/06*.III)

510. Anderson, J.A. of Lambertville, N.J. *The train wire. A discussion of the science of train dispatching.* 2d ed. rev. and enl. New York: Railroad Gazette, 1891. 152 p. 1st ed. Chicago; Railway Age Pub. Co., 1883. 77 p.

511. Anderson, J.L. *Texas and Pacific Railway and its connections; report to His Excellency James L. Kemper with governor's reply. Resolutions of the St. Louis*

Convention. Letters of Frank S. Bond. S.l., s.n., 1875. 15 p.

512. Anderson, Jacob E. *History of the St. Louis Southwestern Railroad Company.* 1939. 109 l. (Thesis, M.S., East Texas State Teachers College.)

513. _____. *A brief history of the St. Louis Southwestern Railway Lines.* St. Louis, Mo., Cotton Belt Route, Public Relations Dept., 1947. 29 p.

514. _____. *80 years of transportation progress: a history of the St. Louis Southwestern Railway.* 2d ed., rev. and enl. Tyler, TX: Story-Wright, 1957. 98 p.

515. Anderson, Lucile. *Railroad transportation through Prescott.* Tucson, AZ: 1934. 105 p. (Thesis, M.A., University of Arizona.)

516. Anderson, Margaret T. *Guide to the corporate record collection of the Chesapeake and Ohio Railway Company at the Chesapeake and Ohio Historical Society.* Clifton Forge, VA: The Society, 1996. 38 p.

517. Anderson, Mark Edward. *The Shepaug Valley Railroad: 1866-1948.* Danbury, CT: 1989. 86 p. Thesis, M.A., Western Connecticut State University

518. Anderson, Norman E. and Chris G. MacDermot. *PA4 locomotive.* Burlingame, CA: Chatham Pub. Co., 1978. 127 p.

519. Anderson, R. T. *A realistic characterization of severe railroad accidents. Case study: tank cars.* Barnwell, SC: Allied-General Nuclear Services, 1978. 14 p.

520. Anderson, Willard V. and others. *Chicago: railroad capital of the world.* Milwaukee. Wisc., Kalmbach Pub. Co., 1948. 64 p.

521. Andover, Karl. *Burlington's Zephyrs fleet.* Osceola, WI: MBI, 2004. 128 p.

521a. Andrescavage, Michael W., John Acton. *Rails around South Jersey* / Dauberville, PA: Outer Station project, 2010-   . v. 1.: Steam and electric era.

522. Andrews, David. *The high country; railroading and me.* Kingsburg, CA: A & A Pub., 1990. 152 p.

523. Andrews, Thomas. *The life of railway axles.* New York, London : Spon & Chamberlain, 1895. 16 p.

524. Angevine, Robert G. *The railroad and the state: war, business, and politics in the United States to 1861* / 1999. 245 l. (Thesis, Ph.D., Duke University)

525. _____. *. The railroad and the state: war, politics, and technology in nineteenth-century America.* Stanford, CA: Stanford University Press, 2004. 351 p.

526. Angier, Jerry. *Bangor and Aroostook railroad in color.* Scotch Plains, NJ: Morning Sun Books, 2004. 127 p.

527. _____. *Bangor and Aroostook: the Maine railroad.* Littleton, ME: Flying Yankee Enterprises, 1986. 272 p.

528. Angus Sinclair (Firm) *Twentieth century locomotives, treating on the designing, construction, repairing and operating of railway machinery.* New York, N.Y., Railway and Locomotive Engineering, 1904. 670 p.

529. Ann Arbor Railroad Company. *Ann Arbor railroad and steamship lines.* Cincinnati, OH: Spencer & Craig Printing Works, 1923. 14 columns.

529a. _____. *Commodity flow matrix/* Lansing; Michigan Department of Transportation, 1975. 12, 60 p. (Mathematical models; forecasting.)

530. _____. *General operating and safety rules: Marine Department employees, Frankfort, Michigan.* Ann Arbor, MI: Ann Arbor Railroad System, 1979. 11 p.

531. _____. *Lumber routes: routes applicable on lumber originating in northern California, Oregon, Washington, Idaho and Montana via Ann Arbor gateways ... /* Dearborn, MI: The Company, 1900s. 14, 16 [i.e. 23] l.

532. _____. *Rules and instructions of the Transportation Department.* S.l., The Company, 1920s. 97 p.

533. _____. *Safety rules: a guide to safe living: maintenance of equipment employees.* Ann Arbor, MI: Ann Arbor Railroad Company, 1979. 42 p.

533a. *Annotated bibliography of Alaska Railroad and related timber bridges/* prepared for Alaska Railroad Corporation; historical consultant, McGinley, Kaslow & Associates LLP, 2008. 29 p.

534. *An annotated bibliography of commuter/regional rail /* Sacramento : California Department of Transportation, Division of Transportation Planning, 1981. 186 p.

534a. *Annotated bibliography of railroad land grants, the Northern Pacific Railroad and its corporate descendants.* Compiled by George Draffan. Spokane, WA: Inland Empire Public Lands Council, 1995. 97 p.

534b. *Annotated bibliography on timber corporations derived from the Northern Pacific Railroad land grant: Weyerhaeuser, Boise Cascade, Potlatch, and Plum Creek.* Compiled by |George Draffan. Spokane, WA: Inland Empire Public Lands Council, 1995. 83 p.

535. *Annual rail carlot shipments of California fruits and vegetables, 1920-1949.* Sacramento, CA: California Bureau of Market News, 1950. 6 l.

536. *Annual report of block signals, automatic train control, and use of train orders; instruction and definitions.* Washington: U.S.G.P.O., 1929-   Annual.

537. *Annual report of Chief Inspector, Bureau of Locomotive Inspection to Interstate Commerce Commission.* Washington: U.S. G.P.O., 1912-1932. Annual.

538. *Annual report of the American Railway Master Mechanics' Association.* S.l., s.n. 1869-1880. 13 v.

539. *Annual report of the Railroad Retirement Board.* Washington, DC: U.S. G.P.O., 1937-   . Annual. http://www.rrb.gov/pdf/opa/AnnualRprt/Annual Report.pdf

540. *Annual report on the statistics of railways in the United States, for the year ended December 31 ...* / Washington, D.C., U.S.G.P.O., 1887-1953. (> *Annual report on transport statistics in the United States for the year ended ...*)

541. *Annual report on transport statistics in the United States for the year ended ...* Washington, D.C.: Interstate Commerce Commission, 1954-1994. Annual. 41 v. (< *Annual report on the statistics of railways in the United States; > Statistics of class I freight railroads in the United States for the year ended ....*)

542. *An anthology of respect : the Pullman porters national historic registry of African-American railroad employees* / Chicago : Hughes Peterson Pub., 2009. 416, 3 p.

543. Anthony, J. T. *Fundamentals of combustion and air supply.* / 3d ed. New York: American Arch Company, 1919. 32 p. (*Bulletin, no. 3.*)

544. _____. *The locomotive heat balance* / New York: American Arch Company, 1920. 32 p. (*Bulletin. no. 5.*)

545. _____. *The mechanism of combustion* / New York: American Arch Company, 1918. 24 p. (*Bulletin no. 2.*)

546. _____. *Radiant heat and fire box design.* Buffalo, NY: Central Railway Club, 1918. 20 p.

547. _____. *The Security arch and locomotive performance* / New York, American Arch Company, 1919. 22 p. (*Bulletin, no. 4.*)

548. Antonetti, Marc A. *The Railway Labor Act: 2009 cumulative supplement (current through 2008).* 2d ed. Arlington, VA: BNA Books, 2009.

549. Antush, Richard M. *The elementary theory of railroad traffic diversion.* 1982. 265 l. (Thesis, Ph.D., Princeton University.) Freight.

550. *Appeal to the California delegation in Congress upon the Goat Island grant to the Central Pacific R.R. Co. with accompanying military and scientific reports, correspondence of Mayor Alvord, veto by Governor Booth of Terminal R.R. bill, etc.*

San Francisco : Alta California Printing House, 1872. 59 p.

551. Appel, Walter A. *Alco official color photography.* Scotch Plains, NJ: Morning Sun Books, 1998. 128 p.

552. _____ *Trackside along the B & O 1957-1958 with Edward P. Griffith.* Scotch Plains, NJ: Morning Sun Books, 2000. 128 p.

553. Applegate, Howard L. and Lyall D Squair. *Delaware, Lackawanna and Western Railroad Company: a register of the corporate records of the Lackawanna Division of the Erie-Lackawanna Railroad Company in the Syracuse University Library.* Syracuse, NY: Manuscript Collections, Syracuse University Library, 1964. 32 l. (*Manuscript register series, register no. 6*)

554. *Appleton's 1865 railroad route maps.* Special reprint ed. Phoenix, AZ: Key Collectors International, 1985. 116 p.

554a. Appleyard, John. *An overview of Pensacola's great lumbering era.* S.l., Bodree Printing Co., 2006.

555. *Applications of electricity to railways. Bibliography of periodical articles appearing in a select list of periodicals covering the period July 1937 to June 1938.* Edmund Arthur Freeman and Douglas Rae Stephenson, compilers. Washington, D.C., Association of American Railroads, Bureau of Railway Economics, 1938. 3 p., 42 l.

556. _____. *Bibliography of periodical articles appearing in a select list of periodicals covering the calendar years 1942-1945.* Edmund Arthur Freeman and Douglas Rae Stephenson, compilers. Washington, D.C., Association of American Railroads, Bureau of Railway Economics, 1946. 87 p.

557. _____. *Bibliography of periodical articles appearing in a select list of periodicals covering the calendar year 1951.* Edmund Arthur Freeman, compiler. Washington, D.C., Association of American Railroads, Bureau of Railway Economics, 1951. 43 p.

558. Arbuckle, J. W. *Cowan Pusher District and Tunnel: the CPD&T, a railroad within a railroad.* Winchester, TN: Herald-Chronicle, 1994. 109 p.

559. _____, and others. *The Mountain Goat: tales of men, locomotives, coal trains, mountain grades, and a lot of memories are woven into a story of the Tracy City branch line of the Nashville, Chattanooga & St. Louis; the Louisville & Nashville; and finally, the CSX Railways.* Johnson City, TN: Overmountain Press, 1992. 123 p.

560. Arcara, Roger. *Elevated and subway cars of the Interborough Rapid Transit Company and its predecessors, 1876-1938.* New York, Arcara, 1973. 23 l.

561. _____. *Westchester's forgotten railway, 1912-1937; the story of a short-lived short line which was at once America's finest railway and its poorest: the New York, Westchester & Boston Railway.* Rev. and expanded ed. New York, NY: Quadrant Press,

1972. 136 p.

562. _____. *When the Westchester was new: a supplement to Westchester's forgotten railway*. S.l., Electric Railroader's Association, 1964. 1 v. (various pagings) (New York, Westchester & Boston Railway.)

563. Archer Automatic Car Coupling Co., *The Archer automatic car coupler*. Saratoga Springs, NY: The Company, 1883. 2 p.

564. Archer, Eric H., ed. *Streamlined steam; a pictorial review of stream styled steam locomotives of thirty-six United State and Canadian railroads*. New York, NY: Quadrant Press, 1973. 54 p. (*Quadrant press review, 1*)

565. Archer, Robert F. *The history of the Lehigh Valley Railroad: "the route of the Black Diamond"*. Berkeley, CA: Howell-North Books, 1977. 371 p. (Reprint: Forest Park, IL: Heimburger House, 1977. 371 p.)

566. Archer, William R. *The Virginian Railway/* Charleston, SC: Arcadia, 2007. 127 p.

567. Architectural and Transportation Barriers Compliance Board. *Intercity rail cars & systems: technical assistance manual*. Washington, D.C.: Architectural & Transportation Barriers Compliance Board, 1992. 34 p.

568. *AREMA bridge inspection handbook*. Lanham, MD: American Railway Engineering and Maintenance of Way Association, 2008. 299 p.

569. Arendt, Morton. *Electric lighting of trains: instruction paper*. Chicago, Ill., American School of Correspondence, 1920. 93 p.

570. *The arguments for and against train-crew legislation*. Washington, DC: Bureau of Railway Economics, 1915. 44 p. (*Bureau of Railway Economics consecutive no. 73; Miscellaneous series no 18.*)

570a. Arizona. Department of Transportation. *Arizona state rail plan*. Phoenix: Arizona Department of Transportation, 2011. 14 p.

571. Armbruster, Frank E., Basil J. Candela. *Research analysis of factors affecting transportation of coal by rail and slurry pipeline: final report*. Croton-on-Hudson, NY: Hudson Institute, 1976. 2 v. (*HI-2409-RR*)

572. Armbruster, Kurt E. *Orphan road: the railroad comes to Seattle, 1853-1911*. Pullman, WA: Washington State University Press, 1999. 271 p.

573. _____. *Whistle down the valley: 100 years of Green River railroading*. Seattle, WA: Northwest Railway and Locomotive Preservation Association, 1991. 80 p.

574. Armitage, Merle *Homage to the Santa Fe*. Yucca Valley, CA: Manzanita Press, 1973. 141 p.

575. _____. *The railroads of America; with more than 400 photos.* Boston, Duell, Sloan and Pierce-Little, Brown, 1952. 319 p.

576. _____, Edwin Cole, P.G. Napolitano. *Operations Santa Fe; Atchison, Topeka & Santa Fe railway system.* New York, N.Y., Duell, Sloan & Pearce, 1948. 263 p.

577. Armitstead, Paul Thompson. *Abandoned short-line railroads of Texas, 1892-1956.* Austin, TX: 1957. 174 l. Thesis, M.A., University of Texas.

578. Armour Research Foundation (U.S.). *Railroad freight car hot boxes: final report* / Chicago : Illinois Institute of Technology, 1954. 2 v. Armour Research Foundation for Association of American Railroads.

579. Armstrong, A.B. *Railway systems in Arkansas.* 1923. 25 l. (Thesis, M.A., University of Arkansas, Fayetteville.)

580. Armstrong, A. H. *The electrification of the Puget Sound lines of the Chicago, Milwaukee & St. Paul railway.* Schenectady, N.Y., General Electric Company, 1915. 8 p.

580a. _____. *The future of our railways.* Schenectady, NY: General Electric Co., 1920. 22 p.

580b. _____. *The last stand of the reciprocating steam engine* / Schenectady, NY: General Electric Co., 1920. 16 p.

581. Armstrong, Donald. *A study of the Boston, Hartford & Erie Railroad Company.* 1935. 1 v. (Thesis, A.B., Honors, Harvard University.)

582. Armstrong, George Buchanan. *The beginnings of the true railway mail service: and the work of George B. Armstrong in founding it.* Chicago, Ill., Lakeside Press, 1906. 85 p.

583. Armstrong, George W. *Locomotive auxiliary power mediums.* New York, American Society of Mechanical Engineers, 1929. 10 p.

584. Armstrong, Jack. *Railfan's guide to New England.* Adams, MA: J. Armstrong, 1987. 73 p.

585. Armstrong, William Patrick. *Fred Harvey, creator of western hospitality.* Bellemont, AZ: Canyonlands Publications, 2000. 30 p.

586. Arnesen, Eric. *Brotherhoods of color: black railroad workers and the struggle for equality.* Cambridge, MA: Harvard University Press, 2001. 332 p.

587. Arnett, William Frances. *Some problems arising out of the conflict between the Brotherhood of Railroad Trainmen and the Switchmen's Union of North America.*

1950. 1 v. (Thesis, M.A., Iowa.)

588. Arnold, Bess. *Union Pacific: crossing Sherman Hill and other railroad stories.* David City, NE: South Platte Press, 1999. 1 v.

589. _____. *Union Pacific: saving a Big Boy and other railroad stories.* David City, NE: South Platte Press, 2004. 56 p.

590. _____, James L Ehernberger. *Union Pacific depot: an elegant legacy to Cheyenne.* Cheyenne, WY: Challenger Press, 2001. 48 p.

591. Arnold, Bion Joseph. *Report on the re-arrangement and development of the steam railroad terminals of the city of Chicago.* Chicago, Ill., 1913. 248 p.

592. Arnold, Ian. *Locomotive, trolley, and rail car builders; an all-time directory.* Los Angeles, CA: Trans-Anglo Books, 1965. 64 p.

593. Arnold, J.M. *Alcohol, paints, varnishes, and lacquers.* Washington, DC: Association of American Railroads, 1946. 1 v. (various pagings) (Railroad Committee for the Study of Transportation)

593a. _____. *Rubber.* Washington, DC: Association of American Railroads, 1946. 119 l. (Group 9. Subcommittee for Economic Study.)

594. *Around the station: the town and the train: focus of a New England town's growth.* Leah Lipton, guest curator. Framingham, Mass., Danforth Museum, 1978. 49 p.

594a. *Around the world with Davenports.* Davenport, Iowa: Davenport Locomotive and Manufacturing Corporation, 1931-?

595. *The Arrow: the Norfolk and Western Historical Society magazine.* S.l., Norfolk & Western Historical Society, 1985-   Bimonthly.

596. *Art deco and the Cincinnati Union Terminal; an exhibition organized by the Art History Department, University of Cincinnati, in cooperation with the Contemporary Arts Center, January 11 to February 10, 1973.* Cincinnati, OH: Contemporary Arts Center, 1973. 48 p.

596a. Arthur, Chester Alan. *Message of the President of the United States, transmitting a communication from the Secretary of the Interior, in reference to the applications of the Chicago, Texas, and Mexican Central, and the Saint Louis and San Francisco Railway Companies, for a right of way across the lands of the Choctaw Nation, in the Indian Territory.* Washington, DC: G.P.O., 1881. 22 p. (Ex. doc; 47th Congress, 1st session, no. 15.

597. Arthur D. Little, Inc., United States. Federal Railroad Administration. *Economic impact of freight car shortages/* Washington, DC: Department of Transportation, Federal Railroad Administration, 1971. 117 p. (FRA/RP-71/1)

598. _____, United States Railway Association. *Factors affecting railroad electrification as applied to CONRAIL: for the United States Railway Association/* Cambridge, MA: Arthur D. Little, Inc., 1975. 108 l.

599. Arthur Koppel (Firm). *Narrow gauge railway materials.* New York, Arthur Koppel, 1901. 104 p.

600. Arthur, Robert Stuart. *Design of a reinforced concrete coaling station.* 1908. 20 l. (Thesis, B.S., University of Illinois.)

601. Artman, L. P. *Florida Keys overseas railroad: history, pictures, construction.* Key West, FL: Florida Keys Printing & Publishing, 19--? 35 p.

602. Asay, Jeff S. *Track and time: an operational history of the Western Pacific Railroad through timetables and maps.* Portola, CA: Feather River Rail Society, 2006. 159 p.
602a. _____. *Union Pacific in the Los Angeles Basin.* Berkeley and Wilton CA: Signature Press, 2012. 496 p.

603. _____ *Union Pacific Northwest: the Oregon-Washington Railroad & Navigation Company: a history.* Edmonds, WA: Pacific Fast Mail, 1991. 335 p.

604. _____ *Western Pacific timetables and operations: a history and compendium.* Crete, NE: J-B Pub. Co., 1983. 110, 81 p.

605. Ascher, John P. *When the Maine Central Railroad went to sea: train boats and boat trains.* Farragut, TN: M.J.A., Inc., 1993. 213 p.

606. *Ashcroft's railway directory for ...: containing an official list of the officers and directors of the rail-roads in the United States and Canadas, together with their financial condition and amount of rolling stock; compiled from official reports by John Ashcroft.* New York NY: J. Ashcroft, 1862?- .

607. Ashe, Sydney Whitmore. *Electric railways, theoretically and practically treated.* New York, NY: Van Nostrand, 1905-1907. 2 v.

607a. Ashiabor, Senanu, Wenbin Wei. *Advancing high-speed rail policy in the United States* / San Jose: Mineta Transportation Institute, College of Business, San José State University, 2012. 72 p.

608. Ashley, W.J., Sir, and George Mortimer Pullman. *The railroad strike of 1894; the statements of the Pullman Company and the report of the Commission, together with an analysis of the issues.* Cambridge, Mass., Church Social Union, 1895. 15, 46, liv p.

609. Ashman, Robert and Charles Milmine. *The Central New England Railroad: boyhood memories of the C.N.E.* Salisbury, CT: Salisbury Association, 1972. 54 p.

610. Ashton Valve Company. *Ashton pop safety and relief valves: pressure and vacuum gauges, locomotive and power plant specialties.* Boston, Mass., The Company, 1924. 176 p.

611. *ASME Rail Transportation Spring Conference proceedings.* New York, NY: American Society of Mechanical Engineers, 1984-1986. Annual. 3 v. (< American Society of Mechanical Engineers. Rail Transportation Division. *Rail transportation proceedings.*)

612. *ASME technical papers.* New York, NY: ASME, 1990-   .

613. Assad, A. *Supply modeling of rail networks: toward a routing/makeup model/* Cambridge, MA: Operations Research Center, Massachusetts Institute of Technology, 1977. 1 v. (Unpaged.)

614. Assad, Arjang Ali. *Modelling rail freight management.* Cambridge, MA: 1978. 293 l.(Thesis, Ph.D., Massachusetts Institute of Technology.)

615. Assarabowksi, Richard J. *Freight car utilization and railroad reliability : an assigned fleet model : final report.* Washington, DC : Freight car Research-Demonstration program, 1978. 170 p. (AAR report, no. CTS 78-1.) CTS: Massachusetts Institute of Technology, Center for Transportation Studies.

616. _____. *High speed rail transportation, New York City to Albany: final report to the New York State Assembly Scientific Staff.* Troy, NY: School of Engineering, Rensselaer Polytechnic Institute, 1974. 48, 31 l.

617. *Assistant train dispatcher.* Syosset, NY: National Learning Corporation, 1995. 1 v. (various pagings)

618. Associated Railroad of Pennsylvania and New Jersey. Executive Committee. *Report of the Executive Committee of Associated Railroad of Pennsylvania and New Jersey : on the campaign to repeal the full crew laws of those states and substitute therefore commission authority over the manning of trains,* Philadelphia. Philadelphia : s.n., 1915. 61 p.

618a. *Association news of the Association of Maintenance of Way and Miscellaneous Foremen, Mechanics and Helpers—The Santa Fe Railway system.* Topeka, KS: The Association, 1925-   . Monthly.

619. Association of American Railroads. *All for one and one for all! More about the railroads' public relations campaign.* S.l., Association of American Railroads, 1936? 8 p.

620. _____. *American railroads and the war.* Washington, D.C., Association of American Railroads, 1943. 76 p.

621. _____. *Car ferries; a list of references, October 1925.* Washington, D.C., AAR,

1925. 24 l.

621a. _____. *Catechism on the standard code.* New York : AAR, 1938. 144 p.

622. _____. *A chronology of American railroads: including mileage by states and by years.* Washington, DC: AAR, 1947-

623. _____. *Coal slurry pipelines: a cost we can't afford: who will benefit? who will be hurt?* Washington, DC: Association of American Railroads, 1970s. 16 p.

624. _____ *Consolidation of railroads.* Washington, D.C., Association of American Railroads, 1945. 93 p.

625. _____. *A chronology of American railroads: including mileage by states and by years.* Washington, D.C., Association of American Railroads, 1951. 9 p.

626. _____. *Directory of freight station accounting codes: including all of North America.* Washington, DC: Economics and Finance Department, Agent Tariff FSAC 6000, Association of American Railroads, 1991-

626a. _____. *Directory of hazardous materials shipping descriptions.* Washington, DC : Association of American railroads, 1994-   . Annual. (Tariff STCC).

627. _____. *The day of two noons.* Washington, D.C. :Association of American Railroads, 1966. 10 p. (Railroad time standards)

628. _____. *Effect of spring travel, height of center of gravity and speed on freight car clearance requirements on curved and tangent track/* Chicago, IL: Association of American Railroads, Research Department, 1963. 25 l.

629. _____. *Field manual of the interchange rules.* Washington, DC: Association of American Railroads, 2010. 807 p. (loose-leaf) Association of American Railroads. Safety and Operations. Rules and Standards.

630. _____. *Final report on failures and performance of main crank pins on steam locomotives.* Chicago, Office of Mechanical Engineer, 1940. 59 l. (Association of American Railroads. Operations and Maintenance Department, Mechanical Division.)

631. _____. *Findings of research program on air conditioning of railroad passenger cars.* Chicago : Association of American Railroads, 1937. ? 1, xix-xxviii p. (Reprinted from Engineering report on air conditioning of railroad passenger cars.)

632. _____. *Freight cars in the United States: railroads and private car lines, 1939-1966.* Washington, D.C.: Association of American Railroads, Economics and Finance Dept., 1967. 15 p.

633. _____. *Growth of railway mileage in the United States, by states and years.* Washington, DC: AAR, 1945. 2 l.

634. _____. *Henry Varnum Poor, 1812-1905; list of his writings and maps ... biographical sketches.* Rev. ed. Washington, D.C., Association of American Railroads, 1941. 12 l.

635. _____ *Highlights of American railroad history.* Washington, D.C., The Association, 1955. 27 p.

636. _____. *Highway-rail grade crossing accident investigation manual.* Washington, DC: Association of American Railroads, 1983. 1 v.

637. _____. *Index of the Interstate Commerce Commission valuation reports.* Compiled by Herbert W. Rice. Washington: Association of American Railroads, 1951. 128 l.

638. _____. *List of maps showing railway lines. Revised.* Washington, D.C., Association of American Railroads, 1955. 24 p.

639. _____. *A list of references to literature relating to the Union Pacific system /* Washington, DC: Association of American Railroads, Bureau of Railway Economics, 1922. 299, 23 p.

640. _____. *List of streamlined passenger trains in the United States, with bibliography.* Washington, DC: Association of American Railroads, 1940. 12 l.

641. _____. *Manual of standards and recommended practices.* Washington, D.C., The Association, 1938. 1 v. (loose-leaf)

642. _____ *Manual of standards and recommended practices.* Washington, DC: Association of American Railroads, 1980- . Issued in parts. Some parts issued in revised editions.

643. _____. *Named passenger trains operated on the railroads of the United States, Canada, and Mexico.* Washington, D.C., Association of American Railroads, 1946. 22 p.

644. _____. *Names and nicknames of freight trains operated on the railroads of the United States and Canada.* Washington, D.C., Association of American Railroads, 1949. 21 p. (Also: 1952. 24 p.)

645. _____. *The Norfolk and Western Railway: a list of references.* Washington, D.C., Bureau of Railway Economics, 1924. 52 ;.

646. _____. *Oil burning locomotives in North America: memorandum listing some reports and articles on the subject.* Washington, D.C., Association of American Railroads, 1943. 7 l.

647. _____. *Passenger traffic study.* Washington, D.C., Association of American Railroads, 1946. 405 l.

648. _____. *Program of the railroads to provide adequate transportation service in ...* New York, NY: The Association, 1923-1924. Annual.

649. _____. *Progress report on failures of driving axles and crank pins on steam locomotives.* Chicago, Association of American Railroads, 1938. 78 p. (Association of American Railroads. Operations and Maintenance Department, Mechanical Division.)

650. _____. *Railroad facts.* Washington, DC: Association of American Railroads, 2009. 84 p.

651. _____. *Railroad histories and sources of historical information about railroads.* Washington, DC: Association of American Railroads, 1940. 16 l.

652. _____. *Railroad passenger stations and freight yards in the United States.* Washington, DC: Association of American Railroads, 1950. 10 p.

653. _____. *Railroad transportation: a statistical record, 1911-1949.* Washington, DC: Association of American Railroads, Bureau of Railway Economics, 1950. 44 p.

654. _____. *Railroad transportation: a statistical record, 1921-1961.* Washington, DC: Association of American Railroads, Bureau of Railway Economics, 1962. 39 p.

655. _____. *The railway mail story.* Washington, D.C.: Association of American Railroads, 1957. 19 p.

656. _____. *Railway mileage by states, December 31, 1934.* Washington, Association of American Railroads, 1935. 62 p.(Further issues appeared in 1952, 1959, 1968, 1974, 1977, and 1982.)

657. _____. *Railroads in this century; a summary of the facts and figures with charts.* Washington, D.C., Association of American Railroads, 1947. 24 p.

658. _____. *Railroads in two wars ...* Washington, D.C., The Association, 1943. 40 p.

659. _____. *Report of Committee on locomotive construction.* Chicago, Association of American Railroads, 1929. 67 p.

660. _____ *Report of Committee on locomotive construction.* Chicago, Association of American Railroads, 1935. 69 p.

661. _____. *Report on road performance of air-conditioned Pullman sleeping cars.* Chicago, IL: Association of American Railroads, 1937. 148 l. (*Report no. 63.*)

662. _____. *The standard code of the Association of American railroads: operating rules, block signal rules, interlocking rules.* New York, The Association, 1940. 854 p.

663. _____. *Supplement to the manual: including drawings for standard cars and trucks adopted by the Association as standard and recommended practice.* Chicago, Ill., Association of American Railroads, 1938. 311 p.

664. _____. *Supplement to the manual, including drawings for standard cars adopted by the Association as standard and recommended practice.* Chicago, Ill., Association of American Railroads, 1940-? 2 v.

665. _____. *Supplemental track tests of twelve locomotives.* Chicago, Ill., Office of Mechanical Engineer, 1944. 131 p.

666. _____. *Specifications for tank cars: standard: effective November 1, 1974.* Washington, D.C., Association of American Railroads, 1974. 209 p.

666a. _____. *Standard transportation commodity code : hazardous materials or substances of hazardous wastes.* Washington, DC : Association of American Railroads, 1991-   . Annual.

667. _____. *Railroad photos: old and new.* Washington, D.C., Association of American Railroads, 1950? 15 p.

668. _____. *The saga of the vanishing caboose.* Washington, D.C., Association of American Railroads, 1986. 6 p.

669. _____. *Transportation conditions and national transportation policy.* Washington: Association of American Railroads, 1950. 1 v.

670. _____. *2006 office manual of the AAR interchange rules.* Washington, DC: Association of American Railroads, 2006. 1 v (various pagings)

671. _____. Bureau of Explosives. *Field guide to tank car identification.* Washington, DC: Association of American Railroads, 1992. 48 p.

672. _____. Car Service Division. *Annual bulletin.* Washington, DC: s.n., 1900s-? Annual. 1923-1926, issued by: American Railway Association.

673. _____. _____. *Cars of revenue freight loaded.* Washington, DC : The Division, 1927-1969. Annual.

674. _____. _____. *Report of the Car Service Division for the year.../* New York, NY: The Division, 1924-   Irregular.(< American Railway Association. *Program of the railroads to provide adequate transportation service in ...*)

675. _____. _____. *Revenue freight loaded and received from connections.* [Statement CS 54-A] Washington, DC: American Railway Association, Car Service Division, Association of American Railroads, Car Service Division, 1921-1970. Weekly. (> Association of American Railroad. Car Service Division. *Revenue freight loaded by commodities and total received from connections* [1970-1979].)

676. _____. _____. *Semi-monthly revenue freight car summary – class I railroads.* Washington, DC: Issues following Sept. 1, 1971 available only to railroad; no longer distributed to libraries. (< Association of American Railroads. Car Service Division. *Home cars on home roads, class one roads, Jan. 1, 1963.* Other title: Freight cars owned and leased; system cars at home, total cars on line – railroad and private. May 1, 1921- Sept. 1934 issued by American Railway Association. Car Service Division.

677. _____. _____. *Semi-monthly statement of revenue freight cars awaiting repairs; class one roads.* Washington, DC: Association of American Railroads, Car Service Division; American Railway Association, Car Service Division, 1900s-? Semimonthly. 1924-1928 by American Railway Association.

678. _____. _____. *Study of empty car mileage.* Washington, AAR, 1924-

679. _____. _____. *Summary of car surplusages and car shortages.* Washington, DC: Association of American Railroads, 1900s-? Weekly.

680. _____. Committee on Motor Transportation. *Survey on trailer-on-flat-car service and operation compiled by Committee on Motor Transportation.* Washington, DC : Association of American Railroads, Freight State Section, 1957. 37 l.

681. _____. Communication and Signal Division. Association of American Railroads, Communication and Signal Division. *Annual meeting*: [proceedings] Washington, DC: The Division, 1970s-1986. Annual. (< Association of American Railroads. Communications and Signal Section. Meeting. *Proceedings of the ... annual meeting*; > Association of American Railroads. Communication and Signal Division. *Technical Conference*; Association of American Railroads. Communication and Signal Division. *Annual Technical Conference*: [proceedings].)

682. _____. _____. *Annual technical conference; proceedings.* Washington, DC: Communication and Signal Division, A.A.R., 1987-1997. (< Association of American Railroads. Communication and Signal Division. *Meeting. Annual meeting*; > American Railway Engineering and Maintenance-of-Way Association. Communications & Signals Functional Group. Technical conference. *Proceedings.*)

683. _____. Communication and Signal Section. *American railway signaling principles and practices.* New York, The Association, 1927-1961. 26 v. "Chapters issued before 1935 by the American Railway Association, Signal Section; 1935-60, by the Signal Section of the Association of American Railroads; 1961- by the Association's Communication and Signal Section."

684. _____. _____. *Proceedings of the ... annual meeting/* Chicago: The Section, 1961-1970s. Annual (< Association of American Railroads. Communications Section. *Proceedings of the ... (annual) session of the Association of American Railroads, Communications Section*; > Association of American Railroads. Communication and Signal Division. *Meeting. Annual meeting. [proceedings]*)

685. _____. _____. *Signal manual of recommended practice: manual parts and drawings.* Washington, DC: The Association, 1912. 2 v. Loose-leaf for annual update.

686. _____. _____. *Typical circuits representing practice for railway signaling/* Washington, DC: The Section, 1971. 1 v. (loose-leaf)

687. _____. Communications Section. *Proceedings.* S.l., The Association, 1919-1960. No meetings held in 1931, 1933, 1938, 1942-45, and 1954. Merged with Association of American Railroads. Signal Section. *Proceedings*, to form: Association of American Railroads. Communication and Signal Section. *Meeting. Proceedings of the ... annual meeting.* (< *Proceedings of the Association of Railway Telegraph Superintendents*)

688. _____. _____. *Proceedings of the ... session of the Association of American Railroads, Communications Section.* S.l., The Sections, 1946-1960. Annual. (< Association of American Railroads. Telegraph and Telephone Section. *Proceedings of the session of the Association of American Railroads ... Telegraph and Telephone Section*; > Association of American Railroads. Signal Section. *Proceedings.* Association of American Railroads. Communications and Signal Section. *Meeting; proceedings of the ... annual meeting. Communication and Signal Section, Association of American Railroads.*)

689. _____. _____. *Railroad radio general and operating rules/* S.l., s.n., 1940? 4 p.

690. _____. Division IV-Engineering. Electrical Section. *Proceedings ... annual meeting.* Washington, DC: Association of American Railroads, 1934-1949. Annual (irregular). Division name varies: 1946-1949, Engineering Division. (< American Railway Association. Division IV-Engineering. Electrical Section. *Proceedings ... annual meeting*; > Association of American Railroads. Mechanical Division. Electrical Section. Engineering Division. Electrical Section. *Proceedings of the joint annual meetings of the Association of American Railroads.*)

691. _____. Division of Equipment Research. *Engineering report on air conditioning of railroad passenger cars* / Chicago, Association of American Railroads, 1937. 316 p.

692. _____. *Findings of research program on air conditioning of railroad passenger cars.* Chicago : Association of American Railroads, 1937? 1, xix-xxviii p.

693. _____. _____. *Report on performance and cost of operation of 1937 Waukesha mechanical compression equipment for air conditioning railroad passenger cars, May 1, 1937.* Chicago : Association of American Railroads, 1937. 26 l.

694. _____. _____. *Summary report on air conditioning of railroad passenger cars* / Chicago : Association of American Railroad, 1936. 68 l.

695. _____. Economics and Finance Department. *Freight cars in the United States: railroads and private car lines, 1939-1966.* Washington, DC: Association of American Railroads, Economics and Finance Department, 1967. 15 p.

696. _____. _____. *Profiles of 475 local and regional railroads*. Washington, DC: Association of American Railroads, 1986. 98 p.

697. _____. Electrical Section. *Proceedings of the annual meeting*. Washington, DC: Association of American Railroads, 1952-1965. (< *Proceedings of the annual meeting of the Electrical Section, Mechanical Division. Proceedings of the annual meeting of the Electrical Section, Engineering Division.*)

698. _____. _____. *Manual of standard and recommended practice*. Chicago: Association of American Railroads, Electrical Section, 1953.. 1 v. (loose-leaf)

699. _____. _____. *Manual of standard and recommended practices*. Chicago : Association of American Railroad, 1958-   . 18 pts. in 2 portfolios.

700. _____. Engineering Division. Mechanical Division. *Electrical manual of standards and recommended practices*. Chicago: American Association of Railroads, 1972. 1 v. (loose-leaf)

701. _____. _____. _____.. *Passenger ride comfort on curved track* / Chicago: Association of American Railroads, Engineering Division, Mechanical Division, 1954. 51, 45 l.

702. _____. Freight Claim and Damage Prevention Division. National Freight Loss and Damage Prevention Committee. *Minimum loading standards for hardboard products in closed cars and protection of equipment* / Chicago: Freight Loading & Container Section, 1974. 30 p. (*General Information series, no. 549.*)

703. _____. Freight Claim Division. *Proceedings of annual session*. Chicago [etc] Association of American Railroads, 1935-1975. Annual. (< American Railway Association. Freight Claim Division. *Proceedings of annual session*; > Association of Am. Railroads. Freight Claim and Damage Prevention Division. *Proceedings.*)

704. _____. Joint Committee on Relation Between Track and Equipment. *Effect of flat wheels on track and equipment* / Chicago : Association of American Railroads, Central Research Laboratory, 1951. 57, 24 l.

705. _____. Mechanical Division. *A.A.R. manual of counterbalance for reciprocating steam locomotives* / Chicago: Association of American Railroads, Mechanical Division, 1945. 29 p..

706. _____. _____. *A.A.R. specifications for the construction of new passenger equipment cars*. S.l., Office of Mechanical Engineers, 1939. 11, 3 l.

707. _____. _____. *Axle research : fatigue tests of freight car axles 5 ½ x 10 inch journals. Second progress report*. Chicago : Association of American Railroads, 1955. 56 l. (*Report no. MR-242.*)

708. _____. _____. *Circular – Association of American Railroads, Mechanical Division.* Chicago: Association of American Railroads, Operations and Maintenance Department, Mechanical Division, 1900s-?

709. _____. _____. *Code of rules governing the condition of, and repairs to, freight and passenger cars for the interchange of traffic.* Chicago: The Association, 1964. 402 p.

710. _____. _____. *Field manual of the interchange rules.* Washington, DC: Association of American Railroads, 1981. 460 p. Annual. Cover title: Field manual of the A.A.R. interchange rules, 1981.

711. _____. _____. *Field manual of the interchange rules.* Washington, DC: Association of American Railroads, 2006. 645 p.

711a. _____. _____. *Final report on failures and performance of main crank pins on steam locomotives.* Chicago: Association of American Railroads, 1940. 59 l.

712. _____. _____. *First progress report of the committee on hot box alarm devices.* Chicago ? AAR, Office of Mechanical Engineer, 1947. 64 l. (*AAR. Mechanical Division. Report no. MR-187.*)

713. _____. _____. *General rules governing the loading of commodities on open top cars and trailers.* Washington, DC: Association of American Railroads, 1960-   .

714. _____. _____. *Inspection and maintenance manual for coupler, coupler parts, and coupler operating mechanism on freight equipment cars : recommended practice adopted 1953.* Chicago : Association of American Railroads, 1954. 29 p.

715. _____. _____. *Investigation of stresses in axle journal area* / Chicago : AAR Central Research Laboratory, Mechanical Research Office, 1951. 6 l. Committee on Axle and Crank Pin Research.

716 _____. _____. *Locomotive counterbalance.* New York? Office of Mechanical Engineer, 1939. 40 l. (A.A.R. Operations and Maintenance Department, Mechanical Division. Counterbalance Committee..)

717. _____. _____. *Lubrication manual.* Washington, DC: Association of American Railroads, 1900s-   .

718. _____. _____. *Maintenance of air brake and air signal equipment on locomotives and cars : adopted as standard 1925 : revised 1933 and 1934.* Washington, DC: Association of American Railroads, 1935. 32 p.

719. _____. _____. *Manual of standard and recommended practices* / Chicago: Association of American Railroads, 1971. 1 v. (loose-leaf)

720. _____. _____. *Manual of standard and recommended practices* / Washington, DC: Association of American Railroads, 1975. 3 v.

721. _____. _____. *Manual of standard and recommended practices*. Washington, DC: The Association, 1976-1981. 15 v.

722. _____. _____. *Manual of standard and recommended practices*. Washington, DC: Association of American Railroads, 1980-

723. _____. _____. *Passenger car axle tests : 5-1/2" x 10" journals : first progress report, May 1, 1938*. Washington, DC: Association of American Railroads, Office of Mechanical Engineer, 1938. 123 l.

724. _____. _____. *Proceedings*. New York and Chicago, The Association, 1919- (No meeting held 1942-1945.) Continues Proceedings of the Master Car Builders' Association and Proceedings of the American Railway Master Mechanics' Association.

725. _____. _____. *Proceedings: annual business meeting, Mechanical Division*. Washington, DC: Association of American Railroads, Operations and Maintenance Department, 1972-   . Annual. (< Association of American Railroads. Mechanical Division. *Proceedings: annual meeting, Mechanical Division*.)

726. _____. _____. *Proceedings of the session of the Association of American Railroads, Operations and Maintenance Department, Mechanical Division*. Chicago: Association of American Railroads, 1935-1989. Title varies lightly.

727. _____. _____. *Progress report on failures of driving axles and crank pins on steam locomotives* / Chicago: Association of American Railroads, 1938. 78 p.

728. _____. _____. *Roller bearing manual*. Washington, DC: Association of American Railroads, 1900s-   . Kept up-to-date between editions by additional and replacement pages. 6th ed. 1977. 112 p.

729. _____. _____. *Rules governing the loading of commodities on open top cars: special supplement containing rules governing the loading of mechanized and motorized Army equipment, also, major caliber guns for the United States Army and Navy, on open top equipment*. S.l., s.n., 1941. 47 p. 18 p. of plates

730. _____. _____. *Rules governing the loading of commodities on open top cars* / Chicago: Association of American Railroads, 1960. 518 p.

731. _____. _____. *Rules governing the loading of Department of Defense materiel on open top cars : adopted by the Master Car Builders' Association as recommended practice, 1896, advanced to standard 1908* / Chicago, Association of American Railroads, 1953. 40 p.

732. _____. _____. *Rules governing the loading of lumber, logs, stone, etc. and loading and carrying structural materials, plates, rails, girders, etc.: adopted by the former Master Car Builders' Association as recommended practice, 1896, advanced to standard 1908, revised 1930, effective January 1, 1931*. New York, The Association,

1930. 365 p.

733. _____. _____. *Rules governing the loading of pipe on open top cars: adopted by the former Master Car Builders' Association as recommended practice, 1896, advanced to standard 1908/* Chicago, IL: Association of American Railroads, 1951. 106 p.

734. _____. _____. *Rules governing the loading of road grading, road making, and farm equipment on open top cars: adopted by the former Master Car Builders' Association as recommended practice, 1896, advanced to standard 1908, effective March 1, 1952.* Chicago, IL: Association of American Railroads, 1952. 154 p.

735. _____. _____. *Specifications for design, fabrication and construction of freight cars* / Chicago: Association of American Railroads, 1966. 263 l.

736. _____. _____. *Specifications for tanks cars, standard.* Washington, DC: Association of American Railroads, 1900s- .(Manual of standards and recommended practices; Section C.)

737. _____. _____. *Specifications for tank cars; standard.* Chicago: Association of American Railroads, Mechanical Division, 1959. 1 v.

738. _____. _____. *Supplement to the manual, including drawings for standard cars adopted by the Association as standard and recommended practice.* Chicago: Association of American Railroads, 1940 . 2 v. Loose-leaf for updating.

739. _____. _____. *Supplement to the manual: including drawings for standard cars and trucks adopted by the Association as standard and recommended practice* / Chicago: The Association, 1938. 311 p.

740. _____. _____. *Wheel and axle manual : recommended practice : adopted, 1928, revised, 1935* / Washington, DC: The Association, 1935. 245 p.

741. _____. _____. *Wheel and axle manual; standards, recommended practices and general information.* 8th ed. Chicago: Association of American Railroads, 1963.

742. _____. _____. *Wheel and axle manual: mandatory standards, recommended practices and general information* / 12th ed. Washington, DC: The Association, 1978. 191 p.

743. _____. _____. Electrical Section. *Proceedings of the session …* Washington, DC: The Association, 1937- . Annual. "The Electrical Section as founded in 1937 as a successor to the Association of Railway Engineers." (< Association of Railway Electrical Engineers. *Proceedings.)*

744. _____. _____. Engineering Division. *Counterbalance tests of locomotives for high speed service.* Chicago: Association of American Railroads, 1944. 313 p. Operations and Maintenance Dept.: Mechanical and Engineering Divisions.

745. _____. _____. Electrical Section. *Proceedings of the joint annual meetings of the Association of American Railroads Mechanical Division, Electrical Section, Engineering Division*. Chicago: Association of American Railroads, 1950-   . Annual. (< Association of American Railroads. Division IV-Engineering. Electrical Section. *Proceedings ... annual meeting*.)

746. _____. _____. _____. *Proceedings of the session*/ Washington, DC: Association of American Railroads, 1937-   . Annual (irregular). (< Association of Railway Electrical Engineers. *Proceedings*.)

747. _____. _____. Equipment Painting Section. *Proceedings*. Chicago, IL: Association of American Railroads, 1800s-1930.

748. _____. Medical and Surgical Section. *Proceedings of the ... annual meeting of the Association of American Railroads Medical and Surgical Section held at ...* New York, NY: Eastern Print. Co., 1935-1900s. Annual. (< American Railway Association. Medical and Surgical Section. Meeting. *Proceedings of the ... Annual meeting of the American Railway Association Medical and Surgical Section held at ...*)

749. _____. Office of Mechanical Engineer. *First progress report of the committee on hot box alarm devices*. Chicago : Association of American Railroads, Office of Mechanical Engineer, 1947. 64 l. (*Association of American Railroads. Mechanical Division. Report no. MR-187.*)

750. _____. Operating-Transportation Division. *Code of rules: governing the interchange of, repairs to, and settlement for, trailers and containers used in trailer-on-flat-car (TOFC) service for the interchange of traffic*/ Chicago, IL: Association of American Railroads, 1966. 44 p.

750a. _____. _____. *Pocket list* (of all railroads freight cars in per diem groups 3-4-5-6-7-8-9). Washington, DC, Association of American Railroads, 1962-   .

751. _____. _____. *The standard code of block signal and interlocking rules, adopted November, 1938*. New York, NY: Association of American Railroads, 1938. 40 p.

752. _____. _____.Freight Station Section. *Proceedings of the session of the Association of American Railroads Operations and Maintenance Department, Operating-Transportation Division, Freight Station Section held at ...* Chicago, IL: Association of American Railroads, Freight Station Section, 1937-1960. Annual. (<American Railway Association. Freight Station Section. *Proceedings of the ... session of the American Railway Association, Division I—Operating, Freight Station Section, held at ...*)

753. _____. Operations and Maintenance Department. Division V: Mechanical Division. *Car owners manual for the inspection and maintenance of double stack container cars*. Rev. ed. Washington, DC: Association of American Railroads, 1995. 1 v.

(various pagings)

754. _____ _____. _____. *List of truck side frames and bolsters approved for use on freight cars in Interchange Service.* Chicago: Association of American Railroads, Operations & Maintenance Department, Mechanical Division, 1950. 22 p. Joint Subcommittee on Side Frames and Bolsters.

755. _____. _____. _____. *List of truck side frames and bolsters approved for use on freight cars in interchange service.* Chicago : Association of American Railroads, operations & Maintenance Department, Mechanical Division, 1952. 47 p. (in various pagings) Joint Subcommittee on Side Frames and Bolsters.

756. _____. _____. _____. *Manual of standards and recommended practices/* Washington, DC: The Association, 1960-   . Section A to Section N.

757. _____. _____. _____. *Manual of standards and recommended practices: section B: couplers and freight car draft components.* Washington, DC: The Association, 1977. 312 p.

758. _____. _____. _____. *Proceedings of the session of the Association of American Railroads, Operations and Maintenance Department, Division V, Mechanical.* Washington, DC: The Association, 1935-1989. Irregular. (< *Proceedings of the session of the American Railway Association, Division V, Mechanical.)*

759. _____. _____. _____. *Specifications for tank cars.* Revised 1940. Effective August 1, 1941. Chicago: Association of American Railroads, 1941. 191 p.

760. _____. _____. _____. *Specifications for tank cars: standard, AAR—effective January 1, 1967; AAR—rev. effective January 1, 1968; I.C.C.—effective as part 79.* Chicago: Association of American Railroads, 1968. 1 v. (various pagings)

761. _____. _____. _____. *Specifications for tank cars: standard: effective November 1, 1974.* Washington, DC: Association of American Railroads, 1974. 385 p.

762. _____. Public Relations Department. Photograph Service. *Railroad photos : old and new /* Washington, DC : Association of American Railroads, 1950s. 15 p. A catalog of 150 photos available for professional purposes. The Department has a collection of 15,000 glossy prints in 8x10-inch size.

763. _____. Purchases and Materials Management Division. *Proceedings.* Chicago, The Association, 1967-1968 2 v.   Annual. 2 v. (No more published.)

764. _____. Purchases and Stores Division.. *Proceedings of the ... annual meeting of the Association of American Railroads, Operations and Maintenance Division, Purchases and Stories Division, held at ...* New York: American Railroad Association, 1935-1966.   Annual. (< American Railway Association. Purchases and Stores Division. *Proceedings of the annual meeting of the American Railway Association. Division VI, Purchases and Stores.*; > Association of American Railroads. Purchases

and Materials Management Division. *Proceedings.*)

764a. _____ Railroad Committee for the Study of Transportation. Subcommittee
on Consolidations. *Consolidation of railroads.* Washington, DC: Association
of American Railroads, 1945. 93 p.

765. _____. _____. Subcommittee on Engineering and Mechanical Research.
The economics of weight reduction in freight carrying railroad cars. Washington, DC:
1946. 1 v. (various pagings).

766. _____. Research and Test Department. *Progress in railroad research :
the program of the Research and Test Department, Association of American Railroads,
1978-1981.* Washington, DC : Association of American Railroads, 1982. 128 p.
Includes list of publications of the Research and Test Dept.

767. _____. Safety and Operations. Association of American Railroads. Rules
and Standards. *Field manual of the interchange rules .* Washington, DC: Association
of American Railroads, 2010. 807 p.

768. _____. *2010 office manual of the A.A.R. interchange rules.* Washington, DC:
Association of American Railroads, 2010. 1 v. (loose-leaf) "Adopted and published
by the Association of American Railroads Safety and Operations Rules and Standards."
"Effective January 1, 2010."

768a. _____. Research Center. *Methods of fireproofing wood bridges and trestles /*
Chicago : Association of American Railroads Research Center, 1961. 14 l.

769. _____. Safety Section. *Proceedings of the ... annual meeting of the Safety Section
...* New York NY: Eastern Printing Corp., 1900s-   Annual.

770. _____. Signal Section. *American railway signaling principles and practices.*
Rev. ed. New York, The Association, 1941. 26 v.

771. _____. _____.*American railway signaling principles and practices.
Chapter 1, History and development of railway signaling.* Chicago, Ill., Signal Section,
A.A.R.,1953. 167 p.

772. _____. _____. *Electric signaling for electric railways.* Bethlehem, PA:
The Association, 1910. 65 p

773. _____. _____. *Manual of recommended practice.* New York, N.Y.,
The Association, 1942- 2 v. in 3

774. _____. Telegraph and Telephone Section. *Proceedings of the session
of the Association of American Railroads ... Telegraph and Telephone Section.* S.l.,
The Association, 1935-1900s. Annual. (< American Railway Association. Telegraph
and Telephone Section. *Proceedings of the session of the American Railway Association.
Telegraph and Telephone Section.*)

775. _____. Transportation Section. *Proceedings of the session of the Association of American Railroads, Operations and Maintenance Department, Division II: Transportation.* Chicago, IL: Association of American Railroads, 1919? -1936. Annual. 11 v. (< American Railway Association. Transportation Division. Proceedings ... of Division II-Transportation. > Continued in part: Association of American Railroads. Operating Transportation Division. *Proceedings of the session.*)

776. Association of Car Lighting Engineers. *Transcript of proceedings of the Association of Car Lighting Engineers.* Chicago: Association of Car Lighting Engineers, 1908. Annual. 1 v. (> Association of Railway Electrical Engineers. *Proceedings of the Association of Railway Electrical Engineers.*)

777. Association of Manufacturers of Chilled Car Wheels, Chicago. *Cast iron chilled car wheels; mode of manufacture and relations they bear to economy in railway practice.* New York : Association of Manufacturers of Chilled car Wheels, 1895. 37 p.

778. _____. *The chilled car wheel /* Chicago : Association of Manufacturers of Chilled Car Wheels, 1952. 63 p.

779. _____. *Chilled tread wheels for industrial and standard railway service: tables, data, designs and specifications also specifications for axles, axle mounting pressures, shop practice.* S.l., s.n., 1928. 104 p.

780. _____. *A general survey of the mechanics of the chilled iron car wheel.* Pittsburgh, Pa., The Association, 1917. 72 p.

781. _____. *Recommended practice for manufacturing chilled car wheels.* Chicago : Association of Manufacturers of Chilled Car Wheels, 1937. 5 v. (1st ed.)

782. _____. *Recommended standards for chilled iron wheels; freight car and engine tender equipment ...* Chicago, Ill., Association of Manufacturers of Chilled Car Wheels, 1917. 42 p.

783. _____. *Theory and practice of mounting railroad wheels on axles.* Chicago : s.n., 1934. 6, 65 p.

784. Association of North American Railroad Superintendents. *Proceedings.* Boston, Rand Avery Supply Co., 1800s-1889. (> *Am. Society of Railroad Superintendents. Proceedings.*)

785. Association of Railway Electrical Engineers. *Proceedings of the Association of Railway Electrical Engineers.* Chicago: The Association, 1908-1934. 22 v.

786. Association of Railway Executives (U.S.) *Statements made by the Association of Railway Executives, Conference Committee on managers, before the United States Railroad Labor Board, Chicago, Illinois ... in connection with the objections of the railroads to the various so-called national agreements, also objections to rules*

and working conditions requested by various organizations [May 17 to June 4, 1920] New York? 1921. 5 v. in 1.

787. Association of Railway Superintendents of Bridges and Buildings (U.S.) *American railway bridges and buildings. Official reports, Association Railway Superintendents Bridges and Buildings.* Compiled and edited by Walter G. Berg. Chicago, IL; Roadmaster, Foreman, 1898. 706 p. "A summary of seven year's reports of the Association of Railway Superintendents of Bridges and Buildings."

788. _____. *Bridge floors: report of the committee to the president and members of the Association of Railway Superintendents of Bridges and Buildings.* S.l., s.n., 1897. 20 p.

789._____. *Proceedings of the ... annual convention of the Association of Railway Superintendents of Bridges and Buildings.* S.l., s.n., 1895-1918. Annual. (< American International Association of Railway Superintendents of Bridges and Buildings. Meeting. *Proceedings of the ... annual meeting of the Am. Int. Assoc. of Railway Superintendents of Bridges and Buildings*; >Proceedings of the ... annual convention of the American Railway Bridge and Building Association.)

790. Association of Railway Telegraph Superintendents. *Proceedings of the annual meeting, Association of Railway Telegraph Superintendents.* Milwaukee, Association of Railway Telegraph Superintendents, 1858-1919. Annual. No meeting held in 1917.

791. _____. Eastern Division. *Proceedings of the annual meeting held at ...* Chicago, Stromber, Allen & Co., Printers, 1800s-1918. Annual. 36th (1918). (> American Railroad Association. Telegraph and Telephone Division. *Proceedings of the session of the American Railroad Association, Telegraph and Telephone Division held at ...*)

792. *At centennial: the modern Southern Pacific, symbol of the new golden empire.* Chicago: Watson Publications, 1955. 70 p.

793. Atack, Jeremy, Fred Bateman, Michael Harris, IL: Robert A. Margo. *Did railroads induce or follow economic growth? Urbanization and population growth in the American Midwest, 1850-60/* Cambridge, MA: National Bureau of Economic Research, 2009. 31 p. Internet file: http://www.nber.org/papers/w14640 (*NBER working paper series, no. 14640.*)

794. _____, Michael R. Haines, Robert A. Margo. *Railroads and the rise of the factory: evidence for the United States, 1850-70.* Cambridge, MA: National Bureau of Economic Research, 2008. 33 p. (*NBER working paper series, no. 14410.*)

795. Atchison, Topeka, and Santa Fe Railway Company. *All aboard Santa Fe: "service all the way" on all Santa Fe tourist sleepers.* Chicago, Santa Fe System Lines, 1935. 10 p.

796. _____. *Barstow, Santa Fe's modern oasis.* S.l., Atchison, Topeka and Santa Fe Railroad, 1980. 14 p.

797. _____. *The California Limited : fifteenth season, 1909-1910* / [Eastern edition]. Chicago : Atchison, Topeka and Santa Fe railway Company, 1909. 24 p.

798. _____. *The California Limited, seventeenth season, 1911-1912*. Chicago ? s.n., Henry O. Shepard Co., 1911. 24 p.

799. _____. *Fred Harvey meal service*. Chicago ? Atchison, Topeka and Santa Fe Railway Co ? , 1924. 48 columns.

800. _____. *Fred Harvey meal service*. Chicago ? : Atchinson, Topeka and Santa Fe Railway Co. ? 1931. 56 columns

801. _____. *Fred Harvey meals : Santa Fe*. Chicago : Poole bros., 1909. 17, 16 p. 16 x 9 cm.

802. _____. *Free sleeping cars for emigrants carried on express trains, and leaving Kansas City both morning and evening on the Santa Fé route*. Topeka, KS: Atchison, Topeka, and Santa Fe Railroad Company, General Passenger and Ticket Department, 1884. 3 p. (*General Passenger and Ticket Department, Circular number 14-1.*)

803. _____. *Freight car classification system*. S.l., Santa Fe Modelers Organization, 1900s 47 l.

804. _____. *In a tourist sleeper*. Chicago, Santa Fe Route, Passenger Department, 1901. 12 l.

805. _____. *Instructions for care and operation of motor cars*. Chicago? The Railway, Operating Department, 1929. 20 p. (*Form 2506 standard.*)

806. _____. *Instructions for enginemen governing the care, maintenance and economical operation of the locomotive*. Chicago? Atchison, Topeka and Santa Fe Railway Company, 1942, c1921. 2d rev. ed.

807. _____. *Instructions for maintaining and operating air brake apparatus. Rev. ed.* Topeka, KS: Santa Fe, 1926. 203 p. 5 folded leaves of plates

808. _____. *The Railroad.* Chicago, Atchison, Topeka and Santa Fe Railway Co., 1941. 38 p.

809. _____. *Record breaking run of the Scott Special*. Chicago, Atchison, Topeka and Santa Fe Railway Company, 1917. 16 p.

810. _____. *Rules and regulations for the maintenance of way and structures, effective November 1, 1911*. Chicago, Ill., The Railway, 1911. 113 p.

811. _____. *Rules: maintenance of way and structures*. Santa Fe, N.M.: The Company, 1952.

812. _____. *Santa Fe car and locomotive plans for model railroads.* S.l., Atchison, Topeka and Santa Fe Railway System, 1948. 1 v.

813. _____. *Santa Fe car and locomotive plans for model railroaders.* S.l., Atchison, Topeka and Santa Fe Railway System, 1953. 42 p.

814. _____. *Santa Fe operating manual: diesel-electric locomotives.* S.l., Atchison, Topeka and Santa Fe Railway Company, 1953. 1 v.

814a. _____. *Santa Fe route: official list of officers, stations, agents, station numbers, etc. of The Atchison, Topeka & Santa Fe Railway, Santa Fe Pacific Railroad, Southern California Railway, Gulf, Colorado & Santa Fe Railway, the Southern Kansas Railway of Texas, Rio Grande & El Paso Railroad.* Chicago : The Atchison, Topeka & Santa Fe Railway Company, 1899. 112 p.

815. _____. *Stresses set up in wheel flanges when striking switch point protector.* Topeka, Kan, Santa Fe System, 1952. 18 l.

816. _____. *Super Chief cook book of famous Fred Harvey recipes.* Chicago? Santa Fe Railway and Fred Harvey Co., 1955? 21 p.

817. _____. *Standing rainbows: railroad promotion of art. The West and its native people: a special exhibition of paintings from the collection of the Atchison, Topeka & Santa Fe Railway.* Topeka, Kansas State Historical Society, 1981. 36 p.

818. _____. *System standards.* Dallas, Kachina Press, 1978. 3 v.

819. _____. *Working for victory on the Santa Fe: a series of wartime advertisements.* Chicago, Santa Fe System Lines, 1944. 24 p.

820. _____, Fred Harvey Hotels. *Fred Harvey meals: Santa Fe.* Chicago, Ill., Poole Bros., 1909. 17, 16 p.

821. *Atchison, Topeka and Santa Fe Railway.* Sacramento, CA: Vanishing Vistas, 1984-? v. 1-

822. Athearn, Robert G. *The Denver and Rio Grande Western Railroad: rebel of the Rockies.* Lincoln, University of Nebraska Press, 1977, c1962. 395 p.

823. _____. *Railroad to a far off country: the Utah and Northern.* s.l., s.n., 1968. 23 p.

824. _____. *Rebel of the Rockies; a history of the Denver and Rio Grande Western Railroad.* New Haven, T: Yale University Press, 1962. 395 p.

825. _____. *Union Pacific country.* Chicago, Rand McNally, 1971. 480 p.

826. A.T. Kearney, Inc., United States Railway Association. *Analysis of railroad*

operated ferry and lighterage operations: United States Railway Association, planning project no. 6. Chicago, Kerney, 1975. 220 l

827. Atkin, Claude F. *Mining, smelting, and railroading in Tooele County.* Tooele, Utah, Tooele County Historical Society, 1986. 135 p.

828. Atkins, Pres T. *When the trains came to Norton, Wise County, in old Virginia in 1891.* Norton, VA: Norton Press, 1994, c1941. 90 p.

829. Atkinson, Pearce. *Steam heating of railroad cars.* 1889. (Thesis, M.E., Lehigh University.)

830. Atkinson, Philip. *The electric transformation of power and its application by the electric motor, including electric railway construction.* New York, D. Van Nostrand Co., 1893. 244 p.

831. Atkinson, Scott E., Joe Kerkvliet. *The Stagger Act and competition in rail transport of Wyoming coal: a report to the University of Wyoming Industrial Fund.* Laramie, WY: University of Wyoming, 1985. 48 p.

832. Atlanta & West Point Railroad Company. *Rules for the government of the operating department: effective January 1st, 1911.* Montgomery, Ala, Brown Printing Co., 1910. 265 p.

833. Atlantic and Great Western Railway Company. *Annual report of the president, directors, and secretary of the Atlantic and Great Western Rail Road Company with the report of the chief engineer.* Cleveland : Sanford & Hayward Steam Printing Est., 1853-   . Annual.

834. _____. *The Atlantic and Great Western Railway; connections, stations, distances, map, &c., &c. : the great through route between East and West, Northwest, South, and Southwest* / New York : H.H. Simmons, 1866. 28 p. Cover title : The oil region of America.

835. _____. *Instructions for the running of trains, etc. on the Atlantic & Great Western Railway Company : takes effect Dec. 18, 1865.* Meadville, Penn., Republican Printing House, 1865. 140 p.

836. _____. *Instructions for the running of trains, etc. on the Atlantic & Great Western rail road. To take effect May 1, 1877.* Cleveland : s.n., 1877. 1 v.

837. _____. *Lease of Atlantic & Great Western to Erie Railway Company, dated 7th day of December, 1868.* New York : General offices of the Company, 1868. 6 p.

838. _____. *Protocol for reorganization of the Atlantic & Great Western Railway Co.* Cleveland ? : s.n., 1860s. 4 f.

839. _____. *Report of the condition of the Atlantic & Great Western Railroad :*

its branches and leased lines and an inventory of the property and effects of every description which have come into the possession or under the control of J.H. Devereux, receiver. Cleveland : Sanford & Co., Printers, 1875. 680, 4 p.

840. _____. *Report of the receiver of the Atlantic & Great Western Railway for the year ending March 31st ...* / New York : Chas. F. Ketcham, 1800s- Annual.

841. Atlantic Coast Line Railroad Company. *The Atlantic Coast Line Railroad: industrial and shippers guide.* Wilmington, N.C., The Traffic Department, 1915. 447 p.

841a._____. [Company records] 298.5 linear ft. Location: University of North Carolina, Chapel Hill,.

842. _____. *A decade of progress, 1939-1948; a four hundred million dollar accomplishment.* Wilmington, N.C., The Company, 1949. 39 p.

843. _____. *Florida and the Coast Line.* Wilmington, N.C., Atlantic Coast Line Railroad Company, 1928. 32 p.

844. _____. *Official directory of industries.* Wilmington, N.C., Atlantic Coast Line Railroad Co., 1940. 264 p.

845. _____. *Official industrial and shippers' directory.* S.l., Traffic Department, 1928. 367 p.

846. _____. *Rules for the government of the Transportation Department of the Atlantic Coast Line in effect January 1st, 1890. 2d* ed. Wilmington, N.C., Jackson & Bell, 1890. 102, 38 p.

847. _____. *Rules for the government of the Transportation Department of the Atlantic Coast Line Railroad Company, in effect October 1st, 1897.*

848. _____. *The story of the Atlantic Coast Line, 1830-1930.* Wilmington, N.C., Atlantic Coast Line Railroad Co., 1933. 20 p.

849. _____. *Vestibuled train to Florida*/ New York, NY: Press of Fleming, Brewster & Alley, 1887. 2 p.

850. Atlantic Terra Cotta Company, New York, NY. *Cincinnati Union Terminal.* New York, N.Y., The Company, 1933. 8 p.

851. Atlas Car & Manufacturing Company. *Atlas electric locomotives: Catalog 1245.* Cleveland, Ohio, Atlas Car & Mfg. Co., 1932. 96 p.

852. *Atlas of properties on Main Line, Pennsylvania Railroad from Overbrook to Paoli : from actual surveys and official plans* / Philadelphia : Bromley, 1926. 1 v.

853. Atterbury, William Wallace. *Employe representation on the Pennsylvania Railroad* /

Chicago : s.n., 1934. 17 p. W.W. Atterbury, president; address before the Chicago General Office Association, May 1, 1934.

854. _____. *Getting back to normal: some real results achieved in six month's efforts to restore this railroad's former standards of freight and passenger service.* Philadephia: Pennsylvania Railroad, 1920. 4 p.

854a. _____. *Let railroad men run the railroad business* / Philadelphia: Pennsylvania Railroad, 1921. 14 p.

854b. _____. *The public can secure the railroad service it wants* / Philadelphia: Pennsylvania Railroad, 1922. 17 p.

855. _____. *The railroad labor situation.* Philadelphia, s.n., 1920. 32 p.

855a. _____. *Railroad rates and railroad wages* / Philadelphia: Pennsylvania Railroad, 1921. 3 p.

856. _____. *Testimony of W.W. Atterbury, vice-resident in charge of operations of the Pennsylvania Railroad Company, before the United States Commission on Industrial Relations, Washington, D.C., May 15, 1915.* S.l., s.n., 1915. 66 p.

857. _____. *Testimony of W.W. Atterbury, vice-president in charge of operations of the Pennsylvania System, before the United States Railroad Labor Board, Chicago, Illinois, march 21, 22, 23, 1921.* Philadelphia? s.n., 1921. 211 p.

858. _____, Myron Morris. Stearns. *The railroads enter aviation*/ Philadelphia, PA: Publicity Bureau, Pennsylvania Railroad, 1929. 30 p. (*Pennsylvania Railroad information, v. 1, no. 2.*)

859. Atwell, Debby and Gene N. Perreault. *I've been working on the railroad: train stories from the people of St. Francis.* Saint Francis, ME: St. Francis Historical Society, 2001. 119 p.

859a. Atwood, Levi Patten. *Railroad and street grade crossing elimination : some problems to be considered by public regulating bodies* / 1916. 45 l. (Thesis, C.E., University of Illinois.)

860. Auchincloss, W.S. *The practical application of the slide and link motion to stationary, portable, locomotive, and marine engines.* New York, D. van Nostrand, 1869. 170 p. (13th ed., 1897.)

861. Austin, Ed. *Spokane, Portland & Seattle color guide to freight and passenger equipment.* Scotch Plains, NJ: Morning Sun Books, 1998. 127 p.

862. _____. *Spokane, Portland & Seattle: diesels of the Northwest's own railroad.* Kutztown, PA: Morning Sun Books, 2007. 128 p.

863. _____. *Union Pacific diesels in color.* Scotch Plains, NJ: Morning Sun Books, 2003- v. 1-

864. _____, Tom Dill. *The Southern Pacific in Oregon.* Edmonds, WA: Pacific Fast Mail, 1987. 319 p.

865. _____, _____. *The Southern Pacific in Oregon pictorial.* Edmonds, WA: Pacific Fast Mail, 1993. 255 p.

866. _____, _____, John R. Signor, Mike Pearsall. *S.P.&S :the Spokane, Portland, & Seattle Railway.* Edmonds, WA: Pacific Fast Mail, 1996. 376 p.

867. Austin, Edwin. *Single-phase electric railways.* New York, Van Nostrand, 1915. 303 p.

868. Austin, Joe. *Taking the train: how graffiti art became an urban crisis in New York City.* New York, NY: Columbia University Press, 2001. 356 p.

869. Austin-Western Company. *Western dump cars in all sizes – for all types of railroad service.* Aurora, IL: The Company, 1948. 2 p.

870. *Automatic block signal progress on the railroads of the United States for the years 1884-1927.* New York: Henry M. Sperry, 1928. 11 p. "Prepared from date submitted by 169 railroads in answer to Interstate Commerce Commission questionnaire of July 22, 1927."

871. *Automatic car coupler question: extracts from the Master Car Builders' annual report.* Boston, W.S. Best Co., 1892. 16 p. Other title: *Howe's automatic car coupler.*

872. Automatic Car Ventilator Company. *Car ventilation* / New York: Automatic Car Ventilator Co., 1900s. 14 p.

873. *Automatic train control. Bulletins no. 1-9.* Washington, DC: American Railway Association, Committee on Automatic Train Control, 1929-1931. 9 v.

874. *Automatic train control in the United States. Bibliography arranged chronologically.* Washington, D.C., Association of American Railroads, 1930. pp. 160-190. (Reprint: American Railway Assoc. Committee on Automatic Train Control. *Automatic train control. Bulletin, no. 1.*)

875. *Avalanche hazard reduction by Burlington Northern Santa Fe Railway in Glacier National Park and Flathead National Park, Montana: final environmental impact statement.* Flathead and Glacier Counties, MT: National Park Service, Waterton-Glacier International Peace Park, 2007. 91 p. http://www.loc.gov/catdir/toc/fy1001/2007467200.html

876. Avery, Derek. *The complete history of North American railways.* Secaucus, NJ: Wellfleet; London: Brian Todd, 1969. 352 p.

877 Aylmer-Small, Sidney. *Electrical railroading or electricity as applied to railroad transportation.* Chicago, Ill., Drake, 1908. 924 p.

878. _____, Calvin F. Swingle, Paul E. Lowe. *Modern electric railway practice: a complete system of practical instruction in electric transportation.* Chicago, Ill., W.V. Wheat Company, 1909. 4 v.

B

879. Babcock, Michael W. *Economic impacts of railroad abandonment on rural Kansas communities.* Topeka, KS: Kansas Department of Transportation, Division of Planning and Development, Bureau of Transportation Planning, 2003. 151 p.

880. _____. *State short line railroads and the rural economy.* Topeka, KS: Kansas Department of Transportation, 1994. 225 p.

881. _____, Eugene Russell, Robert Earl Burns. *Economic development and transportation impacts of railroad branchline abandonment in south central Kansas.* Topeka, KS: Kansas Department of Transportation, 1992. 1 v.

882. _____, James Sanderson. *The impact of jumbo covered hopper cars on Kansas shortline railroads.* Topeka, KS: Kansas Department. of Transportation, 2004. 84 p.

883. _____, Marvin Prater, Eugene Russell. *Long-term profitability of grain dependent short line railroads in the Midwest.* Topeka, KS: Kansas Department of Transportation, 1997. 142 p.

884. Bach, Ira J., Susan Wolfson, assisted by Charles E. Gregersen; photos by Olga Stefanos. *A guide to Chicago's train stations: present and past.* Athens, OH: Ohio University Press/Swallow Press, 1986. 425 p.

885. Bachelder, Peter Dow. *Steam to the summit: the Green Mountain Railway, Bar Harbor's remarkable cog railroad.* Ellsworth, ME: Breakwater Press, 2005. 162 p.

886. Bachman, J.A. *Improved passenger equipment evaluation program: methodology used in the train review: final report.* Washington, DC: Federal Railroad Administration, Office of Research and Development, 1979. 79 p. (*FRA-ORD-8-13.*)

887. *Background document for railroad noise emissions standards* / Washington, DC: EPA, 1975. 624 p. Office of Noise Abatement and Control.

888. *Background on railroad reliability.* Washington, DC: Association of American Railroads, Research and Test Department; Massachusetts Institute of Technology, Center for Transportation Studies, 1992. 98 p. (*Association of American Railroads, Report no. R-803.*)

889. *Background on transportation; coal and the railroads.* Washington, DC: Association of American Railroads, Office of Information and Public Affairs, 1900s-1984. Annual.

890. Bacon, George Morgan, William Henry Schmidt. *Safety appliances on the railroad approach to the Grand Central Station, New York City.* 1893. 25 l. Joint thesis, C.E., Cornell University.)

890a. Bacon, Harlow. *Design for an interlocking system for the Illinois Central Railroad yards at Champaign, Illinois* / 1893. 83 l. (Thesis, B.S., University of Illinois.)

891. Bacon, John L. *Controlled locomotive operation.* New York, Valve Pilot Corporation, 1938. 11 p.

892. Bacon, Lewis Frank. *A report on the proposed electrification of the Illinois Central shops at Mattoon, Illinois* / 1906. 18 l. (Thesis, B.S., University of Illinois.)

893. Bacus, Horace. *The railway labor problem in the United States and public regulation of hours of service of railroad employees*/ 1936. 2 v. (Thesis, Ph.D., American University.)

894 Bade, Walter A. *Railroads in Sheboygan County: a brief history.* Plymouth, WI: W.A. Bade, 1975. 32 p.

895. Baden, Gale, William Reed, John J. Swearingen. *Application of commercial aircraft accident investigation techniques to a railroad derailment.* Ft. Belvoir Defense Technical Information Center, 1973. 37 p.

896. Baehr, George Bernard. *The attempt at a transportation empire in New England: the New York, New Haven and Hartford Railroad, 1872-1913.* 1969. 572 l. (Thesis, University of Notre Dame.)

897. Baer, Christopher T., Coxey, Paul W. Schopp. *The trail of the Blue Comet: a history of the Jersey Central's New Jersey Southern Division.* Palmyra, NJ: West Jersey Chapter of the National Railway Historical Society, 1994. 488 p.

898. _____, John Dziobko. *The Pennsy in the 1950s: the last great decade.* Altoona, PA: Pennsylvania Railroad Technical & Historical Society, 2006. 128 p.

899. _____, and others. *Canals and railroads of the Mid-Atlantic states, 1800-1860.* Wilmington, Del., Regional Economic History Research Center, Eleutherian Mills-Hagley Foundation, 1981. 51, 29 p.

900. Bagdon, Philip V. *Essential Cass: an overview of Cass Scenic Railroad State Park, Cass, West Virginia. Featuring the photography of John W. Farrell.* Hinton, WV: Dog & Pony Show Productions, 1997. 23 p.

901. _____. *Meadow River Lumber Company: West Virginia's last logging railroad.* Lynchburg, VA: TLC Pub., 2002. 76 p.

902. _____. *Shay logging locomotives at Cass, West Virginia, 1900-60.* Forest, VA: TLC Pub., 2001. 103 p.

903. Bagheri, Morteza. *Risk-based model for effective marshalling of dangerous goods railway cars.* Waterloo, ON: University of Waterloo, 2009. 112 p.

904. Bagley, Will. *Always a cowboy: judge Wilson McCarthy and the rescue of the Denver & Rio Grande Western Railroad*/ Logan, Utah State University Press, 2008. 316 p.

904a. Bagwell, Billy MacArthur. *Optimization theory for railroad management: deterministic models*/ 1974. 391 l. (Thesis, Ph.D., University of Mississippi.)

904a. Bahrs, Robert R. *DL&W milk cars*. Ansonia, CT: Bob's Photo, 2005. (Vol. 3 and 4 of Railway milk cars, by Robert A. Liljestrand, John Nehrich and Robert R. Bahrs. Ansonia, CT: Bob's Photo, 2002-2005. 4 v.

905. Baie, John William. *Two track main: a story of the epic mid-twentieth century change from steam to diesel locomotives on America's railroads and its impact on people of those times.* Philadelphia, PA: Xlibris Corp., 2002. 119 p.

906. Bailey, Edd H. *The century of progress; a heritage of service, Union Pacific, 1869-1969.* New York, Newcomen Society in North America, 1969. 24 p.

907. _____ *A life with the Union Pacific: the autobiography of Edd Bailey.* St. Johnsbury, VT: Saltillo Press, 1989. 150 p.

908. Bailey, Sherry Keith. *Fifty years after, 1923-1973: a study of the development of railroad architecture in Columbus, Georgia.* Auburn, GA: Auburn University, 1973. 145 l.

909. Bailey, William Francis. *The story of the first trans-continental railroad; its projectors, construction and history.* Fair Oaks, CA: W.F. Bailey, 1906. 164 p.

910. Bain, David Haward. *Empire express: building the first transcontinental railroad.* New York, Viking, 1999. 797 p.

911. _____. *The old iron road: an epic of rails, roads, and the urge to go West.* New York, Viking, 2004. 434 p.

912. Bain, Robert K. *Tracing the Denver, South Park & Pacific: a detailed, mile-by-mile guide.* West Lafayette, IN: R.K. Bain, 1994. 46 p.

913. Bain, William E. *Frisco folks; stories and pictures of the great steam days of the Frisco Road (St. Louis-San Francisco Railway Company).* Denver, Sage Books, 1961. 272 p.

914. Baird, D. G. *A narrative of some of the events connected with the building by the Lehigh Valley Railroad Company of its railroad line to, and its terminal at New York harbor.* Philadelphia, PA: Lehigh Valley Railroad Company, Secretary's Office, 1915. 68 p.

915. Baird, Robert Ligget. *Review of hinged arch over 30th Street, Phila.* / 1892. 56 l.

5 leaves of folded plates. (Thesis, C.E., Lehigh University.)

916. Baker, Abner D. *The Baker locomotive valve gear.* New York, Pilliod Company, 1925. 70 p.

917. Baker, Bob. *North Western motive power.* Hazel Crest, IL: C&NW Historical Society, 1987. 70 p.

918. _____. *The railfan's guide to Wisconsin and Michigan's Upper Peninsula.* Butler, WI: Wisconsin Chapter, NRHS, 1986. 72 p.

919. _____. *Wisconsin rails: a nostalgic view of railroading in the Badger State (and Michigan's Upper Peninsula).* Butler, WI: Wisconsin Chapter, NRHS, 1987. 155 p.

920. _____. *Wisconsin rails II: a passage of time: growing up with railroading in the Badger State.* Racine, WI: Wisconsin Chapter, NRHS, 1994. 140 p.

921. _____, Joe Piersen, Paul Swanson. *The run of the GE's: the final North Western motive power roster.* Elmhurst, IL: C&NWHS, 1995. 91 p.

922. Baker, Cindy L., Mary L. Maniery. *First in the West: Sacramento Valley Railroad.* Folsom, CA: City of Folsom, Department of Public Works, 1996. 1 v.

923. Baker, Don. *The Montana Railroad: alias, the Jawbone: also known as the Chicago, Milwaukee, St. Paul and Puget Sound, and the Chicago, Milwaukee, St. Paul and Pacific Railroad, and finally as the Milwaukee Road.* Boulder, CO: Pruett, 1990. 96 p.

924. Baker, George Henry. *Locomotive fuel economy.* New York, Railway Educational Association, 1909. 1 v.

925. _____. *A manual of instruction for the economical management of locomotives, for locomotive engineers and firemen.* Chicago, Rand, McNally & Company, 1895. 116 p.

926. _____. *Science of firing locomotives.* New York, Railway Educational Association, 1919. 2 v.

927. _____. *Science of locomotive management.* New York, Railway Educational Association, 1919. 2 v.

928. _____. *Standard signals and rules.* New York, Railway Educational Association, 1913. 61 p.

929. Baker, George P. *The formation of the New England railroad systems; a study of railroad combination in the nineteenth century.* Cambridge, Harvard University Press, 1949, c1937. 283 p. (Reprint: Greenwood Press, 1968)

930. _____. *Railroad combination in New England before 1900.* 1934. (Thesis, Ph.D.,

Harvard University.)

931. Baker, J.B., W.M. Henderson. *Henderson hydraulic brake for railroad cars. : J.B. Baker, president. W.M. Henderson, supt. Descriptive pamphlet issued by the Henderson Hydraulic Car Brake Company. Office: Forrest Building, 119 South Fourth St. Philadelphia, Pa.* Philadelphia : Press of Frame printing House, 4-6-8 North Sixth Street, 1875. 11 , 1 p.

932. Baker, J. Newton. *The segregation of white and colored passengers on interstate trains/* New Haven, CT: Press of S. Z. Field, 1910. 8 p.

933. Baker, John W. *Buffalo Central Terminal : collecting and displaying the memories of a city treasure /* 2001. 82 l. (Thesis, M. Arch., State University of New York, Buffalo.)

934. Baker, Laura. *Overview of computer-based models applicable to freight car utilization.* Washington: Federal Railroad Administration, Office of Policy and Program Development, Transportation Systems Center, 1977. 1 v. (*FRA-OPPD-77-12.)*

935. Baker, Q.A., J.O. Stormant. *Alternate fuels in medium-speed diesel engines: off-specification diesel fuels, simulated coal-derived fuel and methanol /* Washington, DC: Federal Railroad Administration, Office of Research and Development, 1981. 143 p. (*FRA/ORD-80/40.)*

936. Baker, Stanley L. *Railroad collectibles; an illustrated value guide.* 4th ed. Paducah, KY: Collector Books, 1999, c1990.

937. _____. *The railroadiana collector's price guide.* New York, Hawthorn Books, 1977. 128 p.

938. _____, Virginia Brainard Kunz. *The collector's book of railroadiana.* 2d ed. Secaucus, NJ: Castle Books, 1976. 240 p.

939. Balach, Robert. *A history of the Duluth, Missabe and Iron Range Railroad.* 1968. 146 l. (Thesis, M.A., University of Minnesota)

940. Balazik, Ronald F. *The impact of U.S. railroad abandonment on domestic mineral industries.* Washington, D.C., U.S. Department of the Interior, Bureau of Mines, 1980. 18 p. (*Bureau of Mines, Information circular, 8834*)

941. Baldridge, Terry L. *Eastern Kentucky Railway Company.* Charleston, SC: Arcadia, 2007. 128 p.

942. *Baldwin.* Philadelphia, Pa., Baldwin Locomotive Works, Corporation, 1944-1951. 7 v. Quarterly.

943. Baldwin, Clarence Truman. *Proposed electrification of the Pittsburgh and Lake Erie Railroad, Pittsburgh-Youngtown Division.* 1912. 92 l. (Thesis, E.E., Princeton University)

944. Baldwin, Henry Furlong, Abbott Lawrence Rotch. *An application of the steam engine indicator to a locomotive.* 1884. 83, 2 l. (Thesis, B.S., Massachusetts Institute of Technology, Department of Mechanical Engineering.)

945. Baldwin, Karl F. *History and methods of air conditioning on the Baltimore and Ohio Railroad* / 1934. Phi Mu Fraternity, University of Maryland, College Park Chapter, records, 1923-1944. 44 l. Photographs, drawings, and other illustration.

946. Baldwin-Lima-Hamilton. *Baldwin operator's manual, no. DP-108 : diesel-electric passenger locomotive..* Philadelphia, PA: Baldwin-Lima-Hamilton, 195-? 1 v.

947. _____. *4500 HP steam turbine electric freight locomotive with dynamic braking; Norfolk and Western Railroad, no. 2300.* Philadelphia, Pa., Baldwin-Lima-Hamilton, 1953. 89 p. (*Operator's manual, no. STE-1.*)

948. _____. *Operator's manual: diesel-electric locomotives. No. AS-102, 1600-HP road switcher.* Philadelphia, Baldwin-Lima-Hamilton, 1952. 40 p.

949. _____. *Operator's manual. No. DF-104, Diesel-electric freight locomotive.* Philadelphia : Baldwin Locomotive Works, 1948. 1 v. (various pagings).

950 _____. *Operator's manual. No. DF-107A, the RF-16 diesel electric freight locomotive with dynamic braking.* Philadelphia, Baldwin-Lima-Hamilton, 1951. 1 v.

951. _____. *The story of Baldwin-Lima-Hamilton.* Philadelphia, PA: Baldwin-Lima-Hamilton, 1951. 34 p.

952. _____. *The story of Standard Steel Works, division of the Baldwin Locomotive Works, Burnham, Penna., 1795-1945.* Philadelphia? Baldwin-Lima-Hamilton Corporation, 1945. 20 p.

953. Baldwin Locomotive Works. *The actual efficiency of a modern locomotive.* Philadelphia, Pa., Burnham, Williams, 1907. 32 p.

954, _____. *Associated lines.* Philadelphia, Pa., Burnham, Williams, 1906. 24 p. (Code word: Recostaras."

955. _____. *The Atchison, Topeka & Santa Fe railway system.* Clifton Heights, PA: Reprinted with permission of the Baldwin-Lima-Hamilton Corp., by H.P. Albrecht, 1962, c1906. 44 p.

956. _____. *Atlantic type locomotives.* Philadelphia, Pa., Baldwin Locomotive Works, 1900. 84 p.

957. _____. *Atlantic type locomotives.* Philadelphia, Pa., The Works, 1907. 67 p.

958. _____. *Balanced compound locomotives.* Philadelphia, Pa., Burnham, Williams,

1905. 30 p.

959.. _____. *Baldwin diesel-electric locomotives. Operator's manual. No. DRS-100, 1500-hp road switcher.* Philadelphia, Baldwin Locomotive Works, 1949. 44 p.

960. _____. *Baldwin diesel-electric switching locomotives.* Philadelphia, Baldwin Locomotive Works, 1943. 1 v.

961. _____. *Baldwin Locomotive Works.* Philadelphia, J. B. Lippincott Co., 1895. 230 p.

962. _____. _____. Philadelphia, Burnham, Williams, 1907. 251 p.

963. _____. _____. Philadelphia, Burnham, Williams, 190-? 492 p.

964. _____. *Baldwin Locomotive Works: Alaska-Yukon-Pacific Exposition, Seattle, Wash., 1909.* 22 p.

965. _____. *The Baldwin Locomotive Works: catalogue of locomotives.* Philadelphia, Pa., Baldwin Locomotive Works, n.d. 108 p. (Code word: Marksystem.)

966. _____. *The Baldwin Locomotive Works: catalogue of locomotives.* Ocean, NJ: Specialty Press, 1972, 1915. 125 p.

967 _____ *Baldwin Locomotive Works exhibit at the International Universal Exposition, Paris, 1900.* Philadelphia, Pa., Burnham, Williams, 1900. 35 p.

968. _____. *Baldwin Locomotive Works: exhibit at the Trans-Mississippi and International Exposition, Omaha, Neb., June to November, 1898.* Philadelphia, Pa., Burnham, Williams, 1898. 12 p.

969. _____. *Baldwin Locomotive Works; illustrated catalogue, details of locomotives and cable code for duplicate parts.* Philadelphia, Pa., Burnham, Williams, 1906. 251 p.

970. _____. *Baldwin Locomotive Works: illustrated catalogue of locomotives.* Philadelphia, Pa., Press of J.B. Lippincott & Co., 1871. 134 p.

971. _____ *Baldwin Locomotive Works: illustrated catalogue of locomotives. Burnham, Parry, Williams & Co., Philadelphia. George Burnham, Charles T. Parry, Edward H. Williams* (and others). 2d ed. Philadelphia, Pa., Burnham, Williams, 1881. 153 p.

972. _____. *Baldwin Locomotive Works: illustrated catalogue of locomotives and detail parts.* Philadelphia, Pa., Burnham, Williams, 1907. 492 p. (Code word: Meddix.)

973. _____. *Baldwin Locomotive Works: illustrated catalogue of narrow-gauge locomotives.* 3d ed. Philadelphia, Pa., J.B. Lippincott, 1885. 64 p.

974. _____. *Baldwin Locomotive Works: illustrated catalogue of* mine *locomotives and pneumatic locomotives.* Philadelphia, Pa., Lippincott, 1885. 36 p.

975 _____. Baldwin Locomotive Works. *Locomotives for mines, manufacturers, narrow-gauge branches, and other special service.* Philadelphia, M. Baird & Company, 1870. 3 p.

976. _____. *The Baldwin Locomotive Works: logging locomotives.* Ocean, NJ: Specialty Press, 1973, 1913. 59 p.

977. _____. *The Baldwin Locomotive Works, Philadelphia, Pa., U.S.A; completion of the forty-thousandth locomotive, 1913.* Philadelphia, Pa., The Works, 1913. 27 p.

978. _____ (Baldwin Locomotive Works records, 1825-1869) 64 linear feet. Location: Historical Society of Pennsylvania.

979. _____. (Baldwin Locomotive Works register of engines.) Six microfilm reels, 35mm. Location: Smithsonian Institution)

980. _____ *Baldwin Locomotive Works: The Pan-American* Exposition, Buffalo, N.Y., 1901. 32 p.

981. _____ *Baldwin-Westinghouse electric locomotives.* Rev. ed. Philadelphia, Pa., Baldwin Locomotive Works; Westinghouse Electric & Manufacturing Co., 1904. 39 p. (*Circular No. B-W 1000.*)

982. _____. *Baldwin-Westinghouse electric locomotives for interurban freight haulage and switching.* Philadelphia, Pa., Baldwin Locomotive Works; East Pittsburgh, Pa., Westinghouse Electric & Manufacturing Company, 1916. 64 p. (*Circular no. 1516-A*)

983. _____. *Baldwin-Westinghouse electric mine locomotives.* Philadelphia, Pa., The Baldwin Locomotive Works; Westinghouse Electric & Manufacturing Company, 1913. 34 p. (*Publication 1525*)

984. _____. *Baldwin-Westinghouse mine and industrial locomotives.* East Pittsburgh, Pa., Baldwin locomotive Works; Westinghouse, 1929. 24 p.

984a. _____. *Baldwin-Westinghouse steam turbine locomotive.* Philadelphia, Pa., Baldwin Locomotive Works, 1944. 12 unnumbered pages. (*Bulletin 222*)

985. _____ *Caprotti poppet valve gear as applied to locomotive engines.* Philadelphia, Pa., Baldwin Locomotive Works, 1928. 37 p.

986. _____. *Catalogue of locomotives: the Baldwin locomotive Works.* Philadelphia, Pa., Edgell Press, 191-? 121 p. (Code word: Mastichis.)

987. _____. *Catalogue of locomotives: Baldwin Locomotive Works.* Philadelphia, Pa., The Edgell Press, 1908. 103 p. (Code word: Markttages.)

988. _____. *Catalogue of locomotives: the Baldwin Locomotive Works.* New York,

Rand McNally, 1910? 125 p. (Code word: Mazieren.)

989 _____. *Completion of the forty-thousandth locomotive, 1913.* Philadelphia, Pa., Baldwin Locomotive Works, 1913. 27 p.

989a. _____. *Compound locomotives and their steam distribution* / Philadelphia, Pa: Baldwin Locomotive Works, 1904. 11 p.

990. _____. *Compressed air locomotives.* Philadelphia, Pa., Burnham, Williams, 1904. 40 p. (Code word: Recolarias.)

991. _____. *Cotton States and International Exposition, Atlanta, Georgia, U.S.A., September 18 to December 31, 1895.* Philadelphia, Pa., Baldwin Locomotive Works, 1895. 20 p.

992. _____. *Description, method of operation, and maintenance of the Vauclain system of compound locomotives.* Philadelphia, Pa., Baldwin Locomotive Works, 1896. 86 p. (Also: 1900: 91 p.)

993. _____. *Details of locomotives and cable code for duplicate parts. Illustrated catalogue.* Philadelphia, 1895. 230 p.

994. _____. *Details of locomotives and cable code for duplicate parts: Illustrated catalogue.* Philadelphia, Pa., Burnham, Williams & Co., 1907. 251 p.

995. _____. *The development of the eight driving wheel locomotive.* Philadelphia, Pa., Baldwin Locomotive Works, 1917. 28p.

996. _____. *Dimensions, weights, and tractive power of narrow-gauge locomotives manufactured by the Baldwin Locomotive Works.* Philadelphia, Pa., Burnham, Parry, Williams, 1872? 46 p. (Also: 1877: 47 p.)

997. _____. *Electric locomotives. Baldwin Locomotive Works.* Philadelphia, Pa., Burnham, Williams & Co.; Westinghouse Electric and Mfg. Co., 1896. 123 p.

998. _____. *Electric locomotives for mine haulage. Baldwin locomotive Works, Philadelphia; Westinghouse Electric and Manufacturing Company, Pittsburg.* New York, Bartlett & Co., 1901. 75 p.

999. [Engineering files. Detail calculations. 1884-1920. Typescripts, blueprints.] 52 v Location: Purdue University.

1000. _____. *Exhibit of locomotives by Burnham, Parry, Williams & Co., Baldwin Locomotive Works, Philadelphia, U.S.A. The World's Industrial and Cotton Centennial Exposition, New Orleans, 1884-1885.* Philadelphia, Pa., J.B. Lippincott, 1884. 41 p.

1001. _____ *Exhibit of locomotives by the Baldwin Locomotive Works, Burnham, Williams & Co., proprietors, Philadelphia, Pa., U.S.A. World's Columbian Exposition,*

Chicago, Illinois, May-October, 1893. Philadelphia, Pa., 1893. 78 p.

1002. _____. *Exhibit by the Baldwin Locomotive Works and the Standard Steel Works, Philadelphia, Pa., U.S.A.* Philadelphia? Pa., s.n. 1907. 34 p.

1003. _____. *The fifty-thousandth locomotive.* Philadelphia, Pa., Baldwin Locomotive Works, 1918. 25 p. (Code word: Redormir.)

1004. _____. *Forged and rolled steel wheels : manufactured by the Standard Steel Works.* Philadelphia : Burnham, Williams, 1905. 28 p. (*Record of recent construction, no. 52.*)

1005. _____. *Gasoline industrial locomotives.* Philadelphia, Pa., Baldwin Locomotive Works, 1914. 28 p. (Code word: Redanimavi)

1006. _____. *Got there—and got there on time.* Philadelphia, Pa., Innes & Sons, 1918 49 p.

1007. _____. *History of the Baldwin Locomotive Works from 1831 to 1897.* Philadelphia, J.B. Lippincott, 1897. 86 p.

1008. _____. *History of the Baldwin Locomotive Works, 1831-1902.* Philadelphia, The Edgell Co., 1903. 96 p.

1009. _____. *History of the Baldwin Locomotive Works, 1831-1907.* Philadelphia, Pa., The Edgell Co., 1907. 105 p.

1010. _____ *History of the Baldwin Locomotive Works, 1832(!)-1913.* Philadelphia, 1913. 146 p.

1011. _____. *History of the Baldwin Locomotive Works, 1831-1920.* Philadelphia, Pa., Martino-Pflieger Co., 1921? 167 p.

1012. _____. *History of the Baldwin Locomotive Works, 1831-1923.* Philadelphia, Printed by the Bingham Co., 1924? 210 p. ("History of the Standard Steel Works Company", pp. 186-198)

1013. _____. *Illustrated catalogue: details of locomotives; Baldwin Locomotive Works, Burnham, Parry, Williams & Co., Philadelphia.* Philadelphia, s.n., 1885. 100 p. (Press of J.B. Lippincott)

1014. _____. *Illustrated catalogue: details of locomotives and cable code for duplicate parts.* Philadelphia, Pa., Baldwin Locomotive Works, 1919. 140 p.

1015. _____. *Illustrated catalogue of narrow-gauge locomotives: adapted especially to a gauge of 3 feet 6 inches or one metre/* Philadelphia, Pa., Burnham, Williams; Yokohama, Frazar & Co. of Japan, Agents, 1897. 450 p. "Japanese edition"

1016. _____. *Illustrated catalogue of narrow-gauge locomotives, Burnham, Parry, Williams & Co. 3rd ed.* Philadelphia, J.B. Lippincott, 1885. 64 p.

1017. _____. *International exhibition, 1876. Exhibit of locomotives, by Burnham, Parry, Williams, & Co., Baldwin Locomotive Works, Philadelphia.* Philadelphia, Press of J.B. Lippincott & Co., 1876. 29 p. (Centennial Exhibition, 1876, Philadelphia, Pa.)

1018. _____ *Light locomotives.* Philadelphia, Pa., The Works, 1903. 68 p.

1019. _____. *Locomotive; special high grade lubricating oils and greases.* Philadelphia, Pa., The Baldwin Locomotive Works, 1928. 37 p. (*Pamphlet no. F-16.*)

1020. _____. *Locomotive data.* Philadelphia, Pa., Burnham, Williams & Co., 1893. 1 v.

1021. _____. *Locomotive data. 2d ed.* Philadelphia, Pa., Burnham, Williams & Co., 1903? 64 p.

1022. _____. *Locomotive data.* Philadelphia, Pa., Burnham, Williams, & Co., 1904. 80 p.

1023. _____. *Locomotive data.* Philadelphia, Pa., Burnham, Williams & Co., 1907. 90, 24 p.

1024. _____. *Locomotive data.* Philadelphia, Pa., Edgell Press, 1909. 92, 226 p.

1025. _____. *Locomotive data.* Philadelphia, Pa., The Edgell Press, 1912. 108 p.

1026. _____. *Locomotive data.* Philadelphia, Pa., The Edgell Press, 1914. 110 p.

1027. _____. *Locomotive data.* Philadelphia, Pa., Baldwin Locomotive Works, 1920. 120 p.

1028. _____. *Locomotive data.* Philadelphia, Pa., Baldwin Locomotive Works, 1921. 126 p.

1029 _____. *Locomotive data.* Philadelphia, Pa., Bingham Company, 1923. 130, 48, 12 p.

1030. _____. *Locomotive data.* 11th ed. Philadelphia, Pa., 1939. 150 p.

1031. _____. *Locomotive data.* 12th ed. Philadelphia, Pa., 1944. 164 p.

1032. _____. *Locomotive engines.* Philadelphia, Pa., s.n. 1870. 32 p.

1033. _____. *Locomotive number 60,000: an experimental locomotive. Baldwin Locomotive Works.* By Paul T. Warner. Philadelphia, Pa., s.n., 1928. 80 p. (Code word: CUMUW.) Reprint of booklet published in 1927.

1034. _____. *Locomotive: special high grade lubrication oils and greases.* Philadelphia, The Baldwin Locomotive Works, 1928. 37 p.

1034a. _____. *Locomotive steam distribution and valve setting.* Philadelphia, Pa., Baldwin Locomotive Works, 1900-1909? 18 p.

1035. _____ *Locomotives designed and constructed by the Baldwin Locomotive Works, Philadelphia, U.S.A.* Philadelphia, Pa., Baldwin Locomotive Works, 1922. 287 p.

1036. _____ *Locomotives for heavy freight and hump yard service.* Philadelphia, Pa., Baldwin Locomotive Works, 1909. 75 p. (Code word: Mastanabal.)

1037. _____. *Locomotives for industrial and contractors' service: record no. 78, code word, redargutos.* Philadelphia, Pa., Baldwin Locomotive Works, 1914. 31 p. (Reprint: Clifton Heights, Pa., H.P. Albrecht, 1964. 32 p.)

1038. _____. *Locomotives for industrial and contractors' service: record no 86, code word, Redituamos.* Philadelphia, Pa., Baldwin Locomotive Works, 1917. 40 p.

1039. _____. *Locomotives for light road service.* Philadelphia, Pa., Baldwin Locomotive Works, 1916. 32 p. *Record no. 84.* (Code word: Redigimur)

1040. _____ *Locomotives for plantation service.* Philadelphia, Pa., Baldwin Locomotive Works, 1915. 32 p.

1041. _____. *Locomotives recently built for passenger service.* Philadelphia, Baldwin Locomotive Works, 1910. 32 p.

1042. _____. *Logging locomotives.* Philadelphia, Pa., Baldwin Locomotive Works, 1906. 64 p. (Code word: Manigaux.)

1043. _____. *Louisiana Purchase Exposition: St. Louis, Missouri, 1904.* Philadelphia, Pa., Burnham, Williams, 1904. 73 p.

1044. _____. *Mallet articulated locomotives.* Philadelphia, Baldwin Locomotive Works, 1910. 35 p. (Code word: rectitude.)Earlier edition, 1908.

1045. _____. _____. Philadelphia, Pa., Baldwin Locomotive Works, 1918. 44 p. (Code word: Redonnons."

1046. _____. *The motive power situation of American steam railroads.* Philadelphia, Pa., The Baldwin Locomotive Works, 1934. 54 l.

1047. _____. *The narrow gauge locomotives; the Baldwin catalog of 1877. With a foreword by Laurence S. Reid.* New edition. Norman, University of Oklahoma Press, 1967. 47 p.

1048. _____. *Notes on the principles and performances of the balanced compound locomotive.* Philadelphia, Pa., Burnham, Williams, 1905. 42 p. (Code word: Recoquetis.)

1049. _____. *Oil burning locomotives.* Philadelphia, Pa., Baldwin Locomotive Works, 1911. 31 p. (Code word: Recuidar.)

1050. _____. *100 years of locomotive progress. Baldwin Locomotive Works.* Bristol, Conn., Simmons-Boardman, 1931. 170 p. (Reprint of data appearing in *Railway Age,* v. 90, no. 20, May 16, 1931.)

1051. _____. *Operating and maintenance instruction.* Philadelphia, Pa., Baldwin Locomotive Works, Engineering Department, 1928-1949. 2 v.

1052. _____. *Pacific type locomotives.* Philadelphia, Pa., Baldwin Locomotive Works, 1908. 53 p. (Code word: Maschero.)

1053. _____. _____. Clifton Heights, Pa., H.P. Albrecht, 1965, 1914. 39 p.

1054. _____. *The portable boats of early railroad practice, by J. Snowden Bell.* Philadelphia, Pa., s.n., 1920. 35 p.

1055. _____. *Proper handling of compound locomotives. Philadelphia,* Pa., Burnham, Williams, 1903. 32 p.

1056. _____. *Recent development of the locomotive.* Philadelphia, Pa., Baldwin Locomotive Works, 1912. 53 p.

1057. _____ *Record of recent construction: nos. 1-10 inclusive.* Philadelphia, Pa., Baldwin Locomotive Works, Burnham, Williams & Co., 1899. 308 p.

1058. _____. *Record of recent construction, nos 11-20 inclusive.* Philadelphia, Pa., Baldwin Locomotive Works, Burnham, Williams & Co., 1900. 324 p.

1059. _____. *Record of recent construction, nos. 21 to 30 inclusive.* Philadelphia, Pa., Baldwin Locomotive Works, 1900. 322 p.

1060. _____. *Record of recent construction, nos. 31 to 40 inclusive.* Philadelphia, Pa., Baldwin Locomotive Works, 1900? 306 p.

1061. _____. *Report of experiments made with locomotive 82,* in *the burning of crude petroleum.* Philadelphia, Pa., The Company, 1894. 13 p. (*Pamphlet no. 2*)

1062. _____. *Report of tests of compound locomotives on the Northern Pacific Railroad, Western New York and Pennsylvania Railroad, Western Maryland Railroad, and Norfolk and Western Railroad.* Philadelphia, 1892. 79 p.

1063. _____. *Reproduction of Baldwin Locomotive Works. Illustrated catalogue of locomotives.* Berkeley, Calif., Howell-North, 1960. 153 p. (Reprint of item no. 431.)

1064. _____ *Santa Fe type locomotives.* Philadelphia, Pa., Baldwin Locomotive Works, 1917. 36 p.

1065. _____. *Smoke-box superheater.* 1909. 30 p.

1066. _____. *Some notable trains.* Philadelphia, Pa., Burnham, Williams, 1903. 35 p. (Code word: Recobrar.)

1067. _____. *Specification for steel boiler and fire-box plates.* Philadelphia, Pa., Baldwin Locomotive Works, 1894. 20 l.

1068. _____. *Steam locomotive performance.* Philadelphia, Baldwin Locomotive Works, 1940. 11 p.

1068a. _____. *Steam locomotive standards: engineering standards for the design, erection, and production of steam locomotives: updated thru 1949.* Philadelphia, Pa., Baldwin Locomotive Works, Engineering Department, 1900s. 2 v. (Reprint: McCalla, Ala., Little River Press, 2001. 2 v.)

1069. _____. *The story of Eddystone.* Philadelphia, Pa., s.n., 1928. 75 p. (Reprint: Felton Park, Calif., Glenwood Publishers, 1974. 75 p.)

1070. _____. *Testing locomotives on "rollers" Locomotivas em experiencia sobre "rolos."* Philadelphia, Pa., The Works, 1920. 11 p.

1071. _____. *Vauclain system of compound locomotives: an historic reprint.* Ocean, NJ: Specialty Press, 1973, 1900. 91 p. Reprint of item no 448.)

1072. _____. *Walschaerts valve gear.* Revised. Philadelphia, Pa., Baldwin Locomotive Works, 1916. 31 p. (Code word: Recuamento.) (Later ed. in 1921. 34 p.; also 1907, 1906, 32 p.)

1073. _____. *War industries.* Philadelphia, Pa., s.n., 1919. 21 p.

1074. _____ *The World's Columbian Exposition, Chicago, Illinois, May-October, 1893.* Philadelphia, Pa., Lippincott, 1893. 78 p.

1075. Baldwin Locomotive Works. [Engine drawings.] Location: Southern Methodist University, Degolyer Library.

1076. Baldwin Locomotive Works. [Engineering files. Detail calculations.] 52 v. Location: Purdue University.

1077. *Baldwin locomotive Works: erecting drawings at the DeGolyer Library, Southern Methodist University.* Project supervisor, Dawn Letson. Dallas, TX: DeGolyer Library, S.M.U., 1987. 139 p.

1078. *The Baldwin Locomotive Works negative collection.* Benjamin F.G. Kline, Jr.,

Acting Curator. Strasburg, Pa., The Railroad Museum, of Pennsylvania, 1989. 211 p.

1079. *Baldwin locomotives*. Philadelphia, Baldwin Locomotive Works, 1922-1943. 20 v. Quarterly. (> *Baldwin*.)

1080. *Baldwin locomotives* [and] *Baldwin index, 1922-1948*. S.l., Railroadians of America, 1948. 71 l. "Prepared by Thomas T. Taber III [and] Paul T. Warner, November 1948."

1081. Baldwin, Simeon Eben. *Cases on railroad law*. St. Paul: West Pub. Co., 1896. 333 p.

1082. *Baldwin Southwark*. Philadelphia, Baldwin Southwark, Baldwin Locomotive Works, 1936?-1944. Quarterly. (Merged in 1944 with *Baldwin locomotives* to form: *Baldwin*.)

1083. Baldwin, Springfield. *A system of interlocking switches and signals*/ 1896. 23 l. 7 leaves of plates. (Thesis, C.E., Lehigh University.)

1084. Baldwin, W.W. *History of the Chicago, Burlington & Quincy Railroad*. Crete, NE: J-B Publishing Co., 1984-

1085. Baldwin, W. W. (William Wright) *Story of the Burlington*. Chicago, IL: Traffic Department, Burlington Route, 1925. 32 p.

1086. _____, Hale Holden. *The Denver shops of the Chicago, Burlington & Quincy and Colorado and Southern*. Denver? s.n., 1923. 18 p.

1087. Bales, William B. *The Staggers Act—alive and well in the Appalachian coalfields : at the National Coal Association Seminar on the 99th Congress and National Transportation Policies, Houston Texas, February 24-26, 1985*. Houston, TX: National Coal Association, 1985. 16 p.

1088. Balke, Harry Albert. *Design of railroad turntables*/ 1951. 97, 9 l. (Thesis, C.E. University of Kentucky)

1089. Ball, Claire, Norman W. Hanson, John W. Weber. *The Kansas test track*. Washington, DC: Federal Railroad Administration, Office of Research and Development, 1979. 2 v. (*FRA/ORD-79/22*.)

1090. Ball, Don. *America's colorful railroads*. New York, Bonanza Books, 1979, c1978. 210 p.

1091. _____ *America's railroads: the second generation*. New York, Norton, 1980. 216 p.

1092. _____. *Decade of the trains: the 1940s; photo-essay and commentary by Don Ball, Jr; text by Rogers E.M. Whitaker ("E.M. Frimbo")*. Boston: New York Graphic

Society, 1977. 287 p.

1093. _____. *The Pennsylvania Railroad, 1940s-1950s.* Chester, VT: Elm Tree Books; New York, NY: Distributed by W.W. Norton, 1986. 204 p.

1094. _____. *Portrait of the rails; from steam to diesel.* Introduction by David. P. Morgan. Greenwich, CT: New York Graphic Society, 1972. 295 p.

1095. _____. *Rails.* Designed by Hugh O'Neill. New York, NY: W.W. Norton; Toronto, ON: G.J. McLeod, 1981. 150 p.

1096. _____. *Railroads: an American journey.* Boston, MA: New York Graphic Society, 1975. 286 p.

1097. _____. *Railroads.* New York, NY: Norton, 1985. 159 p.

1097a. Ball, Donald L. *George Mansfield and the Billerica and Bedford Railroad /* Blue Springs, Missouri: Aubrey Publications, 2011. 198 p.

1098. Ball, George W.I., Henry S. Drinker. *General railroad and telegraph laws of the State of Pennsylvania : including the acts relating to incline plane railways and street passenger railways , and such acts relative to corporations as affect railroad and telegraph companies, 1816-1883 /* 3rd ed. Special. Philadelphia : Allen, Lane & Scott, 1884.

1099. Balliet, Herbert S. *The invention of the track circuit; the history of Dr. Williams Robinson's invention of the track circuit, the fundamental unit which made possible our present automatic block signaling and interlocking systems.* New York, Signal Section, American Railway Association, 1922. 101 p.

1099a. Ballon Hilary. *Gateway to metropolis: New York's Pennsylvania Stations.* New York: Miriam and Ira D. Wallach Art Gallery, Columbia University in the City of New York, 2000. 8 p.

1100. _____, Norman McGrath. *New York's Pennsylvania Stations.* New York, Norton, 2002. 223 p.

1100a. Baltimore and Ohio Chicago Terminal Railroad Company. *Corporate history of the Baltimore & Ohio Chicago Terminal Railroad Company, as of June 30, 1918.* Baltimore : s.n. 1921. 8, 118, 45 l.

1101. Baltimore and Ohio Railroad Company. *B & O: Baltimore and Ohio Transportation Museum, Baltimore, Maryland.* Baltimore. Md., Baltimore and Ohio Railroad Company, Public Relations Department, 1954. 32 p.

1102. _____. *The Baltimore and Ohio Railroad Company and Reading Company announce the opening November 1, 1926 of the Philadelphia perishable products terminal, Philadelphia, Pa.* Philadelphia : s.n., 1926. 4 p.

1103. _____ *Baltimore and Ohio Railroad corporate histories*. Baltimore, Md., Baltimore and Ohio Railroad Co., Valuation Dept., 1922. 4 v.

1104. _____. *Book of the Royal Blue*. Baltimore: Baltimore and Ohio Railroad Company, 1897-1911. 14 v.

1105. _____. *The catalogue of the centenary exhibition of the Baltimore & Ohio Railroad, 1827-1927*. Baltimore, Waverly Press, 1927. 210 p.

1106. _____. *Concerning the blue china*. S.l., s.n., 1920. 12 p.

1107. _____. *The Fair of the Iron Horse; the centenary pageant of the Baltimore & Ohio Railroad held in Baltimore, Maryland, September 24th to October 16th, 1927*. Baltimore, 1927. 32 p.

1108. _____. *Firemen and brakemen questions and answers: preliminary examination upon operating rules*. Baltimore? B&O Railroad Co., 1944. 15 p.

1109. _____. *The first air-conditioned railroad cars*. Baltimore, MD: The Company, 1931. 1 v.

1110. _____. *Floor plan diagrams of sleeping cars*. Baltimore, Traffic Dept., Baltimore and Ohio Railroad Company, 1951. 9 p.

1110a. _____. *Freight working book* / Baltimore : Baltimore and Ohio Railroad, Transportation Department, 1900s-? Irregular.

1111. _____. *Historical sketch of the Baltimore & Ohio: America's first railroad*. Baltimore, Md., Baltimore & Ohio R.R., 1925. 15 p.

1112. _____. *Locomotive data*. Huntington, W.V: Office Chief Mechanical Officer-Loco, 1971. 20 l.

1113. _____. *The largest Mountain type passenger locomotive in the world*. S.l., Baltimore & Ohio Railroad Company, 1925. 4 p.

1114. _____. *Maintenance of way: standards: Baltimore and Ohio* R.R. S.l., s.n., 1891. 53 l.

1115. _____. *The new Baltimore & Ohio Station in the heart of New York City*. New York, N.Y.? Baltimore and Ohio Railroad Co., 1929. 31 p.

1116. _____. *Papers relative to the recent contracts for motive power*. Baltimore, Printed by J. Lucas & Son, 1857. 58 p.

1117. _____. *Questionnaire for examination of locomotive inspectors*. S.l., Baltimore and Ohio Railroad Co., 1948. 2 v.

1118. _____. *Renumbering and reclassification of locomotives and diesel rail motor cars.* Baltimore, Md., Baltimore and Ohio Railroad, 1956. 41 p.

1118a. _____ *Report of the engineers, on the reconnaissance and surveys, made in reference to the Baltimore and Ohio Rail Road.* Baltimore: W, Woody, 1828,

1119. _____ *Reprint of editorials and magazine articles on the first air-conditioned railroad trains.* Baltimore, s.n., 1932. 70 p.

1120. _____ *Rules and regulations for Baltimore and Ohio system during blackout and air raid alarms, effective November 1, 1942.* S.l., s.n., 1942. 10 p.

1121. _____. *Rules and regulations for the government of the operating Department: to take effect May 1st, 1866.* Baltimore, Md., Baltimore & Ohio Railroad Company, 1886. 106 p.

1122. _____.*Rules and regulations of the Operating Department.* Baltimore, Ms., s.n., 1917. 206 p.

1123. _____. *Rules and regulations of the Operating Department.* Baltimore, Baltimore & Ohio Railroad Company, 1933. 206 p.

1124. _____. *Rules and regulations of the Operating Department: effective January 1, 1948.* S.l., The Railroad, 1948. 248 p.

1125. _____. *Rules and regulations of the Operating Department, effective April 26, 1953.* 169 p.

1126. _____. *Rules for operation of Baltimore and Ohio air-conditioning equipment on passenger cars.* Baltimore? : Baltimore & Ohio Railroad, 1957. 15 p. *(Form 117-A-Rev.)*

1127. _____. *Rules for operation of steam heating systems; Baker Heater and Pintsch Gas.* Baltimore, Md., The Company, 1903. 30 p.

1128. _____. *Rules for the running of trains; Baltimore and Ohio and Washington Branch Rail Roads.* Baltimore? s.n., 1849. 14 p.

1129. _____. *Rules of the Baltimore and Ohio Railroad Company for the government of the Operating Department, to take effect April 1, 1903.* Baltimore, s.n., 1903. 94 p.

1130. _____. *Short history of the Baltimore and Ohio Railroad, also locomotive development and early locomotives since 1827.* Baltimore, s.n., 1937. 48 p.

1131. _____. *Standard plans for maintenance and construction.* Akron, OH: Akron Railroad Club, 1977. 3, 139 p. (Originally published: Baltimore, Md., Office of Chief Engineer, Baltimore and Ohio Railroad, 1907.)

1132. _____. *Statement of performance and cost of locomotive engines employed on the Baltimore & Ohio Railroad.* Baltimore, Baltimore and Ohio Railroad Company, 19--?- (Monthly)

1132a. _____. *Telegraph code.* Baltimore, MD: Baltimore and Ohio Railroad Co., 1889. 240 p.

1133. _____. *Through sleeping car and parlor car lines and space assignments: instructions to city and station ticket agents selling sleeping and parlor car space.* S.l., Baltimore & Ohio Railroad Co.? 1935. 58 p. ("Effective April 28, 1935.)

1134. _____. *Working book, Connellsville (Pa.) terminal.* Baltimore : Baltimore and Ohio Railroad, Office of Chief of Yard and Terminal operations, 1955. 14, 1 l.

1135. _____. Office of Signal Engineer. *Electric interlocking specifications: R.S.A. manual.* Baltimore? Baltimore and Ohio Railroad Company, 1912. 29 p.

1136. _____. Terminal Department. *Train classification/* Baltimore, MD: Baltimore and Ohio Railroad, 1954. 170 p.

1137. _____. Transportation Department. *Clearance tables : showing the maximum dimension for cars and lading that cab be handled over the Baltimore and Ohio Railroad.* Baltimore ? Baltimore and Ohio Railroad Co., 1960. 57 l.

1138. Baltimore and Ohio Railroad Historical Society; Baltimore and Ohio Railroad Company. *Baltimore and Ohio Railroad Company, Mechanical Engineering Department equipment diagrams: locomotives—steam: holdings of archives, Baltimore and Ohio Railroad Historical Society.* Baltimore, MD., The Society, 1984. 1 v.

1139. _____; _____. *Baltimore and Ohio Railroad Company, Mechanical Engineering Department equipment diagrams: passenger cars: holding of archives, Baltimore and Ohio Railroad Historical* Society. Baltimore, MD., The Society, 1985. 1 v.

1140. _____; _____. *Baltimore and Ohio Railroad Historical Society archives holdings of Baltimore and Ohio Railroad Company Mechanical Engineering Department equipment diagrams: locomotives—diesel.* Baltimore, MD., The Society,1987. 1 v.

1141. _____; _____. *Equipment diagrams: the modernized heavyweight Royal Blue trains.* Baltimore, MD., Baltimore and Ohio Railroad Historical Society, 1983. 17 l.

1142. _____. _____. *Equipment diagrams: selected class A-18, A-19, A-20 heavyweight coach diagrams.* Baltimore, MD., Baltimore and Ohio Railroad Historical Society, 1983. 30 l.

1143. *Baltimore & Ohio Railroad.* New York, Crescent Books, 1988. 128 p.

1144. *Baltimore & Ohio Railroad: a scrapbook of old postcard scenes and passenger timetables.* Mountain Top, PA., Ed Gardner, 198-? v. 1-

1145. *The Baltimore and Ohio Railroad Company and its subsidiaries: a bibliography.* Edmund Arthur Freeman, comp. Washington, D.C.: Bureau of Railway Economics Library, 1927. 378 l.

1145a. Baltimore Car Wheel Company. *The central flue system of annealing car wheels* / Baltimore : The Company, 1874. 1 folded sheet

1146 Baltimore Museum of Art; Baltimore and Ohio Railroad Company. *The hand of man: railroads in American prints and photographs: an exhibition to commemorate the 150th anniversary of the Baltimore and Ohio Railroad.* Baltimore, MD., Baltimore Museum of Art, 1978. 22 p.

1147. Bancker, Elbert H., Ernest George Bangratz, James H. Becker, Charles J. Farist, Irwin L. Moore. *A study of the electrification of the suburban zone of the New York, New Haven and Hartford Railroad centering in Boston* / 1920. 1 v. (Various pagings). (Thesis, B.S., Massachusetts Institute of Technology, Department of Electrical Engineering.)

1148. Bancroft, Hubert Howe. *History of the life of Collis P. Huntington.* San Francisco, The History Company, 1890. 110 p.

1149. Bang, Robert A. *The New York, Westchester & Boston Railway, 1906-1946* / Port Chester, NY: Robert A, Bang, 2004. 177 p.

1150. _____. Daniel R. Gallo. *Westchester County's million dollar-a-mile railroad.* S.l., s.n., 1988. 62 p.

1151. _____, John E. Frank, G.W. Kowanski, Otto M. Vondrak. *Forgotten railroads through Westchester County.* Port Chester, NY: P.O. Box 164, s.n., 2007. 168 p. (NYC; NYNH&H; New York, Westchester & Boston Railway)

1152. Bangor and Aroostock Railroad Company. *75 years; the Bangor and Aroostook.* S.l., s.n., 1966. 48 p.

1153. Bangs, George S. *Railroad vs. postal cars. A letter to the post master-general, discussing the question of transportation …* / Washington, G.P.O., 1874. 44 p.

1154. Banks, Richard. *Colorado Midland boomer.* Colorado Springs, CO: Pikes Peak Press, 1987. 255p.

1155. *The Banner.* St. Louis, MO?: Wabash Railroad Historical Society, 1984- Quarterly. (< *Wabash flag*)

1156. Banwart, Donald D. *Rails, rivalry, and romance : a review of Bourbon County, Kansas, and her railroad nostalgia in words and pictures, 1864 thru 1980, including the dramatic railroad construction race to the Indian Territory border*/ Fort Scott, KS: Historic Preservation Association of Bourbon County, 1982. 514 p.

1157. Barbeau, Donald R. *The eccentric crank: steam locomotives in review.* Schenectady, NY: Mohawk & Hudson Chapter, National Railway Historical Society, 1983. 86 p.

1158. Barger, Ralph L. *A century of Pullman cars.* Sykesville, MD: Greenberg Pub. Co., 1987-   v. 1-Alphabetical list; v. 2—The Palace Cars.

1159. _____. *Union Pacific business cars, 1870-1991: including inspection and instruction cars.* Sykesville, Md., Greenberg Pub. Co., 1992. 208 p.

1160. Barkan, Christopher P. L., Theodore S. Glickman, Aviva E. Harvey. *Benefit-cost analysis of using type 105 tanks cars instead of type 111 tank cars to ship environmentally sensitive chemicals /* Washington, DC? ; Association of American Railroads, 1991. 29 p.

1161. Barke, Richard P. *Economic and political determinants of regulatory decisions: the Interstate Commerce Commission and railroad abandonments.* 1980. 236 l. (Thesis, Ph.D., University of Rochester.) Abandonment. Logit models.

1162. Barker, Lesley. *St. Louis Gateway rail: the 1970s.* Charleston, SC: Arcadia Pub., 2006. 127 p.

1163. Barnard, Charles. *Seen from the car: travel as a fine art.* New York, New York Central and Hudson River RR. Co., 1902. 61 p.

1164. Barnard, Eileen Wolford, Julian W. Barnard, Jr. *Catalogue of the Barnard-Wolford collection: a photographic record of Baltimore & Ohio system right-of-way structures and rolling stock, with certain other subjects of possible interest to historians and scale model builders.* Shelby, Ohio, E.W. Barnard and J.W. Barnard, Jr., 1980. 196 l.

1165. _____. *Research workbook: cars of the Baltimore and Ohio Railroad.* Shelby, Ohio, Barnard, 1979. 51, 6, 311 l.

1166. Barnard, W.T. (William Theodore) *The relations of railway managers and employees.* Baltimore, Press of Employees Relief Association, 1886. 42 p.

1167. Barnes, David Leonard. *Iron & steel car construction: memoranda on pressed steel: typescript.* Archival material. 1 v. Location: Crerar Manuscript Collection, University of Chicago. Library. Crerar Ms. 187.

1168. _____. *Electric locomotives. Baldwin Locomotive works, Burnham, William & Co., Philadelphia, Pa., U.S.A., and the Westinghouse Electric and Mfg. Co., Pittsburgh, Pa., U.S.A.* Philadelphia, Pa., J.B. Lippincott Company, 1896. 123 p.

1169. _____, J.C. Whitridge. *Modern locomotives; illustrations, specifications and details of typical American and European steam and electric locomotives.* New York, Railroad Gazette, 1897. 448 p.

1170. Barnes, Fred Asa. *Notes on locomotive rating and run curves for electric service.* Rev. Ithaca, NY: 1913. 24 p.

1171. Barnes, Harold Butler. *The practical solution of the Chicago terminal electrification problem; the storage battery locomotive with the submarine type storage battery and its many advantages over trolley or third rail systems.* Denver, Col., Bradford Publishing Company, 1920. 21 p.

1172. Barney, Peter S. *The Bridgton and Saco River: a technical and pictorial review.* S.l. A&M Pub., 1987. 96 p.

1173. _____. *Bridgton and Saco River Railroad freight cars : photographs and drawings of equipment : a modeler's reference.* O'Fallon, MO : BHI Publications, 2005. 86 p.

1174. _____. *Freight equipment of the Sandy River & Rangeley Lakes: photographs and drawings of equipment : a modeler's reference.* O'Fallon, MO: BHI Publications, 2007. 98 p.

1175. _____ *Handcars, railcars, and railbuses of the Sandy River & Rangeley Lakes R.R..* S.l., A&M Pub., 1990. 64 p.

1176. _____. *The Kennebec Central and Monson railroads.* S.l., A&M Pub., 1986. 64 p.

1177. _____. *Sandy River and Rangeley Lakes passenger cars : ([with special emphasis on the cars that survived) ; photographs and drawings of equipment : a modeler's reference.* O'Fallon, MO : BHI Publications, 2006. 98 p.

1178. _____. *Structures of the Maine two-footers.* S.l., A&M Pub., 1988- v. 1-

1179. _____. *The Wiscasset, Waterville, and Farmington Railway: a technical and pictorial review.* S.l., A&M Pub., 1986. 88 p.

1180. Barnhart, Hugh A. *The business organization of the Pennsylvania Railroad Company.* 1915. 5, 87 l. (Thesis, A.B., Indiana University.)

1181. Barns, James Harry. *Electric railway track.* Columbia, 1906. 18 p. (Thesis, University of Missouri.)

1182. Barr, Howard N. *The 50 best of B & O, book one.* Baltimore, Barnard, Roberts & Company, 1977. 52 p.

1183. _____. *A history of locomotives of the Baltimore and Ohio Railroad.* Baltimore, MD: Baltimore and Ohio Railroad Historical Society, 1986. 10 p.

1183a. Barr, James. *Experimental study of a locomotive link motion /* 1890. 16 l. (Thesis, B.S., University of Illinois.)

1184. Barrett, Richard C. *Boston depots and terminals: a history of Boston's downtown and back railroad stations from 1834 to today.* Railroad Research Publications, 1996. 226 p.

1185. _____, William A. Barringer. *Q; the definitive history of the Baltimore and Ohio Railroad Company's Q-class Mikado locomotives.* With the assistance of Harry C. Eck and Charles S. Roberts. Baltimore, MD: Barnard, Roberts, 1978- v. 1-

1186. Barriger, John Walker, and Walker D. Hines. *The United States of America against the "Anthracite Coal Railroads."* New York, Evening Post Job Printing Office, 1908. 46 p.

1187. _____, _____. *Did Congress intend to give rate-making power to Interstate Commerce Commission? What the Congressional debate shows: extracts from the records.* Louisville, Ky., John P. Morton & Company, 1898. 39 p.

1188. Barriger, John Walker III. (1899-1976) *A corporate history of the Pennsylvania Railroad Company.* 1921. 189 l. (Thesis, B.S., Massachusetts Institute of Technology, Department of Business and Engineering Administration.)

1189. _____. *Development of the Santa Fe, 1935-1948.* Cambridge, MA: Massachusetts Institute of Technology, 1949. 415 l. (Thesis., Ph.D., Massachusetts Institute of Technology.)

1190. _____. *Effect of wheel unbalance, eccentricity, tread contour and track gage on riding quality of railway passenger cars : first progress report.* Chicago : Association of American Railroads, Central Research laboratory, 1950. 83 l.

1191. _____. *Feasibility of atomic energy for use on American railroads: report No. MR-280.* Chicago, IL: AAR Research Center, 1957. 102 l.

1192. _____. *A Hoosier centenarian: "The Monon."* New York, Newcomen Society, American Branch, 1947. 28 p. Chicago, Indianapolis & Louisville Railway Company. (*Newcomen publications, no. 47-2.*)

1193. _____. *The Pennsylvania Railroad.* New York, C. Bullock, 1930. 88 p.

1194. _____. *The Pittsburgh and Lake Erie Railroad: an address ... before the New York Society of Security Analysts, July 22, 1960.* New York, s.n., 1960. 32, 35 l.

1195. _____. *Railroad equities ... a survey.* S.l., s.n., 1930. 8 l.

1196. _____. *Railroads in the Civil War.* S.l., National Railway Historical Society, 1966. 31 p.

1197. _____. *Romance of railroad finance.* Princeton, N.J., Newcomen Society, American Branch, 1939. 24 p. (*Newcomen address, 1939*)

1198. _____. *Super-railroads for a dynamic American economy.* New York, Simmons-Boardman Pub. Corp., 1956. 91 p.

1199. Barriger, Stanley Huntington. *A modern empire builder, Ralph Budd.* 1955. 240 l. (Thesis, B.S., Massachusetts Institute of Technology.)

1200. Barrows, Benjamin H. *The evolution of artificial light from a pine knot to the Pintsch light.* Chicago, Knight, Leonard & Co., Printers, 1893. 107 p. (Reprint: Wethersfield, CT: Rushlight Club, 1986, 1893. 79 p.)

1201. _____. *The evolution of the locomotive from 1813 to 1891, a brief record of great achievement.* Chicago, Knight, Leonard & Co., Printers, 1891. 51 p.

1202. Barry, J.R. *Merchandise directory : list of L.C.L. merchandise cars loaded at stations on the L&N RR : merchandise cars loaded on connecting lines to or via L&N RR : also substituted truck service and coordinated rail-truck service : effective April 1, 1953.* Louisville, KY: Louisville and Nashville Railroad Company, 1953. 17 p.

1203. Barry, Steve. *Rail power.* St. Paul, MN: Voyageur Press, 2006. 192 p.

1204. _____. *Railroad rolling stock/* Minneapolis, MN: Voyageur Press, 2008. 192 p.

1205. _____. *Railroads: the history of the American railroads in 500 photos.* St. Paul, MN: Crestline, 2002. 399 p.

1206. _____. *Trackside around New York City, 1953-1968, with* Robert *Malinoski.* Scotch Plains, NJ: Morning Sun Books, 2001. 126 p.

1206a. Barsom, John M., E.J. Imhof, Jr. *Fatigue and fracture behavior of carbon-steel rails /* Chicago : AAR Technical Center, 1978. 43 p. (*Association of American Railroad, AAR report, no. R-301.*)

1207. Bartels, H. *Betriebs-einrichtungen auf amerikanischen eisenbahnen. Im auftrage seiner excellenz des Herrn ministers fur handel, gewerbe und offentliche arbeiten nach dem eingereichten resiseberichte bearb. und hrsg. von H. Bartels...* Berlin, Ernest & Korn, 1879. 268 p. I. Bahnhofsanlagen und signale. (No more published?)

1208. _____. *Die Organisation der Pennsylvania-Eisenbahn in den Vereinigten Staaten von Nord-Amerika /* Berlin : Ernst & Korn, 1878. 16 p.

1209. Bartels, Michael M. *Missouri Pacific river and prairie rails: the MoPac in Nebraska.* David City, NE: South Platte Press, 1997. 204 p.

1210. _____. *A railfans' guide to Nebraska.* Crete NE: J-B Pub. Co., 1970. 48 p.

1211. _____. *Rock Island town.* David City, NE: South Plate Press, 1999. 80 p.

1212. Bartels, Michael M., James J. Reisdorff. *Ghost railroads of Nebraska—a pictorial.*

David City, NE: South Platte Press, 2002. 96 p.

1213. _____, _____. *Historical railroads of Nebraska.* Chicago, IL: Arcadia, 2002. 128 p.

1214. _____, _____. *Train time in Nebraska: the post card era.* David City, NE: South Platte Press, 2005. 96 p.

1214a. _____, James J. Reisdorff. *Otto Perry and the Union Pacific Nebraska Division,* Grand island, NB: Great Plains Chapter of National Railway Historical Society, 2011. 80 p.

1215. Bartels, Mike. *The C & NW Cowboy Line: a composite by Bartels-Kratville-Mills-Perry.* David City, NE: South Platte Press, 1998. 64 p.

1216. Bartky, Ian R. "The invention of railroad time." Boston; Railway & Locomotive Historical Society, 1983. p. 13-22. *Railroad History,* v. 148. Spring 1983.

1217. _____. *"Sanford Fleming's first essays on time."* Columbia, PA: National Association of Watch and Clock Collectors, 2008. p. 3-11. *NAWCC bulletin,* v. 50, no. 1, whole issue 372.

1218. _____. *Selling the true time: nineteenth-century time keeping in America* / Stanford: Stanford University Press, 2000. 310 p.

1219. Bartholomew, W.S. *Mechanical firing of locomotives: presented before the St. Louis Railway Club at its regular meeting, November 10, 1916, and discussion thereon.* St. Louis, St. Louis Railway Club, 1916. 48 p.

1220. Barton, Carlyle. *Ross Winans, railroad engineer.* 19--? 93 l. Thesis, B.A., Princeton University

1220a. Barton, Timothy. *Chicago and North Western Railway Terminal.* Chicago: Commission of Chicago Historical and Architectural landmarks, 1981. 12 p.

1221. Baruth, Wilma F. *Straight as the crow flies: historical geography of the Kansas Southern Railway Company.* 1986. 180 l.(Thesis, M.A., Kansas State University.)

1222. Barwis, C.W. *An investigation of brake beams for railroad cars* / 1906. 100 l. 7 leaves of plates. (Thesis, C.E., Lehigh University.)

1223. Basford, George Marshall. *Vitalizing locomotives.* New York: New York Railroad Club, 1921. 35 p.

1224. *Basic training manual for brakemen and switchmen.* Omaha, Simmons-Boardman, 1974. 116 p. (2d ed., 2004. 82 p.)

1225. Bass, Charles. *Life on the shiny iron: memories of a mid-century brakeman/*

Middleton, WI: Falconart Media L.L.C., 2009. 191 p.

1225a. Bassett, Edward M. *Report on grade crossing in New York City and the need of change in the grade crossing law*. Albany, NY: J.B. Lyon Company, Printers, 1910. 35 p.

1225b. Bassett, Mark S., J. Joan Bassett. *Nevada Northern Railway*. Charleston, SC: Arcadia Publishing, 2011. 127 p.

1226. Bassily, Fady P., Wesley D. McGuthry. *Development of track maintenance training and maintenance management information system programs*/ Washington, DC: Federal Transit Administration, Office of Technical Assistance and Safety, 1992. v, 15, A-33 leaves. (*FTA-DC-06-0333-92-1*.)

1227. Bateman, Bob. *Big Blackfoot Railway*. 2d ed. Deer Lodge, Mont., Platen Press, 1980. 52 p.

1228. Bates, Beth Tompkins. *Pullman porters and the rise of protest politics in Black Americans, 1925-1945*. Chapel Hill, NC: University of North Carolina Press, 2001. 275 p.

1229. Baugh, Odin A. *John Frank Stevens: American trailblazer*/ Spokane WA: Arthur H. Clark Co., 2005. 251 p.

1230. Baughman, James P. *The maritime and railroads interests of Charles Morgan 1837-1885: a history of the "Morgan Line."* 1963. 294 l. (Thesis, Ph.D., Tulane University.)

1231. Baughman, Jon, Ronald L. Morgan. *From coal to glory : the history of the Huntingdon & Broad Top Mountain Railroad & Coal Co.: including histories of the Bedford Railroad Co. and the Bedford & Bridgeport Railroad Co.* / Saxton, PA: The Authors, 1988. 2 v.

1232. Baumel, C. Philip, John Joseph Miller, Thomas P. Drinka. *An economic analysis of upgrading rail branch lines: a study of 71 lines in Iowa*/ Springfield, VA: National Technical Information Service, 1976. 544 p. (*PB 251-978; DOT-FR-55045*)

1233. Baumes, George J. *Buckets, flanges, and black diamonds: mining and moving coal in Pennsylvania*. Laurys Station, PA: Garrigues House, Publisher, 2008. 1 v.

1234. Baumgardener, T., F.K. Zentmyer. *Test of locomotive no. 2 on the Bellefonte Central Railroad*. 1897. 65 l. (Thesis, B.S., Pennsylvania State College.)

1235. Baumgardener, Floyd G. Hoenstine. *The Allegheny old Portage Railroad, 1834-1854. Building, operation and travel between Hollidaysburg and Johnston, Pennsylvania*. Ebensburg, PA: The Authors, 1952. 90 p.

1235a. Bawden, S.D. *The effect of counter-balance on locomotives* / 1890. 36 l.

(Thesis, B.S., University of Illinois.)

1236. Baxter, Raymond, Arthur G. Adams. *Railroad ferries of the Hudson and stories of a deckhand.* New York, NY: Fordham University Press, 1999. 276 p.

1236a. Baxter, Robert G. *Baxter's USA train travel guide* / Alexandria, VA: Rail-Europe, 1973. 255 p.

1237. Baxter, Sylvester. *Remaking a railway: a study of efficiency, being an appreciation of the new transportation epoch in New England.* Boston : New England Lines, 1910. 40 p. New York, New Haven & Hartford Railroad Company.

1238. Beach, Charles Fisk, Jr. *Commentaries on the law of receivers: with particular reference to the application of that law to railway corporations but including in detail a complete consideration of the whole subject*/ New York, NY: L.K. Strouse, 1887. 796 p.

1239. Beal, Merrill D. *Intermountain railroads, standard and narrow gauge.* Caldwell, ID: Caxton Printers, 1962. 252 p.

1240. _____. *The Utah and Northern Railroad: narrow gauge.* Pocatello, ID: Idaho State University Press, 1980. 81 p.

1241. Beale, Edward Fitzgerald, A.W. Whipple. *Atlantic and Pacific Railroad: route to the Pacific Ocean on the 35th parallel.* New York: Stockholder Job Printing Office, 1867. 8, 20, 15 p.

1242. Beale, Joseph Henry. *The law of innkeepers and hotels including other public houses, theatres, sleeping cars.* Boston, W.J. Nagel, 1906. 621 p.

1243 _____, Bruce Wyman. *The law of railroad rate regulation with special reference to American legislation.* Boston: W.J. Nagel, 1907. 1285 p.

1244. _____, _____. *Railroad rate regulation: with special reference to the powers of the Interstate Commerce Commission under the acts to regulate commerce.* 2d ed. New York, N.Y., Baker, Voorhis, 1915. 1210 p.

1245. Beale, Mildred. *Biography of Charles Teed Pollard*/ 1928. 78 l. (Thesis, M.A., University of Alabama) Railroads-Alabama

1246. Bean, W.L. *Twenty years of electrical operation on the New York, New Haven and Hartford Railroad: report of Committee on Electric Rolling Stock, Mechanical Division, American Railway Association, June 1927* / East Pittsburgh, PA: Westinghouse Electric & Manufacturing Company, 1927. 75 p.

1247. Bearce, Winfield Dexter. *Steam railway electrification*/ Chicago, American School, 1930. 50 p.

1247a. Beard, Henry. *In the matter of the right of the Southern Pacific Railroad Co., California to the odd-numbered tracts of land opposite the first section of its road.* S.l., s.n., 1871. 19 p.

1248. Beasley, David R. *The suppression of the automobile: skullduggery at the crossroads.* New York, Greenwood Press, 1988. 175 p. (*Contributions in economics and economic history, no 81.*)

1248a. Beasley, Harrison E. *Relative merits of a plate girder and a stone arch for a railroad crossing* / 1894. 25 l, 5 folded leaves of plates. (Thesis, B.S., University of Illinois.)

1249. Beatty, Jerome. *Show me the way to go home: the commuter story.* New York, Crowell. 1959. 247 p.

1250. Beatty, W.D. *A review of the Pratt truss skew bridge on the Pennsylvania Railroad, near Pottsville, Pa.* 1888. 74 l. (Thesis, C.E., Lehigh University.)

1251. Beaudette, Edward H. *Central Vermont Railway: operations in the mid-twentieth century.* Newton, NJ: Carstens, 1982. 112 p.

1252. Beaumont, John M. *Locomotive brakes.* 1892. 66 l. (Thesis, M.E., Lehigh University.)

1253. Beauregard, Mark W. *R.R. stations of New England today.* Flanders, NJ: Railroad Avenue Enterprises, 1979- v. 1-

1254. Beaver, Roy C. *The Bessemer and Lake Erie Railroad, 1869-1969.* San Marino, CA: Golden West Books, 1969. 184 p.

1255. _____. *The story of the steam locomotives of the Bessemer and Lake Erie Railroad and predecessor companies.* Pittsburgh, Bessemer and Lake Erie Railroad Co., 1954. 64 p.

1256. Beberdick, Frank H. *The Pullman time line: 1831-1998* / Chicago? F.H. Beberdick, 2000. 16 l. Pullman Company – Chronology.

1256a. Beck, Samuel, Bill Gustason. *Indiana Harbor Belt, in color.* Scotch Plains, NJ: Morning Sun Books, 2011. 128 p.

1256b. Becker, H.C. *The economic design of timber trestle bridges* / 1907. 64 l. (Thesis, C.E., Lehigh University.)

1257. Becker, Sylvanus A. *Design for a turntable and roundhouse for L.&N.E.R.R.* 1903. 49 l. 9 l. of fold. plates. (Thesis, C.E., Lehigh University)

1258. Beckmann, Martin J. *The allocation of switching work in a system of classification yards.* Santa Monica, CA: Rand Corporation, 1953. 11 l.. (*Rand paper series, P-448*)

1259. Beckstrom Paul, David W. Braun. *The Swayne Lumber Company: narrow gauge logging in the Merrimac Forest.* Edmonds, WA: Pacific Fast Mail, 1992. 175 p.

1260. Beckum, W. Forrest, Albert M. Langley. *Central of Georgia Railway album.* North Augusta, SC: Union Station Pub., 1986. 144 p.

1261. _____, Albert M. Langley. *Georgia Railroad album.* North Augusta, SC: Union Station Pub., 1985. 72 p.

1262. Beckwith, E.G. (Edward Griffin). *Report of exploration of a route for the Pacific railroad, near the 38th and 39th parallels of latitude ; from the mouth of the Kansas to Sevier River, in the Great Basin.* Washington : s.n., 1855. 4, 149, 1 p. (*House document. United States. Congress. 33rd Congress, 1st session, no. 129.*)

1263. Bedingfield, Robert E. *The Norfolk and Western strike of 1978.* Edited by Harold S. Taylor. S.l., Norfolk and Western Railway Co., 1979. 149 p.

1264. Bednar, Mike. *Anthracite rebirth: story of the Reading and Northern Railroad.* Laurys Station, PA: Garrigues House, 1998. 124 p.

1265. _____. *Lehigh Valley facilties in color* / Scotch Plains, NJ: Morning Sun Books, 2008- . v. 1. New York Division. v. 2. Wyoming Division. v. 3. Buffalo Division.

1266. _____. *Lehigh Valley Railroad: an illustrated operation history covering the last twenty years of the railroad and the people who were there; the Wyoming and Buffalo Divisions.* Laurys Station, PA; Garrigues House, 2001. 1 v. (Also: Laurys Station, PA: Garrigues House, 1993. 138 p.)

1266a. _____. *Lehigh Valley Railroad: an illustrated operational history covering the last twenty years of the railroad and the people who were there: The New York Division.* Laurys Station, PA: Garrigues House, 1993. 138 p.

1267. _____. *Railroaders in the Lehigh River Valley*/ Hanover, PA: Railroad Press, 2005. 72 p.

1268. Bedwell, Harry. *The boomer.* New York, Editions for the Armed Forces, 1944, c1942. 351 p. (Reissue: Minneapolis, University of Minnesota Press, 2006. 332 p. with an introduction by James D. Porterfield.)

1269. _____. *Priority special.* San Francisco: Southern Pacific Company, 1945. 30 p. (Hospital trains)

1270. Bee, Roger, Gary Browne, John Luecke. *The Chicago Great Western in Minnesota.* Anoka, MN: Blue River Publications, 1984. 107 p.

1271. Beebe, Lucius Morris. *The age of steam; a classic album of American railroading.* New York, Rinehart, 1957. 304 p.

1272. _____. *The Central Pacific & the Southern Pacific Railroads. With 121 photos by Richard Steinheimer.* Berkeley, CA: Howell-North, 1963. 631 p.

1273. _____. *Great railroad photographs, U.S.A.* Berkeley, CA: Howell-North Books, 1964. 243 p.

1274. _____. *High iron; a book of trains.* New York, D. Appleton-Century Co., 1938. 225 p.

1275. _____. *Highball; a pageant of trains.* New York, D. Appleton-Century, 1945. 223 p. (Reprint: New York, NY: Bonanza Books, 1982. 223 p.)

1276. _____. *Highliners; a railroad album.* New York, D. Appleton-Century Co., 1940. 103 p.

1277. _____ *The iron horse in art; the railroad as it has been interpreted by artists of the nineteenth and twentieth centuries.* Fort Worth, TX: Forth Worth Art Center, 1958. 1 v.

1278. _____. *Mansions on rails; the folklore of the private railway car.* Berkeley, CA: Howell-North, 1959. 382 p.

1279. _____. *Mr. Pullman's elegant Palace car; the railway carriage that established a new dimension of luxury and entered the national lexicon as a symbol of splendor.* Garden City, NY: Doubleday, 1961. 574 p.

1280. _____. *Mixed train daily; a book of short-line railroads; with photographs by C.M. Clegg, Jr., and the author and six original oil paintings by Howard Fogg.* New York, E. P. Dutton, 1947. 367 p. (Reprint: New York, Dutton, 1990. 367 p.)

1281. _____. *The Overland Limited.* Berkeley, CA: Howell-North Books, 1963. 157 p.

1282. _____. *Trains in transition.* New York, D. Appleton-Century Co., 1941. 210 p. (Reprint: New York, NY: Hawthorne Books, 1976. 210 p.)

1283. _____. *20th Century; the greatest train in the world.* Berkeley, CA: Howell-North, 1962. 180 p.

1284. _____. *Two trains to remember: the New England Limited, the Air Line Limited.* Virginia City? NV: 1965. 54 p.

1285. _____, Charles M. Clegg. *Hear the train blow; a pictorial epic of America in the railroad age; with ten original drawings by E. S. Hammack and 860 illus.* New York, Dutton, 1952. 407 p.

1286. _____, _____. *Narrow gauge in the Rockies.* Berkeley, CA: Howell-North, 1958. 224 p. (Reprint: Forest Park, IL: Heimburger House, c1993. 224 p.)

1287. _____, _____. *Rio Grande: mainline of the Rockies.* Berkeley, CA: Howell-North, 1962. 380 p.

1288. _____, _____. *Steamcars to the Comstock: the Virginia & Truckee Railroad, the Carson & Colorado Railroad.* 3d ed. Berkeley, CA: Howell-North, 1960. 107 p.

1289. _____, _____. *The trains we rode.* Berkeley, CA: Howell-North, 1965-66. 2 v. (Reprint: New York, Promontory Press, 1990. 976 p.)

1290. _____, _____. *Virginia & Truckee; a story of Virginia City and Comstock times.* Oakland, CA: G.H. Hardy, 1949. 58, 5 p. (5th ed.; Berkeley, CA: Howell-North, 1963. 67 p.)

1291. _____, _____. *When beauty rode the rails; an album of railroad yesterdays.* Garden City, NY: Doubleday, 1962. 222 p.

1292. Beebe, Ralph K. *The worker and social change: the Pullman strike of 1894.* Lexington, MA: Heath, 1970. 138 p.

1293. *Before the United States Railroad Labor Board; exhibit ...* Chicago, IL: American Federation of Labor, Railway Employees Department; United States Railroad Labor Board, 1921. 19 pt. in 2 v.

1294. Behling, Burton N. *Railroad coordination and consolidation, a review of estimated economies.* Washington, DC: Interstate Commerce Commission, 1940. 174 p. (Its *Statement no. 4023.*)

1294a. Behm, Mitch. *Amtrak made significant improvements in its long-term capital planning process.* Washington, D.C.: U.S. Department of Transportation, Office of the Secretary of Transportation, office of Inspector General, 2011. 24 p. http://purl.fdlp.gov/GPO/gpo18757

1295. Behrens, P. L. *The KD line.* Hebron, IL: P.L. Behrens, 1986. 182 p. (C&NW, Kenosha Division)

1296. _____. *Steam trains to Geneva Lake: C & NW's Elgin-Williams Bay branch.* Hebron, IL: P.L. Behrens, 2002. 156 p.

1297. Beier, Glenn. *Steam echoes: the railroad photography of Glenn Beier.* Hillsboro, OR: Timber Times, 2004. 288 p.

1298. Beil, Gail K., Tom McKinney. *The Texas and Pacific depot in Marshall.* Nacogdoches, TX: East Texas Historical Association, 1999. 56 p.

1299. Belcher, C. Francis. *Logging railroads of the White Mountains.* Foreword by Sherman Adams. Boston, MA: Appalachian Mountain Club, 1980. 242 p.

1300. Bell, J. Snowden. *The Baltimore & Ohio Baldwin engine "Dragon"* New York, Angus Sinclair Co.? 1922. 11 p.

1301. _____. *The development of the eight driving wheel locomotive.* Philadelphia, Baldwin Locomotive Works, 1917. 28 p.

1302. _____. *Development of the locomotive.* Massillon, OH: The Central Steel Company, 1925. 64 p.

1303. _____. *The early motive power of the Baltimore and Ohio Railroad.* New York, Angus Sinclair Co., 1912. 4, 157 p. (Reprint: Felton, CA: Glenwood Publishers, 1975. 157 p.)

1304. _____. *Individual paper on feed-water heaters and their development.* New York, J.S. Bell, 1918. 73 p. (American Railway Master Mechanics' Association, Circular No. E /1916-1917.)

1305. _____. *Individual paper on three-cylinder locomotives/* New York? J.S. Bell? 1913. 42 p. (*Circular: American Railway Master Mechanics Association*)

1306. _____. *The modernization of the Baltimore & Ohio Railroad motive power.* New York, Angus Sinclair Company? 1922. 11 p.

1307. Bell, James P. *Steam trains: a modern view of yesterday's railroads.* St. Paul: MN: MBI and Voyageur Press, 2006. 192 p.

1308. Bell, Louis. *Electric railways; a series of papers and discussion presented at the International Electrical Congress in St. Louis, 1904.* New York, McGraw Pub. Co., 1907. 447 p.

1309. _____. *Power distribution for electric railroads.* New York, Street Railway Publishing Company, 1897. 268 p. (3d ed. rev. and enl. 1900. 303 p.)

1310. Bell, N.J. *Railroad recollections for over thirty-eight years.* Atlanta, GA: Franklin Printing and Publishing Co., 1896. 167 p.

1311. _____. *Southern railroad man: conductor N.J. Bell's recollections of the Civil War era.* James A. Ward, ed. DeKalb, IL: Northern Illinois University Press, 1994. 194 p.

1312. Bell, Samuel J. *Design of a modern steel coaling station/* 1919. 21 l. (Thesis, C.E., Iowa State College.)

1313. Bell, Spurgeon. *Postwar earnings of Class I railroads.* Washington, DC: Interstate Commerce Commission, 1946. 104 p. (Its *Statement no. 467.*)

1314. Bell, William Abraham. *New tracks in North America; a journal of travel and adventure whilst engaged in the survey for a southern railroad to the Pacific Ocean during 1867-8.* Albuquerque, NM: Horn and Wallace, 1965. 564 p.

1315. Belle, John, Maxinne RheaLeighton. *Grand Central: gateway to a million lives.* New York, Norton, 2000. 230 p.

1316. Beller, Morris, Meyer Steinberg. *Composite materials for railroad applications: a feasibility study for renovating deteriorating railroad crossties: report/* Washington, D.C.: Federal Railroad Administration, Office of Research, Development, and Demonstrations, 1973. 24 p.

1317. Bellesiles, Michael A. *1877 : America's year of living violently.* New York : New Press, 2010. 386 p.

1318. Bellovich, Steven J. *A geographic appraisal of settlement within the Union Pacific land grant in eastern Nebraska, 1869-1890 /* 1974. 212 l. (Thesis, Ph.D., University of Nebraska.)

1319. Bellovin, Michael, Andre L. DeVillers, Arthur L. Dow. *Improved passenger equipment evaluation program. Technology review: wheels, axles, couplers: final report.* Washington, DC: Federal Railroad Administration, Office of Research and Development, 1976. 58 p. *(FRA-ORD-79-45.)*

1320. Belmont, Norman J. *Railroad hotbox detector /* Washington, DC : Patent and Trademark Office, 1978. 4 l. United States Patent 4,119,284.

1321. Belnap, Hiram W. *Railway accidents, safety appliances, locomotive ash pans, hours of service, investigations of accidents, and inspection of locomotive boilers.* Washington, D.C., G.P.O., 39 p.

1322. Belovarac, Kenneth. *Determinants of line haul reliability.* Washington, DC: Federal Railroad Administration, U.S. Department of Transportation, 1972. 95 p. (Transportation Systems Division, Department of Civil Engineering Massachusetts Institute of Technology: *Studies in railroad operations and economics, v. 3.*)

1323. Bement, A. *The Peabody atlas; shipping, mine and coal railroads in the central commercial district of the United States.* Chicago: Peabody Coal Co., 1906. 149 p.

1324. Ben-Akiva, Moshe E., Takayuki Morikawa. *Ridership attraction of rail compared with bus/* Washington, DC: Urban Mass Transportation Administration, University Research & Training Program, 1991. 38 p. *(UMTA-MA-11-0044-91-1)*

1325. Bendel, A., Ludwig Henz. *Aufsätze betreffend das Eisenbahnwesen in Nord Amerika. Nach Reise-Notizen des geheimen Regierungsrath Henz, bearb. in dem technischen Eisenbahn-Bureau des Königlichen Ministeriums für Handel.* Berlin, Ernst & Korn, 1862. 74 p. and atlas of 40 plates.

1326. Bender, C.W. *Electric train lighting handbook for railway electrical engineers/* Cleveland, OH: Engineering Department of the National Electric Lamp Association, 1910. 342 p.

1327. _____. *Railway electrical engineers' handbook: electric light and illumination.* 2nd ed. rev. and enl. Cleveland, OH: National Electric Lamp Association, 1912. 344 p. (3rd ed., 1917. 456 p.

1328. Bender, E. K., Larry E. Wittig, J. D. Stahr. *Freight train brake system safety study.* Washington, DC: Federal Railroad Administration, Office of Research and Development, 1983. 152 p. (*FRA/ORD-83/18*)

1329. Bender, Henry E. *Southern Pacific Lines: standard design depots.* Berkeley and Wilton CA: Signature Press, 2012.

1329a. _____. *Uintah Railway: the Gilsonite Route.* Berkeley, CA: Howell-North, 1970. 239 p. (Reprint with corrections: Forest Park, IL: Heimburger House, 1998? 240 p.)

1330. Bendersky, Jay. *Brooklyn's waterfront railways: a pictorial journey.* East Meadow, NY: Meatball Productions, 1988. 64 p.

1331. Benison, Saul. *Railroads, land and iron: a phase in the career of Lewis Henry Morgan.* 1953. 361 l. (Thesis, Ph.D., Columbia University) Railroads-Michigan.

1332. Benn, Benjamin Allen. *Hierarchical car pool systems in railroad transportation /* 1966. 150 l. (Thesis, Case Institute of Technology.)

1333. Benn, Howard P. *Living with the "Big Gorilla": the impact of commuter rail operations on other transit operations.* New York, New York City Transit Authority, 1991. 10 l.

1334. Bennett, Gilbert H., Stephen L. Carr. *Railway reflections: a historical review of Utah railroads.* Ogden, UT:, Ogden Union Station Foundation, 1999. 98 p.

1335. Bennett, James William. *The Railway Labor Act of 1926.* 1955. 366, 2 l. (Thesis, Ph.D., University of Florida.)

1336. Bennett, John C., John C. Prokopy, Raymond H. Ellis. *Analysis of intercity modal split models: final report.* Washington, DC: Federal Railroad Administration, 1973. 60 p. (*DOT-FR-20005-5*)

1337. Benschoten, William Henry. *Report of the Commission to investigate the surface railroad situation in the city of New York, on the west side, appointed under chapter 720 of the laws of 1917. Transmitted to the governor and Legislature January 31, 1918.* Albany: J.B. Lyon Company, Printers, 1918. 639 p. {*Legislature, 1918. Assembly doc. 5*].

1338.Benson, Douglas E., Denver D. Tolliver, Frank J. Dooley. *The R-1 railroad database: an application in transportation research: a technical report.* Fargo, ND: Upper Great Plains Transportation Institute, North Dakota State University, 1991. 98 p.

(*UGPTI staff paper, 98.*)

1339. Benson, Gary J. *The art of railroad photography: techniques for taking dynamic trackside pictures.* Waukesha, WI: Kalmbach Books, 1993. 148 p.

1340. _____. *Rolling thunder: a portrait of North American railroading.* New York, W.W. Norton, 1991. 192 p.

1341. Benson, James E. *Along the old Canada road /* Charleston, DC: Arcadia Publishing, 2008. 127 p. Railroad. Roads. Maine.

1342. Benson, Lee. *Merchants, farmers & railroads; railroad regulation and New York politics, 1850-1887.* Cambridge, Harvard University Press, 1955. 310 p. (*Studies in economic history*)

1343. Benson, Ted. *Echoes down the canyon: a Western Pacific journal, 1968-1986.* Glendora, CA: Westrail publications, 1987. 64 p.

1344. _____ *One track mind: photographic essays on Western railroading.* Erin, ON: Boston Mills Press, 1999. 176 p.

1345. _____, and others. *Mother Lode shortline, a Sierra Railroad pictorial.* Burlingame, CA: Chatham Pub. Co., 1970. 48 p.

1346. Bentham, Garret C. *The International Railway Company strike of 1922, in Buffalo, New York: a thesis in history/* 2008. 88 l. (Thesis, M.A., State University College at Buffalo.)

1347. Benton, Eugene D. *Overfire jets and controls for locomotive smoke abatement.* Pittsburgh, Bituminous Coal Research, Inc., 1947. 14 p. (*Bituminous Coal Research, Inc.; Technical report, no. 8.*)

1348. Benton, Thomas Hart. *Discourse of Mr. Benton, of Missouri before the Boston Mercantile Library Association, on the physical geography of the country between the states of Missouri and California, with a view to show its adaptation to settlement, and to the construction of a railroad. Delivered in the Tremont Temple, at Boston ... December 20, 1854.* Washington, D.C.: Printed by J.T. and L. Towers, 1854. 24 p.

1349. Bereskin, Charles Gregory. *A bi-level model of United States railroad costs.* 1983. 220 l. (Thesis, Ph.D., University of Missouri—Columbia.)

1350. Berg, Walter G. *American railway bridges and buildings. Official reports, Association of Railway Superintendents, Bridges and Buildings.* Chicago, Roadmaster, Foreman, 1898. 706 p.

1351. _____. *American railway shop systems.* New York, The Railroad Gazette, 1904. 198 p.

1352. _____. *Berg's complete timber test record; for engineers, architects, inspectors of wood in construction, contractors, bridge men, etc.* Chicago, IL: B.S. Wasson & Co., 1899. 238 p.

1353. _____. *Buildings and structures of American railroads: a reference book for railroad managers, superintendents, master mechanics, engineers, architects, and students.* New York, J. Wiley, 1893. 500 p. (Reprints: New York, J. Wiley in 1900, 1904, 1907, and 1911. Reprint: S.l., Newton K. Gregg, 1977, 1893. 500 p.)

1354. Berge, Stanley. *Railroad passenger service trends, 1950-1960; a compilation of data reported to the Interstate Commerce Commission by representative U.S. class I railroads in the eastern, southern, and western districts.* Evanston, IL: Northwestern University Bookstore, 1961. 1 v.

1355. _____. *Self-propelled diesel cars and multiple-unit trains; a review of recent developments in the United States and overseas.* Chicago, Northwestern University School of Commerce, 1952. 80 p.

1356. Berger, Robert Eugene. *Holding and investment company ownership of railroad securities.* 1951. 314 (Thesis, Ph.D., Columbia University.)

1357. _____, Donald L. Loftus. *Diesel motor trains, an economic evaluation.* Chicago, Northwestern University School of Commerce, 1949. 66 p.

1358. Berglund, Lee. *Wheat belt route: the story of a Dust Bowl railroad.* David City, NE: South Platte Press, 1998. 92 p. (Wichita Northwestern Railway)

1359. Berglund, Mary, Dale Anderson. *Economic impact of rail branch-line abandonment: research procedures employed in a South-Central Nebraska case study.* Lincoln, NE: Agricultural Experiment Station, Institute of Agriculture and Natural Resources, University of Nebraska, Lincoln, 1976. 43 l.

1360. Bergman, Edwin B. *29 years to oblivion: a detailed listing of the last operating trips for nearly 950 railway post offices that were removed from postal service during the period 1948 to 1977, together with a discussion of the causes and effects of this era on the destruction of a vital public transportation service.* Omaha, NB: Mobile Post Office Society, 1980. 79 p.

1361. Bergman, John F. *The history of Reedley's railroads.* 2nd ed. Reedley, CA: Reedley Historical Society, 2000. 61 p.

1362. _____. *The history of the Sunset Railway: including the McKittrick Branch of the Southern Pacific Company.* Bakersfield, CA: Kern County Historical Society, 1994. 114 p.

1362a. _____, John Winfield. *The Southern San Joaquin Valley: a railroad history /* Visalia, CA: Jostens Printing and Publishing, 2009. 216 p.

1363. Berk, Gerald. *Alternative tracks: the constitution of American industrial order, 1865-1917*. Baltimore, MD: Johns Hopkins University Press, 1994. 243 p. (Railroads and state)

1364. Berkman, Pamela, ed. *The history of the Atchison, Topeka & Santa Fe*. New York, NY: Smithmark Publishers, 1994, c1988. 127 p.

1365. Berndt, Ernst R. *Mergers, deregulation and cost savings in the U.S. rail industry/* Cambridge, MA: National Bureau of Economic Research, 1991. 28 p. (*Working paper series, no. 3749.*)

1366. Bernet, Gerard E. *Jersey Central diesels*. Halifax, PA: Withers Pub., 1990. 192 p.

1367. _____. *A colorful look at Conrail's SD-40 and SD40-2's*. Flanders, NJ: RAE Pub., 1996. 48 p.

1368. Bernhardt, Joshua. *The Railroad Labor Board; its history, activities, and organization*. Baltimore, MD: John Hopkins Press, 1923. 83 p. (*Institute for Government Research. Service monographs of the United States government, no. 19.*)

1369. Bernhart, Benjamin L. *Central Railroad of New Jersey: stations, structures, & marine equipment*. Dauberville, PA; Outer Station Project, 2004. 161 p

1370. _____. *The heart of the Reading Railroad: Reading, Pennsylvania*. John L. Bernhart, ed.; additional material by James D. Brownback. Reading, PA: The Author, 1997. 113 p.

1371. _____. *The New York Central Railroad: stations & structures pictorial /* Dauberville, PA: Outer Station Project (1335 Railroad Dr., Dauberville 19533), 2010- . v. 1. – The River Division, Jersey City to Weehawken, New Jersey. Edited by Jay Leinbach and Melissa Bernhart.

1372. _____. *The Outer Station, Reading, Pennsylvania*. John L. Bernhart, ed. Reading, PA: B.L. Bernhart, 1991. 95, 3 p.

1373. _____. *Penn Street: a pictorial look back in time: in honor of Reading's 250th birthday, 1748-1998*. Reading, PA: Outer Station Project, 1998. 30 p.

1374. _____. *Pennsylvania Railroad in the Schuylkill River Valley : along the historic Reading Main Line /* Dauberville, PA: Outer Station Project, 2006. 156 p.

1375. _____. *Reading Railroad station pictorial*. John H.L. Bernhart and Melissa D. Bernhart, editors. Reading, PA: Outer Station Project, 1998-1999. 4 v.

1376. _____. *The Wilmington & Columbia Division of the Reading Railroad: the Schuylkill and Lehigh Branch*. John L. Bernhart, ed. New Tripoli, PA: Outer Station Project, 1994. 53 p.

1377. _____, and others. *The Reading Railroad's North Broad Street Station, Philadelphia, Pennsylvania.* Dauberville, Pa., Outer Station Project, 1999-2007? 24 p.

1378. _____, _____. *Reading steam in action.* Reading, PA: Outer Station Project, 2000. v.<1-2>

1379. Bernstein, David M. *Southern Pacific Railroad in eastern Texas.* Charleston : Arcadia, 2011. 128 p.

1380. Berry Brothers. *Berry Brothers varnishes, finishes & enamels for railway & traction equipment.* Detroit, Berry Bros., 1913? 59 p. with samples.

1381 _____. *Descriptive price list of Berry Brothers' celebrated railway varnishes.* Detroit, Berry Brothers, 1878. 4 p.

1382. Berrick, Cathleen A. *Passenger rail security: enhanced federal leadership needed to prioritize and guide security efforts: testimony before the Committee on Commerce, Science, and Transportation, U.S. Senate.* Washington, DC: U.S. Government Accountability Office, 2005. 48 p.
Internet file: http://purl.access.gpo.gov/GOP/LPS65124

1383. Berry, Dale W., Richard L. Moss. *Economic analysis of narrow gauge rail service between Alamosa, Colorado and Farmington, New Mexico.* Albuquerque, NM: Kirschner Associates Inc., 1969. 114 p. (Prepared for Four Corners Regional Commission)

1383a. Berry, Richard Allen. *A method to estimate the traffic impacts of at-grade light rail crossings.* 1990. 222 l. (Thesis, M.S., University of Texas at Arlington.)

1384. Berte, Leigh Ann Litwiller. *Locomotive subjectivity: the railroad, literature, and the geography of identity in America, 1830-1930.* 2004. 295 l. (Thesis, Ph.D., University of Washington.)

1385. Bessemer and Lake Erie Railroad Company. *The Bessemer story.* Pittsburgh, The Company, 1951. 17 p.

1386. _____. *Rules and regulations.* Pittsburgh, The Company, 1959. 62 p.

1387. _____. *Rules of the Bessemer and Lake Erie Railroad Company for the government of the operating Department, effective November 25, 1946.* Pittsburgh, The Company, 1946. 79 p.

1388. _____. *The story of the steam locomotives of the Bessemer and Lake Erie Railroad and predecessor companies, by Roy C. Beaver, General Manager.* Pittsburgh, Bessemer and Lake Erie Railroad Co., 1954. 64 p.

1389 *Bessemer bulletin.* Pittsburgh, Bessemer and Lake Erie Railroad Company, 1900s-1984. Monthly.

1390. Bessette, Richard P. *Rods down and dropped fires: Illinois Central and the steam age in perspective.* Orland Park, IL: RTN Press, 2004. 594 p.

1391. Bessey, Raymond Duryea. *The railroads in the state of New Jersey; a short synopsis of the railroads passing through the state, and what they do toward the development of the communities served.* Oradell, N.J., 1945. 50 l.

1392. Best. Gerald M. *Early San Francisco locomotives.* San Mateo, CA: Western Railroader, 196-? 21 p. (Booklet 364)

1393. _____. *Iron horses to Promontory. Golden Spike edition.* San Marino, CA: Golden West Books, 1969. 207 p.

1394. _____. *Locomotives of the Dickson Manufacturing Company: their history, reproduction of an 1885 illustrated locomotive catalog, and roster of locomotives erected by the company between 1862 and 1902.* San Marino, CA: Golden West Books, 1966. 176 p.

1395. _____. *Locomotives of the Southern Pacific Company.* Boston, Railway & Locomotive Historical Society, 1941. 116 p.

1396. _____. _____. Boston, Railway & Locomotive Historical Society, 1956. 172 p.

1397. _____. *Minisink Valley express; a history of the Port Jervis, Monticello & New York Railroad and its predecessors. Art work by E.S. Hammack and Frederic Shaw.* Beverly Hills, CA: 1956. 93 p. (Rev. ed: San Marino, CA: Golden West Books, 1967. 96 p.)

1398. _____. *Nevada County narrow gauge.* Berkeley, CA: Howell-North Books, 1965. 214 p. (Reprint: Forest Park, IL: Heimburger House Pub., 1998. 214 p.

1399. _____. *The Pacific Coast Company: ships and narrow gauge rails.* Wilton, CA: Signature Press, 1992, 1964. 153 p.

1400. _____. *Promontory's locomotives. Introduction by Horace M. Albright.* San Marino, CA: Golden West Books, 1980. 43 p.

1401. _____. *Railroads of Hawaii: narrow and standard gauge common carriers.* San Marino, CA: Golden West Books, 1978. 194 p.

1402. _____. *San Bernardino Valley steam dummy lines.* San Mateo, CA: Western Railroader, 1963. 16 p.

1403. _____. *Ships and narrow gauge rails; the story of the Pacific Coast Company.* Berkeley, CA: Howell-North, 1964. 153 p.

1404. _____. *Snowplow: clearing mountain rails.* Berkeley, CA: Howell-North Books, 1966. 119 p.

1405. _____. *Traveltown.* San Mateo, CA: Western Railroader, 1956. 28 p.

1406. _____ *The Ulster and Delaware; railroad through the Catskills,* San Marino, CA: Golden West Books, 1972. 210 p.

1407. Best, Thomas Doniphan. *The role of the Atchison, Topeka, and Santa Fe Railway system in the economic development of Southwestern United States, 1859-1954 /* 1959. 253 l. (Thesis, Northwestern University.)

1408. *The best of the B & M bulletin, 1971-1980.* Littleton, MA: Boston & Maine Railroad Historical Society, 1988. 200 p.

1409. Bethel, Rodman. *Flagler's folly: the railroad that went to sea and was blown away.* Key West, Fla., R. Bethel, 1987. 111 p.

1410. Bethlehem Shipbuilding Corporation. *Bethlehem railway passenger equipment cars.* Bethlehem, PA: Bethlehem Shipbuilding Corporation, 1922. 46 p. Imprint covered by label: Bethlehem Steel Company … Bethlehem, Pa.

1411. Bethlehem Steel Company. *The Bethlehem auxiliary locomotive: six-wheel design.* Bethlehem, Pa., Bethlehem Steel Co.,,, 1926. 4 p.

1412. _____. *Bethlehem light rail trackwork for mines, quarries and industrial plants.* Bethlehem, Pa., Bethlehem Steel Co., 1949. 165 p.

1413. _____. *Bethlehem light weight wrought steel car wheels: 33-inch freight car wheels.* Bethlehem, Pa., Bethlehem Steel Co., 1927. 16 p.

1414. _____. *Bethlehem rolled steel wheels, steel axles and locomotive forgings with profiles, specifications, tables and data relating thereto.* Bethlehem, PA: Bethlehem Steel Co., 1928. 215 p. (*Catalog 100.*)

1415. _____. *Bethlehem Steel Company, Steelton Plant, Frog and Switch Department, Steelton, Pa.* Bethlehem, PA: Bethlehem Steel Co., 1914-1917. 1 v.

1416. _____. *Bethlehem steel mine ties and light rails for mines, industrial and portable track : booklet 71. /* Bethlehem, Pa., Bethlehem Steel Co., 1935. 81 p.

1417. _____. *Bethlehem switch stands for heavy-duty, standard-gage service.* Bethlehem, PA, Bethlehem Steel Co., 1939. 31 p. (*Catalog 149A*)

1418. _____. *Bethlehem wheels and axles /* Bethlehem, PA: Bethlehem Steel Co., 1953. 204 p. (*Handbook 335.*)

1419. _____. *Bethlehem wheels, axles, and circular products ... Catalog /* Bethlehem, PA : Bethlehem Steel Co.,,, 1900s

1420. _____. *Cambria steel cars for freight service: gondola, hopper, ballast, tank, flat, coke, box and special types.* Bethlehem, PA: Bethlehem Steel Co.,, 1924. 36 p.

1421. _____. *Frog and switch track equipment.* Bethlehem, PA: Bethlehem Steel Co., Frog and Switch Department, 1930. 1 v. unpaged, loose leaf.

1422. _____. *Mine and industrial track equipment and other products, catalog K-1.* Bethlehem, Pa., Bethlehem Steel Co.,, 1930. 194 p.

1423. _____. *New century switch stands: two-tie stands throwing parallel to the track: low, intermediate and high models.* Bethlehem, PA: Bethlehem Steel Co., 1921. 35 p.

1424. _____. *Standard structural shapes, shipbuilding and car building shapes.* Bethlehem, Pa., Bethlehem Steel Co.,, 1929. 333 p.

1425. _____. *This winter fight snow before it falls.* Bethlehem, PA: Bethlehem Steel Co.,, 1940. 3 p. (*Folder 436*) Railroad switches.

1426. Betts, James William. *Strategy of the Baltimore & Ohio Railroad, 1930-1932.* Honolulu, James W. Betts & Co., 2006. 74 p.

1427. Betts, Wilson T. *History of the Colorado and Southern Railway system.* 1926. 102 l.(Thesis, M.A., Southwestern University, Georgetown, Texas.)

1428. Beutel, Frederick Keating. *Due "process" applied to railroad valuation.* 1928. 40 l. (Thesis, Harvard Law School.)

1429. Bevan, George Thomas. *A comparison of the operating performances of modern steam and electric locomotives.* 1932. 76 l. (Thesis, M.S., Massachusetts Institute of Technology, Department of Electrical Engineering.)

1430. Beyer, Otto Sternoff. *Report on the extent of low wages and long hours in the railroad industry/* Washington, DC: Office of Federal Coordinator of Transportation, Section of Labor Relations, 1935. 2, 2, 6, vi, 78 p.

1431. _____. *Unemployment compensation for transportation employees.* Washington, DC: Office of Federal Coordinator of Transportation, Section of Labor Relations, 1936. 110 p.

1432. Bezilla, Michael. *Electric traction on the Pennsylvania Railroad, 1895-1968.* University Park, Pennsylvania State University Press, 1980. 233 p.

1433. _____, Jack Rudnicki. *Rails to Penn State: the story of the Bellefonte Central Railroad.* Mechanicsburg, PA: Stackpole Books, 2007. 1 v.

1434. Bhamidipati, Chiranjivi Sarma, Michael J. Demetsky. *Framework for evaluation of system impacts of intermodal terminals using commodity flow data/* Charlottesville, VA: Center for Virginia Transportation Studies at the University of Virginia, 2008.

117 p. (*Research report: UVACTS-14-5-111.*)
http://cts.virginia.edu/docs/UVACTS-14-4-111.pdf

1434a. Bhatti, Majeed Hussain. *Vertical and lateral dynamic response of railway bridges due to nonlinear vehicles and track irregularities* 1982. 141 l. (Thesis, Ph.D., Illinois Institute of Technology.)

1435. Bianculli, Anthony J. *Iron rails in the Garden State: tales of New Jersey railroading.* Bloomington, IN: Indiana University Press, 2008. 208 p.

1436. _____. *Railroad history on American postage stamps.* Mendham, NJ: Astragal Press, 2004. 266 p.

1437. _____. *Trains and technology: the American railroad in the nineteenth century.* Newark, DE: University of Delaware Press, 2001-2003. 4 v. v. 1: Locomotives. v. 2: Cars. v. 3: Track and structures. v. 4: Bridges and tunnels, signals.

1438. Bias, Charles Vernon. *A history of the Chesapeake and Ohio Railway and its predecessors, 1784-1977.* 1979. 429 l. (Thesis, Ph.D., West Virginia University.)

1439. *Bibliography and priced catalogue of early railway books, 1893.* New York, A.M. Kelley, 1965, 1895. 128, 5-36 p.

1440. *A bibliography of federal railroad labor law.* Frank Dooley, Ann Schwabe-Neumayer, compilers. Fargo, ND: Upper Great Plains Transportation Institute, North Dakota State University, 1991. 85 p. (*MPC report/Mountain-Plains Consortium, no. 91-7.*)

1441. *A bibliography of FRA Office of Research and Development technical reports,1974-1980* / Washington, DC: Federal Railroad Administration, Office of Research and Development, 1981. 116 p. (*FRA/ORD-81/39.*)

1442. *A bibliography of FRA Office of Research and Development technical reports, 1980-1984* / Washington, DC : Federal Railroad Administration, Office of Research and Development, 1985. 178 p. (*FRA/ORD-85/07.*)

1443. *Bibliography of industrial relations in the railroad industry.* James O. Morris, compiler. Ithaca, NY: New York State School in Industrial and Labor Relations, Cornell University, 1975. 153 p.

1444. *A bibliography of Michigan railroads.* LeRoy Barnett, compiler. Ann Arbor, MI: Historical Society of Michigan, 1983. 23 p.

1445. *A bibliography of published research reports.* Washington, DC: Federal Railroad Administration; National Technical Information Service, 1972. 59 p.

1446. *A bibliography of railroad and railroad related publications in the Purdue University libraries.* Prepared by: Richard R. Daubert. Lafayette, IN: Krannert Graduate

School of Industrial Administration Library, Purdue University, 1970. 99 p.

1447. *Bibliography of railroad literature*. Washington, DC : Association of American Railroads, 1954. 56 p. (< *Railway literature for young people* and *Railway literature— a bibliography*.)

1448. *Bibliography of railroad literature*. 6th ed. Washington, DC : Association of American Railroads, 1957. 64 p.

1449. *Bibliography of railroad literature* / 7th ed. Washington, DC : Association of American Railroads, 1961. 64 p.

1450. *Bibliography of railroad literature*. 8th ed. Washington, DC : Association of American Railroads, 1966. 64 p.

1451. *A bibliography of railroad literature*. 10th ed. Washington, DC: Association of American Railroads, 1976. 72 p.

1452. *Bibliography of railway history*. Washington, DC : Association of American Railroads, 1940. 16 p. (*Railway information series, no. 9.*)

1453. *Bibliography of railway literature*. 4th ed. Washington, DC: Association of American Railroads, 1950. 48 p. Revised ed. of Railway literature.

1454. *Bibliography of the Nashville, Chattanooga & St. Louis Railway*. Washington, DC: Association of American Railroads; Bureau of Railway Economics, Library, 1922. 27 l.

1455. *A bibliography on rail technology*. Washington, DC: Dept. of Transportation, Federal Railroad Administration, Office of Research and Development, 1977. 531 p.

1456. (Blank entry.)

1457. *A bibliography of railroad development and urbanization of the trans-Mississippi West, circa 1860-1890*. Thomas Nelson, compiler. Monticello, IL: Council of Planning Librarians, 1977. 39 p.

1458. *A bibliography of railroad literature*. Washington, DC : Association of American Railroads, 1937-   . Other titles: Railway literature for young people, 1937-1940; Railway literature, 1942; Bibliography of railway literature, 1950.

1459. *A bibliography of the Baltimore and Ohio Railroad Company, 1827-1879*. Compiled by John Wesley Murray Lee. London, Baltimore, Privately printed by the Chiswick Press for the Author, 1879. 1 v.

1460. *Bibliography of the design, construction, and operation of railroad passenger stations, 1875 to date,(arranged alphabetically by cities)*. By Carl W. Condit. Evanston, IL: C.W. Condit, 1979. 37 l.

1460a. *Bibliography of the Southern Pacific Company:* San Francisco: Southern Pacific Company, Public Relations Department, 1971. 20 l.

1461. *Bibliography on railway signalling, 1960-1972* / Kingston, ON : Canadian Institute of Guided ground Transport, Queen's University, 1973. 50 p.

1462. *Bibliography, rail freight car utilization.* Washington, DC: Reebie Associates; Freight Car Utilization Research-Demonstration Program, 1979. 72 p. (*AAR report: no. R-370.*)

1463. Bice, David A. *The legend of John Henry: the steel drivin' man.* Charleston, WV: Jalamap Publications, 1980. 32 p.

1464. Bick, I Stuart, Robert Teas Wood. *Rail freight of the Tri-State region.* New York, NY: Tri-State Transportation Commission, 1967-

1465. Bickerstaff, T.H. *Air brakes for high-speed ultra-lightweight passenger trains* /New York : American Society of Mechanical Engineers, 1956. 7 p.
(*ASME. Paper no. 56-A-66.*)

1466. Biddle, George, John Rodman Paul. *Acts of Assembly and ordinances relating to Philadelphia passenger railways and steam railroads with the city limits : with a digest of Pennsylvania decisions relating to passenger railways* / S.l., s.n., 1884. 390 p.

1467. *Biennial convention of the Brotherhood Railway Carmen of America.* S.l., Brotherhood Railway Carmen of America, 1900s-1909. (> Brotherhood Railway Carmen
of America. Convention. *Proceedings of the ... convention.*)

1468. Biernacki, D.G. (Daniel G.). *Erie USRA heavy pacifics.* Columbia, NJ: Erie Lackawanna Historical Society, 1992. 78 p.

1469. Biery, Thomas A. *Alcos to Allentown.* Hanover, PA: Railroad Press, 1998. 112 p.

1470. _____. *Chessie System, Cumberland action.* Hanover, PA: Railroad Press, 1999. 112 p.

1471. Bigelow, Lewis S. *The 1913 flood and how it was met by a railroad.* Pittsburgh, Pennsylvania Lines, 1913. 71 p.

1472. Bigler, William. *Speech...on the Pacific railroad bill delivered in the Senate of the United States, January 6, 1859.* Washington, D.C.: Printed at the Congressional Globe Office, 1859. 13 p.

1473. Bilger, Harry Edward. *A history of railroads in Idaho.* 1969. 105 l. (Thesis, M.A., University of Idaho.)

1474. *A bill to increase railway accidents and railway expenses; the proposed legislation to limit freight trains in Illinois to 50 cars, a statement by the railway of Illinois.* Chicago ? 1915. 23 p. Comments on three bill pending before the legislature of Illinois, session of 1915: House bill 239; Senate bill 229 and House bill 108.

1475. *The Billerica & Bedford, 2-ft gauge railroad; a description, with illustrations, of its location, permanent way and rolling stock.* Morristown, NJ: 1950, 1879, 27 p. (Reprinted: New York, Railroad Gazette, 1879; Railroadians of America, Book. no. 4.)

1475a. Billings, Frederick. *Cost of construction and value of land grant* / New York: Northern Pacific Railroad Company, 1880. 6 p.

1476. Billington, David P. *The innovators: the engineering pioneers who made America modern.* New York, NY: Wiley, 1996. 245 p.

1477. Billstein, Arthur E.F. *Signal construction of a modern railroad receiving and classification yard* / 1923. 26 l. (Thesis, B.S. in Electrical Engineering, University of Pennsylvania.)

1478. Bilty, Charles H. *The story of the Hiawatha.* Milwaukee, Milwaukee Road Railfans Association; Milwaukee County Historical Society, 1985. 78 p.

1479. Bing, Alan J. *An assessment of high-speed rail safety issues and research needs/* Washington, DC: Federal Railroad Administration, Office of Research and Development, 19990. 252 p. (*DOT/FRA/ORD-90/04*)

1480. _____. *Safety of high speed magnetic levitation transportation systems: comparison of U.S. and foreign safety requirements for application to U.S. maglev systems/* Washington, DC: Federal Railroad Administration, Office of Research and Development, 1993. 1 v. (various pagings) (*DOT/FRA/ORD-93/10*)

1481. _____, John Harrison, Robert A. Galganski. *Safety of high speed guided transportation systems; collision avoidance and accident survivability* / Washington, DC : Federal Railroad Administration, Office of Research and Development, 1993. 4 v. Performing organizations : Arthur D. Little, Inc., Parsons, Brinckeroff, Quade & Douglas, Inc., and Calspan Corporation.

1482. _____, Shaun R. Berry, Hal B. Henderson. *Design data on suspension systems of selected rail passenger cars/* Washington, DC: U.S. Department of Transportation, Federal Railroad Administration, Office of Research and Development, 1996. 192 p. (*DOT/FRA/ORD/96/11.*)

1483. Bingham, Robert Charles. *The diesel locomotive: a study in innovation.* 1962. 524 l. (Thesis, Ph.D., Northwestern University.)

1484. Bingham, S. H. *The future of Talgo.* S.l., ACF Industries, 1954. 12 p.

1485. Binney, Marcus, David Pearce. *Railway architecture.* New York, Van Nostrand

Reinhold Co., 1980. 256 p.

1486. Biocchetti, Augelli. *High-speed passenger rail: viability, challenges and federal role* / Hauppauge, NY: Nova Science Publishers, 2009. 1 v.

1487. *The biographical directory of the railway officials of America.* Chicago, Railway Age Pub. Co., 1885-1922. 8 v. (>*Who's who in railroading, United States, Canada, Mexico, Cuba.*)

1488. Biondi, Arnold S, Frederick W. Lyman. *Abandoned railroads in Maine: their potential for trail use.* Augusta, ME: Department of Parks & Recreation, 1973. 108 p.

1489. Birchfield, April Denise. *Peonage on the South and Western railway in North Carolina.* 2001. 102 l. (Thesis, M.A., Wake Forest University.)

1489a. Bird, Frederick Joel. *Water supply for locomotives.* 1901. 209 l. (Thesis, B.S., University of Illinois)

1490. Bird, Kenneth L. *Rails to the Osage : the story of the Warsaw Branch of the Missouri Pacific Railroad, including the Sedalia Warsaw & Southern, & the Sedalia, Warsaw & Southwestern railways* / Lincoln, MO: Menwith Productions, 2009. 88, A35 p.

1491. Bishop, David Wendell. *Railroad decisions of the Interstate Commerce Commission: their guiding principles.* Washington, DC: Catholic University of America press, 1961. 193 p. (Thesis, Catholic University of America.)

1492. Bissell, Franklin Brigham. *Vestibule devices for railway cars.* 1892. 199 l. (Thesis, M.E., Cornell University.)

1493. Bisset, Kendrick. *Introduction to North American railway signaling*/ Omaha, NE: Simmons-Boardman Books, 2008. 210 p.

1494. Bitner, Jack. *The Mount Gretna Narrow Gauge Railroad.* Lebanon, PA: Lebanon County Historical Society, 1984. 18 p. (The Lebanon County Historical Society, *Historical papers and addresses, v. 16, no. 3.)*

1495. Bittinger, J.L. *The Railway postal service: originated by William A. Davis of St. Joseph, Mo.: inaugurated on the Hannibal & St. Joseph Railroad in 1862.* S.l., s.n., 1885. 21 p.

1496. Bittner, Van A., W. Jett Lauck. *Before the Interstate Commerce Commission: Docket no. 12530.* Washington, DC: United Mine Workers of America, 1923. 48 p. (Mine railroad cars; coal transportation.)

1497. Bitzan, John D. *The differential effects of rail rate deregulation: U.S. corn, wheat, and soybean markets.* Fargo, ND: Mountain-Plains Consortium, 2003. 50 p.

1498. _____. *Essays examining the impacts of potential U.S. railroad regulatory policies.* 1997. 116 l. (Thesis, Ph.D., University of Wisconsin-Milwaukee.)

1499. _____. *The importance of short line railroads to rural and agricultural America.* Fargo, ND: Upper Great Plains Transportation Institute, North Dakota State University, 2003. 65 p. (*UGPTI Department Publication, no 152*)

1500. _____. *Railroad cost conditions: implication for policy.* Fargo, ND: Upper Great Plains Transportation Institute, North Dakota State University, 1997. 152 p. (*UGPTI Department Publication, no. 137*)

1501. _____. *Railroad cost considerations and the benefits/costs of mergers.* Fargo, ND: Upper Great Plains Transportation Institute, North Dakota State University, 1997. 61 p. (*MPC Report, no. 97-80.*)

1502 _____. *Railroad deregulation: impacts on rates and profitability.* Fargo, ND: Upper Great Plains Transportation Institute, North Dakota State University, 1994. 18 l. (*UGPTI staff paper series, 122.*)

1503. _____, Denver D. Tolliver. *Emerging state rail issues: implications for rail planning in North Dakota: North Dakota rail services planning study.* Fargo, ND: Upper Great Plains Transportation Institute, North Dakota State University, 1990. 17, 2 p. (*UGPTI Staff Paper, no. 101.*)

1504. _____, _____ *North Dakota strategic freight analysis. Item IV: Heavier loading rail cars.* Fargo, ND: Upper Great Plains Transportation Institute, North Dakota State University, 2001. 82 p. (*MPC Report, no. 01-127.4.*)

1505. _____, _____, Douglas E. Benson. *Small railroads: investment needs, financial options, and public benefits.* Fargo, ND: Upper Great Plains Transportation Institute, North Dakota State University, 2002. 97 p. (*UGPTI Departmental Publication, no. 145.*)

1506. _____. Theodore E. Keeler. *Technological innovation, changing work rules, and productivity growth in rail freight since 1980: a farewell to the caboose.* S.l., s..n., 2000. 25 p. Performed by the Upper Great Plains Transportation Institute and the University of California, Berkeley, Department of Economics.

1507. Bjorkman, Thomas A. *The Rutland Railway.* New York, T.A. Bjorkman, 1964. 96 l. (Thesis, M.B.A., New York University.)

1508. Black, Nelson Miles. *The environment and visual requirements of railway enginemen and firemen. Personal observations from an engine cab. Read at the fifty-fifth annual session of the American Medial Association/* Chicago, IL: Press of American Medical Association, 1904? 40 p.

1508a. Black, Paul Vincent. *The development of management personnel policies on the Burlington railroad, 1860-1900/* 1972. 2 v. (Thesis, University of Wisconsin.)

1509. Black, Robert C. *Railroad pathfinder: the life and times of Edward L. Berthoud.* Evergreen CO: Cordillera Press, 1988. 176 p.

1510. _____. *The railroads of the Confederacy.* Chapel Hill, NC: University of North Carolina Press, 1952. 360 p. (Thesis, Ph.D., Columbia University.) (Reprint: Chapel Hill, Univ. of North Carolina Press, 1998. 360 p.)

1511. Black, Robert Lounsbury. *The Little Miami Railroad.* Cincinnati, OH: s.n., 1936. 191 p. "Operated by Pennsylvania Railroad as lessee of Pittsburg, Cincinnati, Chicago and St. Louis Railroad."

1512. Black, Robert Perry. *A critical review of railroad out-of-pocket cost studies.* 1951. 170 l. (Thesis, M.A., University of Virginia.

1513. Black, W. J. *The California Limited: eleventh season, 1905-1906.* Chicago: Atchinson, Topeka & Santa Fe, 1905. (Eastern edition)

1514. Black, William R. *The generation of transportation networks: their growth and structure.* 1969. 203 l. (Thesis, University of Iowa.)

1515. _____. *Growth of the railway network of Maine: a multivariate approach.* Iowa City, Department of Geography, University of Iowa, 1976, 1967. 27 l. (*Discussion Paper, Dept. of Geography, University of Iowa, no. 5*)

1516. _____. *Railroads for rent: the local rail service assistance program.* Bloomington, Indiana University Press, 1986. 341 p.

1517. _____, James F. Runke. *The states and rural rail preservation: alternative strategies (report).* Lexington, KY: Council of State Governments, 1975. 142 p. (National Task Force of Rail Line Abandonment-Curtailment and Rural Development)

1518. *The Black Worker.* New York, Brotherhood of Sleeping Car Porters, 1929-1968. (Quarterly)

1519. Blackman, William Conrad. *Environmental impacts of policies toward the rail- and motor-freight industries in the United States /* 1985. 329 l. (Thesis, D.P.A., University of Colorado at Denver.) Freight. Law.

1520. Blader, F.B. *Analytic studies of the relationship between track geometry variations and derailment potential at low speeds: final report.* Washington, DC: Federal Railroad Administration, Office of Research and Development, 1983. 119/120 p. (*FRA/ORD-83/16; DOT-TSC-FRA-83-3.*)

1521. _____, G.L. Mealy. *Analytic studies of the effects of track geometry variation/* Washington, DC: Federal Railroad Administration, Office of Research and Development, 1985. 76 p. (*DOT/FRA/ORD-85/01; DOT-TSC-FRA-84-3.*)

1522. Blaine, David G. *High green on the passenger main: a review of passenger train brake development.* Wilmerding, Pa., WABCO, 1976. 40 p. (Westinghouse Air Brake Company)

1523. _____. *Inspection and testing of freight train brakes, inbound, outbound: common troubles and remedies.* Omaha, NE: Simmons-Boardman Pub. Corp., 1981. 25 l.

1524. Blair, Albert U., John W. Porter. *Preliminary inventory of the records of the Senate Committee on Interstate Commerce, Subcommittee to Investigate Interstate Railroads, 1935-43: Record Group 46.)/*Washington, DC: National Archives, National Archives and Records Administration, General Services Administration, 1954. 10 p. (*National Archives publication, no. 75.*)

1525. Blair, Henry W. *Texas and Pacific Railroad.* Washington, DC: 1878. 12 p. (*45th Congress, 2d session. House of Representatives. Report 238, pt 2.*)

1526. Blaise, Clark. *Time lord: Sir Sanford Fleming and the creation of standard time /* New York: Vintage Books, 2000. 255 p.

1527. Blake, Henry William, Walter Jackson. *Electric railway transportation.* New York: McGraw-Hill Book Company, 1917. 487 p.

1528. Blake Signal and Manufacturing Company. *The Blake Signal System for electric and steam railroads.* Boston, Blake Signal & Mfg. Co., 1920. 7 p.

1528a. Blakemore, Arthur W. *The abolition of grade crossings in Massachusetts.* Boston : Little, Brown, and Company, 1905. 76 p.

1529. Blakemore, M.N., Richard Hellman, John West. *Fuel economy on railroads of the United States, 1918-1937.* New York, Special Research Section, 1937. 133, 28 p. (National Research Project on Reemployment Opportunities and Recent Changes in Industrial Techniques (U.S.).)

1530. Blakeslee, Philip C. *Lines West: a brief history.* New Haven, CT: Camm Associates, 1974. 32 p.

1531. Blanchard, Leslie F. *Steam locomotives on the Northern Pacific Railway; a historical resume/* S.l., Rail Sound Committee, Puget Sound Railway Historical Association, 1959. 4 p.

1532. Blank, Hartmut. *Der Einfluss der Eisenbahn auf die militarische Beweglichkeit um die Mitte des 19. Jahrhunderts: Kavallerie im Einsatz gegen und für das neue Verkehrssystem Eisenbahn; aufgezeigt am Beispiel des Amerikanischen Bürgerkriegs (1861-1865)/* 2001 260 p., 22 p. of plates. (Thesis, Doctoral, Freie Universität, Berlin, 1999.)

1533. Blanton, Burt C. *400,000 miles by rail: the reminiscences of "professional passenger"* on all types of trains. Berkeley, CA: Howell-North Books, 1972. 183 p.

1533a. Blardone, Charles. *Pennsylvania Railroad advertising art: featuring the Ed Lied collection/* Bryn Mawr, PA: Pennsylvania Railroad Technical & Historical Society; Kutztown, PA: Kutztown Publishing Co., 2013. 284 p.

1533b. _____. *Pennsylvania Railroad business and special cars: a century of Tuscan red deluxe.* Upper Darby, PA: Pennsylvania Railroad Technical and Historical Society, 2007. 148 p.

1534. _____, Peter Tilp. *Pennsylvania Railroad passenger car painting and lettering.* Upper Darby, PA: Pennsylvania Railroad Technical and Historical Society, 1988. 127 p.

1535. Blaszak, Mike, Mike Schafer. *Railroad photography: how to shoot like the pros.* Andover, NJ: Andover Junction Publications, 1993. 62, 3 p.

1536. Blau, Douglas. *Trains: Chris Burden, Jon Kessler, Dennis Oppenheim; December 15, 1990-January 26, 1991/* New York, NY: Michael Klein (Gallery), Inc., 1990. 16 p.

1537. Blay, Joshua K. *Billboard refrigerator cars: a thesis.* 2003. 42 l. (Thesis, M.A., State University of New York College at Oneonta. Cooperstown Graduate Program.)

1538. Blevins, Tim. *Legends, labors & loves: William Jackson Palmer, 1836-1909.* Colorado Springs, Pikes Peak Library District with the Colorado Springs Pioneers Museum & Colorado College, 2009. 405 p.

1539. Blevins, Thomas H. *A brief history of the "Virginia Creeper" : the famed Abingdon branch of the Norfolk and Western Railway* / S.l., s.n., 2003. 15 p.

1540. Bliss, E. F. *Modern electric block signaling.* 1902. 24 l. 16 l. of plates. (Thesis, B.A., University of Nebraska.)

1541. *Block signals on the railroads of the United States and table showing use of the telegraph and the telephone for transmission of train order.* / Washington, D.C., G.P.O., 1908-1913. Annual. (Block Signal and Train Control Board; Interstate Commerce Commission, Division of Safety Appliances.) (> *Tabulation of statistics pertaining to block signals and the telegraph and the telephone for transmission of train orders as used on the railroads of the United States.*)

1541a. Blodget, Bradford G. *Marium Foster's Boston and Albany Railroad: the story of Keene's railroad lady.* Keene, NH: Historical Society of Cheshire County, 2011. 150 p.

1542. Blodgett, Rufus. *Rules and instructions governing the use of automatic block and interlocking signals, New York and Long Branch Railroad.* Rahway, NJ:? Railroadians of America, 1975, 1906. 58 p.

1543. Bloomsburg Car Manufacturing Company. (Bloomsburg, Pa.) *Freight, mine and dump cars and car wheels of every description* ... / Buffalo : Gies & Co., Printers, 1895. 64 p.

1544. Bloss, Ernest K. *The choice of locomotives for the Radford Division of the Norfolk & Western Railway.* 1921. 42 l. (Thesis, E.E., Worcester Polytechnic Institute.)

1545. *The Blue Ridge stemwinder.* DeSoto, MO: John R. Waite, 1988-Quarterly ("A journal of southern Appalachian narrow-gauge railroading."

1546. *BMWE journal.* Detroit, MI: Brotherhood of Maintenance of Way Employes. 1988-2004. Monthly. (< *Railway journal*; > *BMWED journal*.)

1547. *BMWED journal.* Southfield, MI: International Brotherhood of Teamsters; Brotherhood of Maintenance of Way Employes Division; 2005-   . Bimonthly. (< *BMWE journal*.)

1547a. Board, Arley R and others. *Test on C. & N. W. Ry. head end electric lighting system* / 1910. 13, 8l. (Thesis, B.S., Iowa State University.)

1548. Board of Arbitration in the Controversy between the Eastern Railroads and the Order of Railway Conductors and the Brotherhood of Railroad Trainmen, 1913. *Proceedings. Arbitration between the eastern railroads and Order of Railway Conductors and the Brotherhood of Railroad Trainmen. Submitted to arbitration, under the act of July 15, 1913, by agreement dated July 26, 1913. At Manhattan Hotel, New York, Sept. 11-[Oct. 10] 1913* / Seth Low, chairman. New York, Law Reporting Co., 1913. 3 v.

1549. Board of Arbitration in the Controversy between the Western Railroads and the Brotherhood of Locomotive Engineers and the Brotherhood of Locomotive Firemen and Enginemen, 1914-1915. *Proceedings. Arbitration between the Western Railroads and the Brotherhood of Locomotive Engineers and the Brotherhood of Locomotive Firemen and Enginemen submitted to arbitration under the act of July 15, 1913, by agreement dated August 3, 1914.* Jeter C. Pritchard, chairman. Chicago, IL: Law Reporting Co., Official Reports, 1915. 9 v.

1550. Boardman, John Michael. *Industrial development and the modern railway.* 1958. 122 l. (Thesis, M.B.A. in Transportation and Public Utilities, Graduate School of Arts and Sciences, University of Pennsylvania)

1551. Boatner, Victor Vincent. *Report on coordination of railroad terminals: St. Louis – East St. Louis.* Washington, D.C.? Federal Coordinator of Transportation, 1934. 1 v.

1552. _____. *Report on railroad terminal co-ordination, Chicago, Illinois and vicinity.* Chicago, Planographed by Photopress, Inc.,1936. 2 v. (Chicago Terminal Committee; Western Regional Coordinating Committee; United States, Office of Federal Coordinator of Transportation)

1553. _____, A.J. Hammond. *Report on the Minneapolis & St. Louis Railroad* / Chicago: s.n., 1936. 2, 74 l.

1554. Boberg, Kevin B. *Changes in railroad track structure depreciation recognition the United States: their potential economic consequences*/ 1984. 206 l. (Thesis, Ph.D., Business Logistics, Pennsylvania State University.)

1555. Bodt, Barry A., Jerry Thomas. *Statistical modeling of railroad safety performance.* Aberdeen Proving ground, MD: U.S. Army Armament Research and Development Command, Ballistic Research Laboratory, 1983. 36 p. (*Memorandum report, ARBRL-MR-03311.*)

1556. Boehm, William Benedict. *The effect of the Mexican Revolution on El Paso's railroads, 1910-1916.* 1997. 161 l. (Thesis, M.A., New Mexico State University.)

1557. Bogan, R.F. *Technological obsolescence in railroad freight cars, 1945-1960; and, trends in freight car design, 1950-1965.* Chicago, s.n. 1961. 13, 17 l. (Pullman Incorporated. Pullman-Standard Division)

1557a. Bogart, Charles H. *Railroad, trolley, and interurban rail lines of Frankfort, Kentucky.* Frankfort, KY: Yellow Sparks Press, 2010. 237 p.

1557b. _____, William M. Ambrose. *The whiskey route: the Frankfort & Cincinnati Railroad, Frankfort, Kentucky.* Frankfort, KY: Yellow Sparks Press, 2012. 189 p.

1558. Bogart, Mary, William C. Hattan. *Conquering the Appalachians: building the Western Maryland and Carolina, Clinchfield & Ohio Railroads through the Appalachian Mountains; taken from the journals, records and photographs of William C. Hattan, a civil engineer who built much of it.* Rochester, NY: Railroad Research Publications (PMB 266, 3400 Ridge Rd. W., Ste 5, Rochester, NY 14626), 2000. 206 p.

1559. Bogen, Jules Irwin. *Analysis of railroad securities; a guide to the determination of investment values.* New York, Ronald Press, 1928. 449 p.

1560. _____. *The anthracite railroads; a study in American railroad enterprise.* New York, The Ronald Press Company,1927. 281 p. (Thesis, Ph.D., Columbia University.)

1561. Bohn, Dave, Rodolfo Petschek. *Kinsey, photographer: a half century of negatives by Darius and Tabitha May Kinsey, with contributions by son and daughter, J. and Dorothea.* New York, Black Dog & Leventhal Publishers, 1995- 3 v. in 2.

1562. _____, _____, and others. *The locomotive portraits.* San Francisco, Chronicle Books, 1984. 143 p.

1563. Bohnstengel, Walter. *Pulverized coal locomotive vs. hand-fired locomotive.* 1920.

1 v. (Thesis, M.S., University of Kansas.)

1563a. *Boiler attachments : instruction paper with examination questions* / 2nd ed., revised. Scranton, PA: International Textbook Co., 1910. 3 v. Pt. 2. Locomotive lubricators – pt. 3. Sanders and bell ringers.

1564. *Boiler maker and plate fabricator.* Philadelphia, Simmons-Boardman Pub. Corp., 1934-1937. 4 v.

1565. Boland, Kells. *Alaska Canada rail link: phase 1 feasibility study, research report.* Alaska, Yukon: Alaska Canada Rail Link Management Working Group, 2007. 67 p. http://www.alaskacanada rail.org/documents/Research%20Report%2007.pdf

1566. Boldyreff, Alexander W. *Determination of the maximal steady state flow of traffic through a railroad network.* Ft. Belvoir Defense Technical Information Center, 1955. 41 p. (Rand Corporation, Santa Monica, CA.)

1567. Bolema, Theodore Robert. *Railroad common costs and facility abandonments.* 1989. 92 l. (Thesis, Ph.D., Michigan State University.)

1568. Bolen, George Lewis. *The plain facts as to the trusts and the tariff, with chapters on the railroad problem and municipal monopolies.* New York: Macmillan, 1902. 451 p.

1569. Boles, Patrick Parker. *The freight car supply problem and car rental policies.* Washington, DC: Economic Research Service, U.S. Department of Agriculture, 1972. 28 p. (*Marketing research report, no. 953.*)

1570. Bollinger, Edward Taylor. *Rails that climb; the story of the Moffat Road.* Drawings by Wilfred Stedman. Santa Fe, NM: Rydal Press, 1950. 402 p.

1571. _____. *Rails that climb: a narrative history of the Moffat Road.* Edited by William C. Jones. Golden, CO: Colorado Railroad Museum, 1979. 323 p.

1572. Bollinger, Edward Taylor, Frederick Bauer. *The Moffat Road.* Denver, Sage Books, 1962. 359 p. (Reprint: Athens, OH: Ohio University Press, 1981. 359 p.)

1573. Bonbright, James C. *Railroad capitalization: a study of the principles of regulation of railroad securities.* New York, NY: Columbia University, 1920. 206 p. (*Studies in history, economics, and public law, v. XCV, no. 1, whole no. 215.*) Reprint: New York, NY: AMS Press, 1969. 206 p. (Dissertation, Ph.D., Columbia University.)

1574. Bond, Frank Stuart. *Argument made Oct. 7, 1875, at Austin, Texas, before the Committee on Railway Corporation, of the Texas State Constitutional Convention, by Frank S. Bond, vice-president of the Texas & Pacific Railway Company.* Austin : Daily State Gazette, 1875. 12 p.

1575. _____. *Railroad legislation; argument before the Committee on Internal Improvements, House of Representatives, Texas legislature, at Austin, February 15,*

1879. Marshall Tex., Jennings bros. printers, 1879. 26 p.

1576. _____. *Statement and argument of Frank S. Bond, Vice-President Texas and Pacific Railway Company, before the Committee on the Pacific Rail Road, House of Representatives, Jan. 19, 1876*. Washington ? D.C. : s.n., 1876. 29, 16 p.

1577. _____. *Statement and argument of Frank S. Bond, Vice-President Texas & Pacific Rwy Co., made before the Committee on the Judiciary of the House of Representatives, 44th Congress, 1st session : to whom was referred a resolution of inquiry as to matters connected with the Texas & Pacific Railway Co., the passage of its act of incorporation, its contracts and relations with other corporations*. Washington? s.n., 1876. 34 p.

1578. _____. *The Texas and Pacific Railway. Argument and statements of Frank S. Bond ... before the Committee on Pacific Railroads of the U.S. Senate, Washington, D.C., February 15, 1878*. Dallas, TX: J.F. Worley, 1897. 24 p.

1579. _____. *Texas & Pacific Railway. Argument and statements of Frank S. Bond, vice-president Texas and Pacific Railway Company, before the Committee on the Pacific R.R., House of Representatives, Jan. 29, 1878*. Washington? DC: 1878. 33 p.

1580. _____. *The Texas and Pacific Railway Company's relations to the state of Texas, and the character of state legislation in respect to that company* / Marshall, TX: s.n., 1877. 9 p.

1581. _____. *Texas and Pacific Railway. Statement and argument of Frank S. Bond, vice-president of the Texas and Pacific Railway Company, in reply to Mr. Norwood, of Georgia, who appeared as counsel of the Southern Pacific Railroad Company (of California), before the Committee on Pacific Railroads, of the Convention for the promotion of American Commerce, held in New Orleans, December 4th, 1878*. S.l., s.n., 1878. 18 p.

1582. _____. *Texas and Pacific Railway : statements and argument and accompanying papers* / Washington, DC : s.n., 1876. 29, 16, 37 p. To the House Committee on the Pacific Railroad.

1583. _____. *Texas & Pacific Railway : supplemental argument and statements of Frank S. Bond, vice-president Texas and Pacific Railway Co., filed with the Committee on the Pacific Railroad, House of Representatives, Feb. 1, 1878, Washington, D.C.* S.l., s.n., 1878. 9 p.

1584. _____. *Who shall build a southern trans-continental railway on the 32d parallel of latitude?* Philadelphia : Review Printing House, 1876. 13 p. Reply of Frank S. Bond, vice-president Texas & Pacific Railway Company to Collis P. Huntington, Ag't and attorney of the Southern Pacific Railroad Co. of California, January 3d, 1876.

1585. Bonds, Russell S. *Stealing the General: the great locomotive chase and the first Medal of Honor*. Yardley, PA: Westholme Publishing, 2006. 444 p.

1586. Bonenberger, Dan, Michael Caplinger. *The Baltimore & Ohio Railroad main stem.* Morgantown, WV: Institute for the History of Technology and Industrial Archaeology, 2005. 2 v. (*Save America's Treasures, Project 54-02-ML-1258.*)

1587. Boner, Harold A. *The giant's ladder: David H. Moffat and his railroad.* Milwaukee, Kalmbach Pub. Co., 1962. 224 p.

1588. Bonham, John Milton. *Railway secrecy and trusts.* New York, G.P. Putnam's, 1890. 138 p.

1589. Bonnell, Henry F. *Hawaiian rails of yesteryear.* Janet Lorimer and Robert Paoa, editors. Ewa Beach, Hawaii, Hawaiian Railway Society, 1997. 75 p.

1590. Bonney, Charles Carroll. *Rules of law for the carriage and delivery of persons and property by railway* / Chicago : E.B. Myers, 1864. 267 p.

1590a. Bonney, Charles L. *Railway law for railway men: passenger trains, baggage masters, ticket agents, conductors, engineers.* Chicago: Railway Age Publishing Company, 1878. 58 p.

1591. *Book of the Royal Blue.* Baltimore: Baltimore and Ohio Railroad, Co., 1897-1911. 14 v.

1592. Boon, Chris J. *High speed rail tilt train technology: a state of the art survey.* Washington, DC: Federal Railroad Administration, Off ice of Research and Development, 1992. 208 p. (*DOT/FRA/ORD-92/03*)

1593. _____, Brian T. Whitten. *Tilt train technology: a state of the art survey.* Washington, DC: Federal railroad Administration, 1992. 50 p.

1593a. Booth, J. L. *Booth's patent steel tread, duplex steel and iron rails for railways; their manufacture explained, and merits discussed.* Rochester, NY: Benton and Andrews, 1868. 14 p.

1594. Booth, Stephenia L. *Gulf, Mobile, & Ohio Railroad Terminal: Baldwyn House.* 1981. 81 l. (Thesis, B.I.D., Auburn University. _

1595. Boothroyd, Stephen J. *Down at the station: rail lines of southern New England in early postcards.* Watertown, NY: Cranberry Junction, 2002. 121 p.

1596. Booz, Allen & Hamilton. *Analysis of a coordinated rail transportation system for grain between St. Paul and Kansas City : final report.* Washington, DC? : s.n., 1981.

1597. _____. ; Chicago, Milwaukee, St. Paul, and Pacific Railroad Company. *The Milwaukee Road strategic planning studies.* Bethesda, MD: Booz, Allan & Hamilton, Transportation Consulting Division, 1979. 3 v.

1598. Borden, Stanley T. *The Albion Branch, Northwestern Pacific.* San Mateo, CA: Western Railroader, 1961. 32 p.

1599. _____. *Arcata & Mad River: 100 years of railroading in the Redwood Empire.* San Mateo, CA: Western Railroader, 1965. 39 p.

1600. _____. *Caspar Lumber Company: Caspar, South Fork & Eastern Railroad.* San Mateo, CA: Western Railroader, 1966. 34 p.

1601. _____. *Diamond Match Company: Northern California logging operations.* San Mateo, CA: Western Railroader, 1968. 34 p.

1602. _____. *Glen Blair Redwood Company and Cleone tramway.* San Mateo, CA: Western Railroader, 1961. 11 p.

1603. _____. *History and rosters of the Northwestern Pacific Railroad and predecessor lines.* San Mateo, CA: Western Railroader, 1949. 32 p.

1604. _____. *Humboldt logging railroads.* San Mateo, CA: Western Railroader, n.d. 40 p.

1605. _____. *Minarets and Western Railway and the Sugar Pine Lumber Company.* San Mateo, CA: Western Railroader, 1959. 16 p.

1606. _____. *NWP's Carlotta Branch: the California Midland R.R.* San Mateo, CA: Western Railroader, 1958. 12 p.

1607. _____. *Nevada County Narrow Gauge Railroad.* Enl ed. San Mateo, CA: Western Railroader, 1963. 18, 20 p.

1608. _____. *Petaluma & Santa Rosa Electric R.R.* San Mateo, CA: Western Railroader, 1960. 36 p.

1609. _____. *Pre-N.W.P. railroads of Eureka: Oregon & Eureka Railroad and San Francisco & Northwestern.* San Mateo, CA; The Western Railroader, n.d. 16, 23 p.

1610. _____. *Rails for logging: Oregon & Eureka Railroad.* San Mateo, CA: Western Railroader, 1958. 17 p.

1611. _____. *The Western Pacific Railroad Company: Feather River Route.* San Mateo, CA: Western Railroader, 1972. 1 v. (Booklet 361)

1612. _____. *Yreka Western Railroad.* San Mateo, CA: Western Railroader, 1960. 16 p.

1613. Borer, Frank J. *Railway pipe fitter's handbook; pipe fitting in theory and practice for locomotives, passenger and freight cars.* New York, Simmons-Boardman, 1925. 223 p.

1614. Borkin, Joseph. *Robert R. Young, the populist of Wall Street.* New York, NY: Harper & Row, 1969. 236 p. (Finance)

1615. Borkowski, Richard C. *Louisville & Nashville in color.* Scotch Plains, NJ: Morning Sun Books, 2003- v. 1-

1616. _____. *Norfolk Southern Railway/* St. Paul, MN: Voyageur, 2008. 1 v.

1617. _____. *Pittsburgh & Lake Erie Railroad in color.* Scotch Plains, NJ: Morning Sun Books, 2002- v. 1-

1618. _____. *Union Railroad in color.* Scotch Plains, NJ: Morning Sun Books, 2001. 127 p.

1619. Borneman, Walter R. *Marshall Pass*: *Denver & Rio Grande, gateway to the Gunnison country: featuring the Dow Helmers collection.* Colorado Springs, Century One Press, 1980. 160 p.

1620. _____. *Rival rails: the race to build America's greatest transcontinental railroad/* New York, Random House, 2010. 406 p.

1621. Borntrager, Karl A. *Keeping the railroads running: fifty years on the New York Central, an autobiography, and a review of the railroad crisis today.* New York, Hastings House, 1974. 256 p.

1622. Borsvold, David. *Railroading in Conneaut, Ohio.* Chicago, IL: Arcadia, 2003. 128 p.

1623. Borzo, Greg. *The Chicago "L".* Charleston, SC: Arcadia, 2007. 128 p.

1624. Bossler, Craig T. *B&O color guide to freight and passenger equipment.* Edison, NJ: Morning Sun Books, 1996. 1 v.

1625. _____. *CNJ/LV color guide to freight and passenger equipment.* Edison, NJ: Morning Sun Books, 1994. 127 p.

1626. _____. *RDG color guide to freight and passenger equipment.* Edison, NJ: Morning Sun Books, 1993. 127 p.

1627. Boston and Albany Railroad Company. *Classification of locomotives.* 6th ed. Springfield, Mass., Boston And Albany Railroad Co., 1891. 39 p.

1628. _____. *Schedule of instructions and rates of wages affecting road and yard service: to take effect April 1st, 1905.* Written by J.B. Stewart. S.l., Boston & Albany Railroad, 1905.

1629. _____. *Schedule of instructions, rules, and rates of pay governing locomotive engineers, firemen, and hostlers.* S.l., Boston & Albany Railroad, 1922. 55 p.

1630. _____. *Schedule of instructions, rules, and rates of pay governing locomotive engineers, firemen, and hostlers.* S.l., Boston & Albany Railroad, 1924. 60 p.

1631. Boston and Maine Railroad. *Instruction manual: Boston and Maine diesel freight locomotives.* La Grange, Ill., Electro-Motive Division, General Motors Corporation, 1944. 1 v

1632. _____. *Boston and Maine Railroad's snow trains: Sundays and week-ends from North Station.* Boston, MA: Boston and Maine Railroad, 1945. 30, 2 p.

1633. _____. *Instructions and general information for the operation of air conditioning, and its related heating equipments, in passenger service.* Boston, The Railroad, 1937. 67 p.

1634. _____. *Instructions for the government of electric locomotive engineers and firemen in the operation of electric locomotives.* Boston, Office of the General Superintendent of Motive Power, 1938. 34 l, 8 leaves of plates.

1635. _____. *Regulations governing employees upon the main and branch lines of the Boston and Maine Railroad.* Boston, Rand, Avery & Co., 1872. 45 p.

1636. _____. *Rules for the government of the Operating Department, to take effect April 25, 1948.* Boston, Boston and Maine Railroad, 1948. 246 p.

1637. _____. *The snow train: Sundays and week-ends from the North Station.* Boston, Boston and Maine Railroad, 1937. 33 p.

1638. _____. *Winter in New England and the snow train.* Boston, Boston and Maine Railroad, 1936. 46 p.

1639. Boston and Maine Railroad Historical Society. *Hoosac Tunnel centennial, 1873-1973.* Reading, MA: Boston and Maine Railroad Historical Society, Inc., 1973. 19 p.

1640. _____. *Moguls, mountains, and memories: a gallery of New England railroading north and west of Boston.* Reading, MA: Boston & Maine Railroad Historical Society, 1979. 126 p.

1641. Boston (Mass.). City Council. *The railroad jubilee: an account of the celebration commemorative of the opening of railroad communication between Boston and Canada, September 17th, 18th, and 19th, 1851.* Boston, J.H. Eastburn, City Printer, 1852. 288 p.

1641a. Boston (Mass.) Harbor. *Report of the directors of the port of Boston upon the use of water terminals and railroad connections, January 1914.* Boston; Wright & Potter Printing Co., 1914. 27 p.

1642. Boston Elevated Railway Company. *Snow fighting and equipment.* Boston, Boston

Elevated Railway Company, 1917. 111 p.

1643. Botkin, Benjamin Albert, Alvin F. Harlow. *A treasury of railroad folklore; the stories, tall tales, traditions, ballads, songs of the American railroad man.* New York: Crown Publishers, 1953, 530 p.

1644. Botkin, William E., Victor Hand, Ronald C. Hill. *Union Pacific: mainline west.* Golden, CO: Colorado Railroad Museum, 1986. 80 p.

1645._____, Ronald C. Hill, R.H. Kindig. *Union Pacific 3985.* Golden, CO: Colorado Railroad Historical Foundation, 1985. 63 p.

1646. Bottemiller, Charles Edward. *Meat and men in Minnesota; the St. Paul Union Stockyards to 1907.* 1963. 97 l. (Thesis, M.Ed., Macalester College.)

1647. Bourke, Jos. *Modern compound locomotives; a practical treatise on the design, operation and maintenance of Vauclain, Schenectady, Richmond and Rhode Island builds.* Salt Lake City, Utah, Press of the F.W. Gardiner Company, 1902. 138, 7 p.

1648. Bourne, Russell. *Americans on the move: a history of water-ways, railways, and highways with maps and illustrations from the Library of Congress.* Golden, CO: Fulcrum Publishing, 1995.133 p. ("Published in cooperation with the Library of Congress.")

1648a. Bovey, Byron D. *High line of the Camas Prairie Railroad.* Craigmont , ID: Ilo-Vollmer Historical Society, 2007. 96 p.

1649. *Bowden, J.J. Surveying the Texas and Pacific land grant west of the Pecos River.* El Paso, TX: Texas Western Press, 1975. 89 p.

1650. Bowden, Jack. *Railroad logging in the Klamath County.* Hamilton, MT: OSO Pub., 2003. 352 p.

1651. _____, Tom Dill. *The Modoc: Southern Pacific's backdoor to Oregon.* Hamilton, MT: OSO Pub., 2002. 336 p.

1652. Bowden, Jesse Earle, Virginia Parks. *Iron horse in the pinelands: building west Florida's railroad, 1881-1883: a centennial history.* Pensacola, FL: Pensacola Historical Society, 1991. 92, 28 p.

1653. Bowers, Robert G., and James F. Brewer. *Cabooses of the Norfolk and Western.* Forest VA: Norfolk & Western Historical Society, 1994. 247 p.

1654. _____ *Norfolk and Western caboose all-time roster, May2004.* Roanoke, VA: Norfolk and Western Historical Society, 2004. 120 p. (*Data series, no 2.*)

1655. Bowes, Thomas D. *A presentation of modern diesel tugs : 1600 h.p. railroad tugs, 960 h.p. railroad tugs and commercial tugs.* S.l., s.n., 1950-1959. 52 p. Powered by Fairbanks, Morse & Co.; built by RTC Shipbuilding Corporation, Camden, N.J.

1656. Bowman, Bob. *Up and down the line: the centennial history of the Angelina & Neches River Railroad.* Lufkin, TX: Best of East Texas Publishers, 2000. 232 p.

1657. Bowman, Hank Wieand. *Pioneer railroads.* New York, Arco Pub., 1978, 1954. 143 p.

1658. Bowman, Marion. *Railroads: mainlines of Florida, the Orange Belt.* Dade City, FL: Pioneer Florida Museum Association, 197-? 99 p.

1659. *Box, stock & refrigerator cars from the 1931 Car Builders' Cyclopedia.* Novato, CAL Newton K. Gregg, 1972. p. 107-159, 168-194

1660. Boyd, Brian. *The Tallulah Falls Railroad.* Clayton, GA: Fern Creek Press, 1998. 64 p.

1661. Boyd, Jim. *The American freight train.* Osceola, WI: MBI Pub., 2001. 156 p.

1662. _____. *Baldwin diesels.* Scotch Plains, NJ: Morning Sun Books, 2002. 3 v.

1663. _____. *Burlington Northern.* Kutztown, PA: Morning Sun Books, 2007. 128 p.

1664. _____. *Fairbanks-Morse locomotives in color.* Edison, NJ: Morning Sun Books, 1996. 128 p.

1665. _____. *Illinois Central: Monday mornin' rails.* Andover, NJ: Andover Junction Publications, 1994. 128 p.

1666. _____. *Kansas City Southern in color: the era of "streamlined hospitality", 1940-1970.* Scotch Plains, NJ: Morning Sun Books, 2003. 128 p.

1667. _____. *Missouri Pacific in color.* Edison, NJ: Morning Sun Books, 2004- v. 1-

1668. _____. *Outbound trains: in the era before the mergers.* Erin, ON: Boston Mills Press, 2005. 192 p.

1669. _____. *Passenger Alcos in color: the story of the DL109s and PAs.* Scotch Plains, NJ: Morning Sun Books, 2000. 128 p.

1670. _____. *The steam locomotive: a century of North American classics.* New York, MetroBooks, 2002. 144 p.

1670a. _____. *Steamtown in color, from F. Nelson Blount to the National Park Service.* Kutztown, PA: Morning Sun Books, 2011. 128 p.

1671. _____. *Trackside around Granger Country, 1952-1955 with Rich Wilson.* Scotch Plains, NJ: Morning Sun Books, 2004. 128 p.

1672. _____. *Trackside Milwaukee Road east: with Jim Boyd.* Scotch Plains, NJ: Morning Sun Books, 2005. 128 p.

1673. _____. *Trackside Milwaukee Road west: with Jim Boyd.* Scotch Plains, NJ: Morning Sun Books, 2006. 128 p.

1674. _____, Tracy Antz. *Lehigh & Hudson River: in color: history and operations of the L & HR, 1860-1976.* Scotch Plains, NJ: Morning Sun Books, 2001. 128 p.

1675. Boyd, R.H. *The separate or "Jim Crow" car laws or legislative enactments of fourteen southern states: together with the report and order of the Interstate Commerce Commission to segregate negro or "colored" passengers on railroad trains and in railroad stations.* Nashville, TN: National Baptist Pub. Board, 1909. 67 p. "In compliance with a resolution of the National Baptist Convention, September 19, 1908, at Lexington, Ky"

1676. Boyd, William Harland. *The Shasta route, 1863-1887: the railroad link between the Sacramento and the Columbia.* 1942. 116 l. (Thesis, Ph.D., University of California.) (Reprint: New York, Arno Press, 1981.)

1677. Boyden, Henry Paine. *The beginnings of the Cincinnati Southern Railway; a sketch of the years 1869-1878.* Cincinnati, The R. Clarke Co., 1901. 122 p.

1678. Boyer, Dennis. *Prairie whistles: tales of Midwest railroading.* Black Earth, WI: Trails Books, 2001. 128 p.

1679. _____. *Snow on the rails: tales of heartland railroading.* Oregon, WI: Badger Books, 2003. 247 p.

1679a. Boykin, McKinley Edward. *The L & N Railroad : its influence on the development of Alabama/* 1930. 112 l. (Thesis, M.A., George Peabody College for Teachers.)

1680. Boyle, Jonathan J. *Burlington Route: streamlined observation cars.* Forest, VA: TLC Pub., 2004. 80 p.

1681. _____. *Santa Fe Railway's streamlined observation cars.* Forest, VA: TLC Pub., 2004. 76 p.

1682. Boyle, O.D. *History of railroad strikes; a history of the railroad revolt of 1877; the American Railroad Union strike on the Great Northern in 1894 and its participation in the Pullman car strikes of the same year; the eight-hour day strike of 1917 and the runaway switchmen's strike of 1920.* Washington, D.C.: Brotherhood Publishing Co., 1935. 110 p.

1683. Boyles, Berlyn L. *Denver, Longmont and Northwestern.* Denver, The Club, 1952. 35 p. (*Rocky Mountain Railroad Club, v. 5*)

1684. Boynton, James E. *The 4-10-2: three barrels of steam.* Felton, CA: Glenwood Publishers, 1973. 161 p.

1685. _____, and others. *Love affair with iron horse: Jim Boynton's life with on the steel rail.* Quincy, CA: Plumas Community History Project, 1983. 38 p.

1686. Bracken, Jeanne Munn. *Iron horses across America: the trans-continental railroad.* Carlisle, MA: Discovery Enterprises, 1995. 64 p.

1687. Bradford, Armory H. *High speed railroads.* New York: Regional Plan Association, 1965. 14 p. (*Regional plan news, no. 79*)

1688. Bradlee, Francis Boardman Crowninshield. *The Boston and Lowell Railroad, the Nashua and Lowell Railroad, and the Salem and Lowell Railroad.* Melrose, MA: Panorama Publications, 1972. 64 p.

1689. _____. *The Boston and Maine Railroad; a history of the main road, with its tributary lines.* Salem, MA: Essex Institute, 1921. 84 p. (Reprint: Melrose, MA: Panorama Publications, 1972. 84 p.

1690. _____. *The Boston, Revere and Lynn narrow gauge railroad* / Salem, MA: s.n., 1921. 1 v. (various pagings).

1691. _____. *Eastern Railroad; a historical account of early railroading in eastern New England.* 2d ed. Salem, MA: The Essex Institute, 1922. 122 p. (Reprint: Melrose, MA: Panorama Publications, 1972. 122 p.)

1692. Bradley, Bill. *The last of the great stations: 50 years of the Los Angeles Union Passenger Terminal.* Glendale, CA: Interurbans Press, 1989. 120 p. (*Interurbans special, 72.*)

1693. Bradley, Glenn D. *The story of the Santa Fe.* Boston, R.G. Badger, 1920. 288 p. (Thesis, Ph.D., University of Michigan.)

1694. Bradley, James T. *Cabooses of North America.* Irving, TX: Bradley Enterprises, 1990- v. 1-

1695. _____. *North American locomotive production, 1968-1989.* Irving, TX: Bradley Enterprises, 1989. 191 p.

1696. _____ *North American maintenance of way equipment.* Irving, TX: Bradley Enterprises, 1992. 64 p.

1697. _____. *North American non-revenue freight cars.* Irving, TX: Bradley Enterprises, 1992 64 p.

1698. _____. *Wrecks, accidents & collisions.* Irving, TX: Bradley Enterprises, 1991.

94 p.

1699. Bradley, V.J. *The United States railway mail service; a brief sketch of its history and principle features.* Buffalo, N.Y.? National Association Railway Postal Clerks, 1901. 15 p.

1700. Bradshaw, George. *Prevention of railroad accidents* / New York, Norman W. Henley Publishing Company, 1912. 173 p.

1701. Brady, C. *Steel passenger car frame construction.* Montreal? : s.n., 1914. 12 p.

1702. Brady, Jasper Ewing. *Tales of the telegraph: the story of a telegrapher's life and adventures in railroad, commercial and military work.* New York: Doubleday & McClure, 1899. 272 p.

1703. Brady, John Thomas. *The Texas Pacific.* Houston : Telegraph Steam Printing House, 1876. 10 p. Speech of the Hon. John T. Brady, delivered in the Senate of Texas, July 21st, 1876.

1704. Brain, Insley J. *The Milwaukee Road electrification; a review of the first long-distance electrification on main line railroad in North America.* San Mateo, CA: Bay Area Electric Railroad Association and the Western Railroader, 1961. 45 p.

1704a. Bramson, Seth. *Florida East Coast Railway.* Charleston, SC: Arcadia Pub., 2008. 128 p

1704b. _____. *The greatest railroad story ever told: Henry Flagler and the Florida East Coast Railway's Key West extension.* Charleston, SC: History Press, 2011. 160 p.

1705. _____. *Speedway to sunshine*: the story of the Florida East Coast Railway. Erin, ON: Boston Mills Press, 1984. 320 p. (Reprint with revisions: 2003. 347 p.

1706. Brand, Daniel. *Forecasting high speed rail ridership*/ Washington, DC: Transportation Research Board, National Research Council, 1992. 28 p. (Charles River Associates).

1707. Brandeis, Louis Dembitz. *Financial condition of the New York, New Haven & Hartford Railroad Company and of the Boston & Maine Railroad.* Boston, 1907. 77 p.

1708. _____. *Scientific management and railroads: being part of a brief submitted to the Interstate Commerce Commission.* New York, Engineering Magazine, 1911. 92 p.

1709. Brandes, Ely M., Alan E. Lazar. *The future of rail passenger traffic in the West.* Menlo Park, CA: Stanford Research Institute, 1966. 57 p.

1710. _____, Robert C. Brown, Paul S. Jones. *Selected impacts of railroad mergers.* Washington, DC: U.S. Department of Commerce, 1965. 203 p. "Prepared for Department of Commerce by Stanford Research Institute." SRI project no. II-4895.

1711. Brandt, C.A. *The design and proportion of locomotive boilers and superheaters.* New York, The Author, 1928. 43 p.

1711a. Brandt, Marisa Kay. *"Necessary guidance": the Fred Harvey Company presents the Southwest*/2011. 219 l.(Thesis, Ph.D. University of Minnesota.)

1712. Brasher, Larry E. *The one-spot twins.* Derby, KS: Santa Fe Railway Historical & Modeling Society, 2001. 128 p.

1713. _____. *Santa Fe locomotive development: the journey to supreme steam and pioneer diesels.* Berkeley and Wilton, CA: Signature Press, 2006. 304 p.

1714. Braudaway, Douglas Lee. *Railroads of western Texas: San Antonio to El Paso.* Chicago, Arcadia Pub., 2000. 128 p.

1715. Brauer, Peter F. *Records relating to railroads in the cartographic section of the National Archives.* Washington, DC: National Archives and Records Administration, 2010. (*Reference information paper, no. 116.*)

1716. Brautigam, Harold Sylvanus. *United States safety appliances; a practical manual of safety appliance laws, legal decisions, and Interstate Commerce Commission orders and interpretations covering the application of safety appliances to the motive power and rolling stock of steam railway in the United States.* New York, N.Y., Simmons-Boardman Pub. Co., 1924. 246 p. (New ed: New York: Simmons-Boardman, 1927. 232 p)

1717. Bray, Don E., J.R. Salley. *Flaw detection in model railway wheels* / Washington, DC: Federal Railroad Administration, Office of High-Speed Ground Transportation, 1971. 215 p. (*FRA/RT-71/75.*)

1718. _____. M. Najim, L.R. Cornwall. *Optimization of ultrasonic flaw detection in railroad rail : final report.* Washington, DC: Research and Special Programs Administration, U.S. Department of Transportation, 1983. 98, 21 p. (*DOT/RSPA/DMA-50/83/18.*)

1719. Bray, Donald H. *Cog railway: Mount Washington, New Hampshire.* Mount Washington, NH: Mount Washington Railway Company, 1991. 23 p.

1720. _____. *They said it couldn't be done: the Mount Washington* Cog *Railway and its history.* Dubuque, IA: Kendall/Hunt Pub. Co., 1984. 172 p.

1721. Brazeal, Brailsford Reese. *The Brotherhood of Sleeping Car Porters; its origin and development.* New York, London, Harper & Bros., 1946. 258 p. (Thesis, Ph.D., Columbia University, 1942.)

1722. Brazel, James P. *The economic history of the Schuylkill Navigation Canal and its competition with the Philadelphia and Reading Railroad.* 1975. 358 l. (Thesis, M.A., Temple University.)

1723. Brechenser, Donn M. *Railroads of Northern Virginia.* Bernardston, MA: Valley Offset Printing, 1971. 64 p.

1724. Breed, Charles Blaney. *Report on air transportation to Pennsylvania Railroad.* Philadelphia : s.n., 1945. 2 v. Pennsylvania Railroad Company. Committee on Air Transport. Bibliography in v. 2.

1725. Breedlove, Evelyn "Nikki". *Boxcars and candlelight: railroad memories.* Tavares, FL: Artcraft Printing, 1999. 27 p.

1726. Breedlove, John Cromwell. *The development of the use of iron and steel in car construction.* 1902. 69, 5 l. (Thesis, C.E., Cornell University.)

1727. Breen, Denis A. *The Union Pacific/Southern Pacific rail merger; a retrospective on merger benefits.* Washington, DC: Federal Trade Commission, Bureau of Economics, 2004. 46 p. (*Working paper, no 269*)

1728. Breese, Sidney. *Origin and history of the Pacific railroad; the first report in Congress, 1846.* Chicago, IL: E.B. Myers and Company, 1870. 49 p.

1729. Brehm, Frank. *Track charts of the Western Pacific Railroad Company: including branches and subsidiary railroads/* San Jose, CA: San Jose Printing, 2002. 157 p.

1730. Breiner, Charles M., William E. Scott. *A guide to the New York, Ontario & Western Railway's Monticello, Port Jervis& Kingston divisions.* Middletown, NY: Ontario & Western Railway Historical Society, Inc., 2002. 90 p.

1731. _____, _____. *A guide to the New York, Ontario & Western Railway's southern division: Cornwall to Liberty.* Middletown, NY: Ontario & Western Railway Historical Society, 2001. 89 p.

1732. Brennan, Larry. *Railfan's guide to Jacksonville and northeast Florida and southeast Georgia: including a history and maps of all lines* / Jacksonville, FL: Gateway Model Railroad Club, 1994. 32 p.

1733. Brennan, William J. *Trackside in the Erie Lackawanna New Jersey commuter zone with William J. Brennan.* Scotch Plains, NJ: Morning Sun Books, 2005. 128 p.

1734. _____, Walter A, Appel. *Jersey Central Lines in color.* Edison, NJ: Morning Sun Books, 1991-2003. 3 v.

1735. Brenner, Aaron, Benjamin Day, Immanuel Ness. *The encyclopedia of strikes in American history/* Armonk, NY: M.E. Sharpe, 2009. 750 p.

1736. Bretey, Pierre R. *Progress report: Gulf, Mobile and Ohio Railroad Company.*

New York, Hayden, Stone & Co., 1960. 19 p.

1737. _____. *A study of the Gulf, Mobile and Ohio Railroad Company.* New York, Hayden, Stone & CO., 1957. 36 p.

1738. Brewer, James F., Thomas D. Dressler. *Norfolk & Western Railway standards drawings.* Baltimore, MD: Norfolk & Western Historical Society, 1992. 110 l.

1739. Brich, Stephen C. *Investigation of retroreflective sign materials at passive railroad crossings*/ Charlottesville, VA: Virginia Transportation Research Council, 1995. 35 p. (*VTRC-95-R22.*)

1740. Brickle, Barrie. *Passenger rail train-to-train impact test: test procedures, instrumentation, and data.* Washington, DC: Federal Railroad Administration, Office of Research and Development, 2003. 245 p. in various pagings. (*DOT/FRA/ORD-03/17.III.*)

1741. Bricker, L. J. *List of land dealers along the Northern Pacific.* St. Paul : Northern Pacific Railway Company, 1911. 29 p. Land companies- Northwest, Pacific

1742. Bridenstine, Freda L. *The Madison and Indianapolis Railroad.* 1931. 77 l. (Thesis, M.A., Butler University)

1743. *Bridge & building news.* Homewood, IL: American Railway Bridge & Building Association, 1939-

1744. *Bridge architecture and design: railroad bridges, a selected bibliography.* Anthony G. White, comp. Monticello, IL: Vance Bibliographies, 1981. 4 p.

1744a. *Bridge specifications, design of plate girders, design of a highway truss bridge, design of a railroad truss bridge, wooden bridges, roof trusses, bridge piers and abutments, bridge drawing.* Scranton, PA: International Textbook Company, 1908. 1 v. (various pagings)

1745. Bridges, David. *Memories of the Hamp Line: a history of the Starkville Branch.* Joliet, IL: Gulf, Mobile & Ohio Historical Society, 1996. 33 p. (*GM&O Historical Society news, no. 78.*) Starkville (Miss.)

1746. *A brief history of the separation of railroad operating expenses between freight and passenger services.* Washington, DC: Interstate Commerce Commission, Bureau of Transport Economics and Statistics, 1957. 13 p. (*Statement no. 577, file no. 9-E-1.*)

1747. *A brief history of the Washington, Idaho & Montana Railway Company.* S.l., Letah County Historical Society; University of Idaho, 1982. 35 p.

1748. *A brief list of material relating to American railroad songs*/ Washington, DC: Archive of Folk Song, 1971. 2 p.

1749. Briggs, Alton King. *The archeology of 1882 labor camps on the Southern Pacific Railroad, Val Verde County, Texas.* 1974. 210 p. (Thesis, M.A., University of Texas.)

1750. Briggs, Samuel W. *Government regulation of railway transportation: the origin and development of the act to regulate commerce.* Washington, D.C., s.n., 1904. 1 v.

1751. _____. *Regulation of interstate commerce: history of bills and resolutions introduced in Congress respecting Federal regulation of interstate commerce by railways, etc., from the Thirty-seventh Congress to the Sixty-first Congress, inclusive, 1862-1911.* Washington: G.P.O., 1912. 126 p. (United States. Congress. Senate. Committee on Interstate Commerce.)

1752. Brigham, Albert Perry. *From trail to railway through the Appalachians.* Boston, Ginn & Co., 1907. 188 p.

1753. Brignano, Mary, Hax McCullough. *The search for safety: a history of railroad signals and the people who made them.* New York, Union Switch & Signal Division, American Standard Inc., 1981. 199 p.

1753a. Brill, Peter A. *The Maybrook Gateway: linking five railroads with southern New England.* Lansdale, PA: The Anthracite Railroad Historical Society, 2013. 256 p.

1754. Brin, Burton N., Richard S. Prosser. *Spirit of the rails.* Colton, CA: West Colton Press, 1960. 60 p.

1755. Brinegar, Claude S. *Rail service in the Midwest and Northeast region; a report.* Washington, D.C.: Department of Transportation, U.S.G.P.O., 1974. 4 v.

1756. Brink, P.C. *New safety rail road car wheels & axles, letters patent secured.* Camden, NJ : s.n., 1853. 2 l.

1757. Brinton, Caleb Jefferis. *A spatial economic analysis of steam coal exportation from the Rocky Mountains and northern Great Plains to out-of-area power plants.* 1980. 267 l. (Thesis, Ph.D., The University of Utah.)

1758. British Productivity Council. *Diesel locomotives; productivity team report. Report of a visit to the U.S.A in 1950 of a productivity team representing the diesel locomotive industry.* New York, British Productivity Council, 1950. 51 p.

1759. Brittin, Robert P. *Central Vermont, the south end: remembering the "Banana Belt."* David City, NE: South Platte Press, 1995. 84 p.

1760. Britton, Charles C. *The Quanah Route: a Texas short line railroad.* Fort Collins, CO: Joed Books, 1990. 100 p.

1761. Britton, Jack. *Shop hints on locomotive valve setting.* 2d ed. New York, Simmons-Boardman, 1939. 350 p.

1762. *The Broad Street Station building: Pennsylvania Boulevard and the Parkway, Philadelphia,* by the Pennsylvania Railroad and Graham, Anderson, Probst, White. New York, Select Printing Co., 1930. 16 p.

1763. Broadbelt, H.L. *Catalog of original Baldwin Locomotive Works photographs.* Morrisville, PA: The Company, 1966. 101 p.

1764. Brockmann, R. John. *Twisted rails, sunken ships; the rhetoric of nineteenth century steamboat and railroad accident investigation reports, 1833-1879.* Amityville, NY: Baywood Publishing Co., 2004. 273 p. (*Baywood technical communications series*)

1765. Brodhead, Richard. *Speech of Mr. Brodhead, of Pennsylvania, on railroad iron duty: in reply to Mr. Jones, of Tennesseee [sic] delivered in Senate of the United States, February 8, 1855.* Washington: Printed at the Congressional Globe office, 1855. 8 p.

1766. Bromley, Isaac H. *Pacific railroad legislation: 1862-1855.* Boston, Rand, Avery, 1886. 75 p.

1767. Bromley, Joseph, as told to Page Cooper. *Clear the tracks! The story of an old-time locomotive engineer.* New York, NY: Armed Services Editions, 1944, 1943. 288 p. (*Armed Services edition, F-158.*) "Published by arrangement with Whittlesey House, New York and London."

1768. Brooks, Brian B., William Plunkett. *Santa Fe locomotive 3751.* San Bernardino, CA: San Bernardino Railroad Historical Society, 1993. 21 p.

1769. Brooks Locomotive Works. *A catalogue descriptive of simple and compound locomotives.* Buffalo, N.Y., Northrup, 1899. 336 p.

1770. _____. *Catalogue of locomotive details.* Edward Hungerford. Dunkirk, N.Y., Brooks Locomotive Works, 1895. 159 p.

1771. _____. *Catalogue of locomotives.* Dunkirk, N.Y., Brooks Locomotive Works, 1894. 237 p.

1772. _____. *Classification of locomotives.* Dunkirk, N.Y. The Works, 1899. 36 l. of plates.

1773. _____. *Pan-American Exposition, 1901: some notable locomotives.* Dunkirk, N.Y., Brooks Locomotive Works, 1901. 31 p.

1774. _____. *World's Columbian Exposition, Chicago, 1893: exhibit of locomotives made by Brooks Locomotive Works, 1893.* Buffalo, N.Y., The Matthews-Northrup Co.., 1893. 1 v.

1775. Brooks, Michael W. *Subway city: riding the trains.* New Brunswick, NJ: Rutgers University Press, 1997. 252 p.

1776. Brooks, Terrence. *Pennsylvania Railroad: the early days.* Los Angeles, CA: Trans-Anglo Books, 1964. 49 p.

1777. Brookville Locomotive Company. *Brookville locomotives and rail trucks: special models for passenger, express, supplies, light freight and all rail haulage.* Brookville, PA: The Company, 1931. 11 p. (*Bulletin B-3AA-1.*)

1778. _____. *Brookville locomotives BMD series 4, 5, 6, 8, and 10 tons.* Brookville, PA: Brookville Locomotive Company, 1931. 12 p.

1779. _____. *Brookville locomotives for Fordson power : improved Fordson power in improved Brookville locomotives.* Brookville, PA: Brookville Locomotive Company, 1930. 6 p. (*Bulletin B-31.*)

1780. _____. *Brookville locomotives "IB" series in 4 ½, 5, 6, 8, 10, and 12 tons.* Brookville, PA: Brookville Locomotive Company, 1930. 12 p.

1781. _____. *Brookville locomotives with Ford "AA" power : 2, 2 ½. 3. 3 1/2/. and 4 tons.* Brookville, PA: Brookville Locomotive Company, 1930. 8 p. (*Bulletin-B-4-AA-1.*)

1782. Brosius, J. *Erinnerungen an die Eisenbahnen der Vereinigten Staaten von Nord-Amerika.* Wiesbaden, J.F. Bergmamnn, 1885. 2. verm. Aufl. 157 p.

1783. Brotherhood of Locomotive Engineers. *Eighty-ninth anniversary ; official publication* Philadelphia : Division 51, Pennsylvania Railroad, Brotherhood of Locomotive Engineers, 1954. 130 p.

1784. _____. *Locomotive Engineers' 1949 diesel case: the development of the diesel question.* S.l., s.n., 1949. 43 l.

1785. _____. *Rulings: for the government of, and the placing of engineers on the M.K.T. Ry System.* Rev. ed. S.l., s.n., 1933. 14 p.

1786. _____. Pennsylvania Railroad Division 51. *Ninety-fourth anniversary : official publication.* Philadelphia : Division 51, Pennsylvania Railroad, Brotherhood of Locomotive Engineers, 1958. 68 p.

1787. *Brotherhood of Locomotive Engineer's monthly journal.* Rochester, N.Y., Published by the Order of the Grand International Division, 1867-1905. 39 v. Monthly

1788. Brotherhood of Locomotive Firemen and Enginemen. *Catechism of the electric headlight.* Indianapolis, Ind., W.B. Burford, Printer, 1906. 94 p.

1789. _____. *A compilation of rates of pay and rules for engineers, firemen, and hostlers for the Lake Erie and Western District of the New York, Chicago and St. Louis Railroad Company, : Nickel Plate Road.* Peru, IN: Brotherhood of Locomotive Firemen and Enginemen, 1944. 40 p.

1790. _____. *Eastern concerted wage movement, 1912-1913.* n.p., 1913. 1283 p.

1791. _____. *Federal legislation, etc., affecting railroad employees.* January, 1940. Washington? 1940. 247 p.

1792. _____. *Feeding the iron hog; the life and work of a locomotive fireman.* Cleveland, The Brotherhood of Locomotive Firemen and Enginemen, 1927. 100 p.

1793. _____. *General wage and rule agreements.* Cleveland, OH: Brotherhood of Locomotive Firemen and Enginemen, 1941? 596 p.

1794. _____. *Grand Lodge proceedings of the ... biennial convention ... at ....* Toronto, Ont, etc., The Brotherhood, 1898-1904. Biennial. 4 v. (< Brotherhood of Locomotive Firemen. *Journal of proceedings of the ... biennial convention of the Brotherhood of Locomotive Firemen, held in ....; >* Brotherhood of Locomotive Firemen. *Report of the Grand Master of the Brotherhood of Locomotive Firemen to the ... biennial convention.*)

1795. _____. *Journal of proceedings of the ... annual convention of the Brotherhood of Locomotive Firemen.* Terre Haute, IN: The Brotherhood, 1886. Annual. 1 v. (< Brotherhood of Locomotive Firemen. *Journal of proceedings of the ... annual conventions of the Brotherhood of Locomotive Firemen; >* Brotherhood of Locomotive Firemen. *Journal of proceedings of the ... biennial convention of the Brotherhood of Locomotive Firemen, held in ....*)

1796. _____. *Journal of proceedings of the ... annual conventions of the Brotherhood of Locomotive Firemen.* Terre Haute, IN: The Brotherhood, 1885. 1 v. (> Brotherhood of Locomotive Firemen. *Journal of proceedings of the ... annual convention of the Brotherhood of Locomotive Firemen.*

1797. _____. *Journal of proceedings of the ... biennial convention of the Brotherhood of Locomotive Firemen, held in....* Terre Haute, IN: The Brotherhood, 1888-1896. Biennial. 5 v. (< Brotherhood of Locomotive Firemen. *Journal of proceedings of the ... annual convention of the brotherhood of Locomotive Firemen; >* Brotherhood of Locomotive Firemen. *Grand Lodge proceedings of the ... biennial convention ... at ....*)

1798. _____ *The Pennsylvania railroad: schedule of regulations and rates of pay for the government of engineers, firemen, and hostlers in road and yard service.* Philadelphia, 1928. 1063 p.

1799. _____. *Proceedings of the ... biennial convention of the Brotherhood of Locomotive Firemen and Enginemen.* Columbus, OH: The Brotherhood, 1908-1910. Biennial. 2 v. (< Brotherhood of Locomotive Firemen. *Report of the Grand Master of the Brotherhood of Locomotive Firemen to the ... biennial convention;* Brotherhood of Locomotive4 Firemen. *Proceedings of the ... biennial convention of the Brotherhood of Locomotive Firemen; >* Brotherhood of Locomotive Firemen and Enginemen. *Proceedings of the ... convention of the Brotherhood of Locomotive Firemen and Enginemen.)*

1800. _____. *Proceedings of the ... convention of the Brotherhood of Locomotive Firemen and Enginemen.* Washington, DC: etc.: The Brotherhood, 1913-1968. Sexennial, 1937-1968; Triennial, 1913-1931. 14 v. (< Brotherhood of Locomotive Firemen and Enginemen. *Proceedings of the ... biennial convention of the Brotherhood of Locomotive Firemen and Enginemen*; > United Transportation Union. *Proceedings of the convention of the United Transportation Union.*)

1801. _____. *Report covering the wage movement of 1943.* n.p., 1944. 80 p.

1802. _____. *Report of the Grand Master of the Brotherhood of Locomotive Firemen to the ... biennial convention.* Peoria, IL: Edw. Hine & Co., 1902-1906. Biennial. (< Brotherhood of Locomotive Firemen. *Grand Lodge proceedings of the ... biennial convention ... at ....*; > Brotherhood of Locomotive Firemen. *Proceedings of the ... biennial convention of the Brotherhood of Locomotive Firemen*; Brotherhood of Locomotive Firemen and Enginemen. *Proceedings of the ... biennial convention of the Brotherhood of Locomotive Firemen and Enginemen.*)

1803. _____. *State railroad laws relating to full crew qualifications of personnel train lengths.* Cleveland? Brotherhood of Locomotive Firemen and Enginemen, 1939. 46 p.

1804. _____. Grand Lodge. *Schedules of rates of pay and rules and regulations governing locomotive enginemen.* Peoria?: Grand Lodge, Brotherhood of Locomotive Firemen and Enginemen, 1902. 630 p.

1805. *Brotherhood of Locomotive Firemen and Enginemen's magazine.* Terre Haute, Ind., Brotherhood of Locomotive Firemen and Enginemen, 1873-1963. 155 v. (Monthly) (<*Firemen's Magazine,* v. 1-9, 1873-1875; *Locomotive firemen's magazine,* v.10-29, 1886-1900.)

1806. *Brotherhood of Locomotive Firemen's magazine.* Peoria, Ill., The Brotherhood, 1901-1906. 12 v. Monthly

1807. Brotherhood of Maintenance of Way Employes. *Milestones of progress; a brief history of the Brotherhood of Maintenance of Way Employees.* Detroit, The Brotherhood, 1969. 40 p.

1808. _____. *Pictorial history [of] Brotherhood of Maintenance of Way Employes, 1887-1951.* Detroit, MI: Brotherhood of Maintenance of Way Employes, 1951. 64 p.

1809. _____. *Proceedings of the ... regular convention.* Detroit: Brotherhood Press, 1925-   . Quadrennial, 1962-   ; Triennial, 1925-1958.

1810. *Brotherhood of Maintenance of Way Employes journal.* Detroit, MI: Brotherhood of Maintenance of Way Employes, `1931-1975. Monthly. 45 v. (< *Railway maintenance of way employees journal;* > *Railway journal.*)

1811. Brotherhood of Railroad Signalmen of America. *50 years of railroad signaling: a history of the Brotherhood of Railroad Signalmen of America.* Chicago, Ill., Brotherhood of Railroad Signalmen of America, 1951. 32 p.

1812. Brotherhood of Railroad Trainmen. *The Brotherhood of Railroad Trainmen; a brief sketch of its history, functions and accomplishments.* Cleveland, OH: The Brotherhood, 1954. 24 p.

1813. _____. *Federal laws, general wage and rule agreements, decision, awards and orders governing employees engaged in train, yard and dining car service on railroads in the United States.* Cleveland, s.n., 1954. 909 p.

1814. _____. *Main Street, not Wall Street: a reply to the railroad's demands for a wage reduction—1938.* Cleveland, OH: The Brotherhood of Railroad Trainmen, 1938. 482 p.

1815. _____. *Proceedings of the ... biennial convention of the Brotherhood of Railroad Trainmen.* Cleveland, OH: Britton Print. Co., 1800s-1900s. Biennial. 5th, 1901.

1816. _____. *Proceedings of the ... convention of the Brotherhood of Railroad Trainmen.* Miami Beach: Atlantic Printers, 1916?-1968. Frequency varies. (28th, 1946.) (< Brotherhood of Railroad Trainmen. *Proceedings of the ... quadrennial convention of the Brotherhood of Railroad Trainmen* [1935-1939]; > Brotherhood of Railroad Trainmen. *Proceedings of the ... convention of the Brotherhood ...*)

1817. _____. *The pros and cons of compulsory arbitration; a debate manual.* Cleveland, The Brotherhood of Railroad Trainmen, 1965. 194 p.

1818. _____. *Shorter workday: a plea in the public interest.* Cleveland, OH: The Brotherhood of Railroad Trainmen, 1937. 55 p.

1819. Brotherhood of Railway, Airline, and Steamship Clerks, Freight Handlers, Express, and Station Employes. *Proceedings of the ... Regular and ... Quadrennial Convention of Railway, Airline, and Steamship Clerks, Freight Handlers, Express, and Station Employes.* Rockville, MD: BRAC, 1971-1983. 4 v. (> Brotherhood Railway Carmen of the United States and Canada. Convention. *Proceedings.*)

1820. Brotherhood Railway Carmen of America. *Biennial convention of the Brotherhood Railway Carmen of America.* S.l., Brotherhood Railway Carmen of America, 1900s-1909. Biennial. 11th (1909). (> Brotherhood Railway Carmen of America. Convention. *Proceedings of the ... convention.*)

1821. _____. *Caboose and passenger car safety appliances pictured.* Kansas City, Mo., Brotherhood Railway Carmen of America; Trade Educational Bureau, 1921. 48 p.

1822. _____. *Proceedings of the ... convention/* S.l., The Brotherhood, 1905-1900s. Quadrennial, 1950-1958. Frequency varies. Proceedings for 1st-8th conventions in *Railway carmen's journal.*

1823. _____. *Proceedings of the ... convention*. S.l., The Brotherhood, 1913-1968. Quinquennial, 1953-1968. Quadrennial, 1913-1929. Every 6 years, 1935-1941. Quinquennial, 1946. Quadrennial, 1950-1958. 13 v. (< Brotherhood Railway Carmen of America. Convention. *Biennial convention of the Brotherhood Railway Carmen of America* > Brotherhood Railway Carmen of the United States and Canada, Convention. *Proceedings of the ... convention*.)

1824. _____. *Proceedings of the ... convention*. S.l., Brotherhood of Railway Carmen of the United States and Canada, 1973-1983. 3 v. Quinquennial.

1825. _____. Trade Educational Bureau. *The car wheel: compiled.* Kansas City, MO: Brotherhood Railway Carmen of America, Trade Educational Bureau, 1921. 56 p.

1826. Brotherhood of Railway Clerks. *Proceedings ... regular and ... biennial convention of the Brotherhood of Railway Clerks*. S.l., Brotherhood of Railway Clerks, 1900s-1919. (> Brotherhood of Railway and Steamship Clerks, Freight Handlers, Express and Station Employees. Convention. *Proceedings of ... regular and ... triennial convention of the ...*))

1827. Brotherhood of Sleeping Car Porters. *The Pullman porter.* New York, The Brotherhood, 1927. 15 p.

1828. _____. *Report of proceedings of the biennial convention and celebration of the Brotherhood of Sleeping Car Porters*. S.l., Brotherhood of Sleeping Car Porters, 1938-1950. Biennial.

1829. Brotherton, William J. *Burlington Northern adventures: railroading in the days of the caboose.* David City, NE: South Platte Press, 2004. 159 p.

1829a. Brough, Lawrence A. *The electric Pullman: a history of the Niles Car & Manufacturing Company/* Bloomington: Indiana University press, 2013. 113 p.

1830. _____. *From small town to downtown: a history of the Jewett Car Company, 1893-1919.* Bloomington, IN: Indiana University Press, 2004. 255 p.

1831. Brouws, Jeffrey T., Ed Delvers. *Starlight on the rails.* Photographs selected by Jeff Brouws and Ed Delvers; text by Jeff Brouws with an introduction by Richard Steinheimer. New York, Harry N. Abrams, 2000. 137 p. (Catalog of an exhibition held at the Robert Mann Gallery, New York, N.Y., October 26-December 7, 2000.

1832. _____, Ronald C. Hill. *Railroading west: a contemporary glimpse.* Rev. ed. Burbank, CA: Darwin Publications, 1979. 80 p.

1832a. _____, Wendy Burton. *Some vernacular railroad photographs /* New York: W.W. Norton, 2013.

1833. Brovald, Ken C., Michael Aronson, Jacquelyn McGiffert. *Alaska's wilderness rails: from the Taiga to the tundra: a pictorial review of the Alaska Railroad.* Missoula,

MT: Pictorial Histories Pub. Co., 1982. 94 p.

1834. Brown, Albert E. *Locomotives and trains of Kansas City, Southern Louisiana & Arkansas railways.* Leesville, LA: A.E. Brown, 1952. 67 p.

1835. Brown, Cecil Kenneth. *A state movement in railroad development: the story of North Carolina's first effort to establish an east and west trunk line railroad.* Chapel Hill, NC: University of North Carolina Press, 1928. 300 p. (*The University of North Carolina social study series.*)

1836. Brown, Charles Michael, Michael S. Kennedy. *The Alaska Railroad: probing the interior.* Anchorage, AK: Office of Statewide Cultural Programs, Alaska Division of Parks, 1975. 1 v. (*History and archaeology series, no 15*)

1837. Brown, Charles P. *Brownie the boomer; the life story of Chas. P. Brown as a boomer railroad man.* Whittier, CA: Western Printing Corp., 1930. 271 p.

1838. _____. *Brownie the boomer: the life of Charles P Brown, an American railroader.* H. Roger Grant, editor. DeKalb, IL: Northern Illinois University Press, 1991. 259 p.

1839. Brown, Christopher. *Still standing: a century of urban train station design.* Bloomington, IN: Indiana University Press, 2005. 133 p.

1840. Brown, Dee Alexander. *Hear that lonesome whistle blow: railroads in the West.* New York, Holt, Rinehart and Winston, 1977. 311 p. (Reprint: New York, Simon & Schuster, 1994. 311 p.; New York, Henry Holt, 2001. 311 p.)

1840a. Brown, Edward R. *Chug-a-chug-a motion: early years of the railroad* / Beverly Farms, MA: Beverly Historical Society, 2012. 33, 2 p. (Boston and Maine Railroad)

1841. Brown, Ellis. *Electrical equipment of the Philadelphia and Reading Railway Company's locomotive repair plant at Reading, Pennsylvania. Worcester, Mass.* 1903. 44 l. (Thesis, E.E., Worcester Polytechnic Institute.)

1841a. Brown, Frank S., Jonathan Glass. *Eat steel & spit rivets: Norfolk Southern employees reflect on 30 years of change, challenge, and achievement* / Norfolk, VA: Norfolk Southern Corporate Communication Department, 2012. 139 p.

1842. Brown, George Dewitt. *A history of the Blue Ridge Railroad, 1852-1874.* 1967. 120 l. (Thesis, M.A., University of South Carolina.)

1843. Brown, George Lee. *Brown's industrial gazetteer and hand-book of the Atchison, Topeka & Santa Fe R.R.* Topeka, KS: G.L. Brown, 1881. 283 p.

1844. Brown, Grant. *Ninety years crossing Lake Michigan: the history of the Ann Arbor car ferries* / Ann Arbor: University of Michigan Press, 2008. 286 p.

1845. Brown, H.F. *Economic results of diesel electric motive power on the railways of the United States of America.* London, Institution of Mechanical Engineers, 1960. 20 p.

1846. Brown, Harold Owen. *The building of the Texas-Mexican Railroad.* 1937. 81 l. (Thesis, M.A., Texas College of Arts and Industries.)

1847. Brown, Harry Gunnison. *Transportation rates and their regulation: a study of the transportation costs of commerce with especial reference to American railroads.* New York, NY: Macmillan, 1916. 347 p.

1848. Brown, Henry L. (Hank). *Steam locomotives of the Chicago Great Western: 2-8-0 Consolidation type.* Minot, ND: H.L. Brown, 1977. 80 p.

1849. Brown Hoisting Machinery Company. *Brownhoist cranes.* Cleveland, OH: The Company, 1903. 261 p.

1850. _____. *Brownhoist locomotive cranes: catalog of detail parts.* Cleveland, OH: Brown Hoisting Machinery Co., 1918. 44 p. (*Booklet no. 5808.*)

1851. _____. *Brownhoist locomotive cranes.* Cleveland, OH: Brown Hoisting Machinery Co., 1919. 95 p. (*Catalog K 1919.*)

1852. _____. *Brownhoist locomotive cranes.* Cleveland : Brown Hoisting Machinery Co., 1920. 87, 1 p. (*Catalog K 1921.*)

1853. _____. *Cranes.* Cleveland, OH: Brown Hoisting Machinery Co., 1901. 241 p.

1854. Brown, Hubert Leon. *A study of some aspects of the Texas Railroad Commission's crude oil policies and orders.* 1954. 68 l. (Thesis, M.B.A. in Finance and Banking, Graduate School of Arts and Sciences, University of Pennsylvania.)

1855. Brown, Jack, Barbara Rust Brown. *WM color guide to freight and passenger equipment.* Edison, NJ: Morning Sun Books, 1995. 128 p.

1856. Brown, Jim. *A history of the Cincinnati Northern Railroad.* Cataract, WI: Little Falls Press, 2003. 339 p.

1857. Brown, John C.. *Addresses of John C. Brown, president, Texas & Pacific Railway Company, before the Internal Improvement Committee of the Texas House of Representatives at Austin, Saturday, January 26, and Monday, January 28, 1889.* Dallas : Gibson & Worley, 1889. 74 p.

1858. _____. *Argument of John C. Brown, before House Committee on Pacific Railroad, January 25, 1878, in behalf of the Texas and Pacific Railway Company.* Washington, DC: Thomas McGill & Co., 1878. 38 p.

1859. _____. *Argument of John C. Brown before the Judiciary Committee of the House of Representatives : in regard to the title of the Texas and Pacific Railway*

Company to its line between Fort Worth and El Paso, etc., etc. April 17, 1878 / Washington, DC: Thomas McGill & Co., 1878. 26 p.

1860. _____. *Argument of John C. Brown, vice-president Texas and Pacific Railway Compnay, : before the Senate Committee on pacific Railroads, February 22, 1878, in behalf of the Texas and Pacific Railway Co* ... Washington, DC: s.n., 1878. 73 p.

1861. _____. *Reply to Mr. Campbell, before the Judiciary Committee of the House of Representatives, in regard to the title of the Texas & Pacific Railway Company to its line between Fort Worth and El Paso, etc., etc. Filed, by leave of the Committee, April 29, 1878.* Washington, DC: T. McGill, printer, 1878. 23 p

1862. _____. *Texas and Pacific Railway : a letter /* Pulaski, Tenn., 1878. 22 p. "To the people of the South."

1863. _____. *Texas and Pacific Railway : argument of John C. Brown ... before Senate Committee on Railroads, February 7, 1876.* Washington, DC: s.n., 1876. 32 p.

1864. Brown, John K. *The Baldwin Locomotive Works, 1831-1915: a case study in the capital equipment sector.* 1992. 400 l. (Thesis, Ph.D., University of Virginia.)

1865. _____. *The Baldwin Locomotive Works, 1831-1915: a study in American industrial practice.* Baltimore, MD: John Hopkins University Press, 1995. 328 p.

1866. Brown, Joyce S., Robert S. Arnold. *The line: a story of the Providence and Worcester Railroad Company.* Worcester, MA: United Offset Printing Co., 1999. 61 p., 43 p. of plates.

1867. Brown, Margaret Louis. *Asa Whitney and his Pacific railroad publicity campaign.* 1933. 1 v. (Thesis, University of Michigan.)

1868. _____. *Asa Whitney, projector of the Pacific Railroad.* 1930. 147, 7, 9 l. (Thesis, University of Michigan.)

1869. Brown, Nelson Courtland. *Logging transportation: the principles and methods of log transportation in the United States.* New York, J. Wiley & Sons, Inc., 1936. 327 p.

1870. Brown, R.C. (Doc) *Logging railroads of Rusk County, Wisconsin: fifty years of lake state logging railroads, 1883-1935.* Eau Claire, WI: R.C. Brown, 1982. 93 p.

1871. _____. *Rails into the pines, 1883-1910: the Chippewa River and Menomonie Railway.* Eau Claire, WI: R.C. Brown, 1980. 68 p.

1872. Brown, Revelle Wilson. *Daniel Willard (1861-1942):from woodburners to diesels.* New York, Newcomen Society, American Branch, 1948. 32 p.

1873. _____. *Rails and ideals: in U.S.A. and Canada; a Newcomen address in Toronto.*

New York, NY: Newcomen Society in North America, 1949. 32 p.

1874. _____. *The Reading Railroad: an early history.* New York, Newcomen Society, American Branch, 1946. 36 p.

1875. _____. *Some aspects of early railroad transportation in Pennsylvania.* S.l., Pennsylvania Historical Association, 1949. 15 p.

1876. Brown, Richard A. *The Trainset railroad simulation/* Ithaca, NY: Cornell University, Department of Computer Sciences, 1993. 120 p. (*Report no. TR 93-1329*)

1877. Brown, Robert Bruce. *The railroad freight car—development, ownership, and trends.* 1961. 102 l. (Thesis, M.B.A. in Transportation and Public Utilities, Graduate School of Arts and Sciences, University of Pennsylvania)

1878. Brown, Robert C. *The Burlington's Lines west depots: Nebraska, Wyoming, Colorado, South Dakota, Montana, Kansas, Colorado & Southern.* S.l., R.C. Brown, 2001. 144 p.

1879. _____. *The Burlington's Peavine Branch.* S.l., Robert C. Brown, 2001. 44 p.

1880. _____. *Chicago, Burlington & Quincy Railroad Co.: depots and towers, Illinois and Wisconsin' a historical review of the CB&Q Railroad's depots in Illinois and Wisconsin.* S.l., R.C. Brown, 2000. 189 p.

1881. _____. *Chicago, Burlington & Quincy Railroad dispatcher's log books, Ottumwa, Iowa Division, 1886-1947.* Plano, TX: R.C. Brown, 1996. 97 p.

1882. _____ *Chicago, Burlington & Quincy Railroad: dispatchers log books, Ottumwa, Iowa, January, 1886- January 31, 1950.* S.l., R.C. Brown, 1998. 2 v.

1883. _____. *Chicago, Burlington & Quincy Railroad Co.: Missouri depots: a historical review of the railroad's depots in Missouri.* S.l., R.C. Brown, 2000-2001. 2 v.

1884. _____. *Chicago, Burlington & Quincy R.R. Operating Department: employee timetables, Iowa: a historical review of the timetables for trackage in the state of Iowa between 1870 and 1925.* Coralville, IA: R.C. Brown, 1998. 1 v. (unpaged)

1885. _____. *Chicago, Burlington & Quincy, Creston, Iowa Division: telegrapher's employment records, 1900-1906.* Plano, TX: R.C. Brown, 1996. 18 p.

1886. _____. *A historical review of the depots and towers of the Chicago, Burlington & Quincy Railroad in the state of Iowa.* S.l., Robert C. Brown, 1995. 121 p.

1887. _____. *Railroad train orders: Iowa railroads, a historical review of the use of train orders and their importance to the safe operation of trains.* Plano, TX: R.C. Brown, 1998. 87 p.

1888. _____. *The railroads in World War II: an illustrated history.* S.l., Robert C. Brown, 2003. 250 p.

1889. Brown, Robert Ritchie. *Pioneer locomotives of North America.* Boston, Railway & Locomotive Historical Society, 1959. 91 p.

1889a. Brown, Stephen Mark. *Cost-sharing clubs and the private provision of transportation infrastructure.* 1985. 162 l. (Thesis, Ph.D., Washington University.) Railroad terminals – Cost of operation.

1890. Brown, Thomas Pollok. *A check-list of railway literature for adults.* Washington, DC: Association of American Railroads, 1950. 8 p. (*Railway information series, no. 13.*) "Reproduced ... from Book section, San Francisco Chronicle, March 31, 1946."

1891. Brown, W. C. *Report of the Committee on terminals and transportation of the New York State Food Investigating Commission, April 18, 1913.* Albany: J.B. Lyon Co., Printers, 1913. 39 p. (New York (State). Food Investigating Commission. Committee on Terminals and Transportation.) W. C. Brown, chairman.

1892. Brown, William Henry. *The history of the first locomotives in America.* New York, D. Appleton and Co., 1871. 242 p. (Rev. ed., 1874. 246 p. Reprint: Mendham, NJ: Astragal Press, 2003; Whitefish, MT: Kessinger Pub.: 2010. x, [9]-246, [12] p.

1893. _____. *History of the first locomotives in America, together with other interesting information from original documents and testimony of living witnesses. Popular ed.* Philadelphia, Barclay & Co., 1877. 48 p.

1894. Browne, Juanita Kennedy. *A tale of two cities and a train: history of the Nevada County Narrow Gauge Railroad, 1874-1942.* Nevada City, CA: Nevada County Historical Society, 1987. 216 p.

1895. Browne, Thomas E. *An evaluation of electrification of the Eastern railroads— a potential modifier of Diesel oil and coal consumption.* n.d., 164 l. (Thesis, M.S., Pennsylvania State University.)

1896. Brownell, David. *Track Geometry Measurement System software manual/* Washington, DC: Urban Mass Transportation Administration, 1978. 126 p. in various pagings. (*DOT-TSC-UMTA-78-6.*)

1897. Browning Crane & Shovel Company. *Instruction for the erection, care and operation of the Browning locomotive crane.* 6th ed. Cleveland, OH, Browning Crane and Shovel Co., 1943.

1898. Browning Engineering Company. *The Browning locomotive cranes at work.* Cleveland, OH: The Browning Engineering Co., 1903. p. 190-216. (*Bulletin no. 19.*)

1898a. *Brown's gazetteer of the Chicago and Northwestern Railway, and branches, and of the Union Pacific Railroad. A guide and business directory/* Chicago : Bassett

Bros.' Steam Printing House, 1869. 360 p.

1899. Brownson, Howard G. *History of the Illinois Central Railroad to 1870.* 1909. (Thesis, Ph.D., University of Illinois.) (Reprint: New York, Johnson Reprint Co., 1967. 182 p.)

1900. Bruce, Alfred W. *The steam locomotive in America: its development in the twentieth century.* New York, Norton, 1952. 443 p.

1900a. Bruce, George Barclay, Sir; James Forrest. *The Northern Pacific Railroad/* London : Institution of Civil Engineers, 1883. 20 p.

1901. Bruce, Robert V. *1877: year of violence.* Indianapolis, IN: Bobbs-Merrill, 1959. 384 p. (Reprint: Chicago, Quadrangle Books, 1970. 384 p.)

1902. Bruchey, Stuart Weems, and others. *Memoirs of three railroad pioneers.* New York, Arno Press, 1981, 1912. 104 p.

1903. Brueckman, Henry, Jeffrey Moreau. *4449: the queen of steam.* Tiburon, CA: Carbarn Press, 1983. 64 p.

1904. Brueckner, Jan K. *A study in the diffusion of innovation: steel rails in American railroads.* Urbana, IL: College of Commerce and Business Administration, University of Illinois at Urbana-Champaign, 1977. 18 l. (*Faculty working papers, no. 424.*)

1904a. Brugger, Brenda S., Mark C. Stauter, John F. Bradbury. *Guide to the historical records of the St. Louis-San Francisco Railway Company and its predecessor, subsidiary, and constituent companies/* Rolla, Mo: University of Missouri, Western Historical Manuscript Collection-Rolla, 1989. 139 p.

1904b. Brundage, Avery. *Detailed study of specifications for steel bridges /* 1909. 40 l. (Thesis, B.S., University of Illinois.)

1905. Bruner, J.P. *Effect of design variation on service stresses in railroad wheels /* New York : ASME, 1967. 16 p. (*American Society of Mechanical Engineers (Series) : 67-WA/RR-6.*)

1905a. Brush, Douglas C. *Northern Kansas Division, Missouri Pacific Lines : formerly the Central Branch, Union Pacific Railroad /* Great Bend, KS: Golden Belt Printing, 2012. 235 p.

1906. Bryan, Enoch Albert. *Orient meet Occident; the advent of the railways to the Pacific Northwest.* Pullman, WA: The Students Book Corporation, 1936. 269 p.

1906a. Bryan, John A. *Bridging the Mississippi at St. Louis /* St. Louis, MO: Jefferson National Expansion Memorial, U.S. Department of the Interior, National Park Service, 1939. 36 l., 10 leaves of plates.

1907. Bryan, Kemp & Company. *Southern Railway as compared with New York Central, Illinois Central and Norfolk & Western.* Richmond, VA: Bryan, Kemp & Co., 1925. 4 p.

1908. Bryans, William S. *A history of transcontinental railroads and coal mining on the Northern Plains to 1920.* 1987. 253 l. (Thesis, Ph.D., University of Wyoming.)

1909. Bryant, E.T. *Railways; a reader's guide.* Hamden, CT: Archon Books, 1968. 249 p.

1910. Bryant, Keith L. *Arthur E. Stilwell, promoter with a hunch.* Nashville, TN: Vanderbilt University Press, 1971. 256 p.

1911. _____. *History of the Atchison, Topeka and Santa Fe Railway.* New York, Macmillan, 1974. 398 p. (Reprint: Lincoln, University of Nebraska Press, 1982, c 1974. 398 p.)

1912. Bryant, Phyllis Roberts. *The New York and Pennsylvania Railroad.* 1946. 58 l. (Thesis, A.M., Plan B, Cornell University.

1913. Buchan, A.B. *Expansion of the use of freight car scheduling: development of a strategic plan for New England.* Washington, DC: Federal Railroad Administration, Office of Policy, 1981. 108 p.

1914. Buchanan, Lamont. *Steel trails and iron horses: a pageant of American railroading.* New York, NY: Putnam, 1955. 159 p.

1915. Buchanan, Steve. *The impacts on communities of abandonment of railroad service* / Washington, DC: Public Interest Economics Center, 1975. 182 l.

1916. Buchanan, William. *New York Central and Hudson River Railroad, motive power equipment.* S.l., s.n., 1893.

1916a. Buchholz, Charles E. *A design of a double track bridge for an elevated railroad* / 1893. 34 l. (Thesis, B.S., Massachusetts institute of Technology, Department of Civil Engineering.

1917. Buchmann, Heinrich. *Dampflokomitiven in den USA, 1825-1950.* Basel, Birkhauser, 1977-1978. 2 v. (*Eisenbahngeschichte der Vereinigten Staaten von Amerika, Bd. 1-2.*)

1917a. Buchmueller, Roland. *A study of the Union Station layout of the Terminal Railroad Association* / 1918. 1 v. (unpaged). (Thesis, B.S., Washington University, Department of Civil Engineering.) (Signal towers; interlocking mechanisms.)

1918. Buck, Solon J. *The Granger Movement; a study of agricultural organization and its political, economic, and social manifestations, 1870-1880.* Lincoln, NE: University of Nebraska Press, 1963, 1913. 384 p.

1919. Buckley, James J. *Gary railways*. Chicago, IL: Central Electric Railfans' Association, 1975. 36 p.

1920. Buckner, J.B. *Mineral deposits and mining interests along the line of the Nashville, Chattanooga & St. Louis R'y*. Nashville, TN: Nashville, Chattanooga, & St. Louis Railway, Marshall & Bruce, 1900. 47 p. (*Pamphlet, no. 5.*)

1921. Buckner, J.C. *Design for a passenger locomotive boiler from a thermodynamic standpoint*. 1887. 22 l. (Thesis, M.E., Lehigh University.)

1922. Buckwalter, T.V., Oscar John Horger. *Stress analysis of locomotive and other large axles*. Canton, Ohio, Timken Roller Bearing Co., 1936. 12 l.

1923. Buckwell, Lloyd John. *Variable costs for internal management: a case study of a railroad* / 1968. 194 l. (Thesis, Ph.D., University of Minnesota.) Accounting.

1924. Bucyrus Company. *The Bucyrus Company*. South Milwaukee, Bucyrus Company, 1910. 119 p.

1925. _____. *Catalogue no. 2: steam shovels*. South Milwaukee, Bucyrus Co., 1904. 61 p.

1926. _____. *Catalogue no. 3: wrecking cranes and pile drivers*. South Milwaukee, Wis., The Company, 1906. 28 p.

1927. _____. *General catalogue : steam and electric shovels, dipper dredges, dragline excavators, tower excavators, railway wrecking cranes, locomotive pile drivers, unloading plows* / South Milwaukee : Bucyrus Co., 1900s. 42 p. (*Catalogue no. 19.*)

1928. _____. *Placer dredge machinery: steam shovels, dipper dredges, hydraulic dredges, locomotive pile drivers, drag line excavators, railway cranes, rotary snow plows, unloading plows*. South Milwaukee? Bucyrus Company, 1910. 86 p.

1929. _____. *Wrecking cranes and pile drivers*. South Milwaukee, Wisc., The Company, 1904. 30 p.

1930. Bucyrus Steam Shovel & Dredge Co. *Catalogue*. S.l., s.n., 1892. 1 v. (Pt. 1: Steam shovels; Pt. 4: Railroad and locomotive cranes, wrecking cars and pile drivers.)

1930a. Budasuke, Rien. *200 ft. riveted Warren single track railroad bridge loading E65, specification A.R.E.A. 1920* / 1924. 42, 2 l. (Thesis, B.S., Massachusetts Institute of Technology, Department of Civil Engineering.)

1931. Budd Company. *Budd analysis of changes in transportation*. Philadelphia, Edward G. Budd Manufacturing Co., 1940. 2 v.

1932. _____. *Budd Company*. Philadelphia : Budd Co., 1953. 32 p.

1933. _____. *The Budd Company : products and organization.* Philadelphia : The Company, 1957. 8 p.

1934. _____. *Budd railway disc brake.* Philadelphia : Budd Co., 1952. 11 p.

1935. _____. *Budd railway research plan* / Philadelphia: The Company, 1948. 23 p. Railroad passenger cars.

1936. _____. *Budd Siesta coach: enclosed room privacy, comfort and convenience at coach fares.* Philadelphia : Budd Co., 1957. 8 p.

1937. _____. *The Budd system of light-weight construction.* Philadelphia : Edw. G. Budd Mfg. Co., 1936. 26 p.

1938. _____. *The California Zephyrs built by the Budd Company.* S.l., s.n., 194-? 28 p.

1939. _____. *A description in detail of the Santa Fe Super Chief.* Chicago : Railway Age, 1937. 12 l. Reprinted with special permission of May 22, 1937 issue Railway Age.

1940. _____. *Introducing Central of Georgia's "Man-o'-war."* Philadelphia : Budd Co., 1947. 13 p.

1941. _____. *Introducing RDC-1.* Philadelphia : Budd Co., 1949. 12 p.

1942. _____. *The new Pacemaker : designed & built for New York Central System by Budd.* Philadelphia : Budd Co., 1948. 14 p.

1943. _____. *Pennsylvania diners.* Philadelphia : E.G. Budd, 1938. 469-480 l. Reprint: Railroad Age, v. 107, no. 14.

1944. _____. *Presenting a new concept in lightweight passenger car construction: Budd Pioneer III.* Philadelphia : The Company, 1950. 10 p.

1945. _____. *RDC.* Philadelphia : PA: Budd Co., 1956. 24 p.

1946. _____. *RDC comes of age.* Philadelphia : Budd Co., 1953. 24 p.

1947. _____. *RDC goes to work.* Philadelphia : Budd Co., 1951. 20 p.

1948. _____. *Revolution on rails.* Philadelphia, Budd Co., 1950s. 1 v. (unpaged).

1949. _____. *Specification for stainless steel electric multiple unit commuter passenger railway cars for the City of Philadelphia for operation on suburban lines of the Pennsylvania Railroad and the Reading Company.* Philadelphia ? Budd Company, 1961. 227 l. Budd order no. 9677-280.

1950. _____. *Tomorrow's trucks for today's tracks.* Philadelphia : Budd Company, 1960. 8 p.

1951. Budd Company. Technical Center. *Las Vegas to Los Angeles high speed/super speed ground transportation system feasibility study/* Fort Washington, PA: The Center, 1983. 2 v.

1952. _____. _____. *Las Vegas to Los Angeles high speed/super speed ground transportation system feasibility study: executive summary.* Fort Washington, PA: The Center, 1983. 29 p.

1953. Budd, Edward Gowen. [Correspondence with Paul Philippe Cret]. 1936-1939. Archival materials. 2 items. (3 leaves.) Location: University of Pennsylvania Library,

1954. _____. *Edward G. Budd, 1870-1946, "Father of the Streamliners," and the Budd Company.* New York, Newcomen Society in North America, 1950. 28 p.

1955. _____. *A new era has come for the railroads.* Philadelphia : Budd Co., 1944. 10 p.

1956. _____. *The railway outlook : An address before the Railway Club of Pittsburgh at Pittsburgh, Pennsylvania, May 25, 1944 .* Philadelphia : Budd Company, 1944. 23 p.

1957. _____ *A transportation miracle /* Philadelphia : Edward G. Budd Manufacturing Company, 1939. 9, 1 p. Passenger traffic.

1958. Budd, Ralph. *The Burlington Zephyr: America's first diesel all-steel streamlined train: the outstanding achievement in safe, light, railway transportation by the Edward G. Budd Manufacturing Company, Philadelphia, Pa.* New York?: Railway Age, 1934. 20 p.

1959. _____. *John Frank Stevens: died June 2, 1943.* S.l., s.n., 1943. 8 p. Reprint: Railway Age, April 14, 1934.

1960. _____. *The Pacific Northwest and the engineer.* St. Paul, 1931. 16 p.

1961. _____. *Plan for a new northern railway system: a unified operation of Great Northern, Northern Pacific, and Spokane, Portland & Seattle railways, with unified control of Burlington.* Minneapolis? 1927. 18 p.

1962. _____. *Railway routes across the Rocky Mountains.* New York, 1938. 1 v.

1963. _____. *The relation of highway transportation to the railway.* New York, National Automobile Chamber of Commerce, 1926. 28 p.

1964. _____. *Significance of the Rocky Mountains to transcontinental railways.* St. Paul? 1929. 12 p.

1965. _____ *A suggestion for railway consolidation.* Chicago, 1935. 15 p.

1966. _____. *West wind for the railroads* . Philadelphia : Edward G. Budd Manufacturing Co., 1934. 7 p. Description of the trail run of the C.B. & Q. streamlined diesel.

1967. Budd, Ralph, Howard Elliott. *Great Northern Railway Company, Northern Pacific Railway Company; a review of their operations in the period 1916-1923 and a discussion of some of their most difficult problems, with comments on current conditions.* New York, Wood, Struthers, 1924. 131 p.

1968. Buder, Stanley. *Pullman: an experiment in industrial order and community planning, 1880-1930.* 1967. New York, Oxford University Press, 1967. 263 p. (Thesis, Ph.D., Dept. of History, University of Chicago, 1966. 307 l.)

1969. Buell, D.C. *Basic steam locomotive maintenance.* Omaha, NE: Simmons-Boardman Pub., 1980. 333 p.

1970. _____. *Switches, frogs, guard rails and crossings/* Omaha, NB: Railway Educational Bureau, 1938. 53, 31, 21, 23, 45 p.

1971. Buffalo and Susquehanna Railroad Corporation. *Corporate history of Buffalo & Susquehanna Railroad Corporation as of the date of valuation, June 30, 1919 /* Buffalo, NY: Buffalo and Susquehanna Railroad Corporation, 1921. 1 v.

1972. *Buffalo Central Terminal.* Buffalo? s.n., 1929. 12 p.

1972a. *Buffalo Central Terminal master plan 2011 /* Buffalo, NY: Central Terminal Restoration Corporation, Inc., 2011. 24 p.

1973. Buffalo (N.Y.) Grade Crossing and Terminal Station Commission. *Buffalo Central Terminal, dedicated June 22, 1929, opened June 23, 1929.* Buffalo, NY: Grade Crossing and Terminal Station Commission of the City of Buffalo, 1929. 14, 2 p.

1973a. Buffalo, New York and Erie Railroad. Buffalo, New York & Erie R.R. telegraph : instructions for the working of the line, &c., &c. on the Buffalo, New York & Erie R.R. : to go into effect on Thursday, July 1, 1858. Buffalo : Murray, Rockwell & Co., 1858. 14 p.

1974. Buffalo Pitts Company. *"Cheaper than horses": locomotor engines.* Buffalo, N.Y., Buffalo Pitts, 1903. 40 p.

1975. Buffalo, Rochester and Pittsburgh Railway Company. *Engineering Department prohibited unsafe practices.* Buffalo, Buffalo, Rochester and Pittsburgh Railway, 1916. 11 p.

1976. _____. *Industrial and shippers guide, September 1, 1917.* Philadephia, Buffalo, Rochester & Pittsburgh Railway Co., 1917. 197 p.

1977. _____. *Industrial and shippers guide, June 1, 1924 /* Buffalo? NY: Buffalo,

Rochester, and Pittsburgh Railroad Company, 1924. 245 p.

1978. _____. *Maintenance of Equipment Department prohibited unsafe practices.* Buffalo, Buffalo, Rochester and Pittsburgh Railway, 1916. 10 p.

1979. _____. *Transportation Department prohibited unsafe practices.* Buffalo, Buffalo, Rochester and Pittsburgh Railway, 9 p.

1980. Buford, Curtis D. *Trailer Train Company: a unique force in the railroad industry.* New York, Newcomen Society in North America, 1982. 24 p.

1981. *Buildings and structures of American railroads, 1893 (part 5).* Novato, CA; Newton K. Gregg, 1975. 1 v.. (*Train shed cyclopedia, no. 33.*)

1982. Bukovsky, Alexis Paul. *Use and cost of railway fuel and problems in fuel statistics* / Washington, DC: Interstate Commerce Commission, 1944. 108 p. (Its *Statement no. 4428.*)

1983. Bukowski, Richard. *Fire protection systems for rail transportation of class A explosives : final report.* Washington, DC : National Bureau of Standards, 1980. 29 p. (*NBSIR 80-2170.*) Center for Fire Research, National Engineering Laboratory, National Bureau of Standards.)

1984. Bulkeley, George Vicary Owen. *Railway and seaport freight movement, with examples of British and American practice ... with an introduction by His Excellency Sir Edward Grigg.* London : C. Lockwood and Son, 1930. 221 p.

1985. Bulkley, Constance, Carol Eastman. *Brotherhood of Locomotive Firemen and Enginemen records/* Ithaca, NY: New York State School of Industrial and Labor Relations, Cornell University, M.P. Catherwood Library, Labor-Management Documentation Center, 1979. 44 l.

1986. _____, _____. *Order of Railway Conductors and Brakemen records, 1881-1969.* Ithaca NY: New York State School of Industrial and Labor Relations, Cornell University, M.P. Catherwood Library, Labor-Management Documentation Center, 1979? 7 l.

1986a. Bullard, Edwin Elliott, Frederic Hood Emerson. *Cost of hauling express and freight by electric locomotives.* 1906. 22 l. (Thesis, B.S., University of Illinois.)

1987. Bullard, Thomas R. *By bridge to St. Louis.* Oak Park, IL: T.R. Bullard, 1993. 52 p.

1988. Bullerdiek, W.A. *A study to reduce the hazards of tank car transportation/* Washington, DC: Federal Railroad Administration, 1970. 172 p.

1989. *Bulletin.* S.l., American Railway Engineering and Maintenance-of-Way Association, 1900-1911.

1990. *Bulletin*. Chicago, American Railway Engineering Association, 1911-1997. Quarterly.

1991. *The Bulletin*. Allentown, Pa, National Railway Historical Society, 1936-1975.

1992. *Bulletin*. Boston, Railway & Locomotive Historical Society, 1921-1972. (> *Railroad history*.)

1993. *Bulletin of revenues and expenses of steam roads in the United States*. Washington, D.C., Interstate Commerce Commission; Bureau of Transport Economics, 1908-1914.

1994. Bullock, Dale. *The most interesting 100 square mile in America and its impact on Santa Fe*. Santa Fe, NM: El Corral de Santa Fe Westerners, 1981. 18 p.

1995. Bumgarner, Matthew C. *A history of the Atlantic, Tennessee & Ohio Rail Road Company* / Hickory, NC: Tarheel Press, 2010. 104 p.

1995a. _____. *Junebug Lines: Alexander Railroad Company*. Hickory, NC: Hobo Puppy Pub. Co., 1993. 107 p.

1996. _____ *The Lawndale Railway & Industrial Company: with the Southern & Western Air Line*. Hickory, NC: Tarheel Press, 1999. 102 p.

1997. _____. *Legacy of the Carolina & North-Western Railway*. Johnson City, TN: The Overmountain Press, 1996. 190 p.

1998. _____, R. Douglas Walker. *The Watauga & Yadkin River Railroad*. Hickory, NC: Tarheel Press, 2003. 132 p.

1998a. Bunn, Nixon Lawrence. *Design of a plate-girder railroad bridge* / 1913. 26 l. (Thesis, B.S., University of Illinois.)

1999. Bunting, James Whitney. *The distance principle in railroad rate making : an evaluation based upon studies and findings of the Interstate Commerce Commission*. 1947. 95 l. (Thesis, University of Pennsylvania.)

2000. Burch, Edward Parris. *Electric traction for railway trains; a book for students, electrical and mechanical engineers, superintendents of motive power and others*. New York, McGraw-Hill Book Company, 1911. 583 p.

2001. Burch, Franklin Ward. *Alaska's railroad frontier: railroads and federal development policy, 1898-1915*. 1965. 290 l. (Thesis, Ph.D., Catholic University of America.)

2002. Bureau of Railway Economics. (Washington, D.C.) *Albert Fink, October 27, 1827- April 3, 1897: a bibliographical memoir of the father of railway economics and statistics in the United States*: Washington, D.C., October 27, 1927. Washington, D.C., Bureau of Railway Economics, Library, 1927. 23 l.

2003. _____. *Arguments for and against limitation of length of freight trains.* Washington, D.C., Bureau of Railway Economics, 1916. 63 p. (*Bureau of Railway Economics, Consecutive, no. 92; Miscellaneous series, no 23.*)

2004. _____. *Arguments for and against train-crew legislation.* Washington, D.C.: The Bureau, 1915. 44 p. (*Bureau of Railway Economics consecutive no. 73; Miscellaneous series, no. 18.*)

2005. _____. *Bibliography of the Nashville, Chattanooga & St Louis Railway.* Washington, DC: Library, Bureau of Railway Economics, 1922. 27 l.

2006. _____. *A comparative study of railway wages and the cost of living in the United States, the United Kingdom and the principal countries of continental Europe.* Washington, D.C., Bureau of Railway Economics, 1912. 77 p. (*Bulletin no. 34.*)

2007. _____. *The conflict between deferral and state regulation of the railways.* Washington: The Bureau, 1911. 13 p. (*Bulletin no. 15.*)

2008. _____. *Container cars : a transcript of entries from the catalog of the Bureau of Railway Economics Library.* Washington, DC : The Library, 1940. 14 l.

2009. _____. *Descriptive list of Bureau publications.* Washington, D.C., Bureau of Railway Economics, 1929. 8 p.

2009a. _____. *Grade crossings; a list of references to material published 1914-March 1927. Supplementing list of references of 1915.* Washington, DC: Bureau of Railway Economics, 1927. 56 l.

2010. _____. *A guide to railroad cost analysis.* Washington, DC: Association of American Railroads, Bureau of Railway Economics, 1964. 141 p.

2011. _____. *Hump yards.* Washington, DC: Association of American Railroads, Bureau of Railway Economics, 1962. 10 l.

2012. _____. *List of publications of the American Railway Association.* S.l., Association of American Railroads, Bureau of Railway Economics, Library, 1923. 23 l.

2013. _____. *List of references on railway dining cars.* Washington, D.C., Bureau of Railway Economics, 1914. 5 l.(*Supplement*: Washington, D.C.: The Bureau, 1918. 7 l.

2014. _____. *List of references on railway motor cars.* Washington, D.C.: Bureau of Railway Economics, 1915. 1, 37 l.

2015. _____. *List of references on transportation of perishable products.* Washington, DC: The Bureau, 1918. 13 numbered l.

2016. _____. *A list of references to articles on winter service on railroads.* Washington,

D.C., The Bureau, 1918. 53 numbered leaves.

2017. _____. *List of references to books and articles on the Adamson law of September, 1916, revised September 19, 1919.* Washington, D.C.: The Bureau,1919. 22 l.

2018. _____. *List of references to legislation in the United States on minimum train crews and maximum length of trains.* Washington, DC: The Library, 1915. 20 p. + supp. 6 p.

2019. _____. *Locomotives : diesel-electric, oil-electric, etc.* / Washington, DC: The Library, 1940. 4 l. Indexes articles appearing in Railway Mechanical Engineer.

2020. _____ *Locomotives scrapping, retirement: transcript of cards in the Bureau of Railway Economics catalog.* Washington, DC: Association of American Railroads, Bureau of Railway Economics, 1954. 3 l.

2021. _____. *One-man locomotive operation, 1925-March 1960 : some references in BRE Library arranged chronologically.* Washington, DC; Association of American Railroads, Bureau of Economics Library, 1960. 14 l.

2022. _____. *Pullman and sleeping cars: transcript of cards in catalog of Bureau of Railway Economics Library, Association of American Railroads, Washington, D.C., under the following subject or author entries.* Washington, DC: Association of American Railroads, Bureau of Railway Economics Library, 1946. 113 l.

2023. _____. *Railroad mileage by states: December 31, 1959.* Washington, DC: Bureau of Railway Economics, 1960. 64 p.

2024. _____. *Railroad transportation, a statistical record*/ Washington, DC: Association of American Railroads, Bureau of Economics, 1911-1963.

2025. _____. *Railway mileage by states, December 31, 1920.* Washington, DC: Bureau of Railway Economics, 1921. 56 p.

2026. _____. *Railway mileage by states, December 13, 1930.* Washington, DC: Bureau of Railway Economics, 1932. 62 p.

2027. _____. *Railway mileage by states, December 31, 1934.* Washington, DC: Bureau of Railway Economics, 1935. 62 p.

2028. _____. *Railway mileage by states, December 31, 1946.* Washington, DC: Bureau of Railway Economics, 1948.

2029. _____. *Railway mileage by states, December 31, 1950.* Washington, DC: Association of American Railroads, Bureau of Railway Economics, 1952. 79 l.

2030. _____. *Railway motor cars, a list of references, Sept. 1925.* Washington, D.C., Library, Bureau of Railway Economics, 1925. 68 p. and Supplement of 7 pages.

2031. _____. *Railway supplies and capital expenditures.* Washington, D.C.: Bureau of Railway Economics, 1930. 22 p.

2032. _____. *Railways and agriculture, 1900-1910.* Washington, D.C., Bureau of Railway Economics, 1913. 31 p. (*Bulletin; Bureau of Railway Economics, no. 45.*)

2033. _____. *Refrigerator cars and refrigerator service on American railroads: brief list of references to material on history and development.* Washington, D.C.: Library, Bureau of Railway Economics, 1936. 5 p.

2034. _____. *Revised list of references on automatic train control.* Washington, DC: Association of American Railroads, Bureau of Railway Economics, Library, 1922. 32 p.

2034a. _____. *Six-hour day : a list of references.* Washington, DC: Association of American Railways, Bureau of Railway Economics, Library, 1936. 17 l.

2035. *Some references on the Louisville and Nashville Railroad* / Washington, DC: Bureau of Railway Economics, Library, 1916. 7 l.

2036. _____. *Some references to material in the library on separation of railroad grade crossings, 1939-1954.* Washington, DC: Association of American Railroads, Bureau of Railway Economics, 1955. 6 l.

2037. _____. *Some references to material in the Library on the Missouri & North Arkansas Railway.* Washington, DC: Bureau of Railway Economics, Library, 1947. 6 l.

2038. _____. *Statistics of railroad passenger service.* Washington, D.C., Association of American Railroads; Bureau of Railway Economics, 1966. 26 l.

2039. _____. *Statistics of railways.* Washington, D.C., Bureau of Railway Economics, 1914-1918. 5 v.

2040. _____. *Supplemental list of references to legislation in the United States on minimum train crews and maximum length of trains.* Washington, DC: Bureau of Railway Economics, 1915. 6 l.

2041. _____. *Trial bibliography on the New York, New Haven and Hartford Railroad.* Washington, 1915. 149 l.

2041a. Bureau of Railway Signaling Economics. *Railroad highway grade crossing protection statistics, 1925-1936.* New York : Bureau of Railway Signaling Economics, 1938. 7 p. (*Release # 1.*)

2042. Bures, Allen L. *Management audit approach in writing business history : a comparison with Kennedy's technique on railroad history.* New York, NY: Garland Publishing, 1989. 260 p. (Thesis, Ph.D., University of Nebraska, 1980.) (*Garland studies in entrepreneurship*)

2043. Burford, Cary Clive, Guy McIlvaine Smith, Robert McQuown. *The history and romance of Danville Junction: or, When rails were the only trails* / 2d ed. Bismarck, IL: Chicago & Eastern Illinois Railroad Historical Society, 2005. 139 p.

2044. Burg, Thomas E. *The Green Bay & Western steam era: locomotive photos from the Roy Campbell Collection.* Merrill, WI: Merrill Pub. Associates, 2008. 182 p.

2044a. _____. *Green Mountain steam: historic Vermont railroading: photos from the Roy Campbell* collection / Merrill, WI: Merrill Pub. Associates, 2011. 50 p.

2044b. _____. *South Shore steam : locomotives of the Duluth, South Shore & Atlantic Railway and Mineral Range Railroad : photos from the Roy Campbell collection* / Merrill, WI: Merrill Publishing Associates, 2011. 105 p.

2045. _____. *White Pine Route: the history of the Washington, Idaho and Montana Railway Company.* Coeur d'Alene, ID: Museum of North Idaho, 2003. 390 p.

2045a. _____. *Windy City steam: photos from the Roy Campbell collection.* Merrill, WI: Merrill Pub. Associates, 2011. 122 p.

2045b. _____, Bob Storozuk. *Route of the North Woods Hiawatha: the Milwaukee Road's Wisconsin Valley Line.* Merrill, WI: Merrill Pub. Associates, 2010. 113 p.

2046. _____, Roy W. Campbell. *The C&NW steam era in Wisconsin: locomotive photos from the Roy Campbell collection.* Merrill, WI: Merrill Pub. Associates, 2009. 162 p.

2047. _____, _____. *Milwaukee Road: steam in the west: locomotive photos from the Roy Campbell collection* / Merrill, WI: Merrill Pub. Associates, 2006. 127, 1 p.

2048. _____, _____. *Milwaukee Road steam locomotives: F6 class Hudsons: photos from the Roy Campbell collection.* Antioch, IL: Milwaukee Road Historical Association, 2006. 48 p. (The Milwaukee Road Historical Association steam locomotive series, v. 2.)

2049. _____, _____. . *Milwaukee Road steam locomotives: S class Northerns: photos from the Roy Campbell collection.* Antioch, IL: Milwaukee Road Historical Association, 2005. 48 p. (*The Milwaukee Road Historical Association steam locomotive series, v. 1.*)

2049a. Burgess, Edward. *Sustainability of intercity transportation infrastructure: assessing the energy consumption and greenhouse gas emissions of high-speed rail in the U.S.* 2011. 112 p. (Thesis, M.S., Arizona State University.)

2050. Burgess, George Heckman, Miles C. Kennedy with a Foreword by Martin W. Clement. *Centennial history of the Pennsylvania Railroad Company, 1846-1946.*

Philadelphia, Pennsylvania Railroad Company, 1949. 835 p.

2051. Burgess, Glenn. *History of the Kansas City, Mexico and Orient Railroad.* 1962. 57 l. (Thesis, M.A., New Mexico Western College.)

2052. Burgess, Jack A. *Trains to Yosemite.* Berkeley and Wilton, CA: Signature Press, 2004. 364 p.

2053. Burgess, Kenneth Farwell. *An economic measure for railroad rates.* Chicago? 1925. 11 p. ("An address before the Section of Public Utility Law, The American Bar Association, Detroit, Michigan, August 31, 1925.")

2054. Burgess, Stephen R., Robert J. Colucci, Louis P. Rossi. *Solving the branch line problem: a critique of the light-density line analyses of the Preliminary System Plan.* Albany, NY: Railroad Task Force, 1975. 30 p.

2055. Burke, Douglas A., John C. Spychalski, Evelyn A. Thomchick. *The impacts of rail transport on coal inventory levels at power plants /* 2008. 89 l. (Thesis, B.S., Pennsylvania State University.)

2056. Burke, E.P. *List of standard, private and tourist cars : with form number of diagrams used in sale or distribution of space and system of air conditioning : no. 34, canceling no. 33. /* Chicago : The Pullman Press, 1943. 29 p.

2057. Burke, James C. *North Carolina's first railroads, a study in historical geography.* 2008. 427 p. (Thesis, Ph.D., University of North Carolina at Greensboro.)

2057a. _____. *The Wilmington & Weldon Railroad Company in the Civil War /* Jefferson, NC: McFarland & Company, 2013. 262 p.

2058. Burke, Tom, Art Danz, Ted Pannkoke. *The Milwaukee Road in Chicago /* Antioch, IL: Milwaukee Road Historical Association, 2007. 82 p. (*Special publication, no. 6.*)

2059. Burkhalter, Howard J. *Railway stamps.* Milwaukee, American Topical Association, 1971. 83 p. (*Railway stamps.* Milwaukee, WI: American Topical Association, 1981. 103 p. *Supplement.* Johnstown, PA: American Topical Association, 1988. 50 p.

2060. Burkhardt, D.C. Jesse. *The Ann Arbor Railroad.* Charleston, SC: Arcadia, 2005. 128 p.

2061. _____. *Backwoods railroads: branch line and shortlines of western Oregon.* Pullman, WA: Washington State University Press, 1994. 154 p.

2062. _____. *Freight weather: the art of stalking trains.* White Salmon, WA: Rolling Dreams Press, 2001. 120 p.

2063. _____. *Railroads of the Columbia River Gorge.* Charleston, SC: Arcadia, 2004.

128 p.

2064. _____. *Rolling dreams: portraits of the Northwest's railroad heritage*. White Salmon, WA: Rolling Dreams Press, 1997. 86 p.

2065. Burkhardt, Franklin A., Ferne M. Longsworth. *The experience of a Lima ticket agent in the Gay Nineties*. Lima, OH: Allen County Historical and Archaeological Society, 1946. 31 p.

2065a. Burkholder, Kevin. *2012 Vermont rail system: a trackside guide* / White River Junction, VT: Steel Wheels Publishing, 2011. 159 p.

2066. Burleson, Kevin, Gerald Fordham. *Life on the rails: a photographic tour through the archives of the Salamanca Rail Museum*. Salamanca, NY: Salamanca Publications, 1999. 82 p.

2066a. Burley, John M. *First aid to the disabled locomotive : engine, air brake and air signal including the Walchart (sic) valve gear* / Enl. ed. State Line, PA: John M. Burley, 1907. 200 p.

2067. *Burlington Blitzkrieg against Texas*. Fort Worth, TX: Committee Organized to Oppose the Removal of the Fort Worth & Denver Headquarters from Fort Worth and the Closing of the Shops at Childress, 1940. 24 p. Amon Giles Carter, chairman.

2068. *Burlington bulletin*. Bensenville, Il: Burlington Route Historical Society, 1980- . Irregular. Imprint varies.

2068a. *Burlington Escorted Tours*. Chicago : Burlington Escorted Tours, 1934. 65 p. Organized and operated by Burlington Route, Northern Pacific Railway, Great Northern Railway.

2068b. *The Burlington Northern (Chicago, Burlington & Quincy Railroad) roundhouse and shops complex, Aurora, Illinois: a study of alternative uses and their feasibility* / Chicago : Shlaes & Co., 1979. 1 v. (various pagings).

2069. Burlington Northern Railroad Company. *Historical background information: major Burlington Northern predecessor companies*. St. Paul, MN: Burlington Northern Railroad, 1980. 22 p.

2070. [Burlington Northern locomotive diagram book.] St. Paul? Burlington Northern Inc., 1979. 325, 123 p. (Location: Minnesota Historical Society.)

2071. Burlington Northern Santa Fe Railroad. *The history of BNSF: a legacy for the 21st century*. Fort Worth, TX: Burlington Northern Santa Fe Corporation, 1999. 31 p.

2072. Burlington Route Historical Society. *The Burlington Bulletin; No. 33, The S-4 Hudsons*. LaGrange, IL: Burlington Route Historical Society, 1997. 164 p.

2073. *Burlington Route passenger car diagrams.* Godfrey, IL: Railway Production Classics, n.d. 192 p.

2074. *Burlington Route: the "Q": a commemorative pictorial of the final decades of the Chicago, Burlington & Quincy Railroad.* Rockford, IL: National Railway Historical Society, North Western Illinois Chapter, 1990. 24 p.

2075. Burness, Tad. *Classic railroad advertising: riding the rails again.* Iola, WI: Krause Publications, 2001. 224 p.

2076. Burnett, P.H. *Industrial opportunities along the line of the Lehigh Valley Railroad Company.* New York, Industrial Department, Lehigh Valley Railroad Company, 1911. vii, 8-188 p.

2077. Burney, Robert Thomson, Ronald Gregory Mele. *Birmingham Southern Railroad Company: the first century.* Blue Springs, MO: Print House, 1999. 126 p.

2078. Burnham, Douglas G., Greg Proll, Karro Frost. *Non-chemical methods of vegetation management on railroad rights-of-way/* Washington, D.C.: Federal Transit Administration, Office of Research, Demonstration and Innovation, 2003. 55 p.

2079. Burns, Dennis P. *Copper Range Railroad: a historical approach /* Houghton, MI: Burns, 1964? 95, 10 l.

2080. Burns, James Bryan. *The language of merger: corporate combinations in the railroad industry, 1970-1995.* 1996. 424 l. (Thesis, Ph.D., Mississippi State University.)

2081. _____. *Railroad mergers and the language of unification/* Westport, CT: Quorum Books, 1998. 220 p.

2082. Burns, Marc H. *High-speed rail in the rear-view mirror: a final report of the Texas High-Speed Rail Authority /* Austin, TX: M.H. Burns, 1995. 81, 13 p.

2083. Burns, Mary Ray. *A comparative study of four railroad reorganizations: Chicago and North Western Railway Company, Chicago, Milwaukee, St. Paul and Pacific Railroad Company, Minneapolis, St. Paul & Sault Ste. Marie Railway Company.* 1947. 438 l. (Thesis, Ph.D., University of Minnesota.)

2084. Burns, Robert W. *Ex-Baltimore & Ohio lines in northwestern Pennsylvania.* Sheffield, PA: Robert W. Burns, 1999. 68 p.

2085. _____. *Iron trails of North America : 1978-2008.* Atglen, PA: Schiffer, 2009. 174 p.

2086. Burns, W.F. *The Pullman boycott; a complete history of the great R.R. strike.* St. Paul, Minn., McGill Printing Company, 1894. 318 p.

2087. Burr, William Patrick. *The problem of the relocation of the New York Central Railroad tracks on the west side*. New York : Dispatch Press, 1917. 64 p. "Reprinted from the 'Harlem Home News,' June 10, 1917. et. seq."

2088. Burt, Benjamin Chapman. *Railway station service*. New York, J. Wiley & Sons, 1911. 292 p.

2089. Burt, F. Allen. *Mount Washington Cog Railway*. Mount Washington, NH: Mount Washington Cog Railway Company, 1975. 72 p.

2090. Burt, Jesse C., Jr. *The history of the Nashville, Chattanooga and St. Louis Railroad, 1873-1916*. 1950. 15-290 l. (Thesis, Ph.D., Vanderbilt University.)

2091. Burt, Richard E. *Design for an all welded Warren truss railroad bridge*. 1933. 20 p. (Thesis, C.E., Rensselaer Polytechnic Institute.)

2092. Burton, Mark L. *Preserving branch-line railroad capacity in southern West Virginia*. Huntington, WV: Marshall University, Nick J. Rahall, II Appalachian Transportation Institute, 2004. 40 l.

2093. _____. *Railroad deregulation and rail rates: a disaggregated analysis* / 1991. 199 l. (Thesis, Ph.D., University of Tennessee.)

2094. Burwash, Martin. *Cascade Division: a pictorial essay of the BN and Milwaukee Road in the Washington Cascades*. Arvada, CO: Fox Publications, 1995. 124 p.

2095. _____. *The great adventure: the railroad legacy of Stevens Pass*. Arvada, CO: Fox Publications, 1998. 128 p.

2096. Burzillo, David P. *The Boston and Maine Railroad strike of February 12, 1877* / 1992. 169 l. (Thesis, A.L.M., Harvard University.)

2097. Bush & Lobdell. *Bush & Lobdell, Wilmington, Delaware : manufacturers of chilled wheels for rail-road cars and locomotive engines*. Wilmington, Del., John B. Porter, 1851. 14 p.

2098. Bush, H.D. Theodore Cooper. *Discussion on American railroad bridges*. New York? American Society of Civil Engineers, 1889. 1 v.

2098a. Bush, John E. *Building Union Pacific 844: the birth of the FEF-3 steam class* / David City, NB: South Platte Press, 2013. 56 p.

2099. _____, James L. Ehernberger. *Union Pacific steam: Big Boy portraits*. Cheyenne, WY: Challenger Press, 1996. 127 p.

2100. Business Men's League of St. Louis. *The terminals of St. Louis*. St. Louis, Business Men's League, Terminal Facilities Committee, 1903. 30 p.

2101. Business Training Corporation. *Course in Pullman production methods.*
New York, Business Training Corporation, 1926-1927 .6 v. plates

2102. Buss, Dietrich G. *Henry Villard: a study of transatlantic investments and interests, 1870-1895.* 1976. (Thesis, Ph.D., Claremont Graduate School.) Reprint: New York, NY Arno Press, 1978. 196 p. Series: *Dissertations in American economic history.*

2103. Bussing, Irvin. *Railroad debt reduction; outline of a plan for the gradual reduction of railroad debt, tested by application to the financial history of three bankrupt railroads.* New York, NY: Published by the Savings Banks Trust Co., 1937. 37 p.

2104. Butler, Dale M., William M. Graham. *Dismantling railroad freight cars; a study of improved methods with application to other demolition problems.* Rockville, MD: Bureau of Solid Waste Management, 1969. 32 p. (*Report SW-3c,* written for the Bureau of Solid Waste Management under contract no. PH 86-67-100 with Booz, Allen Applied Research, Inc.)

2105. Butler, W.E. (William Edward). *Down among the sugar cane: the story of Louisiana sugar plantations and their railroads.* Baton Rouge, LA: Moran Pub. Corp., 1980. 266 p.

2106. Butler, William Daniel. *The Camas Prairie Railroad: a corporate* history, *1909-1975.* 1979. 282 l. (Thesis, Ph.D., University of Idaho.)

2107. Butler, William R. *The locomotive engine.* 1870. 27 l. (Thesis, M.E., Lehigh University.)

2107a. Butterfield, Francis L. *Illinois high speed rail: historic preservation planning and recommendations* / 2011. 71 l. (Thesis, M.S., School of Art Institute of Chicago.)

2107b. Butts, Edward, J.L. Stubblefield. *The civil engineer's field book: designed for the use of the locating engineer.* 3d ed and rev. ed. New York: J. Wiley & Sons, 1914. 275 p.

2108. Bux, Joe, Ed Crist. *New York, Ontario & Western Railway, Scranton Division.* Middletown, NY: Prior King Press, 1985. 128 p.

2109. Buydos, John F. *High-speed rail transportation* / Washington, DC: Science Reference Section, Science and Technology Division, Library of Congress, 1990. 8 p. (*LC science tracer bullet, TB 90-3.*)

2110. Byberg, Trent, Douglas E. Benson. *The national short line railroad database project, 1996-1997.* Fargo, ND: Upper Great Plains Transportation Institute, North Dakota State University, 1997. 142 p. (Federal Railroad Administration; Upper Great Plains Transportation Institute; American Short Line Railroad Association; Mountain Plains Consortium; University Transportation Centers Program.)

2111. Bye, Ranulph. *The vanishing depot.* Wynnewood, PA: Livingston Publishing

Company, 1973. 113 p. (Rev. ed.: Wayne, PA: Haverford House, 1983. 128 p.)

2112. Byers, Arley. *Bent, zig-zag & crooked: a narrow gauge railroad.* Sycamore Valley, OH: A. Byers, 1974. 231 p. (Bellaire, Zanesville, and Cincinnati Railroad.)

2113. Byers, David E., Amy L. Pressler. *The Federal Valley Railroad Company & its ancestors, 1845-1954.* Westerville, OH: Integrity Press, 2000. 159 p.

2114. Byers, Morton Lewis. *Economics of railway operation.* New York, The Engineering News Publishing Company, 1908. 672 p.

2115. Byington, Mary. *Woman operator on the Milwaukee Railroad during World War II; a memoir.* Timber Lake, SD: M. Byington, 1998. 80 p.

2116. Byrne, C. J. *Rhymes of the rail; songs, poems & stories.* St. Paul: Rhymes of the Rail Company, 1914. 32 p.

2117. Byrne, Kevin Barry. *The United States Railroad Administration, 1917-1920.* 1974. 433 l. (Thesis, Ph.D., Duke University.)

2118. Byrne, Oliver. *The evidence of Oliver Byrne in the patent case of Ross Winans' eight-wheeled car.* Baltimore, Murphy, 1855. 43 p.

2119. _____. *Pocket-book for railroad and civil engineers: containing new, exact and concise methods for laying out railroad curves, switches, frog angles, and crossings; the staking out of work, levelling; the calculation of cuttings and embankments, earthwork, etc.* New York, C. Shepard, 1856. 163 p. (Reissued 1864, 1889.)

2120. Byrne, R. *Railroad axle design factors.* New York : American Society of Mechanical Engineers, 1967. 10 p. (*ASME. Paper no. 67-RR-3.*)

2121. Byron, Carl R. *Boston & Maine trackside with Arthur E. Mitchell.* Scotch Plains, NJ: Morning Sun Books, 1999. 128 p.

2122. _____. *A pinprick of light: the Troy and Greenfield Railroad and its Hoosac Tunnel.* Brattleboro, VT: S. Greene Press, 1978. 71 p.

2123. _____. *Trackside along the Boston & Maine, 1945-1975, with Donald G. Hills.* Scotch Plains, NJ: Morning Sun Books, 2005. 128 p.

2124. _____. *Trackside along the New Haven, 1950-1956, with Arthur E. Mitchell.* Scotch Plains, NJ: Morning Sun Books, 2002. 128 p.

2125. _____. *Trackside around Boston, 1942-1962, with Lawson Hill.* Scotch Plains, NJ: Morning Sun Books, 2000. 128 p.

2126. _____, Robert W. Rediske. *The Pioneer Zephyr: America's first diesel-electric stainless steel streamliner.* Forest Park, IL: Heimburger House Publishing Co.; Museum of Science and Industry, Chicago, 2005. 124 p.

C

2126a. *The C & E.I flyer*. Crestwood, IL: Chicago and Eastern Illinois Railroad Co., 1920s- .

2127. *The C & EI flyer: the magazine of the Chicago & Eastern Illinois Railroad Historical Society*. Crestwood, IL: Chicago and Eastern Illinois Railroad Historical Society, 1990s-? Semiannual. Title varies.

2128. *The C & EI newsletter*. S.l., Chicago and Eastern Illinois Railroad Historical Society, 1900s-2007. (> *Dixie mail.*)

2128a. *C & NW Ry. steam locomotive profiles*. Sheboygan, WI: Northwood Chapter, N.R.H.S., 1985. 1 v.

2129. *C & NW-Rock Island freight car conversion numbers*. Rock Island, IL? Chicago& Northwestern Historical Society, 1999. 1 v.

2129a. *C & O diagrams of passenger cars*. Richmond, VA: Chesapeake and Ohio Railway Co., 1942. 120 l.

2130. *The C. and O. in central Virginia: prepared in connection with the 1979 Annual Convention of the Chesapeake and Ohio Historical Society at Charlottesville, Virginia, July 27, 28, 29, 1979*. Randolph Kean, editor. Alderson, WV: The Society, 1979. 20 p.

2131. C.W. Hunt Company. *C.W. Hunt Company; manufacturers of locomotives, cars, sectional track, and every requisite for the equipment of industrial railways*. New York, C.W. Hunt Co., 1892. 51 p. (*Catalogue 192.*)

2132. _____. *Electric locomotives for manufacturing establishments*. West Brighton, Staten Island, N.Y., C.W. Hunt Company, 1901. 12 p. (*Pamphlet no. 0113.*)

2133. Cabble, George M. *Adhesion between rails and wheels of railway motive power*. 1958. 98 l. (Thesis, University of Illinois.)

2134. _____. *Understanding wheel-rail adhesion* / New York : American Society of Mechanical Engineers, 1960. 7 p. (*ASME. Paper no. 60-RR-3.*)

2135. *Cabin cars of the Pennsylvania and Long Island Railroads*. Hicksville, NY: N.J. International, 1982. 66 p. (*Caboose data book, no. 2.*)

2136. Caboose cars, 1879-1943. Novato, CA: Newton K. Gregg, 1973. 63 p.

2137. *Cabooses of narrow gauge and logging railroads*. Hicksville, NY: N.J. International, 1993. 48 p. (*Caboose data book, no. 3.*)

2138. *Cabooses of the New Haven and New York Central railroads.* Hicksville, NJ: N.J. International, 1982? 48 p. (*Caboose data book, no. 1.*)

2138a. *Cabooses on the Terminal Railroad/* St. Louis: Terminal Railroad Association of St. Louis Historical and Technical Society, 2011. 117 p.

2139. Cackovic, David L., Britto Rajkumar, Vinaya Sharma. *Tank car fatigue crack growth test.* Washington, DC: Federal Railroad Administration, Office of Research and Development, 1993. 156, 4 p. (*DOT/FRA/ORD-93-10.*)

2140. Cafky, Morris. *Colorado Midland.* Denver, Rocky Mountain Railroad Club, 1965. 467 p.

2141. _____. *Rails around Gold Hill.* Denver, Rocky Mountain Railroad Club, 1955. 463 p.

2142. Cagney's Locomotive Works. *Cagney's' Locomotive Works, illustrated catalogue of locomotives, tenders, passenger and freight cars, including rolling stock of all modern improvements, for pleasure resorts, mines, inside and outside, plantations, rolling mills, contractors, logging, or any other service.* New York, Cagney's Locomotive Works, 1901. 32 p.

2143. Blank entry.

2144. _____, Tom Debolski; *North American steam: a photographic history.* Introduction by Bill Yenne. New York, Crescent Books, 1991. 240 p.

2145. Cahill, Marie, Lynne Paide. *The history of the Union Pacific; America's great transcontinental railroad/* New York, NY: Crescent Books, 1989. 127 p.

2146. Caine, Stanley P. *Railroad regulation in Wisconsin, 1903-1910 : as assessment of a progressive reform.* 1967. 353 l. (Thesis, Ph.D., University of Wisconsin.)

2147. Calderhead, Owen Oliver. *Findings of fact, orders and opinions in railroad valuation cases.* Olympia, WA: Public Printer, 1909-1910. 1 v. (various pagings).

2147a. _____. *Physical operating and traffic study of Seattle Terminal.* Olympia, WA: F.M. Lamborn, Public Printer, 1924. 90 p.

2148. Caldes, Charles P. *The steam era in New Jersey, 1930-1945.* Ridgefield, NJ: Journal Square Publishing, 2004. 60 p.

2149. _____. *Steam to diesel in New Jersey.* Charleston, SC: Arcadia, 2002. 128 p.

2150. _____, Joseph Granese, Tim Harris. *Guide to south Jersey abandoned railroads.* Linwood, NJ: Absecon Highlands, TrakEdge Pub., 1995? 1 v.

2151. Caldwell, Linda Damron, Bill Akins, Betty J. Duggan. *Growing up with the L & N:*

life and times in a railroad town. S.l., Etowah Arts Commission, 1989. 64 p.
(McMinn County, Tennessee)

2152. Caldwell, Wilber W. *The courthouse and the depot: the architecture of hope
in an age of despair: a narrative guide to railroad expansion and its impact on public
architecture in Georgia, 1833-1910.* Macon. GA: Mercer University Press, 2001. 613 p.

2153. Calhoun, J. Theodore. *Railroad surgery.* 1859. 1 v. (Thesis, University
of Pennsylvania.)

2154. California. Bureau of State Audits. *High-Speed Rail Authority: it risks delays or an
incomplete system because of inadequate planning, weak oversight, and lax contract
management.* Sacramento, CA: California State Auditor, Bureau of State Audits, 2010.
48 p. (*Report 2009-106*) http://bibpurl.oclc.org/web/39670

2155. California. Department of Forestry. *Railroad fire prevention field guide.*
Sacramento, CA: State of California, Department of Forestry, 1978. 1 v. (U.S. Forest
Service; Bureau of Land Management.)

2156. California. Department of Transportation. *From A to Z by train: the comprehensive
guide to train safety for teens and adults.* S.l., California Department of Transportation
/Amtrak/United States Federal Railroad Administration, 2004. 1 v.

2157. _____. _____. *Los Angeles-Bakersfield high speed ground transportation
feasibility and preliminary engineering study: study information handout, California
Transportation Commission, September 8-9, 1992 meeting, agenda item 2.6a (16)*
Los Angeles? Parsons Brinkerhoff? 1993. 11 l.

2158. _____. _____. *Los Angeles-Bakersfield high speed ground transportation
feasibility study: public participation program: final report.* North Hollywood, CA:
Consensus Planning Group, 1994. 1 v. (various pagings)

2159. _____. _____. *Los Angeles-Bakersfield high speed ground transportation
preliminary engineering feasibility study: draft summary report.* Los Angeles, CA:
California Department of Transportation, District 7, 1994. 70, 7 p.

2160. _____. _____. *Los Angeles-Bakersfield high speed ground transportation
preliminary engineering feasibility study: final report/* Los Angeles, CA: California
Department of Transportation, District 7, 1994. 1 v. (Various pagings)

2161. _____. _____. *Los Angeles-Bakersfield high speed ground transportation
system: preliminary engineering feasibility study: freight compatibility study/* Los
Angeles, CA: California Department of Transportation, District 7, 1994. 1 v. (various
pagings

2162. _____. _____. *Los Angeles-Bakersfield high speed ground transportation
system: request for proposal/* Los Angeles, CA: California Department of Transportation,
District 7, 1993. 61 l.

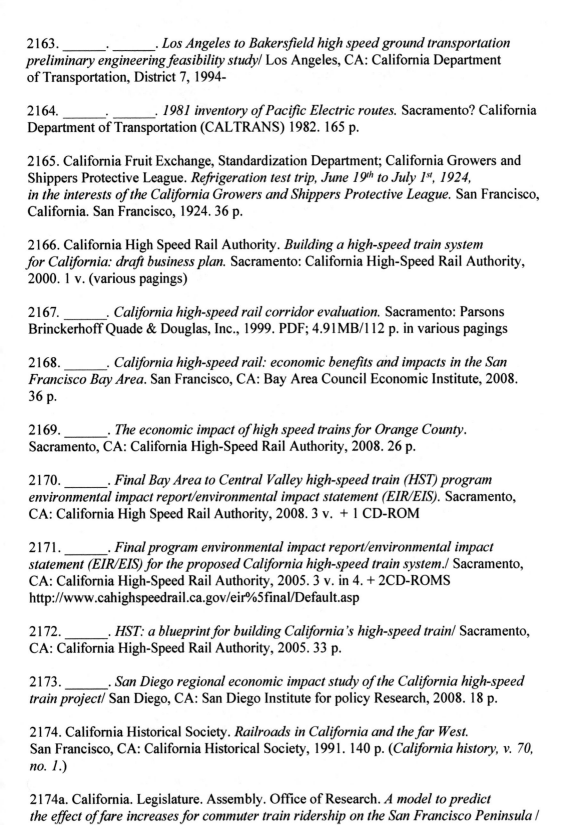

2163. _____. _____. *Los Angeles to Bakersfield high speed ground transportation preliminary engineering feasibility study*/ Los Angeles, CA: California Department of Transportation, District 7, 1994-

2164. _____. _____. *1981 inventory of Pacific Electric routes.* Sacramento? California Department of Transportation (CALTRANS) 1982. 165 p.

2165. California Fruit Exchange, Standardization Department; California Growers and Shippers Protective League. *Refrigeration test trip, June 19th to July 1st, 1924, in the interests of the California Growers and Shippers Protective League.* San Francisco, California. San Francisco, 1924. 36 p.

2166. California High Speed Rail Authority. *Building a high-speed train system for California: draft business plan.* Sacramento: California High-Speed Rail Authority, 2000. 1 v. (various pagings)

2167. _____. *California high-speed rail corridor evaluation.* Sacramento: Parsons Brinckerhoff Quade & Douglas, Inc., 1999. PDF; 4.91MB/112 p. in various pagings

2168. _____. *California high-speed rail: economic benefits and impacts in the San Francisco Bay Area.* San Francisco, CA: Bay Area Council Economic Institute, 2008. 36 p.

2169. _____. *The economic impact of high speed trains for Orange County.* Sacramento, CA: California High-Speed Rail Authority, 2008. 26 p.

2170. _____. *Final Bay Area to Central Valley high-speed train (HST) program environmental impact report/environmental impact statement (EIR/EIS).* Sacramento, CA: California High Speed Rail Authority, 2008. 3 v. + 1 CD-ROM

2171. _____. *Final program environmental impact report/environmental impact statement (EIR/EIS) for the proposed California high-speed train system.*/ Sacramento, CA: California High-Speed Rail Authority, 2005. 3 v. in 4. + 2CD-ROMS
http://www.cahighspeedrail.ca.gov/eir%5final/Default.asp

2172. _____. *HST: a blueprint for building California's high-speed train*/ Sacramento, CA: California High-Speed Rail Authority, 2005. 33 p.

2173. _____. *San Diego regional economic impact study of the California high-speed train project*/ San Diego, CA: San Diego Institute for policy Research, 2008. 18 p.

2174. California Historical Society. *Railroads in California and the far West.* San Francisco, CA: California Historical Society, 1991. 140 p. (*California history, v. 70, no. 1.*)

2174a. California. Legislature. Assembly. Office of Research. *A model to predict the effect of fare increases for commuter train ridership on the San Francisco Peninsula* /

Sacramento : The Office, 1976. 6, 24 l.

2175. California. Legislature. Committee on Public Lands. *Report of committee and statement of Captain Joseph Walker before them on the practicability of a railroad from San Francisco to the United States.* Sacramento? G. Kerr, State Printer, 1853. 7 p.

2176. California Public Utilities Commission. Transportation Division. *The Atchinson, Topeka and Santa Fe Railway Company, application no. 32771 : report on the study of the operating costs and revenues of certain A.T.& S.F. passenger trains in California.* Sacramento ? s.n., 1952. 15 p.

2176a. _____. *Digest of decisions, with a list of all cases that have been the subject of court action: vols 1 to 19, 1912-1927* / San Francisco: Recorder Printing and Publishing Co., 1927. xxxi, 577 p.

2177. _____. _____. *In the matter of proposed discontinuance of the Atchison, Topeka and Santa Fe Railway Company trains 19 and 20 and 23 and 24 : between Chicago and Los Angeles, finance docket no. 24869.* Sacramento ? s.n., 1968. 27 p.

2178. _____. _____. *Pacific Electric Railway Company. Survey of conditions of tracks on lines proposed for abandonment.* Los Angeles, Calif., The Dept., 1949. 27 l.

2179. _____. _____. *Passenger traffic trends and service and mileage estimate for RDC car operation on Northwestern Pacific Railroad Company's passenger trains nos. 3 and 4, application no. 39660: discontinuance of trains nos. 3 and 4 between San Rafael and Willits.* Sacramento? : s.n., 1958. 5 p.

2180. _____. _____. *Report on the "California Zephyr", Western Pacific Railroad trains 17 and 18 : finance docket no. 24277.* Sacramento ? s.n., 1966. 1 v. (various pagings)

2181. _____. _____. *Report on passenger service on Southern Pacific Company's Overland route passenger trains and company's proposed consolidation of "City of San Francisco" trains nos. 101 and 102 with "Overland" trains no. 27 and 28* / San Francisco : The Division, 1960. 17 p.

2182. _____. _____. *Report on passenger service on Southern Pacific Company's Overland route passenger trains, finance docket no. 21946.* Sacramento ? s.n., 1962. 18 p.

2183. _____. _____. *Report on passenger service on Southern Pacific Company's San Francisco-Sacramento route, San Joaquin Valley route, and Peninsula Suburban service: and proposed discontinuance of Sacramento local trains nos. 247, 248, 226 & 241, "West Coast" trains nos. 59 & 60, Peninsula trains nos. 156 & 155 (exc. Sun. & hol.); estimated results of operations on an out-of-the pocket basis for individual passenger trains operated by Southern Pacific Company (exclusive of San Francisco-San Jose local trains) for the year 1958/* San Francisco: California Public Utilities Commission, 1959. 42, 38 p. (*Docket no. 20503*)

2184. _____. _____. *Report on passenger service on Southern Pacific Company's Shasta Route, and proposed discontinuance Shasta Daylight trains nos. 9 and 10, finance docket no. 22905.* Sacramento? : California Public Utilities Commission, Transportation Division, 1964-1965. 3 v.

2185. _____. _____. *Report on passenger service on Southern Pacific' Company's Shasta Route, and proposed tri-weekly service on Shasta Daylight trains nos. 9 and 10: finance docket no. 20444.* Sacramento ? s.n., 1959. 10, 25 p.

2185a. _____. *Report on railroad grade crossing elimination and passenger and freight terminals in Los Angeles.* Sacramento: Railroad Commission of the State of California, 1920. 587 p. (California Railroad Commission. Engineering Department..)

2185b. _____. _____. *Request of Southern Pacific Company to abandon trains nos. 223 and 224 "The Senator" operating between Oakland and Sacramento.* Sacramento? s.n., 1960. 2 v. (Application no. 42468)

2186. _____. _____. *Southern Pacific Company, application no. 32812 : report on the study of the operating costs and revenues of certain Southern Pacific Company passenger trains in California.* Sacramento ? s.n., 1952. 15 p.

2187. _____. _____. *Southern Pacific Company, application no. 36995, for authority to discontinue trains nos. 229 and 246 operating between Sacramento and Oakland Pier.* Sacramento, s.n., 1955. 15 p.

2188. _____. _____. *Southern Pacific Company, application no. 44796 for authority to discontinue "Del Monte" trains nos. 126 and 139 between San Jose and Monterey.* Sacramento ? s.n., 1963. 14 p.

2189. _____. _____. *Southern Pacific Company discontinuance of trains nos. 155 & 156 between San Francisco and San Jose, case no5234, application no. 39719.* Sacramento? : s.n., 1958. 15 p.

2189a. _____. *Southern Pacific Company, San Francisco peninsula suburban service : I.C.C. docket no. 34631.* Sacramento? s.n., 1965. 2 v.

2190. _____. _____. *Supplemental presentation to exhibit no. 21 in proceeding of application no. 36995 for discontinuance of Southern Pacific Company trains nos. 229 and 246 operating between Sacramento and Oakland Pier.* Sacramento? : s.n., 1956. 3 p.

2191. California. Railroad Commission. *Discontinuance of the operation of trains nos. 1 and 2 between San Rafael and Eureka by Northwestern Pacific Railroad Company.* Sacramento? : s.n., 1946. 5, 3 p.

2191a. California. State Board of Horticulture. Fruit-Growers of California. *Transportation, refrigeration, time schedule; action taken by the Fruit-Growers of California at the convention, held in San Francisco, Dec. 3-6, 1901.* San Francisco: State Board of Horticulture, 1902. 20 p. (Report of the Committee on Transportation.))

2192. California Transportation Commission. *Passenger rail grade crossings: report on passenger rail grade crossing inventory guidelines and methodology for prioritizing safety improvements/* Sacramento, California Transportation Commission, 1992. 1 v. (Various pagings)

2193. *The California Zephyr.* Chicago, Poole Brothers, Inc., 1949. 1 v.

2194. Callanan, Thomas Patrick. *Chicago & North Western – Order of Railroad Telegraphers strike: 1962.* 1963. 129 l. (Thesis, M.A., University of Illinois at Urbana-Champaign.)

2195. Calloway, Ernest. *The Red Caps struggle for a livelihood.* Chicago, IL: Educational Department, United Transport Service Employees of America, 194-? 14, 1 l.

2196. Calloway, Warren L. *Atlantic Coast Line: the diesel years.* Halifax, PA: Withers Publishing, 1993. 192 p.

2197. _____, and Paul K. Withers. *Seaboard Air Line Railroad Company: motive power.* Halifax, PA: Withers Publishing, 1988. 256 p.

2198. Caloroso, Bill. *Pennsylvania Railroad's Elmira Branch.* Andover, NJ: Andover Junction Publications, 1993. 96 p.

2199. Calvi, Jim. *Baird & Harper lumber company: Warland, Montana (1906-1926).* Eureka, MT: Jim Calvi, 2011. 43 l.

2199a. _____. *Troy Division Yard on the Great Northern Railway (1890-1926).* Libby, MT: Western Printers, 1997. 85 p.

2200. *Camas Prairie Railroad: a special study/* Boise, ID: Idaho, Transportation Department, Management Services Section;, 1978. 60 p.

2201. Cambria Iron Company. *Cambria Iron and Steel Works at Johnstown: upwards of one million tons of iron and steel rails.* Philadelphia, Cambria Iron and Steel, 1885. 1 v.

2202. _____. *Rail fastenings, splice bars, bolts and nuts, and patented joints, manufactured by Cambria Iron Company, Johnstown, Pennsylvania.* Philadelphia : s.n., 1891. 1 v. (unpaged)

2203. _____. *Sections of iron and steel rails, manufactured by Cambria Iron Company, Johnstown, Pa.* Philadelphia, T. Sinclair, litho., 1890. 17 l.

2204. _____. *Sections of steel and iron rails, manufactured by Cambria Iron Company /* Philadelphia : s.n., 1876. 1 v. (unpaged).

2205. Cambria Steel Company. *Rails: fastenings, guard rails and frog fillers*. Johnstown, Penn., Cambria Steel Co., 1912. 168 p.

2206. Cambria Steel Company. *Cambria steel rails*/ Philadelphia, PA: Cambria Iron Company, 1898.1 v. (Unpaged) (Vol. 2: Girder rails &c for street and electric use.)

2207. _____. *Morrison guard rail*. Johnstown, PA: Cambria Steel Company, 1914. 12 p.

2208. _____. *Rail fastenings*. Johnstown, PA: Cambria Steel Company, 1910. 112 p.

2209. _____. *Rails: fastenings, guard rails and frog fillers*. Johnstown, PA: Cambria Steel Company, 1912. 168 p.

2210. _____. *Sections of steel and iron rails, manufactured by Cambria Iron Company, Johnstown, Pennsylvania. Vol. 1, Steel T rails and fastenings*. Philadelphia, PA: Cambria Iron Company, 1886. 1 v.

2211. _____. *Steel axles and forgings: steel axles, passenger car, freight car, tender truck, engine truck, driving, street car, mine car, etc.: crank pins, piston rods and general forgings* / 2d ed. Philadelphia : Cambria Steel Co., 1903. 70 p.

2212. _____. *"T" rails: fastenings, rail guard and frog filler*. Philadelphia, PA: Cambria Steel Company, 1904. 1 v. (unpaged)

2213. Camisa, Joseph A. *Alexandria's internal improvement struggle and the eventual rise of the Orange and Alexandria Railroad*/ 2008. 114 l. (Thesis, M.A., Central Michigan University.)

2214. Camp, Mark J. *Railroad depots of northeast Ohio* / Charleston, SC: Arcadia Pub., 2007. 127 p.

2215. Camp, Walter Mason. *Notes on track; construction and maintenance*. Chicago, The Author, 1903. 1214 p.

2216. _____. *Railroad transportation at the Universal Exposition. World's Fair number, St. Louis, Missouri*. Chicago, s.n., 1904. 204 p. (Reprint: *The railway and engineering review, special issue, Dec.* 1904, prepared by W.M. Camp, Earl A. Averill and Orville Haydn Reynolds.)

2217. Campbell, Donald G. *Steam locomotives of the Kansas City Southern*. David City: NE: South Platte Press, 2000. 48 p.

2218. Campbell, Donald P. *A history of steam motive power development on the Pennsylvania Railroad*. 1947. 65 l. (Thesis, ME, University of Cincinnati.)

2219. Campbell, E.T. *Tweetsie tales: a collection of reminiscences*. Blowing Rock, NC:

New River Pub. Co., 1989. 74 p.

2220. Campbell, Edward G. *The reorganization of the American railroad system, 1893-1900: a study of the effects of the Panic of 1893, the ensuing depression, and the first years of recovery on railroad organization and financing*/ New York, NY: Columbia University Press, 1938, 366 p. Thesis, Ph.D., Columbia University, 1938. (*Columbia studies in the social sciences, no. 434.*) Published also as *Studies in history, economics and public law*, ed. by the Faculty of Political Science of Columbia University, no. 434. Reprint: New York, AMS Press, 1968.

2221. Campbell, James Hepburn. *Pacific railroad: speech of Hon. J.H. Campbell, of Pennsylvania, in the House of Representatives, Tuesday, April 8, 1862, on the bill to aid in constructing a railroad and telegraph line from the Missouri River to the Pacific Ocean, and to secure to the government the use of the same for postal, military, and other purposes.* Washington, DC: Scammell & Co., 1862. 8 p.

2222. Campbell, Joseph. *California funicular railways.* Los Angeles, CA: Borden Publishers, 1993.89 p.

2222a. Campbell, Neil Nelson, Paul Kautz. *A determination of the comparative values of cross-ties of different materials* / 1910. 48 l. (Thesis, B.S., University of Illinois.)

2223. Campbell, Roy W., Thomas E. Burg. *Soo Line steam: locomotive photos from the Roy Campbell collection* / Merrill, WI: Merrill Pub. Associates, 2005. 155 p.

2224. Campbell, T. C., Sidney Katell. *Long-distance coal transport: unit trains or slurry pipelines* / Washington, DC: U.S. Department of the Interior, Bureau of Mines, 1975. 31 p. (*Information circular. Bureau of Mines, 8690.*)

2225. Campbell, R. L. *Track nuts and bolts.* Buffalo: Joseph King, litho., 1876. 21 p.

2226. Cambridge Systematics; Wilbur Smith and Associates; David Evans Associates; Oregon; Dept. of Transportation. *Oregon rail passenger policy and plan.* Salem, OR: Oregon Dept. of Transportation, 1993. 1 v.

2227. Campbell, Michael H., Edward C. Brewer. *The Railway Labor Act of 1926: a legislative history.* Buffalo, NY: Published for the ABA Section on Labor and Employment Law by W.S. Hein, 1988. 4 v.

2228. Canadian Institute of Guided Ground Transport. *Executive summary: Ridership, economic development, and environmental impacts of super-speed train service for selected sites in the Southern California-Las Vegas Valley corridor*/ Playa Del Rey, CA:; Las Vegas, NV: California-Nevada Super-Speed Ground Transportation Commission, 1989. 18 p.

2229. *Blank entry.*

2230. _____. *Maglev technology assessment: super-speed ground transportation system: Las Vegas/Southern California corridor: phase II.* Kingston, ON: Canadian institute of Guided Ground Transport, Queen's University, 1986. 1 v. (various pagings)

2231. _____. *Ridership, economic development, and environmental impacts of super-speed train service for selected sites in the Southern California-Las Vegas Valley corridor/* Playa Del Rey, CA; Las Vegas, NV: California-Nevada Super-Speed Ground Transportation Commission, 1989. 184 p.

2232. CanagaRetna, Sujit. *High-speed rail: update from the Southern states: an issue alert from the SLC /* Atlanta, GA: Southern Legislative Conference of the Council of State Government, 2009. 4 p.
http://slcatlanta.org/Publications/EconDev/High Speed Rail.pdf

2233. Canfield, John R. *Lackawanna Railroad: in color.* Edison, NJ: Morning Sun Books, 2003. v. 3. v. 1 by David R. Sweetland; v. 2 by Jeremy F. Plant.

2234. _____. *The legendary Lackawanna: a belated tribute to the route of the Phoebe Snow.* S.l., J.R. Canfield, 2007. 48 p.

2235. _____, John T. Morrison. *Trackside in search of northern New England steam with John T. Morrison.* Scotch Plains, NJ: Morning Sun Books, 2006. 128 p.

2236. _____, _____. *Trackside in search of southern New England steam with John T. Morrison /* Scotch Plains, NJ: Morning Sun Books, 2007. 128 p.

2237. _____, Bob Goin, John Dziobko. *Trackside around the Garden State, 1950-1975.* Scotch Plains, NJ: Morning Sun Books, 2009. 128 p.

2238. Cannell, Lewis D. *The freight rate structure and its effect on the price and movement of Northwest wheat.* Pullman, WA: Bureau of Economic and Business Research, Washington State College, 1945. 78 p. (*Bulletin, no. 2.*)

2239. Cannon, Weldon Green. *B.M. Temple: master railroad engineer in Texas/* Temple, TX: W.G. Cannon, 1981. 8 p.

2240. _____. *Bernard Moore Temple: binding Texas with steel rails.* 1987. 145 l. (Thesis, Ph.D., Texas Christian University.)

2240a. Cantine, Edward I. *The location and construction of the Coeur d'Alene Railway and Navigation Company's railroad : from Mullan, Idaho, to the Idaho-Montana boundary line /* 1887. 1 v. (Thesis, B.S., University of Illinois.)

2241. Cantley, W.I. *Official tests of three-cylinder locomotive number 5,000.* S.l., Lehigh Valley Railroad, 1924. 26 p.

2241a. Cantlin, David J. *Tacoma rail /* Charleston, SC: Arcadia Publishing, 2013. 127 p.

2241b. Canton, Wanda, Richard Canton. *Railroad in the sky, 1881-1917* / Lee Vining, CA: Friends of Bodie Railway & Lumber Company, 2012. 109 p.

2242. *The capacity and capital requirements of the railroad industry.* Washington, DC: Interstate Commerce Commission, Bureau of Transport Economics and Statistics, 1952. 1 v. (Its *Statement, no. 5227.*)

2243. Cape, Randall E., Robert G. McKeen. *The ghost trains of SP's Overland Route: trains nos. 21-22, Mail, 1947-1967.* Pasadena, CA: Southern Pacific Historical & Technical Society, 2006. 144 p.

2244. *The capitalist's guide and railway annual for 1859: containing all the railroads completed and in progress in the United States/ Compiled and arranged from late and authentic reports by F.H. Stow.* New York, Samuel T. Callahan, 1859. 537 p.

2245. Cappel, Klaus. *Truck design optimization project, phase II : introductory report.* Washington, DC: Federal Railroad Administration, Office of Research and Development, 1978. 1 v. (various pagings.) (*FRA/ORD-78-53.*)

2246. Capps, Arthur E. *The private tank car: its history, economic regulatory aspects and the ultimate negotiated mileage allowance system.* S.l. s.n, 1980. 54, 6 l. "An original paper submitted in partial fulfillment of the requirements for the certificate of membership in the American Society of Traffic and Transportation Inc." Document location; Northwestern University, Transportation Library.

2247. Capra, Gregory S. *Protecting critical rail infrastructure*/ Maxwell Air Force Base, AL: USAF Counterproliferation Center, Air University, 2006. 52 p. (*Counterproliferation papers, Future warfare series, no. 38.*)

2248. *Car and locomotive cyclopedia of American practice: definitions and illustrations of railroad cars and locomotives and their components built for domestic and export service, and including shop practices and electrical fundamentals.* 1st ed. C.L. Combes, et al editors; Association of American Railroads. New York, Simmons-Boardman, 1966. 1214 p. ("Combining the 22d ed. of the Car Builder's Cyclopedia and the 16th ed. of the Locomotive Cyclopedia.")

2249. *Car and locomotive cyclopedia of American practice...*2d ed. C.L. Combes, et al editors; Association of American Railroads. New York, Simmons-Boardman, 1970. 1074p.

2250. *Car and locomotive cyclopedia of American practice...* 3d ed. C.L. Combes, editor; Association of American Railroads. New York, Simmons-Boardman, 1974. 999 p.

2251. *Car and locomotive cyclopedia of American practices...* 4th ed.; Association of American Railroads. New York, Simmons-Boardman, 1980. 1047 p.

2252. *Car and locomotive cyclopedia of American practices.* 5th ed. Kenneth G. Ellsworth, editor-in-chief; Association of American Railroads, Mechanical Division.

Omaha, NE: Simmons-Boardman, 1984. 755 p.

2253. *Car and locomotive cyclopedia of American practices: combining the Car Builders' Cyclopedia, first published in 1879 as the "Car Builders' Dictionary," and the "Locomotive Cyclopedia," first published in 1906 as the Locomotive Dictionary," combined as the "Car and Locomotive Cyclopedia in 1966.* 6th ed. William W. Kratville, et al, editors. Omaha, NE: Simmons-Boardman, 1997. 1136 p.

2254. *Car builders' cyclopedia of American practice: definitions and typical illustrations of cars, their parts and equipment; descriptions and illustrations of shops and tools employed in their construction and repair; cars built in America for industrial operations and foreign railroads.* 10th ed. Roydon Vincent Wright, editor; Charles Nicholas Winter, joint editor. New York, Simmons-Boardman, 1922. 1192 p.

2255. *Car builders' cyclopedia of American practice…* 11th ed. Roydon Vincent Wright, Managing editor; Robert Clayton Augur, Joint editor. New York, Simmons-Boardman, 1925. 1163 p.

2256. *Car builders' cyclopedia of American practice…* 12th ed. Roydon Vincent Wright, Managing editor, Associate editors: Robert Clayton Augur and H.P. Foster. New York, Simmons-Boardman, 1928. 1288 p.

2257. *Car builders' cyclopedia of American practice…* 13th ed. Roydon Vincent Wright, editor. New York, Simmons-Boardman, 1931. 1260 p.

2258. *Car builders' cyclopedia of American practice…* 14th ed. Roydon Vincent Wright, editor; Robert Clayton Augur, Managing editor; H.P. Foster, Associate editor. New York, Simmons-Boardman, 1937. 1308 p.

2259. *Car builders' cyclopedia of American practice…* 15th ed. Roydon Vincent Wright, editor; Robert Clayton Augur, Managing editor; H.P. Foster, Associate editor. New York, Simmons-Boardman, 1940. 1430 p. (Reprint: Milwaukee, Kalmbach Publishing Co., 1973.)

2260. *Car builders' cyclopedia of American practice…* 16th ed. Roydon Vincent Wright, editor. New York, Simmons-Boardman, 1943. 1328 p.

2261. *Car builders' cyclopedia of American practice…* 17th ed. Roydon Vincent Wright, editor. New York, Simmons-Boardman, 1946. 1446 p.

2262. *Car builders' cyclopedia of American practice…* 18th ed. C.B. Peck, editor. New York, Simmons-Boardman, 1949. 1308 p.

2263   . *Car builders' cyclopedia of American practice…* 19th ed. C.B. Peck, editor. New York, Simmons-Boardman, 1953. 1280 p.

2264. *Car builders' cyclopedia of American Practice…* 20th ed. C.L. Combes, editor.

New York, Simmons-Boardman, 1957.
1114 p.

2265. *Car builders' cyclopedia of American practice...* 21st ed. C.L. Combes, editor.
New York, Simmons-Boardman, 1961. 955 p.(>Car and locomotive cyclopedia
of American practice...1st. ed. New York, Simmons-Boardman, 1966.

2266. *The car-builder's dictionary; an illustrated vocabulary of terms which designate
American railroad cars, their parts and attachments.* Compiled by Matthias N. Forney,
Leander Garey, and Calvin A. Smith. New York, Railroad Gazette, 1879. 491,
84 p. (Reissued: 1881.) (Reprint: New York, Simmons-Boardman, 1949; Kentfield, CA:
N.K. Gregg, 1971.)

2267. *The car-builder's dictionary...* Revised and enlarged edition. New York,
The Railroad Gazette, 1884. xii, 203, 1, E 1-E, 358 p.. (Reissued: 1888; reprint:
Kentfield, CA: Newton K. Gregg, 1971

2268. *The car-builder's dictionary....*Compiled by John Cassan Wait. New York,
The Railroad Gazette, 1895. 151, 393, 16 p.

2269. *The car-builder's dictionary...* Compiled by John Cassan Wait, R.H. Soule, A.E.
Mitchell, Calvin A. Smith. New York, The Railroad Gazette, 1898. 394 p.

2270. *The car builders' dictionary...* Compiled by Rodney Hitt. New York, Railroad
Gazette, 1903. 374, 66 p.

2271. *The car builders' dictionary...* Compiled by Rodney Hitt. New York, Master Car
Builder's Association, 1906. 744 p. (Reprint: Kentfield, CA: N.K. Gregg, 1971.
166, 2, 568 p.)

2272. *The car builders' dictionary...* Compiled by Francis E. Lister. New York, Railway
Age Gazette, 1909. 3, 189, 2, 676 p.

2273. *Car builders' dictionary...* Compiled by Roy V. Wright. New York, Simmons-
Boardman, 1912. 953 p.

2274. *Car builders' dictionary...* Compiled by Roy V. Wright and A.C. Loudon.
New York, Simmons-Boardman, 1916. 2, 1066 p.

2275. *Car builders' dictionary and cyclopedia...* Compiled by Roy V. Wright.
New York, Simmons-Boardman, 1919. 1344 p.

2276. *The car-builder's dictionary...* Kentfield, CA: Newton K. Gregg, n.d. (Reprints
of 1879-1919 editions. 9 v.)

2277. The *car-building industry in Philadephia.* Philadelphia : J.G. Brill Co., 1925. 12 p.

2278. *Car ferries; a list of references, October 1925.* Washington, D.C., Association of American Railroads, 1925. 24 l.

2279. Car Foremen's Association of Chicago. *Proceedings.* Chicago, 1906-

2280. *Car heating.* Scranton, 1940. 1 v.

2281. *Car utility.* Chicago : Car Utility Magazine, 1916-1920s? Monthly.

2282. *Carbuilder.* Chicago, Ill., Pullman, 1926?-

2283. Cardenas, Juan Martin. *An investigation into railroad tapered roller bearing temperature trending using finite element analysis* / 2008. 164 l. (Thesis, M.S., University of Texas-Pan American.)

2284. Cardinal, Joseph W., James H. Feiger, P.C. McKeighan. *Fatigue crack growth equations for TC-128B tank car steel.* San Antonio, TX: Southwest Research Institute, 2006. 9 p. (http://www.volpe.dot.gov/sdd/docs/fatigue-1006-final.pdf)

2285. _____, Peter C. McKeighan, Stephan J. Hudak. *Damage tolerance analysis of tank car stub sill cracking: final report* / San Antonio, TX: Southwest Research Institute, 1998. 1 v. (various pagings)

2286. Carey, Daniel. *An analysis of the equipment lease as a device for securing specialized railroad equipment* / 1965. 22 l. (American Society of Traffic and Transportation.)

2286a. Carey, Henry Charles. *Letters to the people of New Jersey on the frauds, extortions, and oppressions of the railroad monopoly.* Philadelphia: Carey and Hart, 1848. 64 p.

2286b. _____. *The railroad question.* Philadelphia/ s.n., 1865. 16 p.

2287. Carleton, David P., Paul Carleton. *Memories of Norfolk and Western power.* Dunnellon, PA: D. Carleton Railbooks, 1994. 175 p.

2288. Carleton, Paul. *The Erie Lackawanna story.* River Vale, NJ: D. Carleton Rail Books, 1974. 479 p. (Rev. 2d printing: 1978. 478 p.)

2289. _____. *The Erie Railroad story.* Dunnellon, FL: D. Carleton Railbooks, 1988. 223 p.

2290. _____. *The Hudson & Manhattan Railroad revisited.* Dunnellon, FL: D. Carleton Railbooks, 1990. 127 p.

2291. _____. *The Jersey Central story.* River Vale, NJ: D. Carleton Rail Books, 1976. 415 p.

2292. _____. *The Jersey Central story: a locomotive history.* Dunnellon, FL:

D. Carleton Rail Books, 1992. 223 p.

2293. _____. *Locomotives of the Seaboard System: railroad of the South.* Dunnellon, FL: D. Carleton Railbooks, 1987. 207 p.

2294. _____. *Memories of New York Central diesels: electric power too.* River Vale, NJ: D. Carleton Railbooks, 1983. 208 p.

2295. _____. *Memories of O&W power: locomotives of the New York, Ontario & Western Railway.* Dunnellon, FL: D. Carleton Railbooks, 1986. 71 p.

2296. _____. *Memories of Reading Company power, 1833-1976.* Dunnellon, FL: D. Carleton Railbooks, 1985. 144 p.

2297. _____. *A Pennsy diesel power review.* Dunnellon, FL: D. Carleton Railbooks, 1995. 222 p.

2298. _____. *Pennsy steam: a second look.* Dunnellon, FL: D. Carleton Railbooks, 1991. 207 p.

2299. _____. *Rails around Gotham.* River Vale, NJ: D. Carleton Railbooks, 1981. 320 p.

2300. _____. *Under Pennsy wires.* River Vale, NJ: D. Carleton Railbooks, 1977. 319 p.

2301. _____, Daphne Carleton. *Pennsy, A to T.* Fairview, NJ: 1959? 94 p.

2302. *Carload shipments of fruits and melons from stations in the United States for the calendar years...* Washington, D.C., U.S. Dept. of Agriculture, 1923. 1 v. (*Statistical bulletin, U.S. Dept. Of Agriculture, no. 8*)

2303. *Carload shipments of vegetables from stations in the United States for the calendar years...* Washington, D.C., U.S. Dept. of Agriculture, 1923. 1 v. (*Statistical bulletin, U.S. Dept. of Agriculture, no. 9.*)

2304. *Carload waybill analyses: distribution of freight traffic and revenue averages by commodity classes and rate territories/* Washington, DC: Interstate Commerce Commission, Bureau of Transport Economics and Statistics, 1900s-1949. Annual. (*< Carload waybill analyses: territorial distribution, traffic and revenue by commodity classes; > Carload waybill analyses: territorial distribution, traffic and revenue by commodity classes.*)

2305. *Carload waybill analyses: quarterly seasonal comparisons, carloads, tons per car, length of haul (short-line), and revue per hundredweight by commodity classes.* Washington, DC: Interstate Commerce Commission, Bureau of Transport Economics and Statistics, 19 . Annual. (Volume for 1950 covers the years 1947-1950.)

2306. *Carload waybill analyses: state-to-state distribution of all commodities combined traffic and revenue/* Washington, DC: Interstate Commerce Commission, Bureau of Transport Economics and Statistics, 1900s-1951. Annual. (> *Carload waybill statistics: state-to-state distribution of all commodities combined traffic and revenue.*)

2307. *Carload waybill analyses: state-to-state distribution of manufactures and miscellaneous and forwarder traffic (C.L.) traffic and revenue.* Washington, DC: Interstate Commerce Commission, Bureau of Transport Economics and Statistics, 1948-1951. Annual. 4 v. *Statement SS-6.* (> *Carload waybill statistics: state-to-state distribution of manufacturers and miscellaneous and forwarder traffic (C.L.), traffic and revenue.*)

2308. *Carload waybill analyses: state-to-state distribution of products of agriculture traffic and revenue/* Washington, DC: Interstate Commerce Commission, Bureau of Transport Economics and Statistics, 19- . Annual. Information based on 1948 (> *Carload waybill statistics: state-to-sate distribution of products of agriculture traffic and revenue.*)

2309. *Carload waybill analyses: state-to-state distribution of products of forest traffic and revenue/* Washington, DC: Interstate Commerce Commission, Bureau of Transport Economics and Statitistcs, 1900s-1950s. Annual. (> *Carload waybill statistics: state-to-state distribution of products of forest traffic and revenue.*)

2310. *Carload waybill analyses: state-to-state distribution of products of mines traffic and revenue.* Washington, DC: Bureau of Transport Economics and Statistics., 1948- . Annual. (> *Carload waybill statistics: state to-state distribution of products of mines traffic and revenue.*)

2311. *Carload waybill analyses: territorial distribution, traffic and revenue by commodity classes/* Washington, DC: Interstate Commerce Commission, Bureau of Transport Economics and Statistics, 1900s-1951. Annual. (> *Carload waybill statistics: territorial distribution, traffic and revenue by commodity classe*s.)

2312. *Carload waybill analyses: traffic and revenue by commodity class, territorial movement, length of haul (short-line) and type of rate; manufactures and miscellaneous.* Washington, DC: Interstate Commerce Commission, Bureau of Transport Economics and Statistics, 1947-1950. Annual.

2313. *Carload waybill statistics.* Washington, DC: U.S. Department of Transportation, Federal Railroad Administration, Office of Rail Systems Analysis and Information, 1969- . Annual. Statement TD-1.

2314. *Carload waybill statistics: Canadian and Mexican origins: distribution of traffic and revenue by commodity classes. State-to state supplement.* Washington, DC: Interstate Commerce Commission, Bureau of Transport Economics and Statistics, 1900s-?

2315. *Carload waybill statistics: distribution of freight traffic and revenue averages by commodity classes/* Washington, DC: Interstate Commerce Commission, Bureau of Transport Economics and Statistics, 1950s- (< *Carload waybill analyses;*

distribution of freight traffic and revenue averages by commodity classes.)

2316. *Carload waybill statistics: mileage block distribution, traffic and revenue by commodity class, territorial movement, and type of rate.* Washington D.C.: Interstate Commerce Commission, Bureau of Economics, 1950-   . Annual. Issued as *File no. 40-C-13* (1950-1952), and then as its Statement *MB-1-5* (1953-1966).

2317. *Carload waybill statistics: mileage block distribution, traffic and revenue by selected commodity classes, territorial movement, and type of car.* Washington, DC: Interstate Commerce Commission, Bureau of Economics, 1964-   . Supersedes its *Statements MB-1, MB-2, MB-3, MB-4, MB-5, MB-6.*

2318. *Carload waybill statistics: mileage block distribution, traffic and revenue by commodity class, territorial movement and type of rate, animals and products.* Washington, DC: Interstate Commerce Commission, Bureau of Transport Economics and Statistics, 1900s-

2319. *Carload waybill statistics: mileage block distribution of traffic and revenue by commodity class, territorial movement and type of rate: products of agriculture.* Washington, DC: Interstate Commerce Commission, Bureau of Economics; Bureau of Transport Economics and Statistics, 1950-1963. Monographic series. Issued 1954-1963 as Its *Statement SS-2.* (> Its Statements SS-2—SS-7.)

2320. *Carload waybill statistics: mileage block distribution of traffic and revenue by commodity class, territorial movement and type of rate: products of forests.* Washington, DC: Interstate Commerce Commission, Bureau of Economics; Bureau of Transport Economics and Statistics, 1900s-1963. Monographic series. Issued 1953-1963 as the Bureau's *Statement MB-1.* (> *United States. Interstate Commerce Commission. Bureau of Economics. Statement MB-1.* [1964-   ].)

2321. *Carload waybill statistics: mileage block distribution of traffic and revenue by commodity, class, territorial movement and type of rate: products of mines.* Washington, DC: Interstate Commerce Commission, Bureau of Economics; Bureau of Transport Economics and Statistics, 1900s-1963. Monographic series. Superseded by its Statement MB-3 (1964-). (> *United States. Interstate Commerce Commission. Bureau of Economics. Statement MB-1*).

2322. *Carload waybill statistics: mileage block progressions, traffic and revenue by commodity groups and classes.* Washington, DC: Interstate Commerce Commission, Bureau of Economics; Bureau of Transport Economics and Statistics, 1947-

2323. *Carload waybill statistics : mileage distribution of carloads for each commodity class by type of car* / Washington, DC : Interstate Commerce Commission, Bureau of Transport Statistics and Statistics, 1951-1953.

2324. *Carload waybill statistics: mileage distribution of carloads for selected commodity classes by type of car* / Washington, DC: Interstate Commerce Commission, Bureau of Transport Economics and Statistics; Bureau of Economics, 1954-   .

2325. *Carload waybill statistics: quarterly comparisons, traffic and revenue by commodity classes* / Washington, DC: Interstate Commerce Commission, Bureau of Transport Economics and Statistics, 1940s. Quarterly.

2326. *Carload waybill statistics: state-to-state distribution, all commodities, traffic and revenue.* Washington, DC: Interstate Commerce Commission, Bureau of Economics; Bureau of Transport Economics and Statistics, 1949-   .

2327. *Carload waybill statistics: state-to-state distribution, manufactures and miscellaneous and forwarder traffic (C.L.) traffic and revenue.* Washington, D C: Interstate Commerce Commission, Bureau of Economics; Bureau of Transport Economics and Statistics, 1948-1963. Monographic series. Issued 1953-1963 as its *Statement SS-6* (< *Carload waybill analyses: state-to-state distribution of manufacturers and miscellaneous and forwarder traffic (C.L.) traffic and revenue*; > Its *Statements SS2--SS-7*.)

2328. *Carload waybill statistics: state-to-state distribution of all commodities combined traffic and revenue* / Washington, DC: Interstate Commerce Commission, Bureau of Transport Economics and Statistics, 1952-   . < *Carload waybill analyses . State-to-state distribution of all commodities traffic and revenue*; > *Carload waybill statistics: state-to-state distribution, traffic and revenue for all commodities and carloads and tons of revenue freight originated and terminated by states and by commodity* class.)

2329. *Carload waybill statistics: state-to-state distribution of animals and products, traffic and revenue.* Washington, DC: Interstate Commerce Commission, Bureau of Economics; Bureau of Transport Economics and Statistics, 1956-- Monographic series. Issued 1963 as the Bureau's *Statement SS-3*. (< *Carload waybill analyses: state-to-state distribution of animals and products, traffic and revenue*; > Its *Statements SS-2—-SS-7*.

2330. *Carload waybill statistics: state-to state distribution of manufacturers and miscellaneous and forwarder traffic (C.L.) traffic and revenue.* Washington, DC: Interstate Commerce Commission, Bureau of Transport Economics and Statistics. 1952- . Annual.

2331. *Carload waybill analyses: state-to-state distribution of manufacturers and miscellaneous and forwarder traffic (C.L.) traffic and revenue.* Washington, DC: Interstate Commerce Commission, Bureau of Transport Economics and Statistics, 1948-1951. Annual 4 v.

2332. *Carload waybill statistics: state-to-state distribution of products of agriculture traffic and revenue.* Washington, DC: Interstate Commerce Commission, 19--   . Annual. Description based on 1952.

2333. *Carload waybill statistics: state-to-state distribution of products of forest traffic, and revenue.* Washington, DC: Interstate Commerce Commission, Bureau of Transport Economics and Statistics, 1956-   Annual. Issued as *SS-5*. (< *Carload waybill analyses: state-to-state distribution of products of forest traffic and revenue.)*

2334. *Carload waybill statistics: state-to-state distribution, products of mines traffic and revenue.* Washington, DC: Interstate Commerce Commission, Bureau of Economics; Bureau of Transport Economics and Statistics, 1948-1963. Monographic series. Issued 1953-1963 as Its *Statement SS-4.* (< *Carload waybill analyses: state-to-state distribution of products of mines traffic and revenue;* > (Its *Statements SS-2--SS-7.*)

2335. *Carload waybill statistics: state-to-state distribution, traffic and revenue [by commodity and state-to-state movements].* Washington, DC: Interstate Commerce Commission, Bureau of Economics, 1964-   . Monographic series. Its *Statement[s] SS-2, SS-3, SS-4, SS-5, SS-6, SS-7)*

2336. *Carload waybill statistics: state-to-state distribution, traffic and revenue for all commodities and carloads and tons of revenue freight originated and terminated by states and by commodity class.* Washington, DC: Interstate Commerce Commission Bureau of Economics, 1948-   . Its *Statement SS-1.*

2337. *Carload waybill statistics: Statement SS-7, tons of revenue freight originated and tons terminated by states and by commodity class/* Washington, DC: Interstate Commerce Commission, Bureau of Transport Economic s and Statistics, 1953?-19   . Annual. From 1962, issued by the Commission's Bureau of Economics.

2338. *Carload waybill statistics: Statement TD-1, Territorial distribution, traffic, and revenue by commodity classes.* Washington, DC: U.S. Department of Transportation, Federal Railroad Administration, Office of Rail Systems & Information, 1953-1980? Annual. (< *Carload waybill statistics. Territorial distribution, traffic and revenue by commodity classes, terminations in ...*)

2339. *Carload waybill statistics: territorial distribution of carloads for each commodity class by type of car.* Washington, DC: Interstate Commerce Commission, Bureau of Transport Economics and Statistics, 1900s-   . Annual. (Its *Statement TC-3.*) "One percent sample of carload terminations in ..."

2340. *Carload waybill statistics: territorial distribution, traffic and revenue by commodity classes.* Washington, DC: Interstate Commerce Commission, Bureau of Transport Economics and Statistics, 1900s-1951. Annual.

2341. *Carload waybill statistics: tons of revenue freight originated and tons terminated by states and commodity class.* Washington, DC; Interstate Commerce Commission, Bureau of Economics, 1951-1963.. Issued 1953-1963 as the Bureau's *Statement SS-7.* Absorbed in 1964 by its *Statement SS-1.*

2342. *Carload waybill statistics: type of car.* Washington, DC: U.S. G.P.O., 1900s-?

2343. *Carload waybill statistics: weight distribution of carloads for each commodity class by type of car.* Washington, DC: Interstate Commerce Commission, Bureau of Economics; Bureau of Transport Economics and Statistics, 1951-   . Annual.

2344. *Carload waybill statistics: weight distribution of carloads for selected commodity classes by type of car.* Washington, DC: Interstate Commerce Commission, 1947-   .

2344a. *Carlot shipment and unloads of certain fruits and vegetables in 66 cities.* Washington, DC : United States Department of Agriculture, Bureau of Agricultural Economics, market News Service, 1935. Annual 1 v.

2345. *Car-lot shipments and unloads of important fruits and vegetables for the calendar years...* Washington, D.C., U.S. Dept. of Agriculture, 1926-1932. 4 v. Biennial.

2346. *Carlot shipments and unloads of nineteen important fruits and vegetables for the calendar years...* Washington, D.C., U.S. Dept. of Agriculture; Bureau of Agricultural Economics; Division of Fruits and Vegetables, 1934. 1 v. Biennial.

2346a. *Carlot shipments of fresh fruits and vegetables by commodities, states, counties, and stations.* Washington, DC: U.S. Department of Agriculture, Production and Marketing Administration, Fruit and Vegetable Branch, Market News Division, 1949-1953. Annual 5 v. (< *Car-lot shipments of fruits and vegetables from stations in the United States for the calendar years ... ; > Fresh fruit and vegetable carlot shipments by commodities, states, counties, and stations.)*

2346b. *Carlot shipments of fresh fruits and vegetables by commodities, states, counties, and stations : including boat shipments reduced to carlot equivalents.* Washington, DC: U.S. Department of Agriculture, Production and Marketing Administration, Fruit and Vegetable Branch, Market News Division, 1949-1953. Annual. 5 v.

2347. *Car-lot shipments of fruits and vegetables by commodities, states and months...* Washington, D.C. U.S. Dept. of Agriculture, Bureau of Agricultural Economics, Market News Service, 1920-1946. 27 v. Annual.

2348. *Car-lot shipments of fruits and vegetables from stations in the United States for the calendar years...* Washington, D.C., U.S. Dept. of Agriculture, 1927-1948. 12 v. Annual. (*Statistical bulletin.*)

2349. *Car-lot shipments of fruits and vegetables in the United States in...* Washington, D.C., U.S. Department of Agriculture, 1916. (*Bulletin, U.S. Dept. of Agriculture, no. 667.*)

2350. *Carlot unloads of certain fruits and vegetables in 66 cities and imports in 4 cities for Canada.* Washington, D.C., U.S. Department of Agriculture, Bureau of Agricultural Economics; Agricultural Marketing Service, 1935-1939. 5 v. Annual.

2350a. Carlson, Anthony Everett. *Isaac I. Stevens and the Northern Pacific Railroad survey : exploration, diplomacy, and political promotion, 1853-1854* / 2004. 144 l. (Thesis, M.A., University of Tulsa.)

2351. Carlson, Gary R. *New England short lines in color*/ Scotch Plains, NJ: Morning

Sun Books, 2008-2010. 2 v.

2352. _____. *Pennsylvania short lines in color*. Scotch Plains, NJ: Morning Sun Books, 2003-

2353. Carmack, Joe T. *The end of the line*. Texarkana, TX: Carmack, 1989. 7, 27 p. (Memphis and Little Rock Railroad Company)

2354. *The carman.* Chicago, Ill., Railway Educational Press, Inc., 1918-1920. "The American railway car journal" Monthly. Closed with v. 3, no. 4, Apr. 1920.

2355. *The carman's dictionary.* Omaha, Simmons-Boardman, 1979. 135 p.

2356. Carnahan, John Benton. *Highway trailers on railroad flat cars* / 1954. 59 l. (Thesis, M.B.A., University of Pittsburgh.)

2357. Carnegie, Andrew. *Pennsylvania's industries and railroad policy* / Pittsburgh? s.n., 1889. 40 p. "An address delivered before the legislature of Pennsylvania, at Harrisburg, on Monday evening, April 8, 1889..."

2358. Carnegie Steel Company. *Axles and forgings for steam and electric railway service; standard axle designs and specifications.* 7th ed. Pittsburgh : Carnegie Steel Co., 1916. 88 p.

2359. _____. *Gear blanks and miscellaneous circular sections : gear blanks, industrial and mine car wheels, street and interurban railway wheels* / 3rd ed. Pittsburgh : Carnegie Steel Company, 1916. 91 p.

2360. _____. *GEO track construction.* Pittsburgh : Carnegie Steel Company, 1900s-? Serial publication.

2361. _____. *Light rails and fastenings : steel cross ties for mines, quarries, plantation and portable track* / Pittsburgh : Carnegie Steel Co., 1928. 1st ed. 50 p.

2362. _____. *Rails and angle bars.* Pittsburgh, Pa., Carnegie Steel Company, 1926. 10 l.

2363. _____. *Rails and accessories.* 10th ed. Pittsburgh : Carnegie Steel Company, 1913. 177 p.

2364. _____. *Rails and angle bars.* Pittsburgh : Carnegie Steel Co., 1926. 10 l. 132 diagr.

2365. _____. *Shape book containing profiles, tables and data appertaining to the shapes, plates, bars, rails, and track accessories* / 4th ed. Pittsburgh ; s.n., 1911. 1 v.

2366. _____. *Shape book containing profiles, tables and data appertaining to the shapes, plates, bars, rails, and track accessories.* 6th ed. Pittsburgh : Carnegie Steel Co., 1917. 352 p.

2367. _____. *Shape book containing profiles, tables, and data appertaining to the shapes, plates, bars, rails, and track accessories manufactured by Carnegie Steel Company*, Pittsburgh, Pa. Pittsburgh : The Company, 1921. 373 p.

2368 _____. *Shape book : profiles, tables and data for rolled products : shapes, plates, bars and rails manufactured by Carnegie Steel Company, Pittsburgh, Pa.* 9th ed. Pittsburgh : Carnegie Steel Co., 1923. 346 p.

2369. _____. *Shapes manufactured by the Carnegie Steel Company, Limited.* Pittsburgh : Carnegie Steel Company, 1893. 83 p.

2370. _____. *Standard specifications; steel for bridges, buildings, locomotives, cars, and ships, boilers and rivets, concrete reinforcement, wheels and gear blanks, axles and shafts.* 8th ed. Pittsburgh : Carnegie Steel Co., 1920. 146 p.

2371. _____. *Standard steel rails and splice bars* / Pittsburgh : Stevenson & Foster, printers, 1900. 1 v.

2372. _____. *Steel axles and similar forgings for steam and electric railway service. Standard axle designs and specification.* 8th ed. Pittsburgh : Carnegie Steel Company, 1919. 90 p.

2373. _____. *Steel cross tie and Duquesne rail joint.* Pittsburg, PA: The Company; Stevenson & Foster Co., Printers, 1906. 30 p.

2374. _____. *Steel cross ties, Duquesne rail joints, Braddock insulated rail joints* / 7th ed. Pittsburgh : Carnegie Steel Company, 1914. 72 p.

2375. _____. *Steel cross ties for steam and electric railroads, mines, quarries, plantations and portable tracks manufactured by Carnegie Steel Company, Pittsburgh, Pa.* Pittsburgh, Pa., Carnegie Steel Company, 1921. 55 p.

2376. _____. *Steel cross ties for steam, electric and industrial railways.* Pittsburgh : Carnegie Steel Co., 1930. 38 p.

2377. _____. *Supplement no. 13 to shape book, 1903.* Pittsburgh : Carnegie Steel Co., 1910. 345 p.

2378. _____. *Wrought steel wheels and other circular sections, forged steel axles, data, tables and specifications pertaining to designs.* Pittsburgh : Carnegie Steel Co., 1926. 128 p.

2379. Carnes, John K. *The electric locomotive.* Notre Dame, Ind., 1933. 81 p. (Thesis, B.S. in E.E., University of Notre Dame.)

2380. Caron, James Alfred. *The economics of rail freight transportation rate regulation, excess capacity, and competition*/ 1979. 97 l. (Thesis, M.S., Cornell University.)

2380a. Carothers, Alice L. *The history of the Southern Pacific Railroad in the San Joaquin Valley*. 1934. 100 l. (Thesis, M.A., University of Southern California.)

2381. Carpenter, Floyd R., Page Golsan. *The feasibility of operating a light weight, high speed train on the Lehigh Valley Railroad between Wilkes-Barre and New York*/ 1934. 80 l. (Thesis, B.S., Massachusetts Institute of Technology, Department of Business and Engineering Administration.)

2382. Carpenter, G.F., J.M. Wandrisco, D.E. Sonon. *Dynamic behavior and residual stresses in railroad wheels* / Washington, DC: Federal Railroad Administration, Office of Research and Development, 1980. 75 p. (*FRA/ORD-78/54.*)

2383. Carpenter, Richard C. *A railroad atlas of the United States in 1946.* Baltimore, MD: Johns Hopkins University Press, 2003- (v. 1. The Mid-Atlantic states; v. 2. New York & New England; v. 3. Indiana, Lower Michigan, and Ohio; v. 4. Illinois, Wisconsin and Upper Michigan., v.5. Iowa and Minnesota.)

2384. Carpenter, Warwick Stevens. *Official freight shippers' guide and industrial directory of the Delaware and Hudson Company.* Albany, N.Y., Department for Industrial Development, The Delaware and Hudson Company, 1922-

2385. Carr, Albert H. Z. John D. *Rockefeller's secret weapon.* New York: McGraw-Hill, 1962. 383 p. (Union Tank Car)

2386. Carr, Clark E. *History of bringing the Atchison, Topeka & Santa Fe Railway to Galesburg.* Galesburg, Ill., Wagoner, 1913. 85 p.

2387. _____. *The railway mail service; its origin and development.* Chicago, Ill., McClurg, 1909. 49 p.

2388. Carr, Hobart Cecil. *Early history of Iowa railroads.* New York, N.Y., Arno Press, 1981. 98 p.

2389. Carr, Stephen L. *Heber Valley Railroad, the Provo Route: history and mile-by-mile route guide.* Heber City, UT: Heber Valley Historic Railroad Authority, 1999. 32 p.

2390._____, Robert W. Edwards. *Utah ghost rails.* Salt Lake City, UT: Western Epics, 1989. 208 p.

2391. Carranco, Lynwood. *Redwood lumber industry.* San Marino, CA: Golden West Books, 1982. 218 p.

2392. _____, Henry L. Sorenson. *Steam in the redwoods.* Caldwell, ID: Caxton Printers, 1988. 224 p.

2393. _____, John T. Labbe. *Logging the redwoods.* Caldwell, ID: Caxton Printers, 1975. 145 p.

2394. Carrier Engineering Corporation. [Trade catalogs, 1932-1935]. Carrier railroad car pre-cooler for use with ice, [1932]. Carrier heat diffusing units, 1935. Location: Hagley Museum and Library.

2395. Carriker, S. David. *The North Carolina railroad map: a history of North Carolina railroads, 1830-1990.* Rev. ed. Charlotte, NC: Heritage Publishing Co., 1993. 24 l.

2396. _____. *The North Carolina railroad map: explanatory text.* Charlotte, NC: Heritage Publishing Co., 1990. 1 v.

2397. _____, Suzanne Cameron Linder. *Railroading in Richmond County, North Carolina.* Hamlet, NC: Richmond Technical College, 1982. 30 p.

2398. Carroll, Anya A., Janelle L. Helser. *Safety of highway-railroad grade crossings: research needs workshop. Volume 1.* Washington, DC : Federal Railroad Administration, Office of Research and Development, 1996. 142 p. (*DOT/FRA/ORD-95/14.1.*)

2399. _____, Jordan Multer, Debra Williams. *Freight car reflectorization* / Washington, DC: Federal Railroad Administration, Office of Research and Development, 1999. 1 v. (various pagings)

2400. Carroll, Charles. *A history and description of the Baltimore and Ohio Rail Road* / Baltimore : John Murphy & Co., no. 178 Market Street, 1853. 200 p.

2401. Carroll, John M. *Galveston and the Gulf, Colorado and Santa Fe Railroad.* Illustrations, Don Moore, Jose Cisneros. Galveston, TX: Center for Transportation and Commerce, 1985. 164 p.

2401a. Carroll, Todd Davis. *Opportunities and challenges for high-speed rail corridors in Texas.* Austin, TX: 2011. 189l. (Thesis, University of Texas at Austin)

2402. Carrow, Thomas H. *Evidence to show that the passage of the federal full crew bill (S. 4234; H.R. 11012) is without warrant or justification from a safety standpoint / presented by Thomas H. Carrow, Superintendent of Safety, the Pennsylvania Railroad Company.* Philadelphia : Pennsylvania Railroad Co., 1932. 1 v. (various pagings)

2403. *Blank entry.*

2404. *The cars of the Pennsylvania Railroad.* New York, NY: Wayner Publications, 1978. 64 p.

2405. Carson, A.B. *Locomotive management.* Scranton, Pa., International Textbook Co., 1937. 92, 62 p.

2406. Carson, H.M. *Design of an "American" passenger locomotive boiler.* 1889. 20 l.

(Thesis, M.E., Lehigh University.

2407. Carson, Robert Barry. *Main line to oblivion; the disintegration of New York railroads in the twentieth century.* Port Washington, NY: Kennikat Press, 1971. 273 p. (*Kennikat Press National University Publications. Series in American Studies.*)

2408. _____. *New York state railroads in the twentieth century; a study in the decline of an industry.* 1967. 396 l. (Thesis, D.S.S., Syracuse University.)

2409. Carstens, Harold H. *Slim gauge cars.* Newton, NJ: Carstens Publications, 1991. 111 p.

2410. _____, and others. *Circus trains, trucks & models.* Rev. ed. Newton, NJ: Carstens Publications, 1990. 52 p.

2411. Carter, C.S., R.G. Caton, J.L. Guthrie. *Fracture resistance and fatigue crack growth characteristics of railroad wheels and axles : final report.* Washington, DC : Federal Railroad Administration, Office of Research and Development, 1977. 124 p. (*FRA/ORD-77-50.*)

2412. Carter, Charles Frederick. *One hundred years of railroading.* New York? New York Central Railroad, 1926. 19 p.

2412a. _____. *Vagaries of railroad evolution: story of the automatic coupler* / New York: New York Central Railroad, 1928. p. 223-255.
Location: Univ. of Missouri, St. Louis.

2413. _____ *What the railroad has done for America.* New York, New York Central Railroad, 1928. 16 p.

2414. _____. *When the railroads were new.* New York, Henry Holt, 1909. 324 p. (Centenary ed.: New York, Simmons-Boardman Publishing Co., 1926. 324 p.)

2415. Carter, Clive. *Inland Empire electric line: Spokane to Coeur d'Alene and the Palouse* / Cour d'Alene, ID: Museum of North Idaho, 2009. 232 p.

2415a. _____. *The Spokane International Railway: Idaho's main line to Canada* / Coeur d'Alene, ID: Museum of North Idaho, 2012. 214 p.

2415b. Carter, Clive S., David Carter. *Denver & Rio Grande Western depots* / S.l., The Authors, 2013. 3 v.

2416. Carter, James. *Evaluation of concepts for locomotive crew egress.* Washington, DC: Federal Railroad Administration, Office of Research and Development, 2003. 62 p. (*DOT/FRA/ORD-02/07*)

2417. Carter, Kate B. *First transcontinental railroad in picture and story.* Salt Lake City, UT: Daughters of Utah Pioneers, 1969. 56 p.

2418. Carter, Lucian Hugh. *History of railway labor legislation.* 1930. 186 l. (Thesis, University of Virginia.)

2419. Carter T.J. *Railroad progress, transportation and management.* Springfield, IL: State Journal Printers, 1873. 42 p.

2420. Carter, Thad Hillis. *Kansas City Southern Railway /* Charleston, SC: Arcadia Publishing, 2009. 127 p.

2421. _____. *The Kansas City Southern story.* Cassville, MO: Litho Printers, 2004. 112 p.

2422. Cartwright, J. *Pioneer days of steamboats and railroads in Eastern Washington Territory.* Washington, DC: s.n., 1909. 1 v. (unpaged) (Oregon Railway and Navigation Co.; Northern Pacific Railway Co.)

2423. Carver, Hartwell. *Proposal for a charter to build a railroad from Lake Michigan to the Pacific Ocean/* Washington, D.C.: Printed by J. & G.S. Gideon, 1847. 38 p.

2424. Carwardine, William H. *The Pullman strike.* 4th ed. Chicago, C.H. Kerr, 1894. 128 p. (Reprint: Chicago, Illinois Labor History Society, 1971. 126 p.; Reprint of 1st ed. Chicago, Illinois Labor History Society, 1994. Centennial ed.)

2425. Cary, Ferdinand Ellsworth. *Lake Shore & Michigan Southern Railway system/* Buffalo, NY: Biographical Pub. Co., 1900, 947 p.

2426. Cary, John W. *The organization and history of the Chicago, Milwaukee & St. Paul Railway Company.* Milwaukee, Press of Cramer, Aikens & Cramer, 1892. 392 p.

2427. Casavant, Ken, Denver D. Tolliver. *Impacts of heavy axle loads on light density lines in the State of Washington /* Olympia, WA: Washington State Department of Transportation, 2001. 54 p. (*Report: WA-RD499.1.*)

2428. Casdorph, David G. *Auto racks 1: side protection panels, auto rack end doors, modern BN auto racks, ATSF auto rack roster.* Monrovia, CA: Society of Freight Car Historians, 1993.28 p.

2429. _____. *Box car production, 1963-1994.* Monrovia, CA: Society of Freight Car Historians, 1995. 48 p.

2430. _____. *Box cars since 1983.* Monrovia, CA: Society of Freight Car Historians, 1994. 44 p.

2431. _____. *Burlington Northern: color guide to freight and passenger equipment.* Scotch Plains, NJ: Morning Sun Books, 2001. 126 p.

2432. _____. *Burlington Northern's freight cars.* Monrovia, CA; Society of Freight Car

Historians, 1989. 80 p.

2433. _____. *Burlington Northern freight cars today: freight equipment roster data and photos of the contemporary Burlington Northern Railroad.* Monrovia, CA: Society of Freight Car Historians, 1994. 52 p.

2434. _____. *CNW freight car roster and pictorial.* Monrovia, CA: Society of Freight Car Historians, 1991. 36 p.

2435. _____. *CSX freight car review.* Monrovia, CA: Society of Freight Car Historians, 1994. 36 p.

2436. _____. *CSXT 1989 freight car review.* Monrovia, CA: Society of Freight Car Historians, 1989. 36 p.

2437. _____. *Double stack data book: a roster of over 34,000 wells of double-stack containers cars in service operating in the United States.* Monrovia, CA: Society of Freight Car Historians, 1993. 32 p.

2438. _____. *The freight car data book: Trailer Train Company, TTX Company.* Monrovia, CA: Society of Freight Car Historians, 1995. 52 p.

2439. _____. *General Electric's shortline box cars.* Monrovia, CA: Society of Freight Car Historians, 1994. 44 p.

2440. _____. *Grain cars, 1995/96.* Monrovia, CA: Society of Freight Car Historians, 1995. 100 p.

2441. _____. *Modern box car types.* Monrovia, CA: Society of Freight Car Historians, 1997. 80 p.

2442. _____. *Modern flatcars: a pictorial review.* Monrovia, CA: Society of Freight Car Historians, 1989. 36 p.

2443. _____. *Modern 45-foot railroad trailers.* Monrovia, CA: Society of Freight Car Historians, 1994. 31 p.

2444. _____. Modern *freight cars: a photo anthology.* Monrovia, CA: Society of Freight Car Historians, 1992. 72 p.

2445. _____. *Modern piggyback trailers.* Monrovia, CA: Society of Freight Car Historians, 1992. 112 p.

2446. _____. *Modern tank car types.* Monrovia, CA: Society of Freight Car Historians, 1993. 60 p.

2447. _____. *Modern Union Pacific grain hoppers.* Monrovia, CA: Society of Freight Car Historians, 1994. 40 p.

2448. _____. *Molten sulphur tank cars.* Monrovia, CA: Society of Freight Car
Historians, 1994. 28 p.

2449. _____. *Norfolk Southern freight cars today.* Monrovia, CA: Society of Freight
Car Historians, 1994. 60 p.

2450. _____ *On Conrail 52ft gondolas.* Monrovia, CA: Society of Freight Car
Historians, 1994. 37 p.

2451. _____. *Photo supplement to modern tank car types.* Monrovia, CA: Society
of Freight Cat Historians, 1993. 18 p.

2452. _____ *Plastic-pellet hopper cars; a catalog of modern plastics cars.* Monrovia,
CA: Society of Freight Car Historians, 1994. 145 p.

2453. _____. *Railborne highway trailers.* Monrovia, CA: Society of Freight Car
Historians, 1995. 28 p.

2454. _____. *Santa Fe modern freight car pictorial.* Monrovia, CA: Society of Freight
Car Historians, 1991. 31 p.

2455. _____. *60-foot auto parts boxcars: a pictorial review.* Monrovia, CA: Society
of Freight Car Historians, 1988. 91 p.

2456. _____. *Southern Pacific freight cars today.* Monrovia, CA: Society of Freight Car
Historians, 1994. 32 p.

2457. _____. *U.P. freight cars, 1995-96.* Monrovia, CA: Society of Freight Car
Historians, 1995. 116 p.

2458. _____. *Union Pacific freight cars today.* Monrovia, CA: Society of Freight Car
Historians, 1993. 64 p.

2459. _____. *Woodchip cars.* Monrovia, CA: Society of Freight Car Historians, 1995.
72 p.

2460. Case, Mark H. *Tie procurement by the U.S. railroad industry, 1987.* 1988. 57 l.
(Thesis, M.S., Southern Illinois University at Carbondale.)

2461. Case, Stacey Schneyder. *Hogg wild: archaeological analysis of a 19th century
railroad construction camp, Idanha, Oregon.* 2001. 157 l. (Thesis, M.A., Sonoma State
University.)

2462. Case, Theresa Ann. *Free labor on the Southwestern railroads: the 1885-1886
Gould System strikes.* 2002. 359 l. (Thesis, Ph.D., University of Texas, Austin.)

2462a. _____. *The Great Southwest Railroad Strike and free* labor / College Station:

Texas A&M University Press, 2010. 279 p.

2463. *Cases brought in the Commerce Court.* Washington, DC: U.S. G.P.O., 1912. 538 p. (U.S. Department of Justice. U.S. Commerce Court.)

2464. Casey, Robert J., W.A.S. Douglas. *The Lackawanna story; the first hundred years of the Delaware, Lackawanna and Western Railroad.* New York, McGraw-Hill, 1951. 223 p.

2465. _____, _____. *Pioneer railroad: the story of the Chicago and North Western system.* New York, Whittlesey House, 1948. 334 p.

2466. Casler, Walter. *Allegheny Valley logging railroads: locomotives, sawmills, pine timber; Warren, Forest, Venango, Crawford, Erie counties.* Williamsport, PA: Lycoming Printing Co., 1977. 116 p. (*Logging railroad era of lumbering in Pennsylvania*, no. 11.)

2467. ____. Benjamin F.G. Kline, Thomas Townsend Taber. *The logging railroad era of lumbering in Pennsylvania: a history of the lumber, chemical, wood, and tanning companies which used railroads in Pennsylvania: a collection of papers.* Muncy, PA: T.T. Taber III, 1970-1978. (2nd ed.: Strasburg, PA: Railroad Museum of Pennsylvania, 1999.)

2468. Cass, Edward H. *Hidden treasures: the story of the Ohio River & Western Railway.* Hillsboro, OR: TimberTimes, 1997. 248 p.

2469. Cass, Lewis. *Railroads –Atlantic to the Mississippi[pi. Letter from the Secretary of War, transmitting a report in relation to the survey of certain routes for railroads from the Atlantic to the Mississippi ... February 27, 1835 .../* Washington, DC: United States, War Department, 1835. 88 p. (U.S. 23d Congress, 2d session. House, Executive documents, no. 177.)

2470. *The Cass roster: all-time locomotives, all-time rail equipment: Cass Scenic Railroad State Park, Cass, West Virginia.* Compiled by Philip V. Bagdon. Cass, WV: Mountain State Railroad & Logging Historical Association, 1999? 1 v.

2471. Castner, Charles B., Robert E. Chapman, Patrick C. Dorin. *Louisville & Nashville passenger trains: the Pan-American era, 1921-1971.* Lynchburg, VA: TLC Publishing, 1999. 234 p.

2472. _____, Ron Flanary, Lee Gordon. *Louisville & Nashville diesels.* Lynchburg, VA: TLC Publishing, 1998. 168 p.

2473. _____, _____, Patrick Dorin. *Louisville & Nashville Railroad: the old reliable.* Lynchburg, VA: TLC Publishing, 1996. 231 p.

2474. _____, Thomas E. Bailey. *The Dixie Line: Nashville, Chattanooga & St. Louis Railway.* Newton, NJ: Carstens, 1995. 96 p.

2475. Casto, James E. *The Chesapeake and Ohio Railway*. Mount Pleasant, SC: Arcadia Publishing, 2006. 128 p.

2476. *Catalog file of Norfolk & Western Railway...locomotives, rolling stock... in Photographic Services files, General Office Building Annex, Roanoke, Virginia*. 1978. 1 v. Arthur M. Bixby, compiler. (Location: Virginia Tech.)

2477. *Catalog of freight car utilization projects and publications*. Washington, DC: Freight Car Utilization Research-Demonstration Program, 1980. 25 p.

2478. *A catalog of photograph accessions*. 3rd ed., revised. Katherine L.T. Bost, Barry Crossno, Carrie Ramp, compilers. Dallas, TX: DeGolyer Library, Southern Methodist University, 1996. 161 p.

2479. *Catalogue of railroad mortgages* / Washington, DC : s.n., 1919. 163 p. Princeton University. Pliny-Fisk Statistical Library. Bureau of Railway Economics (Washington, D.C.).

2480. *Catalogue of the Otto C. Perry Memorial Collection of Railroad Photographs*. Denver, CO: Western History Department, Denver Public Library, 1977-

2481. *Catalogue: Railroad and Warehouse Commission Library*. Springfield, Ill., Jeffersons Printing Company, 1912. (1st issue). 188 p.

2482. Catella, James. *Our home town railroad (Oneonta, New York)*. Oneonta, NY: J. Catella, 1982. 42 p. (Delaware and Hudson Railroad)

2483. Cates, C Pat, Richard L. Hillman, Sallie Loy. *The Southern Railway: further recollections*. Charleston, SC: Arcadia, 2005. 128 p.

2484. Catlin, George L. *All rail to Long Branch; a work descriptive of the new all-rail route from New York, via the New York & Long Branch R.R. to the sea shore of New Jersey, and the summer metropolis of America...* New York, George L. Catlin; J.W. Pratt, Printer, 1875. 48 p.

2484a. Cator, Thomas Vincent. *The necessity and advantages of national ownership of railroads and telegraphs* / San Francisco : Thomas Howard, 1894. 18 p.

2484a. Catron, F.P. *Texas and Pacific Railway Co. vs. the Southern Pacific Railroad (of New Mexico)*. San Francisco: H.S. Crocker & Co., printers, 1881. 30 p. (F.P. Catron: solicitor, Southern Pacific Railroad Co.)

2485. Catton, William Bruce. *John W. Garrett of the Baltimore & Ohio: a study in seaport and railroad competition, 1820-1874*. 1959. 612 l. (Thesis, Ph.D., Northwestern University.)

2486. Caudill, Edwin G. *Regulatory policy, railroad consolidation and transportation efficiency* / 1968. 293 l. (Thesis, Ph.D., American University.)

2487. Caudle, Robert Emmet, W.L. Maury. *History of the Missouri Pacific Lines: Gulf Coast lines and subsidiaries, International-Great Northern*. Houston, TX: s.n., 1949. 184, [189] l. Mimeographed. Includes corporate history of International Great Northern.

2488. Caughey, Robert Andrew. *Design of a two hinged arch double track railroad bridge* / 1916. 1 v. (Thesis, Civil Engineering, Pennsylvania State College.)

2489. Cauthen, Jeff, Don Munger. *Southern Pacific passenger cars. Volume 4, Dining service cars* / Upland, CA: Southern Pacific Historical & Technical Society, 2010. 1 v.

2489a. _____, _____. *Southern Pacific passenger cars: Volume 5, Lounge, dome & parlor cars* / Upland, CA: Southern Pacific Historical & Technical Society, 2012. 1 v.

2489b. _____, John R. Signor. *Southern Pacific painting and lettering guide; a guide to paint and lettering used on Southern Pacific locomotives and passenger cars from 1913 to 1996* / Upland, CA: Southern Pacific Historical & Technical Society, 2013. 1 v.

2490. Cauthen, Sharron Daniel. *Mississippi railroad heritage: men and iron, steam and diesel* / Madison, MS: China Lamp Pub., 2006. 373 p.

2491. Cavalier, Julian. *Classic American railroad stations*. San Diego, CA: A.S. Barnes, 1980. 212 p.

2492. _____, Frederick Platt. *North American railroad stations*. South Brunswick, A.S. Barnes, 1979. 215 p.

2493. Cavanaugh, Casey. *Trackside with EMD field representative Casey Cavanaugh, 1960-1962*. Scotch Plains, NJ: Morning Sun Books, 2005. 128 p.

2494. Cavanaugh, H.F. *Diesel locomotives of the New Haven Railroad*. Hicksville, NY: N.J. International, 1980. 139 p.

2495. _____. *New York Central System, gone but not forgotten*. Hicksville, NY: N.J. International, 1983. 165 p.

2496. Caves, Douglas W. *Measuring productivity growth in the U.S. railroad industry with an estimate of losses resulting from economic regulation* / 1980. 293 l. (Thesis, Ph.D., University of Wisconsin—Madison.)

2497. _____. Laurits Ray Christensen, Joseph A. Swanson. *Economic performance in regulated and unregulated environments: a comparison of U.S. and Canadian railroads*/ Madison, WI: Social Systems Research Institute, University of Wisconsin-Madison, 1980. 28 l. (*SSRI workshop series, 8004.*)

2498. _____. _____. _____. *Productivity growth, scale economies, and capacity utilization in U.S. railroads, 1955-1974*/ Madison, WI: Social Systems Research Center, University of Wisconsin-Madison, 1980. 26 p. (*SSRI workshop series, 8002.*)

2499. _____, _____, _____. *Productivity in U.S. railroads, 1951-1974/* Madison, WI: Social System Research Institute, University of Wisconsin-Madison, 1978. 23, 15 l. (*SSRI workshop series, 7820.*)

2499a. Cavey, C.A., J.W. Harding. *Locomotive breakdowns and appliances* / Scranton, PA: International Textbook Co., 1943. 40, 69, 71 p.

2500. Cayton, Horace, R., George Sinclair Mitchell. *Black workers and the new unions.* Chapel Hill, NC: The University of North Carolina Press, 1939. 473 p.

2501. Caywood, James A. *Why clean ballast?* Washington, DC: DeLeuw, Cather & Company, 1968. 10 l.

2502. Cedeck, Mark Joseph. *A guide and catalog to the research collections of the Gulf, Mobile & Ohio Historical Society in the John W. Barriger III National Railroad Library: a special collection of the St. Louis Mercantile Library Association* / St. Louis, MO: St. Louis Mercantile Library Association, 1996. 129 l.

2503. _____. *The John W. Barriger III National Railroad Library. St. Louis.* St. Louis Mercantile Library Association, Special Collections, 1989. 12 p.

2504. Celler, Emanuel, Hatton William Sumners. *Reorganization of railroads under the Bankruptcy Act* / Washington, DC: U.S. G.P.O., 1935. 24 p. United States. Congress. House. Committee on the Judiciary.

2505. *Census of manufacturers : 1914. Steam and electric cars, and railroad repair shops. Washington*, DC: U.S. G.P.O., 1917. 23 p. Prepared by: Frank Adams and William M. Steurat, chief statistician for manufacturers.

2506. Center for Railroad Photography and Art. *Representations of railroad work.* Introduction by Mark W. Hemphill. Madison, WI: Center for Railroad Photography, 2005. 39 p. (*Railroad heritage, no. 13.*)

2507. _____. *Ted Rose: the artist's early photography.* Madison, WI: Center for Railroad Photography & Art, 2008. 36 p.

2508. Central Electric Company. *Car lighting fixtures: vol. 1, indirect fixtures no. 1.* Chicago: Central Electric Compnay, 1914. 12 p.

2509._____. . *Car lighting fixtures: vol. 1, no. 2, semi direct fixtures.* Chicago: Central Electric Company, 1914. 16 p.

2510. Central Electric Railfans' Association. *The great third rail.* Chicago, IL: Central Electric Railfans' Association, 1961. 160 p.(*Its bulletin, 105*) (Chicago, Aurora & Elgin Railroad.)

2510a. *Central Illinois rails: color pictorial, 1950s-1970s.* La Mirada, CA: Four Ways

West, 2011. 144 p.

2511. Central New England Railway Company. *Central New England railway system. Poughkeepsie bridge route…* / Hartford, Conn.? Central New England Railway Company, 1903. 48 p. Includes timetable and descriptive material.

2512. _____. *Summer homes among the mountains on the C.N.E.R.* Hartford, Conn., Plimpton Press, 1901. 179 p.

2513. *Central of Georgia magazine.* Savannah, GA: Central of Georgia Railway, 1930-1963. Monthly. (< *Right way magazine;* > *Southern Railway ties.*)

2514. Central of Georgia Railway. *Centennial celebration of the Central of Georgia Railway, December 15th, 1935; and other data concerning Savannah railroads.* Savannah, GA: s.n., 1935. 105 p. "Scrapbook containing pamphlets, newspaper clippings, programs, typed pages relating to the Central of Georgia Railroad and other Savannah railroads."

2514a. _____. *Central of Georgia Railway records.* MS 1362. 557 cubic feet. Location: Georgia Historical Society, Savannah, GA.

2515. _____. *Central of Georgia Railway Company switching costs: Savannah, Macon, Atlanta, Columbus, Albany and Augusta.* Savannah, GA: Central of Georgia Railway Company, 1917. 73 1 p.

2516. _____. *Corporate history: valuation order number 20, February 23, 1916.* Savannah?: s.n., 1916. 2, 95 l.

2517. _____. *The first hundred years: October 12-13, 1843, October 12-13, 1943, Macon, George.* Macon, Ga., Central of Georgia Railway Co., 1943. 11 p.

2518. _____. *Instructions to freight agents and conductors: effective December 1, 1917.* St. Louis, MO: Con. P. Curran Printing Co., 1917. 114 p.

2519. _____. *Official list of officers, agents, attorneys, surgeons, stations, etc.*/ Savannah, GA: The Company, 1949. 69 p. (*Central of Georgia Railway. Official list, no. 51.*)

2520. _____. *The right way: 125th anniversary, 1833-1958; historical issue.* Savannah? Central of Georgia Railway, 1958. 28 p. (Special issue of *Central of Georgia magazine,* Dec. 20, 1958.)

2521. _____. *Rule and regulations of the Transportation Department.* Rev. ed. S.l., s.n., 1917. 153 p.

2522. _____. *Schedule of wages and rules and regulations: conductors, trainmen, and yardmen.* 8th ed. Savannah, Ga.? The Company, 1912. 31 p.

2522a. _____. [W.H. Mims collection of Central of Georgia technical drawings, 1889-1955.] 103 boxes, 8.75 cubic feet. Location: Georgia Historical Society.

2523. Central Pacific Railroad Company. *By-laws of the Central Pacific Railroad Co. of California.* S.l. s.n., 1860-1869? 4 p.

2524. _____. *The Central Pacific Railroad and leased lines, rules and regulations for agents and conductors: in effect July 1st, 1879.* San Francisco: The Company, H.S. Crocker & Co, Printers, 1879. 16 p.

2525. _____. *Central Pacific Railroad and leased lines : rules, regulations and instructions for the use of agents, conductors, etc.* San Francisco: Central Pacific Railroad Company, 1882. 224 p.

2526. _____. *Central Pacific R.R. of California. : Character of the work, its progress, resources, earning, and future prospects.* New York, October, 1865. New York: George Brown, Printer, 37 Park Row, 1866. 14, 2 p.

2527. _____. *Lands of the Central Pacific Railroad company of California.* Sacramento: H.S. Crocker & Co., Printers, 1868. 18 p.

2528. _____. *Lands of the Central Pacific Railroad Company of California.* Sacramento: H.S. Crocker & Co., Printers, 1870. 16 p.

2529. _____. *Lands of the Central Pacific Railroad Co. of California, with general information on the resources of the country through which the railroad takes its way. June 1, 1880.* San Francisco: H.S. Crocker & Co., Printers, 1880. 68 p.

2530. _____. *Oregon branch of the Pacific Railroad.* Washington, DC: McGill & Witherow, Printers & Stereotypers, 1868. 19 p.

2531. _____. *Performance of engines and cost per mile run. Monthly sheet. March 1875.* San Francisco? s.n., 1875. Sheet 85 x 49 cm. fold. to 24 x 11 cm.

2532. _____ *Performance of engines and cost per mile run. Yearly sheet. 1871.* San Francisco? Central Pacific Railroad, Motive Power Department, 1871. Sheet. 68 x 41 cm. fold. to 21 x 9 cm.

2533. _____. *Railroad communication with the Pacific /* New York? s.n., 1867. 25 p.

2534. _____. *Railroad lands in California and Nevada.* S.l., [Central Pacific Railroad Company], Record Printing House, 1872. 34 p.

2535. _____. *Relations between the Central Pacific Railroad Company and the United States government. Summary of facts. 1889.* Prepared by Gerrit L. Lansing. San Francisco: H.S. Crocker & Co., 1889. 70 p.

2536. _____. *Report of the chief engineer on the preliminary survey and cost of construction of the Central Pacific Railroad of California, across the Sierra Nevada mountains, from Sacramento to the eastern boundary of California. Sacramento, October 1, 1861.* S.l., s.n., 1861? 36 p.

2537. _____. *Report of the chief engineer on the preliminary survey, cost of construction and estimated revenue, of the Central Pacific Railroad of California, across the Sierra Nevada Mountains, from Sacramento to the eastern boundary of California. October 22, 1862.* Prepared by: Theodore D. Judah, Chief Engineer. Sacramento: H.S. Crocker & Co., Printers, 1862? 56 p.

2538. _____. *Report of the chief engineer, upon recent surveys, progress of construction, and an approximate estimate of cost of first division of fifty miles of the Central Pacific Railroad of Cal., July 1st, 1863.* Prepared by Theodore D. Judah, Chief Engineer. Sacramento: James Anthony & Co., 1863. 26 p.

2539. _____. *Report of the chief engineer, upon recent surveys, progress of construction, and an approximate estimate of receipts of the Central Pacific Railroad of California.* San Francisco? s.n., 1864-1865. 3 v.

2540. _____. *Report of the chief engineer upon recent surveys, progress of construction, and estimated revenue of the Central Pacific Railroad of California. December, 1864.* S.l., s.n., 1864? 32 p.

2541. _____. *Rules and regulations for employees.* S.l., s.n., 1868. 2 p. Includes timetable for Humboldt Div., called no. 2, 1868.

2542. _____. *Rules, regulations & classification governing the local freight tariff: in force, January 1st, 1876.* Compiled by A.N. Towne and J.C. Stubbs. San Francisco? Central Pacific Railroad, 1878. 1 v. (unpaged)

2543. _____. *Statement of the Central Pacific Comp'y of California to the Committee of the Senate of the United States on the Pacific Railroad, March 25, 1869.* Washington, DC: Gibson Bros., Printers, 1869. 22 p.

2544. *Central Pacific Railroad : the passenger station, Sacramento* / [created by] History West. North Highlands, CA: History West, 1977. 28 p. At head of title: California State Railroad Museum.

2545. Central Railroad Club, Buffalo. *Central railway chronicle.* Buffalo, NY: Central Railway Club of Buffalo, 1931- . Five numbers annually. (< *Official proceedings of the Central Railway Club.*)

2546. _____. *Official proceedings of the Central Railway Club.* Buffalo: Central Railway Club of Buffalo, 1898-1930. Quarterly. 34 v. (< Central Railroad Club of Buffalo. *Proceedings of the ... meeting of the Central Railway Club*; > Central Railway Club of Buffalo. *Central railway chronicle.*)

2547. _____. *Proceedings of the ... meeting of the Central Railway Club.* Buffalo, N.Y.,

Central Railroad Club of Buffalo, 1893-1897. 5 numbers annually. 5 v. (> Central Railway Club. *Official proceedings of the Central Railway Club.*)

2548. _____. *Annual yearbook for the Central Railway Club, Buffalo. Business directory and buyer's guide for the convenience of its 1500 members and railroad employees throughout Buffalo and Western New York.* Buffalo, Central Railway Club, 1933-   . Annual.

2549. Central Railroad of New Jersey. *Announcing the formal opening of the new Newark Baybridge of the Central Railroad Company of New Jersey.* S.l., s.n., 1926. 1 v.

2550. _____. *The Central Railroad Company of New Jersey system valuation docket no. 401; photographs & diagrams of floating equipment.* Jersey City, N.J., Central Railroad of New Jersey, 1917. 140 p.

2551. _____. *Historical highlights: Jersey Central Lines.* New York, The Company, 1949. 16 p.

2552. _____. *Jersey Central Lines annual report, 1949: 100 years of service, 1849-1949.* New York, Central Railroad of New Jersey, 1950. 32 p.

2553. _____. *Official freight shippers' guide of the Central Railroad Company of New Jersey, 1926.* New York, Central Railroad Company of New York, 1926. 230 p.

2554. _____. *The problems facing this railroad and an appraisal of the possible solutions.* New York: Plugfelder, Bampton & Rust, 1945. 4 p.

2554a. _____. *Records.* 1839-1973. 27 linear feet. Location: Hagley Museum and Library.

2555. _____ *Rules of the Central Rail-Road Co. of New Jersey: for the government of the transportation and repairing service.* New York, George Scott Roe, 1852. (Reprint: Dover, NJ: Frank T. Reilly, 1974. 28 p.)

2556. _____. *Rules of the Operating Department.* New York? The Company, 1903. 131 p.

2557. _____. *Specifications of boats built by the System: ledger book.* Jersey City, N.J., The System, n.d. 1 v.

2558. Central Steel Company, Massillon, Ohio. *Development of the locomotive.* Massillon, Ohio, The Central Steel Company, 1925. 64 p.

2559. Central Traffic Association. *Agreement for the division of east-bound dead freight, dressed meats and live stock from Chicago/* Washington, DC: Capital Press, 1894. 8 p.

2560. Central Vermont Railway Company. *Butter notice: on and after Tuesday, May 16th, 1882, the Central Vermont Railroad will run refrigerator cars (provided with ice)* on the special butter train leaving stations on O & L.C., Vermont Central and Rutland Railroads on Tuesday of each week. St. Albans, VT: s.n., 1882. 1 broadside, 41 cm.

2561. _____. *Operating rules and general regulations.* S.l., Central Vermont Railway Co., 1911. 165 p.

2562. *A century of American railway bridges and buildings: a special exhibition of books, manuscripts, prints and photographs honoring the centennial of the American Railway Bridge and Building Association, John W. Barriger III National Railroad Library.* St. Louis, MO: St. Louis Mercantile Library Association, 1991. 18 p.

2563. Cerreño, Allison L. C. de, Daniel M. Evans, Howard Permut. *High speed rail projects in the United States: identifying the elements for success/* San José, CA: Mineta Transportation Institute, College of Business, San Jose State University, 2005. 106 p. (*MTI report, 05-01*)

2564. Chace, Ira M., Lyman E. Bacon. *Steel freight car construction.* 1898. 134 l. (Thesis, B.S., Massachusetts Institute of Technology, Department of Civil Engineering.)

2565. Chalmers, David Mark. *Neither socialism nor monopoly: Theodore Roosevelt and the decision to regulate the railroads.* Philadelphia, Lippincott, 1976. 121 p.

2566. Chamber of Commerce of Pittsburgh. *The insurrection among the railway employees of the United States, and the losses in Pittsburgh resulting therefrom in July 1877 : memorial of the Pittsburgh Chamber of Commerce to the Pennsylvania legislature.* Pittsburgh : Stevenson, Foster & Co., 1877. 16 p.

2567. Chamber of Commerce of the United States of American. *Organization of war transportation control.* Washington, D.C., The Chamber, 1918. 31 p. (Railroad Committee; George A. Post, chairman.)

2568. _____. Transportation and Communication Department. *Train length.* Washington, DC: Chamber of Commerce of the United States, 1937. 16 p.

2569. Chamberlain, Irvin. *Evaluation of effects of alternative western freight rates for coal.* Washington, DC: U.S. Department of Energy, Energy Information Administration, Assistant Administrator for Applied Analysis, 1980. 21 p. (*Analysis report, Energy Information Administration, AR.IA/80-04.*)

2569a. Chamberlin, Oliver Booth. *Industrial switching and allowances, the responsibility of railroads for the delivery or receipt of cars at complex industrial plants /* 1946. 113 l. (Thesis, M.B.A., Graduate School of Arts and Sciences, University of Pennsylvania.)

2570. Chamberlin, Stephen Johnes. *Physical characteristics of railway ballast/* 1931. 118 l. (Thesis, M.S., Iowa State College.)

2571. Chambers, G. J. *A project for the elimination of grade crossings on the Lehigh Valley Railroad at Buffalo, N.Y. /* 1913. 22, 4 l. (Thesis, B.S., Massachusetts Institute of Technology, Department of Civil Engineering.)

2572. Chandler, Alfred Dupont. *Henry Varnum Poor, business editor, analyst, and reformer.* Cambridge, Harvard University Press, 1956. 362 p. (Studies in Entrepreneurial History)

2573. _____. *The railroads: pioneers in modern management.* New York, Arno Press, 1979. 295 p.

2574. _____, Thomas K. McCraw. *The essential Alfred Chandler: essays toward a historical theory of big business.* Boston, Harvard Business School Press, 1988. 538 p.

2575. _____. *The railroads: the Nation's first big business; sources and readings.* New York, Harcourt, Brace & World, 1965. 213 p.

2576. Chandler, Charles Frederick. *Report on water for locomotives and boiler instructions made to the president and directors of the New York Central Railroad /* New York : Trow, 1865. 35 p.

2577. Chandler, Roy F. *A history of Perry County railroads.* New Bloomfield, PA: 1970. 128 p.

2578. Changnon, Stanley A. *Railroads and weather.* Boston, American Meteorological Society, 2006. 136 p.

2579. Changnon, Stanley Alcide. *America's rural hub: railroading in central Illinois in the late twentieth century.* Mohomet, IL: Mayhaven Pub., 1991. 216 p.

2580. _____. *Coal and railroads in Illinois: a unique history and an ever-changing relationship.* Mahomet, IL: Changnon Rails, 2000. 214 p.

2581. _____. *The ghost of the Green Diamond: the Texas Eagle magically appeared during the summer of 2001 on an old Illinois Central line once home of the Green Diamond.* Mohomet, IL: Changnon Rails, 2001. 108 p.

2582. _____ *Prairie crossings: Illinois' exciting rail junctions in the 1990s.* Mahomet, IL: Changnon Rails, 1998. 443 p.

2583. _____. *Railroad bridges in the heartland.* Mohomet, IL: S.A. Changnon, 1997. 216 p.

2584. _____. *The triangle: busy railroading in southern Illinois.* Mahomet, IL: S.A. Changnon, 1991. 104 p.

2585. Channon, Geoffrey. *Railways in Britain and the United States, 1830-1940: studies in economic and business history/* Aldershot, Hants, England; Burlington, VT: Ashgate, 2001. 341 p. (*Modern economic and social history series.*)

2586. Chant, Christopher, John Moore. *Freight by rail.* Rochester, Grange, 2002. 64 p.

2586a. _____. *The history of North American rail* / Edison, NJ: Chartwell Books, 2007. 443 p.

2587. Chantier, Michael. *Socialism and the great railroad strike of 1877* / 1971. 136 l. (Thesis, M.A., Sonoma State College.)

2588. Chapin, George M. *Official souvenir: Key West extension of the Florida East Coast Railway "The Overseas Railroad."* St. Augustine, FL: Record Co., 1912. 78 p. (Issued by Overseas Railroad Extension Celebration Committee of Key West.)

2589. Chapman, Allen. *Ralph in the switch tower: or , Clearing the track*/ New York, NY: Grosset & Dunlap, 1907. 263 p. [Juvenile literature: no specific ages]

2590. _____. *Ralph of the roundhouse: or, Bound to become a railroad man*/ New York, NY: Grosset & Dunlap, 1906. 278, 6 p.

2591. _____. *Ralph on the engine. or, The young fireman of the Limited Mail*/ New York, NY: Grosset & Dunlap, 1909. 250, 2 p.

2592. _____. *Ralph on the Overland Express: or, The trials and trimphs of a young engineer*/ New York, NY: Grosset & Dunlap, 1910. 274 p.

2593. _____. *Ralph, the train dispatcher: or, The mystery of the pay car*/ New York, NY: Grosset & Dunlap, 1911. 272, 12 p.

2594. Chapman, William Williams. *The Great Pacific Northwest and railroad connection: by the Portland, Dalles & Salt Lake Railroad, a through line from Salt Lake to the Columbia River and Portland, Oregon*/ Washington, DC: Jos. L. Pearson, Printer, 1875. 26 p. (*United States. Congress, 43 rd, 1st session, Senate Report, no. 317.*)

2595. Chappell, Gordon S. *Logging along the Denver & Rio Grande: narrow gauge logging railroads of southwestern Colorado and northern New Mexico.* Golden, CO: Colorado Railroad Museum, 1971. 190 p.

2596. _____. *An oasis for railroaders in the Mojave: the history and architecture of the Los Angeles and Salt Lake Railroad depot, restaurant and employees' hotel at Kelso, California, on the Union Pacific System.* Denver, CO: U.S. Department of the Interior, National Park Service, 1998. 488 p.

2597. _____. *Rails to carry copper; a history of the Magma Arizona Railroad.* Boulder, CO: Pruett Publishing Co., 1973. 243 p.

2598. _____. *Steam over Scranton: the locomotives of Steamtown.* Washington, D.C.? U. Department of the Interior, National Park Service, 1991. 304 p.

2599. _____. *To Santa Fe by narrow gauge: the D&RG's "Chili Line".* Golden, CO:

Colorado Railroad Museum, 1981. 56 p.

2600. _____, Cornelius W. Hauck. *Farewell to Cumbres*. Golden, CO: Colorado Railroad Museum, 1967. 32 p. (Colorado Rail Annual, no. 5)

2601 _____, _____. *Narrow gauge transcontinental*. Golden, CO: Colorado Railroad Museum, 1970. 131 p.(Colorado Rail Annual, no 8.)

2602. _____, _____. *Scenic line of the world*. Golden, CO: Colorado Railroad Historical Foundation, 1977 ed. 148 p. (Originally published as Colorado Rail Annual, no 8)

2603. _____, _____ *A short history of steam trains over Cumbres: farewell to Cumbres*. Golden, CO: Colorado Railroad Historical Foundation, 1967. 32 p. (Also published as *Farewell to Cumbres*, Colorado Rail Annual, no. 5, Colorado Railroad Museum, 1967.)

2604. _____, _____, Richard W. Richardson. *The South Park Line: a concise history*. Golden, CO: Colorado Railroad Museum, 1974. 280 p.

2605. *Characterization of 105A tank cars and their usage patterns in transporting hazardous materials: final report* / Washington, DC: Federal Railroad Administration, Office of Research and Development, 1982. 74 p. (Prepared by Dynatrend Incorporated)

2606. *Charles B. Chaney photography collection: Division of Transportation, NMAH, Room 5010*. Washington, D.C., Smithsonian Institution, 1985? 2 v.

2607. *Charles Davenport, 1812-1903*. Cambridge, Mass., Harvard Trust Co., 1931. 15 p.

2608. Charles, Ralph. *Truswell valve gear for steam locomotives*. 1930. 41 l. (Thesis, M.S., New Mexico State University.)

2608a. Charlotte, Columbia, and Augusta Railroad . *Rules & regulations for the movements of trains and the guidance of employees, to take effect Monday morning July 1st, 1878* / Columbia, SC: s.n., 1878. 37 p.

2609. Charlton, E. Harper. *Railway car builders of the United States and Canada*. Indianapolis, IN: Interurbans, 1957. 91 p. (Interurbans special, 24.)

2610. Charlton, Kenody J., *Rails across the land: freight and passenger trains of the 40s and 50s*. Edited and designed by Debra Kenton Incardone. Forest Park, IL: Heimburger House, 1991. 204 p.

2611. Chase, Edward E. *Maine railroads : a history of the development of the Maine railroad system*. Portland ME: A.J. Huston, 1926. 145 p.

2612. Chase, Heman. *Railroad passenger travel: history, recollections, reflections*. Alstead, NH: Chase, 1967. 46 p.

2613. Chateauvert, M. Melinda. *Marching together: women of the Brotherhood of Sleeping Car Porters.* Urbana, University of Illinois Press, 1997. 267 p. (*Women in American History; The Working Class in American History.*) (Ph.D., University of Pennsylvania, 1992. 541 l.)

2614. Chatham, Ruth. *Transcontinental railroad surveys of the 1850s.* 1943. 190 l. (Thesis, M.A., Texas Technological College.)

2614a. Chauvin, Dean. *A digital archive of historical railroad property valuation maps.* Storrs, CT: University of Connecticut, Center for Geographic Information and Analysis, 2008. 9, 3, 1 p.

2615. Chavez, Art. *S.S. Badger: the Lake Michigan car ferry.* Chicago, IL: Arcadia, 2003. 127 p. (Train ferries)

2616. _____. *S.S. City of Midland 41.* Charleston, SC: Arcadia Pub., 2004. 127 p. (Train ferries)

2617. *Check list of publications on American railroads before 1841; a union list of printed books and pamphlets, including state and federal documents, dealing with charters, by-laws, legislative acts, speeches, debates, land grants, officers' and engineers' reports, travel guides, maps, etc.* Compiled by Thomas Richard Thomson. New York, The New York Public Library, 1942. 250 p. "Reprinted with additions from the Bulletin of the New York Public Library of January-July-October 1941."

2618. *A check-list of railway literature for adults* / Washington, DC: Association of American Railroads, 1946. 8 p.

2619. *Checklist of Jackson and Sharp Company photographic collection.* Delaware. Division of Historical and Cultural Affairs. "The record is a checklist of the company's collection of builder's photographs that was given to the Hall of Records when the company ceased business."

2620. Cheever, Bruce Bissell. *The development of railroads in the state of Washington, 1860 to 1948.* Bellingham, Wash., Western Washington College of Education, 1949. 131 l. (Thesis, University of Washington.)

2621. Chen, Chuan-yu Ed. *Estimating cost function for the United States railroads*/ 1972. 105 l. (Thesis, Ph.D., New York University.)

2622. Chen, Jida. *The awards of the National Railroad Adjustment Board.* 1954. 317 l. (Thesis, State University of Iowa.)

2622a. Chen, Lan Sung. *The financial status of the Granger railways of the United States from 1908 to 1915* / 1917. 4, xiv, 157, 4 l, 46 l. of plates.

2623. Chen, Min-Tse, Vijay Kumar Garg. *Analysis of Pratt, Howe, and Warren type railway truss bridges.* Chicago, IL: Association of American Railroads Technical Center, 1978. 43 l. (*Bridge Program, no. 3; R-332.*)

2624. Cheney, Frank, Anthony Mitchell Sammarco. *When Boston rode the EL.* Charleston, SC, Arcadia, 2000. 128 p.

2625. Cheney, Fred D., David R. Sweetland. *Southern Railway in color.* Edison, NJ: Morning Sun Books, 1993-1999. 2 v.

2626. Cheng, Ke Wu. *Railroad passenger terminal operation and management /* 1940. 178 l. (Thesis, M.A. in Economics, Graduate School of Arts and Sciences, University of Pennsylvania.)

2626a. Cheng, Sze. *Locomotive feedwater heaters—a study of their performance and heat transmission.* Thesis, M.S., University of Illinois—Urbana-Champaign, 1926. 139 l.

2627. Cherington, Charles Roberts. *The regulation of railroad abandonments.* Cambridge, Harvard University Press, 1948. 277 p. (*Harvard Political Studies.*)

2628. *Chesapeake and Ohio diesel review.* Compiled and edited by Carl W. Shaver Alderson, WV: Chesapeake & Ohio Historical Society, 1982. 228 p.

2629. *Chesapeake and Ohio historical magazine.* Alderson, WV: The Society, 1986- Monthly. (< *Chesapeake and Ohio historical newsletter.*)

2630. *Chesapeake & Ohio historical newsletter.* Alderson, WV: T.W. Dixon, 1969-1985. Monthly. (> *Chesapeake and Ohio historical magazine.*)

2631. Chesapeake & Ohio Historical Society. *Ride with us on the Chesapeake & Ohio.* Alderson, WV: Chesapeake & Ohio Historical Society, 1985. 9 p.

2632. _____, Chesapeake and Ohio Railway Company. *Pere Marquette District track charts.* Clifton Forge, VA: Chesapeake & Ohio Historical Society, 1940?, 199-? 200 l.

2633. Chesapeake and Ohio Railroad Company. *Central trunk line to the West: a statement showing the superiority of the Chesapeake & Ohio Railroad as a short, constant and economical line of communication between the Atlantic seaboard cities and those of the Ohio and Mississippi valleys and the Pacific Coast: with an account of the present condition and prospects of the enterprise.* New York: Fisk & Hatch, 1870. 28 p.

2634. _____. *The Chesapeake& Ohio Railroad.* New York, 1873. 68 p.

2635. _____. *Chesapeake and Ohio schedules for time freight trains.* Richmond?: Chesapeake and Ohio Railway, 1952. 14 p.

2636. _____. *The coal bin of America.* Cleveland? Chesapeake and Ohio Railway Company, 1937. 25 p.

2637. _____. *Coal mine directory; list of coal mines located on Chesapeake and Ohio lines and lateral lines.* Cleveland, The Company, n.d. 1 v.

2638. _____. *Coal mines on the Chesapeake and Ohio Railway.* S.l., Chesapeake and Ohio Railway Co., 1957. 73 p.

2639. _____. *Freight car equipment of the Chesapeake & Ohio Railway Company: August 1, 1937, with supplemental information provided by the Chesapeake & Ohio Historical Society, Inc.* Carl W. Shaver, editor. Alderson, WV: The Society, 1980. 150 p.

2640. _____. *General specifications for steel bridges.* Richmond, Va., I.N. Jones & Son, 1902. 33 p.

2641. _____. *The George Washington china service, Chesapeake and Ohio.* S.l., Chesapeake and Ohio Railroad Co., 1930s. 16 p.

2642. _____. *The George Washington, the most wonderful train the world : created by the Chesapeake and Ohio to celebrate the two hundredth birthday anniversary of the father of transportation in America, 1732-1932.* S.l., Chesapeake and Ohio Railway Co.? 1932. 12 p.

2642a. _____. *Index of stations and tunnels on the Chesapeake and Ohio Railway/* Clifton Forge, VA: Chesapeake and Ohio Historical Society, Inc., 1969, 2010. 1 v.

2643. _____. *Industry's next great expansion area; the Chessie corridor.* Cleveland, The Chesapeake and Ohio Railway Co., 1941. 56 p.

2644. _____. *Merchandise freight equipment fleet roster.* S.L., Chesapeake and Ohio Railway Company, 1971. 26 p.

2645. _____. *Official industrial and shippers directory* / Cleveland? Chesapeake and Ohio Railway Company, Freight Traffic Department, 1929. 1 v. Includes Hocking Valley Railway Co.

2646. _____. *Official industrial guide and shippers' directory...* Richmond? Chesapeake and Ohio Railway Co., General Freight Department, 1907. 460 p.

2647. _____. *Rules and instructions for train handling.* Richmond, Va.? Chesapeake and Ohio Railway Co./Baltimore and Ohio Railroad Co., 1966. 83 p.

2648. _____. *Stoker coal, Chesapeake and Ohio lines.* Richmond, Va.? The Company, 1935. 61 p.

2649. _____. *Telegraphic cipher code, The Chesapeake & Ohio Railway Company., The Hocking Valley Railway Co., Pere Marquette Railway Co., effective March 1, 1930.* Cincinnati, Ohio, R.H. Vaughan; Richmond, Va., A.P. Gilbert...1930. 171 p.

2649a. _____. *Telephone users guide.* S.L., C&O Railroad/B&O Railroad, 1900s. 11 p.

2650. _____. *Switching instructions for the guidance of engine, train and yard service employees.* Richmond, Va.? C&O Railway Co./B&O Railroad Co., 1964. 8 p.

2651. *Chesapeake and Ohio Lines magazine.* Richmond, VA: Chesapeake and Ohio Railway Public Relations Department, 1930-1931. Monthly. (< *Chesapeake & Ohio, the Hocking Valley employes' magazine*; > *Chesapeake and Ohio magazine*.)

2652. Chesapeake and Ohio Lines magazine: Chesapeake and Ohio, Pere Marquette, Nickel Plate. Huntington, WV: Pere Marquette Railway ; Chesapeake and Ohio Railway, 1938-1943. Monthly. (< *Chesapeake and Ohio Pere Marquette magazine;* > *Tracks.* (Chesapeake and Ohio Railway Co.)

2653. *Chesapeake and Ohio magazine.* Cleveland, OH: Chesapeake and Ohio Railway, 1931-1932. Monthly. (< *Chesapeake and Ohio lines magazine*; > *Pere Marquette magazine*; *Rail.))*

2654. *Chesapeake & Ohio operations on the Nicholas, Fayette & Greenbrier Railroad.* Clifton Forge, VA : Chesapeake & Ohio Historical Society, 2010. 21 l.

2655. *Chesapeake and Ohio Pere Marquette magazine.* Huntington, WV: Pere Marquette Railway : Chesapeake and Ohio Railway, 1900s-? Monthly. (< *The rail.*)

2656. *Chesapeake & Ohio Railway Company employes' magazine.* Richmond, VA: Chesapeake and Ohio Railway Co., 1900s-1920s. Monthly. . (> *Chesapeake and Ohio and Hocking Valley employes' magazine.*)

2657. *The Chesapeake and Ohio, the Hocking Valley employes' magazine.* Richmond, VA: Chesapeake and Ohio Railway Public Relations Department, 1923-1930. Monthly. 8 v. (< *Chesapeake and Ohio Railway Company employes' magazine*; > *Chesapeake and Ohio Lines magazine.*)

2658. Chesser, Al H. *Economic advantages of transporting coal by rail vs. coal slurry pipeline* / Cleveland, OH: United Transportation Union, 1976. 62 p. Research by Ruttenberg, Friedman, Kilgallon, Gutchess & Associates.

2659. Chessie System, Inc. *Freight schedule and classification book.* Baltimore, MD: Chessie System Railroads, 1986. 1 v.

2660. Cheteauvert, M. Melinda. *Marching together: women of the Brotherhood of Sleeping Car Porters, 1925-1957.* 1992. 541 l.(Thesis, Ph.D., University of Pennsylvania.)

2661. Chew, William F. *Nameless builders of the transcontinental railway: the Chinese workers of the Central Pacific Railroad*/ Victoria, BC: Trafford, 2004. 128 p. Also: Heng guan da lu tie lu de wu ming jian she zhe. Shanghai Shi: Shanghai bai jia chu ban she, 2008. 24, 116 p.

2662. Chicago, Ill. City of Chicago. Dept. of Public Works; Dept. of Planning; Chicago Transit Authority. *Master plan for the Loop elevated rehabilitation and historic preservation.* Chicago, IL: City of Chicago…, 1981. 1 v.

2663. Chicago, Ill. City Council. Committee on Local Transportation. *The electrification of railway terminals as a cure for the locomotive smoke evil in Chicago, with special consideration of the Illinois Central Railroad…* Chicago, R.R. Donnelley & Sons Company, 1908. 353 p.

2663a. Chicago. Committee on Co-ordination of Chicago Terminals. *The freight traffic of the Chicago terminal district.* Chicago : s.n., 1927. 117 p.

2664. Chicago and Alton Railroad Company. *Chicago and Alton Railroad Company. Time table for the special train conveying the funeral cortege with the remains of the late President from Chicago to Springfield, Tuesday, May 2, 1865 …* / 1 broadside, 8-1/2 x 13-1/2 in. Signed Robert Hale, General Superintendent. Location:

2665. _____. *Everyman's almanac 1924: containing timely information about the railroads and other matters of general interest.* Compiled by David A. Wallace and Agnes Carroll Hayward. Chicago: Chicago & Alton R.R., 1923. 40 p.

2666. _____. *The flood of 1903.* Chicago: Chicago and Alton Railway, 1903. 66 p.

2667. _____. *A guide to the Chicago Drainage Canal with geological and historical notes to accompany the tourist via the Chicago & Alton Railroad.* Chicago: Chicago and Alton Railroad Company, 1895. 23 p.

2668. _____. *Official business directory of the Chicago & Alton Railroad and the Jacksonville Division.* Cincinnati: J.S. Sheppard & Co., 1870. 318 p.

2669. _____. *Official directory and shippers guide of Chicago and Alton Railway Company.* Chicago: Chicago and Alton Railway Company, General Freight Department, 1902-1903. 83 p.

2670. _____. *Official guide of the Chicago and Alton Railroad: containing the latest revised time cards of the Chicago and Alton Railroad and connections, November 1872.* Chicago: Chicago Evening Journal Printing, 1872. 12 p.

2671. _____. *Rules and regulations governing the road department of the Chicago & Alton Railroad* / Chicago: The J.M.W. Jones stationery & printing co., 1883. 28 p.

2672. _____. *Rules of the Operating Department.* Barrington, IL:? Pantagraph Ptg. & Sta. Co., 1940. 107 p.

2673. _____. *Rules, regulations and rates of pay for conductors, brakemen, baggagemen and flagmen: effective December 1st, 1911.* Chicago? : The Company?, 1911. 28 p.

2674. _____. *Union Station Chicago, 1925.* Chicago: Designed and printed by the Lakeside Press, R.R. Donnelley & Sons Co., 1925. 22 p.

2675. _____. *With paste and shears: a collection of newspaper clippings regarding the parlor and compartment sleeping cars just completed by the Pullman Company for use in Chicago-St. Louis service of Chicago & Alton R.R.* Chicago, IL: Chicago & Alton R.R., 1891. 15 p.

2676. Chicago & Eastern Illinois Railroad Company. *Rules of the Operating Department: effective December 15, 1919.* Danville, Ill., Illinois Printing Co., 1919. 120 p.

2677. Chicago & Eastern Illinois Railroad Historical Society. *Locomotives of the Chicago & Eastern Illinois Railroad. Part 1.* Crestwood, IL: Chicago & Eastern Illinois Railroad Historical Society, 1996. 121 p. (*The C&EI Flyer, v. 15, no. 1-2.*)

2678. _____. *Locomotives of the Chicago & Eastern Illinois Railroad. Part II.* Crestwood, IL: Chicago & Eastern Illinois Railroad Historical Society, 1997. 119 p. (*The C & EI flyer, v. 16, no. 1-2.*)

2679. _____. *Up and down the C&EI, by the Chicago and Eastern Railroad management.* Crestwood, IL: Chicago & Eastern Illinois Railroad Historical Society, 1992. 135 p.

2680. Chicago and Illinois Midland Railway Company. *The Midland story.* Springfield, Ill., Public Relations Department, C&IM Ry. Co., 1954. 44 p.

2681. Chicago & North Western Historical Society. *Abandonments book: lists lines abandoned by the C & NW; also lines formerly owned by CStPM & O., CGW, M&StL., FDDM & S., DM & CI.* Deerfield, IL: J. Piersen, 1999. 1 v.

2682. _____. *C & NW section houses.* Deerfield, IL: Chicago & North Western Historical Society, n.d. 80 p.

2683. _____. *C & NW standards book.* Chicago, The Society, 1998. 68 l.

2684. _____. *North Western lines: 150 years, 1848-1998.* Sheboygan, WI: The Society, 1998. 135 p.

2685. Chicago and North Western Railway Company. *Before the Interstate Commerce Commission: statement of Chicago and North Western Railway Company in relation to proposed discontinuance of passenger trains 161-162 between Green Bay, Wisconsin and Ishpeming, Michigan.* Chicago? The Company? 1960. 1 v. (various pagings)

2686. _____. *Before the Interstate Commerce Commission: statement of Chicago and North Western Railway Company in relation to proposed discontinuance of passenger trains 400-401 between Chicago, Illinois and Minneapolis, Minnesota. and trains 518-519 between Chicago, Illinois and Mankato, Minnesota.* Washington, DC:

Interstate Commerce Commission, 1961. 1 v. (various pagings)

2686a. _____. *C & NW bridge book: from original documents in the archives of the C&NWHS* / S.l., Chicago and North Western Historical Society, 2001. 94 l.

2687. _____. *C & NW Rwy. steam locomotive profiles.* Sheboygan, WI: Northwood Chapter, N.R.H.S., 1985. 258 l.

2687a. _____. *Descriptive list of locomotives* / Chicago : Chicago and North Western Railway, 1885. 1 v. (unpaged)

2687b. _____. *Dimensions and classification of locomotives of the Chicago and North-Western Railway Co.* Chicago : s.n., 1901. 142 p.

2687c. _____. *Iron and copper and where they are found* / Chicago : Traffic Department, Chicago and North-Western Railway, 1901. 51, 5 p.

2688. _____. *List of locomotives, freight cars, passenger cars, miscellaneous equipment, turntables, wye tracks…* Chicago, Ill., The Company, 1964. 52 p.

2689. _____. *Locomotive reports : June 1ˢᵗ 1864 to Dec. 31ˢᵗ 1873.* Chicago : C.&N.W. Ry., 1873. 1 v. (unpaged). 58 x 86 cm.

2689a. _____. *Los Angeles Limited via Chicago & Northwestern, Union Pacific & Salt Lake Route.* Chicago? Chicago and North-Western Railway Co., 1907. 20 p.

2690. _____. *Memorial of the Chicago & North Western and Chicago, Milwaukee & St. Paul Railway Companies to the Senate and Assembly of the state of Wisconsin.* Chicago, IL: Metropolitan, 1875. 48 p.

2691. _____. *Monthly bulletin.* Chicago : Passenger Department, Chicago and North Western Railway Co., 1912- . Monthly.

2692. _____. *The new streamliner: City of Los Angeles.* S.l., North Western-Union Pacific, 1938. 34 p.

2692a. _____. *The new streamliner: City of San Francisco.* Chicago : Rand McNally, 1937. 32 p.

2692b. _____. *The North-Western Limited, electric lighted.* Chicago : s.n., 1903. 16 p.

2693. _____. *The North-Western Limited : between Chicago, St. Paul, Minneapolis, Duluth* / Chicago : Chicago and North Western Railway Company, 1898. 24 p. Cover title: 20ᵗʰ century train—electric lighted.

2694. _____. *The North-Western line gazetteer: containing a business directory of each city and town on the line of the Chicago & North-Western Railway…with a full description of all business, industries, etc. for the use of shippers, investors and merchants generally.* Chicago, Ill., W.P. Dickinson & Co., 1893. 418 p.

2695. _____. *Official directory and atlas naming shippers of staple commodities and giving a list of stations, track scales, etc. on the Chicago & North-Western Ry...* Chicago, Lanward, 1901. 376 p.

2695a. _____. *Passenger terminal, Chicago, U.S.A.* Chicago: Woodward & Tiernan Printing Co., 1911. 38 p.

2696. _____. *The Portland Rose : a triumph in train comfort : only thru train between Chicago and Portland : 200 miles along the scenic Columbia River.* Chicago ? : Chicago & North Western Ry., Union Pacific System, 1900s. 13 p.

2697. _____. *Presenting the streamliners City of Los Angeles: a sailing every third day.* Chicago, Rand McNally, 1941. 32 p.

2698. _____. *The proposed Rock Island mergers: an analysis.* S.l., Chicago and North Western Railway Co., 1965. 27 p.

2699. _____. *Regulations for the guidance of conductors, cooks and waiters of the Chicago & North-Western R'y Co's dining cars.* S.l., s.n., 1883. 12 p.

2699a. _____. *Revised schedule of wages and rules regulating employment of locomotive firemen, hostlers and outside hostler helpers: effective April 1, 1942.* Chicago : Chicago and North Western System, 1942. 167 p.

2699b. _____. *Rules and instructions : dining car employees, effective August 1, 1945 /* Chicago : Chicago & North Western System, 1945. 20 p.

2700. _____. *Rules for the government of employes working in shops, round houses and repair yards.* Chicago, Ill., The Company, 1912. 38 p.

2701. _____. *Rules for the government of the Operating Department, to take effect June 1, 1919. Issued in accordance with the standard code adopted by the American Railway Association, November 17, 1915.* Chicago, s.n., 1919. 262 p.

2702. _____. *Rules governing maintenance of way and structures.* S.l., Chicago and North Western Railway Company, 1929. 131 p.

2702a. _____. *Shippers' guide /* Chicago: Culver, Page, Hoyne & Co., printers, 1880. 116 p.

2703. _____. *Specifications for design and construction of steel railroad bridges, 1912.* S.l., Chicago & North Western Railway Company, 1912. 22 l.

2703a. _____. *Statistics of the Chicago and North Western Railway Company /* New York : Henry Bessey, 1888- . Annual.

2704. _____. *Telegraphic cipher code: effective December 1, 1920.* S.l., Chicago and North Western railway Co., 1920. 121 p.

2705. _____. *Telegraphic cipher code : effective April 1, 1930.* S.l., Chicago and North Western Railway Co., Traffic Department, 1930, ©1920. 123 p. Chicago, St. Paul, Minneapolis & Omaha Railroad, Traffic Department.

2706. *Chicago and North Western Railway Company, a centennial bibliography.* Compiled by Helen R. Richardson. Washington, D.C., Association of American Railroads, Bureau of Railway Economics, Library, 1948. 168 l.

2707. *Chicago & North Western Railway 1975 through 1995: photo archive.* Frank W. Jordan, editor. Hudson, WI: Iconografix, 1997. 126 p.

2708. Chicago Association of Commerce and Industry. Committee on Investigation on Smoke Abatement and Electrification of Railway Terminals. *Smoke abatement and electrification of railway terminals in Chicago...* W.F.M. Goss, chief engineer. Chicago, Rand, McNally, 1915. 1177 p.

2709. _____._____. *Summation of train movements and locomotive coal by elements of route.* Chicago, Ill., The Association, 1912. 1 v.

2709a. Chicago Bridge and Iron Works. *Chicago Bridge and Iron Works, established 1865, engineers, manufacturers, erectors of steel water tanks, steel storage tanks, steel coaling stations, steel smoke stacks, steel railroad bridges.* Chicago: Chicago Bridge and Iron Works, 1917. 23 p.

2710. Chicago, Burlington & Quincy Railroad Company. *The Aristocrat : the West's great train.* S.l., The Railroad, 1932. 15 p. Other title: Aristocrat service directory : Chicago, Omaha, Lincoln, Denver.

2711. _____. *Burlington's new 12-car Denver Zephyrs: America's distinctive trains.* Chicago, Burlington, 1936. 16 p.

2712. _____. *Great Burlington Route, the transcontinental route of America ...* Buffalo, NY: Clay & Richmond, 1884. 24 p. Includes colored illustration of 7 depots and 5 car interiors.

2713. (Blank entry.)

2714. _____. *Industrial properties located on Burling Lines.* Chicago: Chicago, Burlington & Quincy railroad Co., 1950-1960. Monographic series. 139 p.

2715. _____. *Instructions and examinations for engineers in the care and operation of passenger motor cars.* Chicago, Burlington, 1933. 40 p.

2716. _____. *Instructions for enginemen: mechanical examination questions and answers covering locomotive operation.* Chicago, Ill., Chicago, Burlington & Quincy

Railroad Company, 1927. 107 p.

2717. _____. *The mail pay on the Burlington Railroad. Statements of car space and all facilities furnished for the government mails and for express and passengers in all passenger trains on the Chicago, Burlington and Quincy Railroad.* S.l., Chicago, Burlington & Quincy Railroad Company, 1910. 46 p.

2717a. _____. *Official directory and atlas* / Chicago : Lanward Pub. Co., 1901. 304, 14 p.

2718. _____. *Passenger and freight car equipment.* S.l., Chicago, Burlington & Quincy Railroad Co.? 1916. 8 p.

2719. _____. *Press kit: the new Vista Dome Denver Zephyr.* Chicago, Ill., The Company, 1956. 34 l. (Includes floor plans and description of accommodations.)

2720. _____. *Special instructions regarding fuel economy. Economical firing. Economical boiler-feeding. Economical use of steam.* Chicago, Ill., The Purchasing Department, 1901. 108 p.

2721. _____. *The standard code of train rules, block signal and interlocking rules to take effect at twelve o'clock, noon, July 1, 1916.* Chicago, Ill., Rand McNally & Co., 1916. 163 p.

2722. _____. *The standard code of train rules, block signals and interlocking rules.* S.l., s.n., 1928? 156 p.

2723. _____. *Train rules, Operating Department.* Chicago, Ill., H.O. Shepard Co., 1900. 142 p.

2724. _____. *Train rules, signal and interlocking rules.* S.l., s.n., 1951. 191 p.

2725. _____. *The world's record: 1025 miles in 1047 minutes.* Chicago, Ill., The Company, 1897. 8 p.

2725a. _____. *Yellowstone Park Comet : the only solid train from Chicago designed especially for Yellowstone travel.* Chicago? Burlington Route, Northern pacific, 1927. 1 sheet 28 x 86 cm.

2726. _____. *Your most luxurious traveling living room.* Chicago., Ill., Chicago, Burlington & Quincy Railroad, 1928. 16 p.

2726a. *Chicago, Burlington & Quincy roundhouse : Regional Mechanical Engineering Heritage Site, Aurora, Illinois, May 14, 1988.* New York: American Society of Mechanical Engineers, 1988. 7 p.

2727. Chicago Car Heating Company. *Vapor system of car heating, straight steam pressure systems, locomotive equipments, special car heating appliances, hot water specialties.* Chicago, Ill., Chicago Car Heating Company, 1906. 79 p.

2728. Chicago Freight Car and Parts Company. *Freight cars : new cars, repaired cars, rebuilt cars for railroads, for industry.* Chicago : Chicago Freight Car and Parts Company, 1953. 23, 1 p.

2729. *Chicago Great Western Railway Company: a compendium : transportation of motor trucks, trailers and semitrailers, loaded or empty, on their own wheels, loaded on railroad flat cars for shipment between stations on the* C.G.W. Ry. Chicago : R.G. Hawkinson, 1951. 25, 6 l.

2730. *Chicago: if you want to know railroads, you've got to know Chicago.* Waukesha, WI: Trains Magazine, 2003. 106 p.

2731. Chicago, Milwaukee, St. Paul and Pacific Railroad Company. *Car Department hand book: containing procedure, rules and information governing the maintenance of freight and passenger train cars, locomotive tenders, pilots, and cabs; superseding all car maintenance regulations previously issued.* Milwaukee: Chicago, Milwaukee and St. Paul Railway Company, 1922. 384 p.

2731a. _____. *Comparative cost of electrical and steam operation on the Rocky Mountain, Missoula and Coast Divisions as of 1923.* Chicago: Chicago, Milwaukee & St. Paul Railway, 1925. 25 p.

2732. _____. *Descriptive list of locomotives.* Milwaukee, Chicago, Milwaukee, and St. Paul Railway Co., 1889. 44 p.

2733. _____. *Four generations on the line: highlights along the Milwaukee Road's first hundred years.* S.l., Chicago, Milwaukee, St. Paul and Pacific Railroad Co., 1950. 48 p.

2734. _____. *Freight equipment diagrams of cars.* S.l., s.n., 1900s.?

2735. _____. *Instruction book, class EP-2 locomotives; bipolar gearless type for passenger service.* Rev. ed. Chicago, Chicago, Milwaukee, St. Paul, and Pacific Railroad Company, 1928. 1 v.

2736. _____. *List of locomotives on Chicago, Milwaukee, & St. Paul Railway, April 1874.* S.l., Chicago, Milwaukee, and St. Paul Railway Co., 1874. 5 l.

2737. _____. *The Milwaukee Road: America's longest electrified railroad—656 miles of transcontinental line now operated by "white coal."* Chicago, Ill., Chicago, Milwaukee, St. Paul and Pacific Railroad Company, 1930. 51 p.

2738. _____. *More pioneering by the pioneer line: the electrification of the Mountain District of the Chicago, Milwaukee & St. Paul Railway.* Chicago, Poole Bros, 1916. 24 p.

2739. _____. *The new Hiawatha: a new masterpiece.* Chicago, Ill., The Railroad, 1936.

5 p.

2740. _____. *The new Olympian : to Puget Sound electrified.* Chicago : Chicago, Milwaukee, and St. Paul Railway Company, 1927. 4 p.

2741. _____. *The Olympian: Chicago, Milwaukee & St. Paul Railway.* Chicago: Chicago, Milwaukee and St. Paul Railway, 1911. 24 p.

2742. _____. *The Olympian: electrified over four mountain ranges.* Chicago, The Company, 19--? 14 p.

2742a. _____. *The Olympian: new-equipment, unique roller bearings, electrified 660 miles, unparalleled comfort, service: the Chicago, Milwaukee and St. Paul Railway, to Puget Sound electrified.* Chicago: Poole bros., 1927. 24 p.

2743. _____. *The Olympian: the all-steel train over the new steel rail.* Chicago: Chicago, Milwaukee & Puget Sound Railway Company, ca. 1935. 16 p

2744. _____. *Olympians of the past and the Olympian of the present.* Chicago, Ill., Chicago, Milwaukee & St. Paul Ry., 1927. 24 p.

2745. _____. *100 years of locomotive progress.* Chicago, The Railway, 1950. 1 v.

2746. _____. *Rules and regulations for the government of enginemen and inspectors in electric train service and governing the operation of the Westinghouse electric passenger locomotives class EP-3. Revised ed.* Chicago, Chicago, Milwaukee, St. Paul, and Pacific Railroad Company, 1926. 1 v.

2747. _____. *Safety rules: governing electrification line crews, and signal maintainers when working on electrification poles or wires. Revised.* Chicago, Ill.? Chicago, Milwaukee, St. Paul, and Pacific Railroad Co., 1939. 25 p.

2747a. _____. *Sparks from the Milwaukee Road electrification exhibit: a century of progress, Chicago, may 2-Nov. 1, 1933.* Chicago: Gunthorp-Warren Printing Co., 1933. 1 folded sheet (9 p.)

2748. _____. *Statement regarding proposed discontinuance of Milwaukee Road trains no. 15 and 16, the Olympian Hiawatha between Minneapolis and Seattle-Tacoma.* S.l., Chicago, Milwaukee, St. Paul & Pacific Railroad Co., 1960. 6 p.

2748a. Chicago Plan Commission. *The railway terminal situation.* Chicago: Chicago Plan Commission, 1913. 45 p.

2749. *Chicago: railroad capital of the world.* Milwaukee, WI: Kalmbach Pub. Co., 1948. 64 p.

2750. *Chicago Railroad Fair: official guide book and program for the pageant "Wheels a-rolling."* Chicago, Chicago Railroad Fair, 1948. 16 p.

2751. *The Chicago railway review*. Chicago, s.n. 1868-1879. (Weekly)

2752. *The Chicago railway terminal problem*. New York, Jenkins & McGowan, 1892. 147 p. (Chicago Terminal Commission)

2753. Chicago, Rock Island and Pacific Railway Company. *Arkansas, the land of double crops*. Chicago, Passenger Traffic Department, Rock Island Lines, 1910. 48 p.

2753a. _____. *Economic impact of the Rock Island Railroad abandonment in northwest Kansas*. S.l., s.n., 1980. 150 l.

2754. _____. *The garden of Allah: Arizona, California*. Chicago, Ill., Chicago, Rock Island, and Pacific Railway Co., 1936. 36 p.

2755. _____. *General instructions relative to movement of gold and red ball freight*. Chicago, Ill., The Company, 1930. 25 p.

2756. _____. *General roster of officers, agents, attorneys, surgeons, stations, structures, mileage, connections, clearances, equipment, etc*. Chicago, IL: Chicago, Rock Island & Pacific Railway Company, 1929. 296 p. (*No. 67.*)

2757. _____. The *Gulf Coast of Texas: the winter vegetable garden of America*. Chicago, Passenger Traffic Department, Rock Island-Frisco Lines, 1906. 77 p.

2758. _____. *Hotels and boarding houses in California*. San Francisco, Chicago, Rock Island, and Pacific Railway Company, 1915. 74 p.

2758a. _____. *Industrial directory*/ Chicago? Chicago, Rock Island, and Pacific Railroad Co., 1971. 258 p.

2759. _____. *Instructions governing the use and recording of car seals*/ Chicago, IL: The Company, 1924. 12 p.

2759a. _____. *Merchandise loading schedules, package cars and schedules coordinated with Rock Island Motor Transit Company trucks*/ Chicago: Rock Island Lines, 1951. 32 p.

2760. _____. *New Mexico, the land of sunshine; agricultural and mineral resources, irrigation and horticulture, gold, copper, iron and coal, a national sanitarium, playground of the great Southwest*. Chicago, Passenger Department, Rock Island System, 1904. 55 p.

2761. _____. *100 years of progress, 1852-1952*. Chicago, Ill., Chicago, Rock Island and Pacific Railroad Co., 1952. 31 p.

2762. ____, [*Operating Department timetables: B.R. Drew Collection.*] 11 v. University of Iowa Libraries, Special Collections Department.

2763. _____. *Petroleum and natural gas. What the boys and girls learned about these things during a holiday excursion among the oil and gas wells.* Chicago, Ill., J.M.W. Jones Stat. & Ptg. Co., 1887. 79 p.

2763a. _____. *Railroad employes and their pay : facts that speak for themselves.* S.l., Chicago, Rock Island, and pacific Railway Company, 1921. 8 p.

2764. _____. *Rock Island trains to California; season 1906-07.* By John Sebastian. S.l., Rock Island, Press of Wright & Joys Co., 1906. 24 p.

2765. _____. *Rules and instructions governing the operation and maintenance of electric headlight equipments.* Chicago, IL: Faulkner-Ryan Co., 1919. 71 p.

2766. _____. *Rules and regulations for the government of employees of the Operating Department.* Chicago, Ill., Faulkner-Ryan Co., 1910. 142 p.

2767. _____. *The segregated coal and asphalt lands of the Choctaw and Chickasaw nations in Southeastern Oklahoma: which will be opened for settlement by the Department of the Interior.* Chicago, Ill., The Passenger Traffic Department, Rock Island Lines, 1914. 12 p.

2768. _____. *Suggestions effecting efficiency and economy in car, train, and yard operations.* Chicago, Ill., Rock Island Lines, 1924. 7 p.

2769. Chicago, St. Paul, Minneapolis & Omaha Railway Company. *Corporate history of the Chicago, Saint Paul, Minneapolis and Omaha Railway Company: June 30 1917.* S.l., Chicago, St. Paul, Minneapolis & Omaha Railroad, 1920s. 46 p.

2770. _____. *Descriptive list of locomotive engines.* St. Paul: Chicago, St. Paul, Minneapolis & Omaha Railway Company, 1888. 1 v. (unpaged) 11 x 19 cm.

2771. _____. *Rules and regulations of employes in Operating Department.* St. Paul, H.M. Smyth Print. Co., 1892. 131 p.

2772. *The Chicago subways.* Chicago, Ill., F.J. Riley Print. Co., 1943. 31 p. (Issued by: Chicago. Dep't. of Subways and Superhighways.)

2772a. Chicago Terminal Commission. *The Chicago railway terminal problem* / New York : Jenkins & McGowan, 1892. 147 p.

2773. *Chicago to Iowa City intercity passenger rail service: tier 1 service level environmental assessment.* Chicago: Illinois Department of Transportation; Ames, Iowa, Iowa Department of Transportation, 2009. 1 v. (various pagings)

2774. Chicago Union Station Company. *Chicago Union Station: from this huge passenger terminal trains of four great railroads span the nation.* Chicago: Chicago Union Station Company, 1900s. 12 p.

2775. _____. *New Chicago Union Station passenger facilities: executive summary.* Chicago: Metra, 1988. 26 l.

2776. Chiddix, Jim, MacKinnon Simpson. *Next stop Honolulu: Oahu Railway & Land Company, 1889-1971.* Honolulu, Hawai'i, Sugar Cane Press, 2004. 352 p.

2777. Chih, Kenneth Ching-Kang. *A real time dynamic optimal freight car management simulation of the multiple railroad, multiple commodity temporal spatial network flow problem.* 1986. 270 l. (Thesis, Ph.D., Princeton University.)

2778. Childers, W.W. *Work equipment cars.* Norman, OK: Santa Fe Modelers Organization, 1993. 254 p. (*Santa Fe Railway rolling stock reference series, v. 1*)

2779. Chilson, George L. *Passenger train service: theory of decline and plan for survival.* 1963. 204 l. (Thesis, A.B., Princeton University.)

2780. Chilton, Claudius Lysias, D.M. White. *Argument in favor of Senate bill no. 145 (D.M. White) forbidding running of freight trains on Sunday* / Montgomery, Ala : C.L. Chilton?, 1860s. 8 p.

2781. Chinese Historical Society of Southern California. *Portraits of pride.* Los Angeles, CA: Chinese Historical Society of Southern California, 2004. 17-227 p.

2782. Chinn, Barbara. *The history of lands within the Pecos Division of the Texas and Pacific Reservation.* 1967. 124 l. (Thesis, M.A., University of Texas at El Paso.)

2783. Chintala, Latha S. *Recognition of defects in railroad wheels from patterns in acoustic signatures* / 1984. 103 l. (Thesis, M.S., University of Houston, University Park.)

2784. Chittenden, L.E. *Will Congress preserve the national faith in its dealings with the Pacific Railroad Companies?* / Washington, DC: Gibson Brothers, Printers, 1871. 47, 1 p. Written on behalf of the Central Pacific Railroad Co. Presented to the Judiciary Committee of the Senate.

2785. Chiu, Herman B. *When 1,000 words are worth a picture: how newspapers portrayed the Chinese and Irish who built the first transcontinental railroad/* 2004. 241 l. (Thesis, Ph.D., University of Missouri-Columbia.)

2786. Chlorine Institute. *Recommended practices for handling chlorine tank cars* / Washington, DC: Chlorine Institute, 2001. 44 p. (*Chlorine Institute pamphlet, 66.*)

2787. Choctaw Nation. Chickasaw Nation. *Objections of the Choctaw and Chickasaw Nations to House bills 113, 738, 4763, 5868 and Senate bills 544 and 1280, granting to certain railroad companies the right of way through the Indian Territory.* S.l., s.n., 1886. 6, 2 p.

2788. Choda, Kelly. *Thirty pound rails.* Aurora, CO: Filter Press, 1956. 46 p.

2789. Choros, J., I. Gitlin. *Track component property tests: vol. 1, rail, tie, and fasteners/* Washington, DC: Federal Railroad Administration, Office of Research and Development; Association of American Railroads, Research and Test Department, 1979. 54 p. (*FRA/ORD-79/32.*)

2790. _____, _____. *Track component property tests: vol. II: rail, ties, joint bars and fasteners/ interim report/* Washington, DC: Federal Railroad Administration, Office of Research and Development; Association of American Railroads, Research and Test Department, 1980. 45 p. (*FRA/ORD-80-25.*)

2791. Chow, Felton. *Railroad warehousing service.* Shanghai, Printed by Nee Sing Print. Co., 1931. 4, 194 p. (Thesis, Ph.D., University of Pennsylvania, 1931.)

2792. Chrismer, S.M. *Mechanics-based model to predict ballast-related maintenance timing and costs/* 1994. 229 l. (Thesis, Ph.D., University of Massachusetts at Amherst.)

2793. _____. *Recent developments in predicting ballast life and economics.* Chicago, IL: Association of American Railroads, Technical Center, 1988. 30 l. (*Report, Association of American Railroads, no. R-700.*)

2794. _____. *Track surfacing with conventional tamping and stone injection/* Chicago, IL: Association of American Railroads, Technical Center, 1990. 32 p. (*Report, no. R-719.*)

2795. Christiansen, Dennis L. *An evaluation of the need for intercity rail passenger service in Texas /* 1977. 232 l. (Thesis, Ph.D., Texas A & M University.)

2796. _____. *The history of rail passenger service in Texas, 1820-1970.* College Station, TX: Texas Transportation Institute, Texas A & M University System, 1976. 50 p. (*Passenger service evaluation, technical report, 1*)

2797. Christie, Hugh Kidd. *Car anatomy directory; modern box cars.* Chicago, Railway Educational Press, 1920. 25 p. (Published and distributed by the Brotherhood Railway Carmen of America.)

2798. _____. *The carman's helper.* 3d ed. Chicago, Ill., Trade Educational Bureau of the Brotherhood of Railway Carmen of America, 1920. 230 p. (2d ed.: Chicago, Railway Educational Press, 1920. 279 p.)

2799. _____. *The railway foreman and his job.* Chicago, Ill., American Technical Society, 1947, c1943. 385 p.

2800. _____. *Short cut methods for carmen.* New York, N.Y., Simmons-Boardman Pub. Co., 1924. 188 p.

2801. *A chronological list on the history of Florida railroads.* Washington, DC : Bureau of Railway Economics, Library, 1963. 20 p.

2802. *A chronology of American railroads: including mileage by states and by years.* Washington, DC: Association of American Railroads, 1947.

2803. Church, Robert J. *Cab-forward: the story of Southern Pacific articulateds.* Omaha, NE: Kratville Publications, 1968. 216 p. (Revised ed.: Wilton, CA: Central Valley Railroad Publications, 1982. 310 p.

2804. _____. *The 4300 4-8-2s: the story of Southern Pacific Mt class locomotives.* Wilton, CA: Central Valley Railroad Publications, 1980. 150 p. (Revised ed.: Wilton, CA: Signature Press, 1996. 172 p.)

2805. _____. *Snowbound streamliner: rescuing the 1952 City of San Francisco.* Wilton, CA: Signature Press, 2000. 156 p.

2806. _____. *Southern Pacific Daylight locomotives.* Berkeley and Wilton, CA: Signature Press, 2003. 1 v.

2806a. _____ *Southern Pacific : ten-coupled locomotives* / Berkeley and Wilton, CA: Signature Press, 2013.

2807. _____. *Those Daylight 4-8-4s.* Omaha, NE: Kratville Publications, 1976. 97 p. 29 p. of plates.

2807a. _____, Dick Murdock. *Steam days in Dunsmuir: featuring Dick Murdock's Smoke in the Canyon.* Berkeley and Wilton, CA: Signature Press, 2011. 264 p. (Southern Pacific Railroad, Shasta Division.)

2808. Church, S.H. *Corporate history of the Pennsylvania lines west of Pittsburgh.* Baltimore, Md., Friedenwald Co., 1898-1927. 15 v. in 16.

2809. *Churches on wheels: or, chapel-car missions.* Philadelphia, PA: American Baptist Publication Society, 1900-1910? 112 p.

2810. Churchman, John Horace. *Federal regulation of railroad rates, 1880-1898.* 1976. 640 l. (Thesis, Ph.D., University of Wisconsin.)

2811. Churella, Albert J. *Corporate response to technological change: dieselization and the American railway locomotive industry during the twentieth century.* 1994. 2 v.; 552 l. (Thesis, Ph.D., Ohio State University.)

2812. _____. *From steam to diesel: managerial customs and organizational capabilities in the twentieth-century American locomotive industry.* Princeton, NJ: Princeton University Press, 1998. 215 p.

2812a. _____ *The Pennsylvania Railroad.* Philadelphia: University of Pennsylvania Press, 2013- . v. 1. Building an empire, 1846-1917.

2813._____. *Success that didn't last: the decline and fall of the American Locomotive Company in the diesel locomotive industry.* Schenectady, NY: Schenectady Heritage Area, 2001. 48 p.

2814. Cincinnati Frog and Switch Company. *The Cincinnati Frog & Switch Co., manufacturers of frogs, switches, crossing, switch stands, rail braces, curves: and all kinds of special work required for track equipment of steam and electric railroads, mines and mills.* Cincinnati, OH: The Cincinnati Frog & Switch Company, n.d. 131 p. *(Catalogue D-4.)*

2815. Cincinnati Historical Society. *Cincinnati Union Terminal and the artistry of Winold Reiss.* Cincinnati, OH: Cincinnati Historical Society, 1993. 96 p. *(Queen City heritage, v. 51, no. 2-3.)*

2816. _____, Greater Cincinnati Chamber of Commerce. *The Cincinnati Union Terminal: pictorial history: originally published to commemorate the dedication of Cincinnati Union Terminal, March 31, 1933.* Cincinnati, OH: Cincinnati Historical Society, 1987, 1933. 87 p.

2816a. Cincinnati Milling Machine Company. *Locomotive repairs; how Cincinnati millers reduce time on replacement parts* / Cincinnati: The Cincinnati Milling Machine Co., 1921. 32 p.

2817. Cincinnati (Ohio). City Planning Commission. *A plan for facilitating rail freight movements in the Cincinnati area* / Cincinnati, s.n., 1947. 23 p.

2817a. [The Cincinnati Union Terminal Company : 1907-1951. Corporate records.] 5 v. Location: The Chesapeake & Ohio Historical Society, Inc.

2818.*Cincinnati Union Terminal dedication, 1933.* Cincinnati, Ohio, s.n., 1933? 88 p.

2819. *Circular.* Pittsburgh, PA: Westinghouse Electric & Manufacturing Company, 1895-1899. Irregular. No. 1, Sept. 1895 – no. 62, Jan. 1899 also carry title "Catalogue". No. 91-no. 229; the latter later subsequently split off as a separate publication. Each number has a distinctive title. Some issues prepared by various department of the Westinghouse Electric & Manufacturing Company.

2819a. Citizens' Transportation Committee (Nashville, Tenn.) *The Louisville and Nashville Railroad monopoly : its bold defiance of the law and the people of Nashville and in middle Tennessee, the wrong and the remedy.* Nashville, The Committee, 1902. 48 p.

2820. Citizens Union (New York, N.Y.) *Memorandum concerning the proposed relocation of the New York Central Railroad tracks upon the west side of Manhattan Island.* New York : 1916. 16 p. Submitted to the Board of Estimate and Apportionment.

2821. City Club of Chicago. *The railway terminal problem of Chicago* / Chicago : City

Club of Chicago, 1913. 98 p.

2822. *City icons*. London, Phaidon, 1999. 1 v. (Includes: Warren and Wetmore: *Grand Central Terminal, New York City, 1903-13.)*

2823. *The city of New York with the New York Central Railroad Company. Draft form of agreement. Submitted for consideration to the Board of Estimate and Apportionment under the resolution adopted April 6th, 1916.* New York? s.n., 1917. 70 p. West Side Improvement plans.

2824.Civic League of St. Louis. *Report of the Committee on Railroad Electrification, June, 1911.* St. Louis, Civic League of St. Louis, 1911. 14 p.

2825. Claeys, Thomas E., Jr. *Construction of the Pennsylvania Railroad's New York tunnel extension.* 2003. 103 l. (Thesis, M.A., East Stroudsburg University.)

2826. Clamp, Cathy L., C.T. Adams. *Road to riches: the great railroad race to Aspen.* Montrose, CO: Western Reflections Publishing Co., 2003. 180 p. (Fiction)

2827. Clapp, Henry P., S.C. Lore. *High-performance steels in modern railroad freight and passenger-car construction* / New York : American Society of Mechanical Engineers, 1963. 16 p. (*ASME. Paper no. 63-WA-221.*)

2828. Clark, Agnew Hilsman, James F. Clark. *Fifty-one years,1925-1976: a history of early south Georgia railroading.* Fayetteville, GA: J.F. Clark, 1993. 296 p.

2829. Clark, Arthur B. *Review of west span wrought iron railroad bridge across the Delaware River at Portland, Pa.* 1891. 38 l. (Thesis, Lafayette College, Department of Civil Engineering.)

2830. Clark, Charles Hugh. *The railroad safety movement in the United States: origins and development, 1869 to 1893.* 1966. 387 l. (Thesis, Ph.D., University of Illinois.)

2830a. Clark, Charles M., James Herron Westbay. *Fire box design and its relation to boiler performance* / 1917. 43 l. (Thesis, B.S., University of Illinois.)

2831. Clark, David F. *Railroads of Tioga County.* 1989. 74 l. (Thesis, M.Ed., Mansfield University.) (Tioga County, Pennsylvania.)

2832. Clark, D.K. *Railway locomotives: their progress, technical construction and performance, with recent practice in England and America.* Glasgow, Blackie, 1860. 2 v.

2833. _____, Zerah Colburn. *Recent practice in the locomotive engine; being a supplement to "Railway machinery" comprising the latest English improvements, and a treatise on the locomotive engines of the United States.* Glasgow, Blackie and Son, 1860.84 p. 42 l. of plates.

2834. Clark, Edgar E., P.H. Morrisey. *Rates of pay and regulations governing employes in train and yard service on the principal railroads of the United States, Canada and Mexico*/ Cedar Rapids, Iowa: Metcalf, 1900. 375, 3 p.

2835. Clark, Frank D. *Road test of a heavy draft passenger locomotive on the Delaware, Lackawanna & Western Railroad, from Scranton, Pa. to Binghamton, N.Y., and return, May 1900.* 1902. 116, 7 l. 16 leaves of plates. (Thesis, M.E., Cornell University.)

2836. Clark, Frederick C. *State railroad commissions, and how they may be made effective.* Baltimore: American Economic Association, 1891. 110 p. (*Publications of the Am. Econ. Assoc., vol. 6, no. 6.*)

2837. Clark, Ira G. *Then came the railroads; the century from steam to diesel in the Southwest.* Norman, University of Oklahoma Press, 1958. 336 p.

2838. Clark, George Thomas. *Leland Stanford, war governor of California, railroad builder and founder of Stanford University.* Stanford University, CA: Stanford University Press; London, H. Milford, Oxford University Press, 1931. 491 p.

2839. Clark, James G. *Specifications for iron and steel railroad bridges prior to 1905.* Urbana, IL: ESCA Consultants, 1984. 105 l

2840. Clark, John Elwood. *Railroads in the Civil War: the impact of management on victory and defeat.* Baton Rouge, LA: Louisiana State University Press, 2008, 2001. 275 p.

2841. _____. *"To strain every energy": Civil War railroads: a comparison of Union and Confederate war management.* 1997. 353 l. (Thesis, Ph.D., Princeton University.)

2842. Clark, John Maurice. *Standards of reasonableness in local freight discriminations*/ New York, NY: Columbia University Press, 1910. 155 p. (*Studies in history, economics and public law, v. 37, no. 1.*)

2843. Clark, Malcom C. *The birth of an enterprise: Baldwin locomotive, 1831-1842.* S.l., s.n., 197-? 40 l.

2844. Clark, Malcolm Cameron. *The first quarter-century of the Richmond & Danville Railroad, 1847-1871* / 1959. 115 l. (Thesis, M.A., George Washington University.)

2845. Clark, Thomas Dionysius. *The beginning of the L & N; the development of the Louisville and Nashville Railroad and its Memphis branches from 1836 to 1860.* Louisville, Ky., Standard Printing Co., 1933. 107 p.

2846. _____. *A pioneer Southern railroad from New Orleans to Cairo.* Chapel Hill, NC: University of North Carolina Press, 1936. 171 p. (IC)

2847. Clark, William Horace. *Railroads and rivers; the story of inland transportation.* Boston, L.C. Page & Co., 1939. 334 p.

2848. Clark, William L. *George B. Robert's administration of the Pennsylvania Railroad* / 1936. 1 v. (Thesis, A.B., Honors, Harvard University.)

2849. Clarke, Alan R. *The West Virginia and Pittsburgh Railroad: the B & O's road to the hardwoods.* Charleston, SC: Quarrier Press, 2008. 224 p.

2850._____. *The West Virginia Central and Pittsburgh Railway: a Western Maryland predecessor.* Lynchburg, VA: TLC Pub., 2003. 176 p.

2851._____. *West Virginia's Coal & Coke Railway: a B & O predecessor.* Lynchburg, VA: TLC Pub., 2001. 170 p.

2852. Clarke, Allen W. *A.C.F. railroad passenger cars, 1946 models.* S.l., s.n., 1945. 64 p. (American Society of Mechanical Engineers.)

2853. Clarke, David Bruce. *An examination of railroad capacity and its implication for rail-highway intermodal transportation* / 1995. 173 l. (Thesis, Ph.D., University of Tennessee, Knoxville.)

2853a. Clarke, David D. *Narratives of a surveyor and engineer in the pacific Northwest, 1864-1920* / Edited by jerry C. Olson. Vancouver, WA: The Author, 1995. 224 p. (Northern Pacific Railroad Company.)

2854. Clarke, Herman D., Clark Kidder. *Orphan trains & their precious cargo: the life's work of Rev. H.D. Clarke*/ Bowie, MD: Heritage Books, 2001. 368 p.

2855. Clarke, Thomas Curtis, and others. *The American railway, its construction, development, management, and appliances.* Introduction by Thomas M. Cooley. New York, C. Scribner's Sons, 1897. 456 p. Reprinted from Scribner's magazine. Reprint: New York, B. Blom, 1972; New York, Arno Press, 1976; Secaucus, NJ: Castle, 1988.)

2856. *Class I freight line-haul railroads selected earnings data.* Washington, D.C., Interstate Commerce Commission; Bureau of Accounts, 1983. 1 v.444 (Quarterly) (< *Class I line-haul railroads selected earnings data*; > *Class I freight railroads selected earnings data.*)

2857. *Class I freight railroads selected earnings data.* Washington, D.C., Interstate Commerce Commission; Bureau of Accounts, 1983- . Quarterly. (From Nov. 2004, issued as computer file: http://www.stb.dot.gov/econdata.nsf

2858. *Class I line-haul railroads selected earnings data.* Washington, DC: Interstate Commerce Commission, Bureau of Accounts, 1900s-1982. (> *Class I freight line-haul railroads selected earnings data.*)

2859. *Class I railroads: mileage by states.* Washington, D.C., Association of American Railroads; Economics and Finance Department, 1986-   Annual. (< *Railroad mileage by states*.)

2860. *Classic trains*. Waukesha, WI: Kalmbach Pub. Co., 2000-(Quarterly)

2861. *Classified summary, by principal causes and commodities, of freight loss and damage expenditures*. Chicago?: American Railway Association, Freight Claim Division, 1892-1934. Annual. (> Association of American Railroads. Freight Claim Division. *Freight loss and damage*.)

2862. Clause, Shirley, D.C. Royce. *Steel-car repairs; car-shop millwork*. Scranton, Penn., International Textbook Co., 1932. 61, 29, 35, 58 p..

2863. Clayburn, Barbara B. *Prairie stationmaster: the story of one man's railroading career in Nebraska, 1917-1963*. Detroit, Harlo, 1979. 128 p. (CB&Q)

2864. Claycomb, William B. *On the mainlines: railroading in Sedalia, Missouri*. Sedalia, MO: Sedalia Heritage Foundation, 2003. 72 p.

2865. Clayton, P., Roger King Steele. *Wear processes at the wheel/rail interface* / Chicago : Association of American Railroads, Technical Center, 1987. 48 l. (*Report. Association of American Railroads, no. R-613*.)

2866. Clemensen, A. Berle. *Delaware, Lackawanna and Western Railroad Line, Scranton to Slateford Junction, Pennsylvania*. Washington, D.C.? U.S. Department of the Interior, National Park Service, 1991. 114 p.

2867. _____. *Historic resource study: Steamtown National Historic Site, Pennsylvania*. Denver, CO? National Park Service, Denver Service Center, 1988. 149 p.

2867a. Clemons, Marvin, Lyle Key. *Birmingham rails* /Birmingham, AL: Red Mountain Press, 2007. 271 p.

2868. Clerke, Don. *Troop sleepers: hated by a generation of Americans*/ Reading, Mass, Boston & Maine RR Historical Society, 1981. 8 p.

2868a. Cleveland and Pittsburgh Railroad. *Rules and regulations for the running of trains ... to take effect Monday, November 14, 1870*. Wellsville, OH: Printed at the "Wellsville Union office," 1870. 136 p.

2869. Cleveland, Columbus, Cincinnati, and Indianapolis Railway Company; Indianapolis and St. Louis Railway. *Rules and regulations for the running of trains on the C.C.C. & I Ry., and I. & St. l. Ry., and for the guidance of the officers and employees therein referred to*. Cleveland, O., J.B. Savage, printer, 1883. 178 p. "To take effect Monday, February 12, 1883, at 6 o'clock, a.m. Superseding editions of May 29th, 1879, and Jan 2nd, 1882.

2870. Cleveland, Frederick Albert, Fred Wilbur Powell. *Railroad finance*/ New York, NY: D. Appleton and Co., 1912. 462 p.

2871. _____, _____. *Railroad promotion and capitalization in the United States.* New York, Longmans, Green, and Co., 1909. 368 p. (Reprint: New York, Johnson Reprint Corp., 1966. 368 p.)

2871a. Cleveland, Harold Irwin. *A thrilling night's ride on the North-Western Fast Mail /* Chicago : Passenger Department, Chicago and North-Western Railway Co., 1899. 14 p.

2872. Cleveland Machine & Manufacturing Company. *Electric locomotives and industrial cars/* Cleveland, OH: The Company, 1920-1929? 20 p.

2873. Cleveland Union Terminals Company. *The Union Station: a description of the new passenger facilities and surrounding improvements.* Cleveland, OH: Cleveland Union Terminals Company; Cleveland Terminals Building Company, 1930. 30 p.

2873a. Cliburn, William B. *The essentials of railway and commercial telegraphy /* 2nd ed. Newnan, GA: William B. Cliburn, 1926. 238 p.

2874. Clifford, Howard. *Alaska/Yukon railroads: an illustrated history.* Arlington, WA: Oso Pub., 1999. 248 p. (Originally published as Rails north. Seattle, Superior Pub. Co., 1982.)

2875. _____. *Doing the White Pass: the story of the White Pass & Yukon Route and the Klondike gold rush.* Seattle, WA: Sourdough Enterprises, 1983. 88 p.

2876. _____. *Rails north: the railroads of Alaska and the Yukon.* Seattle, WA: Superior Pub. Co., 1981. 200 p.

2877. Climax Manufacturing Company. *The Climax patent geared locomotive. Illustrated catalog.* Cossayuna, N.Y., Builder's Compendium, 1894?1968. 48 p.

2878. _____. *The Climax patent geared locomotives: catalogue "L."* Susquehanna, PA: Starrucca Valley Publications, 1963. 31 p. (Reprint of 1924 edition.)

2879. *The Clinchfield link.* Erwin, TN: Clinchfield Railroad, 1957-1964. Monthly. (< *Clinchfield R.R. Co. news letter.*) Editor: Mrs. Harry Baughman.

2880. *Clinchfield R.R. Co. new letter.* Erwin, TN: Clinchfield Railroad, 1954-1956. Monthly. 3 v. Other title: *Clinchfield Railroad Co. news letter.* Editor: Mrs. Harry Baughman.

2881. Cline, Melinda K. *The impact of information technology investment on productivity improvements in the American railroad industry between, 1986 and 1995.* 2000. 266 l. (Thesis, Ph.D., Florida State University.)

2882. Cline, Richard E. *The influence of the railroads upon economic development in the lower Wabash Valley, 1840-1890.* 1996. 177 l. (Thesis, M.A., Indiana State University.)

2883. Cline, Wayne. *Alabama railroads.* Tuscaloosa, University of Alabama Press, 1997. 314 p.

2883a. Clingman, T. L. *Speech of T.L. Clingman, of North Carolina, on duties on railroad iron and commercial restrictions. Delivered in the House of Representatives, August 21, 1852.* Washington, DC: Towers, printers, 1852. 16 p.

2883a. Clippinger, John Albert. *Sam Johnson: the experience and observations of a railroad telegraph operator.* New York: W.J. Johnston, 1878. 176 (Fiction)

2884. Clock, Paul Michael. *The saga of Pacific Railway & Navigation Co.: Punk Rotten & Nasty.* Portland, OR: Corbett Press, 2000. 127 p.

2885. Clodfelter, Frank. *Fogg and steam: a regional look at steam in North America.* Paintings by Howard Fogg; text by Frank Clodfelter, with contributions by Howard Fogg and others. Boulder, CO: Pruett Publishing Company, 1978. 154 p.

2886. Clutz, J. J. *Unit trains for the future.* S.l., Pennsylvania Railroad Company, 1965. 19 l. (Research Department, PRR, April 6, 1965.)

2887. *Coal and coal trade journal.* New York, Brattleboro, VT: F.E. Saward, 1869-1937. Frequency varies.

2888. *Coal distribution statistics.* Washington, DC: National Coal Association, 1988-1989. Annual. (< *Coal traffic*)

2889. *Coal on the move: via the Virginian Railway.* S.l., Norfolk & Western Historical Society, 1995. 1 v. (unpaged)

2890. *Coal production & transportation: annual conference.* San Francisco: PLM, 1900s-

2891. *Coal tariff report: Unit train/annual volume shipments by originating railroad.* Arlington, VA: Pasha Publications, 1980s-   Quarterly (< *Coal tariff report. Unit train volume shipments by originating carrier.*)

2892. *Coal traffic /* Washington, DC: National Coal Association, 1981-1987. Annual. (< *Coal traffic annual; > Coal distribution statistics; Coal transportation statistics.*)

2893. *Coal traffic annual.* Washington, DC: National Coal Association, 1968-1979. Annual. (> *Coal traffic.*)

2894. *Coal train assessment /* Denver: URS Company; Four Corners Regional Commission, 1976. 2 v.

2895. *Coal transportation statistics.* Washington, DC: National Coal Association, 1988-Annual. (< *Coal traffic.*)

2896. Coates, Wes. *Electric trains to Reading Terminal.* Flanders, NJ: Railroad Avenue Enterprises, 1990. 112 p.

2897. _____. *50th anniversary, 1931-1981: suburban electrification, Delaware, Lackawanna & Western R.R.* Clark, NY: Jersey Central Chapter, National Railway Historical Society, 1981. 32 p.

2897a. Coburn, James Minton. *A model (formula) for deriving a hazard index of rail—highway grade crossings.* 1969. 162 l. (Thesis, Ed. D., Texas A & M university.)

2898. Coccia, Stefano. *Ultrasonic guided waves for structural health monitoring and application to rail inspection prototype for the Federal Railroad Administration.* 281 p. (Thesis, Ph.D., University of California, San Diego.)

2899. Cochran, John Stephens. *Henry Villard and Oregon's transportation development, 1863-1881.* 1961. 2 v. (Thesis, Ph.D., Harvard University.)

2900. Cochran, Thomas Childs. *Railroad leaders, 1845-1890.* New York, N.Y., Russell & Russell, 1966, c1953. 564 p. (Harvard University. Research Center in Entrepreneurial History.)

2901. Cochrane, John. *A description of Cochrane's binary locomotive engine and a defense of its principles, in reply to Ross Winans, Esq.: and a review of the Winan's patent for the use of driving wheels of locomotives with chilled cast iron flanges, also, an exposition of the principles of the cone of the wheel and centrifugal force, in connection with the passage of locomotives through railway curves/* Baltimore, Printed by James Young, 1854. 36 p.

2902. Cockle, George R. *CA-11 cabooses.* Muncie, IN: Overland Models, Inc., 1979. 40 p.

2903. _____. *Giants of the West: a pictorial presentation of Union Pacific's super-powered locomotives.* Muncie, IN: Overland Models, Inc., 1981. 208 p.

2904. _____ *Union Pacific, 1977-1980.* Muncie, IN: Overland Models, Inc., 1980. 208 p.

2905. _____. *Union Pacific's Centennials in action.* Muncie, IN: Overland Models, Inc., 1980. 88 p.

2906. _____, Paul K. Withers, Don Strack. *Union Pacific, 1990.* Halifax, PA: Withers Publishing, 1991. 224 p.

2907. *Code for testing air operated auxiliary devices on locomotives.* New York: Air Brake Association, 1920. 31 p.

2908. *Code of rules governing the condition of, and repairs to, freight and passenger cars for the interchange of traffic.* New York : American Railway Association, Mechanical Division, 1919-1933. Annual.

2909. Codoni, Fred, Paul C. Trimble. *Northwestern Pacific Railroad.* Charleston, SC: Arcadia, 2006. 143 p.

2910. Coffin, Charles Carleton. *The great commercial prize; addressed to every American who values the prosperity of his country/* Boston, A. Williams & Co., 1858. 23 p. (Pacific Railroads)

2911. Cogburn, Lowell T. *Stub sill tank car research project results of a 15,000-mile over-the-road test.* Washington, DC: Federal Railroad Administration, Office of Research and Development, 1995. 170 p. (FRA/ORD/95-11.)

2911a. Coghlan, Byron Kemp. *Design of a gravity railroad switching yard /* 1908. 1, 12, l. (B,S., University of Illinois.)

2912. Cohen, Norm. *Long steel rail: the railroad in American folksong.* Urbana, University of Illinois Press, 1981. 710 p. (2d ed. 2000. 710 p.)

2913. Cohen, Roberta D., Malcolm O. Laughlin, Peat,. Marwick, Mitchell & Co., STV, Inc; Neal Montanus, Inc., *Institutional alternatives for the Penn Station complex, New York City.* Washington, D.C., Federal Railroad Administration; 1975. 1 v. (various foliations) (*DOT-FR-56003.*)

2914. Cohen, Ronald D., Stephen G. McShane. *Moonlight in Duneland: the illustrated story of the Chicago, South Shore and South Bend Railroad.* Bloomington, IN: Indiana University Press, 1998. 139 p.

2915. Cohen, Stan. *Rails across the tundra: a historical album of the Alaska Railroad.* Missoula, MT: Pictorial Histories Pub. Co., 1984. 144 p.

2916. _____. *The White Pass and Yukon Route: a pictorial history.* Missoula, MT: Pictorial Histories Pub. Co., 1980. 104 p.(Revised ed: Missoula, MT: Pictorial histories Pub. Co., 1990. 120 p..)

2917. Cohen, William M. *Lettering guide for early Colorado narrow gauge freight cars.* Denver? Rocky Mountain Region of the National Model Railroad Association, 1970. 95 p.

2918. Cohn, Robert. *The great railroad strike of 1877 : an Ohio perspective /* Gambier, OH: s.n., 1978. 72, 3 l. (Honors thesis, Kenyon.)

2918a. Coiled Spring Fence Co. *Farm, railroad and poultry : coiled spring fencing /* Winchester, IN: The Company, 1902. 40 p.

2919. Colburn, Zerah. *The locomotive engine, including a description of its structure, rules for estimating its capabilities and practical observation on its construction and management.* Boston, Redding, 1851. 120 p. (Later eds.: Philadelphia, H.C. Baird, 1854. 187 p.; Philadelphia, H.C. Baird, 1873: 187 p.

2920. _____. *The throttle lever: to be pulled out, kept open, and always within reach.* New York, NY: John F. Trow, printer, 1856. 41, 14 p.

2921. _____, Charles Manby, James Forrest. *American iron bridges: abstract of the discussion upon a paper/* New York, Van Nostrand, 1867. 15 p.

2922. _____, James Forrest. *American locomotives and rolling stock.* London, W. Clowes and Sons, 1869. 83 p.

2923. _____, Alexander Lyman Holley, Julies Bien. *The permanent way and coal-burning locomotive boilers of European railways; with a comparison of the working economy of European and American lines, and the principles upon which improvement must proceed.* New York, Holley & Colburn, 1858. 168 p.

2924. _____, Daniel Kinnear Clark. *Locomotive engineering, and the mechanism of railways: a treatise on the principles and construction of the locomotive engine, railway carriages, and railway plant...illustrated by sixty-four large engravings and two hundred and forty woodcuts.* New York, John Wiley, 1864. 2 v.

2925. *Colburn's railroad advocate.* New York, Zarah Colburn, 1855-1856. Weekly. (>*Holley's railroad advocate.*)

2926. Cole, Alton Bryant. *A biography of a railroad: the Dummy Line of Old Orchard Beach.* 1969. 85 l. (Thesis, M.A., University of Maine.)

2927. Cole, E.C. *Study of highway-railroad grade separation priority criteria/* San Francisco, CA: California Public Utilities Commission, Transportation Division, Operations and Passenger Branch, Traffic Engineering Section, 1974. 3 l.

2928. _____, William R. Schulte, William H. White. *The effectiveness of automatic protection in reducing accident frequency and severity at public grade crossings in California: a study of 1,552 public grade crossing in California where automatic protection was installed between January 1, 1960 and December 31, 1970, inclusive /* San Francisco: California Public Utilities Commission, Transportation Division, 1973. 94 p.

2929. Cole, Francis Alonzo. *Locomotives of the Chicago & North Western Ry.* Boston, Mass., Railway and Locomotive Historical Society, Inc., Baker Library, Harvard Business School, 1938. 75 p. (*Supplement*: Boston : Railway and Locomotive Historical Society, 1948. 23 p.

2929a. Cole, W. R. *Railroad valuation/* Louisville, KY? Louisville and Nashville Railroad Company? 1930. 21 p.

2930. Cole, Wayne A. *Ghost rails VIII, the Northern sub.* Beaver Falls, PA: ColeBooks,

2011. 312 p. (Baltimore and Ohio Railroad)

2930a. _____. *Ghost rails. V, The PRR Butler Branch and Winfield Railroad* / Darlington, PA: ColeBooks, 2008. 192 p.

2931. _____. *Ghost rails. IV, Industrial shortlines* / Darlington, PA: ColeBooks, 2008. 152 p.

2931a. _____. *Ghost rails, IX, state line legends* / Beaver Falls, PA: ColeBooks, 2012. 232 p. (P&LE Mahoning State line; PY&A Bessemer branch.)

2932. _____. *Ghost rails, 1850-1980. Volume 1: Abandoned railroads, their industries, last runs, eastern Ohio and western Pennsylvania.* Darlington, PA: ColeBooks, 2005. 144 p. v. 4; Industrial shortlines.

2932a. _____. *Ghost rails, X, iron phantoms* / Beaver Falls, PA: ColeBooks, 2013. 336 p. (Jones & Laughlin Steel Corp; Aliquippa and Southern Railroad Co.)

2933. _____. *Rails of dreams: the Youngstown and Southern Railway, the Pittsburgh, Lisbon and Western Railroad, the Pittsburgh Coal Company's private railroad— the Smith Ferry Branch.* Darlington, PA: Wayne A. Cole, 2003. 272 p.

2934. Coleman, Alan. *Railroads of North Carolina*/ Charleston, SC: Arcadia, 2008. 127 p.

2935. Coleman, David M. *Use of geogrids in railroad track: a literature review and synopsis*/ Vicksburg, Miss: U.S. Army Engineer Waterways Experiment Station, 1990. 29, 3 p. (*Miscellaneous paper, GL-90-4.*)

2936. Coleman, Edgard Pierce. *Steel rails and territorial tales: forty months building the Oregon Short Line Railroad through Idaho: a memoir*/ Edited by Philip Sinclair Nicholson; notes and introduction by Merle Wells.. Boise, ID: Limberlost Press, 1994. 108 p.

2937. Coleman, Elizabeth Dabney. *The story of the Virginia Central Railroad, 1850-1860.* 1957. 294 l. (Thesis, Ph.D., University of Virginia.)

2938 Coleman, George L., Robert L. Grandt. *Motive power of the Colorado & Southern.* Oakland, CA: R. Robb, 1986. 224 p.

2939. Coleman, Gilbert Robey. *A model of railroad regulation* / 1982. 113 l. (Thesis, Ph.D., Stanford University.)

2940. Coleman, Lyman, William H. Sayre, Jr. *Guide-book of the Lehigh Valley Railroad and its several branches and connections: with an account, descriptive and historical, of the places along their route: including also a history of the Company from its first organization, and interesting facts concerning the origin and growth of the coal and iron trade in the Lehigh and Wyoming regions*/ Philadelphia, PA: J.B. Lippincott, 1872. 175p.

2941. Coleman, Robert, Karl Knoblauch. *Financial aspects of coal transportation by rail: final report.* Washington, DC: Department of Transportation, Office of the Assistant Secretary for Policy and International Affairs, 1980, 1979. 199 p. Prepared by Input Output Computer Services, Inc.

2942. [A collection of printed and manuscript material pertaining to the New York Central Railroad Company's plans to redevelop the Hudson River waterfront on New York's Upper West Side and Riverside Park, with some other materials]. 1914-1920. 2 boxes (0.7 linear feet) Donor: Douglas Mathewson, Bronx Borough President, 1914-1918. Location: New York Historical Society.

2943. [A collection of printed material pertaining to the rehabilitation of the Hudson River waterfront on New York's Upper West Side and Riverside Park, involving the New York Central Railroad Company and its tracks]. 1916-1917. 10 pieces. Location: New York Historical Society.

2943. Collias, Joe G. *Frisco power: locomotives and trains of the St. Louis-San Francisco Railway, 1903-1953.* Crestwood, MO: MM Books, 1984. 304 p. (2d ed. Springfield, MO: Frisco Railroad Museum, 1997.)

2944. _____. *The last of steam; a billowing pictorial pageant of the waning years of steam railroading in the United States.* Berkeley, CA: Howell-North, 1960. 269 p. (Reprint: Forest Park, IL: Heimburger House Pub. Co., 1994?. 269 p.)

2945. _____. *The Missouri Pacific lines in color.* Crestwood, MO: M M Books, 1993. 142 p.

2946. _____. *Mopac power: Missouri Pacific Lines locomotives and trains, 1905-1955.* San Diego, CA: Howell-North Books, 1980. 351 p.

2947. _____. *The search for steam; a cavalcade of smoky action in steam by the greatest railroad photographers.* Berkeley, CA: Howell-North Books, 1972. 360 p. (Reprint: Forest Park, IL: Heimburger House Pub. Co., 1994? 360 p.)

2948. _____. *The Texas & Pacific Railway: super-power to streamliners, 1925-1975.* Crestwood, MO: M M Books, 1989. 159 p.

2949. _____, Raymond B. George, Jr. *Katy power: locomotives and trains of the Missouri-Kansas-Texas Railroad, 1912-1985.* Crestwood, MO: M M Books, 1986. 268 p.

2950. Collingwood, George Elmer. *Questions and answers based upon the standard code of train rules for single track, for use in the examination of trainmen.* 6th ed. Toledo, OH: Train Dispatchers' Bulletin, 1907. 127 p.

2950a. _____. *Train rule examinations made easy; a complete treatise for train rule instructors, superintendents, trainmasters, conductors, enginemen, brakemen, switchmen,*

train dispatchers, operators and others. New York, The Norman
W. Henley Pub. Co., 1911. 234 p.

2951. _____. *Stoker, superheaters, headlights, train rules.* Scranton, Pa., International
Textbook, 1928. 395 p.

2951a. Collins, Bernard I., Chester H. Bean. *Design of a single track through pin
connected railroad bridge of the Pratt type* / 1908. 34 l. (Thesis, B.S., University
of Maine.)

2952. Collins, Darrell L. *The Jones-Imboden raid: the Confederate attempt to destroy
the Baltimore & Ohio Railroad and retake West Virginia* / Jefferson, NC: McFarland
& Co., 2007. 217 p.

2953. Collins, Frederick Burtrumn. *Charleston and the railroads: a geographic study
of a South Atlantic port and its strategies for developing a railroad system, 1820-1860.*
1977. 128 l. (Thesis, M.S., University of South Carolina.)

2954. Collins, Florence Emily. *The history of the Wisconsin Central Railroad.* 1920. 32 l.
(Thesis, B.A., University of Wisconsin.)

2954a. Collins, Marilyn Harris. *Rogers: the town the Frisco built.* Charleston, SC:
Arcadia Pub., 2002. 160 p. (Rogers, Arkansas)

2955. Collins, Robert. *Arkansas Valley Interurban.* David City, NE: South Platte Press,
1999. 60 p.

2956. _____. *The border tier road: reflection of an industry.* David City, NE: South
Platte Press, 2003. 48 p. (BNSF, Kansas City-Baxter Springs, KS)

2957. _____. *Ghost railroads of Kansas.* David City, NE: South Platte Press, 1997.
80 p. (2d ed.: 1998. 80 p.)

2958. _____. *Kansas Pacific: an illustrated history.* David City, NE: South Platte Press,
1998. 60 p.

2959. _____. *Kansas railroad attractions.* David City, NE: South Platte Press, 2004.
44 p.

2960. _____. *Kansas train tales: a collection of railroad history.* Andover, KS: Create
Space, 2009. 130 p.

2961. _____. *The race to Indian Territory: three railroads, their struggle, and their
ultimate fate.* Andover, KS: Robert Collins, 2005. 72 p.

2962. _____. *A railfan's guide to Kansas attractions.* David City, NE: South Platte
Press, 1996. 56 p.

2962a. Collins, Ryan Michael, John McGlinchey. *Irish gandy dancer: a tale of building the Transcontinental Railroad*. Charleston, SC: CreateSpace, 2011. 174 p.

2963. *The Collis P. Huntington papers, 1856-1901; a guide to the microfilm edition*. Sanford, NC: Microfilming Corp of America, 1979. 56 p.

2964. *Collisions, derailments, and other accidents resulting in injury to persons, equipment, or roadbed, arising from operation of steam railways used in interstate commerce*. Washington: U.S. G.P.O., 1910-1932. Quarterly.

2965. Collman, Charles Albert. *How Wall Street "milked" one railroad: the story of the "Katy" and the millions its investors lost* / S.l., Dearborn Independent, 1922. 10 14, p. Article from: Dearborn Independent, 11 Feb. 1922.

2966. Collman, Russ, Dell A. McCoy. *Over the bridges: Ridgway to Telluride*. Denver, CO: Sundance Publications, 1990. 416 p.(*The R.G.S. story, v. 1.*)

2967. _____, _____. *Telluride, Pandora and the mines above*. Denver, CO: Sundance Publications, 1991. 496 p. (*The R.G.S. story, v. 2.*)

2968. _____, _____. Steven J. Myers. *Trails among the Columbine: a Colorado high country anthology*. Denver, CO: Sundance Publications, 1994. 220 p.

2969. _____, _____, William A. Graves. *Over the bridges: Ophir Loop to Rico*. Denver, CO: Sundance Publications, 1994. 496 p. (*The R.G.S. story, v. 4.*)

2970. _____, _____, _____. *The R.G.S. story: Rio Grande Southern*. Denver, CO: Sundance Books, 1990-   v. 1-6, 8-12>

2971. _____, _____, _____. *Over the bridges: Vance Junction to Ophir*. Denver, CO: Sundance Publications, 1993. 496 p. (*The R.G.S. story, v. 3.*)

2972. _____, Klaas Gunnink. *Colorado railroad structures: from the heart of narrow-gauge country*. Littleton, CO: Great Divide Enterprises, Publications Division, 1987-

2973. Colorado and Southern Railway. *The Colorado & Southern Railway Co. list of bridges, trestles & culverts*. Northern Division. Denver, Chief Engineer's Office, 1923. 93 p.

2974. _____. *The Colorado & Southern Railway Co. list of bridges, trestles & culverts*. South Park Division. Denver, Chief Engineer's Office, 1923. 55 p.

2975. _____. *The standard code of train rules, block signal and interlocking rules*. Chicago, Chicago, Burlington & Quincy Railroad Co., 1921. 177 p. ("Issued in accordance with rules adopted by the American Railway Association, November 17, 1915.")

2976. *Colorado rail bibliography* / Compiled by Robert J. Schoppe. Fairplay, CO : RJS Pub., 2003. 522 p.

2977. Colorado State Historical Society. *Directory of railroad properties in the Colorado state register of historic properties.* 3rd ed. Denver, CO: Office of Archaeology and Historic Preservation; Colorado Historical Society, 2003.

2978. _____. *Railroad and affiliated enterprises: an inventory of the railroad collections in the Stephen H. Hart Library of the Colorado Historical Society.* Denver, CO: Colorado State Historical Society, Library, 1990. 11 p.

2979. Colorado Midland Railway Company. *The Cripple Creek gold fields.* Colorado Springs, Gazette Printing Company, 1892. 34 p.

2980. _____. *Rules and regulations for the information and government of officials employes (sic) of the Operating Department.* Denver, Colo., President's Office, 1898. 52 p.

1981. _____. *Rules and regulations of the Operating* Department; effective May 1, 1906. Denver? The Railway, 1906. 62 p.

2982. Colorado Railroad Museum. *Colorado rail annual.* Golden, CO: Colorado Railroad Museum, 1963-(Other title: *Colorado annual.*)

2983. _____. *A booklet to do with Colorado Railroad history and narrow gauge railroads.* Golden, CO: The Museum, 1961. 32 p. (Prepared by Cornelius W. Hauck.)

2984. _____. *Coal, cinders, and parlor cars: a century of Colorado passenger trains.* Golden, CO: Colorado Railroad Museum, 1991. 238 p. (*Colorado rail annual*, no. 19.)

2985. _____. *The collected Colorado rail annual: reprinted from issues numbers one through seven.* Golden, CO: Colorado Railroad Museum, 1974? 136 p.

2986. _____. *Journeys through western rail history.* Golden, CO: Colorado Railroad Museum, 1997. 168 p. (*Colorado rail annual,* no. 22 .)

2987. _____. *Locomotives of the Rio Grande: a detailed locomotive roster of the Rio Grande system, 1871-1980.* Golden, CO: Colorado Railroad Museum, 1980. 91 p.

2988. _____. *Official roster no 11 of the Denver and Rio Grande Western Railroad system and the Rio Grande Southern Railroad Company, 1923.* Golden, CO: Colorado Railroad Museum, 1998. 160 p.

2989. _____. *Santa Fe in the intermountain West.* Golden, CO: Colorado Railroad Museum, 1998. 296 p. (*Colorado rail annual*, no. 23.)

2990. _____. *Steam in the Rockies; a steam locomotive roster of the Denver Rio Grande.* Golden, CO: Colorado Railroad Museum, 1963. 32 p.

2991. Colquitt, R.E. *Pennsylvania Railroad: passenger equipment roster, October 1, 1954*. S.l., Wahsatch Backshop, 1996. 1 v.

2992. Coltman, Michael, Morrin E. Hazel. *Chlorine tank car puncture resistance evaluation*. Washington, DC : Federal Railroad Administration, Office of Research and Development, 1992. 87 p. (*DOT/FRA/ORD-92/11*.)

2993. Colton, Asa. *The traffic man's handbook; a reference book dealing with subjects of interest to traffic men—industrial and railroad—shippers, shipping clerks and all those interested in shipments: with text of Interstate Commerce Act, and details of express and parcel-post shipment/* Chicago, IL: John C. Winston Company, 1923. 386 p.

2994. Colton, Calvin. *A lecture on the railroad to the Pacific. Delivered August 12, 1850, at the Smithsonian Institute, Washington. At the request of numerous members of both houses of Congress*. New York, NY: A.S. Barnes, 1850. 16 p.

2995. Colton, David Douty, *The octopus speaks: the Colton letters*. Salvador A. Ramirez, editor; with notes and introduction. Carlsbad, CA: Tentacled Press, 1982. 615 p. (Correspondence between Collis Potter Huntington and David D. Colton-Central Pacific Railroad Co.)

2996. Columbia University. Libraries. *The William Barclay Parsons railroad prints; an appreciation and a check list*. New York, Columbia University Library, 1935. 58 p. ("Appreciation by James K. Finch and Faulkner H. Talbot; "Check list" by Laura S. Young.)

2997. Columbus, Hocking Valley, and Toledo Railway Company. *Rules and regulations defining the duties of officers and agents in the Operating Department, and regulating the running of trains and the use of signals on the Columbus, Hocking Valley & Toledo R'y. approved August 30, 1885*. Columbus, OH: Ohio State Journal Job Room, 1885. 150 p.

2998. Colvin, Fred H. *American compound locomotives; a practical explanation of the construction, operation and care of the compound locomotives in use on American railroads*. New York, The Derry-Collard, Co., 1903. 142 p.

2999. _____. *The compound locomotive; a practical pocket book for those interested in their mechanism, operation and repair*. New York, A. Sinclair Co., 1900. 87 p.

3000. _____. *Link motions, valve gears and valve setting*. New York, Derry-Collard; London, Locomotive Publishing Co., 1905. 90 p. (3rd ed. rev. & enl. New York, Henley Pub. Co., 1914? 101 p.

3001. _____. *The railroad pocket-book; a quick reference cyclopedia of railroad information*. New York, Derry-Collard, 1906. 221 p.

3002. Colwick, John M. *Railroad-motor carrier integrations and public policy, 1935-1960.* 79 l. (Thesis, M.B.A., University of Texas.)

3003. Combs, Barry. *Westward to Promontory; building the Union Pacific across the plains and mountains; a pictorial documentary.* Andrew J. Russell, illustrations. Palo Alto, CA: American West Pub. Co., 1969. 77 p.

3004. Combustion Engineering, Inc. *Elesco locomotive feed water heaters: instructions for operation and maintenance.* 5th ed. New York, Superheater Company, 1929. 84 p.

3005. _____. *The Elesco multiple-loop, single-pass superheater.* New York, The Superheater Company, 1929. 6 l.

3006. _____. *Locomotive feed water heaters; a catalog describing and illustrating the theory, construction and application of the Elesco non-contact type.* New York, Superheater Company, 1925. 23 p.

3007. _____. *Locomotive progress.* New York, Superheater Company, 1927. 39 p.

3008. _____. *1928 locomotive progress.* New York, Superheater Company, 1928. 39 p.

3009. _____. *1929 locomotive progress.* New York, The Superheater Co., 1929. 37 p.

3010. _____. *One hundred years, 1786-1926: being a brief story of the locomotive superheater and the part it plays on the American railway of today.* New York, s.n., 1926? 1 v.

3011. _____. *A short story of the locomotive superheater, with particular reference to the history and development of the Elesco locomotive superheater.* New York, The Superheater Company, 1929. 32 p.

3012. _____. *Superheater locomotives: maintenance and operation.* New York, Locomotive Superheater Company, 1911. 12 p.

3012a. Comer, Kevin. *Louisville & Nashville Railroad in south central Kentucky /* Charleston, SC: Arcadia Publishing, 2012. 127 p.

3013. Commerce and Industry Association of New York. *Disposal of West Side railroad tracks; a report to the Merchant's Association of New York.* New York, The Association, 1908. 19 p.

3014. _____. Committee on Harbor, Docks and Terminals. *Report on the proposed plans for the readjustment of the New York Central Railroad tracks upon the west side of Manhattan Island.* New York : The Association, 1916. 33 p.

3015. *The Commercial and financial chronicle.* New York, National News Service, 1896-1976. (Weekly)

3016. *The Commercial & financial chronicle and Hunt's merchants' magazine.* New York, William B. Dana Co., 1871-1896. (Weekly)

3017. *The Commercial & financial chronicle, bankers' gazette, commercial times, railway monitor, and insurance journal.* New York, William B. Dana & Co., 1865-1870. Weekly. (> *Commercial and financial chronicle and Hunt's merchant's magazine.*)

3018. *Commercial and financial chronicle; electric railway section.* New York, W.B. Dana Co., 1908-1924. (<*Commercial and financial chronicle; street railway section.)*

3019. *The Commercial & financial chronicle; railway and industrial compendium.* New York, William B. Dana Co., 1924-1927. (> *Railway and industrial compendium.*)

3020. *The Commercial & financial chronicle; railway and industrial section.* New York, William B. Dana Co., 1903-1923. (Semiannual)

3021. *The Commercial and financial chronicle; railway earnings section.* New York, William B. Dana Co., 1909-1928.

3022. *Commercial atlas & marketing guide.* Chicago, Rand McNally, 1969-1982. (Annual)

3023. Commission on Chicago Landmarks. *Historic Chicago railroad bridges: preliminary landmark recommendation approved by the Commission on Chicago landmarks, September 7, 2006.* Rev. ed. Chicago: Commission on Chicago Landmarks, 2007. 41 p.

3024. _____. *Union Station: 210 S. Canal Street.* Chicago: The Commission, 2000. 10 l.

3025. Commission on Chicago Historical and Architectural Landmarks. *Union Station: summary of information on the Union Station* / Chicago: The Commission, 1981. 4 l.

3026. Committee on Co-ordination of Chicago Terminals. *The freight traffic of the Chicago terminal district.* Chicago, 1927. 175 p.

3027. Committee on Public Relations of the Eastern Railroads. *The Pullman surcharge; what is, why it is, why it should stand.* New York, The Committee, 1927. 7 p.

3027a. Committee on Welded Rail Joints. *Final report, September, 1932.* New York: Office of the Secretary, Engineering Societies Building, 1932. 358 p. (American Bureau of Welding)

3027b. _____. *Progress report.* New York: Office of the Secretary, Engineering Societies Building, 1922-?

3028. *Common Northeastern open top hopper cars of the 1950's and 1960's.* Gibbsboro, NJ: Rail Road Progress, 1985. 38 p.

3029. *Common trailer/container-on-flatcar yard.* Washington, DC: Federal Railroad Administration; Springfield, IL: Department of Transportation; 1981. 26 l. Prepared by: Sverdrup-Envirodyne-Knight.

3030. Commonwealth North (Anchorage, Alaska). *The Alaska Railroad and its future.* Anchorage, AK: Commonwealth North, 1988. 50 p.

3031. _____. *The new Alaska Railroad: an action paper.* Anchorage, AK: Commonwealth North, 1984. 23 p.

3032. Commonwealth Steel Company. *The composite underframe for passenger-train cars.* St. Louis : Commonwealth Steel, 1909. 1 folded sheet 23 x 31 cm. folded to 23 x 11 cm.

3033. *Comparative evaluation of rail and truck fuel efficiency on competitive corridors/* Washington, DC: Federal Railroad Administration, 2009. 1 v. (Various pagings)

3034. *Comparative statement of operating averages.* Washington, D.C., Interstate Commerce Commission; Bureau of Statistics; G.P.O., 1922-1936. (Annual)

3035. *Comparative statement of railway operating statistics.* Washington, D.C., Interstate Commerce Commission; Bureau of Statistics; G.P.O., 1937- Annual)

3036. *Comparative statement of railway operating statistics, individual class 1 steam railways in the United States.* Washington, DC: Interstate Commerce Commission, Bureau of Transport Economics, 1922- Annual.

3037. *A comparative study of railway wages and the cost of living in the United Sates, the United Kingdom and the principal countries of continental Europe.* Washington, DC: Bureau of Railway Economics, 1912. 77 p. (*Bulletin, no. 34.*)

3038. *Competitive transportation review.* Washington, DC: Association of American Railroads, 1949-1954. Monthly.

3039. *Compilation of railroad laws relating to railroad regulation: as amended through May 30, 2008/* Washington, DC: U.S. G.P.O., 2008. 3 v. (*110th Congress, 2nd session. Committee print. September 2008, 110-161.*)

3040. *Compilation of states' laws and regulations on matters affecting rail-highway crossing: final report.* Washington, DC: Federal Railroad Administration; Federal Highway Administration; Association of American Railroads, 1983. 425 p. (*FHWA/TS-83/203*)

3041. *The complete history of North American railways.* London (England), Regency House Pub., 1996, 1989. 352 p.

3042. *The complete roster of heavyweight Pullman cars.* New York, NY: Wayner Publications, 1985. 289 p.

3043. *Comprehensive guide to industrial locomotives.* Jay Reed, editor. Santa Rosa, CA: Rio Hondo, 1995. 298 p.

3044. *Comprehensive guide to industrial locomotives.* Jay Reed editor; military roster by Shane Deemer. 2d ed. Santa Rosa, CA: Rio Hondo, 1998. 198 p.

3044a. Comstock, Arthur Francis. *Details of railroad truss bridges* / 1906. 31 l. (Thesis, B.S., University of Illinois.)

3045. Comstock, Henry B. *The iron horse.* New York, Crowell, 1971. 228 p. (Galahad Books, 1974. 228 p.)

3046. _____. *The iron horse.* 2d ed. Sykesville? MD: Greenberg Pub. Co., 1993. 224 p.

3047. Conant, John H. *Central Nebraska rails: a steam railfan's paradise.* David City, NE: South Platte Press, 1989. 48 p.

3048. Conant, Michael. *Railroad bankruptcies and mergers from Chicago west, 1975-2001; financial analysis and regulatory critique.* Amsterdam, Boston, JAI, 2004. 154 p.

3049. _____. *Railroad mergers and abandonments.* Berkeley, CA: University of California Press, 1964. 212 p.

3050. Condé, Jesse C. *Fowler locomotives in the Kingdom of Hawaii.* Peterborough, England, Narrow Gauge Railway Society, 1993. 48 p. (Special issue of the *Narrow Gauge,* no. 140.)

3051. _____. *Narrow gauge in a kingdom: the Hawaiian Railroad Company, 1978-1897.* Felton, CA: Glenwood Publishers, 1971. 86 p.

3052. _____. *Sugar trains pictorial.* Felton, CA: Glenwood Publishers, 1975. 191 p.

3053._____, Gerald M. Best. *Sugar trains; narrow gauge rails of Hawaii.* Felton, CA: Glenwood Publishers, 1973. 400 p.

3054. Condit, Carl W. *The pioneer stage of railroad electrification.* Philadelphia, American Philosophical Society, 1977. 45 p. (*Transactions, American Philosophical Society,* v. 67, pt. 7.)

3055. _____. *The port of New York: a history of the rail and terminal system from the Grand Central electrification to the present.* Chicago, University of Chicago Press, 1981. 399 p.

3056. _____. *The railroad and the city: a technological and urbanistic history of Cincinnati.* Columbus, Ohio State University Press, 1977. 335 p.

3057. _____ *Sleeping car service provided by railroads of the United States, 1928-1929*. Evanston, IL: C.W. Condit, 1983. 63 l.

3058. Condon, Gregg, Robert Felten, James Nickoll. *The Dinky: C&NW narrow gauge in Wisconsin*. S.l., Marsh Lake Productions, 1993. 80 p.

3059. Condrick, James A. *Federal legislation and decisions on railroad labor conflicts*. 1933. 154 l. (Thesis, Harvard Law School.)

3060. *Conductor and brakeman*. Cedar Rapids, IA: Order of Railway Conductors and Brakemen, 1954-1969. (Monthly)

3061. Confalone, Mike, Joe Posik. *Rails across New England*. Goffstown, NH: Railroad Explorer, 2005-

3062. Conference Committee of Managers. (Railroads of Eastern Territory) 1913. *Summary rates of pay and regulations. eastern, southeastern and western territories. Compiled by Conference Committee of Managers, eastern territory. New York, September, 1913.* New York, 1913. 218 l.

3063. *Conference on car management implications of box car deregulation*. Washington, DC: Association of American Railroads, Freight Car Management Program, 1984. 167, A-14 l. (*AAR publication no. R-563.*)

3064. *Conference Proceedings: Federal Railroad Administration Training Conference: "labor/management/public agency cooperation for railroad employee training," January 31, 1978 through February 2, 1978, Clayton Inn, St. Louis, Missouri.* Washington, DC: Federal Railroad Administration, Office of Policy and Program Development, 1979. 359 p.

3065. *Congressional Symposium, Railroads; 1977 and beyond—problems and promises: proceedings*. Washington, DC: U.S. G.P.O., 1978. 167 p. (Congress. House. Committee on Interstate and Foreign Commerce. Subcommittee on Transportation and Commerce.)

3066. Coniglio, John William. *Steam in the Valley: Tennessee Valley Railroad Museum, 1961-1998*. Chattanooga, TN: Hometown Print Works, 1998. 160 p.

3067. Conklin, Groff. *All about subways*. New York, J. Messner, Inc., 1938. 212 p.

3068. Conkling, Edgar, Andrew B. Gray, T. Butler King. *Southern Pacific Railroad: report of Col. A. B. Gray, chief engineer of the company, and other important information, together with letter of Hon. T. Butler King, with a map, illustrating the course of trade between Europe and Asia, over the continent of America*. Cincinnati: T. Wrightson & Co., 1855. 2, 36, 8 p.

3069. Conkling, Roscoe, William D. Shipman. *The Central Pacific Railroad Company in equitable account with the United States, growing out of the issue of subsidy bonds in aid of construction : a review of the testimony and exhibits presented before the Pacific Railway Commission, appointed according to the act of Congress, approved March 3d, 1887. By Roscoe Conkling and William D. Shipman, of counsel for the Central Pacific R.R. Co.* New York: Henry Bessey, Printer, no. 47 Cedar Street, 1887. 134 p.

3070. Conlon, Peter C., Milton R. Johnson, Michael Grolmes. *Railroad tank car relief valve requirement for liquid PIH lading.* Washington, DC: Federal Railroad Administration, Office of Research and Development, 2003. 34, A-15. (*DOT/FRA/ORD-03/21.*

3071. Conn, Granville Priest. *Report of the Committee on Car Sanitation.* Concord, N.H.: Republican press, 1896. 24 p.

3072. Connecticut. General Assembly. House of Representatives. Special Committee to Investigate the Alleged False Returns of Railroad Companies. *Report of the special committee appointed, March 13, 1878, to investigate the alleged false returns of railroad companies.* Hartford : State of Connecticut, House of Representatives, 1878. 17 p.

3072a. Connecticut River Railroad . *Instructions to passenger trainmen* / Springfield. MA: Cyrus W. Atwood, Printer, 1892. 12 p.

3073. Conner, E.R. *Railroading on the Washington Division.* Manassas, VA: REF Pub., 1986. 143 p. (Southern Railway)

3074. _____. *Washington Division railroad album.* Manassas, VA: REF Pub., 1988. 159 p.

3075. Conners, Pamela A. *The Sugar Pine Railway: history of a Sierran logging railroad.* S.l., U.S. Dept. of Agriculture, Forest Service, Pacific Southwest Region, Stanislaus National Forest, 1997. 429 p.

3076. Connolly, Mary Theresa. *"The Gravity;" history of the Pennsylvania Coal Company Railroad, 1850-1885.* Olyphant, PA: Barrett Pub. Co., 1972. 54 p.

3077. Connolly, Michael J. *Capitalism, politics, and railroads in Jacksonian New England.* Columbia, University of Missouri Press, 2003. 210 p.

3078. Conover, Ted. *Rolling nowhere: riding the rails with America's hoboes.* New York, Viking Press, 1984. 274 p., 2 p. of plates.

3079. Conrad, J. David. *The steam locomotive directory of North America.* Polo, IL: Transportation Trails, 1988. 2 v.

3080. _____. *Steam locomotives on display: their care and maintenance.* Union, IL: Illinois Railway Museum, 1974. 12 p.

3081. *Conrail performance review/* Washington, DC: United States Railway Association, 1981- . Annual.

3082. *Conrail power.* Bob Reid, editor. E. McKeesport, PA: *Rails Northeast,* 1976-
(Annual)

3083. Consolidated Machine Tool Corporation. *Machine tools for the manufacture
and maintenance of railroad equipment.* Rochester, N.Y: The Corporation, 1930. 81 p.

3084. Consolidated Railway Electrical Lighting & Equipment Company. *Consolidated
"axle-light" system bulletin no. 1.* New York : Consolidated Railway Electric Lighting
and Equipment Company, 1905. 19 p.

3085. _____. *The Consolidated axle light system of electric lights and fans for all kinds
of railway passenger cars.* New York, Consolidated Railway Electric Lighting &
Equipment Company, 1904. 6 p.

3086. *Consolidation of railroads: February, 1930.* New York, National City Co., 1930.
16 p.

3087. *Consolidation of railroads, 1930-1958: a list of references.* Compiled by
Helen R. Richardson. Washington, D.C., Bureau of Railway Economics, Library, 1959.
38 p.

3088. *Consolidation of railroads, 1959-July, 1962; a list of references.* Washington, DC:
Bureau of Railway Economics, Library, 1962. 25 p.

3089. *Construction of Chicago's first subway.* Evanston, IL: Western Society
of Engineers, 1944. 99-209 p.

3090. *Contribution of research to railway progress.* Ann Arbor, MI: Edwards Brothers,
1933. 154 p. (American Society of Mechanical Engineers.)

3091. Convention in Favor of a National Rail Road to the Pacific Ocean. *Proceedings
of the Convention in favor of national rail road to the Pacific Ocean through
the territories of the United States, held in Philadelphia, April 1st, 2nd & 3rd, 1850.*
Philadelphia, PA: Crissy & Markley, Printers, 1850. 79 p.

3092. Converse, John W. *Some features of the labor system and management
at the Baldwin Locomotive Works.* Philadelphia, American Academy of Political
Science, 1903. 9 p. (Publications of the Am. Acad. of Political and Social Science,
no. 362.)

3093. *Converting rails to trails: a citizens' manual for transforming abandoned rail
corridors into multipurpose public paths.* Washington, DC: Rails-to-Trails Conservancy,
1987. 65, 35 p.

3093a. Cook, Catherine, Aaron Bobb, Ray Mundy. *Readings in modern railroad
management* / St. Louis: University of Missouri—St. Louis, Center of Transportation
Studies, 2013. 283 p.

3094. Cook, Cecil. *The final steam years: the Milwaukee Road's Dubuque and Illinois Division, 1947-1954*. S.l., C. Cook, 1999. 67 p.

3095. _____. *Marquette: the biography of an Iowa railroad town*. Des Moines, Waukon & Mississippi Press, 1975. 240 p.

3096. Cook, M.P. *Hot boxes: their causes and cure*. Flint, MI : s.n., 1897. 42 p. (Eye Printing Co., Flint, Michigan.)

3097. Cook, Preston. *Before Guilford: the Delaware & Hudson, Boston & Maine, and Maine Central railroads*. Silver Spring, MD: Old Line Graphics, 1988. 128 p.

3098. _____. *Chicago and North Western memories, 1970-1980*. Silver Spring, MD: Old Line Graphics, 1989. 128 p.

3099. _____. *Erie Lackawanna memories: the final years*. Silver Spring. MD: Old Line Graphics, 1987. 127 p.

3100. _____, Jim Boyd. *The railroad night scene*. Silver Spring, MD: Old Line Graphics, 1991. 128 p.

3101. Cook, Richard J. *The beauty of railroad bridges in North America, then and now*. San Marino, CA: Golden West Books, 1987. 208 p.

3102. _____. *A brief history of the Brotherhood of Locomotive Engineers*. Cleveland, Brotherhood of Locomotive Engineers, 1977. 48 p.

3103. _____. *Famous steam locomotives of the United States and Canada*. Cleveland, Brotherhood of Locomotive Engineers, 1974. 96 p.

3104. _____. *New York Central's Mercury: the train of tomorrow*. Lynchburg, VA: TLC Pub., 1991. 60 p.

3105. _____ *Rails across the midlands*. San Marino, CA: Golden West Books, 1964. 144 p.

3106. _____. *Super power steam locomotives*. San Marino, CA: Golden West Books, 1966. 144 p.

3107. _____. *The Twentieth Century Limited, 1938-1967*. Lynchburg, VA: TLC Pub., 1993. 154 p.

3108. _____, Karl Zimmermann. *The Western Maryland Railway: fireballs and black diamonds*. San Diego, CA: Howell-North Books, 1981. 308 p. (2d ed. Laurys Station, PA: Garrigues House, 1992. 332 p.)

3109. Cook, W. George, Dell A. McCoy, Russ Collman. *Over the bridges: Dolores to Mancos*. Denver, CO: Sundance Publications, 2000. 416 p. (*The R.G.S. story*, v. 8.)

3110. _____, _____, _____. *Over the bridges: Grady to Durango.* Denver, CO: Sundance Publications, 2001. 416 p. (*The R.G.S. story*, v. 9.)

3111. _____, William J. Coxey. *Atlantic City Railroad, the royal route to the sea: a history of the Reading's seashore railroad, 1877-1933.* Oaklyn, NJ: West Jersey Chapter, National Railway Historical Society, 1980. 172 p.

3112. Cook, William S. *Building the modern Union Pacific.* New York, Newcomen Society of the U.S., 1985. 24 p.
j
3113. Cooke Locomotive & Machine Company, Paterson, N.J. *Catalogue of locomotives.* Paterson, N.J., Cooke Locomotive and Machine Company, 1895. 17 p., 71 l. of plates.

3114. _____. *Cooke Locomotive & Machine Co., 1901.* Paterson, N.J., The Company, 1901. 102 p.

3115. Cooke, Ralph W. *Freight transportation sales.* Philadelphia : Pennsylvania Railroad, Freight Traffic Department, 1946. 33 p.

3116. Cooley, Thomas McIntyre, Thomas Curtis Clarke. *The railways of America; their construction, development, management, and appliances.* London, J. Murray, 1890. 456 p. (Reprinted from *Scribner's magazine*)

3117. Cooper Bruce Clement. *The classic Western American railroad routes* / New York: Chartwell Books, 2010. 320 p.

3118. _____. *Riding the transcontinental rails: overland travel on the Pacific Railroad, 1865-1881.* Philadelphia, Polyglot Press, 2005. 445 p.

3119. Cooper, Fletcher E. *The trains never came: the story of the Lee & New Haven Railroad.* Litchfield, CT: F.E. Cooper,1990. 28 p. (*Area historical series*, no. 1)

3120. Cooper, Gail Ann. *"Manufactured weather" : a history of air conditioning in the United States, 1902-1955.* 1987. 271 l. (Thesis, Ph.D., University of California, Santa Barbara.)

3121. Cooper, Mason Y. *Norfolk & Western electrics.* Forest, VA: Norfolk & Western Historical Society, 2000. 128 p.

3121a. _____. *Norfolk & Western's Pocahontas Division* / Roanoke, VA: Norfolk & Western Historical Society, 2011. 330 p.

3122. _____. *Norfolk & Western's Shenandoah Valley Line.* Forest, VA: Norfolk & Western Historical Society, 1998. 214 p.

3123. Cooper, Ralph L., Michael R. Johns. *Hogback Road: a history of the Quincy,*

Omaha & Kansas City Railroad Co. S.l., Cooper and M.R. Johns, 1983. 66 p.

3124. Cooper, Stafford S. *Postmortem investigation of the Kansas test track.* Washington, DC: Federal Railroad Administration, Office of Research and Development, 1979. 2 v. (*FRA/ORD-79/09.*)

3125. Cooper, Theodore. *American railroad bridges.* New York, Engineering News Pub. Co., 1889. 60 p.

3126. _____ *General specifications for steel railroad bridges and viaducts.* New and rev. ed. 6th ed. New York, Engineering News, 1901. 34 p.

3127. _____. *Train loadings for railroad bridges.* New York, NY: American Society of Civil Engineers, 1894. 174-220 p. 7 leaves of plates.

3128. *Cooperative research effort among railroads, railroad associations, industry and government: 1974 technical proceedings: 11th annual Railroad Engineering Conference* / Washington, DC: Federal Railroad Administration, 1975. 114 p.

3129. Cooperrider, N.K., E.H. Law, R.H. Fries. *Freight car dynamics : field test and comparison with theory : interim report.* Washington, DC: Federal Railroad Administration, Office of Research and Development, 1981. 143 p. (*FRA/ORD-81/46.*)

3130. Copeland, E. A. *Tank car cleaning and washwater treatment facility* / Omaha, NB: Simmons-Boardman Books, 1984. 339 p.

3131. Copp, Philip. *The Franklin Avenue El/incline.* Maplewood, NJ: Four Oceans Press, 1988. 22 p.

3132. Copper Range Railroad Company. *Rules of the Copper Range Railroad Company for the government of the Operating Department.* S.l., The Company, 1905. 132 p. "To take effect March 1, 1906."

3133. *Copper Range Railroad Company.* Washington, DC: Interstate Commerce Commission, 1922. 16 l. (*Interstate Commerce Commission Valuation Docket, no. 244.*)

3134. Corbett, James W. *The 2-6-0 Mogul on the Southern Pacific.* New enl. ed. Ramsey, NJ: Penn Pub. Co., 1953. 46 p. (*Railroad photo album, no. 5.*)

3135. Corbin, Bernard G. *The Burlington in transition.* Associate editor: Joseph C. Hardy. Red Oak, IA: Corbin Publications, 1967. 208 p. (Reprint: West Burlington, IA: Mile Post 206 Publications, 2003. 208 p.)

3136. _____, F. Hol Wagner. *Creston, Iowa: summit division* point. LeGrange, IL: Burlington Route Historical Society, 1984. 39 p.

3137. _____, Joseph C. Hardy. *Across Iowa on the Keokuk & Western, and the Humeston & Shenandoah railroads.* Red Oak, IA: Corbin Publications, 1986.

144 p.

3138. _____, William Kerka. *Steam locomotives of the Burlington Route.* Red Oak, IA: B.G. Corbin, 1960. 304 p.(Also: New York, Bonanza Books, 1978. 320 p.

3138a. Corbin, Darrell Stephen. *Re-evaluation of the economic consequences of relocation of the Camas Prairie Railroad.* 1969. 166 l. (Thesis, M.A., Washington State University.)

3139. Corbin, J. (John C.) *Correlation of statistical representations of track geometry with physical appearance: final report.* Washington, DC: Federal Railroad Administration, Office of Research and Development, 1978. 67 p. (*FRA/ORD-79/35.*)

3140. _____. *Methods of processing track geometry date to obtain representations of profile and alignment.* Springfield, VA: ENSCO, Inc., 1973. 1 v. (various pagings)

3141. _____. *Statistical representations of track geometry/* Washington, DC: U.S. Department of Transportation, Federal Railroad Administration, Office of Research and Development, 1980. 2 v. (*FRA/ORD-80-4*

3142. _____, J. Lazzaro, C. Peterson. *Locomotive track hazard detector program (LTHD).* Washington, DC: Federal Railroad Administration, Office of Research and Development, 1982. 48 p. (*DOT/FRA/ORD-82/26.*)

3143. Cordes, Bill. *St. Louis Water Works Railway.* Saint Louis, MO: Tower Grove Press, 2004. 79 p.

3143a. Cordes, William. *Minnesota railroad station and depot locations /* Minneapolis: Minnesota Railroad Research project, 1985. 79 p.

3144. Core, H.E. *An employee's view of how the plan of employee representation on the Pennsylvania Railroad actually works.* S.l., s.n., 1920s. 7 p.

3145. _____. *The Pennsylvania Railroad: schedule of regulations and rates of pay for the government of engineers, firemen, and hostlers in road and yard service.* Philadelphia, Pa., General Grievance Committee, Brotherhood of Locomotive Firemen and Enginemen, Pennsylvania Lines East, 1928. 1063 p.

3146. Corliss, Carlton Jonathan. *The American railway industry.* Cambridge, MA: Bellman Pub. Co., 1955. 26 p. (*Vocational and professional monographs, no. 43.*)

3147. _____. *Building the overseas railway to Key West.* S.l., 1953. 21 p.

3148. _____. *Development of railroad transportation in the United States.* Washington, D.C., Association of American Railroads, 1948. 32 p.

3149. _____. *The human side of railroading.* Washington, DC: Association of American Railroads, 1951. 16 p. (*Railway information series, no. 7.*)

3150. _____. *Main line of Mid-America; the story of the Illinois Central.* New York, Creative Age Press, 1950. 490 p.

3151. _____. *Trails to rails, a story of transportation progress in Illinois.* Chicago: s.n., 1934. 48 p.

3151a. Cornell, A.D., Dennis McLerran. *Union Station : landmarks are building that span generations.* Seattle: Union Pacific Realty Co., 1988. 1 v. (unpaged)

3152. Corns, John B. *Nickel Plate Road publicity photos, 1943-1952.* Lynchburg, VA: TLC Pub., 1996. 127 p.

3153. _____. *The Wheeling and Lake Erie Railway.* Lynchburg, VA: TLC Pub., 1991-2002. 2 v. (v. 1, 80 p.; v. 2, 128 p.)

3154. Cornwall, L. Peter. *In the Shore Line's shadow: the six lives of the Danbury & Norwalk Railroad.* Littleton, MA: Flying Yankee Enterprises, 1987. 132 p.

3155. _____, Carol A. Smith. *Names first—rails later: New England's 700-plus railroads and what happened to them.* Stamford, CT: Arden Valley Group, 1989. 132 p. (2d ed.: 2001. 115 p.)

3156. _____, Jack W. Farrell. *Ride the Sandy River; a trip into the past on what was America's largest two-foot gauge railroad.* Edmonds, WA: Pacific Fast Mail, 1973. 248 p.

3157. Cors, Paul B. *Railroads.* Littleton, CO: Libraries Unlimited, 1975. 152 p. (Bibliography)

3157a. Corser, S.T., N.A. Foster. *Rules and regulations for running trains, &c.: June 7, 1858.* Portland, ME: N.A. Foster, Printers, 1858. 22 p. (Grand Trunk Railway Company of Canada, Portland District.)

3158. Corson, Lynn A., Melinda O.I. Jonson. *Report of rail accidents involving cars carrying hazardous materials, State of Michigan, 1977-1982/* East Lansing, MI : Community Development Programs, Lifelong Education programs, Michigan State University, 1983. 15 l.

3159. Cortani, Roger M., Gordon Lloyd, Joseph A. Strapac. *Diesels of the EsPee.* Burlingame, CA: Chatham Pub. Co., 1975- (v. 1: Alco PA's.)

3160. Cortner, Richard C. *The iron horse and the Constitution: the railroads and the transformation of the fourteenth amendment.* Westport CT: Greenwood Press, 1993. 231 p. *(Contributions in legal studies, 68.)*

3161. Cory, W. B. *Hazard connected with the vocation of locomotive firemen and engineers.* Chicago: Brotherhood of Locomotive Firemen and Enginemen, 1915.

54 p.

3161a. Coscia, David. *Pacific Electric Railway and the growth of the San Fernando Valley.* Bellflower, CA: Shade Tree Books, 2011. 240 p.

3162. *Cost and productivity, train & engine service.* Washington, DC: United States Railway Association, 1981. 46 p.

3163. Cotroneo, Ross Ralph. *The history of the Northern Pacific land grant, 1900-1952.* 1967. 468 l. (Thesis, Ph.D., University of Idaho.) (Also: New York, Arno Press, 1979.)

3163a. _____. *The Northern Pacific and government regulation of railroads : development and effects to 1940.* 1962. 135 l. (Thesis, M.A., University of Idaho.)

3164. Cotta, Margaret Mary. *Visalia and the railroad: a study of railroad policy in building through the San Joaquin Valley, 1870-1872.* 1971. 161 l. (Thesis, M.A., University of Santa Clara.)

3165. Cottingham, George R. *Study of rail tiedown gear.* Ft. Belvoir Defense Technical Information Center, 1971. 32 p.

3166. Cotton, Eddy Joe. *Hobo: a young man's thoughts on trains and tramping in America.* New York, Harmony Books, 2002. 287 p.

3167. Cottrell, William Frederick. *The railroader.* Stanford, CA: Stanford University Press, 1940. 145 p. (Reprint: Dubuque, IA: Brown Reprints, 1971.)

3168. _____. *Technological change and labor in the railroad industry; a comparative study.* Lexington, MA: Heath Lexington Books, 1970. 159 p.

3169. Coughlin, Charles Gerald. *The locomotive "Lion."* 1930. (Thesis, B.S. in Mechanical Engineering, University of Maine.)

3170. Coughlin, Eugene W. *Freight car distribution and car handling in the United States.* Washington, D.C., Association of American Railroads, Car Service Division, 1956. 338 p.

3171. Coughlin, Richard T. *Shipper-owned and leased railroad cars /* 1966. 39 l. (American Society of Traffic and Transportation). Document location: Northwestern University, Transportation Library.

3172. Coulter, E. Merton. *The Cincinnati Southern Railroad and the struggle for Southern commerce, 1865-1872.* Chicago, The American Historical Society, Inc., 1922. 68 p.

3173. Council, R. Bruce, Nick Honerkamp. *The Union Railyards site: industrial archaeology in Chattanooga, Tennessee /* Chattanooga, TN: Jeffrey L. Brown Institute of Archaeology, University of Tennessee at Chattanooga, 1984. 201 p. (*Publications in anthropology / The Tennessee Valley Authority, no. 38.*)

3174. County, A.J. *Economic necessity for the Pennsylvania Railroad tunnel extension into New York City.* Philadelphia : American Academy of Political & Social Science, 1907. 18 p.

3175. _____. *The growth of a great transportation system.* Philadelphia? s.n., 1925. 28 p. (Pennsylvania Railroad.).

3176. _____. *The Pennsylvania Railroad Company : its incorporation and organization and the work of the organization, being a view of the Pennsylvania system at present /* Philadelphia : s.n., 1906. 1 v. (various pagings).

3177. Couper, William. *History of the engineering, construction and equipment of the Pennsylvania Railroad Company's New York terminal and approaches.* New York, Isaac H. Blanchard Co., 1912. 131 p.

3178. _____. *A publication descriptive of the development on the lines of the Pennsylvania Railroad, within one hundred miles of New York City Pennsylvania terminal.* New York, Isaac H. Blanchard Co., 1912. 165 p.

3178a. Cournoyer, Brian. *Railroad stations of California's coast.* San Luis Obispo: California Polytechnic State University, 1976. 144 p.

3179. *Course in Pullman production methods.* New York, Business Training Corporation, 1926-1927. 6 v. I. Team leadership – II. Handling men – III. Handling equipment – IV Plant records – V. Planning and organizing – VI. Management.

3180. Coverdale and Colpitts. *The Pennsylvania Railroad Company: corporate, financial and construction history of lines owned, operated and controlled to December 31, 1945.* New York, Coverdale & Colpitts, 1947. 4 v. (v. 1: The Pennsylvania Railroad proper. v. 2: Leased lines east of Pittsburgh. v. 3: Leased lines west of Pittsburgh. v. 4: Affiliated lines, miscellaneous companies; general index.)

3181. _____. *The Pennsylvania Railroad Company : description and history of important bridges and stations.* New York : Coverdale and Colpitts, 1946. 67 l. "Prepared for use in writing the company's centennial history." Limited to an edition of 100 copies.

3182. _____. *Report on Chicago, Milwaukee & St. Paul Railway Company.* New York, Coverdale and Colpitts, 1925. 231, 65 p.

3183. _____. *Report on high-speed trains, Chicago-Twin Cities.* New York, Coverdale and Colpitts, 1935. 22 p.

3184. _____. *Report on light-weight trains of the Zephyr type, January 15, 1935.* New York, Coverdale and Colpitts, 1935. 20 p.

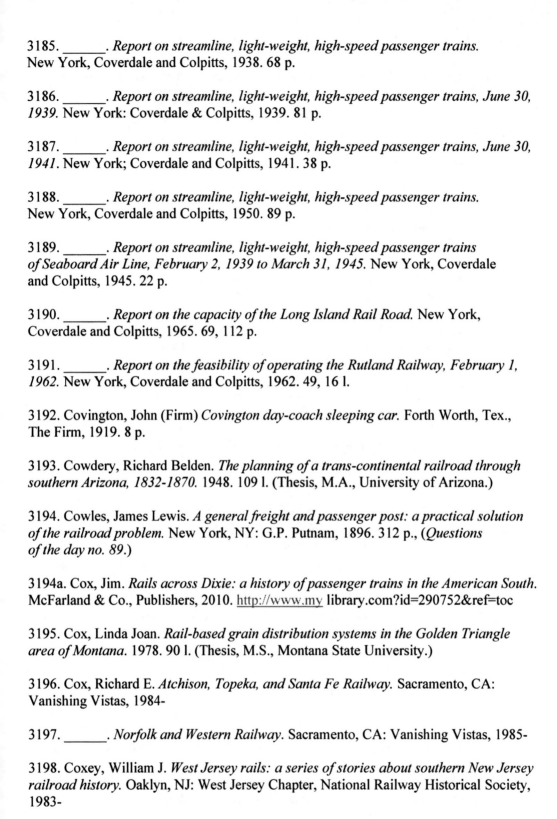

3185. _____. *Report on streamline, light-weight, high-speed passenger trains.*
New York, Coverdale and Colpitts, 1938. 68 p.

3186. _____. *Report on streamline, light-weight, high-speed passenger trains, June 30, 1939.* New York: Coverdale & Colpitts, 1939. 81 p.

3187. _____. *Report on streamline, light-weight, high-speed passenger trains, June 30, 1941.* New York; Coverdale and Colpitts, 1941. 38 p.

3188. _____. *Report on streamline, light-weight, high-speed passenger trains.*
New York, Coverdale and Colpitts, 1950. 89 p.

3189. _____. *Report on streamline, light-weight, high-speed passenger trains of Seaboard Air Line, February 2, 1939 to March 31, 1945.* New York, Coverdale and Colpitts, 1945. 22 p.

3190. _____. *Report on the capacity of the Long Island Rail Road.* New York, Coverdale and Colpitts, 1965. 69, 112 p.

3191. _____. *Report on the feasibility of operating the Rutland Railway, February 1, 1962.* New York, Coverdale and Colpitts, 1962. 49, 16 l.

3192. Covington, John (Firm) *Covington day-coach sleeping car.* Forth Worth, Tex., The Firm, 1919. 8 p.

3193. Cowdery, Richard Belden. *The planning of a trans-continental railroad through southern Arizona, 1832-1870.* 1948. 109 l. (Thesis, M.A., University of Arizona.)

3194. Cowles, James Lewis. *A general freight and passenger post: a practical solution of the railroad problem.* New York, NY: G.P. Putnam, 1896. 312 p., (*Questions of the day no. 89.*)

3194a. Cox, Jim. *Rails across Dixie: a history of passenger trains in the American South.* McFarland & Co., Publishers, 2010. http://www.my library.com?id=290752&ref=toc

3195. Cox, Linda Joan. *Rail-based grain distribution systems in the Golden Triangle area of Montana.* 1978. 90 l. (Thesis, M.S., Montana State University.)

3196. Cox, Richard E. *Atchison, Topeka, and Santa Fe Railway.* Sacramento, CA: Vanishing Vistas, 1984-

3197. _____. *Norfolk and Western Railway.* Sacramento, CA: Vanishing Vistas, 1985-

3198. Coxey, William J. *West Jersey rails: a series of stories about southern New Jersey railroad history.* Oaklyn, NJ: West Jersey Chapter, National Railway Historical Society, 1983-

3199. _____, Frank C. Kozempel, James E. Kranefeld. *The trains to America's playground.* Oaklyn, NJ: West Jersey Chapter, National Railway Historical Society, 1988. 48 p.

3200. _____, James E. Kranefeld. *The Reading Seashore Lines: a pictorial documentary of the Atlantic City Railroad.* Palmyra, NJ: West Jersey Chapter, National Railway Historical Society, 2007. 168 p.

3201. Coy, John R., Robert C. Del Grasso. *Montana's Marias Pass: early GN mileposts and BNSF guide.* Bonners Ferry, ID: Great Northern Pacific Publications, 1996. 144 p.

3202. Cragon, Harvey G. *The Eureka Springs Railway: an automobile tour into the past /* 2d ed. Dallas, TX: Cragon Books, 2007. 46 p. Eureka Springs Railway. Eureka Springs and North Arkansas Railroad.

3203. Craig, Charles L. *How Riverside Park was saved: from Mayor Mitchel, Comptroller Prendergast and the New York Central Railroad : Charles L. Craig, Candidate for Comptroller of New York City : he stood for the citizens of New York against sinister influences that sought to grab their parks and waterfront.* New York : Prepared for publication by the Craig Campaign Committee, 1917. 15, 1 p. Craig, Charles Lacy, 1872-1935; Mitchel, John Purroy, 1879-1918.

3204. _____. *Report on proposed deal between New York Central Railroad and city of New York relating to Riverside Park and North River waterfront.* New York : West End Association, 1916. 22 p.

3205. _____, *Riverside Park improvement : planned by Charles L. Craig, Comptroller.* New York : s.n., 1924. 57 leaves of plates.(New York (N.Y.) Office of the Comptroller.

3206. _____. *The West End Association, organized February 1st, 1884 : Committee on legislation, Law and Schools : re—Senate bill, int. no. 9 : Assembly bill, int. no. 6 : brief in support of bill.* New York : West End Association, 1917. 44 p. February 6, 1917" New York Central Railroad Company; Riverside Park (N.Y.).

3207. _____. *Re—Senate bill, int. no. 9. Assembly bill, int. no. 6.* New York; West End Association, 1917. 4 p. "January 6, 1917"

3208. Cram, George Franklin. *Cram's bankers' and brokers' railroad atlas.* Chicago: George F. Cram, 1898. 590, 38 p.

3209. _____. *Cram's standard American railway system atlas of the world: accompanied with a complete and simple index of the United States/* Chicago: G.F. Cram, 1900. 606, 40 p.

3210. _____. *Cram's standard American railway system atlas of the world: showing all the railway systems in colors and numbers.... Accompanied by a concise and original ready reference index of the United States, Canada, Mexico and Cuba....* New York: G.F. Cram, 1910. 494, 32 p.

3211. Cramer, Barton Emmet. *North American freight rail: regulatory evolution, strategic rejuvenation and the revival of an ailing industry* / 2001. 401 l. (Thesis, Ph.D., University of Iowa.)

3212. Crampton, June Margaret. *A history of the Los Angeles* and *San Pedro Railroad.* 1929. 77 l. (Thesis, M.A., University of Southern California.)

3213. Crandall, Bruce V. *The carman's helper.* Chicago, Railway Educational Press, 1919. 213 p.

3214._____. *Railway equipment primer.* Chicago, Chicago Railway Equipment Company, 1911. 13 p.

3215. _____. *Railway track hand-book.* Chicago, Spencer Otis, 1913. 124 p.

3216. _____. *Terminal cost data.* Chicago, Railway Educational Press, 1919. 104 p.

3217. _____. *Track labor cost data.* Chicago, Kenfield-Leach, 1920. 11-110 p.

3218. Crandall, C.L. (Charles Lee). *Tables for the computation of railway and other earthwork.* 5th ed. New York : J. Wiley and Sons, 1916. 69 p.

3219. *Crane comments.* Bay City, MI: Industrial Works, 1919-1900s. Bimonthly.

3220. Crane, L. Stanley. *Rise from the wreckage: a brief history of Conrail.* New York, Newcomen Society of the United States, 1988. 44 p.

3221. Cranford, Sammy O. *The Fernwood, Columbia and Gulf: a railroad in the Piney Woods of south Mississippi.* New York, Garland Pub., 1989. 372 p. (Also: Thesis, Ph.D., University of Mississippi, 1983.)

3222. Crater, Warren B. *The Central Railroad of New Jersey: an album of Jersey Central photographs with history of construction and acquisition of its roads and lines.* Roselle Park, NJ: Warren B. Crater, 1963. 66 p.

3223. _____. *Locomotives of the Jersey Central: 1 to 999.* Roselle Park, NJ: Railroadians of America, 1978. 105 p.

3224. _____, Arthur E. Owen, Jr., E.T. Moore. *Locomotives of the Jersey Central.* Roselle Park, NJ: W.B. Crater, 1957. 84 p.

3225. Crawford, Golda Mildred. *Railroads of Kansas: a study of local aid, 1859-1930.* 1963. 281 l. (Thesis, D.S.S., Syracuse University.)

3226. Crawford, Jay Boyd. *The Credit Mobilier of America, its origin and history, its work of constructing the Union Pacific Railroad and the relation of members of Congress therewith.* Boston, C.W. Calkins & Co., 1880. 229 p. (Reprint: New York,

Greenwood Press, 1969. 229 p.)

3227. Crawford, Ryan, James E. Lewnard. *C&IM : Chicago & Illinois Midland Railway in color* / Scotch Plains, NJ: Morning Sun Books, 2009. 128 p.

3228. Crawford, Thomas M., Frederick A. Kramer. *Rails along the Hudson: a pictorial review of four decades on the New York Central between New York City and Albany.* New York, Quadrant Press, 1979. 96 p. (Bergen-Rockland Chapter, National Railway Historical Society.)

3229. Creamer, W.G. & Co. *Illustrated catalogue and price list of W.G. Creamer & Co., manufacturers of railway car trimmings, and dealers in car supplies of every description.* Brooklyn : W.G. Creamer & Co., 1887. 100 p.

3230. Creasey, William A., Robert B. Goldberg. *Safety of high speed guided ground transportation systems: potential health benefits of low frequency electromagnetic fields due to maglev and other electric rail systems*/ Washington, DC: Federal Railroad Administration, Office of Research and Development, 1993. 1 v. (Various pagings) (*DOT/FRA/ORD-93/31*)

3231. Credit Mobilier of America; Union Pacific Railroad Company; Massachusetts, Supreme Judicial Court. *The Union Pacific Railroad Co., in equity, vs. The Credit Mobilier of America* Boston, Mass., T.W. Ripley, 1879. 322 p.

3232. Crecer, Ralph, Barry Combs. *Train power: riding the rails to energy independence.* Independence, MO: Independence Press, 1981. 192 p.

3233. Crennan,, C.H. *War adjustments in railroad regulation.* Philadelphia, PA: American Academy of Political and Social Science, 1918. 333 p. (*American Academy of Political and Social Science, Annals, whole no. 165.*)

3234. Crerar, Adams & Co. (Chicago, Ill.) *Railway supplies.* Chicago, Crerar, Adams & Co., 1906. 536 p.

3235. *Crescent Limited : de luxe, all Pullman train : between New Orleans, Mobile, Montgomery, Atlanta, and Washington, Baltimore, Philadephia, New York.* S.l., s.n., 1929. 1 sheet, folded, 10 panels. 23 x 11 cm. Crescent Limited : Louisville & Nashville Railroad; West Point Route; Southern Railway; Pennsylvania Railroad.

3236. Crimmins, Harold. *A history of the Kansas Central Railway, 1871-1935.* Emporia, KS: Graduate Division of the Kansas State Teachers College, 1954. 34 p. (*The Emporia State research studies, v. 2, no. 4.*)

3237. Cripe, Alan R. *Containerization and integral trains.* Richmond, Reynolds Aluminum, 1963. 22 p.

3238. Crippen, Waldo. *The Kansas Pacific Railroad: a cross section of an age of railroad building.* New York, Arno Press, 1981. 63 p. (Thesis, M.A., University of Chicago, 1932.)

3238a. Crise, Steve, Michael A. Patris. *Pacific Electric Railway* / Charlestown, SC: Arcadia Publishing, 2011. 95 p.

3239. Crist, Ed. *Erie memories.* New York, Quadrant Press, 1993. 160 p.

3240. _____, John Krause. *L&HR: Lehigh & Hudson River.* Newton, NJ: Carstens Publications, 1986-(v. 1: *The west end.* v. 2: *The east end.*)

3241. _____, _____. *The Lehigh and New England Railroad.* Edited by Frederick A. Kramer. Newton, NJ: Carstens Publications, 1980. 80 p.

3242. _____, _____, Alvin K. Traz, G.M. Healthcliff. *Delaware & Hudson: Challengers and Northerns.* Hampton, VA: J&D Studios, 1988. 78 p.

3243. _____, Ross Grenard, John Krause. *Ticket to Silverton.* Rockville Centre, NY: Associated Artists of Dixie, 1988. 48 p.

3244. Crist, William Dale. *The role of railroads in the economic development of early Nebraska.* 1962. 115 l. (Thesis, M.A., University of Nebraska.)

3244a. Crittenden, H. Temple. *The two footers.* Boston: R&LHS, 1946. (Reprint: San Francisco: R&LHS, 2001.

3245. Crittenden, J. P., Charles B. Helffrich. *New York securities: a descriptive and statistical manual of the corporations of the New York City and Brooklyn, and the railroads of the United States.* New York: New York Securities, 1893. 2 v.

3246. Crittenden, Katharine Carson. *Get Mears! Frederick Mears, builder of the Alaska Railroad.* Portland, OR: Binford & Mort Pub; Anchorage, AK: Cook Inlet Historical Society, 2002. 285 p.

3247. Crocker, William A. *How to burn coal in locomotive engines.* New York, Wynkoop, Hellenbeck & Thomas, 1857. 39 p.

3248. Cromwell, William Nelson. *In re financial transactions of the New York, New Haven and Hartford Railroad Company.* New York : C.C. Burgoyne, Printer, 1914. 53 p.

3249. Crosby, Oscar Terry, Louis Bell. *The electric railway in theory and practice.* 2d ed. rev. and enl. New York, W.J. Johnston Co., 1896. 1 v.

3250. Cross, Andrew. *Some trains in America.* Munich, New York, Prestel, 2002. 1 v.

3251. Cross, C.S. *Engineer's field book.* 2d ed. New York, Press of Engineering News Pub. Co., 1885. 63 p.

3252. *Cross tie bulletin.* Paterson, NJ: Railway Tie Association, 1920-1968. 49 v.

(Monthly)

3253. *Crossties.* Paterson, NJ: Railway Tie Association, 1968-(Monthly)

3254. *Crossties to the depot.* Compiled and edited by John F. Gilbert. Raleigh, NC: Crossties Press, 1982-(v. 1: *Virginia railroad stations.* v. 2: *South Carolina railroad stations.)*

3255. Crossen, Forest. *The Switzerland trail of America; an illustrated history of the romantic narrow gauge lines running west from Boulder, Colorado: the Greeley, Salt Lake & Pacific, and the Colorado & Northwestern, later the Denver, Boulder & Western.* Boulder, CO: Pruett Press, 1962. 417 p. (Reprint: Fort Collins, CO: Robinson Press, 1978. 422 p.)

3256. Crossley, Rod. *Railway post offices of California and Nevada.* Lake Oswego, OR: La Posta Publications, 1991. 204 p.

3256a. _____. *Chasing the SP in California: 1953-1956.* Upland, CA: Southern Pacific Historical and Technical Society, 2011. 276 p.

3257. Crouch, George. *Erie under Gould and Fisk: a comparison of the past and present management, respectfully dedicated to the stockholders and bondholders generally /* New York: s.n., 1870. 162 p.

3258. Crouse, Chuck. *Budd car: the RDC story.* Mineola, NY: Weekend Chief Publishing, 1990. 226 p.

3259. Crouse-Hinds Company. *Crouse-Hinds imperial arc headlights and Imperial incandescent headlights.* Catalogs nos. 201 and 202/ Syracuse, N.Y. Crouse-Hinds Company, 1917. 1 v.

3260. _____. *Crouse-Hinds Imperial headlights: luminous arc, carbon arc, and incandescent for electric railway service.* Syracuse, N.Y., Crouse-Hinds, 1922. 252 p.

3261. Crouse, Russel. *Casey Jones's profession.* New York, Privately printed for William Bell Wait, 1930. 9 p.

3262. Crowder, Thomas R. *Sanitary regulations for the instruction and guidance of employes.* Chicago : s.n., 1914. 7 p. Pullman Company. Office of the Superintendent of Sanitation. Signed; Thomas R. Crowder, M.D., Superintendent of Sanitation.

3264. _____. *The sanitation of railway cars /* S.l., New York Railroad Club, 1916. 13 p.

3265. _____. *A study of the ventilation of sleeping-cars.* Chicago, Ill., American Medical Association, 1911. 51 p.

3266. _____. *The ventilation of sleeping cars : comparative tests of various types of exhaust ventilators* / S.l., s.n., 1915. 24 p. "Reprinted from the Transactions of the American Society of Heating and Ventilating Engineers."

3267. Crowell, Foster. *Report upon the Buffalo & Susquehanna Railroad*/ New York: Foster Crowell, Consulting Civil Engineer, 1893. 11 p. "Report is addressed to Harvey Fisk & Sons, Bankers, New York."

3268. Crowson, George M. *A lifetime of service: Wayne Johnston and the Illinois Central Railroad.* Chicago, Illinois Central Railroad, 1968. 38 p.

3269. Croxton, Fred C. *Wages and hours of labor in the building and repairing of steam railroad cars: 1890-1912.* Washington, DC: U.S. G.P.O., 1914. 89 p. (*United States Bureau of Labor Statistics. Bulletin. Whole no. 37. Wages and hours of labor series, no. 6.*)

3270. Crull, E.S. *Crull's time and speed chart, for the use of superintendents, train masters, train dispatchers, conductors, engineers*/ Chicago: Rand, McNally & Co., 1889. 71 p.

3271. Crum, Josie Moore. *The Rio Grande Southern Railroad.* Durango, CO: San Juan History, 1961. 431 p.

3272. _____. *The Rio Grande story.* Durango, CO: Railroadiana, 1957. 533 p.

3273. _____. *Three little lines: Silverton Railroad, Silverton, Gladstone & Northerly, Silverton Northern.* Durango, CO: Durango Herald News, 1960. 71 p.

3274. _____, Morris W. Abbott. *The Otto Mears passes.* Rev. ed. Durango, CO: s.n., 1948. 12 p.

3275. Crum, Michael R. *The development and application of an evaluative methodology for proposed railroad mergers.* 1988. 203 l. (Thesis, D.B.A., Indiana University.)

3276. Crumbley, Tony L. *Postal markings of the North Carolina railroads, including station agents, waterway, etc.* Newell, NC: North Carolina Postal History Society, 1994. 74, 5 p. ("Editing, postal marking restorations, Vernon S. Stoupe.")

3277. Crumley, Cy, Kenneth Riddle. *The Cy Crumley collection, with notes by his friend, Kenneth Riddle: his ninety-year photo collection of the East Tennessee and Western North Carolina R.R.* Townsend, TN: Little River Locomotive Company, 2001. 1 v.

3278. Crump, Russell Lee, Stephen M Priest, Cinthia Priest. *Santa Fe locomotive facilities.* Kansas City, MO: Paired Rail Railroad Publications, 2003-

3279. Crump, Spencer. *The California Western "Skunk" Railroad.* 4th ed., rev. Corona del Mar, CA: Zeta Pub., 1998. 1 v.

3280. _____. *Durango to Silverton by narrow gauge rails.* Corona del Mar, CA: Zeta

Pub., 1995. 111 p.

3281. _____. *Henry Huntington and the Pacific Electric: a pictorial album.* Los Angeles, CA: Trans-Anglo Books, 1970. 112 p.

3282. _____. *Rails to Grand Canyon: Santa Fe.* Corona del Mar, CA: Zeta Pub., 199-? 79 p.

3283. _____. *Redwoods, iron horses, and the Pacific: the story of the California Western Railroad.* 5th ed. Corona del Mar, CA: Zeta Pub., 1998. 1 v.

3284. _____. *Ride the big red cars: how trolleys helped build southern California.* 4th ed. Corona del Mar, CA: Trans-Anglo Books, 1970. 256 p.

3285. _____. *Riding the California Western Skunk railroad: Fort Bragg to Willets.* Corona del Mar, CA: Zeta Pub., 1988. 77 p.

3286. _____. *Riding the Cumbres & Toltec Scenic Railroad.* Corona del Mar, CA: Zeta Pub., 1992. 80 p.

3287. _____. *The Skunk Railroad: Fort Bragg to Willits: the story of the California Western.* 5th ed., rev. Corona del Mar, CA: Trans-Anglo Books, 1978. 64 p.

3288. _____ *Western Pacific; the railroad that was built too late.* Los Angeles, Trans-Anglo Books, 1963. 48 p.

3289. Crump, Thomas. *Abraham Lincoln's world: how riverboats, railroads, and Republicans transformed America*/ London, Continuum, 2009. 272 p.

3289a. CSX Transportation. *CSX Transportation locomotive directory.* Halifax, PA: Withers Pub., 2005-

3289b. _____. *CSXT news.* Jacksonville, FL: Corporate Communications Department of CSX Transportation, 1990. 1 v. (> *CSXT today.)*

3289c. _____. *CSXToday.* Jacksonville, FL: CSX Transportation's Communications and Public Affairs Department, 1991-

3289d. _____. *Operating rules.* S.l., CSX Transportation, 1987. 257 p.

3289e. _____. *Rules governing the handling of hazardous materials.* S.l., CSX Transportation, 1889. 7, 2 p.

3289f. _____. *Train accident prevention manual.* Jacksonville, FL: CSX Transportation, 2001. 1 v. (various pagings)

3290. Cudahy, Brian J. *A century of service: the story of public transportation in North*

America. Washington, D.C. American Public Transit Association, 1982. 80 p.

3291. _____. *A century of subways: celebrating 100 years of New York's underground railways.* New York, Fordham University Press, 2003. 388 p.

3292. _____. *Change at Park Street Under; the story of Boston's subways.* Brattleboro, 63 p.

3293. _____. *The Malbone Street wreck.* New York, Fordham University Press, 1999. 120 p.

3294. _____. *The New York subway: its construction and equipment: Interborough Rapid Transit, 1904.* Introduction by Brian J. Cudahy. New York, Fordham University Press, 2004. 150 p. (Originally published: New York, Interborough Rapid Transit Co., 1914.

3295. _____. *Rails under the mighty Hudson: the story of the Hudson Tubes, the Pennsy tunnels, and Manhattan Transfer.* New York, Fordham University Press, 2002. 111 p. (*Hudson Valley heritage series, 2.*)

3296. _____. *Under the sidewalks of New York: the story of the greatest subway system in the world.* Brattleboro, VT: S. Greene Press, 1979. 176 p. (2nd rev. ed. New York, Fordham University Press, 1995. 194 p.)

3297. Culbertson, Charles Allen. *Laws relating to the number of men required on railroad trains/* Washington, DC: U.S. G.P.O., 1909. 7 p. (*60th Congress, 2d session. Senate. Doc. 692*)

3298. Cullen, Elizabeth O. *History of freight cars in this country: memorandum listing 22 books and articles on the subject, published 1832-1958.* Washington, DC: Association of American Railroads, Bureau of Railway Economics, 1959. 4 l.

3299. _____. *Standard time: proposals, adoption, regulation: source material for detailed history, in Bureau of Railway Economics Library.* Washington, D.C.: Association of American Railroads, Bureau of Railway Economics Library, 1957. 25l.

3300. Culotta, Theodore J. *The American Railway Association standard box car of 1932.* San Mateo, CA: Speedwitch Media, 2004. 267 p.

3301. _____. *Steam era freight cards reference manual.* Guilford, CT: Speedwitch Media, 2006-2008. 2 v. (v. 1. Box and automobile cars. v. 2. Tank cars.)

3302. Culp, Edwin D. *Stations west.* Caldwell, ID: Caxton Printers, 1972. 265 p.(Oregon)

3303. _____. *Valley & Siletz Railroad: the Luckiamute River route.* San Mateo, CA: Western Railroader, 1958. 36 p.

3304. Cumming, Joseph B. *A history of Georgia Railroad and Banking Company and its corporate affiliates*, 1833-1958. Augusta, GA: Georgia Railroad and Banking Compnay, 1959. 68 p.

3305. Cumming, Mary G. *Georgia Railroad & Banking Company, 1833-1945; an historic narrative.* Augusta, GA: Walton Printing Company, 1945. 121 p

3305a. Cummings, Andy, Jerry Huddleston. *Dakota, Minnesota and Eastern: a modern Granger railroad.* David City, NE: South Platte Press, 2005.

3306. Cummings, Hubertis, Julia Smith McMillan, Donald H. Kent, S.W. Higginbotham. *The Allegheny Portage Railroad* / Harrisburg : Pennsylvania Historical and Museum Commission, 1957. 4 p. (*Historic Pennsylvania leaflet, no. 19.*)

3307. Cummings, James William. *The Cherokees and the conditional railroad land grants* / 1997. 123 l. (Thesis, M.A., University of Central Oklahoma.)

3308. Cummings, William John. *All aboard! along the tracks in Dickinson County, Michigan.* Iron Mountain, MI: R.W. Secord Press, 1993. 152 p.

3309. Cunney, E.G., J.T. May, H.N. Jones. *The effects of accelerated ballast consolidation*/ Washington, DC: Federal Railroad Administration, 1977. 179 p. (*FRA-OR & D-76-274.*)

3309a. Cunningham, Eckley Samuel. *Mechanical stoking vs. hand firing : the relative merits, costs and efficiencies from actual tests* / 1896. 64 l. (Thesis, M.E., Lehigh University.)

3310. Cunningham, Eileen Smith, Carlton J. Corliss. *Rural railroads, prelude to trails to rails* / Carrolton, IL: Eileen Smith Cunningham Reprints, 1937, 1956. 76 p.

3311. Cunningham, Joseph. *Interborough fleet.* Belleville, NJ: Xplorer Press, 1996. 160 p.

3312. _____. *Second Avenue El in Manhattan.* Hicksville, NY: N.J. International, 1995. 64 p.

3313. _____, Leonard O DeHart. *A history of the New York subway system.* New York? Cunningham, 1976-1977. 3 v.

3313a. Cunningham, Lora Ann. *A forgotten typology: the rediscovery of the train stations on the oldest railroad in the country*/ 2011. 190 l. (Thesis)

3314. Cunningham, Robert G. *Pearls of the prairie: life in small Dakota towns.* Bismarck, ND: Northern Lights, ND Press, 2002. 242 p.

3315. Cunningham, Wm A. *The railroad lantern, 1865 to 1930: the evolution of the railroad hand lantern as reflected by the United States patent records and by lanterns made by Cross, Dane & Westlake, Dane, Westlake & Covert, the Adams*

& *Westlake Manufacturing Co. & the Adams & Westlake Company*. Plano TX: Wm. A. Cunningham, 1997. 69 p.

3316. _____. *Santa Fe lanterns & locks, 1874 to 1928: tall globe hand lanterns and cast locks purchased by the Santa Fe Railroad*. Plano TX: Wm. A. Cunningham, 1997. 45 p.

3317. Cunningham, William James. *The accounting and statistical requirements of the Interstate Commerce Commission*. Washington, DC: Railway Accounting Officers Association, 1923. 8 p.

3318. _____. *American railroads: government control and reconstruction policies*. Chicago: A.W. Shaw, 1922. 409 p.

3319. _____. *The arithmetic of railroads in New England Boston*: New England Railroad Club, 1916. 139 p.

3320. _____. *The present railroad crisis*. Philadelphia: University of Pennsylvania, 1939. 84 p. (The Edward Eugene Loomis Foundation, Lafayette College. Lectures.)

3321. _____ *The Providence Plan for the consolidation of railroads in New England*. Boston: New England Railroad Committee, 1931. 4 p. 86 l.

3322. _____, George P. Baker. *Transportation of commodities*. Cambridge, MA: Harvard University, 1938. 1 v. (various pagings)

3323. Cupper, Dan. *Horseshoe heritage: the story of a great railroad landmark*. 2d ed. Halifax, PA: Withers Pub., 1993. 56 p.

3324. _____. *The Pennsylvania Railroad, its place in history, 1846-1996: a brief history and research guide*. Halifax, PA: Withers Pub., 1996. 32 p.

3325. _____. *Railroad Museum of Pennsylvania: Pennsylvania trail of history guide*. Mechanicsburg, PA: Stackpole Books, 2002. 48 p.

3326. _____. *Rockville Bridge: rails across the Susquehanna*. Halifax, PA: Withers Pub., 2002. 112 p.

3327. Curl, Ray, Robert McQuown. *Passenger train operations: the streamline era begins*. Crestwood, IL: Chicago & Eastern Illinois Railroad Historical Society, 1994. 85 p. (*The C & EI flyer, v. 13, no. 1-2.*)

3327a. Curlee, David. *UP 1998/1999 motive power annual*. La Mirada, CA: Four Ways West Publications, 1999. 160 p.

3328. Curry, Ota Thomas. *The speech of Abraham Lincoln in defense of the Rock Island Bridge in 1857*. 1936. 73 l. (Thesis, M.A., University of Iowa.)

3329. Curtin, D. Thomas. *Men, oil and war*. Chicago: Petroleum Industry Committee,

1946. 360 p.

3330. Curtis, Samuel Ryan. *Proceedings of a Pacific Railroad Convention, at Lacon, Illinois: with the address of Col. Samuel R. Curtis.* Cincinnati, Printed by J.D. Thorpe, 1853. 16 p.

3331. Curtis, Theodore H. *Objections to electric headlights on locomotives: as proposed by House Bill 1294.* Alabama, 1907. 6 p.

3332. _____. *Objections to electric headlights on locomotives: as proposed by House Bill 383.* Louisville, Kentucky, 1911. 106 p.

3333. Curtiss-Wright Corporation. *Speed with profit and comfort; the Curtiss-Wright train for the Pennsylvania Railroad.* Woodridge, NJ: Curtiss-Wright Corporation, 1958. 58 p.

3334. Cushing, Raymond, Jeffrey Moreau. *America's first transcontinental railway: a pictorial history of the Pacific railroad.* Pasadena, CA: Pentrex, 1994. 48 p.

3335. Cushing, William Channing. *Screw-spike and tie-plate test, Pennsylvania Railroad system.* Chicago, American Railway Engineering Association, 1917. 255 p. (*Bulletin of the American railway engineering association, v. 19, no. 200, Oct. 1917.*)

3336. Cushion Car Wheel Co. *The Cushion Car Wheel Co. of Indianapolis, Indiana, U.S.A.* Indianapolis, Ind., Baker-Randolph Litho. and Eng. Co., 1893. 16 p.

3337. *The cutting edge.* Mars. PA: Railway Tie Association, 1990-   (Quarterly)

3338. C.W. Hunt. *Narrow gauge railways.* New York, NY: C.W. Hunt, Press of Moss Engraving Co., 1889. 78 p.

3339. Cyclone Woven Wire Fence Co. *Cyclone Woven Wire Fence Co., Holly, Mich.: fence weaving machinery, fencing material, farm, lawn and railroad fence.* Holly, MI: Cyclone Woven Wire Fence Co., 1898. 16 p.

3340. *Cyclopedia of applied electricity.* Chicago, American Technical Society, 1923. 8 v. (Includes electric railways, railway signaling and car lighting.)

D

3341. *D., T., & I. railroad news.* Dearborn, MI: Ford Motor Co.; D., T., & I. Railroad, 1923-? Semimonthly.

3342. Da Costa, Phil. *Pacific Fruit Express ice refrigerator cars, 1906-1932: prototype specifications, diagrams.* S.l., Apache Press, 1978-

3343. Dabney, Walter D. *The public regulation of railways.* New York, NY: G.P. Putnam's Sons, 1889. 281 p.

3344. Dacus, J.A. *Annals of the great strikes in the United States; a reliable history and graphic description of the causes and thrilling events of the labor strikes and riots of 1877* / Chicago : L.T. Palmer Co.; Philadelphia : W. R. Thomas, 1877. 480 p. (Reprint: New York : B. Franklin, 1969; New York : Arno, 1969.)

3344a. _____. *Revolution in Pennsylvania: a history of the Railroad Union Strike and the "great uprising of 1877."* St. Petersburg, FL: Red and Black Publishers, 2011. 273 p.

3345. Daganzo, Carlos. *Dynamic blocking strategies for railroad yards: a preliminary exploration* / Berkeley" Institute of Transportation Studies, University of California, 1983. 43 p. (*Working paper. Institute of Transportation Studies, UCB-ITS-WP-83-8*)

3346. _____. *Dynamic blocking strategies for railroad yards: heterogeneous traffic* / Berkeley: Institute of Transportation Studies, University of California, 1984. 24 p. (*Research report. Institute of Transportation Studies, UCB-ITS-RR-84-9*)

3347. _____. *Dynamic blocking strategies for railroad yards: homogeneous traffic.* Berkeley: Institute of Transportation Studies, University of California, 1984. 51 p. (*Research report. Institute of Transportation Studies, UCB-ITS-RR-84-7*)

3348. _____. *Static blocking strategies for railroad yards* / Berkeley: Institute of Transportation Studies, University of California, 1983. 26 p. (*Research report. Institute of Transportation Studies, UCB-ITS-RR-83-2*)

3349. _____, Richard G. Dowling, Randolph W. Hall. *Railroad classification yard throughput: the case of multistage triangular sorting.* Berkeley, CA: Institute of Transportation Studies, University of California, 1982. 43 p. (*Research Report. Institute of Transportation Studies, UCB-ITS-RR-82-1.*)

3350. Daggett, Kenneth M., Frederick G. Bailey. *Alcos in Vermont.* Westmoreland, NH: New England Rail Service, 1983. 35 p. (*New England State limited, Vol. 5, no. 1.*)

3351. Daggett, Stuart. *Chapters on the history of the Southern Pacific.* New York, A.M. Kelley, 1966, 1922. 470 p.

3352. _____. *Principles of inland transportation.* 4th ed. New York, Harper, 1955. 788 p.

3353. _____. *Railroad consolidation west of the Mississippi River.* Berkeley, CA: University of California Press, 1933. p. 127-256. (*University of California publications in economics, v. 11, no. 2.*)

3354. _____. *Railroad reorganization.* Boston, Houghton, Mifflin and Co., 1908. 402 p. (*Harvard economic studies, v. IV.*)

3355. _____. *Southern Pacific unmerger; judicial proceedings for the separation of the Central Pacific and Southern Pacific Railroad lines.* Berkeley, CA: 1922. 32 p. (Reprinted from the *University of California chronicle* of October 22, 1922, vol. xxiv, no. 4.)

3356. _____, John Phillip Carter. *The structure of transcontinental railroad rates.* Berkeley, CA: University of California Press, 1947. 165 p.

3357. D'Agostino, Peter. *Coming and going: New York (Subway, Paris (Metro), San Francisco (BART), Washington (METRO).* San Francisco, CA: NFS Press, 1982. 86 p.

3358. Dahl, John C. *Buffalo Central Terminal : construction of a transportation landmark* / Oakland, NJ : Railroad Station Historical Society, 2006. 43 p. (*Railroad station monograph, no. 25.*)

3359. Dahlinger, Fred. *Circus World Museum presents trains of the circus, 1872 through 1956.* Hudson, WI: Iconografix, 2000. 126 p.

3360. _____. *Show trains of the 20th century.* Hudson, WI: Iconografix, 2000. 126 p.

3361. Dahringer, Homer Walston. *Design of a reinforced concrete coaling station*/ 1913. 29 l. (Thesis, B.S., University of Illinois.)

3362. *The daily railway age.* Saratoga Springs, NY: American Railway Master Mechanics' Association; Master Car Builders' Association, 1800s-(>*Railway age gazette.*)

3363. *D&H color guide to freight and passenger equipment: the Bridge Line to New England and Canada.* Jim Odell, et al. in cooperation with the Bridge Line Historical Society. Scotch Plains, NJ: Morning Sun Books, 1997. 127 p.

3364. Dakelman, Mitchell E. *Lehigh Valley 4: in color.* Scotch Plains, NJ: Morning Sun Books, 2007. 128 p.

3365. Dalby, H.A. *Train rules and train dispatching: a practical guide for train dispatchers, enginemen, trainmen and all who have to do with the movement of trains:*

contains the standard rules for both single and double track/ New York: N.W. Henley Pub. Co., 1911. 221 p.

3366. Dalman, John W. *A comparison of steam and electricity as applied to railway transportation, from an economical point of view.* 1896. (Thesis, M.E., Lehigh University.)

3367. *"The damage suit disease." A compilation of editorials, letters and addresses upon personal injury litigation against railroads in Mississippi.* Chicago: Chicago Legal News Press, 1913. 64 p. Claim departments.

3367a. D'Ambrosio, Charles Anthony. *Changes in railroad financial structures, 1929-1958.* 1974? 440 l. (Thesis, University of Illinois.)

3368. *The Dan Patch Railroad: articles about the Dan Patch Railroad.* Bloomington, MN: Bloomington Historical Society, 1964. 37 p. (Minneapolis, Northfield & Southern Railway Company; Minneapolis, St. Paul, Rochester & Dubuque Electric Traction Company.)

3369. Daniel, Jack. *Thoroughbreds of railroading, yesterday and today ...: a pictorial album of Memphis to Chattanooga area, including Memphis & Charleston Railroad, Southern Railway System, Norfolk Southern Corporation* / Memphis, TN: Grandmother Earth Creations, 1999. 308 p.

3370. Daniels, David D. *Railroad industrial development: the influence of selected railroads upon manufacturing locations* / 1974. 181 l. (Thesis, Ph.D., University of North Carolina.)

3371. Daniels, George H. *The center of the first city of the world: concerning the new Grand Central Station, 42nd Street, New York, of the New York Central Lines.* New York, New York Central and Hudson River Railroad Company, Passenger Department, 1904. 62 p. (*Four track series, no. 33*)

3372. Daniels, Richard K. *Freight car equipment (includes cabooses), 1945-1960: a summary of B&O summary of equipment books issued during that time.* Baltimore, MD: Baltimore and Ohio Railroad Historical Society, 1987. 19 p.

3373. Daniels, Rudolph L. *Sioux City railroads.* Charleston, SC: Arcadia, 2008. 127 p.

3374. _____. *Trains across the continent: North American railroad history.* Foreword by Roger Cameron, Thomas C. White, Frank N. Wilner. 2nd ed. Bloomington, IN: Indiana University Press, 2000. 257 p.

3375. Daniels, Winthrop More. *American railroads: four phases of their history.* Princeton, NJ: Princeton University Press, 1932. 120 p. ("Four lectures delivered at Princeton University in 1932 on the Stafford Little lectureship on public affairs.")

3376. _____. *The price of transportation service; a theory of American railroad rates.*

New York, Harper & Brothers, 1932. 86 p.

3377. Daniels, Wylie Johnston. *The village at the end of the road, a chapter in early Indiana railroad history.* Indianapolis, IN: Indiana Historical Society, 1938. 112 p. (*Indiana Historical Society publications, v. 13, no. 1.*)

3378. Danielson, Clarence L., Ralph W. Danielson. *Basalt: Colorado Midland town.* Boulder, CO: Pruett Pub. Co., 1965. 373 p. (2d ed.: Boulder, CO: Pruett Pub. Co., 1971. 382 p.)

3379. Danly, Susan. *The railroad in the American landscape, 1850-1950. Susan Danly Walther, guest curator; the Wellesley College Museum, Wellesley, Massachusetts, 15 April-8 June 1981.* Wellesley, MA:: Wellesley College, Jewett Art Center, 1981. 144 p.

3380. _____, Leo Marx. *The railroad in American art: representations of technological change.* Cambridge, MA: MIT Press, 1988. 218 p.

3381. Danneman, Herbert. *Rio Grande narrow gauge varnish: a Denver & Rio Grande narrow gauge passenger train car roster, 1871-1981.* Golden, CO: Colorado Railroad Museum, 2003. (*Colorado rail annual, no. 25.*) 328 p.

3382. _____. *A ticket to ride the narrow gauge: a chronological history of Denver & Rio Grande narrow gauge passenger trains and their equipment, 1871-1981.* Golden, CO: Colorado Railroad Museum, 2000. 272 p. (*Colorado rail annual, no. 24.*)

3383. _____. *Rio Grande through the Rockies.* Waukesha, WI: Kalmbach Pub., 2002. 128 p.

3383a. Danniel, Randall R., Marian L. Reis, Joseph R Douda. *The Burlington waycars /* West Burlington, IA: Mile Post 206 Publishing, 2012. 757 p.

3384. Danzig, Jerry C. *Procedures for analyzing the economic costs of railroad roadway for pricing purposes/* Washington, DC: Federal Railroad Administration, 1976. 2 v. (*DOT-FR-30028*)

3385. Darbee, Jeffrey T. *Taking the cars : a history of Columbus Union Station /* Columbus, OH: Columbus Historical Society, 2003. 60 p.

3385a. _____. *A tale of three cities : the union stations of Cleveland, Columbus, and Cincinnati /* Indiana: Indiana Historical Society, 2003. 24 l.

3386. Darlington, James W. *A railroad geography: the New York, Ontario and Western Railway.* 1974. 143 l. (Thesis, M.A., Syracuse University.)

3387. Darnall, Diane Thomas. *The Southwestern Indian detours: the story of the Fred Harvey/Santa Fe experiment in detourism.* Phoenix, AZ: Hunter Publishing Co., 1978. 327 p.

3388. D'Ambrosio, Charles A. *Changes in railroad financial structures, 1929-1958.* 1862. 440 l. (Thesis, Ph.D., University of Illinois.)

3389. Darr, Richard K. *A history of the Nashua and Lowell Railroad Corporation, 1835-1880.* 1956. 389 l.(Thesis, Ph.D., University of Nebraska.)

3390. Dart, Robert C., Karen Shockley, Roseann Schwaderer. *Contracting for coal transportation: rail service agreement under the Staggers Act* / Washington, DC: McGraw-Hill, 1982. 113 p.

3391. Darrow, Clarence. *Ex parte Eugene V. Debs et al., habeas corpus.* Washington, DC: s.n., 1894. 97 p. (United States. Supreme Court. United States. Circuit Court (Illinois, Northern District.) Pullman strike (1894).

3392. Darwin, Robert. *The history of the Union Pacific Railroad in Cheyenne: a pictorial odyssey to the Mecca of steam.* Carmel Valley, CA: Express Press, 1987. 386 p.

3393. daSilva, Marco P. *Railroad infrastructure trespass detection performance guidelines.* Washington, DC : Federal Railroad Administration, Office of Research and Development, 2011. 1 v. (various pagings)

3394. Dauchan, Davy. *Railtalk: a pocket guide to railroad slang and terminology/* Oakland, CA: Railtalk, 2000. 17 p.

3395. Daughen, Joseph R., Peter Binzen. *The wreck of the Penn Central.* Boston, Little, Brown, 1971. 365 p. (2d. ed.: Washington, DC: Beard Books, 1999. 365 p.)

3396. Daughety, Andrew F. *A hybrid cost function: an integration of "statistical" and "engineering" approaches to cost analysis for railroads/* Evanston, IL: Northwestern University, The Transportation Center, 1978-1979? 20 p.

3397. D'Autremont, Hugh. *Rails north.* Los Angeles, CA: Vantage Press, 1989. 273 p. (Railroad travel, 1918-1932.)

3398. Davenport Locomotive & Manufacturing Corporation. *Davenport steam locomotive repair parts.* Davenport, Iowa, Davenport Locomotive & Manufacturing Corporation, 19--? 42 p.

3399. Davenport Locomotive Works. *Rod locomotive catalog.* 10th ed. Davenport, Iowa, The Company, 1905. 72 p.

3400. Davidson, Bruce. *Subway.* New York, Aperture, 1986. 83 p.

3401. Davidson, Janet F. *Women and the railroad: the gendering of work during the First World War era, 1917-1920.* 2000. 405 l.(Thesis, P.D., University of Delaware.)

3402. Davidson, John Leander, Carl Fred Phillips. *A study of the locomotive water supply situation on the main line of the New York Central Railroad with respect to the utilization of larger tenders and their relation to track pan location.* Atlanta, 1928. 94 l. Thesis, Georgia Institute of Technology.

3403. Davies, Gerald Keith. *Rates and costs of grain transportation by railroad.* 1972. 209 l. (Thesis, Ph.D., Washington State University.)

3404. Davies, Greg B. *Union Pacific Railroad passenger cars.* Omaha, NE: G.B. Davies & Associates, 1976. 333 p.

3405. _____. *Union Pacific Railroad: freight cars of the 1950s.* Fremont, NE: Mid-America Publications, 1979. 98 p.

3406. Davies, Harold. *North American steam locomotive builders & their insignia.* Marceline, MO: Walsworth Pub. Co., 2005. 266 p.

3406a. Davies, John Vipond, J. Hollis Wells. *Terminal stations* / New York : Evening Post Job Printing Office, 1909. 24 l.

3407. Davis, A.L. *Rail failures for the trackman, with notes on rail specifications, rail manufacture, and rail sections.* Chicago, Hall-Stockton, 1919. 155 p.

3408. Davis, Burke. *The Southern Railway: road of the innovators.* Chapel Hill, NC: University of North Carolina Press, 1985. 309 p.

3409. Davis, C. S., G. F. Fowler, E. A. Phillips. *Railroad tank car safety assessment* / Chicago: Association of American Railroads, Technical Center, 1990. 12 l. "Railroad Tank Car Safety Research and Test Project." (*Report, Association of American Railroads, no. R-751.)*

3410. Davis, Champion McDowell. *Atlantic Coast Line, fragments of its history during over a century.* New York, Newcomen Society in North America, 1950. 28 p.

3411. Davis, Colin John. *Bitter storm: the 1922 National Railroad Shopmen's Strike.* 1989. 389 l. (Thesis, Ph.D., State University of New York at Binghamton.)

3412. Davis, David, Don Guillen, Charity Sasaoka, Satya Singh. *A review of turnout design and current practices/* Baltimore, MD: Transportation Technology Center, Inc., 2002. 1 v. (various pagings)

3413. Davis, David, and others. *Track-related research.* Washington, D.C., National Academy Press, 2001-(*Transit Cooperative Research Program; TCRP report, 71.)*

3414..Davis, David E. *Class I railroad labor markets: deregulation, mergers, and union bargaining.* 1998. 107 l. (Thesis, Ph.D., University of Oregon.)

3415. _____., Wesley W. Wilson. *Wages in rail markets: deregulation, mergers, and changing networks characteristics.* Fargo, ND: Upper Great Plains Transportation

Institute, North Dakota State University, 2002. 42 p. (*UGPTI departmental publications, no. 146.*)

3416. Davis, E.O. *The first five years of the railroad era in Colorado, June 19, 1867, to June 19, 1872, Julesburg to Pueblo in five years.* Golden, CO: Sage Books, 1948. 214 p.

3416a. Davis, F. Eugene. [Spokane, Portland, and Seattle Railway main line photograph album, 1938-1954.] .29 cubic feet. 160 black and white photographs in 1 album

3417. Davis, Gherardi, G. Morgan Browne. *Car trusts in the United States: a brief statement of the law of contracts of conditional sale of rolling stock to railroads*/ New York, NY: Evening Post Job Printing Office, 1894. 49 p.

3418. Davis, J. Frank. *Sam Houston, David Crockett, James Bowie : an appreciation of three immortal Texans for whom have been named the three new air-cooled dining cars of the Missouri-Kansas-Texas Lines, pioneer railroad of the great Southwest* / Dallas, TX : M-K-T Lines, 1931. 16 p.

3418a. Davis, J. Woodbridge. *Formulae for the calculation of railroad excavation and embankment*/ New York: Gilliss, 1877.106 p.   .

3419. Davis, James Leslie. *The elevated system and the growth* of *northern Chicago.* Evanston, IL: Department of Geography, Northwestern University, 1965. 180 p. (*Northwestern University studies in geography, no. 10.*)

3420. Davis, Jefferson. *Report of the Secretary of War on the several Pacific railroad explorations.* Washington, D.C.: A.O.P. Nicholson, n.d. 43 p.

3421. _____. *Report of the Secretary of War communicating the several Pacific railroad explorations. In three volumes.* Washington: A.O.P. Nicholson, Printer, 1855. 4 v. (33d Congress. 1st session. House Ex. doc: 129: serial no. 736-739.)

3422. _____. Speech *of the Hon. Jefferson Davis, of Mississippi, on the Pacific Railroad Bill, delivered to the Senate of the United States, January, 1859.* Baltimore, Printed by J. Murphy & Co., 1859. 36 p.

3423. Davis, Jeffery C., D. H. Stone. *Revised railroad tank car damage assessment guidelines for pressure tank cars* / Washington, DC: Federal Railroad Administration, Office of Research and Development, 2004. 1 v. (various pagings) (*DOT/FRA/ORD-03/22.*)

3424. Davis, John, L.A. Stockwell. *Public ownership of railroads*/ Girard, Kan., J.A. Wayland, 1898. 96 p. (*One-hoss philosophy, no. 6.*)

3425. Davis, John G. *Railroad to the Pacific. Speech of Hon. John G. Davis, of Indiana, in the House of Representatives, June 13, 1854.* Washington, D.C.: Printed at the Congressional Globe Office, 1854. 8 p.

3426. Davis, John P. *The Union Pacific Railway: a study in railway politics, history, and economics.* Chicago, IL: S.C. Griggs and Company, 1894. 247 p. (Reprint: New York, Arno Press, 1973. 247 p.)

3427. Davis, Leonard M. *Roseville's Pacific Fruit Express from 1900 to 1996.* Roseville, CA: Roseville Historical Society, 1997. 37 p.

3428. Davis, Llewellyn Clark. *The folded two stage railway classification yard.* 1967. 89 l. (Thesis, M.B.A., University of Pennsylvania)

3429. Davis, Mary Gillett. *Railroad consolidation in the United States, 1920-1944/* 1944. 324 l. (Thesis, Departmental Honors in Economics, Wheaton College.)

3430. Davis, Milton A. *The 50 best of PRR. A portfolio of the favorite fifty photographs from the camera and collection of the well-known PRR photo-historian. Book One.* Baltimore, MD: Barnard, Roberts, 1978. 52 l.

3431. _____, Charles S. Roberts. *B&O salute.* Baltimore, MD: Barnard, Roberts, 1987. 64 p.

3432. Davis, Patricia Talbot. *End of the line: Alexander J. Cassatt and the Pennsylvania Railroad.* New York, Neale Watson Academic Publications, 1978. 208 p.

3433. _____. *The railroad general: William Wallace Atterbury.* Atlanta, GA: Metro Printing, 1994. 205 p.

3434. Davis, W.D. (William Doyle) *Valuation study of the Pottawatomie Reserve lands sold by the United States of America to the Atchinson, Topeka & Santa Fe Railroad Company, August 7, 1868.* Kansas City, MO: Farm Management Association, 1949, c 1950. 154 (i.e. 166) l.

3434[a]. Davis Railroad Club (University of California, Davis). *A call for an investigation of the adequacy of rail passenger service between California and Oregon.* Davis, CA: s.n., 1967. 42 l.

3434b. _____. *A call for restoration to service of the Shasta Daylight passenger train between San Francisco, California and Portland, Oregon and a call for an investigation of Southern Pacific passenger service.* Davis, CA: Happy Train Free Press, 1967. 94 l.

3435. Dawson, Henry, Dulce Glober. *Trips in the life of a locomotive engineer.* New York, J. Bradburn, 1863. 224 p.

3436. Dawson, Philip. *Electric traction on railways.* New York, The D. Van Nostrand Co., 1910. 856 p.

3437. Day & Zimmermann; ConRail; United States. Federal Railroad Administration. *Providence & Worcester Railroad Company: acquisition of the Conrail Lines in Connecticut and Rhode Island.* Woonsocket, RI: Day and Zimmermann, Inc., 1981. 1 v..

3438. Day, Jerry B., Robert L. Grandt. *Denver and Rio Grande Western work equipment: OA to OZ.* Oakland, CA: R. Robb, 1989. 224 p. (*Narrow gauge pictorial, 7.*)

3439. Day, Leonard. *Signalling systems for electric railways and an attempt to meet existing requirements, particularly in third rail installations.* 1907. 28 l. (Thesis, Professional Degree, E.E., Worcester Polytechnic Institute.)

3440. Dayton Art Institute. *The railroad in painting: an exhibition of paintings shown at the Dayton Art Institute, April 19-May 22, 1949.* Dayton, OH: Dayton Art Institute, 1949. 20 p.

3441. Dayton Manufacturing Company. *Dayton car lighting fixtures; electric, gas, oil, candle, glassware and accessories.* Dayton, Ohio, Dayton Manufacturing Company, 19--? 158 p. (*Catalogue, no. 166.*)

3442. _____. *Dayton car trimming,: passenger car hardware and lighting fixtures, water and dry closets, washstands and saloon fittings, vestibule and platform trimmings, brake handles, sash fixtures, basket racks, headlights/* Dayton, Ohio, Dayton Manufacturing Company, 1916. 1600 p. (Catalog no. 200.)

3443. _____. *The Dayton Manufacturing Co., Dayton, Ohio, manufacturers and dealers in every description of furnishing for railway cars /* Dayton, Ohio, Dayton Manufacturing Company, 1903. 1073 p.

3444. Dayton, Mark R. *Economic viability of Conrail.* Washington, D.C., Congress of the United States; Congressional Budget Office, 1986. 85 p.

3445. De Borchgrave, Alexandra Villard, John Cullen. *Villard: the life and times of an American titan.* New York, Nan. A. Talese, 2001. 414 p.

3446. De Decker, Francis Joseph. *A study of ballast and ballasting/* 1948. 50 l. (Thesis, B.S., Michigan State College of Agriculture and Applied Science.)

3447. De Ford, Paul Victor. *In defense of empire : the Southern Pacific versus the Texas and Pacific.* 1948. 125 l. (Thesis, M.A., University of California.)

3447a. De Leuw, Cather & Company. *Proposal to the City of Chicago Department of Development and Planning for a study of downtown Chicago terminal alternatives for the Chicago Rock Island and Pacific Railroad commuter services.* Chicago: De Leuw, Cather & Co., 1975. 1 v. (various pagings)

3448. De Merritt, E. B. *Operation of trains by signal indication on a section of single track on the Central of Georgia Railway/* Swissvale, PA: Union Switch and Signal Company, 1928. 23 p. (*Bulletin, 127*)

3449. De Simone, Peter George. *Railroad spark fire liability: a problem in nineteenth century tort law.* 1977. 70 l. (Thesis, M.A., University of Virginia.)

3450. Dean, Albert G. *The new 160 mph trains: presented before the 57th convention of the Air Brake Association, September 14, 1965.* Philadelphia, PA: Railway Division, Budd Co., 1965. 19 p.

3451. _____. *Practical considerations in new railway passenger car designs* / New York : American Society of Mechanical Engineers, 1955. 14, 6 p. (*ASME. Paper no. 55-A-134.*)

3452. Dean, Francis E. *Concrete and wood tie performance through 425 MGT.* Pueblo, Co: Transportation Test Center, 1981. x, 63, A-2 p. (*FRA/TTC-81/06.*)

3453. _____. *The effect of service loading on the bending strength of concrete ties: interim report.* Pueblo, CO: Transportation Test Center, 1981. 28 p.

3454. _____. *Measurements of rail/tie and fastener clip strains.* Pueblo, CO: Transportation test Center, 1981. 26, A-5 p. (*FRA/TTC-81/03.*)

3455. _____, Robert H. Prause. *Concrete and wood tie track performance through 150 million gross tons/* Pueblo, CO: Facility for Accelerated Service Testing, Transportation Test Center, 1980. 61 p.

3455a. Dean, Harold Churchill. *A review of the problem of the electrification of the Saint Clair Tunnel on the Grand Trunk Railway* / 1909. 38 l. (Thesis, B.S., University of Illinois.)

3456. Dean, William H. *Coal, steamboats, timber, and trains: the early industrial history of St. Albans, West Virginia & the coal river, 1850-1925.* Charleston, WV: Pictorial Histories Pub., 2007. 250 p.(Distributed by the Coal River Navigation Co. (Saint Albans and Coal River, West Virginia)

3457. Dean, William Worth. *The significance of technology for the railroad freight services.* 1968. 137 l. (Thesis, M.B.A. in Transportation and Public Utilities, Graduate School of Arts and Sciences, University of Pennsylvania)

3458. Dearinger, Ryan L. *Frontiers of progress and paradox: building canals, railroads, and manhood in the American West.* 2009. 302 l. (Thesis, Ph.D., Department of History, University of Utah)

3459. Dearstyne, Bruce W. *Railroads and railroad regulations in New York State, 1900-1913.* New York, Garland, 1986. 393 p. (*American legal and constitutional history.*) (Thesis, Ph.D., Syracuse University, 1974.)

3460. Debebe, Fekru. *Nonlinear estimation of variability ratios for rail rate regulation under the Staggers Act.* 1985. 128 l. (Thesis, Ph.D., Colorado State University.)

3461. DeBoer, David J. *Piggyback and containers: a history of rail intermodal on America's steel highway*. San Marino, CA: Golden West Books, 1992. 192 p.

3462. DeBow, James Dunwoody Brownson. *Legal history of the entire system of Nashville, Chattanooga & St. Louis Ry. and possessions*. Nashville, TN: Press of Marshall & Bruce Co., 1900. 985 (i.e. 989) p.

3463. Debs, Eugene V. *You railroad men*. Chicago? Charles H. Kerr & Co., 1900s. 32 p.

3464. DeButts, Harry A. *Men of vision "who served the South!"* New York, Newcomen Society in North America, 1955. 24 p.(Southern Railway)

3465. Decco, Nora Breckenridge, Ida May B. Lundin. *Up & down hill on the Rocky Mountain Division*. Forest Grove, MT: Ida May B. Lundin, 1986. 132 p. (Chicago, Milwaukee, and St. Paul Railway Company.)
i
3466. Decker, H.L. *Strength requirements for special cars to transport 40-ft. trailers* / New York : American Society of Mechanical Engineers, 1959. 8 p. (*ASME. Paper no. 60-WA-263.*)

3467. Decker, Harry Lichliter. *Comparative tests of the Walschaerts gear and the Caprotti gear for locomotives*. 1930. 284 l. (Thesis, M.E., University of Nebraska, Lincoln.)

3468. Decker, Leslie Edward. *Railroads, lands, and politics; the taxation of the railroad land grants, 1864-1897*. Providence, RI: Brown University Press, 1964. 435 p. (Thesis, Cornell University)

3469. *Dedication, Buffalo Central Terminal : United Buffalo luncheon given by the Buffalo Chamber of Commerce, Saturday, June 22, 1929* / Buffalo : Press of Turner & Porter, 1929. 12 p.

3470. Deely, Nicholas. *Alaska Railroad*. Denver, CO: Sundance Publications, 1988- (v. 1: *The great Denali trek*.)

3471. _____. *Tanana Valley Railroad: the Gold Dust Line*, Alaska. Fairbanks, AK: Denali Designs, 1996. 161 p.

3472. *Defects of M.C.B. couplers and their cures; being a few notes on the weak points and mechanical defects of the present M.C.B. couplers as commonly used; with notes on the Hien double automatic coupler, which overcomes such defects*. Chicago: Railroad Supply Co., 1898. 44 p.

3473. Defense Transport Administration (U.S.) *The tank car story*. Washington, D.C., 1951. 48 p.

3474. Deforest, Walter Suffern. *The periodical press and the Pullman Strike: an analysis of the coverage and interpretation of the railroad boycott of 1894 by eight journals of opinion and reportage.* 1973. 227 l. (Thesis, M.A., University of Wisconsin-Madison.)

3474a. *Defunct Idaho railroads* / Memphis, TN: Books LLC, 2010. 133 p.

3475. DeGolyer, Everett L. *Texas railroads: the end of an era.* Dallas, TX: DeGolyer Foundation, 1970. 1 v. *(DeGolyer Foundation. Library. Occasional publication, no. 6.)*

3476. _____. *The track going back.* Fort Worth, TX: Amon Carter Museum of Western Art, 1969. 7 p. 103 plates. (In commemoration of the 100th anniversary of the completion of the first transcontinental railway.)

3477. Degrand, P.P.F. *Petition of P.P.F. Degrand and others praying a charter for the purpose of constructing a railroad and establishing a line of telegraph from St. Louis to San Francisco.* Washington, D.C.: s.n., 1850. (31st Congress, 1st session. Senate. Misc. doc. 28.)

3478. _____. *Proceedings of the friends of a rail-road to San Francisco at their public meeting, held at the U.S. Hotel, in Boston, April 18, 1849; including an address to the people of the United States; showing ... P.P.F. Degrand's plan. 4th ed.* Boston, Dutton and Wentworth, 1849. 24 p.

3479. DeGraw Ronald, G. Mac Sebree. *Pig & Whistle: the story of the Philadelphia & Western Railway.* Chicago, IL: Central Electric Railfans Association, 2007. 224 p.

3480. Deimling, Gene. *Southern Pacific switchers of the Pacific Lines.* Los Altos, CA: Benchmark Publications, 1987. 96 p.

3481. Del Grosso, Robert C. *BNSF Northwest: a part of the whole; the BNSF Railway in the Pacific Northwest.* Bonners Ferry, ID: Great Northern Pacific Publications, 2002. 128 p.

3482. _____. *Burlington Northern & Montana Rail Link locomotive directory, 1994.* Bonners Ferry, ID: Great Northern Pacific Publications, 1994. 104 p.

3483. _____. *Burlington Northern & Santa Fe, 2000-2001 locomotive and business car review.* Bonners Ferry, ID: Great Northern Pacific Publications, 2000. 176 p.

3484. _____. *Burlington Northern and Santa Fe Railway, 1997 annual: historical profile and motive power summary.* Bonners Ferry, ID: Great Northern Pacific Publications, 1998. 128 p.

3485. _____. *Burlington Northern and Santa Fe Railway: 1997 motive power review.* Bonners Ferry, ID: Great Northern Pacific Publications, 1998. 192 p.

3486. _____. *Burlington Northern and Santa Fe Railway: 1998-1999 motive power review.* Bonners Ferry, ID: Great Northern Pacific Publications, 1999. 192 p.

3487. _____. *Burlington Northern and Santa Fe Railway, 1999 annual.* Bonners Ferry,

ID: Great Northern Pacific Publications, 2000. 128 p.

3488. _____. *Burlington Northern & Santa Fe 2000-2001 locomotive and business car review* / Bonners Ferry, ID : Great Northern Pacific Publications, 2000. 176 p.

3489. _____. *Burlington Northern caboose book.* Revised ed. Bonners Ferry, ID: Great Northern Pacific Publications, 1994, c1993.

3490. _____. *Burlington Northern, railroad giant of the Pacific Northwest: a traveler's guide to all its subdivisions.* Bonners Ferry, ID: Great Northern Pacific Publications, 1994. 209 p.

3491. _____. *Burlington Northern Railroad locomotives, 1970-1996.* Bonners Ferry, ID: Great Northern Pacific Publications, 1999. 232 p.

3492. _____. *Burlington Northern trackside guide from Pasco to Marias Pass.* Bonners Ferry, ID: Great Northern Pacific Publications, 1991. 48 p.

3493. _____. *Burlington Northern trackside guide to the Columbia River Gorge.* Bonners Ferry, ID: Great Northern Pacific Publications, 1990. 34 p.

3494. _____. *Railfan's guide to Stampede and Stevens Pass.* Bonners Ferry, ID: Great Northern Pacific Publications, 1997.
124 p.

3495. _____, Joseph W. Shine. *Burlington Northern Santa Fe 1994 annual.* La Mirada, CA: Four Ways West Publications, 1995. 158 p.

3496. _____, Patrick C. Dorin. *The Burlington Northern Railroad in 1993.* Bonners Ferry, ID: Great Northern Pacific Publications, 1994. 128 p.

3497. _____, Richard Yaremko. *Montana Rail Link locomotives and rolling stock, 2000.* Bonners Ferry, ID: Great Northern Pacific Publications, 2000. 128 p.

3498. Del Vecchio, Michael J. *Iron horses: the illustrated history of the tracks and trains of North America.* Philadelphia, PA: Courage books, 2000. 176 p.

3499. _____. *Lackawanna Railroad trackside with Henry Peterson.* Scotch Plains, NJ: Morning Sun Books, 1999. 128 p.

3500. _____. *Pictorial history of America's railroads.* Osceola, WI: MBI Publications, 1998. 224 p.

3501. _____. *Railroads across America: a celebration of 150 years of railroading.* Osceola, WI: MBI Publications, 1998. 224 p.

3501a. Delano, Frederic Adrian. *Chicago railway terminals : a suggested solution for the Chicago terminal problem* / Chicago : Printed for private distribution, 1906. 12 p.

(Chicago Real Estate Board)

3502. Delaware and Hudson Company. *A century of progress; history of the Delaware and Hudson Company, 1823-1923.* Albany, NY: J.B. Lyon Company, Printers, 1925. 755 p.

3503. _____. *A century of steam locomotive development: August 8, 1829 –August 8, 1929.* Honesdale, PA: Delaware and Hudson Company, 1929. 8 p.

3504. _____. *Motive power on the Delaware and Hudson.* Albany? Press of the Delaware and Hudson Co., 1926. 105 p.

3505. _____ *Passenger and freight stations on the Delaware and Hudson.* Albany, N.Y., The Company, 1928. 360 p. (Reprint: Niskayuna, NY: Bridge Line Historical Society, 1999, 1928. 360 p.)

3506. _____. *Passenger, freight and work equipment on the Delaware and Hudson.* Albany? Press of the Delaware and Hudson Company, 1927. 126 p. (Reprint: Monrovia, CA: Society of Freight Car Historians, 1989, 1927. 126 p.: *Freight cars journal; monograph, no. 4.)*

3507. _____. *Rules for the government of the Transportation Department.* Albany? The Company, Brandow Printing, 1919. 185 p.

3508. *The Delaware and Hudson Company bulletin.* Albany, NY: The Company, 1900s-1930. (> *Delaware and Hudson Railroad bulletin.)*

3509. *The Delaware and Hudson Railroad bulletin.* Albany, NY? : Delaware and Hudson Railroad Corporation, 1930-? Monthly. (< *Delaware and Hudson Company bulletin.)*

3510. Delaware and Hudson Railroad Corporation. *Industrial development.* Albany? The Corporation, 1931. 166 p.

3511. _____. *Inspection of lines.* Albany? Delaware and Hudson, 1927. 126 p. (Types of freight and passenger cars.)

3512. _____. *Motive power, passenger, freight, and work equipment, 1926-1936.* Albany, N.Y., Press of the Delaware and Hudson Railroad, 1936. 126 p.

3513. Delaware, Lackawanna and Western Railroad Company. *The Delaware Lackawanna and Western Railroad Company's Terminal at Hoboken.* S.l., s.n., 1908. 52 p.

3514. _____. *Lackawanna, the route of the Phoebe Snow: brief history of the railroad with photographs and description of its motive power.* New York? Delaware, Lackawanna and Western Railroad Company, 1952. 24 p.

3515. _____. *List of officers, agents, stations, equipment and facilities, etc.* S.l., s.n.,

1909. 1 v.

3516. _____. *Rules of the Operating Department: effective* April *27, 1952.* S.l., s.n., 1952. 202 p.

3517. _____. *Rules of the Transportation Department.* New York, N.Y., Press of C.H. Jones & Co., 1901. 132 p.

3518. *Delaware, Lackawanna and Western Railroad Company: a register of the corporate records of the Lackawanna Division of the Erie-Lackawanna Company in the Syracuse University Library.* Edited by Howard L. Applegate and Lyall D. Squair. Syracuse, NY: Syracuse University Library, 1964. 32 l. (*Syracuse University. Library. Manuscript register series, no. 6.*)

3519. Delker, Ed. *Trains to Saint Louis: guide to train watching in the St. Louis area.* Wentzville, MO: E. Delker, 2001. 28 p.

3520. Dellinger, Clyde J. *Tweetsie and the Clinchfield Railroads: crossing the Blue Ridge Mountains.* 2d ed. Morganton, NC: News Herald Press, 1975. 75 p.

3521. Dellums, C.L., Joyce A. Henderson. *C.L. Dellums, International President of the Brotherhood of Sleeping Car Porters, and civil rights leader.* Berkeley, CA: Regents of the University of California, 1973. 159 l. (*The Bancroft Library, University of California, Berkeley, Regional Oral History Office, Earl Warren History Project.*)

3522. DeLong, Thomas Stover. *Logging railroads and their history in the coastal plain of North Carolina.* 1947. 28 l. (Thesis, M.F., Duke University.)

3523. Delquadro, David M. *The railroad retirement system: benefits and financing.* Washington, D.C.: Congress of the U.S., Congressional Budget Office, 1982. 43 p.

3523a. Demarest, Theodore F.C. *The rise and growth of elevated railroad law.* New York: Baker, Voorhis, 1894. 278 p.

3524. D'Emilio, Sandra, Suzan Campbell. *Visions & visionaries: the art & artists of the Santa Fe Railway.* Layton, UT: Gibbs Smith, 1991. 147 p.

3525. Demorro, Harre W. *California's electric railways : an illustrated review /* Glendale, CA: Interurban Press, 1986. 214 p. (*Interurbans special, 100.*)

3526. _____. *Electric railway pioneer; commuting on the Northwestern Pacific, 1903-1941.* Glendale, CA: Interurban Press, 1983. 127 p.

3527. _____. *The Key Route: transbay commuting by train and ferry.* Glendale, CA: Interurban Press, 1985. 2 v.

3528. _____. *Sacramento Northern.* Berkeley and Wilton, CA: Signature Press, 2009. 352 p.

3529. _____ *Southern Pacific Bay Area steam.* Burlingame, CA: Chatham Publishing Company, 1979. 143 p.

3530. _____, Vernon J. Sappers. *Rails to San Francisco Bay.* New York, Quadrant Press, 1992. 96 p.

3531. DeNevi, Don. *America's fighting railroads: a World War II pictorial history.* Missoula, MT: Pictorial Histories Publishing Company, 1996. 135 p.

3532. _____. *Tragic train: "the City of San Francisco."* Seattle, Superior Pub. Co., 1977. 188 p.

3533. _____. *The Western Pacific, Feather River route: railroading yesterday, today and tomorrow.* Seattle, Superior Pub. Co., 1978. 157 p.

3534. _____. *Western train robberies.* Millbrae, CA: Celestial Arts, 1976. 201 p.

3535. _____, Bob Hall. *United States Military Railway Service: America's soldier-railroaders in WW II.* Toronto, Stoddart, 1993. 160 p.

3536. Denney, C.E. *The Northern Pacific: first of the northern transcontinentals.* New York, Newcomen Society in North America, 1949. 24 p.

3537. Denney, John D. *Trains of the Pennsylvania Dutch country: Pennsylvania, Reading, Western Maryland, Strasburg, Stewartstown, Maryland & Pennsylvania, Wanamaker Kempton & Southern, and others.* Columbia? PA: s.n., 1966. 60 p.

3538. Dennis, Scott M. *Economic analysis of an end-to-end railroad merger/* Washington, DC: National Research Council, Transportation Research Board, 1988. 36 l.

3539. _____. *The effect of end-to-end railroad mergers on economic welfare.* 1985. 205 l. (Thesis, Ph.D., Economics, Northwestern University.)

3540. _____, Wayne Kenneth Talley. *Railroad economics/* Ámsterdam, Oxford: Elsevier JAI, 2007. 281 p.

3541. Dennis, William Jefferson. *The traveling post office; history and incidents of the railway mail service.* Des Moines, Homestead Printing Company, 1916. 128 p.

3542. *Denver & Rio Grande Western narrow gauge : alternative study /* Washington, DC: U.S. Department of the Interior, National Park Service, Western Service Center, 1970s. 32 p.

3542a. Denver and Rio Grande Railroad. Rio Grande Southern Railroad. *Danger warning to employes : list of obstructions and points of danger concerning employes engaged in train, engine, and switching service.* Denver : Denver and Rio Grande Railroad

Company, 1904. 34 p.

3543. Denver and Rio Grande Western Railway. *The Denver & Rio Grande Western Railroad Co. summary of equipment, ...* Denver, The Company, 1800s-? Rolling stock.

3544. _____. *Official directory of industries.* Denver; Denver & Rio Grande Western Railroad, 1900s-? Issued by Freight Traffic Dept.

3545. _____. *Railroad red book.* Denver, Denver and Rio Grande Railroad and Western Pacific Railway, 1884-1925.

3546. _____. *Rules and regulations of the Operating Department.* Denver, The Company, 1907. 104 p.

3547. _____ *Rules and regulations of the Operating Department.* Denver, The Company, 1938. 147 p.

3547a. _____. *Safety rules.* Denver : W.H. Kistler Stat'y Co., 1937. 54 p.

3548. Denver and Salt Lake Railroad. *Maintenance of way and structures.* Denver? The Company, 1929. 120 p.

3549. _____. *Rules and regulations of the Operating* Department, 1929. Denver? The Company, 1929. 188 p.

3550. _____. *Train rules, Operating Department.* Denver? The Company, 1913. 160 p.

3551. DePaola, Pier Luigi Gregory. *Management and organized labor relations of the Louisville and Nashville Railroad during the depression year 1893.* 1971. 119 l. (Thesis, M.A., University of Louisville.)

3552. Depew, Chauncey (Mitchell). *A retrospect of 25 years with the New York Central Railroad and its allied lines* / New York : s.n., 1892. 17 p.

3553. _____. *The state and the railroads. Argument of Chauncey M. Depew, General Counsel of the New York Central and Hudson River Railroad Co., before the Special Investigating Committee f the New York Assembly, at the Chamber of Commerce, November 28 and 29, 1879.* New York: Evening Post Steam Presses, 1880. (New York State.)

3554. DeRamus, Troy L. *Up and down the Red River and Gulf Railroad.* Alexandria, LA: Mpress Printing and Publishing, 1989. 166 p.

3555. Derby, E.H. *The overland route to the Pacific; a report on the condition, capacity and resources of the Union Pacific and Central Pacific railways, October, 1869.* Boston, Lee & Shepard, 1869. 97 p.

3556. Derleth, August William. *The Milwaukee Road; its first hundred years.* New York, Creative Age Press, 1948. 330 p.

3557. DeRouin, Edward M. *Chicago Union Station: a look at its history and operations before Amtrak* / Elmhurst, IL: Pixels Pub., 2003. 96 p.

3558. _____. *Moving mail and express by rail.* La Fox, IL: Pixels Pub., 2007. 224 p.

3559. _____. *The Pennsy in Chicago.* La Fox, IL: Pixels Pub., 2009. 256 p. (*Midwestern rail series, no. 3.)*

3560. _____. *Trackside around Chicago, 1957-1965, with George G. Speir.* Scotch Plains, NJ: Morning Sun Books, 1999. 128 p.

3561. Derr, William L. *Block signal operation.; a practical manual.* New York, D. Van Nostrand, 1897. 270 p. (2d ed., 1902. 270 p.)

3562. Derrick, Peter. *Tunneling to the future: the story of the great subway expansion that saved New York.* New York, New York University Press, 2001. 442 p.

3563. _____, David W. Kiehl, Kirsten Jensen. *Around town underground: the New York City subway in prints: from the collection of Reba and Dave Williams.* Stamford, CT: The Print Research Foundation, 2004. 26 p.

3564. Derrick, Samuel Melanchthon. *Centennial history of South Carolina Railroad.* Columbia, SC: State Company, 1930. 335 p.

3564a. Derry, Harold W. *History of the Louisville and Nashville Railroad in Tennessee.* Knoxville, TN: H. W. Derry, 1939. 51 l.

3565. Desai, Samir A., James Anderson. *Rail transportation requirements for coal movement in 1980.* Washington, DXC: United States. Department of Transportation, 1976. 212 p. (*Report. Transportation Systems Center, no. DOT-TSC-OST-76-32.*)

3566. *Descriptive circular of sleeping, hotel, dining, private and hunting cars, for charter to special parties, with diagrams, rates, etc.* Chicago, IL: Pullman's Palace Car Company, 1870s- ?

3567. DeskMap Systems, Inc. *Professional railroad atlas of North America: United States, Canada, Mexico.* 3rd ed. Austin, TX: DeskMap Systems, Inc., 2004. 112 p.

3567a. *Determining counterbalancing effects on C. & N.W. Railway locomotives by rail stress measurements* / Chicago : Chicago and North Western Railway Co., Association of American Railroads, Operations and Maintenance Department, Mechanical and Engineering Divisions, 1941. 91 p.

3568. Detroit, Toledo and Ironton Railroad. *Rules and regulations for the government of the Operating Department.* S.l, The Company, 1925. 171 p.

3569. _____. *Uniform alphabetical car reporting marks.* S.l., Detroit, Toledo and Ironton Railroad Co., 1900s

3569a. *Detroit, Toledo, and Ironton Railroad photographs subseries, 1922-1923.* Detroit: Ford Motor Company. Engineering Photographic Department. 2 cubic feet. Location: The Henry Ford.

3570. Detwyler, Carl A., Peter Brill, John Deserto. *That Unionville train: a look at the Middletown & Unionville/Middletown & New Jersey and its connection with the New York, Ontario & Western.* Middleton, NY:? Ontario & Western Railway Historical Society, 2003. 115 p.

3571. Deutsch, Reena. *San Diego and Arizona Railway : the impossible railroad.* Charleston, SC : Arcadia Pub., 2011. 127 p.

3572. *Development and present status of city planning in New York City* / New York: Board of Estimate and Apportionment, Committee on the City Plan, 1914. 76 p. Being the report of the Committee on the City Plan, December 31, 1914, together with papers presented at a meeting of the Advisory Committee on City Plan, December 17, 1914. Includes: Development of port and terminal facilities, by E. P. Goodrich.

3573. *Development of mechanized loading refrigerator cars.* Ft. Belvoir Defense Technical Information Center, 1948. 71 l. *(Report 2.304040-1.)*

3574. Deverell, William Francis. *Building an octopus; railroads and society in the late nineteenth century Far West.* 1989. 460 l. (Thesis, Ph.D., Princeton University.)

3575. _____. *Railroad crossing: Californians and the railroad, 1850-1910.* Berkeley, University of California Press, 1994. 278 p.

3576. Devine, David. *Slavery, scandal, and steel rails.* New York, iUniverse, 2004. 266 p.

3577. Devoe, D. B. *An analysis of the job of railroad train dispatcher.* Washington, DC: Federal Railroad Administration, 1974. 276 p. *(FRA-ORD&D-74-37; DOT-TSC-FRA-73-13.)*

3578. Devoe, Donald B., C.N. Abernethy. *Maintaining alertness in railroad locomotive crews: final report.* Washington, DC: Federal Railroad Administration, Office of Research and Development, 1977. 56 p. *(FRA-ORD-77-22.)*

3579. DeVos, Jerry. *The Sandy River and Rangeley Lakes Railroad and predecessors* / Towaco, NJ: Stonybrook Press, 2009. 282 p.

3580. Devulapally, Ranga Rao V. *Laboratory investigation on the effects of heavy axle loads on settlement and degradation of ballast*/ 1993. 199 l. (Thesis, M.S., University of Massachusetts.)

3581. Dew, Lee A. *The JLC&E; the story of an Arkansas Railroad.* State University, Arkansas State University Press, 1968. 121 p. (Jonesboro, Lake City and Eastern Railroad Company.)

3582. Dewey, Ralph L. *The long and short haul principle of rate regulation.* Columbus, OH: The Ohio State University, 1935. 287 p. (*Contribution in economics, no. 1.*)

3583. Dewhurst, Paul Coulthard. *The Norris locomotives.* Boston, Railway & Locomotive Historical Society, 1950. 80 p. (Railway and Locomotive Historical Society, Bulletin, no. 79.)

3584. De Witt, Philip H. *Coal cars of the L.V.R.R. Co.* 1888. 40 l. (Thesis, C.E., Lehigh University.)

3585. Dewsnup, Ernest R. *Freight classification*/ Chicago, Ill., La Salle Extension University, 1920. 4 v.

3586. _____. *Railway organization and working; a series of lectures delivered before the railway classes of the University of Chicago*/ Chicago, Ill., The University of Chicago Press, 1906. 498 p.

3587. DeYoung, Larry. *Conrail color guide to freight equipment.* Scotch Plains, NJ: Morning Sun Books, 2000-

3588. _____. *EL color guide to freight and passenger equipment.* Edison, NJ: Morning Sun Books, 1995. 128 p.

3589. _____. *Erie Lackawanna in color.* Edison, NJ: Morning Sun Books, 1991-2004. 5 v.

3590. _____. *Erie Railroad trackside with Robert F. Collins.* Scotch Plains, NJ: Morning Sun Books, 1998. 126 p.

3591. _____, Mike Del Vecchio. *Erie/DL&W color guide to freight and passenger equipment.* Scotch Plains, NJ: Morning Sun Books, 2001. 128 p.

3591a. Diacont, Dale W. *Yesterday's trains across the Commonwealth* / Lynchburg, VA: Blackwell press, 2012. 118 p.

3592. Dial, Denise Lorraine. *Railroad promotion in Davis and Appanoose Counties, Iowa, 1865-1880.* 1992. 77 l. (Thesis, M.A., Northeast Missouri State University.)

3593. Diamond, Jay G. *Car loadings of Montana agricultural commodities.* Helena, MT: Agricultural Marketing Service, 1939. 33 p.

3594. Dick, Fairman R. *Modern railroad box cars and the American system of free competitive enterprise : a presentation of facts given at the second Railroad Economics dinner, New York City, Nov. 19, 1952* / New York : Graphics Group, 1952. 29 p.

3595. Dick, Trevor J.O. *An economic theory of technological change; the case of patents and the United States railroads, 1871-1950.* 1970. 145 l. (Thesis, Ph.D., University of Washington.) (New York, NY: Arno Press, 1978, c1970. 145 p.)

3596. Dicken, Bruce K., Eric E. Hirsimaki, James M. Semon. *Reflections, the Nickel Plate years, Lake Erie & Western.* Cleveland, OH: Nickel Plate Road Historical & Technical Society, 1982. 59 p.

3597. Dickens, Laurie C. *Wreck on the Wabash.* Blissfield, MI: Made for Ewe, 2001. 132 p.

3598. Dickerman, William C. *43 hours: my era in railway equipment life.* Princeton, Printed at the Princeton University Press, 1943. 40 p.

3599. _____. *The locomotive on the railroads' battlefield.* Princeton, NJ: Printed at the Princeton University Press, 1931. 36 p. ("An address before Princeton University in the Cyrus Fogg Brackett lectureship in applied engineering and technology delivered on April 14, 1931.")

3600. _____. *The modern freight car.* 1896. 70 l. 20 mounted photographs of freight cars. (Thesis, M.E. Lehigh University.)

3601. _____. *Modern trends in railway motive power; an address before the New York Railroad Club delivered on April 21, 1933.* New York, N.Y., Reprinted by American Locomotive Company, 1933. 48 p.

3602. _____. *Steam and the railroads*/ Princeton, The Princeton University Press, 1936. 22 p.

3603. Dickinson, A. Bray, Roy Graves, Ted Wurm, Alvin C. Graves. *Narrow gauge to the Redwoods: the story of the North Pacific Coast Railroad and San Francisco Bay paddle-wheel ferries.* 2d ed. Glendale, CA: Trans-Anglo Books, 1981.

3604. Dickinson, Jack L. *Better take two guns : the N&Ws special agents (railroad detectives) and their W. VA. cases.* Huntington, WV: J.L. Dickinson, 2008. 211 p.

3605. _____. *Wheels aflame, whistle wide open : train wrecks of the N&W Railroad, 1892-1959* / Huntington, WV : J.L. Dickinson, 2010. 299 p.

3606. _____, Kay Stamper Dickinson. *Trail of the Powhatan Arrow : The N & W's Big Sandy Line, Kenova to Williamson, W.Va.* / Huntington, WV: J.L. Dickinson, 2007. 301 p. N & W Railway. Yellow Poplar Lumber Co.

3607. Dickinson, Thorn. *A design for a new terminal in East Boston, Massachusetts for the Boston, Revere Beach and Lynn Railroad* / 1914. 49, 4 l. (Thesis, B.S., Massachusetts Institute of Technology, Department of Civil Engineering.)

3608. Dickinson, William Penn. *The social saving generated by the Richmond & Danville Railroad: 1859* / 1975. 126 l. (Thesis, M.A., University of Virginia.)

3609. Dickman, Howard Leigh. *James Jerome Hill and the agricultural development of the Northwest.* 1977. 410 l. (Thesis, Ph.D., University of Michigan.)

3610. Dickon, Chris. *Eastern Shore Railroad.* Charleston, SC: Arcadia, 2006. 128 p. (New York, Philadelphia & Norfolk Railroad.)

3611. Dickson Manufacturing Company. *Illustrated catalogue of locomotives.* New York, N.Y., Unz & Company, 1898. 72 p.

3612. _____. *Illustrated catalogue of locomotives manufactured by the Dickson Manufacturing Company, Scranton and Wilkes-Barre, Pa. and 112 Liberty Street, New York, U.S.A.* Scranton, Pa., s.n. 1886. 272 p.

3613. _____. *Illustrated catalogue of narrow-gauge locomotives.* Scranton, Pa., Dickson Manufacturing Company, 1885. 128 p.

3614. _____. *Illustrated catalogue of standard gauge locomotives manufactured by the Dickson Manufacturing Company, Scranton, Pa. and 112 Liberty Street, New York, U.S.A.* Scranton, Pa., Dickson Manufacturing Company, 1885. 143 p.

3615. *Dictionary of car and locomotive terms.* Omaha, NE: The Railway Educational Bureau, 1974. 48 p.

3616. *A dictionary of electric railway material.* Edited by the staff of Electric Railway journal. 4th ed. New York, McGraw Publishing Company, 1908. 184 p.

3617. *A dictionary of railroad terms.* Compiled by W.E. (Bill) Wood. Belen, NM: W.E. Wood, 1990. 1 v.

3618. *The dictionary of railway track terms.* Compiled by Christopher F. Schulte. Philadelphia, PA: RCON Services, 1989. 187 p. (2d ed. Omaha, NE: Simmons-Boardman Books, 1993. 225 p.)

3619. *Dictionary of standard terms.* Chicago, IL: Association of American Railroads, Operations and Maintenance Department, Damage Prevention Section, 1982. 93 p.

3620. Diebert, Timothy S., Joseph A. Strapac. *Southern Pacific Company steam locomotive compendium.* Huntington Beach, CA: Shade Tree Books, 1987. 426 p.

3620a. Dieckmann, Thomas Wilbur. *The possibilities of freight transportation by interurban electric railways* / 1915. 48 l. (Thesis, B.A., University of Illinois.)

3621. Diehl, John Christopher. *A study of reducing the helper grade at Horn, Renovo Div., P.R.R.* / 1910. 32 2 l. (Thesis, B.S. Massachusetts Institute of Technology,

Department of Civil Engineering.)

3622. Diehl, Lorraine B. *The late, great Pennsylvania Station*. New York, American Heritage, 1985. 168 p. (New York, Four Walls Eight Windows, 1996. 168 p.)

3623. _____. *Subways: the tracks that built New York City*. New York, Clarkson Potter/Publishers, 2004. 123 p.

3623a. Diehl, Thomas. *The shops of the East Broad Top Railroad: at Rockhill Furnace, Pennsylvania*. Charleston, SC: CreateSpace Independent Publishing Platform, 2011. 64 p.

3624. Diemer, Hugo. *Self-propelled railway cars*. Chicago, American School of Correspondence, 1910. 16 p.

3625. Dienemann, P. *Analysis of railway operating costs for class I line-haul railroads /* Bethesda, MD: Resource Management Corporation (RMC), 1973. 1 v. (*RMC report no. UR-215*.)

3625a. Diers, John W. *St. Paul Union Depot /* Minneapolis: University of Minnesota press, 2013. 285 p.

3626. *Diesel-electric locomotive handbook; a basic reference book for enginemen, maintenance men and other railroad personnel engaged in operating and maintaining diesel-electric locomotives*. New York, Simmons-Boardman Publishing Corporation, 1951. 2 v.

3627. *Diesel-electrics—how to keep 'em rolling: the complete series as it appeared in Railway Locomotives and Cars*. A.G. Oehler, editor. New York, Simmons-Boardman Publishing Corporation, 1954. 139 p.

3628. *Diesel locomotive, rail diesel car and gas electric car diagram book*. 2d ed. Montgomery, AL: The New Haven Railroad Historical and Technical Association, 1978. 24 p.

3629. *Diesel locomotives; increasing use and future outlook for diesel engines on American railroads, and their "off line" usages*. Chicago, IL: Diesel Engine Manufacturers Association, 1945. 7 p.

3630. *Diesel and gas turbine progress*. Milwaukee WI: Diesel Engines, 1957-

3631. *Diesel progress*. New York, s.n., 1935-1957. 23 v.

3632. Dietrich, William E. Feero, William L. Jacobs. *Safety of high speed guided ground transportation systems: comparison of magnetic and electric fields of conventional and advanced electrified transportation systems/* Washington, DC: Federal Railroad Administration, Off ice of Research and Development, 1993. 70 p. (*DOT/FRA/ORD-93/07*)

3633. Dietz, Paul C. *Firing on the Pennsy: a fireman on the Pennsylvania Railroad describes the "last hurrah" of the steam engine, 1943-1947*. Baltimore, MD: Gateway Press, 2001. 97 p.

3634. Dietz, Paul T. *Operation of the railroads by the United States government during the Civil War, 1861-1865*. 1950. 1 v. (unpaged) (Thesis, M.A., Marquette University.)

3635. Digerness, David S., John W. Maxwell, Richard A Ronzio. *The Mineral Belt: an illustrated history, featuring the Denver, South Park & Pacific Railroad, and the gold-and-silver mining industry of the fabulous Mineral Belt of Colorado.* Silverton, CO: Sundance Books, 1977-

3636. Dill, Tom. *Southern Pacific's colorful Shasta Route*. La Mirada, CA: Four Ways West Publications, 1996. 126 p.

3637. _____. *Southern Pacific's Overland Route*. La Mirada, CA: Four Ways West Publications, 1999. 127 p.

3638. _____. *Southern Pacific's San Joaquin Valley Line*. La Mirada, CA: Four Ways West Publications, 2001. 127 p.

3639. _____. *Southern Pacific's Sunset Route: including the Golden State Route, El Paso to Tucumcari, New Mexico* / La Mirada, CA: Four Ways West Publications, 2009. 128 p.

3640. _____, Walter R. Grande. *The red electrics: Southern Pacific's Oregon interurban*. Edmonds, WA Pacific Fast Mail, 1994. 135 p.

3641. Dillon, John Forrest, Theos French. *Pacific railroad laws, including charters and acts of Congress, relating to or affecting the Union Pacific Railroad, the Kansas Pacific Railway, the Denver Pacific Railway, the Central Pacific Railroad, the Atlantic & Pacific Railroad and the Texas & Pacific Railroad, the Northern Pacific Railroad...* New York: Printed for the Union Pacific Railway Co. [E.C. Miles, publisher and printer], 1890. 269 p.

3642. Dillon, Sydney, J. Proctor Knott. *Letter of president of Union Pacific Railroad company relative to a settlement of its indebtedness to the United States*. Washington, DC: U.S. G.P.O., 1876. 5 p. J. Proctor Knott, chairman of the Committee on the Judiciary, U.S. House of Representatives.

3643. Dils, Lenore. *Horny Toad man*. El Paso? TX: Boots and Saddle Press, 190 p. (AT&SF)

3644. Dilts, James D. *The great road: the building of the Baltimore and Ohio, the nation's first railroad, 1828-1853*. Stanford, CA: Stanford University Press, 1993. 472 p.

3645. Dilts, Larry D. *Union Pacific's Plainville Branch : an illustrated history.* Colby, KS : L.D.D. Publications, 2010. 395 p.

3646. DiMasi, Frank P. *Engineering data characterizing the fleet of U.S. railway rolling stock: final report.* Washington, D.C., Federal Railroad Administration, Office of Research and Development, 1981. 2 v. (v. 1: User's guide; v. 2: Methodology and data.) (FRA/ORD-81/75.1 and 81/75.2.)

3647. Dimmick, Luther Fraser. *A discourse on the moral influence of rail-roads/* Boston, Tappan & Dennet, 1841. 125 p. (Railroads and Sunday legislation)

3648. *The Dinky: C&NW narrow gauge in Wisconsin.* Gregg Condon, Robert Felten, James Nickoll. S.l., Marsh Lake Productions 1993. 80 p.

3649. Dineen, John. *GE transportation: 100 years growing forward.* Exton: The Newcomen Society of the United States, 2007. 16 p. (*Newcomen publication, no. 1615.*)

3650. *Directory of freight station accounting codes: including all of North America.* Washington, DC: Economics and Finance Dept., Agent Tariff FSAC 6000, Association of American Railroads, 1991-   Annual.

3651. *Directory of industries and historical and statistical data: Chicago and North Western Railway; Chicago, St. Paul, Minneapolis and Omaha Railway.* Dayton, OH: Reynolds & Reynolds, 1941. 596 p.

3652. *The directory of North American railroads, association, societies, archives, libraries, museums and their collections.* Holly T. Hansen, compiler. Croydon, UT: H.T. Hansen, 1999. 131 p.

3653. *Directory of the Cumberland Valley Railroad main line : Harrisburg, Pa. to Hagerstown, Md.* / Newburgh, NY: Breed Pub. Co., 1900-1920s. Biennial.

3654. *Directory of the New York, Ontario and Western Railway from Cornwall to Norwich : and branches for the year 1890 : embracing a general directory of the adult population of the cities, villages and stations on the main line from Cornwall Landing to Norwich : and the Ellenville, Delhi and New Berlin Branches.* Newburgh, NY: Thompson & Breed, 1890. 710 p.

3655. *Directory of the New York, Ontario and Western Railway from Norwich to Oswego, for the year 1891.* Newburgh, NY: Thompson & Breed, 1892. 302 p.

3656. *Directory of the New York, Ontario and Western Railway from Norwich to Oswego, for the year 1900.* 6th ed. Newburgh, NY: Thompson & Breed, 1900.

3657. *Directory of the New York, Ontario and Western Railway from Norwich to Oswego, for the year 1905.* 7th ed. Newburgh, NY: Thompson & Breed, 1905. 371 p.

3658. *Directory of the West Shore Railroad from Kingston to Albany ... containing an advertisers' classified business directory.* Newburgh, NY: J.H. Topping & Co., 1892-

3659. Dirkes, Rod. *The Reading's T-1 Locomotive: an unusual Northern.* Andover, NJ: Andover Junction Publications, 1987.
64 p.

3660. _____, John Krause with the assistance of Robert F. Collins. *The route of the Erie Limited: from Chicago—to Jersey City.* Featuring photographs by Robert F. Collins and Paul Slager. Hampton, VA: Three Star Productions, K-C Publications, 1986. 48 p.

3660a. *Disaster relief by railroads, 1906-1930.* Washington, DC: Bureau of Railway Economics, Library, 1930.

3661. Diski, Jenny. *Stranger on a train: daydreaming and smoking around America with interruptions.* New York, Picador USA, 2002. 280 p.

3662. Disman, Martha J. *Rail freight systems.* [proceedings of the Carnegie-Mellon Conference on Rail Freight Systems, May 22-23, 1978]. Pittsburgh, Transportation Research Institute, Carnegie-Mellon University, 1978. 8, 163 p.

3663. *The disposal of discarded railroad wood crossties: a method of analyzing alternatives/* Washington, DC: Association of American Railroads, 1984. 145 p.

3664. *Distribution of the rail revenue contribution by commodity groups/* Washington, DC: Interstate Commerce Commission, Bureau of Accounts, Cost Finding and Valuation, 1947- . Annual.

3665. Disturnell, John. *Disturnell's railroad, steamboat, and telegraph book: being a guide through the middle, northern, and eastern states and Canada: also giving the great lines of travel south and west and the ocean steam packet arrangements, containing tables of distances, &c. telegraph lines and charges, list of hotels, express offices, &c. &c.* New York, NY: J. Disturnell, 1849. 87, 8 p. (New York, NY: J. Disturnell, 1850. 103, 5 p.

3666. Ditto, Susan C. *Comings and goings: the history of the Oxford railroad depot /* Oxford, MS: University of Mississippi, 2004. 54 p.

3667. *The Dixie Line: official publication of the Louisville & Nashville Historical Society.* Glenwood, IL: The Society, 1983- . Bimonthly.

3668. *Dixie mail: the newsletter of the C & EI RR Historical Society.* S.l., The Society, 2007- . Irregular.

3669. Dixon, Dick, Russ Collman. *Trails among the Columbine: the D & RG's Calumet Branch and the Turret Mining Area.* Denver, CO: Sundance Publications, 1995. 320 p.

3670. Dixon, Frank Haigh. *State railroad control, with a history of its development in*

Iowa. New York, T.Y. Crowell & Co., 1896. 251 p.

3671. _____, Julius H. Parmelee. *War administration of the railways in the United States and Great Britain/* New York, NY: Oxford University Press, 1919. 203 p.

3672. Dixon, Jefferson Max. *The Central Railroad of Georgia, 1833-1892.* 1953. 362 l. (Thesis, Ph.D., George Peabody College for Teachers.)

3673. _____. *Georgia railroad growth and consolidation, 1860-1917.* 1949. 144 l. (Thesis, M.A., Emory University.)

3674. Dixon, John E. *Lima-Hamilton: its historical past, 1869, 1845, and later.* New York, Newcomen Society, American Branch, 1948. 40 p.

3675. Dixon, O.O. *Distinctive features of track equipment of the New York subways.* New York, N.Y., Railroad Club, 1914. 10 p.

3676. Dixon, Stuart P. *The Honesdale Branch of the Delaware & Hudson Railroad: rails through Canaan.* Washington, D.C., U.S. Department of Justice, Federal Bureau of Prisons; Pennsylvania Historical and Museum Commission; Louis Berger Group, 2004. 86 p. (Includes "The Gravity Railroad of the Delaware & Hudson Coal Company.")

3677. Dixon, Thomas W. *Appalachian coal mines & railroads.* Lynchburg, VA: TLC Publishing, 1994. 74 p.

3678. _____. *Baltimore & Ohio steam locomotives: the last 30 years: 1938-1958.* Lynchburg, VA: TLC Publishing, 2003. 1 v.

3679. _____. *Baltimore & Ohio's magnificent 2-8-8-4 EM-1 articulated locomotive.* Lynchburg, VA: TLC Publishing, 2008. 74 p.

3680. _____. *C & O for progress: the Chesapeake & Ohio at mid-century.* Clifton Forge, VA: Chesapeake & Ohio Historical Society, 2008. 176 p.

3681. _____. *Chesapeake & Ohio Alleghany Subdivision.* Alderson, WV: Chesapeake and Ohio Historical Society, 1985. 143 p.

3682. _____. *Chesapeake and Ohio H7 series.* Annapolis, MD: Published for N.J. International, Inc. by Leeward Publications, 1979. 54 p.

3683. _____. *The Chesapeake & Ohio in color.* Lynchburg, VA: TLC Publishing, 1992. 86 p.

3684. _____. *Chesapeake & Ohio in the coal fields.* Clifton Forge, VA: Chesapeake & Ohio Historical Society, 1995. 1 v.

3685. _____. *Chesapeake and Ohio: main lines & mine runs in West Virginia.* Rockville

Centre, NY: Associated Artists of Dixie, 1988. 80 p.

3685a. _____. *The Chesapeake & Ohio Railway: a concise history and fact guide.* Clifton Forge, VA: The Chesapeake & Ohio Historical Society, 2012. 160 p.

3686. _____. *The Chesapeake & Ohio Railway at Hawks Nest, West Virginia.* Clifton Forge, VA: Chesapeake & Ohio Historical Society, 200. 24 p.

3687. _____. *Chesapeake & Ohio Railway in the coal fields of West Virginia and Kentucky, mines, towns, trains.* Clifton Forge, VA: Chesapeake & Ohio Historical Society, 2006, 2008. 108 p.

3688. _____. *Chesapeake & Ohio Railway in West Virginia—photos, 1940-1960.* Clifton Forge, VA: Chesapeake & Ohio Historical Society, 2005. 80 p.

3689. _____. *Chesapeake & Ohio standard structures.* Clifton Forge, VA: Chesapeake & Ohio Historical Society, 1991. 64 p.

3690. _____. *Chesapeake & Ohio: superpower to diesels.* Newton, NJ: Carstens Publications, Inc., 1984. 128 p.

3691. _____. *The Chesapeake & Ohio Railway's Craig Valley Branch.* Clifton Forge, VA: Chesapeake & Ohio Historical Society, 1991. 16 p.

3692. _____. *Chesapeake & Ohio's Pere Marquettes: America's first post-war streamliners, 1946-1971.* Lynchburg, VA: TLC Publishing, 2003. 1 v.

3693. _____. *The Chessie era.* Lloyd D. Lewis, editor. Sterling, VA: TLC Publishing, 1990. 64 p.

3694. _____. *Chessie: the railroad kitten.* Sterling, VA: TLC Publishing, 1988. 64 p.

3695. _____. *Early diesels: Chesapeake and Ohio.* Designed and edited by John Krause and Ed Crist. Andover, NJ: Andover Junction Publications, 1988. 64 p.

3695a. _____. *Lima Super power steam locomotives.* Forest, VA: TLC Publishers, 2010. 144 p.

3696. _____. *Norfolk & Western's Powhatan Arrow/* Forest, VA: TLC Pub., 2009. 113 p.

3697. _____. *Steam locomotive coaling stations and diesel locomotive fueling facilities.* Lynchburg, VA: TLC Publishing, 2002. 80 p.

3697a. _____. *West Virginia railroads: Chesapeake & Ohio Railway* / Forest, VA: TLC Pub., 2010. 144 p. (Volume 2)

3698. _____. *West Virginia railroads: railroading in the Mountain State.* Forest, VA:

TLC Pub, Inc., 2009. 128 p.

3698a. _____. *West Virginia railroads: geared logging locomotives.* Forest, VA: TLC Publishing, 2013. 112 p. (Volume 5)

3699. _____, Art Million;. *Pere Marquette power.* Edited by Carl W. Shaver Alderson, WV: Chesapeake and Ohio Historical Society, 1984. 244 p.

3700. _____, Bob Withers. *Baltimore & Ohio's magnificent 2-8-8-2 EM-1 articulated locomotive.* Forest, VA: TLC Publishing, 2008. 69 p.

3700a. _____, Allen Eckle, William E. Simonton. *The Chesapeake & Ohio Railway in Hinton, West Virginia* / Clifton Forge, VA: Chesapeake & Ohio Historical Society, 2011. 80 p.

3701. _____, John Krause, Ed Crist. *Chesapeake and Ohio early diesels.* Andover, NJ: Andover Junction Publications, 1988. 64 p.

3702. _____, _____, _____. *Old Dominion steam, C & O.* Hampton, VA: J&D Studios, 1988. 62 p.

3702a. _____, Karen Parker. *The Van Sweringen railroad empire : studies in the development of the Van Sweringen railroad empire emphasizing its effect on operations, rolling stock, and locomotive design for the Chesapeake & Ohio, Erie, Pere Marquette, and Nickel Plate railroads.* Clifton Forge, VA: Chesapeake & Ohio Historical Society, 2006. 150 p.

3703. _____, Robert L. Hundman. *Chesapeake & Ohio K-2, K-3 and K-3a 2-8-2s.* Edmonds, WA: Pacific Fast Mail, 1978. 40 p.

3704. Doane, Thomas. *Report on the question of bridging the Missouri River.* Boston: Press of T.R. Marvin & Son, 1868. 11 , 1 p. "Report to James F. Joy, President, Burlington & Missouri River Railroad Company."

3705. Dobbin, Frank. *Forging industrial policy: the United States, Britain, and France in the railway age*/ Cambridge, New York, Cambridge University Press, 1994. 262 p.

3706. Dobnick, Otto P., Steve Glischinski. *Wisconsin Central: railroad success story.* Waukesha, WI: Kalmbach Books, 1997. 160 p.

3707. Dobson, J.V., F.C. Hanker. *A history of the development of the single-phase system.* East Pittsburgh, Pa., Westinghouse Electric & Manufacturing Company, 1929. 9 p.

3707a. Dockweller, John Francis. *Railroad Commission of the State of California.* 1922. 39, 1 l. (Thesis, Harvard University, School of law.)

3708. *Documents relating to Ross Winan's patent for the eight-wheeled car.* New York,

J.W. Amerman, Printer, 1856. 47 p.

3709. Dodd, Townsend Foster, William Frederick Schroeder. *Determination of power consumption in truck center-bearings* / 1907. 11 l. 14 leaves of plates. (Thesis, B.S., University of Illinois.)

3710. Dodge, Grenville Mellen. *How we built the Union Pacific Railway, and other railway papers and addresses.* Washington, D.C., U.S. Govt. Printing Office, 1910. 136 p. (U.S. 61st Congress, 2d sess. Senate Doc. 447.) (Reprint: Denver, CO: Sage Books, 1965. 171 p.)

3711. _____. *Personal biography of Major Grenville Mellen Dodge, 1831-1870.* Cedar Rapids, IA : Heritage Museum, 2007. 4 microfilm reels. 35 mm. pos.

3712. _____. *Report of Gen. G.M. Dodge, chief engineer, 1874.* New York, G.W. Wheat, 1880. 146 p. (Texas and Pacific Railway Company)

3713. _____. *Report of the chief engineer, with accompanying reports of division engineers, for 1866.* Washington, D.C., Philp & Solomons, 1868. 123 p. (Union Pacific Railroad Company)

3714. _____. *Romantic realities. The story of the building of the Pacific roads.* Omaha, Neb., s.n., 1889. 24 p.

3715. _____. *Texas and Pacific Railway Company : report of Gen. G.M. Dodge, chief engineer, 1874.* New York : Geo. W. Wheat, Fine Mercantile printer, 1880. 146 p.

3716. _____. *The Union Pacific Railroad. Report of the Gen. G.M. Dodge, chief engineer, on lines crossing the Rocky Mountains.* New York, W.C. Bryant, 1867. 33 p.

3717. _____. *Union Pacific Railroad. Report of G.M. Dodge, chief engineer, to the Board of Directors, on a branch railroad line from the Union Pacific Railroad to Idaho, Montana, Oregon, and Puget's Sound.* Washington, D.C., Philp & Solomons, 1868. 13 p.

3718. _____. *Union Pacific Railroad. Report of the Engineer on bridging the Missouri River.* New York, Van Nostrand, 1867. 18 p.

3719. _____, Sidney Dillon. *Three studies in railroading.* Omaha, NB., Union Pacific Railroad Company, Passenger Department, 1896. 90 p. (Previous issue: 1893. 80 p.)

3720. Dodge, John W. *Electric railroading in Central California.* San Marino, CA: Pacific Railway Journal, 1956. 35 p. ("Third anniversary special issue.")

3721. Dodge, Richard V. *Rails of the Silver Gate; the Spreckels San Diego empire.* San Marino, CA: Pacific Railway Journal, 1960. 143 p.

3722. _____, R.P. Middlebrook. *The California Southern Railroad: a rail drama of the Southwest.* Boston, Mass., Railway and Locomotive Historical Society, 195-? 1 v.

3723. Dodgson, F.L. *The A.P. block system for single track* steam *railroads.* Rochester, NY: General Railway Signal Co., 1912. 28 p. (*Bulletin. General Railway Signal Company, 128.*)

3724. Doering, David J. *Burlington Northern Santa Fe : last train to Wymore : the story of a prairie local.* David City, NE: South Platte Press, 2008. 56 p.

3725. Doezema, William R. *Maneuvering within the system: railroad responses to state federal regulation, 1870-1916 /* 1978. 323 l. (Thesis, Ph.D., Kent State University.)

3726. *Doggett's railroad guide and gazetteer for—1848—with sectional maps of the great routes of travel.* New York, NY: John Doggett, Jr. Proprietor, 64 Liberty Street, 1848. 128 p.

3727. *Doggett's United States railroad and ocean steam navigation guide.* New York: John Doggett, Jr., S.W. Benedict, Stereotyper and Printer, 1848. 132 p.

3728. Doherty, Timothy Scott, Brian Solomon. *Conrail.* St. Paul, MN: MBI, 2004. 144 p.

3729. Dolan, Thomas J. *An investigation of wrought steel railway car wheels.* Urbana Ill., Engineering Experiment Station, University of Illinois, 1939. 1 v. (*Bulletin series. Engineering Experiment Station, University of Illinois, 312.*)

3730. Dolby, A. J. *The disposal of discarded railroad wood cross ties: a study of alternatives /* Washington, DC: Association of American Railroads, Research and Test Department, 1975. 80, 20 l.

3731. Dolengo-Kozerovsky, Victor Paul. *Development & design of turbo-locomotives.* Cincinnati, 1928. 58 l. Thesis (M.E.) University of Cincinnati.

3732. Dolzall, Gary W., Michael Danneman. *The spirit of railroading: a color celebration of North American trains.* Waukesha, WI: Kalmbach Publishing Company, 1991. 193 p.

3733. _____, _____. *Steel rails across America: the drama of railroading in spectacular photos.* Waukesha, WI: Kalmbach Publishing Company, 1989. 205 p.

3734. _____, Stephen F. Dolzall. *Diesels from Eddystone: the story of Baldwin diesel locomotives.* Milwaukee, WI: Kalmbach Publishing Company, 1984. 152 p.

3735. _____, _____. *Monon: the Hoosier Line.* Glendale, CA: Interurban Press, 1987. 206 p. (2d ed. rev.: Bloomington, Indiana University Press, 2002. 201 p.)

3736. *Domestic containerization ; a preliminary feasibility study/* prepared by Temple, Barker & Sloane, Inc. for the Association of American Railroads. Washington, DC: Association of American Railroads, 1986. 200 p. (Association of American Railroads.

Research and Test Department. Freight Equipment Management Program.)

3737. Dominy, Arthur L., Rudolph A. Morgenfruh. *A collector's guide to railroad dining car flatware patterns* / 3 rd ed. S.l., The Authors, 1975. 23 p.

3738. _____. *Silver at your service: a collector's guide to railroad dining car flatware patterns.* Del Mar, CA: D&M Pub., 1987. 191 p.

3738a. Donaldson, Stephen E. *Trains to Newport.* Huntington Beach, CA: Southern pacific Historical and Technical Society, 1985. 12 p.
3739. _____, William A. Myers. *Errata and footnotes for Rails through the orange groves, volumes I & II.* Glendale, CA: Trans-Anglo Books, 1991. 70 p.

3740. _____, _____. *Rails through the orange groves: a centennial look at the railroads of Orange County.* Glendale, CA: Trans-Anglo Books, 1989-1990. 2 v.

3741. Donat, Richard R. *Southern Pacific piggyback service from San Francisco-Los Angeles. Individual research project, Stanford Graduate School of Business, Spring quarter, 1957.* Stanford, CA: s.n., 1957. 60 l.

3742. Donely, George A. *The construction of the Union Pacific Railway by the Credit Mobilier of America; an historical, political, economic report and analysis.* New York, NY: 1958. 126 l. (Thesis, M.A., Economics. Columbia University.)

3743. Donley, Mark G. *Thermal buckling of curved railroad tracks.* Newark, DE: Department of Civil Engineering, University of Delaware, 1981. 110 p. (Thesis, M.C.E., University of Delaware.)

3744. Donley, Mary E. *Thermal sensing unit test for railroad car journal bearings; final report* / Washington, DC: Federal Railroad Administration, Office of Research and Development, 1980. 24 p. (*FRA/ORD-80/76.*)

3744a. Donnelly, Charles. *The facts about the Northern Pacific land grant.* St. Paul, MN: Northern Pacific Railway Co., 1924. 24 p.

3745. Donovan, Frank Pierce. *The Burlington in Iowa.* Iowa City, State Historical Society, 1969. 481-544 p. (Special Burlington edition.)

3746. _____. *Mileposts on the prairie; the story of the Minneapolis & St. Louis Railway.* New York, Simmons-Boardman, 1950. 310 p.

3747. _____. *Harry Bedwell, last of the great railroad storytellers.* Minneapolis, MI: Ross & Haines, 1959. 119 p.1951.

3748. _____. *Harry Bedwell—railroad raconteur.* Iowa City, State Historical Society, 1958. 209-240 p. (Includes bibliography of Bedwell's published works.)

3749. _____. *Iowa railroads: the essays of Frank P. Donovan, Jr.* Edited by H. Roger

Grant. Iowa City, University of Iowa Press, 2000. 330 p.

3750. _____. *The Manchester & Oneida Railway, 1901-1951.* Iowa City, State Historical Society of Iowa, 1957. 48 p.

3751. _____. *Minneapolis & St. Louis.* Plandome, NY: s.n., 1942. 1 v (unpaged)

3752. _____. *The railroad in literature; a brief survey of railroad fiction, poetry, songs, biography, essays, travel and drama in the English language, particularly emphasizing its place in American literature.* Boston, MA: The Railway & Locomotive Historical Society, Baker Library, Harvard Business School, 1940. 138 p.

3753. _____. *Railroads of America.* Milwaukee, WI: Kalmbach Publishing Company, 1949. 244 p.

3754. _____. *The Wabash in Iowa.* Iowa City, State Historical Society, 1964, 369-400 p.

3755. _____, Robert Selph Henry. *Headlights and markers: an anthology of railroad stories.* New York, Creative Age Press, 1946. 406 p. (Reissue: San Marino, CA: Golden West Books, 1968. 396 p.

3756. Dooley, Frank J. *Economies of size and density for short line railroads.* Fargo, ND: Upper Great Plains Transportation Institute, North Dakota State University, 1991. 118 p. (*MPC report / Mountain-Plains Consortium, no. 91-2.*)

3757. _____. *Post-Staggers productivity for class 1 railroads*/ Springfield, VA: U.S. Department of Commerce, National Technical Information Service, 1992. 1microfiche (67 p.) Fargo, ND: Upper Great Plains Transportation Institute, North Dakota State University, 1991. 67 p. (*MPC report / Mountain-Plains Consortium, no. 91-6.*)

3758. _____, Ann Schwabe-Neumayer. *A bibliography of federal railroad labor law.* Fargo, ND: Upper Great Plains Transportation Institute, North Dakota State University, 1991. 85 p. (*MPC report / /Mountain-Plains Consortium, no. 91-7.*)

3759. _____, William E. Thoms. *Railroad law a decade after deregulation.* Westport, CN: Quorum Books, 1994. 187 p.

3760. Dooner, Richard T. *Super Chief, Santa Fe.* Philadelphia, PA: Edw. G. Budd Manufacturing Co., 1937. 17 l.

3761. Dorflinger, Don. *Phoebe Snow: the lady and the train.* Bernardsville, NJ: Hill Press, 1979. 12 p.

3761a. Dorin, Patrick C. *American passenger train equipment 1940s-1980s* / Hudson, WI: Iconografix, 2010. 126 p.

3762. _____. *American passenger trains: WWII to Amtrak*/ Hudson, WI: Iconografix, 2009. 126 p.

3763. _____. *Amtrak trains and travel.* Seattle, WA: Superior Pub. Co., 1979. 184 p.

3764. _____. *The Chesapeake and Ohio Railway; George Washington's railroad.* Seattle, WA: Superior Pub. Co., 1981. 232 p.

3765. _____. *Chicago & North Western freight trains and equipment.* Lynchburg, VA: TLC Publishing, 2003. 117 p.

3766. _____. *Chicago and North Western passenger service: the postwar years.* Lynchburg, VA: TLC Publishing, 2000. 124 p.

3767. _____. *Chicago & North Western passenger train equipment.* Lynchburg, VA: TLC Publishing, 2001. 52 p.

3768. _____. *Chicago and North Western power; modern steam and diesel, 1900 to 1971.* Seattle, WA: Superior Pub. Co., 1972. 192 p.

3769. _____. *Coach trains and travel.* Seattle, WA: Superior Pub. Co., 1975. 192 p.

3770. _____. *Commuter railroads; a pictorial review of the most traveled railroads.* Seattle, WA: Superior Pub. Co., 1970. 192 p.

3771. _____. *The domeliners; a pictorial history of the penthouse trains.* Seattle, WA: Superior Pub. Co., 1973. 224 p.

3772. _____. *The Elgin, Joliet and Eastern railway: around not thru Chicago.* Berkeley and Wilton, CA: Signature Press, 2009. 175 p.

3773. _____. *Everywhere West: the Burlington Route.* Seattle, WA: Superior Pub. Co., 1976. 171 p.

3774. _____. *The Grand Trunk Western Railroad: a Canadian national railway.* Seattle, WA: Superior Pub. Co., 1977. 174 p.

3775. _____. *The Great Northern Railway, lines east.* Burbank, CA: Superior Pub. Co., 1985. 1 v.

3775a. _____. *An illustrated guide to American freight train equipment/* Hudson, WI: Enthusiast Books, 2013. 127 p.

3776. _____. *The Lake Superior iron ore railroads.* Seattle, WA: Superior Pub. Co., 1969. 144 p.

3777. _____. *Lines east—Great Northern.* Burbank, CA: Superior Pub. Co., 1989. 231 p.

3778. _____. *Michigan-Ontario iron ore railroads.* Lynchburg, VA: TLC Publishing, 2002. 103 p.

3779. _____. *The Milwaukee Road east: America's resourceful railroad.* Seattle, WA: Superior Pub. Co., 1978. 175 p.

3780. _____. *The Milwaukee Road passenger train services: from the Hiawatha era to Amtrak and beyond.* Forest, VA: TLC Publishing, 2004. 143 p.

3781. _____. *Missouri Pacific freight trains and equipment.* Lynchburg, VA: TLC Publishing, 2001. 136 p.

3782. _____. *Missouri Pacific passenger trains: the postwar years.* Lynchburg, VA: TLC Publishing, 2003. 118 p.

3783. _____. *Pacific Coast commuter railroads: from San Diego to Anchorage.* Hudson, WI: Iconografix, 2008. 110 p.

3784. _____. *Santa Fe passenger trains in the streamlined era.* Forest VA: TLC Publishing, 2004. 142 p.

3785. _____. *The Soo Line.* Seattle, WA: Superior Pub. Co., 1979. 192 p.

3786. _____. *The Super Chief and the El Capitan: all the way on the Santa Fe.* Forest, VA: TLC Publishing, 2005. 92 p.

3787. _____. *Union Pacific's Challenger: an unusual passenger train, 1935-1971.* Lynchburg, VA: TLC Publishing, 2001. 70 p.

3788. _____. *Western Pacific locomotives and cars: steam diesel, passenger, freight.* Lynchburg, VA: TLC Publishing, 1998-2006. 2 v.

3789. _____, Joe Salisbury. *Train watchers' log.* Seattle, WA: Superior Pub. Co., 1981. 1 v.

3790. _____, Richard H. Hendrickson, Staffan Ehnbom. *Great Northern lines east.* 2d ed. Berkeley, CA: Signature Press, 2001. 304 p.

3791 _____, Robert C. Del Grasso. *Burlington Northern and Santa Fe Railway, 1996: an historical profile and motive power roster.* Bonners Ferry, ID: Great Northern Pacific Publications, 1997. 288 p.

3792. _____, _____. *Burlington Northern Railroad: coal hauler and coal country trackside guide.* Bonners Ferry, ID: Great Northern Pacific Publications, 1995. 194 p.

3793. Dorman, Richard L. *Alamosa/Salida and the Valley Line.* Santa Fe, NM: R.D. Publications, 1991. 223 p.

3794. _____. *Chama/Cumbres with a little Chili. 2d ed.* Santa Fe, NM: R.D. Publications, 1993. 222 p.

3795. _____. *The Chili Line and Santa Fe, the city different.* Santa Fe, NM: R.D. Publications, 1996. 215 p.

3796. _____. *Durango: always a railroad town.* Santa Fe, NM: R.D. Publications, 1987. 184 p.

3797. _____. *Gunnison: covering Marshall Pass, Lake City, Crested Butte thru to Ouray.* Santa Fe, NM: R.D. Publications, 1993. 223 p.

3798. _____. *The Rio Grande Southern: an ultimate pictorial study.* Santa Fe, NM: R.D. Publications, 1990. 279 p.

3799. _____. *The Rio Grande Southern II: an ultimate pictorial study.* Santa Fe, NM: R.D. Publications, 1994. 344 p.

3800. _____. *Rocky Mountain railroads: Rio Grande Southern.* Santa Fe, NM: R.D. Publications, 1999. 90 p.

3801. _____. *The Southern: a narrow gauge odyssey.* Santa Fe, NM: R.D. Publications, 1986. 153 p.

3802. _____, Bob Hayden. *D&RGW: Durango to Alamosa and Salida.* Santa Fe, NM: R.D. Publications, 2005. 174 p.

3803. _____, Charles R. Lively. *Chama/Cumbres: with a little Chili.* 1st ed. Santa Fe, NM: R.D. Publications, 1988. 206 p.

3804. Doran, John T., R.C. Bailey. *Explanations of switch and signal circuits/* New York, NY: Doran & Kasner, 1907. 140 p.

3805. Dorr, Lawrence Daniel. *Penn Central corporate strategy since 1963.* 1971. 68 l. Professional report, M.B.A., University of Texas, Austin.

3806. Dorsey, Edward Bates, and others. *English and American railroads compared.* New York, J. Wiley & Sons, 1887. 142 p.

3807. Doster, James Fletcher. *Railroads in Alabama politics, 1875-1914.* University, AL: University of Alabama, 1957. 273 p.(*University of Alabama studies, no. 12.*)

3808. Dothan Landmarks Foundation. *Railroading around Dothan and the Wiregrass Region.* Charleston, SC: Arcadia Pub., 2004. 128 p.

3809. Dotson, Irma McGinnis. *Danville Branch of the Oakland, Antioch & Eastern Railway.* Danville, CA: Museum of the San Ramon Valley, 1996. 212 p.

3810. _____. *San Ramon Branch Line of the Southern Pacific.* Danville, CA: Museum of the San Ramon Valley, 1991. 288 p.

3811. *The double-stack container car manual.* Omaha, NE: Railway Educational Bureau, 2004. 75 p.

3812. *Double stack container systems: implications for U.S. railroads and ports: bibliography.* Washington, D.C., U.S. Department of Transportation, 1990. 40 p.

3813. Dougherty, Peter J. *Tracks of the New York City subway/* 3rd ed. New York, NY: The Author, 2002. 100 p.

3814. Dougherty, Samuel A. *Call the big hook.* Sam Marino, CA: Golden West Books, 1984. 256 p.

3815. _____. *Railroad tall tales (and other B.S.).* Grand Junction, CO: Printed by Printmasters, 154 p.

3816. Doughty, Geoffrey H. *Chicago North Shore and Milwaukee Railway in color: North Shore Line.* Scotch Plains, NJ: Morning Sun Books, 2006. 2 v.

3817. _____. *The early Zephyrs: Burlington Route.* Lynchburg, VA: TLC Publishing, 2002. 118 p.

3818. _____. *Michigan Central trackside with Emery Gulash.* Scotch Plains, NJ: Morning Sun Books, 2001. 128 p.

3819. _____. *New Haven in color.* Scotch Plains, NJ: Morning Sun Books, 2003. 2 v.

3820. _____. *The New Haven Railroad in the streamline era.* Lynchburg, VA: TLC Publishing, 1998. 120 p.

3821. _____. *The New Haven Railroad's streamline passenger fleet, 1934-1953.* Lynchburg, VA: TLC Publishing, 2000. 136 p.

3822. _____. *New York Central and the trains of the future.* Lynchburg, VA: TLC Publishing, 1997. 102 p.

3823. _____. *New York Central facilities in color: New York Central System.* Scotch Plains, NJ: Morning Sun Books, 2002. 127 p.

3824. _____. *New York Central in color.* Scotch Plains, NJ: Morning Sun Books, 2001-

3825. _____. *New York Central's great steel fleet, 1948-1967.* Lynchburg, VA: TLC Publishing, 1995. 120 p.

3826. _____. *New York Central's lightweight passenger cars, trains and travel.* Lynchburg, CA: TLC Publishing, 1997. 151 p.

3827. _____ *New York Central's stations and terminals.* Lynchburg, VA: TLC Publishing, 1999. 168 p.

3827a. _____. *Northern Pacific through passenger service* / Scotch Plains, NJ: Morning Sun Books, 2013. 126 p.

3827a. _____. *Penn Central through passenger service* / Scotch Plains, NJ: Morning Sun Books, 2012. 128 p.

3828. _____. *Way of the Zephyrs: the postwar years, Burlington Route.* Lynchburg, VA: TLC Publishing, 2005. 156 p.

3829. _____, Ed Nowak. *New York Central through passenger service in color. New York Central System. Volume 1: hope and glory, 1943-1950.* Scotch Plains, NJ: Morning Sun Books, 2008. 128 p.

3830. Douglas, George H. *All aboard! The railroad in American life.* New York, Paragon House, 1992. 462 p.

3831. _____. *Rail city, Chicago, USA.* San Diego, CA: Howell-North Books, 1981. 338 p.

3832. Douglas, Jack H. *The narrow gauge Silverton train.* Salt Lake City, UT: Douglas Models, 1972. 52 p.

3833. Douglas, Kenneth L., Peter C. Weiglin. *Pennsy diesels, 1924-1968, A-6 to EF36.* Mukilteo, WA: Hundman Publishing, 2002. 256 p.

3833a. Douglas, Percy Gordon. *A discussion of the practice and design in railroad timber trestle bridges* / 1906. 101 l. (Thesis, C.E., Cornell University.)

3834. Dover, Alfred Thomas. *Electric motors and control systems: a treatise on electric traction motors and their control.* New York, Pitman & Sons, 1918. 372 p.

3835. Dow, Andrew. *Dow's dictionary of railway quotations.* Baltimore, MD: Johns Hopkins University Press, 2009. 1 v. (Also: 2006. 354 p.)

3836. _____. *Norfolk and Western coal cars from 1881 to 1998.* Lynchburg, VA: TLC Publishing, 1998. 248 p.

3837. Dow, Arthur L. *Improved passenger equipment evaluation program: technology review/* Washington, DC : Federal Railroad Administration, Office of Research and Development, 1977. 27 p. (Unified Industries, Incorporated) (*FRA/ORD-77-74.*)

3838. Dow, Marcus A. *Safety and short trains/* New York: Kempster Printing, 1915.

30 p. "In substance an argument against the 'Short train' bill introduced in Illinois, made by Mr. Dow before the Public Utilities Committee in the House of Representatives at Springfield on May 6, 1915." Intro.

3839. Dowd, Charles Ferdinand. *System of national time and its application, by means of hour and minute indexes, to the national railway timetable; also a railway time gazetteer, containing all the railways in the United States and Canada, alphabetically arranged, with their stations indexed in from for the national railway time-table.* Albany, NY: Weed, Parsons and Company, Printers, 1870. 16 p.

3840. Dowd, Mary-Jane M. *Preliminary inventory of the records of the National Mediation Board, record group. 13.* Washington, D.C.: National Archives and Records, Service, 1974. 39 p.

3841. Dowling, Thomas H. *Memorial of Thomas H. Dowling, and accompanying papers in regard to his claim to the Island of Yerba Buena, in the harbor of San Francisco, California.* Washington, DC: W.H. Moore, 1869. 34 p.

3842. _____. *Memorial of Thos. H. Dowling, and accompanying papers, in regard to his claim to the Island of Yerba Buena, in the harbor of San Francisco, California.* S.l., s.n., 1868. 14 p.

3843. *Blank entry*

3844. Down, S.G. *Contribution of the air brake to modern transportation.* Pittsburgh, Pa., Westinghouse Air Brake Co., 1930. 46 p.

3845. Downey, Clifford J. *Chicago and the Illinois Central Railroad.* Charleston, SC: Arcadia, 2007. 128 p.

3846. _____. *Illinois Central color pictorial.* La Mirada, CA: Four Ways West Publications, 2002. 128 p.

3847. _____. *Kentucky and the Illinois Central Railroad* / Charleston, SC: Arcadia Pub., 2010. 127 p.

3848. _____. *Tennessee Central: the Nashville Route.* Lynchburg, VA: TLC Publishing, 2005. 156 p.

3849. Downing, Kenneth Wentworth. *With a cinder in my eye; a layman's memories and sketches of American trains.* Moline, ILL: s.n. 1951. 43 p.

3850. Downs, Virginia C. *Life by the tracks: when passenger trains steamed through the Notch.* Canaan, NH: Phoenix Pub., 1983. 113 p. (Crawford Notch, NH.)

3851. Dowty, Robert R. *Rebirth of the Jupiter and the 119: building the replica locomotives at Golden Spike.* Tuscon, AZ: Southwest Parks & Monuments Association, 1994. 48 p.

3852. Doyle, Jerry. *Chesapeake & Ohio diesel locomotives in color, 1949-1971.* Clifton Forge, VA: Chesapeake & Ohio Historical Society, 2006. 122 p.

3853. _____. *Chessie System diesel locomotives.* Lynchburg, VA: TLC Publishing, 1999. 108 p..

3854. Doyle, Theodore F. *Oriental Limited.* Burnsville, MN: Great Northern Railway Historical Society, 2006. 56 p. (*Reference sheet, no. 335.*)

3855. _____. *Transcontinental passenger service, 1886-1929.* Burnsville, MN: Great Northern Railway Historical Society, 1999-

3856. Dozier, Howard Douglas. *A history of the Atlantic Coast Line Railroad.* Boston, New York, Houghton Mifflin Company, 1920. 198 p. (Reprint: New York, A.M. Kelley, 1971. 197 p.)

3856a. Drabelle, Dennis. *The great American railroad war: how Ambrose Bierce and Frank Norris took on the notorious Central Pacific Railroad* / New York: St. Martin's Press, 2012. 306 p.

3857. Draine, Edwin H. *Import traffic of Chicago and its hinterland.* Chicago, Department of Geography, University of Chicago, 1963. 138 p. (*Department of Geography research paper, no. 81.*)

3858. Draney, John. *Diesel locomotives, electrical equipment; a practical treatise on the operation and maintenance of railway diesel locomotives.* Chicago, American Technical Society, 1944. 388 p.

3859. _____. *Diesel locomotives: mechanical and electrical fundamentals.* Chicago, American Technical Society, 1954. 344 p.

3860. _____. *Diesel locomotives, mechanical equipment; a practical treatise on the operation and maintenance of railway diesel locomotives.* Chicago, American Technical Society, 1943. 472 p.

3861. Drayton, Charles D. *Transportation under two masters: devitalizing vital agencies.* Washington, National Law Book Co., 1946. 210 p.

3862. Dredge, James. *The Pennsylvania Railroad; its organization, construction, and management ... with eighty-two plates and numerous illustrations. Chiefly reproduced from "Engineering."* New York, J. Wiley; London, Offices of "Engineering," 1879. xiv, 274 p., lxxxii leaves of plates.

3863. _____. *A record of the transportation exhibits at the World's Columbian Exposition of 1893.* London, Office of "Engineering," New York, J. Wiley & Sons, 1894. 779 p.

3864. Dreimiller, David. *Signal lights: a collector's reference to railroad signal lamps and highway warning devices.* Solon OH: D. Dreimiller, 1990. 101 p.

3865. Drennan, Carl Mac. *ABC's of air brakes, with air brake dictionary.* New York, Simmons-Boardman, 1971. 213 p.

3866. _____. *Air compressors and compressor governors; a practical textbook for the instruction of locomotive engineers and firemen.* Chicago, American Technical Society, 1946. 76 p.

3867. _____. *Car air brakes.* New York, Simmons-Boardman, 1972. 153 p.

3868. _____. *Car inspection manual.* Kansas City, MO: Brotherhood Railway Carmen of the United States and Canada, 1949. 304 p.

3869. _____. *Enginemen's questions & answers. Firemen's' first year examinations; second year examinations; third year examination.* 3rd ed. Fort Worth Tex., Printed by the Fort Worth Vocational School 1929. 118 p.

3870. _____, *"HSC" high-speed brake equipment for types "A", "B", and "C" diesel locomotive units and cars with individual speed governor control; a practical textbook for the instruction of locomotive engineers and firemen. Prepared under the supervision and with the approval of the Westinghouse Air Brake Company.* Chicago, American Technical Society, 1944. 68 p.

3871. _____. *Inspection and maintenance of freight and passenger car brake equipment; a practical textbook for the instruction of locomotive engineers and firemen.* Chicago, American Technical Society, 1946. 47 p.

3872. _____. *Inspection of locomotive brake and signal equipment/* Chicago, American Technical Society, 1946. 11 p.

3873. _____. *Locomotive air brakes.* New York, Simmons-Boardman, 1972. 300 p.

3874. _____. *Modern railway air brakes/* Chicago, American Technical Society, 1945-1946. 14 parts in 2 v.

3875. _____. *No. 6-ET locomotive brake equipment/* Chicago, American Technical Society, 1946. 71 p.

3876. _____. *No. 8-ET locomotive brake equipment/* Chicago, American Technical Society, 1946. 46 p.

3877. _____. *No. 14-EL equipment for diesel-electric switching locomotives/* Chicago, American Technical Society, 1946. 50 p.

3878. _____. *Railway air conditioning : principles of operation and possible troubles of air conditioning equipment on passenger cars* / Kansas City, MO: Brotherhood Railway Carmen of America, 1940. 88 p.

3879. _____. *The train air signal equipment*/ Chicago, American Technical Society, 1946. 11 p.

3880. _____. *Type AB freight car brake equipment*/ Chicago, American Technical Society, 1946. 56 p.

3881. _____. *Type AB-8 automatic empty and load freight car brake equipment*/ Chicago, American Technical Society, 1946. 15 p.

3882. _____. *Type AB-4-12 freight car brake equipment*/ Chicago, American Technical Society, 1946. 10 p.

3883. _____. *Type D-22-P passenger car brake equipment with D-22-AR control valve*/ Chicago, American Technical Society, 1946. 43 p.

3884. _____. *Questions and answers. Firemen's first year examination. Second year examination. Third year examination. Engineer's re-examination on air brakes.* Winfield, Kan., Printed by Evening Free Press, 1917. 112 p.

3885. _____. *Universal control passenger car brake equipment with U-12-BD universal valve.* Chicago, American Technical Society, 1946. 32 p.

3886. *Dressel Railway Signal Lamp & Signal Company: 1926 catalog of railway lighting equipment.* Hiram, Ohio, Hiram Press, 1995. 216 p.

3887. Dressler, Thomas. *The first Northerns: Northern Pacific A Class 4-8-4.* Hicksville, NY: N.J. International, 1980. 100 p.

3888. _____, Edward W. King. *USRA 2-8-8-2 series. 2nd ed.* Hicksville, NY: N.J. International, 1980. 150 p. *(Classic power, 3A.)*

3889. Drew, Stephen E. *Brief histories of the Virginia & Truckee Railroad equipment owned by the State of Nevada.* Oakland, CA: Drew, 1974. 101 l.

3889a. _____. *Carson & Colorado Railroad equipment roster and pictorial, 1880-1900: 8 locomotives, 10 passenger cars, 194 freight cars and maintenance-of-way.* Reno, NV: Virginia & Truckee Historical Society, 2013. 43 p.

3890. _____. *Restoration feasibility investigation on Virginia & Truckee Railroad locomotives nos. 18 "Dayton" and 22 "Inyo."* Arcadia, CA: Short Line Enterprises, 1979. 185 l.

3891. _____. *Virginia & Truckee Railroad Brill cars nos. 11 and 12: restoration feasibility investigation.* Arcadia, CA: Short Line Enterprises, 1984. 123 l.

3892. _____. *Virginia & Truckee Railway, McKeen motor car no. 22: restoration feasibility investigation.* Carson City, NV: Friends of the Nevada State Railroad Museum, 1997. 124 l.

3893. _____, Walter P. Gray. *Official guidebook: California State Railroad Museum.* San Francisco? Pacific Coast Chapter of the Railway & Locomotive Historical Society, 1981. 1 v.

3894. _____, _____. *Virginia & Truckee Railroad Carson City shops; an interpretive evaluation.* Sacramento, CA: s.n., 1981. 29, 28 l.

3895. _____, William A. Oden. *Central of Georgia Railway Company private car no. 100 "the Gold Coast."* Oakland, CA: s.n. 1976. 1 v.

3896. _____, _____. *Virginia & Truckee Railroad Company locomotive no. 12 "Genoa."* Oakland, CA: s.n., 1976. 1 v.

3897. Dreyfuss, Henry. *The Mercury* / New York : New York Central System : Designed and printed by Bodley printers, 1936. 12 p.

3898. _____. *New York Central lights a train* / Chicago : Luminator, Inc., 1936. 13 p. Interior lighting designs for the Mercury (Cleveland-Detroit).

3899. Drinka, Thomas P., C. Phillip Baumel, John J. Miller. *Estimating rail transport costs for grain and fertilizer* / Columbia, MO: University of Missouri-Columbia, College of Agriculture, Agricultural Experiment Station, 1978. 24 p. (*Research bulletin. University of Missouri-Columbia, Agricultural Experiment Station, 1028.*)

3900. Driscoll, Barbara A. *El programa de braceros ferroviarios.* Tijuana, Baja California: Centro de Estudios Fronterizos del Norte de México, 198-¿ 45 p.

3901. _____. *Me voy pa'Penisilvania por no andar en la vagancia: los ferrocarrileros mexicanos en Estados Unidos durante la Segunda Guerra Mundial/* Mexico, D.F., Consejo Nacional para la Cultura y las Artes : Universidad Nacional Autónoma de México, Centro de Investigaciones sobre América del Norte, 1996. 278 p.

3902. _____. *The railroad bracero program of World War II.* 1980. 235 l. (Thesis, Ph.D., University of Notre Dame.)

3903. _____. *The tracks north: the railroad bracero program of World War II.* Austin, TX: CMAS Books, Center for Mexican American Studies, University of Texas at Austin, 1999. 236 p. (*CMAS border & migration studies series.*)

3904. Droege, John Albert. *Freight terminals and trains, including a revision of Yards and Terminals.* New York, McGraw-Hill Book Company, 1912. 465 p.

3905. _____ *Freight terminals and trains. 2d ed.* New York, McGraw-Hill Book Company, 1925. 567 p. (reprint: Chattanooga, TN: National Model Railroad Association,

1998, 1925. 567 p.)

3906. _____. *Passenger terminals and trains*. New York, McGraw-Hill, 1916. 410 p. (Reprint: Milwaukee, Kalmbach Publishing Company, 1969, 1916. 410 p.)

3907. _____. *Yards and terminals and their operations*. New York, Railroad Gazette, 1906. 285 p.

3908. Drone, Craig Alan. *On to the orient: the history, restoration and preservation of the Kansas City, Mexico and Orient Railway Depot in San Angelo, Texas* / 1990. 233 l. (Thesis, M. of Arch., Texas Tech University.)

3909. Drury, George H. *Guide to North American steam locomotives*. Waukesha, WI: Kalmbach Books, 1993. 448 p.

3910. _____. *The historical guide to North American railroads. 2nd ed.* Waukesha, WI: Kalmbach Books, 2000. 480 p.

3911. _____. *New York Central in the Hudson Valley: the water level route in steam and diesel*. Waukesha, WI: Kalmbach Books, 1995. 127 p.

3912. _____. *Santa Fe in the mountains: three passes of the West—Raton, Cajon, and Tehachapi*. Waukesha, WI: Kalmbach Books, 1995. 127 p.

3913. _____. *Southern Pacific in the Bay Area: the San Francisco-Sacramento-Stockton triangle*. Waukesha, WI: Kalmbach Books, 1996. 128 p.

3914. _____. *Union Pacific across Sherman Hill: Big Boys, Challengers and streamliners*. Waukesha, WI: Kalmbach Books, 2000. 128 p.

3915. _____, Bob Hayden. *The train-watcher's guide to North American railroads. 2d ed.* Waukesha, WI: Kalmbach Books, 1992. 288 p.

3916. Du Bois, Chester Buck, Robert Morton Campbell. *Comparative test, piston versus slide valve locomotives on the D. & H., Co's Ry.* 1902. 71 l. (Thesis, M.E., Cornell University.)

3917. Duback, Steven R. *The Wisconsin farmer faces the railroads, 1840-1875.* 1966. 139 l. (Thesis, B.A., Princeton University.)

3918. Dubin, Arthur D. *More classic trains*. Milwaukee, Kalmbach Books, 1974. 512 p.

3919. _____. *Pullman paint and lettering notebook: a guide to the colors used on Pullman cars from 1933 to 1969*. Waukesha, WI: Kalmbach Pub., 1997. 160 p.

3920. _____. *Some classic trains*. Milwaukee, Kalmbach, 1964. 434 p.

3921. _____. [Railroad collection] Indiana Historical Society. 24 series, in folders, alphabetically by line and route. Articles, brochures, timetable, photographs, etc. Collection guide available.

3922. Ducker, James H. *Men of the steel rails: workers on the Atchison, Topeka & Santa Fe Railroad, 1869-1900.* 1980. 464 l. (Thesis, Ph.D., University of Illinois, Urbana-Champaign) Lincoln, University of Nebraska Press, 1983. 220 p.

3923. _____ *Ships, trains & automobiles: transportation in Alaska's past.* Anchorage, AK: Alaska Historical Society, 2000. 72 p. (*Alaska history, v. 15, no. 1.*)

3924. Duddy, Edward A., David A. Revzan. *The use of transportation facilities in the Chicago fruit and vegetable market.* Chicago, The University of Chicago Press, 1940. 86 p. (*University of Chicago. Graduate School of Business. Studies in business administration, v. 10, no. 4.*)

3925. Dudley, Arthur S. *The economics of railroad valuation.* Chicago, Ill., J.J. Collins & Son Company, 1928. 94 p.

3926. Dudley, Charles Benjamin. *Passenger car ventilation system of the Pennsylvania Railroad Company* / Altoona : The Pennsylvania Railroad Company, 1904. 24 p., 4 leaves of plates.

3927. Dudley, Samuel William. *Brake performance on modern steam railroad passenger trains: a discussion of the Pennsylvania Railroad brake tests, 1913*/ Pittsburgh, PA: Westinghouse Air Brake Company, 1914. 156 p. (*Special publication, no. 9031.*)

3928. Dudley, Wray. *Electric traction: a comparison of steam and electricity as a motive power for railroads.* 1905. 21 p. (Thesis, University of Missouri, Columbia.)

3929. Due, John Fitzgerald. *The causes and failure of small and regional railroads.* Champaign, IL: Bureau of Economic and Business Research, College of Commerce and Business Administration, University of Illinois at Urbana-Champaign, 1988. 38 p. (*BEBR working paper, no. 21.*)

3930. _____ *The experience of local enterprises formed to take over railway lines abandoned by major systems.* Urbana, College of Commerce and Business Administration, Bureau of Economic and Business Research, University of Illinois, Urbana-Champaign, 1982. 54 p. (*BEBR faculty working paper, no. 896.*)

3931. _____ *The nationwide experience with new small railroads formed to take over abandoned lines, 1971-1984.* Urbana, Bureau of Economic and Business Research, College of Commerce and Business Administration, University of Illinois at Urbana-Champaign, 1984. 150 p. (*BEBR working paper, no. 7.*)

3932. _____ *Railroads: an endangered species and the possibility of a fatal mistake.* Iowa City, Institute of Urban and Regional Research, University of Iowa, 1980. 35 p. (*University of Iowa. Institute of Urban and Regional Research. Working paper, no. 24.*)

3933. _____. *The San Francisco and Alameda Railroad.* San Marino, CA: Southern California Chapter, Railway & Locomotive Historical Society and the Pacific Railroad Society, 1956. 8 p.

3934. _____. *Short line railroad operations as an alternative to loss of rail service; pros and cons.* Lexington, KY: Council of State Governments, 1976. 36 p. (Based on a report prepared for the Wisconsin Department of Transportation.)

3935. _____, Giles French. *Rails to the mid-Columbia wheat lands: the Columbia Southern and Great Southern railroads and the development of Sherman and Wasco Counties, Oregon.* Washington, D.C., University Press of America, 1979. 297 p.

3936. _____, Francis Juris Rush. *Rails to the Ochoco country: the City of Prineville Railway.* Introduction by Tom McCall. San Marino, CA: Golden West Books, 1968. 236 p.

3937. _____, _____. *Roads and rails south from the Columbia: transportation and economic development in Mid Columbia and central Oregon.* Bend OR: Maverick Publications, 1991. 187 p.

3938. Duerwachter, Robert. *The whistle didn't blow long enough : a history of the Chicago & Lake Superior Railroad : the shortest common carrier railroad in Wisconsin* / Summit Lake, WI: WinPress, 2007. 118 p.

3938a. Duffy, Edward W. *Philadelphia : a railroad history* / Philadelphia: Camino Books, 2013. 164 p.

3939. Dufour, William Damian. *The early black labor movement: the case of the Brotherhood of Sleeping Car Porters.* 1972. 89 l. (Thesis, M.A., West Virginia University.)

3940. Dufwa, Thamar E. *Transcontinental railroad legislation, 1835-1862.* 1933. 174 l. (Thesis, M.A., University of North Dakota. (Reprint: New York: Arno Press, 1981. 161 p.)

3941. Duin, Edgar Charles. *The emigration propaganda of the Northern Pacific Railroad.* Washington, 1950. 139 l.

3942. Dukarm, Ronald R. *Erie and D.L.&W. wreck trains*/ Harleysville, PA: Erie Lackawanna Historical Society, 2009. 96 p.

3943. Duke, Donald. *Electric railways around San Francisco Bay.* San Marino, CA: Golden West Books, 1999-2000. 2 v.

3944. _____. *Fred Harvey, civilizer of the American Southwest.* Arcadia, CA: Pregel Press, 1995. 64 p.

3945. _____. *Incline railways of Los Angeles and Southern California.* San Marino, CA:

Golden West Books, 1998. 240 p.

3946. _____. *Mount Lowe Railway.* Rev. ed. Los Angeles, Railway & Locomotive Historical Society, Southern California Chapter, 1955. 12 p.

3947. _____. *Night train.* San Marino, CA: Pacific Railway Journal, 1961. 127 p.

3948. _____. *Pacific Electric Railway: a pictorial album of electric railroading.* San Marino, CA: Golden West Books, 1958. 62 p. (Reprint from *Pacific Electric Journal, v. 2, no. 7.*)

3949. _____. *Pacific Electric Railway.* San Marino, CA: Golden West Books, 2001-2003. 4 v.

3950. _____. *Santa Fe: the railroad gateway to the American West.* San Marino, CA: Golden West Books, 1995-1997. 2 v.

3951. _____. *Santa Maria Valley RR: a thriving short line.* Los Angeles, CA: Pacific Railway journal, 19--? 7 p. (*Pacific Railway Journal, v. 1, no. 6.*)

3952. _____. *Southern Pacific steam locomotives; a pictorial anthology of western railroading.* 2d ed. San Marino, CA: Golden West Books, 1965. 88 p.

3953. _____. *Two angels on a string: the story of Angels Flight, Los Angeles' funicular railway.* San Marino, CA: Pacific Railway Journal, 1958. 12 p. (*Pacific Railway Journal, v. 2, no. 5.*)

3954. _____. *Union Pacific in Southern California.* San Marino, CA: Golden West Books, 2005. 154 p.

3955. _____, Edmund Keilty. *RDC: the Budd rail diesel car.* San Marino, CA: Golden West Books, 1990. 278 p.

3956. _____, Stan Kistler. *Santa Fe: steel rails through California.* San Marino, CA: Golden West Books, 1963. 184 p.

3957. Duke, Jason. *Tennessee coal mining, railroading & logging in Cumberland, Fentress, Overton, and Putnam Counties.* Paducah, KY: Turner Publishing Co., 2003. 120 p.

3958. Dukesmith, Frank H. *Modern airbrake practice: its use and abuse: a book of instruction on the automatic and straight air brakes/* Chicago, Ill., Frederick J. Drake & Company, 1904. 312 p.

3959. Duluth & Iron Range Railroad Company. *Transportation of iron ore.* Duluth, MN: s.n., 1927. 56 p.

3960. Duluth and Winnipeg Railway Company. *The Duluth and Winnipeg Railroad Company*. Boston: Rockwell & Churchill, Printers, 1881. 48 p. (Central Trust Company of New York. Duluth & Iron Range Railroad Company.)

3961. Duluth, Missabe, and Iron Range Railway. *Celebrating 100 years, 1892-1992:* Duluth, Missabe & Iron Range Railway Company. Minnesota, The Company, 1992. 16 p.

3962. _____. *The Missabe story, 1892-1967*. Duluth, MN: Duluth, Missabe & Iron Range Railway, 1967. 16 p.

3963. _____. *Two Harbors storage and shiploading facility, Port of Two Harbors, Minnesota*. S.l., Duluth, Missabe and Iron Range Railway, 1979. 8 p.

3964. Duluth, Missabe & Northern Railway Company. *The Missabe Road*. Duluth: The Railway, 1927. 20 p.

3965. Duluth, South Shore, and Atlantic Railroad Company. *Rules and regulations for the government of employes of the Operating Department*. Marquette, MI: Mining Journal, 1919. 143 p.

3966. Dunaway, Robert William. *Current railroad reorganization proposals* / 1937. 193 l. (Thesis, M.B.A. in Finance and Banking, Graduate School of Arts and Sciences, University of Pennsylvania.)

3967. Duncan, Carson S. *Getting railroad facts straight: 1. About wages. 2. About maintenance. 3. About valuation*. New York, NY: Association of Railway Executives, 1922. 51 p.

3968. Dunbar, Willis Frederick. *All aboard! A history of railroads in Michigan*. Grand Rapids, MI: W.B. Eerdmans Pub. Co., 1966. 308 p.

3969. Dunham, Walter. *Railway car shop maintenance, especially prepared for the education and training of railway carmen*. Chicago, American Technical Society, 1942. 244 p.

3970. Dunk, Frank Everton. *The Chicago and Alton railroad shopmen's strike*. 1939. 71 l. (Thesis, M.A., University of Colorado)

3971. Dunlap, Thomas. *Wiley's American iron trade manual of the leading iron industries of the United States, with a description of the iron ore regions, blast furnaces, rolling mills, Bessemer steel works, crucible steel works, car wheel and car works, locomotive works, steam engine and machine works, iron bridge works, iron ship yard, pipe and tube works, and stove foundries of the country, giving their location and capacity of product*. New York, J. Wiley and Son, 1874. 9-554, 172 p.

3972. Dunlavy, Colleen A. *Politics and industrialization: early railroads in the United States and Prussia*. Princeton, NJ: Princeton University Press, 1994. 303 p.

3973. Dunn, Edward T. *A history of railroads in western New York.* Buffalo, NY: Canisius College Press, 2000. 345 p.

3973a. Dunn, Marshall. *The Southern Pacific System: a railroad in renaissance* / New York : Wood, Struthers & Co., 1959. 24 p.

3974. Dunn Samuel Orace. *American railways and the war*/ St. Louis: J.W. Steele & Co., 1917. 15 p.

3975. _____. *Current railway problems.* New York, NY: Railway Age Gazette, 1911. 85 p.

3976. _____. *The decline of railroad employment*/ Bristol, Conn? Simmons-Boardman Pub. Co., 1930. 11 p.

3977. _____. *Government ownership of railways*/ New York: D. Appleton & Co., 1913. 400 p.

3978. _____. *The Interstate Commerce Commission and the railroads*/ New York: American Academy of Political and Social Science, 1916. 18 p.

3979. _____. *Some often overlooked points regarding government ownership of railways*/ Chicago? s.n., 1912. 25 p. (Address before the Traffic Club of New England at Boston, Mass, December 6, 1912.)

3980. Dunnavant, Robert. *The railroad war: N.B. Forrest's 1864 raid through northern Alabama and middle Tennessee.* Athens, AL: Pea Ridge Press, 1994. 180 p.

3981.Dunning, Glenna. *The Amtrak railway system: a periodical bibliography of an inter-city transportation network.* Monticello, IL: Vance Bibliographies, 1985. 41 p.

3982. _____. *The "red cars" of Southern California: bibliography of an urban transportation network.* Monticello, IL: Vance Bibliographies, 1981. 20 p.

3982a. Dunning, William Neil. *Concrete work on the Illinois Central Railroad* / 1902. 35 l. (Thesis, B.S., University of Illinois.)

3983. Dunscomb, Guy L. *Album of Western locomotives.* S.l., The author, 1950. 56 p.

3984. _____. *A century of Southern Pacific steam locomotives, 1862-1962.* Modesto, CA: s.n., 1963. 480 p. (2d ed. Modesto, CA: s.n. 1967. 496 p.)

3985. _____. *Division maps of the Southern Pacific Company.* Modesto, CA: Rose Lithographic Co., 1949. 50 p.

3986. _____, Donald K. Dunscomb, Robert A. Pecotich. *Southern Pacific steam pictorial.* Riverbank, CA: G.L. Dunscomb, D.K. Dunscomb, G. Milford, 1991-

(v.1: 100 series to 2800 series.)

3987. _____, Fred A. Stindt. *Western Pacific steam locomotives, passenger trains, and cars.* Modesto, CA: G.L. Dunscomb; Kelseyville, CA: F.A. Stindt, 1980. 376 p.

3988. _____, Donald K. Dunscomb. *Western steam pictorial.* Modesto, CA: Railroad Books, 1988. 112 p.

3988a. Dunsmore, Jaymes Phillip. The next great American station: Union Station and downtown Los Angeles in the twenty-first century / 2011. 160 p. (Thesis, M.C.P., Massachusetts Institute of Technology, Department of Urban Studies and Planning.)

3989. Dupont, Thomas L. ed. *U.S. railroads : issues, regulations, and safety* / New York : Nova Science Publishers, 2011. 202 p.

3990. Durham, Howard Ellis. *The American Railway Union strike of 1894.* 1933. 189 l. (Thesis, M.A., University of Washington.)

3991. Durham, Robert K. *The Chicago, Milwaukee, St. Paul and Pacific Railroad.* Auburn, PA: R.K. Durham, 1998. 66 p.

3992. _____. *The Erie Railroad.* Auburn, PA: R.K. Durham 1995. 56 p.

3993. _____. *The Great Northern and Northern Pacific railroads.* Friedensburg, PA: Robert K. Durham, 1999. 74 p.

3994. _____. *The Jersey Central Railroad.* Auburn, PA: R.K. Durham, 1996. 52 p.

3995. _____. *The Pennsylvania Railroad.* Auburn, PA: R.K. Durham, 1995. 80 p.

3996. _____. *The Reading Railroad* / Friedensburg, PA : Robert K. Durham, 1997. 71 p.

3997. Duriez, Philip. *The effects of make-work rules on railroad revenue.* 1962. 171 l. (Thesis, Ph.D., Louisiana State University.) Full crew rules. Featherbedding. Chicago and Illinois Midland Railway Company.

3998. Durr, Frederick R.E. *Economic and social effects of railway abandonments: with special reference to land use and taxation.* 1961. 320 l. (Thesis, Ph.D., Ohio State University.) (Also: Columbus, OH: Transportation Engineering Center, Engineering Experiment Station, Ohio State University, 1961. 319 p.

3999. Durrant, A.E. *The Mallet locomotive.* Newton Abbott, Eng., David & Charles, 1974. 144 p.

4000. DuVal, Miles P., Jr. *John Frank Stevens, 1853-1943: civil engineer, explorer, diplomat and statesman*/ S.l., John F. Stevens Hall of Fame Committee, 1976. 19, 1 p.

4001. Dwight P. Robinson & Company. *Locomotive terminals.* New York, D.,P.

Robinson & Co, Inc., 1921. 33 p.

4002. Dwyer, Jim. *Subway lives: 24 hours in the life of the New York subway.* New York, Crown, 1991. 312 p.

4003. Dye, Victoria E. *All aboard for Santa Fe: railway promotion of the Southwest, 1890s to 1930s.* Albuquerque, University of New Mexico Press, 2005. 163 p.

4004. Dzeda, Bruce. *Railroad town ; Kent and the Erie Railroad* / Kent, OH : Kent Historical Society Press, 2011. 42 p.

4005. Dziadaszek, Beverly. *Adaptive reuse of railroad stations : a case study of the Central Terminal, Buffalo, New York* / 1998. 102 l. (Thesis, M.U.P., State University of New York at Buffalo.)

E

4006. E. I. Du Pont de Nemours Export Company. *Du Pont Duco is working on the railroad helping to sell transportation.* Parlin, NJ: E. I. du Pont de Nemours & Co., Chemical Products Division, Railway Sales Department, 1927. 1 folded sheet ([3]) p. Document location: Hagley Museum and Library

4007. _____. *Harrison paints for marine, railway and machine finishing and refinishing.* New York: E. I. du Pont de Nemours Export Co., 1919. 20 p. illus., mounted color samples.

4007a. *The Eads bridge: an exhibition.* Princeton, NJ: Art Museum, Princeton University, 1974. 84 p. (Princeton University: Department of Civil and geological Engineering; St. Louis Art Museum; Princeton University: Art Museum.)

4008. Eager, Jim. *Rio Grande: color guide to freight and passenger equipment.* Edison, NJ: Morning Sun Books, 1996. 128 p.

4009. _____ *Western Pacific: color guide to freight and passenger equipment.* Scotch Plains, NJ: Morning Sun Books, 2001. 128 p.

4010. *The eagle/* Webster Groves, MO: Missouri Pacific Historical Society, 1900s-   . Quarterly.

4011. Eagleson, Mike. *Motive power of the Jersey Central.* New York, Quadrant Press, 1978. 64 p. (*Quadrant Press review, 7*)

4012. _____. *Steam on the anthracite roads.* New York, Quadrant Press, 1974. 96 p.

4013. Eakin, Kelly. *A study of competition in the U.S. freight railroad industry and analysis of proposals that might enhance competition.* Washington, DC: Surface Transportation Board, 2008. 3 v. (PDF file) (Laurits R. Christensen Association, Inc.)

4014. Eames Vacuum Brake Company. *Locomotive driver-brakes.* Watertown, N.Y., Eames Vacuum Brake Company, 1883. 22 p.

4015. Earle, Huber Dale. *A study of the traffic of the Florida East Coast Railway.* 1933. 97 l. (Thesis, M.A., University of Florida.)

4016. Earle, Valerie A., Chester B. Earle. *Taxing the Southern Railway in Alabama/* University: Published for ICP by University of Alabama Press, 1960. (*ICP Case series, no. 18.*) (Inter-university Case program.)

4017. Early, J.D. *A metallurgical analysis of an ASTM, a 212-B steel tank car head plate.* Washington, DC : Federal Railroad Administration, Office of Research and Development, 1981. 51 p. (*FRA/ORD-81/32.*)

4018. *Early diesel-electric locomotives*. Omaha, NE: Simmons-Boardman Pub. Corp., 1983. 105 p.

4019. Early, J. G., C. G. Interrante. *A metallurgical evaluation of two AAR M-128 steel tank car head plates used in switchyard impact tests* / Washington, DC: Federal Railroad Administration, Office of Research and Development, National Bureau of Standards, 1981. 1 v. (various pagings)

4020. _____, _____. *A metallurgical investigation of a full-scale insulated rail tank car filled with LPG subjected to a fire environment* / Washington, DC: Federal Railroad Administration, Office of Research and Development, 1975. 64 p. (*FRA-ORD & D-75-52.*)

4021. *Early railways: a selection of papers from the First International Early Railways Conference.* Edited by. Andy Guy and Jim Rees. London, Newcomen Society, 2001. 360 p. (St. John's College, City of Durham, England.)

4022. East Tennessee and Western North Carolina Railroad. *The scenic route through the heart of the Blue Ridge.* Chicago, Ill., Poole Brothers, 1916. 14 p.

4023. Eastern Maintenance of Way Association. *Proceedings of the annual convention.* Providence, RI: The Association, 1882-1901. 19 v. (Issued 1882-1898 [vols. 1-16] under its earlier name: New England Roadmasters' Association.)

4024. Eastlake, Keith. *Great train disasters.* Osceola, WI: Motorbooks International, 1997. 96 p.

4025. Eastman, Arthur Fessenden. *A proposed system of electrification for the lines of the New York, New Haven and Hartford Railroad from Boston to Providence.* 1924. 28 l. (Thesis, B.S., in Electrical Engineering, University of Maine.)

4026. Eastman, H.B. *Experiments with railway cross-ties.* Washington, DC: s.n., 1908. 22 p. (*Forest Service Circ. No. 146.*)

4027. Eastman, Joseph B. *The extent of low wages and long hours in the railroad industry.* Washington, DC: U.S. Federal Coordinator of Transportation, 1936. 142 p.

4028. Easton, Kerner. *Report of the Secretary to the Committee on Port and Terminal Facilities of the Board of Estimate and Apportionment.* New York? The Committee, 1915. 61 p. Includes N.Y.C. R.R. tracks, Manhattan.)

4029. Easton, Larry E. *Soo Line standards.* S.l., Soo Line Historical & Technical Society, Archives Committee, 2000. 3 v.

4030. Eaton, James Shirley. *Education for efficiency in railroad service.* Washington, DC: U.S.G.P.O., 1909. 159 p. (*Bulletin. United States Bureau of Education, 1909, no. 10.*)

4031. _____. *Railroad operations; how to know them from a study of the accounts and statistics*/ New York: The Railroad Gazette, 1900. 313 p.

4032. Eaton, Walter Prichard. *4/34 hours of de luxe travel between New York and Boston: the Yankee Clipper*. New York, New York, New Haven and Hartford Railroad, Passenger Traffic Department, 1930. 28 p.

4033. *ECAP outlook for freight cars*. Bala Cynwyd, PA: WEFA Group, 1900s-1992. (> *Outlook for freight cars.)*

4034. Eck, Harry Carl, J.C. Kissinger. *The modern locomotive handbook: a textbook on the operation of today's locomotives*. 3rd ed. Pontoon Beach, IL: International Association of Railway and Operating Officers, 1994. 256 p.

4035. Eck, William John. *Alternating current block signals on the Southern Railways*. Rochester, N.Y.: General Railway Signal Company, 1913. 51 p. (Its *Bulletin, 126.)* (2d ed. 1925. 97 p.; Its *Bulletin, 146.)*

4036. Eckenrode, H.J., Pocahontas Wight Edmunds. *E.H. Harriman: the little giant of Wall Street*. New York, NY: Arno Press, 1981, 1933. 242 p.

4037. Eckes, Ruth Trueblood. *Blow the whistle softly: an anthology of railroad stories*. Orting, WA: Heritage Quest Press, 1996. 184 p. (Northern Pacific Railway Company)

4038. _____. *Whistles in the night: an anthology of railroad stories*. Orting, WA: All Color Printing, 1997. 184 p. (Northern Pacific Railway Company)

4039. *The economic ABZ's of the railroad industry*. Washington, D.C., Economics and Finance Department, Association of American Railroads, 1980-1983. Annual. (>*Railroad ten-year trends.)*

4040. *Economic costing of railroad operations: proceedings of a conference held December 8-9, 1960, Knickerbocker Hotel, Chicago, Illinois*. Chicago, IL: Railway Systems and Management Association, 1960. 96 p.

4041. Economic Education Council of St. Louis. *The railroads of St. Louis*. St. Louis, MO: Economic Education Council of Greater St. Louis, 1959. 23 p.

4042. *Economic impact of freight car shortages* / Washington, DC : Federal Railroad Administration, 1971. 117 p. (*FRA/RP-71/1*)

4043. Economic Research Council, Michigan; Upper Great Lakes Regional Commission. *Area economic significance of rail car ferry service across the Straits of Mackinac*. Washington, D.C., The Council, 1971. 59 l.

4043a. *The economics of running more trains: a case study of the Louisville and Nashville Railroad*/ Cambridge, MA: Multisystems, Inc., 1979. 1 v. (various pagings)

4044. *Economics of transportation in the United States; some essential sources.* Elizabeth O. Cullen, compiler. Washington, D.C., Bureau of Railway Economics, Library, 1954. 29 l.

4045. *The economics of weight reduction in freight carrying railroad cars.* Washington, DC: Association of American Railroads, Railroad Committee for the Study of Transportation, Subcommittee on Engineering and Mechanical Research, 1946. 1 v. (various pagings)

4046. *Economy in the generation of steam with some suggestions upon the proposed substitution of coal for wood upon railroads.* Boston, Bazlin and Chandler, 1857. 45 p.

4047. Edaburn, Sharon L. *The archeological study and interpretation of western railroads.* 1981. 3 v. (Thesis, M.A., California State University, Sacramento.)

4047a. Eddy, Clarence L. *Design of reinforced concrete engine house* / 1909. 32 l., 5 l. of plates. (Thesis, University of Illinois.)

4048. Eddy, Harry L. *Railroads 100 years old, 1945-1955; a list of names of railroads which were chartered and built in the United States...between the years 1845 and 1855.* Washington, D.C., Association of American Railroads; Bureau of Railway Economics, Library, 1948. 9 l.

4049. Edelman, A.D. *Loan and life relationship of roller bearings as applied to railroad journals.* New York : American Society of Mechanical Engineers, 1959. 7 p. (*ASME. Paper no. 59-RR-1.*)

4050. Edfeldt, Theodore Roosevelt. *Motor operation by or for class I railroads, 1944.* Washington, D.C., 1948. 199 p.

4051. _____. *Motor operations of class I railroads.* Washington, D.C., 1953. 200 p.

4052. Edgar Thomson Steel Works; Carnegie Brothers & Company, Limited. *Sections of standard patterns of steel rails manufactured by Carnegie Brothers & Company, Limited at the Edgar Thomson Steel Works, Bessemer, Penn'a.* Pittsburgh ? Pa., s.n. 1891. 1 v.

4053. Edmonson, Harold A. *Journey to Amtrak; the year history rode the passenger train.* With special commentary by David P. Morgan, and others. Maps by Robert Wegner. Milwaukee, WI: Kalmbach Pub. Co., 1972. 104 p.

4054. _____. *Steam on Q.* Chicago? Ill., Illini Railroad Club, 1960. 40 p. (CB&Q)

4055. _____, David Goodheart. *Union Pacific's 8444.* Chicago, IL: Goodheart Publications, 1989. 16 p.

4056. _____, David Goodheart. *Zephyrs thru the Rockies.* Chicago, IL: Goodheart Publications, 1986. 128 p.

4057. Edson, William D. *Diesel locomotives of the New York Central System..* Cleveland, New York Central System Historical Society, 1978. 169 p

4058. _____. *Keystone steam & electric: a record of steam and electric locomotives built for the Pennsylvania Railroad since 1906.* New York, Wayner Publications, 1974. 137 p.

4059. _____. *Locomotives of the New York Central Lines.* Irvington-on-Hudson, s.n., 1966. 136 p.

4060. _____ *New York Central diesel locomotives.* Lynchburg, VA: TLC Pub., 1995. 1 v.

4061. _____. *Railroad names: a directory of common carrier railroads operating in the United States, 1826-1982.* 1st ed. Potomac, MD: W.D. Edson, 1984. 144 p. (2d ed., 1989. 144 p.; 3rd ed., 1993. 168 p.; 4th ed., 1999. 179 p.)

4062. _____. *Steam locomotives of the Baltimore & Ohio: an all-time roster.* Potomac, MD: W.D. Edson, 1992. 221 p.

4063. _____, Edward L. May. *Steam and electric locomotives of the New York Central Lines; numbering and classification.* Irving-on-Hudson, NY: s.n., 1966. 136 p.

4064. _____, Edward L. May, H.L. Vail. *Steam locomotives of the New York Central Lines.* Cleveland, OH: New York Central Historical Society, 1997-2002. 2 v.

4065. _____, H.L. Vail, C.M. Smith. *New York Central System diesel locomotives.* Lynchburg, VA: TLC Pub., 1995. 212 p.

4066. _____, John H. White. *Illinois Central.* Boston, MA: Railway & Locomotive Historical Society, 1979. 146 p. (Locomotive rosters)

4067. Edward B. Smith & Company. *A decade of progress. Expenditures and improvement of the Pennsylvania Railroad Company, 1896-1907.* Philadelphia : s.n., 1908. 20 p.

4068. Edward G. Budd Manufacturing Company. *The Budd system of light-weight construction.* Philadelphia : Edw. G. Budd Mfg. Co., 1936. 26 p.

4069. _____. *The Burlington Zephyr : America's first diesel all-steel streamlined train : the outstanding achievement in safe, light, railway transportation by the Edward G. Budd Manufacturing Company.* Philadephia : Railway Age, 1934. 18 p. "Reprinted from Railway Age, April 14, 1934."

4070. _____. {Correspondence with Paul Philippe Cret]. 2 items, 3 leaves. "Correspondence concerns trains designed for the Budd Company, Work No. 278." Location:

4071. _____. *A description of the new 12 car Denver Zephyrs of the Chicago, Burlington & Quincy R.R.* / Philadelphia : Edward G. Budd Company, 1936. 4 p.

4072. _____. *A new era has come for the railroads* / Philadelphia : Budd Company, 1944. 10 p.

4073. _____. *The new Flying Yankee*. Philadelphia: Edward G. Budd Manufacturing Company, 1935. 12 p.

4074. _____. *Pennsylvania 4688-4698*. Philadelphia : Edward G. Budd Manufacturing Company, 1935. 4 l. Streamlined trains.

4075. _____. *Reading "65"*. Philadelphia : Edward G. Budd Manufacturing Company, 1932. 4 l. "The Budd-Micheline pneumatic-tired rail cars of stainless steel for suburban, main and branch line use on American railways."

4076. _____. *Stainless steel trains and the defense program*. Philadelphia: Edward G. Budd Manufacturing Company, 1941. 4 p.

4077. _____. *U.S. patents issued to Edward G. Budd : March 1899 to November 1946*. Philadelphia : s.n., 1948. 1 v. (various pagings). Location:

4078. Edwards Electric Headlight Company. *Catalogue of locomotive electric headlight equipment*. Chicago, IL: Edwards Electric Headlight Company; Franklin Co. Engravers and Printers,1900-1910? 13 p.

4079. Edwards, Emory. *Modern American locomotive engines; their design, construction and management. A practical work for practical men*. Philadelphia, Henry Carey Baird; London, S. Low, Marston, Searle & Rivington, 1883. 383 p. (Also: 1895. 383 p., and 1903.)

4080. Edwards Railway Motor Car Company. *Edwards gasoline rail cars*. Milwaukee, WI: Old Line Publishers, 1970. 28 p.(Reprint of the 1936 ed.)

4081. _____. *Edwards gasoline rails cars: model 10 new and improved design*. Sanford, N.C., The Company, 1927. 8 p.

4082. _____. *Edwards gasoline rail cars: model 20; new and improved design*. Milwaukee, WI: Old Line Publishers, 1970. 19 p. (Reprint of the 1926 ed.)

4083. *Effect of heavy axle loads on track*/ Washington, DC: Federal Railroad Administration, Office of Research and Development, 1975. 167 p. (*FRA/ORD&D-76-243.*)

4084. *Effects of rail vehicle size : special bibliography*. Washington, DC : Federal Railroad Administration, Office of Research and Development, 1979. 46 p. National Research Council (U.S.). Railroad Research Information Service.

4085. Egbert, Ercell Jane. *Kentucky's interest in the Pacific railroad question from 1830 to 1865*. 1930. 135 l. (Thesis, M.A., Graduate School of Arts and Sciences, University of Pennsylvania.)

4086. Eggert, Gerald G. *Railroad labor disputes: the beginnings of Federal strike policy*. Ann Arbor, University of Michigan Press, 1967. 313 p.

4087. Eggerton, Albert S. *Out of the past into the future; the bicentennial story of Southern Railway*. Washington, D.C., Southern Railway System, 1977. 19 p.

4088. Ehernberger, James L. *Locomotives, snow plows, flangers and passenger and freight car equipment: June 1, 1885: and includes subsidiary lines, Colorado Central...and a photographic rendezvous*. Cheyenne, WY: J.L. Ehernberger, 1989. 56 p.

4089. _____ *Sunset on the Rio Grande Southern*. Cheyenne, WY: Challenger Press, 1996-1998. 2 v.

4090. _____. *Union Pacific common standard drawings: bridges and buildings*. Cheyenne, WY: Challenger Press, 1994. 80 p.

4091. _____. *Union Pacific common standard drawings: roadway signs*. Cheyenne, WY: Challenger Press, 1994. 80 p.

4092. _____. *Union Pacific common standard drawings: roundhouse, turntables and water tanks /* Cheyenne, WY: Challenger Press, 1994. 80 p.

4093. _____. *Union Pacific common standard drawings: signals and track*. Cheyenne, WY: Challenger Press, 1994. 80 p.

4094. _____. *Union Pacific prototype locomotive photos*. Cheyenne, WY: Produced and published by the Union Pacific Historical Society, 2006-   . 38 v.

4095. _____. *Union Pacific steam: Challenger portraits*. Cheyenne, WY: Challenger Press, 1993. 127 p.

4096. _____, Francis G. Gschwind. *Colorado & Southern, Northern Division*. Callaway, NE: E. & G. Publications, 1966. 64 p.

4097. _____, _____. *Sherman Hill, Union Pacific*. Callaway, NE: E. & G. Publications, 1973. 128 p.

4098. _____, _____. *Smoke above the plains: Union Pacific, Kansas Division*. Callaway, NE: E. & G. Publications, 1965. 64 p.

4099. _____, _____. *Smoke across the prairie, Union Pacific, Nebraska Division.* Golden, CO: Intermountain Chapter, National Railway Historical Society, 1964. 61 p. (2d ed., 1975. 72 p.)

4100. _____, _____. *Smoke along the Columbia: Union Pacific, Oregon Division.* Callaway, NE: E. & G. Publications, 1968. 64 p.

4101. _____, _____. *Smoke down the canyons: Union Pacific, Idaho Division.* Callaway, NE: E. &. G. Publications, 1966. 64 p.

4102. _____, _____. *Smoke over the Divide: Union Pacific, Wyoming Division.* Callaway, NE: E. & G. Publications, 1965. 64 p.

4103. _____, _____. *Union Pacific steam: Eastern District.* Callaway, NE: E. & G. Publications, 1975. 200 p.

4103a. Ehlert, Willis J. *The Wisconsin &Northern Railroad: the building of a railroad, 1906-1921* / Madison, WI: State House Pub., 2010. 97 p.

4104. Ehnbom, Staffan. *Great Northern box cars: numbers 11875-17999.* Burnsville, MN: Great Northern Railway Historical Society, 2005. 16 p. (*Reference sheet no. 331.*)

4105. Eichelberger, George. *Southern Railway equipment drawings & photographs: Volume 1, Book 1: 40' steel box cars.* Spencer, NC: Southern Railway Historical Association, 2004. v.1-

4106. E.I.du Pont de Nemours & Company. Chemical Products Division. Railway Sales Department. *Duco for motor cars, railway furniture and many other articles: a booklet of general information on the uses and application of this remarkable product.* Parlin, NJ: E.I. du Pont de Nemours & Company, 1926. 24 p.

4107. _____. *"I never knew a locomotive could be so beautiful."* Parlin, NJ: E.I. du Pont de Nemours & Co., 1925. 4 p.

4108. Eisenhart, Harry Weiser. *Design of a freight locomotive boiler.* 1903. 16 l. (Thesis, M.E., Lehigh University.)

4109. El-Aini, Yehia M. *The effect of imperfections on the vertical buckling of railroad tracks/* Washington, DC: Federal Railroad Administration, Office of Research and Development, 1976. 33 p. (*FRA-Or & D-76-09.*)

4110. El-Hajjar, Rani Fayez. *Structural response of railroad tank cars during acoustic emission testing* / 2000. 110 l. (Thesis, M.S., University of Texas at Austin.)

4111. El Paso and Southwestern Railroad. *Locomotive diagrams. Revised.* El Paso, Tex., El Paso & Southwestern, Motive Power Department, 1919. 42 l.

4112. El-Sibaie, Magdy A. *Coupler angling under in-train loads : modeling and validation* / Pueblo, CO : Association of American Railroads, Transportation Test Center, 1991. 27 p. (*AAR. report, no. R-722.*)

4113. Elazar, Daniel J. *Federal-state relations in Minnesota: a study of railroad construction and development* / 1957. 1 v. (Thesis, University of Chicago.)

4114. Elder, Cyrus. *Steel rails, the railroads, and the people.* Johnstown, Pa., s.n. 1888. 12 p. (Steel industry, rails)

4115. Eldredge, Andrew T. *Railroads of Cape Cod and the Islands.* Charleston, SC: Arcadia, 2003. 128 p.

4116. Electric Axle Light and Power Company. *Train electric lighting and car refrigeration from the axle.* New York, Electric Axle Light and Power Company, 1900. 40 p.

4117. *Electric car heating and lighting.* Scranton, International Textbook Company, 1940. 1 v.

4118. *Electric locking, including a number of chapters which appeared originally in the Railway Signal Engineer.* New York, Chicago, Simmons-Boardman Publishing Co., 1918. 219 p.

4119. *Electric locomotive plan and photo book.* Hicksville, NY: N.J. International, Inc., 1987. 1 v.

4120. *Electric locomotives.* Scranton, Pa., International Textbook Company, 1909. 74 p.

4121. *Electric motor cars, 1888-1928.* Novato, CA: Newton K. Gregg, 1974. 1 v.

4122. Electric Railway Historical Society. *Bulletin.* Chicago: Electric Railway Historical Society, 1952-   .

4123. _____. *Railway equipments and locomotives in the Far West.* Chicago, The Society, 1962. 1 v.

4124. *Electric railway systems; electric-railway line construction; track construction; electric-railway calculations; railway motors; electric-car equipment; speed control; efficiency tests, switch gear; electric stations; electric substations; operation of electrical machinery.* Scranton, Pa., International Textbook Co., 1908. 1 v. (Also 1915 and 1923. 1 v.)

4125. *Electric railways.* Milwaukee, Kalmbach Publishing Co., 1944. 2 p., 20 l. of plates (*Trains album of photographs, no. 7.*)

4126. *Electric railways.* Washington, D.C., Interstate Commerce Commission, Bureau of Statistics, 1917-1935. Annual.

4127. *Electric railways.* Washington, D.C., Interstate Commerce Commission, Bureau of Transport Economics and Statistics, 1962. 1 v. (*Transport statistics in the United States, year ended December 31, 1961, part 4.*)

4128. Electric Service Supplies Company. *Electric car equipment and supplies.* Philadelphia, Pa., The Company, 1923. 687 p.

4129. _____ *Electric railway overhead line and track supplies.* Philadelphia, Electric Service Supplies Company, 1911. 698 p.

4130. _____. *Golden Glow: headlights, searchlights and projectors.* Philadelphia, Electric Service Supplies Company, 1916. 19 p.

4131. Electric Storage Battery Company. *Exide ironclad batteries for railway car lighting.* Philadelphia, Pa., The Electric Storage Battery Company, 1924. 11 p.

4132. *Electric trunk line age.* New York, Muralt & Co., 1907-1910. Monthly. (>*Railway electrical engineer.*)

4133. *Electrification of steam railways: electrification in all countries with special reference to the United States and the extensive program of the Pennsylvania Railroad.* New York, NY: Liquidating Committee of the National Electric Light Association, 1933. 80 p. (Its *Publication, no. 247.*)

4134. Electromagnetic Compatibility Analysis Center. *Railroad electromagnetic compatibility.* Washington, DC: Federal Railroad Administration, Office of Research and Development, 1978-   . (*FRA/ORD 77/77.I; FRA/ORD 77/77.II.*)

4135. *Elements of arithmetic, fractions, decimals, car lighting, car heating, Southern Locomotive valve gear, Franklin steam grate shaker, Franklin automatic fire door, Ragonnet reverse gears, Young locomotive valve gear. Scranton, Pa., International Textbook Company, 1922. 1 v.*

4136. *The elements of railroad engineering.* Scranton, Pa., The Colliery Engineer Company, 1897. 5 v.

4137. Elgin National Watch Company. *Timemakers and timekeepers.* Philadelphia: N.W. Ayer & Son, 1900s. 27 p.

4137a. Elkind, Ethan N. *Railtown; the fight for the Los Angeles metro rail and the future of the city* / Berkeley: University of California Press, 2014. 292p.

4138. Eller, Ronald D. *Mountain road: a study of the construction of the Chesapeake and Ohio Railroad in southern West Virginia, 1887-1873.* 1973. 96 l. (Thesis, M.A., University of North Carolina.)

4139. Ellet, Charles. *Cost of transportation on railroads*/ Philadelphia, PA: s.n., 1844.

4, 24, 34 p. (Reprinted from the *Journal of the Franklin Institute*.)

4140. _____. *Report of the location of the western portion of the Baltimore and Ohio Rail Road, to a committee of the city council of Wheeling* / Philadelphia : Printed by John C. Clark, 60 Dock Street, 1850. 87 p.

4141. _____. *Second report on the location of the western portion of the Baltimore and Ohio Rail-Road, to a committee of the city council of Wheeling* / Philadelphia : John C. Clark, printer, 68 Dock Street, 1850. 111 p.

4142. Ellington, Frank M. *Caboose cars of the Santa Fe Railway.* Colfax, IA: Railroad Car Press, 1977. 88 p. (2d ed., 1978. 99 p.)

4143. _____. *Santa Fe depots of the Plains.* Colfax, IA: Railroad Car Press, 1984. 97 p.

4144. _____. *Steam locomotives of the Santa Fe: a former shopman's scrapbook.* Colfax, IA: Railroad Car Press, 1989. 276 p.

4145. _____, John Berry, Loren Martens. *Stock cars of the Santa Fe Railway.* Los Angeles: Reprinted and distributed by the Santa Fe Railway Historical Society, 1986. 132 p. (Originally published: Colfax, IA: Railroad Car Press, 1981.)

4146. _____, Joseph W. Shine. *Business and special purpose cars.* Colfax, IA: Railcar Press, 1975. 177 p. (Revised and updated ed.: Midwest, OK: Santa Fe Railway Historical & Modeling Society, 2008. 248 p.

4147. _____, _____. *Passenger train equipment of the Atchison, Topeka and Santa Fe, 1870-1975.* Colfax, IA: Railcar Press, 1973-1975. 2 v. (v. 1: Head end cars. v.2: Business and special purpose cars.)

4148. Ellingwood, Albert R., Whitney Coombs. *The government and railroad transportation*/ Boston: Ginn, 1930. 642 p.

4149. Elliot Frog and Switch Co. *Elliot Frog and Switch Co., East St. Louis: manufacturers of Elliot's patent steel rail frogs and crossings, split switches, lap and stub switches, switch stands, bridle rods, head chairs, rail braces, replacing frogs, and every description of railroad iron work.* East St. Louis, Il: Elliot Switch and Frog Company, 1915. 155 p.

4150. Elliot, Paul. *Nondestructive techniques for measuring the longitudinal force in rails: proceedings of the joint government-industry conference held in Washington, DC, February 26-27, 1979.* Washington, DC: Federal Railroad Administration, Office of Research and Development, 1908. 186 p. (FRA/ORD-80/50.)

4151. Elliott, Byron K., William F. Elliott. *A treatise on the law of railroads*/ 2d ed. Indianapolis, The Bobbs-Merrill Co., 1907. 5 v.

4152. Elliott, Frank Nelson. *The causes and the growth of railroad regulation in Wisconsin, 1848-1876.* 1956. 325 l. (Thesis, Ph.D., University of Wisconsin.)

4153. _____. *When the railroad was king: the nineteenth-century railroad era in Michigan.* Lansing, Michigan Historical Commission, 1966. 68 p. (2d ed.: Lansing, Bureau of History, Michigan Department of State, 1988. 68 p.)

4154. Elliott, Howard. *The case for the railroads: the significance of the surrender of Congress to the brotherhoods as seen by a railroad president.* New York: 1918. 16 p. "From the New York Times, magazine section, September 10, 1916."

4155. _____. *Connecticut and the New Haven road: address to the Chamber of Commerce of New Haven.* New Haven, CT: s.n., 1913. 19 p.

4156. _____. *Efficient railway management; extracts from an address by Howard Elliott...* St. Paul, Minn., 1911. 7, 1 p.

4157. _____. *Jay Cooke, Duluth and the Northern Pacific Company.* New York? s.n., 1921. 15 p.

4158. _____. *A mile of railroad and a country store.* Saint Paul? Minn., McGill-Warner Co., 1911. 14 p. (North Dakota)

4159. _____. *Minnesota: the railways and advertising: address.* St. Paul, Minn., McGill-Warner Co., 1911. 16 p.

4160. _____. *The railways and the government: address.* New York, NY: Railway Business Association, 1913. 14 p.

4161. _____. *Relation between the farmer and the railroad.* St. Paul? 1912. 19 p.

4162. _____. *The relation of the railway to community and state-wide advertising /* Saint Paul, MN: McGill-Warner Co., Printers? 1910. 14 p.

4163. _____. *The truth about the railroads.* Boston, Houghton Mifflin Co., 1913. 260 p.

4164. Elliott, Joyce Randolph Blackstock. *The Gunnison Branch of the Denver, South Park and Pacific Railroad.* 1951. 64 l. (Thesis, M.A., Western State College of Colorado.)

4165. Elliott, W.H. *Block and interlocking signals.* New York, Locomotive Engineering, 1896. 277 p.

4166. Ellis, Cuthbert Hamilton. *The lore of the train.* New York, Barnes & Noble, 1995, c1971. 240 p.

4167. _____. *Railway art.* Edited by Susan Hyman. Boston, New York Graphic Society, 1977. 144 p.

4168. Ellis, Edward. *Compound locomotives adapted to all classes of service.* Schenectady, N.Y., Schenectady Locomotive Works, 1892. 44 p.

4169. Ellis, Erl H. *A broad gauge tail on a narrow gauge dog: standard gauge days on the Farmington Branch of the Denver & Rio Grande RR.* Albuquerque, NM: Railroad Club of New Mexico, 1965. 1 v.

4170. Ellis, James Calvin. *The decline of the passenger train in America, 1920-1939.* 1971. 163 l. (Thesis, M.A., Mississippi State University.)

4171. Ellis, M. Fred. *The transportation of Illinois coal* / Springfield: Illinois Department of Energy and Natural Resources, Office of Research and Planning, Office of Coal Development and Planning, 1990. 283 p. (*ILENR/RE-ER-90/07*)

4172. Ellis, Raymond H., John C. Prokopy. *Development of a demand forecasting framework for ten intercity corridors within the United States: final report.* Washington, DC: Department of Transportation, Federal Railroad Administration, Office of Research and Development, 1973. 68 p. (*DOT-FR-2005-6*)

4173. _____, _____. *Variations in travel forecasts for improved high speed rail services in the Northeast Corridor; final report.* Washington, DC: Federal Railroad Administration, 1973. 44 p. (*DOT-FR-20005-4*)

4174. Ellis, Susan Elizabeth. *"The route of scenic charm" : a case study of the Delaware, Lackawanna, and Western Railroad in the American landscape, 1880-1940.* 1990. 161 l. (Thesis, M.S. in Historic Preservation, Graduate School of Arts and Sciences, University of Pennsylvania.)

4175. Ellwanger, Charles H. *1986 guide to diesel locomotives.* New York, Simmons-Boardman Publishing Company, 1986. 73 p.

4176. _____. *1990 guide to diesel locomotives: the industrial sector.* New York, Simmons-Boardman Publishing Corporation, 1990. 78 p.

4177. Elmer, W. *Climatical ventilation for dwellings ... railroad cars, etc.* New York : 1863. 1 v.

4178. Elmont, Earl V. *Basalt and the Frying Pan: legacy of the Colorado Midland Railroad.* Basalt, CO: WHO Press, 2004. 158 p.

4179. Elstein, Steven. *State issues in rail transportation of coal.* Lexington, KY: Council of State Governments, 1978. 11 p.

4180. Elting, Mary. *All aboard! The railroad trains that built America.* Rev. ed. New York, Four Winds Press, 1970, c1969. 127 p.

4180a. Elve, Steven D. *Rails across the water: the story of the Ann Arbor car ferries*/ Lowell, MI: Elve, 1984. 126 p.

4181. Elwood, Warren, Patricia Bick. *The Milwaukee Road: Harlowton's historic district.* Harlowton, MT: s.n., 1988. 4 p.

4182. Ely, James W. *Railroads and American law*. Lawrence, KS: University Press of Kansas, 2002. 365 p.

4183. Ely, Theo N. *Specifications for cabin car color.* Altoona : Pennsylvania Railroad Co., Motive Power Department, 1887. 1 sheet.

4184. _____, J. Elfreth Watkins. *Catalogue of the exhibit of the Pennsylvania Railroad Company at the World's Columbian Exposition, Chicago, 1893* / Chicago : Pennsylvania Railroad Company, 1893. 158 p., 50 leaves, 32 p. of plates.

4185. *Ely's "Railroad Day."* Salt Lake City : Press of the Century Printing Co., 1906. 1 v. (unpaged) In celebration of the completion of Nevada Northern Railway from Cobre to Ely, Nevada.

4186. Emeka, Mauris Lee Porter. *Amtraking: a guide to enjoyable train travel.* Port orchard, WA: Apollo, 1994. 116 p.

4187. _____. *Getting the most from train travel: a publication for train travelers.* Port Orchard, WA: Emeka, 1991. 32 p.

4188. _____. *Heart & soul of the train: personal travel notes from an Amtrak attendant.* Port Orchard, WA: Apollo Pub. International, 1999. 101 p.

4189. *Emergency response training: hazardous materials operations.* Pueblo, CO: Association of American Railroads, Transportation Technology Center, 2000. 1 v. (various pagings)

4190. Emerick, William J. Brennan. *Trackside on the New York Central road to the future with William J. Brennan.* Scotch Plains, NJ: Morning Sun Books, 2010. 126 p.

4190a. Emerson, Frank Collins. *A forecast of railroad freight traffic over the Union Pacific system*/ 1936. 58 l. (Thesis, University of Wyoming.)

4191. Emerson, Harrington. *Col. J.M. Schoonmaker and the Pittsburgh & Lake Erie Railroad: a study of personality and ideals.* New York, Engineering Magazine Company, 1913. 152 p.

4192. _____. *The railroad situation; why 30 per cent rate increase is not enough.* New York, NY: Emerson Engineers, 1920. 48 p.

4193. _____. *Securing efficiency in railroad work; story of an attempt to apply scientific management to some departments. A lecture delivered at Harvard, November 16th, 1910.* New York, 1910. 38 p.

4194. Emerson, Robert L. *The Pennsylvania Railroad Historical Collection, 1939-1989/* Strasburg, PA: Friends of the Railroad Museum of Pennsylvania, 1989. 11 p.

4194a. Emge, Kyle J. *National passenger policies and the effect on investment, ridership, and congestion/* 2013. 75 l. (Thesis, Master of Science, University of Massachusetts, Boston.)

4195. Emmett, Rowland. *The early morning milk train: the cream of Emmett railway drawings.* Brattleboro, VT: S. Greene Press, 1977. 112 p.

4196. Emmons, Robert A. *Del luxe : the tale of the Blue Comet.* 2009. 69 l. + 1 DVD (93 min.). Blue Comet (Express train)—Central Railroad of New Jersey. (Thesis (D.Litt.) -- Drew University, 2009.)

4196a. Emory, William H., John G. Parke. *Report of explorations for that portion of a railway route near the 32nd parallel of latitude, lying between Dona Ana, on the Rio Grande, and Pimas Villages, on the Gila /* Washington, DC: G.P.O., 1855. 53 p. (United States War Department. Report of the Secretary of War communicating the several Pacific Railroad explorations. Washington, DC, 1855. Volume 3, Report 8.)

4197. Empire State Railway Museum. *Empire State Railway Museum's tourist trains: 41st annual guide to tourist railroads and museums.* Waukesha, WI: Kalmbach Books, 2006. 454 p.

4198. Empire Transportation Company. *Theory and practice of the American system of through fast freight transportation as illustrated in the operations of the Empire Transportation Company.* Philadelphia, Penn., Press of Helfenstein, Lewis & Greene, 1876. 48 p.

4199. *Encyclopedia of North American railroads.* Edited by William D. Middleton, George M. Smerk, and Roberta L. Diehl. Bloomington, Indiana University Press, 2007. 1280 p.

4200. *Encyclopedia of railroading.* Chicago, National Textbook Company, 1910. 6 v.

4201. *The encyclopedia of trains & locomotives.* New York, MetroBooks, 1995 and 2002. C.J. Riley, editor. 224 p.

4202. *The encyclopedia of trains and locomotives: the comprehensive guide to over 900 steam, diesel, and electric locomotives from 1825 to the present day.* David Ross, General editor,. San Diego, CA: Thunder Bay Press, 2003. 544 p.

4203. *Energy study of railroad freight transportation /* Washington, DC: U.S. Department of Energy, Division of Transportation Energy Conservation, 1979. 4 v.

4204. English, Robert Edward. *The probabilistic design of a railroad hump yard.* 1982. 139 l. (Thesis, M.S.M.E, West Virginia University.)

4205. Engelbourg, Saul, Leonard Bushkoff. *The man who found the money: John Steward Kennedy and the financing of the western railroads.* East Lansing, MI: Michigan State University Press, 1996. 257 p.

4206. Engelhardt, Carroll L. *Gateway to the Northern Plains: railroads and the birth of Fargo and Moorhead.* Minneapolis, University of Minnesota Press, 2007. 366 p.. (NP and GN)

4207. *Engineering and design of railway brake systems/* Chicago: Air Brake Association, 1975. 1 v. (various pagings)

4208. *Engineering manual of the American Electric Railway Engineering Association.* New York, American Electric Railway Engineering Association, 1914-1929. (Annual) (>American Transit Engineering Association. *Engineering manual.)*

4209. *Engineering news.* New York, McGraw-Hill Pub. Co., 1902-1917. 30 v. Weekly. (>*Engineering news-record.*)

4210. English, Robert Edward. *The probabilistic design of a railroad hump yard/* 1982. 139 l. (Thesis, M.S.M.E., West Virginia University)

4211. Engwall, Richard L. *The railroad car manufacturing industry* / S.l., s.n., 1961. 67 l.

4212. Ennis, Joseph Burroughs. *The last fifty years—and the next!* New York, Newcomen Society of England, American Branch, 1945. 20 p. (Locomotives)

4213. *Ensuring railroad tank car safety; a government and industry partnership* / Washington, DC: National Academy Press, 1994. 152 p. (*National Research Council (U.S.), Transportation Research Board. Committee for the Study of the Railroad Tank Car Design Process. Special report, 243.*)

4214. *Environmental compliance manual for the road and rail transportation industries.* New York, NY: McGraw-Hill, 1998. 382 p.

4215. Eppler, Paul R., Richard N. Mansley. *The history of the Wilmington and Northern Railroad.* Wilmington, DE: s.n., 1996. 211 p.

4216. Epstein, Ralph Cecil. *GATX: a history of the General American Transportation Corporation, 1898-1948.* New York, North River Press, 1948. 198 p. (Reprint: New York, Arno Press, 1981. 198 p.)

4217. *Equipment diagrams: selected class A-18, A-19, A-20 heavyweight coach diagrams.* Baltimore, MD: Baltimore and Ohio Railroad Historical Society, 1983. 30 l.

4218. Erbesen, Wayne. *Singing rails: railroadin' songs, jokes, & stories.* Pacific, MO: Mel Bay Pub., 1999. 79 p. (Music)

4219. Erickson, Eric, Walter Taubeneck. *Mile post : a history of the Arlington-*

Darrington branch of the Northern Pacific Railway : 1899-2009. Anacortes, WA: [The authors], 2009. A-4, B-21, 238 p.

4220. Erickson, Hazel Cushman. *I grew up with the narrow gauge.* New York, Carlton Press, 1971. 48 p. (Maine)

4220a. Erickson, Thomas F. *A railroad manifesto: fifty short articles on railroad economics, operations, and management.* Lanham: University Press of America, 2011. 262 p.

4221. Erie and Western Transportation Co. *Anchor Line : the Great lakes route.* Buffalo, NY: Erie & Western Transportation Co., 1910. 19 p. "Pennsylvania Railroad steamers." Cover.

4222. Erie Lackawanna Dining Car Preservation Society, Inc. *Recipes of the Erie Lackawanna: dinner in the diner, 1964-1970.* Parsippany, NJ: Erie Lackawanna Dining Car Preservation Society, Inc., 2002. 27 p.

4223. Erie Railroad Company. *The Erie Limited: new 25-hour service, New York-Chicago and companion trains.* New York? Erie Railroad System, 1929. 24 p.

4224. _____. *Erie Railroad: its beginnings, 1851.* New York, Erie Railroad, 1951. 28 p.

4225. _____. *Instructions for the running of trains, etc. on the Erie Railway: to go into effect on Wednesday, January 1,1862.* New York, Press of the Erie Railway Company, 1862.106 p.

4226. _____. *One hundred years of the locomotive, 1815-1915. A book of old prints and unusual photographs.* New York, s.n., 1915. 32 p.

4227. _____. *Rules of the Operating Department, November 1, 1908.* New York, s.n., 1908. 146 p.

4228. *Erie Railroad employes' magazine.* New York, etc.: Erie Railroad Company, 1905-1916. Monthly. (> *Erie Railroad magazine.*)

4229. *Erie Railroad magazine.* New York, etc: Erie Railroad Company, 1916- . Monthly. (< *Erie Railroad employes' magazine.*)

4230. Ernest, Dale S. *The Chesapeake & Ohio Railway in Thurmond, West Virginia.* Clifton Forge, VA: Chesapeake & Ohio Historical Society, 2004. 48 p.

4231. Ernst & Ernst; Iowa Department of Transportation. *The state role in railroad restructuring.* Washington, D.C., Ernst & Ernst, 1978. 109 p.

4232. Ernst Wiener Company. *Gasoline locomotives.* New York, The Company, 1909. 7 p. (*Bulletin, no. 150.*)

4233. Estabrook, Harry M. *A history of the Barney & Smith Car Company of Dayton Ohio. With short biographical sketches of some of the men...connected with the company, together with reminiscences of some interesting events.* Ohio? Press of the J.W. Johnson Company, 1911. 89 p. (Dayton, OH: Curt Dalton, 1997, 1911. 107 p.)

4234. Estaville, Lawrence E. *Confederate neckties: Louisiana railroads in the Civil War.* Ruston, LA: McGinty Publications; Department of History, Louisiana Tech University, 1989. 123 p. (*The McGinty monograph series.)*

4235. Esterline Company. *Golden glow electric lamps.* Indianapolis, Esterline Company, 1914. 15 p.

4236. _____. *Golden glow headlights for railway service.* Indianapolis, The Company, 1914. 19 p.

4237. Estes, George. *Railway employees united: a story of railroad brotherhoods.* Portland, OR: G. Estes, 1931. 5, 13-79 p. (Telegraph operators, Southern Pacific Lines; Order of Railroad Telegraphers.)

4238. _____. *The rawhide railroad.* Canby OR: Publishing House of the Clackamas County News, 1916. 54 p. (Walla Walla and Columbia River Railroad Company.) (Reprint: Seattle, WA: Shorey Book Store, 1974. 54 p.

4239. EuDaly, Kevin. *The complete book of North American railroading/* Minneapolis, MN: MBI, 2009. 1 v.

4240. _____. *Missouri Pacific diesel power.* Kansas City, MO: White River Productions, 1994. 192 p.

4241. _____. *Santa Fe 1993-1994 annual.* Ferndale, WA: Hyrail Productions, 1994. 144 p.

4242. _____, Eugene L. Huddleston. *The Chesapeake & Ohio Railway: west end, PM District, Chicago Division, Cincinnati& Russell Divisions.* Hart, MO: White River Productions, 1999. 111 p.

4243. _____, Mark W. Hemphill. *Santa Fe 1992 annual.* Denver CO: Hyrail Productions, 1992. 144 p.

4243a. Eure, Bruce Thomas. *An operating concept for increasing the efficiency of bulk commodity railroad freight cars as evaluated by computerized simulation/* 1976. 135 l. (Thesis, Ph.D., University of Georgia)

4244. Eusebio, Victor E. *Economic impacts of rail line abandonment on rural communities in Kansas.* Topeka: Kansas Department of Transportation, Bureau of Rail Affairs, 1992. 38 p.

4245. _____. *Railroad pricing behavior for export wheat in selected areas in Kansas: the pre- and post Staggers eras*. 1988. 193 l. (Thesis, Ph.D., Kansas State University)

4246. _____. *A survival analysis of light density rail branch lines in Kansas/* Topeka: Kansas Department of Transportation, Bureau of Rail Affairs, 1991. 32 p.

4247. _____, Stephen J. Rindom. *The impact of rail branch abandonment on rural highways: the case of south-central Kansas*. Topeka? Kansas Department of Transportation, Bureau of Rail Affairs, 1989. 54 p.

4248. _____, _____, Ali Abderrezak. *Economic impacts of changes in rail pricing for export wheat in Kansas/* Topeka: Kansas Department of Transportation, Bureau of Rail Affairs, 1993. 25 p.

4248a. Eustis, Percy Sprague. *Homeward through America*. Chicago : Poole Bros., printers, 1887. 32 p. (Railroad travel)

4249. *Evaluation of retroreflective markings to increase rail car conspicuity: safety of highway-railroad grade crossings*. Washington, DC: U.S. Dept. of Transportation, Research and Special Programs Administration, 1999. 1 v.(various pagings)

4249a. *Evaluation of Southern Pacific Land Company's mineral resources in Southern California* / San Francisco : Dames & Moore, 1980. 1 v.

4250. *Evaluation of the costs and benefits of railroad electrification*. Washington, DC: Federal Railroad Administration, 1977. 211 p.

4251. Evans, Anthony Walton White. *American v. English locomotives: correspondence, criticism and commentary respecting their relative merits*. New York, E.K. Pease, Printer, 1880. 78 p.

4252. Evans, Cerinda W. *Collis Potter Huntington*. Newport News, VA: Mariners' Museum, 1954. 2 v.

4253. Evans, Edward S. *"Off again-on again" railroad*. S.l., Popular Mechanics, 1944. 160 p. (Railroad motor cars)

4253a. Evans, Gerry, Peter Bush. *Good morning USA : by train through America* Auckland, NZ: David Ling Pub., 2004. 182 p.

4254. Evans, Lynn Barkley. *Study of the lubrication of railway locomotives and car journals, with special reference to the packing used*. 1918. 27 p. (Thesis, University of Kentucky)

4255. Evans Products Company. *Evans Auto-Railer: dual-purpose transportation units*. Detroit, MI: Evans Products Co., 1936. 18 p.

4256. Evans W.W. *Chapters on locomotives and iron bridges from a letter to the chief of the Bureau of Statistics of the United States.* New York, G.F. Nesbitt & Company, 1885. 24 p.

4257. _____, Benj H. Latrobe. *Letters on the railway gauge question* / New York: Evans, 1874. 116 p.

4257a. Evans, Walker, William Earle Williams. *Walker Evans in color: railroad photographs.* Haverford, PA: Haverford College, 2011. 63 p.
(Atrium Gallery, Haverford College, Haverford, PA., Oct. 21-Dec. 2011.)

4258 Evans, Walter. *Many are called. With an introduction by James Agee.* Boston, Houghton Mifflin, 1966. 178 p. (Subways-New York.) (Also: New Haven: CT: Yale University Press; New York, Metropolitan Museum of Art, 2004. 207 p.)

4259. Evans, Walton W. *A letter on crank-axles in locomotives and their demerits.* New York, s.n., 1884. 11 p.

4260. Evenson, James L. *Capability in decline: a historical analysis of the post-World War II degradation of domestic railroads and the impact on the United States military.* Fort Leavenworth, KS: USA Army Command and General Staff College, 2008. 1 v. http://cgsc.cdmhost.com/u?/p4013coll2,1807

4261. _____. *Intermodal war: assessing containerized power projection.* Ft. Belvoir: Defense Technical Information Center, 2009. 31 p.

4262. Everett, George G. *The cavalcade of railroads in central Colorado.* Denver, CO: Golden Bell Press, 1966. 235 p.

4263. Evers, Henry. *Steam and the locomotive engine.* New York, Putnam, 1873. 160 p.

4263a. Evers, Kathleen. *Railroads in Minneapolis* / Minneapolis: City Planning Department, 1981. 54 p.

4264. *Every time with no complaint.* Lenoir, NC: ET&WNCRR Historical Society, 2008- . Semiannual.

4265. Ewalt, John W. *The last hurrah of the P.R.R.* New York, Vantage Press, 1992. 156 p.

4266. Ewart, Field and Morrison. *Railway mail service systems of railway transportation. Ninth Division.* Springfield, Mass., Home Correspondence School, 1909. 64 p. (Ninth Division = lower peninsula of Michigan.)

4267. Ewert, Henry. *Great Northern's third route to the Pacific: Spokane to Vancouver, B.C.* Burnsville, MN: Great Northern Railway Historical Society, 2005. 8 p.

4268. Ewing, David, William Gallagher. *Intercity passenger rail transportation.* Washington, D.C., American Association of State Highway and Transportation Officials,

Standing Committee on Rail Transportation, 2002. 151 p.

4269. Ewing, James H., Harry Slep. *History of the city of Altoona and Blair County: including sketches of the shops of the Pennsylvania Railroad Co.* Altoona, Penn., H. Slep's Mirror Print House,1880. 262 p. 6 leaves of plates.

4269a. Ewoldt, Ruth H. *Content analysis of local news in six selected country weeklies in a period from 1830 to 1883 prior to and following the advent of the railroad/* 1981. 92 l. (Thesis, M.A., California State University, Fullerton.)

4270. *Extra 220 south: the locomotive newsmagazine.* Blaine, WA: s.n., 1961- Quarterly.

F

4270a. F.M. Pease. *We own and offer 300 refrigerator cars in first-class condition* / Chicago; The Company, 1900. 4 p.

4271. F.W. Devoe & Co. *Samples and priced list of coach and car colors, and fine varnishes, manufactured by F.W. Devoe & Co.* New York : F.W. Devoe & Co., 1880. 1 v. (unpaged).

4272. Fabing, Horace W. *Watsonville Transportation Company.* San Mateo, CA: Western Railroader, 1966. 16 p. (Port Rogers, Calif.)

4273. _____, Rick Hamman. *Steinbeck country narrow gauge.* Boulder, CO: Pruett, 1985. 236 p. (2d ed.: Santa Cruz, CA: Otter B Books, 2004. 236 p.) (Pajaro Valley Consolidated Railroad.)

4273a. *Facts about railroad use of motor vehicles: results of Second Annual Survey, with facts largely supplied by railroad officials, are made public.* New York: National Automobile Chamber of Commerce, National Motor truck Committee, 1925. 11 p. (*Co-ordinated transportation series, no. 12.*)

4274, Fagan, James O. *The autobiography of an individualist*/ Boston: Houghton Mifflin Co., 1912. 290 p.

4275. _____. *Confessions of a railroad signalman*/ Boston and New York: Houghton Mifflin Co., 1908. 181 p. (Published in part in Atlantic Monthly, Jan-July, 1908.

4276. _____. *Labor and the railroads.* Boston, Houghton Mifflin Company, 1909. 164 p.

4277. Fagen, Edward A. *The engine's moan: American steam whistles.* Mendham, NJ: Astragal Press, 2001. 277 p.

4278. _____, Hugh Gibb, Brian Woodcock. *Motive power roster of the Wilmington & Western Railroad.* Wilmington, DE: HRCV, 1981. 3 p.

4279. Fahey, John. *Inland Empire; D.C. Corbin and Spokane.* Seattle, University of Washington Press, 1965. 270 p.

4280. Fahmy, Mahmoud N. *Inspection of railroad wheels by impact generated rim waves* / 1984. 211 l. (Thesis, Ph.D., University of Houston.)

4280a. Fahy, Anna Louis. *Borderland Chinese : community identity and cultural change* / 2006. 139 l. (Thesis, M.A., University of Texas at El Paso.) El Paso. Southern Pacific Railroad Co.

4281. Fair, James R. *The Louisiana and Arkansas Railway: the story of a regional line.* DeKalb: Northern Illinois University Press, 1997. 158 p.

4282. _____. *The North Arkansas line: the story of the Missouri & North Arkansas Railroad.* Berkeley, CA: Howell-North Books, 1969. 304 p.

4283. Fairbanks, Morse and Company. *Cut operating expenses by using Sheffield Section Motor Car no. 14./* Chicago? S.n., 1905. 4 p.

4284. _____. *Fairbanks-Morse diesel electric locomotives: enginemen's manual.* Beloit, Wisc: Fairbanks-Morse, 194-? 108 p. (*Bulletin No. 1114J;*

4285. _____. *Fairbanks-Morse diesel electric locomotives: enginemen's manual.* Beloit, WI: Fairbanks-Morse, 1951. 1 v. (*Bulletin no. 1705, April, 1951.)* "Manual for operating Fairbanks-Morse "Consolidation-Line" diesel electric locomotives."

4286. _____. *Fairbanks-Morse diesel electric locomotives: enginemen's manual.* Chicago, IL: Fairbanks-Morse, 1955. 1 v. (*Bulletin no. 1502; Feb., 1955.)* (For 1600HP all-purpose locomotives.)

4287. _____. *Fairbanks-Morse diesel engines: comparison of diesel engine principles, operation and construction.* Chicago, Ill., The Company, 1930. 23 p. (*Bulletin no. 3020.)*

4288. _____. *Fairbanks-Morse diesels.* Chicago, Ill., Fairbanks, Morse & Co., 1936. 11 l.

4289. _____. *The Fairbanks-Morse O.P. diesel engine for locomotive power.* Chicago, Ill., Fairbanks-Morse, 1940-? 16 p.

4290. _____. *The Fairbanks-Morse O.P. diesel engine: for passenger, freight and switching service.* Chicago, Ill., Fairbanks, Morse & Co., 1948. 23 p.

4291. _____. *Locomotive coaling stations: Construction Department.* Chicago, Ill., Fairbanks, Morse & Co., 1905. 16 p.(*Catalogue no. 103.)*

4292. _____. *Locomotive coaling stations: yard storage systems, cinder conveyors, sand plants.* Sterling, VA: TLC Pub., 1989? (Reprint of ca1935 ed.)

4293. _____. *Pioneers in industry; the story of Fairbanks, Morse & Co., 1830-1945.* Chicago, Ill., Fairbanks, Morse & Co., 1945. 1 v.

4294. _____. *Railroad service: water and track.* Chicago, IL: Fairbanks, Morse & Co., 1918. 80 p. (*Catalogue No. 126D.)*

4295. _____. *Railway hand cars and push cars.* Three Rivers, Mich., Sheffield Car Company, 1907. 16 p. (*Catalogue no. 105A.)*

4296. _____. *Railway supplies; Railroad Department.* Chicago, Ill., Fairbanks, Morse and Company, 1906. 430 p. (*Catalogue number 52A.*)

4297._____. *Sheffield 40 motor car: a powerful puller for heavy section work.* Chicago, IL: Fairbanks, Morse & Company, 1918. 2 p.

4298. _____. *Sheffield 41 motor car: the kerosene car that's safe.* Chicago, IL: Fairbanks, Morse and Company, 1918. 2 p.

4299. _____. *Sheffield 42 inspection car: like covering the lines in your automobile.* Chicago, IL: Fairbanks, Morse & Company, 1919. 2 p.

4300. _____. *Sheffield gasoline motor cars* / Chicago : The Company, 1905. 16 p. (*Catalogue 101A.*)

4301. _____ *Sheffield hand cars—push cars.* Chicago, Fairbanks & Morse, 1917. 12 p. (*Bulletin 105F.*)

4302. _____. *Sheffield pressed steel wheels for motor cars, trailers, hand cars and push cars.* Chicago : Fairbanks, Morse and Company, 1927. 16 p.

4303. _____. *Sheffield 38 motor car: it runs successfully on common kerosene.* Chicago, IL: Fairbanks Morse & Company, 1916. 2 p.

4304. _____. *Sheffield 36 motor car: a light, powerful one-man inspection car.* Chicago, Il: Fairbanks, Morse & Company, 1917. 2 p.

4305. _____. *Sheffield 32 motor car: everything you wanted in a section car*/ Chicago: Fairbanks Morse & Co., 1916. 2 p.

4306. _____. *Sheffield gasoline motor cars.* Chicago, The Company, 1905. 16 p. (*Catalogue no. 101A.*)

4307. _____. *Sheffield hand cars—push cars.* Chicago, IL: Fairbanks, Morse & Company, 1917. 12 p. (*Bulletin 105F.*)

4308. _____. *Sheffield velocipede cars*/ Chicago, IL: Fairbanks, Morse and Company, 1917. 4 p. (*Bulletin 106G.*)

4309. _____. *Track appliances: hand cars and push cars; railway velocipedes and motor cars, track jacks and rail drills, track tools, Sheffield cattle guards.* Chicago, Ill., Fairbanks, Morse & Co., 1907. 32 p. (*Catalogue No. 127.*)

4310. *Fairbanks' pocket atlas of the United States, and miniature railway guide, with illustrations and descriptions of Fairbanks' standard platform & counter scales.* New York: Schonberg, 1859. 59 p.

4310a. Faircio, George Cassius. *Design of a steel coal-tower* / 1902. 17 l. (Thesis, B.S.,

University of Illinois.)

4310b. [Fair lane railroad business car collection, 1920-1989.] 6 cubic feet and 9 oversize boxes. Location: The Henry Ford Museum.

4311. Fairmont Railway Motors. *Fairmont M9, series C: one-man inspection car.* Fairmont, Minn., Fairmont Railway Motors, Inc., 1938. 8 p.

4312. _____. *Fairmont M9, series D: one man inspection car.* Fairmont, Minn., Fairmont Railway Motors, Inc., 1938. 8 p. (*Bulletin 391, M9 car, series D.*)

4313. _____. *Fairmont M9, series F: spring mounted one man inspection car.* Fairmont, Minn., Fairmont Railway Motors, Inc., 1945. 8 p. (*Bulletin 527, M9 car, series F.*)

4314. _____. *The Fairmont M19, series E; one to four man inspection car.* Fairmont, Minn., Fairmont Railway Motors, Inc., 1938. 8 p. (*Bulletin 396, M19, series E.*)

4315. _____. *Fairmont railway motor cars.* Fairmont, Minn., Fairmont Railway Motors, Inc., 1915. 20 p.

4316. _____. *Fairmont railway motor cars.* Fairmont, Minn., Fairmont Railway Motors, Inc., 1919. 18 p.

4317. _____. *Fairmont railway motor cars and work equipment.* Fairmont, Minn., Fairmont Railway Motors, Inc., 1944. 34 p. (*Bulletin 515.*)

4318. _____. *Fairmont railway motor cars and work equipment.* Fairmont, Minn., Fairmont Railway Motors, Inc., 1952. 51 p. (*Bulletin 660.*)

4319. _____ *Fairmont Railway Motors, Inc.* Fairmont, Minn, Fairmont Railway Motors, Inc., 1931. 28, 104 p.

4320. _____. *Fairmont S2 motor car F-3-38 instructions and spare parts list.* Fairmont, Minn., The Company, 1941. 60 p.

4321. _____. *The Fairmont 2110: official inspection coach.* Fairmont, Minn., Fairmont Railway Motors, Inc., 1929. 12 p. (*Bulletin 250C, 2100 cars.*)

4322. _____. *Motor car performance by Fairmont.* Fairmont, Minn., Fairmont Railway Motors, Inc., 1945. 2 l.

4323. Fales, Henry Hammett. *Stresses in locomotive connecting rods.* 1903. 37 l. (Thesis, B.S., Massachusetts Institute of Technology, Department of Mechanical Engineeering)

4324. Falkenau, A. *Illustrated catalogue of narrow-gauge locomotives.* Scranton, Pa., Dickson Manufacturing Company, 1895. 128 p.

4325. Falkenberg, Ruth, John Hankey. *Railroad depot acquisition and development/*

Washington, DC: National Trust for Historic Preservation, 1989. 15 p. (*Information series, 44.*)

4326. Fallberg, Carl. *Fiddletown & Copperopolis; the life and times of an uncommon carrier.* Foreword by Lucius Beebe. Reseda, CA: Hungerford Press, 1960. 1 v. (2d ed.: River Forest, IL: Heimburger House Pub. Co., 1985. 72 p.)

4327. Faller, John D., Jr. *The South Pennsylvania Railroad* / New York ? 1935. 30 l.

4328. Fallon, W.J., N.K. Cooperrider, E.H. Law. *An investigation of techniques for validation of railcar dynamic analyses* / Washington, DC: Federal Railroad Administration, Office of Research and Development, 1978. 105 p. (*FRA-OR&D-78/19.*)

4329. Fambro, Daniel, Michael M. Beitler, Sarah M. Hubbard. *Enhancements to passive warning devices at railroad-highway grade crossings.* Rev. ed. College Station, TX: Texas Transportation Institute, Texas A & M University System, 1994. (*Research report: 1273-1.*)

4330. Fanning, Leonard M. *John Stevens: father of American railroads*/ New York, NY: Mercer Pub. Co., 1956. 10 p. (*Fathers of industry series*)

4331.Farewell, R.C. *Rio Grande: ruler of the Rockies.* Glendale, CA: Trans-Anglo Books, 1987. 168 p.

4332. *The far-famed Georgetown Loop: the grandest of all one day trips.* Denver, Colo., Smith-Brooks Press, 1911? 23 p.

4333. Faricy, William T. *A.A.R., the story behind a symbol.* New York, Newcomen Society in North America, 1951. 28 p.

4334. _____. *Freight car supply and effective transportation capacity*/ Washington, DC: Association of American Railroads, 1950. 17 p.

4335. _____. *Gauge of railroads in the United States.* Washington, D.C., Association of American Railroads, 1947. 4 p.(*Document number 70470.*)

4336. _____. *Wartime problems of the domestic railroads.* Washington, D.C., Industrial College of the Armed Forces, 1949. 19 p. (*Publication no. L50-57.*)

4337. Faris, Charles L., Don Dopf. *Charles L. Faris; western railroad engineer.* Boise, ID: Writers Press, 2001. 125 p. (Union Pacific Railroad; Camas Prairie Railroad.)

4338. Farnsworth, JoAnn. *Montpelier and the Oregon Short Line.* Montpelier, ID:? J. Farnsworth, 1993. 85 p.

4339. Farnsworth, M.M., G.W. Baughman. *History of Union Switch & Signal.* S.l., s.n., 1947. 113 l.

4340. Farooqi, A. Masood. *Ridership studies for the proposed Florida high speed rail system/* 1990. 120 l. (Thesis, M.S., Florida International University)

4341. Farr, Edwin H. *Accident severity prediction formula for rail-highway crossings.* Washington, DC: Federal Highway Administration, 1984. 31, A-9 p.

4342. _____. *Summary of the DOT rail-highway crossing resource allocation procedure—revised: final report.* Washington, DC: Federal Railroad Administration, Office of Safety, Office of Safety Analysis, 1987. 30 p.

4343. _____, John S. Hitz. *Effectiveness of motorist warning devices at rail-highway crossings.* Washington, DC: Federal Highway Administration, Office of Research, Development and Technology, 1985. 98 p. (*FHWA/RD-85/015.*)

4344. Farrell, Jack W. *The Berkshire and Texas types.* Edmonds, WA: Pacific Fast Mail, 1988. 191 p.

4345. _____. *The Mountains.* Edmonds, WA: Pacific Fast Mail, 1977. 381 p.

4346. _____, and Mike Pearsall. *The Northerns.* Edmonds, WA: Pacific Fast Mail, 1975. 248 p.

4347. Farrell, Joseph F. *The illustrated guide to Peter Grey railroad hardware/* Worcester, MA: Farrell Railroad Consulting, 1994. 180 p. (Lanterns, equipment & supplies.)

4348. Farrington, S. Kip. *Railroading coast to coast: riding the locomotive cabs—steam, electric, and diesel, 1923-1950.* New York, Bonanza Books, 1981, c1976. 305 p.

4349. _____. *Railroading from the head end.* Garden City, NY: Doubleday, Doran & Co., 1943. 296 p.

4350. _____. *Railroading from the rear end.* New York, Coward, McCann, Inc., 1946. 430 p.

4351. _____. *Railroading the modern way.* New York, Coward-McCann, Inc., 1951. 395 p.

4352. _____. *Railroads at war.* New York, Coward-McCann, Inc., 1944. 320 p.

4353. _____. *Railroads of the hour.* New York, Coward-McCann, Inc., 1958. 333 p.

4354. _____. *Railroads of today.* New York, Coward-McCann, 1949. 306 p.

4355. _____. *The Santa Fe's big three; the life story of a trio of the world's greatest locomotives.* New York, D. McKay Company, 1972. 287 p.

4356. _____, Glen Thomas. *Giants of the rails.* Garden City, NY: Garden City Pub. Co.,

1944. 26 p.

4357. Farris, J.K. *The Harrison riot, or, The reign of the mob on the Missouri and North Arkansas Railroad* / Wynne, AR: Rev. J.K. Farris, 1924. 195 p. (Missouri and North Arkansas Railroad Strike, Arkansas, 1921-1923.

4358. Farrow, Edward S. *Equalized trucks for heavy electric and steam service* / New York : Office of Edward S. Farrow, Consulting Railroad and Mining Engineer, 1905. 1 v.

4359. *FAST Engineering Conference, Denver, Colorado, November 4 & 5, 1981: proceedings.* Washington, DC: Federal Railroad Administration; Association of American Railroads, 1982. 282 p. (*FRA/TTC-82/01.*)

4360. *The Fast mail.* New York : Twentieth Century Railroad Club, 1971-   . Monthly.

4361. *Fast tracks in the Golden State: symposia on California high-speed rail: proceedings summary.* San Jose, CA: Mineta Transportation Institute, San José State University, 2003. 100 p. (*FHWA/CA/OR-2002-33*)

4362. Fastenrath, William. *Locomotive safety.* Nashville, Tenn., J. Withers, Printers, 1902. 189 p.

4363. Fate-Root-Heath Company. *Plymouth gas electric and oil electric locomotives: model WE 50-ton electric and OE 60-ton oil electric.* Plymouth, Ohio, The Company, 1929. 12 p.

4364. Fath, J.M. *Measurements of railroad noise—line operations, yard boundaries and retarders.* Washington: Applied Acoustics Section, Institute for Basic Standards, National Bureau of Standards, 1974. 104 p. (*NBSIR74-488; EPA-550/9-007; COM-75-10088.*)

4365. Faulk, Paul. *Atlantic Coast Line color guide to freight and passenger equipment.* Scotch Plains, NJ: Morning Sun Books, 2000. 128 p.

4366. _____. *Seaboard Air Line color guide to freight and passenger equipment.* Scotch Plains, NJ: Morning Sun Books, 1998. 127 p.

4367. _____. *Trackside around Atlanta, 1956-1976, with Howard Robins.* Scotch Plains, NJ: Morning Sun Books, 2004. 128 p.

4368. Faus, H.W. *The effect of improved draft gears and spring dampened truck on freight car shocks.* New York : American Society of Mechanical Engineers, 1957. 5 p. (ASME. Paper no. 56-A-80.)

4369. Favour, Alpheus H. *In the matter of the hearing on the report of the committee on Port and Terminal Facilities in connection with the relocation and improvement of the West Side tracks on the New York Central Railroad, within the city of New York :*

pursuant to chapter 777 of the laws of 1911. New York : Board of Estimate and Apportionment, 1916. 9 p.

4370. Feagans, Raymond J. *The railroad that ran by the tide; Ilwaco Railroad & Navigation Co. of the State of Washington.* Berkeley, CA: Howell-North Books, 1972. 146 p.

4371. *Feasibility of developing a hopper-bottom boxcar for railroad transportation of grain and soybeans* / Washington, DC: Department of Agriculture, Agricultural Research Service, 1974. 1 v. (various pagings)

4372. *"Featherbedding:" a list of references arranged chronologically with index of authors.* Washington, DC: Bureau of Railway Economics, Library, Association of American Railroads, 1950. 16 l.

4373. Fec, M.C. *Hot spots on railroad wheels generated during dynamometer tests* / Chicago : Association of American Railroads, Technical Center, 1983. 14 l. (*Report, no. R-556>*)

4374. *Federal rail safety improvements.* Washington, DC: U.S. G.P.O., 2008. 123 p.

4375. *Federal Railroad Administration Northeast Corridor Improvement Project Electrification: New Haven, Connecticut to Boston, Massachusetts.* Cranston, RI: Allied Court Reporters, 1993. 97 l.

4376. *The Federal railway digest.* Chicago: Federal Law Book Co., 1916-1919. Quarterly.

4377. Federal Reserve Bank of Boston; Business History and Economic Life Program, Inc. *Towpaths to oblivion: the Middlesex Canal and the coming of the railroad, 1792-1853.* Boston, MA: Business History and Economic Life Program, Inc., 1975. 22 p.

4378. Feick, Fred L. *The life of railway men: together with a brief sketch and history of the great railway organizations, their aims and purposes; also a true and scientific solution of the great labor problem as seen from the Inside.* Chicago, Ill., Press of the H.O. Shepard Co., 1905. 184 p.

4379. Feiger, James H. *Small fatigue crack growth from notches in Ti-AI-4V under constant and variable amplitude loading* / 1999. 95 l. (Thesis, M.S., University of Idaho.)

4380. _____, P.C. McKeighan. *Variable amplitude fatigue crack growth characteristics of railroad tank car steel.* Washington, DC: Federal Railroad Administration, Office of Research and Development, 2006. 3 v.

4381. Feighney, Al. *Missouri, Kansas and Texas Railroad* / 1938. 60 l. (Thesis, Oklahoma Agricultural and Mechanical College.)

4382. Feitz, Leland. *Cripple Creek railroads; a quick history of the great gold camps railroads*. Denver, CO: Golden Bell Press, 1968. 30 p.

4383. Fellows, David S. *The Cut-Off and Fellows station: a local rail history of Rock County, Wisconsin*. Evansville, WI: Star Printing Co., 2004. 251 p. (C&NW)

4384. Felthousen, D.N. *Industrial directory of the Pennsylvania Railroad system; the Pennsylvania Railroad Company, West Jersey & Seashore Railroad Company, Waynesburg & Washington Railroad Company, the Ohio River & Western Railway Company*. Oak Park, Ill., Delmont Railroad Advertising Agency, Printers, 1926. 572 p.

4385. Felton, John Richard. *The economics of freight car supply*. Lincoln, University of Nebraska Press, 1976. 118 p.

4386. _____. *The problem of freight car supply*. Lincoln, University of Nebraska, College of Agriculture and Home Economics, Agricultural Experiment Station, 1970. 20 p. (*Agricultural Experiment Station, 25*.)

4387. Felton, Paul Ellsworth. *The history of the Atlantic and Great Western railroad* / 1943. 235 l (Thesis, Ph.D., University of Pittsburgh.)

4388. Felton, S.M. *Steel rails, axles and forgings: testimony to their economy and safety; from leading railways, and from other sources*. Philadelphia, Review Printing House, cor. Walnut & Fourth Sts, 1870. 24 p.

4389. Felton, Samuel M. *Railroad passenger car standard floor plans*. New York, American Railway Car Institute, 1949. 8 l. 27 x 42 cm. S.M. Felton : President, American Railway Car Institute.

4389a. Feng, Kaimin Kay. *Stresses in railway structures on curves* / 1916. 103 l. (Thesis, M.S., University of Illinois

4390. Fenlon, Paul E. *The struggle for control of the Florida Central Railroad (1867-1882), a case study of business enterprise in post-Civil War Florida*. 1955. 198 l. (Thesis, Ph.D., University of Florida.)

4391. Ferguson, Allen R. *Community impacts of abandonment of railroad service*. Washington, D.C., Public Interest Economics Center, 1974. 219 p. (Prepared for the United States Railway Association by the Public Interest Economics Center.)

4392. Ferguson, John Alan. *Unit train transportation of coal* / 1975. 64 l. (Thesis, M.S., University of Illinois at Urbana-Champaign.)

4393. Ferguson, Robert T. *Mathematical modeling of the railroad switching process*. 1993. 114 l. (Thesis, Ph.D., University of Virginia.)

4394. Fernon, Thomas Sargent. *On the transportation tactics of the Pennsylvania R.R. Co*. Philadelphia, s.n., 1870. 8 p.

4395. _____. *Thomas A. Scott as a pledge-breaker and salary grabber.* Philadelphia: s.n., 1878. 7 p. Pennsylvania Railroad Co.

4396. Fernow, B.E. *Report on the relation of railroads to forest supplies and forestry : together with appendices on the structures of some timber ties, their behavior, and the cause of their decay in the road bed, on wood preservation, on metal ties, and on the use of spark arrestors.* Washington, DC: U.S. Department of Agriculture, Forestry Division, 1887. 149 p. (Bulletin. Forestry Division, no. 1.)

4397. Ferrarini, Alessia. *Railway stations: from the Gare de l'est to Penn Station.* Milan, Electa Architecture, 2005. 217 p.

4398. Ferrell, Mallory Hope. *Argent: last of the swamp rats.* Edmonds, WA: Pacific Fast Mail, 1994. 143 p.

4399. _____. *C & S ng: Colorado & Southern narrow gauge: the bear trap stack era.* Richard B. Jackson, photographer. Boulder, CO: Pruett Publishing Company, 1981. 238 p.

4400. _____. *Colorful East Broad Top.* Forest Park, IL: Heimburger House, 1993. 84 p.

4401. _____. *A description of locomotives manufactured.* [Grant Locomotive Works catalog. New York, J. Sutton & Company, 1871.] Boulder, CO: Pruett Publishing Company, 1971, 1871. 1 v.

4402. _____. *El Dorado narrow gauge: the Diamond & Caldor Railway.* Edmonds, WA: Pacific Fast Mail, 1990. 159 p.

4403. _____. *The Gilpin gold tram, Colorado's unique narrow-gauge.* Boulder, CO: Pruett Publishing Company, 1970. 112 p.(2d ed.: Forest Park, IL: Heimburger House Pub. Co., 1992. 120 p.)

4404. _____. *Narrow gauge country, 1870-1970.* Forest Park, IL: Heimburger House, 2006. 371 p.

4405. _____. *Nevada Central ; sagebrush narrow gauge.* Forest Park, IL: Heimburger House, 2010. 204 p.

4406. _____. *Norfolk & Western : steam's last stand.* Mukilteo, WA: Hundman Pub., 2007. 319 p.

4406a. _____. *Rails around Lake Tahoe: steam trains and steamboats of the Tahoe region* / Berkeley and Wilton, CA: Signature Press, 2011. 256 p.

4407. _____. *Rails, sagebrush, and pine; a garland of railroad and logging days in Oregon's Sumpter Valley.* San Marino, CA: Golden West Books, 1967. 128 p.

4408. _____ *Silver San Juan: the Rio Grande Southern.* Boulder, CO: Pruett Publishing

Company, 1973. 645 p.

4409. _____. *Slow trains down South: --daily 'cept Sunday/* Mukilteo, WA: Hundman Pub., 2005-

4410. _____. *The South Park Line.* Mukilteo, WA: Hundman Pub., 2003. 368 p.

4411. _____. *Southern Pacific narrow gauge.* Edmonds, WA: Pacific Fast Mail, 1982. 272 p. (Carson and Colorado Railroad)

4412. _____. *Tweetsie Country: the East Tennessee & Western North Carolina Railroad.* Illustrations by Mike Pearsall and Casey Holtzinger. Boulder, CO: Pruett Publishing Company, 1976. 219 p. (2d ed.: Johnson City, TN: Overmountain Press, 1991. 219 p.)

4413. _____. *Virginia & Truckee: the bonanza road.* Mukilteo, WA: Hundman Pub., 1999. 300 p.

4414. _____. *West Side, narrow gauge in the Sierra.* illustrations by Howard Fogg, Jim Finnell, Mike Pearsall. Edmonds, WA: Pacific Fast Mail, 1979. 319 p.

4415. Ferris, Sally A. *Federal subsidies to rail passenger service: an assessment of Amtrak.* Washington, DC: Congressional Budget Office, 1982. 85, 1 p.

4416. Fetters, Thomas T. *The Charleston & Hamburg: a South Carolina railroad and an American legacy.* Charleston, SC: History Press, 2008. 156 p.

4417. _____. *Logging railroads of South Carolina.* Forest Park, IL: Heimburger House Pub. Co., 1990. 246 p.

4417a. _____. *Logging railroads of the Blue Ridge and Smoky Mountains* / Hillsboro, OR: Timber Times, 2010. 2 v.

4418. _____, Peter W. Swanson. *Piedmont and Northern; the great electric system of the South.* San Marino, CA: Golden West Books, 1974. 175 p.

4419. *A few reasons why Senate Bill 159, granting "Yerba Buena" island to the Western Pacific Railroad Co. should not be passed.* S.l,, s.n., 1868. 1 folder (4 p.)

4420. Fickewirth, Alvin A. *California railroads: an encyclopedia of cable car, common carrier, horsecar, industrial, interurban, logging, monorail, motor road, shortlines, streetcar, switching, and terminal railroads in California, 1851-1992.* San Marino, CA: Golden West Books, 1992. 194 p.

4421. Fiedler, George Joseph. *Railway electrification and its application to the Chicago and Illinois Midland Railroad.* 1932. 1 v. (Thesis, M.S., Electrical Engineering, University of Kansas.)

4422. *Field manual of the interchange rules.* Washington, D.C., Association of American Railroads, 2006. 645 p.

4423. Field, Stephen J., Lorenzo Sawyer. *The taxation of property of railroad companies in California as affected by the Fourteenth Amendment of the Federal Constitution.* San Francisco: United States, Circuit Court (9th Circuit); Santa Clara County, 1883. 96 p.

4424. Fielder, Mildred. *Railroads of the Black Hills.* Seattle, WA: Superior Publishing Company, 1964. 176 p. (Reprint: Deadwood, SD: Dakota Graphics, 1993, 1964. 176 p.

4425. Fields, Randall K. *Chessie System color guide to freight equipment.* Scotch Plains, NJ: Morning Sun Books, 2003. 126 p.

4426. Fields, Richard A. *Range of opportunity: a historic study of the Copper Range Company.* Hancock, MI: Published by Quincy Mine Hoist Association in cooperation with The Program in Industrial History and Archaeology, Department of Social Science, Michigan Technological University: Produced by Book Concern Printers, 1997. 126 p. (Copper Range Company. Copper Range Railroad Company.)

4427. *50 years of railroading in Southern California: 1936-1986 plus updates through 1996.* Edited by Tom A. Nelson. Santa Fe Springs, CA: Pacific Railroad Society, 2001. 1 v.

4428. *Final environmental assessment for the proposed super-speed ground transportation system, Las Vegas/Southern California corridor, phase II/* San Bernardino, CA: URS Co., 1986. 3 v. Prepared for the Department of Super-Speed Train Development, Las Vegas, NV.

4429. *Final environmental impact statement, finance docket no. 33388: Proposed Conrail acquisition, CSX Corporation and CSX Transportation, Inc., Norfolk Southern Corporation and Norfolk Southern Railway Company, control and operating leases/agreements, Conrail, inc., and Consolidated Rail Corporation/* Washington, DC: Surface Transportation Board, Section of Environmental Analysis, 1998. 11 v.

4430. *Final environmental impact statement: Florida high-speed rail, Tampa to Orlando/* S.l., Federal Railroad Administration, 2005. Computer file 2 CD-ROMs

4431. *Final environmental impact statement for the proposed Canadian National Railway Company acquisition of the Elgin, Joliet & Eastern Railway Company/* Washington, DC: Surface Transportation Board, Section of Environment Analysis, 2008, 6 v.

4432. *Final environmental impact statement/report and 4(f) statement. Volume 1. Northeast Corridor Improvement Project: electrification, New Haven, CT to Boston, MA.* Washington, DC: Federal Railroad Administration, Office of Railroad Development, 1994. 1 v (various pagings). (*DOT-VNTSC-FRA-94-5.*)

4433. *Final environmental impact statement/report. Volume II, Technical studies:*

Northeast Corridor Improvement Project: electrification, New Haven, CT to Boston, MA. Washington, DC: Federal Railroad Administration, Office of Railroad Development, 1994. 478 p. (*DOT-VNTSC-FRA-94-6.*)

4434. *Final environmental impact statement report. Volume III. Responses to comments on draft environmental impact statement/report: Northeast Corridor Improvement project: electrification, New Haven, CT to Boston, MA.* Washington, DC: Federal Railroad Administration, Office of Railroad Development, 1994. 354 p. (*DOT-VNTSC-FRA-94-7.*)

4435. *Final environmental impact statement/report: Northeast Corridor Improvement Project: electrification,-New Haven, CT to Boston, MA.* Washington, DC: Federal Railroad Administration, 1994. 38 p. (Massachusetts EOEA number-9134)

4436. *Final report on the National Maglev Initiative* / Washington, DC: Federal Railroad Administration; Army Corps of Engineers, 1983. 1 v (various pagings) (*DOT/FRA/NMI-93/03*)

4437. *Financial and operating statistics for the six months ending... Class I railroads.* Washington, D.C., Interstate Commerce Commission, Bureau of Accounts, 1971- Semiannual. (<*Operating revenues and operating expenses of class I railroads in the United States.* (1957-1970); *Selected income and balance sheet items of class I railroads in the United States.* (1956-   ); *Selected income and balance-sheet items of class I steam railways in the United States.* (1900s-1956);

4438. *The financial review.* New York, NY: W.B. Dana Co., 1874-1921. Annual.

4439. Finch, C.W. *The CGW Winston tunnel and its ghost.* Newell, IA: Bireline Publishing Co., 1985. 90 p.

4440. _____. *The depot agent: the history of the C.G.W. Railroad as seen through the eyes of an agent.* Apple River, IL: North-West Associates, 1984. 174 p.

4441. _____. *The old railroad depot.* S.l., s.n., 19--? 198 l.(CGW)

4442. _____. *Our American railroads: the way it was.* Dubuque, IA: C.W. Finch, 1988. 444 p.

4443. _____. *The railroad man: past, present, future.* East Dubuque, Ill., C.W. Finch, 1992. 235 p.

4444. _____. *Railroads: it's the men who made them famous: the Chicago Great Western Railroad Company in Elizabeth, Jo Davies County, Illinois.* S.l. s.n., 1900? 1 v.

4445. Findlay, Charles Owen. *Review of the wrought iron railroad bridge across the Bushkill at Walter's Mill* . 1891. 41 l. (Thesis, Lafayette College (Easton, Pa.), Department of Civil Engineering.)

4446. Fink, Albert. *Cost of railroad transportation, railroad accounts, and governmental regulations of railroad tariffs/* New York: Evening Post Job Printing Office, 1882. 29 p.

4446a. _____. *Investigation into the cost of passenger traffic on American railroads with special reference to cost of mail service and its compensation.* Louisville, Printed by J.P. Morton and Company, 1876. 59, 20 p.

4447. _____. *An investigation into the cost of transportation on American railroad: with deductions for its cheapening.* Louisville, KY: J.P. Morton, 1874. 44, 16 p.

4448. _____. *The railroad problem and its solution.* New York, Russell Brothers, Printers, 1880. 80 p.

4449. Fink, Tiffany Marie Haggard. *The Fort Worth and Denver City Railway: settlement, development, and decline on the Texas High Plains.* 2004. 260 l. (Thesis, Ph.D., Texas Tech University.)

4450. *Final standards, classification, and designation of lines of Class I railroads in the United States: a report.* Washington, DC: Department of Transportation, Federal Railroad Administration, 1976. 2 v. (v. 2. issued June 1977.)

4451. *The financial review: finance, crops, railroads, trade, commerce.* New York: W.B. Dana & Co., 1860-1921. Annual. Subtitle varies.

4451a. Finney, E. C. *The Northern Pacific land grant* / Washington, DC: G.P.O., 1925. 10 p. (United States. Congress. Joint Committee on Investigation of the Northern Pacific Railroad Land Grant.)

4452. Fiore, David J. *The Chicago Great Western in Du Page County, Ill./* Villa Park, IL: D.J. Fiore, 1988. 11 l.

4453. _____. *The Chicago Great Western Railway.* Charleston, SC: Arcadia, 2006. 127 p.

4454. *Fire and flammability characteristics of materials used in rail passenger cars: a literature survey.* Compiled by: John A. Rakaczky. Aberdeen Proving Ground, MD: U.S. Army Armament Research and Development Command, Ballistic Research Laboratory, 1980. 100 p. (*ARBRL-MR-03009.*)

4455. *Firemen and oilers' journal.* Omaha, NE: International Brotherhood of Firemen and Oilers, 1919-19-- ?

4456. *Firemen's magazine.* Terre Haute, IN: Brotherhood of Locomotive Firemen, 1882-1885. Monthly

4457. *First in the West: Sacramento Valley Railroad, of 100 years ago, oldest link in SP's Western lines.* San Francisco, Calif., Public Relations Department, Southern Pacific Company, 1955. 16 p.

4457a. Fiscella, John M. *San Diego & Arizona Railway main line route passenger service: the agony and the odyssey* / San Diego: Rail History Pub, in conjunction with San Diego Model Railroad Museum, 2010. 364 p.

4458. Fischer, Ian S. *PRR color guide to freight and passenger equipment, vol. 2 and 3.* Edison, NJ: Morning Sun Books, 1996-2002. 2 v. (Vol. 1- See entry 7124.).)

4459. Fischer, John W. *Maglev as a high speed ground transportation alternative: background and developments.* Washington, DC: Congressional Research Service, Library of Congress, 2000. 6 p. (Major studies and issue briefs of the Congressional Research Service; Supplement. 2000, reel 9, fr. 0601.)

4460. Fischer, Philip Anthony, John D. Bitzan. *Analysis of economies of size and density for short line railroads.* Fargo, ND: North Dakota State University; Mountain Plains Consortium, 2001, 65 p. Thesis, M.S., North Dakota State University, 2000. 64 l. (*MPC report, no. 01-128.*)

4461. Fischler, Stan. *Long Island Rail Road.* St, Paul, MN: MBI, 2007. 160 p.

4462. _____. *Next stop Grand Central: a trip through time on New York's metropolitan area commuter railroads.* Erin, ON: The Boston Mills Press, 1986. 175 p.

4463. _____. *The subway: a trip through time on New York's rapid transit.* New York, J&M Productions II, 1997. 256 p.

4464. _____. *Uptown, downtown: a trip through time on New York's subways.* New York, Hawthorn Books, 1976. 271 p.

4465. _____, John Henderson. *The subway and the city: celebrating a century.* Syosset, NY: Frank Merriwell, Inc., 2004. 547 p.

4466. Fish, Frederick P. *Railroads and railroad labor*/ Philadelphia, PA: Railway Business Association, 1922. 16 p.

4466a. Fischer, Louis Engelmann. *Economics of interurban railways.* Boulder, CO: University Libraries, University of Colorado at Boulder, 2011, 1914. 116 p. (Originally published; New York: McGraw-Hill Book Co., 1914.)

4467. Fischer, Robert F. *Only yesterday on the Lehigh & New England Railroad: a photographic remembrance* / Englewood, FL: R.F. Fischer, 2004. 158 p.

4468. Fisher, Bill. *30 years over Donner: railroading "family style" over Southern Pacific's Donner Pass, through the eyes of a company signal engineer.* Glendale, CA: Trans-Anglo Books, 1991. 198 p.

4469. Fisher, Charles Eben. *The Galena and Chicago Union Railroad.* Boston, Mass., The Railway and Locomotive Historical Society, Inc., Baker Library, Harvard Business

School, 1932. 32 p. (*Bulletin no. 27.*)

4470. _____. *A little story of the Boston & Providence Railroad Company.* Federalsburg, MD: J.W. Stowell Printing Company, 1917. 16 p.

4471. _____. *Locomotives of the Chicago, Burlington* & Quincy *Railroad.* Boston, Mass., The Railway and Locomotive Historical Society, Inc., 1936- (*Supplement, August 1, 1948.* 8 p.)

4472. _____. *Philadelphia, Wilmington & Baltimore Railroad Company.* Boston, Mass., The Railway and Locomotive Historical Society, Inc., 1930. 36 p. (*Bulletin, no. 21.*)

4473. _____. *Steam locomotives of the New Haven Railroad.* New York, N.Y., National Railway Publishing Company, 1981. 171 p. (Reprints from Its *Bulletin, nos. 40, 41, 43, 44, 46, 47, 49, 50, 52.*)

4474. _____. *The story of the Old Colony Railroad.* Taunton, Mass., C.A. Hack & Son, Printers, 1919. 196 p.

4475. _____. *Whistler's railroad: the western railroad of Massachusetts.* Boston, MA: The Railway & Locomotive Historical Society, Inc., 1958. 103 p. (*Bulletin, no. 69.*) (Western Railway Corporation.)

4476. _____, Cornelius W. Hauck, John H. White. *Our first locomotives.* San Francisco, CA: The Railway & Locomotive Historical Society, 1998. 40 p.(*Bulletin, no. 62.*)

4477. _____, Frank P. Dubiel. *The story of the Old Colony Railroad.* Revised, enlarged and published by Frank P. Dubiel. Fall River, MA: Dubiel, 1974. 104 p.

4478. Fisher, Clyde Otto. *Use of federal power in settlement of railway labor disputes.* Washington, DC: U.S. G.P.O., 1922. 121 1 p. (*Bulletin of the United States Bureau of Labor Statistics, no. 303. Conciliation and arbitration series.*)

4479. Fisher, Franklin G., Edward L. Rogers, Anthony J. Maiale. *Computerized weighing of railroad freight cars coupled in-motion.* New York : American Society of Mechanical Engineers, 1966. 11 p. (*ASME. Paper no. 66-RR-2.*)

4480. _____, R.K. Allen. *Adhesion, how much? : an investigation of the causes of low wheel-to-rail adhesion and possible methods of improving it* / New York : American Society of Mechanical Engineers, 1955. 14 p. (*ASME. Paper no. 55-A-132.*)

4481. Fisher, John Sterling, Chase Mellen. *A builder of the West: the life of General William Jackson Palmer.* Caldwell, Idaho, The Caxton Printers, 1939. 332 p. (Reprint: New York, Arno Press, 1981? 332 p.)

4482. Fisher, John Warren. *Comparison of different types of frogs and switches from the point of view of the maintenance of way department.* 1904. 67 1. 5 leaves of folded pl. (Thesis, C.E., Lehigh University.)

4483. Fisher, Joseph Anton. *The Reading.* Philadelphia ? Reading Lines, 1958. 60 p.

4484. _____. *The Reading's heritage, 1833-1958; 125th anniversary of a pioneer railroad.* New York, Newcomen Society in North America, 1958. 32 p.

4485. Fisher, Kay. *A baggage car with lace curtains.* Colfax, CA: B & K Fisher, 1979. 167 p. (Southern Pacific Company)

4486. Fisher, Ralph E. *Vanishing markers: memories of Boston and Maine railroading, 1946-1952.* Brattleboro, VT: S. Greene Press, 1976. 128 p.

4487. Fisher, Theodore W. *Ventilation of railroad cars : with chemical analysis.* Boston : Wright & Potter, 1875. 1 v.

4488. Fishlow, Albert. *American railroads and the transformation of the antebellum economy.* Cambridge, MA: Harvard University Press, 1966. 452 p. (*Harvard economic studies, v. 127.*)

4489. Fisk, Dale, Don Dopf. *The Idaho Northern Railway* / Cambridge, ID : Cambridge Litho, Inc., 2010. 208 p.

4490. _____, _____. *P & IN to the golden heart of Idaho: the story of the Pacific & Idaho Northern Railway.* Boise, ID: Writers Press, 2001. 147 p.

4491. Fisk, James, Jr. *James Fisk, Jr., against the Union Pacific Railroad Company et al. Motion for stay.* New York, N.Y., P.W. Derham, 1869. 42 p.

4491a. _____. *James Fisk, Jr. against the Union Pacific Railroad Company et al.: motion papers.* New York: Evening Post Steam Presses, 1870. 24 p.

4492 . Fitch, Benjamin Franklin. *Immediate relief for New York's congested port terminal* / New York, I.H. Blanchard Company, 1921. 24 p. (New York, New Jersey Port and Harbor Development Commission.)

4493. Fitchburg Railroad. Car Department. *Specifications for first-class coaches.* S.l., s.n., 1890. 6 p.

4494. Fitch, Edwin M. *The Alaska Railroad.* New York, Praeger, 1967. 326 p.

4495. Fitt, William C. *Southern Ps-4 class Pacific locomotive drawings.* Cadillac, MI: Wildwood Publications, 1973. 32 p.

4496. Fitzgerald, Joan. *Reviving the U.S. rail and transit industry : investments and job creation.* Washington, DC : WorldWatch Institute, 2010. 38 p.

4497. Flagg, Thomas R. *New York harbor railroads in color.* Scotch Plains, NJ: Morning Sun Books, 2000-2002. 2 v.

4498. Flamboe, Eugene E., J. Ouelett. *Multidisciplinary accident investigation: school bus locomotive-caboose collision.* Washington, D.C., National Highway Traffic Safety Administration, 1977. 139 p. (*NHTSA technical report, no. DOT HS-803 237.*)

4499. Flanary, Ron. *The Louisville & Nashville Cumberland Valley Division album, 1945-1985.* Silver Spring, MD: Old Line Graphics, 1999. 192 p.

4500. Flanary, Ron. *The tracks of my years.* Big Stone Gap, VA: Crawdad Publications, 2002. 120 p. (L&N)

4501. _____, Dave Oroszi, Garland McKee. *The Louisville and Nashville in the Appalachians.* Silver Spring, MD: Old Line Graphics, 1990. 128 p.

4502. Flanders, Ralph E. *Locomotive building.* New York, The Industrial Press, 1911-1912. 6pts. (Reprint: Los Angeles : Periscope Film LLC, 2010.)

4503. Flandrau, Grace. *The story of Marias Pass.* St. Paul? Minn., Great Northern Railway, 1925. 22 p. (Reprint: Seattle, Shorey Book Store, 1971. 21 p.)

4504. Flat-Top Directory Company, Bluefield, W. Va. *Directory of N. & W. coal fields, embracing all coal mining and lumber companies reached by the Norfolk and Western Railway system in southwest Virginia and southern West Virginia, containing a complete map of the Flat-Top coal field.* Roanoke, VA: The Stone Printing and Manufacturing Co., 1902. 101 p.

4504a. Fleckenstine, L.S., Martin Miller. *Fleckenstine & Miller automatic car coupling: Patent obtained August 11th, 1874.* Lancaster, Pa? 1874. 1 sheet {2 p.} 20 x 30 cm.

4505. Fleming, Dale. *The South Park sketchbook.* Canton, OH: Railhead Publications, 1988. 1 v.

4506. Fleming, Howard. *Narrow gauge railways in America: embracing a sketch of the rise, progress and success of the new system, and valuable statistics as to grades, curves, weight of rail, locomotives, cars, etc.; also a directory of narrow gauge railways in North America.* Lancaster, Pa., Inquirer Printing and Publishing Company, 1875. 79 p. (2d ed.: Lancaster, Pa., Press of the Inquirer Printing and Publishing Company, 1876. 104 p.)

4507. _____. *Narrow gauge railways in America; edited by Grahame Hardy and Paul Darrell; foreword by Lucius Beebe. Including a list of narrow gauge railways in America, 1871to 1949, compiled by Brian Thompson. Decorations by E.S. Hammack.* Oakland, Calif., G. H. Hardy, 1949. 101, 39 p.(Reprint: Canton, OH: Daring Press, 1981, and 1983, 1876 ed. Includes updated list of narrow gauge railroads, James Eakin, compiler. 101, 38 p.; 31 p. of plates.)

4508. Fleming, L.D. *Impact fracture properties of reconditioned yokes and couplers* / Chicago : Association of American Railroad, Technical Center, 1983. 31 l. (*Report no.*

R-548.)

4509. Fleming, Susan A. *High speed passenger rail: effectively using Recovery Act funds for high speed rail projects: testimony before the Subcommittee on Surface Transportation and Merchant Marine Infrastructure, Safety, and Security, Committee on Commerce, Science and Transportation, U.S. Senate.* Washington, DC: U.S. Government Accountability Office, 2009. 4 p. (*GAO-09-786T*)

4509a. Fletcher, Cassius Paul. *The valuation of railroads* / 1914. 35, 1 l. (Thesis, B.S., University of Illinois.)

4510. Fletcher, John Cameron. *A Delphi evaluation of a railroad's social costs and benefits.* 1981. 230 l. (Thesis, M.B.A., University of Colorado, Boulder.)

4511. Fletcher, Malcolm, John Taylor. *Railways: the pioneer years.* Secaucus, NJ: Chartwell Books, 1990. 320 p.

4511a. Fletcher, Robert. *A history of wooden bridges, especially as developed in the United States.* New York, s.n., 1931-1933. 4 v.
4512. [The Fletcher report] Washington, DC: Railroad Committee for the Study of Transportation, 1947. 8 v.

4512a. Flick, Michael W., Dennis J. Kogan, Terry W. Lehmann. *Sleeping cars of the Santa Fe.* Midwest City, OK: Santa Fe Railway Historical and Modeling Society, 2012. 406 p. (*Santa Fe passenger car reference series, v. 5.*)

4513. Flinchum, Russell. *Henry Dreyfuss and American industrial design.* 1998. 296 l. (Thesis, Ph.D., University of New York)

4514. _____.*Henry Dreyfuss: industrial designer: the man in the brown suit.* New York: Cooper-Hewitt, National Design Museum, Smithsonian Institution and Rizzoli, 1997. 222 p.

4515. Flint, Henry M. *The railroads of the United States: their history and statistic comprising the progress and present condition of the various lines with their earnings and expenses: to which are added a synopsis of the railroad laws of the United States, and an article on the comparative merits of iron and steel rails/s* Philadelphia, John E. Potter and Co., Nos. 614 and 617 Sansom Street, 1868. 452, 6 p. (Reprint: New York, Arno Press, 1976.)

4516. Flint, William Parker. *A study of the balancing of the drivers of the eight-wheel locomotive by means of counter-weights.* 1890. (Thesis, B.S., Massachusetts Institute of Technology, Department of Mechanical Engineering.)

4517. Flood & Conklin Company. *The F. & C. line, "it goes everywhere;" being a careful description of Flood & Conklin Co.'s systems of surfacers for railway cars – wooden and metal – with suggestions as to effective methods of application.* Newark, NJ: Flood & Conklin Co., 1909. 28 p.

4518. Florence and Cripple Creek Railroad Co. *Diagrams 3 rail split switches.* S.l., s.n., 1897 1 v. 9 x 23 cm.

4519. Florida. Department of Transportation. *High-speed rail corridor by corridor: environmental considerations/* Orlando: Department of Transportation/Florida Overland Express, 1998. 1 v. (various pagings)

4520. Florida East Coast Railway. *A brief history of the Florida East Coast Railway and associated enterprises. Centennial edition.* S.l., s.n., 1996. 40 p.

4520a,. _____. *Key West extension.* St. Augustine, Fla., The Railway, 1912. 36 p.

4521. _____. *Key West extension, Florida East Coast Railway, opened January 22, 1912.* Buffalo, N.Y., Matthews Northrop Works, 1912. 1 v.

4522. _____. *Official industrial and development directory of the Florida East Coast Railway Compnay /* 1926-1927. Serial publication. Compiler by D.N. Felthousen.

4523. _____. *Rules for the government of the Transportation Department.* Jacksonville, Fla., H. & W.B. Drew Co., 1896. 89 p.(Signal diagrams, p. 55-89.)

4524. _____. *Rules of the Transportation Department.* St. Augustine, Fla., Florida East Coast Railway, 1905. 137 p.

4525. _____. *Rules of the Transportation Department.* Revised edition. St. Augustine, Fla., The Record Company, 1923. 180 p.

4526. _____. *The story of a pioneer; a brief history of the Florida East Coast Railway and its part in the remarkable development of the Florida East Coast.* St. Augustine, Fla., Florida East Coast Railway, 1946. 39 p.

4527. Florida. Environmental and Planning Advisory Committee. *Report to the Florida High Speed Rail Transportation Commission on the high speed rail applications.* S.l.,: The Committee, 1989. 1 v. (various pagings)

4528. Florida High Speed Rail Transportation Commission. *Florida High Speed Rail Transportation Commission.* Tallahassee: The Commission, 1989. 1 v. (various pagings)

4529. _____. *Preliminary report on Florida High Speed Rail Corporation & TGV of Florida, Inc.* Tallahassee: Environmental & Planning Advisory Committee, 1989. 118, 9, 16 p.

4530. Florida High Speed Transportation Program. *Florida intercity passenger rail service vision plan: executive summary.* Tallahassee: Florida Department of Transportation, High Speed Transportation Program, 2000. 19 p. (Prepared by National Railroad Passenger Corporation.)

4531. (Blank entry)

4532. Florida Overland Express. *Florida high speed transportation system: executive summary*/ Orlando: Florida Overland Express 1996. 23 1, p.

4533. *Florida: Pennsylvania R.R., Southern Railway, Florida Central & Peninsular R.R., Florida East Coast R'y.* New York, Frank Presbrey, 1899. 12 p. (New York and Florida Limited.)

4534. Florida Transportation Commission. *Independent review of Florida's high speed rail ridership forecasts*/ Tallahassee, FL: Florida Transportation Commission, 1998. 28 p.

4535. Florom, Robert L. *Roller bearing failure mechanisms research.* Washington, DC : federal Railroad Administration, Office of Research and Development, 1994. 45 p. (*DOT/FRA/ORD-94/21.*)

4536. _____. Britto R. Rajkumar. *Roller bearing failure mechanisms and wheel anomaly test report.* Washington, DC: Federal Railroad Administration, Office of Research and Development, 1992. 103, H-II-86 p.(*DOT/FRA/ORD-92/08.*)

4537. Flynn, George J., Carroll O Bickelhaupt. *Puritan Valley Line.* S.l., Privately printed by Carroll O. Bickelhaupt, 1948. 16 p. (Shepaug Valley Railroad)

4538. Flynn, James R. *The railroad shopmen's strike of 1922 on the industry, company, and community levels.* 1993. 345 l. (Thesis, Ph.D., Northern Illinois University) Strikes and lockouts--CB&Q--Illinois

4539. Flynn, John J. *The privately owned freight car: past, present, and future.* 1967. 23 l. (American Society of Traffic and Transportation.) Document location: Northwestern University, Transportation Library.

4540. Flynn W.H. *Locomotive maintenance.* New York, New York Central Railroad, 1925. 13 p.

4541. (Blank entry)

4542. Foell, Charles F., Maurice Eugene Thompson. *Diesel-electric locomotive.* New York, Diesel Publications, 1946. 1 v.

4543. Fogel, Robert William. *Railroads and American economic growth: essays in econometric history.* Baltimore. MD: Johns Hopkins Press, 1964. 296 p.

4544. _____. *The Union Pacific Railroad; a case in premature enterprise.* Baltimore, MD: Johns Hopkins Press, 1960. 129 p. (*The Johns Hopkins University studies in historical and political science, series 78, no. 2.*)

4545. Fogg, Howard. *Along the right-of-way: a portfolio of paintings depicting mostly*

scenes along the Pittsburgh and Lake Erie Railroad, New York Central System.
Pittsburgh? PA: Pittsburgh and Lake Erie Railroad Company, 1964. 2 p., 32 p. of plates.

4546. _____. *Road to the future: the Pittsburgh and Lake Erie Railroad.* Pittsburgh?
PA: Pittsburgh and Lake Erie Railroad Company, 1964. 1 v.

4547. Foit-Albert, Beverly. *New York Central Terminal : a studio in historic preservation
and adaptive reuse of the New York Central Terminal, Buffalo, New York* / Buffalo : State
University of New York at Buffalo, 1990. 42 p. (*State University of New York
at Buffalo. School of Architecture and Planning; Projects, 2.*)

4547a. Follis, John W. *Long Island Rail Road transportation hub integration study: final
report* / New York : Buckhurst Fish & Jaquemart, 1995. 2 v.

4548. Follmar, A. Joseph. *Locomotive facilities, C&NW and CStPM&O.* Elmhurst, IL:
Chicago & North Western Historical Society, 1996-2001. 2 v. (v.1: Engine terminals.
v. 2: Fuel and water stations.)

4549. _____. *Grand crossings: railroading and people in La Crosse, WI.* La Crosse,
WI: 4000 Foundation, 1992. 95 p.

4550. Folsom, Moses. *National railway fireman's hand book and pocket guide.* St. Paul,
Minn., National Railway Publishing Company, 1907. 43 p.

4551. Foner, Philip Sheldon. *The great labor uprising of 1877.* New York, Monad Press,
1977. 288 p.

4552. _____, Ronald L. Lewis. *The Black worker during the era of the American
Federation of Labor and the railroad brother-hoods.* Philadelphia, Temple University
press, 1979. 402 p. (*The Black worker: a documentary history from colonial times to
the present, v. 4.*)

4553. Fontaine, Joseph Auguste. *The American mountain railroad.* New York,
Macdonald & Swank, 1867. 1 v.

4554. Foote, Allen Ripley. *Taxation of railroads in the United States.* Columbus, OH:
National Tax Association, 1911. 2, 51 p.

4555. Forbes, John Murray, Sarah Forbes Hughes. *Letters and recollections of John
Murray Forbes.* Boston: Houghton, Mifflin and Co., 1989. 2 v.

4556. Ford, Bacon, and Davis. *Specifications covering steel car bodies for Lackawanna
& Wyoming Valley Railroad Company, Scranton, PA.* New York : Ford, Bacon & Davis,
1923. 1 v. (unpaged)

4557. Ford, Chris H. *ET & WNC railroad aerial photos, 1952-1955* / s.l., C.H. Ford,
2010. Computer file. Contains 35 (1200 dpi) scans of 9"x 9" contact prints.

4558. Ford, Nancy, Edward T. Myers. *The modern Great Northern...20th century empire builder*. Chicago, Ill., Modern Railroads, 65-210 p. (Reprinted from *Modern Railroad*, May 1926, v. 11, no. 5.)

4559. Ford, Robert E, Stephen H. Richards, John C. Hungerford. *Evaluation of retroreflective marking to increase rail car conspicuity*. Washington, D.C., Department of Transportation, Research and Special programs, 1998. 228 p. (*DOT-VNTSC-RR897-PM-98-22*.)

4560. Ford, Robert S. *Red trains in the East Bay: the history of the Southern Pacific transbay train and ferry system*. Glendale, CA: Interurbans Books, 1977. 351 p. (*Interurbans special, 65*.)

4561. _____. *Red trains remembered*. Glendale, CA: Interurbans Books, 1980. 104 p. (*Interurbans special, no. 75*.)

4562. Foreman, Milton J. *The electrification of railway terminals as a cure for the locomotive smoke evil in Chicago, with special consideration of the Illinois Central Railroad*. Chicago: R.R. Donnelley & Sons, 1908. 353 p. (Chicago (Ill.). City Council. Committee on Local Transportation.)

4563. Forkenbrock, David J. *External costs of truck and rail freight transportation*. Iowa City IA: Public Policy Center, University of Iowa, 1996. 55 p.

4564. Forman, Harry Willard. *Rights of trains*. 4th ed. New York, Simmons-Boardman, 1951. 397 p.

4565. _____. *Rights of trains on single track: a complete examination for employees on the standard code and other recommended train rules*. New York, The Railroad Gazette, 1904. 477 p.

4566. *Foremen's advance advocate*. St. Louis, MO: Brotherhood of Railway Trackmen of America? 1890-1919. Monthly. 28 v. (> *Railway maintenance of way employes journal.)*

4567. Formichella, Joe. *The wreck of the Twilight Limited*. San Francisco, MacAdam/Cage Pub., 2004. 266 p. (Fiction)

4568. *Formula for use in determining rail freight service costs*. Washington, DC: Interstate Commerce Commission, 1948-   (*Statement. Interstate Commerce Commission. Bureau of Accounts*.)

4569. Forney, Matthias Nace. *Catechism of the locomotive*. 2d ed., rev. and enl. New York, Railroad Gazette, 1875. 709 p. (2d ed. Revised and enlarged. New York, The Railroad Gazette, 1891. 709 p.) (See also: 4577)

4570. _____. *Forney's catechism of the locomotive*. 3d ed., rev. and enl. by George L. Fowler. New York, The Railroad Gazette, 1911. 2 v.

4571. _____ *Improved tank locomotives.* New York, M.N. Forney, 1880. 33 p.

4572. _____. *Locomotives and locomotive building, being a brief sketch of various improvements in locomotive building during the last century, together with a history of the origin and growth of the Rogers Locomotive and Machine Works, Paterson, New Jersey, from 1831 to 1876.* New York, J.W. Pratt, Printer, 1876. 149 p.

4573. _____ *Locomotives and locomotive building, being a brief sketch of the growth of the railroad system and of the various improvements in locomotive building in America, together with a history of the origin and growth of the Rogers Locomotive and Machine Works, Paterson, New Jersey, from 1831 to 1886.* New York, Gottsberger, 1886. 200 p.

4574. _____ *Locomotives for rapid transit railroads.* New York, s.n., 1881. 31 p.

4575. _____. *M.N. Forney's tank locomotive.* New York, Waterman & Coby, Steam Printers, 1867. 15 p.

4576. _____. *Memoir of Horatio Allen.* S.l., Printed by the Burr Printing House, 1890. 47 p.

4577. Forney, Matthias N., Georg Kosak. *Catechism of the locomotive.* Bridgeport, Conn., F. Keppy, 1874. 609 p. (Based on Georg Kosak's "Katechismus ... der locomotive.")

4578. _____, Leander Garey, Calvin A. Smith. *The railroad car builder's pictorial dictionary.* New York, Dover Publications, 1974, 1879. (1st ed. reprint) 493, 84 p. See also: Entries 2248-2276..

4579. Forrest, Kenton. *The railroads of Coors Field: a brief history of railroading in the vicinity of Coors Field.* Golden, CO: Colorado Railroad Museum, 1995. 44 p.

4580. _____, Charles Albi. *Denver's railroads: the story of Union Station and the railroads of Denver.* Golden, CO: Colorado Railroad Museum, 1986. 256 p.

4581. _____, Gene McKeever, Charles Albi. *Rio Grande freight travel guide, 1951.* Denver, CO: Tramway Press, 1983, 1951. 99 p.

4582. Forsythe, Edwin James. *The Gould strikes and Missouri newspaper opinion.* 1949. 144 l. (Thesis, M.A., University of Missouri, Columbia.)

4583. Fortenbery, T, Randall, Gail L. Cramer, Bruce R. Beattie. *Highways and railroads in Montana: problems and opportunities.* Bozeman, MT: Montana Agricultural Experiment Station, 1982. 22 p.

4584. Foss, Charles R. *Evening before the diesel: a pictorial history of steam and first generation diesel motive power on the Grand Trunk Western Railroad, 1938-1961.*

Boulder, CO: Pruett Publishing Company, 1980. 444 p.

4585. Foster, George H., Peter C. Weiglin. *The Harvey House cookbook: memories of dining along the Santa Fe Railroad.* Atlanta, GA: Longstreet Press, 1992. 193 p.

4586. _____, _____. *Splendor sailed the Sound: the New Haven Railroad and the Fall River Line.* San Mateo, CA: Potential Group; Tuscon, AZ: Mid-State Associates, 1989. 384 p.

4587. Foster, Gerald L. *A field guide to trains of North America.* Boston, Houghton Mifflin, 1996. 160 p.

4587a. Foster, J. W. *Report upon the mineral resources of the Illinois Central Railroad, made at the request of the president* / New York: G. S. Roe, printer, 1856. 29 p.

4588. Foster, William Z. *The railroad workers and the War*/ New York, NY: Workers Library Publishers, 1941. 15 p.

4589. _____. *Railroad workers forward!* New York, NY: Workers Library, 1937. 61 p.

4590. Foster, Wolcott C. *A treatise on wooden trestle bridges : according to the present practice on American railroads* / 3rd ed. rev. and enl ed. New York : J. Wiley, 1908. 255 p.

4591. _____. *A treatise on wooden trestle bridges and their concrete substitutes, according to the present practice on American railroads.* 4th ed., rev. and enl. New York, J. Wiley, 1913. 440 p. (1st ed., 1891. 160 p.; 2nd ed. 1900. 255 p.)

4591a. Foster-Barham, Alkman Henryson. *American railway investments exemplified: land grant railways; example 1, Missouri, Kansas, and Texas Railway.* London: Effingham Wilson, Royal Exchange, 1873. 44 p.

4591b. Fostik, John A. Amtrak across America: an illustrated history. Hudson, WI: Iconografix, 2012. 127 p.

4592. *4-8-4's and other heavy passenger locos, 1927-1941.* Novato, CA: Newton K. Gregg, 1973. 1 v.

4593. Four Wheel Drive Auto Company. *FWD railroad equipment.* Clintonville, Wisc., Four Wheel Drive Auto Company, 1921. 12 p. (Reprint: Milwaukee, WI: Old Line Publishers, 1971. 12 p.)

4594. Fourer, Robert. *Models of railroad passenger-car requirements in the Northeast Corridor*/ Washington, DC: Federal Railroad Administration, Northeast Corridor Project office, 1976. 2 v. (*FRA-NEPCO-76-21*)

4595. *4th International Conference on Contact Mechanics and Wear of Rail/Wheel Systems* / Joseph Kalousek, guest editor. New York : Elsevier Science, Inc., 1996. 286 p.

4595b. Foust, Clifford M. *John Frank Stevens: civil engineer* / Bloomington: Indiana University Press, 2013. 337 p.

4596. Foutch, Douglas A. *National Workshop on Railway Bridge Research Needs: summary report.* Chicago, IL: Association of American Railroads, Technical Center, 1989. 55 p. (*Report, no. R-710.*)

4596a. Fowler, David J. *All aboard! : railroads and New Jersey, 1812-1930 : exhibition catalog* / New Brunswick, NJ: Special Collections & University Archives, Rutgers University Libraries, 2011. 680 p.

4597. Fowler, E.C. *Career of Samuel Rea; a review of his life and an appreciation of his character and public service* / Philadelphia : Pennsylvania Railroad, 1925. 18 p. "Pennsylvania railroad information ... October, 1925.")

4598. Fowler, Gary Jefferson. *Fatigue crack initiation and propagation in pearlitic rail steels* / 1976. 382 l. (Thesis, Ph.D., University of California, Los Angeles.)

4599. Fowler, George Little. *The car wheel; giving the results of a series of investigations.* Pittsburgh, Pa., Schoen Steel Wheel Company, 1907. 161 p.

4600. _____. *Compressed gas and electric car lighting.* New York, Safety Car Heating and Lighting Company, 1909. 18 p.

4601. _____. *Locomotive breakdowns, emergencies and their remedies.* New York, N.W. Henley Publishing Company, 1903. 244 p. (New York, Norman W. Henley Pub. Co., 1916. 8th rev. and enl. ed. 301 p.)

4602. _____, Carl J. Mellin. *Locomotive design.* New York, Industrial Press, 1910. 2 v.

4603. Fox, Charles Douglas, Francis Fox, James Forrest. *The Pennsylvania Railroad; with remarks on American railway construction and management.* London, Printed by W. Clowes and Sons, 1874. 66 p.

4604. Fox, Charles Philip. *Circus trains.* Milwaukee, Kalmbach Pub. Co., 1947. 2 p., 19 leaves of plates.

4605. Fox, Gerald B. *Optimism derailed: the economic impact of the Burlington & Lamoille Railroad.* 1993. 181 l. (Thesis, M.A., University of Vermont.)

4606. Fox, Wesley. *Golden State rails: a California railroading pictorial.* Brisbane, CA: Fox, 1980. 72 p.

4607. _____. *Montana Rail Link: the main street of southern Montana.* Arvada, CO: Fox Publications, 1997. 96 p.

4608. _____. *Northwestern Pacific pictorial.* Naperville, IL: W. Fox, 1983. 80 p.

4609. _____. *Northwestern Pacific Railroad and its successors.* Arvada, CO: Fox Publications, 1995. 112 p.

4610. _____. *Overland to the Rockies.* Lakewood, CO: W. Fox, 1984. 104 p.

4611. _____. *Powder River coal and the BN's Denver Division.* Arvada, CO: Fox Publications, 1993. 96 p.

4612. _____ *Santa Fe across the Southwest.* Lakewood, CO: Fox Publications, .1991. 80 p.

4613. _____. *Santa Fe out West.* Arvada, CO: Fox Publications, 1998. 160 p.

4614. _____. *Southern Pacific: across the Southwest.* Lakewood, CO: Fox Publications, 1990. 80 p.

4615. _____. *Southern Pacific in the West.* Denver, CO: Fox Publications, 1994-1996. 2 v.

4616. _____. *Sugar country shortline.* Lakewood, CO: Fox Publications, 1989. 64 p. (Great Western Railway)

4617. *FRA 2000: a report to the nation/* Washington, DC: Federal Railroad Administration, 2000. 16 p.

4618. Frailey, Fred W. *A quarter century of Santa Fe consists.* Godfrey, IL: RPC Publications, 1974. 208 p.

4619. _____. *Southern Pacific's Blue Streak Merchandise: six decades of the great American freight train.* Waukesha, WI: Kalmbach Pub. Co., 1991. 168 p.

4620. _____. *Twilight of the great trains.* Waukesha, WI: Kalmbach Pub. Co., 1998. 192 p. (Also: Bloomington: Indiana University Press, 2010. 211 p.)

4621. _____. *Zephyrs, Chiefs & other orphans.* Godfrey, Ill: RPC Publications, 1977. 260 p.

4622. Fraim, E.T. *Illustrated and descriptive list of padlocks, designed and constructed expressly for railroad use.* Lancaster, PA: Examiner Print., 1897. 18 p. (Keystone Lock Works, Lancaster Pa.)

4623. Frame, William S. *History of the Schenectady plant of the American Locomotive Company.* Schenectady, NY: American Locomotive Company, 1943. 45 p.

4624. Francaviglia, Richard V. *Over the Range: a history of the Promontory Summit route of the Pacific railroad.* Logan: Utah State University Press, 2008. 333 p.

4625. Franch, John. *Robber Baron: the life of Charles Tyson Yerkes*. Urbana, University of Illinois Press, 2006. 374 p.

4626. Francis, George Blinn. *The New York tunnel extension of the Pennsylvania Railroad. Certain engineering structures of the New York terminal area*. New York : s.n., 1911. 152-225 p. Reprinted from the Transactions of the American Society of Civil Engineers, v. LXIX, paper no. 1164, 1911.)

4626a. Francis, Mark Steven. *Empire: the development of the timber industry in Tuolumne County, the Standard Lumber Company and its railroads, 1850-1920 /* Berkeley, CA: Wheelhorse Press, 2011. 410, 198 p.

4627. Franckey, William A. *Cathedral of steel: an intimate look inside Galesburg's "Q" roundhouse /* s.l., W.A. Franckey, 1999. 122 p.

4628. Franklin Institute. *The compound locomotive of the Rhode Island Locomotive Works, Providence, R.I.* Philadelphia, Franklin Institute, 1892. 46 p. 24 l. of plates.

4629. Franklin Railway Supply Company. *.Dynamometer tests of the locomotive booster*. Chicago, Ill., Franklin Railway Supply Company, n.d. 8 p.

4630. _____. *The locomotive booster speeds railroad operation*. New York, Franklin Railway Supply Company, Inc.,1922. 16 p.

4631. _____. *The locomotive booster: speeds railroad operation, first resume*. New York, Franklin Railway Supply Company, 1923. 14 p.

4632. _____ *The locomotive booster type C-2; parts catalog no. 2, long cut-off.* New York, Franklin Railway Supply Company, 1927. 22 p.

4633. _____. *The locomotive booster types C-1 and C-2: instruction book no. 102.* New York, Franklin Railway Supply Company, Inc., 1927. 114 p.

4634. _____. *New locomotives can work on 30% less fuel: some questions railroad men are asking about the limited cut-off.* New York, Franklin Railway Supply Company, 1925. 9 p.

4635. _____. *The Pennsylvania Railroad's T-1 class locomotives equipped with the Franklin system of steam distribution*. New York: Franklin Railway Supply Company, Inc., 1940s. 8 p. (*Bulletin, no. 26.)*

4636. _____. *Power makes money: the locomotive booster provides more power for every locomotive*. New York, Franklin Railway Supply Company, Inc., 1928. 35 p.

4637. Franklin, Walter Simonds. *The Long Island Rail Road—its problems and future.* New York: Long island Rail Road Company, 1942. 60 p.

4638. _____. *The Pennsylvania Railroad and the Long Island Rail Road : a review of their relations and the present situation : a statement to the stockholders of the Pennsylvania Railroad.* Philadelphia : s.n., 1951. 20 p.

4639. Fraser, Donald Vincent. *"Katy," pioneer railroad of the Southwest! 1865.* New York, Newcomen Society in North America, 1953. 28 p.

4640. Fraternal Order of Empire Builders. Great Northern Historical Society & Scale Replica Railway Association. *Report of proceedings – Fraternal order of Empire Builders.* Evanston, IL: Great Northern Historical Society & Scale Replica Railway Association, 1974- . Quarterly.

4641. Frattasio, Marc J. *Dining on the Shore Line Route: the history and recipes of the New Haven Railroad Dining Car Department.* Lynchburg, VA: TLC Publishing, 2003. 106 p.

4642. _____. *New Haven Railroad in the McGinnis era.* Hart, MO: Whiteriver Productions, 2003. 256 p.

4643. Fravert, Jack, Rick Tipton. *Trackside around Louisville (East) 1948-1958 with Jack Fravert.* Scotch Plains, NJ: Morning Sun Books, 2005. 128 p.

4644. Fred Harvey (Firm) *Hospitality cookbook : famous recipes were served along the Santa Fe Railroad route from Kansas to California by Fred Harvey.* Grand Canyon, AZ : Fred Harvey Co., 1990s. 30 p.

4644a. [Fred Harvey collection] 1,700 black-and-white photographs and 3,300 color slides. Location : Northern Arizona University, Flagstaff.

4644b. [Fred Harvey hotels collection] 1896-1945. 8.3 ft. Approx. 2,000 black and white photographs, exterior and interior views, eating houses, railroad stations and newsstands operated by Fred Harvey. Location: University of Arizona.

4645. Frederick, Douglas Weldon. *Reconsidering the theory of capture: an empirical examination of the Texas Railroad Commission* / 1994. 186 l. (Thesis, Ph.D., University of Texas at Dallas.)

4646. Frederick, John H. *Federal regulation of railway securities under the Transportation Act of 1920.* Philadelphia, Westbrook Pub. Co., 1927. 120 p. (Thesis, Ph.D., University of Pennsylvania, 1927.)

4647. Fredericks, Harold S. *The Wilkes-Barre and Eastern Railroad.* Livingston, NJ: Railroadians of America, 1986. 108 p.

4648. Frederickson, Arthur C., Lucy F. Frederickson. *Frederickson's history of the Ann Arbor auto and train ferries.* Frankfort, MI: Gulls Nest Pub., 1994. 156 p.

4649. _____, _____. *Pictorial history of the C & O train and auto ferries and Pere Marquette Line steamers.* Rev. ed. Ludington, MI: Lakeside Printing Co., 1965, c1955.

74 p.

4650. Fredrickson, Jim. *Rairoad shutterbug: Jim Fredrickson's Northern Pacific.* Pullman, Washington State University Press, 2000. 160 p.

4651. _____. *Steam to diesel: Jim Fredrickson's railroading journal.* Pullman, Washington State University Press, 2001. 160 p.

4652. _____. *Railscapes: a Northern Pacific brasspounder's album.* Pullman, Washington State University Press, 2003. 154 p.

4653. Freed, Clyde H. *The story of railroad passenger fares.* Washington, DC: 1942. 299 p.

4653a. Freedman, Bernard I. *How to get cheap farms : the land-colonization policies of the Great Northern Railway and its progenitors in Minnesota* / 1947. 73 l. (Thesis, M.A., Brooklyn College.)

4654. Freeman, Edmund Arthur. *Applications of electricity to railways.* Washington, DC: Association of American Railroad, Bureau of Railway Economics, Library, 1933- ? Bibliography.

4655. _____. *"The largest railroad library in the United States."* Washington, DC: Association of American Railroads, Bureau of Railway Economics, Library, 1936 11 l.

4655a. Freese, Zachary. *Off the tracks!: deadly railway accidents, markets, and morality, 1850-1893.* 2013. 125 l. (Thesis, M.A., University of Wisconsin, Eau Claire.)

4656. *Freight and passenger service operating statistics of class I steam railways in the United States.* Washington, D.C., Interstate Commerce Commission, Bureau of Statistics, 1925-   Monthly. (<*Freight and passenger service operating statistics of class I steam roads in the United States.)*

4657. *Freight and passenger service operating statistics, class I steam roads by regions* / Washington, D.C., Bureau of Railway Economics, 1930-

4658. *Freight and passenger service operating statistics, class I steam roads by regions. (1920-1930).* Washington, D.C., Bureau of Railway Economics, 1931. 13 p.

4659. *Freight and passenger train service unit costs (selected expense accounts) of class I steam roads in the United States including a proportion of mixed-train and special-train service.* Washington, D.C., Interstate Commerce Commission, Bureau of Statistics, ?-1924. Monthly.

4660. *Freight car and caboose trucks.* Omaha, NE: Simmons-Boardman, 1980. 86 p.

4661. *Freight car couplers.* Omaha, NE: Simmons-Boardman, 1974. 36 p.

4662. *Freight car demand information and forecasting research project : industry report* / Washington, DC: Federal Railroad Administration, 1978. 85 p. (*FRA-OPPD-78-13.*)

4663. *Freight car outlook.* Waltham, MA: Global Insight, 2000? Quarterly. (*<Outlook for freight cars [2002]*)

4664. *Freight car reflectorization : safety of highway-railroad grade crossings* / [Anya A. Carroll ... et al.] Washington, DC: Federal Railroad Administration, Office of Research and Development, 1999. 190 p. in various pagings. (*DOT-VNTSC-FRA-97-2.*)

4665. *Freight car truck design optimization* / Washington, DC: Federal Railroad Administration, Office of Research and Development, 1978-   (*FRA/ORD-78/12/1-VI*)

4666. Freight Car Utilization Research-Demonstration Program. *Analysis of car service rules, orders, and directives: the impact of car service rules on car utilization.* Washington, D.C., The Program, 1979. 19 p. (*Report AAR-A-369.*)

4667. _____. *Freight car utilization and railroad reliability: case studies: final report.* Washington, D.C., The Program, 1977. 379 p. (*Report AAR no. R-283.*)

4668. *Freight car yearbook & buyers' guide.* Chicago, IL: Murphy-Richter Publishing Company, 1989-1990? Annual.(*>Progressive railroading's car & locomotive yearbook & buyers' guide.* 1991-)

4669. *Freight cars.* Omaha, NE: Simmons-Boardman Publishing Corporation, 1977. 28 l.

4670. *Freight cars.* Friday Harbor, WA: Phoenix Pub., 1991-v. 1-

4671. *Freight cars journal.* Monrovia, CA: Freight Car Historical Section, MTTHS, 198-?-

4672. *Freight cars journal. Monograph.* Monrovia, CA: Modern Transport Technical & Historical Society, 1985-

4673. *Freight cars: lettering and marking.* Omaha, NE: Simmons-Boardman, 1983. 40 p.

4674. *Freight commodity statistics.* Washington, D.C., Association of American Railroads, Economics and Finance Department, 1980-   Annual. (< *Freight commodity statistics: U.S. class I railroads.*)

4675. *Freight commodity statistics, class I railroads in the United States for the year ended December 31.../* Washington, D.C., Interstate Commerce Commission, Bureau of Transport Economics and Statistics, 1956-1979. Annual.(< *Freight commodity statistics, class I steam railways in the United States for the year ended December 31...; 1924-1955.;>Freight commodity statistics, U.S. class I railroads*; 1979-)

4676. *Freight commodity statistics: class 1 steam railways in the United States.*
Washington, DC: Interstate Commerce Commission, Bureau of Statistics, 1937-1940.
Annual.

4677. *Freight commodity statistics, class I steam railways in the United States
for the year ended December 31.../* Washington, D.C., Interstate Commerce
Commission, Bureau of Statistics, 1924-1955. Annual. (>*Freight commodity statistics,
class I railroads in the United States for the year ended December 31...; 1956-1979.)*

4678. *Freight commodity statistics of class I railroads in the United States/* Washington,
D.C., Interstate Commerce Commission, Bureau of Accounts, 1956- .Quarterly.
(<*Freight commodity statistics of class I steam railways in the United* States; 1900s-
1955?)

4679. *Freight commodity statistics of class I steam railways in the United States.*
Washington, D.C., Interstate Commerce Commission, Bureau of Transport Economics
and Statistics, 1900s-1955?. Quarterly. (>*Freight commodity statistics of class I railroads
in the United States; >Freight commodity statistics.*)

4680. *Freight commodity statistics, U.S. class I railroads /* Springfield, VA: National
Technical Information Service, 1979. Annual. (Federal Railroad Administration;
Interstate Commerce Commission. Bureau of Accounts.) (<*Freight commodity statistics
of class I railroads in the United States for the year ended...; >Freight commodity
statistics.*)

4681. *Freight loss and damage.* Washington, DC: Association of American Railroads,
Freight Claim Division, 1892-1934. (< American Railway Association. Freight Claim
Division. *Classified summary, by principle causes and commodities.)*

4682. *Freight revenue and value of commodities transported on Class I steam railways
in the United States, calendar year ... /* Washington, DC: Interstate Commerce
Commission, Bureau of Statistics, 1930?-   Annual.

4683. *Freight: the shippers' forum.* New York, NY Freight Commodity Pub. Co., 1904-
1912. Monthly. 12 v. (> *Trade and transportation.)*

4684. *The Freight traffic red book.* New York, Traffic Publishing Company, 1920-?

4685. *Freight train performance of class I steam railways in the United States.*
Washington, D.C., Interstate Commerce Commission, Bureau of Statistics, 1936-   .
Monthly. "Switching and terminal companies not included."

4686. French, Charles D. *Industrial development program of the New Haven
and Baltimore and Ohio railroad s/* 1947. 82 l. (Thesis, M.B.A., Graduate School
of Arts and Sciences, University of Pennsylvania)

4687. French, Chauncey Del. *Railroadman.* New York, NY: Macmillan Co., 1938. 292 p.

4688. French Ezra B. *Resolutions of the legislature of Maine, in favor of a railroad from lake Michigan to the Pacific, on the plan proposed by Mr. Whitney.* Washington, DC: Tippin & Streeper, Printer, 1847. 2 p.

4689. French, Frank C. *State railroad taxation*/ Ames, IA: Iowa State College Engineering Experiment Station, 1905. 38 p. (*Bulletin. Iowa State College. Engineering Experiment Station, vol. III, no. 2 [whole no. 14].*

4689a. French, Gerald. *When steam was king: railroads of the Central Mother Lode Region of California: Sierra Railway, Pickering Lumber Company, West Side Lumber.* Petaluma, CA: Eureka Pub., 2006. 241 p.

4689b. French, Henry Heim, James Aiken Wilson. *A code for conducting steam locomotive tests* / 1914. 95 l. (Thesis, B.S., University of Illinois.)

4690. French, Kenneth. *Railroads of Hoboken and Jersey City.* Charleston. SC: Arcadia, 2002. 128 p.

4691. French, Michael T. *Occupational safety regulation and economic efficiency: the railroad industry.* 1986. 110 l. (Thesis, Ph.D., Boston College.)

4691a. *Fresh fruit and vegetable carlot shipments by states, commodities, counties and stations.* Washington, DC: U.S. Department of Agriculture, Agricultural Marketing Service, Fruit and Vegetable Division, Market News Branch, 1954-1959. Annual. 6 v. (*< Carlot shipments of fresh fruits and vegetables by commodities, states, counties and stations; > Fresh fruit and vegetable shipments by states, commodities, counties, stations.*)

4691b. *Fresh fruit and vegetable shipments by commodities, states and months* / Washington, DC: U.S. Department of Agriculture, Agricultural Marketing Service, Fruit and Vegetable Division, Market News Branch, 1954-   . Annual. (*< Carlot shipments of fresh fruits and vegetables by commodities, states and months.; Fresh fruit and vegetable shipments by states, commodities, counties, stations.*)

4691c. *Fresh fruit and vegetable shipments by states, commodities, counties, stations.* Washington, DC: U.S. Department of Agriculture, Agricultural Marketing Service, Fruit and Vegetable Division, Market News Branch, 1960-1977. Annual.) *< Fresh fruit and vegetable carlot shipments by states, commodities, counties, and stations; > Fresh fruit and vegetable shipments by commodities, states, months.*)

4691d. *Fresh fruit and vegetable unloads in western cities by commodities, states, and months* / Washington, DC: U.S. Department of Agriculture, 1900s-1981. Annual.

4692. *Fresh lamb transported by refrigerated rail cars and piggyback trailers* / Washington, DC: Agricultural Marketing Service, U.S. Department of Agriculture, 1962. 19 p. (*Marketing research report, no. 553.*)

4693. Frey, Elmer J., Charles E. Theobald. *Grade crossing accident injury minimization study* / Washington, DC: Federal Railroad Administration, Office of Research and Development, 1980. 1 v. (various pagings)

4694. Frey, Robert Lovell. *A technological history of the locomotives of the Northern Pacific Railway Company.* 1970. 2 v. (Thesis, Ph.D., University of Minnesota.)

4695. _____, Lorenz P. Schrenk. *Northern Pacific Railway.* San Marino, CA: Golden West Books, 1985-1988. 2 v.

4696. Freytag, Dean, Ted Wetterrstroem. *Chesapeake & Ohio freight cars prior to 1945.* Louisville, KY: Bob Brown Enterprises, 1974. 51 p.

4697. Friebel, Guido, Gerard John McCullough, Laura Padilla. *Patterns of restructuring: the U.S. class 1 railroads from 1884 to 2004/* London, England: Centre for Economic Policy Research, 2008. 15, 1 p. (*Discussion paper/ Centre for Economic Policy Research, no. 6836.*)

4698. Fried. Krupp AG. *The Krupp system of American standard steel-tired wheels. Cast-steel works of Fried. Krupp, Essen, Germany. Represented by Thos. Prosser & Son.* New York, 1885. 28 p.

4699. Fried, Stephen. *Appetite for America: how visionary businessman Fred Harvey built a railroad hospitality empire that civilized the Wild West.* New York, NY: Bantam Books, 2010. 518 p.

4700. Friedlaender, Ann Fetter, Richard H. Spady. *Freight transport regulation; equity, efficiency, and competition in the rail and trucking industries.* Cambridge, MA: MIT Press, 1981. 366 p. (*MIT Press series on the regulation of economic activity, 1.*)

4701. _____. *Technical change in the railroad industry.* Cambridge, MA: Center for Transportation Studies, Massachusetts Institute of Technology, 1980. 249 p. (NSF/PRA-761739/1/ (Piggybacking and intermodalism)

4702. _____. *Technical change in the railroad industry.* Cambridge, MA: Center for Transportation Studies, Massachusetts Institute of Technology, 1980. 203 p. (NSF/PRA-7617394/2) (Unit trains)

4703. _____. *Technical change in the railroad industry: executive summary.* Cambridge, MA: Center for Transportation Studies, Massachusetts Institute of Technology, 1980. 14 p.

4704. _____, et al. *Rail costs and capital adjustments in a quasi-regulated environment/* Cambridge, MA: National Bureau of Economic Research, 1991. 38, 4 p. (*Working paper series, no. 3841.*)

4705. Friedlander, Amy. *Emerging infrastructure: the growth of railroads.* Reston, VA: Corporation for National Research Initiatives, 1995. 74 p. (*History of infrastructure, v. 1.*)

4706. Friedman, Jesse J. *Economic aspects of the proposed merger of Seaboard Air Line Railroad and Atlantic Coast Line Railroad.* Washington, D.C., Jesse J. Friedman & Associates, 1961. 166 p. (Southern Railway System; Jesse J. Friedman & Associates; Interstate Commerce Commission.)

4707. Friedricks, William Ben. *Henry E. Huntington and metropolitan entrepreneurship in Southern California, 1898-1917.* 1986. 367 l. (Thesis, Ph.D., University of Southern California.)

4708. _____. *Henry E. Huntington and the creation of Southern California.* Columbus, Ohio State University Press, 1992. 229 p. (*Historical perspectives on business enterprise series.*)

4709. Friends of the High Line. *Designing the High Line; Gansevoort Street to 30th Street.* New York, NY: Friends of the High Line, 2008. 160 p.

4710. Friends of the Nevada Northern Railway. *Nevada Northern Railway and the copper camps of White Pine County, Nevada.* East Ely, NV: Friends of the Nevada Northern Railway, 1991. 176 p.

4711. Friends of the Railroad Museum of Pennsylvania. *The Kline collection catalogue: negatives from the collection of Benjamin F.G. Kline, Jr.* Strasburg, PA: Friends of the Railroad Museum of Pennsylvania, 1997. 54 p.

4712. Frier, B.E. *The development of the GP-30 locomotive.* New York, Society of Automotive Engineers, 1963. 9 p. (Preprint: Automotive Engineering Congress, Detroit, MI. SAE-641A.)

4713. Fries, William. *The Baltimore and Ohio Railroad: stations and towers along the Niagara Division.* New Port Richey, FL: W. Fries, 1996. 95 p.

4714. _____. *Train wrecks & disasters: a pictorial & chronological history as reported by the press: Rochester & State Line, Rochester & Pittsburgh, Buffalo, Rochester & Pittsburgh, Baltimore & Ohio.* New Port Richey, FL: W. Fries, 1994. 148 p.

4715. Frignet, Ernest. *Etudes financieres sur les chemins de fer Americains. I: Missouri, Kansas and Texas Railway.* Paris, Imprimerie de D. Jouaust, 1873. 97 p.

4716. Frink, Gerald. *Partial design of a logging locomotive.* 1900. 34 l. (Thesis, B.S., Massachusetts Institute of Technology, Department of Mechanical Engineering.)

4716a. *Frisco first.* St. Louis? St. Louis-San Francisco Railway Company, 1946- .

4716b. *The Frisco employes' magazine.* St. Louis, MO: St. Louis-San Francisco Railway Company, 1923-1935.

4716c. *Frisco Railroad car paint diagram book.* S.l., s.n., 1900s. 39' x 14"

Location: Special Collections and Archives, Missouri State University.

4717. Fritts, W.N., M. Blomberg. *Diesel locomotives, trucks, draft rigging.* Scranton, Pa., International Textbook, 1945. 56, 67 p.

4718. Frizzi, Daniel L. *An American railroad portrait: people, places and Pultney: a history of the development of railroads in Pultney Township of Belmont County, Ohio, and in particular the city of Bellaire.* Bellaire, OH: D.L. Frizzi, Jr., 1993. 272 p.

4719. *The Frost dry carburetor system of car lighting : the greatest light of the age for passenger and other railroad cars.* Philadelphia : Railroad Lighting and Manufacturing Co., 1893. 61 p. 21 leaves of plates.

4720. Frost Wire Fence Company. *The Frost Wire Fence Company : manufacturers of the Frost farm and railroad field erected and woven fence : the Frost coiled spring wire : the Frost steel farm and lawn gates.* Cleveland : Frost Wire Fence Co., 1896. 31, 1 p.

4721. Fry, Howard. [Letters and statement to Baldwin Locomotive Works concerning performance of "Class I" consolidation-type locomotives. Philadelphia : s.n., 1878. [4] p. (Pennsylvania Railroad Company)

4722. Fry, Lawford H. *Steam distribution of the Vauclain compound locomotive.* Philadelphia, Pa., Burnham, Williams, 1903. 16 p. (Baldwin Locomotive Works. *Record of recent construction, no. 42.*)

4723. _____. *A study of the locomotive boiler.* New York, Simmons-Boardman, 1924. 157 p.

4724. _____. *The steam locomotive of the future.* Philadelphia, Baldwin Locomotive Works, 1907. 36 p. (*Record of recent construction, no. 61*; reprinted from *Magazine*, January, 1907.

4724a. Frye, Albert Irwin. *Two-hinged steel arch bridge for standard four-track railroad* / 1898. 50 l. (Thesis, B.S., Massachusetts Institute of Technology, Department of Civil Engineering.)

4725. Frye, Harry A. *Minuteman steam: Boston & Maine steam locomotives, 1911-1958.* Littleton, MA: Boston and Maine Railroad Historical Society, 1982. 163 p.

4726. Fu, Paul, Suzanne Cameron Linder. *Railroads in Hoke County.* Hamlet, NC: Richmond Technical College, 1982. 26 p.

4726a. Fuchs, H.O. *Design and development of an automatic refrigerator car heater: a case history* / Los Angeles, CA: Department of Engineering, University of California, 1963. 95 p. (*EDP* report, no. I-63.)

4726b. Fuchs, Steve, Rick Acton. *My C&O* / Dayton, OH: St Alban Media, 2011. 160 p.

4727. *Fuel and power statistics of class I railroads in the United States.* Washington, D.C., Interstate Commerce Commission, Bureau of Transport Economics and Statistics, 1925-1963. Quarterly, 1961-1963. Formerly: Monthly, 1925-1960. Other titles: *Fuel for road locomotives in freight and passenger train service*, 1925-27; *Fuel for locomotives*, 1928-35; *Fuel and power for locomotives and rail motor cars*, 1936-48.

4728. *Full steam ahead: East Broad Top Railroad, national historic landmark.* Altoona, PA: EBT Partnership, 1995. 28 p. (EBT Partnership; East Broad Top Railroad and Coal Company.)

4729. Fuller, Dudley D., Beno Sternlicht. *Preliminary investigation of minimum oil-feed rate for fluid-film conditions in journal bearings* / New York : American Society of Mechanical Engineers, 1954. 5, 3 p. (*ASME. Paper no. 54-A-107.*)

4730. Fuller, E.O. *Cheyenne looking north.* Laramie, WY: E.O. Fuller, 1951. 59 p.

4731. Fuller, Justin. *History of the Tennessee Coal, Iron, and Railroad Company, 1852-1907.* 1958. 98 l. (Thesis, M.A., Emory University.)

4732. _____. *History of the Tennessee Coal, Iron, and Railroad Company, 1852-1907.* 1966. 414 l. (Thesis, Ph.D., University of North Carolina at Chapel Hill.)

4733. Fuller, Willard B. *A design for a car wheel plant.* 1898. 41 l. 8 leaves of plates. (Thesis, M.E., Lehigh University.)

4734. Fulton, Robert Lardin. *Epic of the Overland.* San Francisco, A.M. Robertson, 1924. 100 p.

4735. Fulton Sylphon Company. Railway Equipment Division. *Sylphon control system for railroad car air conditioning.* Philadephia ; Fulton Sylphon Co., Railway Equipment Division, 1938. 1 v. (various pagings), blueprints (some folded). 29 cm.

4736. *Fundamentals of the steam locomotive.* Omaha, NE: Rail Heritage, 1983. 41 p. (Also: Omaha, NE: Simmons-Boardman, 1992. 41 p.)

4737. Furrer, J.R. *History and development of the ACF Talgo* / New York : American Society of Mechanical Engineers, 1955. 10 p. (*ASME. Paper no. 55-A-131.*)

4738. Furukawa, Sam. *Cumbres & Toltec : a photographic tribute to America's most spectacular scenic railway* / San Carlos, CA: Narrow Gauge Preservation Foundation, 2007. 175 p.

4739. _____, Bob Hayden. *Durango & Silverton : a photographic celebration of America's favorite narrow gauge train ride* / San Carlos, CA: Narrow Gauge Preservation Foundation, 2009. 175 p.

4740. Fusco, Michael. *The Third Avenue El demolition in the Bronx* / San Bernardino,

G

4741. *G. M. & N. news*. Mobile, AL: Gulf, Mobile and Northern Railroad Company, 1925-

4742. *GM & O historical society news*. Joliet, IL: etc. Gulf, Mobile and Ohio Historical Society, 1900s-   . Quarterly. Other title: Gulf, Mobile and Ohio historical society news.

4743. Gabel, Christopher R. *Railroad generalship: foundations of Civil War strategy*. Fort Leavenworth, KS: U.S. Army Command and General Staff College, Combat Studies Institute, 1997. 1 v. (Also: Computer file:http://purl.access.gpo.gov/GPO/LPS59065.)

4744. _____. *Rails to oblivion: the battle of Confederate railroads in the Civil War*. Fort Leavenworth, KS: U.S. Army Command and General Staff College Press, 2002. 29 p. (Also: Computer file: http://purl.access.gpo.gov/GPO/LPS59067.)

4745. Gaertner, John T. *The Duluth, South Shore & Atlantic Railway: D.S.S.& A: a history of the Lake Superior District's pioneer iron ore hauler*. Bloomington: Indiana University Press, 2009. 349 p.

4746. _____. *North Bank Road: Spokane, Portland & Seattle Railway*. 2nd printing, revised. Pullman, WA: Washington State University Press, 1992, c1990. 246 p.

4746a. Gaffney, T. J. *Rails around the Thumb* / Charleston, SC: Arcadia Publishing, 2012. 127 p. (Michigan—Thumb District)

4747. Gagarin, Gregory. *Brake system design for high-speed passenger locomotives*. Chicago, IL: Air Brake Association, 1995. 31, 14 p.

4748. Gage, Norris L. *The relations of Kansas railroad to the state of Kansas*. Topeka, KS: Kansas Publishing House: T.D. Thacher, State printer, 1884. 27 p.

4749. Gairns, John Francis. *Locomotive compounding and superheating; a practical text-book for the use of railway and locomotive engineers, students, and draughtsmen*. Philadelphia, J.B. Lippincott Co., 1907. 189 p.

4750. *Galbraith's railway mail service maps, Missouri*. Chicago, McEwen Map Company; U.S. Railway Mail Service, 1897. 180 x 240 cm. Scale not given. Computer file:http://hdl.loc.gov/loc.gmd/g4161.rr002460 (Maps for most states.)

4751. Gallagher, Dan. *Florida's great ocean railway: building the Key West extension*. Sarasota, FL: Pineapple Press, 2003. 197 p.

4752. _____. *Marathon: heart of the Key West extension*. Marathon, FL: Pigeon Key Foundation, 1999. 108 p.

4753. Gallagher, James P., Jacques Kelly. *Trackside Maryland: from railyard to main line.* Sykesville, MD: Greenberg Publishing Co., 1992. 224 p. (Reissue: Johns Hopkins University Press, 2003.)

4754. Gallagher, James R., Karen Roberts, William H. Crown *A detailed methodology for railroad costs; prepared for the Economics Development Administration, U.S. Department of Commerce, and the Federal Railroad Administration, U.S. Department of Transportation.* Washington, DC: Economic Development Administration, 1980. 208 p. (*Economic Development Administration. Report no. 24.*)

4755. Gallo, Daniel R., Frederick A. Kramer. *The Putnam Division: New York Central's bygone route through Westchester County.* New York, Quadrant Press, 1981. 80 p.

4756. Gallo, Tom. *Chattahoochee Valley Railway.* Charleston, SC: Arcadia, 1999. 128 p.

4757. _____. *Henry Hudson Trail: Central RR of NJ's Seashore Branch.* Charleston, SC: Arcadia, 1999. 128 p.

4758. _____. *Railroads of Monmouth County.* Charleston, SC: Arcadia, 2007. 128 p. (New Jersey)

4759. Galloupe, Francis E. *Certain points in the development and practice of modern American locomotive engineering.* Philadelphia, Pa., Wm. P. Kildare, Printer, 1877. 63 p.

4760. Galloway, A.K. *The 0-4-0 locomotive and switcher on the B & O. New enl. ed.* Ramsey, NJ: Pennsylvania Publishing Co., 1953. 46 p.

4761. Galloway, Duane, Jim Wrinn. *Southern Railway's Spencer Shops.* Lynchburg, VA: TLC Pub., 1996. 105 p.

4762. Galloway, John Debo. *The first transcontinental railroad: Central Pacific, Union Pacific.* New York, Simmons-Boardman, 1950. 319 p. (Reprint: New York, Arno Press, 1981, c1950. 319, 33 p. of plates; Westport, CCT: Greenwood Press, 1983, c1950. 319, 32 p. of plates; New York, Dorset Press, 1989, c1950. 319, 32 p. of plates.)

4763. Galloway, Roderick S. *Comparative test data of locomotive performance, featuring "the Worthington Feedwater heater", "the Bethlehem auxiliary locomotive", and other tests.* 1927. 35 l.(Thesis, B.S., Iowa State College.)

4764. Galton, Douglas, Georges Marié. *The effect of brakes upon railway trains.* Pittsburgh, Pa., Westinghouse Air Brake Company, 1894. 1 v. (217 p. in various pagings.) Excerpt minutes of Proceedings of the meetings of the Institution of Mechanical Engineers, Paris, June 1878, Manchester, Oct. 1878, and London, Apr. 1879.

4764a. Gamal el-Din, Mohammed Kamel. *Evaluation of the factors affecting capacity and operating efficiency of gravity-type railroad classification yards.* 1968. 111 l.

(Thesis, University of Illinois.)

4765. Gamble, Bonnie L. *The Nashville, Chattanooga and St. Louis Railroad, 1845-1880: preservation of a railroad landscape.* 1993. 1 v. (Thesis, M.A., Middle Tennessee State University.)

4766. Gamst, Frederick C. *The hoghead: an industrial ethnology of the locomotive engineer.* New York, NY: Holt, Rinehart and Winston, 1980. 142 p.

4767. Gant, S.C. *Proposed system of underground railroad communication for Philadelphia : also, floating and tidal docks, with surface and elevated rail connections, quays, embankments, etc.* / Philadelphia : s.n., 1881. 20 p.

4768. Gantt, Robert. *A study of congestion in the Kansas City Southern Railway System.* Leavenworth, KS : Army Command and General Staff College, 1998. 95 p. (*Series: AD-a350 009*)

4769. Garbe, Robert, Leslie Stephen Robertson. *The application of highly superheated steam to locomotives; being a reprint from a series of articles appearing in "The Engineer."* New York, The N.W. Henley Publishing Company, 1908. 70 p.

4769a. García, David L. *Southern Pacific car roster: as of January 31, 1956. 3rd. ed.* Pasadena, CA: Southern Pacific Historical and Technical Society, 1995. 1 v. (various pagings).

4769b. _____, Joseph A. Strapac. *Pacific Electric cars: a pictorial journey, 1911-1953* / Upland, CA: Southern Pacific Historical & Technical Society, 2013. (Includes roster)

4770. Garcia, Gregory A. *Railroad tank car nondestructive methods evaluation* / Washington, DC: Federal Railroad Administration, Office of Research and Development, 2002. 108 p. (*DOT/FRA/ORD-01/04.*)

4771. Garcilazo, Jeffrey Marcos. *Mexican track workers and Americanization, 1900-1970.* Irving, CA: Center for Research on Latinos in a Global Society, University of California, Irving, 1997. 18 l. (*Working paper series, no. 12.*)

4772. _____. *Traqueros: Mexican railroad workers in the United States, 1870-1930.* 1995. 374 l. (Thesis, Ph.D., University of California, Santa Barbara.) Denton, TX: UNT Press, 2012. 235 p. (Mexican American Studies; 6)

4773. Gard, Lura Mary. *East St. Louis and the railroads to 1875.* 1947. (Thesis, A.M. Washington University, Department of History.)

4773a.. *Gardiner Campbell and Sons, Centennial Bell Foundry ; manufacturers of the celebrated church, school, court house, factory, city hall, academy, fire alarm, locomotive and other bells* / Milwaukee : Gardiner Campbell and Sons, 1888. 47, 24 p.

4774. Gardner, Ed. *Along the Lackawanna Railroad.* Wilkes-Barre, PA: Gardner, 1975. 3 v.

4775. _____. *Central New England Railway: a pictorial review.* 2d ed. Mountaintop, PA: Ruth Gardener, 1981. 114 p

4776. _____. *An early Lackawanna scrapbook.* Mountain Top, PA: Ed Gardner, 197-? 24 p.

4777. _____. *Lehigh Valley Railroad: a pictorial review.* Mountaintop. PA: E. Gardener, 1972?-1976. 4 v.

4778. _____. *Pennsylvania Railroad, the standard railroad of the world: through train service between the East and the West.* Mountain Top, PA: E. Gardner, 1967. 138 p.

4779. _____. *A pictorial review: the Milwaukee Road.* Mountain Top, PA: Ed Gardner, 1980-1983. v. 1-

4780. _____. *A pictorial review: New Jersey Central, the Reading, Mauch Chunk Switch Back Ry* / Wilkes-Barre, PAS: E. Gardner, 1970s. 96 p.

4781. Gardner, Franklin B. *The painters' encylopaedia: containing definitions of all important words in the art of plain and artistic painting ... coach, carriage, railway car* / New York: M.T. Richardson, 1887. 427 p.

4782. Gardner, Ruth. *Missouri-Kansas-Texas lines, Missouri-Kansas-Texas Railroad Company: postcard views and passenger time tables.* Mountaintop, PA: R. Gardner, 1990. 80 p.

4783. _____ *Rutland Railroad postcard scenes and passenger timetables.* Mountaintop, PA: Ruth Gardener, 198-? 90 p.

4784. Garforth, Harry. *Rails through Manayunk.* Telford PA: Silver Brook Junction Publishing Company, 1999. 72 p.

4785. Garg, V. K. *Locomotive track hunting model: mathematical model.* S.l., Government-Industry Research Program on Track Train Dynamics, 1976. 91 p. (*Government-Industry Research program on Track Train Dynamics, R-219.*)

4786. Garin, Paul V. *Improving rail adhesion for diesel locomotives* / New York : American Society of Mechanical Engineers, 1957. 16 p. (*ASME. Paper no. 57-A-268.*)

4787. Garmany, John Bonds. *Southern Pacific dieselization. Introduction by Richard Stenheimer; rosters by Richard E. Buike.* Edmonds, WA: Pacific Fast Mail, 1985. 400 p.

4788. Garratt, Colin Dennis. *The last of steam.* Chicago, Swallow Press, 1980, c1977. 127 p.

4789. _____. *Steam trains: an American portrait.* New York, Mallard Press, 1989.

239 p.

4790. Garrett, Charles Wilbur. *Pennsylvania lines west of Pittsburgh; a history of the flood of March, 1913.* Pittsburgh, Pa., Press of Wm. G. Johnston & Co., 1913. 257 p.

4791. _____, C.W. Bate, H.E. Custar. *Experiences of the Pennsylvania Railroad System with employee representation : convention addresses.* New York : National personnel Association, 1922. 14 p.

4792. Garrett, Klink. *Ten turtles to Tucumcari: a personal history of the Railway Express Agency.* With Toby Smith. Albuquerque, University of New Mexico Press, 2003. 172 p.

4793. Garrity, Norman Edward. *A study of railroad mergers with emphasis on the proposed Pennsylvania and New York Central Railroad merger /* 1964. 119 l. (Thesis, M.S., Economics and Business Administration, Bucknell University.)

4794. Gartner, Michael. *Riding the Pennsy to ruin; a Wall Street Journal chronicle of the Penn Central debacle.* Princeton, NJ: Dow Jones Books, 1971. 90 p.

4795. Garver, Thomas H. *The last steam railroad in America.* Photographs by O. Winston Link. New York, H.N. Abrams, 1995. 144 p.

4796. _____. *O. Winston Link: the man and the museum.* Edited by O. Winston Link Museum staff and volunteers. Roanoke, VA: O. Winston Link Museum, 2004. 42 p.

4797. *Gas light in traveling conveyances : Hill & Demarest's patent apparatus for lighting railroad cars, steamboats, omnibuses, etc. with gas : patented November 6th, 1855.* Chicago : Democratic Press Book & Job Office, 1857. 8 p.

4798. Gastman, Roger, Darin Rowland, Ian Sattler. *Freight train graffiti.* New York, Abrams, 2006. 349 p.

4799. Gates, Orus Ethan, Ludwig Kummer. *The development of a method of maintaining constant voltage on the lights of an electric car /* 1910. 82 l. (Thesis, B.S., University of Illinois.)

4800. Gates, Paul Wallace. *History of public land law development.* Washington, DC: U.S.G.P.O., 1968. 828 p.

4801. _____. *The Illinois Central Railroad and its colonization work.* Cambridge, Harvard University Press, 1934. 374 p. (*Harvard economic studies, vol. XLII.*)

4801a. Gaugh, William J. *Locomotive control : the valve pilot and how it increases efficiency in the operation of locomotives /* New York? New York University College of Engineering? 1944. 4 p.

4802. Gautreau, Marshall B. *The New Orleans, Opelousas and Great Western Railroad, 1850-1960*. 1955. 78 l. (Thesis, M.A., Louisiana State University.)

4803. Gaynor, Joseph F.N. *Comparative operating results of steam, diesel electric, and electric motive power on the Great Northern Railway electrification.* New York, American Institute of Electrical Engineers, 1947. 8 p.

4804. *Gazette.* North Freedom, WI: Mid-Continent Railway Historical Society, 1971-1975. Monthly 5 v. (< *Railway gazette.* North Freedom, Wisc.); > *Railway gazette,* North Freedom, Wisc.)

4805. Geer, Charles, Phyllis R. Fenner. *Open throttle: stories of railroads and railroad men.* New York, Morrow, 1966. 222 p.

4806. Geertz, A.O. *Pennsylvania Railroad locomotives and cars, stations, bridges and structures ; information and data book.* Yardley, PA: Edwin P. Alexander, 1949. 25 p.

4806a. Geletzke, Charles H., Jr., Wilbur E. Hague. *The Detroit & Toledo Shore Line railroad : "expressway for industry"* / Kutztown, PA: Kutztown Pub. Co., 2011. 264 p.

4807. Gellman Research Associates. *An analysis of the impacts of the acquisition of the Monon Railroad by the Louisville & Nashville Railroad Company.* Jenkintown, PA: Gellman Research Associates, 1976. 35 p. Prepared for Federal Railroad Administration.

4808. General American Car Company. *Modern transportation of dairy products: patented, glass-lined, seamless, refrigerator milk cars/* Chicago, IL: s.n., 1928. 50 p.

4809. General American Transportation Corporation. *General American tank car journeys: where industrial liquids come from and where they go.* Chicago, GATC, 1931. 189 p.

4810. _____. *General American tank car manual.* Chicago? General American Transportation Corporation, 1961. 85 p.

4811. _____ *Imagination at work.* Chicago, The Corporation, 1961. 63 p.

4812. _____. *Tank car manual.* 2d ed. Chicago, The Corporation, 1966. 176 p.

4813. _____. *GATX tank car manual.* 3rd ed. Chicago, The Corporation, 1972. 150 p.

4814. _____. *GATX tank car manual.* 4th ed. Chicago: The Corporation, 1979. 179 p.

4815. _____ *GATX tank car manual.* 5th ed. Chicago: General American Transportation Corporation, 1985. 165, 7 p.

4816. _____. *GATX tank and freight car manual.* 6th ed. Chicago: General American

Transportation Corporation, 1994. 265 p.

4817. General Electric Company. *Building locomotives for the world's railroads*. Erie, PA: General Electric, 1956. 19 p. (Locomotive and Car Equipment Department.)

4817a. _____. *Cleveland Union Terminal electrification*. Schenectady, NY: General Electric Company, 1930. 11 p.

4818. _____. *C.M. & St. P. Ry. electric locomotive exhibit*. S.l., General Electric Company, 1900s. 1 v (unpaged)

4819. _____. *Diesel-electrics for industrial switching*. Schenectady, NY: s.n., 1942. 15 p.

4820. _____. *Diesel engine mechanical service manual: diesel-electric locomotive*. Erie, PA: General Electric, n.d. 166 p.

4821. _____. *Educational manual: model U33 diesel-electric locomotive*. Erie, PA: General Electric, n.d. 156 p.

4822. _____ *The electric divisions of the Chicago, Milwaukee & St. Paul Railway*. Schenectady, NY: General Electric Company, 1927. 44 p. (*Bulletin GEA 150A.*)

4823. _____. *Electric haulage*. Schenectady, NY: General Electric Company, 1896. 137 p. 2 l. (Power and Mining Department.)

4824. _____. *Electrical equipment for the Puget Sound lines of the Chicago, Milwaukee and St. Paul Railway*. New York, s.n. 1915. 12 p. (*Bulletin no. 44012.*)

4825. _____. *Electricity in the service of steam railroads*. S.l., s.n., 1911. 1 v.

4826. _____. *Electricity on the New York Central*. New York? The Company, 1913. 15 p.

4827. _____. *Electrification by GE*. Chicago, Central Electric Railfans' Association; General Electric Company, 1976. 1 v.

4828. _____. *The electrification of the Butte, Anaconda & Pacific Railway*. Schenectady, NY: 1914. 1 v. (*Bulletin no. 44011, July, 1914.*)

4829. _____. *The electrification of the West Jersey & Seashore Railroad*. Schenectady, NY: General Electric Company, 1907. 23 p.

4830. _____. *The electrification of the West Shore Railroad*. Schenectady, NY: General Electric Company, 1907. 21 p. (*Bulletin No. 4546.*)

4831. _____. *An epoch in railway electrification*. S.l., s.n., 1916. 30 p. (*Bulletin no. 44013.*)

4832. _____. *Erie works : welcomes you!* Erie, PA ? : General Electric Co., 1948. 20 p.

4833. _____. *Essentials of train lighting.* Cleveland, Ohio, The Company, 1916. 14 p.

4834. _____. *44 tons of railroad motive power.* S.l., s.n., 1945. 18 p.

4835. _____. *The gas turbine electric locomotive: opening a new chapter in the history of railroad motive power.* S.l., Alco-GE, 1949. 5 p.

4836. _____. *G.E. Edison mazda lamps for Standard train lighting Service.* Schenectady, NY: General Electric Co., 1911. 10 p. (*Bulletin no. 4897.*)

4837. _____. *G-E 70 ton locomotive. 600 horsepower.* Schenectady, NY: Apparatus Department, General Electric Company, 1950. 15 p.

4838. _____. *GE locomotives.* Erie, Pa., General Electric Transportation Systems, 1989. 27 p. (*Report TS-6348.*)

4839. _____. *General Electric and transportation.* Schenectady, NY: General Electric Company, 1928. 26 p.

4840. _____. *General Electric Railroad.* Schenectady, NY: s.n., 1902. 22 p.

4841. _____. *High speed locomotive tests at Erie, Pa., December 4-5. 1923.* Schenectady, NY: General Electric Company, 1923. 14 p.

4842. _____. *Hot-box detector with wire or carrier current mode remote recording : for automatic instantaneous pin-pointing of overheated journals before costly trouble results.* Waynesboro, VA: General Electric Company, 1959. 7 p.

4843. _____. *The New York Central electrification.* Schenectady, NY: General Electric Company, 1929. 36 p.

4844. _____. *Oil-electric locomotives manufactured by General Electric Company, American Locomotive Company, Ingersoll-Rand Company.* 4th ed. New York, Ingersoll-Rand, 1925. 12 l.

4845. _____. *The oil-electric locomotive.* 5th ed. New York, General Electric Company; American Locomotive Company, Ingersoll-Rand Company, 1926. 12 l.

4846. _____. *Operating manual: General Electric diesel-electric locomotives.* Erie, PA: Transportation Systems Division, General Electric, 1968. 58 p. (*GEJ-3856/2-68.*)

4847. _____. *Parade of modern high-speed diesel-electric trains.* Schenectady, NY: General Electric, 1936. 12 p.

4848. _____. *Pennsylvania Railroad , electric and multiple-car replacement.* Erie, PA:

General Electric Company, 1959. 1 v.

4849. _____. *The Pennsylvania Railroad electrification, New York-Washington.* Schenectady, NY: General Electric, 1935. 23 p.

4850. _____. *Profiles of American railroading.* Schenectady? N.Y., s.n. 1965. 48 p.

4851. _____. *Radio telephone equipment for train communication* / Schenectady, NY: General Electric Co., 1928. 8 p. (*Bulletin GEA-944A*)

4852. _____. *Railway apparatus and supplies: catalogue and price list.* Schenectady, NY: Supply Department, General Electric Company, 1896. 226 p. (*No. 7510.*)

4853. _____. *Railway supplies.* Schenectady, NY: Supply Department, General Electric Company, 1910. 437 p.

4854. _____. *Railway supplies.* Schenectady, NY: General Electric Company, 1922. 505 p.

4855. _____. *60-ton oil-electric locomotive.* Schenectady, NY: General Electric Company, 192-? 8 p. (General Electric Company; American Locomotive Company; Ingersoll-Rand Company.)

4856. _____. *Some results of the B.A. & P Railway electrification.* Schenectady, NY: General Electric Company, 1914. 11 p. (Butte, Anaconda & Pacific)

4857. _____. *Specifications for electric locomotives proposed for New York Central and Hudson River Railroad Company leased and operated lines, Electrical Department.* Schenectady, NY: General Electric Company, 1903. 78 l.

4858. _____. *Specifications for electric locomotives proposed for New York, New Haven and Hartford Railroad. Submitted by General Electric Company, Schenectady, N.Y.* Schenectady, NY: 1905. 157 l.

4859. _____. *Specifications for railway motors proposed for New York Central and Hudson River Railroad Company leased and operated lines, Electrical Department.* Schenectady, NY: 1905. 17 l.

4860. _____. *Specifications for Sprague-General Electric multiple unit control equipments proposed for New York Central and Hudson River Railroad Company, leased and operated lines. Electrical Department.* Schenectady : General Electric Company, 1905. 22 l.

4861. *General Electric Company review.* Schenectady, NY: General Electric Company, 1903-1907. Monthly.

4862. *General Electric review.* Schenectady, NY: General Electric Company, 1907-1958. 54 v. Bimonthly.

4863. General Machinery Corporation. *Niles 90-inch balanced quartering & crank pin turning machine for right hand lead locomotives.* Hamilton, Ohio: General Machinery Corp., Niles Tool Works Division, 1936. 7 p.

4864. General Motors Corporation. Electro-Motive Division. *Analysis of future motive power requirements / electrified territory / Pennsylvania Railroad.* La Grange, IL: Electro-Motive Division, 1959. 102 p.

4865 _____. _____. *Decades of the diesel: the 30-year history of General Motors diesel-electric locomotives.* Detroit, MI: General Motors Corp., 1964. 24 p.

4866. _____. *Diesel locomotive operating manual for model GP35. 3rd ed.* Omaha, NE: Railway Educational Bureau, 1965.

4867. _____. *Diesel locomotive operating manual no. 2308A for model F3.* La Grange, IL: General Motors, n.d. 1 v.

4868. _____. *Diesel locomotive operating manual no. 2310 for freight-passenger locomotive models F7 and FP7 with vapor steam generator and Elseco steam generator.* Milwaukee, WI: Old Line Publishers, 197-? 120 p. (Reprint of the 194-? edition published by the Electro-Motive Division, General Motors Corp.)

4869. _____. *Diesel locomotive operating manual no. 2318, for model GP9.* 3rd ed. Omaha, NE: Railway Educational Bureau, 1957. 1 v.

4870. _____. *The diesel locomotive, preface of a new era.* La Grange, IL: General Motors Corporation, Electro-Motive Division, 194-? 30 p.

4871. _____. *83,000 miles; the story behind the Diesel freight locomotive.* La Grange, IL: s.n. 1941. 50 p.

4872. _____. *The Electro-Motive story.* Detroit, MI: The Corporation, 1961. 23 p.

4873. _____. *EMD's 60 series: steppingstone to the 21st century.* Halifax, PA: Withers Publ., 1996. 152, 6 p.

4874. _____. *Evolution on the rails: the story of the 25,000th General Motors locomotive.* La Grange, IL: The Corporation, 1962. 16 p.

4875. _____. *General Motors diesels in review, 1934-1944; 10th anniversary of diesel road power on American railroads.* La Grange, IL: The Corporation, 1944. 24 p.

4876. _____. *GM/Electro-Motive diesels--; a history of being first—a future dedicated to it.* La Grange, IL: Electro-Motive Division, General Motors, 1983. 10 p,

4877. _____. *How complete dieselization pays off: a study based upon operating experience of United States railroads.* La Grange, IL: Electro-Motive Division, General Motors, 1953. 26 p.

4878. _____. *Instruction manual: diesel freight locomotives.* La Grange, IL: Electro-Motive Division, General Motors Corp., 1945. 1 v.

4879. _____. *Instruction manual for the operation of railway equipment.* La Grange, Ill., Electro-Motive Division, General Motors, 1944. 1 v.

4880. _____. *The locomotive industry and General Motors.* New York, Bar Press, 1973. 78 p.

4881. _____. *Locomotive operation and maintenance Union Pacific Railroad diesel electric passenger locomotives 7M1, 7M2, 8M1, 8M2, 9M1 & 9M2 (AMC 1136 to 1141 – E-333).* La Grange, IL: Electro-Motive Division, General Motors, 1941. 1 v (*Its Bulletin, 177.*)

4882. _____ *Locomotive reference book: delivery history through 1990: domestic and export.* La Grange, IL: Electro-Motive Division, General Motors, 1991. 196 p.

4883. _____. *On the road trouble-shooting: 1500H.P.-F-3 and F-7 units.* La Grange, IL: Electro-Motive Division, General Motors, 1949. 16 p.

4884. _____. *Operating manual, models 4501-4516-4517-5301-5302.* Milwaukee, WI: Old Line Publishers, 1963. 1 v. (Krauss-Maffei Diesel hydraulic ML-400 C' C'.)

4884a. _____. *Operation and maintenance instructions for 1000 HP. switching locomotives with 12-567 diesel engines (E.M.C. model NW-2)* / La Grange, IL: Electro-Motive Corp., 1941. 1 v. (*Bulletin 153 Rev. A.*)

4885. _____. *Pull—the tractive effort of diesel locomotives.* La Grange, IL: Electro-Motive Division, General Motors Corp., n.d. 18 p.

4886. _____. *SD40-2 locomotive service manual.* 6th ed. La Grange, IL: General Motors, 1978. 1 v.

4887. _____. *600 HP & 1200 HP switching locomotive: operating manual no. 2303, models SW-1 & SW-7, 567 series engines.* 5th ed. Omaha, NE: Railway Education Bureau, 1950. 1 v.

4888. _____. *Train of tomorrow.* Detroit?: General Motors Corp., 1947. 20 p.

4888a. _____. *Water – its use in diesel locomotives.* La Grange, IL: Electro-Motive Division, General Motors Corp., 1948. 15, 1 p.

4889. _____. *Why we built the Train of Tomorrow.* By Paul Garrett, and William A. Gosling. S.l., General Motors, 1947? 2, 16, 2 p.

4890. General Railway Signal Company. *A.P.B. absolute permissive block system for single track railways.* Rochester, NY: General Railway Signal Co., 1916. 27, 1 p. (*Bulletin, 128A.*)

4891. _____. *Absolute permissive block system circuits.* Rochester, NY: General Railway Signal Co., 1919. 15, 1 p. 7 l. of plates. (*Bulletin, 135.*)

4892. _____. *Advance description of the cab signal and speed control system designed by the General Railway Signal Company for installation on the lines of the New York Municipal Railway Corporation.* Rochester, NY: General Railway Signal Company, 1916. 46 p.

4893. _____. *Automatic block signaling for steam roads.* Rochester, NY: The Company, 1908. 132 p.

4893a. _____. *Bright side of Blue Island : a brief description of a recent hump classification yard on the Indiana harbor Belt Railroad operated by a G-R-S all-electric car retarder system.* Rochester, NY: General railway Signal Co., 1927. 1 v. (Bulletin 148.)

4894. _____. *Catalogue and price list of assembled layouts of derails, switches and movable point frogs for mechanical interlocking: made by the General Railway Signal Company of Rochester, N.Y.* Rochester, NY: The Company, 1907. 140 p.

4895. _____. *Catalogue and price-list of electric interlocking and signaling devices made by the General Railway Signal Company of Buffalo, N.Y.* Buffalo, NY: General Railway Signal Company, 1905. 2 v.

4896. _____. *Centralized traffic control.* Rochester, NY: General Railway Signal Company, 1938. 54 p. (*Bulletin, 169*)

4897. _____. *Electric interlocking handbook* / by the Engineering staff of the General Railway Signal Company, with an introduction by Wilmer W. Salmon, Henry M. Sperry, editor; Paul E. Carter, assistant editor. Rochester, NY: General Railway Signal Company, 1913. 435 p.

4898. _____. *Elements of railway signaling.* Rochester, N.Y., General Railway Signal Company, 1954. 1 v. (*Handbook, 50.*)

4899. _____. *G-R-S automatic train control.* Rochester, NY: General Railway Signal Company, 1922. 61 p. (*Bulletin, no. 138.*)

4900. _____. *G-R-S automatic train control, continuous inductive single phase, two speed system.* Rochester, NY: General Railway Signal Company, 1926. 38 p. (*Pamphlet 528.*)

4901. _____. *G-R-S automatic train control: continuous inductive single phase, two speed system: installation, maintenance, and ordering information.* 2d ed. Rochester,

NY: General Railway Signal Company, 1928. 127 p. (*Handbook no. 5, March 1928.*)

4902. _____. *G-R-S automatic train control: intermittent inductive auto-manual system: installation and maintenance and catalog.* 2d ed. Rochester, NY: General Railway Signal Company, 1928. (*Handbook, no. 6.*)

4903. _____. *G-R-S centralized traffic control: type F, class M, duplex, coded system.* Rochester, NY: General Railway Signal Company, 1937. 53 p. (*Bulletin, 170.*)

4904. _____. *G-R-S centralized traffic control: type K2, class M, coded system.* Rochester, NY: General Railway Signal Company, 1955. 166 p. (*Handbook, no. 45.*)

4905. _____. *G-R-S coded cab signals.* Rochester, NY: General Railway Signal Company, 1937. 52 p. (*Bulletin, 171.*)

4906. _____. *G.R.S. model 2A signal: booklet 1003A,* December, 1918. Rochester, NY: General Railway Signal Co., 1918. 72 p.

4907. _____. *G-R-S model 9: hand-operated switch machine: complete hand-switch facilities all in one unit.* Rochester, NY: General Railway Signal Co., 1949. 21 p.

4908. _____. *G.R.S. model 9 switch machine: operation, installation, maintenance.* Rochester, N.Y., General Railway Signal Company, 1949. 52 p. (*Handbook, 32.)*

4909. _____. *G-R-S model 9A: electric switch lock.* Rochester, NY: General Railway Signal Co., 1949. 47 p. (*Bulletin, 181.)*

4910. _____. *G-R-S model 10: electric switch lock.* Rochester, NY: General Railway Signal Co., 1952. 22 p. (*Bulletin, 187.)*

4911. _____. *G.R.S. railway signal appliances.* Rochester, NY: General Railway Signal Company, 1952. 87 p. *(Pamphlet 751.)*

4912. _____. *The GRS way to electronic railroading.* Rochester, NY: General Railway Signal Company, 1963. 28 p. (*Bulletin 203.)*

4913. _____. *History of General Railway Signal Company.* Rochester, NY: General Railway Signal Company, 1979. 35 p.

4914. _____. *Mechanical signal appliances: General Railway Signal Company.* Rochester, NY: General Railway Signal Co., 1915. 1 v.

4915. _____. *Paul J. Neff Yard, Missouri Pacific Lines.* S.l., s.n., 1960. 1 v. (unpaged)

4916. _____. *Railway signal engineering.* Rochester, N.Y., s.n., 192-? 1 v.

4917. _____. *Technical library catalog of books.* Rochester, NY: The Library, 1976. 49 p.

4918. _____. *Type SA color-light signal, search-light type; installation, operation, maintenance.* Rochester, NY: s.n., 1947. 36 p. (*Handbook 29.*)

4919. _____. *Type SC color-light signal, searchlight type, description, operation, installation, maintenance.* Rochester, NY: General Railway Signal Company, 1946. 57 p.

4919a. _____. *The way is clear* / Rochester, NY: General Railway Signal Co., 1912. 31 p.

4920. *General statement of the affairs of the New York, New Haven, and Hartford Railroad Company.* S.l., s.n., 1894-1914. 21 v. (> *Statement of the affairs of the New York, New Haven and Hartford Railroad Company.*)

4921. General Ticket and Passenger Agents' Association. *Proceedings of Convention of the General Ticket and Passengers Agents' Association.* S.l., The Association, 1873-1878. 6 v. (< National General Ticket Agents' Association. Convention. *Proceedings…*; (> National Association of General Passenger and Ticket Agents. Convention. *Proceedings…*)

4922. Gentzel, Robert Allen. *A comparison of rail yard queuing models: analytic queuing models versus computer simulation: a thesis*/ 1981. 173 l. (Thesis, M.S. in Transportation, Northwestern University)

4923.George, Charles B. *Forty years on the rail.* Chicago, Ill., R.R. Donnelley, 1887. 262 p. ("Reminiscences of a veteran conductor.")

4924. George Eastman House. *Tracks, the railroad in photographs from the George Eastman House collection*/ Rochester, NY: George Eastman House, 2008. 8 p.

4925. George, Herbert. *Change at Ozone Park: a history and description of the Long Island Rail Road Rockaway branches.* Flanders, NJ: RAE Pub., 1993. 79 p.

4926. George, Michael. *Louisville and Nashville's Atlanta Division.* Apison, TN: Blue Ridge Historics, 2000. 192 p.

4927. _____. *Southern Railway's Murphy Branch.* Collegedale, TN, College Press, 1996. 119 p.

4928. _____, Frank Strack. *Passage through time: a milepost guide for the Great Smoky Mountains Railroad.* Collegedale, TN: College Press, 2000. 176 p. (2d ed.: 2005. 177 p.)

4929. George, Preston, Sylvan Rupert Wood. *The railroads of Oklahoma.* Boston, Mass., Railway & Locomotive Historical Society, Baker Library, Harvard Business School, 1900, 1943. 81 p.

4930. George, Raymond B. *Missouri-Kansas-Texas Lines: in color.* Edison, NJ:

Morning Sun Books, 1994. 128 p.

4931. Georgia Historical Society. *Central of Georgia Railway, collection #1362: collection description.* Savannah, GA: Georgia Historical Society, 1990. 1 v.

4932. Georgia Southern & Florida Railway Company. *Rules for the government of employes of the Georgia Southern & Florida Railroad: superseding all existing rules inconsistent therewith.* Macon, GA: J.W. Burke, 1889. 108 p.

4933. Gerard, Felix Roy. *The Lehigh Valley Railroad, 1846-1946: a centenary address.* New York, Newcomen Society of England, American Branch, 1946. 28 p. (*Newcomen address, 1946.*)

4934. Gerber, Rudolph Joseph, Peg Hogan. *Grand Canyon Railroad: illustrated guidebook.* Phoenix, AZ: Primer Publishers, 1990. 75 p.

4935. Gerber, Rudy J. *The railroad and the canyon.* Gretna, LA: Pelican Pub. Co., 1995. 127 p. (Grand Canyon Region)

4936. Gerhart, Robert R. *Night trains.* Greensboro, NC: Art Department, University of North Carolina, 1975. 89 l.

4937. Gerland, Jonathan Kirk. *Steam in the pines: a history of the Texas State Railroad.* Nacogdoches, TX: East Texas Historical Association, 2004. 66 p. (*Ann and Lee Lawrence East Texas history series, no. 6.*)

4938. German-American Portland Cement Works. *Big Muddy Bridge: Illinois Central System.* Chicago: G.E. Cole & Co., 1903. 34 p.

4939. Gerstner, Franz Anton, Ritter von, Frederick C. Gamst. *Early American railroads: Franz Anton Ritter von Gerstner's Die inner Communicationen (1842-1843).* Stanford, CA: Stanford University Press, 1997. 844 p.

4940. _____, L. Klein. *Die inner communicationen der Vereinigten Staaten von Nordamerika.* Wien, L. Forster's Artistische Anstalt, 1842-1843. 2 v. and 35 plates.

4941. Gertier, Judith B. *Selection of railroad dispatcher candidates/* Washington, DC: Federal Railroad Administration, Office of Research and Development, 2003. 107 p. (DOT/FRA/ORD-03-09)

4942. _____. *A study of state programs for rail-highway grade crossing improvements/* Washington, DC: Office of Rail Systems Analysis and Information, 1978. 1 v. (various pagings). (*FRA-OPPD-78-7.*)

4943. _____, Alex Viale. *Work schedules and sleep patterns of railroad maintenance of way workers.* Washington, DC: Federal Railroad Administration, 2006. 77 p. Internet resource: http://www.fra.dot.gov/downloads/research/ord0625.pdf)

4944. _____, _____. *Work schedules and sleep patterns of railroad signalmen.* Washington, DC: Federal Railroad Administration, 2006. 75 p. (Internet resource: http://www.fra.dot.gov/downloads/reseaqrch/ord0619.pdf)

4945. Gertler, J., S. Reinach, George I. Kuehn. *Non-accident release of hazmat from railroad tank cars: training issues.* Washington, DC: Federal Railroad Administration, Office of Research and Development, 1999. 75 p. *(DOT/FR)A/ORD-99/05.*

4946. Ghate, Purva. *Making sustainable and resilient urban neighborhoods : new connections : Central Terminal to Broadway market* / 2008. 57 l. Project, M.Arch., State University of New York at Buffalo. (New York Central Terminal, Buffalo, New York.)

4947. Ghega Carl, Ritter von. *Die Baltimore-Ohio Eisenbahn über das Alleghany-Gebirg, mit besonderer Berücksichtigung der Steigungs-und Krümmungsverhältnisse.* Wien, Kaukfuss Witwe, Prandel & Comp., 1844. 264 p.+ atlas.

4948. *Ghost tracks : the official newsletter of the Nevada Northern Railway Museum.* East Ely, NV: White pine Historical Railroad Foundation d.b.a. as Nevada Northern Railway Museum, 1900s-   . Quarterly.

4949. *Ghost train! American railroad ghosts legends, as collected and retold by Tony Reevy.* Lynchburg, VA: TLC Publishing, 1998. 166 p.

4950. *Giants of the rails: an articulated steam pictorial.* New York, NY: Wayner Publications, 197-? 48 p.

4951. Gibbings, Alfred Horswill. *Oil fuel equipment for locomotives and principles of application.* New York, Van Nostrand, 1915. 125 p.

4951a. Gibbons, William M. *Plan of reorganization for Chicago, Rock Island and Pacific Railroad Company*/ Chicago: United States District Court for the Northeastern District of Illinois Eastern District, 1979. 50 l. (Docket no. 75B2697, before the Interstate Commerce Commission.)

4952. Gibbs, Alfred W. *The problem of reducing smoke on railroads* / S.l., s.n., 1910. 21, 28 p. 7 leaves of plates. Alfred W. Gibbs: General Superintendent of Motive Power, Pennsylvania Railroad Company.

4953. Gibbs & Hill. *Penn Central electrification: New York tunnels, 25 kV vs. 12.5/25 kV*/ Washington, DC: Federal Railroad Administration, 1975. 85 p. *(FRA-ONECD-75-51.)*

4954. _____. *The Pennsylvania Railroad Company : an engineering and economic study of motive power replacement with evaluation of electrification* / New York : Gibb & Hill, 1955. 35 p.

4955. _____. *Railroad electrification: its economic advantages to the railroads and its relationship to the coal and power markets.* New York, Gibbs & Hill, Inc., 1954. 5 l., 15 p., 6 l. of plates.

4956. Gibbs, George. *Synopsis of the report of the Chicago Association of Commerce Committee on Smoke Abatement and Electrification of Railway Terminals.* New York, New York Railroad Club, 1916. 59 p. 6 l. of plates.

4957. _____. *The Virginian Railway electrification.* S.l., s.n., 1926. 59 p.

4958. Gibson, David William. *Truck design optimization project, phase II : friction snubber force measurement system field test report* / Washington, DC: Federal Railroad Administration, Office of Research and Development, 1979. 61 p. in various pagings. (FRA-ORD=79/24.)

4959. Gibson, James Anderson Beirne, Bascom Sale Pribble. *United States safety appliances for all classes of cars and locomotives. 4th ed. rev.* Richmond, Va., Gibson, Pribble & Company, 1914. 62 p.

4959a. Gibson, James K. *Southern Pacific Company investigation of passenger service : Peninsula commute operations between San Francisco and San Jose* / San Francisco : California Public Utilities Commission, Transportation Division, 1975. 7 l. (Case no. 5234; Application no. 38951.)

4960. _____, William F. Hibbard. *The Atchison, Topeka and Santa Fe Railway Company proposed elimination of trains 6 and 61* / Los Angeles : California Public Utilities Commission, Transportation Division, Traffic, Operations, and Safety Branch, 1958. 28 l. (Application no. 39616.)

4961. _____, William R. Peters. *Report on the investigation of Southern Pacific Company's passenger service in California.* San Francisco,: California Public Utilities Commission, Transportation Division, 1958. 78 p. (Case no. 5829)

4962. Gibson, Pribble & Company, Richmond, Virginia. *United States safety appliances for all classes of cars and locomotives. M.C.B. edition.* Richmond, Va., Published for the Master Car Builders' Association by Gibson, Pribble & Company, 1915. 111 p.

4963. Gibson, William Oliver. *Journal of a Santa Fe wire twister: 100 years of family railroading.* Grants Pass, OR: W. O. Gibson, 1988. 135 p.

4964. _____. *Journal of a Santa Fe wire twister, final entries.* David City, NE: South Platte Press, 1991. 36 p.

4965. _____. *Santa Fe engine picture taker.* David City, NE: South Platte Press, 1993. 36 p.

4966. _____. *Topeka rails.* David City, NE: South Platte Press, 2000. 44 p.

4966a. Giddings, Franklin Henry. *Railroads and telegraphs : who shall control them?* Springfield. MA: Manufacturer and Industrial Gazette, 1881. 12 p.

4967. Giesking, Paul F. *Covered ore cars and automatic loading, unloading, and weighing features* / New York : American Society of Mechanical Engineers, 1965. 4 p.

4968. Gifford, Adam. *The impact of unionism on annual earnings: a case study involving locomotive engineers and firemen and telephone linemen and servicemen.* 1955. 262 l. (Thesis, Ph.D., University of Washington.)

4969. Gilbert, A.M. & Co. *The improved Howe railroad track scales, iron frame, with protected steel bearings (patented) ... : an illustrated comparison of the mechanism of scales* / Chicago ? : A. M. Gilbert & Co., 1877. 18 p.

4970. Gilbert, Bradford L., and others. *Sketch portfolio of railroad stations and kindred structures, with nearly two hundred illustrations.* 5th ed. New York, Railroad Gazette, 1895. 70 l.

4971. Gilbert Car Works. *The Mann Boudoir car.* New York: Mann's Boudoir Car Company, n.d. 19 p. 25 x 35 cm. ill. diagrs. floor plans and arrangement of furniture.

4971a. Gilbert Frank, John McAuley Palmer. *Railway law in Illinois*/ Chicago; Callaghan and Company, 1873. 337 p.

4972. Gilbert, Gilbert H., Lucius I. Wightman, W.L. Saunders. *The subways and tunnels of New York, methods and costs.* New York, J. Wiley & Sons, 1912. 372 p.

4973. Gilbert, H. E., W. P. Kennedy. *Railroad safety—long trains: before the Interstate Commerce Commission, H. E. Gilbert, President of the Brotherhood of Locomotive Firemen and Enginemen, and W. P. Kennedy: petition for promulgation and enforcement of rules, standards, and instructions for installation, inspection, maintenance and repair of power brakes.* Chicago?; The Brotherhood of Locomotive Firemen and the Brotherhood of Railroad Trainmen? 1955. 62 p.

4974. Gilbert, John F. *Blue Ridge crossties: steam, depots & diesels in the mountains of North Carolina.* Raleigh, NC: Crossties Press Books, 2003. 76 l.

4975. _____. *Crossties to the depot.* Raleigh, NC: Crossties Press Books, 1982- (Railroad stations-Southern states)

4976. _____. *N&W crossties in the North Carolina heartland: an album of Norfolk & Western Railway depots and trains in the days before diesels.* Raleigh, NC: Crossties Press Books, 2005. 40 l.

4977. _____. *South Carolina railroad stations: ACL, SAL, Southern & related rrs.* Raleigh, NC: Gilbert Design, Inc., Crossties Press Books, 2000. 88 l.

4978. _____. *Virginia railroad stations.* Raleigh, NC: Crossties Press, 1982. 56 p.

4979. _____, Grady Jefferys. *Crossties over Saluda; a portrait of Southern Railway power on the nation's steepest, standard gauge, main line railway grade.* Compiled and edited by John F. Gilbert. Text by Grady Jefferys. Raleigh, NC: Crossties Press, 1971. 36 p. (Rev. ed.: 1982. 36 p.)

4980. _____, _____ *Crossties through Carolina; the story of North Carolina's early day railroads.* Raleigh, NC: Helios Press, 1969. 88 p. (2d ed.: Raleigh, NC: Crossties Press, 1982. 88 p.)

4981. _____, _____. *The tree of life; a history of the North Carolina Railroad.* Raleigh, NC: North Carolina Railroad Co., 1972. 96 p.

4982. Gilbert, Tim. *Boston & Maine cabooses: a history of development & use, 1914-1955.* Amesbury, MA: Salisbury Point Railroad Historical Society, 1999. 22 l.

4983. Gildersleeve, Tom, Nils Huxtable. *Narrow gauge—then and now.* West Vancouver, B.C., Steamscenes, 1993. 47 p. (D&RGW)

4983a. Gilfillan, John B. *Forfeiture of Northern Pacific land grant* / Washington, DC: s.n., 1886. 23 p.

4984. Gillanders, J. David, Thomas J. Parsons. *Bridges constructed from railroad cars : software operation manual : draft version 1* / Little Rock, AR : Arkansas State Highway and Transportation Department, 1991. 24 l. (*Highway research project---TRC8901.*)

4984a. Gillespie, Michael. *Old time railroad stories : an anthology of true adventures, humorous tales, and high melodrama written by those who lived the era* / Stoddard, WI: Great River Publishing, 2013. 160 p.

4985. Gillespie, Mike. *The best school I ever attended: once upon our depot platform.* S.l., Michael C. Gillespie, 2003. 113 p. (Railroad stations-Georgetown, KY.)

4986. Gillette, Edward. *Locating the iron trail.* Boston, The Christopher Publishing House, 1925. 172 p. (Railroads-Surveying.)

4987. Gillette, Jack H. *The Cheyenne Line.* Greeley, CO: J.H. Gillette, 1977. 242 p. (CB&Q)

4988. Gilpin, William. *The central gold region. The grain, pastoral and gold regions of North America. With some new views of its physical geography; and observations on the Pacific railroad.* Philadelphia, PA: Barnes & Co., St. Louis, E.K. Woodward, 1860. 194 p.

4988a. Gingerich, Barton. *A wilderness road: Isaac Merrill in West Virginia, 1873.* 2011. 105 l. (Thesis, B.A., Patrick Henry College.) Chesapeake and Ohio Railroad Co.

4989. Githens, Herbert J. *A photographic recording and architectural description of the ferry portion of the CRRNJ Maritime Terminal, Liberty State Park, Jersey City, Hudson County, New Jersey.* Newton, NJ: Historic Conservation & Interpretation, 1981. 78 p.

4990. Givens, Charles H. *Diagrams, common standard passenger train cars, Southern Pacific Lines, as of March 1, 1933.* 6th ed. Pasadena, CA: Southern Pacific Historical & Technical Society, 1997. 1 v. (various pagings)

4991. Gjevre, John A. *Chili Line: the narrow rail trail to Santa Fe; the story of the narrow gauge Denver and Rio Grande Western's Santa Fe branch, 1880-1941.* Espanola, NM: Printed by the Rio Grande Sun Press, 1969. 82 p. (3rd ed.: Espanola, NM: Las Trampas Press, 1984. 100 p.)

4992. _____. *Saga of the Soo, three generations west: an illustrated history of the Soo Line Railroad Company and its predecessors in Minnesota, The Dakotas, and Montana* Moorhead, MN: Agassiz Publications, 1995. 224 p.(2d ed.: Moorhead, MN: Gjevre Books, 1990- v.1-

4993. _____. *Saga of the Soo, west from Shoreham; an illustrated history of the Soo Line Railroad Company and its predecessors in Minnesota, the Dakotas, and Montana.* La Crosse, WI: Printed by the Molzahn Printing Company, 1973. 111 p.

4994. _____, George A. Forero, Stuart J. Nelson. *Saga of the Soo: an illustrated history of the Soo Line and the Wisconsin Central with special emphasis on their relation to the Canadian Pacific Railway.* Moorhead, MN: Agassiz Publications, 2006. 240 p. (Vol. 3: East, West and to the North.)

4995. Glaab, Charles Nelson. *Kansas City and the railroads: community policy in the growth of a regional metropolis.* Lawrence, KS: University Press of Kansas, 1993. 260 p.

4996. _____. *Local railroad promotion in Kansas City, 1855-1889.* 1958. (Thesis, Ph.D., University of Missouri.)

4996a. Glancey, Jonathan. *The train: a photographic history* / London: Carlton Books, 2009. 256 p.

4997. Glaser, Tom W. *A guide to the collection of John Insley Blair: mss 40, Fikes Hall of Special Collections and DeGolyer Library*/ Dallas, TX? The Library, 1985. 73 p.

4998. Glasscock, Carl B. *Man-hunt; bandits and the Southern Pacific.* New York, Grosset & Dunlap, 1929. 294 p.

4999. Glassell, A.M. *A review of the Lehigh Valley Rail Road bridge over the Delaware River at Easton, Pa.* 1879. 49 l. (Thesis, C.E., Lehigh University.)

5000. Gleed, Charles S. *The rehabilitation of the Santa Fe Railway system.* Chicago? Ill., s.n. 1912. 26 p. (Reprinted from the *Santa Fe employees' magazine*, Dec., 1912.)

5001. Glendinning, Gene V. *The Chicago & Alton Railroad: the only way.* DeKalb, IL: Northern Illinois University Press, 2002. 274 p.

5002. Gleysteen, Jan. *Symphony in steam; the history and development of the 4-4-0 or American type locomotive.* Scottdale, PA: Trogon Publications, 1966. 112 p.

5003. Glick, William L. *Burlington passenger car photo album.* San Jose, CA: Quincy House, 2007. 324 p.

5004. _____. *Passenger cars of the Burlington, 1869 to1930's.* San Jose, CA: Quincy House, 1986. 166 p.

5005. _____ *Passenger equipment register of the Chicago, Burlington & Quincy Railroad: approximate dates, 1869 to the 1930's.* Rev. ed. San Jose, CA: Quincy House, 1987. 130 p.

5006. Glischinski, Steve. *Burlington Northern and its heritage.* Andover, NJ: Andover Junction Publications, 1992. 192 p. (Also: Osceola, WI: Motorbooks International, 1996. 192 p.)

5007. _____. *Milwaukee Road 261: a steam locomotive for the 21st century.* David City, NE: South Platte Press, 2004. 80 p.

5008. _____. *Minnesota railroad guide: a guide to Minnesota's railroads, railroad museums, rail historical societies and more.* Shoreview, MN: Minnesota Railroad Guide, 2001. 165 p.

5008a. _____. *Minnesota railroads: a photographic history, 1940-2012* / Minneapolis: University of Minnesota press, 2012. 288 p.

5009. _____. *Regional railroads of America: Midwest.* St. Paul, MN: Voyageur Press, 2007. 160 p.

5010. _____. *Santa Fe Railway.* Osceola, WI: Motorbooks International, 1997. 128 p.

5011. _____. *Santa Fe Railway.* Minneapolis, MN: Voyageur Press, 2008. 160 p.

5011a. _____, Jeff Terry. *Official guidebook, Lake Superior Railroad Museum and North Shore Scenic Railroad* / Duluth, MN: Lake Superior Railroad Museum, 2013. 76 p.

5012. Glover, James Edward. *The click of the rails.* Jackson, Tenn., The Railroader, 1929. 180 p.

5013. Glover, Thomas O., Melvin E. Hinkle, Harold L. Riley. *Unit train transportation of coal: technology and description of nine representative operations.* Washington, DC: U.S. Bureau of Mines, 1970. 109 p. (*Bureau of Mines information circular, 8444.*)

5014. Glover, Vernon J. *A brief history of the logging railroads of the Saginaw & Manistee Lumber Company: Kaibab and Coconino National Forests, Arizona.* Alburquerque, NM: V.J. Glover, 1983. 9 l. (Includes locomotive roster.)

5015. _____. *Jemez Mountains railroads: Santa Fe National Forest, New Mexico.* Albuquerque NM: USDA Forest Service, Southwestern Region, 1990. 77 p. (*Cultural resources management report no. 9.*)

5016. _____. *Logging railroads of Arizona.* 1990. 58 l. (Arizona Lumber & Timber Company; Central Arizona Railway.)

5017. _____. *Logging railroads of the Lincoln National Forest, New Mexico.* Albuquerque, NM: USDA Forest Service, Southwestern Region, 1989, 1984. 65 p. (*Cultural resources management report, no. 4.*)

5018. _____. *The railroad collection.* Santa Fe, NM: Museum of New Mexico, 1977. 86 p. (V. 1: Santa Fe Railroad; Atlantic & Pacific, New Mexico Central, Mexican Central.)

5019. _____. *Zuni Mountain railroads: Cibola National Forest, New Mexico.* Albuquerque, NM: USDA Forest Service, Southwestern Region, 1986. 88 p. (*Cultural resources management report, no. 6.*)

5020. *GM & O historical society news.* Joliet, IL: Gulf, Mobile and Ohio Historical Society, 1900s-   . Quarterly. Other title: Gulf, Mobile and Ohio historical society news.

5021. *GM & O news.* Mobile, AL: Gulf, Mobile and Ohio Railroad, 1900s. Monthly. Other titles: GM and O news; G M and O news; G M & O news; Gulf, Mobile and Ohio news.

5022. Goddard, Charles Backus, Joseph S. Hawkins. *Resolution of the legislature of Ohio, in favor of the construction of a railroad from Lake Michigan to the Pacific Ocean, on the plan of Asa Whitney.* Washington, DC: Tippin & Streeper, Printers, 1848. 2 p.

5023. Goddard, Stephen B. *Getting there: the epic struggle between road and rail in the American century.* New York, Basic Books, 1994. 351 p. (Also: Chicago, University of Chicago Press, 1996. 351 p.)

5024. Godfrey, Aaron Austin. *Government operation of the railroads, 1918-1920; its necessity, success, and consequences.* Austin, TX: Jenkins Publishing Company, 1974. 190 p.

5025. Godwin, H.C. *Railroad engineers' field-book and explorers' guide/* New York, J. Wiley & Sons, 1890. 358 p.

5026. Goebel, G.L. *Highway trailer rail service /* New York : American Society of Mechanical Engineers, 1951. 19, 15 p. (*Paper no. 81-A-82.*)

5027. Goellner, Don. *Safety of high speed guided ground transportation systems: broadband magnetic fields, their possible role in EMF-associated bioeffects/* Washington, DC: Federal Railroad Administration, Office of Research and Development, 1993. 220 p. in various pagings. (*DOT/FRA/ORD-93/29*)

5028. _____. *Safety of high speed guided ground transportation systems: review of existing EMF guidelines, standards and regulations.* Washington, DC: Federal Railroad Administration, Office of Research and Development, 1993. 74 p. (*DOT/FRA/ORD-93/27*)

5029. Goen, Steve Allen. *Cotton Belt color pictorial.* La Mirada, CA: Four Ways West Publications, 199-? 126 p.

5030. _____. *"Down south" on the Rock Island: a color pictorial, 1940-1969.* La Mirada, CA: Four Ways West Publications, 2002. 128 p.

5031. _____. *Fort Worth & Denver: color pictorial.* La Mirada, CA: Four Ways West Publishing, 1996. 128 p.

5032. _____. *Kansas City Southern color pictorial.* La Mirada, CA: Four Ways West Publishing, 1999. 128 p.

5033. _____. *Miss Katy in the Lone Star State.* La Mirada CA: Four Ways West Publishing, 2006- (v. 1: The good old days, 1942-1960.)

5034. _____. *Santa Fe in the Lone Star State color pictorial; 1949-1969.* La Mirada, CA: Four Ways West Publishing, 2000- 144 p. (v.1: 1949-1960.)

5035. _____. *Texas & New Orleans color pictorial, 1944-1961: Southern Pacific's Texas and Louisiana lines.* La Mirada, CA: Four Ways West Publishing, 2004. 128 p.

5036. _____. *Texas & Pacific color pictorial.* La Mirada, CA: Four Ways West Publishing, 1997. 127 p.

5037. Goforth, James A. *Building the Clinchfield: a construction history of America's most unusual railroad.* 2d ed. Erwin, TN: Gem Publishers, 1989. 122 p. (1st ed.: Gem Publishers, 1983. 106 p.)

5038. _____. *When steam ran the Clinchfield.* Johnson City, TN: Overmountain Press, 1998, 1991. 105 p. (Locomotive roster compiled by Charles K. Marsh.) (2d ed.: Erwin, TN: Gem Publishers, 1993. 105 [.)

5039. Gohmann, John W. *Air and rail labor relations: a judicial history of the Railway Labor Act.* Dubuque, IA: Kendall/Hunt Publishing Company, 1979, 1976. 373 p.

5040. _____. *Arbitration and representation: applications in air and rail labor relations.* Dubuque, IA: Kendall/Hunt Publishing Company, 1981. 276 p.

5040a. _____. *Rail industry advertising during the Great Era.* Libertyville. IL: 14047 Petronella Dr., Ste. 201, Libertyville 60048: Railmode Press, Gohmann & Associates, 2011. 2 v.

5041. _____. *The Railway Labor Act: a judicial history.* Chicago, IL: Lake Shore Litho, 1976. 321 p.

5042. *Going places: workshop proceedings from the 4th National Rails-to-Trails Conference, September 29-October 2, 1993. Concord, California.* Washington, DC: Rails-to-Trails Conservancy, 1994.

5042a. Golay, Michael. *Railroad stations, depots and roundhouses* / New York : Barnes & Noble, 2000. 144 p.

5043. Gold Car Heating Company. *The "Gold" system of car heating is the standard of perfection...catalogue 1899-1900.* New York, Charles F. Bloom, Printer, 1899. 79 p.

5044. _____. *The "Gold systems" of car heating represent the highest development of the art.* New York, 1905. 1 v.

5045. Goldberg, Bruce. *Amtrak—the first decade.* Silver Spring, MD: Alan Books, 1981. 244 p.

5046. Goldberg, Robert G., William A. Creasey, Kenneth R. Foster. *Safety of high speed guided ground transportation systems: an overview of biological effects and mechanisms relevant to EMF exposures from mass transit and electric rail systems*/ Washington, DC: Federal Railroad Administration, Office of Research and Development, 1993. 176 p. (*DOT-VNTSC-FRA-93-19*)

5047. Goldberg, Susan Galloway, Malcolm R. Lovell, Beverly Prior Smaby. *CSX and the railway unions: in search of new solutions.* Washington, D.C., U.S. Department of Labor, Bureau of Labor-Management Relations and Cooperative Systems, 1990. 52 p. (*BLMR 140.*)

5048. Golden, James Reed. *Investment behavior by United States railroads, 1870-1914.* New York, NY: Arno Press, 1975. 301 p. (Thesis, Ph.D., Harvard University, 1972.)

5049. Golden Spike Symposium, University of Utah, 1969. *The golden spike.* David E. Miller, editor. Salt Lake City, Utah State Historical Society, 1973. 153 p.

5049a. *The Golden way : the journal of the Pullman Society.* Leatherhead : Pullman Society, 1980s-   . Quarterly.

5050. Goldmeer, Helen. *The New York, New Haven and Hartford Railroad in the twentieth century* / South Hadley, MA: s.n., 1938. 100, xliv leaves. (Honors Paper, Mount Holyoke College. Department of Economics and Sociology.)

5051. Goldsack, Bob. *Those wonderful, colorful, and exciting carnival trains.* Nashua, NH: Midway Museum Publications, 1991. 120 p.

5051a. Goldstein, Horace. *Design of a locomotive coaling station and comparison of costs of wooden and reinforced concrete structures* 1909. 42 l. (Thesis, M.S., University of Pennsylvania.)

5052. Goltra, W.F. *Characteristics of the Lake Erie & Western Railroad System, as existing January 1st, 1895.* Indianapolis, Ind., Press of Level Brothers & Co., 1895. 102 p.

5053. _____. *Some facts about treating railroad ties.* Cleveland, Ohio, Press of the J.B. Savage Company, 1912-1913. 6 v.

5054. Gomez, Manuel. *Trends in locomotive loadings as they affect bridge design*/ 1941. (M.S. Engineering, University of Florida.)

5055. Gooden, Orville Thrasher. *The Missouri and North Arkansas Railroad strike.* New York, Columbia University Press, 1926. 274 p. (*Studies in history, economics and public law, no. 275.*)

5056. Goodman, Edward C. *Writing the rails: train adventures by the world's best –loved writers.* New York, Black Dog & Levanthal: Distributed by Workman Publishing, 2001. 368 p.

5057. Goodman, Nan. *Shifting the blame: literature, law, and the theory of accidents in nineteenth-century America.* Princeton, Princeton University Press, 1998. 198 p.

5058. Goodnow, William T. *Investigation of the Lehigh Valley coal stocking grounds at Perth Amboy, N.J.* 1883. 40 l. (Thesis, C.E., Lehigh University.)

5059. Goodrich, Carter. *Government promotion of American canals and railroads, 1800-1890.* New York: Columbia University Press, 1960. 382 p.

5060. Goodrich, Carter Lyman. *Earnings and standard of living of 1,000 railway employees during the Depression.* Washington, DC: U.S. G.P.O., 1934. 56 p. (United States. Bureau of Labor Statistics. United States. Children's Bureau. United States. Women's Bureau.)

5061. Goodrich, Carter Lyman. *A survey of 1,000 families during the Great Depression: changes in the standard of living for railway workers*/ American Fork, Utah, Seven Suns Distribution, 2008, 1934. 91 p. (United States. Bureau of Labor Statistics; United States. Children's Bureau; United States. Women's Bureau.)

5062. Goodrich, Charles F. *The Martinez-Benica Bridge: a double track railroad structure 5803 feet long completed in 1930; a description of the design and erection of the steel superstructure built for Southern Pacific Company by American Bridge*

Company. S.l., American Bridge Co., United States Steel Corp., 1930. 35 p.

5063. Goodrich, Ernest Payson, Harry P. Nichols. *Report upon the elimination of surface freight railroad tracks of the New York Central and Hudson River Railroad : and A general scheme of improved freight handling facilities at the port of New York /* New York : M.B. Brown Printing and Binding, 1911. 107 p.

5064. Goodrich, Frederick "Abe". *Abe's ABC of the Texas-type locomotive.* Floreffe, Penn., The Author? 1945. 69 p.

5065. Goodrick, Sanford, William C. Janssen, Bill Marvel. *Under Milwaukee wires: the color photography of Sanford Goodrick and William C. Janssen.* Edison, NJ: Morning Sun Books, 1996. 128 p.

5066. Goodwin Car Company. *Goodwin patent steel gravity dumping car, especially adapted to the coal and ore trade'* operated by compressed air apparatus or by hand power ... / New York, Goodwin Car Co., 1889? 32 l. (Steel construction.)

5067. Goolsby, Larry. *Atlanta, Birmingham & Coast.* Valrico, FL: Atlantic Coast Line & Seaboard Ail Line Railroads Historical Society, 2000. 248 p.

5068. _____. *Atlantic Coast Line passenger service: the postwar years.* Lynchburg, VA: TLC Publishing, 1999. 142 p.

5069. Goolsby, James H., Hugh M. Comer, Albert M. Langley. *Central of Georgia Railway steam locomotives and trains.* N. Augusta, SC: Union Station, 2006. 68 p.

5070. Gordon, Alexander. *Accidents at grade crossing and to trespassers.* San Francisco : Southern Pacific Railway Company, 1916. 23 p.

5071. Gordon, Sarah. *Passage to Union: how the railroads transformed American life, 1829-1929.* Chicago, Ivan R. Dee, 1996. 403 p.

5072. _____. *A society of passengers: rail travel 1865 to 1910.* 1981. (Thesis, Ph.D., University of Chicago, Department of History.)

5073. Gordon, William Reed. *Stories and history of the Erie Railroad, Rochester Division; steam and diesels, 1854-1964, electric from 1907-1934: 110 years of Erie service in the Genesee Valley.* Rochester? NY: 1965. 144 p.

5074. _____. *The story of the Buffalo, Lockport, and Rochester Railway, 1908-1919; the Rochester, Lockport and Buffalo Corporation, April 1919-April 30, 1931. With trackage rights over the International Railway Company, Lockport Division to Buffalo, Niagara Falls and Olcott Beach.* Rochester, N.Y., 1963. 84 p.

5075. Gorman, J.E. *On the human side of railroading.* Chicago, Rock Island and Pacific Railway Co., 1929. 15 p.

5076. Gorman, Roscoe W. *The flight of the midnight mail.* Atlanta, Dittler Bros, 1930, 1905. 42 p. (Atlanta & West Point Railroad Co.) "First published as articles in Atlanta Constitution, Atlanta Journal and Atlanta News, 1905."

5077. Gormley, M. J. *Adequacy and efficiency of railway equipment.* Washington, DC: American Railway Association, Car Service Division, 1929. 11 p.

5078. Gorzoch, Jerry, Jack Polaritz, Joe Sparico. *Freight car equipment of the Pittsburgh & Lake Erie Railroad.* New Kent, VA: Kahndog Publications, 2003- (v.1: P&LE's gondola cars.)

5079. Goss, W.F.M. (William Freeman Myrick) *High steam-pressures in locomotive service.* Washington, D.C., Carnegie Institution of Washington, 1907. 6, 144 p. (*Carnegie Institution of Washington publication, no. 66.*)

5080. _____. *Locomotive performance; the result of a series of researches conducted by the Engineering Laboratory of Purdue University.* New York, Wiley, 1907. 439 p.

5081. _____. *Locomotive sparks.* New York, J. Wiley & Sons, 1902. 172 p. (Reissue: New York, J. Wiley & Sons, 1907. 172 p.)

5082. _____. *Locomotive tests: from a publication of the Pennsylvania Railroad entitled Locomotive tests and exhibits, the Pennsylvania Railroad system at the Louisiana Purchase Exposition: a compilation.* New York, American Locomotive Company, 1906. 55 p. (Code word: CALDERILLA.)

5082a. [Scientific and technical papers] 1891-1927. 2 v. Location: Purdue University.

5083. _____. *Smoke abatement and electrification of railway terminals in Chicago; report of the Chicago Association of Commerce, Committee of Investigation on Smoke Abatement and Electrification of Railway Terminals.* Chicago, Rand McNally, 1915. 1177 p. (Reprint with added commentary: See entry 4225.)

5084. _____. *Superheated steam in locomotive service.* Washington, D.C., Carnegie Institution of Washington, 1910. 144 p. (*Carnegie Institution of Washington publication, no. 127.*)

5085. _____. *Tests of a Jacobs-Shupert boiler in comparison with a radial-stay boiler.* Coatesville, Pa., Jacobs-Shupert United States Firebox Company, 1912. 171 p.

5086. _____. *The utilization of fuel in locomotive practice.* Washington, D.C., GPO, 1909. 28 p. (*Geological Survey (U.S.) bulletin, 402.*)

5087. Gossard, Gloria Hine. *Tehachapi* / Charleston, SC: Arcadia Pub., 2007. 127 p.

5088. Gossard, Steve. *A history of the Chicago & Alton Railroad stations in Bloomington-Normal, Illinois.* Bloomington, IL: Steve Gossard, 1991. 44 p.

5089. Gould C. Dale. *Blackie's railroad handbook: all you ever wanted to know about railroad slang (lingo), signs, signals and definitions but didn't know who to ask/* Yorba Linda, CA: Railroad Lingo, 1976. 32 p.

5090. Gould, Charles D., Ross Winans. *To [blank}. On the 1st October, 1834, letters patent were issued to Ross Winans, of Baltimore, Maryland, "for a new and useful improvement in the construction of cars or carriages intended to run on railroad, "known as the eight wheel railroad car... "* Albany, NY: s.n., 1851. 4 p. (the last 3 p. blank).

5091. Gould, Jay. *The Union Pacific Railroad Company, in equity, vs. The Credit Mobilier of America; plaintiff's brief.* Suffolk County, N.Y., s.n., 1875. 28 p.

5092. Gould, William John Gilbert. *My life on mountain railroads.* William R. Gould, editor. Logan, UT: Utah State University Press, 1995. 250 p.

5093. Gove, Bill. *J.E. Henry's logging railroads: the history of the East Branch & Lincoln and the Zealand Valley railroads.* Littleton, NH: Bondcliff Books, 1998. 187 p. (Rev. and expanded ed.: 2012. 293 p.)

5094. _____. *Logging railroads of New Hampshire's north country.* Littleton, NH : Bondcliff Books, 2010. 159 p.

5095. _____. *Logging railroads of the Adirondacks.* Syracuse, NY: Syracuse University Press, 2006. 256 p.

5096. _____ *Logging railroads of the Saco River Valley.* Littleton, NH: Bondcliff Books, 2001. 141 p.

5097. _____. *Sky Route to the quarries: history of the Barre Railroad.* Barre? VT: Quarry View Pub., 2004. 97 p.

5098. *Government ownership and operation of railroads. Formal action as taken by national, regional, state and local business organizations, 1936. S. 2573, H.R. 10,595.* Chicago, IL: Printed by the Railway Business Association, 1936. 742 p.

5099. *Government ownership of railways : a list of publications, 1938-May 1939 /* Washington, DC: Bureau of Railway Economics, Library, 1939. 21 l.

5100. Gowan, F.D., B.A. Widell, A. Bredenberg. *A new electric locomotive for the Pennsylvania Railroad /* New York : AIEE, 1951. 14, 8 p. (*AIEE Technical paper, 52-53.*)

5101. Gowen, Franklin B. *Philadelphia & Reading Railroad Company.* Philadelphia, Penn., Jackson Brothers, 1881. 62 p.

5102. _____ *The railway problem. Address of Mr. Franklin B. Gowen, on the position which the city of Philadelphia should occupy to the commonwealth of Pennsylvania, to its transportation lines, and to the railway problem of the day.* Philadelphia : Jackson Bros, Printers, 1881. 61 p.

5103. _____, *Statement of the present condition of the Philadelphia & Reading Railroad Co., and the Philadelphia & Reading Coal and Iron Co.: with plan for the financial re-organization.* Philadelphia : Jackson Bros, Printers, 1880. 81 p.

5103a. Gowen, Sumner. *Computations for railroad bridge, single track – span 440 ft. /* 1897. 46 l. (Thesis, B.S., Massachusetts Institute of Technology, Department of Civil Engineering.)

5104. *The GP20 and SD24: EMD's turbocharged duo.* Halifax, PA: Withers Pub., 1998. 136 p. (*Diesel era*)

5105. Grace, Patricia Elizabeth. *A history of railroad pensions in the United States, 1875-1937: a case study in reform.* 1967. 91 l. (Thesis, M.A., Ohio State University.)

5106. *Grade crossing technologies—the new millennium.* College Station TX: Texas A&M University System, Texas Transportation Institute, 2000. 209 p. Conference proceedings, October 17-19, Texas Transportation Institute, Texas A&M University,)

5107. *Grade separation; a report compiled by the Chamber of Commerce of the United States, Civic Development Department, John Ihlder, Manager.* 13 p.

5108. *Grafton Greenough; a brief sketch of his life.* (Written by his sister.) Philadelphia ? s.n., 1926. 33 p. (Baldwin Locomotive Works)

5109. Graham, F. Stewart. *The locomotives of the Delaware, Lackawanna and Western Railroad.* Boston, Mass., The Railway & Locomotive Historical Society, 1948. 143 p. (Its *Bulletin, no. 72.*)

5110. Graham, Kenneth Ralph. *Strategy, management change, and economic perfor-mance in rail-based holding companies /* 1985. 128 l. (Thesis, Ph.D., Pennsylvania State University.)

5111. Graham, Lloyd J., Jim F. Martin. *Ultrasonic inspection of railroad rails by electromagnetic acoustic tranducers (EMATS).* Washington, DC: Federal Railroad Administration, office of Research and Development, 1986. 239 p. (*FRA/ORD-86/09.*)

5112. Graham, Maury, Robert J. Hemming. *Tales of the iron road: my life as king of the hobos.* New York, Paragon House, 1990. 222 p.

5113. Graham, Thomas H. *The development of later types of locomotives used by the Baltimore and Ohio Railroad Company.* College Park, MD: 1929. 6, 8 l. (Records of Phi Mu, University of Maryland at College Park Libraries.)

5114. Graham-White, Sean. *GE Evolution locomotives.* St. Paul, MBI, 2007. 144 p.

5115.. *Grand Central alternative: Long Island Rail Road East Midtown Terminal.* New York, Parsons Brinckerhoff-Gibbs & Hill; Metropolitan Transportation Authority, 1982, 1976. 116 l.

5116. *Grand Central Terminal: city within the city.* Deborah Nevins, general editor. Foreword by Jacqueline Kenney Onassis, essays by Deborah Nevins... [et al.] [New York] : Municipal Art Society of New York, 1982. 145 p.

5117. *Grand Central Terminal, New York City: The New York Central System.* [New York: New York Central System, ca. 1947.12 p.

5118. *Grand Lodge proceedings of the...biennial convention...at...*Toronto, etc., The Brotherhood of Locomotive Firemen and Enginemen, 1898-1904. 4 v. (*<Journal of proceedings of the ...biennial convention of the Brotherhood of Locomotive Firemen, held in...> Report of the Grand Master of the Brotherhood of Locomotive Firemen to the...biennial convention.*)

5119. Grande, Walter R. *The Northwest's own railway: Spokane, Portland & Seattle Railway and its subsidiaries.* Portland, OR: Grand Press, 1992-1997. 2 v.

5120. _____, Richard F. Lind. *Rails to the Pacific Northwest.* Boulder, CO: R.F. Lind, 1964. 130 p.

5121. *Grande gold: photos by Andy M. Payne; edited by James S. Eakin.* Canton, OH: Railhead Publications, 1989. 120 p.

5121a. Grandpré, Ambrose Goulet. *A study of elevated railroad* structures / 1906. 54 l. (Thesis, B.S., University of Illinois.)

5122. Grandt, Robert L. *Gondolas, boxcars and flatcars of the D & RGW.* Oakland, CA: R. Robb, 1984. 208 p.(*Narrow gauge pictorial, v. 3.*)

5123. _____. *The Grande Mountains: the standard gauge 4-8-2s of the Denver and Rio Grande Western.* S.l., R.L. Grandt, 1998. 188 p.

5124. _____. *Locomotives of the D & RGW.* Oakland, CA: R. Robb, 1997. 192 p. (*Narrow gauge pictorial, v. 11.*)

5125. _____. *Numbered work cars of the D & RGW.* Oakland, CA: R. Robb, 1993. 1 v. (*Narrow gauge pictorial, v. 10.*)

5126. _____. *Passenger cars of the D & RGW.* Oakland, CA: R. Robb, 1982. 191 p. (*Narrow gauge pictorial, v. 2.*)

5127. _____. *Refrigerator cars, stock cars, and tank cars.* Oakland, CA: R. Robb, 1985. 176 p. (*Narrow gauge pictorial, v. 4.*)

5128. _____. *Rio Grande Southern and D & RGW motive power.* Oakland, CA:

R. Robb, 1981. 176 p. (*Narrow gauge pictorial, v. 1.*)

5129. _____. *Rio Grande Southern right-of-way and structures, Rico to Durango.* Oakland, CA: R. Robb, 1992. 160 p. (*Narrow gauge pictorial, v. 9.*)

5130. _____, J.L. Hubbard, John W. Maxwell. *Cabooses of the D & RGW.* Oakland, CA: R. Robb, 1987. 160 p. (*Narrow gauge pictorial, v. 5.*)

5131. Granger, J.T. *A brief biographical sketch of the life of Major-General Grenville M. Dodge/* New York, Press of Styles & Cash, 1893. 128 p. (Reprint: New York, Arno Press, 1981. 128 p.)

5132. Grant, Arthur W., Casimer J. Welligen, John J. Raby. *Hot box sensor /* Washington, DC : Patent and Trademark Office, 1970. 3 l. United States Patent : 3,540, 459.

5133. Grant, H. Roger. *The Corn Belt Route: a history of the Chicago Great Western Railroad Company.* DeKalb, IL: Northern Illinois University Press, 1984. 231 p.

5134. _____. *Erie Lackawanna: death of an American railroad, 1938-1992.* Stanford, CA: Stanford University Press, 1994. 284 p.

5135. _____. *"Follow the flag." A history of the Wabash Railroad Company.* DeKalb, IL: Northern Illinois University Press, 2004. 291 p.

5136. _____. *Kansas depots.* Topeka, KS: Kansas State Historical Society, 1990. 117 p.

5137. _____. *Living in the depot: the two-story railroad station.* Iowa City, IA: University of Iowa Press, 1993. 131 p. (American land and life series.)

5138. _____. *The North Western: a history of the Chicago & North Western Railway system.* DeKalb, IL: Northern Illinois University Press, 1996. 292 p.

5139. _____. *Ohio's railway age in postcards.* Akron, OH: University of Akron Press, 1996. 203 p.

5140. _____. *The railroad: the life story of a technology.* Westport, CT: Greenwood Press, 2005. 182 p.

5141. _____. *Railroad postcards in the age of steam.* Iowa City, IA: University of Iowa Press, 1994. 208 p.

5141a. _____. *Railroads and the American people /* Bloomington; Indiana University press, 2012. 309 p.

5142. _____. *Railroads in the heartland: steam and traction in the golden age of postcards.* Iowa City, IA: University of Iowa Press, 1997. 181 p.

5143. _____. *Rails through the wiregrass: a history of the Georgia & Florida Railroad.* DeKalb, IL: Northern Illinois University Press, 2006. 223 p.

5144. _____. *Richard C. Overton: railroad historian.* Lexington, KY: The Lexington Group, 1998. 120 p.

5145. _____. *Twilight rails: the final era of railroad building in the Midwest /* Minneapolis: University of Minnesota Press, 2010. 275 p.

5146. _____. *Visionary railroader: Jervis Langdon Jr. and the transportation revolution.* Bloomington, Indiana University Press, 2008. 258 p. (*Railroads past and present.*)

5147. _____. *We took the train.* DeKalb, IL: Northern Illinois University Press, 1990. 175 p.

5148. _____, Charles W. Bohi. *The country railroad station in America.* Boulder, CO: Pruett Publishing Company, 1978. (Revised and enlarged edition: Sioux Falls, SD: Center for Western Studies, Augustana College, 1988. 183 p.

5149. _____, Donovan L. Hofsommer, Osmund Overby. *St. Louis Union Station: a place for people, a place for trains.* St. Louis, MO: St. Louis Mercantile Library, 1994. 127 p.

5150. _____, Ronald J. Manheimer, Sylvia Riggs Liroff. *We got there on the train: railroads in the lives of the American people.* Washington, D.C., National Council on the Aging, 1989. 197 p. (*Discovery through the humanities.*)

5151. Grant, John. *Great American rail journeys: the companion to the public television programs.* Guilford, CT: Globe Pequot Press, 2000. 194 p.

5152. Grant Locomotive Works. *A description of locomotives manufactured by the Grant Locomotive Works of Peterson, N.J.* New York, J. Sutton & Company, 1871. 16 l. (Reprint: Boulder, CO: Pruett Publishing Company, 1971. 1 v.)

5153. Grasso, Jack. *Diamondbugs: the story of the rail motor cars on the Erie Railroad.* Flanders, NJ: RAE Publishing, 1999. 64 p.

5154. _____. *Operation CUT—the first 30 years: the story of the rail operations out of Cleveland Union Terminal in "railroading's golden age".* Flanders, NJ: RAE Publishing, 2003. 72 p.

5155. Gratz, David E. *The Monongahela Railway: its history and operation /* S.l., D.E. Gratz, 1997. 76 p.

5156. _____, Terry E. Arbogast. *The Monongahela Railway /* Washingtonville, OH: M2FQ Publications, 2003. 212 p.

5157. Graves, Albert H., Gerald L. Kline. *Loading boxcars at country elevators in the hard winter wheat area/* Washington, D.C., USDA, Agricultural Research Service, 1964. 32 p. (*Kansas Agricultural Experiment Station. Marketing research report, no. 676.*)

5158. Gravity Measuring Coal Chute Company. *Coaling stations for locomotives.* Roanoke, Va., Stone Printing & Manufacturing Company, 1911. 24 p.

5159. Gray, A.B. *Southern Pacific Railroad: survey of a route for the Southern Pacific R.R., on the 32nd parallel … for the Texas Western R.R. Company.* Cincinnati, OH: Wrightson & Co's … Print., 1856. 110 p. 36 leaves of plates.

5160. Gray, Carl R. *The Lincoln car on Union Pacific, 1865.* Princeton, N.J., Princeton University Press, 1937. 22 p.

5160a. Gray, George. *The law which determines the rights of the Northern Pacific R.R. Co. to its land grant.* New York: E.W. Sackett & Rankin, 1882. 8 p.

5161. Gray, Henry L. *Historic railroads of Washington.* Seattle, s.n., 1971. 26 p.

5162. Gray, J.R. (Bob) Gray. *Depots and maintenance shops along the C & G Railway, Mississippi* / Mississippi State, MS : MSU Printing, 2009. 33 p. Columbus and Greenville Railway.

5163. Gray, Richard Henry. *Railway connections and junction points; a systematic compilation, showing conjointly information as to passenger and freight connections between various railroads in the United States* / Baltimore, H.K. Camman, 1917.

5164. _____. *Railway connections and junction points.* S.l., s.n., 1916. 1 v.

5165. Gray, Thomas C. *Pullman-Standard's train X.* Chicago, IL: Pullman-Standard Manufacturing Company, 1955. 26 p.

5166 _____. *Realistic goals for railway passenger car design* / New York : American Society of Mechanical Engineers, 1954. 8 p. (*ASME. Paper no. 54-A-49.*)

5167. Gray, Walter P., John P. Hankey. *Pictorial history of North American railroads.* Contributing writers: Paul Hammond, Jim Wrinn, and Karl Zimmermann. Lincolnwood, IL: Publications International, 1996. 312 p.

5168. _____, Michael V. Speer, Stephen E. Drew. *Steam train to Sacramento: Walnut Grove branch line acquisition feasibility study.* Sacramento, CA: California State Railroad Museum, 1980. 67 p.

5169. Gray, William Enoch, C.W. Messersmith. *Development of draft gears for American freight cars.* Lafayette, Ind., Purdue University, 1936. 149 p.

5170. Graybeal, Johnny. *Along the ET&WNC.* Hickory, NC: Tarheal Press, 2001-

(v. 1: Early narrow gauge locomotives. v. 2: The ten wheelers.)

5171. _____. *The railroads of Johnson City* / Hickory, NC: Tarheel Press, 2007. 202 p. (Johnson City, Tennessee. East Tennessee & Western North Carolina Railroad. East Tennessee and Virginia Railroad Company. Clinchfield Railroad.

5172. Great Britain. Consulate. Philadelphia. *Report to Her Majesty's government on the Pennsylvania Railroad* / London : Printed by Harrison and Sons, 1884. 4, 9-93 p. (*Commercial. No. 38, 1884.* "Report from Her Majesty's diplomatic and consular officers abroad on subjects of commercial and general interest; pt. IV.")

5173. Great Northern Railway Company. *The autobiography of an engine: the story of the William Cooke and its big brother no. 2500.* St. Paul, Minn., Great Northern Railway, 1925. 16 p.(Also: 1939. 23 p.)

5174. _____ *The Cascade Mountain crossing of the Great Northern Railway.* St. Paul? Minn., Great Northern Railway, 1929. 14 p.

5175. _____. *The Empire Builder.* St. Paul? Minn., The Railway, 1929? 31 p.

5175a. _____. Engineering Department. [Records] 1882-1970. 105 cubic feet. Location: Minnesota Historical Society.

5175b. _____. _____. [Drawings of structures] 1882-1964. 15 map drawers, ca 1,000 drawings. Location:

5176. _____. *Great Northern Railway long tunnel through Cascade Range.* St. Paul? Minn., Great Northern Railway, 1926. 16 p.

5177. _____. *Last year of the "Switch-back" ...* / 2d ed. St. Paul : Great Northern Railway, Passenger Department, 1900. 19 p. (*Great Northern pocket-book, no. 7.*)

5178. _____. *Locomotive diagrams.* St. Paul, Minn., Great Northern Railway, 1921. 173 l. Plans.

5179. _____. *Locomotive diagrams.* St. Paul, Minn., Great Northern Railway Company, Motor Power Department, 1941. 282 l. Plans.

5179a. [Mechanical Department, records. 1879-1969.] 127.5 cubic feet. Mechanical drawings and other records. Location: Minnesota Historical Society.

5180. _____. *New Cascade Tunnel.* St. Paul? Minn., Great Northern Railway, 1929? 14 p.

5181. _____. *Official directory and atlas: giving alphabetical list of stations, stock yards, track scales, etc., and list of shippers and dealers in staple commodities on lines, owned, leased, or operated by the Great Northern Railway line*/ Saint Paul? Minn., The Company, 1903. 260 p. 6 p. of plates. (General Freight Department.)

5181a. _____. Operating Department. [Records] 1874-1969. 90 cubic feet. Location: Minnesota Historical Society

5182. _____. *The Oriental Limited.* Saint Paul, Minn., Great Northern Railway, 1914. 14 p.

5183. _____ *Origin of station names in Montana.* S.l., s.n., 1937. 20 l.

5184. _____. *Rules and information for the handling of oil burning locomotives, stationary boilers and oil tank cars.* S.l., Great Northern Railway Co., 1924. 22 p. "Printed June 1st, 1911. Revised May 16, 1924."

5186. _____. *Rules and instructions for the maintenance of way and structures, electrical, signal, telegraph and telephone employees.* St. Paul, Minn., The Company, 1945. 96 p.

5187. _____. *Statement of origin of station names: lines west of Williston.* S.l., s.n., 1940? (Engineering Division.)

5188. _____. *Steam locomotive diagrams.* Chula Vista, CA: J.W. Sheets, 1952. vi l., 100 l. of plates, chiefly plans.

5188a. _____. [Steam locomotive record books] 1901-1956. 1 v. on 1 microfilm reel. Location: Minnesota Historical Society.

5189. _____. [Magazine and newspaper advertisements, 1884-1970; magazine and newspaper articles and other publicity, 1911-1943.] St. Paul, Minn., Minnesota Historical Society, 1980. (Great Northern Railway Company: Advertising and Publicity Department.)

5189a. _____, Western Pacific Railroad Company. *The application of the Great Northern and the Western Pacific for permission to connect their two railroads* / San Francisco: Great Northern Railway and the Western Pacific Railway, 1929. 15 p.

5190. *Great Northern bulletin.* St. Paul: Great Northern Railway Co., General Passenger Department, 1890-1919. Monthly.

5191. *The Great Northern goat.* Mankato, MN: Great Northern Railway Historical Society, 1982-   . Quarterly. (< Fraternal Order of Empire Builders. *Report of proceedings.)*

5192. *The Great Northern goat.* St. Paul, MN: Great Northern Railway, 1924-1970. 40 v. Frequency varies. (< Fraternal Order of Empire Builders. *Report of proceedings.*)

5193. *Great Northern Pacific Steamship Company : operating the floating palaces of the Pacific.* San Francisco: The Company, 1914? 15 p.

5194. *The Great Northern Railway electrification.* S.l., Great Northern Railway Historical Society, 1985, 1929. 23 p. (Originally published: East Pittsburgh, Pa., Westinghouse Electric & Manufacturing Company, 1929.)

5195. *Great Northern Railway, 1945-1970: photo archive.* Edited with introduction by Byron D. Olsen. Osceola, WI: Iconografix, 1996. 126 p.

5196. *Great Northern Railway photograph catalogue: steam, diesel, electric, maintenance of way & miscellaneous equipment.* Lompoc? CA: The Organization, 1973- (Fraternal Order of Empire Builders; Great Northern Historical Society & Scale Replica Railway Association.)

5197. *Great Northern semaphore.* Saint Paul: Great Northern Railway, 1925-1900s. Monthly.

5198. *Great railroad paintings.* Edited and with an introduction by Robert Goldsborough. New York, Peacock Press/Bantam Book, 1976. 96 p.

5199. *Great railroad photographs from the collection of the Smithsonian Institution.* Compiled by John Winthrop Adams. Philadelphia, PA: Courage Books, 1994. 128 p. (Smithsonian Institution; National Museum of American History, Division of Transportation.)

5200. *The Great Southwest of the Fred Harvey Company and the Santa Fe Railway.* Edited by Marta Weigle and Barbara A. Babcock. Phoenix, AZ: Heard Museum; Tucson, AZ: Distributed by the University of Arizona Press, 1996. 254 p.

5201. *The Great Western magazine.* Chicago: Chicago Great Western Railroad Company, 1922-? Monthly.

5202. Greater Pittsburgh Chamber of Commerce. *The insurrection among the railway employees of the United States, and the losses in Pittsburgh resulting therefrom, in July 1877 : memorial of the Pittsburgh Chamber of commerce, to the Pennsylvania Legislature.* Pittsburgh : Stevenson, Foster & Co., 1877. 16 p.

5203. Greater San Francisco Chamber of Commerce. *Central Pacific-Southern Pacific dismemberment. Transportation chaos is threatened if present unified railway system is torn apart.* San Francisco: Greater San Francisco Chamber of Commerce; Committee of the Business Interests of California, 1922. 8 p.

5204. Greco, Thomas J., Karl D. Spence. *Dining on the B&O: recipes and sidelights from a bygone age.* Baltimore, MD: Johns Hopkins University Press, 2009. 170 p.

5205. Green Bay and Western Railroad Company; Kewaunee, Green Bay and Western Railroad Company. *Rules and instruction for the government of employees of the Transportation Department.* Green Bay, WI: The Companies, 1950. 110 p.

5205a. Green, DeLeon Fillyaw. *Atlantic Coast Line Railway and North Carolina truckers*

/ Thesis, B.A., 11 l. 1907. University of North Carolina, Chapel Hill.

5206. *Green diamond* / S.l., Illinois Central Historical Society, 1900s- Three times a year. Former: Irregular.

5207. Green, Gene. *Chicago & North Western official color photography*. Scotch Plains, NJ: Morning Sun Books, 1999. 128 p.

5208. _____. *Chicago Great Western color guide to freight and passenger equipment*. Scotch Plains, NJ: Morning Sun Books, 1998. 127 p.

5209. _____. *Minneapolis & St. Louis in color: Minneapolis & St. Louis Railway, the Peoria Gateway*. Edison, NJ: Morning Sun Books, 1996. 128 p.

5210. _____. *Refrigerator car color guide*. Scotch Plains, NJ: Morning Sun Books, 2005. 128 p.

5211. *Green light*. Denver: Colorado Historical Society, 1940-?

5212. *Green light*. Denver; Denver and Rio Grande Western Railroad Company, 1957- . Bimonthly. Other title: Rio Grande green light.

5213. *Green light: the newsletter of the Rio Grande Modeling & Historical Society*. Colorado Springs: RGMHS, 2000s-   . Bimonthly.

5214. Green, Richard. *The Northern Pacific Railway of McGee and Nixon: classic photographs of equipment and environment during the 1930-1955 period*. Seattle, WA: Northwest Short Line, 1985. 270 p. (2d ed.: Seattle, WA: Northwest Short Lines, 1995. 270 p.)

5215. Green, Stanley C. *The history of the Tex Mex Railway*. 2d ed. Laredo, TX: Border Studies Center, 1996. (Webb County Heritage Foundation.)

5216. Green, William. *Problems of railroad workers*/ Washington, DC: American Federation of Labor, 1930. 21 p.

5217. Green, Winford L. *Railroading on the Illinois Central*/ Philadelphia, Xlibris Corp, 2007. 253 p.

5218. Greenawald, G. Dale. *The railroad era: business competition and the public interest*. Boulder, CO: Social Science Education Consortium, 1991. 67 p. (*Public issues series.*)

5219. Greenberg, Dolores. *Financiers and railroads, 1869-1889: a study of Morton, Bliss & Company*. Newark, University of Delaware Press, 1980. 286 p.

5220. Greenberg, William T., Frederick A. Kramer, Frederick A. Gleichmann. *The handsomest trains in the world: passenger service on the Lehigh Valley Railroad.*

Westfield, NJ: Bells & Whistles, 1978. 120 p.

5221. _____, Robert F. Fischer. *The Lehigh Valley Railroad: east of Mauch Chunk.* Warren, NJ: Gingerbread Shop, 1997. 192 p.

5221a. Greenberger, Daniel. *As honest as the sun : Thomas Durant and the building of the Union Pacific Railroad.* 1986. 46 l. (Thesis, M.F.A., Columbia University.)

5221b. Greene, O. C. *Cipher book* / Saint Paul, MN: Northern Pacific Railroad Company, 1892. 206 p. (Cipher and telegraph codes)

5222 Greenhill, Ralph Donor. *Pan-American Express: the new train between New York and Buffalo and Niagara Falls.* Buffalo : Matthews-Northrup, 1901. 32 p. (*Four track series, no. 15.*) New York and Hudson River Railroad Company.

5223. Greenough, Grafton. *Log of the "Philadelphia", with Mr. Samuel M. Vauclain and party to the South and South-west, April 4-April 26, 1923.* Philadelphia, s.n. 1923. 87 p.

5224. _____. *Mallet articulated compound locomotives.* Philadelphia, Pa., Baldwin Locomotive Works, Burnham, Williams & Co., 1908. 44 p. (*Record of recent construction, no. 65.*)

5225. _____. *To Boulder and back; trip of Samuel M. Vauclain and party through the middle West, May 21-30, 1923.* Philadelphia, s.n., 1923. 66 p.

5226. Greenough, Jones & Company. *The American railway and supply directory of 1873: containing an official list of the officers and directors of the railroads in United States and Canada, together with their financial conditions, amount of rolling stock, etc./* Boston, Greenough, Jones & Co., 1873. 536, 58 p. ("Also, a railway supply directory of all the principal dealers in railway supplies in the United States, arranged under appropriate headings, lists of master car builders, master mechanics, railroad societies. &c.")

5227. Greenough, Sarah. *Walker Evans, subways and streets.* Washington, D.C., National Gallery of Art, 1991. 132 p.

5228. Greenville Steel Car Company. *Greenville freight cars.* Greenville, PA: Greenville Steel Car Co., 1949. 60, 3 p.

5229. _____. *Greenville GV-1 triple hopper car.* Greenville, PA : Greenville Steel Car Co., 1900s. 24 p.

5230. _____. *A pictorial record of Pittsburgh Forgings Company and the Greenville Steel Car Company.* Greenville, PA: Greenville Steel Car Company, 1946. 61 p.

5231. Greenwood, H.E., C.J. Girvin. *Locomotive test on East Broad Top Railroad.* 1893. 69 l. (Thesis, B.A., Pennsylvania State College.)

5232. Greever, William S. *Arid domain: the Santa Fe Railway and its western land grant.* Stanford, CA: Stanford University Press, 1954. 184 p.

5233. Grefe, Dana L. *The Iowa railfan guide.* Grimes, IA: D.L. Grefe, 12996. 124, 79 p.

5234. _____. *Trainwatcher's guide for the C&NW.* Grimes, IA: Dana L. Grefe, 1994. 100 p.

5235. Gregg, Robert. *Origin and development of the Tennessee Coal, Iron and Railroad Company.* New York, Newcomen Society of England, American Branch, 1948. 40 p.

5235a. Gregg, Washington Parker, Benjamin Pond. *The railroad laws and charters of the United States/* Boston: C.C. Little and J. Brown, 1851. 2 v. in 4.

5236. Gregory, Julian Arthur. *Improved and economic freight service for Manhattan, universal inland freight stations and industrial terminal building. August, 1925. The Port of New York Authority.* New York, W.P. Hukill, 1925. 25 p.

5237. Greller, James C. *New York subway cars.* Belleville, NJ: Xplorer Press, 1995. 160 p.

5238. _____. *Subway cars of the BMT.* Belleville, NJ: Xplorer Press, 1995? 170 p. (Brooklyn-Manhattan Transit Company.)

5239. _____, Edward B. Watson. *The Brooklyn Elevated.* Hicksville, NY: N.J. International, 198-? 118 p.

5240. Grenard, Ross. *Colorado & Southern: a personal memory of the standard gauge.* Designed and edited by John Krause and Ed Crist. Andover, NJ: Andover Junction Publications, 1987. 64 p.

5241. _____. *Requiem for the narrow gauge.* Canton, OH: Railhead Publications, 1985. 125 p. (D&RGW, Alamosa Division.)

5242. _____, Frederick A. Kramer. *East Broad Top to the mines and back.* Newton, NJ: Carstens Publications, 1980. 80 p.

5243. _____, James Sandrin. *Rio Grande: in color.* Edison, NJ: Morning Sun Books, 1992-2001. 3 v.

5244. _____, John Krause, Ed Crist. *Steam in the Alleghenies: Western Maryland.* Photography by Robert F. Collins and William P. Price. S.l., Carstens Publications, 1988. 82 p.

5245. Grensten, Ray. *Tracks of the iron horse.* Lewiston, MT: Grensten, 1979. 132 p. (Milwaukee Road)

5246. Gressette, Robert B. *A history of the Ocmulgee and Flint Railroad: also known as the Brisbane Railroad.* Tilton, GA: RB Publishing Company, 2002. 112 p.

5247. Grewer, Hazel E. *The new Oriental Limited, Great Northern Railway.* Saint Paul, Minn., Great Northern Railway, 192-? 24 p.

5248. Grey, Alan Hopwood. *A railroad across the mountains: choosing the route of the Union Pacific over the Eastern Rockies.* 1963. 199 l. (Thesis, Ph.D., University of Wisconsin, Madison.)

5249. Grice & Long. *Steam versus horse: Evidences of the practical and successful operation of Grice & Long's steam passenger cars for city and suburban railways.* New York, Baker & Godwin, Printers, 1865. 36 p.

5250. Grieshop, Anne M. *The machine in the roundhouse: American locomotive decoration, 1830-1875.* 1986. (Thesis, M.A., Bowling Green State University.)

5250a. Griffin, Clare E. *Some phases of the railway history of Illinois since* 1870 / 1918. 2, 164 [i.e. 168] 1 l. (Thesis, Ph.D., University of Illinois.)

5251. Griffin, Gene C., Byron L. Dorgan. *Hearing on rail freight transportation in North Dakota* / Fargo, ND: North Dakota State University, Upper Great Plains Transportation Institute, 2002. 14 l. (*UGPTI staff paper, no. 147.*) United States Senate, Committee on Commerce, Science, and Transportation. Bismarck, ND, March 27, 2002. Senator Byron Dorgan presiding.

5252. Griffin, J.F. *Streamlining effect on air resistance and smoke lifting on steam locomotives.* New York, American Society of Mechanical Engineers, 1948, 1 v.

5253. Griffin, James R. *Rio Grande Railroad.* St. Paul, MN: MBI, 2003. 142 p.

5254. Griffin, William E., Jr. *All lines north of Raleigh: a history of the Seaboard Air Lines Railway's Virginia Division.* S.l., W.E. Griffin, 1991. 160 p.

5255. _____. *Along the RF&P in Prince William County.* Prince William, VA: Prince William County Historical Commission, 1991. 30 p.

5256. _____. *The Atlantic and Danville Railway Company: the railroad of southside Virginia.* Richmond, VA: W.E. Griffin, Jr., 1987. 152 p. (Also: Osceola, WI: Voyageur Press. 108 p.; TLC Pub, 2006. 107 p.)

5257. _____. *Atlantic Coast Line: standard railroad of the South.* Lynchburg, VA: TLC Publishing, Inc., 2001. 216 p.

5258. _____. *One hundred fifty years of history: along the Richmond, Fredericksburg and Potomac Railroad.* Richmond? VA: RF&P, 1984. 168 p.

5259. _____. *Richmond, Fredericksburg and Potomac Railroad: passenger service,*

1935-1975. Lynchburg, VA: TLC Pub., 2000.106 p.

5260. _____. *Richmond, Fredericksburg & Potomac Railroad: the Capital Cities Route.* Lynchburg, VA: TLC Pub., 1994. 204 p.

5261. _____. *Seaboard Air Line Railway: the route of courteous service.* Lynchburg, VA: TLC Pub., 1999. 222 p.

5262. _____. *Seaboard Coast Line & Family Lines Railroad: 1967-1986, a CSX predecessor.* Forest, VA: TLC Pub., 2004. 171 p.

5262a. _____, Thomas W. Dixon. *Virginia railroads* / Forest, VA: TLC Pub., 2010- v. 1. Railroading in the Old Dominion – v. 2.Chesapeake & Ohio.

5263. Griffith, Henry Maynard. *A design for an installation of signaling to provide for abnormal operating conditions, and to increase the capacity of the single track, at Tehachapi Pass, on the San Joaquin Division of the Southern Pacific Company, California.* 1914. 1 v. various pagings (Thesis, M.I.T., Department of General Science.)

5264. Griffith, Louis E., Robert Alexander Hemmes. *The stabilization of high speed railroad trains and other vehicles* / 1956. 89 l. (Thesis, M.S., Massachusetts Institute of Technology, Department of Aeronautical Engineering.)

5265. Griffiths, Henry R., Arthur A. Hart. *Steam trains in Idaho in the nineteenth and twentieth centuries.* Boise: Idaho State Historical Society, 1966. 28 p.

5266. Grigg, Steven L. *Reflections, the Nickel Plate years: Clover Leaf District.* New Haven, IN: Nickel Plate Road Historical & Technical Society, 1996. 58 p.

5267. Grille, A., H. Falconnet. *Les chemins de fer à l'Exposition de Chicago.* Paris, E. Bernard, 1894-1895. 2 v. (v. 1: *Locomotives.*-v. 2: *Voies, signaux, matériel roulant et tramways.)*

5268. Grimland, Wade M. *The Kansas City, Mexico & Orient Railway.* 1924. 18 l. (Thesis, B.B.A., University of Texas.)

5269. Grimm, Curtis Martin. *Strategic motives and competitive effects in railroad mergers: a public policy analysis.* 1983. 141 l. (Thesis, Ph.D., University of California, Berkeley.) Consolidation. Freight.

5270. Grimm, Curtis M., Robert G. Harris. *A discrete choice analysis of rail routings: implications for vertical foreclosure & competition.* Berkeley, CA: Center for Research in Management, University of California, Berkeley Business School, 1987. 31 p. (*Economic analysis & policy working paper, no. EAP-21.*)

5271. _____, _____. *The effects of railroad mergers on industry productivity and performance.* Berkeley: Institute of Transportation Studies, University of California, 1985. 30 p. (*Working paper, Institute of Transportation UCB-ITS-WP-85-4)*

5272. _____, _____. *Vertical foreclosure in the rail freight industry: economic analysis and policy prescriptions.* Berkeley: Institute of Transportation Studies, University of California, 1982. 38 p. (*Working paper, Institute of Transportation Studies, UCB-ITS-WP-82-7*)

5273. Grimmons, John A., S. Murray Jones, Decker G. McAllister, A.L. Welford. *The proposed electrification of the Boston division and main line to Providence, of the New York, New Haven and Hartford Railroad* / 1921. 1 v. (various pagings) (Thesis, B.S., Massachusetts Institute of Technology, Department of Electrical Engineering.)

5274. Grimshaw, Robert. *The locomotive catechism: containing nearly 1,300 questions and answers concerning designing and constructing, repairing and running various kinds of locomotive engines*/ New York, Henley, 1893. 362 p. (27th ed.: entirely revised, enlarged and reset, New York, W. Henley, 1908. 817 p. Reprint: Anaheim, CA: Locomotive Reprints, 1978. 817 p.; 30th revised and greatly enlarged edition, New York, The Norman W. Henley Publishing Company, 1923. 958 p.)

5275. Grimsley, George Perry. *The Baltimore and Ohio Railroad.* Washington, D.C., National Capital Press, 1933. 79 p.

5276. Grinnell, Hugh. *Chester, Montana: the saga of a railroad town during the early steam years.* Burnsville, MN: Great Northern Railway Historical Society, 2004. 20 p.

5277. Griswold, P.R. *The Alpine Tunnel story: a 21st century look at a 19th century engineering marvel.* 2d ed. Brighton, CO: Sherm Conners Pub., 2003. 16 p.

5278. _____. *Arizona's railroads: exploring the state by rail.* Frederick, CO: Renaissance House, 1992. 48 p.

5279. _____. *Before the Moffat Tunnel: celebrating the centennial arrival of the first train to Tolland, Colorado, June 1904.* Brighton, CO: Sherm Connors, 2004. 13 p.

5280. _____. *Colorado's loneliest railroad: the San Luis Southern.* Boulder, CO: Pruett Publishing Company, 1980. 190 p.

5281. _____. *David Moffat's Denver, Northwestern and Pacific: "the Moffat Road."* Denver, CO: Rocky Mountain Railroad Club, 1995. 1 v.

5282. _____. *The Denver and Salt Lake Railroad, 1913-1926.* Denver, CO: Rocky Mountain Railroad Club, 1996. 242 p.

5283. _____. *The Grand Canyon Railway* / Brighton, CO: Sherm Conners, 2006. 11, 28 p. of plates.

5284. _____. *The Morrison Branch of the Denver, South Park and Pacific Railroad.* Revised edition. Brighton, CO: Sherm Conners Publishing, 2003. 16 p.

5285. _____. *Railroads of California: seeing the state by rail.* Frederick, CO: Renaissance House, 1992. 47 p.

5286. _____ *Railroads of Colorado: a guide to modern and narrow gauge trains.* Frederick, CO: Renaissance House, 1988. 48 p.

5287. _____. *Rio Grande: along the Rio Grande.* Denver, CO: P.R. Griswold, 1986. 243 p.

5288. _____. *Tracks along the Chili Line: memories of a unique railroad in southern Colorado and northern New Mexico.* Brighton, C: Sherm Conners Pub., 2006. 12 p., 31 p. of plates.

5289. _____. *Rio Grande Southern pictorial: a collection o old and rare photos of America's most scenic railroad* / Brighton, CO: Sherm Conners Publishing, 2006.

5290. _____, Richard H. Kindig, Cynthia Trombly. *Georgetown and the Loop.* Denver, CO: Rocky Mountain Railroad Club, 1988. 254 p.

5291. Griswold, Wesley S. *Train wreck!* Brattleboro, VT: S. Greene Press, 1969. 158 p.

5292. _____. *A work of giants: building the first transcontinental railroad.* New York, McGraw-Hill, 1962. 367 p.

5293. Grodinsky, Julius. *Federal regulation of railroad security issues.* 1925. Philadelphia, Westbrook Pub. Co., 1925. 71 p (Thesis, Ph.D., University of Pennsylvania, 1925.)

5294. _____. *The Iowa Pool, a study in railroad competition, 1870-84.* Chicago, IL: University of Chicago Press, 1950. 184 p.(Reprint: New York, Arno Press, 1981.)

5295. _____. *Jay Gould, his business career, 1867-1892.* Philadelphia, University of Pennsylvania Press, 1957. 627 p.(Reprint: New York, Arno Press, 1981. 627 p.)

5296. _____. *Railroad consolidation, its economics and controlling principles.* New York, D. Appleton and Co., 1930. 333 p. (Reprint: Beard Books, 1999. 333 p.)

5297. _____. *Transcontinental railway strategy, 1869-1893; a study of businessmen.* Philadelphia, University of Pennsylvania Press, 1962. 443 p.

5298. Groff, Garth G. *Off the track in Ivy: the wreck of the Old Dominion Express.* Charlottesville, VA: Drop Leaf Press, 1992. 16 p. (C&O)

5299. _____. *Soapstone shortline: Alberene stone and its railroads.* Charlottesville. VA: Drop Leaf Press, 1991. 52 p. (Nelson & Albemarle Railway Company.)

5300. Grogan, Louis V. *The coming of the New York and Harlem Railroad.* Pawling, NY:

L.V. Grogan, 1989. 364 p.

5301. Groh, Kenneth Robert. *Safety of high speed guided ground transportation systems: the biological effects of Maglev magnetic field exposures*/ Washington, DC: Federal Railroad Administration, Office of Research and Development, 1993. 56 p. in various pagings)

5302. Groner, Alex. *PACCAR: the pursuit of quality*. Bellevue, WA: Documentary Book Publishers Co., 1981. 243 p. (2d ed.: Woodinville, WA: Documentary Book Publishers, 1996. 280 p.;3rd ed. Seattle, WA: Documentary Book Publishers, 1998. 280 p.; 4th ed. Seattle, WA: Documentary Media LLC., 2005. 328 p.)

5303. Groom, J.J. *Determination of residual stress in rails*/ Washington, DC: Federal Railroad Administration, Office of Research and Development, 1983. 66 p. (DOT/FRA/ORD-83/05.)

5304. Gross, Joseph. *Railroads of North America*. 3rd ed. Rochester, NY: Railroad Research Publications, 2000. 274 p.

5305. _____, Dick Barrett. *Railroad locks and keys. Vol. 1, The Adams & Westlake Company*. Rochester, NY: Railroad Research Publications, 1998. 246 p.

5306. Grossman, Peter Z. *Contract and conflict: a study of the express cartel*. 1992. 167 l. (Thesis, Ph.D., Washington University.)

5306a. Grover, Oscar Llwellyn. *Design of standard masonry arches*/ 1909. 10 l. (Thesis, University of Maine.)

5307. Grow, Lawrence. *On the 8:02: an informal history of commuting by rail in America*. New York, Mayflower Books, 1979. 176 p.

5308 _____. *Waiting for the 5:05: terminal, stations, and depot in America*. New York, Main Street/Universe Books, 1977. 128 p. ("Based on an exhibition prepared by the Historic American Building Survey and the Historic American Engineering Record".)

5309. Gruber, John E. *Classic steam: timeless photographs of North American steam railroading*/ New York: Fall River Press, 2009. 224 p.

5310. _____. *Focus on rails*/ Introduction by Bill Withuhn. North Freedom, WI: Mid-Continent Railway Historical Society, 1989. 49 p.

5311. _____. *GBW, Wisconsin's historic east-west railroad*. North Freedom, WI: Mid-Continent Railway Historical Society, 1986. 24 p.

5312. _____. *The Milwaukee Road's Hiawathas*. St. Paul, MN: Motorbooks, 2006. 1 v.

5313. _____. *Railroads & photography: 150 years of great images.* Madison, WI: Center for Railroad Photography and Art, 2001. 15 p.

5314. _____, Michael E. Zega. *Lucius Beebe & Charles Clegg railroading journeys: a special retrospective devoted to their life and times/* Madison, WI: Center for Railroad Photography & Art, 2007. 32 p. (*Railroad heritage, no. 18, 2007*)

5315. _____, Steve VanDenburgh, Daniel Thielen. *Railroads and photography: 150 years of great images.* Carson City, Nev., Nevada State Railroad Museum, 2001. 24 p.

5316. Grzyb, Gerard Jerome. *Death of a craftsman: the impact of rationalization in the railroad industry on the occupational community and occupational culture of operating railroaders.* 1977. 300 l. (Thesis, Washington University.)

5317. Gschwind, Francis G. *Kearney & Black Hills: a historic branch of the Union Pacific Railroad.* David City, NE: South Platte Press, 1990. 415 p.

5318. *GT reporter.* Detroit, MI: Grand Trunk Western Railroad Company, 1900s-1986. (> *GTC reporter.*)

5319. *GTC reporter.* Detroit, MI: Grand Trunk Corporation, 1986-1987. 2 v. (< *GT reporter; > GTC today.*)

5320. *GTC today.* Detroit, MI: Grand Trunk Corporation, 1988- . (< *GTC reporter.*) "Published for employees of Grand Trunk Corporation railroads: Grand Trunk Western/Central Vermont/ Duluth, Winnipeg & Pacific."

5321. Guerin, Jules. *Grand Central, the greatest railway terminal in the world.* New York, Warren & Wetmore? 191-? 20 p.

5322. Guest, William J. *The duty on steel rails, the case for the manufacturers, at a hearing before the Ways and Means Committee, of the House of Representatives, at Washington, February 3, 4, and 5, 1880.* Philadelphia, Pa., American Iron and Steel Association, 1880. 76, 16 p.

5323. Guggenheim, Hans, Richard Vieira, John H. White. *The Pioneer: light passenger locomotive of 1851.* Minneapolis, MN: Tonka Corporation, 1974. 24 p.

5324. *Guide-book of the Central Railroad of New Jersey, and its connection through the coal-fields of Pennsylvania.* New York: Harper & Brothers, 1864. 120 p. (Reprint: Louisville, KY: Los Cause Press, 1972. Microfiche, 5 sheets.)

5325. *Guide for writers and photographers/* Waukesha, WI: Trains Magazine, 2009. 7 p.

5326. *Guide to a microfilm edition of the Northern Pacific Land Department records.* St. Paul, MN: Minnesota Historical Society, 1983. 71 p.

5327. *Guide to coupler and draft gear systems for freight cars.* Omaha: Railway Educational Bureau, 2000. 1 v. (Loose-leaf) (*Freight car maintenance series*)

5328. *Guide to freight car trucks.* Omaha, NE: Railway Education Bureau, 2001. 1 v.

5329. *Guide to railroad collections in the intermountain West.* Ronald G. Watt, editor. Salt Lake City, UT: Conference of Intermountain Archivists, 1984. 98 l.

5330. *Guide to railroad historical resources, United States and Canada.* Muncy, PA: T.T. Taber III, 1993. 4 v.

5331. *Guide to railroad historical resources. Addenda, 1992-2003.* Muncy, PA: T.T. Taber III, 2004. 6, 63 p.

5332. *Guide to records of the Northern Pacific branch lines, subsidiaries, and related companies in the Minnesota Historical Society.* St. Paul, MN: The Society, 1977. 13 p.

5333. *Guide to the Burlington archives in the Newberry Library, 1851-1901.* Elisabeth Coleman Jackson and Carolyn Curtis, compilers. Chicago, Ill., Newberry Library, 1949. 374 p.

5334. *A guide to the collection of John Insley Blair: mss 40, Fikes Hall of Special Collections and DeGolyer Library.* Tom W. Gläser, compiler. Dallas, TX? The Library, 1985. 73 p.

5335. (Blank entry)

5336. *Guide to the historical records of the St. Louis-San Francisco Railway Company and its predecessors, subsidiary, and constituent companies.* Brenda S. Brugger, compiler; Mark C. Stauter, editor and project director; John F. Bradbury, Jr., project advisor. Rolla, MO: University of Missouri, Western Historical Manuscript Collection-Rolla, 1989. 139 p.

5337. *Guide to the Illinois Central archives in the Newberry Library, 1851-1906.* Carolyn Curtis Mohr, compiler. Chicago, Ill., Newberry Library, 1951. 210 p.

5338. *A guide to the John W. Barriger III papers in the John W. Barriger III National Railroad Library: a special collection of the St. Louis Mercantile Library Association.* St. Louis? MO: The Association, 1997. 2 v.

5339. *Guide to the Pullman Company archives.* By Martha T. Briggs and Cynthia H. Peters. Chicago, IL: Newberry Library, 1995. 794 p.

5340. *Guidelines for evaluating the feasibility of short line operations/* Washington, DC: Interstate Commerce Commission, Rail Services Planning Office, 1985. 26 p.

5341. *Guidelines for trainyard inspection of freight cars.* Rev. Omaha, NE: Railway Education Bureau, 1996. 88 p.

5342. Guild, William. *A chart and description of the rail-road from Boston to New York: via Worchester, Springfield, Hartford, and New Haven ... with numerous illustrations ...* / Boston, MA: Bradbury & Guild, 1850, 84 p, (*Bradbury's & Guild's rail-road charts, no. 2.*)

5343. *Guilford XPRESS.* Portland, ME: Guilford Transportation Industries, 1984- . Published by the railroads of Guilford Transportation Industries: Boston and Maine Corporation, Delaware and Hudson Railway Company and Maine Central Railroad Company.

5343a. Guillaudeu, David A. *Washington & Old Dominion Railroad* / Charleston, SC: Arcadia Publishing, 2013. 127 p.

5344. Guillot, Frank. *New 2000-bhp diesel-electric road locomotives for the New York, New Haven & Hartford Railroad.* Erie, Pa., General Electric Company, 1942. 6 p.

5345. Guise, Byron E. *First steam west of the Big Muddy.* Marysville, KS: Marysville Pub. Co., 1970. 51 p. (St. Joseph and Grand Island Railway Company)

5346. Gulf, Colorado, and Santa Fe Railroad. *The cattle route of Texas: a round-up of facts.* Galveston, TX: Clark & Courts, Stationers, Lithographers and Printers, 1884. 6 p.

5347. Gulliford, Andrew, John Stilgoe. *High iron: a series of exhibits exploring the effect of the railway industry on the Lima, Ohio, community.* Lima, OH: American House, 1987. 39 p.

5348. Gunn, J. T. *A special coupler-pin development for measuring railroad-locomotive drawbar forces.* Berkeley, CA: Lawrence Berkeley Laboratory, 1982. 6 p.

5349. Gunnell, Bruce C. *The use of steel wheels in freight service* / New York : American Society of Mechanical Engineers, 1953. 5 p. (ASME. Paper no. 53-A-119.)

5350. Gunnison, J.W. *Central Pacific railroad. Letter from the Secretary of War, transmitting a report relative to Captain Gunnison's survey, &c...* Washington, D.C., s.n., 1854. 10 p.

5351. Gurley, F.G. *A new idea and how it grew : why the new "Hi-Level" El Capitan was developed.* S.l., Atchison, Topeka, and Santa Fe Railway Company, 1955. 9 p.

5352. _____. *New Mexico and the Santa Fe Railway.* New York, Newcomen Society in North America, 1950. 32 p.

5353. Gusano, Teodora. *The devil's shortline: Mt. Diablo & San Jose Railroad, a forgotten California narrow gauge.* Albany, CA: Ross Valley Books, 1988. 12 p. (Contra Costa County)

5354. Gustafson, Lee, Philip C. Serpico. *Coast Line depots: Los Angeles Division.* Palmdale, CA: Omni Publications, 1992. 332 p. (AT&SF)

5355. _____, _____. *Coast Line depots: Valley Division.* Palmdale, CA: Omni Publications, 1996. 240 p. (AT&SF)

5356. Guthrie, Carol. *All aboard for Glacier: the Great Northern Railway and Glacier National Park.* Helena, MT: Farcountry Press, 2004. 96 p.

5356a. Gutkowski, Richard M., Abdalla M.T. Shigidi, An Vinh Tran. *Field investigation of a strengthened timber trestle railroad bridge* / Fargo, ND: Mountain-Plains Consortium, 2003. 54 p. (*MPC report, no. 03-147.*)

5356b. _____, Geoffrey Robinson, Abdalla Shigidi. *Field load tests of open-deck timber trestle railroad bridges* / Fort Collins, CO: Colorado State University, Mountain-Plains Consortium, 2001. 110 p. (*MPC report, no. 01-125.*)

5357. Gutohrlein, Adolf. *Rayonier, Inc.: railroading in the Northwest pines.* Los Angeles, CA: Trans-Anglo Books, 1964. 33 p.

5358. _____. *Rails in the Mother Lode.* Omaha, NE: Kratville Publications, 1969. 205 p.

5359. Gypsy Moon. *Done and been: steel rail chronicles of American hobos.* Bloomington, Indiana University Press, 1996. 199 p.

H

5360. H.K. Porter. *Compressed air haulage: a system of H.K. Porter Company, builders of light locomotives, steam and compressed air.* Pittsburg, Pa., H.K. Porter, 1911. 81 p.

5361. _____. *Compressed air haulage system of H.K. Porter Company, builders of light locomotives, steam and compressed air.* Pittsburg, The Company, 1904. 82 p.

5362. _____. *H.K. Porter Company, builders of light locomotives, steam and compressed air. 10th ed.* Pittsburg, Pa., H.K. Porter, 1908. 224 p.

5363. _____. *Light locomotives. 5th ed.* Pittsburg, Pa., H.K. Porter & Company, 1885. 111 p.

5364. _____. *Light locomotives. 6th ed.* Buffalo, N.Y., Matthews, Northrup & Co, Art-Printing Works, 1889. 147 p.

5365. _____. *Light locomotives. 7th ed.* Buffalo, N.Y., The Matthews-Northrup Company, 1892. 170 p.

5366. _____. *Light locomotives. 8th ed.* Pittsburg, Pa., The Company, 1890. 216 p.

5367. _____. *Light locomotives. 9th ed.* New York, Chasmar-Winchell Press, 1900. 1 v.

5368. _____. *Light locomotives, steam and compressed air /* 10th ed. Pittsburg, H.K. Porter Co., 1908. 224 p.

5369. _____. *Modern compressed air locomotives: a descriptive catalogue of two-stage compressed air locomotives and the necessary auxiliary apparatus for successful operation and maintenance. 2d ed.* Pittsburg, Pa., H.K. Porter Company, 1914. 80 p.

5370. _____. *Porter diesel-electric locomotives.* Pittsburg, Pa., H.K. Porter Company, 1944. 44 p.

5371 _____. *Porter locomotives.* Pittsburg, Pa., The Company, 1929. 56 p. (Porter fireless steam locomotive with engineering data)

5372. _____. *Porter steam locomotives.* Pittsburg, Pa., H.K. Porter Company, 1943. 68 p.

5373. _____. *Porter steam locomotives, light and heavy. 11th ed.* Pittsburg, Pa., H.K. Porter Company, 1915. 151 p.

5374. _____. *Porter steam locomotives, light and heavy. 12th ed.* Pittsburg, Pa., H.K. Porter Company, 191-?

5375. _____. *Porter steam locomotives, light and heavy. 13th ed.* Pittsburg, Pa., H.K. Porter, 19--? 152 p.

5376. _____. *Steam locomotive repair parts.* Pittsburg, Pa., H.K. Porter Company, 1913. 83 p.

5377. _____. [Records of H.K. Porter & Company] Location: University of Pittsburgh.

5378. Haber, William. *Maintenance of way employment on U.S. railroads; an analysis of the sources of instability and remedial measures.* Detroit, Brotherhood of Maintenance of Way Employees, 1957. 237 p.

5379. Haberman, Ian S. *The Van Sweringens of Cleveland: the biography of an empire.* Cleveland, Western Reserve Historical Society, 1979. 202 p. (*Publication. Western Reserve Historical Society, no. 148.*)

5380. Hackworth, Werter Shipp. *Over a century of railroad service.* Nashville, TN: Cullom & Ghertner, 1953. 24 p. (Nashville, Chattanooga, and St. Louis Railway)

5381. Hadcock, Carryl E., Alfred J.J. Holck. *Burlington Route depot life.* David City, NE: South Platte Press, 1996. 44 p.

5382. Hadden, J. *Shared right-of-way safety issues.* Washington, DC: Federal Railroad Administration, Office of Research and Development, 1992. 1 v. (various pagings)

5383. Haddock, David Dewaide. *Regulation of railroads by commission* / 1980. 92 l. (Thesis, Ph.D., University of Chicago.)

5384. Haddock, Keith. *Bucyrus: making the earth move for 125 years.* St. Paul, MN: MBI, 2005. 160 p.

5385. Hadley, Arthur Twining. *The meaning of valuation* / Evanston, IL: American Economic Association, 1928. 1 v.

5386. _____. *Railroad transportation, its history and its laws.* New York, NY: G.P. Putnam's Sons, 1903. 269 p. (Reprint: New York, NY: Johnson Reprint Corp., 1968.)

5387. _____. *Report of the Railroad Securities Commission to the president and letter of the president transmitting the report to the Congress.* Washington, DC: U.S. G.P.O., 1911. 42 p. (^2nd Congress, 2d session. House Doc. 256.) Committee on Interstate and Foreign Commerce/ Arthur T. Hadley, chairman.

5387a. Haeg, Lawrence Peter. *Harriman vs. Hill: Wall Street's great railroad war.* Minneapolis: University of Minnesota Press, 2013. 375 p.

5388. Hafen, Le Roy Reuben. *The overland mail, 1849-1869: promoter of settlement, precursor of railroads.* Cleveland, OH: A.H. Clark, 1926. 361 p.

5389. Hagen, J.M., Harry K. McClintock. *Railroad songs of yesterday*/ New York: Shapiro, Bernstein & Co., 1943. 48 p.

5390. Hager, David C. *Next stop Kalamazoo! A history of railroading in Kalamazoo County.* Kalamazoo, MI: Kalamazoo Public Museum, 1976. 34 p.

5391. Haghani, Ali E. *A combined model of train routing, makeup, and empty car distribution.* 1986. 395 l. (Thesis, Ph.D., Northwestern University)

5392. Hahn, Barbara. *Union Terminal: businessmen, railroads and city planning in Cincinnati, 1869-1933.* Cincinnati, 2000. 105 p. (Thesis, M.A., University of Cincinnati.)

5393. Hahn, John D., Paul K. Withers *Pennsylvania Railroad diesel locomotive pictorial.* Halifax, PA: Withers Publishing, 1996-v. 1-

5394. Haig, M.H. *The design of large locomotives.* New York, American Society of Mechanical Engineers, 1921. 28 p.

5395. Haig, Maham H. *Railway shop up to date: a reference book of up to date American railway shop practice.* Chicago, Crandall Publishing Company, 1907. 243 p.

5395a. Hain, Peter Murray. *Frank K. Hain and the Manhattan Railway Company: the elevated railway, 1875-1903.* Jefferson, NC: McFarland, 2011. 176 p.

5396. Haine, Edgar A. *Railroad wrecks.* New York, Cornwall Books, 1993. 235 p.

5397. _____. *Seven railroads.* South Brunswick, NJ: A.S. Barnes, 1979. 291 p.

5398. _____. *The steam locomotive.* New York, Cornwall Books, 1990. 674 p.

5399. Haines, Henry S. *American railway management. Addresses delivered before the American railway association, and miscellaneous addresses and papers.* New York, NY: J. Wiley, 1897. 368 p.

5400. _____. *Efficient railway operation.* New York, Macmillan Company, 1919. 709 p.

5401. _____ *Problems in railway regulations.* New York, NY: Macmillan, 1911. 582 p.

5402. _____. *The railroad and the state.* Savannah; Savannah Morning News, 1879? 23 p.

5403. _____. *Railway corporations as public servants.* New York: The Macmillan Company, 1907. 233 p.

5404. _____. *Restrictive railway legislation.* New York: The Macmillan Company, 1905. 355 p.

5405. Haines, Michael R., Robert A. Margo. *Railroads and local economic development: the United States in the 1850s*/ Cambridge, MA: National Bureau of Economic Research, 2006. 36 p. (*NBER working paper series, no. 12381.*)

5406. Haines, William L. R. *The modern freight terminal of the Pennsylvania Railroad in Chicago* / S.l., American Society of Civil Engineers, 1923. 11 p.

5406a. Halagera, Raymond T., Carol Johnson. *The potential benefits of railroad facility consolidation* / Chicago : Chicago Area Transportation Study, 1972. 68 p.

5407. Halberstadt, Hans. *Classic trains*. New York, MetroBooks, 2001. 144 p.

5408. _____. *Modern diesel locomotives*. Osceola, WI: Motorbooks International, 1996. 96 p.

5409. _____ *Working steam: vintage locomotives today*. New York, MetroBooks, 1999. 120 p.

5410. _____, April Halberstadt. *Great American train stations: classic terminals and depots*. New York, Barnes & Noble, 1997, c1995. 192 p.

5411. _____, _____ *Train depots and roundhouses*. St. Paul MN: MBI Pub. Co., 2002. 192 p.

5412. Hale E. Hawk (Firm). *Hawk's safety self-coupling for freight and passenger cars*. Kansas City, MO: Hale E. Hawk, 1884. 1 sheet

5413. Hale, Robert Lee. *Valuation and rate-making*/ New York, NY: Columbia University Press, 1918. 156 p.

5414. Hale, Robert O., Donald Duke. *Railroad photography: Western states*. San Marino, CA: Golden West Books, 2004. 117 p.

5415. Hall, Charles Gilbert. *The Cincinnati Southern Railway: a history: a complete and concise history of the events attending the building and operation of the road*. Cincinnati, Ohio, The McDonald Press, 1902. 231 p.

5416. Hall, John A. *The great strike on the "Q," with a history of the organization and growth of the Brotherhood of Locomotive Engineers, Brotherhood of Locomotive Firemen, and Switchmen's Mutual Aid Association of North America*. Chicago and Philadelphia, Elliott & Beezley, 1889. 7-124 p.

5417. Hall, John W. *Reading Company cabooses*. Reading, PA: Reading Company Technical & Historical Society, 2001. 270 p.

5418. Hall, Randolph W. *Railroad train blocking for fuel efficiency*/ Berkeley: Institute of Transportation Studies, University of California, 1981. 18 l. (*Graduate report: UCB-*

ITS-GR-81-8.)

5419. Hall, Richard E., Greg M. Ajamian. *Some company service cars of the P W & B, P B & W, PRR and related lines* / Wilmington, DE: Wilmington Chapter of the National Railway Historical Society, 2005. 166 p.

5420. Hall, Ronald, Robert Wuchert. *Memories of the New Haven.* Wallingford, CT: Cedar Hill Productions, 1983-

5421. Hall, W.E. *Car lubrication.* New York, J. Wiley & Sons, 1891. 66 p. (2d ed. 1895. 73 p.; 3d ed. rev.: New York, Wiley, 1901. 81 p.)

5421a. Hall, Ward, Ford K. Edwards. *Report on the subject of delays in transbay rail service following the inauguration of the service over the San Francisco-Oakland Bay Bridge* / San Francisco: California Railroad Commission, Transportation Department, 1935. 37 l.

5421b. _____, James K. Gibson. *Southern Pacific Company investigation of passenger service, San Francisco-Sacramento* / San Francisco : California Public Utilities Commission, Transportation Department, 1961. 54 l. (Case no. 5234; Application no. 31304.)

5422. Hallgren, Harley K., John Fitzgerald Due. *United Railways of Oregon.* San Marino, CA: Pacific Railway Journal, 1961. 34 p.

5423. Hallowell, Susan Fraley. *Optimal dispatching under uncertainty: with application to railroad scheduling*/ 1993? 179 p. (Thesis, Ph.D., University of Pennsylvania.)

5424. Halsey, Frederick A. *The locomotive link motion.* New York, NY: Press of Railway and Locomotive Engineering, 1898. 86 p.

5425. _____ *Slide valve gears* / 5th ed. New York, Van Nostrand, 1889. 135 p.

5426. Halsey, William. *William Halsey locomotive drawings collection.* Dallas, TX : Southern Methodist University, 2009. Internet \Resource. 2-D image. 84 image files. JPEG2000 files. col. http;//www.lib.utexas. edu/taro/smu/0079/smu-0079.html

5427. Halstead, Murat, J. Frank Beale, Willis Fletcher Johnson. *Life of Jay Gould: how he made his millions.* Philadelphia, Pa, Edgewood Pub. Co., 1892. 490 p.

5428. Ham, John M., Robert K. Bucenec. *The grand old stations and steam locomotives of the Ulster & Delaware.* Hunter, NY: Stony Clove & Catskill Mountain Press, 2005. 1 v.

5429. _____, _____. *Light rail and short ties through the Notch: The Stony Clove & Catskill Mountain Railroad and her steam legacy.* Hunter, NY: Stony Clove & Catskill Mountain Press, 2002. 1 v.

5430. _____, _____. *The "Old Up and Down": Catskill Mountain Branch of the New York Central.* Hunter, NY: Stony Clove & Catskill Mountain Press, 2003. 263 p.

5431. Harnack, Art. *The Milwaukee Road's beer line.* Antioch, IL: Milwaukee Road Historical Association, 2003. 38 p. (*Special Publication, 5*)

5431a. Hamada, Tracy, Craig Hamada. *Southern Pacific diesel power guide /* Wilmington, NC: LCW Productions, 2006. 59 l.

5432. Hamblen, Herbert Elliott. *The general manager's story; old-time reminiscences of railroading in the United States.* New York, Macmillan Company, 1898. 311 p. (Reprint: Upper Saddle River, NJ: Literature House, 1970.)

5433. Hamburg, James Fredric. *The influence of railroads upon the processes and patterns of settlement in South Dakota.* New York, Arno Press, 1981, c1970. 287 p. (Thesis, University of North Carolina, 1969.)

5434. Hamid, Abdul. *Analytical descriptions of track geometry variations/* Washington, DC: Federal Railroad Administration, Office of Research and Development, 1983. 2 v. (*DOT/FRA/ORD-83/03.1.*)

5435. _____. *A prototype maintenance-of-way planning system.* Washington, D.C.: U.S. Department of Transportation, Federal Railroad Administration, Office of Research and Development, 1980- . (*FRA/ORD-80-47.1*)

5436. _____, R. Owings, M. Kenworthy. *Characterization of relatively large track geometry variations: final report.* Washington, DC: U.S. Department of Transportation, Federal Railroad Administration, Office of Rail Safety Research, 1982. 148 p. (*FRA/ORD-82/13; DOT-TSC-FRA-81-18.*)

5437. Hamilton Houston Lownie Architects. *Buffalo Central Terminal : existing conditions engineering study ; technical report /* Buffalo, NY: The Architects, 1996. 1 v. (various pagings).

5438. Hamilton, Kristi D. *The railroad roundhouse of Frankfort, Indiana.* 2005. 178 l. (Thesis, M.S.H.P., Ball State University.)

5439. Hamilton, W.G., George Whitney. *Improvement in metals, for car wheels, under patents of W.G. Hamilton and George Whitney.* New York, Van Nostrand, 1876. 20 p. (Hamilton Steeled Wheel Company) Also: Philadelphia : s.n., 1874. 15 p.)

5440. _____. *Useful information for railway men.* Compiled for the Ramapo Wheel and Foundry Co. 11th ed. rev. and enl. New York, D. Van Nostrand, 1898. 577 p.

5441. Hamilton-Dann, Mary. *Rochester and Genesee Valley rails.* Rochester, NY: Railroad Research Publications, 2001. 170 p.

5442. _____. *Upstate odyssey: the Lehigh Valley Railroad in western New York.*

Rochester, NY: Railroad Research Publications, 1997. 136 p.

5442a. Hamilton Watch Company. *The Hamilton watch: the railroad timekeeper of America.* Lancaster, PA: The Hamilton Watch Company, 1920. 7 p.

5442b. _____. *The timekeeper.* Lancaster, PA: The Hamilton Watch Company, 1911. 43 p.

5443. Hamman, Rick. *California central coast railways.* Boulder, CO: Pruett Pub. Co., 1980. 309 p.

5444. Hammell, Alfred L. *Wm. Frederick Hamden (1813-1845) founder of the express business in America!* New York, Newcomen Society in North America, 1954. 28 p.

5445. Hammer, Kenneth. *Dakota railroads.* 1966. 2 v. (Thesis, South Dakota State University.)

5446. Hammesfahr, Roy D. *A simulation model for the analysis of railway intermodal terminal operations.* 1981. 225, 2 l. (Thesis, Ph.D., Virginia Polytechnic Institute and State University.)

5447. Hammitt, Andrew G. *Aerodynamic forces on various configurations of railroad cars for carrying trailers and containers : final report* / Washington, DC : Federal Railroad Administration, Office of Research and Development, 1979. 85 p. (*FRA/ORD-79-39.*)

5448. _____, Prakash B. Joshi. *Aerodynamic forces on freight trains: final report.* Washington, DC: Federal Railroad Administration, Office of Research and Development, 1978. 3 v. (Tests of containers and trailers on flatcars.) (*FRA-ORD&D-76-295. I, II, III.*)

5449. Hammond, M.B. *Railway rate theories of the Interstate Commerce Commission.* Cambridge, Mass., Harvard University, 1911. 200 p.

5450. Hammond, Paul. *Railway odyssey: a guidebook to the Orange Empire Railway Museum, Perris, California.* Perris, CA: The Museum, 1987. 95 p.

5451. Hammond, Stevens H. *Materials handling in railroad service shops* / New York: American Society of Mechanical Engineers, 1949. 11, 7 l. (*Paper, no. 49-A-90.*)

5451a. Han Xiangdong. *Evaluation of ballast materials based on ballast particle characteristics and functions.* 1998. 167 l. (Thesis, Ph.D., University of Massachusetts at Amherst.)

5451b. Hand, Victor, Don Phillips. *A steam odyssey : the railroad photographs of Victor Hand.* New York : W.W. Norton, 2013. 224 p.

5452. *The hand of man: railroads in American prints and photographs: an exhibition to commemorate the 150th anniversary of the building of the Baltimore and Ohio Railroad.* Baltimore, MD: Baltimore Museum of Art, 1978. 24 p.

5452a. *Hand book of American railroad repair facilities : location, size and function: shops and roundhouses : class 1 railroads of the United States* / New York : Railway Mechanical Engineer, 1922. 193 p.

5453. *Hand-book of railroad securities.* New York, W.B. Dana & Company, 1883-1907. Semiannual (*<Value of railroad securities; >Hand-book of securities*)

5454. *A hand book of U.S. safety appliance standards: instructions for application to freight cars in inter-state traffic.* Cleveland, OH: J.D. MacAlpine, 1913. 31 p.

5455. *Handbook of sanitation of dining cars in operation: standards of sanitation for operation and maintenance of food and drink service facilities on railroad passenger cars.* Washington, DC: United Public Health Service, Division of Engineering Services, 1959. 11 p. (*PHS publication no. 83.*)

5456. *Handbook on sanitation of railroad passenger cars* / Washington, DC: U.S. G.P.O., 1964. 18 p. (U.S. Public Health Service. Division of Environmental Engineering and Food protection.)

5457. *Handy railroad atlas of the United States, 1928: showing all railroad and interurban lines with their names and mileages; principal cities, towns, junction points; list of all railroads with their abbreviations.* Milwaukee, WI: Kalmbach, 1928, c1923. 48 p.

5458. Haney, Lewis H. *The business of railway transportation, traffic, rates, regulation.* New York, The Ronald Press, 1924. 613 p.

5459. _____. *A congressional history of railways in the United States.* New York, A.M. Kelley, 1968, 1908. 2 v.

5460. Hanft, H.H. *A-C air conditioning for railroad passenger cars* / New York : American Institute of Electrical Engineers, 1947. 6 p. (*AIEE miscellaneous paper, no. 48-51.*)

5461. Hanft, Robert M. *Pine across the mountain: California's McCloud River Railroad.* San Marino, CA: Golden West Books, 1971. 224 p.

5462. _____. *Railroad picture list.* Berkeley, CA: R. Hanft, 1946. 22 p.

5463. _____. *Red River: Paul Bunyan's own lumber company and its railroads.* Chico, CA: Center for Business and Economic Research, California State University: Chico, 1980. 304 p.

5464. _____. *San Diego & Arizona: the impossible railroad.* Glendale, CA: Trans-Anglo Books, 1984. 224 p. (Rev. ed.: 1988. 224 p.)

5465. Hanger, E. Sterling. *Chesapeake and Ohio dining car recipes*. Clifton Forge, VA: Chesapeake & Ohio Historical Society, 1995. 152 p.

5466. Hankey, John P. *The Baltimore and Ohio railroad Martinsburg shop complex: historic structure report*. Martinsburg, WV: Grove & Dall'Olio Architects, 2000. 1 v.

5467. _____. *The diesel-powered National Limited, streamlined 1940: modernized heavyweight trains equipment diagram portfolio*. Baltimore, MD: Baltimore and Ohio Railroad Historical Society, 1987. 1 v.

5468. Hankins, Caneta Skelley. *Chattanooga, Tennessee: train town*. Washington, DC: National Trust for Historic Preservation, 1996. 12 p. Internet resource: http://www.cr.nps.gov/nr/twhp/wwwlps/lessons/52chattanooga/52/chattanooga.htm

5469. Hanks, David, Anne Hoy. *American streamlined design : the world of tomorrow* / New York : Thames and Hudson, 2005. 279 p.

5470. Hanna, Amir N. *State-of-the-art report on prestressed concrete ties for North American railroads*. Skokie, IL: Portland Cement Association, 1980. 16 p.

5471. Hanna, Thomas C. *P.R.R. Centennial* / Philadelphia : Mutual Benefit Association of Pennsylvania Railroad Employees, 1946. 136 p.

5472. Hannauer, George. *Safety appliances and their care*. Washington: Govt. Print. Off., 1904. 8 p. (United States. Congress. House. Committee on Interstate and Foreign Commerce.)

5473. Hannum, James S. *The Ann Arbor Railroad: abandoned early lines*. Olympia, WA: Hannum House Publications, 2004. 34 p.

5474. _____, Carol B. Hannum. *Delusions of grandeur : the Olympia & Tenino Railroad* / Olympia, WA: Hannum House Publications, 2009. 169 p.

5475. _____, _____. *Gone but not forgotten: abandoned railroads of Thurston County, Washington*. Olympia,. WA: Hannum House Publications, 2002. 245 p.

5476. _____, _____. *South Puget Sound railroad mania*. Olympia, WA: Hannum House Publications, 2006. 284 p.

5477. Hanover, E. Robert. *American shadows: a history of the Promontory Branch of the Southern Pacific Railroad*. Omaha, 2001. 158 l. (Thesis, M.A., University of Nebraska, Omaha.)

5478. Hansen, Max L. Railroads : *U.S. access and competition issues* / New York : Nova Science Publisher's, 2010. 230 p.

5479. Hansen, Walter J. *State aid to railroads in Michigan during the early statehood period.* Ann Arbor, 1941. 357 l. (Thesis, Ph.D., University of Michigan.)

5480. Hanson, Erie C. *The true story of the California and Nevada Railroad.* Walnut Creek, CA: Erie C. Hanson, 1988. 65 p. (3rd ed.: 1994. 65 p.)

5481. Hanson, M.A. *Available and potential developments in design for standard AAR solid bearing assemblies* / New York : American Society of Mechanical Engineers, 1958. 5 p. (*ASME. Paper no. 58-RR-3.*)

5482. Hanson, Melvin Arthur. *The impact of trailer on flatcar on transportation pricing.* 1960. 147 l. (Thesis, M.B.A., University of Minnesota.)

5483. Hanson, Robert H. *Safety, courtesy, service: history of the Georgia Railroad.* Johnson City, TN: Overmountain Press, 1996. 206 p.

5484. _____. *The West Point Route: the Atlanta & West Point Rail Road and the Western Railway of Alabama.* Forest, VA: TLC Pub. Inc., 2006. 191 p.

5485. Hanson, Warren D., Theodore Wurm. *San Francisco Water and Power: a history of the Municipal Water Department and Hetch Hetchy System.* San Francisco, CA: Hetch Hetchy Water and Power System, 1984. 47 p. (Hetch Hetchy Railroad)

5486. Hanstein, Carl Menelaus. *Review of the Peoria and Eastern Railway shops at Urbana, Ill.* / 1905. 44 2 l. (Thesis, B.S., University of Illinois.)

5487. Haran, S., S.M. Rocha, R.D. Finch. *Evaluation of a prototype acoustic signature inspection system for railroad wheels* / Washington, DC: Federal Railroad Administration, Office of Research and Development, 1985. 148 p. (*DOT/FRA/ORD-84/19.*)

5488. Harding, C. Francis. *Electric railway engineering.* New York, McGraw-Hill Book Company, 1911. 336 p. (2d ed.:1916. 416 p.; 3d ed. 1926. 489 p.)

5489. _____. *Locomotive headlight tests.* Worcester, MA: Worcester Polytechnic Institute, 1910. 67 l. (Thesis, E.E., Worcester Polytechnic Institute.)

5490. Harding, Carroll Rede. *George M. Pullman, 1831-1897, and the Pullman Company.* New York: Newcomen Society in North America, 1951. 44 p. (*Newcomen address, 1951.*)

5491. Harding, Glenn T., Cindy Lee. *Rails to the Rio.* Raymondville TX: Glen Harding, 2003. 168 p. (St. Louis, Brownsville and Mexico Railway)

5492. Harding, J.W. (Joseph Whitehead) *Air-brake troubles.* Scranton, Pa., International Textbook Company, 1939. 1 v.

5493. _____. *Baker locomotive valve gear.* Scranton, Pa., International Textbook Company, 1943.

5494. _____. *Brake equipments for high-speed trains.* Scranton, Pa., International Textbook Company, 1942. 94 p.

5495. _____. *Car heating, train control.* Scranton, Pa., International Textbook Company, 1919. 1 v.

5496. _____. *Freight-car brake equipment.* Scranton, Pa., International Textbook Company, 1935. 47, 72 p.

5497. _____. *Hand firing and locomotive boiler attachments/* Scranton, Pa., International Textbook Company, 1928. 1 v.

5498. _____. *Hand firing of locomotives, heat and superheaters.* Scranton, Pa., International Textbook Company, 1920. 268 p.

5499. _____. *Locomotive appliances.* Scranton, Pa., International Textbook Company, 1943. 2 v.

5500. _____. *Locomotive boilers.* Scranton, Pa., International Textbook Company, 1935. 49, 96 p.

5501. _____. *Locomotive brake equipments. Air brake, vol. I.* Scranton, International Textbook Company, 1926. 365 p.

5502. _____. *Locomotive injectors.* Scranton, Pa., International Textbook Company, 1941, c1937. 79 p.

5503. _____. *Locomotive stokers.* Scranton, Pa., International Textbook Company, 1943, c1939. 83 p.

5504. _____. *Locomotive valves and valve gears.* Scranton, Pa., International Textbook Company, 1937. 1 v.

5505. _____. *Lubricators and headlights.* Scranton, Pa., International Textbook Company, 1933. 51, 61 p.

5506. _____. *No. 6 and no. 8 ET brake equipment.* Scranton, Pa., International Textbook Company, 1939. 87 p.

5507. _____. *Passenger and freight-car brake equipments; Air brake, vol. II.* Scranton, Pa., International Textbook Company, 1926. 355 p.

5508. _____. *Southern locomotive valve gear.* Scranton, Pa., International Textbook Company, 1942, c1925. 23 p.

5509. _____. *The steam locomotive.* Scranton, Pa., International Textbook Company, 1934. 123, 153 p.

5510. _____. *Type C-2 locomotive booster*. Scranton, Pa., International Textbook Company, 1943, c1928. 38 p.

5511. _____. *Type D duplex stoker*. Scranton, Pa., International Textbook Company, 1943, c1922. 62 p.

5512. _____. *Walschaert and Baker valve gears*. Scranton, Pa., International Textbook Company, 1940. 44, 56, 57 p.

5513. _____. *Walschaert valve gear*. Scranton, Pa., International Textbook Company, 1942-1943. 2 v.

5514. _____, Frank Williams. *Locomotive valve gears*. Scranton, Pa., International Textbook Company, 1925. 428 p.

5515. _____, G.V. Williamson. *Locomotive boiler-feeding devices*. Scranton, Pa., International Textbook Company, 1935. 51, 48, 76 p.

5516. _____, H.H. Ketcham. *Lubricators and headlights*. Scranton, Pa., International Textbook Company, 1943. 159 p.

5517. _____, John T. Gill. *Passenger brake equipment*. Scranton, Pa., International Textbook Company, 1936. 38, 47, 78 p.

5518 Hardy, Grahame H., Paul Darrell. *American locomotives, 1871-1881/* Decorations by E.S. Hammack. Oakland, CA: G. Hardy, 1950. 1 v.

5519. Hardy, Joseph C. *Burlington Route West: a personal journey*. Davis City, NE: South Platte Press, 2000. 88 p.

5519a. Hare, Charles T., Karl J. Springer. *Exhaust emissions from uncontrolled vehicles and related equipment using internal combustion engines : final report. part 1 : Locomotive diesel engines and marine counterparts* / Ann Arbor MI: U.S. Environmental protection Agency, \Office of Air and Water programs, office of Mobile Source Air Pollution Control, 1972. 1 v. (various pagings)

5520. Hare, Jay Veeder. *History of the North Pennsylvania Railroad*. Philadelphia, Pa., Reading Company, 1944. 31 p.

5521. _____. *History of The Reading*. Philadelphia : Reading Railway Department, Young Men's Christian Association, 1909? 392 p.

5522. Hargrave, Frank Flavius. *A pioneer Indiana railroad; the origin and development of the Monon*. Indianapolis, Wm. B. Burford Printing Company, 1932. 3, 5-229 p.

5523. Harkness, Leroy Thompson. *In the matter of the tracks of the New York Central Railroad Company on the west side of the Borough of Manhattan in the city of New York.*

Albany? : 1925. 16 p.

5523a. _____. George McAneny. *The grade crossing problem in the City of New York and its solution: report to Transit Commission* / New York : M.B. Brown Printing and Binding Co., 1925. 34 p.

5524. Harlan, George H. *Those amazing cab forwards.* Greenbrae, CA: G.H. Harlan, 1983. 159 p.

5525. Harlan, James Shanklin. *New York, New Haven & Hartford Railroad Co.* Washington, D.C., U.S.G.P.O., 1914. 2 v. (Interstate Commerce Commission; 63d Cong., 2d sess. Senate Doc. 543) " ... a report concerning the financial transactions of the New York, New Haven & Hartford Railroad Co.,"

5526. Harlan and Hollingsworth Corporation. *Catalogue of narrow gauge passenger equipment.* Wilmington, Del., The Corporation, 1900. 21 p.

5527. _____. *The Harlan & Hollingsworth Co., ship and car builders; their plant and operations.* Wilmington, Del., The Corporation, 1898. 31 l.

5528. _____. *Semi-Centennial memoir of the Harlan & Hollingsworth Company, Wilmington, Delaware, U.S.A., 1886.* Wilmington, Del., The Corporation, 1886. 490 p.

5529. _____. *Specification "A" for building two double-screw steel-hulled ferry boats: for the Central Railroad of New Jersey.* Wilmington, Del., Mercantile Printing Company, 1892. 43 p.

5530. _____. *Specification of a double screw steel ferryboat: for the Central Railroad Co. of New Jersey.* Wilmington, Del., Star Printing, 1912. 60 p.

5531. _____. *Specifications for a steel screw tug boat: for the Pennsylvania Railroad Co., Lighterage Department.* Wilmington, Del., Chas. L. Story, Printer, 1889. 68 l. Hull Nos. 315, 316, 317. Completed vessels named; Wilmington, Harrisburg, Johnstown.

5532. _____. *Specifications for one (1) steel steam propelled lighter: for the Central Railroad Co. of New Jersey/* Wilmington, Del., Star Printing Company, 1912. 60 p.

5533. _____. *Specifications for the construction of a steel harbor tow boat for the Southern Pacific Company, Atlantic Steamship :Lines: S.P Tug No. 2.* Wilmington, Del., Mercantile Printing Company, 1906. 179 l. (*El Chico.* Hull No. 376.)

5534. _____. *Specifications for the construction of a steel tow boat for the Southern Pacific Company, Atlantic Steamship Lines: S.P. Tug No. 1.* Wilmington, Del., Mercantile Printing Company, 1906. 179 l. (Hull No. 375.)

5535. _____. *Specification for the hull on an iron ferry boat : for the Pennsylvania R.R. Co.* / Wilmington, Del., Ferris Bros., Printers, 1881. 14 l. (Hull Nos. 193, 194.)

5536. _____. *Specifications for three steel tug boats: for the Central Railroad Co of New Jersey.* Wilmington, Del., Star Printing Company, 1906. 91 p. (*Ashley*; Hull 366; *Brigeton*, Hull 367; *Sea Bright*, Hull 368.)

5537. _____. *Specifications for two iron tug boats: to be built for the New York, New Haven and Hartford Railroad Company*/ Wilmington, Del., Delaware Printing Company, 1887. 39 p. (Hull Nos. 235, 236.)

5538. _____. *Specifications of a steel screw steamer for the Central Railroad Company of Vermont : for freight service on Long Island Sound* / Wilmington, Del., New Amstel Press, 1908. 96 p. "Completed vessels named: New London, New York. Hull nos. 392, 393."

5539. Harland Bartholomew & Associates. *A preliminary report on railroad and water-borne transportation facilities for Rochester, New York.* St. Louis, MO: Harland Bartholomew & Associates, 1930. 197, 13 l., 31 l. of plates, ill, maps.

5540. Harleman, Samuel Thomas. *Locomotive coaling stations: design of a 600-ton coaling station for L.V.R.R. at South Easton, Pa.* 1901. 63 l. (Thesis, M.E., Lehigh University.)

5541. Harley, E.T. *Pennsy Q Class.* Hicksville, NY: N.J. International, 1982, 88 p.(*Classic power 5.*)

5542. Harmon, Shirley A., Arley Byers. *An index to Bent, Zig-Zag & Crooked: a narrow gauge story by Arley Byers, 1974.* Woodsfield, OH: Monroe County Historical Society, 1984. 14 l.

5543. Harnsberger, John Lewis. *Jay Cooke and Minnesota: the formative years of the Northern Pacific Railroad, 1868-1873.* New York, Arno Press, 1981. 348 p. (Thesis, Ph.D., University of Minnesota, 1958.)

5544. _____, Fred C. Stoes. *The American railroad album: Fred C. Stoes photography, 1935-1975.* McGregor, TX: Yesteryear Depot, 2008. 1 CD-ROM

5545. Harncourt, Paul. *The planter's railway: excitement and Civil War years.* Arab, AL: Heritage, 1995. 295 p. Southern States/Alabama/Memphis and Charleston Railway Co.

5546. Harper, Carl. *Movements toward railroad building on the South Plains of Texas, 1907-1914.* 1935. 210 l. (Thesis, M.A., Texas Technological College.)

5547. Harper, Jared V. *Santa Fe's Raton Pass.* Foreword by R.H. Kindig. Dallas, TX: Kachina Press, 1983. 144 p.

5548. Harper, John Baskin. *Locomotives of the Missouri Pacific System.* Webster Groves, MO: Missouri Pacific Historical Society, 1976-

5549. Harpster, Jack. *The railroad tycoon who built Chicago: a biography of William B. Ogden.* Carbondale, IL: Southern Illinois University Press, 2009. 309 p.

5550. Harrell, John M. *Proceedings of the National Railroad Convention at St. Louis, Mo., November 23 and 24, 1875, in regard to the construction of the Texas & Pacific Railway as a southern transcontinental line from the Mississippi Valley to the Pacific Ocean on the thirty-second parallel of latitude.* John M. Harrell, secretary. St. Louis, MO: Woodward, Tiernan & Hale, Printers, 1875. 208 p.

5551. Harriman, E. Roland. *The golden spike: a centennial remembrance.* New York, NY: American Geographical Society of New York, 1969. 118 p. (Its *Occasional publication, no. 3.*)

5552. Harriman, George W.R. *Railroad evaluations; a treatise on methods for the valuation of property of common carriers, based on the specifications of the Valuation Act and the decisions of the United States Supreme Court.* Wright & Potter Print Co., 1915. 1 v.

5553. Harrington, Clinton O. *Locomotive cab signals.* 1905. 1 v. (Thesis, B.S., Massachusetts Institute of Technology, Dept. of Civil Engineering.)

5554. Harris, Forbes & Company. *The Hill roads; a short history and description of the railroads comprising the Hill system.* New York, Harris, Forbes & Co., 1921. 19 p.

5555. Harris, J.E., W.E. Pierce. *Vibration testing of railroad tank car specimens : final report* / Washington, DC: Federal Railroad Administration, Office of Research and Development, 1982. 58 p. (FRA/ORD-82/28.)

5556. Harris, Nelson. *Norfolk and Western Railway.* Charleston, SC: Arcadia, 2003. 128 p.

5557. _____. *Norfolk and Western Railway stations and depots*/ Charleston, SC: Arcadia, 2009. 127 p.
.

5558. Harris Palatial Car Company. *Prospectus.* New York, NY: Harris Palatial Car Compnay, 1905. 16 p

5559. Harris, Robert G., Theodore E. Keeler. *Determinant of railroad profitability: an econometric study.* Berkeley, CA: Department of Economics, University of California, 1980. 28 l.(*Working paper. Dept. of Economics. No. SL-8001.*)

5560. _____. *An empirical and institutional analysis of excess capacity in the rail freight industry.* Berkeley: Department of Economics, University of California, 1976. 38 p. (*Working paper, Workshop in Transportation Economics, no. SL-7602*)

5561. _____. *Rationalizing the rail freight industry: a case study in institutional failure and proposals for reform.* Berkeley: Department of Economics, University of California, 1977. 147 p. (*Working paper, Workshop In Transportation Economics, no. SL-7705*)

5562. _____. *Restructuring the railroads: cost savings for branchline abandonments: final report.* Washington, DC: Federal Railroad Administration, Office of Policy and Program Development, 1981? 89 p. (*FRA-OPPD-80-6.)*

5563. _____. *The simple analytics of rail costs and disinvestment criteria.* Berkeley: Institute of Transportation and Traffic Engineering, University of California, 1976. (*Working paper, Institute of Transportation Studies, UCB-ITS-WP-78-1*)

5564. _____, Theodore E. Keller. *Determinants of railroad profitability: an econometric study.* Berkeley: Department of Economics, University of California, 1980. 24, 4 l. (*Working paper/Department of Economics, no. SL-8001*)

5565. Harris, W.M., Joe D. Rice. *Logging with steam: steam logging in the 1880s.* Traverse City, MI: Village Press, 1996. 294 p.

5566. Harris, William Hamilton. *Keeping the faith. Philip Randolph, Milton P. Webster, and the Brotherhood of Sleeping Car Porters, 1925-1937.* .) Urbana, University of Illinois Press, 1977. 252 p.) (Thesis, Ph.D., Indiana University, 1973.)

5567. _____, Blair Hydrick, Martin Paul Schipper. *Records of the Brotherhood of Sleeping Car Porters. Series A. Holdings of the Chicago Historical Society and the Newberry Library, 1925-1969.* Bethesda, MD: University Publications of America, 1990-1994. 50 microfilm reels. 35 mm. (*Black studies research sources*)

5568. Harris, William J. *Report on equipment issues: a report on the equipment proposed for use in the Texas high-speed rail corridors* / College Station, TX: Texas Transportation Institute, Texas A & M University, 1991. 11 l.

5569. Harrison Bros. & Co. *Harrisons' paints and varnishes for railways.* Philadelphia, PA: Harrisons' Bros. & Co., 1889. 72 p.

5570. _____. *Harrison's paint and varnish for railroads.* Philadelphia, PA: Harrison Bros & Co., 1890. 39 p. mounted color samples.

5571. Harrison, Frederick G. *Cinders and timber; a bird's-eye view of logging railroads in northeastern Minnesota yesterday and today.* S.l., s.n., 1967. 49 p.

5572. _____. *Fading glory; a pictorial review of steam railroading in the boom days of the Upper Midwest.* Indian Rocks Beach, FL: Books Unlimited, 1971. 1 v.

5572a. Harrison, James H. *Sacramento Northern gallery*/ Bellflower, CA: Shade Tree Books, 2002. 96 p.

5573. Harrison, Joseph. *The locomotive engine, and Philadelphia's share in its early improvements.* Rev. ed. Philadelphia, G. Gebbie, 1872. 86 p.

5574. Harrison, Richard J. *Long Island Railroad memories: the making of a steam locomotive engineer.* New York, Quadrant Press, 1981. 64 p.

5574a. Harrison, Robert, James R. Blaze. *The potential for improving rail international intermodal services in Texas and the Southeast Region of the United States/* Austin, TX: Southwest Region University Transportation Center, Center for Transporation Research, University of Texas at Austin, 2011. 59 p.

5575. Harshaw, Lou. *Trains, trestles, & tunnels: railroads of the Southern Appalachians.* Lakemont, GA: Copple House Books, 1980, c1977. 93 p.

5576. Hart, Arthur A., Henry R. Griffiths. *Steam trains in Idaho in the nineteenth and twentieth centuries.* Boise, Idaho State Historical Society, 1972. 12 l.

5577. Hart, George M. *History of the locomotives of the Reading Company.* Boston, Mass., Railway & Locomotive Historical Society, 1946. 124 p. (*Bulletin, no. 67.*)

5578. Harter, Henry A. *Fairy tale railroad: the Mohawk and Malone: from the Mohawk, through the Adirondacks to the St. Lawrence.* Utica, NY: North Country Books, 1992, c1979. 310 p.

5579. Harter, Jim. *American railroads of the nineteenth centry: a pictorial history in Victorian wood engravings/* Lubbock, TX: Texas Tech University Press, 1998. 320 p.

5580. Hartley, Eugene F. *Fourteenth census of the United States manufacturers: 1919: steam and electric cars, and railroad repair shops* / Washington, DC: U.S. G.P.O., 1922. 21 p. Eugene F. Hartley, chief statistician for manufactures; Department of Commerce, Bureau of the Census.

5581. Hartley, Scott. *Conrail/* Piscataway, NJ: Railpace Company, 1990. 2 v.

5582. _____. *Guilford: five years of change.* Piscataway, NJ: Railpace, 1989. 112 p. (Guildford Transportation Industries)

5583. _____. *New England Alcos in twilight.* Homewood, IL: PTJ, 1984. 72 p.

5584. _____. *New Haven Railroad: the final decades.* Piscataway, NJ: Railpace, 1992. 160 p.

5585. Hartley, W.M.B., James Harrison. *Harrison's automatic whistle for locomotives.* New York, Wynkoop, Hallenbeck & Thomas, 1857. 22 p.

5586. Hartough, E.W. *The car inspector's handbook.* New York, Simmons-Boardman Pub. Co., 1924. 284 p.

5587. _____. *Handbook of steel car repairs.* New York, Simmons-Boardman, 1925. 292 p.

5588. _____ *Handbook of wooden car repairs.* New York, Simmons-Boardman Pub.

Co., 1925. 276 p.

5589. Hartshorne, Francis Cope. *The railroads and the Commerce clause*. Philadelphia: University of Pennsylvania Press, 1892. 165 p.

5590. Hartzler, John G. *The 'ol hook & eye: a history of the Kishacoquillas Valley Railroad Co.* Belleville, PA: J.G. Hartzler, 1988. 170 p.

5591. Harvard Trust. *Charles Davenport: 1812-1903*. Cambridge, MA: Harvard Trust Co., 1931. 15 p.

5592. Harvey Fisk & Sons. *Information concerning the Central of Georgia Railway. July 22d, 1897.* New York?: s.n., 1897. 5 p.

5593. _____. *Tennessee Central Railway, east and west gateway to Nashville/* New York: H. Fisk, 1928. 16 p.

5594. Harvey, Fred. *The great Southwest along the Santa Fe.* Kansas City, Mo., F. Harvey, 1900. 67 p. (9th ed.: 1926.)

5594a. Harvey Willard A. *Railroads of the Ohio Valley, 1947-1960* / Telford, PA: Silver Brook Junction Publishing, 1995-   . <5 v.>

5595. Harvey, William Morgan. *Chicago, Milwaukee and St. Paul Railway Company.* Chicago, Ill., Faithorn Company, 1912. 202 p.

5596. _____. *Frisco Lines.* Chicago, Ill., Press of Faithorn Company, 1912. 202 p.

5597. Harwood, Herbert H. *Chesapeake & Ohio lightweight passenger equipment, 1946-1972.* Alderson, WV: Chesapeake & Ohio Historical Society, 1973. 18 p.

5598. _____. *The 50 best of B & O, book two.* Baltimore, MD: Barnard, Roberts & Co., 1977. 52 p.

5599. _____. *The 50 best of PRR, book three.* Baltimore, Barnard, Roberts, 1978. 51 l.

5600. _____. *The first 50 best of New York Central System.* Baltimore, Barnard, Roberts, 1977-

5601. _____. *Impossible challenge: the Baltimore and Ohio Railroad in Maryland.* Baltimore, Barnard, Roberts, 1979. 497 p.

5602. _____. *Impossible challenge II: Baltimore to Washington and Harpers Ferry from 1828 to 1994.* 2d rev. ed. Baltimore, Barnard, Roberts, 1994. 431 p.

5603. _____. *Invisible giants: the empires of Cleveland's Van Sweringen brothers.* Bloomington, Indiana University Press, 2003. 342 p.

5604. _____. *The New York, Westchester & Boston Railway: J.P. Morgan's magnificent mistake*. Bloomington, Indiana University Press, 2008. 168 p.

5605. _____. *Philadelphia's Victorian suburban stations*. Crete, NE: J-B Pub. Co., 1975. 48 p.

5606. _____. *The railroad that never was : Vanderbilt, Morgan, and the South Pennsylvania Railroad* / Bloomington : Indiana University Press, 2010. 1 v.

5607. _____. *Rails to the Blue Ridge*. 2d ed. Falls Church, VA: Pioneer American Society, 1969. 112 p. (Washington and Old Dominion Railroad.) 4th ed. Fairfax Station, VA: Northern Virginia Regional Park Authority, 2009. 160 p.

5608. _____. *Royal Blue Line*. Sykesville, MD: Greenberg Pub. Co., 1990. 199 p.

5609. _____ *Royal Blue Line: the classic B & O train between Washington and New York*. Baltimore, The Johns Hopkins University Press, 2002, c 1990. 197 p.

5610. _____ Robert S. Korach. *The Lake Shore Electric Railway story*. Bloomington, Indiana University Press, 2000. 297 p.

5610a. *Haskell and Barker Car Company, Michigan City, Indiana; photographic collection. Catalog prepared and edited by William D. Edson*. Washington, DC: Smithsonian Institution, 1991. 40 p.

5611. Haskell, Charles Frederick Beals, Daniel Carl Haskell. *On reconnaissance for the Great Northern; letters of C.F.B. Haskell, 1889-1891*. New York, New York Public Library, 1948. 40 p.

5612. Hassler, Charles William. *Railroad rings and the their relation to the railroad question in this country*. New York, NY: D.H. Gildersleeve & Co., Printers, 1876. 29 p.

5613. Hastings, Philip R. *Chicago Great Western Railway*. Newton, NJ: Carstens, 1980. 80 p.

5614. _____. *Remember the Rock*. Walt Lankenau, editor. Andover, NJ: Andover Junction Publications, 1987. 47 p.

5615. _____. *Philip Ross Hastings: the Boston & Maine, a photographic essay*. Text by Frank Kyper. Introduction by William B. Stewart. S.l., Locomotive & Railway Preservation, 1989. 206 p.

5616. _____ *Grand Trunk heritage: steam in New England*. Edited and designed by John Krause and Ed Crist. New York, Railroad Heritage Press, 1978. 48 p. (Enlarged edition: Newton, NJ: Carstens Publications, 1987. 64 p.

5617. Hatch, Henry D, George L. Andrews. *Red cap*. S.l., Federal Writers' Project, 1980, 1939. 19 l.

5618. Hatch, P.H., R.P. Turnbull. *Winter aspects of electric railroad operation/*
New York, NY: American Institute of Electrical Engineers, 1961. 7 p. (*AIEE Conference Paper: CP62-160.*)

5619. Hathaway, William T., Jason Baker, N. Albert Mousa. *Fire safety countermeasures for urban rail vehicles* / Washington, DC: Federal Rail Transit Administration, 1992. 76 p. (*FTA-MA-0200-92-1.*)

5620. Hatt, William Kendrick. *Holding force of railroad spikes in wooden ties.* Washington, D.C., U.S.G.P.O., 1906. (*United States Department of Agriculture, Forest Service. Circular, 46.*)

5621. Hauck, Cornelius. *Narrow gauge to Central and Silver Plume.* Golden, CO: Colorado Railroad Museum, 1972. 223 p.

5622. _____, Charles Albi, Robert W. Richardson. *Colorado railroads and the Colorado Railroad Museum.* Golden, CO: The Museum, 1989. 63 p.

5623. _____, Mallory Hope Ferrell, Rex C. Myers. *Idaho- Montana issue.* Golden, CO: Colorado Railroad Museum, 1981. 215 p.

5624. _____, Robert W. Richardson. *Locomotives of the Rio Grande.* Golden, CO: Colorado Railroad Museum, 1983. 100 p.

5625. Hauer, E.R., C.M. Angel. *Mobile axle flaw detector unit carrier and method used to ferret out defective car journals on the Chesapeake and Ohio* / New York : American Institute of Electrical Engineers, 1956. 5, 10 p. (*AIEE Conference paper, CP-56-978.*)

5626. _____, _____. *Mobile reflectoscopic inspection of railroad car axles on the Chesapeake and Ohio Railway* / New York : American Institute of Electrical Engineers, 1956. 3, 8 p. (*Transactions papers, no. 58-238.*)

5627. Hauff, Steve, Jim Gertz. *The Willamette locomotive.* Portland, OR: Binford & Mort, 1977. 182 p. (Willamette Iron and Steel Works.) (Reissue: Arlington, WA: Oso Pub., 1997. 182 p.)

5628. Haupt, Herman *The coal business on the Pennsylvania Railroad; a communication addressed to the president, directors, and stockholders of the Pennsylvania Railroad, on the cost of transportation* / Philadelphia: T.K. and P.G. Collins, 1857. 33 p.

5629. _____. *General theory of bridge construction* / Lexington, KY : BiblioLife, 2010, 1886. 268 p.

5630. _____. *Reminiscences of General Herman Haupt.* Milwaukee, Wright & Joys, 1901. 331 p. (Reprint: New York, NY: Arno Press, 1981.)

5630a. Hauser, Chad Allan. *Building iron rails to their future: examination* of Davenports, Iowa's antebellum relationship with the Rock island Line and Missouri

railroads / 2012. 98 p. (Thesis, M.A., Iowa State University.)

5631. Hauser, Gilbert B. *Development of the aluminum tank car*. New York: American Society of Mechanical Engineers, 1950. 15 p. (*Paper. American Society of Mechanical Engineers, 50-A-118.*)

5632. _____. *The expanding use of aluminum in railroad cars* / New York : American Society of Mechanical Engineers, 1957. 5 p. (*ASME. Paper no. 57-RR-2.*)

5633. Hawkes, Paine & Company. *Hawkes & Paine's spark and smoke consuming apparatus for locomotives*. Providence, R.I., The Company, 1873. 8 p.

5634. Hawkes, William M. *The electrification of the Delaware, Lackawanna and Western Railroad*. 1933. 87, 1 l. (Thesis, B.S. in E.E., University of Notre Dame.)

5634a. Hawkins, Gary. *U.S.A. by bus and train* / New York : Pantheon Books, 1985. 396 p.

5635. Hawkins, Jeff. *Richmond railroads*. Charleston, SC: Arcadia, 2010. 127 p.

5636. Hawkins, Susan, Lawrence Bender, William E. Thoms. *End of the line… after abandonment, then what?* Fargo, NG: Upper Great Plains Transportation Institute, North Dakota State University, 1982. 78 p. (*TLS 12.*)

5637. *Hawkins index-digest-analysis of decisions under the Interstate Commerce Act*, [rail carrier service]. Arlington, VA: Hawkins Pub. Co., 1930s-   (loose-leaf)

5638. Hawks, Donald Ray. *Railroad equipment trust market: a relative importance study*. 1975. 79 l. (Thesis, M.A., San Francisco State University.)

5639. Hawthorne, J.W. *The history, design and experience of the railroad freight car roller bearing on the Atlantic Coast Line Railroad* / Jacksonville, FL: Atlantic Coast Line Railroad Company, 1963. 43, 8 l. 37 leaves of plates.

5640. _____. *Hot boxes : some fundamental problems* / New York : American Society of Mechanical Engineers, 1953. 7, 2 p. (*ASME. Paper no. 53-A-104.*)

5641. Hawthorne, V. R. *Dome covers approved by Committee on Tank Cars, American Railway Association, Division V-Mechanical*. Chicago: American Railway Association, Sub-Committee on Dome Covers and Safety Valves, 1933. 12 l. "Lists designs submitted by: American Car and Foundry Co., Canadian Car & Foundry Co., General American Tank Car Corp., Petroleum Iron Works Co. of Ohio, Pressed Steel Car Co., Standard Steel Car Corp., Standard Tank Car Corp., Tidal Refining Co., and Union Tank Car Co.

5642. Hawxhurst, Thomas Erie. *Road to ruin: the New Orleans Tehuantepec Railroad Company, 1849-1852, and United States-Mexican Isthmian policy*/ 1993. 103 l.

(Thesis, M.A., Auburn University.)

5643. Hay, W.W., R. Baugher, A.J. Reinschmidt. *A study of railroad ballast economics.* Washington, D.C., Federal Railroad Administration; Office of Research and Development, 1977. 91 p. (*National Institute of Standards and Technology, no. FRA-ORD-77/64.*)

5644. Hay, William Walter. *Effects of weather upon railroad operation, maintenance, and construction/* 1956. 332 l. (Thesis, Ph.D., University of Illinois at Urbana-Champaign.)

5645. _____. *Lateral stability of ballast: Ballast and Foundation Research program/* Washington, DC: Federal Railroad Administration, Office of Research and Development, 1977. 46 p. (*FRA-ORD-77-61*)

5646. _____. *Railroad engineering.* 2nd ed. New York, NY: Wiley, 1982. 758 p.

5647. Hayden, Bob. *Diesel locomotives.* Milwaukee, WI: Kalmbach Pub. Co., 1980. 160 p. (*Model Railroader cyclopedia, v. 2*)

5648. Hayden, Stone & Company. *A study of Chicago, Rock Island and Pacific Railroad.* New York, Hayden, Stone, 1959. 43 p.

5649. _____. *A study of Southern Railway Company.* New York, Hayden, Stone, 1958. 30 p.

5650. _____. *A study of the Chicago & Eastern Illinois Railroad* Company. S.l., s.n., 1956. 27 p.

5651. _____. *A study of the Great Northern Railway Company.* New York, Hayden, Stone, 1958. 25 p.

5652. _____. *A study of the Minneapolis & St. Louis Railway Company.* New York, Hayden, Stone, 1957. 21 p.

5653. _____ *A study of the Missouri Pacific System.* New York, Hayden, Stone, 1956. 34 p.

5654. _____. *A study of the Norfolk and Western Railway Company.* New York, Hayden, Stone, 1959. 38 p.

5655. _____ *A study of the Western Pacific Railroad Company.* New York, Hayden, Stone, 1959. 43 p.

5656. Hayes, Derek. *Historical atlas of the North American railroad.* Berkeley : University of California Press, 2010. 224 p.

5657. Hayes, W. F. *Update of super-speed ground transportation technology development status and performance capabilities*/ Kingston, ON: Canadian Institute of Guided ground Transport/California-Nevada Super-Speed Ground Transportation Commission, 1990. 1 v. (various pagings) (*CIGGT project no. PRJ-838*)

5658. Hayes, William Edward. *Iron road to empire: the history of 100 years of the progress and achievements of the Rock Island Lines.* New York: Simmons-Boardman, 1953. 306 p.

5659. Haymes, Max. *Railroadin' some: railroads in the early blues.* York, Music Mentor, 2006. 390 p.

5660. Haymond, Creed. *The Central Pacific Railroad. Its relations with the government. It has performed all its obligations. Argument of Creed Haymond, its general solicitor, made to a select committee of the U.S. Senate ... March 17th and 26th, and April 7th, 1888. Reported by James L. Andem ...* Washington, DC: Judd & Detweiler, Printers, 1888. 181 p.

5661. Haynes, Thomas Francis. *Crawford underfeed mechanical stoker.* 1918. 87 p. (Thesis, M.E., University of Kentucky.)

5661a. Hays, Douglas L., Jr. *Locomotives of the Milwaukee & Mississippi Railroad and the Milwaukee & Prairie du Chien Railway, 1850-1867* / Baton Rouge, LA: American Printing Center, 2013. 216 p.

5662. Hayward, James, Stephen Harriman Long, Edward H. Robbins. *Report of the directors of internal improvement on the subject of rail roads.* Boston, Dutton and Wentworth, Printers to the State, 1830. 61 p. (Massachusetts. Board of Internal Improvement.

5663. Hayward, Walt. *A glossary of words, terms and expressions used by trainmen during the days of steam railroads.* Kanarravile, Utah, Acorn Creations, 1990. 14 p.

5664. Hazard, Rowland. *The Credit Mobilier of America; a paper read before the Rhode Island Historical Society, Tuesday evening, February 22, 1881.* Providence, S.S. Rider, 1881. 42 p.

5665. *Hazardous material tank cars – tank head protective "shield" or "bumper" design.* Washington, DC: Federal Railroad Administration, 1971. 1 v. (various pagings)

5666. Hazel, M.E. *The U.S. train performance simulator*/ Washington, DC: Federal Railroad Administration, Office of Research and Development, 1978. 46 p. "Final report. Research and Special Programs Administration, Transportation Systems Center. September 1978. 46 p. in various pagings. (*FRA/ORD-77/48*)

5667. Hazel, Morrin E. *Tank car accident data analysis.* Washington, DC: Federal Railroad Administration, Office of Research and Development, 1991. 154 p. (*DOT/FRA/ORD-91/05.*)

5667a. Hazen, John Munger. *Railway contractor's hand-book* / Minneapolis; Press of Kimball & Storer Co., 1900. 139 p.

5668. *Hazmat Transport '94: a national conference on the transportation of hazardous materials and wastes, June 17-19, 1991.* Evanston, IL: Northwestern University, Transportation Center, 1991. 851 p.

5668a. Headley, Scott A. *The Denver Pacific Railroad, the Union Colony, and the creation of a middle-class community at Greeley, Colorado, 1869-1880/* 2005. 137 l. (Thesis, M.A., University of Northern Colorado.)

5668a. *Headlight.* Cincinnati, OH: Louisville and Nashville Railroad Co., 1800s-?

5669. *The Headlight.* Larkspur, CA: Northwestern Pacific Railroad Historical Society, 1980s- . Bimonthly, 1995-. Former,: Monthly.

5670. *Headlight.* New York : Public Relations Department, New York Central System, 1940- . Other titles: New York Central headlight; Central headlight. v. 1-10, no. 8, 1940-Sept. 1949.

5671. Heald, Bruce D. *Boston & Maine in the 19ᵗʰ century.* Charleston, SC: Arcadia, 2001. 128 p.

5672. _____. *Boston & Maine in the 20ᵗʰ century.* Charleston, SC: Arcadia, 2001. 128 p.

5673. _____. *Boston & Maine locomotives.* Charleston, SC: Arcadia, 2002. 128 p.

5674. _____. *Boston & Maine trains and services.* Charleston, SC: Arcadia, 2005. 128 p.

5675. _____. *A history of the Boston & Maine Railroad: exploring New Hampshire's rugged heart by rail.* Charleston, SC: The History Press, 2007. 128 p.

5675a. _____. *The Mount Washington Cog Railway : climbing the White Mountains of New Hampshire* / Charleston, SC: History Press, 2011. 127 p.

5676. _____. *Railways and waterways: through the White Mountains.* Charleston, SC: Arcadia, 1999. 128 p.

5677. Healy, Kent Tenney. *Economies of electrification of the Boston-New Haven-Springfield New Haven-Maybrook Divisions of the New York, New Haven, and Hartford Railroad.* 1923. 55 l. (Thesis, B.S., Massachusetts Institute of Technology, Department of Electrical Engineering.)

5678. _____. *Electrification of steam railroads.* New York, McGraw-Hill Book Company, 1929. 395 p.

5679. _____. *Performance of the U.S. railroads since World War II: a quarter century of private operation.* New York, Vantage Press, 1985. 295 p.

5680. Heap, Gwinn Harris. *Central route to the Pacific. With related material on railroad explorations and Indian affairs by Edward F. Beale, Thomas H. Benton, Kit Carson, and E.A. Hitchcock, and in other documents, 1851-54.* Edited with an introd. and notes by LeRoy R. Hafen and Ann W. Hafen. Glendale, CA: Arthur H. Clark Co., 1957. 346 p. (*The Far West and the Rockies historical series, 1820-1875, v. 7.*)

5681. Heath & Milligan Manufacturing Company. *The 1-2-3 method of railway painting : (invented by Geo. R. Cassie, originator of the A-B-C system)* / Chicago: Heath & Milligan Mfg. Co., 1890s. 16 p.

5682. Heath, Erie. *Seventy-five years of progress: historical sketch of the Southern Pacific.* San Francisco, Southern Pacific Bureau of News, 1945. 51 p.

5683. Heathcliff, G.M., Alvin K. Traz. *Rails along the Schuylkill.* Highland Mills, NY: GRIT Commercial Printing, 1989. 72 p.

5684. *Heavy traction, 1922-1941.* Novato, CA: Newton K. Gregg, 1974. 1 v.

5685. Hecker, JayEtta Z. *Intercity passenger rail: Congress faces critical decisions in developing a national policy.* Washington, DC: U.S. General Accounting office, 2002. http://purl.access.gpo.gov/GPO/LPS38593

5686. _____. *Freight railroads: updated information on rates and other industry trends: testimony before the Subcommittee on Surface Transportation and Merchant Marine, Committee on Commerce, Science, and Transportation, U.S. Senate*/ Washington, DC: U.S. Government Accountability Office, 2007. 27 p. http://purl.access.gpo.gov/GPO/LPS88038

5687. _____. *Intercity passenger rail: the Congress faces critical decisions about the role of and funding for intercity passenger rail systems*/ Washington, DC: U.S. General Accounting Office, 2001.(*GAO-01-820 T*) *http://purl/access.gpo.gove/GPO/LPS47506*

5688. _____. *Passenger rail security: evaluating foreign security practices and risk can help guide security efforts: testimony before the Committee on Transportation and Infrastructure, Subcommittee on Highways, Transit, and Pipelines, House of Representatives*/ Washington, D.C.: U.S. Government Accountability Office, 2006. 27 p. Internet file: *http://purl.access.gpo.gov/GPO/LPS70486*

5689. Hecteman, Kevin W. *Sacramento Southern Railroad.* Charleston, SC: Arcadia Publishing, 2009. 127 p.

5690. _____. *Sacramento's Southern Pacific shops.* Charleston, SC: Arcadia Pub. Co., 2010. 127 p.

5691. Hedge, John W., Geoffrey S. Dawson. *The San Antonio and Aransas Pass Railway: the story of the famous "SAP" railway of Texas*. Waco, TX: AMA Graphics, 1983. 148 p.

5692. Hedge, Thomas. *Charles Elliott Perkins/* Manchester-by-the-Sea, 1931. 40 p.

5693. Hedges, James Blaine. *Factors in the development of transportation in the Pacific Northwest, 1860-1893, as reflected in the career of Henry Villard.* 1924. 1 v. (Thesis, Ph.D., Harvard University.)

5694._____. *Henry Villard and the railways of the Northwest*. New Haven, Yale University Press, 1930. 224 p.(Reprint: New York, Russell & Russell, 1967. 224 p.)

5695. Hedgpeth, J. Pete. *5 miles of family ties: its recollections of Missouri's family-operated Rock Port, Langdon & Northern Railway*. James J. Reisdorff, editor. David City, NE: South Platte Press, 1988. 72 p.

5696. _____. *Terminal tales: memories of a Rock Island Chicago Division trainmaster, 1961-1964*. Newton, IA: C.P.M., the Railway Book People, 2004. 136 p.

5697. Hedin, Robert. *The great machines: poems and songs of the American railroad.* Iowa City, University of Iowa Press, 1996. 251 p.

5698. Hedrick, J.K. *Performance limits of rail passenger vehicles: stability/curving trade-offs and model evaluation/* Washington, DC: U.S. Department of Transportation, Office of the Secretary of Transportation, 1985. 1 v. (various pagings) (*DOT/OST/P-34/85-014.*)

5699. Hegne, Barbara. *Stories centered around the Virginia & Truckee Railroad.* Sparks, NV: B. Hegne, 2006. 73 p.

5700. Heidelmark, William J., Sylvia Adams, Michael Chiffolo. *Taxation of railroads, other transportation companies, and other businesses: a survey of state laws: summary report/* Albany, NY: Program Analysis and Development Unit, New York State Division of Equalization and Assessment, 1983. 60 p.

5700a. Heiling, Frank J., Billy R. Bishop, Billy A. Miller. *Missouri-Kansas-Texas Railroad Company manual of freight car and diesel locomotive equipment*. S.l., Missouri-Kansas-Texas Railroad, 1969. 55 p.

5701. Heilman, H., C. Kahrs, G. Williams. *A multipurpose train performance calculator/* Washington, DC: Federal Railroad Administration, Office of Passenger Systems, 1978. 2 v. (*FRA/ORD-79/17.I; FRA/ORD-79/17.II*)

5702. Heimburger, Donald J. *Along the East Broad Top*. River Forest, IL: Heimburger House Pub. Co., 1987. 248 p.

5703. _____. *Denver & Rio Grande Western narrow gauge plans: interesting locomotive, car and work equipment plans for railfans and modelers.* Tolono, IL: Heimburger, 1976. 56 p.

5704. _____. *Illinois Central: main line of Mid-America.* Forest Park, IL: Heimburger House, 1995. 128 p.

5705. _____. *Rio Grande steam locomotives: standard gauge.* River Forest, IL: Heimburger House Pub. Co., 1981. 200 p.

5706. _____ *Trains of America: all-color railroad photography featuring the late steam and early diesel era.* Forest Park, IL: Heimburger House Pub. Co., 1989. 204 p.

5707. _____. *Wabash.* River Forest, IL: Heimburger House Pub. Co., 1984. 320 p.

5708. _____. *Wabash standard plans and reference.* Forest Park, IL: Heimburger House Pub. Co., 1993. 128 p.

5709. _____, Carl R. Byron. *The American streamliner: postwar* years. Forest Park, IL: Heimburger House Pub. Co., 2001. 200 p.

5710. _____, _____. *The American streamliner: prewar years.* Forest Park, IL: Heimburger House Pub. Co., 1996. 176 p.

5711. _____, John Kelly. *Trains to victory: America's railroads in World War II: including foreign theater operations/* Forest Park, IL: Heimburger House, 2009. 380 p.

5712. Heinemann, Adelbert Lewis. *Trade apprenticeship education in the railroad shop /* 1917. 1 v. (Thesis, M.E., Pennsylvania State College.)

5713. Heinigk, Penelope Pearl. *The other side of the tracks: representations of gender in early railroad turmoil.* 2001. 207 l. (Thesis, University of Oregon, Eugene)

5714. Heirman, Bob. *A railroad runs through it: reflections from Everett to Darrington.* Snohomish, WA: Cloudcap, 1998. 115 p.

5715. Heisler, Charles L. *Heisler's geared locomotives.* Philadelphia, The Company, 1907. 12 p.

5716.Heisler Locomotive Works. *Heisler fireless locomotives.* Erie, Pa., The Company, 1930. 1 v.

5717. _____. *Heisler geared locomotives.* Erie, Pa., Heisler Locomotive Works, 1923. 23 p.

5718. _____. *Heisler geared locomotives: an illustrated catalogue describing the construction in detail of the patented Heisler geared locomotive.* Erie, Pa., Heisler Locomotive Works, 1908. 47 p. (*Heisler Locomotive Works, no. 108.*)

5719. _____. *Heisler geared locomotives: an illustrated catalogue describing in detail the patented construction.* Erie, Pa., Heisler Locomotive Works, 1912. 47 p. (*Heisler Locomotive Works, no. 115.*)

5720. _____. *Heisler geared locomotives: description of the patented construction.* Erie, Pa., Heisler Locomotive Works, 1923. 11 p. (Heisler Locomotive Works, no. 4763.)

5721. _____. *Heisler geared locomotives.* Erie, Pa., Heisler Locomotive Works, 1908. 16 p. (1908 repair list)

5722. _____. *Why you can haul at least 30% more per ton of locomotive with the modern Heisler: hauling at a lower cost-per-ton without sacrificing required speed.* Hillsboro, OR: Timber Times, 1995, 1920. 32 p. (Also: Edmonds, WA: Pacific Fast Mail, 1973. 32 p.)

5723. *The Heisler locomotive, 1891-1941.* Lancaster, Pa., Benjamin F. Kline, 1982. 199 p.

5724. Heiss, Ralph A. *The Lehigh Valley Railroad across New Jersey.* Charleston, SC: Arcadia, 2009. 128 p.

5724a. Hellen, Joseph. *East-Southwest Texas on the Texas and New Orleans Railroad.* Houston. TX: s.n. 1909. 93 p.

5725. Heller, James N. *Coal transportation and deregulation: an impact analysis of the Staggers Act/* New York, NY: Energy Bureau; Washington, DC: Serif Press, 1983. 190 p.

5726. Heller, Frank J. *Evolution of tank car design through engineering.* S.l., s.n., 1970? 24, 5 p. "Presented before the 1970 annual ASME Petroleum Conference, September 15, 1970 at Denver, Colorado."

5727. Heller, John. *Pacific Electric stations.* Long Beach, CA: Electric Railway Historical Association of Southern California, 1998. 250 p.

5728. Heller, Vivian. *The city beneath us: building the New York subways.* New York, W.W. Norton, 2004. 247 p.

5729. Helm, Robert A. *The Clinchfield Railroad in the coal fields.* Lynchburg, VA: TLC Pub., 2004. 120 p.

5730. Helmer, William F. *A Catskill souvenir: scenes on the line of the Ulster and Delaware Railroad.* Cornwallville, NY: Hope Farm Press, 1969, 1879. 25 p.

5731. _____. *O. & W.; the long life and slow death of the New York, Ontario & Western Railway.* Berkeley, CA: Howell-North, 1959. 211 p. (Also: Hensonville, NY: Black Dome Press, 2000. 213 p.)

5732. _____. *Rip Van Winkle railroads: Canajoharie & Catskill R.R., Catskill Mountain Ry., Otis Elevating Ry., Catskill & Tannersville Ry.* Berkeley, CA: Howell-North Books, 1970. 146 p.

5733. Helmers, Dow. *Historical Alpine tunnel.* Denver, CO: Sage Books, 1963. 200 p. (Also: Chicago, Sage Books, 1971. 208 p.

5734. _____. *Tragedy at Eden.* Pueblo, CO: s.n., 1971. 149 p.

5734. Helmholtz, Henry. *Mechanical and air brake examination for firemen; first, second and third year.* Chicago, H. Helmholtz, 1938. 413 p.

5735. Helser, J.L., A.A. Carroll. *Safety of Highway-Railroad Grade Crossings Research Needs Workshop.* Washington, DC: Federal Railroad Administration, Office of Research and Development, 1996. 2 v. (*DOT/FRA/ORD-98/14.1 and 14.2*)

5736. Hemenway, Scott. *Anthracite collieries and railroads of the Western Middle Field.* Laurys Station, PA: Garrigues House, 2008. 1 v.

5737. Hemphill, Hugh. *The railroads of San Antonio and south central Texas.* San Antonio, TX: Maverick Pub. Co., 2006. 101 p.

5738. Hemphill, Mark W. *Union Pacific Salt Lake route.* North York, ON: Stoddart, 1995. 176 p.

5739. Henck, John Benjamin. *Field-book for railroad engineers*/ New York, D. Appleton, 1854. 243 p. (2d ed.: 1896. 312 p.)

5740. Hender, Arthur C. *A brief history of the Sierra Railroad.* San Mateo, CA: The Western Railroader, 1955. 38 p. (*The Western Railroader, v. 18, no. 6, April 1955.*)

5741. Henderson, George R. *The cost of locomotive operation.* New York, The Railroad Gazette, 1906. 198 p.

5742. _____. *Locomotive operation, a technical and practical analysis.* Chicago, Railway Age, 1904. 528 p. (2d ed. Chicago, Wilson Company, 1907. 532 p.)

5743. _____. *Recent development of the locomotive.* Philadelphia, Pa., Baldwin Locomotive Works, 1912. 53 p.

5744. Henderson Hydraulic Car Brake Company. *Henderson hydraulic brake for railroad cars : descriptive pamphlet* / Philadephia : Henderson Hydraulic Car Brake Company, Press of Fame Print. House, 1875. 11 p.

5745. Henderson, James M., Clem C. Linnenberg. *Shifts in rail and truck transportation of fresh fruits and vegetables.* Washington, D.C., U. Dept of Agriculture, Agricultural Marketing Services, Marketing Research Division, 1958. 52 p.

5746. Henderson, Jennifer Sturbois. *Belonging in the American West: dining by Mimbreno railroad china in the twentieth century.* 1994. 88 l. (Thesis, M.A., State University of New York at Oneonta.)

5747. Henderson, John *Blue diesels & black diamonds: the operation of the West End of the Cumberland Division in the Baltimore and Ohio's diesel era.* Flushing, NY: H&M Publications, 1991. 83 p.

5748. _____. *Cabins, crummies & hacks: a pageant of the little red caboose behind the train.* Flushing, NY: H&M Productions, 1991-1993. 4 v.

5749. _____. *Classic freight cars: a symphony of box cars in wood and steel.* Flushing NY: H&M Productions, 1992- . v. <1-5, 9>

5750. _____. *4 great divisions of the New York Central, Erie-Lackawanna & Northern Pacific.* Flushing, NY: H&M Productions, 1992. 111 p.

5751. _____. *Gotham turnstiles: a visual depiction of rapid transit in the New York Metropolitan area from 1958-1968.* Flushing, NY: H&M Productions, 1992. 96 p.

5752. _____. *Jersey City westbound.* Flushing, NY: H&M Productions, 1990. 1 v. (CNJ)

5753. Hendrex, James. *Milwaukee Road through Missouri.* 1954. 97 l. (Thesis, M.A., Northeast Missouri State Teachers College.)

5754. Hendrickson, Richard H. *Furniture and automobile box cars, 1887-1997.* Highlands Ranch, CO: Santa Fe Railway Historical and Modeling Society, 1997. 157 p. (*Santa Fe Railway rolling stock reference series, v. 3.*)

5755. _____. *Santa Fe Railway painting and lettering guide for model railroaders.* Dallas, TX: Santa Fe Modelers Organization, 1990-

5756. _____, Edward S. Kaminski. *Billboard refrigerator cars/* Berkeley, CA: Signature Press, 2008. 224 p.

5757. _____, Richard W. Pelouze. *Santa Fe tank cars/* Midwest City, OK: Santa Fe Railway Historical and Modeling Society, 2004. 120 p. (*Santa Fe rolling stock reference series, v. 5.*)

5758. Hendy, Anne-Marie. *American railroad stock certificates.* London, Gibbons, 1980. 168 p.

5759. Hengeveld, Henry John (1860-) C.P. Disney, William James Miskella. *Practical railway painting and lacquering, a handbook for railroad men.* Chicago, IL: Finishing Research Laboratories, 1929. 242 p. (*Practical finishing series, vol. IV.)*

5760. Henry, Joseph, Spencer Fullerton Baird. *Reports of explorations and surveys,*

to ascertain the most practicable and economical route for a railroad
from the Mississippi River to the Pacific Ocean. Made under the direction
of the Secretary of War in 1853-[6]... Washington, A.O.P. Nicholson, Printer, 1855-1860. 12 v. in 13

5760a. Henry, Lyell D. *The National Association of Railroad Passengers: a case study of the formation, organization, and political effectiveness of a consumer interest group.* 1973. 302 l. (Thesis, Ph.D., University of Iowa.)

5761. Henry, Robert Selph. *Civil War railroads.* Iowa City , IA: State University of Iowa, 1961. 1 v.

5762. _____. *The railroad land grant legend in American history texts.* Cedar Rapids, IA: Torch Press, 1945. 1v. (Reprinted from the *Mississippi Valley historical review, v. 32,no. 2, Sept. '45.*)

5763. _____. *This fascinating railroad business.* Indianapolis, IN: Bobbs-Merrill Company, 1942. 520 p. (3d ed. rev.; 1946. 621 p.)

5764. _____, Otto Kuhler. *On the railroad.* Akron, OH: Saalfield Publishing Company, 1949. 21 p.

5765. _____, _____. *Portraits of the iron horse; the American locomotive in pictures and story.* Chicago, New York, Rand, MacNally & Company, 1937. 80 p. (Reprint: Santa Fe, NM: Sunstone Press, 1976, 1937. 80 p.

5766. Hensel, Gary. *The Pullman effect* / 1997. 41 l. (Thesis, M.A., California State University, Dominguez Hills.) The Pullman method.

5767. Hensler, Donald Paul. *Fallen by the wayside : the unfulfilled promise of Patrick McGinnis and the New Haven Railroad* / 2008. 94 l. (Thesis, M.S., Trinity College, Hartford, Conn.)

5768. Henson, Stephen Ray. *Industrial workers in the mid-nineteenth-century South: Atlanta railwaymen, 1840-1870.* 1982. 238 l. (Thesis, Ph.D., Emory University.)

5769. Henwood, James N.J. *A short haul to the bay; a history of the Narragansett Pier Railroad.* Brattleboro, VT: Stephen Green Press, 1969. 48 p.

5770. Hepburn, A. Barton. *Proceedings of the Special Committee on railroads, appointed under a resolution of the Assembly to investigate alleged abuses in the management of railroads chartered by the state Of New York.* New York : Evening Post Steam Presses, 1879-1880. 8 v. (New York State. Legislature. Assembly. Special Committee on Railroads.)

5771. Hepler, Al. *CSX Transportation: Volume one: freight equipment; freight motive power and cars in color; EMD General Motors diesel locomotives, road slugs and visitors, cabooses, transfer cars, open and covered hoppers.* Crawfordsville, IN:

Howell Publications, 2001. 70 p.

5772. Hepler, James Leslie. *The Southern Railway remembered.* Lynchburg, VA: TLC Pub. Co., 2001. 108 p.

5772a. Heppner, Frank H. *Railroads of Rhode island: shaping the Ocean State's railways* / Charleston, SC: History Press, 2012. 204 p.

5773. Herbert, Hilary A., John K. Luttrell. *The true Southern Pacific versus the Texas Pacific Railroad.* New York : M.W. Gilmore, 1878. 47 p.

5774. Herbert, Lee Carrington, K. Edward Lay. *Norfolk & Western depots of the Shenandoah Valley.* Charlottesville, VA: School of Architecture, University of Virginia, 1991. 43 l. (*Architecture in Virginia, no. 107.*)

5775. Herdman, William Curry. *An analysis of the development of the accounting aspects of depreciation in the railroad industry.* 1959. 87 l. (Thesis, M.B.A. in Accounting, Graduate School of Arts and Sciences, University of Pennsylvania.)

5776. Hereford, Joseph P. *Rotary snowplows on the Cumbres & Toltec Scenic Railroad.* Albuquerque, NM: Windy Point Press, 1995. 72 p.

5777. Hering, Carl. *Recent progress in electric railways; being a summary of current periodical literature relating to electric railway construction, operation, systems, machinery, appliances, etc.* New York, The W.J. Johnston Company, Ltd., 1892. 289 p.

5778. Hermann, H.E. *Dynamic balancing car wheels for the train of tomorrow* / Rock island, IL: Bear Manufacturing Co., 1948-1949? 20 l.

5779. Herne, Shawn M. *The railroad timekeepers.* Baltimore, B & O Railroad Museum, 1999. 32 p.

5780. Hernick, James L. *Railroad timekeeping: based on the exhibit at the NAWCC Seminar in Rockford, IL, October 24-26, 1966.* Chicago? NAWCC Chicagoland Chapter #3, Midwest Regional Convention, 1996. 68 p.

5781. Herow, William C. *Riding the rails: tourist guide to America's scenic train rides.* Aura, CO: Roundabout Publications, 1996. 256 p.

5782. Herr, Kincaid A. *The Louisville & Nashville Railroad, 1850-1941, 1941-1959.* 3d ed. Louisville, KY: L & N Magazine, 1959. 234 p.

5783. _____. *The Louisville & Nashville Railroad, 1850-1963.* 5th ed. Louisville, Public Relations Department, L & N., 1964. 402 p. (Reissued: Lexington, KY: University Press of Kentucky, 2000. 402 p.)

5784. Herr, Steven C. *Effects of per diem rates on railroad operations and freight car ownership* / 1983. 165 l. (Thesis, M.S., Northwestern University.)

5785. Herrick, Albert Bledsoe. *Practical electric railway hand book.* New York, Street Railway Publishing Company, 1901. 407 p. (2d ed.: New York, McGraw Publishing Company, 1906. 460 p.)

5786. _____, Edward C. Boyton. *American electric railway practice.* New York, McGraw Publishing Company, 1907. 403 p.

5787. Herrick, Mark F., James N. Glover. *The latest type streamline air brake high speed control with train controls used on locomotives 4, 5 and 6, City of San Francisco.* Boone, Iowa, M.F. Herrick, 1944. 42 p.

5788. Herron, Edward A. *Alaska's railroad builder, Mike Heney.* New York, Messner, 1960. 192 p.

5789. Hersh, Lawrence K. *Central Pacific Railroad across Nevada, 1867 & 1997.* North Hollywood, CA: Lawrence K. Hersh, 2000. 127 p.

5790. Hertel, D.W. *History of the Brotherhood of Maintenance of Way Employees: its birth and growth, 1887-1955.* Washington, DC: Ransdell, 1955. 308 p. 24 leaves of plates.

5791. Hess, Ralph Henry. *Outlines of American railway transportation.* Madison, Wis., Democrat Printing Co., 1915. 208 p.

5792. Hewings, Geoffrey, John J.Y. Seo. *Economic impact of the transportation sector in the Chicago economy 1970-2021 and the potential impact of freight transportation capacity limitations on the Chicago, Illinois and US economies.* Urbana, IL: Regional Economics Applications Laboratory, 2001. 32 p.

5793. Heyns, Francois. *Railway track drainage design techniques.* 2000. 354 l. (Thesis, Ph.D., University of Massachusetts at Amherst.)

5794. Heywood, Frank A. *The Norfolk & Southern Railroad and its commercial tributaries.* Norfolk, Norfolk Landmark Pub. Co., 1891. 64 p.

5795. *Hiawatha: first of the Speedliners: C.M.St.P. & P.R.R. passenger equipment built by: the Milwaukee Shops, 1934-1935.* Carl W. Solheim, editor. Milwaukee, WI: Milwaukee Shops, 1993. 139 p.

5795a. Hibbard, George B. *Land Department of the Northern Pacific Railroad Company : Bureau of Immigration for soldiers and sailors/* New York : s.n., 1871. 7, 1 p.

5796. Hibbard, Herbert Wade. *Locomotive driving-wheel connecting rods; a brief history of their development, an account of the present methods of manufacture and fitting, and a review of many of the various modifications in use upon American locomotives.* 1891. 196 l. (Thesis, M.E., Cornell University.)

5797. Hibbard, William F. *Pacific Electric Railway Company substitution of motor coach service for rail service: Los Angeles-Van Nuys and Los Angeles-West Hollywood lines. Los Angeles,* California Public Utilities Commission, Transportation Department, 1952. 25 l.

5797a. Hichborn, Franklin. *Why the corporations win before the State Railroad Commission.* Santa Clara? CA: s.n., 1926. 32 p.

5798. Hicho, George E. *Fracture mechanics evaluation of railroad tank cars containing circumferential cracks* / Gaithersburg, MD: National Institute of Standards and Technology, 1993. 22 p. (*Report no. 27.*)

5799. _____, C. H. Brady. *Hazardous materials tank cars: evaluation of tank car shell construction material* / Washington, DC: Federal Railroad Administration, Office of Research and Development, 1975. 34 p. (*FRA-ORD & D-75-46.*)

5800. Hickcox, David H. *Chesapeake and Ohio color guide to freight and passenger equipment.* Edison, NJ: Morning Sun Books, 1998. 126 p.

5801. _____. *GN color guide to freight and passenger equipment.* Edison, NJ: Morning Sun Books, 1995. 128 p.

5802. _____. *Great Northern in color.* Kutztown, PA: Morning Sun Books, 2006. 128 p. v. 1, Lines West.

5803. _____. *Great Northern steam & electric in color.* Scotch Plains, NJ: Morning Sun Books, 1999. 128 p.

5804. _____, Dale A. DeVene. *Detroit, Toledo and Ironton Railroad in color.* Scotch Plains, NJ: Morning Sun Books, 2001. 128 p.

5805. Hickman, Barbara J. *Japanese railroad workers in Wyoming, 1891-1941: an interdisciplinary study.* 1989. 72 l. (Thesis, M.A., University of Wyoming.)

5806. Hicks, Charles C. *The Bangor and Aroostook Railroad and the development of northern Maine.* 1940. 101 l. (Thesis, M.A., in Economics and Sociology, University of Maine.)

5807. Hicks, E.C. *Citrus fruits.* Washington, D.C., Railroad Committee for the Study of Transportation, Association of American Railroads, 1946. 1 v.

5808. Hicks, Frederick C., Charles Francis Adams. *High finance in the sixties: chapters from the early history of the Erie Railway.* New Haven, Yale University Press, 1929. 410 p.

5809. Hicks, W. Raymond, and others. *The 50 best of B & O.* Baltimore, MD: Barnard, Roberts & Co., 1977-1979. 5 v. (52 leaves each)

5810. _____. *The 50 best of Western Maryland, Fast Freight Lines, book two.* Baltimore, MD: Barnard, Roberts, 1978. 52 l.

5811. Hidy, Ralph Willard, Muriel E. Hidy, and Roy V. Scott, with Don L. Hofsommer; editorial assistance from Elizabeth A. Burnham. *The Great Northern Railway: a history.* Boston, Harvard Business School Press, 1988. 360 p. (1st University of Minnesota Press ed. Minneapolis, University of Minnesota Press, 2004. 360 p.)

5812. Hielscher, Udo. *Der Pionier: Commodore Cornelius Vanderbilt: Dampfschifffahrts-Pionier und Eisenbahn-Tycoon*/ München, FinanzBuch, 2006. 242 p.

5813. Higa, Seiko. *Effect of motor carrier competition on railroad rates.* 1966. 211 l. (Thesis, Ph.D., Northwestern University.)

5814. Higgins, J. Wallace. *The Orient Road: a history of the Kansas City, Mexico and Orient Railroad.* Boston, Railway and Locomotive Historical Society, 1956. 43 p. (Its *Bulletin, no. 95.)*

5815. Higgins, Neal Owen. *The early pension plans of the Baltimore and Ohio and the Pennsylvania railroads, 1880-1937.* 1974. 1 v. (Thesis, Ph.D., University of Nebraska, Lincoln.)

5816. Higgins, R.L., B.R. Rajkumar. *Evaluation of two prototypical devices for non-destructively measuring stresses in railroad wheels.* Washington, DC: Federal Railroad Administration, Office of Research and Development, 1992. 175 p. (*DOT/FRA/ORD-92/15/TD3.15:92/15.)*

5817. *High finance in the sixties : chapters from the early history of the Erie Railway /* by Charles Francis Adams, Jr. ... [et al.]; edited, with an introduction, by Frederick C. Hicks. New Haven: Yale University Press, 1929. 410 p.

5818. *Highlights of American railroad history.* Illustrations by Gary Gaynor. Washington, D.C., Association of American Railroads, 1955. 27 p.

5818a. *High Line.* Bryn Mawr, PA: Pennsylvania Railroad Technical and Historical Society, 1900s-   Quarterly. (Volume 5 published in 1984/85)

5819. *Highline: a journal of redwood logging history.* Willits, CA: Roots of Motive Power, 2006-

5820. *High-speed ground transportation for America: overview report.* Washington, DC: Federal Railroad Administration, 1996. 48 p.

5820a. *High speed ground transportation journal.* Durham, NC: Planning-Transport Associates, 1967-1978. (> *Journal of advanced transportation.)*

5821. *High-speed ground transportation: proceedings of the Carnegie-Mellon Conference on High-Speed Ground Transportation, Pittsburgh, Pennsylvania, 1969.*

Pittsburgh: Transportation research Institute, Carnegie-Mellon University, 1969. 335 p.

5822. *High-speed passenger rail corridor conference: March 26-27, 1996, Washington, DC.* Washington, DC: Federal Railroad Administration, 1996. 1 v. (various pagings)

5823. *High-speed passenger rail corridor conference: September 26, 1996, Bloomington, Minnesota.* Washington, DC: Federal Railroad Administration, 1996. 1 v. (various pagings)

5824. *High-speed passenger rail corridor conference: September 24-25, 1997, Indianapolis, Indiana.* Washington, DC: Federal Railroad Administration, 1997. 1 v. (various pagings)

5825. *High-speed passenger rail corridor conference: March 25-26, 1998, Biloxi, Mississippi.* Washington, DC; Federal Railroad Administration, 1998. 232 l. in various foliations

5826. *High speed rail: a bibliography for U.S. decision-makers* / Compiled by Chris Thompson, Tim Bawden, Dave Lyons. Chicago: Council of Planning Librarians, 1992. 30 p. (*CPL bibliography, no. 287*)

5827. *High-Speed Rail Association. International Convention of High-Speed Rail ; proceedings.* Washington, DC: High-Speed Rail Association, 1987- . Annual.

5828. *High-speed rail strategic plan: the American Recovery and Reinvestment Act.* Washington, DC: Federal Railroad Administration, 2009. 17 p.

5829. *High speed rail tilt train technology: a state of the art survey: final report.* Washington, DC: Federal Railroad Administration, office of Research and Development, 1993. 1 v.

5830. *High/super speed rail in Southern California: projects, technology, finance and public policy considerations.* Beverly Hills, CA: Edmund G. "Pat" Brown Institute of Government Affairs, 1984. 43 p.

5830a. *Highway operation an obligation of New Haven Railroad.* New York: National Automobile Chamber of Commerce, 1925. 15 p. (*Co-ordinated transportation series, no. 18.*)

5831. *Highway-rail crossing accident/incident and inventory bulletin* / Washington, DC: Federal Railroad Administration, Office of Safety, 1992-1990s. Annual. (< *Rail-highway crossing accident/incident and inventory bulletin; > Accident/incident bulletin; Trespasser bulletin; Railroad safety statistics.*)

5832. *Highway-rail crossing and trespasser initiatives: FRA is working to improve crossing safety and prevent trespassing.* Washington, DC: Federal Railroad Administration, 1994. 6 p.

5833. *Highway-rail crossing consolidation and elimination: a public safety initiative.* Washington, DC: Federal Railroad Administration, 1995. 11 p.

5834. *Highway-rail crossing elimination and consolidation: a public safety initiative: National Conference of State Railway Officials; Railroad Industry Ad Hoc Committee on Crossing Elimination and Consolidation; American Association of State Highway and Transportation Officials, Standing Committee on Railways.* Washington, DC: American Association of State Highway and Transportation Officials, 1994. 74 p.

5835. Hildebrand, Jesse Richardson. *Trains of today—and tomorrow.* Washington, D.C., The National Geographic Society, 1936. 55 p. (Reprint from the *National Geographic Magazine, v. 70, no. 5, November 1936.*)

5836. Hildebrand, John R. *Iron horses in the valley: the Valley and Shenandoah Valley Railroads, 1866-1882.* Shippensburg, PA: Burd Street Press; Roanoke, VA: History Museum and Historical Society of Western Virginia; Salem, VA: Salem Historical Society, 2001. 128 p.

5837. Blank entry.

5838. Hildrup, William T. *History and organization of the Harrisburg Car Manufacturing Company*/ Harrisburg, Pa., Edwin K. Meyers, Printer, 1890. 68 p.

5839. Hile, Steve, David H. Hickcox, Todd Miller. *Rock Island color guide to freight and passenger equipment.* Edison, NJ: Morning Sun Books, 1996. 124 p.

5840. Hill & Demarest. *Gas light in traveling conveyances : Hill & Demarest's patent apparatus for lighting railroad cars, steamboats, omnibuses, etc, with gas : patented November 6th, 1855.* Chicago : Democratic Press Book & Job Office, 1857. 8 p.

5841. Hill, Arthur Cyrus. *The history of dining car employees unions in the Upper Midwest and the impact of railroad abandonments, consolidations and mergers on dining car unions.* 1968. 195 l. (Thesis, M.A., University of Minnesota.)

5842. Hill, Barry T. *Interstate Commerce Commission: budget and other impacts of eliminating or transferring functions* /Washington, D.C., The Office (P.O. Box 6015, Gaithersburg, MD 20884-6015), 1995. 12 2 p. (*GAO/T-RCED-95-111.*)

5843. Hill, C.V., L.P. Hibbits, D.B. Clarke. *The Nevada railroad system; physical, operational, and accident characteristics.* Las Vegas, NV: U.S. Department of Energy, Yucca Mountain Site Characterization Project Office, 1991. 1 v. *(Report no: YMP-91-19.)*

5844. (Blank entry)

5845. Hill, Dorothy. *A costing methodology for freight cars* / Washington, DC: Federal Railroad Administration, Office of Policy and Program Development, 1978. 2 v.

(*FRA-OPPD-78-17-I-II.*)

5846. Hill, E. Rowland. *Railroad electrification—its accomplishment and outlook* / New York : Gibbs & Hill, consulting engineers, 1938. 16, 9 p.

5847. Hill, Edwin Conger, Charles Kenyon, John Russell. *The iron horse.* New York, Grosset & Dunlap, 1923. 329 p.

5848. Hill, Forest G. *Roads, rails and waterways: The Army Engineers and early transportation.* Norman: University of Oklahoma Press, 1957. 248 p.

5849. Hill, Frederick P. *Report of the trial of Frederick P. Hill, late a conductor on the Philadelphia & Reading Railroad, on a charge of embezzling funds of that company in his capacity as conductor.* Chicago : G.H. Fergus, 1864. 60 p.

5850. Hill, Howard G. *Riding the Limited's locomotives.* Seattle, WA: Superior Publishing Company, 1972. 175 p.

5851. Hill Jack. *The Cambria and Indiana Railroad : 90 years, 1904-1994* / Charleston, SC: CreateSpace, 2011, 210. 111 p.

5852. Hill, James Jerome. *The country's need of greater railway facilities and terminals: address.* New York? Railway Business Association? 1912. 28 p.

5853. _____.*Highways of progress.* New York, Doubleday, Page & Co., 1910. 353 p.

5853a. _____. *Traffic growth and terminal needs.* Minneapolis: s.n., 1910. 11 p.

5854. Hill, John Alexander. *Jim Skeever's object lessons on railroading for railroaders.* New York, Press of Railway and Locomotive Engineering, 1899. 159 p.

5855. _____. *Jim Wainright's kid, and other stories of the railroad.* Chicago, Ill., Jamieson-Higgins, 1901. 225 p.

5856. _____. *Progressive examinations of locomotive engineers and firemen.* New York, J.A. Hill, 1891. 78 p.

5857. _____. *Stories of the railroad.* New York, Doubleday& McClure, 1899. 297 p.

5858. Hill, May Davis. *Telltale photographs: the Stoner Railroad Collection, the Michigan Historical Collection.* Ann Arbor, MI: Michigan Historical Collections/Bentley Historical Library, University of Michigan, 1981. 32 p. (*Bulletin, Michigan Historical Collections, no. 30.*)

5859. Hill, R.G. *Comparative efficiency of wire-basket bunkers* in *refrigerator cars.* Washington, D.C., U.S. Department of Agriculture, 1926. 11 p. (*Department bulletin, no. 1398.*)

5860. _____. W.S. Graham, R.C. Wright. *The efficiency of a short-type refrigerator car.* Washington, D.C., U.S. Department of Agriculture, 1925. 28 p. (*Department bulletin, no. 1353.*)

5861. Hill, Richard Elias. *Railroad operation of motor trucks/* 1949. 115 l. (Thesis, M.B.A. in Transportation and Public Utilities, Graduate School of Arts and Sciences, University of Pennsylvania)

5862. Hill, Ronald C. *Colorful Colorado railroads in the 1960's.* Golden, CO: Colorado Railroad Historical Foundation; Colorado Railroad Museum, 1992. 112 p.

5863. _____. *Mountain mainlines of the West.* Golden, CO: Colorado Railroad Historical Foundation; Colorado Railroad Museum, 1988. 64 p.

5864. _____. *Rio Grande in the Rockies: a contemporary glimpse.* Golden, CO: Colorado Railroad Museum, 1977. 80 p.

5865. _____. *Rio Grande: memories of the final years.* Golden, CO: Colorado Railroad Museum, 2007. 112 p. (*Colorado rail annual, no. 28.*)

5866. _____. *Rio Grande West: a contemporary glimpse.* Golden, CO: Colorado Railroad Museum, 1982. 80 p.

5867. _____, Al Chione. *The railroad artistry of Howard Fogg.* Edited by G. Mac Sebree. San Rafael, CA: Cedco Publishing, 1999. 168 p.

5868. _____, Dave Stanley. *Rails in the Northwest: a contemporary glimpse.* Golden, CO: Colorado Railroad Museum, 1978. 80 p.

5869. Hille, Stanley James. *Marketing research in United States class I railroads, with special emphasis on western transcontinental railroads.* 1966. (Thesis, Ph.D., University of Minnesota.)

5870. Hillegas, Barry D., Lloyd M. Pernela, D. Chandler Lewis. *The Alaska Railroad's future freight market.* Washington, DC: Federal Railroad Administration, 1976-1977. 3 v. (*Report no. RP-3010; FRA/ARR-77/01-II; FRA/ARR-77/01-III.*)

5871. Hillman, Jordan Jay. *Competition and railroad price discrimination: legal precedent and economic policy.* Evanston, IL: Transportation Center at Northwestern University, 1968. 164 p.

5872. Hillstrom, Kevin, Laurie Collier Hillstrom. *The industrial revolution in America: railroads. {Volume 2}.* Santa Barbara, CA: ABC-CLIO, 2005. 289 p.

5873. Hillyer, Clair Richards. *Procedure before the Interstate Commerce Commission, and grounds of proof in rate cases.* Chicago, IL: La Salle Extension University, 1924. 3, 55, 43, 61 p.

5874. Hilton, George Woodman. *American narrow gauge railroads.* Stanford, CA: Stanford University Press, 1990. 580 p.

5875. _____. *Amtrak: the National Railroad Passenger Corporation.* Washington, D.C., American Enterprise Institute for Public Policy Research, 1980. 80 p.

5876. _____. *Cable car days in Baltimore.* Springfield? VA: s.n., 1965. 9 p.

5877. _____. *The cable car in America; a new treatise upon cable or rope traction as applied to the working of street and other railways.* Cartography by James A. Bier. Berkeley, CA: Howell-North Books, 1971. 484 p. (2d ed. San Diego, CA: Howell-North Books, 1982. 484 p. Revised ed.: Stanford, CA: Stanford University Press, 1997. 484 p.)

5878. _____. *Cable railways of Chicago.* Chicago, IL: Electric Railway Historical Society, 1954. 43 p.

5879. _____. *The Ma & Pa; a history of the Maryland & Pennsylvania Railroad.* Berkeley, CA: Howell-North Books, 1963. 183 p. (2d ed.: San Diego, CA: Howell-North Books, 1980. 220 p.; 2d ed. revised. Baltimore, MD: Johns Hopkins University Press, 1999. 228 p.)

5880. _____. *Monon Route.* Berkeley, CA: Howell-North Books, 1978. 323 p.

5881. _____. *The Northeast railroad problem.* Washington, D.C., American Enterprise Institute for Public Policy Research, 1975. 59 p.

5882. _____. *The Toledo, Port Clinton and Lakeside Railway.* Chicago, IL: Electric Railway Historical Society, 1964. 59 p.(Also: Montevallo, AL: Montevallo Historical Press, 1997. 62 p.)

5883. _____, John Fitzgerald Due. *The electric interurban rail-ways in America.* Stanford, CA: Stanford University Press, 1960. 463 p. (Reprint: Stanford, CA: Stanford University Press,1964. 463 p; Stanford, CA: Stanford University Press, 2000. 463 p.)

5884. Hilton, John J. *The Virginia Central Railway; a short history.* Bethesda, MD: National Capital Historical Museum of Transportation, 1970. 12 p.

5885 _____, Randolph Kean. *Steam days on the Virginia Blue Ridge Railway.* Arlington, VA: National Capital Historical Museum of Transportation, 1975. 23 p.

5886. Himmelberg, Robert F. *Growth of the regulatory state, 1900-1917: state and federal regulation of railroads and other enterprises.* New York, Garland Publications, 1994, 1967. 405 p.

5887. _____. *The rise of big business and the beginnings of antitrust and railroad regulation, 1870-1900.* New York, Garland Publications, 1994. 423 p.

5888. Hinckley, Isaac. *Postal cars or no postal cars? A question to be settled by the action or inaction of Congress.* Philadelphia, Pa., Allen, Lane & Scott, 1874. 35 p.

5889. Hinckley, Thomas K. *Transcontinental rails/* Palmer Lake, CO: Filter Press, 1969. 48 p. (Pacific railroads)

5890. Hinds, Russell H., Harold D. Jonson, Robert C. Haldeman. *A performance test of refrigerated rail cars transporting frozen food /* Washington, DC: U.S. Department of Agriculture, Agricultural Marketing Service, Marketing Research Division, 1957. 26 p. (*Marketing research report, no. 182.*)

5891. _____, William George Chace. *Piggyback transportation of Florida citrus fruit: problems, methods, equipment /* Washington, DC: U.S. Department of Agriculture, Agricultural marketing Service, Transportation and Facilities Research Division and Market Quality Research Division, 1962. 21 p.

5892. Hine, Charles De Lano. *Letter from an old railway official to his son, a division superintendent.* Chicago, Ill., The Railway Age, 1904. 179 p.

5892a. Hines, Edward Warren. *Corporate history of the Louisville and Nashville Railroad Company, and roads in its system/* Louisville, KY: J.P. Morton, 1905. 445 p.

5893. Hines, Walker D.. *Consolidation of railroads: opening statement before the Interstate Commerce* Commission. S.l, s.n.,1922. 19 p.

5894. _____. *Report to the President by Walker D. Hines, Director General of Railroads, for fourteen months ended March 1, 1920.* Washington, D.C., Federal Railroad Administration, 1920. 48 p.

5895. _____. *War history of American railroads/* New Haven, CT: Yale University Press, 1928. 327 p. (Reprint: Englewood, NJ: J.S. Ozer, 1974. 327 p.)

5896. _____, John Walker Barriger. *Car service rules: their reasonableness and necessity upheld and approved by the Courts.* S.l., s.n., 1902. 12 p.

5897. _____, _____. *Interstate Commerce commission makes extravagant demands far beyond what Congress intended : the powers demanded are unnecessary, unreasonable, and dangerous /* S.l., s.n., 1898. 23 l.

5898. _____, _____. *Legislative regulation of railroad rates: paper before American Economic Association, Philadelphia, December 27, 1902.* Louisville, Ky., s.n., 1902. 18 p.

5899. _____, _____. . *The public interest in railroad unification and consolidation.* New York, Academy of Political Science,1929. 14 p.

5900. _____, _____. *Railway regulation : the English system contrasted with the demands of the Interstate Commerce Commission.* S.l., s.n., 1898. 8 l.

5901. Hinman, Roger C. *Merchants Despatch : its history and equipment.* Berkeley and Wilton, CA : Signature Press, 2011.

5902. Hinsdale, Alizur Brace. *History of the Long Island Railroad Company, 1834-1898.* New York, The Evening Post Job Printing House, 1898. 34 p.

5903. Hinshaw, David. *Stop, look and listen; railroad transportation in the United States.* Garden City, N.Y., Doubleday, Doran & Company, 1932. 293 p.

5904. Hipes, Steve, Dave Oroszi. *Pennsylvania Railroad lines west.* Hanover, PA: Railroad Press, 2004-

5905. Hirsch, Susan E. *After the strike: a century of labor struggle at Pullman.* Urbana, University of Illinois Press, 2003. 292 p.

5906. Hirschey, Mark John *An incentive contract methodology for subsidized railroad freight services/* 1977. 254 l. (Thesis, University of Wisconsin.)

5907. _____. *The structure of railroad freight service costs/* Madison, WI: Graduate School of Business, University of Wisconsin-Madison, 1977. 20 l. (*Wisconsin working paper, 9-77-32.*)

5908. Hirschfeld, Charles. *The great railroad conspiracy; the social history of railroad war.* East Lansing, MI: Michigan State College Press, 1953. 128 p. (Michigan Central Railroad Company)

5910. Hirsimaki, Eric. *The Alco Line.* N. Olmsted, OH: Mileposts Pub., 1993. 128 p. (C&NW)

5911. _____. *Black gold, black diamonds: the Pennsylvania Railroad and dieselization.* N. Olmsted, OH: Mileposts Pub., 1997-

5912. _____. *Chicago and North Western system: the Michigan ore lines.* Montoursville, PA: Paulhamus Litho, 2002. 56 p.

5913. _____. *The Huron Hustler.* Cincinnati, OH: NKPHTS, 1988. 42 p. (Wheeling and Lake Erie Railroad Company)

5914. _____. *Lima: the history.* Edmonds, WA: Hundman Pub.,1986. 351 p.

5915. _____. *The Nickel Plate years.* N. Olmsted, OH: Mileposts Pub. Co., 1989. 144 p.

5916. *Historic American Engineering Record: Central of Georgia Railway: Savannah repair shop & terminal facilities.* Washington, DC: HAER, 1975-1976? 133 p.

5917. *Historic railroad stations: a selected inventory.* H. Ward Jandl, Jan Thorman,

Katherine H. Stevenson, compilers. Washington, D.C., National Register of Historic Places, Office of Archaeology and Historic Preservation, National Park Service, 1974. 100 p.

5918. *Historic Southern Pacific cars.* New York, Wayner Publications, n.d. 1 v.

5919. *Historical bulletin.* S.l., M.F. Lyon, 1978-   . (Katy Railroad Historical Society.)

5920. *Historical inventory of the Union Pacific Railroad, 1946.* Denver, CO: Intermountain Chapter, National Railway Historical Society, 1991. 297 columns.

5921. *Historical sketch and views of Mauch Chunk : the Switchback Railroad, Summit Hill and Panther Creek Valley.* New York : Union News Co., 1900? 1, 23 p. of plates.

5922. *History of CB&Q RR and C. E. Perkins. Theses of students of R.C. Overton.* London, Ont., University of Western Ontario, History Department, 1965. 1 v. "Xerox copies of papers delivered in the History 564 seminar, spring 1965, given by R.C. Overton."

5923. *History of the anti-separate coach movement of Kentucky; containing half-tone cuts and biographical sketches ... /* Evansville, IN: National Afro-American Journal and Directory, 1895. 220 p. 30 leaves of plates. "The case in full of W.H. Anderson vs. L & N Railroad Company."

5924. *The history of the Baltimore & Ohio: America's first railroad.* Edited by Timothy Jacobs. New York, Crescent Books, 1989. 128 p.

5925. *History of the Chicago, Milwaukee & St. Paul Railway Co., and representative employees.* Chicago, Ill., Railroad Historical Company, 1901. 653 p.

5926. *History of the Norfolk & Southern Railroad Company : and of its constituent companies.* Norfolk, VA: W.T. Barron, 1905. 316 p. (various pagings)

5927. *History of the Norris Locomotive Works.* S.l., s.n., 1928? 1 v.

5928. *History of the Old Colony Railroad: a complete history of the Old Colony Railroad from 1844 to the present.* Boston, Hager & Handy, 1893. 512 p.

5929. *A history of the railway mail service, together with a brief account of the origin and growth of the post office service and a sketch showing the daily life of a railway mail clerk.* Washington, D.C., Columbian Correspondence College, 1903. 123 p.

5929a. *History of the anti-separate coach movement of Kentucky containing half-tone cuts and biographical sketches/* Evansville, IN: National Afro-American Journal and Directory, 1895. 220 p. (Louisville and Nashville Railroad Company)

5930. *The history of the Union Pacific: America's great transcontinental railroad.* Edited by Marie Cahill and Lynne Paide. New York, Crescent Books, 1989. 127 p.

5931. History West; Southern Pacific Company. *Golden State Route: the direct line between the Middle West and Southern California...between Los Angeles and Chicago, along the first trails of the great Southwest.* North Highland, CA: History West, 1981. 150 p.

5932. _____, _____. *Overland Route, Lake Tahoe Line: shortest route across the center of the country, Chicago-San Francisco...line of first transcontinental railroad.* North Highlands, CA: History West, 1981. 150 p.

5933. _____, _____. *Rail and water: a colorful story of railroad building, Central Pacific Railroad, forerunner of the Southern Pacific Company.* North Highland, CA, History West, 1981. 150 p.

5934. _____, _____. *Shasta Route, between Pacific Northwest and California...story of railroad progress of Southern Pacific Company.* North Highlands, CA: History West, 1981. 150 p.

5935 _____, _____. *Sunset Route: by sea, New York to New Orleans, thence by rail to San Francisco...a colorful story of railroad building and progress of Southern Pacific Company.* North Highlands, CA: History West, 1981. 150 p.

5936. Hitchcock, Lyman C. *Locomotive running repairs.* Terre Haute, Ind., Debs Publishing Company, 1893. 108 p.

5937. Hitt, Rodney. *Electric railway dictionary; definitions and illustrations of the parts and equipment of electric railway cars and trucks; compiled under the direction of a committee appointed by the American Electric Railway Association.* New York, McGraw, 1911. 63, 292 p.

5938. Hobbah, Reginald Vyvyan. *Railroad transit privileges.* Chicago, University of Chicago Press, 1944. 104 p.(*Studies in business administration, v. 14, no. 3;* Thesis, Ph.D., University of Chicago.) Freight rates.

5939. Hobbie, Richard, Richard Rimkunas. *Why is the railroad unemployment insurance program insolvent?* Washington, DC: Congressional Research Service, Library of Congress, 1983. 1 v. (*Major studies and issue briefs of the Congressional Research Service,; Supplement, 1983-84. Reel 12, fr. 0433.)*

5940. Hobbs, Paul T. *Spokane, Portland & Seattle Railway cabooses: a history.* Bonners Ferry, Idaho, Great Northern Pacific Publications, 1996. 104 p.

5941. Hobson, Anthony. *Lanterns that lit our world: how to identify, date, and restore old railroad, marine, fire, carriage, farm, and other lanterns.* Spencertown, NU: Golden Hill Press, 1991-1997. 2 v. (v. 1: 231 p.; v. 2: 232 p.)

5942. Hochschild, Harold K. *Adirondack railroads, real and phantom.* Blue Mountain Lake, NY: Adirondack Museum, 1962. 21 p.

5943. _____. *Doctor Durant and his iron horse*. Blue Mountain Lake, NY: Adirondack Museum, 1961. 17 p.

5944. Hocking Valley Railway Company. General Freight Department. *The Hocking Valley Railway official shippers' guide and general business directory: 1901-1903.* Toledo, OH: The Railway, Press of the Hadley Printing Co., 1901. 76 p.

5945. _____, Toledo and Ohio Central Railway Company, Kanawha & Michigan Railway Company. *Joint rules and instructions for the government of employes in the Operating Department.* S.l., The Companies, 1902. 144 p.

5946. Hockridge, W.S. *Facts and fancies in rhyme: taken from life at West Albany shops.* Rensselaer, NY: Mintline, 1900. 13 p.(Poetry)

5946a. Hodges, Michael H. *Michigan's historic railroad stations* / Detroit: Wayne State University Press, 2012. 186 p.

5947. Hodges, Robert F., Peter Dennis. *American Civil War railroad tactics*. Osprey Publishing, 2009. 64 p.

5948. Hodnette, J.K. *The gas turbine as railroad motive power*. S.l., Westinghouse Electric 1953. 9 l.

5949. Hoerl, Henry Gordon. *Development of the Illinois Central Railroad System in Mississippi, 1865-1892* / 1975. 159 l. (Thesis, M.A., University of Mississippi.)

5950. Hoess, J. *Braking system for advanced high-speed passenger trains*. Washington, DC: Federal Railroad Administration, 1979. 1 v. (various pagings)

5951. Hoffman, Gilbert H. *Dummy lines through the longleaf: a history of the sawmills and logging railroads of southwest Mississippi*. Oxford, Center for the Study of Southern Culture, University of Mississippi, 1992. 1 v. (2d ed. Brookhaven, MS: Quentin Press, 1999. 308 p.)

5952. _____. *Steam whistles in the Piney woods: a history of the sawmills and logging railroads of Forrest and Lamar* Counties, *Mississippi.* Hattiesburg, Miss., Longleaf Press, 1998-

5953. Hoffman, Glen, Richard E. Bussard. *Building a great railroad: a history of the Atlantic Coast Line Railroad Company.* S.l., CSX Corporate Communications and Public Affairs, 1998. 326 p.

5954. Hoffman, Linwood A. *The economic effects of demand-sensitive railroad rates upon the storage and transportation system for U.S. feed grains* / 1980. 305 l. (Thesis, Ph.D., University of Illinois at Urbana-Champaign.)

5955. _____., Lowell D. Hill, Mack N. Leath. *A flexible rail rate policy:*

impacts on U.S. feed grains/ Washington, DC: U.S. Department of Agriculture, Economic Research Service, 1985. 34 p. (*Technical bulletin, no. 1701.*)

5956. Hofsommer, Donovan L. *Grand Trunk Corporation: Canadian National Railway in the United States, 1971-1992.* East Lansing, Michigan State University Press, 1995. 219 p.

5957. _____. *The Hook & Eye: a history of the Iowa Central Railway.* Minneapolis, University of Minnesota Press, 2005. 151 p.

5958. _____. *Katy Northwest: a case study of branch line railroading.* 1973. 1 v. (Thesis, Ph.D., Oklahoma State University.)

5959. _____ *Katy Northwest: the story of a branch line railroad.* Foreword by John W. Barriger. Boulder, CO: Pruett Publishing Company, 1976. 305 p.

5960. _____. *Katy Northwest: the story of a branch line* W. Frailey. Bloomington, Indiana University Press, 1999. 305 p.

5961. _____. *The Minneapolis & St. Louis Railway: a photographic history.* Minneapolis, MN: University of Minnesota Press, 2009. 277 p.

5962. _____. *Minneapolis and the age of railways.* Minneapolis, University of Minnesota Press, 2005. 337 p.

5962a. _____. *Off the main lines: a photographic odyssey* / Bloomington: Indiana University Press, 2013. 306 p.

5963. _____. *Prairie oasis: the railroads, steamboats, and resorts of Iowa's Spirit Lake country.* Des Moines, Waukon & Mississippi Press, 1975. 159 p.

5964. _____. *The Quanah Route: a history of the Quanah, Acme & Pacific Railway.* College Station, TX: Texas A&M University Press, 1991. 215 p.

5965. _____. *Railroads in Oklahoma.* Oklahoma City, Oklahoma Historical Society, 1977. 171 p. (*The Oklahoma series, v. 7.*)

5966. _____. *Railroads in the West.* Manhattan, KS: Sunflower University Press, 1978. 120 p.

5967. _____. *Railroads of the trans-Mississippi West: a selected bibliography.* Plainview, TX: Wayland College, 1974. 45 p. (3d ed.: Plainview, TX: Llano Estacado Museum, Wayland College, 1976. 92 p.)

5968. _____. *The Southern Pacific, 1901-1985.* Foreword by Richard C. Overton. College Station, TX: Texas A&M University Press, 1986. 373 p.

5969. _____. *Steel trails of Hawkeyeland: Iowa's railroad experience.* Bloomington,

Indiana University Press, 2005. 353 p.

5970. _____. *The Tootin' Louie: a history of the Minneapolis & St. Louis Railway.* Minneapolis, University of Minnesota Press, 2005. 374 p.

5971. _____, H. Roger Grant. *Iowa's railroads: an album.* Bloomington, IN: Indiana University Press, 2009. 320 p.

5972. Hofvendahl, Russ. *A land so fair and bright: the true story of a young man's adventures across Depression America.* Dobbs Ferry, NY: Sheridan House, 1991. 303 p. (Railroad travel)

5973. Hogan, Edmond K. *The work of the railway carmen.* Chicago, Ill., United States Railroad Labor Board; American Federation of Labor; Railway Employees Department, Brotherhood Railway Carmen of America, 1921. 201 p.

5974. Hogg, Garry. *Union Pacific; the building of the first transcontinental railroad.* New York, Walker, 1969, c1967. 166 p.

5975. Hohenemser, K.H. *Computer simulation of tank car head puncture mechanisms : classification yard accidents* / Washington, DC: Federal Railroad Administration, 1975. 75 p. (*FRA-ORD & D-75-23.)*

5976. Hojnacki, Kenneth L. *Steam railroads of central New York.* Marcellus, NY: Central New York Chapter, National Railway Historical Society, Inc., 1973. 35 p.

5977. Holbrook, Daniel P., Steven D. Lorenz. *Waycars of the Chicago, Burlington & Quincy RR.* Danvers, MA: Prototype Modeler, 1978. 107 p.

5978. Holbrook, Stewart Hall. *The age of moguls*/ Garden City, NY: Doubleday, 1953. 373 p. (Reprint: New York, Arno Press, 1981. 373 p.)

5979. _____. *James J. Hill, a great life in brief.* New York, Knopf, 1955. 205 p.

5980. _____. *The story of American railroads.* New York, Crown Publishers, 1947. 468 p. (Reprint: New York, American Legacy Press, 1981, c1947. 468 p.)

5981. Holck, Alfred J.J. *Burlington Route color pictorial.* La Mirada, CA: Four Ways West Publications, 1994-

5982. _____. *The hub of Burlington Lines West: Lincoln and* the *Lincoln Division of the Burlington Route.* 2d ed. David City, NE: South Platte Press, 1992, c1991. 380 p.

5983. Holcomb, Kenneth Johnson. *History, description and economic analysis of trailer-on-flatcar (piggyback) transportation.* Fayetteville, AR: University of Arkansas, 1962. 315 l. (Thesis, Ph.D., University of Arkansas.)

5983a. Holcomb, Russell. *Miami Transit Center* / 1988. 130 l. (Thesis, B.Arch., Roger

Williams College.)

5984. Holderness, Herbert O. *The reminiscences of a Pullman conductor, or, Character sketches of life in a Pullman car.* Chicago : s.n., 1901. 229, 1 p. 5 leaves of plates

5985. Holdom, James, Harrison B. Riley. *Abstract of report of the Chicago Association of Commerce Committee of Investigation on Smoke Abatement and Electrification of* Railway *Terminals.* Chicago, Chicago Association of Commerce and Industry, 1915. 18 p.

5986. Holland, James Wendell. *A history of railroad enterprise in east Tennessee, 1836-1860.* 1930. 448 l. (Thesis, M.A., University of Tennessee, Knoxville.

5987. Holland, Kevin J. *Berkshires of the Nickel Plate Road.* Lynchburg, VA: TLC Publishing, 1998. 124 p.

5988. _____. *Chicago South Shore & South Bend: in color.* Scotch Plains, NJ: Morning Sun Books, 2005-

5989. _____. *Classic American railroad terminals.* Osceola, WI: MBI Pub., 2001. 156 p.

5990. _____ *Nickel Plate Road diesel locomotives.* Lynchburg, VA: TLC Pub., 1998. 124 p.

5991. _____. *Nickel Plate Road passenger service.* Lynchburg, VA: TLC Pub.,1997. 128 p.

5992. _____. *Passenger trains of northern New England in the streamline era.* Lynchburg, VA: TLC Pub., 2004. 152 p.

5993. _____. *The streamliners: streamlined steam locomotives and the American passenger train.* Lynchburg, VA: TLC Pub., 2002. 155 p.

5994. _____. *Trackside in the Heartland, 1946-1959: with Vincent A. Purn and John A. Knauff.* Scotch Plains, NJ: Morning Sun Books, 2008. 128 p.

5995. _____, Robert J. Yanosey. *Trackside in the Northeast, 1946-1959 with Vincent A. Purn and John A. Knauff.* Kutztown, PA: Morning Sun Books, 2007. 128 p.

5996. Holland, Rupert Sargent. *Historic railroads.* Philadelphia, Macrae Smith Co., 1927. 343 p.

5997. Hollander. *The Cincinnati Southern Railway: a study in municipal activity.* Baltimore, John Hopkins Press, 1894. 116 p. (Reprint: New York, Johnson Reprint, 1973.)

5998. Hollenback, Frank R. *The Argentine Central: a Colorado narrow gauge.* Denver,

Sage Books, 1959. 80 p.

5999. _____. *The Gilpin tram.* Denver, Sage Books, 1958. 64 p.

6000. _____. *The Laramie Plains Line, Laramie, Wyoming to Coalmont, Colorado.* Denver, Sage Books, 1960. 94 p.

6001. _____, William Russell, Jr. *Pike's Peak by rail.* Denver, Sage Books, 1962. 91 p.

6002. Hollenback, John Joseph. *Economic causes of the Penn Central bankruptcy.* 1972. 85 p. (Thesis, M.A., California State University, Sacramento.)

6003. Holley, Alexander Lyman. *American and European railway practice in the economical generation of steam/* New York, D. Van Nostrand, 1867, c1860. 1 v.

6004. Holley, Noel T. *The Milwaukee electrics.* Hicksville, NY: N.J. International, 1987. 310 p.

6005. _____. *The Milwaukee electrics: an inside look at locomotives and railroading.* 2d ed. Edmonds, WA: Hundman Publishing Company, 1999. 304 p. (3rd ed.: Mukilteo, WA: Hundman Publishing Company, 2002. 304 p.)

6006. _____. *Milwaukee Road bi-polar electrics.* Annapolis, MD: N.J. International, 1979. 54 p.

6007. *Holley's railroad advocate.* New York, Holley & Cochrane, 1856-1857. (>*American engineer.*)

6007a. Holliday, Alex R. *Design of a single track riveted R.R. bridge /* 1899. 54 l. (Thesis, B.S., Massachusetts Institute of Technology, Department of Civil Engineering.)

6007b. Hollinger, Chris A. *The Railway Labor Act /* 3rd ed. Arlington, VA: Bloomberg BNA, 2012. 967 p.

6008. Hollingsworth, J.B. *American railroads.* New York, Gallery Books, 1984. 63 p.

6009. _____. *The history of American railroads.* New York, Exeter Books, 1983. 256 p.

6010. _____. *The illustrated encyclopedia of North American locomotives: a historical directory of America's greatest locomotives from 1830 to the present day.* New York, Crescent Books, 1984. 208 p.

6011._____. *North American railways.* London, Hamlyn, 1977. 190 p.

6012. _____, P.B. Whitehouse. *American railroads.* London (England), Bison Books Ltd., 1977. 190 p.

6013. Hollis, Jeffrey R., Charles S. Roberts. *East End: Harpers Ferry to Cumberland,*

1842-1992. 223 p. (Baltimore and Ohio Railroad Company) (2d ed.: Baltimore, MD: Barnard, Roberts & Co., 2003. 224 p.)

6014. Hollister, Will C. *Dinner in the diner.* 4th ed. Glendale, CA: Trans-Anglo Books, 1984. 144 p.

6015. Holloway, Robert M. *Fundamentals and design of freight car brake riggings.* Chicago: Air Brake Association, 1956. 88 p.

6016. Holman, Frank Newton. *Record breaking run of the Scott Special: Los Angeles to Chicago, 44 hours & 54 minutes.* Chicago, Ill., A.T.&S.F. Ry. System, 1905. 30 p. (Yosemite, CA: Flying Spur Press, 1972.)

6017. Holt, Marilyn Irvin. *The orphan trains: placing out in America.* Lincoln University of Nebraska Press, 1994, 1992. 248 p.

6018. Holmes, Dennis E. *Depots on the Minneapolis & St. Louis Railway* / Ethel, MO: Chicago & North Western Historical Society, 2009. 104 p.

6019. Holmes, Norman W. *California's Tidewater shortlines; railroads that touched the Western Pacific between Stockton and San Francisco*/ Bellflower, CA: Shade Tree Books, 2009. 128 p. (Tidewater Southern Railway. Central California Traction Company. Stockton Terminal & Eastern Railroad.)

6019a. _____*My Western Pacific Railroad: an engineer's journey.* Reno, NV: Steel Rails West Publishing, 1996. 128 p.

6020. _____. *Prune country railroading: steel rails to San Jose.* Huntington Beach, CA: Shade Tree Books, 1985. 191 p.

6021. Holt, Jeff. *The Grand Trunk in New England.* Toronto, ON: Railfare Enterprises, 1986. 176 p.

6021a. Holt, Robert C., Bob McElwee. *St. Louis Station : a city within a city* / Charleston, IL: Family Journeys, 2003. 48 p.

6022. Holter, Russell, and others. *Rails to paradise: the history of the Tacoma Eastern Railroad, 1890-1919.* Rochester, WA: Gorham Printing, 2005. 538 p.

6023. Holterhoff, G. *Historical review of the Atchison, Topeka and Santa Fe Railway Company*/ Hawthorne, CA: Omni Publications, 1986, 1914. 12 p.

6024. Holton, James L. *The Reading Railroad: history of a coal age empire.* Laury's Station, PA: Garrigues House, 1989-1992. 2 v.

6025. *Home cars on home roads, class one roads.* Washington, DC: Association of American Railroads, Car Service Division; American Railway Association, Car Service Division, 1921-1962. Monthly, Nov. 1932-May 1940, Jan. 1962-Dec. 1962;

Semimonthly, Oct 15, 1921-Dec. 15, 1931; June 1, 1940-Dec. 15, 1961. (> Association of American Railroads. Car Service Division. *Semimonthly revenue freight car summary – class I railroads.*)

6026. Honeyman, Joel S. *A method for assessing the impact of railroad abandonment on rural communities.* Fargo, ND: Upper Great Plains Transportation Institute, North Dakota State University, 1995. 84 p. (Thesis, M.S., North Dakota State University, 1995.)

6027. Hood, Clifton. *722 miles: the building of the subways and how they transformed New York.* New York, Simon & Schuster, 1993. 335 p.

6028. Hoogenboom, Ari Arthur, Olive Hoogenboom. *The gilded age/* Englewood Cliffs, NJ: Prentice-Hall, 1967. 187 p.

6029. Hook, Henry Hudson. *Dynamometer car tests of 1905-1906 /* 1906. 18 l. (Thesis, B.S., University of Illinois.)

6030. *Hoosac Tunnel and Mountain.* Boston, s.n., 1866. 99 p.(Troy and Greenfield Railroad Company)

6030a. *The Hoosier Line.* S.l., Monon Railroad Historical-Technical Society, 1900s-Quarterly.

6031. Hoover, D.N. *A mathematical model for railway control systems.* Hampton, VA: Langley Research Center, 1996. 39 p. (*NASA Contractor Report, 205087.*)

6032. Hoover, John Lynn. *The Pennsylvania Railroad Company, the organization /* 1935. 424, 2 l. (Thesis, M.A., University of Kentucky.)

6033. Hoover Medal Board of Award. *John Frank Stevens, third Hoover medalist/* New York, NY: Hoover Medal Board of Award, 1938. 22 p.

6034. Hopkins, Irving L. *The history and development of locomotive feed water heaters.* 1927. 58 l. (Thesis, B.S., Massachusetts Institute of Technology.)

6035. Hopkins, John B. *Enhancement of train visibility.* Washington, DC: Federal Railroad Administration, 1973. 81 p. (*FRA-ORD & D-74-15.*)

6036. _____. *Grade crossing protection in high-speed, high density, passenger-service rail corridors/* Washington, DC: Federal Railroad Administration, Office of Research and Development, Development and Demonstrations, 1973. 42 p. (*FRA-ORD & D-74-14.*)

6037. _____. *Guidelines for enhancement of visual conspicuity of the trailing end of trains.* Washington, DC: Federal Railroad Administration, National Institute of Standards and Technology, 1974. 1 v.

6038. _____. *Operational testing of locomotive-mounted strobe lights.* Cambridge, MA: United States Office of Rail Safety Research; Transportation Systems Center, 1980. 26 p. (*DOT-TSC-FRA-80-48*)

6039. _____. *Railroads and the environment; estimation of fuel consumptions in rail transportation.* Washington, DC: Federal Railroad Administration, Office of Research and Development, Transportation Systems Center, 1977- 3 v.

6040. _____. A.T. Newfell. *Guidelines for enhancement of visual conspicuity of trains at grade crossings.* Washington, DC: Federal Railroad Administration, National Institute of Standards and Technology, 1975. 47 p.

6041. _____, Morrin E. Hazel. *Technological innovation in grade crossing protective systems.* Cambridge, MA: Transportation Systems Center, 1971. 62 p. (*DOT-TSC-FRA-71-3*)

6042. Hopkins, Zelle G. *The 90 year trail.* Clayton, MO: Z. Hopkins, 1960? (Public relations)

6043. Hoppe, C.W., W.M. Hart. *Potential economies and improvements in performance resulting from improvement in railroad terminal operations/* Washington, DC: Federal Railroad Administration, Office of Policy and Program Development, 1977. 1 v. (various pagings) (*FRA-OPPD-78-4*)

6044. Hopper, Gordon E. *The Victory Branch Railroad of Vermont: a spirited lumbering line that helped develop the Northeast.* River Forest, IL: Heimburger House, 1989. 32 p.

6045. Horger, Oscar J., *An economic study of roller bearings on freight cars* / New York : American Society of Mechanical Engineers, 1951. 23, 21 p. (*ASME. Paper no. 51-A.152.*)

6045a. _____. *Fatigue investigation of railroad axles and crank pins.* 1941. 1 v. (Dissertation, University of Michigan.)

6046. _____., W.I. Cantley. *Design of crankpins for locomotives.* New York, American Society of Mechanical Engineers, 1945. 17 p.

6047. Horine, J.W., H.S. Ogden. *The Pennsylvania Railroad class GG-1 electric locomotives* / New York : American Institute for Electrical Engineers, 1959. 12 p. (*AIEE Transactions paper, 60-48.*)

6048. _____, D.R. MacLeod. *Rectifier type locomotive for the Pennsylvania Railroad* / New York : American Institute of Electrical Engineers, 1962. 7, 2 p. (*AIEE Conference paper, CP 62-269.*)

6049. Horn, Julie. *Viaducts, bridges, and ghost trains: Air Line Railroad Archaeological District, Colchester and East Hampton, Connecticut.* Westport, CT: Historical Perspectives, 2004. 24 p. (New York and Boston Railroad Company)

6050. Hornblower & Weeks. *A brief history of the New York, New Haven & Hartford Railroad Company during the past twenty years.* Boston, Hornblower & Weeks, 1926. 19 p.

6051. Hornstein, Hugh A. *The Haywire: a brief history of the Manistique & Lake Superior Railroad.* East Lansing, MI: Michigan State University, 2004. 122 p.

6052. Horowitz, Morris Aaron. *Manpower utilization in the railroad industry: an analysis of working rules and practices.* Boston, Bureau of Business and Economic Research, Northeastern University, 1960. 68 p. (*Publications of the Bureau of Business and Economic Research*)

6053. Horst, Elias Vander. *The interlocking switches on Lehigh Valley Railroad at South Bethlehem, Penna.* / 1891. 32 l. (Thesis, C.E., Lehigh University.)

6054. Horst, Paul R. *The Midland Branch* (C&NW). Lincoln, NE: iUniverse, 2007. 90 p.

6055. Horton, George Roswell. *Railroad unification.* 1962. 174 l. (Thesis, University of Virginia.)

6056. Horton, Gertrude Fitch. *The Delaware & Northern and the towns it served.* Fleischmanns, NY: Purple Mountain Press, 144 p.

6057. Hoskins, T.J. *The locomotive headlight; a review of their development and aid to train movement, with especial reference to a reduction of the dangers involved. The merits of different lights by those who know.* Nashville, Tenn., Marshall & Bruce Company Printing, 1911. 48 p. (Brotherhood of Locomotive Engineers [Tenn.])

6058. *Hot-box detection with the GRS versatile wheel thermo-scanner unit.* Rochester, NY: General Railway Signal Co., 1966. 27 p.

6059. *Hot-box detector with wire or carrier current remote recording : for automatic instantaneous pin-pointing of overheated journals before costly trouble results.* Waynesboro, VA: General Electric Co., 1959. 7 p. (*GEA-6950.*)

6060. *Hot box warning device for continuous monitoring to detect overheated journal bearings.* Chicago : AAR Research Center, 1965. 18 l. (*AAR. Mechanical Division. Report no. MR-441.*)

6060a. *Hot spots guidebook* / Waukesha. WI" Kalmbach Books, 2012. 271 p.

6061. Hosmer, Howard. *Railroad passenger train deficit.* Washington, DC: Interstate Commerce Commission, 1958. 72, 7 p.

6062. Houck, Malcolm, John Taibi. *Ridin' the rails: passenger equipment of the N. Y. O. & W. Ry.* S.l., Ontario & Western Railway Historical Society, 2007. *(Volume, 42, number*

6062a. Houghton, Daniel Eugene, W. P. Wood. *Study of the operating characteristics of the Westinghouse locomotive headlight turbo-generator set.* 1926. 35 l. (Thesis, B.S., University of Pennsylvania.)

6063. Houk, Rose. *Golden Spike National Historic Site.* Tuscon, AZ: Southwest Parks and Monuments Association, 1990. 14 p.

6064. Houlahan, Patrick Henry. *Houlahan's railroad hand book.* Kansas City, Missouri, Press of Hudson-Kimberly Pub. Co. 1891. 130 p.

6065. Houshower, Hans. *Working at the Lima Loco: the Lima Locomotive Works and its workers, an exhibit exploring the shaping of an industrial culture in Lima, Ohio.* Lima, OH: American House, 1988. 22 p.

6066. Hover, John Calvin. *Marketing of Class I intercity railroad passenger service.* 1967. 122 l. (Thesis, M.B.A. in Marketing, Graduate School of Arts and Sciences, University of Pennsylvania.)

6067. Hovey, William Simmons. *Electrical equipment of the Rochester Branch of the Lehigh Valley Railroad.* 1897. 39 l. 22 plans. (Thesis, M.E. in E.E., Cornell University.)

6068. How, James F. *The protection of railroad interests.* Chicago: Railway Age and Northwestern Railroads, 1893. 9 p.

6069. *How to be a first class trainmaster!* New York, The Railroad Age Gazette, 1909. 56 p.

6070. Howard, Ernest. *A new story of American railroad wrecking; Denver and Rio Grande, Western Pacific and the Missouri Pacific's part in the affair!* New York? s.n., 1918. 60 p.

6071. _____. *Wall Street fifty years after Erie: being a comparative account of the making and breaking of the Jay Gould railroad fortune.* Boston, Mass., Stratford Company, 1923. 181 p.

6072. Howard, J.J. *The Union Pacific Railroad from Omaha to Promontory.* Omaha, Barkalow Brothers, 1869. 12 p.

6073. Howard, Jacob Merritt. *In the Senate of the United States : the sub-committee of the Pacific Railroad Committee, to whom was referred, for the purpose of investigation, a bill "incorporating the Southern Transcontinental Railway Company and granting the right of way to lands in aid of its construction," presented to the committee the flowing report, accompanied by the testimony and statements laid before them: "Memphis, El Paso and Pacific Railroad Company of Texas.* S.l., s.n., 1870. 102 p. (*United States. 41st Congress, 2d session, 1869-1870. Senate. Miscellaneous document, no. 121.*)

6074. Howard, Kathleen L., Diana F. Pardue. *Inventing the Southwest: the Fred Harvey Company and Native American art.* Flagstaff, AZ: Northland Pub., 1996. 150 p.

6075. Howard, Robert West. *The great iron trail: the story of the first transcontinental railroad.* New York, Putnam, 1962. 376 p.

6076. Howard, S.M., L.C. Gill, P.J. Wong. *Railroad energy management: train performance calculator, a survey and assessment.* Washington, D.C. Federal Railroad Administration, Office of Research and Development, 1981. 60 p. (*FRA/ORD-81/02*)

6076a. Howard Watch and Clock Company. *Fine regulators : clocks for banks, railroads, private residences, and public buildings, 1889.* Exeter, NH: Adams, Brown, 1889. 43 p.

6077. Howden, Joseph Russell. *The boys' book of locomotives: with over one hundred illustrations from photographs.* New York, N.Y., The McClure Company, 1907. 264 p.

6077a. Howe, Horace Joseph. *Design of a railroad bridge of 324 feet span* / 1879. 59 l. (Thesis, B.S., Massachusetts institute of Technology, Department of Civil Engineering,)

6078. Howe, Roger W., James S. Gillespie, Joseph A Matteo. *A study of the proposed Virginia Rail Transportation Development Authority.* Charlottesville, VA: Virginia Transportation Research Council, 2004. 121 p.

6079. Howe Scale Company of New York. *The Howe railroad track scale.* New York : Marchbanks Press, 1900s. 12 p.

6080. Howell, R. P. *Northeast corridor high speed rail passenger service improvement project, Task 22: program plan for track development and demonstration/* Washington, DC: U.S. Department of Transportation, Federal Railroad Administration, 1976. 146 l. (*FRA-NECPO-76-08*)

6081. Howell, Spencer P., J.E. Crawshaw. *Sparks from steam shovels and locomotives as caused of premature explosion.* Washington, D.C., U.S. Department of the Interior, Bureau of Mines, 1920. 22 p. (*Report of investigations, Bureau of Mines, 2187.*)

6082. Howerter, E.D. *Track geometry measurement system/* Washington, DC: Federal Railroad Administration, office of Research and Development, 1980. 78, 16 p. (*FRA/ORD-80/80)*

6083. Howerton, Joseph B. *The valuation records of the Interstate Commission as a source of statistical data relating to American railroads during the 19th century/* Washington, DC: National Archives and Records Service, General Services Administration, 1973. 36 p.

6084. Howitz, A.A. *Efficiency of the locomotive boiler.* 1894. 43 l. (Thesis, M.E., Lehigh

University.)

6085. Howland, Elvin. *Rails across Michigan*. Cadillac, MI: Zosma Publishing, 1999. 59 p.

6086. Howland, S.A. *Steamboat disasters and railroad accidents in the United States*. 2d ed. Worcester, Mass., Dorr, Howland, 1840. 408 p.

6087. Hoxsie, Charles. *Pocket companion for locomotive engineers and firemen: containing general rules and suggestions for the management of an engine under all circumstances*. 5th ed. Albany, N.Y., Weed, Parson, 1876. 104 p.

6088. Hoy, William S. *Railroad stations in the Gallatin area, Montana*. Montgomery Village, MD: Keystone Press, 1998. 124 p.

6089. Hoyt, J. K. *Pen and pencil pictures on the Delaware, Lackawanna, and Western Railroad*. New York: W.H. Cadwell, 1874. 287 p.

6090. Hridaya, Neha. *Development of an environmental consequence model for assessing the impact of hazardous chemical spills from railroad tank cars on groundwater cleanup times and cost* / 2008. 64 l. (Thesis, M.S., University of Illinois at Urbana-Champaign.)

6091. Hsieh, Wen Lung. *Railroad safety problems, federal safety legislation and administration*/ Shanghai, Printed at T. Chu, 1930. 140, 4 p. (Thesis, Ph.D., University of Pennsylvania.)

6092. Hsu, Chao-Luan. *Railroad passenger terminal management*. 1932. 112, 5 l. (Thesis, M.B.A. in Transportation and Public Utilities, Graduate School of Arts and Sciences, University of Pennsylvania.)

6093. Hsu, Jen Chieh. *Effect of motor transportation on the railroad business*. 1925. 123 l. (Thesis, M.B.A. in Transportation and Public Utilities, Graduate School of Arts and Sciences, University of Pennsylvania.)

6094. Hsu, C.Y. *A study of locomotive superheaters*. 1918. 43 l. (Thesis, B.S., Massachusetts Institute of Technology.)

6095. Hsu, Tung-Kuang. *Railroad car draft gear model for modeling dynamic impacts*/ 1977. 54 l. (Thesis, M.S., Washington University, Department of Mechanical Engineering.

6096. Hu, Dickson Jenyu. *A study of railroad freight yards and terminals*. 1925. 1 v. (Thesis, M.C.E., Cornell University.)

6097. Huang, Annian.. *Chen mo de suo dao ding: jian she Bei Mei tie lu de hua gong. The silent spikes: Chinese laborers and the construction of North American railroads*/ Beijing; Wu zhou chuan bo chu ban she/China Intercontinental Press, 2006. 173 p. Translated by Zhang Juguo. (Central Pacific Railroad)

6097a. _____. *Dao ding, bu zai chen mo: jian she bei Mei tie lu de Hua gong*. Shenyang Shi: Bai Shan chu ban she, 2010. 3, 5, 352 p. (Central Pacific Railroad)

6098. Huang, Hsien-Ju. *State taxation of railways in the United States/* New York: Columbia University Press, 1928. 209 p. (Thesis, Ph.D., Columbia University, 1928.)

6099. Hubbard, Elbert. *A little journey over the Buffalo, Rochester and Pittsburgh Ry.* East Aurora, N.Y., The Roycrofters, 1914. 31 p.

6100. Hubbard, Freeman. *Encyclopedia of North American railroading: 150 years of railroading in the United States and Canada*. New York, McGraw-Hill, 1981. 377 p.

6101. _____ *Railroad Avenue; great stories and legends of American railroading*. New York, McGraw-Hill Book Company, 1945. 374 p. (Revised edition: San Marino, CA: Golden West Books, 1964. 444 p.)

6102. Hubbard, Howard Archibald. *A chapter in early Arizona transportation history: the Arizona Narrow Gauge Railroad Company* / Tuscon, AZ: University of Arizona, 1934. 69 p. (*University of Arizona. Social science bulletin, no. 6.)*

6103. Hubbard, J.R. *Locomotive and equipment maintenance: unsung heroes in shops and roundhouses keep 'em rolling on the Santa Fe*. S.l., s.n, 1943. 25 p.

6103a. Hubbard, Oliver P. *Circular on Magoon's patent feed water heater for locomotives* / St. Johnsbury, VY: R. Hale, Magoon & Co., 1855. 17 p.

6104. Hubbell, William Wheeler, Ross Winans, Orsamus Eaton. *Arguments of William W. Hubbell on behalf of the defendants, before Hon. Samuel Nelson, in the case of Ross Winans vs. Orsamus Eaton, et al., in the Circuit Court of the United States of the Northern District of New York, against a motion for an injunction to restrain the defendants from constructing and vending the railroads cars, commonly known as the "Eight-wheeled railroad car." alleged to infringe Ross Winan's patent of Oct. 1, 1834*. Albany, N.Y., Weed, Parson & Company, Printers, 1853. 200 p.

6105. Hubler, Robert. *B & O caboose diagram book*. Baltimore, MD: Baltimore and Ohio Railroad Historical Society, 1982. 30 p.

6106. _____, John P. Hankey. *Cabooses of the Baltimore & Ohio Railroad*. Baltimore, MD: Baltimore and Ohio Railroad Historical Society, 1994. 176 p.

6107. Huckel, Samuel, William J. Wilgus. *General specification of the work and materials required in the alteration and additions in the Grand Central Station, New York City*. New York, New York Central and Hudson River Railroad Company, 1899. 60 p.

6108. Huddleston, Eugene L. *Appalachian conquest: C & O, N & W, Virginian and Clinchfield cross the mountains*. Lynchburg, VA: TLC Pub., 2002. 138 p.

6109. _____. *Appalachian crossing: the Pocahontas roads.* Sterling, VA: TLC, 1989. 65 p.

6110. _____. *Chesapeake & Ohio super power steam locomotives.* Clifton Forge, VA: Chesapeake & Ohio Historical Society, 2005. 168 p.

6111. _____. *Riding that New River train: the story of the Chesapeake & Ohio Railway through the New River Gorge of West Virginia.* Alderson, WV: Chesapeake & Ohio Historical Society, 1989. 132 p.

6112. _____. *The role of the Virginia Central in the North Anna campaign, May, 1864.* Clifton Forge, VA: Chesapeake & Ohio Historical Society, 1993. 10 p.

6113. _____. *Uncle Sam's locomotives: the USRA and the nation's railroads.* Bloomington, Indiana University Press, 2002. 215 p.

6114. _____. *The Van Sweringen Berkshires.* Hicksville, NY: N.J. International, 1986. 147 p. (*Classic power, 7*)

6115. _____. *The world's greatest mallets: C & O H-8 versus N & W class A.* Alderson, WV: Chesapeake & Ohio Historical Society, 1986. 42 p.

6116. _____. *World's greatest steam locomotives: C & O 2-6-6-6, Virginian 2-6-6-6, N & W 2-6-6-4, UP 4-8-8-4.* Lynchburg, VA: TLC Publishing; The Chesapeake & Ohio Historical Society, 2001. 132 p.

6117. _____, Edward Stokes Miller. *Trackside in Appalachia with Gene Huddleston.* Scotch Plains, NJ: Morning Sun Books, 2006. 128 p.

6118. _____, John Joseph, Everett Young. *Chesapeake & Ohio, coal and color.* Clifton Forge, VA: Chesapeake & Ohio Historical Society, 1997. 120 p.

6119. _____. Thomas W. Dixon. *The Allegheny: Lima's finest on the Chesapeake & Ohio and the Virginian.* Edmonds, WA: Hundman Publishing, 1984. 245 p. (Reprint: Mukilteo, WA: Hundman Publishing, 1996. 244 p.)

6120. Hudson, Charles M. *The design of a railroad interlocking switch and signal system at Riverside, Mass.* 1916. 1 v. (Thesis, B.S., Massachusetts Institute of Technology, Department of Electrical Engineering.)

6121. Hudson, F.K. *Diesel and electric locomotive specifications: locomotives in service including locomotives currently or recently in production.* Ocean, NJ: Specialty Press, 1981. 96 p.

6122. _____. *Pocket guide to diesel and electric locomotives in service/* Ocean, NJ: Specialty Press, 1974. 224 p.

6123. Hudson, James F. *The railways and the republic.* New York, NY: Harper, 1886. 489 p. (3d ed. 1889. 532 p.)

6124. Hudson, John W. II, Suzanne C. Hudson. *Scenes along the rails: the Delaware, Lackawanna & Western Railroad's Syracuse Division.* Loveland, OH: Depot Square Publishing, 2001. 144 p.

6125. Hudson Suspension Bridge and New England Railway Company. *Agreement between the Hudson Suspension Bridge and New England Railway Company, and, the Lehigh Valley Railroad Company, September 18ᵗʰ, 1888.* New York, s.n., 1888. 12 p.

6126. Hudson, William S. *Locomotives and locomotive building...together with a history of the origin and growth of the Rogers Locomotive and Machine Works, from 1831 to 1876.* New York, J. W. Pratt, 1876. 149 p.

6127. Hudson Coal Company; Delaware and Hudson Company. *The mining and preparation of D & H anthracite.* Scranton, Pa., Hudson Coal Co., 1944. 1 v.

6128. Hudson Highland Suspension Bridge and New England Railway Company. *The Hudson Suspension Bridge and New England Railway Company.* New York, The Company, 1870. 26 p.

6129.*The Hudson Highland Suspension Bridge, connecting the West and East, via the Erie and New England Railroad : general remarks, report of the board of Consulting Engineers, the bridge charter, railroad prospectus, ferry charter, maps, &c.* New York : Haskins & Co., [1869?]

6130. Hudson River Museum. *Next stop Westchester!: people and the railroad.* Yonkers, NY: Hudson River Museum of Westchester, 1996. 28 p.

6131. Huebner, Grover Gerhardt, *The fundamentals of traffic: a series of fifty-two lectures on traffic and traffic management.* Chicago, The Traffic Service Corporation, 1925. 276 p.

6132. _____, Emory R. Johnson. *The railroad freight service.* New York, D. Appleton and Co., 1926. 589 p. (*Appleton's railway series.*)

6133. Huffman, Eldridge. *Rail and derails: or railroaders on the job.* Pendleton, OR: East Oregonian, 1946. 1 v.

6134. Hufstetler, Mark. *South Dakota's railroads: an historic context.* Pierre, SD: South Dakota State Historical Society, 1998. 72 p.

6135. Hughes, Lyn. *An anthology of respect : the Pullman porters national historic registry of African-American railroad employees* / Chicago : Hughes Peterson Pub., 2007. 414 p.

6136. Hughes, Maria Jon. *Social relations in a railroad town: the locomotive engineers, locomotive firemen, and switchmen of Galesburg, Illinois and the Burlington strike of 1888.* 1996. 2 v. (Thesis, Ph.D., University of Maryland at College Park.)

6137. Huibregtse, Jon Roland. *American railroad labor and the genesis of the New Deal, 1919-1935.* Gainesville: University Press of Florida, 2010. 172 p. (*Working in the Americas*)

6138. _____. *Years of transition: American railroad labor, 1919-1934.* 1995. 265 l. (Thesis, Ph.D., University of Akron, Department of History.)

6139. Hulbert, Archer Butler, John Moody. *The highways of commerce. Part 1: The paths of inland commerce, by Archer B. Hulbert. Part 2: The railroad builders.* New Haven, Yale University Press, 1920. 211 p. (The chronicles of America series [Benjamin Franklin edition] v. 17.)

6140. Hulbert, S. *Research locomotive and train handling evaluator definition: concept 1.* Washington, DC: Department of Transportation, Federal Railroad Administration, Office of Research and Development, 1978, 1977. 1 v. *(FRA/ORD-77/47)*

6141. Hull, Clifton E. *Railroad stations and trains through Arkansas and the Southwest.* Hart, MO: Whiteriver Productions, Inc., 1997. 120 p.

6142. _____. *Shortline railroads of Arkansas.* Norman, University of Oklahoma Press, 1969. 416 p. (Also: Conway, AR: University of Central Arkansas Press, 1988, 1969. 432 p.)

6143. _____. *Steamcars to Waterloo.* N. Little Rock, AR: C.E. Hull, 1993. 1 v. (Reader Railroad)

6144. _____, Bill Pollard. *The Dardanelle & Russellville Railroad.* Conway, AR: UCA Press, 1995. 536 p.

6145. Hulson Grate Company. *The Hulson locomotive grate: its construction, its shaking action and the economies derived from its adoption as standard equipment.* Keokuk, Iowa, Hulson Grate Company, 1924. 19 p.

6146. Hultgren, Thor. *Agricultural production compared with railway traffic in farm products during the Depression/* Washington, DC: U.S. Department of Agriculture, Bureau of Agricultural Economics, 1934. 28, 7 p.

6147. _____. *Illustrative comparisons between freight rates on and retail prices of farm products.* Washington, DC: U.S. Department of Agriculture, Bureau of Agricultural Economics, 1934. 14 p.

6148. _____. *Railroad travel and the state of business/* New York, NY: National Bureau of Economic Research, 1943. 2, 35 p. (National Bureau of Economic Research. *Occasional paper, 13.*)

6149. _____. *Railway freight traffic in prosperity and depression.* New York, National Bureau of Economic Research, 1942. 51 p. (National Bureau of Economic Research. *Occasional paper, 5.)*

6150. _____. *Railway traffic expansion and use of resources in World War II.* New York, National Bureau of Economic Research, 1944. 31 p. (National Bureau of Economic Research. *Occasional paper, 15.)*

6151. _____, Sam George Spal. *Freight rates on bituminous coal, with index numbers, 1929-1940.* Washington, DC: Interstate Commerce Commission, Bureau of Transport Economics and Statitistcs, 1941. 132 p. (Its *Statement, no. 413.)*

6151a. *Humors of the railroad kings; authentic and original anecdotes of prominent railroad men.* New York: Office of "Wild Oates," 1872. 31 p.

6152. *Hump yards: list of references in the BRE Library.* Washington, D.C., Association of American Railroads, 1962. 10 l.

6153. Humphrey, Clarice John, Clarice Audrey Richards. *Railroad tie decay; comprising The Decay of ties in storage, by C.J. Humphrey ... Defects in cross ties, caused by fungi, by C. Audrey Richards.* Washington, DC: American Wood-Preservers' Association, 1939. 54 p.

6154. Humphrey, Todd E., John W. Humphrey. *Southern Tier lines.* East Syracuse, NY: Rainy Day Books, 1992. 96 p.

6155. Humphreys, Andrew Akinson, Gouverneur Kimble Warren. *An examination by direction of the Hon. Jefferson Davis, Secretary of War, of the reports of explorations for railroad routes from the Mississippi to the Pacific, made under the orders of the War Department in 1853-'54, and of the explorations made previous to that time, which have a bearing on the subject.* Washington, D.C.: Printed by A,O,P, Nicholson, 1855. 116, 1 p. (United States. Army. Corps of Topographical Engineers.)

6156. Hundhausen, A.J. *Cougars, Utes, and Columbines: an illustrated catalog of Colorado Midland advertising publications.* Colorado Springs, CO: Colorado Midland Quarterly, 1991. 76 p.

6157. Huneke, William F. *The heavy hand: the government and the Union Pacific, 1862-1898.* New York, Garland Publications, 1985. 166 p. (Thesis, Ph.D., University of Virginia, 1983.)

6157a. _____. *The road to ruin : the Union Pacific and the government, 1862-1878/* 1979. 85 l. (Thesis, M.A., University of Virginia.)

6158. _____. *Study of railroad rates, 1985-2007.* Washington, DC: Surface Transportation Board, Office of Economics, Environmental Analysis & Administration, Section of Economics, 2009. 13 p.

6159. Hungerford, Edward. *The American railroad in laboratory; a brief digest of research and experimentation, conducted by railroads individually and collectively through the American Railway Association in the interest of constant improvement of their facilities and service.* Washington, DC; American Railway Association, 1933. 544 p.

6160. _____. *Book of the pageant: Railroads on parade.* S.l., Eastern Railroad Presidents Conference, 1940. 16 p. (World's Fair, New York, 1940.)

6161. _____. *Catalogue of locomotive details.* Dunkirk, N.Y., Brooks Locomotive Works, 1895. 159 p.

6162. _____. *Daniel Willard rides the line: the story of a great railroad man.* New York, G.P. Putnam's Sons, 1938. 301 p.

6163. _____. *From covered wagon to streamliner.* New York, The Greystone Press, 1941. 64 p.

6164. _____. *Locomotives on parade.* New York, Crowell, 1940. 236 p.

6165. _____. *Men and iron: the history of New York Central.* New York, Thomas Y. Crowell Co., 1938. 424 p.

6166. _____. *Men of Erie, a story of human effort.* New York, Random House, 1946. 346 p.

6167. _____. *The modern railroad.* Chicago, A.C. McClurg, 1911. 476 p.

6168. _____. *Our railroads to-morrow.* New York, Century Company, 1922. 332 p.

6169. _____. *Pattern for a railroad for tomorrow.* Milwaukee, Kalmbach Publishing, 1945. 323 p.

6170. _____. *The railroad problem.* Chicago, A.C. McClurg, 1917, 265 p.

6171. _____. *The run of the Twentieth Century.* New York, New York Central Lines, 1930. 110 p. (Reprint: New York, Wayner Publications, 1970. 111 p.)

6172. _____. *The story of the Baltimore & Ohio Railroad, 1827-1927.* New York, G.P. Putnam's Sons, 1928. 2 v.(Reprint: Freeport, NY: Books for Libraries Press, 1972. 2 v.)

6173. _____ *The story of the Rome, Watertown and Ogdensburgh Railroad.* New York, R.M. McBride & Company, 1922. 269 p.

6174. _____. *Transport for war, 1942-1943.* New York, E.P. Dutton, 1943. 272 p.

6175. _____, and others. *Vermont Central-Central Vermont, a study in human effort.*

Boston, Mass., The Railway & Locomotive Historical Society, Inc., Baker Library, Harvard Business School, 1942. 104 p. (*Bulletin, no. 58A.*) (Reprint: St. Albans, VT: L.G. Printing, 2003. 100 p.)

6176. _____ *Wings of a century: the romance of transportation.* Chicago, Century of Progress International Exposition, 1934. 16 p.

6177. Hungerford, John B. *Cab-in-front; the half-century story of an unconventional locomotive.* Reseda, CA: Hungerford Press, 1959. 35 p. (Reprint: Edmonds, WA: Pacific Fast Mail, 1974. 35 p.)

6178. _____. *Hawaiian railroads; a memoir of the common carriers of the fiftieth state.* Reseda, CA: Hungerford Press, 1963. 80 p.

6179. _____. *Narrow gauge to Silverton.* 2d ed. Reseda, CA: Hungerford Press, 1956. 36 p.

6180. _____. *The slim Princess; the story of the Southern Pacific narrow gauge.* Reseda, CA: Hungerford Press, 1956. 32 p.

6181. Hungerford, L.S. *Instructions for employees on cars of the Pullman Company.* Chicago? The Pullman Company, 1906. 74 p.

6182. Hungry Wolf, Adolf. *Off on a wild caboose chase—true adventures, folklore, and a farewell to the old train caboose b ya writer who lives aboard one.* New York, Morrow, 1989. 205 p.

6182a. Hunt, Jarvis. *Proposal for a central passenger and freight terminal for Chicago's railroads.* Chicago : City Club of Chicago, 1913. 13 p.

6183. Hunt, Louie. *The Silverton train; a story of southwestern Colorado's narrow gauges.* Leucadia, CA: s.n., 1955. 70 p.

6184. Hunt, Robert S. *Law and locomotives: the impact of the railroad on Wisconsin law in the nineteenth century.* Madison, WI: State Historical Society of Wisconsin, 1958. 292 p.

6185. Hunter, Chris. *Ocean Shore Railroad.* Charleston, SC: Arcadia, 2004. 127 p.

6185a. Hunter, Don. *Highballing in high style.* Colorado Springs, CO: Villa Publishing Syndicate, 1983. 91 l. (Rolling stock; locomotives—patents)

6186. Hunter J.G. *Preliminary report of the transportation problem in the State of California as it affects war industries/* San Francisco, CA: California Railroad Commission, 1942. 13 l. (*File 040).*

6186a. _____. *Progress in grade crossing regulation in California.* San Francisco, CA: California Railroad Commission, Transportation Division, 1929. 2, 48 l.

6187. _____, E.F. McNaughton. *Report on financial, operating and service condition of the Pacific Electric Railway Company.* Los Angeles, California Railroad Commission, Transportation Division, 1928. 172 l.

6188. _____, Ward Hall. *Progress in grade separation construction in California, 1860 to 1929, inclusive/* San Francisco, California Railroad Commission, Transportation Division, 1931. 12 l.

6189. Huntingdon and Broad Top Mountain Railroad and Coal Company. *Rules for the government of the Transportation Department /* Pennsylvania? Huntingdon and Broad Top Mountain Railroad and Coal Co., 1910. 50 p.

6190. Huntington, Collis Potter. *The Central Pacific R.R. of California. Character of the work, its progress, resources, earnings, and future prospects/* New York, NY: G. Brown, Printer, 1866. 14 p.

6191. _____. *The Collis P. Huntington papers, 1856-1901 : a guide to the microfilm edition.* Sanford, NC: Microfilming Corp. of America, 1979. 56 p.

6192. _____. *In the matter of the payment for surveys and the taxation of granted lands. Letter to Hon. P.B. Plumb, chairman Committee on Public Lands, United States Senate.* New York, 1885. 7 p.

6193. _____ *Thirty-second parallel Pacific railroad: remarks of C.P. Huntington, agent and attorney of the Southern Pacific Railroad Co's, before the Committee on Public Lands of the U.S. Senate (February 23d, 1884) on House Bill 3933, declaring a forfeiture of the lands granted to the Texas Pacific Railroad Company, its successors and assigns.* New York, NY: J.C. Rankin, Jr., Printer & Stationer, 1884. 19 p.

6194. _____. *The Pacific rail road companies; their relations to the government growing out of advances of bonds in aid of construction. Letter of the vice-president Central Pacific R.R. Company, to the chairman, Pacific Railroad Committee, House of Representatives.* New York, s.n., 1886. 25 p.

6195. _____. *Report of discussion between the House and Senate committees on Pacific Railroads and C.P. Huntington, vice-president of the Central Pacific Railroad Company, in relation to a settlement between the government and the Central and Union Pacific Railroad companies : House of Representatives and Senate, January 23 and 24, 1890.* New York : Evening Post Job Print, 1890. 27 p. (United States. Congress. House. Committee on Pacific Railroads. United States. Congress. Senate. Committee on Pacific Railroads.)

6196. _____. *Southern Pacific Railroad (of California). Description, progress and business.* New York, NY: Evening Post Steam Presses, 1875. 21 p. (…"in opposition to bill to extend the time for completing the Texas Pacific Road, and acquiring the public lands in the territories west of Texas.")

6197. _____, David Douty Colton. *As to refunding the Central Pacific debt.* S.l., s.n., 1878. 10 p. "Extracts from Mr. Huntington's letters to Colton during the three years between May, 1875, and January 1878."

6198. _____, _____. *The octopus speaks : the Colton letters* / Edited with notes and introduction by Salvador A. Ramirez. Carlsbad, CA: Tentacled Press, 1992. 6, 615, 5 p., 33 leaves of plates.

6199. _____, James H. Storrs. *Thirty-second parallel Pacific railroad : remarks of C.P. Huntington and argument of James H. Storrs in behalf of the Southern Pacific Railroad, before the Committee on the Pacific Railroads, House of Representatives, forty-fifth Congress ... January 31ˢᵗ, 1878.* Washington, D.C.: Judd & Detweiler, Printers, 1878. 62 p. (United States. Congress. House. Committee on Pacific Railroads; United States. Congress. Senate. Committee on Railroads.)

6200. _____, John Tyler Morgan. *Pacific railroads: views of the minority to accompany S. 119.* Washington, D.C.: U.S. G.P.O., 1897. 352 p. (*Report. 55ᵗʰ Congress, 1ˢᵗ session, Senate, 20, pt. 2.*)

6201. Huntington, William S. *The roadmaster's assistant and section-master's guide; a manual of reference for all having to do with the permanent way of American railroads, and containing the best results of experience and minute directions for tracklaying, ballasting and keeping track in good repair.* Chicago, Ill., A.N. Kellogg, 1871. 95 p. (Rev. and enl ed.: 1878. 286 p. Enlarged by Charles Latimer; 11ᵗʰ ed.: New York, N.Y., Railroad Gazette, 1884. 282 p.)

6202. *Hunt's merchants' magazine.* New York, NY: Freeman Hunt, 1839-1848. Monthly. 18 v. (> *Hunt's merchants' magazine and commercial review.*)

6203. *Hunt's merchants' magazine and commercial review.* New York, NY: Freeman Hunt, 1848-1861. Monthly 26 v. (< *Hunt's merchants' magazine;* > *Merchants' magazine and commercial review.*)

6204. Hurley, L.M. *Newton, Kansas, a railroad town: history, facilities and operations, 1871-1971.* North Newton, KS: Mennonite Press, 1985. 185 p.

6205. Hurt, Gordon Gilmer. *The future of railroad passenger traffic from a marketing standpoint.* 1947. 127 l. (Thesis, M.B.A. in Marketing, Graduate School of Arts and Sciences, University of Pennsylvania.)

6206. Husband, Joseph. *The story of the Pullman car.* Chicago, A.C. McClurg & Company, 1917. 9, 161, 31 l. of plates. (Reprint: New York, Arno Press, 1972. Grand Rapids, MI: Black Letter Press, 1974.)

6207. Husing, John E. *California high speed train system's impact on the Inland Empire, 2030.* Redlands, CA: Economics & Politics, Inc., 2008. 18 p.

6208. Huston, Harvey. *Thunder Lake Narrow Gauge, '93-'41.* Winnetka, IL: s.n., 1961. 145 p. (2d ed.: 1982. 151 p.)

6209. _____ *The Roddis Line; the Roddis Lumber & Veneer Co. Railroad and the Dells & Northeastern Railway.* Winnetka, IL: 1972. 150 p.

6209a. Hutchings, Carleton B. *Transportation of dairy products* / Chicago: The American Institute of Agriculture, 1923. 36 p. (marketing dairy products, lesson 8.)

6210. Hutchins, George A. *The manufacture of steam railroad cars.* Washington, D.C., Bureau of the Census, 1902. 29 p. (*Census bulletin, no. 214; Twelfth Census.*)

6211. Hutchins, J. Lee. *A stochastic analysis system for urban railroad transportation investments* / 1979. 226 l. (Thesis, D.S., Washington University.)

6212. Hutchins, John C. *The Blueberry Express: a history of the Suncook Valley Railroad.* Littleton, MA: Flying Yankee Enterprises, 1985. 113 p.

6213. Hutchinson, Cary Talcott. *Sectionalization arrangement for sections of the Virginian Railway between Princeton, W. Va., and narrows, Va., and between Eggleston, Va., and Whitethorne, Va.* New York, 192-.

6214. Hutchinson, G.C. *A feed-water heater for locomotives.* 1894. 30 l. (Thesis M.E., Lehigh University.)

6215. Hutchinson, Veronica S. *Tales of the rails*/ Cleveland: World Pub. Co., 1952. 329 p. (Anecdotes, facetiae, satire, etc.)

6216. Hutter, Bridget M. *Regulation and risk: occupational health and safety on the railways*/ New York, NY: Oxford University Press, 2001. 356 p.

6217. Huxtable, Nils. *Classic North American steam.* New York, Gallery Books, 1990. 128 p. (Reprint: New York, MetroBooks, 2001. 128 p.)

6218. Hwang, Shyh-Lin. *Railroad refrigeration service of fruits and vegetables in the United States.* 1941. 151 l. (Thesis, M.B.A. in Transportation and Public Utilities, Graduate School of Arts and Sciences, University of Pennsylvania)

6220. Hyde, Frederick W. *The Milwaukee Road.* Denver, CO: Hyrail Productions, 1990. 192 p.

6221. _____, Dale Sanders. *The Milwaukee Road: diesel power.* Antioch, IL: The Milwaukee Road Historical Association, 2009. 256 p.

6222. Hyde, Ted Evans. *An economic comparison between the coal slurry pipeline proposed by Houston Natural Gas Corporation and two comparable unit train models* / Austin TX: Center for Energy Studies, University of Texas at Austin, 1979. 197 p. (*Public information report, no. 5.*)

6223. Hydell, Richard Paul. *A study of technological diffusion: the replacement of steam by diesel locomotives in the United States.* 1977. 309 l. (Thesis, Ph.D., Massachusetts Institute of Technology, Department of Economics.)

6224. Hydrick, Blair, and others. *A guide to the microfilm edition of Records of the Brotherhood of Sleeping Car Porters. Series A, Holdings of the Chicago Historical Society and the Newberry Library, 1925-1969.* Bethesda, MD: University Publications of America, 1993-1994. 3 v. (*Black studies research sources*)

6225. Hypps, Frank T. *Federal regulation of railroad construction and abandonment under the Transportation Act of 1920.* 1929. 82 p. (Thesis, Ph.D., University of Pennsylvania.)

6226. Hyslip, James P. *Ground penetrating radar for railroad track substructure evaluation.* Washington, DC: Federal Railroad Administration, Office of Research and Development, 2005. 39 p. (*DOT/FRA/ORD-05/04.*)

6227. Hyson, Ray. '*High ballers': classic railroad cartoons.* Chino, CA: The Author, 1978. 150 p.

I

6228. *I like trains, 1940-1954: great reading from the magazine of railroading; selected by David Morgan.* Milwaukee, WI: Kalmbach Pub. Co., 1980. 104 p.

6229. Iakisch, John Rudolph. *Studies of freight train operation on proposed ruling grades in the Milwaukee track elevation project, Chicago, Milwaukee and St. Paul; Railway.*1911. 48 l. (Thesis, C.E., University of Wisconsin, Madison.)

6229a. Idaho. Transportation Department. *The Camas Prairie Railroad : a special study /* Boise, ID: Management Services Section, 1978. 60 p.

6230. _____. Transportation Planning Division; Wilbur Smith and Associates. *Idaho state rail plan.* Boise, ID: The Department, 1996. 1 v.

6231. *IEEE ... Railroad Technical Conference.* New York, NY: Institute of Electronics and Electrical Incorporated Engineers, 1900s-1975. Annual.

6232. *IEEE technical papers presented at the ... Joint ASME/IEEE Railroad Conference.* New York, NY: Institute of Electrical and Electronics Engineers, 1981-1986. Annual. 8 v. (< Joint ASME/IEEE/AAR Railroad Conference; *IEEE technical papers presented at the ... Joint ASME/IEEE/AAR Railroad Conference*; > Joint ASME/IEEE Railroad Conference; *Technical papers presented at the ... IEEE/ASME Joint Railroad Conference.*)

6233. *IEEE technical papers presented at the ... Joint ASME/IEEE/AAR Railroad Conference.* New York, NY: Institute of Electrical and Electronics Engineers, 1977-1980. Annual. (< Joint ASME/IEEE Railroad Technical Conference.)

6234. *Illinois Central employees' magazine.* Chicago: Illinois Central Railroad Company, 1900s. Monthly. L.B. Mackenzie, editor. ((> *Illinois Central magazine.)*

6235. *Illinois Central Gulf news.* Chicago: Illinois Central Gulf Railroad, 1972-1900s. Monthly. (< *Illinois Central magazine; > Main Line news.*)

6236. Illinois Central Gulf Railroad Company. *Freight car diagrams.* S.l., Illinois Central Gulf, 1982. 1, 43, 352 l.

6237. _____. *Interpretations and explanations of operating rules /* Chicago: Illinois Central Gulf Railroad Company, 1977. 288 p.

6238. _____. *Recognizing and identifying hazardous material /* Chicago: Illinois Central Gulf Railroad Company, 1982. 26 p.

6239. _____. *Refrigerated container services: efficient transportation of quick-frozen and fresh perishable merchandise by rail /* Chicago? : Research and Development

Bureau, Illinois Central Gulf Railroad Company, 1941. 18, 17 l.

6240. Illinois Central Historical Society. *Membership newsletter* / Lombard, IL: The Society, 1984-?

6241. _____. *Where the Southern crosses the Yellow Dog.* Paxton, IL: Illinois Central Historical Society, 2004. 72 p. (Special issue of the Green Diamond.

6242. *Illinois Central magazine.* Chicago: Illinois Central Railroad Co., 1912-1900s. Monthly. (*< Illinois Central employee's magazine; > Illinois Central Gulf news.)*

6243. Illinois Central Railroad Company. *A brief outline of the 100 year evolution of the dining car.* Chicago : Illinois Central Railroad Company, 1962. 1 folder (10 p.)

6244. _____. *Centennial report: the financial story of our first hundred years, 1851-1951.* Chicago, Illinois Central Railroad Company, 1951. 45 p.

6245. _____. *The de luxe all-Pullman Panama Limited.* Chicago, Ill., Poole Brothers, 194-? 15 p.

6246. _____. *Florida: Illinois Central via Birmingham, Columbus, Albany to Jacksonville.* Chicago, Ill., Rand McNally, 1916. 14 p. (Seminole Limited)

6247. _____. *The Floridian: the de luxe train.* Chicago, Ill., Poole Brothers, 1924. 15 p.

6248. _____. *Instructions for trainmen and mechanical department employees governing heating, lighting, etc. of passenger train equipment.* S.l., s.n., 1921. 19 p.

6249. _____. *List of locomotives, freight cars, passenger cars, miscellaneous equipment, floating equipment, turntable, wye tracks.* Chicago, Ill., The Company, 1946. 74 p.

6250. _____ *List of locomotives, freight cars, passenger cars, miscellaneous equipment, floating equipment, turntables, wye tracts* / Chicago ? The Company, 1954. 74 p. *(Equipment list/Illinois Central Railroad, no. 15.)*

6251. _____: *List of stations: (alphabetically and by divisions and districts), location of districts named in list, station agents, joint freight agencies, freight car equipment, switching charges via intermediate lines, track connections and junction points, track scales, maximum load diagrams, numerical list of accounting stations numbers; no. 2, April 1945.* Chicago: Illinois Central System, 1945. 95 p.

6252. _____. *A look into the heart of one of the problems of railway operation in the state of Mississippi.* Chicago: Illinois Central Railroad Co., 1914. 32 p. Railroad accidents.

6253. _____. *Organization and traffic of the Illinois Central System.* Chicago, Ill., Illinois Central Railroad Company, 1938. 526 p.

6253a. _____. *Progress of reconstruction and electrification of the Chicago terminal.* S.l., s.n., 1926. 12 p., 7 leaves of plates.

6254. _____. *Report upon the mineral resources of the Illinois Central Railroad: made at the request of the president.* Prepared by J.W. Foster, March 4th, 1856. New York: George Scott Roe, Printer and Stationer, 19 & 21 Merchants' Exchange, 1856. 29 p.

6255. _____. *Rules and instructions covering maintenance & operation of lighting equipment on locomotives and passenger train cars, except M.U. electric suburban cars.* Chicago, Ill., Illinois Central Railroad Company, 1926. 33 p.

6256. _____. *Rules and regulations governing air brakes and air signals, effective May 1st, 1920* / Chicago: Illinois Central Railroad Co., 1920. 36 p.

6257. _____. *Rules for the maintenance of way and structures.* Rev. ed. Chicago, Illinois Central Railroad Co., 1925. 1 v. (various pagings) (Illinois Central Railroad Company, the Yazoo & Mississippi Valley Railroad Company, Gulf and Ship Island Railroad Company.)

6258. _____. *Smart, swift, thrifty: America's great new dayliner: "City of New Orleans"* Chicago, Illinois Central, 194-? 11 p.

6259. _____. *Table of mileages: between freight stations on Illinois Central Railroad, northern and western lines: also freight connections and junction points.* Chicago, Ill., F.C. Furry, 1930. 129 p.

6260. _____. *This is our railroad: the Illinois Central family book.* S.l., Illinois Central Railroad, 1948. 37 p.

6261. _____. *Whistle in the night: the story of Illinois Central, main line of mid-America.* Chicago, Ill., Illinois Central Railroad, 1949. 28 p.

6262. *Illinois Central Railroad Company: a centennial bibliography, 1851-1951.* Compiled by Helen R. Richardson. Washington, D.C., Association of American Railroads, 1950. 239 p.

6263. *The Illinois Central Railroad Company: a graphic study of this standard trunk line.* New York, National City Company, 1919. 23 p.

6264. Illinois. Department of Conservation. Hoffman Williams Lafen and Fletcher (Firm) *Illinois rail-trails developer's handbook.* Springfield, IL: Illinois Department of Conservation, 1990. 61, 14, 1 p.

6264a. Illinois. General Assembly. Legislative Investigating Commission. *The Burlington Northern & St. Louis-San Francisco Railway merger: a report to the Illinois General Assembly.* Chicago: The Commission, 1980. 85 p.

6265. Illinois Steel Company, Chicago. *Rails and accessories.* Chicago, Ill., Illinois Steel Company, 1914. 177 p.

6266. _____. Carnegie Steel Company. *Standard steel rails & fastenings* / New York and Pittsburgh : Chasmar-Winchell Press, 1905. 141, vii p.

6267. Illinois. University. Engineering Experiment Station. *The economical use of coal in railway locomotives.* Urbana, The University of Illinois, 1918. 76 p.

6268. *The illustrated encyclopedia of railroad lighting.* Text by Richard Barrett. Research by Richard Barrett and Joseph Gross. Rochester, N.Y., Railroad Research Publications, 1994- v. 1: *The railroad lantern.*

6269. *Illustrated treasury of Baldwin locomotives, 1831-1956.* Compiled by James W. Kerr. Alburg, VT: DPA-LTA Enterprises, 1983. 226 p.

6270. *Illustrated history of Budd railway passenger cars: world's foremost builder of railway passenger cars.* Compiled by J.W. Kerr. Montreal, Delta Publications Associates, 1979. 84 p.

6271. *Illustrated treasury of Budd railway passenger cars: world's foremost builder of railway passenger cars, 1931-1981, fiftieth anniversary.* Compiled by James W. Kerr. Alburg, VT:; Montreal: Delta Publications Associates Division, DPA-LTA Enterprises, 1981. 250 p.

6272. *Illustrated modern freight cars of North America.* Alburg, VT: DPA-LTA Enterprises, 1982. 119 p.

6273. *Impact of data link technology on railroad dispatching operations: human factors in railroad operations.* Cambridge, MA. John A. Volpe National Transportation Systems Center, 2005, 2004. 62 p. (*DOT/FRA/ORD-04/11*)

6274. *The impact of freight car design and serviceability on freight car utilization* / Chicago : Association of American Railroads, Freight Car Utilization Research Demonstration Program, 1980. 1 v. (various pagings). (*AAR-R-438.*)

6275. *Implementing high-speed rail in Wisconsin: peer exchange, June 2-4, 2009.* Madison, WI: Wisconsin Department of Transportation Investment Management, 2009. 30 p.

6276. *The improved Howe railroad track scales : iron frame, with protected steel bearings (patented), improvements and advantages : an illustrated comparison of the mechanism of scales.* Chicago : Published and presented by A.M. Gilbert & Co., 1876. 16 p.

6277. *Improved passenger equipment evaluation program: train system review report/* Washington, DC: Federal Railroad Administration, Office of research and Development,

6278. *Improved passenger train service: proceedings of the Carnegie-Mellon Conference on Improved Passenger Train Service, December 2-4, 1975.* Edited by Marie T. Hlasnick. Pittsburgh, PA : Transportation Research Institute, Carnegie-Mellon University, 1976. 358 p.

6279. *Improving the service life of cross ties.* Chicago : Association of American Railroads, National Lumber Manufacturers Association, 1948-1952. 4 v. Monographic series.

6280. *In pursuit of speed: new options for intercity passenger transport.* Washington, DC: Transportation Research Board, National Research Council, 1991. 179 p. (*Special report, 233*)

6281. *Inception and creation of the Grand Central Terminal.* New York, Privately printed for Allen H. Stem and Alfred Fellheimer, successors to Read & Stern, architects. New York, Robert L. Stillson Company, [1913?]

6282. *Index-digest-analysis of decision under part I of the Interstate Commerce Act.* Mayo, MD: Hawkins Pub. Co., 1928- 10 v. (loose-leaf)

6283. *Index of papers and subjects discussed by railway clubs.* New York : 1902?-1915? Serial.

6284. *Index of proceedings of the Master Car-Builders' Association : from Volume 1 to volume 34, inclusive* / Chicago : H.O. Shepard Company, 1902. 243 p. Compiled by George L. Fowler.

6285. *Index of stations and tunnels on the Chesapeake and Ohio Railway* / Clifton Forge, VA : Chesapeake & Ohio Historical Society, 2010, 1969. 1 v. (various pagings)

6286. *Index to engineering periodicals, 1883 to 1887 inclusive: comprising engineering, railroads, science, manufactures and trade.* Boston, Mass., Engineering News Publishing Company, 1888. 294 p.

6287. *Index to photographs of the Southern Pacific Transportation Company, and related lines at the Kalmbach Memorial Library.* Chattanooga, TN: The Library, National Model Railroad Association, 1989. 17 p.

6288. *Index to signal literature.* Bethlehem, Pa., Times Publishing Company, 1911. 185 p.

6289. *Indexed county and railroad pocket map and shipper's guide of Pennsylvania* / Chicago and New York : Rand McNally and Company, 1907. 126 p.

6290. *Indexes of average freight rates on railroad carload traffic* / Washington, DC: Interstate Commerce Commission, Bureau of Transport Economics and Statistics, 1950-.

Annual.

6291. *Indexes of railroad material prices and wage rates. Railroads of Class 1.* Washington, DC: Association of American Railroads, Bureau of Railway Economics, 1900s-1967. Quarterly. (> *Indexes of railroad material prices and wage rates.*)

6292. *Indexes of railroad material prices and wage rates. Railroads of Class 1.* Washington, DC: Association of American Railroads, Economics and Finance Department, 1968-1981. (< *Indexes of railroad material prices and wage rates;* > *AAR railroad cost recovery index.*)

6293. Indiana Harbor Belt Railroad Company. *Dimensions and classification of locomotives of the Indiana Harbor Belt Railroad Co. Book no. 55.* 1924. 36 l. (Technical drawings and specifications on blueprint)

6293a. *Indiana Railway Museum: a visitor's guide & historical publication.* French Lick:: Indiana Railway Museum, 2011. 50 p.

6294. Indianapolis Switch and Frog Company. *The Indianapolis Switch and Frog Co., Springfield, Ohio.* [Catalogue.} Springfield, OH: Indianapolis Switch and Frog Co., 1910. 84 p.

6295. Industrial Works, Bay City, Michigan. *Cranes & special railway appliances /* Bay City, Mich., Industrial Works, 1900-1909? 107 p.

6296. _____. *Cranes : rail, traction and crawling locomotive cranes, wrecking cranes, wharf, barge, and gantry cranes, transfer and pillar cranes, railway pile drivers, combination carne pile drivers, portable rail saws, transfer tables, steam pile hammers, grab buckets.* Bay City, MI: Industrial Works, 1923. 161 p. (Fiftieth anniversary edition. Book 115.)

6297. _____. *Fiftieth anniversary of the Industrial Works, 1873-1923.* 1923. 24 p.

6298. (blank entry)

6299. _____. *Industrial Works: manufacturers of steam railway wrecking and locomotive cranes for all purposes and pile drivers.* Bay City, Mich., Industrial Works, 1899. 14 p.

6300. *An industry perspective on Maglev.* Washington, DC: Federal Railroad Administration, Office of Research and Development, 1990. 17 p. (*DOT/FRA/ORD-90/07*)

6301. Industry Task Force of Reliability Studies; Massachusetts Institute of Technology. *Railroad reliability and freight car utilization: an introduction.* Cambridge, Massachusetts Institute of Technology, Center for Transportation Studies, 1975. 58 p.

(*Massachusetts Institute of Technology; Center for Transportation Studies, CTS report, no. 75-8.) Prepared for the Freight Car Utilization Research-Demonstration Program, Association of American Railroads.*

6302. *The influence of coal transportation cost on the optimal distribution of coal and the optimal location of electric power generation plants* / Washington, DC: U.S. Department of Transportation, Office of University Research; West Virginia University, Regional Research Institute, 1979. 79 p. (*DOT/RSPA/DPB-50/79/36.*)

6303. *Influence of materials on crash-worthiness of rail car bodies* / Washington, DC: Federal Railroad Administration, 1978. 17, 3 p. Prepared by Louis T. Klauder and Associates.

6304. *Info*. Omaha, NE: Union Pacific Railroad Co., 1900s-1983. Monthly. Other title: Union Pacific info.

6305. *InfoMagazine*. Omaha, NE: Union Pacific System, 1984-   . Monthly. (< *Infonews.)*

6306. *Infonews: the magazine of the Union Pacific System*. Omaha, NE: Union Pacific Railroad Co., Missouri Pacific Railroad Co., 1983-1984.2 v. (> Union Pacific System. *InfoMagazine.*)

6307. *Information for employes and the public*. Philadelphia : Pennsylvania Railroad System, 1913-1920. Irregular. (> *Pennsylvania railroad information.*)

6308. *Information for the public and employes* / Philadelphia : Pennsylvania Railroad Co., 1922-1925. (< *Pennsylvania Railroad information* (1925); > *Pennsylvania Railroad information for the public and employes.*)

6309. *Ingalls diesel-electric locomotives.* Pascagoula, Miss., Ingalls Shipbuilding Corporation, 1900s-? 8 p.

6310. Ingels, Margaret. *Willis Haviland Carrier, father of air conditioning*. Garden City, NY: Country Life Press, 1952. 170 p. Chronological table: p. 107-156. Bibliography, p. 157-170.

6310a. Ingles, Dave, Denny E. Hamilton, Bill Metzger. *Cincinnati railroad heritage* / La Mirada, CA: Four-Ways West, 2012. 144 p.

6311. Ingraffea, A.R. *Technical summary and database for guidelines for pipelines crossing railroads and highways*. Chicago : Gas Research Institute, 1991. 517 p. (*GRI-91/0285.)*

6312. Ingersoll-Rand Company. *Diesel electric locomotives in the United States*. New York, Ingersoll-Rand, 1936. 39 l.

6313. _____. *Ingersoll-Rand diesel electric locomotives and rail cars*. New York,

Ingersoll-Rand, 1935. 1 v.

6314. Ingles, J. David. *Guide to North American railroad hot spots*. Waukesha, WI: Kalmbach Books, 2001. 208 p.

6315. *Injured railroad workers: know your rights; a brief outline of railroad workers' rights under the Federal Employees' Liability Act: how to protect them*. New York? Brotherhood of Locomotive Engineers; New York Legislative Board; Brotherhood of Locomotive Firemen and Enginemen; Order of Railway Conductors and Brakemen, 1964. 12 p.

6316. *Inland Empire rail quarterly*. Spokane, WA: Inland Empire Railway Historical Society, 197-

6317. *Innovation in classification yard technology : proceedings of the third railroad classification yard workshop*. Washington, DC: Transportation Research Board, 1983. 67 p. (*Transportation research record, 927.*)

6318. Institute of Public Administration. *Suburbs to Grand Central: a study of the feasibility of reorganizing the suburban services of the New York Central and New Haven Railroads under a public agency*. New York, The Institute, 1963. 1 v.

6319. *Instructions respecting the handling of oil burning locomotives*. San Francisco, Printed by Pacific Coast Merchant, 1917. 24 p.

6320. *Intelligent transportation systems and their implication for railroads: proceedings of a joint FRA-ITS America Technical Symposium, Washington, D.C., June 4 and 5, 1997*. Washington, DC: U.S. Department of Transportation, 1997. 1 v. (Various pagings)

6321. Interborough Rapid Transit: *the New York subway; its construction and equipment*. New York, Arno Press, 1969, 1904. 150 p; New York, Fordham University Press, 1991, 1904. 150 p.)

6322. *Interchange*. Washington, DC: Brotherhood of Railway, Airline, and Steamship Clerks, Freight Handlers, Express Employees, 1985-2005. Bimonthly. (< *Railway clerk interchange*.)

6323. *Intercity passenger rail*. Washington, DC: American Association of State Highway and Transportation officials, 2009. 24 p. *http://downloads.transportation.org/IPRT-2.pdf*

6324. *Intercity passenger rail; freight rail; and track design and maintenance*. Washington, D.C.: National Academy Press, 2001. 96 p. (*Transportation research record. Rail, no. 1742.*)

6325. *International convention on high-speed rail: proceedings*. Washington, DC: High-Speed Rail Association, 1987-   . Annual.

6326. *International heavy haul railway conference*. Virginia Beach, VA: International

Heavy Haul Association, 1991. 295 p.

6327. International Motor Company; Mack Trucks, Incorporated. *Mack catalog no. R91.* New York, The Company, 1928. 105 p.

6328. _____. *Mack rail cars.* New York, The Company, 1928. 15 p. (Reprint: Milwaukee, WI: Old Line Publishers, 1971. 15 p.)

6329. International Nickel Company. *The modern material for modern railroads: nickel stainless steel.* New York, International Nickel Company, 1967. 11 p.

6330. _____ *Nickel alloys in railroad equipment.* New York, International Nickel Company, 1947. 32 p.

6331. _____. *Nickel containing materials in the railroad industry.* New York, International Nickel Company, 1963. 31 p.

6332. International Railway Fuel Association. *Proceedings of the ... annual convention of the International Railway Fuel Association.* Chicago, Ill., The Association, 1909-1930. Annual.

6333. Interrante, C. G. *Impact properties of steels taken from four failed tank cars /* Washington, DC: Federal Railroad Administration, 1976. 150 p. (*FRA-ORD & D-75-51.*)

6334. *Interstate Commerce Commission reports. Decisions of the Interstate Commerce Commission of the United States. Valuation reports.* Washington, DC: U.S. G.P.O., 1929-1964. Irregular. 36 v. Title varies.

6335. *Interstate Commerce Commission reports: reports and decision of the Interstate Commerce Commission of the United States.* New York, N.Y., L.K. Strouse, 1888-1995. 377 v.

6336 *An introduction to railroads in east Tennessee and western North Carolina. 1975 N.R.H.S. Convention, Knoxville, Tennessee, Old Smoky Chapter.* Knoxville, TN: 1975. 54 p.

6337. *An introduction to the uniform rail costing system,; its development, functions and regulatory role.* Washington, DC: Interstate Commerce Commission, 1981? 59 p.

6338. *Inventory of railroad structures in Iowa as represented in the photograph collection of the State Historical Society of Iowa,* Compiled by James Beranek. Iowa City. Iowa City, The Society, 1990. 1 v.

6339. *An inventory of the photographs of the Denver & Rio Grande Railroad, the Denver & Rio Grande Western Railroad: a holding of the Library of the Colorado Historical Society.* Denver, CO: Colorado Historical Society, 1996. 65 p.

6340. Iowa. Department of Transportation. Planning and Research Division.

The economic feasibility of rail diesel car passenger service in Iowa: a study for Governor Robert D. Ray. Ames, IA: Iowa Department of Transportation, 1977. 18 p.

6341. Iowa Engineering Experiment Station. *Locomotive tests with Iowa and Illinois coals.* Ames, Ia., Iowa State College of Agriculture and Mechanic Arts, 1917. 40 p. *(Engineering Experiment Station, bulletin no. 44.)*

6342. Iowa. Executive Council. *Statistical abstracts of Iowa railroads (supplement to railroad assessment report) Comp. by A.H. Davison, secretary of the Executive Council and A.U. Swan, assistant secretary. From data complied form reports made to the Executive Council and Railroad Commission, and other state reports.* Des Moines, E.H. English, State Printer, 1907. 63 p.

6343. Iowa. Rail and Water Division. *Review of capital expenses for equipment, facilities & stations and annual operating expenses & revenues in Amtrak's Chicago to Omaha 403 (B) route study/* Ames, IA: The Division, 1992. 19 p.

6344. Iowa. Railroad Commissioners. *Schedule of reasonable maximum rates for the transportation of freight and cars on each of the railroads in the state of Iowa. Together with a classification of freights, prepared by the Railroad Commissioners, in accordance with section 17, of chapter 28, of the acts of the twenty-second General Assembly.* Des Moines : G.H. Ragsdale, State printer, 1890. 43 p.

6345. Iowa. Wilbur Smith and Associates. *1995 Iowa rail plan.* Ames, IA: Iowa Department of Transportation, 1995. 1 v.

6345a. Irion, Thomas H. *An historical geography of the Sacramento Northern Railway/* 1997. 171 l. (Thesis, M.A., California State University, Hayward.)

6346. *The iron horse in art: the railroad as it has been interpreted by artists of the nineteenth and twentieth centuries.* Foreword by Lucius Beebe. Drawings by Nancy Romine Gillis. Forth Worth, TX: Fort Worth Art Association, 1958. 44 p. (Shown at the Fort Worth Art Center January 6-March 2, 1958.)

6347. *Iron icon: the railroad in American art, April 22-23, 2004: proceedings of a conference at the John W. Barriger III National Library.* St. Louis, MO: John W. Barriger III National Railroad Library, 2005. 72 p. ("Funded by a grant from the Burlington Northern Santa Fe Foundation." *Railroad heritage, no. 14, 2005.*)

6348. *Iron Mountain railroad shops in Carondelet, Missouri.* St. Louis : Carondelet Historical Society, 2011. 11 p.

6349. *Iron ore industry and mines on the C&NW.* Deerfield, IL: Archives Committee of the Chicago & North Western Historical Society, 1999. 66 l.

6350. Irvine, Thomas Richard. *The effect of uncertainty on the profitability of empty railroad car distribution decisions.* 1984. 42 l. (Thesis, M. Eng., Virginia Polytechnic Institute and State University.)

6351. Irwin, Leonard Bertram. *Pacific railways and nationalism in the Canadian-American Northwest, 1845-1873.* New York, Greenwood Press, 1968. c1939. 246 p.

6352. Isham, Edward Swift. *Pullman's Palace Car Company, appellant, vs. The Missouri Pacific Railway Company and the St. Louis, Iron Mountain and Southern Railway Company, appellees. Appeal from the eastern District of Missouri. Argument of Edward S. Isham, counsel for appellant.* Chicago : Barnard & Gunthorp, 1885. 42 p. "In the Supreme Court of the United States, October term, A.D. 1884."

6353. Israelowitz, Oscar, Brian Merlis. *Subways of New York in vintage photographs.* Brooklyn, NY: Israelowitz Publishing,2004. 246 p.

6353a.*Issues in railway law: limiting carrier liability and litigating the railroad crossing case.* Chicago : Tort and Insurance Practice Section, American Bar Association, 1990. 251 p.

6354. ITT Rayonier. *End of an era.* San Francisco, Rayonier, 1959. 1 v. (Locomotives)

6355. Itzkoff, Donald Martin. *Off the track: the decline of the intercity passenger train in the United States.* Westport, CT: Greenwood Press, 1985. 161 p. 12 p. of plates. (*Contributions in economics and economic history, no. 62.*)

6356. _____. *Where have all the trains gone? The decline of the long-distance passenger railroad in the United States.* 1983. 180 l. (Thesis, Department of History, Honors, Brown University)

6357. Ivaldi, Marc, Gerard John McCullough. *Welfare trade-offs in US rail mergers.* London: Centre for Economic Policy Research, 2005. 29 p. (*Discussion paper, no. 5000.*)

6358. Ivey, Paul Wesley. *The Pere Marquette Railroad Company: an historical study of the growth and development of one of Michigan's most important railway systems.* Lansing, MI: Michigan Historical Commission, 1919. 259 p. (Thesis, Ph.D., University of Michigan, 1917.)

6359. Ivory, Karen. *Eight great American rail journeys.* Guilford, CT: Globe Pequot Press, 2000. 90 p.

6360. Iwnicki, Simon . *Handbook of railway vehicle dynamics.* Boca Raton: CRC/Taylor & Francis, 2006. 535 p.

J

6361. J. G. Brill Company. *The car-building industry in Philadelphia.* Philadelphia, J. G. Brill Co., 1925. 12 p.

6362. J. G. White Engineering Corporation. *Report on the Long Island Railroad.* New York: J.G. White Engineering Corp., 1942. 4 v.

6363. Jackman, William T. *Economics of transportation.* Chicago: A.W. Shaw, 1926. 818 p.

6364. Jackson & Moreland. *Memorandum on manufacturers' proposals and engineering estimates in connection with the proposed Scranton grade electrification of the Delaware, Lackawanna and Western Railroad.* Boston, Jackson & Moreland, 1923? 1 v.

6365. *The Jackson and Sharp Co.; Delaware Car Works.* Wilmington, Delaware, The Jackson and Sharp Co., 1894. 84 p.

6366. Jackson and Sharp Company. [Job files, 1898-1905]. 2.6 linear ft. Location: Hagley Museum and Library.

6367. Jackson and Sharp Company. [Order books and photographs] Location: Smithsonian Archives Center, National Museum of American History, Washington, D.C.

6368. *Jackson and Sharp photograph collection checklist* [glass plate negatives] Dover, State of Delaware, Division of Historical and Cultural Affairs, Hall of Records, 1978. 9 microfiches. (Record group 9015; document number: 20-06-78-02-09.)

6369. Jackson, Dugald C. *Methods of electric lighting for railway trains.* Chicago, Ill., Western Society of Engineers, 1907. 40 p.

6370. Jackson, Jill Carlson. *Along came a spider: visions and realities of railroad development in Fort Worth, Texas, 1873-1923; a cartographic approach.* 1996. 187 l. (Thesis, M.A., University of Texas at Arlington.)

6370a. Jackson, Louise A., Carl Switzer. *The Visalia Electric Railroad: stories of the early years* / Visalia, CA: Tulare County Historical Society, 2012. 79 p.

6371. Jackson, R.C. *A sketch of the railway mail service from its initial to its present terminal station from the standpoint of the Second Division: comprising New York, New Jersey, Pennsylvania, Delaware, Eastern Shore of Maryland with pencilings by the way to the railway postal clerks of this division.* New York, Wynkoop & Hallenbeck, 1884. 48 p.

6371a. Jackson, Robert W. *Rails across the Mississippi : a history of the St. Louis bridge*

/ Urbana: University of Illinois Press, 2001. 265 p.

6371a. Jackson, Roy V., M. Fred Lyon. *Early steam engines and passenger equipment, 1900-1920s.* 2nd ed. / S.l., Katy Railroad Historical Society, 2009. 142 p.

6372. Jackson, William Henry. *William Henry Jackson's Rocky Mountain railroad album: steam and steel across the Great Divide.* Introductory remarks by Terry Wm. Mangan; photo-graphic captions by Russ Collman and Dell A. McCoy; edited by Jackson C. Thode. Silverton, CO: Sundance Publications, 1976. 6 p., 76 leaves of plates.

6373. Jackson, Willis F. *An advanced communication system for application to railroad security.* Aberdeen Proving Ground, MD: U.S. Army Ballistic Research Laboratory, 1983. 126 p. (*Report: ARBRL-MR-03267.*)

6373a. Jacobs, Charles M., Lawrence Portnoy. *The Hudson River tunnels of the Hudson and Manhattan Railroad Company.* London: Institution of Civil Engineers, 1910. 92 p.

6374. Jacobs, H.W. *Betterment briefs: a collection of published papers on organized industrial efficiency.* New York, NY: John Wiley, 1909. 270 p. (Improving efficiency in railroad shops; commercial tool methods in railroad shops; high-speed steel in railroad shops, etc.)

6375. Jacobs, Nathan L. *The Interstate Commerce Commission and interstate railroad organizations.* 1931. 50 l. (Thesis, Harvard Law School.)

6376. Jacobs, William W. *The railroad hero in the United States*/ 1975. 116 l. (Honors paper, Macalester College, Department of History.)

6377. Jacobs-Shupert United States Firebox Company. *The Jacobs-Shupert sectional firebox* / New York, Redfield Brothers, 1911. 101 p.

6378. _____. *Some recent Jacobs-Shupert fireboxes.* New York, Publishers Printing Company, 1911. 3 p.

6379. Jacobs, Timothy. *The history of the Baltimore & Ohio: America's first railroad.* New York, Crescent Books, 1989. 128 p. (Also: New York, Smithmark Publishers, 1994. 128 p.)

6380. _____. *The history of the Pennsylvania Railroad.* Greenwich, CT: Bonanza, 1988. 128 p. (Also: New York, Smithmark Publishers, 1995. 128 p.)

6381. Jacobson, Albert Herman. *Railroad consolidations and transportation policy*/ 1976. (Thesis, Ph.D., Graduate Division Special Programs, Management Engineering, Stanford University.

6382. Jaenicke, Paul W., Ralph A. Eisenbrandt. *Elgin, Joilet, and Eastern Railway.* Charleston, SC: Arcadia, 2007. 127 p.

6383. Jahn, Richard W., John D.L. Johnson. *Western Maryland diesels.* Ambler, PA: Crusader Press, 1979. 114 p.

6384. Jain, Ranjit Singh. *Design of high speed direct current railway generator* / 1915. 4, 14 l. (Thesis, B.S., University of Illinois.)

6385. Jakubauskas, Edward B. *The impact of technological change on railroad employment: 1947-1958.* 1961. 232 l. (Thesis, Ph.D., University of Wisconsin.)

6386. James, David C. *Grisdale, last of the logging camps: a photo story of Simpson camps from 1890 into 1986: centennial supplement, an album of big logs and old locomotives.* Fairfield, WA: Ye Galleon Press, 1988. 1 v. (Camp Grisdale, Mason County, Wash.)

6387. *The James Jerome Hill papers.* Project director, W. Thomas White. Frederick, MD: University Publications of America, 1984-1985. 54 microfilm reels

6388. James, Robert L. *Major legislative transportation issues facing the Northeast : assessment of the Northeast rail corridor as an economic development spine, and introduction to railroad and trucking deregulations issues* / Washington: CONEG Policy Research Center, 1979, 1980. 50 p. (Research report series; CONEG Policy Research Center, no. 4.) CONEG : Coalition of Northeastern Governors.

6389. James, Thomas Lemuel. *The railway mail service.* New York? s.n., 1888. 40 p.

6390. Jamieson, Sandy. *President Harding railroad car restoration. Phase 1. The Denali* / Anchorage, AK: Samuel, Duff, Combs, 1985. 1 v. (various pagings) Prepared for the City of Fairbanks; architect, Samuel, Duff, Combs, AIA.

6391. Janeway, R.N. *Analytical study of railroad car equipment; a staff memorandum.* Washington, D.C., National Resources Planning Board, 1940. 67 p., 19 l., 16 leaves of plates. (*National Resources Planning Board reports and records, 1934-1943; NRPB 181.*)

6392. Jankovich, John P. *Human factors survey of locomotive cabs.* Washington, D.C., Federal Railroad Administration, U.S. Department of Transportation, 1972. 225 p. (*FRA-OPP-73-1.*)

6393. Janney, Eli H. *Improvement in car-couplings: specification forming parts of Letters Patent No. 138,405 dated April 29, 1873, application filed April 1, 1873.* S.l., s.n., 2 p. 1 leaf of plates. cm. At head of title: United States Patent Office.

6394. Jansen, Arthur. *Diesel locomotive ownership compared with total locomotive ownership, Class I railroads (as of June 30, 1948).* New York, s.n., 1948. 59 l.

6395. Janson, Richard H. *The railroad passenger train : architecture, machinery and motion, 1830 to 1950* / 1958. 278 l. (Thesis, Yale University.)

6396. Janus, James Anthony. *The Santa Fe's Super Chief: the transcontinental train deluxe as an aesthetic object.* 1978. 171 l. (Thesis, M.A., George Washington University.)

6397. Japiot, Marcel. *Les chemins de fer américains: material et traction.* Paris, H. Dunod et E. Pinat, 1907. 406 p. (Extrait de *Annales des Mines, 2e semester 1906 et 1er semester 1907.*)

6398. Jaros, Tom, Rick W. Mills. *All aboard the 1880 train between Hill City & Keystone, South Dakota: a guide to the history, equipment & operations of the Black Hills Central Railroad.* Hill City, SD: Black Hills Central Railroad, 2002. 31 p.

6398a. Jarrett, Donald Steven. *St. Louis Station: contributor to the physical, cultural and economic development of St. Louis, Missouri* / 1988. 179 l. (Thesis, M.A., San Francisco State University.)

6399. Jasper, Margaret C. *Transportation law: passenger rights and responsibilities* New York, NY: Oceana, 2009. 140 p.

6399a. Jeffers, William Thomas. *"A mill to the mile": James B. Duke, Charles Christian Hook, and the impact of the Piedmont and Northern Railroad on industrial development in the Piedmont region of North and South Carolina* / 2011. 90 l. (Thesis, M.A., University of North Carolina at Charlotte, Department of History.)

6400. Jefferys, Grady, John F. Gilbert. *Crossties over Saluda: a portrait of Southern Railway power on the Nation's steepest, standard gauge, main line railway grade, with a 2000 update of post-merger NS motive power.* Rev. ed. Raleigh, NC: J.F. Gilbert; Gilbert Design/Crossties Press Books, 2001. 36 l.

6401. _____, _____. *Crossties through Carolina: the story of North Carolina's early day railroads.* Raleigh, NC: Crossties Press, 1982. 88 p.

6402. Jeffrey, Jonathan, Michael Dowell. *L & N: bittersweet: the Louisville & Nashville Railroad and Warren County, Kentucky.* Bowling Green, KY: Landmark Association, 2001. 58 p.

6403. Jeffrey Manufacturing Company. *Jeffrey electric locomotives.* Columbus, Ohio, The Company, 1901. 1 v (*Catalog no. 18.*)

6404. _____. *Jeffrey electric locomotives for industrial haulage.* Columbus, OH: Jeffrey Manufacturing Company, 1908. 32 p. (*Bulletin no. 13.*)

6405. Jeffries, Lewis I. *N & W.: giant of steam.* Boulder, CO: Pruett Publishing Company, 1980. 333 p. (Rev. ed.: Roanoke, VA: Norfolk and Western Historical Society, 2005. 350 p.)

6406. Jehrio, Peter. *Niagara by rail—I.-III.* Boalsburg, PA: Coldwaters Press, 1991-1993.

3 v.

6407. Jehrio, Peter, Terry Sprague. *Baltimore & Ohio steam locomotives: the last 30 years, 1928-1958.* Lynchburg, VA: TLC, 2003. 128 p.

6408. Jenkins, Arthur C. *Compilation of statistical data relating to decline in railroad passenger traffic and upward trend in passenger volume on competitive modes of travel.* San Francisco, CA: Jenkins, 1957. 39 l. (*Report no. 13-571.* Application no. 38982 before the California Public Utilities Commission.)

6409. Jenkins, Brian Michael, Bruce R. Butterworth. *Selective screening of passengers.* San Jose, CA: Mineta Transportation Institute, College of Business, San Jose State University, 2007. 76 p (Internetresource:http://transweb.sjsu.edu/mtiportal/reseaarch/publications/documents/06-07/pdf/MTI-06-07.pdf)

6410. Jenkins, Dale. *The Illinois Terminal Railroad: the road of personalized services.* Hart, MO: Whiteriver Productions, 2005. 328 p.

6411. _____, Mark Barnett James Reese. *Illinois Terminal Railroad spotter's guide.* S.l., Bruggenjohann/Reese, Inc., Illinois Traction Society, 2001-

6412. Jenks, Robert Darrah. *A study of the development of the Pennsylvania Railroad System from its incorporation to 1882 : prepared under the direction of professor F.W. Taussig as part of Economics 20.* Cambridge, Mass : s.n., 1897. 1 v. Harvard students' essays.

6413. Jenks, S.H. *Switches, frogs and crossings/* 1888. 70 l, 11 l. of plates (Thesis, C.E., Lehigh University.)

6414. Jennings, C. W. *The effect of weld length on the surface stress in a railroad tank car bolster area.* 1979. 96 l. (Thesis, M.S. in Mechanical Engineering, Louisiana Tech University.)

6415. Jennings, Dorothy. *Railroad development in Missouri before the Civil War.* 1930. 117 l. (Thesis, A.M., Department of History, Washington University.)

6416. Jenness, James W. *Human factors guidance for intelligent transportation systems at the highway-rail intersection.* Washington, DC: Federal Railroad Administration, Office of Research and Development, 2006. 192 p. (DOT/FRA/ORD-06/26.)

6417. Jennings, L. Stephen. *Compilation of state laws and regulations affecting highway-rail grade crossings/* 3rd ed. Washington, DC: Federal Railroad Administration, 2000. 1 v (Various pagings)

6418. Jennings, Larry, Henry E. Bender, Bill Farmer. *Remaining California railroad depots.* Crete, NE: Railroad Station Historical Society, 1989. 25 p. (*Railroad station monograph, no. 17.*)

6419. Jennison, Brian, Victor Neves. *Southern Pacific Oregon Division* / Mukilteo, WA: Hundman Pub., 1997. 128 p.

6419a. Jenny, L. Alfred. *Report on the plan for bringing the New Jersey railroads into a union passenger terminal in New York* / Trenton, NJ: State of New Jersey, Department of Economic Development, 1946. 22, 33, 4 p.

6420. Jensen, Derrick, George Draffan, John Osborn. *Railroads and clearcuts: legacy of Congress's 1864 Northern Pacific Railroad land grant.* Spokane, WA: Inland Empire Public Lands Council; Sandpoint, ID: Distributed by Keokee Co. Pub., 1995. 198 p.

6420a. Jensen, H.P. *Design for a curved chord single track R.R. bridge, span 200 ft.* / 1899. 34 l. (Thesis, B.S., Massachusetts Institute of Technology, Department of Civil Engineering.)

6421. Jensen, Jens. *Report to the Women's League for the protection of Riverside Park on the proposed plan for changes in the New York Ventral Railroad along the Hudson, November 29, 1916* / New York? 1916. 10 p.

6422. Jensen, Kathleen Rachel. *Trains in America: machine and metaphor.* 1993. 17 l. (Thesis, M.A., California State University, Dominquez Hills.)

6423. Jensen, Larry. *The movie railroads.* Burbank, CA: Darwin Publications, 1981. 257 p.

6424. Jensen, Oliver Ormerod. *The American Heritage history of railroads in America.* New York, American Heritage Pub. Co., 1981, c1975. 320 p.

6425. Jensen, William H., Gary Kohler, Darryl Sleszynski. *Two-foot cyclopedia* / Washingtonville, OH: M2FQ Publications, 1999- (Originally published: Coon Valley, WI: Flag Stop, 1977.)

6426. Jeong, David Y, Gopal Samavedam, Andrew Kish. *Determination of track lateral resistance from lateral pull tests/* Washington, DC: Federal Railroad Administration, Office of Research and Development, 1986. 40 p. (*DOT/FRA/ORD-85/06*)

6427. _____, Y H Tang, A Benjamin Perlman. *Evaluation of semi-empirical analyses for railroad tank car puncture velocity* / Washington, DC : Federal Railroad Administration, Office of Research and Development, 2001. 2 v. Pt. 1 – Correlations with experimental data. Pt. 2 – Correlations with engineering analyses. (DOT/FRA/ORD-01/21.I; DOT/FRA/ORD-01/21.II

6428. Jeppson, Lew E. *Decision to federalize: conditions that led to federal operation of United States railways commencing in 1917.* 1992. 90 l. (Thesis, M.S., Department of Economics, University of Utah.)

6429. Jepsen, Thomas C., Mattie C. Kuhn. *Ma Kiley: the life of a railroad telegrapher/*

El Paso, TX: Texas Western Press, 1997. 138 p. (*Southwestern studies, no. 104.*)

6430. Jervey, Theodore D. *The railroad, the conqueror.* Columbia, SC: State Co., 1913. 44 p.

6430a. Jervis, Paul. *Details of railroad truss-bridges* / 1910. 35 l. (Thesis, B.S., University of Illinois.)

6431. Jessen, Kenneth Christian. *Railroads of northern Colorado.* Boulder, CO: Pruett Pub. Co., 1982. 287 p.

6432. _____. *The Wyoming/Colorado Railroad.* Loveland, CO: The Author, 1982. 40 p. (Laramie, Hahn's Peak, and Pacific Railway Company.)

6433. _____, Hendrik Vandenberg. *Built to haul sugar beets: the Great Western Railway Co.* Loveland, CO: JV Publications, 1984. 23 p.

6434. Jester, W. Albert. *Analytic and experimental investigation of a 1/5 scale rail vehicle simulator.* 1989. 100 l. (Thesis, M.S., Virginia Polytechnic Institute and State University.)

6435. Jeter, W. D. *The Fort Worth and Denver South Plains Railway* / 1949. 119 l. (Thesis, M.A. Texas Technological College.)

6436. Jewell, B, M. *Memorandum on real wages of railroad employees : an analysis of monthly expense accounts* / Chicago: Research Bureau, Railway Employees' Department, American Federation of Labor, 1921. 45 l.

6437. _____, George M. Cucich. *Historical development of the railroad wage structure.* Chicago: Railway Employees' Department, American Federation of Labor, 1941. 85 p.

6438. Jewell, Donald V. *Southern Pacific motive power annual.* Burlingame, CA: Chatham Pub. Co., 1967-

6438a. Jewell, Hubert H., Jr. *Working on the Richmond, Fredericksburg & Potomac Railroad : the memories of Hubert H. Jewell, Jr.* Fredericksburg, VA: Richmond, Fredericksburg & Potomac Railroad Historical Society, 2010. 126 p.

6439. Jewett, Harrison L. *Comparison of electric locomotive control systems.* 1933. 45, 23 l. (Thesis, B.S., Massachusetts Institute of Technology, Department of Electrical Engineering.)

6440. John Fritz Medal. Board of Award. *John Fritz medal: biographies of Guglielmo Marconi, medalist for 1923, Ambrose Swasey, medalist for 1924, John F. Stevens, medalist for 1925, Edward Dean Adams, medalist of 1926.* New York, NY: Printed by the Devinne-Hallenbeck Compnay, 1926. 23 p.

6441. _____. *Presentation of the John Fritz gold medal to John Frank Stevens.* New York, NY: Engineering Societies Building, 1926. 61 p.

6442. John Gall & Company (Philadelphia). *Stone arch bridge, no. 78, Coatesville, Pa. : built for the Pennsylvania Railroad Co.* Philadelphia : s.n., 1904. 11 l. plates.

6443. John Nuveen & Company (Chicago, Ill.) *Tollroads, rail-roads and piggyback operations.* Chicago, John Nuveen & Co., 1954. 10 l.

6444. John W. Masury (Firm). *Samples of ready-made "rail road" colors : for painting houses, barns, fences, out-buildings, rail road cars, rail road depots, bridges &c. which will be found economical, reliable and durable /* New York : John W. Masury, 1880. 1 sheet : col. samples : 15 x 19 cm. Includes 20 color samples.

6445. Johns-Manville, Incorporated. *J-M asbestos, magnesia and electrical railroad supplies.* New York, The Company, 1911. 342 p.

6446. _____. *Johns-Manville service to railroads; asbestos roofings, packings and insulations; steam and electrical railroad supplies.* New York, Akron, 1923. 264 p.

6447. Johns, Michael R. *Remembering southwest Iowa's Peavine: a rail line with beginnings as a narrow gauge, then converted to standard gauge; affiliations with the Santa Fe and the Burlington systems: a history covering the years 1871-1981 /* Chillicothe, MO: Milepost 208 Publications, 2009. 100 p.

6448. Johns, Michael R., Ralph L. Cooper. *Quincy Route: a history of the Quincy, Omaha, and Kansas City Railroad & the Iowa and St. Louis Railway/* Chillicothe, MO: Milepost 208 Publications, 2008. 116 p.

6449. Johnsen, A.M. *Wrought-steel passenger-car wheels from a consumer's standpoint /* New York : American Society of mechanical Engineers, 1953. 5 p. (*ASME. Paper, 53-A-113.*)

6450. Johnsen, Kenneth G. *Daylight: 4449's family album.* Renton, WA: K.G. Johnsen, 1984. 112 p.

6451. _____. *Southern Pacific: 2472's family album.* Glendale, CA: Interurban Press, 1990. 134 p.

6452. _____. *Washington steam locomotives.* Burlingame, CA: Chatham Pub. Co., 1978. 79 p.

6453. Johnson, A.L. *Timber physics series: economical designing of timber trestle bridges.* Washington, DC: U.S. G.P.O., 1896-1902. 2 v. (*Forest Service Bulletin, no. 12.*)

6454. Johnson, Aldin William. *The Cumbres & Toltec Scenic Railroad.* Bozeman, MT: Montana State University, 1985. 141 p.

6455. Johnson, Arthur Menzies, Barry Supple. *Boston capitalists and Western railroads; a study in the nineteenth century railroad investment process.* Cambridge, MA: Harvard University Press, 1967. 392 p. (*Harvard studies in business history, 23.*)

6456. Johnson Automatic Refrigerator Company. *A description of the Johnson system of refrigerator cars and cold storage.* Chicago, Ill., Johnson Automatic Refrigerator Company, 1903. 38 p.

6457. Johnson, Carla J. *A history of the Union Pacific passenger stations in Omaha, Nebraska, 1854-1931.* 1997. 133 l. (Thesis, M.A., University of Nebraska, Omaha.)

6458. _____. *Union Pacific and Omaha Union Station.* David City, NE: South Platte Press, 2001. 84 p.

6459. Johnson, Clint. *From rails to roads: the history of Perley Thomas Car Works and Thomas Built Buses.* Raleigh, NC: Lifescapes Corporation, 1996. 114 p. (*A Lifescapes corporate biography.*)

6460. Johnson, David F. *The history and economics of Utah railroads.* 1947. 151 l. (Thesis, M.S., University of Utah.)

6461. Johnson, Dennis Myron. *An investigation into the Scranton railroad riots of 1877 /* 1969. 89 l. (Thesis, M.A., University of Scranton.)

6462. Johnson, Dudley Sady. *The railroads of Florida, 1865-1900.* 1965. 296 l. (Thesis, Ph.D., Florida State University.)

6463. Johnson, Edwin Ferry. *Railroad to the Pacific. Northern route. Its general character, relative merits, etc.* New York: Railroad Journal Job Printing Office, 1854. 5-166 i.e. 176 p.

6464. _____. *Trans-continental railways of the United States.* Hartford, CT: Lockwood & Brainard, 1871. 36 p.

6465. _____, Ira Spaulding, James Tilton. *Northern Pacific Railroad : report of Edwin F. Johnson, engineer-in-chief, to the Board of Directors, April, 1869, and reports of surveys /* Hartford, CT: Lockwood & Brainard, 1869. 77 p.

6466. Johnson, Emory Richard. *American railway transportation.* New York, D. Appleton and Company, 1903. 434 p. (Revised ed., 1904.)

6467. _____. *Elements of transportation: a discussion of steam railroad, electric railway, and ocean and inland water transportation.* New York and London, D. Appleton, 1909. 360 p.

6468. _____. *Government regulation of transportation.* New York and London : D. Appleton-Century Co., 1938. 680 p.

6469. _____. *Railroad traffic associations* / Chicago : La Salle Extension University, 1910. 1 v. "Technical lectures in the course in interstate commerce."

6470. _____. *The railroads and public welfare; their problems and policies* / New York: Simmons-Boardman Pub. Corp., 1944. 336 p.

6471. _____, Grover G. Huebner. *Railroad traffic and rates* / New York and London: D. Appleton and Co., 1911. 2 v.(970 p.) v. 1. The freight service.—v.2. Passenger, express, and mail service.

6472. _____, Thurman W. Van Metre. *Principles of railroad transportation.* New York, D. Appleton and Company, 1916. 619 p. (*Appleton's railway series*)

6473. Johnson, Enid. *Rails across the continent; the story of the first transcontinental railroad.* New York, J. Messner, 1965. 190 p.

6474. Johnson, F.H. *Brief record of the development of the Milwaukee Road: from the chartering of its first predecessor company in February 1847 to date, July, 1944.* Chicago, Ill., Public Relations Department, Milwaukee Road, 1944. 52 p.

6475. Johnson, Freddie Lee. *The tracks of war: Confederate strategic rail policy and the struggle for the Baltimore and Ohio* / 1999. 365 l. (Thesis, Ph.D., Kent State University.)

6475a. Johnson, Frederick Dawson. *Dynamometer car tests, 1902-03.* 1903. 50 l. (Thesis, B.S., University of Illinois.)

6476. Johnson, Harley A. *AB brake tests.* S.l., s.n., 1933. 1 v. Tests conducted by the Am. Railway Assoc. on the Sang Hollow Extension Branch of the Pennsylvania Railroad, and brake trials on the Chesapeake & Ohio Railway.

6477. Johnson, Harold D., R.W. Penney, Robert F. Guilfoy. *Rail car and 'piggyback' transportation of freshly killed beef* / Washington, DC: Marketing Research Division, Agricultural Marketing Service, U.S. Department of Agriculture, 1959. 32 p. (*Marketing research report, no. 339.*)

6478. _____, Robert F. Guilfoy, R.W. Penney. *Transportation of hanging beef by refrigerated rail cars and 'piggyback' trailers* / Washington, DC: Agricultural Marketing Service, U.S. Department of Agriculture, 1961. 23 p. (*Marketing research report, no. 485.*)

6477a. _____, William L. Arnold, C.E. Carner. *Refrigeration rules & regulations for government shipments of perishable products.* Washington? War Food Administration. office of Distribution, 1944. 92 p.

6479. Johnson, Harold L. *An economic analysis of "Piggyback" transportation.* Atlanta, University of Georgia, 1956. 11 p.

6480. _____. *Piggyback transportation; an economic analysis.* Atlanta, Division of Business Research, School of Business Administration, Georgia State College of Business Administration, 1956. 54 p. (*Studies in business and economics, no. 1.*)

6481. Johnson, Kaylene, Roy Corral. *Portrait of the Alaska Railroad.* Anchorage, Alaska Northwest Books, 2002. 94 p.

6482. Johnson, Larry E. *Breakdown from within: Virginia railroads during the Civil War era.* 2004. 169 l. (Thesis, M.A., University of Louisville.)

6483. Johnson, Lynn, Michael O'Leary. *All aboard! Images from the golden age of rail travel.* San Francisco, Chronicle Books, 1999. 131p. (Advertising/marketing)

6484. Johnson, M.R. *Temperatures, pressures and liquid levels of tank cars engulfed in fires* /Washington, DC: Federal Railroad Administration, Office of Research and Development, 1984.

6485. _____, E. A. Phillips. *Study of railroad tank car thickness minimums* / Chicago: Association of American Railroads, Technical Center, 1989. 46 l. (*Report, no. R-726.*)

6486. Johnson, Marc A. *Community evaluation of railroad branch lines: principles and procedures.* East Lansing, MI: Michigan State University Center for Rural Manpower and Public Affairs, 1975. 111 p. (*Report no. 38.*)

6486a. _____. *Market and social investment and disinvestment in railroad branch lines: evaluation procedures and decision criteria* / 1975. 276 l. (Thesis, Ph.D., Michigan State University, Department of Agricultural Economics.)

6487. _____. *Oklahoma railroads and freight service.* Stillwater, Agricultural Experiment Station, Oklahoma State University, 1977. 74 p. (*Research report: Agricultural Experiment Station, Oklahoma State University, P-757*)

6488. _____, Elton Li, Gordon Empting. *The Oklahoma Railroad Analysis and Information Library System (ORAILS).* Stillwater, Agricultural Experiment Station, Oklahoma State University, 1978. 98 p. (*Research report, P-779.*)

6489. Johnson, Marion M. *Preliminary inventory of the records of the Commissioner of Railroads: record group 193.* Washington, D.C.: National Archives, National Archives and Records Service, General Services Administration, 1964. 18 p.

6490. _____. *Preliminary inventory of the records of the Presidential Railroad Commission: record group 220.* Washington, DC: General Services Administration, National Archives and Records Service, National Archives, 1965. 4 p.

6491. Johnson, Milton R. *Analysis of railroad car truck and wheel fatigue* / Chicago : IIT Research Institute, 1973. 57 l. (*Interim report J6284.*)

6492._____. *Freight train brake system safety study*. Washington, DC: Federal Railroad Administration, 1984. 116 p. (*DOT/FRA/ORD-84/16*)

6493. _____. *Railroad wheel back rim face failures : III. Residual stress calculations on 33" one-wear freight car wheels* / Chicago : Association of American Railroad, Technical Center, 1983. 29 l. (*Report no. R-560.*)

6494. _____. *Results from the car coupling impact tests of intermodal trailers and containers*. Washington, DC: Federal Railroad Administration, Office of Research and Development, 1988. 36 p. (*DOT/FRA/ORD-88/08.*)

6495. _____. *Structural adequacy of freight car truck casting and wheels*. Washington, D.C., Federal Railroad Administration, Office of Research and Development, 1977. 74 p. (*Report no. FRA/ORD-77/51.*)

6496. _____. *TCFIRE: a model for prediction of fire effects on tank cars* / Washington, DC: Association of American Railroads, Research and Test Department, 1995. 80 p. + 1 computer disk. (*Report no. SD-053*)

6497. _____. *Temperatures, pressures and liquid levels of tank cars engulfed in fires* / Washington, DC: Federal Railroad Administration, 1984. 2 v. v. 1. Results of parametric analyses. – v. 2. Description of analytical procedure. (*FRA-ORD-84-08; NTIS. PB85 156859.*)

6498. _____, E.A. Phillips. *Study of railroad tank car thickness minimums* / Chicago : Association of American Railroads, Technical Center, 1989. 46 l. (*AAR. Report no, R-726.*)

6499. _____, O. J. Viergutz. *Selected topics in railroad tank car safety research*. Washington, DC: Federal Railroad Administration, Office of Research and Development, 1978. 2 v. (*FRA/ORD-78/32, I and 32, II*)

6500. _____, R.A. Evans, S. Guins. *Hopper vs. tank car truck loads: final report* / / Washington, DC: Federal Railroad Administration, 1981. 1 v. (various pagings) Freight car trucks-Testing

6501. _____, Rhees R. Robinson. *Improved safety of railroad car wheels*. Aberdeen Proving Ground, MD: Ballistic Research Laboratory, 1981. 96 p. (*Report ARBRL-CR-00475.*)

6502. Johnson, Philip Cornwall. *Fortieth year of the Milwaukee Road Rocky Mountain electrification*. Missoula, MT: s.n., 1979. 129 l.

6503. Johnson Railroad Signal Company. *Catalogue of interlocking and railroad signaling appliances*. New York, Mitchel & Miller, 1889. 140 p.

6504. Johnson, Ralph Paine. *The steam locomotive, its theory, operation and economics, including comparison with Diesel-electric locomotives*. New York, Simmons-Boardman

Pub.. Corp., 1942. 502 p. (2d ed.: 1944. 564 p.; 1981, 564 p.)

6505. Johnson, Richard. *Railroad technology and manpower in the 1970s.* Washington, DC: U.S. G.P.O., 1972. (United States. Bureau of Labor Statistics. Its *Bulletin, 1717.)*

6505a. Johnson, Richard C. *A case study of the Dearborn railway station in the South Loop* / 1977. 36, 37 l. (Thesis, M.A., Governors State University.)

6506. Johnson, Richard E. *The Montana Eastern Railway Company, 1912-1935: Great Northern's second main line.* Burnsville, MN: Great Northern Railway Historical Society, 1993. 16 p. (*Reference sheet, no. 207.)*

6507. Johnson, Robert L. *The steam locomotive "Yankee": a survey and research report.* 1989. 115 p. (Michigan Historical Museum, Michigan Department of State, Bureau of History.)

6508. Johnson, Robert Wayne. *Through the heart of the South: the Seaboard Air line Railroad story.* Toronto, ON: Stoddart, 1995. 160 p.

6509. Johnson, Ron. *The best of Maine railroads.* South Portland, s.n., 1985. 144 p.

6510. _____. *Maine Central R.R., Mountain Division.* South Portland, ME: 470 Railroad Club, 1985. 328 p.

6511. _____. *New Hampshire and Vermont railroads: classic to contemporary scenic action.* South Portland, R. Johnson, 1986. 79 p.

6512. _____. *Northern rails.* Portland, ME: 470 Railroad Club, 1978. 32 p.

6513. Johnson, Simeon M. *A letter to the President about the title to Yerba-Buena Island, Bay of San Francisco, with an analysis of the report of the Senate Pacific Railroad Committee upon the same.* Washington, DC: M'Gill & Witherow, 1870. 10, 4 p.

6514. Johnson, Stanley W. *The Milwaukee Road in Idaho: a guide to sites and locations.* Coeur d'Alene, ID: Museum of North Idaho, 1997. 220 p. (Enl. and rev. ed.: 2003. 357 p.)

6515. _____. *The Milwaukee Road Olympian: a ride to remember.* Coeur d'Alene, ID: Museum of North Idaho, 2001. 333 p.

6516. _____. *The Milwaukee Road revisited.* Moscow, ID: University of Idaho Press, 1997. 239 p.

6517. _____. *The Milwaukee Road's western extension: the building of a transcontinental railroad.* Coeur d'Alene, ID: Museum of North Idaho, 2007. 548 p.

6518. Johnson, Steven D. *Louisville & Nashville color guide to freight and passenger equipment*. Scotch Plains, NJ: Morning Sun Books, 2000-2004. 2 v.

6519. Johnston, Angus James. *Virginia railroads in the Civil War, 1861-1865*. 1959. 472 l. (Thesis, Ph.D., Northwestern University.))Also: Chapel Hill, Published for the Virginia Historical Society by the University of North Carolina Press, 1961. 336 p. Reissued in 2012.

6520. Johnston, Bob, Joe Welsh, Mike Schafer. *The art of the streamliner.* New York, Metro Books, 2001. 144 p.

6521. Johnston, David Raymond. *Railroad stations of Northern Arizona, their history and architecture: historical research.* 1985. 349 l. (Thesis, M.A., Northern Arizona University.

6522. Johnston, Hank. *The railroad that lighted Southern California.* Los Angles, CA: Trans-Anglo Books, 1965. 128 p.(2d ed.: 1966. 128 p.; 3rd ed. 1970. 128 p.)

6523. _____ *Railroads of the Yosemite Valley.* Long Beach, CA: Johnston-Howe Publications, 1963. 206 p. (2d ed.: Los Angeles, Trans-Anglo Books, 1966. 206 p.; 3rd ed.: Corona del Mar, CA: Trans-Anglo Books, 1980? 206 p.)

6524. _____. *Rails to the Minarets: the story of the Sugar Pine Lumber Company.* Corona del Mar, CA: Trans-Anglo Books, 1980. 128 p.

6525. _____. *Short line to paradise; the story of the Yosemite Valley Railroad.* Long Beach, CA: Johnston & Howe, 1962. 86 p. (3rd ed.: Yosemite, CA: Flying Spur Press, 1971, c1962.)

6526. _____ *They felled the redwoods; a saga of flumes and rails in the High Sierra.* Los Angeles, Trans-Anglo Books, 1966. 160 p. (3rd ed.: Los Angeles, Trans-Anglo Books, 1969, c 1966. 160 p.)

6527. _____. *Thunder in the mountains; the life and times of Madera Sugar Pine.* Los Angeles, Trans-Anglo Books, 1968. 128 p.

6528. _____. *The whistles blow no more; railroad logging in the Sierra Nevada, 1874-1942.* Glendale, CA: Trans-Anglo Books, 1984. 160 p.

6529. Johnston, Howard E. *The New Jersey short line railroads; photo album.* Plainfield, NJ: 1959. 20 p.

6529a. Johnston, J. Fletcher. *Digest of proceedings in the Fifty-ninth Congress, first session, relating to the regulation of railroad rates (H.R. 12987) with index to the remarks of senators and representatives on that subject/* Washington, DC: Government Printing Office, 1908. 52 p. (United States. Interstate Commerce Commission.)

6530. Johnston, J.H. *Leavenworth's Santa Fe depot diner.* Leavenworth, KS: J.H. Johnston III, 2000? 20 p.

6531. Johnston, John W. *The true Southern Pacific railroad versus the Texas Pacific railroad. Speech of Hon. John W. Johnston, of Virginia, in the Senate of the United States, June 5, 1878, contrasting the plan of a genuine southern transcontinental railroad, as laid down in S. bill 1186, with the scheme of Col. T.A. Scott to extend the feeders and connections of the Pennsylvania Railroad to the Pacific Ocean.* Washington : s.n., 1878. 24 p.

6532. Johnston, Richard M. *Coal car distribution and handling in the Pocahontas Region.* 1959. 170 l. (Thesis, M.B.A., University of Pennsylvania.)

6533. Johnston, Wayne Andrew. *The Illinois Central heritage, 1851-1951; a centenary address.* New York, Newcomen Society in North America, 1951. 32 p.

6534. Jones, Arthur. *Vocational education as applied to railroad shop apprentices* / 1916. 1 v. (Thesis, M.E., Pennsylvania State College.)

6535. Jones, C. Clyde. *The agricultural development program of the Chicago, Burlington & Quincy Railroad.* 1954. 374 l. (Thesis, Ph.D., Northwestern University.)

6536. Jones, C.T. *Mathematical modeling of DODX railcars: final report.* Washington, DC: Federal Railroad Administration, Office of Research and Development, 1980. 150 p. (*FRA-ORD-78-47.*)

6537. Jones, Clark F. *LP gas tank car fire* / Boston : National Fire Protection Association, 1954. 8 p. (*Fire loss bulletin; Series 1954-1.*)

6538. Jones, David Dylan. *The joy and thunder days: Michigan railroads during the twentieth century in the days of the steam locomotive.* 1991. 122 l. (Thesis, M.A., Michigan State University.)

6539. Jones, David Louis. *Diesel engines, marine, locomotive, stationary* / New York, The Norman W. Henley Publishing Company, 1926. 565 p.

6540. Jones, Dwight. *Baltimore & Ohio cabooses.* Lynchburg, VA: TLC Publishing, 1998. 124 p.

6541. _____. *C and O for progress, B&O cabooses: display and private owner cars.* Columbus, OH: B&O Caboose Publishers, 2001-

6542. _____. *Steel cabooses of the Chesapeake & Ohio, 1937-1987.* Alderson, WV: Chesapeake & Ohio Historical Society, 1987. 120 p.

6543. _____. *Western Maryland cabooses.* Union Bridge, MD: Western Maryland Historical Society, 1991. 192 p.

6544._____, Phil Samuel. *Chesapeake & Ohio cabooses, 90700 series*. Gambier, OH: Kokosing Gap Trail, 2000. 48 p.

6545. Jones, Eliot. *Principles of railway transportation*. New York, NY: Macmillan, 1927. 607 p.

6546._____, Homer Bews Vanderblue, eds. *Railroads : cases and selections*. New York, The Macmillan Company, 1925. 882 p.

6547. Jones, Franklin D. *Railway repair shop practice* / New York, The Industrial Press, 1912. 40 p. ("From the Trenton shops of the Pennsylvania Railroad.")

6548. Jones, Frederic Paul, Ralph Erie Sawyer. *An investigation of steam railroad electrification with particular reference and application to the Bangor & Aroostook Railroad*. 1917. 33 l. (Thesis, B.S., University of Maine.)

6549. Jones, Harry E. *Railroad wages and labor relations, 1900-1946, an historical survey and summary of results*. New York, Bureau of Information of the Eastern Railways, 1947. 351 p.

6550._____. *Wages and labor relations in the railroad industry, 1900-1941; an historical survey and summary of results*. New York, NY: Bureau of Information of the Eastern Railways, 1942. 358 p.

6551. Jones, Helen Hinckley. *Rails from the West: a biography of Theodore D. Judah*. San Marino, CA: Golden West Books, 1969. 207 p.

6552. Jones, Ivor Vaughan. *The wartime transport of petroleum with especial reference to movements in the eastern seaboard*. 1953. 146 l. (Thesis, M.B.A. in Transportation and Public Utilities, Graduate School of Arts and Sciences, University of Pennsylvania)

6553. Jones, James B., Jr. *Early railroad development in Tennessee, 1820s-1865*. Nashville, TH: Tennessee Historical Commission, 1986. 44 p. (*Study unit, no. 4.)*

6554._____. *Railroad development in Tennessee, 1865-1920*. Nashville, TN: Tennessee Historical Commission, State Historic Preservation Office, 1987. 64 p.

6555. Jones, James Robert. *Denver & New Orleans: in the shadow of the Rockies*. Denver, CO: Sundance Publications, 1997. 376 p.

6556._____, Russ Collman. *Sterling, Colorado: crossroads on the prairie*. Denver, CO: Sundance Publications, 2000. 351 p.(CB&Q)

6557. Jones, Leonard A. *The legal nature of the rolling-stock of railroads*. St. Louis, MO: G.I. Jones, 1878. 42 p.

6558._____. *A treatise on the law of railroad and other corporation securities, including municipal aid bonds*. Boston, Houghton, Osgood, 1879. 707 p.

6559. Jones, Lloyd W. *Humor along the Katy Lines.* Dallas, TX: Southwest Railroad Historical Society, 1970. 51 p.

6559a. Jones, Michael E. *Lost at Thaxton: the dramatic true story of Virginia's forgotten train wreck /* Lugoff, SC: Thaxton press, 2013. 215 p.

6560. Jones, Neason. *Tom Keenan, locomotive engineer; a story of fifty years on the rail as told by himself.* Compiled by Neason Jones. New York, NY: Fleming H. Revell, 1904. 12, 15-280 p. "New ed.: " New Rochelle, NY: Knickerbocker Press, 1926. 283 p.

6561. Jones, Peter d'Alroy. *The robber barons revisited.* Boston, Heath, 1968. 128 p.

6562. Jones, Phillip Andrew. *Railroad financial reporting and auditor responsibility.* 1968. 4, vii, 179 l. (Thesis, Ph.D., Michigan State University.) Accounting. Finance.

6563. Jones, Robert C. *The Central Vermont Railway: a Yankee tradition.* Silverton, CO: Sundance Publications, 1981. 6 v.

6564. _____. *Railroads of Vermont.* Shelburne, VT: New England Press, 1993. 2 v.

6565. _____. *Two feet between the rails.* Silverton, CO: Sundance Publications, 1979-1980. 2 v.

6566. _____. *Two feet to the lakes: the Bridgton & Saco River Railroad.* Edmonds, WA: Pacific Fast Mail, 1993. 255 p.

6567. _____. *Two feet to the quarries: the Monson Railroad.* Burlington, VT: Evergreen Press, 1998. 1 v.

6568. _____. *Two feet to Togus: the Kennebec Central Railroad.* Burlington, VT: Evergreen Press, 1999. 198 p.

6569. _____. David L. Register. *Two feet to tidewater: the Wiscasset, Waterville & Farmington Railway.* Boulder, CO: Pruett Publishing Co., 1987. 269 p. (Expanded and updated ed.: Burlington, VT: Evergreen Press, 2002. 386 p.)

6570. _____, Whitney J. Maxfield, William G. Gove. *Vermont's granite railroads: the Montpelier & Wells River and the Barre & Chelsea.* Boulder, CO: Pruett Publishing Co., 1985. 277 p.

6571. Jones, Robert Willoughby. *Boston and Albany: the New York Central in New England.* Los Angeles, CA: Pine Tree Press, 1997-

6572. _____. *Boston and Maine: city and shore.* Los Angeles, CA: Pine Tree Press, 1999. 192 p.

6573. _____. *Boston and Maine: forest, river, and mountain.* Los Angeles, CA:

Pine Tree Press, 2000. 224 p.

6574. _____. *Boston and Maine: three colorful decades of New England railroading.* Los Angeles, CA: Pine Tree Press, 1999, 1991. 210 p.

6575. _____ *Green Mountain rails: Vermont's colorful trains.* Los Angeles, CA: Pine Tree Press, 1994. 176 p.

6576. Jones, W.S. *Items of interest on ties and tie plates, being a discussion on the present and future of ties and tie renewals from actual conditions on existing roads.* Chicago, Ill., Corbitt & Butterfields Company, 1897. 32 p.

6577. Jones, Wilson E. *The Pascack Valley Line: a history of the New Jersey and New York Railroad.* Madison, NJ: Railroadians of America, 1996. 114, 46 p.

6578. Jonnes, Jill. *Conquering Gotham: a Gilded Age epic: the construction of Penn Station and its tunnels.* New York, NY: Viking, 2007. 368 p.

6579. Jordan, Amy Stanton, Alison Stone, K. Edward Lay. *Architecture of the railroad stations of the late nineteenth and early twentieth century: a study of the Chesapeake and Ohio Railway and the Southern Railway in six counties of Virginia.* Charlottesville, VA: School of Architecture, University of Virginia, 1983. 102 l.

6580. Jordan, C. Keith. *Refrigerator cars: ice bunker cars, 1884-1979.* Norman, OK: Santa Fe Modelers Organization, 1994. 288 p. (*Santa Fe rolling stock reference series, v. 2.*)

6581. Jordan, Julie M., Barbara Foster. *Rail transport of spent fuel and high-level waste/* Denver, CO: National Conference of State Legislatures, 1986. 16 p. (State legislative report, v. 11, no. 2.)

6582. Jordan, Leonard Crouch. *Steel framed box car.* 1906. 42 l. (Thesis, B.S., University of Colorado.)

6583. Jordan, Mildred L. *Railroads in the El Paso area.* 1957. 221 l. (Thesis, M.A., University of Texas, El Paso.)

6584. Jordan, Phillip R. *Rails beyond the Rutland.* Newton, NJ: Carstens Publications, 1988. 76 p. (Vermont Railway, Green Mountain Railroad, Clarendon & Pittsford.)

6585. Jordan, William C. *The impact of uncertain demand and supply on empty railroad car distribution.* 1982. 173 l. (Thesis, Ph.D., Cornell University.)

6586. Josephson, H.R. *An economic evaluation of the use of treated wood ties and concrete ties on U.S. railroads; energy requirement for wood and concrete ties.* S.l., Railway Tie Association, 1977. 1 v.

6587. Josephson, Matthew. *The robber barons; the great American capitalists, 1861-*

1901. New York, Harcourt, Brace and Company, 1934. 474 p.

6588. Joshi, Prakash B. *Aerodynamic forces on freight trains* / Washington, DC : Federal Railroad Administration, Office of Freight Systems, 1978. 1 v. (*FRA/ORD-76-295.*)

6589. Joslin, Richard S. *Sylvester Marsh and the cog railway.* Tilton, NH: Sant Bani Press for the Mount Washington Railway Company, 2000. 43 p.

6590. Joslyn, David Lindsay. *The romance of the railroads entering Sacramento.* Boston, Mass., Railway & Locomotive Historical Society, 1939. 42 p. (*R&LHS Bulletin, no. 48.*)

6591. Josserand, Peter, Harry Willard Forman. *Rights of trains.* 5th ed. New York, Simmons-Boardman Pub. Corp., 1987. 459 p.

6591a. Joubert, William H. *A history of the Seaboard Air Line Railway Company.* 1935. 258 l. (Thesis, M.A., University of Florida.)

6591a. Jouett, Edward S. *The unfair competition between railroads and motor carriers for hire*/ Louisville, KY: Louisville and Nashville Railroad Co., 1931. 20 p.

6592. *Journal failure report.* Washington, DC: Federal Railroad Administration, 1972. 19 p.

6592a. *Journal of advanced transportation.* Durham, NC: Institute for Transportation, 1979-   Quarterly.

6593. *Journal of proceedings of the ... annual conventions of the Brotherhood of Locomotive Firemen.* Terre Haute, Ind: The Brotherhood, 1885. 1 v. 1st twelve, from 1874-1855, inclusive.(>*Journal of proceedings of the...annual convention of the Brotherhood of Locomotive Firemen.*)

6594. *Journal of proceedings of the...annual convention of the Brotherhood of Locomotive Firemen.* Terre Haute, Ind: The Brotherhood, 1886. 1 v. 13th, 1886. (>*Journal of proceedings of the...biennial convention of the Brotherhood of Locomotive Firemen, held in*...[1888-1896])

6595. *Journal of proceedings of the...biennial convention of the Brotherhood of Locomotive Firemen, held in*... Terre Haute, Ind: The Brotherhood, 1888-1896. Biennial. 5 v. (<*Journal of proceedings of the ...annual convention of the Brotherhood of Locomotive Firemen* [1886] >*Grand Lodge proceedings of the..biennial convention...at*...[1898-1904])

6596. *The journal of railroad car heating, lighting and ventilating.* New York, Railroad Car Heating pub. Co., 1890-1891.Monthly. (>*The railroad car journal,* 1891-1900.)

6597. *The journal of railway appliances and railway price current.* New York, s.n., 1892- Monthly. (<*American journal of railway appliances*; > *Railway machinery.*)

6598. *Journal of railway tank cars*. Monrovia, CA: Society of Freight Car Historians, 1990- . Semiannual.

6599. *Journal of the Railway Signal Association*. Bethlehem, Pa., The Association, 1901-1918. Quarterly. Became the Signal Division of the American Railroad Association in 1919.

6600. *Journal of the Switchmen's Union*. Buffalo, NY: The Union, 1898- . Monthly (Switchmen's Union of North America. Other title: Journal of the Switchmen's Union of North America.)

6600a. *Journal of transportation law, logistics, and policy*. Gaithersburg, MD: Association for Transportation Law, Logistics, and Policy, 1994- Quarterly. (< *Transportation practitioners journal.*)

6601. *Journeys through Western rail history*. Golden, CO: Colorado Railroad Museum, 1997. 168 p. (*Colorado rail; annual, no. 22.*)

6602. Jovanovic, Dejan. *Improving railroad on-time performance: models, algorithms, and applications*. 1989. 151 l. (Thesis, Ph.D., University of Pennsylvania.)

6603. Joyce, John W. *A study of the factors involved in converting the Boston, Revere Beach and Lynn Railroad into a rapid transit system* / 1928. 27, 5 l. (Thesis, B.S., Massachusetts Institute of Technology, Department of Electrical Engineering.)

6604. Joyce, T. Frank. *The Boston and Maine. A cross section of New England—past history—present usefulness, 1830-1925*. Boston, E.L. Grimes Printing Company, 1925. 23 p.

6605. J.S. Coffin, Jr., Company. *The Coffin feed water heater system*. S.l., s.n., 1926. 1 v. (*Bulletin no. 101.*)

6606. _____. *The new Coffin feed water heater system*. S.l., s.n., 1938. 1 v.

6607. Judah, Theodore D. *A practical plan for building the Pacific railroad: San Francisco, January 1, 1857*. Washington, D.C.: H. Polkinhorn, 1857. 31 p.

6608. _____. *Report of the chief engineer on the preliminary survey and cost of construction of the Central Pacific Railroad, of California, across the Sierra Nevada Mountains, from Sacramento the eastern boundary of California. Sacramento, October 1, 1861*. Sacramento? 1861. 36 p.

6609. _____. *Report of the chief engineer upon the preliminary survey, revenue, and cost of construction, of the San Francisco and Sacramento Rail Road*. San Francisco, Printed by Whitton, Towne, 1856. 32, 8 p.

6610. *Junction and journey: trains and film: essays* // by Laurence Kardish ... [et al.] New York: Museum of Modern Art, 1991. 48 p. (The Museum of Modern Art,

Department of Film. Laurence Kardish, Curator.)

6610a. Junkersfeld, Peter. *Power supply for terminal electrification of railways entering Chicago* / 1909. 13, 16, l, 12 folded leaves of plates. (Thesis, University of Illinois.)

6611. Juran, Robert A. *Steel rails across America: the short line and regional railroads, past and present, of the U.S. and Canada.* Oregon City OR: Paradise Press, 2005. 521 p.

6612. Jurgensen, Delbert Frederick. *Railroad accidents, their causes and remedy.* Minneapolis, MN: Syndicate Printing Company, 1912. 18 p.

6612a. Juris, Frances, Ron Halvorson. *City of Prineville Railway* / Pineville, OR: Crook County Historical Society, 2012. 51 p.

6612a. Jutton, Lee. *Design of a round house* / 1902. 20 l. (Thesis, B.S., University of Illinois.)

K.

6613. Kachadourian, George. *Laboratory tests of two 100-ton covered hopper cars.* Washington, DC: Federal Railroad Administration, Office of Research and Development, 1985. 1 v. (various pagings). (*DOT/FRA/ORD-85/13.*)

6614. Kahn, Allan Paul, Jack May. *The tracks of New York.* New York, Electric Railroaders' Association, 1973-1977. 3 v.

6615. Kahn, Otto Hermann. *Government ownership of railroads, and war taxation.* S.l., s.n., 1918. 50 p. "An address before the National Industrial Conference Boards, New York, October 10, 1918.

6616. Kaiser Aluminum & Chemical Sales, Inc. *Engineering, fabrication and welding of aluminum railroad equipment* / Skokie, IL: Kaiser Aluminum, 1966. 35 l.

6617. _____. *Welded, aluminum bodied railroad gondola car (70 ton)* / Chicago : Kaiser Aluminum & Chemical Sales, Inc., 1957. 4, 11 p.

6618. Kaiser, W.D. *Rail inspection systems analysis and technology survey.* Washington, DC: Federal Railroad Administration, Office of Research and Development, 1977. 214 p. (*FRA/ORD-77/39.*)

6619. Kaitz, Gary M. *An economic history of five Midwestern railroads.* Washington, D.C., Department of Transportation, Office of University Research, 1976. 79 p. (*Report, Dept. of Transportation DOT-TST-77-73.*) Prepared for the University Research Program, United States Department of Transportation by the Department of Urban Studies and Planning, Massachusetts Institute of Technology, Contract no. DOT-OS-30104.

6620. Kalamazoo Railroad Velocipede Company. *Kalamazoo Railroad Velocipede Co., Kalamazoo, Michigan, U.S.A. manufactures of steel railroad velocipedes, section, telegraph, push and inspection hand cars; also, steel baggage, express and warehouse trucks ...* / Chicago ? : s.n., 1886. 32 p.

6621. Kalay, Semih, Albert Joseph Reinschmidt. *An overview of wheel/rail load environment caused by freight car suspension dynamics*/ Chicago, IL: Association of American Railroads, Technical Center, 1990. 57 l. (*Report, no. R-741.*)

6622. _____. Ali Tajaddini, Satya P. Singh. *Heavy axle load characterization tests*/ Chicago, IL: Association of American Railroads, Technical Center, 19990. 266 p. (*Report, No. R-720.*)

6623. Kalisher, Simpson. *Railroad men: a book of photographs and collected stories. With an introduction by Jonathan Williams.* New York, Clarke & Way, 1961. 83 p.

6624. Kalmanovich, M.Z., S.I Sokolov, Yu N. Dymant. *Railroad passenger car body.*

Ft. Belvoir Defense Technical Information Center, 1974. 10 p.

6625. Kalmbach, Albert Carpenter. *Baltimore & Ohio Railroad.* Milwaukee, Wis., Kalmbach Pub. Co., 1946. 20 l. (*Trains album of photographs, book 13.)*

6626. _____. *Colorado railroads.* Milwaukee, Wis., Kalmbach Pub. Co., 1942. 2 p. 41 illus. (*Trains album of photographs, book 4.)*

6627. _____. *Far western railroads.* Milwaukee, Wis., Kalmbach Pub. Co., 1942. 24 p. (*Trains album of photographs, book 2.*)

6628. _____. *Grand Central Terminal, New York City; the New York Central System.* S.l., s.n., 19--? 12 p. (Reprinted from *Trains & Travel.*)

6629. _____. *The Model Railroader cyclopedia: railroad equipment prototype plans.* Milwaukee, Wis., Kalmbach Pub. Co., 1936-1949. 6 v.

6630. _____. *Railroad panorama.* Milwaukee, Wis., Kalmbach Pub. Co., 1944. 6 p.

6631. _____. *Southern Pacific Lines.* Milwaukee, Wis., Kalmbach Pub. Co., 1945. 1 v. (*Trains album of photographs, book 11.*)

6632. _____. *Trains; album of photographs.* Milwaukee, Wis., Kalmbach Pub. Co., 1942. 15 v. (v. 1 *Eastern railroads.* v. 2 *Far western railroads.* v. 3 *Midwestern railroads.* v. 4 *Colorado railroads.* v. 5 *Southern railroads.* v. 6 *New England railroads.* v. 7 *Electric railways.* v. 8 *Pennsylvania Railroad.* v. 9 *New York Central Railroad.* v. 10 *Modern steam locomotives.* v. 11 *Southern Pacific Lines.* v. 12 *Santa Fe Railway.* v. 13 *Baltimore & Ohio Railroad.* v. 14 *Erie Railroad.* v. 15 *Great Northern Railway.*)

6633. Kalt, William D, III. *Tuscon was a railroad town.* Mountlake Terrace, WA: VTD Rail Publishing, 2007. 345 p.

6634. Kamat, Ganpat Jaiwantrao. *An analysis of the dynamics of locomotives and railway cars.* 1951. 1 v. (Thesis, University of Illinois.)

6635. Kamholz, Edward J., Jim Blain, Gregory Kamholz. *The Oregon-American Lumber Company: ain't no more.* Stanford, CA: Stanford University Press, 2003. 362 p.

6636. Kaminski, Edward S. *American Car & Foundry: a centennial history, 1899-1999.* Wilton, CA: Signature Press, 1999. 362 p.

6637. _____. *The Magor Car Corporation.* Berkeley, CA: Signature Press, 2000. 200 p.

6637a. _____. *New York, Susquehanna & Western Railroad in New Jersey* / Charleston, SC: Arcadia, 2010. 127 p.

6638. _____. *Pullman-Standard freight cars, 1900-1960.* Berkeley and Wilton, CA: Signature Press, 2007. 192 p..

6639. _____. *Tank cars: American Car & Foundry, 1865-1955.* Berkeley and Wilton, CA: Signature Press, 2003. 1 v.

6640. Kamm, Al, Jr. *D&RGW passenger car plan set.* phoenix, AZ : Coronado Scale Models, 1900s. 1 v.

6641. Kane, J.A., C.E. Waldman. *Railroad financial evaluation model : description and computer users' manual : final report.* Washington, DC: Federal Railroad Administration, Office of Research and Development, 1981. 53, A-35 p. (*FRA/ORD-81/25.II*)

6642. Kanely, Edna A. *Baltimore and Ohio railroad employees: 1842 and 1852, 1855 and 1857/* Westminster, MD: Heritage Books, 2008, 1982. 348 p. (Wages-19th Century)

6642a. Kang, Seung Kyu. *Development of geometric design standards to accommodate low-clearance vehicles: a microcomputer software approach/* 1991. 204 l. (Thesis, Ph.D., West Virginia University.)

6643. Kanner, Donald R. *Red doesn't always mean stop: a layman's guide to the understanding and interpretation of track side railroad signals.* Chicago, Donald R. Kanner & Sons, 1993. 76 p.

6644. Kansas. Department of Transportation. Division of Planning and Development. *1982 Kansas state rail plan. Light density line analysis, 1982.* Topeka, KS: The Division, 1982. 1 v. (various pagings)

6644a. Kansas City Northwestern Railroad. *Bridges, water stations, culverts, overhead railway and highway crossing bridges on the Kansas City Northwestern R.R. Co. and branch lines.* St. Louis : R.P. Studley & Co., 1895. 62, 1 p.

6644a. Kao, Si-Chin. *The tractive resistance and machine friction of steam locomotives.* 1931. 126 l. (Thesis, M.S., University of Illinois, Urbana-Champaign.)

6645. Kaplan, Bob, Deane E. Mellander. *The Richmond, Fredericksburg & Potomac Railroad: linking North and South.* Silver Spring, MD: Old Line Graphics, 1990. 128 p.

6646. Kaplan, Michael David. *Otto Mears: Colorado's transportation king.* 1975. 439 l. (Thesis, Ph.D., University of Colorado.)

6647. Kaplan, Stan. *Rail transportation of coal to power plants: reliability issues/* Washington, DC: Congressional Research Service, Library of Congress, 2007. 89 p. (*Major studies and issue briefs of the Congressional Research Service. Supplement, 2007, 07-RL-34186.*)

6648. _____. *Rail transportation of coal to Texas /* Austin: Public Utility Commission of Texas, 1985. 15, 4 p. (*Public Utility Commission of Texas working paper series, no. 85-5.*)

6648a. Kapsch, Robert J. *Over the Alleghenies: early canals and railroads of Pennsylvania* / Morgantown: WV: West Virginia University Press, 2013. 449 p.

6649. Kar, Abdülkerim. *Fundamental properties and performance of generic passenger rail vehicles.* 1980. 229 l. (Thesis, Ph.D., Massachusetts Institute of Technology, Department of Mechanical Engineering.)

6650. Karam, Duane, Jeff Ainsworth. *Santa Fe Northern 4-8-4 pictorial.* La Crescenta, CA: Monte Vista Publishing, 2000. 58 p.

6651. _____. *Southern Pacific Mogul 2-6-0 pictorial.* Rialto, CA: Monte Vista Publishing, 1998. 74 p.

6652. Kardes, Fabian Edward. *Railway locomotive maintenance: a practical textbook for the instruction of locomotive machinists, engineers and firemen, hostlers, and others in railway employ, interested in the operation, care, and maintenance of freight and passenger locomotives.* Chicago, Ill., American Technical Society, 1944-1945. 4 v.

6653. Karig, Martin Robert III. *Coal cars: the first three hundred years.* Scranton, PA: University of Scranton Press, 2007. 400 p.

6654. _____. *Hard coal and coal cars: hauling anthracite on the New York, Ontario & Western Railway.* Scranton, PA: University of Scranton Press, 2006. 210 p.

6655. Karlawish, John Waters. *Financial aspects of railroad diversification.* 1961. 76 l. (Thesis, M.B.A. in Finance and Banking, Graduate School of Arts and Sciences, University of Pennsylvania.)

6656. Karlewicz, Ken, Scott Hartley. *Susquehanna: from short-lines to stack packs.* Piscataway, NJ: Railpace Co., 1987. 104 p.

6656a. Karmel, Amir. *Analytical and experimental studies of derailment processes of railway vehicles/* 1982. 184 l. (Thesis, Ph.D., Princeton University.)

6657. Karr, Ronald Dale. *Amtrak, ten years of controversy: a guide to the literature.* Evanston, IL: Transportation Center, Northwestern University, 1982. 68 p.

6658. _____. *Chicago's transit, 1850-1982.* Chicago, IL: R.D. Karr, 1985. 1 v.

6659. _____. *Lost railroads of New England.* Pepperell, MA: Branch Line Press, 1989. 143 p. (2nd ed.: 1996. 167 p.)

6660. _____. *Rail abandonments in New England, 1845-1981.* Chicago, IL: R.D. Karr, 1983. 12 p.

6661. _____. *The rail lines of southern New England: a handbook of railroad history.*

Pepperell, MA: Branch Line Press, 1995. 383 p.

6661a. Kassabian, Nomi. *Light rail transit: planning, design, and operating experience.* Washington, DC: national Academy Press, 1992. 359 p.

6662. Kassander, Leopold. *Injectors, hydrostatic lubricators, mechanical lubricator and other important locomotive accessories* / New York: Nathan Manufacturing Company, 1927. 150 p.

6662a. _____. *Valveless mechanical lubricator; booklet of instructions.* New York: Nathan Manufacturing Company, 1927. 38 p.

6663. *Katy employes' magazine.* St. Louis: M.K.& T. Railway System, 1913-1956. Monthly: 1913-Aug. 1956. Bimonthly Sept/Oct. 1956-   . Other title: 1913-1945 – *M.K. and T. employes' magazine.*

6664. *The Katy flyer.* St. Charles, MO: Katy Railroad Historical Society, 1978-   . Quarterly.

6665. Katz, Daniel. *Productivity, supervision and morale among railroad workers.* Ann Arbor, Survey Research Center; Institute for Social Research, University of Michigan, 1951. 61 p. (*Survey Research Center series, no. 5.*)

6666. Katz, S.H., Edward George Meiter. *Temperatures in cabs of freight locomotives passing through tunnels of the Chesapeake & Ohio Railway.* Washington, D.C., U.S. Department of the Interior, Bureau of Mines, 1924. 8 p.

6667. Katz, Stanley M. *A three-dimensional demand model of the competition between regulated rail and motor transportation in the United States*/ 1980. 206 l. (Thesis, Ph.D., University of Pennsylvania.)

6668. Kaufman, Jacob Joseph. *Collective bargaining in the railroad industry.* New York, King's Crown Press, 1954. 235 p.

6669. Kaufman, Lawrence. *Leaders count: the story of the BNSF Railway.* Austin, TX: Texas Monthly Custom Publishing; distributed by Texas A&M University Press, 2005. 384 p.

6669a. Kaufman, William H., Michelle S. Kaufman. *The State Belt: San Francisco's waterfront railroad* / Berkeley and Winton, CA: Signature Press, 2013.

6670. Kauke, Phillips C. *The Visalia Electric Railroad: Southern Pacific's Orange Grove route.* Berkeley and Wilton, CA: Signature Press, 2004. 168 p.

6671. Kavanaugh, Kelli B. *Detroit's Michigan Central Station.* Charleston, SC: Arcadia, 2001. 128 p.

6672. Kavanaugh, William Harrison. *Economy of compound locomotives.* 1894. 70 l.

(Thesis, M.E., Lehigh University.)

6673. Kay, Dale M. *Robotic applications in environmentally undesirable car maintenance operations*. Washington, D.C.: United States Mass Transportation Administration, Long Island Railroad Company, Industrial Engineering Department, 1986. 41 l.

6674. Kay, John L. *Directory of route agent routes, 1837-1882: a listing of the route agent routes, operated by the United States Post Office Department over railroads and waterways, including the dates of establishment, discontinuances and changes of names and operation/* Chicago, IL: Mobile Post Office Society, 1990. 170 p.

6675. Kaysen, James P. *The railroads of Wisconsin, 1827-1937*. Boston, Mass., Railway and Locomotive Historical Society, 1937. 72 p.

6676. Keating, Ann Durkin. *Chicagoland: city and suburbs in the railroad age*. Chicago, University of Chicago Press, 2005. 262 p. (*Historical studies of urban America.*)

6677. Keaton, Mark Hiazlip. *Optimizing railroad operations*. 1985. 261 l. (Thesis, Ph.D., University of Wisconsin, Madison.) Railroad yards – Mathematical models. Scheduling – mathematical models.

6678. Kedzie, R.C. *Ventilation of railroad cars*. Lansing, Mich., W.W. George & Co., State Printers and Binders, 1876. 2, 133-140 p. (Michigan. State Board of Health. Annual report of the Secretary of the State Board of Health.)

6679. Keefer, Ellen Eloise. *The Chicago, Burlington and Quincy in the early history of Nebraska, 1860-1885*. 1929. 14 p., 84 l. (Thesis, M.A., University of Nebraska, Lincoln.)

6680. Keekley, Harold. *Big blows: Union Pacific's super turbines*. Omaha, NE: George R. Cockle and Associates, 1975. 64 p.

6681. _____. *Roaring U50's—Union Pacific's twin diesels*. Omaha, NE: George R. Cockle and Associates, 1978. 80 p.

6682. Keeler, Theodore E. *Freight rate deregulation and the financial viability of the railroad industry*. Berkeley, CA: s.n., 1980. 29, 2 p. Brookings Institution; University of California, Berkeley, Department of Economics.

6683. _____. *On the economic impact of railroad freight regulation*. Berkeley, CA: Department of Economics, University of California, 1976. 54 p. (*Working paper; Workshop in Transportation Economics, no. SL-7601.*)

6684. _____. *Railroad cost functions: an empirical study*. 1967. 99 l. (Thesis, B.A., Reed College.)

6685. _____. *Railroad costs, returns to scale, and excess capacity: a neoclassical* *analysis/*Berkeley, CA: Department of Economics, University of California, 1973. 29 p. (*Working paper, no. 35.)*

6686. _____. *Railroads, freight and public policy.* Washington, D.C.: Brookings Institution, 1983. 180 p. (*Studies in the regulation of economic activity.*)

6687. _____. *Resource allocation in intercity passenger transportation.* 1971. 311 l. (Thesis, Ph.D., Massachusetts Institute of Technology)

6687a. *Keeling's railway, telegraph, and steamship directory, for 1866.* New York : J.S. Keeling, 1866. 173 p.

6688. Keenan, Sharon K. Sommerlad. *The history of the Railroad of New Jersey Maritime Terminal in Jersey City, New Jersey: commemorating its centennial, 1889-1989.* 1990. 499 l. (Thesis, M.S., Virginia Polytechnic Institute and State University.)

6689. Keenan, James D. *Growth of unions among the railroad workers of America/* 1952. 50 l. (Thesis, M.A., St. Bonaventure University.)

6689a. *Keepin' track.* Chicago : Atchison, Topeka and Santa Fe Railway, Company Information Department, 1900s- . Monthly.

6689b. *Keeping track.* Portland, OR: Oregon Railroad Association, 1964-   . Irregular.

6690. Kehoe, Jeff. *Milwaukee Roads rib-side cabooses.* Madison, WI: Milwaukee Road Historical Association, 1995. 39 p. (Rev. and updated ed: 2012. 47 p.)

6691. _____. *Milwaukee Road's steel cabooses.* Antioch, IL: Milwaukee Road Historical Association, 1998. 39 p. (*Milwaukee Road special publication, no. 2.*)

6692. _____. *Milwaukee Road's wooden cabooses.* Antioch, IL: Milwaukee Road Historical Association, 2003. 39 p. (*Milwaukee Road special publication, no. 4.*)

6692a. Keillor, Steven J. *Erik Ramstad and the empire builder* / Minot, ND: North American heritage press, 2002. 151 p.

6693. Keilty, Edmund. *Doodlebug country: the rail motorcar on the Class 1 railroads of the United States.* Glendale, CA: Interurban Press, 1982. 184 p.

6694. _____. *Interurbans without wires: the rail motorcar in the United States.* Glendale, CA: Interurbans, 1979. 198 p.(*Interurbans special, no. 66.*)

6695. _____. *The short line doodlebug: Galloping Geese and other rail critters.* Glendale, CA: Interurban Press, 1988. 152 p.

6696. Keith, Herbert F. *Cheap coal, or, The Boston and Northwestern, Massachusetts Central, and Boston and Poughkeepsie Railroads : their relations to Massachusetts, the coal fields of Pennsylvania, and the commerce of Boston* / Boston : Franklin Press :

Rand, Avery, & Company, 1877. 21 p.

6697. Keith, Jean Edwin. *The role of the Louisville and Nashville Railroad in the development of coal and iron in Alabama, Tennessee, and Kentucky, 1873-1893.* 1959. 167 l. (Thesis, M.A., Johns Hopkins University.)

6698. Keith, Tom, Sharon Curran Wescott, *A comparison of unit train and slurry pipeline transportation of coal* / Denver, CO: Federation of Rocky Mountain States, 1977. 57 p. (*Regional background paper.*)

6699. Kelchner, William Hayes. *A study of the signal system of the Northern Central Division of the Pennsylvania Railroad* / 1915. 37 l. (Thesis, C.E., Lehigh University.)

6700. Keliher, Alice Virginia, Franz Hess, Marion LeBron, Rudolf Modley. *Railroad workers.* New York, NY: Harper & Brothers, 1941. 56 p. (*Picture fact books, Group II.*)

6701. Kell, C.M. *Railroad lanterns: an easy to use buying guide with price references.* Marietta, PA: Mabius Marketing Systems, 1981. 32 p.

6702. Kell, Elmer Andrew. *Early travel and communication in Southern California.* 1940. 106 l. (Thesis, M.A., University of Southern California.)

6703. Keller, David. *The Long Island Rail Road: 1925-1975.* Charleston, SC: Arcadia, 2004. 128 p.

6704. _____. *Revisiting the Long Island Rail Road, 1925-1975.* Charleston, SC: Arcadia, 2005. 128 p.

6705. Keller, Leo E. *History of eight-hour day and overtime payments for Sundays and holidays.* Detroit, MI: United Brotherhoods of Maintenance of Way Employees and Railway Shop Laborers, 1924. 10 p.

6706. _____. *Training and skill of track and roadway section men.* Detroit, MI: Brotherhood of Maintenance of Way Employes, 1929. 44 p.

6706a. _____. *Training and skill of trackmen; argument before the Board of Arbitration on Louisville & Nashville Railroad in support the claim of employes that trackmen are not common laborers*/ S.l., s.n., 1927. 32 p.

6707. Keller, W.M. *Feasibility of atomic energy for use on American railroads.* Chicago, IL: Association of American Railroads, 1957. 102 l. (*Armour Research Foundation; ARF project no. A666; Its report, no. MR-280.*)

6708. Kelley, Edward, Peggy Conaway. *Railroads of Los Gatos.* Charleston, SC: Arcadia, 2006. 128 p.

6709. Kelley, Frederick Williams. *Car heating.* Ithaca, N.Y., s.n., 1893. 46 l. (Thesis)

6710. Kelley, George L. *Life and work of Edward G. Budd : an address* / Philadelphia ? : s.n., 1949. 1 v. E.G. Budd (1870-1946).

6711. Kellogg, James Eugene. *The decline of railroad passenger travel in Kansas, 1950-1969.* 1971. 54 l. (Thesis, M.A., Department of Geography, University of Kansas.)

6712. _____. *The impact of the railroad upon a frontier region: the case of Alaska and the Yukon.* 1975. 160 l. (Thesis, Ph.D., Indiana State University.)

6713. Kelly, Henry. *Railroading in Hopkins County.* 1903. 192 l. (Kentucky)

6714. Kelly, James Anthony. *Tales of the trackwalker.* New York, American Locomotive Company; General Electric Company, 1944. 36 p. (Railroad advertising)

6715. Kelly, Joe. *The train doesn't stop in Wagner, Montana, anymore and neither do I: travels in America.* Utica, NY: Good Times Publishing, 1995. 240 p.

6716. Kelly, John. *Burlington Zephyrs: photo archive: America's distinctive trains.* Hudson, WI: Icongrafix, 2004. 126 p. (*Photo archive series*)

6717. _____. *Chicago & North Western passenger trains of the 400 fleet: photo archive.* Hudson, WI: Iconografix, 2006. 126 p. (*Photo archive series*)

6717a. _____. *Chicago postwar passenger and commuter trains* / Hudson, WI: Iconografix, 2012. 126 p.

6718. _____. *Chicago stations & trains photo archive.* Hudson, WI: Iconografix, 2008. 126 p.

6719. _____. *Classic streamliners photo archive: the trains and the designers.* Hudson, WI: Icongrafix, 2004. 126 p. (*Photo archive series*)

6720. _____. *Freight trains of the upper Mississippi River: photo archive.* Hudson, WI: Iconografix, 2005. 126 p. (*Photo archive series*)

6720a. _____. *Great Northern Railway: route of the Empire Builder.* Hudson, WI: Iconografix, 2013. 127 p.

6721. _____. *Northern Pacific Railway.* Hudson, WI: Iconografix, 2007. 126 p.

6722. _____. *Pennsylvania railroad locomotives : photo archive : steam, diesel & electric.* Hudson, WI: Iconografix, 2008. 126 p.

6723. _____. *Railroad freight cars—slogans and heralds.* Hudson, WI : Iconografix, 2011. 1 v.

6724. _____. *Rio Grande locomotives photo archive* / Hudson, WI: Iconografix, 2009. 126 p.

6725. _____. *Santa Fe Railway photo archive* / Hudson, WI: Iconografix, 2010. 126 p.

6726. _____. *Streamliners to the Twin Cities: photo archive. 400, Twin Zephyrs & Hiawatha trains.* Hudson, WI: Icongrafix, 2002. 126 p. (*Photo archive series*)

6727. _____. *Union Pacific Railroad: passenger trains of the City Fleet photo archives*/ Hudson, WI: Iconografix, 2009. 126 p.

6728. Kelly, John C. *The 50 best of B & O, book three.* Baltimore, MD: Barnard, Roberts, 1977. 52 l.

6729. Kelly Michael C. *Wabash in color.* Kutztown, PA: Morning Sun Books, 2007. 2 v.

6730. Kelsey, Kerck. *Prairie lightning : the rise and fall of William Drew Washburn .* Lakeville, MN : Pogo Press, 2010. 187 p. (Railroads -Middle West)

6731. Kemble, John Haskell. *Railroad car facts : statistics on car building and car repairing, 1956.* New York : American Railway Car Institute, 1957. 1 v. (various pagings)

6732. _____. *Railroad car facts : statistics on car building & car repairing, 1958.* New York : American Railway Car Institute, 1959. 1 v (various pagings)

6733. Kemp, Willard E. *A standardized covered hopper car for special situations* / New York : ASME, 1965. 5 p. (American Society of mechanical Engineers (Series) : 65-WA/RR-7.)

6734. Kendall, W. F. *Automatic car-couplers.* 1885. 18 l. 4 leaves of pl. (Thesis, B.S., University of Illinois.)

6735. Kenefick, John C. *Union Pacific and the building of the West.* New York, Newcomen Society of the United States, 1985. 18 p. (*Newcomen publication, no. 1251.*)

6736. Kenison, Arthur M. *Frederic C. Dumaine: office boy to tycoon*/Manchester, NH: Saint Anselm College Press, 2000. 277 p. (Amoskeag Manufacturing Co.; American Waltham Match Co.; New York, New Haven, and Hartford Railroad Co.)

6737. Keniston, H.E. *Railroad coal, aggregate and ore cars : yesterday, today and tomorrow* / Dearborn, MI: Society of Manufacturing Engineers, 1975. 14 p.

6738. Kennan, George. *The Chicago & Alton case; a misunderstood transaction.* Garden City, NY: Country Life Press, 1916. 3-57 p.

6739. _____. *Misrepresentation in railroad affairs*/ New York, Arno Press, 1981. 59 p.

6739a. Kennebeck, William, Kurt Ikrath. *Use of railroad tracks for carrier telephony and as long-wire antennas for transmission of long-wave radio signals.* Ft. Belvoir Defense Technical Information Center, 1967. 27 p.

6740. Kennedy and Company, New York, N.Y. *A salute to railroading: prints, etchings and water colors showing the development of a great American industry.* New York, Kennedy & Company, 1952. 11 p.

6740a. Kennedy, Harold W. *The rate base and the California Railroad Commission /* 1925. 44 l. (Thesis, J.D., University of California, Berkeley, School of Law.

6741. Kennedy, Ian G., Julian Treuherz. *The railway: art in the age of steam.* New Haven: Yale University Press, 2008. 287 p. ("Catalog of an exhibition entitled: "Art in the Age of steam: Europe, America and the Railway, 1830-1960,' at the Walker Art Gallery, National Museums, Liverpool, Apr. 18-Aug. 10, 2008 and at The Nelson-Atkins Museum of Art, Kansas City, Missouri, Sept. 13, 2008-Jan. 18, 2009 / Includes bibliographical references [p. 274-279] and index.'

6742. Kennedy, James. *The valve-setter's guide; a treatise on the construction and adjustment of the principal valve gearing used on American locomotives /* New York, A. Sinclair Company, 1910. 60 p. (2d ed. New York, A. Sinclair Company, 1915. 100 p.)

6743. Kennedy, Maurus A. *The reorganization of the Erie Railroad Company : 1938-1941.* 1946. 90 l. (Thesis, M.B.A. in Finance and Banking, Graduate School of Arts and Sciences, University of Pennsylvania.)

6744. Kennedy, Randy. *Subwayland: adventures in the world beneath New York.* New York, St. Martin's Griffin, 2004. 226 p.

6745. Kennedy, Valerie Eva. *Switching tracks: organizational change in the railroad industry/* 1995. 280 l. (Thesis, Ph.D., Cornell University.)

6746. Kenney, Dennis Jay. *Crime, fear, and the New York City subways: the role of citizen action.* New York, Praeger, 1987. 136 p.

6747. Kent, Otis Beall. *A digest of decisions <including dicta> under the Federal safety appliance and Hours of service acts ... with references to or excerpts from additional cases in which acts have been construed; orders and administrative rulings of the Interstate Commerce Commission.* Washington: Govt. Print. Off., 1915. 281 p.

6748. _____. *An index-digest of decisions under the Federal safety appliance acts: act of March 2, 1893, 27 Stat. L., 531, as amended by act of April 1, 1896, 29 Stat. L., 85, and act of March 2, 1903, 32 Stat. L., 943; together with relevant excerpts from other cases in which the acts have been construed.* Washington: Govt. Print. Off., 1910. 294 p.

6748a. Kentucky. Circuit Court. *Sunday trains/* Kentucky? s.n., 1881. (Louisville and Nashville Railroad Co.)

6749. *Kentucky coal rail loading facilities*. Lexington, KY: Kentucky Energy Cabinet, 1985. 121 p, in various pagings. (Kentucky Coal Marketing Information System; Appalachian Regional Commission.)

6750. Kenyon, Otis Allen, Lewis Buckley Stilwell. *Steel cars, side-truss construction, L.B. Stillwell, consulting engineer* / New York, Chalmar-Winchell Press, 1912. 32 p. 18 ½ x 31 cm.

6751. Kerby, William Charles. *An economic analysis of the impact of piggyback to the Far Western railroads.* 1961. 178 p. (Thesis, M.A., California State University, Sacramento.)

6752. Kerley, James William. *The failure of railway labor leadership: a chapter in railroad labor relations, 1900-1932.* 1959. 261 l. (Thesis, Ph.D., Columbia University.)

6753. Kernan, Charles R. *Rails to weeds: searching out the ghost railroads around Wilmington* / Wilmington, NC: The Author, 1995. 28 p.

6754. _____. *The story of the Atlantic Coast Line: 1830-1930.* Wilmington, NC: Wilmington Railroad Museum, 1990. 28 p.

6755. Kerr, Arnold D. *Effect of torsional fastener resistance on the lateral response of a rail-tie structure.* Washington, DC: Federal Railroad Administration, Office of Research and Development, 1978. 21 p. (*FRA/ORD-78-35.*)

6756. _____. *Fundamentals of railway track engineering.* Omaha, NE: Simmons-Boardman Books, Inc., 2003. 1 v.

6757. _____. *The lateral buckling of railroad tracks due to constrained thermal expansions/* Washington, DC: Federal Railroad Administration, Office of Research Development and Demonstrations, 1975. 37 p.

6758. _____. *On the stability of the railroad track in the vertical plane.* Washington, DC: Federal Railroad Administration, 1972. 36 l.

6759. _____. *On the stress analysis of rails and ties/* Washington, DC: U.S. Department of Transportation, Federal Railroad Administration; Princeton University, Department of Civil and Geological Engineering, 1976. 40 p. (*FRA/OR&D-76-284.*)

6760. _____. *Railroad track mechanics and technology: proceedings of a symposium held at Princeton University, April 21-23, 1975.* New York, NY: Pergamon Press, 1978. 431 p.

6761. _____. *Thermal buckling of straight tracks fundamentals, analysis and preventive measures.* Washington, DC: Federal Railroad Administration, 1978. 50 p. (*FRA-ORD-78-49*)

6762. _____, Alain L. Kornhauser. *Productivity in U.S. railroads: proceedings of a symposium held at Princeton University, July 27-28, 1977.* Elmsford, NY: Pergamon Press, 1980. 143 p. (*Pergamon policy studies on business.*)

6763. Kerr, Charles, Jr., John S. Newton, W.A. Brecht. *The geared-turbine steam locomotive* / Pittsburgh, Pa., Westinghouse Electric & Manufacturing Company, 1945. 8 p.

6764. _____, T.J. Putz, T.L. Weybrew. *Operating record of the Westinghouse-Baldwin gas turbine locomotives.* New York, American Society of Mechanical Engineers, 1952. 8 l.

6765. Kerr, Duncan J. *The story of the Great Northern Railway Company, and James J. Hill.* Princeton? NJ: Newcomen Society, American Branch, 1939. 43 p.

6766. Kerr, James W. *General Electric advanced generation diesel-electric and electric locomotives.* Alburg, VT; Montreal, Delta Publications Associations Division, DPA-LTA Enterprises, 1989. 250 p.

6767. _____. *General Motors advanced generation diesel-electric and electric locomotives: the second and third generation locomotives.* Alburg, VT; Montréal, Delta Publications Associates, DPA-LTA Enterprises, 1987. 240 p.

6768. _____. *General Motors: first generation diesel-electric locomotives.* Montreal, Alburg, VT: Delta Publications, 1982. 2 v.

6769. _____. *General Motors phenomenal SD40 series diesel-electric locomotives.* Montreal, Delta Publications, 1980. 100 p.

6770. _____. *Illustrated modern freight cars of North America.* Alburg, VT: Montreal: DA-LTA, 1982. 119 p.

6771. _____. *The 1989 locomotive rosters: U.S.A. & Canada: after mega-mergers and renumberings of the 20 largest systems.* Alburg, VT: DPA-LTA Enterprises, 1989. 1 v.

6772. Kerr, John Leeds. *A brief analysis and history of the Kansas City, Mexico, and Orient Railway* / New York: Railway Research Society, 1928. 4 p.

6773. _____. *History of Western railroads.* Seattle, Railway & Marine News Publishing Company, 1924. 33 p.

6774. _____. *The railroad problem in 1932.* New York: Railway Research Society, 1932. 28 l. (Prepared for the National Transportation Committee [U.S.].)

6775. _____. *The story of a Southern carrier: the Louisville & Nashville; an outline history.* New York, Young & Ottley, Inc., 1933. 67 p.

6776. _____. *The story of a western pioneer: The Missouri Pacific; an outline history.* New York, Railway Research Society, 1928. 54 p.

6777. _____. *Destination Topolobampo; the Kansas City, Mexico & Orient Railway.* San Marino, CA: Golden West Books, 1968. 270 p.

6777a. Kerr, Joseph G. *Historical development of the Louisville and Nashville Railroad system.* Louisville: s.n., 1926. 195 p.

6778. Kerr, Joseph G. *Supplement to Historical development of the Louisville and Nashville Railroad system.* Louisville, KY: Louisville and Nashville Railroad Company, 1928. 38 l. Covers the period, June 30, 1917 to December 31, 1927.

6778a. Kerr, K. Austin. *American railroad politics, 1914-1920.* 1965. 321 l. (Thesis, University of Pittsburgh.)

6779. Kerr, O.M. *Centennial treasury of General Electric locomotives.* Alburg, VT; Montreal, Delta Publications, 1981. 2 v.

6780. _____. *General Electric industrial locomotives, 1924-1978.* Lewiston, NY; St. Davids, ON: DPA-LTA Enterprises, 2004. 1 v.

6781. _____. *Illustrated history of General Electric locomotives.* Montreal; Alburg, VT: Delta Publications, 1979. 96 p.

6782. _____. *Illustrated treasury of Pullman-Standard railway passenger cars; since 1945.* Montreal; Alburg, VT: Delta Publications, 1981. 2 v.

6783. _____. *Illustrated treasury of the American Locomotive Company. Foreword by H. Stafford Bryant, Jr.* New York, Norton, 1990. 263 p.

6784. _____. *Illustrated treasury of the American Locomotive Company, 1837 to 1969: includes continued Bombardier production in Montreal, Canada, until 1979.* St. David's, ON: DPA-LTA Enterprises, 2001. 224 p.

6785. Kerr, K. Austin. *American railroad politics, 1914, 1920: rates, wages and efficiency.* Pittsburgh: University of Pittsburgh Press, 1968. 250 p.

6786. Kerr, Peter A. *Models for investigating train connection reliability at rail classification yards: final report.* Cambridge, MA: Department of Civil Engineering, Massachusetts Institute of Technology, 1976. 128 p. (*Department of Civil Engineering, Massachusetts Institute Of Technology, Studies in railroad operations and economics, v. 14; R76-44.)*

6787. Kerr, Robert E. *Tiedown handbook for rail movements/* 3rd ed. Newport News, VA: Military Traffic Management Command, Transportation Engineering Agency, 1995. 1 v (various pagings).

6788. Kerr, Walter Craig. *Disposal of West side railroad tracks: a report of the Merchants' Association of New York by its Committee on Disposal of West Side Railroad Tracks. November 25, 1908* / New York: Merchants' Association of New York, 1908. 19 p.

6789. Kersten, Andrew Edmund. *A. Philip Randolph: a life in the vanguard.* Lanham, MD: Rowman & Littlefield Publishers, 2007. 1 v.

6790. Kesler, Kevin, Chris Tinto. *Performance of degraded roller bearings.* Washington, DC: Federal Railroad Administration, Office of Research and Development, 1990. 114 p. (*DOT-FR-89-09.*)

6791. Kester, Scott. *The Pennsylvania Coal Company Gravity Railroad* / 2000. 129 l. (Thesis, M.A., University of Scranton.)

6792. Ketcham, Henry Hendricks. *Locomotive headlights.* Scranton, PA: 1943. 70 p.

6793. Kettering, E.W. *History and development of the 567 series General Motors locomotive engine.* La Grange, IL: Electro-Motive Division, General Motors Corporation, 1951. 83 p.

6794. *The Kettle turn: selections from Inland Empire Rail Quarterly.* Spokane, WA: Inland Empire Railway Historical Society, 1977. 28 p.

6795. Key, R. Lyle. *Midwest Florida sunliners.* Godfrey, IL: RPC Publications, 1979. 160 p.

6796. Keyes, Fred H, John W. Logan. *Experiments on the application of brakes to the truck of a locomotive.* 1893. 1 v. (Thesis, M.E., Massachusetts Institute of Technology.)

6797. Keyser, Lloyd A. *Chicago & North Western, in color.* Scotch Plains, NJ: Morning Sun Books, 1997. 2 v.

6798. Keyserling, Leon H. *The move toward railroad mergers, a great national problem.* Washington, DC: Railway Labor Executives' Association, 1962. 102 p.

6799. *The Keystone : official publication of the Pennsylvania Railroad Technical and Historical Society.* Pittsburgh: The Society, 1968-   . Quarterly. Other titles: Official Publication of the Pennsylvania Research & Information Association, Apr. 1968-Mar. 1974.

6800/ Keystone Bridge Company. *Descriptive catalogue of wrought-iron bridges; fire-proof columns and floor girders, wrought-iron roof trusses, wrought-iron turntables, pivot bridges, park bridges, suspension bridges, columns, links, and bridge bolts.* Pittsburgh, PA: s.n., 1874. 48 p.

6801. Keystone Spring and Metal Works. *Keystone Spring and Metal Works, K.W. Blackwell, manufacturer of spiral and elliptic springs, for railway cars and locomotives* / Philadelphia, Pa., s.n., 1882. 59 p.

6802. Kiang, R.L. *Railroad classification yard technology: assessment of car speed control systems.* Washington, D.C., Federal Railroad Administration; Office of Research and Development, 1980. 1 v. (*Report: FRA/ORD-80/90*)

6803. Kibbey, Mead B. *The railroad photographs of Alfred A. Hart, artist* [1816-1908] Edited by Peter E. Palmquist. Sacramento, CA: California State Library Foundation, 1996. 238 p.

6804. Kidd, Howard Carson. *Railroad consolidations and the state of Pennsylvania : a study of the probable effects of grouping of railroads proposed by the Interstate Commerce Commission upon varied interests of the Commonwealth of Pennsylvania* / Harrisburg : The Public Service Commission of the Commonwealth of Pennsylvania, 1930. 158 p.

6805. Kidd, James Franklin. *The electrification of steam railroads.* 1906. 35 l. (Thesis, University of Missouri, Columbia.)

6806. Kidwell, Edgar, Carlton F. Moore. *Wooden beams and columns; tables showing safe loads, deflections, etc., based on allowable working unit stresses recommended by "Committee on Strength of Bridge and Trestle Timbers," of the Association of Railway Superintendents of Bridges and Buildings, October, 1895 ...*/ New York, NY: Engineering News Publishing Company, 1899. 57 p.

6807. Kidwell, Mr. *Supplementary report in reply to the comments of the Secretary of War upon the minority report of the Select Committee on the Pacific Railroad.* Washington, D.C.: Cornelius Wendell, 1857. 16 p. (*House of Representatives. 34th Congress, 3d session, 1856-1857. Misc. Doc. No. 44.*)

6807a. Kieckhefer, Guy N., Thomas J. Kehoss. *Architectural styling, description and written history of the former Wisconsin Central roundhouse at Waukesha, Wisconsin.* Rosemont, IL: Wisconsin Central Ltd. 1994. 1 v. (various pagings). "Chiefly photographs."

6808. Kiefer, Paul Walter. *The Hudson type passenger locomotive.* New York : Franklin Railway Supply Co., Inc., 1929. 8 p.

6809._____. *A practical evaluation of railroad motive power.* New York, Simmons-Boardman Pub. Corp., 1948. 65 p.

6809a. Kifle, Beniam, Nathan Goodman. *Roaring Camp railroads* / Charleston, SC: Arcadia Publishing, 2013. 127 p. (Felton, CA; Santa Cruz County)

6810. Kilian, Len, Jim Odell. *Trackside in the Albany, N.Y. gateway, 1949-1974 with Gerrit Bruins.* Scotch Plains, NJ: Morning Sun Books, 1998. 127 p.

6811. Kilian, Lincoln. *A dog's life: Boomer Jack of the Northwestern Pacific.* Willits, CA: Mendocino County Museum, 1998. 24 p. (*Mendocino County Museum Grassroots History Publication, no. 18.*)

6812. Kilic, Nuri. *Historic and current economic developments of refrigerated rail transport of perishable good in the United States and Europe.* 1951. 99 l. (Thesis, M.S. in M.E., University of Texas, Austin.)

6813. Killam, Howard D. *Frisco Railway stations in Kansas.* Crete, NE: Railroad Station Historical Society, 1984. 21 p. (*Monograph, no. 11.*)

6814. _____. *Missouri-Kansas-Texas stations in Kansas* / Crete, NE: J-B Pub. Co., 1987. 19 p. (*The railway history monograph, v. 14, no. 3-4.*)

6815. _____. *Rock Island stations in Kansas.* Crete, NE: Railroad Historical Society, 1982. 15 p.

6816. Killingstad, Ralph. *Shipping point refrigeration: do our transportation facilities meet the demand of fresh fruit and vegetable industry?* New York, N.Y., American Society of Refrigerating Engineers, 1939. 5 p.

6817. Killough, E.M. *History of the Western Maryland Railway Company, including biographies of the presidents.* Revised ed. Baltimore, MD: 1940. 128 p.

6818. Kilmcr, Lawrence W. *Bradford & Foster Brook, peg leg railroad: plus trains & trolleys in McKean and Cattaraugus Counties.* Olean, NY: Lawrence W. Kilmer, 1974. 206 p.(Also: Interlaken, NY: Empire State Books, 1993. 206 p.) (Narrow gauge)

6819. _____ *Erie Railroad, 1863-1976: Bradford Branch.* Olean, NY: L.W. Kilmer, n.d. 208 p.

6820. _____ *Iron rails in Seneca land.* New Port Richey, FL: William J. Fries, 1999. 243 p.

6821. Kim, George Monte. *The Southern Pacific Railroad and the making of place and community in California.* 2004. 386 l. (Thesis, Ph.D., University of California, Santa Barbara.)

6821a. Kim, Seung Jai. *A model building concept for facilitating the application of existing railroad network simulation models*/ 1974. 193 l. (Thesis, Ph.D., University of Illinois at Urbana-Champaign.)

6821b. Kim, Sung Kun. *The experimental analysis of the fatigue life of full depth asphalt railway roadbeds.* 1983. 197 l. (Thesis, Ph.D., University of Maryland.)

6822. Kim, Sung-uk. *Accident risk and railroad worker compensation: an historical study, 1880-1945* / 1988. 174, 23 l. (Thesis, Ph.D., University of Georgia.)

6823. Kimball, John, Hollis Stambaugh. *Special report: rail emergencies.* Emmitsburg, MD: Federal Emergency Management Agency; U.S. Fire Administration, National Fire Data Center, 2003. 29 p. (*Technical report series: USFA-TR-094.*)

6823a. Kimball. Robert Haskell. *A statistical analysis of the detailed operating earnings and expenses of a railroad* / 1906. 39 l, 25 l. of plates. (Thesis, B.A., University of Illinois.)

6824. Kindelan, Joseph.. *The trackman's helper: a book of instruction for track foremen. 3rd ed., rev. and enl. With new illustrations and tables.* Chicago, IL: Roadmaster & Foremen, 1898, 1894. 281 p. (*Twentieth Century edition*: Chicago, Ill., Roadmaster and Foreman,1900. 334 p.)

6825. _____. *The trackman's helper. A pocket companion for track foremen generally* Mitchell, SD: The Mitchell Printing Company, 1888. 299 p.

6826. _____, Frederick A. Smith, F.R. Coates, Jerry Sullivan, Richard T. Dana, Alexander F. Trimble. *The trackman's helper, a handbook for foremen, supervisors and engineers.* New York, Clark Book Co., 1917. 410 p.

6827. Kindig, Richard H. *Pictorial supplement to Denver, South Park & Pacific.* Denver, Rocky Mountain Railroad Club, 1959. 467 p. (Also: Lakewood, CO: Trowbridge Press, 1986. 467 p.)

6828. _____. Ronald C. Hill. *Union Pacific 8444.* Golden, CO: Colorado Railroad Museum, 1978. 1 v.

6829. Kinert, Reed. *Early American steam locomotives: 1st seven decades, 1830-1900.* Seattle, WA; Superior Publishing Company, 1962. 158 p. (Reprint: Minneola, NY: Dover Publications, 2005. 158 p.)

6830. Kinetic Chemicals, Incorporated. *Air. conditioned train inaugurated on the C & O. : freon, is specified for new type equipment* / Wilmington, DE: Kinetic Chemicals, Inc., 1932. 5 p.

6831. _____. *Baltimore & Ohio R.R. equips cars for better air conditioning : freon, is specified for new equipment, developed and manufactured by Kinetic Chemicals, Inc.* Wilmington, DE: Kinetic Chemicals, Inc., 1932. 4 p.

6832. _____. *Illinois Central air conditions its "Daylight Special" : freon, is specified for new equipment, developed and manufactured by Kinetic Chemical Inc.* Wilmington, DE: Kinetic Chemicals, Inc., 1932. 4 p.

6833. King, Andrew. *Safety of life on railroads*/ Washington: F. & J. Rives & G.A. Bailey, reporters and printers of the debates of Congress, 1873. 13 p.

6834. King, Charles. *A tame surrender; a story of the Chicago strike.* Philadelphia, Pa., J. B. Lippincott Company, 1896. 277 p.(Pullman Strike, 1894-Fiction.)

6835. King, Cheryl S. *Union Pacific freight station, Boise, Idaho.* 1990. 127 l. (Thesis, B. Arch., University of Idaho.)

6836. King, Ed. *The A: Norfolk & Western's Mercedes of steam.* Glendale, CA: Trans-Anglo Books, 1989. 176 p.

6837. _____. *Norfolk & Western in the Appalachians: from the Blue Ridge to the Big Sandy.* Waukesha, WI: Kalmbach Publishing Co., 1998. 128 p.

6838. King, Ernest La Marr, as told by Robert E. Mahaffay. *Main line; fifty years of railroading with the Southern Pacific.* Garden City, N.Y., Doubleday, 1948. 271 p.

6839. King, Everett Edgar. *Railway signaling.* New York, McGraw-Hill Book Company, 1921. 371 p.

6840. King, Frank Alexander. *Locomotives of the Duluth, Missabe & Iron Range.* Edmonds, WA: Pacific Fast Mail, 1984. 319 p.

6841. _____. *Minnesota logging railroads: a pictorial history of the era when white pine and the logging railroad reigned supreme.* San Marino, CA: Golden West Books, 1981. 206 p.(Also: Minneapolis, University of Minnesota Press, 2003. 202 p.)

6842. _____. *The Missabe Road; the Duluth, Missabe and Iron Range Railway.* San Marino, CA: Golden West Books, 1972. 224 p. (Also: Minneapolis, University of Minnesota Press, 2003. 224 p.)

6843. _____. *Our story of steam.* Duluth? Duluth, Missabe & Iron Range Railway Company, 1961. 50 p.

6844. King, G.E. *Radiation protection aspects of the movement of radioactive liquid waste in railroad tank cars.* Richland, WA : Pacific Northwest Laboratory, 1969. 11 l. (*U.S. Atomic Energy Commission, Report no. BNWL-966.*)

6845. King, G.E., Charles Andrew Wrigley. *The New York Central Lines; examinations for firemen, first, second and third years.* Rev. ed. Toledo, Toledo Type-Setting Company, 1915. 113 p.

6846. King, John, J.G. McCullough. *Instructions for operating the Westinghouse quick-acting automatic air brake, compressed air train signal, steam heat and gas lighting system, December 1st, 1893.* New York, M.B. Brown, Railroad Printers, 1893. 48 p. (Chicago & Erie Railroad)

6847. King, Robert A. *Trails to rails: a history of Wyoming's railroads.* Casper, WY: Endeavor Books, 2003. 125 p.

6848. King, Shelden S. *The route of Phoebe Snow: a story of the Delaware, Lackawanna and Western Railroad.* Elmira Heights, NY: S.S. King, 1974. 165 p.

6849. King, Shih-Hsuan. *Railroad freight car service: control by the Car Service Division of the American Railroad Association.* 1927. 89 l. (Thesis, Ph.D., University of Pennsylvania.)

6850. King, Spencer Bidwell. *Railroads of western North Carolina.* 1936. 164 l. (Thesis, M.A., George Peabody College for Teachers.)

6851. King, Stephen L. *Locomotive gyrating warning lights.* 3d ed. Auburn, NY: S.L. King, 2001. 1 v.

6852. King, Steve. *Clinchfield country.* Silver Spring, MD: Old Line Graphics, 1988. 127 p.

6853. King, William F. *The Pennsylvania tunnel franchise : some of the reasons why it should be granted* / New York : s.n., 1902. 10 p.

6854. *King's railway directory for 1867.* York, NY: A.H. King, 1867. 238 p Advertising material p. 174-238. ("Containing an official list of the officers and directors of the railroads in the United States and Canada, together with their financial condition and amount of rolling stock.")

6855. Kingsbury, Samuel. *Kingsbury's practical instructor in questions and answers for locomotive firemen, engineers and trainmen.* Sacramento, Cal.: s.n., 1893. 109 p.

6855a. Kingsbury, W.S., Jerome Madden. *The lands of the Southern Pacific Railroad Company of California : with general information on the resources of Southern California* / London : s.n., 1876. 136 p. W.G. Kingsbury, General European Agent, 41, Finsbury Pavement, London, England.

6856. Kinkaid, James. *C&NW color guide to freight and passenger equipment.* Scotch Plains, NJ: Morning Sun Books, 2008. 128 p. (v. 1-Passenger cars, cabooses and acquired roads. V. 2-Revenue freight cars.)

6857. _____. *IC/GM&O color guide to freight and passenger equipment.* Scotch Plains, NJ: Morning Sun Books, 2002. 128 p.

6858. _____. *Missouri Pacific color guide to freight and passenger equipment.* Scotch Plains, NJ: Morning Sun Books, 2004. 128 p.

6859. _____ *Penn Central color guide to freight and passenger equipment.* Scotch Plains, NJ: Morning Sun Books, 1998. 128 p.

6860. _____ *Post 1970 aggregate hoppers.* Monrovia, CA: Society of Freight Car Historians, 1993. 20 p.

6861. _____. *The Pullman-Standard builders photo collection.* Monrovia, CA: Society of Freight Car Historians, 1995. v. <2-> (*Freight cars journal; Monograph no. 67.*)

6862. _____. *Pullman-Standard color guide to freight equipment: the decade of color, 1960-1970.* Edison, NJ: Morning Sun Books, 1995. 127 p.

6863. _____. *Southern Railway color guide to freight and passenger equipment.* Edison, NJ: Morning Sun Books, 1996. 102 p.

6864. _____. *Wabash Nickel Plate DT&I: color guide to freight and passenger equipment.* Scotch Plains, NJ: Morning Sun Books, 2007. 128 p.

6864a. Kinney, John J. *Captain Jack and the Dalton Gang: the life and times of a railroad detective.* Lawrence: University press of Kansas, 2005. 270 p.

6865. Kinsey, Geo. *The cattle transportation problem/* Cincinnati, OH: Parlor Cattle Car, 1880s. 15 p.

6865a. Kinsman Block System Company. *Kinsman automatic stop for steam and electric railways /* New York: Kinsman Block System Co., 1907. 8 p.

6866. Kinzer, Howard A. *A study of the economies to be obtained by the operation of gas and oil-electric rail motor cars on the Boston and Maine Railroad /* 1933. 90 l. (Thesis, M.S., Massachusetts Institute of Technology, Department of Civil and Sanitary Engineering.)

6867. Kirby, Lynne. *Parallel tracks: the railroad and silent cinema.* Durham, NC: Duke University Press, 1997. 338 p.

6868. Kirk, George. *A history of the San Pedro, Los Angeles and Salt Lake Railroad.* 1935. 71 l. (Thesis, M.A., University of California, Berkeley.)

6869. Kirkland, D. F. *Destruction of railroads by excessive and unwise governmental regulation and strangulation.* Augusta, GA: Georgia & Florida Railway; Augusta Southern Railroad Company, 1917. 7 p.

6870. Kirkland, Edward Chase. *Men, cities and transportation; a study in New England history, 1820-1900.* Cambridge, Mass., Harvard University Press, 1948. 2 v.

6871. Kirkland, John F. *Dawn of the diesel age: the history of the diesel locomotive in America.* Glendale, CA: Interurbans Publications, 1983. 199 p.

6872. _____. *The diesel builders.* Glendale, CA: Interurban Press, 1985. 2 v. (*Interurbans special, 98, 110.*)

6873. Kirkman, Marshall Monroe. *Air brake. Supplement to "The science of railways."* New York, World Railway Pub. Co., 1900. 70 p.

6874. _____. *The air brake, its construction and working* / Chicago, Cropley Phillips Company, 1917. 1 v.

6875. _____. *Baggage, express and mail business.* Chicago, World Railway Publishing Co., 1894. 406 p. (*The science of railways, v. 6.*)

6876. _____. *The Baker valve gear; supplement to Kirkman's Science of railways.* Chicago, Cropley Phillips Company, 1914. 31 p.

6877. _____. *The Baker-Pilliod valve gear; supplement to The science of railways.* Chicago, Cropley Phillips Company, 1912. 13 p.

6878. _____. *Basis of railway rates and private vs. governmental management of railroads, forming one of the series of volumes in the rev. and enl ed. of The science of railways.* New York, The World Railway Publishing Co., 1905. 350 p.

6879. _____. *Cars, their construction and handling.* Chicago, Cropley Phillips Company, 1923. 644 p. Also: New York; World Railway Pub. Co., 1907. 435, 279 p.)

6880. _____. *Examinations for firemen (New York Central Lines) Supplement o the volume Engineer's and firemen's handbook of the Science of railways.* Chicago, Cropley Phillips Company, 1914. 92 p.

6881. _____. *The four-cylinder balanced compound locomotive* / New York, World Railway Pub. Co., 1904. 31 p.

6882. _____. *How oil is used for fuel on locomotive s*/ New York, World Railway Pub. Co., 1904. 71 p.

6883. _____. *Kirkman's "Science of railways" portfolio 1.* Chicago, Cropley Phillips Company, 1911. 1 v. plates. (Also 1915, and 1919.

6884. _____. *The locomotive* / New York, World Railway Pub. Co., 1908. 185, 246 p. (Also: Chicago, Cropley Phillips, 1917. 2 v.)

6885. _____. *Locomotive appliances* / New York, The World Railway Pub. Co., 1902. 490 p.

6886. _____. *Mallet locomotives* / Chicago, Cropley Phillips company, 1914. 296 p.

6887. _____ *Motive power: the locomotive and its supervision* / New York, World Railway Pub. Co., 1907. 2 v.

6888. _____. *The Pyle-National electric headlight equipments.* Chicago, Cropley Phillips Company, 1919. 24 p.

6889. _____. *Railway service: trains and stations describing the manner of operating trains, and the duties of train and station officials*/ New York: Railroad gazette, 1878. 277 p.

6890. _____. *The science of railways*. New York, The World Railway Pub. Co., 1904. 20 v. (Rev. ed. 1906-1911 19 v.)

6891. _____. *Shops and shop practice*. Rev. and enl. ed. Chicago, Ill., Cropley Philips, 1923. 2 v. (701 p.)

6892. Kirkpatrick, Ollie H. *Working on the railroad*. Philadelphia, Dorrance, 1949. 301 p.

6893. Kirkpatrick, S. Roger. *Captive cabeese in America: a reference to 7500+ caboose locations*/ Expanded 2nd ed. St. Louis, MO: American Railway Caboose Historical Educational Society, 2008. 300 p.

6894. Kirsch, Richard. *Scenic Western Maryland Railroad travel guide*. S.l., Western Maryland Chapter, National Railway Historical Association, 2000. 12 p.

6895. Kiscaden, Lester James. *A history of the Strasburg Rail Road, 1832-1862*. Lancaster, PA: Lancaster County Historical Society, 1973. 25 p. (*Journal of the Lancaster County Historical Society, v. 77, no. 1*.)

6896. Kiser, A.B. *Coal cutters, loaders, trackwork*. Scranton, Pa., International Textbook Company, 1929. 39, 59 p.

6897. Kish, A. (Andrew) *Analysis of Phase III dynamic buckling tests*/ Washington, DC: Federal Railroad Administration, Office of Research and Development, 1990. 1 v. (*DOT/FRA/ORD-89/08.*)

6897a. _____. *On the nonlinear bending-torsional equations for railroad track analyses*/ 1974. 102, 17 l. (Thesis, New York University.)

6898. _____. *Track structures performance: comparative analysis of specific systems and component performance*/ Washington, DC: U.S. Department of Transportation, Federal Railroad Administration, 1977. 142 p. (*FRA/ORD-77-29.*)

6899. _____, G. Samavedam. *Dynamic buckling tests analyses of a high degree CWR track*/ Washington, DC: Federal Railroad Administration, Office of Research and Development, 1991. ix/x, 23/24, A-6, R-1/R-2. (*DOT/FRA/ORD-90/13*)

6900. _____, _____, D.N. Wormley. *New track shift safety limits for high-speed rail applications*. Cambridge, MA: John A. Volpe National Transportation Systems Center, 2007. 20 p.

6901. _____, _____, _____. *Influence of vehicle induced loads on the lateral stability of CWR track*/ Washington, DC: Federal Railroad Administration, Office of Research and Development, 1985. 94 p. (*DOT/FRA/ORD-85/03.*)

6902. _____, _____, David Jeong. *Analysis of thermal buckling tests on U.S. railroads/* Washington, DC: Federal Railroad Administration, Office of Research and Development, 1982. 101 p. in various pagings. (*FRA/ORD-82/45; DOT-TSC-FRA-82-6.*)

6903. _____, Theodore R. Sussmann, Michael J. Trosino. *Effects of maintenance operations on track buckling potential.* Cambridge, MA: John A Volpe National Transportation Systems Center, 2007. 6 p.
Computer file: http://www volpe. dot.gov/sdd/pubs-buckle.html

6904. Kisor, Henry. *Zephyr: tracking a dream across America.* New York, TimesBooks/Random House, 1994. 338 p.

6905. Kistler, Richard C. *Discontinued depots of Nebraska: 1919-June 30, 1970.* Crete, NE: J-B Publishing Company, 1972. 24 p.

6906. _____ *The Wymore story: a history of the Wymore Division of the Chicago, Burlington and Quincy Railroad.* 2d ed. David City, NE: South Platte Press, 1984, 1970. 64 p. (3d ed. ed.: 1987. 72 p.)

6907. _____, James J. Reisdorf. *The High Plains route: a history of the McCook Division of the Chicago, Burlington and* Quincy Railroad. 3rd ed. David City, NE: South Platte Press, 1987, 1986. 112 p.

6908. _____, Joseph C. Hardy. *Alliance and everywhere west.* David City, NE: South Platte Press, 1990. 164 p.

6909. Kistler, Stan, John R. Signor. *Stan Kistler's Santa Fe in black and white* / Midwest City, OK: Santa Fe Railway Historical and Modeling Society, 2009. 180 p.

6910. Kistler, Thelma. *The rise of railroads in the Connecticut River Valley.* Northampton, MA: The Department of History of Smith College, 1938. 289 p. (*Smith College studies in history, v. 22, no. 1-4.*)

6911. Klaiber, Teresa Lynn Martin. *Scioto Division, Norfolk & Western Railroad: life and limb, 1895-1928.* Rush, KY: Family Lineage Investigations, 2003. 270 p. (Railroad accidents and medical care)

6912. Klamka, Andrew. *The GN Fargo passenger depot.* Burnsville, MN: Great Northern Railway Historical Society, 2004. 22 p.

6913. Klamkin, Charles. *Railroadiana: the collector's guide to railroad memorabilia.* New York, Funk & Wagnalls, 1976. 274 p.

6914. Klein, Aaron E. *Encyclopedia of North American railroads.* Secaucus, NJ: Chartwell Books, 1994, c1985. 256 p.

6915. _____. *The men who built the railroads.* New York, Gallery Books, 1986. 111 p.

6916. _____. *New York Central.* New York, Bonanza Books, 1985. 128 p.

6917. Klein, Maury. *The great Richmond Terminal: a study in businessmen and business strategy.* Charlottesville, Published for the Eleutherian Mills-Hagley Foundation; University Press of Virginia, 1970. 323 p.

6918. _____. *History of the Louisville & Nashville Railroad.* New York, Macmillan, 1972. 572 p.

6919. _____. *The life & legend of E.H. Harriman.* Chapel Hill, NC: University of North Carolina Press, 2000. 521 p.

6920. _____. *The life and legend of Jay Gould.* Baltimore, MD: Johns Hopkins University press, 1986. 595 p.

6921. _____. *Source notes for Union Pacific: birth of a railroad, 1852-1893.* New York, Doubleday; Omaha, NE: Distributed by the Union Pacific Museum, 1987. 117 p.

6922. _____. *Unfinished business: the railroad in American life.* Hanover, University of Rhode Island; University Press of New England, 1994. 226 p.

6923. _____ *Union Pacific.* Garden City, NY: Doubleday, 1987. 2 v. (Reprint: Minneapolis, University Press, 2006. 2 v.)

6924. _____. *Union Pacific : the reconfiguration/* New York : Oxford University Press, 2011. 508 p.

6925. Kleihans, Frank Brasil. *Locomotive boiler construction; a practical treatise for boilermakers, boilers users and inspectors/* New York, The Norman W. Henley Publishing Company, 1912. 421 p. (2d ed. 1913. 462 p.)

6926. Klindworth, Keith A. *Impacts of rail deregulation on marketing of Kansas wheat/* Washington, DC? U.S. Department of Transportation, Office of Transportation, 1985. 52 p.

6927. _____, John A. Batson. *Economic impact of proposed Kansas rail abandonments.* Washington, D.C., U.S. Department of Agriculture, Agricultural Marketing Service, Transportation and Marketing Division, 1991. 38 p.

6928. Kline, Benjamin F.G. *Dinkies, dams, and sawdust: the logging railroads of West Central Pennsylvania: BuBois, Clearfield, Brookville, Brockway, Penfield, Ebensburg, Punxsutawney/* 2d ed. Strasburg, PA., Friends of the Railroad Museum of Pennsylvania; Pennsylvania Historical & Museum Commission, 1999. 104 p.

6929. _____. *The Heisler locomotive, 1891-1941.* Lancaster, PA., B.F.G. Kline, 1982. 199 p.

6930. _____. *"Little, old and slow" The life and trials of the Peach Bottom and Lancaster, Oxford and Southern railroads.* Lancaster, PA., B.F.G. Kline, 1985. 86 p.

6931. _____. *The odyssey of five locomotives, 1835-1965.* S.l., s.n., 1965. 14 p.

6932. _____. *"Stemwinders" in the Laurel Highlands; the logging railroads of southwestern Pennsylvania: Somerset, Fayette, Westmoreland, Cambria, Bedford, Blair counties.* Williamsport, PA: Lycoming Printing Company, 1973. 112 p. (*Logging railroad era of lumbering in Pennsylvania, no. 13.*)

6933. _____. *Tall pines and winding rivers: the logging railroads of Maryland* / S.l., s.n., 1976. 100 p. (*The logging railroad era of lumbering in Maryland.*)

6934. _____. *"Wild catting" on the mountain: the William Whitmer & Sons Company and the Whitmer-Steele Company operations in Cambria, Centre, Clearfield and Union counties, Pennsylvania and Cornwall, Rockbridge County, Virginia*/ 2d ed. Strasburg, PA: Friends of the Railroad Museum of Pennsylvania, Pennsylvania Historical & Museum Commission, 1999. 56, 4 p. (*Logging railroad era of lumbering in Pennsylvania, no. 2.*)

6935. Kline, Larry, Ted Culotta. *The postwar freight car fleet.* Chattanooga, TN: NMRA, 2006. 1 v.

6936. Klinger, Tom, Denise Klinger. *C&S high line memories and then some.* Boulder, CO: Johnson Printing, 2004. 280 p.

6937. Klingler, Karl. *Modernizing journal lubrication* / New York: American Society of Mechanical Engineers, 1953. 4, 1 p. (*ASME. Paper no. 53-A-110.*)

6937a. Klink, William Lee. *Modern passenger schedules and their development* / 1918. 47, 1 l. (Thesis, B.A., University of Illinois.)

6938. Klobucar, Barbara J. *The influence of Pullman : railroad passenger coach colors, 1900-1940* / 2000. 146 l. : 23 paint samples in pocket. (Thesis, M.A., Goucher College.)

6939. Klohn, Charles H. *Proceedings of the Conference on Joint usage of Utility and Transportation Corridors, September 24-25, 1981*/ New York, NY: American Society of Civil Engineers, 1981. 121 p.

6940. Kloop, Richard W., Steven W. Kirkpatrick, D. A. Shockey. *Damage assessment of railroad tank cars involved in accidents: phase II—modeling and validation* / Washington, DC: Federal Railroad Administration, Office of Research and Development, 2002. 99, 18 p. (*DOT/FRA/ORD-02/04.*)

6941. Klopp, Richard W., Steven W. Kirkpatrick, Donald A. Shockey. *Damage assessment of railroad tank cars involved in accidents. Phases II. Modeling and variation* / Washington, DC : Federal Railroad Administration, Office of Research and Development, 2002. 1 v. (various pagings) (*DOT/FRA/ORD-02/04.*)

6942. Klug, Adam, John S. Landon-Lane, Eugene Nelson White. *How could everyone have been so wrong? Forecasting the Great Depression with the railroads*/ Cambridge, MA: National Bureau of Economic Research, 2002. 30 p. (http://papers.nber.org/papers/W9011.pdf)

6943. Kluksdahl, James H. *Right on track : the narrow gauge trolley of the Pacific Coast Oil Company : a detailed account of industrial archaeology and railroad pioneering in Contra Costa County, California* / Pleasant Hill, CA : s.n., 1997. 30 p.

6944. Knapke, William F. *The little red caboose.* Dayton, OH: Carillon Park, 1980s. 12 p.

6945. _____. *The railroad caboose; its 100-year history; legend and lore.* With Freeman Hubbard. San Marino, CA: Golden West Books, 1968. 237 p.

6946. Knapp, Martin Augustine. *Principles of railway legislation.* Chicago: The Railway Review, 1893. 16 p.

6947. _____. *Report of the Interstate Commerce Commission on block-signal systems and appliances for the automatic control of railway trains.* Washington, DC: U.S. G.P.O., 1907. 77 p. (*59th Cong., 2d sess. Senate. Doc. 342.*)

6948. Knapp, Michael J. *A study of evaluation criteria for high speed rail corridors.* 1983. 96 l. (Thesis, M.L.A., Kansas State University)

6949. Kneafsey, James F. *Costing in railroad operations: a proposed methodology: final report*/ Cambridge, MA: Transportation Systems Division, Department of Civil Engineering, Massachusetts Institute of Technology, 1975. 72 p. (*MIT. Transportation Systems Division. MIT report, no. R75-15.*; *Studies in railroad operations and economics, v. 13.*)

6949a. _____. *An economic evaluation of mergers in the railroad industry : t he C&O/B&O consolidation ; a case study*/ 1971. 2222 l. (Thesis, Ph.D., Ohio State University.)

6950. Kneass, Strikland. *Report on the eastern terminus of the Pennsylvania Railroad.* Philadelphia : Crissy & Markley, Printers, 1859. 15 p.

6951. Kneiss, Gilbert H. *Bonanza railroads.* Stanford, Stanford University Press, 1954. 187 p.

6952. _____ *Pineapples, sugar and war.* Boston, s.n., 1957. 15 p. (Oahu Railway and Land Company)

6953. _____. *Redwood railways; a story of redwoods, picnics and commuters.* Berkeley, CA: Howell-North, 1956. 165 p. (Northwestern Pacific Railroad Company)

6954. _____. *The Virginia and Truckee Railway*. Boston, Railway and Locomotive Historical Society, Baker Library, Harvard Business School, 1938. 32 p. (*Railway & Locomotive Historical Society, Bulletin no. 45.*)

6955. Knight, J. (Jonathan), Benj. H. Latrobe. *Report upon the locomotive engines and the police and management of several of the principal rail roads in the northern and middle states, being a sequel to the Report of the 8th of January, 1838 upon railway structures*. Baltimore, Md., Lucas & Deaver, 1838. 36 p.

6956. _____, _____. *Report upon the plan of construction of several of the principal rail roads in the northern and middle states, and upon a railway structure for a new track on the Baltimore and Ohio Rail Road*. Baltimore, Md., Printed by Lucas & Deaver, 1838. 79 p.

6957. Knight, Thomas R. *Railroad branch line service in the Midwest: examining alternative approaches*. 1982. 138 l. (Thesis, M.B.A., University of Texas at Austin.)

6958. Knight, William George. *Practical locomotive management: a complete and practical work on the locomotive treating on combustion and firing, injectors, lubricators, steam gages, safety valves, air pumps and brakes*. 2d ed. rev. and enl. New York, Norman W. Henley Publishing Company, 1921. 541 p.

6959. _____. *Practical questions on locomotive operating*. Boston, E.L. Grimes Company, 1913. 246 p.

6960. Knispel, Alfred. *Die Bedeutung der Eisenbahnen für den Hafen von New York; eine verkehrsgeographische Untersuchung*. 1957. Berlin-Dahlem, Ernst-Reuter, 65 p. (Inaug.-Dis Frei Universitat, Berlin.)

6960a. Knoll, Bob. *Bob Knoll's Southern Pacific: the Southern Pacific Railroad photos of J.R. Knoll*. Pasadena, CAL Southern Pacific Historical and Technical Society, 2005. 116 p.

6961. Knoll, Charles M. *Go Pullman: life and times: the man, the company, products, services and contemporaries*. Rochester, NY: Rochester Chapter, National Railway Historical Society, 1995. 230 p.

6962. _____. *The Water Level Route: a pictorial essay, with text and illustrations*. 2d ed. Rochester, NY: Rochester Chapter, National Railway Historical Society, 1984. 64 p.

6963. Knoll, John R. *Steel trails: chasing Arizona trains in the 1950's*. Tuscon: FriendlySP, 2008. 116 p.

6964. Knous, Bill, Sue Knous. *Railroadiana: the official price guide for the year 2000 and beyond*. Denver, CO: RRM Pub., 2000. 350 p.

6965. Knowles, Henry P. *Railroad-motor carrier integrations and public policy*. 1961.

522 l. (Thesis, Ph.D., Stanford University.)

6966. Knowles, J. Harris, Frederick Humphreys. *A flight in spring in the car Lucania from New York to the Pacific coast, during April and May, 1898.* New York: Press of J.J. Little & Co., 1898. 204 p.

6967. Knudsen, Charles T. *Chicago and North Western Railway steam power, 1848-1956, classes A-Z.* Chicago, IL: Knudsen Publications, 1965. 187 p.

6968. Knudsen, Daniel C. *Modeling change in a commodity flow system: an examination of U.S. rail freight flows, 1971-1981/* 1984. 118 l. (Thesis, Ph.D., Indiana University.)

6969. Knutson, Reid Merray. *Factors influencing the repeated load behavior of railway ballast.* 1976. 183 l. (Thesis, University of Illinois.)

6969a. _____. *Material evaluation study: Ballast and Foundation Materials Research Program/* Washington, DC: Federal Railroad Administration, Office of Research and Development, 1977. 310 p. *(FRA-OR & D-77-02.)*

6970. Kobbé, Gustav. *The Central Railroad of New Jersey: an illustrated guide-book, with road maps.* New York: G. Kobbé, 1890. 108 p. 44 leaves of plates.

6971. Kobus, Ken, Jack Consoli. *The Pennsy in the steel city: 150 years of the Pennsylvania Railroad in Pittsburgh.* Upper Darby, PA: Pennsylvania Railroad Technical and Historical Society, 1997. 87 p.

6972. _____, _____. *The Pennsylvania Railroad's Golden Triangle: main line panorama in the Pittsburgh area.* Upper Darby, PA: Pennsylvania Railroad Technical and Historical Society, 1998. 91 p.

6973. Koch, Kevin W. *In-service, over-the-road testing of one car for tank car operating environment study (phase IIA) test results.* Washington, DC: Federal Railroad Administration, Office of Research and Development, 2007. 47 p. (DOT/FRA/ORD-07/23.)

6974. _____. *Tank car operating environment study: phase 1/* Washington, DC: Federal Railroad Administration, Office of Research and Development, 2007. 78 p. *(DOT/FRA/ORD-07/22.)*

6975. Koch, Michael. *The Shay locomotive: titan of the timber.* Denver, CO: World Press, 1971. 488 p.

6976. _____. *Steam & thunder in the timber: saga of the forest railroads.* Denver, World Press, 1979. 528 p.

6977. Koehler, Arthur. *Guidebook for the identification of woods used for ties and timbers.* Washington, D.C., U.S.G.P.O., 1917. 79 p. (Forest Products Laboratory)

6978. Koeller, Jeffrey, William F. Stauss. *The Milwaukee Road: in color*. Edison, NJ: Morning Sun Books, 1995- v. 1-

6979. Koenig, Alan R. *Ironclads on rails: American Civil War railroad weapons, 1861-65*. 1995. 327 l. (Thesis, Ph.D., University of Nebraska.)

6980. Koenig, Karl R. *Sugar Pine Railway*. Burlingame, CA: Chatham Pub. Co., 1971. 15 p. (Pickering Lumber Company.)

6981. _____. *Virginia & Truckee locomotives*. Burlingame, CA: Chatham Pub. Co., 1980. 87 p.

6982. Koenig, Stephan M. *South Buffalo Railway: Bethlehem Steel Company railroad operations in Lackawanna*, New York. David City, NE: South Platte Press, 2004. 120 p.

6983. _____, and others. *Trackside around Buffalo, 1953-1976, with Ray Richards, Reg Button & Devan Lawton*. Scotch Plains, NJ: Morning Sun Books, 2001. 128 p.

6984. Kogan, Dennis J., Larry Occhiello, Nelson H. McCormick. *Santa Fe's hi-level cars*. Danvers, MA: Prototype Modeler, 1975. 35 p.

6985. Koglin, Thomas John. *The advantages and liabilities of assigning freight cars to the service of automobile manufacturers: a thesis*. 1973. 156 l. (Thesis, M.S. in Transportation, Northwestern University.)

6986. Kohn, Lawrence Frederick. *Single route service advantage: making a case for end-to-end railroad mergers: a thesis*. 1981. 66 l. (Thesis, M.S. in Transportation, Northwestern University.)

6987. Kokkins, S. J. (Stephen) *Locomotive crashworthiness research : locomotive crew egress evaluation* / Washington, DC : Federal Railroad Administration, Office of Research and Development, 2002. 183 p. (*DOT/FRA/ORD-02/03.*)

6988. _____. *Safety of high-speed ground transportation systems: thermal effects and related safety issues of typical maglev steel guideways*/ Washington, DC: Federal Railroad Administration, Office of Research and Development, 1994. 89 p. (*DOT/FRA/ORD-94/10*)

6988a. Kolp, John G. *The Chicago, Burlington & Quincy Railroad roundhouse and backshop complex, Aurora, Illinois* / Iowa City: Dennett, Muessig, Ryan Associates for National Park Service, Division of Cultural Programs, 1983. 127 l.

6989. Komelski, Peter L. *26 miles to Jersey City*. Flanders, NJ: Railroad Avenue Enterprises, 1983. 82 p. (Central Railroad of New Jersey.)

6990. Koo, Won W., Thomas P. Drinka. *Alternatives for future rail grain transportation in Montana: cost and benefit analysis*. Bozeman,: Montana Agricultural Experiment Station, Montana State University, 1979. 31 p. (*Research report, no. 146.*)

6991. _____. *U,S. grain railroad rate structure and deregulation.* Fargo, Department of Agricultural Economics, Agricultural Experiment Station, North Dakota State University, 1982. 37 p. (*Agricultural economics report, no. 152.*)

6992. _____, Linda Cox. *Grain distribution by rail.* Bozeman, Montana Agricultural Experiment Station, Montana State University, 1979. 38 p. (*Bulletin, Montana Agricultural Experiment Station, Montana State University, 707.*)

6993. Kooistra, Bill, Jim Belmont, Dave Gayer. *Crossroads of the West: a photographic look at fifty years of railroading in Utah.* Pasadena, Pentrex Media Group, 1998. 160 p.

6994. Koontz, Jason. *Interbay Locomotive Shop: a tradition of excellence.* Seattle? The Shop, 1998. 80 p.

6995. Koppell, G. Oliver. *Public hearing on the inadequacy of rail freight access to New York City : May 10, 1979.* New York: EN-DE Reporting Services, 1979. 304 l. (New York (State). Legislature. Assembly. Committee on Corporation, Authorities, and Commissions.)

6996. Kornhauser, Alain L., Evdokia Adamidou. *User and system optimal formulation and solution to the shared rail fleet management problem.* Princeton, NJ: Transportation Program, Princeton University, 1986. 24 p.

6997. Kornweibel, Theodore. *No crystal stair: Black life and the Messenger, 1917-1928.* Westport CT: Greenwood Press, 1975. 306 p. (Brotherhood of Sleeping Car Porters)

6998. _____. *Railroads in the African American experience: a photographic journey/* Baltimore, MD: Johns Hopkins University Press, 2010. 557 p.

6999. Korve, Hans W. *Integration of light rail transit into city streets /* Washington, DC: National Academy Press, 1996. 1 v. (various pagings)

7000. Korpics, Frank J. *Track-train dynamics suspension dynamics /* Chicago : Association of American Railroads, Technical Center, 1976- . v. 1. Truck suspension.

7001. Koschinske, E.A. *Vapor-Clarkson steam generator for diesel locomotives, type, OK 4625.* Scranton, Pa., International Textbook Company, 1954. 87 p.

7002. Koval, Francis V. *A pioneering railroad: its first century, Chicago and North Western since 1948.* Chicago, Chicago and North Western Railway System, 1948. 24 p.

7002a. Kozak, Daniel J. *Employee job and income protection in the railroad industry/* 1981. 287 l. (Thesis, Ph.D., University of Maryland.)

7003. Kozempel, Frank C., W.G. Dorwart, Henry Owen. *The Camden & Amboy Railroad: 150 years of service.* Bryn Mawr, PA. C. Blardone, 1985. 28 p.

7004. Kozu, R. Allan. *A brief history of federal financial assistance to railroads.* Washington, DC: United States Railway Association, Office of Rail Use Valuation, 1978. 14, 27 l.

7005. Kraemer, Ken. *Buffalo Central Terminal: a photo album.* Cumberland, MD: RR Trax Studios, 2004. 71 p.

7006. _____. *The Lehigh Valley Railroad: a photo album.* Cumberland, MD: RR Trax Studios, 2008. 116 p.

7007. Krambeck, J. Wesley, William D. Edson, Jack W. Farrell. *Rock Island steam power.* Potomac, MD: Edson Publications, 2002. 139 p.

7008. Kramer, Bernardus Josephus Maria. *Dutch investments in railroads of the Southwest.* 1959. 111 l. (Thesis, M.A., University of Texas at Austin.)

7009. Kramer, Frederick A. *Building the Independent Subway.* New York, Quadrant Press, 1990. 80 p. (Eighth Avenue Line)

7010. _____. *Horseshoe Curve remembered: a cavalcade of trains and motive power/* Westfield, NJ: Bells & Whistles, 1993. 15 p.

7011. _____. *Long Island Rail Road.* Photography by John Krause. Newton, NJ: Carstens Publications, 1978. 94 p.

7012. _____. *Penny K-4's remembered.* Westfield, NJ: Bells & Whistles, 1992. 32 p.

7013. _____. *Pennsylvania-Reading Seashore Lines: an illustrated history of South Jersey's jointly-owned railroad.* Ambler, PA: Crusader Press, 1980. 104 p.

7014. _____. *Southern Railway panorama.* New York, Quadrant Press, 1978. 55 p.

7015. _____. *Subway to the World's Fair.* Westfield, NJ: Bells & Whistles, 1991. 32 p.

7016. _____. *Twilight on the narrow gauge: Rio Grande scenes of the fifties.* New York, Quadrant Press, 1978. 64 p.

7017. _____. *Unifying the subways: New York City's rapid transit system from unification to the Transit Authority.* S.l., RAE Publications, 2001. 72 p.

7018. _____, John Krause. *Cass Scenic Railroad of West Virginia.* Fredon, NJ: Carstens Publications, 1977. 40 p.

7019. Kramer, Melissa. *The inclines of Cincinnati/* Charleston, SC: Arcadia, 2009. 127 p.

7020. Kramer, Roland Laird. *The history of export and import railroad rates and their effect upon the foreign trade of the United States/* Philadelphia, PA: Printed by Westbrook Pub. Co., 1923. 120 p. (Thesis, Ph.D., University of Pennsylvania, 1923.)

7021. Kratville, William W. *Big Boy*. Omaha, NE: Barnhart Press, 1963. 96 p. (Reprint: Omaha, Kratville Publications, 1972. 96 p.; 2004, 96 p.)

7022. _____. *The Challenger locomotives*. Omaha, NE: Kratville Publications, 1980. 144 p.

7023. _____. *Golden rails*. Omaha, NE: Kratville Publications, 1965. 314 p.

7024. _____. *Little look at Big Boy*. Omaha, NE: Wm. W. Kratville, 1992. 1 v.

7025. _____. *Little look at the Challengers*. Omaha, NE: Wm. W. Kratville, 1993. 1 v.

7026. _____. *The mighty 800*. Omaha, NE: Kratville Publications, 1967. 136 p.

7027. _____. *Passenger car catalog: Pullman operated equipment, 1912-1949*. Omaha, NE: Kratville Publications, 1968. 176 p.

7028. _____. *Pullman-Standard classics*. Omaha NE: The Author, 1962. 23 p.

7029. _____. *Railroads of Omaha and Council Bluffs*. Chicago, IL: Arcadia, 2002. 128 p.

7030. _____. *Steam, steel & limiteds*. Omaha, NE: Barnhart Press, 1962. 416 p. (4th ed.: Omaha, NE: Kratville Publications, 1983. 413 p.)

7031. _____. *The war engines*. Omaha, NE: W.W. Kratville, 1986. 64 p.

7032. _____, and Harold E. Ranks. *Motive power of the Union Pacific*. Omaha, NE: Barnhart Press, 1958. 253, 73 p. (5th ed.: Omaha, NE: Barnhart Press, 1966. 147 p.)

7033. _____, _____. *Union Pacific equipment*. Omaha, NE: Kratville Pub. Co., 1969. 143 p.

7034. _____, _____. *Union Pacific locomotives*. Omaha, NE: Barnhart Press, 1960. 2 v.

7035. _____, John E. Bush. *The Union Pacific type: the story of the Union Pacific's three cylinder locomotives*. Omaha, NE: AutoLiner, 1990-1995. 2 v.

7036. Kratz, Charles G. *American railroad china, image and experience: the Jay W. Christopher transportation china collection*. Valparaiso, IN: Brauer Museum of Art, Valparaiso University, 2008. 71 p.

7037. Kraus, George. *High road to Promontory; building the Central Pacific (now the Southern Pacific) across the High Sierra*. Palo Alto, CA: American West Pub. Co., 1969. 317 p.

7037a. Krause, John. [Photograph collection] .5 linear ft. 51 photographic prints.

Location: Denver Public Library.

7038. Krause, John, Donald Duke. *American narrow gauge*. San Marino, CA: Golden West Books, 1978. 238 p.

7039. _____, Ed Crist. *Baltimore & Ohio heritage, 1945-1955*. Newton, NJ: Carstens Publications, 1986. 48 p. (*Carstens heritage series, 2.*)

7040. _____, _____. *The final years: New York, Ontario & Western Ry.* Fredon, NJ: Carstens Publications, 1977. 98 p.

7041. _____, _____. *Lackawanna heritage, 1947-1952*. Newton, NJ: Carstens Publications, 1986. 48 p. (*Carstens heritage series, 1.*)

7042. _____, _____. *Susquehanna: New York, Susquehanna & Western RR*. Newton, NJ: Carstens Publications, 1991. 98 p.

7043. _____, Fred Bailey. *Trains of northern New England*. New York, Quadrant Press, 1977. 96 p.

7044. _____, H. Reid. *Rails through Dixie*. San Marino, CA: Golden West Books, 1970. 176 p.

7045. _____, Ross Grenard. *Colorado memories of the narrow gauge circle*. Newton, NJ: Carstens Publications, n.d. 130 p.

7046. _____, _____. *The Overland Route: Union Pacific Railroad*. Newton, NJ: Carstens Publications, n.d. 82 p.

7047. Krauss-Maffei AG. *Operating manual road locomotives, model ML4000C'C*. Milwaukee, Old Line Publishers, 1963. 1 v.

7048. Krauter, Allan I., Richard L. Smith. *A methodology for evaluating the maintenance of high speed passenger train trucks* / Washington, DC : Federal Railroad Administration, 1978. 1 v. (various pagings). (*FRA/ORD-78/73*.)

7049. Krawczyk. *The City of Louisville and the Louisville and Nashville Railroad Company, 1850-1855*. 1978. 170 l. (Thesis, M.A., University of Louisville.)

7050. Kresse, Alfred L., Carl W. Schaver. *Chesapeake & Ohio freight cars, 1937-1965*. Clifton Forge, VA: Chesapeake & Ohio Historical Society, 1996- (v. 1- Hopper and gondola cars.)

7051. Krick, Charles S. *Review of the deck span of the iron truss bridge of the Central R.R. of New Jersey over the Lehigh River at Easton, Pa.* 1887. 63 l. (Thesis, Department of Civil Engineering, Lafayette college (Easton, Pa.))

7052. Krieger, J.L., Glen Icanberry. *Valley Division vignettes*. Hanford, CA: Valley Rail

Press, 1983. 254 p. (AT&SF, Central Valley, California.)

7053. Krieger, Karen Lynn. *Time on a chain: railroaders, technological change and time.* 1991. 84 p. (Thesis, M.S., Utah State University.)

7054. Krieger, Michael J. *Where rails meet the sea: America's connections between ships & trains.* New York, MetroBooks, 1998. 176 p.

7055. Krist, Gary. *The white Cascade: the Great Northern Railway disaster and America's deadliest avalanche.* New York, Henry Holt and Company, 2007. 336 p.

7056. Krolick, Reuben Harrison. *A study of the changing economic status of skilled occupations: railroad engineers and airline pilots.* 1966. 347 l. (Thesis, Ph.D., Stanford University.)

7057. Kroner, Jack L. *Minor disputes under the Railway Labor Act: a critical appraisal.* 1962. 168 l. (Thesis, S.J.D., New York University.)

7058. Krueger, Frederick J. *Freight car equipment; a reference book for car men on freight car work* / Detroit, s.n., 1910. 202 p.

7058a. Krug, James N. *Benjamin Franklin Yoakum and the St. Louis, Brownsville, and Mexico Railroad.* 1999. 81 l. (Thesis, M.A., Texas A&M University, Kingsville.)

7059. Kruttschnitt, Julius. *The operating organization of the Union Pacific and Southern Pacific systems.* Chicago: s.n., 1909. 1 v.

7059a. _____. *Supplement to Remedial railroad legislation, 1919 : containing testimony before Senate Committee on Interstate Commerce* / New York : Association of Railway Executives, 1919. 98 p.

7060. Kubat, Tim A. *Locomotives and motor cars of the M&NA.* Springfield, MO: Quick Print, 2004. 106 p. (Missouri and North Arkansas Railroad.)

7061. Kübeck von Kübau, Maximillian. *Reiseskizzen aus den Vereinigten Staaten von Nordamerika...Amerikanisches Communications-Wesen. Mit mehreren Holzschnitten.* Wien, C. Gerold's Sohn, 1872. 2p. 66, 2 p.

7062. Kudish, Michael. *Railroads of the Adirondacks: a history.* Fleischmanns, NY: Purple Mountain Press, 1996. 496 p.

7063. _____. *Where did the tracks go: following railroad grades in the Adirondacks.* Saranac Lake, NY: Chauncy Press, 1985. 148 p.

7064. _____. *Where did the tracks go in the central Adirondacks?* Fleishmanns, NY: Purple Mountain Press, 2007. 1 v. (*Mountain railroads of New York State, v. 2.*)

7065. _____. *Where did the tracks do in the eastern Adirondacks?* Fleishmanns, NY:

Purple Mountain Press, 2007. 1 v. (*Mountain railroads of New York State, v. 3.)*

7066. _____. *Where did the tracks go in the western Adirondacks?* Fleishmanns, NY: Purple Mountain Press, 2005. 263 p. (*Mountain railroads of New York State, v. 1.*)

7066a. _____. *Where did the tracks go in the eastern Adirondacks?* Fleishmanns, NY: Purple Mountain press, 2011. (*Mountain railroads of new York State, v. 4.*)

7067. Kuebler, William R. *The Vista Dome North Coast Limited: the story of the Northern Pacific Railway's famous domeliner.* Hamilton, MT: Oso Pub., 2004. 333 p.

7068. Kuehn, George I. *Enginemen stress and fatigue: pilot study*/ Washington, DC: Federal Railroad Administration, 1992. 26, 46 p. (*FRA-ORD-92-17.*)

7069. Kuhler, Otto. *Appeal design in railroad equipment.* New York, New York Railroad Club, 193-? 15 p. (Reprint: Official proceedings, New York Railroad Club, Nov. 1, 1935.)

7070. _____. *My iron journey: an autobiography of a life with steam and steel.* Denver, Intermountain Chapter, National Railway Historical Society, 1967. 244 p.

7071. Kujawa, Roger. *Toledo, Peoria & Western in color.* Kutztown, PA: Morning Sun Books, 2006. 128 p.

7072. Kullman, Brian Charles. *A model of rail/truck competition in the intercity freight market: final report.* Cambridge, MA: Department of Civil Engineering, School of Engineering, Massachusetts Institute of Technology, 1973. 316 l. (*Studies in railroad operations and economics, v. 15.; M.I.T. Department of Civil Engineering, MIT report, no. R74-35, Studies in railroad operations and economics.*)

7073. Kulp, Randolph. *History of Lehigh and New England Railroad Company.* Allentown, PA: Lehigh Valley Chapter, National Railway Historical Society, Inc., 1972. 144 p.

7074. _____. *History of Mack rail motor cars and locomotives.* Allentown, PA: Lehigh Valley Chapter, National Railway Historical Society, 1959. 68 p.

7075 _____. *Railroads in the Lehigh River Valley: steam operations 1836-1953.* Allentown, PA: Lehigh Valley Chapter, National Railway Historical Society, Inc., 1956. 44 p. (Rev. ed.: 1996. 128 p.)

7075a. Kulpa, Algis R. *Design stress analysis of railroad rails*/ 1994. 101 l. (Thesis, (M. Eng.), Cooper Union for the Advancement of Science and Art.)

7076. Kuniyasu, Uichi. *A modern gas-electric motor car.* 1909. 34 l. (Thesis, E.E., University of Washington.)

7077. Kunkle, H. *Reefer refrigerator systems for meat transportation.* St. Joseph, American Society of Agricultural Engineers, 1976. 11 p. (*Papers. ASAE, no. 6004.*)

7078. Kupka, P.F. *Amerikanische Eisenbahnen*/ Wien, Lehmann & Wentzel, 1877. 108 p.

7079. Kurtz, C.M. *Track and turnout engineering. A handbook on design details of railroad turnouts and crossings, with mathematical treatments of track layouts and connections.* New York, NY: Simmons-Boardman, 1945. 461 p. (Originally published in 1910 as: *Modern location of standard turnouts.*)

7080. Kurz, Frank. *Identification and categorization of accidents and injuries in cabs of locomotives: summary report.* Silver Springs, MD: Central Technology, Inc., 1972. 12, 55 l.

7081. Kusner, George S., Nicholas Seman. *Pennsylvania Railroad compendium: freight car lettering arrangements.* New Cumberland, PA: Middle Division, 1989-   . v. 1 no. 1. 1954-1968.

7082. Kvasnicka, Robert M. *The Trans-Mississippi West, 1804-1912.* Washington, D.C.: National Archives and Records Administration, 1993-   v. >1-4 in 6.< (Pt. 4—A guide to records of the Department of the Interior for the territorial period. Sec. 1. Records of the Offices of the Secretary of the Interior and the Commissioner of Railroads.)

7083. Kwon, Yong Woo. *Differential pricing in rail transport of wheat in Kansas after rail deregulation: a pooled cross-sectional time-series analysis.* 1992. 119, 3 l (Thesis, Ph.D., Kansas State University)

7084. Kyper, Frank. *Narrow gauge to Boston: a nostalgic window on the Boston, Revere Beach & Lynn Railroad.* David City, NE: South Platte Press, 2010. 112 p.

7084a. _____. *The railroad that came out at night: a book of railroading in and around Boston.* Brattleboro, VT: S. Greene Press, 1977. 160 p.

7085. _____. *A ramble into the past on the East Broad Top Railroad, Rockhill Furnace, Pennsylvania. Official EBT souvenir booklet.* Rockhill Furnace, PA: East Broad Top Railroad and Coal Company, 1971. 62 p.

7086. _____. *The rise and abrupt fall of the Rutland Railroad.* Rutland, VT: Rutland Historical Society, 1986. 15 p. (*Rutland historical society quarterly, v. 16, no. 1.*)

L

7087. *L & N and NC&StL memories*. St. Louis, MO: Terminal Railroad Association of St Louis Historical and Technical Society, 2001. 43 p. (*Newsletter*. Issue 57-58, Winter/Spring 2001.)

7088. *L & N magazine*. Louisville, KY: Louisville and Nashville Railroad, 1939-1970s. Bimonthly. Monthly, 1939- ; Bimonthly, 1972-

7089. *L & N magazine* / Louisville, KY: Louisville & Nashville Railroad Historical Society, 2005-   . Quarterly. Merger of Dixie line, Old reliable (Louisville, Ky.), and: Company store. (< Dixie line; Old reliable; Company store.)

7090. La Salle Extension University. *Atlas of traffic maps*. Prepared by Wayne Butterbaugh. Chicago, La Salle Extension University, 1925. 184 p.

7091. Labaree, Benjamin. *New Budd diesel railroad car RDC with torque converter transmission* / New York : Society of Automotive Engineers, 1950. 15 p. 4 leaves of plates. "For presentation at the SAE National Diesel Engine meeting. Hotel Knickerbocker, Chicago, November 2-3, 1950."

7092. Labbe, John T., and Peter J. Replinger. *Logging to the salt chuck: over 100 years of railroad logging in Mason County, Washington: pictorial history of Simpson Timber Company associated logging railroad operations including Arcata & Mad River Railroad*. Seattle, WA: North West Short Lines, 1990. 187 p.

7093. _____, Vernon Goe. *Railroads in the* woods. Berkeley, CA: Howell-North, 1961. 269 p. (Also: Arlington, WA: OSO Pub. Co., 1995. 258 p.)

7094. *Labor/management/public policy agency cooperation for railroad employee training: conference proceedings, Federal Railroad Administration Conference, Jan. 31 through Feb. 2, 1978, Clayton Inn, St. Louis, MO*. Washington, DC: U.S. Federal Railroad Administration, 1978. 359 p.

7095. Labra, John J. *An elastically stressed railroad track on an elastic continuum subjected to a moving load*. Washington, DC: Federal Railroad Administration; New York University, Department of Aeronautics and Astronautics, 1974. 30 p. (NYU-AA-72-37.)

7096. Lacher, Walter S. *Cincinnati's new Union Terminal now in service*. Cincinnati, Merton Co., 1996, 1933. 1 v.

7097. Lachatanere, Diana. *Blacks in the railroad industry collection, 1946-1954*. Wilmington, DE: Scholarly Resources Inc., 1995. 1 microfilm reel, 35 mm. ("Microfilmed from collections in the Schomburg Center for Research in Black Culture, New York Public Library.)

7097a. Lachaussee, Jerry G. *L & N stations in Jackson County, Mississippi*. Jacksonville, FL:[i.e. Mobile, AL]: The Author, 1986. 18 l.

7098. Lacher, Walter S. *Noteworthy passenger terminal completed at Chicago: Union Station provided for Pennsylvania, Burlington, St. Paul and Alton roads* / Bristol, CT: Simmons-Boardman, 1925. 100 p.
v
7099. Laciak, John A. *Private railroad hopper cars (chemical/plastic) : an analysis of leasing versus ownership* / 1974. 18 l. American Society of Traffic and Transportation, Inc.)

7100. Lackawanna Iron and Steel Company. *The Lackawanna Iron & Steel Co.: sections of rails and splice bars*. Scranton? Pa., The Company? 1899. 81 p.

7101. *Lackawanna route in central New York*. Marcellus, Central New York Chapter, National Railway Historical Society, 1977. 32 p.

7102. Lackawanna Steel Company. *Rails and fastening, 1916*. Lackawanna, NY: Lackawanna Steel Company, 1915. 146 p.

7103. Laconia Car Company. *Laconia car Company : manufacturers of all types of steam and electric railway cars for freight and passenger service : car trucks, malleable iron castings, grey iron castings, car forgings, car pressings*. Laconia, NH: Laconia Car Company, 1917. 21 l.

7104. Ladd, Dwight R. *Cost data for the management of railroad passenger service*. Boston, Harvard University, Graduate School of Business Administration, Division of Research, 1957. 345 p.

7105. Ladd, Harry. *U.S. railroad traffic atlas*. Orange, CA: Ladd Publications, 1995. 98 p.

7106. Ladenheim, Jules C. *The Jarrett-Palmer Express of 1876: coast to coast in eighty-three hours*. Westminster, MD: Heritage Books, 2008. 89 p.

7107. Ladner, Hubert. *Ride this train: people of the Piney Woods*. Bloomington, IN: 1stBooks Library, 2003. 142 p. (Mississippi Southern Railroad)

7107a. Lafferty, Maude Ward. *A pioneer railway of the West*. Lexington, KY: University of Kentucky, College of Mechanical and Electrical Engineering, 1916. 29 p. (Lexington and Ohio Rail Road Company; Louisville and Nashville Railroad Co.)

7108. Lai, Yung-Cheng. *Increasing railway efficiency and capacity through improved operations, control and planning*. 2008. 173 l. (Thesis, Ph.D., University of Illinois at Urbana-Champaign.)

7109. Lake Shore and Michigan Southern Railway Company. *Dimensions and classification of the locomotives of the Lake Shore & Michigan Southern Railway*

Company. Cleveland, s.n., 1900. 1 v.

7110. _____. *Dimensions and classification of locomotives of the Lake Shore
& Michigan Southern Railway, Lake Erie & Western Railroad, Chicago, Indiana
& Southern Railroad, Lake Erie, Alliance & Wheeling Railroad.* Cleveland, A.S.
Gilman Printing Company, 1907. 163 p.

7111. _____. *Rules for the government of the Transportation Department.* Cleveland,
A.S. Gilman Company, 1909. 144 p.

7112. _____. *Lake Shore & Michigan Southern Ry.; route of the 20th Century Limited.*
New York, New York Central Lines, 1907. 19 p.

7113. Blank entry.

7114. Laman, Jeffrey A. *Heavy axle study: impact of higher rail car weight limits
on short-line railroads.* University Park, Pennsylvania Transportation Institute,
Pennsylvania State University, 2002. 2 v. *(PTI 2001-26-1.; FHWA-PA-2001-011-97-4.)*

7114a. Lamb, Cody. *The Northern Pacific Railroad and Helena's emergence as a social,
economic, and political center, 1883-1894* / Helena: Cody Lamb, 2009. 29 p.
Bibliographical references (p. 26-29.)

7115. Lamb, J. Parker. *Classic diesels of the South: a railfan's odyssey.* Lynchburg, VA:
TLC Pub., 1997. 117 p.

7116. _____. *Evolution of the American diesel locomotive.* Bloomington, Indiana
University Press, 2007. 208 p.

7117. _____. *Katy: diesels to the Gulf.* Andover, NJ: Andover Junction Publications,
1991. 108 p.

7118. _____. *Perfecting the American steam locomotive.* Bloomington, Indiana
University Press, 2003. 197 p.

7118a. _____. *Railroads of Meridian.* Bloomington: Indiana University Press, 2012.
176 p. (Meridian, Mississippi)

7119. _____. *Steel wheels rolling: a personal journey of railroad photography.* Erin,
ON: Boston Mills Press, 2001. 176 p.

7120. Lambert, Anthony J. *Steam locomotives.* Edison, NJ: Chartwell Books, 2005. 6 p.,
36 p. of plates.

7120a. Lambert, W.C. *Design for a double track railroad bridge* / 1893. 70 l.
(Thesis, B.S., Massachusetts Institute of Technology, Department of Civil Engineering.)

7121. Lambert Point Coal Exchange. *Alphabetical list of coal mines on the Norfolk*

& Western Railway and connections, including Carolina, Clinchfield & Ohio, Interstate, Norton & Northern, with consigning pool numbers / Roanoke, VA: s.n., 1920. 19 p.

7122. Lambie, Joseph T. *From mine to market; the history of coal transportation on the Norfolk and Western Railway*. New York, New York University Press, 1954. 380 p. (*Graduate School of Business Administration, Business history series.*) (Reprint: 1980)

7123. Lambrecht, James W. *The Fond du Lac community and the Chicago and North Western Railway, 1851-1876*. 1978. 50 l. (Thesis, M.A., University of Wisconsin, Oshkosh.)

7124. Lampert, Lyndon, Robert W. McLeod. *Little Book Cliff Railway; the life and times of a Colorado narrow gauge*. Boulder, CO: Pruett Pub. Co., 1984. 191 p.

7125. Lancaster, Clay. *The far-out island railroad, 1879-1918: Nantucket's old summer narrow-gauge*. Nantucket, MA: Pleasant Publications, 1972. 135 p.

7126. Lander, F.W. *Practicability of railroad through the South Pass : letter from the Secretary of the Interior, transmitting a report from F.W. Lander, relative to the practicability of a railroad through the South Pass*. Washington, DC: U.S. G.P.O., 1858. 20 p. Submitted 13 February 1858. (*35th Congress, 1st sess. house. Ex. doc. no. 70.*)

7127. _____. *Remarks on the construction of a first class double track railway to the Pacific, and the difficulties attending its solution as a practical and scientific problem*. Washington: H. Polkinhorn, 1854. 14 p.

7128. Landis, Charles Kline. *Rails over the horizon*. Harrisburg, PA: Stackpole Sons, 1938. 171 p. (Locomotives-History)

7129. Landow, Herbert Trask. *The elimination of random car sequence in trains*. 1961. 141 l. (Thesis, M.B.A. in Transportation and Public Utilities, Graduate School of Arts and Sciences, University of Pennsylvania)

7129a. Lane, Chris. *Slim gauge cars*. 2nd ed. Newton, NJ: Carstens Publications, 2011. 128 p.

7130. Lane, James Edward. *The public interest in railroad consolidations/* 1962. 411 l. (Thesis, D.B.A. Indiana University.)

7131. Lang, A.S. (Sheffer), Carl D. Martland. *Reliability in railroad operations*. Washington, DC: Federal Railroad Administration, 1972. 88 p. (Transportation Systems Division, Department of Civil Engineering, Massachusetts Institute of Technology.)

7132. Langan, Martin Thomas. *The role of the railroad car ferry in freight transportation*. 1953. 1 v. (Thesis, M.B.A., University of New Mexico.)

7133. Langan, Timothy. *High-strength, lightweight car bodies for high-speed rail vehicles: final report for High-Speed Rail IDEA Project 32* / Washington, DC: IDEA Programs, Transportation Research Board, 2004. 24 p.

7134. Lange, E. A., L. D. Fleming, D. H. Stone. *Fracture properties of couplers and yokes*/ Chicago: Association of American Railroads, Technical Center, 1981. 25 l. (*Report. Association of American Railroads, no. R-500*)

7135. Langley, Albert M. *Atlantic Coast Line Railroad album: the standard railroad of the South*/ North Augusta, DC: Union Station, 2007. 110 p.

7136. _____. *Georgia & Florida Railroad album* / North Augusta, SC: Union Station, 2004. 56 p.

7137. _____. *Georgia short line railroad album.* North Augusta, SC: Union Station, 2005. 60 p.

7138._____. *Southern Railroad system : a history of the premier carrier of the South : the Southern serves the South.* North Augusta, SC: Union Station Pub., 2010. 140 p.

7139. Langley, Mary L., Albert M. Langley, Jr. *The railroad comes of age: the historic South Carolina Canal; and Rail Road and the Best Friend of Charleston.* Augusta, GA: Augusta Chapter, National Railway Historical Society, 1970. 26 p.

7140. Langone, Louis C. *Railroad days: memories of the Delaware, Lackawanna and Western Railroad and Erie-Lackawanna Railway Company, the Utica Division/Branch.* Waterville, NY: Hickory Hill Books, 2006. 204 p.

7141. Langsdorf, Robert Gordon. *Railroad freight car shortages* / 1974. 244 l. (Thesis, M.A., San Diego State University.)

7142. Langstroth, Charles S., Wilson Stilz. *Railway co-operation: an investigation of railway traffic associations and a discussion of the degree and form of co-operation that should be granted competing railways in the United States.* Philadelphia, University of Pennsylvania, 1899. 210 p. (Publications of the University of Pennsylvania. Series in political economy and public law, no. 15.)

7143. Laning, Paul F. *The history of the Lake Shore and Michigan Southern Railway in Ohio.* 1938. 95 l. (Thesis, M.A., Ohio Sate University.)

7144. Lanning, Harold K. *Electrical equipment of diesel locomotives.* Scranton, Pa., International Textbook Company, 1945. 2 v.

7145. Lanning, Steven G. *Exploiting limited time series: estimating a railroad firm's cost function using interpolation and distribution* / 1981. 143 l. (Thesis, Ph.D., Northwestern University.)

7146. Lansing, G. L. *Relations between the Central Pacific Railroad Company and the United States Government. Summary of facts.* Francisco: H.S. Crocker & Company, 1869. 70 p.

7147. Lanz, Daniel J., Elizabeth R. Holmes, Candice Dexheimer. *Railroads of southern and southwestern Wisconsin: development to decline.* Monroe, Wis., D. Lanz., 1986. 186 p.

7148. Lanza, Gaetano. *Details of an eight-wheel locomotive: plates.* Boston, J.S. Cushing, 1892. 22 l. of plates

7149. _____. *Details of an eight-wheel locomotive: text.* Boston, J.S. Cushing, 1892. 33 p.

7150. _____. *Heating passenger cars by steam from the locomotive.* Boston, Board of Railroad Commissioners, 1888. 27 p.

7151. _____. *Notes on locomotive engineering.* Boston, s.n., 1890? 2 v.

7152. _____. *The progress in testing full-size pieces under practical conditions; together with locomotive testing in the United States.* Philadelphia, J.B. Lippincott Co., 1912. 1 v.

7153. Lanzilotta, Edward J., Thomas B. Sheridan. *Human factors phase III: effects of train control technology on operator performance/* Washington, DC: Federal Railroad Administration, 2005. 72 p. (*DOT/FRA/ORD-04/18.*)

7154. _____, _____. *Human factors phase IV: risk analysis tool for new train control technology/* Cambridge, MA: John A. Volpe National Transportation Systems Center, 2005. 78 p. (DOT/FRA/ORD-04/17)

7155. Lapp, Charles Joseph. *An empirical study of some relationships between technological innovations and organizational characteristics in eight railroads.* 1966. 169 l. (Thesis, M.S., Northwestern University.)

7156. Laramie, Hahn's Peak, and Pacific Railway Company. *L.H.P. and P. Ry. standard practice.* S.l., s.n., 1910s. 30 l.

7157. _____. *Laramie, Hahns Peak and Pacific Railway System : the direct gateway to southern Wyoming, northern Colorado, and eastern Utah.* Laramie, Wyo : The Company, 1910? (Boston : Tudor Press) 204 p.

7158. Lardner, Dionysius. *Investigation of the causes of the explosion of the locomotive engine, "Richmond," near Reading, Pa. on the 2d Sept. 1844.* New York, Herald Book and Job Printing Office, 1844. 23 p.

7159. _____. *Railway economy : a treatise on the new art of transport, its management prospects, and relations, commercial, financial, and social : with an exposition of the practical results of the railways in operation in the United Kingdom, on the continent, and in America.* New York, NY: Harper & Bros., 1850. 442 p.

7160. Larimer, James McCormick. *Bucyrus, the railroad wrecker*/Muskogee, Okla., Muskogee Print. Co., 1909. 96 p.

7161. Larkin, F. Daniel. *Pioneer American railroads: The Mohawk and Hudson & the Saratoga and Schenectady.* Fleischmanns, NY: Purple Mountain Press, 1995. 95 p.

7162. Larkin, George V. *Operating and financial policy of the New York, New Haven and Hartford Railroad, 1921-1926* / 1928. 45, xliv leaves (Thesis, B.S., Massachusetts Institute of Technology, Department of Business & Engineering Administration.)

7163. Larkin, Michael Joseph. *Moral aspects of railroad valuation* / 1927. 105 p. (Thesis, Ph.D., Catholic University of America.)

7164. Larrabee, William. *The railroad question; a historical and practical treatise on railroads, and remedies for their abuses.* Chicago, IL: The Schulte Publishing Company, 1893. 457, xvii, 477-488 p.

7165. Larson, John Lauritz. *Bonds of enterprise: John Murray Forbes and western development in America's railway age.* Iowa City, University of Iowa Press, 2001. 257 p.

7166. _____. *John Murray Forbes and the Burlington Route: enterprise and culture in the railway age, 1813-1898.* 1981. 392 l. (Thesis, Ph.D., Brown University.)

7167. Larson, Robert K. *Effect of worn brake components on brake forces in a freight car brake rigging.* Washington, DC: Federal Railroad Administration, Office of Research and Development, 1992. 154 p. (*FRA/ORD-92/16.)*

7168. _____, Britto R. Rajkumar. *Controlled tank car impact tests.* Washington, DC: Federal Railroad Administration, Office of Research and Development, 1992. 79 p. (*FRA/ORD-92/28.*)

7169. _____, M.N. McCulloch, J.C. Davis. *Field product removal methods for tank cars.* Washington, DC: Federal Railroad Administration, Office of Research and Development, 1993. 162 p. /*FRA/ORD-92/27.*)

7170. _____. Robert L. Florom, Britto R. Rajkumar. *Field testing of a wayside wheel crack detection system.* Washington, DC: Federal Railroad Administration, Office of Research and Development, 1992. 82 p. (*FRA/ORD-92/07.*)

7171. Larson, William G. *Aluminum/cold temperature tank car puncture resistance tests: data report.* Washington, DC: Federal Railroad Administration, Office of Research and Development, 1992. 112 p. (*FRA/ORD-92/29.)*

7172. _____. *Fire tests on insulation for aluminum tank cars : an evaluation of glass fiber, ceramic fiber, and mineral fiber materials in torch-fire and pool-fire environments*

/ Washington, DC : Federal Railroad Administration, Office of Research and Development, 1987. 28 p. (*FRA/ORD-87/04.*)

7173. Lash, Jeffrey N. *Destroyer of the iron horse: General Joseph E. Johnston and Confederate rail transport, 1861-1865.* Kent, OH: Kent State University Press, 1991. 228 p.

7174. *The last spike is driven.* S.l., Utah Historical Quarterly; Golden Spike Centennial Celebration Commission, 1969. 143 p.(Reprint: *Utah Historical Quarterly, v. 37 (1), Winter 1969.*)

7175. Lathrop, Gilbert A. *Little engines and big men.* Caldwell, Idaho, Caxton Printers, 1954. 326 p. (Colorado narrow gauge)

7176. _____. *Rio Grande glory days.* San Marino, CA: Golden West Books, 1976. 352 p.

7177. Latimer, Charles. *Profiles, maps and alignment of main tracks, yards, switches and side tracks of New York, Pennsylvania & Ohio Rail Road and its branch lines : together with information referring to bridges, water supply, railroad and road crossings, culverts, grades and curves* / New York : s.n., 1883. 1 v.

7178. Latimer, James Brandt. *Railway signaling in theory and practice.* Chicago, Mackenzie-Klink Publishing Company, 1909. 420 p.

7179. Latrobe, Benj H. *A letter on the railway gauge question.* New York, George F. Nesbitt, 1873. 44 p.

7180. _____. *Report on the preliminary surveys made for the Cincinnati, Hillsborough and Parkersburg Railway, the Ohio link in the through line from Baltimore to St. Louis.* Cincinnati, Cincinnati Gazette Co Print., 1852. 45 p.

7181. _____. *Report upon the surveys for the extension of the Baltimore and Ohio Rail Road from its present termination near Harper's Ferry on the Potomac to Wheeling and Pittsburg on the Ohio River.* Baltimore, Printed by Lucas & Deaver, 1838. 1 v.

7182. Latrobe Steel Company. *Tires for locomotive and car wheels; weldless rolled steel flanges, forged and rolled steel,, crusher rings.* Philadelphia, Latrobe Steel Company, n.d. 14 p.

7183. Latta, Samuel W. *Rest houses for railroad men. How the railroad men regard such conveniences; a model hospital car.* New York, National Civic Federation, Welfare Department, 1906. 29 p. (*National Civic Federation. Welfare Department ,pamphlet no. 5.*)

7184. Lauck, W. Jett. *Financial performance of American railroads*/ Chicago, United States Labor Board, 1921. 4 pt, in 5. (His Before the United States Railroad Labor Board, Exhibit no. [6].)

7185. _____. *Inadequacies of railway management. Prepared by Bureau of Research, Railway Employees' Department, American Federation of Labor. Presented by W. Jett Lauck, in behalf of B.M. Jewell, president, Railway Employees' Department, American Federation of Labor.* Chicago, IL: 1921. 4 pts.

7186. _____. *Industrial relations on railroads prior to 1917; presenting evidence relating to certain conditions existing under non-contractual relations in 1899-1900 and on the Pennsylvania Railroad in 1914-1915.* Chicago, IL: American Federation of Labor; Railway Employees Department, 1921. 36 p.

7187. _____. *Occupation hazard of railway shopmen.* Chicago, IL: s.n., 1921. 14 p. (American Federation of Labor; Railway Employees Department; United States Railroad Labor Board.)

7188. _____. *The unity of the American railway system.* Chicago: Railway Employees' Department, American Federation of Labor, 1921. 31 p.

7189. _____, C.S. Watts. *Railroad boards of labor adjustment.* Chicago: Railway Employees' Department, American Federation of Labor, 1921. 13 p.

7190. Laudig, J.J. *What causes car journals to burn off?* New York : American Society of Mechanical Engineers, 1953. 4 , 1 p.

7191. Laughlin, Rosemary. *The Pullman strike of 1894 : American labor comes of age* / Greensboro, NC: Morgan Reynolds, 1999. 112 p.

7192. Laundy, J. H. *The problem of railway passenger fares and train services.* Chicago: Davies, 1949. 18 p.

7193. Laut, Agnes C. *The romance of the rails.* New York, R.M. McBride, 1929. 2 v. (Reprint: New York, Tudor, 1936. 590 p.; Freeport, NY: Books for Libraries Press, 1972. 2 v.)

7193a. Lautala, Pasi T. *Development of university-industry partnerships in railroad engineering education.* 2007. 231, 58 p. (Thesis, Ph.D., Michigan Technology University.)

7194. Lavallée, Omer. *Canadian Pacific to the East: the International of Maine Division.* Ottawa, ON: Bytown Railway Society, 2007. 336 p.

7195. Lavarack, Frederick Charles. *Locking; being an elementary treatise on the mechanisms in interlocking lever machines by which the movements of the levers are restricted to certain predetermined ways, rendering it impossible to operate conflicting switches and signals on railways.* East Orange, N.J., F.C. Lavarack, 1907. 83 p.

7196. Lavender, David Sievert. *The great persuader.* Garden City, NY: Doubleday, 1970.

444 p. (Collis P. Huntington)

7197. Lavis, Fred, Maurice E. Griest. *Building the new rapid transit system of New York City.* New York, 1915. 73 p.

7198. Lavoinne, E., E. Pontzen. *Les chemins de fer Amérique.* Paris, Dunod, 1880-1882. 4 v.

7199. Law, E.H. *Analysis of the nonlinear dynamics of a railway vehicle wheelset /* 1971. 54 l. (Thesis, Ph.D., University of Cleveland.)

7200._____, J.A. Hadden, N.K. Cooperrider. *General models for lateral stability analyses of railway freight vehicles.* Washington, DC: Federal Railroad Administration, 1977. 220 p. (*FRA/ORD-77-36.*)

7201. _____, N.K. Cooperrider. *Freight car dynamics: final report.* Washington, D.C.: Federal Railroad Administration; Office of Research and Development, 1981. 1 v. (Various pagings) (*FRA/ORD-81/47.*)

7202. Lawall, E.H., R.T.. Morrow. *On a proposed railroad from Bethlehem, Pa., to ore washeries and Nazareth, Pa.* 1882. 24 l. (Thesis, C.E., Lehigh University.)

7203. Lawrence, David I., David H. Kurtzman. *Report and recommendations on proposed Pennsylvania Railroad-New York Central merger.* Harrisburg : Interdepartmental Committee to Study Proposed Pennsylvania-New York Central Merger (Pa.), 1963. 12 , 1 l.

7204. Lawrence, Elrond G. *Route 66 railway: the story of Route 66 and the Santa Fe Railway in the American Southwest/* Los Angeles: Los Angeles Railroad Heritage Foundation, 2008. 176 p.

7205. Lawrence, J.J. *Rules for the government of the Transportation Department of the Allegheny Valley Railroad /* Pittsburgh : Ptd. by W.S. Haven & Co., 1870. 95 p.

7206. *Laws relating to interstate and foreign commerce.* Washington, DC: U.S. G.P.O., 1900s- (Compiled by ... Superintendent, Document Room, House of Representatives.)

7207. Lawson, Audrey Kathleen. *Charles Elliott Perkins, was he a robber baron?* 1990. 144 l. (Thesis, M.A., Western Illinois University.)

7208. Lawson, L.J., W.T. Curran. *Dual-mode locomotive application to a typical U.S. rail system. Final report.* Los Angeles, CA: Garrett, AiResearch Manufacturing Co., 1982. 61 l.

7209. Lawson, Thomas, Jr. *Logging railroads of Alabama.* Birmingham, AL: Cabbage Stack Publ., 1996. 277 p.

7210. _____. *Shay; the supplement.* Birmingham, AL: Cabbage Stack Publ., 1998. 95 p.

7211. Lay, Charles Downing. *Report to the West Side Track Committee of the West End Association on the proposed plan for changes in the New York Central Railroad along the Hudson.* New York, Office of Charles Downing Lay, 1910s. 7 p. (West End Association, New York; West Side Track Committee.) Revised 2d ed. released on May 30th, 1916. 7 p.

7211a. Layng, J.D. *Rules for the movement of trains by telegraph.* Chicago: Chicago and North-Western Railway, Office of General Superintendent, 1882. 15 p.

7212. Lazar, Joseph. *Due process in disciplinary hearings: decisions of the National Railroad Adjustment Board.* Los Angeles: Institute of Industrial Relations, University of California, 1980. 459 p. (*Monograph series, Institute of Industrial Relations, University of California, Los Angeles, 25.*)

7213. _____. *Due process on the railroads: disciplinary grievance procedures before the National Railroad Adjustment Board, First Division.* Los Angeles, Institute of Industrial Relations, University of California, 1953. 38 p. (Rev. and enl. Ed.: 1958. 66 p.)

7214. *L.C.L.* Philadelphia : Pennsylvania Railroad Company, Traffic Department, 1940-1900s. Monthly.

7215. Le Van, William Barnet. *60 miles in 60 minutes on our present roadbeds.* Philadelphia, s.n., 1883. 23 p.

7216. Lea, Albert Miller. *A Pacific railway/* Knoxville, Tenn: s.n., 1858. 16 p.

7217. Lea, Clarence Frederick, Burton K. Wheeler. *Transportation Act of 1940/* Washington, DC: U.S. G.P.O., 1940. 95 p.

7218. Leatherwood, Guy H. *Quaint tales of mail on wheels.* Ashville, OH: G.H. Leatherwood, 1993. 98 p.

7219. Leavitt, Dan. *Potential for improved intercity passenger rail service in California: study of corridors/* Berkeley: University of California Transportation Center, 1994. 113, 5 p. (*California high speed rail series. Working paper/ University of California Transportation Center, no. 222.*)

7220. Leavitt, Linda Lee. *James John Hagerman: study of a pioneer businessman.* 1980. 139, 1 l. (Thesis, M.A. University of Northern Colorado.) Colorado Midland Railway Company.

7221. Leavy, Michael. *The New York Central System.* Charleston, SC: Arcadia, 2007. 128 p.

7222. _____. *Railroads of the Civil War : an illustrated history* / Yardley, PA:

Westholme, 2010. 275 p.

7223. LeBeau, Bryan F. *Wheels and deals: railroads and the American West: a symposium, December 7, 1985, Omaha, Neb.* Kansas City, MO: National Archives and Records Administration, Kansas City Branch, 1985. 59 l.

7224. Lecht, Leonard Abe. *Experience under railway labor legislation.* New York, Columbia University Press, 1954. 254 p. Thesis, Columbia University. (*Columbia studies in the social sciences, no. 587.*) (Reprint: New York, AMS Press, 1968.)

7225. Lee, Chas. S. *The making of a railroad man: the chances for office men.* Boston: J.A. Lowell & Co., 1900. 8 p. Lehigh Valley Railroad. Reprinted from the Philadelphia Saturday Evening Post, May 13, 1900.

7226. Lee, Dan. *The L&N Railroad in the Civil War : a vital north-south link and the struggle to control it* / Jefferson, NC : McFarland & Co., 2011.

7227. Lee, Elisha. *How a railroad uses motor cars.* Philadelphia, Timken, 1926. 4 p. Reprinted from "Timken Magazine." At head of title: Pennsylvania Railroad information, July 12, 1926.

7228. _____. *Railroads and steel: the part of transportation in the growth and progress of modern industry.* Philadelphia, PA: Pennsylvania Railroad System, 1925. 9 p.

7229. Lee, Ernest L. *Railroad lingo and other outrageous language: a collection of words and phrases, popularly used by rail workers, with a few brief notes mixed in.* Ft. Worth, TX: Lee, 1983. 79 p.

7230. Lee, Harvey Shui-Hong. *Assessment of potential aerodynamic effects of high-speed passenger trains on other trains*/ Washington, DC: Federal Railroad Administration, Office of Research and Development, 1999. 43 p.

7231. _____. *Assessment of potential aerodynamic effects on personnel and equipment in proximity to high-speed train operations; safety of high-speed ground transportation systems.* Washington, DC: Federal Railroad Administration, Office of Research and Development, 1999. 43 p. (*DOT/FRA/ORD-99/11*)

7232. Lee, Ivy L. *Human nature and railroads.* Philadelphia, PA: E.S. Nash & Co., 1915. 129 p.

7233. Lee, J. L. *Lima "Super Power" steam locomotive: Texas & Pacific class I-1a, 2-10-4, no. 610.* New York, American Society of Mechanical Engineers, 1989. 12 p.

7234. _____. *Pullman sleeping car Glengyle: a National Historic Mechanical Engineering Landmark: the Age of Steam Railroad Museum, Southwest Railroad Historical Society, Dallas, Texas, August 27, 1987.* New York, American Society of Mechanical Engineers, 1987. 8 p. (*HH1287*)

7235. Lee, May. *A study of car services of railroads in the United States.* 1950. 205 l. (Thesis, M.B.A., University of Texas, Austin.)

7236. Lee, Thos R. *Rock Island westward.* Clay Center, KS: T. Lee Publications, 1998. 2 v.

7237. _____. *Turbines westward.* Manhattan, KS: T. Lee Publications, 1975. 160 p. (2d ed.: 1990. 184 p.)

7238. Lee, Tenpao. *The cost structure of U.S. railroad industry, 1980-81.* 1984. 133 l. (Thesis, Ph.D., Iowa State University.)

7238a. Lee, Thomas R., John B. Signor. *Union Pacific's M-10000 and the early Streamliner era, 1934-1941.* Cheyenne, WY: Union Pacific Historical Society; Manhattan, KS: AgPress, 2012. 208 p.

7239. Lee, Warren F. *Down along the old Bel-Del: the history of the Belvedere Delaware Railroad Company, a Pennsylvania Railroad Company.* Albuquerque, NM: Bel-Del Enterprises, 1987. 366 p.

7239a. Leech, Harper. *The freight traffic of the Chicago terminal district.* Chicago: Committee on Co-ordination of Chicago Terminals, 1927. 175 p.

7240. Leen, Daniel. *The complete freighthopper's manual for North America.* S.l., Revisionist Jackanapes Press in cooperation with Seriatim Publications, 1978. 103 p.

7241. _____. *The freight hopper's manual for North America: hoboing in the 1980s/* London, Travelaid, 1981. 95 p.

7242. _____. *The freighthopper's manual for North America: hoboing in the 21st century.* Seattle, WA: Ecodesigns Northwest Publishers, 1992. 111 p.

7243. Leet, Merwin A., James B. Hale. *Railway mail postmarks of Wisconsin and Upper Michigan.* Madison, WI: Wisconsin Postal History Society, 1978. 107 p. (*Bulletin. Wisconsin Postal History Society, no. 12.*)

7244. Lefton, James A. *Selling Pennsylvania Railroad freight service.* 1948. 119 l. (Thesis, M.B.A., University of Pennsylvania.)

7245. *Legislative history of the Louisville & Nashville R.R. Co. and roads in its system.* Louisville, KY: John P. Morton & Co., Printers, 1881. 39 p.

7246. Lehigh and New England Railroad Company. *Finding the facts.* Bethlehem, PA: Traffic Department, Lehigh and New England Railroad Co., 1922. 48 p. Factories on the line.

7247. _____. *Industrial and shippers guide: containing alphabetical and geographical lists of stations, shippers and receivers of freight, and information pertaining* to the commercial resources and advantages of the principal towns on its line. Bethlehem, PA: Freight Traffic Department, 1929. 100 p.

7248. _____. *Locating the factory*. Bethlehem, PA: Lehigh and New England Railroad Company, Traffic Department, 1922. 39 p.

7249. *Lehigh Valley comet : a quarterly devoted to the diversified industries of the Lehigh, Wyoming and Susquehanna Valleys*. Bethlehem, PA: Robert M. Kaufman, Chomitzky's Printing Service of Bethlehem, 1888-1894. L.V.R.R. documents.

7250. Lehigh Valley Railroad Company. *Centennial 1846-1946. History of 100 years*. Lehigh Valley, PA: Lehigh Valley Railroad Company, 1946. 12 p.

7251. _____. *Centennial year Lehigh Valley Railroad 1946: fiftieth anniversary of the Black Diamond*. S.l., s.n., 1947. 8 p.

7252. _____. *Fuel and steam economy*. South Bethlehem, Pa., Lehigh Valley Railroad Company, 1909. 106 p.

7253. _____. *Guide around the switch-back: and history of the discovery of coal in the Lehigh Valley*. Mauch Chunk, Pa., Joe Lynn, Printer, 1870. 32 p.

7254. _____. *Lease / the Lehigh Valley Railroad Company to the Philadelphia and Reading Railroad Company* / Philadelphia : Allen, Lane & Scott, 1892. 23 p.

7255. _____. *Lehigh Valley Railroad centennial, 1846-1946: the Route of the Black Diamond.*. S.l., Lehigh Valley Railroad Company, 1946. 12 p.

7256. _____. *Lehigh Valley Railroad, the black diamond route, between New York, Philadelphia, and Buffalo, Niagra [sic] Falls*. New York, NY: Rand McNally, 1912. 45 p.

7257. _____. *Lehigh Valley System : cipher code*. New York : s.n., 1902. 110 p.

7258. _____. *Rules for the government of the Operating Department*. Easton, Pa., The Company, 1940. 204 p.

7259. _____. *Rules of the Lehigh Valley Railroad and associated lines for the governing of the Operating Department. To take effect May 17, 1903 ...*/ Philadelphia? S.n., 1903. 172 p.

7260. _____. *Specifications for a single screw steel sea-going tugboat for Lehigh Valley Railroad Co., February 1912: built by the Staten island Shipbuilding Company*. S.l., s.n., 1912. 81 l. (Hull 563, Engine 84, Boiler 206.)

7260a. *Lehigh Valley diesel pictorial* / Newton, NJ: Carstens Publications, 2013. 112 p.

7261. *The Lehigh Valley Railroad*. Boston: Railway and Locomotive Historical Society,

1937. 64 p. (*Bulletin. Railway and Locomotive Historical Society, no. 42.*)

7262. Leider, David J. *The Wisconsin Central in Illinois*. Prospect Heights, IL: D. Leider, Sooauthor Publishing, 2010. 269 p.

7263. Leigh, Edward Baker. *Brake beams and foundation rigging. The requirements from the standpoint of safety and emergency*. Chicago, Ill., [Master Car Builders' Association, Committee on Brake Beams], 1906. 33 p.

7264. Leigh, Frederick J. *American passenger locomotives*. London, 1901. 11 p.

7265. Leighton, Hudson. *Minnesota railroad station & depot locations; fourth interim report, November 1, 1994*. Minneapolis, MN: Minnesota Railroad Research Project, 1994. 79 p.

7266. Leilich, Robert H. *A study of the economics of short trains/* Washington, DC: Peat, Marwick, Mitchell, 1974. 34 l.

7267. _____, John Williams. *Railroad freight car requirements for transporting energy, 1974-1985*. Washington, Peat, Marwick, Mitchell & Co., 1974. 97 p. (United States. Federal Energy Administration; Department of Commerce; Department of Transportation.)

7268. Leipf, Dieter. *Rivers and rails: a milepost guide to the Thunder Mountain Line*. Meridian, Idaho, Forgotten Rails; Middleton, Idaho, Printed by CHJ Pub., 2001. 75 p. (Pacific and Northern Idaho Railway)

7269. Leland, Charles Godfrey. *The Union Pacific Railway, Eastern Division; or, Three thousand miles in a railway car*. Philadelphia, Ringwalt & Brown, 1867. 95 p.

7270. Leland, William E. *An experimental study of a method of determining the vertical throw in the drivers of a locomotive*. 1891. 1 v. (Thesis, B.S., Department of Mechanical Engineering, Massachusetts Institute of Technology.)

7271. LeMassena, R.A. *American steam*. Denver, CO: Sundance Books, 1987-1989. 2 v.

7272. _____. *America's workhorse locomotive: the 2-8-2*. New York, Quadrant Press, 1993. 80 p.

7273. _____. *Articulated steam locomotives of North America*. Silverton, CO: Sundance Books, 1979-1991. 2 v.

7274. _____. *Colorado's mountain railroads*. Golden, CO: Smoking Stack Press, 1963-1968. 5 v. (Rev. ed.: Denver, CO: Sundance Publications, 1984. 383 p.)

7275. _____. *Denver and Rio Grande Western: superpower railroad of the Rockies*. Lynchburg, VA: TLC Pub., 1999. 103 p.

7276. _____. *Lackawanna-superpower railroad of the Northeast.* Lynchburg, VA: TLC Pub., 1998. 102 p.

7277. _____. *Rio Grande...to the Pacific.* Denver, Sundance, 1974. 416 p.

7278. _____. *Union Pacific in Colorado, 1867-1967.* Denver, Printed by Hotchkiss and Nelson, 1967. 40 p.

7279. _____, Robert J. Yanosey, Lou Schmitz, eds.. *Union Pacific: official color photography.* Edison, NJ: Morning Sun Books, 1993-1999. 2 v.

7279a. Lemberger, Michael W. *Railroads of southeast Iowa: photos from the Lemberger Collection.* Ottumwa, IA: PBL Limited, 2012. 197 p.

7280. Lemke, Kenneth Michael. *The economic impacts of rail mergers and abandonments on Kansas export wheat rail rates and costs.* 1989. 180 l. (Thesis, Ph.D., Kansas State University)

7281. Lemly, James Hutton. *The Gulf-Mobile and Ohio; a railroad that had to expand or expire.* Homewood, IL: R.D. Irwin, 1953. 347 p.

7282. _____. *History and economic analysis of the growth of the Gulf, Mobile and Ohio Railroad Company.* 1952. 13, 463 l. (Thesis, D.C.S.., Indiana University.)

7283. Lemmerich, Gustave E. *The design of modern locomotive repair shops.* Cleveland, Ohio, Austin Company, 1919. 6 p.

7284. Lennon, J. *Establishing trails on rights-of-way.* Washington, Department of the Interior, Bureau of Outdoor Recreation, 1971. 54 p.

7285. Lentz, Harry David. *Old Switchback Railroad.* Lebanon, PA: s.n., 1946. 29 p. (Mauch Chunk Switchback Railway.)

7286. Leonard, Edward A. *Railroads and highways at the Pass of the North: a historical survey.* El Paso, TX: El Paso Community Foundation, 2005. 24 p. (Rev. ed.: El Paso, Texas Western Press, 1981. 60 p. *{Southwestern studies, monograph no. 63.})*

7287. Leonard, James H., Theodore Wurm. *San Francisco Water and Power.* San Francisco, Hetch Hetchy Water and Power System, 1979. 48 p.

7288. Leonard, John R. *The fish car era.* Washington, Department of the Interior, U.S. Fish and Wildlife Service, 1979. 16 p.

7289. Leonard, Levi O., Jack T. Johnson. *A railroad to the sea.* Iowa City, IA: Midland House, 1939. 277 p. (Union Pacific Railroad)

7290. Leonard, Robert C. *The rivalry between the Pennsylvania and the Baltimore and Ohio railroads through the Civil War.* 1959. 102 l. (Thesis, M.A., West Virginia University.)

7291. Leonard, William N. *Estimates of railroad freight requirements and other traffic data.* Washington, DC: War Production Board, 1943. 233 l.

7292. _____. *Railroad consolidation under the Transportation Act of 1920.* New York, NY: AMS Press, 1968, 1943. 350 p. (*Colombia studies in history, economics and public law, no. 522.*)

7293. Leopard, John. *Duluth, Missabe & Iron Range Railway.* St. Paul MN: MBI, 2005. 160 p.

7294. _____. *Windy City to the Twin Cities: a Burlington Northern color pictorial.* La Mirada, CA: Four Ways West Publications, 2004. 128 p.

7295. _____. *Wisconsin Central heritage.* La Mirada, CA: Four Ways West Publications, 2007. 128 p.

7296. LePage, R G. *Analysis of the behavioral relationships of railroad track maintenance spending: final report.* Washington, DC: Federal Railroad Administration, Office of Research and Development, 1982. 200 p.

7297. Le Pak, Gregory. *Limited edition of Rails to the Rockies.* Littleton, CO: Alpine Publishing, 1976. 126 p.

7298. _____. *The limited edition of vanishing varnish; Denver & Rio Grande R.R., scenic line of the world.* Littleton, CO: Alpine Publishing, 1978. 256 p.

7299. _____. *Rails to the Rockies.* Littleton, CO: Alpine Publishing, 1976. 126 p.

7300. Lerner, Marc. *Guide to coal rail contracts.* Arlington, VA: Pasha Publications, 1982. 140 p.

7301. Lesher, Robert A. *Railroad lighterage and carfloat service in New York harbor : description of facilities and equipment used and the more important operations conducted : statement of costs of marine service and rail and water distances /* Jersey

City, NJ: s.n., 1930. 183 l.

7302. Lesley, Lewis Burt. *The struggle of San Diego for a southern transcontinental railroad connection, 1854-1891.* 1933. 392 l. (Thesis, Ph.D., University of California, Berkeley.)

7303. Leslie Brothers Manufacturing Company. *America's famous snow plow.* Paterson, N.J., Leslie Bros. Mfg. Co.,1893. 4 p.

7304. Leslie, Douglas L. *The Railway Labor Act.* Washington, D.C., Bureau of National

Affairs, 1995. 617 p. (American Bar Association. Railway and Airline Labor Law Committee.)

7305. Leslie, Frank, Richard Reinhardt. *Out west on the overland train; across-the-continent excursion with Leslie's Magazine in 1877, and the overland trip in 1967.* Palo Alto, CA: American West Pub., 1967. 207 p.

7306. Leslie, Vernon. *Honesdale and the Stourbridge Lion.* Honesdale, PA: Stourbridge Lion Sesquicentennial Corporation, 1979. 140 p.

7307. Lessley, Donald E. *The Paducah gateway: the record of railroads in western Kentucky.* Paducah, KY: Troll Pub. Co., 1978. 299 p.

7308. Letourneau, Peter A. *Chicago, St. Paul, Minneapolis & Omaha Railway, 1880-1940: photo archive; photographs from the State Historical Society of Wisconsin.* Osceola, WI: Iconografix, 1997. 125 p.

7309. _____. *Milwaukee Road, 1850 through 1960: photo archive; photographs from the State Historical Society of Wisconsin.* Osceola, WI: Iconografix, 1996. 125 p.

7310. _____. *Wisconsin Central, 1871 through 1909: photo archive.* Hudson, WI: Iconografix, 1998. 126 p.

7311. Letson, Dawn. *Baldwin Locomotive Works: Erecting drawings at the DeGolyer Library, Southern Methodist University.* Dallas, TX: DeGolyer Library, 1987. 139 p. (2d ed.: 1991. 201 p.)

7312. _____. *A catalog of manuscript accessions in the DeGolyer Library*/ Dallas, TX: DeGolyer Library, Southern Methodist University, 1983. 53 l.

7313. *Letters, papers and data in reference to the merits, value and economy of the American cast iron chilled disc railway wheels: and more particularly, wheels made of pure Salisbury iron of Connecticut* / New York, Egbert K. Pease, 1877. 20 p. Responsibility; Barnum, Richardson Company.

7314. Leu, George E. *A hoghead's random railroad reminiscences.* New York, Vantage Press, 1995. 140 p.

7315. Leuthner, Stuart. *The railroaders.* New York, Random House, 1983. 152 p.

7316. Leuthner, Stuart G. *A visual communication piece: concerning the remaining steam locomotives of the Pennsylvania Railroad located at Northumberland, Pennsylvania.* 1965. 50 l. (Thesis, M.F.A., Rochester Institute of Technology.)

7317. Leverett, Frances. *Arthur E. Stilwell, 1859-1928.* 1955. 128 l. (Thesis, M.A., University of Texas.)

7318. Leverty, Maureen Joyce. *Guide to records of the Northern Pacific branch lines, subsidiaries, and related companies in the Minnesota Historical Society.* St. Paul, The Society, 1977. 13 p.

7319. Levine, Donald, David M. Dancer. *Fire protection of railroad tank cars carrying hazardous materials – Analytical calculations and laboratory screening of thermal insulation candidates* / White Oak, MD: Ft. Belvoir Defense Technical Information Center, 1972. 59 p. (NOLTR-72-142.)

7320. Levin, Laura. *To pass the time away : why the 1877 railroad strike never roared in Detroit.* Detroit : ? L. Levin? 1986. 64 l. "Senior essay, American studies."

7321. Levine, Harvey A. *Economics of scale in the railroad industry: state-of-the art, 1979.* Washington, DC: Association of American Railroads, Economics and Finance Department, 1979. 36 l.

7322. _____. *Small railroads.* Chelsea, MI: Book Crafters, 1982. 421 p.

7323. _____. *Statistics of regional and local railroads/* Washington, DC: Association of American Railroads, Economics and Finance Department, 1988. 294 p.

7324. (Blank entry)

7325. Levine, Robert. *History of New York, New Haven and Hartford Railroad Company, 1842-1913.* 1931. 162 l. (Thesis, M.A., Clark University.)

7326. Levitas, Susan. *Railroad ties: industry and culture in Hagerstown, Maryland.* Crownsville, MD: Maryland Historical Trust Press, 1994. 64 p.

7327. Levy, Norman J. *The demise of the Delaware and Hudson Railway and its impact on New York State.* Albany, NY: New York; Legislative Commission on Critical Transportation Choices, 1988. 51 p.

7328. _____. *New York City suburban area rail consolidation; a more economical and efficient system? A report to the Legislature.* Albany, N.Y., Legislative Commission on Critical Transportation Choices, 1989. 50 p.

7329. _____. *New York State's gains and losses in the public sale of Conrail.* Albany, NY: Legislative Commission on Critical Transportation Choices, 1987. 1 v.

7330. Lewie, Chris J. *Two generations on the Allegheny Portage Railroad: the first railroad to cross the Allegheny Mountains.* Shippensburg, PA: Burd Street Press, 2001. 178 p.

7331. Lewin, Kurt I. *The reorganization of the Missouri Pacific Railroad.* 1955. 1 v. (Thesis, M.A., Columbia University.)

7332. Lewis, Allan C. *Colorado & Southern Railway: Clear Creek narrow gauge.* Charleston, SC: Arcadia, 2004. 128 p.

7333. _____. *Florence & Cripple Creek Railroad: forty miles to fortune: a history of the fabulous narrow-gauge Florence & Cripple Creek Railroad and America's greatest gold-mining region...the amazing Cripple Creek District.* Denver, CO: Sundance Publications, 2002. 416 p.

7334 _____. *Railroads of the Pike's Peak region, 1870-1900.* Charleston, SC: Arcadia, 2004. 128 p.

7335. _____. *Rails around Denver.* Charleston, SC: Arcadia, 2007. 127 p.

7336. _____. *Rails around Durango.* Charleston, SC: Arcadia, 2006. 127 p.

7337. Lewis, E.R. *Winter track work.* Chicago, Ill., Railway Educational Press, 1917. 166 p.

7338. Lewis, Edward A. *American shortline railway guide.* 5th ed. Waukesha, WI: Kalmbach Pub. Co., 1996. 368 p.

7339. _____. *Arcade & Attica Railroad.* 2d ed. Arcade, NY: The Baggage Car, 1972. 104 p.

7340. _____. *The Blackstone Valley Line: the story of the Blackstone Canal Company and the Providence & Worcester Railroad.* Seekonk, MA: The Baggage Car, 1973. 80 p.

7341. _____. *The "do" lines: Gettysburg Railroad, Hillsdale County Railway, Lackawaxen & Stourbridge Railroad.* Strasburg, PA: The Baggage Car, 124 p.

7342. _____. *New England country depots.* Arcade, NY: The Baggage Car, 1973. 160 p.

7343. _____. *Reading's Victorian stations.* Strasburg, PA: The Baggage Car, 1976. 120 p.

7344. _____. *Vermont's covered bridge road: the story of the St. Johnsbury & Lamoille County Railroad.* Strasburg, PA: The Baggage Car, 1974. 131 p.

7345. _____ *Wellsville, Addison and Galeton Railroad: "Sole Leather Line."* Arcade NY: Short Tracks Development Corporation, 1971. 40 p.

7346. Lewis, Eugene M. *12,000 days on the North Western Line: the life and time of a railroad civil engineer, 1947-1980.* Deerfield, IL: Chicago & North Western Historical Society, 2005. 961 p.

7347. Lewis, George Henry. *National consolidation of the railways of the United States.* New York: Dodd, Mead, 1893. 326 p.

7348. Lewis, Hugh M.L. *Design for an iron Pratt truss.* 1893. 15 l. (Thesis, B.C.E., University of Maine.)

7349. Lewis, Joe. *Date nails, brought up to date; [a pictorial guide to the identification and classification of date nails].* Nacogdoches, TX: P & G Press, 1973. 108 p.

7350. Lewis, Leonard P. *Railway signal engineering (mechanical).* 2d ed. New York, D. Van Nostrand Company, 1920. 358 p.

7351. Lewis, Lloyd, Stanley McCrory Pargellis. *Granger country; a pictorial social history of the Burlington Railroad.* Boston, Little, Brown, 1949. 1 v. (unpaged)

7352. Lewis, Lloyd D. *The Virginian era.* Lynchburg, VA: TLC Pub., 1992. 60 p.

7353. _____. *Virginian Railway locomotives.* Lynchburg, VA: TLC Pub., 1993. 76 p.

7353a. _____. *West Virginia railroads: Virginian Railway.* . Lynchburg, VA: TLC Pub., 2011. 1 v.

7354. Lewis, John Edward. *Reservation narrow gauge, Omak Creek Railroad (Bow & Arrow Short Line): The last narrow gauge logging railroad in Washington State: a chronicle of Biles- Coleman Lumber Company's narrow gauge.* York, PA: Lewis, 1980. 133 p.

7354a. Lewis, Lloyd, Stanley McCrory Pargellis. *Granger country: a pictorial social history of the Burlington Railroad.* Boston, Little, Brown, 1949. 1 v. (unpaged)

7355. Lewis, Oscar. *The big four; the story of Huntington, Stanford, Hopkins, and Crocker, and the building of the Central Pacific.* New York, A.A. Knopf, 1938. 418 p.

7356. Lewis, Robert G. *The handbook of American railroads.* New York, Simmons-Boardman Pub. Corp., 1951. 242 p.(2d ed.: 1956. 251 p.)

7357. _____, and others. *Off the beaten track: a railroader's life in pictures.* Omaha, NE: Simmons-Boardman Pub. Corp., 2004. 192 p.

7358. Lewis, Ronald L. *Railroads, deforestation, and the trans-formation of agriculture in the West Virginia back counties, 1880-1920.* Morgantown, WV: West Virginia University, Regional Research Institute, 1994. 42 p. (*Research paper, 9402.*)

7359. Lewis, S. L. *Durability of wood crossties, phase I/* Chicago: Association of American Railroads, 1987. 113 l.
(*Report. Association of American Railroads, no. R-702.*)

7360. Lewis, Sherman Leland. *History of the New York, New Haven and Hartford Railroad to 1917 /* 1932. 1 v. (Thesis, A.B., Honors, Harvard University.)

7361. Lewis, Thomas R., Jr. *The era of railroad development in Connecticut: a systematic study in historical geography.* 1964. 67 l. (Thesis, M.S., Central Connecticut

State University.)

7362. Lewnard, James. *Monon in color.* Scotch Plains, NJ: Morning Sun Books, 2002. 128 p.

7362a. _____. *Trackside in the Land of Lincoln with Richard Ward* . Scotch Plains, NJ: Morning Sun Books, 2011. 127 p.

7363. Lewty, Peter J. *Across the Columbian Plain: railroad expansion in the interior Northwest, 1885-1893.* Pullman, WA: Washington State University Press, 1995. 326 p.

7364. _____. *To the Columbia gateway: the Oregon Railway and the Northern Pacific, 1879-1884.* Pullman, WA: Washington State University Press, 1987. 202 p.

7365. *Lexington quarterly.* Plainview, TX: Lexington Group in Transportation History, 1986- Quarterly.

7366. Leyendecker, Liston E. *Palace Car prince: a biography of George Mortimer Pullman.* Niwot, CO: University Press of Colorado, 1992. 323 p.

7367. Lezette, Doug. *Delaware & Hudson passenger trains: the final decade.* Goffstown, NH: Railroad Explorer, 2002. 74 p.

7368. Library of Congress. *Railroad maps of North America: the first hundred years.* Compiled by Andrew Modelski. Washington, Library of Congress, 1984. 186 p.

7369. _____. *Railroad maps of the United States: a selective annotated bibliography of original 19th-century maps in the Geography and Map Division of the Library of Congress.* Compiled by Andrew M. Modelski. Washington, The Library. 1975. 112 p.

7370. _____. Division of Bibliography. *Railways in the United States; a bibliographical list.* Compiled by Ellen Fay Chamberlin, under the direction of Florence S. Hellman, acting chief bibliographer. Washington, 1933. 38 p.

7371. *A library of railway books suggested by the editors of Railway Age, Railway Mechanical Engineer, Railway Electrical Engineer, Railway Signal Engineer, Railway Maintenance Engineer.* New York, N.Y., Simmons-Boardman Publishing Company, 1921. 32 p.

7372. Licht, Walter. *Nineteenth-century American railwaymen: a study in the nature and organization of work.* 1977. 486 l. (Thesis, Ph.D., Princeton University.)

7373. _____. *Working for the railroad: the organization of work in the nineteenth century.* Princeton, N.J., Princeton University Press, 1983. 328 p.

7374. Lidgerwood Manufacturing Company. *An illustrated description of a new device known as the rapid unloader used for unloading dirt, ballast, etc., from flat cars, manufactured under patent Sept. 20, 1892.* New York : Lidgerwood Manufacturing Co.,

1892. 40 p.

7375. _____. *Rapid unloader for discharging dirt, ballast, ore, etc. from flat cars in railroad work ... Manufactured exclusively by Lidgerwood Manufacturing Company under an exclusive license from the Rapid Unloader & Equipment Co. of New York City ...* / 2d ed. New York : Duyster Press, 1903. 48 p.

7376. Lieberman, Richard K., Lisa M. Sita. *Tracks and tunnels: the New York City subway system.* Long Island City, NY: La Guardia Community College, LaGuardia and Wagner Archives, 2006. 40 p.

7377. *Life and times of the Central Pacific Railroad.* Edited by David F. Myrick. San Francisco, Printed by L. and A. Kennedy, 1969. 12 folders in case.

7378. Liggett, Barbara. *A history of the adoption of standard time in the United States, 1869-1883.* 1960. 116 l. (Thesis, M.A., University of Texas at Austin.)

7379. *Light iron & short ties.* Rockville, MD?: Three Rivers Narrow Gauge Historical Society, 1982?-

7379a. *Light rail transit* / Washington, DC: Transportation Research Board, 1989. 667 p.

7379b. *Light rail transit: planning, design, and implementation* / Washington, DC: Transportation Research Board, 1982. 175 p.

7379c. *Light rail transit: system design for cost-effectiveness* / Washington, DC: Transportation Research Board, 1985. 240 p.

7380. Lightner, David L. *Labor on the Illinois Central Railroad, 1852-1900: the evolution of an industrial environment.* New York, Arno Press, 1977. 437 p. (Thesis, Cornell University, 1969.)

7381. Liljestrand, Bob. *Alco reference #1.* Hanover, PA: Railroad Press, 1998. 224 p. (American Locomotive Company)

7382. Liljestrand, Robert A. *Boston, Revere Beach & Lynn Railroad* / Ansonia, CT: Bob's Photo, 2002. 48 p.

7383. _____. *New England 1930's steam action, Worcester.* Hanover, PA: Railroad Press, 2000. 47 p.

7384. _____. *New Haven Railroad, Midland Division* / Framers, KY: Bob's Photo, 2007. 48 p.

7385. _____. *The New Haven Railroad's Boston Division.* Ansonia, CT: Bob's Photo, 2001. 48 p.

7386. _____. *The New Haven Railroad's Old Colony Division.* Ansonia, CT:

Bob's Photo, 2000. 48 p.

7387. _____. *Rails across Boston.* Ansonia, CT: Bob's Photo, 2000? 2 v.

7388. _____. *Rolling stock of New England.* Ansonia, CT: Bob's Photo, 2001. 2 v.
v. 1-Cranes. Snow fighting equipment. Work service boxcars. Other work cars. Highway
vehicles. v. 2 – Steel boxcars. Gondola cars. Hopper cars. Covered hoppers. Flatcars.
Cabooses.

7388a. _____, David R. Sweetland. *Atlantic Coast Line freight cars.* Ansonia, CT:
Bob's Photo, 2004. 48 p.

7389. _____, _____. Boston ,Revere Beach & Lynn Railroad. Mansfield, OH: Book
Masters, 2003. 1 v.

7390. _____,. _____. *Equipment of the Virginian Railway.* Roanoke, VA: Norfolk
and Western Historical Society, 2005-   . (v. 1-Steam locomotives. v. 2- Electric
and diesel-electric locomotives.)

7391. _____, _____. *New Haven diesel locomotives.* Ansonia, CT: Bob's Photo, 2000?
(v. 1-Switchers and road switchers.)

7392. _____, _____. *Passenger cars of New England.* Hanover, PA: Railroad Press,
2000- (v. 1-Boston & Maine; v. 2-Bangor & Aroostook and Maine Central; v. 3- Central
Vermont and Rutland.)

7393. _____, _____. *Passenger equipment of the Pennsylvania Railroad.* Hanover,
PA: Railroad Press, 2001-   . <1> v.

7393a. _____, _____. *Pennsylvania Railroad baggage and mail cars.* Ansonia, CT:
Bob's Photo, 2005. 48 p.

7393b. _____, _____. *Pennsylvania Railroad dining cars.* Ansonia, CT: Bob's Photo,
2007. 48 p.

7393c. _____, _____. *Pennsylvania parlor cars* / S.l., s.n., 2000s. 48 p.

7394. _____, _____. *Philadelphia* / Farmers, KY: Bob's Photo, 2008. 48 p.
(*Railroad cities, v. 1.)*

7395 _____, _____. *Railroad cities: Concord, New Hampshire.* Ansonia, CT: Bob's
Photo, 2001. 48 p.

7396. _____, _____. *Railroad cities: Providence, Rhode Island.* Ansonia, CT: Bob's
Photo, 2000? 1 v.

7397. _____, _____. *Railroad cities: Springfield, Massachusetts.* Ansonia, CT: Bob's
Photo, 2001. 48 p.

7397a. _____, John Nehrich, Robert R. Bahrs. *Railway milk cars* / Ansonia, Conn: Bob's Photo, 2002-2005. 4 v.

7398. _____, Richard Abramson. *The New Haven Railroad's electrified zone*. Higham, MA: BSRA Publications, 2000? 48 p.

7399. Lillo, Sarah Marie. *Evaluation of passive railroad grade crossing warning devices/* 1992. 103 l. (Thesis, M.S., Texas A & M University.)

7400. Lilly, Douglas, David C. Augsburger. *The Lehigh and New England Railroad : a color retrospect*. Bridgeport PA: Anthracite Railroads Historical Society; Laurys Stations, PA: Garrigues House, 1988. 136 p.

7401. *The Lima legacy: railroaders in the community*. Lima, OH: American House, 1989. 32 p.

7402. Lima-Hamilton. *Operators manual: diesel electric transfer locomotive*. Lima, Ohio, Lima-Hamilton Corporation, 1945. 62 p.

7403. _____. *Operators manual; 800 & 1200 HP diesel electric switching locomotive*. Lima, Ohio, Lima-Hamilton Corp, 1945. 48 p.

7404. _____. *Operators manual; 1000 HP diesel electric switching locomotive*. Lima, Ohio, Lima-Hamilton Corporation, 1945. 44 p.

7405. Lima Locomotive and Machine Works. *Instructions for the care of Shay geared locomotives, manufactured by the Lima Locomotive and Machine Company, Lima, Ohio*. Parsons, WV: McClain Print. Co., 1972. 1 v.

7406._____. *Lima locomotives*. Lima, Ohio, The Company, 1911. 48 p. (*Catalog number sixteen.*) (Reprint: San Marino, CA: Golden West Books, 1960; San Marino, CA: Pacific Railroad Publications, 1961; San Marino, CA: Golden West Books, 1964.)

7407. _____. *Shay geared and rod locomotives*. Lima, Ohio, The Lima Locomotive and Machine Company, 1907. 78 p.*(Catalogue number fifteen.)*

7408. _____. *Shay patent geared locomotives; World's Fair, St. Louis, 1904, Louisiana Purchase Exposition*. Lima, Ohio, Lima Locomotive & Machine Company, 1904. 30 p.

7409. _____. *Shay patent locomotive engine; built by the Lima Locomotive and Machine Co*. Lima, Ohio, The Company, 1892. 42 p.

7410. Lima Locomotive Works, Incorporated. *Bulletin*. Lima, Ohio, Lima Locomotive Works, 1917-

7411. _____. *Lima super-power steam locomotives*. Lima, Ohio, Lima Locomotive Works, 1942. 39 p. (Also: 1946. 49 p.;1947, 53 p.)

7412. _____. *Locomotives.* Lima, Ohio, 193-? 4 v. of plates.

7413. _____. *1919 Shay locomotive catalog.* Edmonds, WA: Pacific Fast Mail, 1979, 1919. 27 p.

7414. _____. *1921 Shay repair parts catalog.* Edmonds, WA: Pacific Fast Mail, 1979, 1921. 50 p.

7415. _____. *Repair parts for Shay geared locomotives.* Parson, WV: McClain Printing Company, 1969, 1908. 55 p.

7416. _____. *Repair parts Shay geared locomotives,* Lima, Ohio, The Works, 1921. 50 p. (*Catalogue no. X2.)*

7417. _____. *Shay geared locomotives.* Lima, Ohio, Lima Locomotive Works, 1925. 28 p. *(Catalogue no. S-4.)*

7418. _____. *Shay geared locomotives for industrial service.* Lima, Ohio, Lima Locomotive Works, 1921. *(Catalogue no. S-3.)*

7418a. _____. *Shay instruction sheets.* Parsons, WV: McClain Printing Co., 1975. 38 p.

7419. _____. *Shay patent and direct locomotives; logging cars, car wheels, axles, railroad and machinery castings.* Parson, WV: McClain Printing Company, 1971. 62 p. Reprint of Lima Locomotive & Machine Company catalog.

7420. *The Lima Shays on the Greenbrier, Cheat & Elk Railroad Company.* Parson, WV: McClain Printing Co., 1969. 32 p.

7421. Limas, Peter. *Southern Pacific rails: a motive power finale.* Hart, MO: White River Productions, 1998. 157 p.

7422. *Limiting the length of trains by law: an editor's opinion and the railroads' viewpoint.* Washington, DC: Association of American Railroads, 1937. 15 p.

7423. Lincoln, Clifford F. *Railroad signals.* 1911. 50 l. (Thesis, C.E., Lehigh University.)

7424. Lincoln, John J. *The bridges on the Lehigh and Lackawanna Rail Road between Bethlehem and Bath /* 1889. 32 l. 3 leaves of folded plates. (Thesis, C.E., Lehigh University.)

7424a. Lincoln, Paul Martyn. *Report on Santa Fe Electrification.* S.l., s.n., 1919. 100 l. (Concerning possible electrification between Winslow, Arizona and Barstow, California.)

7425. Lind, Alan R. *Chicago surface lines: an illustrated history.* Park Forest, IL: Transport History Press, 1974. 400 p.

7426. _____ *From horsecars to streamliners: an illustrated history of the St. Louis Car Company.* Park Forest, IL: Transport History Press, 1978. 400 p.

7427. _____. *From the Lakes to the Gulf: the Illinois Central story: an illustrated history of the 'main line of mid-America.'* Park Forest, IL: Transport History Press, 1993. 384 p.

7428. _____. *Limiteds along the lakefront: the Illinois Central in Chicago.* Park Forest, IL: Transport History Press, 1986. 144 p.

7429. Lind, Richard F. *Narrow gauge country.* Boulder, CO: The Author, 1963. 132 p.

7430. _____. *Rails along the foothills.* Barrington, IL: The Author, 1966. 82 p.

7431. _____. *Rails to the high country.* Boulder, CO: The Author, 1961. 122 p.

7432. _____. *Steam with variation.* Barrington, IL: Richard F. Lind, 1965. 110 p.

7433. Lindahl, Martin L. *The New England railroads.* Boston, New England Economic Research Foundation, 1965. 169 p.

7433a. Lindberg, Edward Ferdinand Jacob. *A report of the development of railway signal systems* / 1909. 48 l. (Thesis, B.S., University of Illinois.)

7434. Linder, Suzanne Cameron. *They came by train and chose to remain: the importance of Moore County railroads, 1850-1900.* Hamlet, NC: Richmond Technical College, 1982. 20 p.

7435. Lindahl, Martin Leroy. *Cooperation between the Interstate Commerce Commission and the state commissions in railroad regulation.* 1935. 1 v. (Thesis, University of Michigan.)

7436. _____. *The New England railroads* / Boston, MA: New England Economic Research Foundation, 1965.169 p.

7437. _____. *Railroad freight rates and New England's competitive position.* Boston, New England Governor's Committee on Public Transportation, 1957. 77 l.

7438. Lindley, Daniel. *Ambrose Pierce takes on the railroads: the journalist as muckraker and cynic.* Westport, CT: Praeger, 1999. 152 p.

7439. Lindsay, Robert M, Jr. *The wartime and postwar railroad general freight rate increases.* 1950. 1 v. (Thesis, M.B.A., University of Pennsylvania.)

7440. Lindsell, Robert M. *The rail lines of northern New England: a handbook of railroad history.* Pepperell, Mass, Branch Line Press, 2000. 414 p.

7441. Lindsey, Almont. *The Pullman Strike; the story of a unique experiment and of a great labor upheaval.* Chicago, University of Chicago Press, 1942. 385 p. (Reprint: 1964)

7442. Lindsey, Scott. *Norfolk Southern 1995 review.* Mukilteo, WA: Hundman Publishing, 1995. 144 p.

7443. Lingo, C.L. *Bases for freight charges/* Chicago, IL: La Salle Extension University, 1914. 62 p.

7444. Link-Belt Company. *Link-Belt rotary railroad car dumper.* S.l., Link-Belt Company, 1900s. 7 p.

7445._____. *Modern methods applied to the coaling of locomotives, disposing of cinders, and to the handling of freight in railroad depots, steamship docks and warehouses.* New York, Link-Belt, 1903. 96 p.

7446. Link, Jay. *Electric locomotives.* Osceola, WI: MBI. 2003. 96 p.

7447. Link, O. Winston. *Ghost trains: railroad photographs of the 1950s.* Norfolk, VA: Chrysler Museum, 1983. 50 p.

7448._____. *"Night trick" on the Norfolk and Western Railway.* New York, The Author, 1957. 16 p.

7449._____. *Night trick: photographs of the Norfolk &* Western *Railway, 1955-60.* By O. Winston Link; edited with an introduction by Rupert Martin. London, Published by the Photographers Gallery in conjunction with the National Museum of Photography, Film & Television, Bradford, and the National Railway Museum, York, 1983. 24 p.

7450._____. *O. Winston Link's sounds of steam railroading.* Volumes 1-6. Roanoke, VA: O. Winston Link Railway Productions, Roanoke Division, 2004. 5 sound discs.

7451._____, Thomas H. Garver. *The last steam railroad in America: from Tidewater to Whitetop.* New York, H,N, Abrams, 1995. 144 p. (2008 ed. : 144 p.)

7452._____, Timothy Hensley. *Steam, steel & stars: America's last steam railroad.* Afterword by Thomas H. Garver. New York, Abrams, 1987. 144 p. (Reprint: 1994 and 1998.)

7453. Link, P.K., E. Chilton. Phoenix. *Rock, rails & trails.* 2d ed. Pocatello, Idaho, Idaho Museum of Natural History, 1996. (Idaho: Pocatello; Snake River Plain)

7454. Link, Theodore C., Bertram Allen Atwater. *Saint Louis Union Station.* Chicago : B.A. Atwater, 1895. 30 p.

7455. Linnaus, Vernon F. *A real, live railroad: the 40-year saga of the ill-fated Yankton-Norfolk line.* David City, NE: South Platte Press, 2003. 64 p. (*Midwest rail monograph, no. 2.*) (Nebraska; South Dakota)

7456. Linksy, Benjamin, W.F.M. Goss. *The Chicago report on smoke abatement; a landmark survey of the technology and history of air pollution control.* Elmsford, NY: Maxwell Reprint, 1971. 1 v.

7457. Linroth, Ralph W. *The history of the CB&Q Illinois Pea-Vine, the Galesburg to Savanna Branch* / S.l., Ralph W. Linroth, 2009. 286 p. (2d ed. 2010. 275 p.)

7458. Lipetz, Alphonse. *Diesel engine potentialities and possibilities in rail transportation.* Lafayette, Ind., Purdue University,1935. 47 p. (*Engineering Experiment Station, Purdue University, Research bulletin, no. 49; Engineering bulletin, Purdue University, vol. 19, no. 2, March, 1935.*)

7459. Lippian, Joseph M. *The transportation of hazardous materials : transport of benzene by tank car.* Ft. Belvoir Defense Technical Information Center, 1973. 94 p. (Army Material Command, Texarkana, Tex, Intern Training Center.)

7460. Lipsey, John Johnson, Edith Powell. *The lives of James John Hagerman: the builder of the Colorado Midland Railway.* Denver, CO: Golden Bell Press, 1968. 281 p.

7461. List, G.F., H.L. Bongaardt. *Freight car scheduling benefits projection on Conrail : the Pittsburgh to St. Louis corridor* / Washington, DC : Federal Railroad Administration, Office of policy, 1981. 104 p. (*FRA/ORRP-81/9.*)

7462. *A list of books, with references to periodicals, relating to railroads in the relation to the government and the public.* Compiled by Appleton P.C. Griffin.Washington, U.S.G.P.O., 1907. 131 p. (Library of Congress. Division of Bibliography.)

7462a. *A list of government and railroad lands open to pre-emption, or homestead, or to purchase along the lines of the Central Pacific, and the California and Oregon railroads.* New York : New York General Agency, 1886. 96 p.

7463. *List of maps showing railway lines.* Washington, D.C., Association of American Railroads, 1948- Irregular. (*Railway information series, no. 8.*)

7464. *List of publications of the American Railway Association.* S.l., Association of American Railroads, Bureau of Railway Economics, Library, 1923. 23 l.

7465. *List of railroad companies which have filed applications for further extension of time within which to equip their cars with safety appliances for period of a year or until January 1, 1901.* Washington ? s.n., 1901. 8 p.

7466. *List of references on American railway accounting.* Washington, DC: Bureau of Railway Economics, Library, 1924. 2, 159 l.

7466a. *List of references on Atlantic Coast Line system.* Washington, DC: Bureau of Railway Economics, Library, 1920. 8 l.

7467. *List of references on locomotive mechanical stokers.* Washington, D.C., Bureau of Railway Economics, Library, 1915. 9 l.

7468. *List of references on maximum railway passenger fares* / Washington DC: Bureau of Railway Economics, 1915. 14 l.

7469. *List of references on oil burning locomotives and fuel oil for locomotives.* Washington, D.C., Bureau of Railway Economics, Library, 1919. 3 l.

7470. *List of references on railway motor cars.* Washington, D.C., Bureau of Railway Economics, Library, 1915. 37 l.

7471. *A list of references on the proposed consolidation of railroads (chronologically arranged).* Washington, DC: Association of American Railroads, Bureau of Railway Economics, Library, 1923. 1 v.

7472. *List of references on the use of railroads in the war.* Washington, D.C., Bureau of Railway Economics, Library, 1915. 34 l.

7473. *List of references on transportation of perishable products.* Washington, D.C., Bureau of Railway Economics, 1918. 13 l.

7474. *List of references on valuation of steam railways.* Chicago, American Railway Engineering Association, 1916. 154 p. (*Bulletin of the American Railway Engineering Association, v. 18, no. 190, October, 1916.*)

7475. *List of references relating to the eight-hour working day and to limitations of working hours in the United States, with special reference to railway labor* / Washington, DC : Bureau of Railway Economics, 1917. 30 l.

7476. *List of references to books and articles on the Adamson eight-hour law of September, 1916.* Washington, D.C., Bureau of Railway Economics, 1919. Revised ed. 22 l.

7477. *A list of references to literature relating to the Union Pacific System, August 15, 1922.* Newton, Mass, Crofton Pub. Corp., 1922. 299, 23 p. (Bureau of Railway Economics, Association of American Railroads)

7478. *List of selected references to material emphasizing the economic aspects of electrification of railroads in the U.S.* Washington, D.C., Bureau of Railway Economics, 1924. 17 l.

7479. *A list of references to the more important books and articles on government control and operation of railroads.* Washington, Bureau of Railway Economics, Library, 1919. 52, 14, 17 l.

7480. *List of steam locomotives in the United States: a locations guide for railroad historians, photographers and railfans.* Denver, CO: Centennial Rail Ltd., 1987. 30 p.

7481. *List of works in the New York Public Library relating to government control of railroads, rates, regulations, etc.* New York, New York Public Library, 1906. 26 p.

7482. Litch, Jno. E. *The manufacture of rails in the United States.* 1890. 50 l. (Thesis, M.E., Lehigh University.)

7483. Litteer, Loren K. *The Leavenworth, Lawrence, & Ft. Gibson Railroad; Kansas' first railroad south of the Kaw.* Baldwin, KS: Champion Pub., 1991. 44 p.

7484. *The little giant: the official publication of the Pittsburgh & Lake Erie Railroad Historical Society.* Moon Township, PA: Pittsburgh and Lake Erie Railroad Historical Society, 2003- . Quarterly.

7485. Little, Norman M. *History of the building of the Chicago and Alton Railroad in Missouri from 1837 to 1879 /* 1952. 83 l. (Thesis, M.A. Northeast Missouri State Teachers College.)

7486. Little, Patrick, Carl D. Martland. *Improving railroad car maintenance by using knowledge based systems /* Cambridge, MA: Center for Transportation Studies, Massachusetts Institute of Technology, 1989. 57 p.

7487. Littlejohn, Duffy. *Hopping freight trains in America.* Los Osos, CA: Sand River Press, 1993. 353 p.

7488. _____. *Lonesome whistle.* Jack Rummel, editor. Silver City, NM: Zephyr Rhoades Press, 2002. 174 p. (Railroad stories)

7489. Liu, Shuangqin. *Finite element analysis of residual stresses in railroad car wheel /* 2006. 150 l. (Thesis, Tufts University.)

7490. Lively, Edith Hall. *The Pullman Company/* 1950. 195 l. (Thesis, M.B.A., Wharton School, University of Pennsylvania.)

7491. Livingood, James Weston. *The Chattanooga country: gateway to history; the Nashville to Atlanta rail corridor of the 1860's.* Chattanooga, TN: The Chattanooga Area Historical Association, 1995. 698 p.

7492. Livingstone, John. *How to save 50 percent now spent on coal; also the utility of hollow stay bolts as stays and as factors bettering combustions /* New York, Printed by Roy Press, 1905. 62 p.

7493. Livingston, John. *The perils of the nation; bribery, dishonesty, usurpations and despotism of the railway corporations, and their relation to the politics of the day, the remedy to be used, read, discuss, diffuse.* New York, NY: Evening Post, 1877. 88 p.

7494. Llano, Antonio. *Standard specifications for carbon steel car and tender axles. Test as adopted by the American Society for Testing Materials. Rev. 1918.* Washington, DC: U.S. G.P.O., 1919. 15 p. (*United States. Bureau of Foreign and Domestic Commerce. Industrial standards, no. 14.*)

7495. Lloyd, Gordon, Louis A, Marre. *Conrail motive power review.* Glendale, CA: Interurban Press, 1992-(v. 1- *The first ten years, 1976-1986.*)

7496. Lloyd, Gordon E. *Illinois Terminal in color.* Scotch Plains, NJ: Morning Sun Books, 1998-2001. 2 v.

7497. Lloyd, J.G., Roger M. Cortani, Joseph A. Strapac. *Diesels of the Espee.* Burlingame, CA: Chatham Pub. Co., 1975-

7498. Lloyd, J.T. *Reminiscences of the two Vanderbilts, "Corneel" and "Bill" /* Abridged ed. Boston : Lloyd Publishing Company, 1887. 45 p.

7499. *Lloyd's American railroad weekly.* New York, J.T. Lloyd, 1860-18--?

7500. Llewellyn, Neil Samuel. *The piggy-back service.* 1956. (Thesis, M.B.A. Transportation and Public Utilities, Graduate School of Arts and Sciences, University of Pennsylvania)

7501. *Loading and unloading of trailers on railroad flatcars.* Chicago : National Safety Council, 1990. 3, 1 p. (*Data sheet 1-672 reaf. 90.)*

7502. Lobdell Car Wheel Company. Wilmington, Del. *Car wheels manufactured by Lobdell Car Wheel Co., Wilmington, Delaware,.* Philadelphia: Allen, Lane & Scott, Printers, 1892. 53 p.

7503. _____. *Catalogue.* Philadelphia : Allen, Lane & Scott, 1892?

7504. _____. *Lobdell Car Wheel Co.: the oldest car wheel establishment in the country : capacity 300 wheels per day.* Wilmington, Del.: The Company, 1876. 3 p.

7505. _____. *[Papers, 1817-1929].* 30 linear ft. Location: Historical Society of Pennsylvania.

7506. Lobosco, Nicholas. *New York (Buffalo) Central Terminal : the programming and revitalization of the property /* 2006. 55 l. (Thesis, M.Arch., State University of New York at Buffalo.)

7507. Lochhead, Herbert James. *The failure and reorganization of the Missouri, Kansas and Texas Railroad.* 1926. 1 v. (Thesis, Columbia University.)

7508. Locke, Marvin Elliott. *A history of the Nevada County Narrow Gauge Railroad.* 1962. 143 l. (Thesis, M.A., UCLA.)

7509. Lockhart, Charles F. *Lockhart's book of instructions for locomotive firemen.*

Cleveland, Ohio, C.F. Fulton, 1908. 180 p.

7510. _____. *Practical instructor and reference book for locomotive firemen and engineers* / New York, Norman W. Henley Pub. Co., 1911. 362 p. (Also: 1917. 362, 22 p.)

7511. Locklin, D. Philip *Regulation of security issues by the Interstate Commerce Commission*/ Urbana, IL: University of Illinois, 1926. 189 p. (Thesis, Ph.D., University of Illinois, 1926.)

7512. Lockwood, Ryland Leonard. *Report on technical improvement in railroad equipment, roadway, and structures.* Washington, DC: Office of Federal Coordinator of Transportation, Section of Purchases, 1935. 2, 31 p.

7513. *Loco.* Schenectady, N.Y., Locomotive Club, 1910-1919. 10 v. Quarterly.

7514. *Loco Mania.* S.l., 7FX; Distributed by Wizard Works/Atari, 2007. Windows 2000/XP Computer file 1 computer optical disc; s.d., col. (*Part # 27519CD*)

7515. *Loco 1, the diesel.* Compiled by the staff of Railroad Model Craftsmen. Editor, Harold H. Carstens. Ramsey, NJ: Model Craftsman Pub. Corp, 1966. 142 p.

7516. *The locomotive.* Hartford, Conn., Hartford Steam Boiler Inspection and Insurance Company, 1867-   Quarterly.

7517. *Locomotive and railway data.* New York, Industrial Press, 1910. 39 p.

7518. *Locomotive & railway preservation.* Richmond, VT: Mark Smith, 1986-1997. Bimonthly.

7519. *Locomotive advertising in America, 1850-1900.* Scotia, NY: Americana Review, 1960. 30 p. (Reprint: Maynard, MA: Chandler Press, 1989. 32 p.)

7520. *Locomotive coaling stations: cinder and sand stations, water tanks.* Birmingham, Ala.; Chicago, Roberts and Schaefer Company, 1907. 12 p.

7521. *The locomotive cyclopedia.* [Compiled by the editors of Mainline modeler magazine.] Mukilteo, WA: Hundman Publishing, 1998-

7522. *Locomotive cyclopedia of American practice.* New York, Simmons-Boardman Pub. Corp, 1906-1956. 15 v. (*<Car builders' cyclopedia of American practice. > Car and locomotive cyclopedia of American practice.* Other title: *Locomotive dictionary*: 1909-1919.)

7523. *Locomotive cyclopedia of American practice. Definitions and typical illustrations of locomotives, their parts and equipment.* 6th ed. Editor: Roy V. Wright. New York, Simmons-Boardman Pub. Co., 1922. 1155 p.

7524. *Locomotive cyclopedia of American practice; definitions and typical illustrations of locomotives, their parts and equipment; descriptions and illustrations of the tools and methods employed in their construction and repair; locomotives built in America for industrial operations and for foreign railroads.* 7th ed. Edited by Roydon Vincent Wright. Managing editor, Robert Clayton Augur. New York, Simmons-Boardman Pub. Co., 1925. 1131 p. (Compiled and edited for the American Railway Association, Division V, formerly American Railway Master Mechanics Association. Reprint: Novato, CA: Newton K. Gregg, 1973 and 1985.)

7525. *Locomotive cyclopedia of American practice/* 8th ed. Edited by Roydon Vincent Wright. New York, Simmons-Boardman Pub. Co., 1927. 1372 p.

7526. *Locomotive cyclopedia of American practice.* 9th ed. Edited by Roydon Vincent Wright. New York, Simmons-Boardman Pub. Co., 1930. 1440 p. (Reprint: Novato, CA: Newton KJ. Gregg, 1985, 1930. 1440 p.)

7527. *Locomotive cyclopedia of American practice.* 10th ed. New York, Simmons-Boardman, 1938. 1232 p.

7528. *Locomotive cyclopedia of American practice.* 11th ed. Edited by Roydon Vincent Wright. New York, Simmons-Boardman Pub. Co., 1941. 1312 p. (Reprint: Milwaukee, WI: Kalmbach Pub. Co., 1974, 1941. 1312 p.)

7529. *Locomotive cyclopedia of American practice; definitions and typical illustrations of steam, electric and internal-combustion locomotives for railroad and industrial service; their parts and equipment; also locomotives built in America for operation in foreign countries, including a section on locomotive shops and engine terminals.* 12th ed. Edited by Roydon Vincent Wright. New York, Simmons-Boardman, 1944.

7530. *Locomotive cyclopedia of American practice; definitionsand typical illustrations of steam, turbine, electric and diesel locomotives for railroads and industrial service.* 13th ed. New York, Simmons-Boardman Pub. Corp., 1947. 1418 p.

7531. *Locomotive cyclopedia of American practice, 1950-1952: definitions, drawings and illustrations of diesel, steam, electric and turbine locomotives for railroad, industrial and foreign service, their parts and equipment, descriptions and illustrations of locomotive shops and servicing facilities.* Editor, C.B. Peck. Compiled and edited for the Association of American Railroads, Mechanical Division. 14th ed. New York, Simmons-Boardman Pub. Corp., 1950. 1028 p.

7532. *Locomotive cyclopedia of American practice; definitions, drawings and illustrations of Diesel, electric and turbine locomotives.* 15th ed. New York, Simmons-Boardman Pub. Corp., 1956. 728 p.

7533. *Locomotive dictionary.* Compiled and edited for the American Railway Master Mechanics Association. New York, The Railroad Gazette, 1906-1919. 5 v.

7534. *Locomotive dictionary; an illustrated vocabulary of terms which designate*

American railroad locomotives, their parts, attachments and details of construction, with definitions and illustrations of typical British locomotive practice; five thousand one hundred and forty-eight illustrations. Edited by George Little Fowler. New York, The Railroad Gazette, 1906. 523 p.
(Reprint: Novato, CA: Newton K. Gregg, 1972.)

7535. *Locomotive dictionary* / 2d ed. Compiled by George L. Fowler. New York, Railroad Age Gazette, 1909. 539, 266 p.

7536. *Locomotive dictionary* / 3rd ed. New York, Simmons-Boardman Pub. Co., 1912. 901 p.

7537. *Locomotive dictionary; definitions and illustrations of American locomotives, their parts and equipment, together with typical illustrations of machine tools and devices used in their maintenance and repair.* 4th ed. Compiled by Roy V. Wright. New York, Simmons-Boardman Pub. Co., 1916. 991 p. (> *Locomotive dictionary and cyclopedia.*)

7538. *Locomotive dictionary and cyclopedia.* 5th ed. Compiled and edited for the American Railway Master Mechanics Association by Roy V. Wright. New York, Simmons-Boardman Pub. Co., 1919. 1284 p.

7539. *Locomotive draft gears.* Omaha, NE: Simmons-Boardman, 1982. 53 p.

7540. *Locomotive economy devices.* New York, International Railway Supply Company, 1936. 30 l.

7541. *Locomotive Engine Safety Truck Company vs. the Pennsylvania Railroad Company : in equity : defendant's proofs on accounting [taken before] Robert N. Wilson, esq, Master.* S.l., s.n., 1877. 479 p. 58 leaves of plates.

7542. *The locomotive engineer.* New York, American Machinists Pub. Co., 1888-1891. 4 v. Monthly. (>*Railway and locomotive engineering*)

7543. *The locomotive engineer.* Cleveland, Brotherhood of Locomotive Engineers, 1960-1986. Semimonthly. (<*Locomotive engineers' journal*; > *Locomotive engineer newsletter.)*

7544. *The locomotive engineer newsletter.* Cleveland, OH: Brotherhood of Locomotive Engineers, 1987-

7545. *Locomotive engineering: a practical journal of railway motive power and rolling stock.* New York, A. Sinclair, 1892-1900. Monthly. (< *Locomotive engineer*, 1888-1891; > *Railway and locomotive engineering, 1901-1928.)*

7546. *Locomotive engineers & trainmen journal.* Cleveland, Ohio, Brotherhood of Locomotive Engineers, 2004-2005. 2 v. Quarterly. (>*Rail teamster*)

7547. *Locomotive engineers journal.* Cleveland, Ohio, Brotherhood of Locomotive

Engineers, 1907-1959. 53 v. Monthly.(< *Brotherhood of locomotive engineers journal*; > *Locomotive engineer.*)

7548. *Locomotive engineers journal.* Cleveland, Ohio, Brotherhood of Locomotive Engineers, 1987-2003. 17 v. Quarterly. (> *Locomotive engineers & trainmen journal.*)

7549. *Locomotive engineer's monthly journal.* Cleveland, Ohio, Brotherhood of Locomotive Engineers, 1867-1871. 5 v. Monthly.

7550. *Locomotive equipment.* Washington, DC: Association of American Railroads, Car Service Division, 1921-1950. Monthly Jan. 1936-June 1950; Semi-monthly, Oct. 15, 1921-Dec. 1935.(>*Summary of locomotive ownership and condition reports.*)

7551. *Locomotive firemen's magazine.* Terre Haute, Ind., 1800s-1900. Monthly. (>*Brotherhood of locomotive firemen's* magazine.)

7552. *The locomotive headlight: a review of their development and aid to train movement.* Nashville, Marshall & Bruce Co. Print., 1911. 47, 1 p.

7552a. *Locomotive headlights: the Pyle-National electric headlight : instruction paper with examination questions /* Scranton, PA: International Textbook Co., 1912. 1 v. (various pagings)

7553. *Locomotive historical review.* Auburn, Ind., American Association for Railroad and Locomotive History, 1933-1934. 2 v.

7554. Locomotive Maintenance Officers Association (U.S.) *Proceedings ... annual meeting of the Locomotive Maintenance Officers Association /* Huntington, WV: LMOA, 1939-   .

7555. *Locomotive ownership.* Washington, DC: Association of American Railroads, Car Service Division, 1923-1950.

7556. *Locomotive progress, 1910-1930.* New York, Superheater Company, 1930. 71 p.

7557. *Locomotive quarterly.* Mount Vernon, NY: Metaphor, 1976-2006. Quarterly.

7558. *Locomotive rosters of North America.* Champlain, NY: DPA-LTA Enterprises, 1996. 1 v.

7559. Locomotive Stoker Company. *Description and instructions covering oiling, handling and inspection of type B Street locomotive stoker: with 3 ½ x 3 ½ constant speed engine/* New York: Locomotive Stoker Company, 1914. 45 p.

7559a. _____. *Duplex locomotive stoker type "D".* Pittsburgh: Locomotive Stoker Co., 1919. 19 p.

7560. _____. *Duplex locomotive stoker, type "D-2": instructions for operating.*

Pittsburgh: Locomotive Stoker Co., 1923. 10 p.

7561. _____. *The Elvin mechanical stoker, "Saves as it serves"; road service hand book*. Pittsburgh: Locomotive Stoker Co, 1925. 55 p.

7561a. _____. *Instructions for operating, oiling and maintaining type C Street locomotive stoker : with 4 x 3 ½ variable speed engine and friction clutch* / New York : Locomotive Stoker Company, 1914. 48 p. (*Publication no. 12.*)

7562. _____. *Locomotive Stoker Company: manufacturers of Street and Duplex stokers, and mechanical coal pushers*. Pittsburgh, Locomotive Stoker Co., 1917. 22 p.

7563. _____. *Mechanical coal pushers for locomotive tenders*. New York: Locomotive Stoker Company, 1916. 19 p.

7564. _____. *Screw conveyor for types B & C stokers*. New York: Locomotive Stoker Company, 1916. 9 p.

7564a. _____. *Stoker fired locomotives equipped with duplex and Street stokers*. Pittsburgh : Locomotive Stoker Company, 1919. 96 p. (*Catalogue no. 14-D.*)

7565. _____. *Street locomotive stoker*. New York: Locomotive Stoker Co., 1915. 17 p.

7566. _____. *Street locomotive stoker* / New York: Locomotive Stoker Co., 1915. 49 p. (*Catalogue no. 14-B.*)

7566a. _____. *Street locomotive stoker backhead fittings* / New York : Locomotive Stoker Company, 1919. 17 p.

7567. _____. *Street locomotive stoker; type C, patents pending*. New York, Locomotive Stoker Co., 1923. 23 p.

7568. (Blank entry)

7569. Locomotive Superheater Company. *The use of highly superheated steam in locomotive practice*. New York, Locomotive Superheater Company, 1912. 28 p.

7570. *Locomotive truck assemblies*. Omaha, NE: Simmons-Boardman, 1981. 124 p.

7571. *The locomotive world*. Lima, Ohio, Franklin Type and Printing Company, 1909- Monthly. (v. 8=1916.)

7572.. *Locomotives and their operation* / Scranton, Pa., International Textbook Company, 1926. 3 v.

7573. *Locomotives of the Chicago & North Western Railway, supplement*. Boston, Mass., Railway & Locomotive Historical Society, 1948. 23 p.

7574. *Locomotives of the Pennsylvania Railroad.* Milwaukee, Kalmbach, 1940? 2 p. 20 l. of plates.

7575. *Locomotives of the Western Pacific.* Santa Barbara, CA: H.S. Thorne, n.d. 138 p.

7576. Lodge, Stuart W., Linda Ingram. *The Atlanta railfan guide.* Atlanta, GA: Crossroads Atlanta'95, 1994. 191 p.

7577. Loeb, Betty Wagner. *Altoona and the Pennsylvania Railroad: between a roar and a whimper.* Altoona, PA: Pennsylvania Railroad Technical & Historical Society, 1999. 99 p.

7578. Loewy, Raymond Fernand. *Industrial design* / Woodstock, NY: Overlook Press, 1979. 250 p.

7579. _____. *The locomotive.* London, The Studio, Ltd.; New York, The Studio Publications, Inc., 1937. 108 p. (Reprint: New York, NY: Universe, 1988, c1987.)

7580. _____. *Never leave well enough alone* / Baltimore : Johns Hopkins Press, 2002, 1951. 377 p.

7581. Loftus-Otway, Lisa Dawn. *Protecting and preserving rail corridors against encroachment of incompatible uses.* Austin, TX: Center for Transportation Research, 2008. 182 p.

7582. *The Log train: journal of the Mountain State Railroad & Logging Historical Association.* Cass, WV: The Association, 1982-

7583. Logan, John W., Archibald H. Kinghorn, John T. Elliott. *Energy consumption and traffic conditions of the Philadelphia-Paoli electrification of the Pennsylvania Railroad* / 1920. 1 v. (various pagings) (Thesis, B.S., Massachusetts Institute of Technology, Department of Electrical Engineering.)

7583a. *Logan's railway business directory from Saint Louis to Galveston via the Missouri pacific Railroad (to Sedalia), Missouri, Kansas & Texas R.W., Houston & Texas Central R.W., Galveston Houston & Henderson R.W.* St. Louis : A.L. Logan & Co., 1873. 200 p.

7583b. Lohse, Richard E. *Memories of the cab forwards: a personal view* / Upland, CA: Southern Pacific Historical & Technical Society, 2013.

7584. Lomax, E.L. *The evolution of the locomotive from 1813 to 1891: a brief record of great achievements.* Chicago, Ill., Knight, Leonard & Co., Printers, 1891. 31 p.

7585. Lomazzi, Brad S. *Railroad timetables, travel brochures & posters: a history and guide for collectors.* Spencertown, NY: Golden Hill Press, 1995. 194 p.

7586. Lombard, Albert Eaton. *Locomotive coaling stations.* 1902. 1 v. (Thesis, B.S.,

Massachusetts Institute of Technology, Department of Civil Engineering.)

7587. London, Jack. *The road.* New York, Macmillan, 1907. 224 p.

7588. Long, Bryant Alden. *Mail by rail; the story of the Postal Transportation Service.* With William Jefferson Dennis. New York, Simmons-Boardman, 1951. 414 p.

7589. Long Island Rail Road Company. *The Long Island Rail Road Co. safety rules; maintenance of way and structures employees, effective November 1, 1959.* New York, Long Island Rail Road Company, 1959. 129 p.

7590. Long Island Railroad Company. *Description of the construction of the First Division of the Long Island Railroad.* New York, Printed by G. Mitchell, 1838. 31 p.

7591. _____. *Locomotive classification and register; corrected to May 1st, 1917.* Richmond Hill, Long Island, Office, Superintendent of Motive Power, 1917. 19 l.

7592. _____. *Rules of the Operating Department, effective...May 1, 1903.* New York? Long Island Railroad Company, 1903. 140 p.

7592a. *The Long Island Railroad and the industrial development of Long Island, New York.* Brooklyn : Eagle Press, 1901. 20 p.

7593. Long, Lennart, and others. *Optical automatic car identification (OACI).* Washington, D.C., Federal Railroad Administration, Office of Research and Development, 1978. 4 v. (*Report no. FRA/ORD-78/15 (1-IV).*)

7593a. Long, Raphael F. *Red car era: an album : memories of Los Angeles and the Pacific Electric.* Charleston, SC: CreateSpace, 2010. 142 p.

7594. Long, Stephen Harriman. *Rail road manual; or, a brief exposition of principles and deductions applicable in tracing the route of a rail road.* Baltimore, Md., W. Woody, Printer, 1828-1829. 2 v.

7595. _____. *Specifications of certain improvements in the locomotive engine, and in the mode of transferring loaded carriages from one level to another, in their passage upon rail-ways.* Philadelphia, 1826. 12 p.

7596. Long, W. Alva. *Catalogue of steam locomotive types.* 2d ed. Easton, MD: Printed by Economy Printing Co., 1973. 64 p.

7597. _____. *A pictorial catalog of steam locomotive types and wheel arrangement.* Easton, MD: Printed by the Easton Pub. Co., 1971. 1 v.

7598. Longenecker, David, Christopher Fallon. *The Sunbury Canal and Water-Power Company and Sunbury Lumber and Car Manufacturing Company.* Philadelphia : McLaughlin Bros Book and Job Print Office, 1854. 15 p.

7599. Longest, David E. *The Monon Railroad in southern Indiana*. Charleston, SC: Arcadia Pub., 2008. 127 p.

7600. _____. *The railroad depots of northern Indiana*. Charleston, SC: Arcadia, 2007. 128 p.

7601. _____. *The railroad depots of southern Indiana*. Charleston, SC: Arcadia, 2005. 128 p.

7602. Longhurst, Lyle. *The Gilmore & Pittsburgh: Lemhi County's only railroad*. 1989. 172 l. (Thesis, M.S., University of Idaho.)

7603. Longini, Arthur. *Chicago-Chicago Heights industrial economic blueprint*. Chicago, IL: Chicago & Eastern Illinois Railroad, 1957. 346, 247 p. ("Directory of establishments served directly by railroads in the Chicago rate base area.")

7604. _____. *Economic atlas of the Pittsburgh-Youngstown economic area*. Foreword by John W. Barriger. Pittsburgh, Pittsburgh and Lake Erie Railroad, 1960. 45 p.

7605. _____. *Industrial potentialities of the lower Wabash River Valley; a report*. Chicago, Chicago & Eastern Illinois Railroad Company, 1954. 299, 145 p.

7606. _____. *Region of opportunity: industrial potential along the Pittsburgh-Youngstown Axis*. Pittsburgh, Pittsburgh and Lake Erie Railroad Company, 1961. 1 v.

7607. Lonon, J.L. *Tall tales of the rails, on the Carolina, Clinchfield & Ohio*. Johnson City, TN: Overmountain Press, 1989. 215 p. (Clinchfield Railroad)

7608. Lontz, Mary Belle. *Early railroads of Union County, Pennsylvania*. Lewisburg, PA: M.B. Lontz, 2002. 155 p.

7609. Loomis, Earl Hiram. *Industrial relations on the Pennsylvania Railroad*. 1923. 1 v. (Masters essay. Columbia University, Business & Economics.)

7610. Loomis, Jim. *All aboard! The complete North American train travel guide*. Rocklin, CA: prima Pub., 1995. 390 p.

7611. Loomis, Nelson Henry. *Asa Whitney; father of Pacific railroads*. Lincoln, Neb., s.n., 1912? 12 p.

7612. Loosbrock, Richard D. *Living with the octopus: life, work, and community in a western railroad town*. 2005. 275 l. (Thesis, Ph.D., University of New Mexico.) (CB&Q)

7613. Lopata, Edwin Lee. *Local aid to railroads in Missouri*. New York, Parnassus Press, 1937. 153 p.

7614. Lorain Steel Company. *Girder rails: catalogue number 22*. Johnstown, Penn,

Lorain Steel Company, 1927. 126 p.

7615. _____. *Standard tee rail construction for steam railroad and industrial railway track and switch work.* Johnstown, PA: Lorain Steel Co., 1912. 155 p. (*Catalogue, no. 17.*)

7616. _____. *Standard tee rail construction for steam rail road and industrial railway track and switch work.* Johnstown, PA: Lorain Steel Co., 1921. 212 p. (*Catalogue no. 21.*)

7617. Lord, Carroll J. *The doctrine of reasonableness in railroad rate regulation.* 1911. 62 l. (Thesis, LL.M., Yale Law School.)

7618. Lord, Eleazar. *A historical review of the New York and Erie Railroad.* New York: Mason, 1855. 223 p.

7619. Lord, Francis. *Lincoln's railroad man: Hermann Haupt.* Rutherford, NJ: Fairleigh Dickinson University Press, 1969. 325 p.

7620. Loree, Leonor Fresel. *The business depression and its effect on the railways; address of L.F. Loree, president, Delaware* and Hudson Railroad Corporation/ New York? 1931. 17 p.

7621. _____. *Locomotives, past and present.* New York, 1933. 13 p.

7622. _____. *Our American railroads: today and tomorrow.* New York, Institute of Arts and Sciences, Columbia University, 1935. 22 p.

7623. _____. *Railroad freight transportation.* New York, D. Appleton and Company, 1922. 771 p. (2d ed.: New York, D. Appleton and Co., 1929. 771 p.)

7624. _____. *Track.* Madison, Wis., University of Wisconsin, 1894. 24 p. (*University. of Wisconsin, bulletin, engineering series, v. 1, no. 1.*)

7625. _____. *The transportation significance of the steam railroad; an address delivered on November 23, 1926...Holland Society of New York.* New York, 1926. 13 p.

7626. Loree, J.T. *Transportation; the Delaware and Hudson Company.* Albany, N.Y., Press of the Delaware and Hudson Company, 1929. 101 p.

7627. Lorenz, Bob. *The 50 best of PRR, book four.* Baltimore, MD: Barnard, Roberts, 1979. 52 l.

7628. _____. *The 50 best of B & O, book five.* Baltimore, MD: Barnard, Roberts, 1979. 52 l.

7629. Lorenz, Max Otto. *Territorial variation in the cost of carload freight service on steam railways in the United States for the year 1928.* Washington, DC: Interstate

Commerce Commission, 1930. 12 p.

7630. _____. *Variation in cost of carload freight service among Class I steam railways 1928.* Washington, DC: Interstate Commerce Commission, Bureau of Statistics, 1930. 13 p. (Its *Statement no. 3120.*)

7631. Lorenzo, Robert V., Nathan S. Clark. *Bessemer and Lake Erie Railroad.* Edison, NJ: Morning Sun Books, 1994. 128 p.

7632. Lorenzon, Dimitri. *Residual stresses in railroad car axles resulting from manufacturing and service loads* / 1996. 1 v. (Thesis, M.S., Tufts University.)

7633. Lorenzsonn, Axel S. *Steam and cinders: the advent of railroads in Wisconsin, 1831-1861.* Madison: Wisconsin Historical Society Press, 2009. 342 p.

7634. Los Angeles & Salt Lake Railroad Company. *Rules and instructions of the Transportation Department.* S.l., Los Angeles and Salt Lake Railroad, 1919. 135 p.

7634a. *The Los Angeles Limited via Chicago & Northwestern, Union Pacific & Salt Lake route: every day in the year between Chicago and Southern California, electric lighted.* Chicago?: Chicago and North-Western Railway Co., 1907. 20 p.

7634b. [Los Angeles Union Station Collection. 1913-1969]. 22 linear feet. Location: Regional History Collection, Special Collections, University of Southern California.

7635. Lothbridge, Kenneth. *A conductor tells unauthorized train stories.* S.l., Working Title Publishing, 2006. 152 p.

7636. Lotz, David E. *The Burlington & Western and Burlington & Northwestern narrow gauge branch line.* LaGrange, IL: Burlington Route Historical Society, 1994. 57, 16 p. (Special issue of *Burlington Bulletin, no. 30.*)

7637. _____. *Burlington, Iowa: heart of the CB&Q.* LaGrange, IL: Burlington Route Historical Society, 1991. 123 p. (Special issue of *Burlington bulletin, no. 23.*)

7638. _____. *Burlington, Iowa, shops.* LaGrange, IL: Burlington Route Historical Society, 1992. 94 p.

7639. Loughborough, John. *The Pacific telegraph and railway, an examination of all the projects for the construction of these works with a proposition for harmonizing all sections and parties of the Union, and rendering these great works truly national in their character.* Saint Louis, Printed by Charles & Hammond, 1849. 80 p.

7639a. Loughran, Patrick H. *Special privilege in the public lands : the original grant of 43,159,428.04 acres to the Northern Pacific Railway Company, and the subsequent and additional grants to that company under "special and advantageous" scrip laws* / Washington, DC: P.H. Loughran, 1913. 24 p.

7640. Louisiana Purchase Exposition (1904, Saint Louis, Mo.) Electric Railway Test Commission. *Report of the Electric Railway Test Commission to the president of the Louisiana Purchase Exposition. Members of the commission: J.G. White, chairman, Geo. F. McCulloch, James H. McGraw, H.H. Vreeland, W.J. Wilgus.* Edited by Henry H. Norris and Bernard Victor Swenson. New York, McGraw, 1906. 621 p.

7641. Louisiana and Arkansas Railway Company. *Louisiana & Arkansas Railway Co.: transportation rules.* Parson, KS: Commercial Publishers, 1930. 136 p.

7642. _____. *Rules and instructions for the maintenance of way and structures, effective September 1, 1931.* S.l., Louisiana and Arkansas Railway Company, 1931. 33 p.

7642a. *Louisville and Great Southern monthly railway guide.* Louisville: Louisville and Nashville and Great Southern Railroad, 1874-? Monthly.

7643. *Louisville & Nashville employes' magazine.* Louisville, KY: Louisville and Nashville Railroad Company, 1925-1938. Monthly. (> *L & N magazine.*)

7643a. Louisville and Nashville Historical Society. *The Old Reliable/* Louisville, KY: The Society, 1900s-   Quarterly.

7644. Louisville and Nashville Railroad Company. *A book about the L & N (Louisville & Nashville R.R..)* Louisville? KY: The Company, 1923. 54 p.

7645. _____. *Coal mines served by the L & N Railroad.* S.l., Louisville and Nashville Railroad Company, 1966. 1 v.

7645a. _____. *Industrial and freight shippers directory.* S.l., Railroad Advertising Agency,1900s-

7645b. _____. *The L & N: one hundred years of progress.* Louisville, KY: 1950. 104 p.

7645c. _____. *Rules and instructions for the government of Trackmen of the Louisville & Nashville R.R.: 1891.* Louisville, KY: Bradley & Gilbert, 1891. 45 p.

7646. _____. *Rules for the government of the Operating Department: effective May 1st, 1909.* Louisville, Ky., John P. Morton, 1909. 209 p.

7647. _____. *Rules governing the use of manual block, controlled manual block, automatic block and interlocking systems.* Louisville, KY: Louisville and Nashville Railroad Company, 1910. 67 p.

7648. _____. *Safety rules: train and yard employees: effective February 11, 1931.* Louisville. KY: s.n., 1931. 19 p.

7649. _____. *Safety rules.* Louisville, KY: Louisville & Nashville Railroad Company, 1977. 46 p.

7649a. _____. *Specifications for steel railroad bridges.* Louisville, KY: Bradley & gilbert Co., 1912.

7650. _____. *The story of L. & N. motive power.* Louisville? Louisville and Nashville Railroad Company, 194-? 11 p.

7651. _____. *The story of L. & N. motive power.* Louisville? Louisville and Nashville Railroad Company, 1961. 16 p.

7652. _____. *Telegraph code.* Louisville, KY: Louisville and Nashville Railroad Company, 1912. 36 p.

7653. _____, Public Relations Department. *Handbook of railroad information/* Louisville, KY: The Company, `1924. 89 p.

7655. Louisville Car-Wheel and Railway Supply Co. *Statement of individual mileage of each wheel of Louisville Car-Wheel and Railway Supply Co.'s make, taken from under engines and tenders, passenger, baggage, mail, express, postal, and sleeping cars for the years 1876 and 1877.* Louisville, Ky., John P. Morton & Company, Printers, 1878. 12 p. Also issued in 1881.

7656. Love, Jean, Wendell Cox, Stephen Moore. *Amtrak at twenty-five: end of the line for taxpayer subsidies.* Washington, DC: Cato Institute, 1996. 31 p. (*Policy analysis (Cato Institute), no. 266.*)

7657. Love, John Joseph. *A demand-responsive approach to railroad track maintenance management/* 1981. 224 l. (Thesis, M.S., Massachusetts Institute of Technology, Department of Civil Engineering.)

7658. Lovegrove, Keith. *Railroad: identity, design and culture.* New York, Rizzoli, 2005. 160 p.

7659. Lovelace, Jeff. *Mount Mitchell: its railroad and toll road.* Johnson City, TN: Overmountain Press, 1994. 86 p. (North Carolina)

7660. Loveland, Jim A. *Dinner is served; fine dining aboard the Southern Pacific.* San Marino, CA: Golden West Books, 1996. 241 p.

7661. Lovell, D.H. *Practical switch work; a handbook for track foremen. 10th ed.* Philadelphia, PA:, Allen, Lane & Scott's Printing House, 1909. 174 p. (First ed, 1891. 174 p.)

7662. Lovell, F.H. & Company. *Railroad marine lighting appliances and fixtures.* S.l., Rushlight Club, 1983, 1916. 64 p. (Partial reprint of catalogue no. 500.)

7663. Lovell, Joseph D. *List of locomotives built at Altoona machine shops, Pennsylvania Railroad.* 1939. 87 p. ("Lists engines with construction nos. from 1 to 2289, built between 1866 and 1904.") (Location: University of Illinois.)

7664. _____. *Pennsylvania Railroad Altoona machine shops: construction number list, 1866-1904*. S.l., Library of American Transportation, 1984. 113 p.

7665. _____, Paul T. Warner. *1946. Pennsylvania Railroad System locomotive rosters /* S.l., s.n. 1946. Archival material. 0.6 linear feet. Document
Location: Hagley Museum & Library.

7665a. Lovett, Thomas D. *Report on the progress of work, cost of construction, etc., of the Cincinnati Southern Railway*. Cincinnati : Wrightson & Co., 1875. 85 p.

7666. Lovette, P.M., J. Thivierge. *Train make-up manual/* Chicago: Association of American Railroads/Track Train Dynamics Implementation Officers, 1992. 57 p. (*AAR report, R-802*)

7667. Loving, Rush. *The men who loved trains: the story of men who battled greed to save an ailing industry*. Bloomington, Indiana University Press, 2006. 360 p.

7668. Low, E.M., Vijay Kumar Garg. *Programming manual: train operation simulator*. Chicago, IL: Association of American Railroads, 1979. 163 p. (*AAR report no. R-359*)

7669. Low, William. *Old Penn Station*. New York, Henry Holt and Company, 2007. 40 p. Grades 3-6.

7670. Lowe, Ida Marie Williams. *The role of the railroads in the settlement of the Texas Panhandle*. 1962. 102 l. (Thesis, M.A. West Texas State College.)

7671 Lowe, Paul Emilius. *Electric railway troubles and how to find them; a comprehensive treatise on motors, motor operation, motor repairs, car break-downs, control systems, repairing of control, air brakes, air brake troubles, and electric railway operation generally*. Chicago, F.J. Drake and Company, 1909. 367 p.

7672. Lowenthal, Larry, William T. Greenburg. *The Lackawanna Railroad in northwest New Jersey*. Morristown, NJ: Tri-State Railway Historical Society, 1987. 244 p.

7673. Lowenthal, Max. *The investor pays*. New York, A.A. Knopf, 1933. 406 p. (Milwaukee Road)

7674. *Low's railway and telegraph directory for 1865 /* New York : J.S. Keeling, No. 16 Broadway, 1865. 220 p.

7674a. *Low's railway directory for ...; compiled from official reports*. S.l., s.n., 1858-1863. 6 v. (New York, Wynkoop, Hallenbeck & Thomas).

7675. Loy, Sallie, Richard L. Hillman, C. Pat Cates. *The Southern Railway*. Charleston, SC: Arcadia, 2004. 128 p.

7676. Lozier, John William. *Taunton and Mason: cotton machinery and locomotive manufacturer in Taunton, Massachusetts.* New York, Garland, 1986. 549 p. (Thesis, Ohio State University.)

7677. LS Transit Systems, Inc.; Vermont. Agency of Transportation. *Vermont rail feasibility study: final report.* Vermont, Vermont Agency of Transportation, 1993. 1 v.

7677a. *Lubbock: the railroad center of the Plains.* Lubbock, TX: Bledsoe & Price, 1910. 26 p.

7678. Lubetkin, M. John. *Jay Cooke's gamble: the Northern Pacific Railroad, the Sioux, and the Panic of 1873.* Norman, University of Oklahoma Press, 2006. 380 p.

7679. Lubin, Isador. *Report of the Railroad Marine Workers Commission.* New York, NY: Railroad Marine Workers Commission, 1962. 64, 26 p.

7680. Lubliner, Paul. *The New York, Ontario & Western, in color.* Scotch Plains, NJ: Morning Sun Books, 1997. 128 p.

7681. Lucas Walter Arndt. *From the hills to the Hudson; a history of the Paterson and Hudson River Rail Road and its associates, the Paterson and Ramapo, and the Union Railroad.* New York, Mullens-Tutrone Company, 1944. 319 p. (Reprint: Railroadians of America, 1950. 319 p.) Paterson and Hudson River Rail Road Company. Paterson and Ramapo Railroad Company. Union Railroad Company. Erie Railroad Company.

7682. _____. *The history of the New York, Susquehanna and Western Railroad.* New York, Railroadians of America, 1939. 116 p. (*Railroadians of America, v. 1, no. 1.*) (2d ed. New York, Railroadians of America, 1980. 195 p.)

7683. _____. *An illustrated record of the motive power and growth of the Delaware and Hudson Railroad; originally printed in two books published by the Company entitled: Motive power on the Delaware and Hudson, 1926.* New York, Railroadians of America, 1941? (*Railroadians of America, no. 3.)*

7684. _____. *Locomotives and cars since 1900.* New York, Simmons-Boardman Pub. Corp., 1959. 119 p.

7685. _____. *100 years of railroad cars.* New York, Simmons-Boardman Pub. Corp., 1958. 196 p.

7686. _____. *100 years of steam locomotives.* Contributing editors: Paul Needham, C.L. Combes, C.A. Phelps. New York, Simmons-Boardman Pub. Corp., 1957. 278 p.

7687. _____. *Pocket guide to American locomotives.* New York, Simmons-Boardman Pub. Corp., 1953. 290 p.

7688. _____. *Popular picture and plan book of railroad cars and locomotives.* New York, Simmons-Boardman Pub. Corp., 1951. 288 p.

7689. _____, Paul T. Warner. *Book no. 2: Exit, the Sixth Avenue Elevated Line; Compound locomotives. Norris Brothers, locomotive builders.* New York, Railroadians of America, 1940. 76 p. (*Railroadians of America, no. 2.*)

7690. Luce, Robert. *Electric railways and the electric transmission of power described in plain terms.* Boston, W.I. Harris & Company, 1886. 106 p.

7691. Luckin, Richard W. *Dining on rails; an encyclopedia of railroad china.* Denver, RK Publishing, 1983- (2d ed. Golden: CO: RK Pub., 1990- ; 3d ed. 1994. 416 p.; 4th ed.: 1998.)

7692. _____. *Mimbres to mimbreño; a study of Santa Fe's famous china pattern.* Golden, CO: RK Publishing, 1992. 88 p.

7693. _____. *Santa Fe's California poppy china pattern.* Sacramento, CA: California State Railroad Museum Foundation, 2002. 21 p.

7694. _____. *Teapot treasury (and related items).* Denver, RK Pub., 1987. 152 p.

7695. Ludlow, Donald B. *State rail planning best practices.* Washington, DC: American Association of State Highway and Transportation Officials, 2009. 84 p.

7696. Ludwig, Armin K. *The transportation structure of the lower Wabash Valley: a study of an area as a generator, recipient, and corridor for commodity movements by railroad, highway, waterway, and pipeline /* 1962. 217 l. (Thesis, Ph.D., University of Illinois.)

7697. Ludwig, Charles Herbert. *The history and methods of electrification of the Pennsylvania Railroad between Baltimore and Washington, D.C.* In: Records of Phi Mu, University of Maryland at College Park Libraries. 1934. 35 l.

7698. Ludy, Llewellyn V. *Air brakes; an up-to-date treatise on the Westinghouse air brake as designed for passenger and freight service and for electric cars, with rules for care and operation.* Chicago, American Technical Society, 1917. 200 p.

7699. _____. *Air brakes.* Chicago, American School of Correspondence, 1922. 2 v.

7700. _____. *Locomotive boilers and engines: a practical treatise on locomotive boilers and engine design, construction and operation.* Chicago, American School of Correspondence, 1913. 1 v. (Also: 1920. 192 p..)

7701. _____. *Steam engine indicators and valve gears; a practical presentation of modern testing appliances and methods used to produce maximum efficiency as applied to the steam engine.* Chicago, American Technical Society, 1918. 1 v.

7702. _____. *Valve gears.* Chicago, American School of Correspondence, 1912. 1 v.

7703. Luebke, Robert W. *Investigation of boxcar vibrations* / Washington, DC: Office of High-Speed Ground Transportation, Department of Transportation, 1970. 176 p.

7704. Luecke, John C. *The Chicago and North Western in Minnesota*. Eagan, MN: Grenadier Publications, 1990. 250 p.

7705. _____. *Dreams, disasters, and demise: the Milwaukee Road in Minnesota.* Eagan, MN: Grenadier Publications, 1988. 227 p.

7706. _____. *The Great Northern in Minnesota: the foundations of an empire.* St. Paul, MN: Grenadier Publications, 1997. 289 p.

7707. _____. *More Chicago Great Western in Minnesota* / Saint Paul, MN: Grenadier Publications, 2009. 208 p.

7708. _____. *The Northern Pacific in Minnesota.* St. Paul, MN: Grenadier Publications, 2005. 449 p.

7708a. _____. *The Rock island in Minnesota* / Eagan, MN: Grenadier Publications, 2011. 250 p.

7709. Luedeke, Jonathan F. *Safety of high speed ground transportation systems: analytical methodology for safety validation of computer controlled subsystems/* Washington, DC: Federal Railroad Administration, Office of Research and Development, 1995. 2 v. (*DOT/FRA/ORD-95/10*)

7710. Luisi, Vincent G. *Railroading in Pinellas County* / |Charleston, SC : Arcadia, 2010. 127 p. Florida – Pinellas County.

7711. Luminator, Inc. *Art and science light a modern fleet*. Chicago : Luminator, Inc., 1938. 9 l. Lighting for the Broadway Limited and Liberty Limited by Paul Philippe Cret and Raymond Loewy.

7712. Luna, Henry J. *Niles Canyon railways*. Charleston, SC: Arcadia, 2005. 128 p.

7713. Lund, George W., Sarah F. Schwenk. *Chicago and Alton Depot, Independence, Missouri: evaluation and feasibility study*. Kansas City, MO: Western Blue Print Co., 1993. 51 l.

7714. Lund, John Herbert, Robert F. McCullough. *Herb's hot box of railroad slang, plus Heroes of American railroading/* Chicago, IL: J. Herbert Pub. Co., 1975. 215 p.

7715. Lund, Leonard. *The commuter problem in the New York area: a consideration of past efforts and a proposed solution for the present problem.* 1962. 370 l. (Thesis, Ph.D., New York University.)

7716. Lundien, Jerry R. *Feasibility study for railroad embankment evaluation with radar measurements.* Washington, DC: Federal Railroad Administration, Office of Research and Development, 1979. 40 p.

7717. Lundy, Robert F. *The economics of loyalty-incentive rates in the railroad industry of the United States.* Pullman, Washington State University Press, 1963. 144 p. *(Washington State University. Bureau of Economic and Business research, Bulletin, no. 37.)*

7718. Luo, Yu. *Chinese railroad workers in the western U.S.,1860s./* 2000. 87 l. (Thesis, M.A., University of Wyoming.)

7719. Luttgens, Henry A. *A treatise upon the ordinary draft appliances of a locomotive boiler as superseded by more rational means.* Paterson, NJ: Press Printing and Publishing Company, 1891. 19 p.

7720. Luttrell, Norm .W. *Train operations simulator mathematical model: user's manual.* S.l., Government-Industry Research program on Track Train Dynamics, 1976. 1 v. (various pagings (*Government-Industry Research program on Track Train Dynamics, R-198*)

7721. _____. *Train operations simulator user's manual track-train dynamics : release 4.26 /* Chicago : Association of American Railroads, Technical Center, 1983. 183 p. *(Report no. R-564.)*

7722. _____. *User's manual: train operations simulator.* Chicago, IL: Association of American Railroads, 1976. 1 v (various pagings) (*AAR report no. R-198*)

7723. Lutz, Charles A. *Classification of revenues and expenses of sleeping car operations, of auxiliary operations and of other properties for sleeping car companies as prescribed by the Interstate Commerce Commission in accordance with section 20 of the Act to regulate commerce. First rev. issue.* Washington, DC: G.P.O., 1912. 41 p.

7723a. Lutz, Delos A. *The railroad is to blame : perceptions of Ogden's decline /* Ogden: Weber State University, 2012. 26 p.

7724. Luzzi, Anthony Reno, Joseph M. Sussman. *A systems dynamics model of the U.S. rail industry.* 1976. 2 v. (607 l.) (Thesis, M.S., Massachusetts Institute of Technology, Department of Civil Engineering.)

7725. Lyden, Anne M. *Railroad vision: photography, travel, and perception.* Los Angeles, The J, Paul Getty Museum, 2003. 164 p.

7726. Lydiatt, Sara Maud. *Transcontinental travels: two American limited trains, 1900-1914.* 2001. 84 l. (Thesis, M.A., Bard Graduate Center for Studies in the Decorative Arts.) (North Coast Limited; Oriental Limited.)

7726a. Lyford, W.H. *Co-operation versus competition between motor truck and railroad transportation.* New York: National Automobile Chamber of Commerce, 1955. 19 p.

7727. Lyle, Katie Letcher. *Scalded to death by the steam: authentic stories of railroad disasters and the ballads that were written about them.* Chapel Hill, NC: Algonquin Books, 1983. 212 p. (Reissued 1988.)

7728. Lyles, Mortimer Lee. *The railroad.* Chicago: Atchison, Topeka and Santa Fe Railway Co., 1939. 31 p.

7728a. Lyman, Henry M. *Electro-motors and their application to railways/* 1887. 47 l. (Thesis, B.S., University of Illinois.)

7729. Lynch, P.J. *Instructions to conductors pertaining to the handling of perishable freight/* Rev. ed. S.l., Union Pacific Railroad Company, 1944. 11 p. (*Circular, no. R-65*)

7730. (Blank entry.)

7731. Lynch, Peter E. *New Haven Railroad.* St. Paul, MN: MBI, 2003. 160 p.

7732. _____. *New Haven Railroad passenger trains.* St. Paul, MN: MBI, 2005. 160 p.

7733. _____. *Penn Central Railroad.* St. Paul, MN: MBI, 2004. 160 p.

7734. Lynch, Terry. *Railroads of Kansas City.* Boulder, CO: Pruett Pub. Co., 1984. 142 p.

7735. _____, W.D. Caileff, Jr. *The Kansas City Southern: route of the Southern Belle.* Boulder, CO: Pruett Pub. Co., 1987. 223 p.

7736. Lynch, Thomas A. *An analysis of the economic impacts of Florida high-speed rail/* Tampa: University of South Florida, Center for Economic Forecasting and Analysis; Center for Urban Transportation Research, 1997. 1 v. (various pagings)

7737. _____. *High speed rail in the U.S.: super trains for the millennium /* Amsterdam: Gordon and Breach Science Publishers, 1998. 163 p.

7738. _____. *Travel time, safety, energy and air quality impacts of Florida high-speed rail/* Tampa: University of South Florida, Center for Economic Forecasting and Analysis; Center for Urban Transportation Research, 1997. 44, A-14, B-3 p.

7739. Lynde, Francis, Jay Hambidge. *Empire builders.* Indianapolis, The Bobbs-Merrill Co., 1907. 377 p. (Stories)

7740. Lyndon, George W., Frederick K. Vial. *The chilled iron car wheel /* Chicago : Association of Manufacturers of Chilled Car Wheels, 1917. 32 p.

7741. Lynn, Robert W. *Death by electrocution? The Chicago, Milwaukee, Saint Paul, and Pacific Railroad choice of electrical motors over steam engines in Montana, 1914-1974.* 2004. 184 l. (Thesis, M.A., University of Montana.)

7742. Lyon, Arion Everett. *The first 75: history of the Brotherhood of Railroad Signalmen, 1901-1976.* Mount Prospect, IL: Brotherhood of Railroad Signalmen, 1976. 325 p.

7743. Lyon, Carl V. *A survey of the freight car shortage in the United States.* 1951. 120 l. (Thesis, M.A., American University.)

7744. Lyon, James. *Where steam still serves: the picture story of the Great Western Railway serving the sugar centers of northern Colorado: starring Old No. 90.* Denver, CO: Great Western Sugar Company, 1961. 46 p.

7745. Lyon, Peter. *To hell in a day coach; an exasperated look at American railroads.* Philadelphia, PA: Lippincott, 1967. 324 p.

7746. Lyon, Tracy, C.A. Read, B.J. Arnold. *The Oelwein shops of the Chicago Great Western Railway.* Chicago : Arnold E.P.S. Co., 1900. 13 p. (*Arnold E.P.S. Co., Bulletin no. 4.*)

7746a. Lyons, Robert Donlan. *A compilation of the laws of the forty-eight States relating to the protection of the public at points where railroads intersect highway at grade, including grade crossing elimination acts.* Washington, DC: Bureau of Public Lands, 1931. 391 l.

M

7747. *M.K. and T. employes' magazine*. St. Louis, Missouri-Kansas-Texas Railroad, 1913- Monthly. Title varies slightly.

7748. M. Ray Perryman Consultants. *The economic impact of the Texas High-Speed Rail Project: an analysis of construction, operation, tourism, and potential contributions to economic development: a technical memorandum* / Waco, TX: Perryman Consultants, 1980s. 50 l.

7749. Mabee, Carleton. *Bridging the Hudson: the Poughkeepsie Railroad Bridge and its connecting rail lines: a many-faceted history*. Fleischmanns, NY: Purple Mountain Press, 2001. 296 p.

7750. _____, John K. Jacobs. *Listen to the whistle: an anecdotal history of the Walkill Valley Railroad in Ulster and Orange counties, New York*. Fleischmanns, NY: Purple Mountain Press, 1995. 166 p.

7751. Mac Publishing. *Railroad maps*. Colorado Springs, Mac Publishing, 1980. 5 v. ("Maps originally prepared for the Department of Transportation.")

7752. MacAlpine, John Douglas. *A catechism of the A.R.A. rules and the general instructions, A.R.A. loading rules*. Cleveland, Ohio, McConway & Torley Co., American Railway Association, 1922. 117 p. Published by authority of the McConway & Torley Co. of Pittsburgh, Pa. by J.D. MacAlpine.

7753. MacAvoy, Paul W. The *economic effects of regulation: the trunk-line railroad cartels and the Interstate Commerce Commission before 1900*. Cambridge, MA: M.I.T. Press, 1965. 275 p.

7754. _____, James Sloss. *Regulation of transport innovation; the ICC and unit coal trains to the East Coast*. New York, Random House, 1967. 143 p. (*Random House series in industrial economics*)

7755. _____, John W. Snow. *Railroad revitalization and regulatory reform*. Washington, D.C., American Enterprise Institute, 1977. 246 p. (*AEI studies, 173.*)

7756. MacBain, Donald Robertson. *Locomotive management, break-downs and their cures, including questions and answers for first, second and third years examinations for promotion, and studies on Mallet compounds and electric head-light*. Cleveland, The Britton Printing Company, 1917, 1900. 192 p.

7757. MacCurdy, William K. *Impact tests of cushion underframes and hydrafriction and standard draft gears* / Stanford, CA: Stanford Research Institute, 1954. 25 p. (*Final Report Project 1226, February 1955.*

7758. MacDonald, Frederick D., John L. Kay. *Catalog of New Jersey railway postal markings.* Holmdel, NJ: New Jersey Postal History Society, 1984. 136 p. ("A basic history of railway mail routes in New Jersey.)

7759. MacDonald, J.R. *Treatise covering operation, defects and remedies of the locomotive, Westinghouse and New York air brake.* 2d ed. S.l., J.R. MacDonald, 1926. 290 p.

7760. MacDonald, James M. *Effects of railroad deregulation on grain transportation /* Washington, DC: U.S. Department of Agriculture, Economic Research Service, 1989. 52 p.

7761. MacDonald, Robert. *In quest of Maine narrow gauge: 1938-1950.* Grey, ME? Robert MacDonald, 1999. 111 p.(Wiscasset, Waterville, and Framington Railway; Sandy River and Rangeley Lakes Railroad.)

7762. _____. *Maine narrow gauge railroads.* Charleston, SC: Arcadia, 2003. 128 p.

7762a. Macdonald, Stuart H. *Evaluation of recreational reuse of abandoned railroad rights-of-way /* 1979. 187 l. (Thesis, M.L.A., Utah State University.)

7763. MacFarland, H.B. *Superheater tests; comparative road tests of Jacobs high and low pressure superheaters as applied to Santa Fe type tandem compound locomotives.* Chicago, Ill., Atchison, Topeka and Santa Fe Railway Company, 1910. 116 l.

7764. Macfarlane, Robert S. *Henry Villard and the Northern Pacific.* New York, Newcomen Society in North America, 1954. 28 p.

7765. MacGregor, Bruce A. *The birth of California narrow gauge: a regional study of the technology of Thomas and Martin Carter.* Stanford, CA: Stanford University Press, 2003. 673 p.

7766. _____. *Narrow gauge portrait: South Pacific Coast.* Felton, CA: Glenwood Publishers, 1975. 187 p.

7767. _____. *South Pacific Coast; an illustrated history of the narrow gauge South Pacific Coast Railroad.* Berkeley, CA: Howell-North Books, 1968. 280 p.

7768. _____, Ted Benson. *Portrait of a silver lady: the train they called the California Zephyr.* Boulder, CO: Pruett Pub. Co., 1977. 357 p.

7769. _____, Richard Truesdale. *South Pacific Coast, a centennial.* Boulder, CO: Pruett Pub. Co., 1982. 351 p.

7769a. Macidull, Joseph Charles. *A proposed methodology for subjectively evaluating an intrastate railroad network/* 1978. 255 l. (Thesis, Ph.D., University of Austin.)

7769b. Macie, T.W. *Selective bibliography of world literature on electric traction for railroads, 1970-1976.* Washington, DC: Department of Transportation, Federal Railroad Administration, Office of Research and Development, 1977. 141 p.

7770. Mack, J.S. *Forms of rail-road rails and their relation to the forms of the wheel flanges* / 1888. 60 l. 9 leaves of plates. (Thesis, C.E., Lehigh University.)

7771. Mack Trucks, Inc. *Mack catalog no. R91: gas-electric railcars and locomotives.* New York, Mack Trucks; International Motor Company, 1928. 105 p.

7772. _____. *The new Mack gas-electric 60-ton switcher (405 H.P.).* New York, The Company, 1928. 4 p.

7773. _____. *12-ton gas-electric locomotive.* New York, Mack Trucks, Inc., 1928. 4 p.

7774. MacKavanagh, Kelvin Lawrence. *An analysis of Pennsylvania Railroad freight service since 1946.* 1961. 124 l. (Thesis, M.B.A. in Transportation and Public Utilities, Graduate School of Arts and Sciences, University of Pennsylvania.)

7775. _____. *An analysis of Pennsylvania Railroad piggyback service* / 1961 18 l. Paper submitted in partial fulfillment of the requirements for the certificate of membership in the American Society of Traffic and Transportation, Inc.

7776. MacRae, Albert, C.L. Hamil. *An illustrated biographical directory of officials of the Atchison, Topeka & Santa Fe Railway System.* Chicago, Ill., Railway Exchange, 1908. 116 p.

7777. *Mad River & Nickel Plate Railroad Society Museum : anthology.* Bellevue, OH : Bellevue Gazette, 2010. 132 p. Compiled by Dale D. Owens. (Mad River and Lake Erie Railroad Company.)

7777a. Madden, Jerome. *The lands of the Southern Pacific Railroad Company of California: with general information on the resources of Southern California.* San Francisco: Southern Pacific Co., 1882. 151 p.

7778. Madden, Tom, Mallory Hope Ferrell. *Narrow gauge Oregon railroads* / San Mateo, CA: The Western Railroader, 1964, 1962. 12, 13 p.

7779. Maddock, Don, Jim Sinclair. *The history and development of the Ann Arbor Railroad's central terminal.* Grand Rapids, MI: Ann Arbor Railroad Technical and Historical Association, 2002-

7780. Maddox, Kenneth. *Intruder into Eden: the train in the nineteenth-century American landscape.* 1999. 509 l. (Thesis, Ph.D., Columbia University.)

7780a. Madi, Vijay Narayan. *Transformation behavior and weldability of alloy steel rails.* 1988. 253 l. (Thesis, Ph.D., Illinois Institute of Technology.)

7780b. Madison, Marshall Pierce. *The Railroad Commission of the state of California;*

its powers and jurisdiction. San Francisco? Peman-Walsh Printing Co., 1920. 61 p. (Thesis, J.D., University of California, Berkeley.)

7781. Madson, Hal. *Railroads of the Santa Maria Valley: three California railroads, three different gauges.* Los Olivos, CA: Olive Press Publications, 2001. 184 p.

7782. Maertens, Thomas Brock, Jr. *The relationships of climate and terrain to maintenance of way on the Norfolk Southern Railroad Between Norfolk, Virginia, and Portsmouth, Ohio.* 1990. 228 l. (Thesis, Ph.D., University of Tennessee.)

7783. Maffett, Everett L. *Silver banquet: a compendium on railroad dining car silver serving pieces.* Eaton, OH: Silver Press, 1980-1990. 2 v.

7784. Magee, G.M. *Survey of railroad rail and wheel contour studies* / Chicago : Association of American Railroads, Technical Center, 1981. 79 l. (*Report. Association of American Railroads, Technical Center, no. R-504.*)

7785. *Maglev deployment program: final programmatic environmental impact statement/* Washington, DC: John A. Volpe National Transportation Systems Center, 2001. 2 v. (*DOT/FRA/RDV-00/02. DOT-VNTSC-FRA-00-04*)

7786. Magnus Metal Corporation. *Current economics of solid bearing operation in freight service* / S.l., Magnus Metal Corp., 1962. 38 l.

7786a. Magoc, Chris Joseph. *The selling of wonderland : Yellowstone National Park, the Northern Pacific Railroad, and the culture of consumption, 1872-1903* / 1992. 2 v., 467 l. (Thesis, Ph.D., University of New Mexico.)

7787. Magor Car Corporation. *Railway cars, steel freight cars; standard American and European designs; cars also built to purchasers' requirements.* Passaic, NJ: Magor Car Corporation, 1921. 156 p.

7788. Maguire, Jack. *Katy's baby: the story of Denison, Texas.* Austin, TX: Nortex Press, 1991.

7789. Mahan, Charles T. *The 50 best of beloved Ma & Pa, book one.* Baltimore, MD: Barnard, Roberts, 1979. 52 l.

7790. Mahoney, E.S. *Prince Ivory: the switchman detective and chief of the secret service of the Texas & Pacific Railway.* St. Louis, MO: Nixon-Jones, 1892. 128 p. (Fiction)

7791. Mahoney, John E. *Monitoring rail freight* / New York: Tri-State Planning Commission, 1978. 1, 27 p. (*Analysis notes, 2612.*)

7792. Mahoney, John H. *Intermodal freight transportation.* Westport, CT: Eno Foundation for Transportation, 1985. 214 p.

7793. Maiken, Peter T. *Night trains: the Pullman system in the golden years of American rail travel*. Chicago, IL: Lakme Press, 1989. 415 p. (Also: Baltimore, John Hopkins University Press, 1992. 415 p.)

7794. Mailer, Stan. *Green Bay & Western: the first 111 years*. Edmonds, WA: Hundman, 1989. 349 p.

7795. _____. *The Omaha Road: Chicago, St. Paul, Minneapolis & Omaha*. Mukilteo, WA: Hundman, 2004. 311 p.

7796. *Main Line news*. Chicago: Illinois Central Gulf Railroad Co., 1900s-? Bimonthly. (< *Illinois Central Gulf news*.)

7797. *Maine Central magazine*. Portland, ME: Maine Central Railroad, 1924- . Monthly.

7798. Maine Central Railroad Company. *Agreement between the Maine Central Railroad Company and Pullman's palace Car Company. Dated April 1st, 1893. Expires April 1st, 1918*. S.l., s.n., 1893. 9 p.

7799. _____. *Corporate history of the Maine Central Railroad Company: March 15, 1916*. S.l., s.n., 1915. 110 l.

7800. _____. *Maine Central Railroad: a century of service to the state Of Maine, 1862-1962*. Portland? ME: Maine Central Railroad Co., 1962. 20 p.

7801. _____. *Official directory and atlas: Maine Central R.R., St. Johnsbury & Lake Champlain R.R., Boston & Maine R.R.* S.l., s.n., 1898. 201 p.

7802. _____. *Regulations for the movement & management of trains, to take effect Monday, May 1, 1876*. S.l., s.n., n.d. 1 v. (unpaged)

7803. _____. *Stations, bridges, and culverts*. S.l., Maine Central Railroad, 1904. 3 v.

7804. _____. *Official directory and atlas: Maine Central R.R., St. Johnsbury & Lake Champlain R.R., Boston & Maine R.R.* S.l., s.n., 1898. 201 p.

7805. Maine. Department of Transportation. *Maine Central Railroad inventory and line evaluation report*. Augusta, ME: Maine Department of Transportation, 1975. 1 v. (various pagings)

7806. *The Mainstreeter*/ Minneapolis, MN: The Northern Pacific Railway Historical Association, 1980s-- Quarterly.

7807. *Maintenance of way bulletin*. Sterling, IL: Roadmasters' and Maintenance of Way Association of America, 1900s-?

7808. *Maintenance of way cyclopedia: a reference book covering definitions, descriptions, illustrations, and methods of use of the materials, equipment, and devices employed in the maintenance of the tracks, bridges, buildings, water stations, signals, and other fixed properties of railways.* Howson, E.T. 1st ed. New York, Simmons-Boardman, 1921. 860 p.(> *Railway engineering and maintenance cyclopedia, 2d-7th ed.)*

7809. Makley, Michael J. *The infamous king of the Comstock: William Sharon and the Gilded Age of the West.* Reno, University of Nevada Press, 2006. 291 p.

7810. Malan, Roland M. *Review of the LIRR's performance in providing adequate temperature control* / New York : Metropolitan Transportation Authority, Office of the Inspector General, 1998. 4, 29, 11 p. (*MTA/IG 98-14.)*

7810a. *Malibu rails and roads* / Thomas W. Doyle, et al. Malibu, CA: Malibu Lagoon Museum, 2012. Updated ed. 100 p.

7811. Malinoski, Robert R. *A golden decade of trains: the 1950's, in color.* Edison, NJ: Morning Sun Books, 1991. 128 p.

7811a. Mall, Burt W. *Steam's last season: a portfolio of steam locomotive photographs from the late 1950s* / Long Grove, IL: Grate Rail Publishing, 2013. 206 p.

7812. Mallet, Anatole. *Compound engines.* New York, Van Nostrand, 1874. 82 p. *Van Nostrand science series, no. 10.)*

7813. Malone, Micheal P. *James J. Hill: empire builder of the Northwest.* Norman, University of Oklahoma Press, 1996. 306 p. (*The Oklahoma western biographies, v. 12.*)

7814. Mandel, Francis Milton. *The feasibility of railroad electrification in the United States.* 1970. 32 l. (Thesis, M.A., San Francisco State College.)

7814a. Mangurian, George Nishan. *A study of railroad and highway grade crossings, including types of construction and methods of protection* / 1928. 61 l. (Thesis, B.S., Massachusetts Institute of Technology, Department of Civil and Sanitary Engineering.)

7815. *Manitou and Pike's Peak Railway Company. Pikes Peak by rail: cog wheel route.* Manitou, CO: Manitou and Pikes Peak Railway, 19--? 16 p.

7816. Mann, Ann, Herbert Finch, Constance Buckley. *Switchmen's Union of North America records, 1894-1971: finding guide.* Ithaca, NY: Joint Railway Labor History Project, 1972. 312 p.

7817. Mann, James Robert. *Block signals and appliances for the automatic control of railway trains ... Report.* <To accompany H.J. Res. 153.> (*59th Congress., 1st. sess. House. Rept. 4637.*)

7818. Mann, Robert W. *Rails 'neath the palms.* Burbank, CA: Darwin Publications, 1983. 220 p. (Florida)

7819. Mann, Tina. *The old Chicago and Alton train depot of Fulton, Missouri: "the nicest and prettiest depot on the C & A line."* Fulton, MO: William Woods University, 1994. 58, 12 p.

7820. Mannello, Timothy A. *Problem drinking among railroad workers: extent, impact, and solutions.* Washington, DC: University Research Corporation, 1979. 69 p. (*Monograph series, no. 4.*)

7821. _____, F.J. Seaman. *Prevalence, costs, and handling of drinking problems on seven railroads: final report.* Washington, DC: Federal Railroad Administration; University Research Corporation, 1979. 219 p.

7822. Manning, David F. *The West Side improvement.* New York: Committee on Port and Terminal Facilities of the Board of Estimate and Apportionment, 1917. 6 p. (Justice Manning's decision, April 19, 1917.)

7823. Manning, Thomas G. *The Chicago Strike of 1894; industrial labor in the late nineteenth century.* New York, Holt, 1960. 65 p. (*Select problems in historical interpretation, 4.*)

7824. Manson, Arthur James. *Railroad electrification and the electric locomotive/* New York, Simmons-Boardman Pub. Co., 1923. 332 p. (2d ed.: 1925. 332 p.)

7825. *Manual for railway engineering.* Washington, D.C., American Railway Engineering Association. 1996. 4 v.

7826. *Manual for railway engineering.* St. Louis, MO: Mira Digital Pub., 2002- (American Railway Engineering and Maintenance-of-Way Association.)

7827. *Manual of recommended practice for railway engineering and maintenance-of-way.* Chicago, Ill., American Railway Engineering and Maintenance-of-Way Association, 1905-1907. 2 v.

7828. *Manual of standard and recommended practice.* New York, American Railway Association, 1922. 12 pt. in 1 vol. (American Railway Association. Mechanical Division.)

7829. *Manual of standards and recommended practices for rail passenger equipment.* Washington, DC: American Public Transportation Association (APTA), 1999. 682 p. (Loose leaf)

7830. *Manual of the railroads of the United States.* New York, H.V. & H.W. Poor, 1869-1894. 27 v. Annual. (>*Poor's manual of the railroads of the United States.*)

7831. *Manual on the railroad spike industry.* Washington, D.C., Federal Railroad Administration; Minority Business Resource Center, U.S. Dept. of Transportation, 1980. 1 v. (various pagings)

7831a. *Manufacturer's Railway: a century of service, 1887-1987*. St. Louis: National Railway Historical Society, St. Louis Chapter, 2012. 32 p.

7832. Manufacturers Trust Company (New York, N.Y.) *Pennsylvania, the station, the tunnels, the connecting railroad, the company, and its workers*. New York : Manufacturers Trust Company, 1921. 33, 1 p.

7833. Manufacturing Chemists' Association (U.S.). *Loading and unloading corrosive liquids—tank cars: recommended practice*. Washington, DC: manufacturing Chemists' Association, 1975. 13 p. (*Technical bulletin, TC-27.*)

7834. _____. *Loading and unloading flammable liquid chemicals—tank cars: recommended practice*. Washington, DC: Manufacturing Chemists' Association, 1975. 13 p. (*Technical bulletin, TC-29.*)

7835. Many, William V., George W. Sizer. *Report of the trial in the case of William V. Many vs. George W. Sizer et al. for the infringement of a patent for a railroad car wheel, commonly known as the wolf wheel : before Judge Sprague and a jury, at Boston, in the Circuit Court of the United States, for the Massachusetts District, January, 1849*. Boston : C.C.P. Moody, 1849. 361 p.

7836. Mao, Chi-Kuo, Carl D. Martland, Joseph Martin Sussman. *The relationship between power availability and freight car utilization : final report*. Cambridge : Center for Transportation Studies, Massachusetts Institute of Technology, 1980. 72 p. (*Studies in railroad operations and economics, v. 30. CTS report 80-4.*)

7837. Mapes, Mark G. *Losing steam; the decision-making process in the dieselization of the Pennsylvania Railroad*. 2000. 369 p. (Thesis, Ph.D., University of Delaware.)

7837a. Mapother, W. L. *The railroad and economic progress : brief review of the railroad situation since the enactment of the Transportation Act of 1920*/ Louisville: Louisville and Nashville Railroad Co., 1924. 15 p.

7838. *Maps of the Southern Pacific*. Compiled by Guy Dunscomb and Al Rose. Modesto, CA: Rose Lithograph Co., 1949.

7839. Marcham, David, John Marcham. *Lehigh Valley memories: a tour of the Lehigh Valley Railroad in New York's Finger Lake Region, 1941-1959*. Ithaca, NY: DeWitt Historical Society of Tompkins County, 1998. 88 p.

7839a. Marchant, Frederick, Stephen Massengill, C. Vernon Vallance. *Richmond County and the Seaboard Air Line Railway*. Charleston, SC: Arcadia, 2005. 128 p.

7840. Margler, Lawrence William. *Some environmental impact of coal transportation by slurry and unit train*. 1979. 133 l. (Thesis, D. Env., University of California, Environmental Science and Engineering.)

7841. Marin, Edward J., Elvin Sydney Ketchum, Edward G. Ward. *Interstate commerce law; act to regulate commerce.* Chicago: American Commerce Association, 1917. 3 v. "Prepared under the direction of the Advisory Traffic Council of the America Commerce Association."

7842. *Marine and locomotive work; steam fitting.* Chicago, Ill., American School, 1908. 530 p. (Modern engineering practice, v. 8.)

7843. *Marine line equipment.* Middletown, NY: Ontario & Western Railway Historical Society, 1992. 76 p. (*Observer, no. 27, nos. 1-9.*)

7844. Marion, H.S., E.E. Place. *Electric locomotive tests made at the Hoosac Tunnel, North Adams, Mass.* 1915. 1 v. (Thesis, B.S., Massachusetts Institute of Technology.)

7845. Maris, James Clyde. *Locomotive design and construction.* 1919. 1 v. (Thesis, University of Kansas, Mechanical Engineering.)

7846. *Market analysis of high speed rail services in Ohio/* Arlington, VA: Transmode, Inc., 1985. 1 v. (various foliations) "Prepared for Ohio High Speed Rail Task Force in conjunction with the Ohio Department of Transportation."

7846a. Markle, William D., S. Michael Corlett. *The Rock Island terminal relocation study; a study of downtown terminal alternatives for the Chicago, Rock Island and Pacific Railroad commuter services/* Chicago: Westenhoff and Novick, 1977. 145 p.

7847. Markos, Stephanie H. *Recommended emergency preparedness guidelines for passenger trains. Final report.* Washington, DC: U.S. Dept. of Transportation, Federal Railroad Administration, Office of Research and Development, 1993. 1 v.

7848. Marks, Kevin Otis. *Railroad-highway grade crossing safety knowledge: perspectives in driver education /* 1982. 249 l. (Thesis, H.S.D., Indiana University.)

7849. Marks, Marcus M. *The position of Hon. Marcus M. Marks, President of the Borough of Manhattan, City of New York, in relation to the proposed West Side agreement between the City of New York and the New York Central Railway Company.* New York : Published by the Conference Committee of Organizations Interested in the Matter of the New York Central Railroad Company's West Side Track System, 1916. 8 p. Addressed to the Board of Estimate and Apportionment. "May 17, 1916"

7849a. Marquette, Judson Henry Gougler. *The lay-out and equipment of a locomotive repair shop /* 1912. 51 l. (Thesis, B.S., University of Illinois.)

7850. Marquez, Ernest. *Port Los Angeles: a phenomenon of the railroad era.* San Marino, CA: Golden West Books, 1975.143 p.

7851. Marquis, Franklin Wales. *A discussion of train resistance with special reference to the effect of variations in loading on the resistance of freight trains /* 1909. 120 l.

11 leaves of plates. (Thesis, M.E., University of Illinois.)

7852. Marre, Louis A. *Diesel locomotives: the first 50 years; a guide to diesels built before 1972.* Waukesha, WI: Kalmbach Pub. Co., 1995. 479 p.

7853 _____. *Rock Island diesel locomotives, 1930-1980.* Cincinnati, OH: Railfax, 1982. 146 p.

7854. _____. Gregory J. Sommers. *Frisco in color.* Edison, NJ: Morning Sun Books, 1995. 125 p.

7855. _____, _____ *Kansas City Southern in the Deramus era.* Halifax, PA: Withers Pub., 1999. 232 p.

7856. _____, _____. *Kansas City Southern lines.* Kansas City, MO: Paired RR Publications, 2005. 192 p.

7857. _____, Gregory J. Sommers. *Katy recollections/* Kansas City, MO: Paired RR Publications, 2007. 192 p.

7858. _____. Jerry A. Pinkepank, George H. Drury. *The contemporary diesel spotter's guide.* Milwaukee, WI: Kalmbach Books, 1989. 336 p.

7859. _____, _____, _____. *The contemporary diesel spotter's guide: a comprehensive reference manual to locomotives since 1972.* 2d ed. Waukesha, WI: Kalmbach Books, 1995.

7860. _____, John Baskin Harper. *Frisco diesel power.* Glendale, CA: Interurban Press, 1984. 147 p.

7861. _____, Paul K. Withers. *The contemporary diesel spotters guide.* 1st ed. Halifax, PA: Withers Pub., 2000. 224 p. (Also: 2008, 248 p.)

7862. Marrs, Aaron W. *Railroads in the old South: pursuing progress in a slave society.* Baltimore, MD: Johns Hopkins University Press, 2009. 288 p.

7863. Marsano, Italo. *Railway roadbed and its improvement.* 1947. 116 p. (Thesis, M.S., University of Minnesota.)

7864. Marsh, C.K. *Clinchfield in color.* Scotch Plains, NJ: Morning Sun Books, 2004. 128 p.

7865. Marsh, James C. *A pictorial history of the Holly River & Addison RR and West Virginia Midland RR, 1890-1931 and Webster Springs/* Buckhannon, WV: Ralston Press, 2008. 54 p.

7866. Marsh, Kenneth L., Robin L. Marsh. *Lavish silence; a pictorial chronicle of vanished Curry, Alaska: a unique Alaska railroad community.* Trapper Creek, AK:

Trapper Creek Museum Sluice Box Productions, 2003. 130 p.

7867. Marshall, C.D. *Construction and investigation of Brinton ribbed arch over Turtle Creek, Pittsburgh Div. P.R.R.* 1888. 87 l. 12 leaves of folded plates. (Thesis, C.E., Lehigh University.)

7868. Marshall, Charles K. *The Texas and Pacific Railway : an address delivered by request before the members of the legislature of Mississippi and the Cotton Exchange of Vicksburg* / Vicksburg, Miss.: Rogers & Groome, 1876. 20 p.

7869. _____. *Texas Pacific Railway—Senate Committee* / S.l., s.n., 1870s. 10 p.

7870. Marshall, Charles Richard. *Economic analysis of the freight car manufacturing industry of the United States; a thesis in industrial management.* 1953. 52 p. (Thesis, M.B.A., University of Pennsylvania.)

7871. Marshall, David. *Grand Central.* New York, Whittlesey House, McGraw-Hill Book Co., 1946. 280 p.

7872. Marshall, James Leslie. *Santa Fe; the railroad that built an empire.* New York, Random House, 1945. 465 p.

7873. Marshall, Mauel, Pamela A. Conners. *Sugar Pine memories; recollections of a steam engineer.* Sonora, CA: Tuolumne County Historical Society, 1991. 122 p. (Sugar Pine Railway Company)

7874. Marshall, Merrill G. *Standard and special flatcars* / Scranton, PA : International Correspondence Schools, 1962. 66, 2 p. (*Serial 6611.*)

7875. Marshall, Ralph William. *The early history of the Galena and Chicago Union Railroad* / 1937. 69 l. (Thesis, M.A., University of Chicago.)

7876. Marshall, William. *Protection of metal equipment* / New York: New York Railroad Club, 1910. 17 p. "Discusses the painting and varnishing of metal railroad cars; compares the durability of wooden and metal cars."

7877. Marson, G. Donald, Brian L. Jennison. *Railroads of the Pine Tree State.* Editor, Joe Shine; associate editor, Ernie Towler. La Mirada, CA: Four Ways West Publications, 1999. v. 1-

7878. Marta, Henry A., K.D. Mels. *Wheel-rail adhesion* / New York : ASME, 1968. 8 p. (*American Society of Mechanical Engineers (Series), 68-WA/RR-1.*)

7879. Martell, SueAnn, Western Mining and Railway Museum. *Rails around Helper (UT).* Charleston, SC: Arcadia, 2007. 128 p.

7880. Martin, Albro. *James J. Hill and the opening of the Northwest.* New York, Oxford

University Press, 1976. 676 p.(Reprint: St. Paul, MN: Minnesota Historical Society Press, 1991, 1976. 676 p.)

7881. _____. *Enterprise denied; American railroads in the Progressive Era, 1898-1917.* 1970. 522 l. (Thesis, Ph.D., Columbia University.) (New York, Columbia University Press, 1971. 402 p.)

7882. _____. *Railroads triumphant; the growth, rejection, and rebirth of a vital American force.* New York, Oxford University Press, 1992. 428 p.

7883. Martin, Charles Francis. *Locomotives of the empire builder; a rail buff's primer of steam on the Great Northern Railway.* Chicago, Normandie House, 1972. 1 v.

7884. _____. *Official employees' shop diagrams for in-service freight cars & cabooses.* Chicago, Normandie House, 19--?. 1 v. of 94 sheets.

7885. Martin, Cy. *Gold Rush narrow gauge: the story of the White Pass and Yukon Route.* Corona del Mar, CA: Trans-Anglo Books, 1974. 96 p.

7886. Martin, Edward Winslow. *Behind the scenes in Washington: being a complete and graphic account of the Credit Mobilier Investigation.* New York, Continental Publishing Company, 1873. 518 p. (Reprint: New York, Arno Press, 1974. 518 p.; Whitefish, MT: Kessinger Publishing, 2007. 520 p.

7886a. Martin Gregory Clarke. *The influence of wheel-rail contact forces on the formation of rail shells.* 1971. 124 l. (Thesis, Ph.D., University of Illinois at Urbana-Champaign.)

7887. _____, William Walter Hay. *Method of analysis for determining the coupler forces and longitudinal motion of a long freight train in over-the-road operations/* Urbana, IL: University of Illinois at Urbana-Champaign, Department of Civil Engineering, Engineering Experiment Station; New York Central Railroad Company, 1967. 33 l.

7888. Martin, James A. *Diagrams, common standard passenger trains cars, Southern Pacific, as of 1924.* Pasadena, CA: Southern Pacific Historical & Technical Society, 1996. 1 v. (unpaged)

7889. _____. *Diagrams, common standard rail motor cars, Southern Pacific Lines : as of 1937.* Pasadena, CA: Southern Pacific Historical & Technical Society, 1996. 1 v. (unpaged)

7890. Martin, John J. *Technology assessment: diesel-electric locomotives for the year 2000/* Washington, DC: Association of American Railroads, 1984. 50 p. (*AAR publication R-578.*)

7891. Martin, John Welborn. *Henry M. Flagler, 1830-1913; Florida's east coast is his monument.* New York, Newcomen Society in North America, 1956. 24 p.

7892. Martin, M.A., Warder Cumming, A.A. Talmage. *Bridges, buildings, water stations, &c: January 1, 1884.* St. Louis, MO: Time Printing House, 1884. 123 p. (Texas & Pacific Railway)

7893. Martin P. Catherwood Library; Labor Management Documentation Center. *Brotherhood of Railroad Trainmen records/* Ithaca, NY: The Center, 1979. 34 l.

7894. Martin, Robert E. *Track rehabilitation research and development: a basis for program planning: final report.* Washington, DC: Federal Railroad Administration, Office of Research and Development, 1980. 323 p. (*FRA/ORD-80-10.*)

7895. Martin, Robert N. *Rail atlas of Indiana.* Bloomington: Center for Urban and Regional Analysis, Indiana University, 1976. 150 l. (*Rail planning and policy series. Research paper, no. 2.*)

7896. Martin, Roy L. *History of the Wisconsin Central.* Boston, Railway and Locomotive Historical Society, 1941. 169 p. (*Railway and Locomotive Historical Society, Bulletin, no. 54.*)

7897. Martinelli, Raymond Constantin, J. T. Gier. *Measurement of thermal resistances of typical wall and roof sections for refrigerator cars of the Pacific Fruit Express Co.* San Francisco: Pacific Fruit Express Co., 1940s? 53 l.

7898. Martino, Michael. *The role of the Interstate Commerce Commission in regulating railroad passenger train service, 1958-1976: a thesis/* 1977. 167 l. (Thesis, M.S. in Transportation, Northwestern University.)

7899. Martland, Carl D. *Improving freight car distribution performance: overcoming organizational and institutional barriers to change.* Cambridge, MA: Center for Transportation Studies, Massachusetts Institute of Technology, 1982. 75 p. (*Studies in railroad operations and economics, v. 36.*)

7900. _____. *Procedures for improving railroad reliability.* Cambridge, MA: Massachusetts Institute of Technology, Transportation Systems Division, 1974. 77 p. (*Studies in railroad operations and research, v. 12. Department of Civil Engineering; MIT report no. R-74-30.*)

7901. _____. *Rail service planning : a case study of the Santa Fe /* Cambridge, MA: Center for Transportation Studies, Massachusetts Institute of Technology, 1981. 61 p. (*Report. Association of American Railroads, no. R-494.*)

7902. _____. *Rail trip time reliability: evaluation of performance measures and analysis of trip time data.* Washington, DC: Federal Railroad Administration, U.S. Department of Transportation, 1972. 100 p. (Transportation Systems Division, Department of Civil Engineering, Massachusetts Institute of Technology: *Studies in railroad operations, v. 2.*)

7903. _____, Henry S. Marcus, George B. Raymond. *Improving railroad terminal control systems : budgeting techniques, probabilistic train connection analysis and microcomputer applications* / Cambridge, MA: Center for Transportation Studies, Massachusetts Institute of Technology, 1983. 1 v. (various pagings) (*Studies in railroad operations and economics, v. 37..*)

7904. _____, Marc N. Terziev. *Railroad rationalization methodology: final report.* Cambridge, MA: Department of Civil Engineering, Massachusetts Institute of Technology, 1976. 147 p. (*M.I.T. report; no. R77-12.*)

7905. Marvel, Bill. *New York Central trackside with Eugene Van Dusen.* Scotch Plains, NJ: Morning Sun Books, 1997. 127 p.

7905a. _____. *Rock Island in color.* Edison, NJ: Morning Sun Books, 1995. 128 p.

7905b. _____. *The Rock Island Line* / Bloomington: Indiana University Press, 2013. 169 p.

7906. _____. *Santa Fe all the way.* Scotch Plains, NJ: Morning Sun Books, 1998. v. 1-

7907. _____. *Under Milwaukee wires; the color photography of Sanford Goodrick and William C. Jansen.* Edison, NJ: Morning Sun Books, 1996. 128 p.

7908. Marvin, Walter Rumsey. *Columbus and the railroads of central Ohio before the Civil War.* 1953. 349 l. (Thesis, Ph.D., Ohio State University.)

7909. Marx, Leo. *The machine in the garden: technology and the pastoral ideal in America.* Rev. ed. New York: Oxford University Press, 2000. 392 p.

7910. Marx, Thomas George. *The diesel-electric locomotive industry: a study in market failures.* 1973. 287 l. (Thesis, University of Pennsylvania.)

7911. Maryland and Pennsylvania Railroad Company. *Rules for the government of the Operating Department : effective March 1, 1951.* S.l., s.n., 1951. 72 p.

7912. Maschi, A.P., J.J. Driscoll. *A study of the possibility of using low voltage A.C. on the third rail system entering the Pennsylvania terminal* / 1926. 97 l. (Thesis, B.S., Massachusetts Institute of technology, Department of Electrical Engineering.)

7913. Masden, Steve, Burlyn Pike. *Railroad town: a pictorial history of Lebanon Junction, Kentucky.* Lebanon Junction, KY: Lebanon Junction Branch, Peoples Bank of Bullitt Country, 1991. 212 p.

7914. Mason Machine Works Company, Taunton, Mass. *The Mason Machine Works, Taunton, Massachusetts; builders of locomotives of all kinds and cotton machinery.* S.l., s.n., 1879. 29 p.

7915. Massachusetts. Board of Railroad Commissioners. *Report of Massachusetts*

Railroad Commissioners on the Boston & Maine railroad strike of February 12, 1877. Boston? s.n., 1877. 17 p. (*General Court, 1877. House Doc. no. 102.*)

7916. _____. _____. *Steel rails.* S.l., s.n., 1870. (*Senate (Series) Massachusetts. General Court 1870, no. 47.*)

7917. _____. General Court. *Hearings in opposition to the approval of the lease of the Boston & Albany Railroad to the New York Central & Hudson River Railroad Company, before the joint Standing Committee on Railroads, 1900.* Boston : s.n., 1900. 1, 352 p.

7918. _____. _____. Committee on Railroads. *Lease of the Boston & Albany R.R. to the New York Central R.R. Hearing by the Committee on Railroads* / Boston: s.n. 1900. 168 p. (House Bill no. 36.)

7919. Massari, S.C., R.W. Lindsay. *The microstructure of chilled car wheel iron and its relation to physical properties.* Chicago : Association of Manufacturers of Chilled Car Wheels, 1940. 66 p.

7920. Massey, Mary Meeth. *The historical and legislative background of the Maintenance of Way Railway Employees.* 1949. 1 v. (Thesis, M.A., Iowa.)

7921. Master Car and Locomotive Painters' Association of the United States and Canada *Proceedings of the 1st-48th annual convention.* Reading Mass., W.E. & E.J. Twombly, 1870-1919. Annual. (> American Railway Association. Equipment Painting Section. *Proceedings of the session of the American Railway Association. Division V-Mechanical Equipment Painting Section.*)

7922. Master Car Builders' Association. *Abstract and index.* 1919.

7923. _____. *Annual report of the proceedings of the Master Car-Builders' Association.* New York, N.Y., S.W. Green, 1873-1877. 5 v. Annual. (<*History and early reports*; >*Report of the proceedings of the…annual convention of the Master Car-Builders' Association.*)

7924. _____. *Circular.* Chicago : Master Car Builders' Association, 1900s. Irregular. (Office of the Secretary.)

7925. _____. *Code of rules governing the condition of, and repairs to: freight cars for the interchange of traffic, adopted by the Master Car Builders' Association. Revised at Alexandria Bay, N.Y., June, 1895.* Chicago, The Association, 1895. 50 p.

7926. _____. *Code of rules; governing the condition of, and repairs to, freight cars for the interchange of traffic* / Chicago, The Association, 1908. 109 p.

7927. _____. *Code of rules governing the condition of, and repairs to: freight cars for the interchange of traffic, adopted by the Master Car Builders' Association. revised at Atlantic City, N.J., June, 1913.* Chicago, The Association, 1913. 154 p.

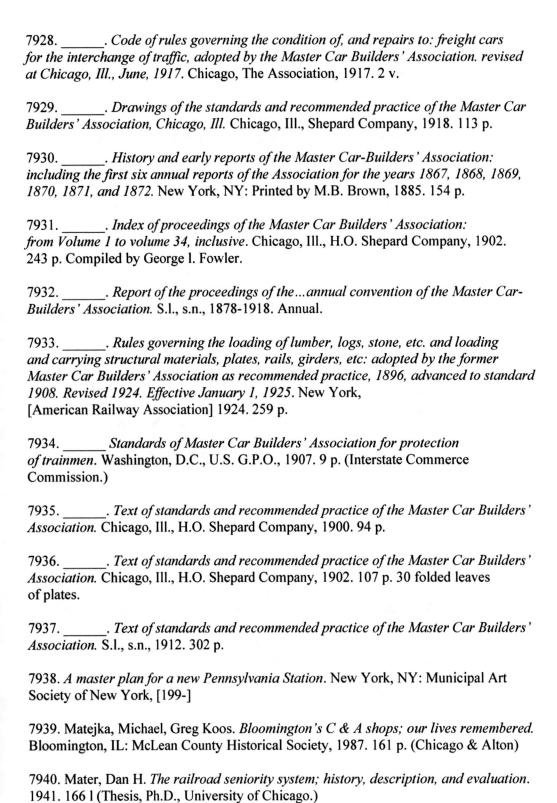

7928. _____. *Code of rules governing the condition of, and repairs to: freight cars for the interchange of traffic, adopted by the Master Car Builders' Association. revised at Chicago, Ill., June, 1917.* Chicago, The Association, 1917. 2 v.

7929. _____. *Drawings of the standards and recommended practice of the Master Car Builders' Association, Chicago, Ill.* Chicago, Ill., Shepard Company, 1918. 113 p.

7930. _____. *History and early reports of the Master Car-Builders' Association: including the first six annual reports of the Association for the years 1867, 1868, 1869, 1870, 1871, and 1872.* New York, NY: Printed by M.B. Brown, 1885. 154 p.

7931. _____. *Index of proceedings of the Master Car Builders' Association: from Volume 1 to volume 34, inclusive.* Chicago, Ill., H.O. Shepard Company, 1902. 243 p. Compiled by George l. Fowler.

7932. _____. *Report of the proceedings of the...annual convention of the Master Car-Builders' Association.* S.l., s.n., 1878-1918. Annual.

7933. _____. *Rules governing the loading of lumber, logs, stone, etc. and loading and carrying structural materials, plates, rails, girders, etc: adopted by the former Master Car Builders' Association as recommended practice, 1896, advanced to standard 1908. Revised 1924. Effective January 1, 1925.* New York, [American Railway Association] 1924. 259 p.

7934. _____ *Standards of Master Car Builders' Association for protection of trainmen.* Washington, D.C., U.S. G.P.O., 1907. 9 p. (Interstate Commerce Commission.)

7935. _____. *Text of standards and recommended practice of the Master Car Builders' Association.* Chicago, Ill., H.O. Shepard Company, 1900. 94 p.

7936. _____. *Text of standards and recommended practice of the Master Car Builders' Association.* Chicago, Ill., H.O. Shepard Company, 1902. 107 p. 30 folded leaves of plates.

7937. _____. *Text of standards and recommended practice of the Master Car Builders' Association.* S.l., s.n., 1912. 302 p.

7938. *A master plan for a new Pennsylvania Station.* New York, NY: Municipal Art Society of New York, [199-]

7939. Matejka, Michael, Greg Koos. *Bloomington's C & A shops; our lives remembered.* Bloomington, IL: McLean County Historical Society, 1987. 161 p. (Chicago & Alton)

7940. Mater, Dan H. *The railroad seniority system; history, description, and evaluation.* 1941. 166 l (Thesis, Ph.D., University of Chicago.)

7941. Mathers, Michael H. *Riding the rails.* Boston, Gambit, 1973. 138 p. (Tramps)

7942. Mathewson, J.S. *Spark arresters, ash pans, and forest fires.* S.l., s.n., 1922. 3 p. 66 l. (Forest Products Laboratory (U.S.))

7943. Mathewson, Jon C. *"The face of time is becoming wondrously strange" : changing views of time and the history of Standard Time in the United States.* 1989. 114 l. (Thesis, M.A., University of Vermont.)

7944. Matthew, David. *David Matthew's patents for spark arresters: together with certificates of their utility and economy in fuel and repairs.* Philadelphia, Pa., Printed by H. Evans, 1856. 26 p.

7945. _____. *A pictorial history of the pioneer locomotives; where they were first put on rail.* San Francisco, D. Matthew, 1887. 31 p.

7946. Matthews, Fred. *Sierra and desert rails.* Philadelphia, PA: Xlibris, 2006. 1 v.

7947. Matthews, Fred H. *Northern California railroads; the silver age.* Denver, CO: Sundance, 1982-

7947a. Mathews, John Hays. *Railroad Commission of California.* 1923. 63 l. (Thesis, Harvard University, Law School.)

7948. Mattison, Peter D., Douglas W. Palmer, P. Ranganath Nayak. *A report on investigation into rail passenger safety : final report.* Washington, DC: Federal Railroad Administration, Office of Research and Development, 1980. 85 p. (*FRA/ORD-80/65.*)

7949. Matzzie, Donald E., Barry D. Hillegas, Thomas R. Bell. *Railroad corridor consolidation: analyses and implications.* Pittsburgh, PA: CONSAD Research Corporation, 1979. 239 p.

7949a. Maw, William Henry. *Modern examples of road and railway bridges; illustrating the most recent practice of leading engineers in Europe and America.* London: Published at the offices of "Engineering," 1872. 180 p.

7950. Mawdsley, Alar. *Iron men & iron horses.* Pratt, KS: First Marketing, 1995. 214 p. (Railroad employees)

7951. Maxwell, John W., Charles S. Small. *Rio Grande narrow gauge in the summer of 1941.* Canton, OH: Railroad Publications, 1986. 124 p.

7952. Maxwell, Robert S. *Whistle in the Piney Woods: Paul Bremond and the Houston, East and West Texas Railway.* S.l., Texas Gulf Coast Historical Association, 1963. 77 p. (Publication series, v. 7., no. 2.) (Rev. ed.: Denton, TX: East Texas Historical Association; University of North Texas Press, 1998. 128 p.)

7953. May, Edward L., Richard L. Stoving. *New York Central power along the Hudson.*

Hanover, PA: Railroad Press, 2005. 2 v. (v. 2—Oscawana to Albany)

7954. May, Herbert S. *A series of tests on car heating from the locomotive.* 1902. 29 l. (Thesis, B.S., Massachusetts Institute of Technology.)

7955. Maybee, Rolland Harper. *Railroad competition and the oil trade, 1855-1873.* Mount Pleasant, Mich., Extension Press, Central State Teachers College, 1940. (Thesis, Columbia University.) (Reprint: Philadelphia, Pa., Porcupine Press, 1974, 1940. 451 p.

7956. Maydew, Brian J. *Prospects for contract rail rates from Kansas county elevators /* 1982. 87 l. (Thesis, M.S., Kansas State University)

7957. Mayer, Harold M. *The changing railroad pattern of the United States.* Milwaukee, Urban Research Center, University of Wisconsin-Milwaukee, 1979. 51 p.

7958. _____. *The railway pattern of metropolitan Chicago.* 1943. 168 p. (Thesis, Ph.D., University of Chicago.)

7959. Mayer, Lynne Rhodes, Kenneth E. Vose. *Makin' tracks: the story of the transcontinental railroad in the pictures and words of the men who were there.* New York, Praeger, 1975. 216 p.

7960. Maynard, Neil Arthur. *Marketing of Diesel-electric locomotives: an analysis.* 1955. 98 p. (Thesis, M.A., Boston University.

7961. Maynard, Peter. *The Brunswick roundhouse in the age of steam.* Brunswick, MD: Brunswick Historical Press, 2002. 35 p.

7962. _____. *Roundhouse: the heart of the B & O.* Brunswick, MD: Brunswick Press, 1992. 16 p.

7963. Mays, Richard David. *That versatile diesel and its maintenance facilities.* 1950. 59 l. (Thesis, University of Cincinnati.)

7964. Mayville, Ronald A. *Crashworthiness design modifications for locomotive and cab car anticlimbing systems /* Washington, DC : Federal Railroad Administration, Office of Research and Development, 2003. 86 p. Performed by Arthur D. Little, Inc. (under contract to John A. Volpe National Transportation Systems Center). (*DOT/FRA/ORD-03/05; DOT-VNTSC-FRA-03-01.)*

7965. _____. *Locomotive crashworthiness research.* Washington, DC : Federal Railroad Administration, Office of Research and Development, 1995. 5 v.

7966. _____, Randolph P. Hammond, Kent N. Johnson. *Evaluation of railroad cab car end beam designs: rail passenger equipment collision tests/* Washington, DC : U.S. Department of Transportation, Federal Railroad Administration, Office of Research and Development, 2003. 39 p. (*DOT/FRA/ORD-02/08.)*

7967. Maywald, Henry. *Memories of the Boston and Maine*. Hicksville, NY: N.J. International, 1984. 40 p.

7968. _____. *E units: the standard bearer of America's passenger trains*. Hicksville, NY: N.J. International, 1988. 1 v.

7969. Mazer, Nathan H., John J. Stewart. *The driving of the Golden Spike: an authentic pictorial history of May 10, 1869 and May 10, 1969*. Salt Lake City, UT; Wheelwright Press, 1970. 32 p.

7970. Mazlish, Bruce. *The railroad and the space program: an exploration in historical analogy*. Cambridge, M.I.T. Press, 1965. 223 p.

7971. Mazziotti, Donald F., Mark C. Meyer, Kenneth J. Dueker. *Railroad abandonment and re-use planning: relationship with statewide transportation planning and citizen participation*. Rev. ed. Iowa City, IA: Institute of Urban and Regional Research, University of Iowa, 1974. 45 p.

7972. McAdoo, William Gibbs. *Extension of tenure of government control of railroads*. Washington: G.P.O., 1919. 124 p. (McAdoo served as Secretary of the Treasury and Director General of Railroads.)

7973. _____. *Government control and operations of railroads*. Washington, G.P.O., 1918. 89 p.

7974. _____. *Railroads & shipping*. Washington: G.P.O., 1918. 2 v.

7975. McAfee, Ward. *California's railroad era*. San Marino, CA: Golden West Books, 1973. 256 p.

7976. _____. *Local interests and railroad regulation in nineteenth century California*. 1965. 207 l. (Thesis, Stanford University.)

7977. McAlister, Samuel Betram. *The building of the Texas and Pacific Railway*. 1926. 154 l. (Thesis, M.A., University of Texas.)

7978. McAlpine, R.W. *The life and times of Col. James Fisk, Jr*. New York, NY: New York Book Co., 1872. 504 p. (Reprint: New York, Arno Press, 1981. 504 p.)

7979. McArdle, Fred. *Everything behind the engine for conductors and brakemen; a complete treatise on the duties of conductors and brakemen* / Chicago, F. McArdle, 1910. 336 p.

7980. _____, Henry Helmholtz. *Air brake test for engineers and firemen; a complete treatise on the Westinghouse and New York air brake and signal systems, air brake practice and train handling*. Chicago, F. McArdle and H. Helmholtz, 1909. 375 p.

7981. _____, _____. *Locomotive text for engineers and firemen; a complete treatise on the engine, electric headlight and standard code of train rules.* Chicago, F. McArdle and H. Helmholtz, 1909. 452 p.

7982. McArdle, Golda Mary. *The Ponchartrain Railroad, pioneer in the South* / 1931. 67 l. (Thesis, M.A., Tulane University of Louisiana.)

7983. McAuliffe, Eugene. *Railway fuel; the coal problem in its relation to the transportation and use of coal and coal substitutes by steam railroads.* New York, Simmons-Boardman, 1927. 468 p.

7984. McBride, Daunis, Homer Richey. *Richey's Federal Employers' Liability, Safety Appliances, and Hours of Service Acts.* Charlottesville, VA: Michie, 1916. 795 p.

7985. McBride, Harry Alexander. *Trains rolling; stories on railroads at home and abroad with 237 illustrations.* New York, Macmillan, 1953. 269 p.

7986. McCabe, Douglas M. *The crew size dispute in the railroad industry.* Washington, DC: U.S. Department of Transportation, Federal Railroad Administration, 1977. 693 p.

7987. _____. *Railroad manpower adjustments to technological change through collective bargaining: crew consist on the Illinois Central Railroad.* Ithaca, NY: New York State School of Industrial and Labor Relations, Cornell University, 1977. 693 p. (Thesis, Cornell University)

7988. McCabe, James Dabney. *Behind the scenes in Washington: being a complete and graphic account of the Credit Mobilier investigation, the congressional rings, political intrigues, working of the lobbies ...* New York, Continental Publishing Company, 1873. 518 p.

7989. _____. *History of the Grange Movement; or, The farmer's war against monopolies.* Philadelphia, National Pub. Co., 1873. 539 p.

7990. _____. *The history of great riots; being a full and authentic account of the strikes and riots on the various railroads of the United States and in the mining regions* / Philadelphia, National Publishing Company, 1877. 516 p.

7991. McCaleb, Charles S. *The San Jose railroads: centennial, 1868-1968.* Los Altos Hills, CA: Foothill Junior College District. 88 p.

7992. McCaleb, Walter Flavius. *Brotherhood of Railroad Trainmen; with special reference to the life of Alexander F. Whitney.* New York, A. & C. Boni, 1936. 273 p.

7993. McCaleb, Willis A., Bruce K. Dicken, James M. Semon. *Baltimore & Ohio trackside with Willis A. McCaleb.* Scotch Plains, NJ: Morning Sun Books, 1998. 128 p.

7994. _____, and others. *Nickel Plate: color photography of Willis A. McCaleb.* Edison, NJ: Morning Sun Books, 1995-1997. 3 v.

7995. McCall, John B. *Coach, cabbage & caboose; Santa Fe mixed train service: a one-hundred year history of Santa Fe mixed train service from 1869 to 1971 in words, photographs, equipment rosters, and timetable schedules.* Dallas, TX: Kachina Press, 1979. 256 p.

7995a. _____. *Coach, smoker and chair car genealogy.* Midwest City, OK: Santa Fe Railway Historical and Modeling Society, 2005. 284 p. (*Santa Fe Railway passenger car reference series, v. 2.*)

7996. _____. *The doodlebugs: a word and picture history of over six decades of self-propelled passenger car service on America's most colorful major railroad.* Dallas, TX: Kachina Press, 1977. 255 p.

7997. _____. *An economic study of railroad passenger service; the Santa Fe and Southern Pacific Railroads, 1950-1965.* 1968. 155 l. (Thesis, Oklahoma State University.)

7998. _____. *Katy southwest: steam and diesel pictorial.* Dallas, TX: Kachina Press, 1985. 130 p.

7999. _____. *Santa Fe's early diesel daze, 1935-1953: the story of the first generation diesel power on the Santa Fe Railway and the process by which they brought about the honorable retirement of the steam locomotive.* Dallas. TX: Kachina Press, 1980. 272 p.

8000. _____. *Son of doodlebug: a pictorial supplement.* Derby, KS: Santa Fe Railway Historical & Modelling Society, 1977. 128 p.

8001. _____, Frank A. Schultz. *Frisco southwest, late steam, early diesel pictorial.* Dallas, TX: Kachina Press, 1982. 120 p.

8002. John T. McCall. *Shovel and throttle; or My fireman and I. With hints.* Baltimore, MD: The Sun Book and Job Printing Off., 1893. 278 p.

8003. McCall, R. David. *"Every thing in its place." Gender and space on America's railroads, 1830-1899.* 1999. 95 l. (Thesis, M.A., Virginia Polytechnic Institute and State University.)

8004. McCalley, R.G. *The man behind the throttle; a hundred years of railroadin'.* Mountain Home, ID: R.G. McCalley, 1981. 112 p. (Oregon, Southern Pacific)

8005. McCallum, George E. *New techniques in railroad ratemaking.* 1965. 316 l. (Thesis, Ph.D., University of California, Berkeley.)

8006. McCaque, James. *Moguls and iron men; the story of the first transcontinental railroad.* New York, Harper & Row, 1964. 392 p.

8007. McCarter, Steve. *Guide to the Milwaukee Road in Montana.* Helena, MT: Montana

Historical Society Press, 1992. 104 p.

8008. McCarthy, Joseph H., Joseph M. McCarthy, John A. McCarthy. *Erie Lackawanna: trackside with the McCarthys*. Kutztown, PA: Morning Sun Books, 2006. 128 p.

8009. McCartney, Everett Fortune. *The history of the San Jose Railroad Company*. 1959. 81 l. (Thesis, M.A., University of Southern California.)

8010. McCarty, Richard J. *Federal valuation of railroad property*. Kansas City, Mo., Tiernan-Dart Printing Co., 1915. 103 p.

8011. McCauley, Peter E. *Boston Revere Beach & Lynn Railroad: meet you at the station, the narrow gauge railroad* / Revere, MA: Peter E. McCauley, Inc., 2001. 143 p.

8012. McCawley, Paul Leland. *Agitation for a Pacific railroad: 1832-1862*/ 1937. 3, xiii, 120 l. (Thesis, M.A., Colorado State College of Education, Department of History.)

8013. McChesney, Chris, Jerry DeVos, Gary Kohler. *Narrow gauge in the Sheepscot Valley: a comprehensive guide to the Wiscasset, Waterville & Farmington Railway*. Washingtonville, OH: M2FQ Publications, 2001-2203. 3 v.

8013a. McClelland, Patrick C. *The effects of technological change on working knowledge in rail switching*. 1981. 331 l. (Thesis, Ph.D., American University.)

8014. McClement, J.H. *Past history, present condition and future prospects of the Chicago Great Western Railway Company* / St. Paul : s.n., 1900. 106 p.

8015. McClintic, H.H. *Masonry bridges for railroad purposes* / 1888. 67 l. 9 leaves of folded plates. (Thesis, C.E. Lehigh University.)

8016. McClintic-Marshall Company. *Steel structures for railroads*. Pittsburgh, PA: The Company, 1921. 12 p.

8017. McClintic, William A. *Roadrailers; a combination rail-highway service*. Chicago, IL: Murphy-Richter Pub. Co., 1963. 1 v.

8018. McClintock Manufacturing Company. *McClintock automatic block systems: locomotive telegraph, locomotive telephone, automatic stop, cab signals, electric car signals, railway switch and crossing signals*. St. Paul, MN: McClintock Manufacturing Co., 1906. 25 p. 6 l. of plates. (*Bulletin no. 5*.)

8019. McClintock, William R. *Early railroad regulation in Michigan, 1850-1863*. 1976. 220 l. (Thesis, Ph.D., University of Wyoming.)

8019a. McClosky, Peter J. *A working list of books and booklets on the Southern Pacific and related subsidiaries*. 5th ed. Pasadena, CA: SPH&TS, 1995. 36 l.

8020. McClure, Louis Charles, Frank S Thayer. *The trail of the iron horse: a trip over the Continental Divide of the Rocky Mountains by the Moffat Line, from photographs.* Denver, CO: Frank S. Thayer; The Colorado News Co., 1905. 24 p. (Denver and Salt Lake Railroad)

8021. McClure, Louis Charles. *Photo by McClure: the railroad, cityscape, and landscape photographs of L.C. McClure.* Compiled by William C. Jones and Elizabeth B. Jones. Boulder, CO: Pruett Pub. Co., 1983. 254 p.

8022. McClure, William G. *Norfolk & Western facilities in color* / Scotch Plains, NJ : Morning Sun Books, 2010. v. 1 – Eastern lines.

8023. McClure, William G., III, Jeremy F. Plant. *Norfolk and Western steam in color* / Scotch Plains, NJ: Morning Sun Books, 2007. 128 p.

8024. _____, _____. *Virginian Railway in color.* Scotch Plains, NJ: Morning Sun Books, 2005. 127 p.

8025. McColley, Grant. *Railway and transit equipment, 1940-45.* Washington, D.C., Defense Production Administration, 1951. 21 p. (*War Production Board. Historical reports on war administration.*)

8026. McCommons, James. *Waiting on a train: the embattled future of passenger rail service.* White River Junction, VT: Chelsea Green Pub. Co., 2009. 285 p.

8027. McConnell, Thomas Otto. *An historical perspective of the impact of railroad freight car rental rates.* 1976. 132, 32 l. (Thesis, Georgia State University.)

8028. _____. *Railroad freight car rental rates: their impact on railroad management decisions as to investment in and utilization of the freight car fleet.* 1979. 350 l. (Thesis, Ph.D., Georgia State University.)

8029. McConway & Torley Company. *Car interchange guide and ready reference tables.* Pittsburgh, Pa., McConway & Torley, 1915. 51 p.

8030. _____. *A catechism of the M.C.B. rules.* Pittsburgh, Pa., McConway & Torley Company, 1899. 99 p. Corrected ed.

8031. _____. *The evolution of car couplings // L'evolution des enclanchements d"attelage.* Pittsburgh, Pa., E.C. Baum Company, 1905. 38 p.

8032. _____. *The Janney coupler for passenger cars, freight cars, and locomotives* / Pittsburgh? s.n., 1899. 99 p.

8033. _____. *The Janney-Penn coupler; catalogue C.* Pittsburgh, s.n., 1919- 1 v.

8034. _____. *The McConway & Torley Co.: manufacturers of M.C.B. couplers for passenger cars, freight cars, and locomotives, malleable iron castings and steel castings.* Pittsburgh, Pa., s.n., 1905. 152 p.

8035. _____. *The McConway & Torley Co.: sole manufacturers of the Janney coupler for passenger cars, freight cars, and locomotives.* Pittsburgh, PA: The Company, 1899. 99 p.

8035a. _____. [Records of the McConway and Torely Company, 1889-1948]. 3.75 ft. Location: University of Pittsburgh, Archives Service Center.

8036. McCourry, Donald L. *The railroad; the last years, Clinchfield steamers.* Marion? NC: s.n., 1989. 77 p.

8037. _____. *Railroading in North Carolina: Clinchfield.* Marion? NC: s.n., 1989. 56 p.

8038. _____. *Trains and tracks.* Mitchell County, NC: Appalachian Eagle, 1989. 34 p.

8039. McCoy, Dell A., Russ Collman. *"The Crystal River pictorial."* Denver, CO: Sundance Ltd., 1972. 224 p.

8040. _____, _____. *Over the bridges...Ridgway to Durango.* Denver, CO: Sundance Publications, 2003. 416 p. (Rio Grande Southern)

8041. _____, _____. *Rico to Dolores.* Denver, CO: Sundance Publications, 1997. 480 p.(Rio Grande Southern)

8042. _____, _____. *The Rio Grande pictorial, 1871-1971; one-hundred years of railroading thru the Rockies.* Denver, CO: Sundance Ltd., 1971. 216 p.

8043. _____, _____, and others. *Locomotives and rolling stock.* Denver, CO: Sundance Books, 2006. 416 p. (Rio Grande Southern)

8044. _____, _____, Robert W. McLeod. *Durango and the Perins Peak branch.* Denver, CO: Sundance Publications, 2005. 416 p. (Rio Grande Southern)

8045. _____, _____, William A. Graves. *Rico and the mines* / Denver, CO: Sundance Publications, 1996. 496 p. (Rio Grande Southern)

8046. _____, W. George Cook, Russ Collman. *Dolores and McPhee* / Denver, CO: Sundance Publications, 1998. 496 p. (Rio Grande Southern)

8047. McCoy, V.E. *A new mechanical oiler for car journals* / New York : American Society of Mechanical Engineers, 1953. 3 , 1 p. (*ASME. Paper no. 53-A-109.*)

8048. McCreath, Andrew S. *The mineral wealth of Virginia tributary to the lines of the Norfolk and Western and Shenandoah Valley Railroad.* Harrisburg, Pa., L.S. Hart, Printer and Binder, 1884. 157 p.

8049. McCulloh, *Steam roster for the Union Pacific System, 1915-1988* / S.l., Smokerise

Publications, 1988. 80 l. (2d ed. 1990. 82 l., 32 l. of plates)

8050. McCune, Joseph C. *Fundamentals involved in stopping trains.* Pittsburgh, Pa., Westinghouse Air Brake Company, 1938. 30 p. (*Publication no. 9086*)

8051. McDaniel, J.C. *Racing for the mail; the origin of Train No. 7, the Katy Fast Mail.* Fort Scott, KS: Katy Railroad Historical Society, 1991. 45 p. (*Bulletin, Katy Railroad Historical Society, no. 3.*)

8052. McDaniel, Robert H. *The contribution of an anthropologist to social impact assessment: a case study of railroad abandonment* / 1984. 242 l. (Thesis, Ph.D., Washington State University.)

8053. McDannold, Thomas Allen *Train watching in the Tehachapi Pass.* Keene, CA: Heritage West Books, 2003. 88 p.

8054. McDermott, Paul D., Ronald E. Grim, Philip Mobley. *Eye of the explorer : views of the Northern Pacific Railroad survey, 1853-54* / Missoula: Mountain Press, 2010. 210 p.

8055. McDermott, William P. *Dutchess County railroads.* Clinton Corners, NY: Clinton Historical Society, 1996. 64 p.

8056. McDonald, Charles W. *Diesel locomotive rosters: United States, Canada, Mexico.* Editor, George H. Drury. Milwaukee, WI: Kalmbach Books, 1982. 123 p. (2d ed.: 1986. 168 p.; 3rd ed. 1992. 239 p.)

8057. McDonald, Garreth M. *A chronology of railroad building in North Carolina, 1832-1935* / Pleasant Garden, NC:G. McDonald, 2002. 1 v.

8058. _____. *150 years of common carrier railroads in North Carolina*/ Pleasant Garden, NC: G. McDonald, 2004. 36 p.

8059. McDonald, Paul R., Jules Hansink. *Forty-one years in the D.C. & H.: Jules Hansink and his career in the Dining Car and Hotel Department of the Union Pacific Railroad.* Cedar Falls, Iowa, P.R. McDonald, 1983. 74 p.

8060. McDonnell, Greg. *Field guide to modern diesel locomotives.* Waukesha, WI: Kalmbach Pub., 2002. 208 p.

8061. _____. *Heartland* / Toronto, Stoddart, 1993. 176 p.

8062. _____. *U-boats.* Toronto, Stoddart, 1994. 192 p.

8063. McDugald, John Curtis. *Computer simulation of rail freight management on a line of stations network.* 1979. 77 l. (Thesis, M.S., Massachusetts Institute of Technology, Department of Civil Engineering/Alfred P. Sloan School of Management)

8064. McEvoy, Stephen A. *The classic railway signal tower: New Haven railroad S.S.44/Berk.* S.l., InstantPublisher.com, 2007. 166 p. (1155 Cardinal Dr. West Chester, PA 19382; *samvevoy@aol.com*)

8065. McEwen, Isaac H. *Train orders, rules and signals: a manual of reference for train dispatchers, road-masters, conductors, etc.* Buffalo, The Railroad Herald, 1884. 1 v.

8066. McFall, Robert James. *Railway monopoly and rate regulation/* New York, NY: Columbia University Press, 1`916. 223 p. (*Studies in history, economics and public law, vol. LXIX, no. 1, whole no. 164.*)

8067. McFarland, Edward M. *The Cripple Creek Road: a Midland Terminal guide and data book.* Boulder, CO: Pruett Pub. Co., 1984. 214 p.

8068. _____. *Midland Route: a Colorado Midland guide and data book.* Boulder, CO: Pruett Pub. Co., 1980. 350 p.

8069. _____. *Railroads of Old Colorado City /* Colorado Springs: Old Colorado City Historical Society, 2006. 19 p. (Cripple Creek District Railway; Colorado Midland Railway Co.; Midland Terminal Railway Co.)

8070. McFarland, Henry. *Ramsey pricing inputs with downstream monopoly power and regulation: implications for railroad rate setting/* Washington, DC: U.S. Department of Justice, Antitrust Division, Economics Policy Office, 1985. 18 p. (*Economic Policy Office discussion paper, EPO 85-2.*)

8071. McFarland, Henry Bernard. *The estimation of railroad cost function.* 1979. 182, 37 l. (Thesis, Ph.D., Northwestern University.)

8072. McGehee, C. Coleman. *I've been working on the railroad: the saga of the Richmond, Fredericksburg and Potomac Railroad Company.* 1992. 180 l. (Thesis, M.A., University of Richmond.)

8073. McGinnis, Leo George. *Railroad reorganization under the Mahaffie act.* 1950. 157 l. (Thesis, M.B.A., Graduate School of Arts and Sciences, University of Pennsylvania.)

8074. McGinnis, Richard G. *The benefits and costs of a program to reflectorize the U.S. fleet of railroad rolling stock.* Washington: Federal Railroad Administration, Office of Policy and Program Development; Bucknell University, Dept. of Civil Engineering, 1979. 72 p. (*FRA-OPPD-79-12.*)

8075. McGonigal, Robert S. *Dream trains 2: the last, best streamliners, 1946-1956.* Waukesha, WI: Kalmbach Pub. Co., 2009. 106 p .(Special collectors ed.)

8075a. _____. *Heart of the Pennsylvania Railroad: the main line, Philadelphia to Pittsburgh.* Waukesha, WI: Kalmbach Books, 1996. 127 p. (*Golden years of railroading, 4.*)

8075b. _____. *Streamliner pioneers : bold new trains of the 1930s* / Waukesha, WI: Kalmbach Pub. Co., 2004. 114 p. (*Classic trains special edition, no. 3.*)

8075c. _____. *Working on the railroad: life on the rails in the age of steam and diesels.* Waukesha, WI: Kalmbach Pub. Co., 2011. 107 p.

8075d. _____, William R. Hough. *Fantastic 4-8-4 locomotives: fast, powerful giants from the zenith of steam* / Waukesha, WI: Kalmbach Publishing Co., 2012. (*Classic trains special edition, no. 12, 2012.*)

8076. McGowan, George F. *Diesel-electric locomotive handbook; a basic reference book for enginemen, maintenance men and other railroad personnel engaged in operating and maintaining diesel-electric locomotives.* New York, Simmons-Boardman, 1951. 2 v.

8077. McGowan, Joseph P., Walter Frame. *Sacramento and the first transcontinental railroad, 1856-1864.* Sacramento, CA: Sacramento County Historical Society, 1969. 19 p.

8078. McGrath, John Edward. *Piggyback: transportation of trailers on flat cars.* 1956. 68 l. (Thesis, D.B.A., Indiana University.)

8079. McGuinn, Doug. *The lopsided three : a history of railroading, logging & mining in the Holston, Doe, & Watauga Valleys of northeast Tennessee* / Boone, NC: Bamboo Books, 2010. 101 p.

8079a. _____. *The railroad to nowhere: the Deep Gap Tie & Lumber Co. Railroad and other northwestern North Carolina business ventures*/ Boone, NC: Bamboo Books, 2009. 63 p.

8080. _____. *The "Virginia Creeper": remembering the Virginia-Carolina Railway.* Rev. ed. S.l., Bamboo Books, 2008. 81 p.

8081. McGuinness, Marci Lynn. *Along the Baltimore & Ohio Railroad; from Cumberland to Uniontown.* Charleston, SC: Arcadia, 2004. 128 p.

8082. McGuire, C.B. *Steam locomotive availability and terminal facilities.* Santa Monica, CA: Rand Corporation, 1955. 26 l. (*Research memorandum, RM-1592.*)

8083. McGuire-Cummings Manufacturing Company. *Trolley cars and locomotives of the McGuire-Cummings Manufacturing Company.* Los Angeles, : Penscope Film LLC, 2010, 1911. 1 v. (unpaged)

8084. McGuirk, Martin J. *Baltimore & Ohio Railroad in the Potomac Valley.* Waukesha, WI: Kalmbach Books, 2001. 128 p.

8085. _____. *The New Haven Railroad along the shoreline; the thoroughfare from New York City to Boston.* Waukesha, WI: Kalmbach Pub. Co., 1999. 128 p.

8086. McHenry, E.H., Halbert Powers Gillette. *Rules for railway location and construction used on the Northern Pacific Railway.* New York, Engineering News Pub. Co., 1903. 88 p.

8087. McHenry, George. *Philadelphia and Reading Railroad Company.* London, Wertheimer, Lea and Co., 1878. 43 p.

8088. _____. *Philadelphia and Reading Railroad Company; its financial history.* 3rd ed., rev. Philadelphia : s.n., 1881. 43 p. "...with the suppressed report of the committee of directors.../

8089. McHenry, James. *"Stealing a railway" : the Atlantic and Great Western now called the New York, Pennsylvania and Ohio Railway : postscript to the statement* / S.l., s.n., 1800s-? Read by James McHenry, esq. at the City Terminus Hotel, Cannon Street, London on Monday, May 10th, 1886.

8090. McInnes, Allen T. *The railroad equipment industry.* 1960. 50 l. (Thesis, M.B.A., University of Texas.)

8090a. McIntire, William Raphael. *Investigation of a reinforced concrete railroad bridge* / 1912. 16 l. (Thesis, B.S., University of Illinois.)

8091. McIntyre, Douglas W. *The official guide to railroad dining car china.* Lockport, NY: D.W. McIntyre, 1990. 24 p. (*Update #1.* 1992. 22 p.; *Update #2.* 1995. 24 p.)

8092. McIntyre, Elyssa. *Transporting fictions: Burlington Route advertising and passenger experiences, 1934-1964.* St. Paul MN: Macalester College, Department of History, 1999. 98 l.

8093. McIsaac, Archibald. *The Order of Railroad Telegraphers; a study in trade unionism and collective bargaining.* Princeton, Princeton University Press, 1933. 284 p. (Thesis, Ph.D., Princeton University. 2 v.)

8094. McKamey, Matthew. *Analysis of rail rates for wheat rail transportation in Montana* / 2009. Computer file. (Thesis, M.A.B., Kansas State University.) http://hdl.handle.net/2097/1701

8095. McKay, Dave. *Trackside around Cleveland, 1965-1979 with Dave McKay.* Scotch Plains, NJ: Morning Sun Books, 2005. 128 p.

8096. McKean, John, Stuart Durant, Steven Parissien. *Lost masterpieces: Joseph Paxton: Crystal Palace; Ferdinand Dutert: Palais des Machines; McKim, Mead and White: Pennsylvania Station.* London, Phaidon, 2000. 1 v.

8097. McKee, Leo A., Alfred L. Lewis. *Railroad post office history.* Pleasantville, NY: Mobile Post Office Society, 1972. 218 p.

8098. McKee, Roger Curtis. *The collective bargaining history of the Order of Railroad Telegraphers from 1932-1956.* 1959. 136 l. (Thesis, M.A., University of Illinois at Urbana-Champaign.)

8099. McKeelway, Ben. *In the cab of the Congressional Limited* / Philadelphia : Pennsylvania Railroad, 1927. 8 p. (*Pennsylvania Railroad Information, 1927, Jan. 17.*)

8100. McKeen Motor Car Company. *McKeen gasoline motor cars; mechanical transmission.* Omaha, Neb., McKeen Motor Car Company, 1912. 74 p.

8101. _____. *McKeen Motor Car Co.: 124 cars in service, 1912, Omaha, Neb. U.S.A.* Milwaukee, WI: Old Line Publishers, 1972. 74 p.

8102. _____. *Two latest additions to the transportation world.* Omaha, Neb., McKeen Motor Car Company, 1915. 16 p.

8103. McKeighan, P.C., James H. Feiger. *Fatigue crack growth behavior of railroad tank car steel TC-128B subjected to various environments.* Washington, DC: Federal Railroad Administration, Office of Research and Development, 2006. 2 v.. (*DOT/FRA/ORD-06/04..I, II.*)

8104. McKenzie, David R., Mark C. North, Daniel S. Smith. *Intermodal transportation: the whole story.* Omaha, NE: Simmons-Boardman, 1989. 289 p.

8105. McKenzie, William A. *Dining car line to the Pacific: an illustrated history of the NP Railway's "famously good" food, with 150 authentic recipes.* St. Paul, MI: Minnesota Historical Society Press, 1990. 164 p. (Reissue: Minneapolis, University of Minnesota Press, 2004. 164 p.)

8106. McKenzie, William H. *The Colorado Midland Railway: its role in the transcontinental ambitions of the western trunk line railroads, 1883-1894.* 1970. 360 l. (Thesis, M.A., Colorado College.)

8107. _____. *Mountain to mill: the Colorado and Wyoming Railway.* Colorado Springs, CO: MAC Publishing, 1982. 199 p.

8108. _____. *Opening the rail gateway to the west: constructing the Pacific Railroad of Missouri.* St. Louis, MO: St. Louis Chapter, National Railway Historical Society, 2001. 64 p. (Missouri Pacific Railroad)

8109. McKeon, Jacquie. *"If that don't beat the devil." The story of the American Baptist chapel cars.* S.l., s.n., 1975. 44 p.

8110. McKeon, Owen F. *The railroads and steamers of Lake Tahoe.* San Mateo, CA: The Western Railroader, 1946. 22 p.

8111. McKinney, Alexis, and others. *Narrow gauge byways in the San Juans: private cars, Lake City, Creede.* Golden, CO: Colorado Railroad Museum, 1979. 232 p.

8112. McKinney, Tom Watson. *A history of the Nacogdoches and Southwestern Railroad, 1904-1954.* 1996. 116 p. (Thesis, M.A., Stephen F. Austin State University.)

8112a. McKinney, Wayne. *Roanoke locomotive shops and the Norfolk & Western Railroad* / Charleston, SC: Arcadia, 2014. 127 p.

8112a. McKisick, L.D. *Refund or foreclose? How the enormous privileges of the Central Pacific Railroad were obtained*/ San Francisco: s.n., 1896. 15 p.

8113. McKissack, Pat, Frederick McKissack. *A long, hard journey: the story of the Pullman porter.* New York, Walker, 1989. 144 p.

8114. McKnight, R. Patrick. *Steamtown National Historic Site: the nation's living railroad museum.* Lawrenceburg, IN: Creative Company, 2001. 34 p.

8115. McLaughlin, Edward J. *The library & empire of David H. Moffat, Jr.*/ S.l., Historic Blooming Grove Association, 1987. 112 p.

8116. McLaughlin, Mark. *Western train adventures: the good, the bad & the ugly.* Lake Tahoe, CA: Mic Mac Publishing, 2003. 208 p.

8117. McLaughlin, Patrick O'Shea. *Vanishing varnish: business and private railroad cars.* Danville, VA: POM Publishing Company, 198-? 1 v.

8118. McLean, Francis G., Ronald D. Williams, Robert C. Turnbell. *The Kansas test track: non conventional track structures, design report*/ Washington, DC: Federal Railroad Administration, 1972. 156 p. (FRA-RT-73-9.)

8119. McLean, Harold H. *Pittsburgh and Lake Erie R.R.* San Marino, CA: Golden West Books, 1980. 236 p.

8120. McLellan, David, Bill Warrick. *The Lake Shore & Michigan Southern Railway.* Polo, IL: Transportation Trails, 1989. 208 p.

8121. McLennan, A.D. *Texas & New Orleans: SP's lines in Texas and Louisiana.* Wilton CA: Signature Press, 2008. 386 p.

8122. McLeod Car Heating & Ventilating Company. *The McLeod safety pneumatic system of heating, cooling and ventilating railway cars, cars, steamboats, etc. : pure air heated without cost of fuel.* Boston : McLeod Car Heating and ventilating Co., 1890-1899? 24 p. 11 leaves of plates.

8123. McLin, William H. *The twenty-four-inch gauge railroad at Bridgton, Maine the life cycle of a unit of transportation.* 1949. 105 l. (Thesis, M.Ed., Rhode Island College of Education.)

8124. McIlhenny, David Robert. *Early history of Pennsylvania railroads* / 1932. 90 l.

(Thesis, M.A., Pennsylvania State College.)

8125. McIlnay, Dennis P. *The Horseshoe Curve: sabotage and subversion in the railroad city*. Hollidaysburg, PA: Seven Oaks Press, 2007. 455 p.

8126. _____. *The wreck of the Red Arrow: An American train tragedy*/ Hollidaysburg, PA: Seven Oaks Press, 2010. 1 v.

8127. McLuhan, T.C., William E. Kopplin. *Dream tracks: the railroad and the American Indian, 1890-1930*. New York, Abrams, 1985. 208 p.

8128. McMaster, Fraser J., Guadalupe B. Robledo. *Fatigue behavior of AAR (Association of American Railroads) Class A railroad wheel steel at ambient and elevated temperatures* / Washington, DC: Federal Railroad Administration, Office of Research and Development, 2006. 47 p. (http://www.fra.dot.gov/downloads/Research/ord0615.pdf)

8129. McMaster, Rose. *Origin and development of the Kansas City Southern Railway Company*. 1936. 108 p. (Thesis, M.A., University of Missouri.)

8130. McMillan, Joe. *High green to Marceline*. Woodridge, IL: McMillan Publications, 1989. 192 p. (AT&SF)

8131. _____. *Route of the Warbonnets*. Chicago, IL: McMillan, 1977. 176 p. (AT&SF)

8132. _____. *Santa Fe motive power*. Woodridge, IL: McMillan Publishing, 1985. 164 p.

8133. _____. *Santa Fe's diesel fleet*. Burlingame, CA: Chatham Pub. Co., 1975. 143 p.

8134. _____. *Tumbleweeds and fast freights*. Arvada, CO: McMillan Publications, 2008. 248 p. (Santa Fe)

8135. _____. *Warbonnets and Bluebonnets*. Woodridge, IL: McMillan Publications, 2004. 240 p.(AT&SF)

8136. _____. *Wheat lines and super freights*. Woodridge, IL: McMillan Publications, 1992. 238 p. (AT&SF)

8137. _____, Robert P. Olmsted. *The Peoria way*. Woodridge, IL: McMillan Publications, 1984. 136 p.

8138. McMillan, Marvin D. *Recent financial history of the Chicago and North Western Railway Company*. 1941. 1 v. (Thesis, M.B.A., Northwestern University.)

8139. McMillan, Stephen. *Alco's Century series*. Halifax, PA: Withers Pub., 2003-

8139a. McMillen, George Burr. *Railway wages in the United States, 1908-1914* / 1917. 90 l. (Thesis, M.A., University of Illinois.)

8139b. _____. *Some economic aspects of railway electrification* / 1915. 58 l. (Thesis, B.A., University of Illinois.)

8140. McMullen, Glenn L. *Manuscript sources for railroad history at Carol M. Newman Library, Virginia Tech.* Blacksburg, VA: University Libraries, Virginia Polytechnic Institute and State University, 1986. 26 p.

8141. _____. *The Norfolk and Western Railway archival collection: a guide.* Blacksburg, VA: Special Collections Division, University Libraries, Virginia Polytechnic Institute and State University, 1983. 124 l.

8142. McMullen, J.A., John Walker Barriger, III. *A study of the operating organization and working methods of the Pennsylvania Railroad Company of America* / Philadephia : s.n., 1937. 134 l. 38 leaves of plates.

8143. McMurray, T.S. *The Colorado and Southern Railway Company; corporate history.* 1916. 100 l. (Interstate Commerce Commission. Valuation 20.)

8144. McMurty, Walter L. *Wartime problems of American railroads.* 1983. 3 v. (Thesis, Ph.D., University of New Mexico.)

8145. McMyler Manufacturing Co. *Locomotive cranes, bridge conveyers, grab buckets, car dumpers.* Cleveland, A.C. Rogers Co., 1907. 75 p.

8146. McNatt, Emmett B. *Employee representation in the Lehigh Valley Railroad shops; a case study in company unionism.* 1932. 227 l. (Thesis, Ph.D., Cornell University.)

8147. McNeel, William Price. *The Durbin Route: the Greenbrier Division of the Chesapeake & Ohio Railway.* Charleston, WV: Pictorial Histories Pub. Co., 1985. 142 p.

8147a. McNichols, Timothy E. *A high speed rail terminal for the city of Miami* / 1988. 45 l. (Thesis, M.A., Harvard University.)

8148. McNulty, A.J. *The road of the dashing commuter.* Smithtown, NY: Exposition Press, 1980. 76 p. (Long Island Rail Road)

8149. McPherson, James Alan, Miller Williams. *Railroad: trains and train people in American culture.* New York, NY: Random House, 1976. 185 p.

8150. McPherson, Logan Grant. *Abstract of annual reports of the Baltimore & Ohio Railroad Company, 1827-1901.* Baltimore, Baltimore and Ohio Railroad Company, 1902. 68 p.

8151. _____. *The farmer, the manufacturer and the railroad.* New York, NY: North American Review Pub. Co., 13 p.

8152. _____. *The hand-book of the Pennsylvania Lines*. Chicago? Pennsylvania R.R., 1888. 81 p.

8153. _____. *Railroad freight rates in relation to the industry and commerce of the United States*. New York, H. Holt, 1909. 441 p.

8154. McPherson, William H. *Employee representation for shop craft employees on the Pennsylvania Railroad System* / 1924. 84 l. (Thesis, M.A., Ohio State University.)

8154a. McPike, Eugene Fairfield. *On the Railroad Refrigerator Service Association, its origin and its aims*. Paris, Secretariat General, 1908. 7 p. (International Congress of Refrigerating Industries, 1st, 1908, Paris.)

8155. _____. *Transportation of perishable freight in America*. S.l., s.n., 1910. 1 v.

8156. McQuigg, Tammy Galloway, Scott McIntosh. *Central of Georgia Railway*. Charleston, SC: Arcadia, 1998. 126 p.

8157 McShane, Charles Leo. *The locomotive up to date*. Chicago, Ill., Griffin & Winters, 1899. 711 p.

8158. _____, *The locomotive up to date*. Rev. ed. Chicago, Ill., Griffin & Winters, 1925, 1927. 893 p.

8159. _____. *Modern air brakes*. Chicago, Ill., Griffin & Winters, 1924. 532 p.

8160. _____, *Modern locomotive valves and valve gears*. Chicago, Ill., Griffin & Winters, 1917. 339 p.

8162. _____, John T. Hoar. *New York and Westinghouse air brakes*. Chicago, Ill., Griffin & Winters, 1905. 206 p.

8162a. McVey, Frank LeRond. *Railroad transportation; some phases of it history, operation and regulation* . Minneapolis: Cree Publishing, 1910. 408 p.

8163. Meacham, Howard C. *Carbody structural technology for intercity passenger trains* / Washington, DC: Federal Railroad A ministration, 1979. 31, 2 p.(*Working paper : improved passenger equipment evaluation program, no. 5.2*)

8164. Mead, Edgar Thorn, Jr. *The Bridgton narrow gauge*. Canton, OH: Railhead Publications, 1985. 1 v.

8165. _____. *"Busted and still running:" the famous two-foot gauge railroad of Bridgton, Maine*. Brattleboro, VT: S. Greene Press, 1968. 58 p.

8166. _____. *The Concord & Claremont Railroad: a scenic branch of the Boston & Maine*. Sunapee, NH: SooNipi Pub. Co., 1998. 76 p.

8167. _____. *Over the hills to Woodstock: the saga of the Woodstock Railroad.* Brattleboro, VY: S. Greene Press, 1967. 43 p.

8168. _____. *Through covered bridges to Concord: a recollection of the Concord & Claremont RR (NH).* Brattleboro, VT: S. Greene Press, 1970. 51 p.

8169. _____. *The up-country line: Boston, Concord & Montreal RR to the New Hampshire lakes and White Mountains.* Brattleboro, VT: S. Greene Press, 1975. 64 p.

8170. _____. *The Woodstock Railroad, 1863-1933: Woodstock, Vermont to White River Junction, Vermont.* Sunapee, NH: SooNipi Pub. Co., 1999. 64 p.

8171. Mead, Kenneth M. *High speed ground transportation: strategic approach needed fro introduction of HSGT: statement of Kenneth M. Mead, Director, Transportation Issues, Resources, Community, and Economic Development Division, before the Subcommittee on Transportation and Hazardous Materials, Committee of Energy and Commerce, House of Representatives* / Washington, DC: General Accounting Office, 1993. 14, 4 p. (*GAO/T-RCED-93-35.*)

8172. Meadows, David Stanley. *Locomotive coaling stations*/ 1908. 46 l. (Thesis, B.S., University of Illinois.)

8173. Means, Richard Nathaniel Griffith. *Empire, progress, and the American Southwest: the Texas and Pacific Railroad, 1850-1882.* 2001. 525 l. (Thesis, Ph.D., University of Southern Mississippi.)

8174. Measors, William H. *Politics, performance and perception of the United States Railroad Administration.* 1996. 85 l. (Thesis, B.A., Williams College, Dept. of History.)

8175. *Measures of effectiveness, railroad-highway grade crossings, and visibility: 9 reports prepared for the 54th annual meeting of the Transportation Research Board.* Washington, DC: Transportation Research Board, 1976. 106 p. (*Transportation research record, 562.*)

8175a. Medaugh, Frederick Wilbur. *Railroad vertical curves and spirals*/ Baltimore: F. W. Medaugh, 1926. 34 p.

8176. Medding, Walter L., H.E. Strout. *An investigation of the relative economy of various types of locomotive coaling stations.* 1917. 44 l. (Thesis, B.S., Massachusetts Institute of Technology.)

8177. Mee, Brian E. *Overview of railroad bridges and assessment of methods to monitor railroad bridge integrity* / Washington, DC : Federal Railroad Administration, Office of Research and Development, 1994. 143 p. (DOT/FRA/ORD-94/20.)

8178. _____. *Ride quality evaluation of high speed trains on the Northeast Corridor.* Washington, DC: Federal Railroad Administration, 1996. 1 v. (various pagings). (*DOT/FRA/ORD-96/07.*)

8179. Meeker, R.F., D.C. McGahey. *A review of some recent advances in lubrication of railway car journal plain bearings* / New York : American Society of Mechanical Engineers, 1958. 12 p. (*ASME. Paper no. 58-A-266.*)

8180. Meeker, Royal. *Wages and hours of labor in the building and repairing of steam railroad cars: 1907 to 1913.* Washington, DC: U.S. G.P.O., Bureau of labor Statistics, 1915. 58 p. (*Bulletin of the United States Bureau of Labor Statitistcs, whole no. 163. Wages and hours of labor series, no. 15.*)

8181. Meeks, Carroll L. V. *The railroad station: an architectural history.* New Haven., Conn., Yale University Press, 1956. 203 p. (*Yale historical publications. History of art. 11.*) (Reprint: Secaucus, NJ: Castle Books, 1978, 1956. 203 p; New York, Dover Publications, 1995. 203 p.)

8182. Meeks, Harold Austin. *The growth of Minnesota railroads, 1857-1957.* 1957. 55 l. (Thesis, M.A., University of Minnesota.)

8183. *Meet the Maine Central: the Pine Tree Route.* Portland, ME: The 470 Club, 1981. 64 p.

8184. *Meet the new Texas Special streamliners.* St. Louis, St. Louis-San Francisco Railway, 1948. 14 p.

8185. Mehls, Steven F. *David H. Moffat, Jr., early Colorado business leader.* New York NY: Garland Pub., 1989. 366 p. (*Garland studies in entrepreneurship.*)

8186. Mehrer, Jim. *Cross-reference guide to United States railway post office postmarks.* Rock Island, IL: J. Mehrer, 1993. 100 p.

8187. _____. *Guide to identifying U.S. route and station agent postmarks.* Rock Island, IL: J. Mehrer, 1994. 110 p.

8189. Meints, Graydon M. *Along the tracks: a directory of named places on Michigan railroads.* Mount Pleasant, Clarke Historical Library, Central Michigan University, 1987. 303 p.

8189a. _____. *Indiana railroad lines* / Bloomington: Indiana University Press, 2011. 402 p. (Includes interurban lines)

8190. _____. *Michigan railroad lines.* East Lansing, MI: Michigan State University Press, 2005. 2 v.

8191. _____. *Michigan railroads and railroad companies.* East Lansing, MI: Michigan State University Press, 1992. 305 p.

8191a. _____. *Railroads for Michigan* / East Lansing: Michigan State University Press, 2013. 523 p.

8192. _____ *Telegraph calls of the New York Central lines.* Kalamazoo, MI: Michigan Classic Railroad Reprints, 1980. 26 p.

8193. Mele, Ronald Gregory. *Birmingham Southern Railroad Company: the first century.* 2d ed. S.l., Rail Images, 2000. 136 p.

8194. Mellander, Deane E. *The Cumberland & Pennsylvania Railroad: western Maryland's historic coal carrier.* Newton, NJ: Carstens, 1981. 64 p.

8195. _____. *East Broad Top: slim gauge survivor.* Silver Spring, MD: Old Line Graphics, 1995. 128 p.

8196. _____. *Rails to the big vein: the short lines of Allegany County, Maryland: the Cumberland and Pennsylvania RR, the Georges Creek and Cumberland RR, the Cumberland and Westernport Electric.* S.l., Potomac Chapter, National Railway Historical Society, 1981. 1 v.

8197. _____, Bob Kaplan. *B&O steam finale.* Photography by William P. Price. Kensington, MD: Potomac Chapter, National Railway Historical Society, 1986-1988. 2 v.

8198. _____, Frederick A. Kramer, Theodore F. Gleichmann. *B & O thunder in the Alleghenies.* Newton, NJ: Carstens, 1983. 80 p.

8199. Meller, Russell D., Kevin R. Gue. *A model to design a national high-speed network for freight distribution.* Fayetteville, AR: Mack-Blackwell Transportation Center, University of Arkansas, 2008. 44 l.

8200. Mellin, Carl Johan. *Articulated compound locomotives: a paper read before the American Society of Mechanical Engineers, New York City, December, 1908.* New York, American Locomotive Company, 1908. 40 p. (*Pamphlet no. 10034*) Code word: Calectasie.

8200a. Melrose, M.F., T.E. De Vilbiss. *Mobile reflectoscope inspection of railway car axles under rolling equipment on the Chesapeake and Ohio Railway Company/* 1959. 9 p. (*American Society of Mechanical Engineers. Paper no. 59-A-228.*)

8201. Melvin, George F. *Bangor and Aroostook in color.* Scotch Plains, NJ : Morning Sun Books, 2010. 128 p. 2 v.

8202. _____, Jeremy F. Plant. *Central Vermont, in color.* Scotch Plains, NJ: Morning Sun Books, 2000. 128 p.

8202a. _____, Katherine Melvin. *Bangor and Aroostook stations and structures /* Readfield, ME: Melvin Photos, 2013. 144 p.

8203. _____, _____, Preston Johnson. *Boston and Maine memories: featuring the photography and career of Preston Johnson /* Readfield, ME: Melvin Photos, 2010.

111 p.

8204. Melzer, Richard. *Fred Harvey Houses of the Southwest* / Charleston, SC: Arcadia Pub., 2008. 127 p.

8205. *A memorial against refunding the claims of the United States upon the Central Pacific Railroad Company for $77,000,000.* San Francisco: s.n., 1894. 14 p. Signed: Chas. A. Sumner, J.M. Bassett, Frederic B. Perkins. Addressed to the Senate and House of Representatives of the United States.

8206. Mencken, August. *The railroad passenger car: illustrated history of the first hundred years, with accounts of contemporary passengers.* Baltimore, Johns Hopkins Press, 1957. 209 p. (Reprint: Baltimore, Johns Hopkins University Press, 2000. 209 p.)

8207. Meneely, George R., T.W. Getman. *Hopkins' patent journal bearings for railway cars and engines, and of all kinds of bronze machinery castings* / Albany, NY: Weed, Parson and Co., 1877. 17 p.

8207a. Menke, Arnold S. *Diagrams of tenders: Southern Pacific Lines as of 6-1-50.* Upland, CA: Southern Pacific Historical and Technical Society, 1998. 1 v. (Unpaged)

8208. Mennem, Gary M. *Effects of railroad abandonment on grain producers and grain elevator supply areas in North Central Kansas.* 1974. 142 l. (Thesis, Ph.D., Kansas State University.)

8209. Mercer, Lloyd J. *The Central Pacific system: an estimate of social and private rates of return for a land-grant aided railroad system.* 1967. 201 l. (Thesis, Ph.D., University of Washington.)

8210. _____. *E.H. Harriman, master railroader.* Boston, Twayne Publishers, 1985. 188 p. (*The evolution of American business*) (Reprint: Washington, D.C., Beard Books, 2003.)

8211. _____. *Railroads and land grant policy; a study in government intervention.* New York, Academic Press, 1982. 268 p. (Reprint: Washington, D.C., Beard Books, 2002.)

8212. Merchant's Association of New York. *The Pennsylvania tunnel franchise : some of the reasons why it should be granted* / New York : Economist press, 1902. 10 p.

8213. _____. Committee on Disposal of West Side Railroad Tracks. *Disposal of West Side railroad tracks; a report to the Merchants' Association of New York by its Committee on Disposal of West Side Railroad Tracks, November 25, 1908* / New York : The Merchants' Association of New York, 1908. 19 p. Walter C. Kerr, chairman.

8214. _____. Committee on Domestic Commerce. *Report of the plans under consideration by the Board of Estimate and Apportionment of the city of New York for the reorganization of the railroad terminals upon the Hudson River waterfront.* New York : 1911. 11 p.

8215. _____. Committee on Harbor, Docks and Terminals. *Report on the proposed plans for the readjustment of the New York Central Railroad tracks upon the west side of Manhattan Island.* New York: Merchants' Association of New York, 1916. 33 p.

8215a. Merchants' Exchange of St. Louis. Transportation Committee. Iowa. Railroad Commissioners. Western Classification Committee. *The car-load rate discrimination against the wholesale interests of St. Louis, Chicago and Milwaukee.* St. Louis? 1885. 19 p.

8216. *The Merchants' magazine and commercial review.* New York, Freeman Hunt, 1861-1870. 20 v. Monthly. (*<Hunt's merchants' magazine and commercial review.; >Commercial and financial chronicle and Hunt's merchants' magazine.*)

8217. Meredith, Roy, Arthur Meredith. *Mr. Lincoln's military railroads: a pictorial history of United States Civil War railroads.* New York, Norton, 1979. 253 p.

8218. *Mergent transportation manual.* New York, Mergent, Inc., 2001-2002. Annual. 2 v. *<Moody's transportation manual; >Mergent public utility manual.*)

8219. *Mergent public utility & transportation manual.* New York, NY: Mergent, Inc., 2003- Annual. (*<Mergent public utility manual.)*

8220. *Mergent public utility manual.* New York, NY: Mergent, Inc., 2001-2002. Annual. 2 v. (*>Mergent public utility & transportation manual.*)

8221. *Mergent transportation news reports.* New York, Mergent, Weekly. (*<Moody's transportation news reports, 1999-2001.*)

8222. Merriam, Charles Allen. *An investigation of the stresses in locomotive connecting rods with tests on full-sized specimens.* 1906. 1 v. (Thesis, B.S., Massachusetts Institute of Technology.)

8223. Merrill, E. D. *An estimate of the cost of improving and extending the Boston, Revere Beach & Lynn Railroad* / 1909. 19 4 l. (Thesis, B.S., Massachusetts Institute of Technology, Department of Civil Engineering.)

8224. Merrill, T.D. *Catechism on safety appliances for freight car, passenger coach and steam locomotives: suggestions for electric locomotives, gas, gasoline and gas-electric motor cars used in railway service.* Minneapolis, Minn., s.n., 1926. 75 p.

8225. Merrill, William E. *Iron truss bridges for railroads. Methods of calculating strains, with a comparison of the most prominent truss bridges, and new formulas for bridge computations.* 3d ed. New York, D. Van Nostrand, 1875. 130 p.

8225a. Merritt, Harold Thomas. *The Chicago and Eastern Illinois railroad yards at Mitchell, Illinois* / 1907. 23 l. 6 l. of plates. (Thesis, B.S., University of Illinois.)

8226. Merritt, Raymond H. *Engineering in American society, 1850-1875*. Lexington: University Press of Kentucky, 1969.

8227. Messenger, C.W., O.E. Stewart. *Chicago, Burlington& Quincy R.R., Ottumwa, Iowa, 1891-1899; instructions and information for train dispatchers from the Chief Dispatcher and Superintendent*. Compiled by Robert C. Brown. Plano, TX: R.C. Brown, 1998. 149 p.

8228. *The messenger*. New York, N.Y., Messenger Publishing Company, 1917-1928. Monthly. (Brotherhood of Sleeping Car Porters)

8229. Messer, David W., Charles S. Roberts. *Triumph II: Philadelphia to Harrisburg, 1828-1998*. Baltimore, MD: Barnard, Roberts and Co., 1999. 399 p.

8230. _____, _____. *Triumph III: Philadelphia terminal, 1838-2000*. Baltimore, MD: Barnard, Roberts and Co., 2000. 397 p.

8231. _____, _____. *Triumph IV: Harrisburg to Altoona, 1846-2001*. Baltimore, MD: Barnard, Roberts and Co., 2001. 397 p.

8232. _____, _____. *Triumph V: Philadelphia to New York, 1830-2002*. Baltimore, MD: Barnard, Roberts and Co., 2002. 399 p.
 Company)

8232a. Messer, John S. *Adequacy of railroad passenger service : report and recommended order* / Washington, DC: U.S. G.P.O., 1969. 45 p. (Southern Pacific Company)

8232a. Messina, Lynn Marie. *Trains of thought: the railroad and consciousness in selected works by Hawthorne, James, and Cather*. 1997. 213 l. (Thesis, Ph.D., The City University of New York.)

8233. Messner, Michael Gerard. *A system for controlling a railroad's on-line freight car cycle* / 1980. 143 l. (Thesis, M.S., Massachusetts Institute of technology, Department of Civil Engineering.)

8234. Metcalfe, Terry. *Steam era freight car lettering diagrams*. Englewood, CO: Metcalfe Publications, n.d. 6 sheets in envelope.(Union Pacific)

8235. _____. *Union Pacific diesel painting and lettering*. Englewood, CO: Metcalfe Publications, 1972-1973. 8 sheets in envelope.

8236. _____. *Union Pacific freight cars, mechanical design drawings*. Englewood, CO: Metcalfe Publications, n.d. 8 sheets in envelope.

8237. _____. *Union Pacific freight cars, 1936-51.* 2d ed. Englewood, CO: Metcalfe Publications, 1989. 217 p.

8238. Metheny, Orvil Cranfill. *Container service: coordinated highway-rail-water transportation.* 1959. 93 l. (Thesis, M.B.A. in Transportation and Public Utilities, Graduate School of Arts and Sciences, University of Pennsylvania)

8239. Metro-North Railroad. *A history of Grand Central Terminal.* New York, Metro-North Railroad, 1998. 1 v.

8240. Metzman, Gustav. *Cincinnati and Ohio, their early railroads.* New York, Newcomen Society, American Branch, 1948. 32 p.

8241. _____. *Faith, facts and freight cars.* New York, American Railway Car Institute, 1954. 9 p.

8242. _____. *Rail transportation: its equipment problems.* New York, American Rail Car Institute, 1954. 11 p.

8243. _____. *The simple arithmetic of transportation* / S.l., New York Central System, 1949. 14 p.

8244. Meurer, Richard Charles. *Improvements in railroad freight classification yards.* 1957. 234 l. (Thesis, M.B.A. in Transportation and Public Utilities, Graduate School of Arts and Sciences, University of Pennsylvania)

8245. Meyer, Balthasar Henry. *A history of early railroad legislation in Wisconsin.* Madison, State Historical Society of Wisconsin, 1908. 1 v.

8246. _____. *Railway legislation in the United States.* New York, N.Y., Macmillan Company, 1903. 329 p.

8247. _____, Caroline E. MacGill. *History of transportation in the United States before 1860/* New York, NY: P. Smith, 1948. 678 p. (*Carnegie Institution of Washington, Publication no. 215C.*)

8248. Meyer, Dan, Dawn Holmberg, Hudson Leighton. *Minnesota railroad station & depot locations; third interim report, November 1, 1993.* Minneapolis, MN: Minnesota Railroad Research Project, 1993. 87 p.

8249. Meyer, Frederic L. *Twentieth century manual of railway and commercial telegraphy.* 2nd. Ed. Chicago, IL: Rand McNally & Company, 1902. 249 p.

8250. _____. *Twentieth century manual of railway station service; freight, baggage and passenger department.* Chicago: Rand, McNally & Company, 1911. 271 p. First published 1906.)

8251. Meyer, Jacob G Arnold. *Modern locomotive construction.* New York, J. Wiley and Sons, 1892. 658 p. (Reprint: Bradley, IL: Lindsay Publications, 1994. 658 p.)

8252. Meyers, Steven J., Dell A. McCoy. *Trails among the Columbine: a Colorado high country anthology.* Denver, CO: Sundance Pub. Ltd., 1987. 160 p. (Cumbres and Toltec Scenic Railroad)

8252a. *Miami's railway terminal problem.* Miami: City Planning Board of Miami, 1941. 19 l., 12 l. of plates.

8253. Mian, Zahid F. *Automated wheel inspection station* / Washington, DC : Transportation Research Board, National Research Council, 1997. 10 p. (*Report of investigation, no. 3.*)

8254. Michalski, Adam T. *Unfulfilled promise : electrification and the Chicago, Milwaukee & St. Paul Railroad.* 2009. 117 l. Computer file. (Thesis, M.A., University of Missouri—St. Louis.) http://etd.umsl.edu/r4564

8255. Michaud, Marie-Christine. *From steel tracks to gold-paved streets: the Italian immigrants and the railroad in the North Central states*/ New York, NY: Center for Migration Studies, 2005. 204 p.

8256. Michels, G.J., G.L. Semon. *Cabooses of the Missouri Pacific Lines.* Foreword by Joe G. Collias. S.l., Missouri Pacific Historical Society, 1996. 376 p.

8257. Michigan Bridge and Construction Company. *The Michigan Bridge & Construction Co., Detroit: manufacturers of iron, wooden, combination and suspension bridges, trestles, roofs, turntables, water-stations, &c.: engineers and contractors for the location and construction of rail roads and other public works.* Detroit, MI: O.S. Gulley's Steam Presses, 1871. 40 p.

8258. Michigan Central Railroad Company. *An explanation of the Michigan Central system of dispatching trains by telegraph.* Detroit, Mich., s.n., 1888. 17 p.

8259. _____. *General rules and regulations for handling freight and passenger traffic. Effective June 1, 1923.* S.l., s.n., 1923.500 p.

8260. _____. *Instructions to signalmen on the operation of interlocking plants.* S.l., The Michigan Central Railroad Company, 1926. 26 p.

8261. _____. *Manual block signal rules.* S.l., The Michigan Central Railroad Company, 1914. 14 p.

8262. _____. *The North Shore Limited and the New York and Chicago Limited: two great limited trains.* Chicago: Rand, McNally & Co., 1893. 36 p.

8263. _____. *Rules for the government of the conducting transportation department. Effective April 1, 1906; revised January 2, 1907.* Detroit : W. S. Gilkey Printing Co., 1917. 147 p.

8264. _____. *Rules for the government of the Operating Department*. S.l., s.n., 1920. 176 p.

8265. _____. *Rules of the Maintenance of Way Department, to take effect August 1, 1915*. Detroit, Mich., The Michigan Central Railroad Company, 1915. 102 p.

8266. _____. *Statement of expenses connected with car movements in Detroit terminals: explanatory statement*. Detroit? E.C. Taylor, 1917. 65 p.

8267. Michigan. Department of State. *Steel, steam & smoke: Michigan's railroad heritage*. Lansing, MI: Michigan History Center, 1993. 72 p.

8268. _____. Department of State Highways and Transportation. *Economic benefits of Lake Michigan car ferry service*. Arlington, VA: TERA, Inc., 1976. 2 v.

8269 _____. Department of Transportation; Michigan Sesquicentennial Commission. *150 years of Michigan's railroad history*. Lansing, MI: Michigan Department of Transportation, 1987. 36 p.

8270. *Michigan railroad history*. Crete, NE: J-B Pub. Co., 1985. 36 p. (*Railway history monographs, v. 14, no. 3/4.*)

8271. *Michigan railroad history: a selected bibliography*. Compiled by Graydon M. Meints. S.l., s.n., 1991. 21 l.

8271a. Mickelson, Siegfried. *Promotional activities of the Northern Pacific Railroad's Land and Immigration Departments, 1870 to 1902; a case study of commercial propaganda in the nineteenth century/* 1940. 257 l. (Thesis, M.A., University of Minnesota.)

8272. Mickey, M., D. Warfel. *Lehigh Valley Railroad passenger cars*. Flanders, NJ: Railroad Avenue Enterprises, 1980. 64 p. (*Photo and diagram book, no. 1.*)

8273. *Microsoft Train Simulator*. Redmond, WA: Microsoft Corporation. Computer file. Computer program 2 CD-ROMs. Quickstart guide, 15 p.

8274. *Microsoft train simulator: Sybex official strategies & secrets*. Alameda, CA: Sybex Inc., 2001. 304 p.

8275. *Mid-Continent railway gazette*. Brookfield, WI: Mid-Continent Railway Historical Society, Inc., 1963-1965. Monthly 3 v. (< *Monthly newsletter of your Society;* > *Railway gazette*. Milwaukee.)

8276. *Mid-Continent railway gazette*. North Freedom, WI: Mid-Continent Railway Historical Society, 1987-   . (< *Railway gazette*.)

8277. Mid-Continent Railway Historical Society. *Mid-Continent compendium:*

a guidebook for the Mid-Continent Railway Museum. North Freedom, WI: Mid-Continent Railway Historical Society, 2005. 103 p.

8278. Middlebrook, R.P. *The Fallbrook Branch; how a main line in a dry wash became a branch line.* San Marino, CA: Pacific Railway Journal, 1957. 8 p. (AT&SF; California Southern RR)

8279 _____. *The high iron to La Jolla: the story of a railroad.* San Diego, San Diego Historical Society, 1961. 13 p. (*San Diego Historical Society Quarterly, v. 7, no. 1.)*

8280. _____, Richard V. Dodge. *San Diego's first railroad; Pacific Coast Steamship Company.* San Mateo, Western Railroader, 1957. 15 p.

8281. Middleton, Kenneth R. *Early Pacific locomotives of the Great Northern.* Burnsville, MN: Great Northern Railway Historical Society, 2004. 22 p.

8282. _____. *Great Northern air dump cars.* Burnsville, MN: Great Northern Railway Historical Society, 2007. 24 p. (*Reference sheet, no. 339.)*

8283. _____. *Great Northern official and business cars* / Burnsville, MN: Great Northern Railway Historical Society, 2006. 64 p. (*Reference sheet no. 333.)*

8284. _____. *Great Northern research references.* Burnsville, MN: Great Northern Railway Historical Society, 2005. 4 p.

8285. _____. *Great Northern steam locomotive cab side data.* Burnsville, MN: Great Northern Railway Historical Society, 2006. 12 p.

8286. _____, John R. Westley. *Great Northern official and business cars.* Burnsville, MN: Great Northern Railway Historical Society, 2006. 64 p.

8287. _____, Norman F. Priebe. *Steam locomotives of the Great Northern Railway.* Stevens Point, WI: Great Northern Railway Historical Society, 2010. 544 p.

8288. Middleton, P. Harvey. *Freight transport in the United States; prewar, war, and postwar.* Chicago, Ill., Railway Business Association, 1945. 98 p.

8289. _____. *Oil industry and transportation, prewar and postwar.* Chicago, Ill., Railway Business Association, 1943. 60 p.

8290. _____. *Railways and organized labor.* Chicago, Ill., Railway Business Association, 1941. 136 p.

8291. _____. *Railways and public opinion; eleven decades.* Chicago, Ill., Railway Business Association, 1941. 169 p.

8292. _____. *Railways and the equipment and supply industry.* 2d ed. Chicago, Ill., Railway Business Association, 1941. 142 p.

8293. Middleton, William D. *Frank Julian Sprague: electrical inventor and engineer/* Bloomington, IN: Indiana University Press, 2009. 314 p.

8294. _____. *Grand Central, the world's greatest railway terminal.* San Marino, CA: Golden West Books, 1977. 160 p.

8295. _____. *Landmarks on the iron road: two centuries of North American railroad engineering.* Bloomington, IN: Indiana University Press, 1999. 194 p.

8296. _____. *Manhattan gateway: New York's Pennsylvania Station.* Waukesha, WI: Kalmbach Books, 1996. 159 p.

8296a. _____. *Metropolitan railways : rapid transit in America* / Bloomington: Indiana University Press,2003. 275 p.

8297. _____. *The Pennsylvania Railroad under wire.* Waukesha, WI: Kalmbach Books, 2002. 128 p.

8298. _____. *The railroad scene.* San Marino, CA: Golden West Books, 1969. 144 p.

8298a. _____. *South Shore, the last interurban.* San Marino, CA: Golden West Books, 1970. 176 p.

8299. _____. *When the steam railroads electrified.* Milwaukee, Kalmbach Books, 1974. 439 p.
(2d ed.: Bloomington, Indiana University Press, 2001. 467 p. Foreword by John W. Barriger, III.)

8300. *Middletown: home of the O&W and the O&WRHS.* Middletown, NY: Ontario & Western Railway Historical Society, 1991. 102 p. (*Observer, v. 26, no. 1-9, Jan-Sept. 1991.*)

8301. Midgley, J.W. *The effect of restrictive legislation upon the railways of Wisconsin and the material interest of the state/* Chicago, IL: Culver, Page, Hoyne & Co, Printers, 1876. 20 p.

8302. *Midland Terminal.* Denver: Rocky Mountain Railroad Club, 1949. 4 p. (*Rocky Mountain Railroad Club, vol. II, No. 1.*)

8303. Midvale Steel Company. *Rolled steel wheels.* Philadelphia : s.n., 1910. 68 p. (*Series no. 27.*)

8304. _____. *Steel axles and locomotive forgings.* Philadelphia : Midvale Cambria Steel and Ordinance Co., 1920. 122 p.

8305. *Midwest railroader.* Ft. Wayne, IN: R.W. Carlson, 1957-Monthly. (Title varies

8306. *Midwest railroader remembers—the Frisco and steam.* Shelby, OH: Hallmark Books, 1982. 94 p. (*Midwest Railroader Magazine*)

8307. *Midwestern railroads.* Milwaukee, Kalmbach Pub. Co., 1942. 2 p. 23 l. of plates. (*Trains album of photographs, no. 3.*)

8308. Milener, Eugene D. *How the railroad from Albany to Binghamton affected the economic development of Oneonta, New York, 1891.* 1971. 313 l. (Thesis, Ph.D., New York University.)

8309. _____. *Oneonta: the development of a railroad town.* Oneonta, NY: E.D. Milener, 1983. 558 p.

8309a. Millar, Peter. *All gone to look for America.* London, U.K., Arcadia, 2009. 319 p. (Railroad travel)

8310. Millard, James Kemper. *Chesapeake and Ohio streamliners: second to none. Volume 1, the cars.* Clifton Forge, VA: Chesapeake and Ohio Historical Society, 1994-

8311. Miller, Bernard Ernest. *Painting of railway equipment.* New York: Simmons-Boardman Pub. Co., 1924. 1 v. (various pagings)

8312. Miller, D.J., P.R. Houghton. *Performance of western softwood species as crossties in mainline railroad track.* Chicago, IL: Association of American Railroads, Technical Center, 1988. 35 l. (*Report/AAR: no. R-698.*)

8313. Miller, Darrel. *Life in a railroad town.* Downs, KS: Cellar Door Publications, 1996. 159 p. (Downs, Kansas)

8314. _____. *Life on the Central Branch.* Down, KS: Cellar Door Publications, 1999. 144 p. (Down, Kansas; Union Pacific Railroad.)

8315. Miller E. *Miller's trussed platforms, compression buffers, and automatic couplers for railroad cars.* New York: Baker & Godwin, 1868. 29 p.

8316. _____. *Miller's trussed platforms, compression buffers and automatic couplers. The standard American system of making up railroad passenger trains* / New York, Baker & Godwin, 1873. 49 p.

8317. Miller, E. Spencer. *Maine Central Railroad, 1940-1978.* New York, Newcomen Society in North America, 1979. 52 p. (*Newcomen publication, no. 1110.*)

8318. Miller, Edward H. *The Hocking Valley Railway.* Southgate? MI: Chesapeake & Ohio Historical Society, 1984. 16 p.

8319. _____. *The Hocking Valley Railway.* Athens, OH: Ohio University Press, 2007. 347 p.

8320. Miller, Eugene A. *Railroad 1869: along the historic Union Pacific*/ Mill Valley, CA: Antelope Press, 2009. 1 v.

8321. Miller, Frederic P., Agnes F. Vandome, John McBrewster. *Long Island Rail Road* / Mauritius : Alphascript Pub., 2009. 110 p.

8322. Miller George H. *The Granger laws: a study of the origins of state railway control in the Upper Mississippi Valley*. 1951. 348 l. (Thesis, Ph.D., University of Michigan.)

8323. _____. *Railroads and the Granger laws*. Madison, University of Wisconsin Press, 1971. 296 p.

8324. Miller, Harry W. *Trains of the Broadway Limited route, 1922-1977*. Washington, DC: Rail Ways of the Americas, 1977. 41 p

8324a. Miller, Henry, Thomas M. Pierce. *The romance of Eads Bridge; the truth about the terminal* / St. Louis: Terminal Railroad Association of St. Louis, 1931. 29 p.

8325. Miller, Ivor. *Aerosol kingdom: subway painters of New York City*. Jackson, Miss., University Press of Mississippi, 2002. 218 p.

8326. Miller, J. Meredith. *Railroad turntables about Bethlehem Penn'a. and a design of a new one*. 1904. 53 l., 7 l. of fold. plates. (Thesis, C.E., Lehigh University.)

8327. Miller, John, Barclay F. Thorn, Jason S. Beaton. *Update on status of proposed TransDominion Express (TDX) passenger rail service*. Charlottesville, VA: Virginia Transportation Research Council, 2007. 40 p. (*VTRC, 07-R23*.)

8328. Miller, John David. *A railroad terminal evaluation methodology*. 1985. 166 l. (Thesis, Ph.D., West Virginia University.)

8329. Miller, Kenneth L. *Norfolk and Western class J: the finest steam passenger locomotive*. Roanoke, VA: Roanoke Chapter, National Railway Historical Society, 2000. 131 p.

8330. Miller, Laura. *Tracks and travelers: the visual culture of tourism and the National Parks*. 2001. 54 l. (Thesis, M.A., University of St. Thomas , Saint Paul, MN.)

8331. Miller, Paul E. *Financial history of the Chicago Great Western Railroad Company*. 1924. 1 v. (Thesis, M.B.A., Northwestern University.)

8332. Miller, Robert N. *The design of a steel truck for 100,000 capacity cars* / 1909. 16 l. (Thesis, M.E., Lehigh University.)

8333. Miller, Sidney Lincoln. *Inland transportation, principles and policies; a revision and extension of "Railway transportation"*. New York, NY: McGraw-Hill Book Co., 1933. 822 p.

8334. _____. *Railway transportation, principles and point of view.* Chicago, IL: A.W. Shaw, 1924. 905 p.

8335. _____. *The railways and labor: what price peace?* Chicago, IL: Associated Traffic Clubs of America, 1941. 49, 1 p.

8336. _____. *Tomorrow in West Texas: economic opportunities along the Texas and Pacific Railway.* Lubbock, TX: Texas Tech Press, 1956. 643 p. (West Texas Chamber of Commerce.)

8337. _____, Virgil Dale Cover. *Rates of return: class I line-haul railways of the United States; an analysis and an appraisal embodying a comparison with other industries regulated and unregulated.* Pittsburgh, University of Pittsburgh Press, 1950. 211 p.

8338. Miller Signal Company. *The first practical block signal placed in the cab of a locomotive: a revolution in block signaling*/ Chicago: Miller Signal Compnay, 1901. 3 p.

8339. Miller, Ted R., John B. Douglass, Nancy Pindus. *Railroad injury: causes, costs, and comparisons with other transport modes.* Washington, D.C., Urban Institute; Federal Railroad Administration, 1992. 33 p.

8340. Miller, William Grant. *A design for a five panel Pratt bridge across the Bushkill River, Easton, Pa.* 1891. 57 l. (Thesis, Lafayette College (Easton, Pa.), Department of Civil Engineering.)

8341. Millichap, Joseph R. *Dixie Limited: railroads, culture, and the Southern renaissance.* Lexington, KY: University Press of Kentucky, 2002. 146 p.

8342. Million, Art. *Pere Marquette passenger car pictorial.* Edited by Sigrid K. Powell. Grand Haven, MI: Pere Marquette Historical Society, 2002. 299 p.

8343. _____, John C. Paton. *Pere Marquette revenue freight cars.* Mukilteo, WA: Hundman Pub., 2001. 170 p.

8344. _____. Thomas W. Dixon, Carl W. Shaver. *Pere Marquette power.* 2d ed. Alderson, WV: Chesapeake and Ohio Historical Society, 1985. 244 p.

8345. Million, John Wilson. *State aid to railways in Missouri.* Chicago, Ill., University of Chicago Press, 1896. (Reprint: New York, Arno Press, 1981. 264 p.)

8345a. Mills, Donald L. *The Kanawha & Michigan Railroad : bridgeline to the Lakes, 1888-1922.* Huntington, WV: Mid-Atlantic Highlands, 2010. 218 p.

8345a. Mills, Eve. *Rail and water: a colorful story of railroad building—Central Pacific Railroad* / North Highlands, CA: History West, 1981. 134, 26 p.

8346. Mills, George. *The little man with the long shadow: the life and times of Frederick

M. Hubbell. Ames, Iowa: Iowa State University Press, 1988, 1955. 262 p. (*Iowa heritage collection.*)

8347. Mills, John William. *Analysis and design of a steel wheel and rail profilometer /* 1980. 278 l. (Thesis, M.S., Massachusetts Institute of Technology, Department of Mechanical Engineering.)

8348. Mills, Randall V. *Railroads down the valleys; some short lines of the Oregon country.* Palo Alto, CA: Pacific Books, 1950. 151 p.

8349. Mills, Rick W. *The high, dry, and dusty: memories of the Cowboy Line.* David City, NE: South Platte Press, 1992. 168 p.

8350. _____. *Making the grade: a century of Black Hills railroading.* Rapid City? R.W. Mills, 1985. 154 p.

8351. _____. *The Milwaukee Road in Dakota.* Hermosa, SD: Battle Creek Pub. Co., 1998. 155 p.

8352. _____. *North Western rails: a pictorial essay of the C&NW's Western Divisions, 1868-1988.* Rapid City, SD: R.W. Mills, 1988. 194 p.

8353. _____. *125 years of Black Hills railroading.* Hermosa, SD: Battle Creek Pub. Co., 2004. 201 p.

8354. _____. *Railroading in the land of infinite variety: a history of South Dakota's railroads.* Hermosa, SD: Battle Creek Pub. Co., 1990. 238 p.

8355. Mills, Robert. *Report* [of] *the Committee on Public lands, to whom was refereed the "memorial of Robert Mills, proposing a plan for a railroad and telegraphic communication with the Pacific Ocean".* Washington, D.C. s.n., 1852. 17 p. (United States, Congress. Senate. Committee on Public Lands.)

8356. Mills, William H. *In the matter of survey and taxation of land granted to the Pacific Railroads Companies/* San Francisco, s.n., 1884. 11 p. (Binder title: *Railroad briefs before Congress, vol. 1.*)

8357. Mills, William Wirt. *The Pennsylvania Railroad tunnels and terminals in New York City.* New York : Moses King, 1904. 14 l. Also: New York, A.S. Cameron Steam Pump Works, 1907. 28 p.

8358. _____. *Tunnels and terminals in greater* New York. New York : A.S. Cameron Steam Pump Works, 1907. 31 p. Caption title; The Pennsylvania Railroad tunnels.

8359. Milsk, Laura Elaine. *Meet me at the station: the culture and aesthetics of Chicago's railroad terminals, 1871-1930.* 2003. 237 l. (Thesis, Ph.D., Loyola University, Chicago.)

8359a. Milton, Ann. *Powering up : a history of the women of the Union Pacific in North Platte, Nebraska.* North Platte, NE: Odd Duck Press, 2011. 120 p.

8360. *The Milwaukee employees' magazine.* Chicago: Chicago, Milwaukee & St. Paul Railway System, 1919-1923. V. 7-10. Monthly. (< *Milwaukee railway system employees' magazine;* > *Milwaukee magazine.*)

8361. Milwaukee Locomotive Manufacturing Company. *Gasolene driven locomotives: for service in manufacturing plants, mills, lumber yards and camps, mines, plantations, quarries, railroad, electric railway, tunnel and canal construction, general freight and passenger transportation.* Milwaukee, Wis., The Company, 1909. 28 p. (*Publication no. 100.*)

8362. _____. *Milwaukee gasoline locomotives. Type H8-C. Parts catalog no. 162.* Milwaukee, Wis., The Company, 1931. 19 p.

8363. _____. *Vanguard gasolene and alcohol locomotives.* Milwaukee, Wis., The Company, 1908. 12 p.

8364. *The Milwaukee magazine.* Chicago: Chicago, Milwaukee, St. Paul, and Pacific Railway System, 1923-1950. Monthly. 28 v. (< *The Milwaukee employees' magazine;* > *Milwaukee Road magazine.*)

8365. *The Milwaukee railroader.* Wauwatosa, WI: Milwaukee Road Railfan's Association, 1970s- . Quarterly. Later publisher: Milwaukee Road Historical Association, Milwaukee. Supplement: *Hiawathagram.*

8366. *The Milwaukee Railway System employees' magazine.* Chicago: Chicago, Milwaukee and St. Paul Railway System, 1913-1919. Monthly. 6 v. Vol. 1, no. 1 (April 1913) – v. 6, no. 12 (Mar. 1919.) (> *Milwaukee employees' magazine.*)

8367. Milwaukee Road Historical Association. *First call to (a Milwaukee Road) dinner.* Collierville, TN : Fundcraft Publishing, 1997, 1960. 1 v. (Recipe book.)

8368. *Milwaukee Road Historical Association newsletter.* Waukesha, WI: The Association, 1991- . Three times a year.

8369. *The Milwaukee Road magazine.* Chicago: Chicago, Milwaukee, St. Paul, and Pacific Railroad Company, 1950-1977. Quarterly. 29 v. Monthly: Feb. 1950-1958. Bimonthly, Mar./Apr. 1958-1976. (< *Milwaukee magazine.*)

8369a. Mims, J.E. *Makin' tracks : a history of railroad stations in Texas* / 1978. 92 l. (Thesis, University of Houston, College of Architecture)

8370. Mine Hill and Schuylkill Haven Railroad Company. *Act of Incorporation of the Mine Hill & Schuylkill Haven Railroad Road Co.: with the supplements and by-laws.* Philadelphia : J & W. Kite, Printers, 1836. 32 p.

8371. _____. *Mine Hill and Schuylkill Haven Railroad.* S.l., s.n., 1845. 6 p.

8372. _____. *Rules & regulations for the engineers, conductors, and brakemen, on the Mine Hill & Schuylkill Haven Rail Road.* S.l, s.n., 1840. 7 p.

8373. Miner, H. Craig. *The Border Tier Line; a history of the Missouri River, Fort Scott and Gulf Railroad, 1865-1870.* 1967. 139 l. (Thesis, M.A., Wichita State University.)

8374. _____. *A most magnificent machine : America adopts the railroad, 1825-1862.* Lawrence : University Press of Kansas, 2010. 325 p.

8375. _____. *The rebirth of the Missouri Pacific, 1956-1983.* College Station, Texas A&M University Press, 1983. 236 p.

8376. _____. *The St. Louis-San Francisco transcontinental railroad; the thirty-fifth parallel project, 1853-1890.* Lawrence, University Press of Kansas, 1972. 236 p. (St. Louis-San Francisco Railway Company)

8376a. _____. *The thirty-fifth parallel project: the formation of a St. Louis-San Francisco railway system, 1853-1890 /* 1970. 362 l. (Thesis, Ph.D., University of Colorado.)

8377. Ming, Dennis R. *An analysis of shipper leased rail equipment in North Dakota.* Fargo, ND: Agricultural Economics Department, North Dakota Agricultural Experiment Station and Upper Great Plains Transportation Institute, North Dakota State University, 1983. 67 p. (*UGPTI report, no. 45.)*

8378. _____. *Use of leased rail equipment in North Dakota.* Fargo, ND: Upper Great Plains Transportation Institute, North Dakota State University, 1982. 6 l.

8379. _____, Daniel L. Zink. *Rail line abandonment.* Fargo, ND: Upper Great Plains Transportation Institute, North Dakota State University, 1982. 7 l. (*UGPTI staff paper series; staff paper no. 26.*)

8380. _____., Denver D. Tolliver. *An analysis of rail rates for grain in North Dakota: an alternative to the Crow's Nest Pass rates?* Fargo, ND: Upper Great Plains Transportation Institute, North Dakota State University, 1984. 14 l. (*UGPTI staff paper series; staff paper no. 62.*)

8381. Minneapolis & St. Louis Railroad. *The Minneapolis & St. Louis Railroad Company: plan of reorganization dated as of May 1, 1939.* Minneapolis: Court Printing Company, 1939. 43, 1 p.

8382. _____. *The Minneapolis & St. Louis Railroad Company: second amended plan of reorganization dated June 27, 1940.* Minneapolis: Court Printing Company, 1940. 56, 1 p.

8383. *The Minneapolis & St. Louis Railroad Company: analysis of railroad and plan of reorganization.* New York: A. W. Benkert & Co., 1939. 8 p.

8384. Minneapolis-Honeywell Regulator Company. Railway Controls Division. *All aboard for comfort unlimited.* Minneapolis, s.n., 1948. 9 p.

8385. Minneapolis, St. Paul & Sault Ste. Marie Railway Company. *Instructions to ticket agents, conductors, station and train baggage men: in effect June 1, 1900.* Minneapolis, The Company, 1900. 59 p.

8386. _____. *List of stations and table of distances; between stations on the Minneapolis, St. Paul & Sault Ste. Marie Railway.* Minneapolis, A.R. Hayward, 1928. 111 p.

8387. _____. *Official blue book and atlas of Minneapolis, St. Paul & Sault Ste. Marie Ry. and Duluth, South Shore & Atlantic Railway, for use of shippers and buyers, 1899-1900.* S.l., s.n., 1898. 100 p.

8388. _____. *Rules of the Operating Department; effective May 1, 1912.* S.l., The Company, 1912. 241 p.

8389. _____. *Rules of the Operating Department; effective May 1, 1928.* S.l., The Company, 1928. 121 p.

8390. Minnesota. Department of Natural Resources. *Milwaukee Road corridor study.* St. Paul, MN: Minnesota Department of Natural Resources, 1979-1980. 12 v.

8390a. _____. Department of Transportation. *Freight rail development study* / St. Paul: Minnesota Department of Transportation, 2013. 28 p.

8390b. _____. _____. *Southeastern Minnesota freight rail capacity study : feasibility and alternative analysis study* / St. Paul: Minnesota Department of Transportation, 2013. 2 v.
8391. _____. State Planning Agency. *Reuse of abandoned railroad rights-of-way.* St. Paul, The Agency, 1978. 87 p.

8392. *The Milwaukee Road's first hundred years.* S.l., s.n., 1950. 28 p. (Reprint: *Railway Age, Milwaukee centennial issue.*)

8393. Minnigerode, Meade. *Certain rich men; Stephen Girard, John Jacob Astor, Jay Cooke, Daniel Drew, Cornelius Vanderbilt, Jay Gould, Jim Fisk.* Freeport, NY: Books for Libraries Press, 1970, 1927. (*Essay index reprint series.*)

8394. Minor, Benjamin S., Hugh B. Rowland. *Before the Interstate Commerce Commission, in the matter of private cars, docket no. 4906: brief on behalf of certain carriers.* Washington: Byron S. Adams, 1915. 65 p.

8395. _____, _____. *Before the Interstate Commerce Commission, in the matter of private cars, docket no. 4906: testimony on behalf of certain carriers, and exhibits thereto/* S.l., s.n., 1915. 134 p.

8396. Minter, Patricia Hagler. *The codification of Jim Crow: the origins of segregated railroad transit in the South, 1865-1910* / 1994. 253 l. (Thesis, Ph.D., University of Virginia.)

8397. Minter, Roy. *The White Pass: gateway to the Klondike.* Fairbanks, AK: University of Alaska Press, 1987. 394 p. (White Pass & Yukon Route)

8398. Mintz, Marianne. *Hazardous materials emergencies in railyards: preparedness guidance for railroads and adjacent communities* / Argonne, IL: Argonne National Laboratory, 1991. 15 p. (ANPL/CP-72161.)

8399. Minus, Jennifer Sue Voightschild. *Dressing for the railroad: the uniforms of railway workers from the Civil War to World War I.* 2003. 39 l. (Thesis, M.A. Rutgers University.)

8400. *Minutes of the 1996 North American tank car research coordination meeting, November 19, 1996, Washington, D.C.* / Hockessin, Del., RPI-AAR Railroad Tank Car Safety Research and Test Project, 1997. 1 v. (various pagings).

8401. Miranda-Naón, Alejandra, and others. *America's great road: the impact of the Baltimore & Ohio Railroad on the Baltimore region.* Baltimore, MD: B&O Railroad Museum Education Department, 1995. 75 p.

8402. Mironer, mark, Michael Coltman, Robert McCown. *Assessment of risks for high-speed rail grade crossing on the Empire Corridor: the next generation high-speed rail program/* Washington, DC: Federal Railroad Administration, 2000. iv, 38, A-1, R-1 p. (*DOT/FRA/RDV-00/05; DOT-VNTSC-FRA-00-03*)

8403. Mississippi. Agricultural and Industrial Board *The Illinois Central railroad in Mississippi.* Jackson? Mississippi Agricultural and Industrial Board? 1953. 24 p.

8404. Missouri. Bureau of Labor Statistics. *The official history of the great strike of 1886 of the Southwestern railway system.* Jefferson City, MO: Tribune Printing Co., State Printers and Binders, 1886. 117 p.(Missouri Pacific Railroad Company. Texas & Pacific Railway)

8405. Missouri-Kansas-Texas Railroad. *Condensed report of operations.* New York and St. Louis? Missouri-Kansas-Texas Railroad, 1923-…. Annual.

8406. _____.*Freight and passenger train handling instructions/* S.l., Missouri-Kansas-Texas Lines, 1936. 37 p. (*Form 298 [rev.]*)

8406a. ____. *Freight train handling instructions/* S.l., Missouri-Kansas-Texas Lines, 1933. 23 p.

8407. _____. *Hours of Service Act: information for guidance of officers and employes.*

Dallas, TX: Missouri-Kansas-Texas Lines, 1929. 17 p.

8408. _____. *Instructions on train handling with diesel electric locomotives for enginemen and trainmen.* S.l., Missouri-Kansas-Texas Lines, 194-? 41 p.

8409. _____. *The Katy Flyer: a brief history of a famous southwestern train.* Parsons, KS: Missouri-Kansas-Texas Lines, 1900s. 7 p.

8410. _____. *Katy standard plans.* Compiled by Leon Sapp. Colorado Springs, CO: Mac Pub., 1981. 128 p.

8411. _____. *Missouri, Kansas & Texas Railway Company reorganization, 1915.* S.l., s.n., 1915. 5 pts. in 10 v.

8411a. _____. *Official list of station and agents: with alphabetical list of stations.* 2nd ed. /
St. Louis, MO: Woodward & Tierman Printing Co., 1889. 33 p.

8412. _____. *The opening of the great Southwest, 1870-1945. A brief history of the origin and development of the Missouri, Kansas & Texas Railway, better known as the Katy Lines.* S.l., Missouri, Kansas and Texas Railway Company, 1945. 29 p.

8412a. _____. *Questions and answers on diesel electric locomotives for the purpose of examining firemen for promotion.* S.L., Missouri-Kansas-Texas Lines, 1900s. 36 p.

8413. _____. *Rules and instructions governing the operation of a railroad radio communication system.* S.l., Missouri-Kansas-Texas Lines, 1952. 4 p.

8414. _____. *Safety rules.* Dallas TX: Missouri-Kansas-Texas Lines, 1943. 44 p.

8415. Missouri, Kansas and Texas Railway. *Official industrial and freight shippers directory.* Chicago : Railroad Advertising Agency, 1900s- ?

8415a. _____. *Official list of stations and agents: with alphabetical list of stations.* 2d ed. St. Louis: Woodward & Tierman Printing Co., 1889. 33 p. (Includes junction points, location of track scales, cotton compresses, stock yards, stock pens, etc.)

8416. _____. *Official list of stations and agents with alphabetical list of stations.* St. Louis : Woodward & Tierman Printing Co., 1894. 47 p.

8417. _____. *Official list of stations and agents : with alphabetical list of stations /* 2d ed. St. Louis: Woodward & Tierman Printing Co., 1889. 33 p. Includes Junction points and railroad crossings, showing location and track connection, railroad crossings, location of track scales, location of cotton compresses, location of stock yards, stock pens, etc.

8418. _____. *To old Mexico via the MK and T, in through Pullman sleeping cars without change: new route, standard gauge all the way.* St. Louis? Missouri, Kansas

& Texas R'y, 1900-1910? 40 p.

8418a. _____. *"Trade follows the flag", travel follows good eating houses*. St. Louis: Buxton & Skinner, 1900s. 47 p.

8419. *Missouri Pacific annual.* Compiled by John Eagen. Danvers, MA: Protoype Modeler, 1975?- Annual.

8420. *Missouri Pacific lines magazine.* St. Louis: Missouri Pacific Railroad Co., 1926-1963. Bimonthly. 34 v. Monthly, 1926-1957. (< *Missouri Pacific system lines magazine;* > *MoPac magazine.*)

8421. Missouri Pacific Railroad Company. *A brief outline of the history of the Missouri Pacific Lines.* St. Louis, MO: Public Relations Department, Missouri Pacific Lines, 1961. 13 l. Typescript.

8422. _____. *A few facts about the reorganized Missouri Pacific Railroad Company.* St. Louis: The Company, 1956. 56 p. Report to the stockholders.

8423. _____. *Freight train classification book.* St. Louis : Missouri Pacific Railroad Company, 1925. 1 v. (various pagings)

8424. _____. *General specifications for steel railroad bridges.* St. Louis: Missouri Pacific Railway Co., St. Louis, Iron Mountain, and Southern Railway Company, 1911. 15 p.

8425. _____. *Handbook of ports served by the Missouri Pacific Railroad. Foreign shipping procedure.* St. Louis: Missouri Pacific Railroad Co., 1960. 56 p.

8426. _____. *History of the Pacific Railroad of Missouri, from its inception to its final completion.* St. Louis, Printed at the Democrat Office, 1865. 28 p.

8427. _____. *Mineral resources along the Missouri Pacific Railroad.* St. Louis: Missouri Pacific Railroad, 1928-1929. 4 v. (Industrial Development Department.)

8428. _____. *MoPac proposal for freight car scheduling system : technical/management proposal* / St. Louis : Mo-Pac, 1974. 1 v. (various pagings) Federal Railroad Administration.

8429. _____. *A new freight station for St. Louis.* S.l., Missouri Pacific Lines, 1952. 19 p.

8430. _____. *Official correspondence relative to the strike on the Missouri Pacific Railway, March 6th to May 4th, 1886.* St. Louis? s.n., 1886. (St. Louis: Nixon-Jones Printing) 82 p. Jay Gould. Terence Vincent Powderly. Knights of Labor.

8430a. _____. *Official industrial and shippers directory* / Chicago : Railroad Publicity Bureau, 1900s-?

8431. _____. *Official list of stations and agents, with alphabetical list of stations.* 9th ed. St. Louis : Missouri Pacific Railway Company, 1889. 60 p.

8432. _____. *Paul J. Neff yard: yard automation by the general Railway Signal Company for the Missouri Pacific Railroad.* St. Louis: Missouri Pacific Railroad Co., 1960. 44 p.

8433. _____. *Rules and rates of pay for boilermakers, helpers, and apprentices* / S.l., s.n., 1919. 14 p.

8434. _____. *Rules and regulations for enginemen and shopmen on operation and maintenance of air brake, air signal and steam heat apparatus, effective July 1, 1925.* St. Louis, Mo., Missouri Pacific Railroad Company, 1925. 128 p.

8435. _____ *Rules and regulations for the Maintenance of way and structures.* S.l., Missouri Pacific Railroad Company, 1941. 192, 16 p.

8436. _____. *Safety rules* / S.l., Missouri Pacific Railroad Company, 1930. 24 p.

8437. _____. *Service : a pageant of progress : 75 years of service, diamond jubilee, 1851-1926.* St. Louis, The Lines, 1926. 32 p.

8438. *Missouri Pacific system lines magazine.* St. Louis: Missouri Pacific Railroad, 1925. Monthly 2 v. (< *Missouri Pacific magazine; > Missouri Pacific lines magazine.*)

8439. *Missouri Pacific's computerized freight car scheduling system : advanced systems study* / Washington : Federal Railroad Administration, Office of Policy and Program Development, 1980. 131 p. (*FRA-OPPD-80-4.*)

8440. *Missouri Pacific's computerized freight car scheduling system : orientation module* / Washington, DC: Federal Railroad Administration, Office of Policy and Program Development, 1980. 130 p. (*FRA-OPPD-80-2.*)

8441. *Missouri Pacific's computerized freight car scheduling system: state of the art survey: a cooperative effort of private industry and government.* Washington, DC: Federal Railroad Administration, Office of Policy and Program Development, 1976. 278 p. (*FRA-OPPD-76-5.*)

8442. *Missouri Pacific's computerized freight car scheduling system : system functional requirements.* Washington, DC: Federal Railroad Administration, Office of Policy and Program Development, 1977. 175 p. in various pagings. (*FRA/OPPD-77-10.*)

8443. *Missouri Pacific's computerized freight car scheduling system : system performance measurement* / Washington, DC : Federal Railroad Administration, Office of Policy and Program Development, 1978. 40 p. (*FRA-OPPD-78-9.*)

8444. *Missouri Pacific's computerized freight car scheduling system: system performance measurement report/* Washington, DC: Federal Railroad Administration, 1981. 57 p. (*FRA/ORRP-81-3*)

8445. Mitchel, John Purroy, William Ambrose Prendergast. *Report upon organization of rail terminal facilities upon the west side of Manhattan and the elimination of surface operation by the New York Central Railroad Company upon the streets of the city.* New York : M.B. Brown Co., 1913. 47 p. Board of Estimate and Apportionment. Committee on Terminal Improvements.

8446. Mitchell, E.T. *Steam powered passenger trains of yesteryear.* Paoli, PA: The Author, 1972. 96 p.

8447. Mitchell, Patricia. *Dining cars and depots; train food in America.* Chatham, VA: P.B. Mitchell, 1992. 37 p.

8448. Mittal, Ram K. *Energy intensity of intercity passenger rail: final report.* Schenectady, NY: Union College, Transportation Program, 1977. 274 l.

8449. _____, Axel Rose. *Traffic data characteristics for New York City to Buffalo corridor.* Washington, D.C., Department of Transportation, Research and Special Programs Directorate, Transportation Programs Bureau, 1977. 49 p. (*Report no: DOT-RSPD-DPB-50-77-9.*)

8450. _____, Joseph Santamaria. *State of the art in passenger rail rolling stock equipment.* Washington, D.C., U.S. Department of Transportation, Research and Special Programs Administration, Office of University Research, 1977. 197 p. in various pagings. (*Report no.: DOT/RSPD/DPB/50-77/10.*)

8451. Mobarak, Christyn. *Buffalo as an architectural museum : the rehabilitation of the Buffalo State Hospital and the New York Central Terminal of Buffalo : a thesis in History /* 2005. 199 l. (Thesis, M.A., State University College at Buffalo, Department of History.) Also: Buffalo : Monroe Fordham Regional History Center, State University College at Buffalo, 2006. 131 p.)

8452. Mobile and Northwestern Railroad Company. *The Mobile and North-Western . Railroad project.* New York: S.W. Green, Printer, 1871. 48 p.

8453. Mobile Post Office Society. *A history of the railway mail service, together with a brief account of the origin and growth of the post office service, and a sketch showing the daily life of a railway mail clerk.* Omaha, NE: Mobile Post Office Society, 1977, 1903. 33 p. (Originally published: Wash., D.C., Columbian Correspondence College, 1903.)

8454. Modders, Nick. *Soo Line Railroad Company locomotive roster no. 1; effective 12:01 a.m. Central Standard Time, Wednesday, July 15, 1987.* Neenah, WI: Soo Line Historical and Technical Society, 1987. 30 p.

8455. _____. *Soo Line Railroad Company locomotive roster no. 2; effective 12:01 a.m.*

Central Standard Time, Sunday, April 10, 1990. Neenah, WI: Soo Line Historical and Technical Society, 1990. 33 p.

8456. *The Model Railroader cyclopedia.* Milwaukee, Kalmbach Publishing Co., 1936-1949. 6 v.

8457. Modelski, Andrew M. *Railroad maps of North America: the first hundred years.* Washington, D.C., Library of Congress, 1984. 186 p. (Reprint: New York, Bonanza Books, 1987, 1984. 186 p.)

8458. _____. *Railroad maps of the United States: a selective annotated bibliography of original 19ᵗʰ-century maps in the Geography and Map Division of the Library of Congress.* Washington, D.C., Library of Congress, 1975. 112 p.

8459. *Modern American railway practice: a complete system of practical instruction in railway transportation.* Editor-in-chief, Calvin F. Swingle. Chicago, Ill., National Institute of Practical Mechanics, 1908. 10 v.

8460. *Modern electric railway practice: a complete system of practical instruction in electric transportation.* Chicago, Ill., W.V. Wheat, 1909. 4 v. (Reissued: Chicago, Ill., National Institute of Practical Mechanics, 1915. 4 v.)

8461. *The modern freight-car truck.* Chicago: American Steel Foundries, 1940s. 12 p.

8462. *Modern railroads.* Des Plaines, IL: Cahners Pub. Co., 1982-1991. Monthly. (Absorbed by *Railway age,* July 1991.)

8463. *Modern railroads: short lines and regionals.* Chicago, IL: International Thomson Transport Press, 1988- Monthly.

8464. *The modern railway car as illustrated by the exhibition car built for Railway Age: by Pullman's Palace Car Company, from specimens of the best materials and appliances, furnished by leading manufacturers and dealers.* Chicago, Ill., Railway Age Company, 1883. 62 p.

8465. *Modern steam locomotives.* Milwaukee, Kalmbach Pub. Co., 1945. 2 p., 20 l. of plates. (*Trains album of photographs, no. 10.*)

8466. Modjeski, Ralph. *Northern Pacific Railway Company final report [to] Ralph Modjeski, consulting engineer / by [the] resident engineer [of the Bismarck Bridge].* Bismarck, ND: s.n., 1906. 1 v. (various pagings).

8467. _____. *The Vancouver-Portland bridges : a report to Mr. Howard Elliott, president of the Northern Pacific Railway Company, and to Mr. John F. Stevens, president of the Spokane, Portland & Seattle Railway Company.* Chicago: H.G. Sherman & Co., Printers, 1910. 30 p. 58 plates.

8467a. Moebs, J.J. *Computations for a single track through bridge span = 300 ft. /* 1898.

52 l. (Thesis, B.S., Massachusetts Institute of Technology, Department of Civil Engineering.)

8468. Moelker, William Jack. *The crazy passenger train.* Bloomington, IN: Author House, 2004. 164 p.

8469. Moffat, Bruce. *The Chicago tunnel story: exploring the railroad "forty feet below."* Chicago, IL: Central Electric Railfans' Association, 2002. 232 p. (*Bulletin. Central Electric Railfans' Assoc, no. 135.*)

8470. _____. *Forty feet below: the story of Chicago's freight tunnels.* Glendale, CA: Interurban Press, 1982. 84 p.

8471. _____. *The "L." The development of Chicago's rapid transit system, 1888-1932.* Chicago, IL: Central Electric Railfans' Association, 1995. 305 p. (*Bulletin. Central Electric Railfans' Assoc., no. 131.*)

8472. *Moguls, mountains, and memories: a gallery of New England railroading north and west of Boston.* Reading, MA: Boston & Maine Railroad Historical Society, 1979. 128 p.

8473. Mohler, Charles K. *Chicago railway development: city of Chicago steam railway maps showing development of railroads in Chicago.* Chicago, s.n., 1912. 1 atlas. (Maps printed by Rand McNally & Co. Compiled by the City Club of Chicago.)

8474. _____. *Report on passenger subway and elevated railroad development in Chicago: prepared for the Committee on Traffic and Transportation of the City Club of Chicago.* Chicago, City Club of Chicago, 1912. 44 p.

8475. Mohney, Kirk Franklin. *Along the rails: a survey of Maine's historic railroad buildings.* Portland, ME: Maine Preservations, 2000. 156 p.

8476. Mohowski, Robert E. *Lehigh & Hudson River Railway Company and Lehigh & New England Railroad Company; estimated results of joint management.* S.l., PRR Research Department, 1958. 1 v.

8477. _____. *The New York, Ontario & Western Railway and the dairy industry in central New York State: milk cans, mixed trains, and motor cars.* Laurys Station, PA: Garrigues House, Publishers, 1995. 356 p.

8478. _____. *New York, Ontario & Western in the diesel age.* Andover, NJ: Andover Junction Publications, 1994. 96 p.

8479. _____. *The New York, Susquehanna & Western Railroad.* Baltimore, MD: John Hopkins University Press, 2003. 205 p.

8479a. Mohr, Nicolaus. *Ein Streifug durch den Nordwestern Amerikas. Festfahrt zur Northern Pacific-Bahn im herbste, 1883.* Berlin : R. Oppenheim, 1884. 394 p.

8479a. Moller, Abraham G. *The iron horse, American railroads and the Queen City: an introduction of American railroads and their impact on Cincinnati*. Cincinnati: Abraham G. Moller, 2011. 173 p.

8480. Moller & Schumann. *Descriptive catalogue of fine coach and railway varnishes : wood filler, japans and liquid dryers* / Brooklyn, NY: Moller & Schumann, 1881. 1 folded sheet. 40 x 48 cm. folded to 14 x 8 cm.

8481. Möller, Kurt. *Something on the peculiarities of American and British railway English*/ S.l., Stockholms Universitet, Engelska Institutionen, 1968. 61 l.

8482. Molloy, Robert T. *Railroad tax workshop*/ New York: Practising Law Institute, 1981. 368 p. (*Tax law and estate planning series; tax law and practice course handbook series, no. 164*.)

8483. Molo, Nicholas John. *Frisco/Katy: color guide to freight equipment*. Scotch Plains, NJ: Morning Sun Books, 2003. 128 p.

8483a. Molony, Bill. *The Illinois Central Railroad and the Civil War*. Lockport, IL: Will County Historical Society, 2011. 16 p.

8484. Monarch Parlor-Sleeping Car Company. *Prospectus of the Monarch Parlor-Sleeping Car Co*. New York, Monarch Parlor-Sleeping Car Company, 1885. 12 p.

8485. Monette, Clarence J. *The Copper Range Railroad*. Lake Linden, MI: C.J. Monette, 1989. 120 p.

8486. _____. *The Mineral Range Railroad*. Lake Linden, MI: C.J. Monette, 1993. 128 p.

8487. *Monon outlook*. Chicago: Chicago, Indianapolis and Louisville Railway Co., 1939-? Quarterly.

8488. Monongahela Railway Company. *Corporate history of the Monogahela Railway Company, as of the date of valuation, June 30, 1916*. Philadelphia, s.n., 1916. 16 l. (Interstate Commerce Commission.)

8488a. _____. [Photograph collection, David E. Gratz] 1903-1993. 9470 items. Location: Archives Service Center, University of Pittsburgh.

8489. Monroe, Gregory. *Colorado's modern narrow gauge circle*. Arvada, CO: Fox Publications, 1994. 96 p.

8490. _____. *Moffat! Rio Grande-Southern Pacific-Union Pacific west of Denver, Colorado*. Arvada, CO: Fox Publications, 1997. 128 p.

8491. Monroe, Joseph Elmer. *Railroad men and wages*/ Washington, DC: Bureau of Railway Economics, Association of American Railroads, 1947. 155 p.

8492. Montague, Samuel S. *Reports of the president and chief engineer, upon recent surveys, progress of construction, and estimated revenue of the Central Pacific railroad of California. December 1865.* Sacramento? Central Pacific Railroad Company, 1886. 22 p. Signed: Sam S. Montague, chief engineer.

8493. Montana. Department of Agriculture. *Prospectus for providing continuing rail service on Milwaukee lines located between Miles City, MT and Marengo, WA.* Helena, MT: Department of Agriculture, 1980. 28 p.

8494. Montana. Supreme Court. *Decisions under the Hours of Service Act. Sate v. Northern Pacific Railway Co.* S.l., s.n., 1908? 7 p.

8495. Montange, Charles H. *Preserving abandoned railroad rights-of-way for public use: a legal manual.* Washington, DC: Rails-to-Trails Conservancy, 1989. 154, 39 p.

8496. Monteiro, Bren. *Heritage railways : historic railroads and museums of Colorado, Florida and Georgia.* s.l., Six Degrees Books, 2010. 91 p.

8496a. Montesi, Al., Richard Deposki. *St. Louis Union Station* / Chicago : Arcadia, 2002. 128 p.

8497. Montgomery, Raymond W. *Iron horses and iron men; the golden era of railroad passenger service and railway mail service.* Findlay, OH: Lowell Montgomery Pub., 1990. 3 v. (587 p.)

8498. *Monthly benefit statistics.* Chicago, IL: Railroad Retirement Board, Bureau of Research, 1900s-1996. Monthly. (>*Quarterly benefit statistics.*)

8498a. *Monthly bulletin.* Chicago : Passenger Department, Chicago and North Western Railway Co., 1912-   . Monthly.

8498b. *Monthly bulletin.* Chicago : Traffic Department, Chicago and North Western Railway Co., 1912-   . Monthly.

8499. *Monthly earnings record.* New York, William B. Dana Company, 1928-1949. Monthly. (<*Commercial and financial chronicle. Railway earnings section.*)

8500. *The monthly newsletter of your Society.* Milwaukee, WI: Railway Historical Society of Milwaukee, 1962. Bimonthly. 1 v. (< *Progress report.* Mid-Continent Railway Museum; > *Mid-Continent railway gazette.*)

8501. *Monthly review – Railroad Retirement Board.* Chicago, IL: Railroad Retirement Board, 1940-1968. Monthly. (> *RRB quarterly review.*)

8502. *Monthly statement of revenue freight cars in unserviceable condition, class I railroads.* Washington, DC: Association of American Railroad, Car Service Division,

Monthly. Aug. 15, 1927-Sept. 1934 issued by American Railway Association, Car Service Division. *Monthly statement of revenue freight cars awaiting repairs, class one roads.*

8503. *Monthly summary of railway revenues and expenses.* Washington, D.C., Bureau of Railway Economics, 1918-1920. 26 v. Monthly. (<*Revenues and expenses of steam roads in the United States*; >*Railway revenues and expenses.*)

8504. Montour Iron and Steel Company. *Rail sections.* Danville, PA: The Company, n.d. 45 l.

8505. Moody, Don. *America's worst train disaster: the 1910 Wellington tragedy.* Plano. TX: Abique, 1998. 184 p. (King County, Washington State)

8506. Moody, Eric N. *Flanigan: anatomy of a railroad ghost town.* Susanville, CA: Lahontan Images, 1985. 121 p. (Flanigan, Nevada)

8507. Moody, John. *How to analyze railroad reports/* New York: Analyses Pub. Co., 1912. 224 p. (5th ed.: 1919.)

8508. _____. *The Pennsylvania system.* New York: Potter, Choate & Prentice, 1908. 47 p.

8509. _____. *The railroad builders: a chronicle of the welding of the states.* New Haven, CT: Yale University Press, 1919. 257 p. (*The Chronicle of America series, v. 38.)* (Reprint: New York, United States Publishers Association, 1974.)

8510. _____. *The Union Pacific system.* New York, Potter, Choate & Prentice, 1908. 73 p.

8511. Moody, Linwood. *Edaville Railroad: the Cranberry Belt.* South Carver, MA: E.D. Atwood, 1947. 80 p.

8512. _____. *The Maine two-footers; the story of the two-foot gauge railroads of Maine.* Berkeley, CA: Howell-North, 1959. 203 p. (2d ed.: Forest Park, IL: Heimburger House, 1998. 240 p.)

8513. Moody, Thomas W. *Here comes Frisco: a story of the St. Louis-San Francisco Railway and its predecessor railroads to Pensacola.* Pensacola, FL: s.n., 1992. 27 p.

8514. _____. *Railroads of Santa Rosa County: from Arcadia to Amtrak.* Milton, FL: West Florida Railroad Museum, 2003. 68 p.

8515. _____. *Those railroadin' McLaughlins: Pensacola's forgotten visionaries.* Milton, FL: T.W. Moody, 2001. 22 p.

8516. *Moody's analyses of railroad investments, by John Moody.* New York, Analyses Pub. Co., 1909-1912. Annual. 3 v. (> *Moody's analyses of investments. Part I, steam railroads.)*

8517. *Moody's analyses of investments and security rating books. Part I, Railroad investments.* New York: Moody's Investors Service, 1921-1923. Annual 3 v. (< *Moody's analyses of investments and security rating books. Railroad securities; > Moody's analyses of investments and security rating books. Railroad securities.*)

8518. *Moody's analyses of investments and security rating books. Railroad securities.* New York, Moody's Investors Service, 1921-1925. Annual. 5 v.

8519. *Moody's analyses of investments. Part I: Railroad investments.* New York, Moody's Investors Service, 1920. Annual. 1 v.

8520. *Moody's analyses of investments. Part I: Steam railroads.* New York, Analyses Pub. Co., 1913-1919. Annual. 7 v.

8521. *Moody's manual of investments: American and foreign.* New York: Moody's Investors Service, 1909-1954. 188 v.

8522. *Moody's manual of investments, American and foreign. Railroad securities.* New York, NY: Moody's Investors Service, 1928-1951. Annual. 24 v. (<*Moody's manual of investments and security rating service. Railroad securities*; >*Moody's manual of investments, American and foreign. Transportation.*)

8523. *Moody's manual of investments, American and foreign. Transportation.* New York, NY: Moody's Investors Service, 1952-1953. Annual. 2 v. (<*Moody's manual of investments, American and Foreign. Railroad securities*; > *Moody's transportation manual.)*

8524. *Moody's analyses of investments and security rating books. Part I, Railroad investments.* New York: Moody's Investor Service, 1921-1923. Annual. 3 v. (< *Moody's analyses of investments. Part I, Railroad investments*; > *Moody's analyses of investments and security rating books. Railroad securities.*)

8525. *Moody's analyses of investments and security rating books. Railroad securities.* New York; Moody's Investors Service, 1924-1925. Annual. 2 v. *(< Moody's analyses of investments and security rating books. Part I, Railroad investments; > Moody's manual of investments and security rating service. Railroad securities.*)

8526. *Moody's manual of investments and security rating service. Railroad securities.* New York, Moody's Investors *Service*, 1926-1927. 2 v. Annual. (<*Moody's analyses of investments and security rating books. Railroad securities*; >*Moody's manual of investments. American and foreign. Railroad securities.*)

8527. *Moody's manual of railroads and corporation securities.* New York, Moody Pub. Co., 1900-1924. Annual. 43 v. (> *Poor's manual of railroads.*)

8528. *Moody's railroads.* New York, Moody's Investors Service, 1930-1952. 23 v.

Semiweekly.(>*Moody's transportation.)*

8529. *Moody's transportation.* New York, Moody's Investors Service, 1952-1964. 13 v. Semiweekly. (>*Moody's transportation news.*)

8530. *Moody's transportation manual.* New York, NY: Mergent FIS, 1954-2000. Annual 47 v. (<*Moody's manual of investments, American and foreign. Transportation*; >*Mergent transportation manual.*)

8531. *Moody's transportation news.* New York, Moody's Investors Service, 1964-1970. Semiweekly. (< *Moody's transportation*; > *Transportation news reports)*

8532. *Moody's transportation news reports.* New York, Moody's Investors Service, 1970-1999. Weekly. (>*Moody's transportation news reports.*)

8533. *Moody's transportation news reports.* New York, Financial Information Services, 1999-2001. Weekly. (>*Mergent transportation news reports.*)

8534. Moomaw, W. Hugh. *Virginia's Belt Line Railroad: the Norfolk & Portsmouth, 1898-1997.* Gloucester Point, VA: Hallmark Pub. Co., 1998. 202 p. (Norfolk and Portsmouth Belt Line Railroad Co.)

8535. Moon, Albert E., Paul S. Jones. *The merger between the Seaboard Air Line and Atlantic Coast Line railroads: a case study: final report.* Washington, DC: Federal Railroad Administration, 1979. 89 p. (*FRA-OPPD-79-5.)*

8536. Moon, Germaine L. Ramounachou. *Barstow depots and Harvey Houses.* Barstow, CA: Mojave River Valley Museum Association, 1980. 36 p.

8537. Moor, Brenda J. *Social and cultural themes in late nineteenth century central Great Plains railroad literature.* 2002. 110 l. (Thesis, M.A., University of Montana.)

8537a. Moore, Barbara. *The destruction of Penn Station.* New York; Distributed Art Publishers, 2000.

8538. Moore, Ernest Carroll. *Report on the removal of the New York Central Railroad tracks from the surface of Eleventh Avenue and the Improvement of the New York Central Railroad tracks between West 60th and Spuyten Duyvil; also, the relation of these improvements to the general question of freight handling to the west side.* New York: s.n., 1910. 24 p. New York (N.Y.). Committee to Consider the Formulation of Plans for the Elimination of Surface Freight Tracks on the West Side of the City.

8539. Moore, Hagan. *Fair by eleven: railroading in Oregon and other early adventures.* Klamath Falls, OR: Gardner Press, 1987. 87 p. (Railroad police; 1929 Depression)

8540. Moore, Herbert F., Nereus H. Ropy, Bernard B. Betty. *A study of stresses in car axles under service conditions* / Urbana, IL: University of Illinois, Engineering Experiment Station, 1932. 80 p. (*University of Illinois. Engineering Experiments Station.*

Bulletin no. 244.)

8541. _____, Stuart Wellington Lyon, Norville James Alleman. *A study of fatigue cracks in car axles* / Urbana, IL: University of Illinois, Engineering Experiment Station, 1927-1929. 2 v. (*University of Illinois. Engineering Experiment Station. Bulletin, no. 165, 197.*)

8542. Moore, Hilmar Guenther. *The railroads and Western railroad towns.* 1971. 43 l. (Thesis, M.A., University of Texas at Austin.)

8542a. Moore, Jeff. *Oregon & Northeastern Railroad* / Charleston, SC: Arcadia, 2013. 127 p.

8542b. Moore, Milton M. *Report on St. Louis-San Francisco Railway Company.* Washington, DC: Reconstruction Finance Corporation, Railroad Division, 1934. 1 v.

8543. Moore, James. *The first passenger train run in the state of Pennsylvania; drawn by the first locomotive built in the United States, the "Old Ironsides."* Philadelphia, Pa., Hoopes & Townsend, 1887. 10 p.

8544. Moore, John B. *Mechanical refrigerator cars and insulated refrigerator cars of the Santa Fe Railway, 1949-1988.* Midwest City, OK: Santa Fe Railway Historical & Modeling Society, 2007. 192 p. (*Santa Fe Railway rolling stock reference series, v. 6.*)

8545. Moore Patent Car Co. *Perishable products transported scientifically, economically w/supplement.* St. Paul. MN: s.n., 1912. 1 v.

8546. Moore, Paul Howard. *The Alaska Railroad; an American experiment in government ownership.* 1960. 119 l. (Thesis, M.B.A. in Transportation and Public Utilities, Graduate School of Arts and Sciences, University of Pennsylvania)

8547. Moore, Peter, Eric P. Nash, Lorraine B. Diehl. *The destruction of Penn Station: photographs by Peter Moore.* New York, D.A.P., 2000. 127 p.

8548. Moore, William Herbert. *The reorganization of railroad corporations, a study of public interest.* Washington, DC: American Council on Public Affairs, 1941. 173 p.

8549. *MoPac magazine.* St. Louis: Missouri Pacific Railroad Co., 1963-1965. Bimonthly. 2 v. (< *Missouri Pacific lines magazine;* > *Mo Pac news.)*

8550. *Mo-Pac news.* St. Louis: Missouri Pacific Railroad Co., 1970-1983.*Monthly.* (< *MoPac magazine;* > *Info-news.*)

8551. Moran, William T. *Santa Fe and the Chisolm Trail at Newton.* Newton, KS: Moran, 1970. 98 p.

8552. Morchower, Scott M. *A study of a high speed locomotive powered by multiple regenerated gas turbine engines and an energy storage system.* 1995. 69 l.

(Thesis, M.S.M.E., University of Washington.)

8553. Mordecai, Gratz. *A report on the terminal facilities for handling freight of the railroads entering the port of New York; especially those railroads having direct western connections.* New York, Railroad Gazette, 1885. 68 p.

8554. Mordecai, John B. *A brief history of the Richmond, Fredericksburg and Potomac Railroad.* Richmond, VA: Old Dominion Press, 1941. 86 p. (Reprint: Richmond, VA: Childress Print. Co., 1972. 86 p.)

8555. Morden Frog and Crossing Works. *Light rail catalogue : standard and narrow gauge track material.* Chicago Heights, IL: Morden Frog and Crossing Works, 1900s. 32 p.

8555a. _____. *Manufacturers of frogs, switches, switch stands, crossings, guard rails, guard rail clamps, compromise joints, tie bars, rail braces, etc. and all kinds of standard and special track work for steam, electric and industrial railroads : Bessemer or open hearth rail and manganese steel catalog H.* Chicago Heights, IL: Morden Frog and Crossing Works, 1918. 231 p.

8555b. _____. *Morden's patents and railway supplies in general* / Chicago : s.n., 1885. 2 v.

8556. *More rail classics.* Edited by William C. Jones and Charles Albi. Denver CO: Intermountain Chapter, National Railway Historical Society, 1976. 736 p.

8557. Morel, J.J. (Julian John). *Pullman, the Pullman Car Company ; its services, cars, and traditions.* Newton Abbott, Devon ; North Pomfret, VT : David & Charles, 1983. 224 p.

8558. Moreland, D.W.H. *Berry Brothers varnishes, finishes & enamels for railway & traction equipment.* Detroit, Berry Bros., 192-? 59 p.

8559. Morey, A.H., R.A. Williamson. *A 4500 H.P. gas turbine electric locomotive.* New York, American Society of Mechanical Engineers, 1949. 7 p.

8560. Morgan, Curtis Alan. *Abandoned rail corridors in Texas: a policy and infrastructure evaluation.* College Station, TX: Texas Transportation Institute, Texas A & M University System, 2011. 268 p.

8560a. _____. *Potential development of an intercity passenger transit system in Texas : final project report* / College Station, TX : Texas Transportation Institute, Texas A & M University System, 2010. 195 p. (*Technical report, no. 5930-2.*)

8561. Morgan, David Page. *The Burlington story.* Milwaukee, WI: Kalmbach Pub. Co., 1955. 1 v. (Originally published in 2 parts: *Trains,* Nov., Dec. 1955.)

8562. _____. *Confessions of a train-watcher: four decades of railroad writing, from the pages of Trains Magazine.* Edited by George H. Drury. Waukesha, WI: Kalmbach Pub., 1996. 160 p.

8563. _____. *Diesels west! The evolution of power on the Burlington.* Milwaukee, Kalmbach Pub. Co., 1963. 164 p.

8564. _____. *Fast mail, the first 75 years; a history of the Burlington's Railroad's mail service between Chicago and Council Bluffs, Omaha, 1884-1959.* Chicago, s.n., 1959. 38 p.

8565. _____. *I like trains, 1940-1954; great reading from the magazine of railroading.* Milwaukee, Kalmbach Pub. Co., 1980. 104 p. (Previously published in *Trains and Travel.*

8565a. _____. *In search of steam: the final quest for the last great locomotives. Volume III, 1955.* Waukesha, WI: Kalmbach Pub. Co., 2011. 98 p. (Special collector's edition)

8566. _____. *Locomotive 4501.* Milwaukee, Kalmbach Pub. Co., 1968. 127 p.

8567. _____. *The Mohawk that refused to abdicate, and other tales.* Milwaukee, Kalmbach Books, 1975. 304 p.

8568. _____. *Steam's finest hour.* Milwaukee, Kalmbach Pub. Co., 1959. 126 p. (Reprint: 1979.)

8569. _____. *True adventures of railroaders.* New York, Grosset, 1954. 209 p.

8570. Morgan, Edward James. *Sources of capital for railroads in the Old Northwest before the Civil War.* 1964. 481 l. (Thesis, Ph.D., University of Wisconsin.)

8571. Morgan, Gary. *The Georgetown Loop: Colorado's scenic wonder.* Rev. ed. Ft. Collins, CO: Centennial Publications, 1984. 40 p.

8572. _____. *Rails around the Loop: the story of the Georgetown Loop.* Ft. Collins, CO: Centennial Publications, 1976. 40 p.

8573. _____. *Sugar tramp; Colorado's Great Western Railway.* Ft. Collins, CO: Centennial Publications, 1975. 97 p.

8574. _____. *Three foot rails; a quick history of the Colorado Central Railroad.* Colorado Springs, CO: Little London Press, 1974. 38 p.

8575. Morgan, Ric. *The train of tomorrow.* Bloomington, University of Indiana Press, 2007. 1 v.

8576. Morgenbesser, Martin J. *The relationship between railroad work and operating plans.* Cambridge, MA: Center for Transportation Studies, Massachusetts Institute of Technology, 1978. 74 p. (*Studies in railroad operations and economics, v. 26.*)

8577. Morgenstern, Wes. *Working on the Western Maryland Railroad: a collection of employee interviews.* Union Bridge, MD: Western Maryland Railway Historical Society, 1999. 176 p.

8578. Morgret, Charles O. *Brosnan: the railroads' messiah/* New York, NY: Vantage Press, 1996. 2 v.

8579. Morley, Alfred Charels. *The consolidation of the Van Sweringen railroad interests.* 1950. 88 l. (Thesis, M.A., West Virginia University.)

8580. Morlok, Edward K., Stephanie P. Riddle. *Estimating the capacity of transportation systems: a model with applications to freight transportation: a report/* University Park, PA: Pennsylvania State University, Pennsylvania Transportation Institute, 1998. 31 p.

8581. Morrell, Daniel J. *United States Revenue Commission :the manufacture of railroad iron.* Philadelphia? American Iron and Steel Association, 1866. 20 p.

8582. Moore, Arthur Scudder, Clifton Allison Hall. *A power distribution study of the Boston, Revere Beach and Lynn Railroad /* 1910. 18 l. (Thesis, B.S. in Electrical Engineering, University of Maine.)

8583. Morris, Charles D. *The farmers and the railroads.* Chicago: Western Railways Committee on Public Relations, 1925. 16 p.

8584. Morris, Charles R. *The tycoons: how Andrew Carnegie, John D. Rockefeller, Jay Gould, and J.P. Morgan invented the American supereconomy.* New York, Times Books, 2005. 382 p.

8585. Morris, Cyril J. *Conversion by railroads to Diesel-electric motive power.* 1949. 153 l. (Thesis, M.C.E., Cornell University.)

8586. Morris, Ellwood, Benj H. Latrobe. *Report on the preliminary surveys made for the Cincinnati, Hillsborough and Parkersburg Railway; the Ohio link in the through line from Baltimore to St. Louis.* Cincinnati, Ohio, Cincinnati Gazette Company Printing, 1852. 48 p.

8587. Morris, Joe Dale. *Serving the golden empire: branch-line style: a look at Southern Pacific's Clovis (Friant) Branch.* Pasadena, CA: Southern Pacific Historical and Technical Society, 2002. 56 p.

8587a. _____. *Southern Pacific's Slim Princess in the sunset: 1940-1960 /* Pasadena: Southern Pacific Historical & Technical Society, 2008. 1 v.

8587b. _____, George C. Werner. *Southern Pacific across Texas and Louisiana, 1934-1961.* Upland, CA: Southern Pacific Historical & Technical Society, 2012. 496 p.

8587c. _____, Rod Crossley. *Southern Pacific golden empire, 1954-1958: the color photography of John B. Hungerford and Harold F. Stewart.* Upland, CA: Southern Pacific Historical and Technical Society, 2011. 296 p.

8587c. Morris, Ray. *Railroad administration.* New York: D. Appleton and Co., 1910. 309 p.

8587d. Morris, Timothy. *Trackside on the Union Pacific, 1960-1982 with Emery Gulash /* Scotch Plains, NJ: Morning Sun Books, 2012. 126 p.

8588. Morrison, Bruce F. *The influence of the railroad on the rural settlement landscape of Sumter County, South Carolina, 1848-1978.* 1980. 159 l. (Thesis, M.A., University of South Carolina.)

8589. Morrison, David D. *Long Island Rail Road steam locomotive pictorial: a collection of photographs.* Hicksville, NY: Cannon Ball Publications, 1987. 60 p.

8590. _____, Valerie Pakaluk. *Long Island Rail Road stations.* Chicago, Arcadia, 2003. 128 p.

8591. Morrison, James D. *The northern railroads and the development of the new Northwest.* 1931. 83 l. (Thesis, M.A., University of Oklahoma.)

8591a. Morrison, Robert G. *Recollections of Wheeling & Lake Erie at Norwalk, Ohio.* Cleveland, s.n., 1970. 36 p.

8592. Morrissette, James P., Richard C. Sherrard. *Soo Line steam power.* Minneapolis, MN: Locomotives, 1964. 3 l. 53 plates.

8593. Morse, Edward Sylvester. *The steam whistle a menace to public health.* Salem, Mass., Newcomb and Gauss, Printers, 1905. 14 p.

8594. Morse, Frank Philip. *Cavalcade of the rails.* New York, E.P. Dutton & Co., 1940. 370 p.

8595. Morse-Kahn, Deborah, Joe Trnka. *Clinton, Iowa: railroad town.* Des Moines, IA: Iowa Department of Transportation, 2003. 48 p.

8596. Morton, A.C. *Report on the St. Lawrence and Atlantic Railroad, its influence on the trade of the St. Lawrence, and statistics of the cost and traffic of the New York and Massachusetts Rail-Roads.* Portland, ME: C.W. Pennell & Co, Printers, 1849. 30 p.

8597. Morton, Joseph H. *Fast freight to DeCoursey.* Louisville, KY: Louisville and Nashville Railroad Historical Society, 1997. 103 p.

8598. Morton, Margaret. *The tunnel: the underground homeless of New York City/* New Haven, CT: Yale University Press, 2008. 148 p. (*The architecture of despair.)*

8599. Moseley, Edward A. *Arbitration as applied to railway corporations and their employees*. Washington, D.C.: W. F. Roberts, 1893. 26, 3 p.

8600. Moses, Carl Jonathan. *The Washington State Railroad Commission, 1905-1911: a history of a progressive reform* / 1984. 329, 1 l. (Thesis, Ph.D., University of Washington.)

8601. Moses, Leon N. *Union Pacific Corporation, Pacific Rail System, Inc., and Union Pacific Railroad Company – control - Missouri Pacific Corporation and Missouri Pacific Railroad Company [and] Union Pacific Corporation, Pacific Rail System, Inc., and Union Pacific Railroad Company – control – the Western Pacific Railroad Company : related applications ; verified statement of Leon N. Moses*. St. Paul, MN: Burlington Northern, Inc., 1981. 2 v. (various foliations)

8602. Mosher, James Elliott. *Railroad finance and the Baltimore and Ohio Railroad.* 1960. 172 l. (Thesis, M.B.A. in Finance and Banking, Graduate School of Arts and Sciences, University of Pennsylvania.)

8603. Moss, Eduardo. *Investigation of the finite element method for computing wheel/rail contact forces in steady curving* / 1987. 109 l. (Thesis, M.S., Virginia Polytechnic Institute and State University.)

8604. *Most economically feasible alternative methods to open burning in the dismantling of railroad cars* /New York ? Foster D. Snell, Inc; Booz Allen Applied Research Inc., 1969. 13 l. Presented by Foster D. Snell, Inc. … at the Special Solid Wastes Symposium, held January 29, 1969, in Albany, New York, [sponsored by the New York State Department of Health, Bureau of Solid Wastes Engineering].

8605. Motes, William Calvin. *Effects of changes in transportation costs on the location of the meat packing industry.* 1960. 174 l. (Thesis, Ph.D., Iowa State University.)

8607. *Motive power and car equipment-averages; railways of class I including class I switching and terminal companies.* Washington, D.C., Bureau of Railway Economics, 1947-

8608. *Motive power and car equipment of class I railroads in the United States.* Washington, D.C., Bureau of Transport Economics and Statistics, 1957-197-? Quarterly. (> *Operating revenues and operating expenses of class I railroads in the United States.*)

8609. *Motive power and car equipment of class I steam railways in the United States.* Washington, D.C., Bureau of Transport Economics and Statistics, 1936-1956. Monthly. 21 v. (> *Motive power and car equipment of class I railroads in the United States.*)

8610. *Motive power of the Union Pacific system: all types, 1869-1974.* Omaha, NE: Kratville Publications, 1975. 48 p.

8611. *Motive power review.* Denver, CO: Motive Power Services, 1977-   . (Union Pacific Railroad)

8611a. Mott, A.G., P.E. Dufour. *Report of service and operation, Southern Pacific vehicular ferry service*/ San Francisco: California Railroad Commission, Transportation Division, 1925. 47 p. (Oakland; San Francisco Bay.)

8612. Mott, Edward Harold. *Between the ocean and the lakes: the story of Erie.* New York, Collins, 1899. 511, 157 p.

8613. Moul, Edward W. *Stations along the Reading Company's Philadelphia to Williamsport, Pennsylvania, line.* Crete, NE: Railroad Station Historical Society, 1974. 10 p. (*Railroad station monograph, no. 5.*)

8614. Mould, David H. *Canals and railroads in the Hocking Valley Region of Ohio, 1825-1875.* 1989. 426 l. (Thesis, Ph.D., Ohio University.)

8615. _____. *Dividing lines: canals, railroads and urban rivalry in Ohio's Hocking Valley, 1825-1875.* Dayton, OH: Wright State University Press, 1994. 306 p.

8616. Moulton, Harold Glenn. *The American transportation problem.* Washington, DC: Brookings Institution, 1933. 915 p.

8617. _____. *Waterways versus railroads.* Boston, Houghton Mifflin Co., 1912. 468 p. (Thesis, Ph.D., University of Chicago.)

8618. Mount Vernon Car Manufacturing Company. *Freight cars of every description, pressed steel parts for cars, cast iron car wheels, casting, forgings.* Mount Vernon, Ill., Mount Vernon Car Manufacturing Company, 1921. 1 v.

8619. Mountfield, David. *The railway barons.* New York, Norton, 1979. 224 p.

8620. Moyar, Gerald J., S.K. Punwani. *Railroad journal roller bearing failure and detection* / New York : American Society of Mechanical Engineers, 1988. 126 p. (*RTD, vol. 1.*) RTD: Railroad Transportation Division, ASME.

8620a. Mrozek, David J. *Railroad depots of Michigan : 1910-1920.* Charleston, SC: Arcadia, 2008. 127 p.

8621. Muhlenberg, John D. *Resistance of a freight rain to forward motion.* Washington, DC: Federal Railroad Administration, Office of Research and Development, 1981. <3> v. (*FRA-ORD-78.I; FRA-ORD-78/04.II; FRA-ORD-78/04.III; FRA-ORD-78/04.IV.*)

8622. Muhlfeld, John Erhardt. *Discussion of Mr. W.E. Woodard's general specifications for a steam locomotive for light-weight, high-speed, passenger trains: general conditions.* New York, Muhlfeld, 1934. 53 p.

8623. _____. *The economics of railway motive power and train service.* New York, s.n., 1935. 28 p.

8624. _____. *Large steam and electric locomotives; a paper read before the New York*

Railroad Club. New York, American Locomotive Company, 1906. 28 p.

8625. _____. *Pulverized fuel for locomotives.* New York, American Society of Mechanical Engineers, 1916. 68 p.

8626. _____. *Relative advantages of modern steam and electric locomotives* / New York, Railway and Industrial Engineers, Inc., 1920. 65 p.

8627. _____. *Tractive power and hauling capacity of steam locomotives.* New York, Muhlfeld, 1924. 22 p.

8628. Muir, Allan H. *Cost effectiveness review of railroad electrification.* Washington, DC: Pan-Technology Consulting Corporation, 1973. 135 p. (*Federal Railroad Administration. Report no. FRA-RT-73-31*)

8629. Muir, Andrew Forest. *The Thirty-Second Parallel Pacific Railroad in Texas [to] 1872.* Austin, TX: 1949? 238 l. (Thesis, University of Texas))

8630. Mulhearn, Daniel J. *General Motor's F-units: the locomotives that revolutionized railroading.* New York, Quadrant Press, 1982. 80 p.

8631. Mulina, Tim. *Colorado & Southern narrow gauge Baggage mail 13: era 1880-present.* Blue Springs, MO: BHI Rail Systems, 2003. 94 p.

8632. _____. *Colorado & Southern narrow gauge Coach 76.* Blue Springs, MO: BHI Rail Systems, 2003. 94 p.

8633. _____. *Denver & Rio Grande Western 3000 series boxcars.* Blue Springs, MO: BHI Rail Systems, 2002. 42 p.

8634. Mullaly, Larry, Bruce Petty. *The Southern Pacific in Los Angeles, 1873-1996.* San Marino, CA: Golden West Books; Los Angeles Railroad Heritage Foundation, 2002. 280 p.

8635. Mullenix, Andrea, Carolee Williams, Matthias E. Kayhoe. *Union Station, Charlottesville, Virginia.* Charlottesville, VA: University of Virginia, School of Architecture, 1981. 1 v.

8636. Mullett, Alfred, Leonard Merritt. *Sumpter Valley Railway*/ Charleston, SC: Arcadia Pub., 2009. 127 p.

8636a. _____, Leonard Merritt. *Sumpter Valley logging railroads* / Charleston, SC: Arcadia, 2011. 127 p.

8637. Multer, Jordan, Robert Rudich, Kevin Yearwood. *Human factors guidelines for locomotive cabs.* Washington, D.C., U.S. Department of Transportation, Federal Railroad Administration, Office of Research and Development, 1998. 197 p. (*DOT-VNTSC-FRA-98-8.*)

8638. *Multiple unit operation.* Omaha, NE: Simmons-Boardman Pub., 1978. 46 p.

8639. Mulvey, Frank P. *Amtrak; an experiment in rail service.* Washington, D.C., National Transportation Policy Study Commission, 1978. 202 p.

8640. _____. *The economic future of Amtrak.* 1974. 474 l. (Thesis, Ph.D., Washington State University.)

8641. _____. *Predatory pricing in intercity passenger transportation markets: Amtrak vs. Greyhound.* Iowa City, IA: Institute of Urban and Regional Research, University of Iowa, 1981. 30 p. (*Working paper, University of Iowa, Institute of Urban and Regional Research, 35.*)

8642. Mumford, Brian D., F.J. Schneider. *The Glenfield & Western Railroad: a history of the "Old Gee Whiz" and its environs.* S.l., Frederick J. Schneider, 2003. 119 p. (Logging railroads—New York (State))

8643. Mumford, Theo L. *The Switzerland of America : historical sketch of the Switch Back Railroad, the discovery of anthracite coal, and an account of the rise and growth of the Lehigh Coal and Navigation Company* / New York : American Bank Note Co., 1886. 40 p.

8644. Munday, Jessie. *The railroads of Kentucky, 1861-1865.* 1925. 53 l. (Thesis, M.A., University of Louisville.)

8645. Mundy, Floyd W. *History of the Atchison, Topeka & Santa Fe Railway.* 1898. 69 l. (Thesis, A.B., Cornell University.)

8646. _____. *The value of a railroad security*/ Boston, MA: American Institute of Finance, 1922. 56,4 p.

8647. *Mundy's earning power of railroads.* New York, Jas. H. Oliphant & Company, 1920s-1946?. Annual. (< *Earning power of railroads [1902-].* > *Oliphant's earning power of railroads.*)

8648. Municipal Art Society of New York, Committee on West Side Readjustment. *Hearing before Board of Estimate and Apportionment on the report of it Terminal Committee as to Manhattan West Side (N.Y. Central) re-adjustment, May 27, 1913.* New York : s.n., 1913. 14 p.

8649. Munse, William Herman, James Edward Stallmeyer, Freeman Pierce Drew. *Structural fatigue and steel railroad bridges; proceedings of AREA seminar*/ Chicago, IL: American Railway Engineering Association; American Railway Engineering Association, Committee on Iron and Steel Structures, 1968. 152 p.

8649a. Munsell, Joel. *The origin, progress and vicissitudes of the Mohawk and Hudson Rail Road* / Albany: NY: J. Munsell, 1875. 20 p.

8650. Munski, Douglas Charles. *Modeling the historical geography of the Chicago & Eastern Illinois Railroad, 1849-1969.* 1978. 258 l. (Thesis, Ph.D., University of Illinois at Urbana-Champaign.)

8651. Munzert, Rodger. *Railway infrastructure management in the United States of America.* Darmstadt, Technische Universitat Darmstadt, Institute für Volks-wirtschaftslehre, 2000. 64 p.. (*Darmstadt discussion papers in economics, nr. 98.*)

8652. Murchison, Kenneth M. *Passenger terminals and stations.* New York, Murchison, 1921. 57 p.(New York, Redfield-Kendrick-Odell Co.)

8653. Murdaugh, Herbert C. *The Ripley Railroad : Mississippi's only narrow-gauge common carrier.* Jackson, TN: s.n., 1968. 28 l.

8654. Murdock, Dick. *Bill Knapke, a railroad legend: sketches from the life of an old-time boomer.* Ross, CA: May-Murdock Publications, 1996. 143 p.

8655. _____. *Early call for the perishables: a day at the throttle.* Ross, CA: May-Murdock Publications, 1983. 21 p. (Reprint: 1985.) Fiction.

8656. _____. *Hogheads & highballs: railroad lore and humor.* Ross, CA: May-Murdock Publications, 1979. 62 p.

8657. _____. *Love affair with steam.* Ross, CA: May-Murdock Publications, 1985. 33 p.

8658. _____. *Port Costa, 1879-1941: a saga of sails, sacks, and rails.* Port Costa, CA: Murdock-Endom Publications, 1977. 40 p.

8659. _____. *Smoke in the canyon: my steam days in Dunsmuir.* Ross, CA: May-Murdock Publishers, 1986. 140 p.

8660. _____. *Walnut Creek's unique old station, a short, colorful history.* Walnut Creek, CA: JD Graphics Enterprises, 1974. 23 p.

8661. Murdock, R. Ken. *Outline history of central Florida railroads.* 4th ed. Winter Garden, FL: Central Florida Chapter, National Railway Historical Society, 1997. 27 p.

8662. Mure, Julien. *Implication of high speed rail on the length of commuting trips/* 2005. 59 l. (Thesis, M.S., Northwestern University)

8663. Mureen, E.W. *A history of the Fulton County Narrow Gauge Railway, the Spoon River "Peavine."* Boston, Railway & Locomotive Historical Society; Baker Library, Harvard Business School, 1943. 77 p. (Its *Bulletin, no. 61A.*) (Reprint: S.l., Amaquonsippi Chapter, National Society of Daughters of the American Revolution, 1979. 76 p) 2d ed.: Chicago, IL: The Chicago Chapter, The Railway & Locomotive Historical Society, 1988. 120 p. (*R&LHS Bulletin, no. 61A-Revised.*)

8664. Murphy, Ared Maurice. *The Big Four railroad in Indiana.* Bloomington, Department of History, Indiana University, 1925. 1 v. (Cleveland, Cincinnati, Chicago, and St. Louis Railway Company.) (Originally appeared in: *Indiana magazine of history,* v. 21, nos 2-3.)

8665. Murphy, Janice K. *A history of local steam railroads of Los Angeles, 1870-1900.* 1936. 70 l. (Thesis, M.A., University of Southern California.)

8666. Murphy, Jim. *Across America on an emigrant train.* New York, Clarion Books, 1993. 150 p.

8666a. Murphy Maurice Elzin. *The railroads and the industrial development of southern Illinois* / 1916. 113 l. (Thesis, M.A., University of Illinois.)

8667. Murphy Varnish Company. *Descriptive price list of the Murphy railway varnishes* / Newark, NJ : Murphy & Co., 1875-1876. 5 items. Consists of 2 descriptive price lists and 3 circulars. "In Cleveland, Ohio firm is also known as 'Murphy, Sherwin & Co.' " Location:

8668. _____. *Murphy finishing system with ABC surfacers for wooden railway and street cars and Murphy finishing system with steel-car surfacers for steel railway and street cars* / Newark, NJ: Murphy Varnish Co., 1900. 23 p.

8668a. Murray, Don. *The identification of views on safety held by the employees of the Union Pacific Railroad.* 1992. 93 l. (Thesis, Southern Illinois at Carbondale.)

8669. Murray. Michael S., Robert J. Yanosey. *Trackside on the PRR north of Washington with Wayne Sherwin.* Scotch Plains, NJ: Morning Sun Books, 2001. 128 p. (*Trackside series, no. 20.*)

8670. Murray, Tom. *Chicago & North Western Railway*/ Minneapolis, MN: Voyageur press, 2008. 160 p.

8671. _____. *Illinois Central Railroad.* St. Paul, MN: MBI Pub. Co., 2006. 1 v.

8672. _____. *The Milwaukee Road.* St. Paul, MN: MBI Pub. Co., 2005. 160 p.

8673. Musa, Mohammad. *Representing a railroad signal block by a data structure.* 1993. 63 l. (Thesis, M.S., Memphis State University.)

8674. Muscalus, John Anthony. *Locomotive engravings on state bank notes and scrip, 1832-1875.* Bridgeport, PA: Historical Paper Money Research Institute, 1964. 40 p.

8675. Musolf, Lloyd D. *Uncle Sam's private profitseeking corporations: Comsat, Fannie Mae, Amtrak, and Conrail.* Lexington, MA: Lexington Books, 1983. 126 p.

8676. Mutschler, Chas V. *Wired for success: a history of the Butte, Anaconda & Pacific Railway, 1892-1895.* Pullman, WA: Washington State University Press, 2002. 135 p.

(Thesis, Ph.D., Washington State University, 1999. 293 l.)

8677. Myers, Clint, Randal O'Toole. *The Northwest's own locomotive: the history and restoration of the SP&S 700.* 2d ed. Portland, OR: Pacific Railroad Preservation Association, 1993. 23 p.

8678. Meyers, Gustavus. *History of the great American fortunes/* Chicago, IL: C.H. Kerr & Co., 1910. 3 v. Vol. 3: "Great fortunes from railroads". Reprint: Nabu Public Domain Reprints, 2012.

8679. Mutschler, Paul H., Robert J. Evans, Gary M. Larwood. *Comparative transportation costs of supplying low-sulfur fuels to Midwestern and eastern domestic energy markets.* Washington, DC: U. S. Bureau of Mines, 1973. 54 p. (*United States. Bureau of Mines information circular, 8614.*)

8680. Myers, Robert C. *Locomotives along the lakeshore : railroads of Berrien County, Michigan.* Berrien Springs, MI: Berrien County Historical Association, 2010. 174 p.

8680a. Myers, Stephen G., Michael J. Connor. *Buffalo railroads* / Charleston, SC: Arcadia, 2011. 127 p.

8681. Myrick, David F. *A brief survey of the histories of pioneer Arizona railroads.* Golden, CO: Colorado Railroad Museum, 1968? 29 p.

8682. _____. *Life and times of the Central Pacific Railroad.* San Francisco, CA: Printed by L. & A. Kennedy, 1969. 12 folders in case. Published for its members by the Book Club of California; Keepsake series.

8683. _____. *New Mexico's railroads; an historical survey.* Golden, CO: Colorado Railroad Museum, 1970. 197 p. (Revised ed.: Golden, CO: Colorado Railroad Museum, 1990. 276 p.)

8684. _____. *Railroads of Arizona.* Berkeley, CA: Howell-North Books, 1975-1984. 6 v. (v. 3: Glendale, CA : Trans-Anglo Books; v. 6: Wilton, CA : Signature Press.)

8685. _____. *Railroads of Nevada and eastern California.* Berkeley, CA: Howell-North Books, 1962-2007.. 3 v. (v.1—The northern roads; v. 2—The southern roads; v. 3— More on the northern roads.) (Reprint: Reno, University of Nevada Press, 1992. v. 1-2: 933 p.)

8686. _____. *Rails around the Bohemian Grove.* San Francisco, CA: Printed by L. and A. Kennedy, 1973. 39 p.

8687. _____. *Refinancing and rebuilding the Central Pacific, 1899-1910* (includes appendix and footnotes). Salt Lake City, University of Utah, 1969. 42, 20 l. (Golden Spike Symposium, May 6-7, 1969, University of Utah.)

8688. _____. *Santa Fe to Phoenix.* Berkeley, CA: Signature Press, 2001. 275 p.

(*Railroads of Arizona, v. 5.*)

8689. _____. *Southern Pacific water lines: marine, bay & river operations of the Southern Pacific system*. Pasadena, CA: Southern Pacific Historical & Technical Society, 2007. 132 p.

8690. _____. *Ventura County railroads: a centennial history*. Ventura, CA: Ventura County Historical Society, 1987. 2 v. (*Ventura County Historical Society quarterly, v. 33, no. 1-3.*)

8691. _____. *Western Pacific: the last transcontinental railroad*. Golden, CO: Colorado Railroad Museum, 2006. 232 p. (*Colorado rail annual, no. 27.*)

8692. _____, Charles F. Outland. *The determined Mrs. Rindge and her legendary railroad: a history of the Hueneme, Malibu and Port Los Angeles Railway*. Ventura, CA: Ventura County Historical Society, 1996. 53 p. (*Ventura County Historical Society quarterly, v. 41, no. 3.*)

N

8693. Nadenicek, Daniel, Eliza Pennypacker, David Goldberg, Priya Bhatia. *The cultural landscapes of the East Broad Top Railroad* / University Park, PA: Penn State, College of Arts & Architecture, Department of Landscape Architecture, 1995. 215 p.

8694. Naeder, G.I., G. Koeppert, H. Schulze. *Lubricating oil for axle friction bearings* / Ft. Belvoir Defense Technical Information Center, 1972. 8 p.

8695. Nagel, Karen A. *The wreck of the Penn Central*. 1987. 69 l. (Thesis, M.S.A., University of New Haven.)

8696. Nagle, J.C. *A field manual for railroad engineers*. 3d ed. New York, John Wiley & Sons, 1917. 499 p.

8697. *Named passenger trains*. Washington, D.C., Association of American Railroads, 1950. 24 p.

8698. *Named passenger trains*. Washington, DC: Association of American Railroads, 1952. 24 p.

8699. *Named passenger trains in the United States*. Washington, DC: Association of American Railroads, 1946. 8 p.

8700. *Named passenger trains operated on the railroads of the United States, Canada, and Mexico*. Washington, DC: Association of American Railroads, 1946. 1, 22 p. (*Railway information series, no. 4.*) Title varies.

8701. *Named passenger trains operated on the railroads of the United States, Canada, and Mexico*. Washington, DC: Association of American Railroads, 1948. 37 p. (*Railway information series, no. 4.*)

8702. *Names and nicknames of freight trains operated on the railroads of the United States*. Washington, DC; Association of American Railroads, 1946. 8 p. (*Railway information series, no. 12.*)

8703. *Names and nicknames of freight trains operated on the railroads of the United States and Canada*. Washington, DC: Association of American Railroads, 1949. 2, 19 p. (*Railway information series, no. 12.*)

8704. *Names and nicknames of freight trains operated on the railroads of the United States and Canada*. Washington, DC: Association of American Railroads, 1952. 2, 22 p.

8705. Napper, Paul S. *Effects of railroad accidents on railroad engineers* / 1998. 123 l. (Thesis, Massachusetts School of Professional Psychology.)

8706. *Narrow gauge land.* Edited by James S. Eakin. Canton, OH: Railhead Publications, 1982. 136 p.

8707. *Narrow gauge railroads: their history and progress; the Kennebec and Wiscasset Railroad: the first narrow gauge enterprise in Maine.* Augusta, ME: Sprague, Owen & Nash, printers, 1872. 35 p.

8708. *Narrow gauge transcontinental; through Gunnison country & Black Canon revisited.* Golden, CO: Colorado Railroad Museum, 1971. 63 p.

8709. Nash, Andrew. *Best practices in shared-use high-speed rail systems/* San Jose, CA: Mineta Transportation institute, College of Business, San José State University, 2003. 106 p. (*FHWA/CA/OR-2002/26*)

8710. Nash, Ray. *Boston and Maine rail, bus: railroad "minute man service."* Boston, Boston and Main Railroad, 1945. 43 p.

8711. Nashua Iron and Steel Company. *Great improvements in truck, tender and car wheels / James A. Woodbury's patented wheels.* Boston : Nashua Iron and Steel Company, 1877. 2 l.

8712. Nashville, Chattanooga, & St. Louis Railway. *Corporate history of the Nashville, Chattanooga 7 St. Louis Railway /* Nashville, TN: Nashville, Chattanooga, and St. Louis Railway, 1916. 1 v.

8713. _____. *Engine General: captured by Andrews' party and recaptured by Confederates, April 12, 1862 /* Nashville, James J. Ambrose, Printer, 1897. 30, 2 p.

8714. _____. [List of locomotives and rail cars received from the State of George by the Nashville, Chattanooga, and St. Louis Railway]. Nashville, TN?: Nashville, Chattanooga, and St. Louis Railway? 1890. 6 p.

8715. _____. *Rules governing the Operating Department, July, 1906.* Nashville, TN: Marshall & Bruce Co., 1906. 93 p.

8716. _____. *The seventy-fifth anniversary of the Nashville, Chattanooga & St. Louis Railway, 1848-1923.* Nashville? TN: The Railway, 1923. 32 p.

8717. _____. *The story of L. & N. motive power /* Rev. ed. S.l., s.n., 1956. Revision of reprint: L & N magazine, July 1949.

8718. _____. *The story of the "General", 1862.* Nashville, TN: Passenger Department of the Nashville, Chattanooga & St. Louis Railway, 1933. 27 p.

8719. _____. *Timber resources along the line of the N.C. and S. Ry. ...* Nashville, TN: Nashville, Chattanooga, and St. Louis Railway, 1901. 20 p. (*Pamphlet, no. 4.*)

8720. _____; Western & Atlantic Railroad. *The Capture of a locomotive : a brilliant exploit of the war.* Atlanta, GA: Franklin Print. & pub., 1895. 20 p.

8721. _____, ._____. *The story of the "General," 1862.* Rev. ed. Nashville, The Railroads, 1909. 24 p.

8722. Nathan, Adele Gutman, Margaret S. Ernst. *The iron horse.* New enl. ed. New York, Knopf, 1937. 44 p.

8723. Nathan Manufacturing Company. *Catalogue of injectors, injector attachments, lubricators, oilers, engine and boiler fittings.* New York, Nathan Manufacturing Company, 1907. 175 p.

8724. _____. *Illustrated and descriptive catalogue of Nathan Manufacturing Co.* New York, Nathan Manufacturing Company, 1892. 48 p., 9 l. of plates.

8725. National Association for the Advancement of Colored People. *NAACP 1940-55. General office file. Labor: Dining service employees.* Frederick, MD: University Publications of America, 1991. 1 microfilm reel. ("Regarding discriminatory rules, wages, hours protested for black dining car workers on New York Central Railroad." Group II, Box A-333.

8726. National Association of Car Service Managers (U.S.) *Proceedings of the annual convention of the National Association of Car Service Managers/* Scranton, PA: People Printing Co., 1893-1907. Annual. 15 v. (< National Association of Car Service Managers (U.S.). *Proceedings of the semi-annual meeting of the National Association of Car Service Managers*; > American Association of Demurrage Officers. *Proceedings of the ... annual convention of the American Association of Demurrage officers.*)

8727. _____. *Proceedings of the National Association of Car Service Managers.* Scranton, PA: Scranton Republican, Printing, Lithographing, Binding, 1890s-1891. Quarterly. (> National Association of Car Service Managers (U.S.). *Proceedings of the semi-annual meeting of the National Association of Car Service Managers.*)

8728. _____. *Proceedings of the semi-annual meeting of the National Association of Car Service Managers ...* Scranton, PA: People Printing Co., 1891-1892. Semiannual (< National Association of Car Service Managers (U.S.). *Proceedings of the National Association of Car Service managers*; > National Association of Car Service Managers (U.S.). *Proceedings of the annual convention of the National Association of Car Service Managers ...*)

8729. National Association of General Passenger and Ticket Agents. *Proceedings.* Cleveland, OH., Short & Forman, 1879-1888. Annual. (< *Proceedings of convention of the General Ticket and Passenger Agents' Association*; > American Association of General Passenger and Ticket Agents. *Proceedings.*)

8730. National Association of Owners of Railroad Securities. *Condensed report of conference between Committee of the National Association of Owners of Railroad*

*Securities and Committee of American Railway Association : relating to more efficient
and economical distribution, repair and standardization of classes of interchange freight
cars through pooling.* Baltimore, MD: National Association of Owners of Railroad
Securities, 1924. 105 p.

8731. _____. *Proposal for more serviceable and economical distribution
and conservation of freight cars.* Washington, DC : 1902. 1 v.

8732. National Association of Railroad and Utilities Commissioners. *Proceedings.*
Washington, DC: National Association of Railroad and Utilities Commissioners, 1946-
1966. Annual. 21 v. (< National Association of Railroad and Utilities Commissioners.
Convention. *Proceedings of ... annual convention;* > National Association of Regulatory
Utility Commissioners. Convention. *Proceedings.*)

8733. _____. *Proceedings of ... annual convention.* New York, NY: State Law
Reporting Company, 1922. Annual. 1 v. (< National Association of Railway and Utilities
Commissioners (U.S.). Convention. *Proceedings of the ... annual convention;* > National
Association of Railroad and Utilities Commissioners. Convention. *Proceedings of ...
annual convention.*)

8734. *Proceedings of ... annual convention/* New York, NY: Ronald Press, 1923-1945.
Annual. 23 v. (< National Association of Railway and Utilities Commissioners (U.S.).
Convention. *Proceedings of the ... annual convention;* > National Association
of Railroad and Utilities Commissioners. Convention. *Proceedings.*)

8735. National Association of Railroad Passengers. *The Southern Pacific and railroad
passenger service.* Chicago, IL: National Association of Railroad Passengers, 1967. 1 v.

8736. National Association of Railway and Utilities Commissioners (U.S.). *Proceedings
of ... annual convention.* New York, NY: Law Reporting Co., 1918-1921. Annual 4 v.
(< National Association of Railway Commissioners (U.S.) *Proceedings of ... annual
Convention;* > National Association of Railroad and Utilities Commissioners.
Convention. *Proceedings of the ... annual convention.*)

8737. National Association of Railway and Utilities Commissioners (U.S.) *Proceedings
of ... annual convention.* New York, NY: State Law Reporting Co., 1922. Annual 1 v.
(< National Association of Railway and Utilities Commissioners (U.S.). Convention.
Proceedings of the ... annual convention; > National Association of Railroad
and Utilities Commissioners. Convention. *Proceedings of ... annual convention.*)

8738. National Association of Railway Commissioners (U.S.). *Proceedings of the ...
annual convention.* Washington, DC: G.P.O., 1901-1917. Annual. 17 v. (< National
Convention of Railroad Commissioners. *Proceedings of the National Convention
of Railroad Commissioners.;* > National Association of Railway and Utilities
Commissioners (U.S.). Convention. *Proceedings of the ... annual convention/*)

8739. National Association of Regulatory Utility Commissioners. *Handbook
and program of the National Convention of Railroad Commissioners, Denver, Colo.,*

August 10, 1899., containing the program and proceedings of the eleventh annual convention, with reports of committees. A synopsis of the railroad laws and rules of practice of the Interstate Commerce Commission and all state railroad commissions, together with half-tone portraits of railroad commissioners and secretaries. Chicago, IL: J.F. Higgins, Printer, 1899. 208 p.

8740. _____. *Proceedings.* Washington, DC: National Association of Regulatory Utility Commissioners, 1967-1972. Annual. 6 v. (< National Association of Railroad and Utilities Commissioners. Convention. *Proceedings*; > National Association of Regulatory Commissioners. *Proceedings, regulatory symposium, annual convention*)

8741. _____. *Proceedings, regulatory symposium…annual convention.* Washington, DC: National Association of Regulatory Utility Commissioners, 1973. Annual. 1 v. (> National Association of Regulatory Utility Commissioners. Convention and Regulatory Symposium. *Proceedings.*)

8742. National Automobile Chamber of Commerce. *Trucks replace freight trains: Pennsylvania Railroad contracts its short-haul business to private carriers who use autos.* New York: National Automobile Chamber of Commerce, 1924. 4 p. (*Coordinated transportation series, no. 2*)

8743. *National car and locomotive builder: devoted to the interests of railway rolling stock.* New York, R.M. Van Arsdale, etc., 1886-1895. v. 17-26. Monthly. (<*National car builder; devoted to the interests of railway rolling stock.* 1870-1885; >*American engineer and railroad journal,* 1893-1911.)

8744. *National car builder.* New York, s.n., 1870-1885. v. 1-16. (>*National car and locomotive builder*)

8745. National Civic Federation. *Shall the government own and operate the railroads, the telegraph and telephone systems? Shall the municipalities own their utilities? The affirmative side.* New York, NY: The National Civic Federation, 1915. 108 p.

8745a. *National Conference on Prevention of Railroad-Highway Crossing Accidents.* S.l., National Association of Railroad and Utilities Commissioners, 1924. 140 p.

8746. National Commission of Productivity and Work Quality. *Keeping railroads on track: a condensation of improving railroad productivity, the final report of the Task Force on Railroad Productivity.* Washington, D.C., National Commission of Productivity and Work Quality, 1976. 30 p.

8747. *National conference on critical issues for the future of intercity passenger rail.* Washington, DC: Transportation Research Board, National Research Council, 1998. 78 p. (*Transportation research circular, no. 484.*)

8748. *National Cooperative Freight Research Program: a status report.* Washington, DC: National Research Council, Transportation Research Board, 2010. 4 p. (*Research results/digest / National Cooperative Freight Research program, 2*)

8748a. *National Cooperative Freight Research program: a status report.* Washington, D.C.: National Research Council, Transportation Research Board, 2011. 5 p. (Research results digest, 3.)

8749. National Electric Lamp Association. *Mazda train-lighting lamps.* Cleveland, Ohio, Engineering Department, National Electric Lamp Association, 1912. 14 p. (*Bulletin, Engineering Department of the National Electric Lamp Association, 10C superseding Bulletin 10B.)* "Showing the performance and characteristics of Mazda lamps designed for steam railway use."

8750. National Electric Light Association. *Serial report : electrification of steam railroad committee, 1928-1929.* New York; National Electric Light Association, 1929. 77 p.

8751. _____. Electrification of Steam Railroads Committee. *Electrification of steam railroads: continuing the statistical and economic studies of changes from steam to electric motive power* / New York: Charles Francis Press, 1930. 73 p. (*NELA publication no. 079.)*

8752. _____. _____. *Report of subcommittee for study of the electrification of western railroads.* S.I., National Electric Light Association, 1930. 113 l.

8753. _____. Railway Electrification Committee.. *Electrification of steam railroads; bringing up to date the extensive researches on changes from steam to electric power for the propulsion of trains.* Prepared by the Railway Electrification Committee. New York, National Electric Light Association, 1931. 74 p. (*Publication no. 165.)*

8754. _____. _____. *Electrification of steam railways: electrification in all countries with special reference to the United States and the extensive program of the Pennsylvania Railroad.* New York: Liquidating Committee of the National Electric Light Association, 1933. 80 p. (Its *Publication, no. 247.)*

8754a. *The National Elgin Watch Company illustrated almanac.* New York : National Elgin Watch Company, 1872. 8, 32, 8 p.

8755 .*National forecast of quarterly freight car requirements for ... principal commodities, based upon estimates and reports of trade conditions furnished by commodity committees of the shippers' advisory boards with regional jurisdiction covering the entire United States.* Washington, DC: American Railway Association, Car Service Division, 1928- . Quarterly. (< *Quarterly forecast of anticipated freight car requirements, of principal commodities, as reported by commodity committees, regional advisory boards, to the Car Service Division; > National forecast of the regional shippers advisory boards.)*

8756. *National forecast of the regional shippers advisory boards.* Washington, DC: Association of American Railroads, Car Service Division, 1927-1970. Other title: Quarterly forecast of anticipated freight car requirements; 1927. Volumes for 1927-1934 issued by the association under its earlier name: American Railway Association.

8757. National General Ticket Agents' Association. *Proceedings of Convention of National General Ticket Agents' Association.* S.l., The Association, 1856-1872. 17 v. (< Convention of General Ticket Agents'. *Proceedings of Convention of General Ticket Agents' Association*; General Ticket and Passenger Agents' Association. Convention. *Proceedings of Convention of the General Ticket and Passenger Agents' Association.*)

8758. National Hardwood Lumber Association. *Standard specifications for grades of hardwoods and cypress lumber for freight cars and locomotives, in accordance with Association of American Railroads, recommended practice rev. 1933 and conforming to American lumber standards.* Chicago: National Hardwood Lumber Association, 1935. 31 p.

8759. National Industrial Conference Board. *The consolidation of railroads in the United States.* New York, National Industrial Conference Board, 1923. 107 p. (*Research report, no. 56.*)

8760. _____. *Individual and collective bargaining in public utilities and on railroads, October, 1934.* New York, NT: National Industrial Conference Board, 1934. 16 p.

8761. _____. *The present railroad situation.* New York, NY: National Industrial Conference Board, 1923. 32 p.

8762. _____. *Railroad equipment.* New York, National Industrial Conference Board, 1952. 1 v.

8763. _____. *Railroad performance* / New York, National Industrial Conference Board, 1924. 60 p. (*Research report, no. 71.*)

8764. _____. *Railroad wages and working rules.* New York, NY: Century Company, 1922. 130 p. (*Research report, no. 46.*)

8765. _____. *Wages, hours and employment of railroad workers.* New York, National Industrial Conference Board, 1924. 80 p. (*Research report, no. 70.*)

8766. National Institute of Social Science. *Government versus private railroads.* New York, The Institute, 1919. 247 p.

8767. National Learning Corporation. *Motorman/* Plainview, NY: National Learning Corporation, 1972. 1 v. (various pagings)

8768. _____ *Signal maintainer: test Preparation study guide, questions & answers.* Syosset, NY: National Learning Corp., 2007. 1 v. (various pagings)

8769. National Malleable and Steel Castings Company. *National tight lock passenger coupler.* Cleveland, OH: National Malleable and Steel Castings Co., 1936. 17 p. (*Report no. 2763*)

8770. National Museum of American History. Smithsonian Institution. *Charles B. Chaney railroad photography collection.* Washington, D.C., National Museum of American History, Division of Transportation; Smithsonian Institution, 1989. 402 p.

8771. _____, _____. *Clayton H. Hall railroad photographic collection.* Washington, D.C., National Museum of American History, Division of Transportation, Smithsonian Institution, 1988. 20 p.

8772. _____, _____. *Harry A. McBride railroad photographic collection.* Washington, D.C., National Museum of American History, Division of Transportation, Smithsonian Institution, 1990. 99 p.

8773. _____, _____. *Photographs from the Division of Transportation railroad collection.* Washington, D.C., National Museum of American History, Division of Transportation, Smithsonian Institution, 1988. 32 p.

8774. _____, _____. *Photographs from the Division of Transportation's railroad collection: railroad cars.* Washington, D.C., National Museum of American History, Division of Transportation, Smithsonian Institution, 1988. 23 p.

8775. National Postal Transport Association. *Proceedings of the National Postal Transport Association.* Washington, D.C., National Postal Transport Association, 1900s-1960. Biennial.

8776. _____. *The railway postal clerk and the Railway Mail Association.* S.l., s.n., 1923. 8 p.

8777. *National rail freight infrastructure capacity and investment study.* Cambridge, MA: Cambridge Systematics, 2007. 69 p.

8778. National Rail Planning Conference (1975*). Proceedings of the 1975 National Rail Planning Conference, New Orleans, Louisiana, May 19-22, 1976.* Edited by JoAnne McGowan, Hoy A. Richards. Washington, DC: U.S. G.P.O., 1975. 92 p.

8779. *National Railroad Accident Investigation Symposium, July 30, 31, August 1, 1984, Washington, DC.* Washington, DC: U.S. National Transportation Safety Board, 1985. 269 p.

8780. *National railway bulletin.* Allentown, PA: National Railway Historical Society, 1976- 2004. Bimonthly. 29 v. (<*The Bulletin.* 1936-1975; >*NRHS bulletin,* 2005-) *Cumulative index, volumes 1-50, 1936-1985.* Compiled by Hugh R. Gibb. Philadelphia, PA: National Railway Historical Society, 1986. 91 p.

8781. National Railway Historical Society. *ALCO historic photos: a catalog of ALCO locomotive photo negatives from the period ca. 1880 to 1969 in the Library of the National Railway Historical Society, including a short history of ALCO and its predecessor companies.* 3d ed. Schenectady, NY: The Chapter, 1984. 107 p.

(Mohawk & Hudson Chapter. National Railway Historical Society.)

8782. _____. *Burlington Route: the "Q:" a commemorative pictorial of the final decades of the Chicago, Burlington & Quincy Railroad*. Rockford, IL: The Chapter, 1990. 24 p. (North Western Illinois Chapter. National Railway Historical Society.)

8783. _____. *Directory of rolling stock*. Rochester, NY: Rochester Chapter, National Railway Historical Society, 1986. 16 l. (Rochester & Genesee Valley Railroad Museum)

8784. _____. *Lackawanna route in central New York*. Marcellus, NY: Central New York Chapter, National Railway Historical Society, 1977. 32 p.

8785. _____. *A railfan's guide to Washington State*. Tacoma, WA: Tacoma Chapter, National Railway Historical Society, 1968. 1 v.

8786. _____. *The railroads that serve Buffalo*. Getzville, NY: Buffalo Chapter, National Railway Historical Society, 1982, 1927. 79 p. (Reprint: Originally published: Buffalo, N.Y., Manufacturers & Traders; People Trust Co., 1927.)

8787. _____. *Rails north: Lehigh Valley Railroad*. Marcellus, NY: Central New York Chapter, National Railway Historical Society, 1990, 1971. 50 p. (Partial reprint)

8788. National Research Council. *Compensating injured railroad workers under the Federal Employers' Liability Act/* Washington, DC: National Academy Press, 1994. 188 p. (*National Research Council, Transportation Research Board, special report, 241*.)

8789. _____. *Ensuring railroad tank car safety; a government and industry partnership*. Washington, D.C., National Academy Press, 2005, 1997. 152 p. Committee for the Study of the Railroad Tank Car Design Process. (*National Research Council, Transportation Research Board, special report, 243*.)

8790. _____. *Innovation in classification yard technology: proceedings of the Third Railroad Classification Yard Workshop*. Washington, D.C., Transportation Research Board, National Research Council, National Academy of Sciences, 1983. 67 p. (*Transportation research record, 927.*)

8791. _____. *Intercity passenger rail; freight rail; and track design and maintenance*. Washington, DC: National Academy Press, 2001. 96 p. "Papers…presented at the 80th Annual Meeting of the Transportation Research Board in January 2001."

8792. _____. *Local rail services program: perspectives of states and railroads*. Washington, DC: National Research Council; Transportation Research Board, 1979. 16, 1 p. (*Transportation research circular, no. 209.*)

8793. _____. *National conference on critical issues for the future of intercity passenger rail*. Washington, DC: Transportation Research Board, National Research Council, 1998. 78 p. (*Transportation research circular, no. 484.*)

8794. _____. *Performance of aggregates in railroads and other track performance issues.* Washington, D.C., Transportation Research Board, National Research Council, 1987. 106 p.

8795. _____. *Rail and motor carrier freight.* Washington, DC: Transportation Research Board, National Research Council, 1984. 47 p. (*Transportation research record, 966.*)

8796. _____. *Rail freight.* Washington, DC: Transportation Research Board, National Research Council, 1983. 49 p. (*Transportation research record, no. 917.*)

8797. _____. *Rail passenger service, electrification, and training.* Washington, DC: Transportation Research Board, National Research Council, 1985. 48 p. (*Transportation research record, 1023.*)

8798. _____. *Rail planning/* Washington, DC: National Academy of Sciences, 1977. 72 p. (*Transportation research record, 656.*)

8799. _____. *Rail, track and structures.* Washington, D.C., Transportation Research Board, National Research Council, 1986. 80 p. (*Transportation research record, 1071.*)

8800. _____. *Rail transport research needs: final report of the railroad research study conducted by the Transportation Research Board and sponsored by the Federal Railroad Administration, U.S. Department of Transportation, and the Association of American Railroads/* Washington, DC: National Research Council, Committee on the Railroad Research Study, 1977. 77 p. (*Special report. Transportation Research Board. National Research Council, 174.*

8801. _____. *Railroad freight transportation research needs: proceedings of a conference, Bethesda, Maryland, July 12-14, 1993.* Washington, DC: Transportation Research Board, Association of American Railroads, Federal Railroad Administration, 1994. 149 p . (*Conference proceedings, 2.*)

8802. _____. *Railroad issues.* Washington, DC: National Research Council, 1992. 82 p. (*Transportation research record, no. 1341.*)

8803. _____. *Railroad productivity.* Washington, DC: Transportation Research Board, National Research Council, 1985. (*Transportation research record, 1029.*)

8804. _____. *Railroad research topics: costs of high-speed rail, communications-based control and track research.* Washington, DC: National Academy Press, 1997. 45 p. (*Transportation research record, no. 1584.*)

8805. _____. *Railroad safety and environmental research.* Washington, DC: National Academy Press, 1996. 34 p. (*Transportation research record, no. 1531.*)

8806. _____. *Railroad track and electrification studies.* Washington, D.C., National Academy of Sciences, 1978. 72 p. (*Transportation research record, 694.*)

8807. _____. *Railroad track and facilities.* Washington, D.C., National Academy of Sciences, 1980. 66 p. (*Transportation research record, 744.*)

8808. _____. *Railroad track engineering and maintenance; passenger rail planning and operations.* Washington, D.C., National Academy Press, 2000. 55 p. (*Transportation research record, 1713.*)

8809. _____. *Railroad track structure, electrification, and operations management.* Washington, D.C., National Academy of Sciences, 1981. 85 p. (*Transportation research record, 802.*)

8810. _____. *Railroad transportation issues.* Washington, DC: Transportation Research Board, National Research Council, 1989. 52 p. (*Transportation research record, 1241.*)

8811. _____. *Railroads: high-speed passenger rail, railway bridges, and track design and maintenance.* Washington, DC: Transportation Research Board, 2004. 98 p. (*Transportation research record, no. 1863.*)

8812. _____. *Recent issues in rail research.* Washington, DC: National Academy Press, 1993. 59 p. (*Transportation research record, no. 1381.*)

8813. _____. *Research issues in intercity rail passenger systems and railroad track structure design.* Washington, D.C., National Academy Press, 1999. 56 p. (*Transportation research record, 1691.*)

8814. _____. *Review of rail transport research needs/* Washington, DC: National Academy of Sciences, 1980. 78 p. (*Special report. Transportation Research Board, National Research Council, 188.*)

8815. _____. *Safety factors related to high-speed rail passenger systems.* Washington, DC: Transportation Research Board, National Research Council, 1989. 26 p. (*Transportation research circular, no. 351.*)

8816. _____. *Science and technology in the railroad industry: a report to the Secretary of Commerce.* Washington, DC: National Academy of Science-National Research Council, 1963. 130 p.

8817. _____. *Surface transport regulation and railroad planning/* Washington, DC: Transportation Research Board, National Research Council, 1978. 58 p. (*Transportation research record, 687.*)

8818. _____. *Track design and construction.* Washington, D.C., Transportation Research Board, National Research Council, 1985. 60 p. (*Transportation research record, 1006.*)

8819. _____. *Track design and railroad electrification.* Washington, D.C., Transportation Research Board, National Research Council, National Academy of Sciences, 1983. 54 p. (*Transportation research record, 939.*)

8820. _____. *Track maintenance and classification yards.* Washington, D.C., Transportation Research Board, National Research Council, 1985. 48 p. (*Transportation research record, 1030.*)

8821. _____. *Track systems and other related railroad topics.* Washington, D.C., Commission of Sociotechnical Systems, National Research Council, National Academy of Sciences, 1977. 65 p. (*Transportation research record, 653.*)

8822. _____. *Traffic control devices, visibility, and railroad grade crossings.* Washington, DC: Transportation Research Board, National Research Council, 1995. 170 p. (*Transportation research record, no. 1495.*)

8823. _____. *Transportation characteristics of truck, rail, and water freight: 5 reports prepared for the 54th annual meeting of the Transportation Research Board.* Washington, DC: Transportation Research Board, National Research Council, 1976. 44 p. (*Transportation research record, 577.*)

8823a. National Watch Company. *Railroad time-keepers manufactured by the National Watch Co., of Elgin, Illinois* / Chicago, s.n., 1870. 8 p.

8824. *Nationalization of railways, 1939-1949 : a list of references* / Washington, DC: Association of American Railroads, Bureau of Railway Economics, Library, 1949. 30 l. Issued as a supplement to the Bureau's Bulletin no. 62.

8825. *Natural partners for progress: an analysis of the proposed North Western-Milwaukee Road consolidation.* Milwaukee? s.n. 1967. 31 p.

8826. Navarro, Lariza A. *Thermal analysis of railroad bearings : effect of wheel heating* / 2010. 102 l. (Thesis, M.S., Mechanical Engineering, University of Texas-Pan American.)

8827. Nayak, P. Ranganath. *Coal unit trains: operations, maintenance, and technology.* Palo Alto, CA: The Institute, 1984. 5 v. (*Electric Power Research Institute*: *EPRI: EA-3769*)

8828. _____, Donald B. Rosenfield, John H. Hagoplan. *Event probabilities and impact zones for hazardous materials accidents on railroads.* Cambridge, MA: Arthur D. Little, Inc., 1983. 296 p. (*DOT-TSC-FRA-83-5*)

8829. _____, Douglas W. Palmer. *Issues and dimensions of freight car size: a compendium.* Washington, DC: Federal Railroad Administration, Office of Research and Development, 1980. 299 p. (Various pagings) (*FRA/ORD-79/56*)

8830. _____, Peter D. Mattison. *Bullet train from Los Angeles to San Diego: forecast of Ridership and revenues*/ Cambridge, MA: Arthur D. Little, Inc., 1982. 1 v. (various foliations)

8831. Naylor, David. *Railroad stations; the building that linked the nation* / New York :

W.W. Norton, 2012. 336 p.

8833. Neal, Dorothy Jensen. *The cloud-climbing railroad: a story of timber, trestles, and trains.* Alamogordo, NM: Alamogordo Printing Company, 1966. 81 p. (Alamogordo and Sacramento Mountain Railroad)

8834. _____. *The cloud-climbing railroad: highest point on the Southern Pacific.* El Paso, TX: Texas Western Press, 1998. 135 p.

8835. Neal, Ray. *The American railroad: life after death (Memories and milestones).* Miami, FL: Minerva, 2000. 317 p.

8836. Neal, Robert Niller. *High green and the Bark Peelers; the story of Engineman Henry A. Beaulieu and his Boston and Maine Railroad.* New York, Duell, Sloan and Pearce, 1950. 275 p.

8837. Neale, D.H. *Recent locomotives* / New York, The Railroad Gazette, 1886. 112 p.

8838. Neary-Owens, Veronica. *An in-depth analysis of the impact of traumatic stress exposure on railroad employees.* 2001. 194, 32 l. (Thesis, Ph.D., Bryn Mawr College.)

8839. Needs, S.J. *Tests of oil-film journal bearings for railroad cars* / S.l., American Society of Mechanical Engineers, 1945. 12 p.

8840. Neighbors, Kyle. *The Lima shays on the Greenbrier, Cheat & Elk Railroad Company.* Parsons, WV: McClain Printing Company, 1969. 32 p.

8841. Neill, Charles Patrick. *Mediation and arbitration of railway labor disputes in the United States.* Washington, Bureau of Labor, 1912. 63 p. (*Bulletin, no. 98.*)

8842. Nelligan, Tom. *Bluebirds & Minutemen: Boston & Maine, 1974-1984.* Woodridge, IL: McMillan Publications, 1986. 151 p.

8843. _____. *Commuter trains to Grand Central Terminal.* New York, Quadrant Press, 1986. 64 p. (*Quadrant Press review, 10.*)

8844. _____. *New England shortlines, 1970-1980.* New York, Railroad Heritage Press, 1982. 48 p.

8845. _____. *The Valley Railroad story: the Connecticut Valley Line.* New York, Quadrant Press, 1983. 40 p.

8846. _____, Scott Hartley. *Route of the Minute Man: the Boston and Maine, 1969-1979.* New York, Quadrant Press, 1980. 64 p.

8847. _____, _____. *Trains of the Northeast Corridor.* New York, Quadrant Press, 1982. 96 p.

8848. Nellis, F. M. *Brakes in railroad and street car service*. New York: New York Railroad Club, 1901. 47 p.

8849. Nelson, Andrew S. *Green Bay & Western color pictorial: the Green Bay Route*. La Mirada, CA: Four Ways West Publications, 2003. 128 p.

8850. Nelson, Douglas M, Philip R. Hastings. *Philip R. Hastings: portrait of the Pennsylvania Railroad*. Foreword by Kevin P. Keefe; afterword by Jim Shaughnessy.; Los Angeles Pine Tree Press, 2002. 128 p. ("Photographs from the collection of the California State Railroad Museum.")

8851. Nelson, Edwin Fritijof. *A complete course in locomotive firing*. Minneapolis, Minn., s.n., 1915. 1 v.

8852. Nelson, James C. *Railroad transportation and public policy*. Washington, DC: Brooking Institution, 1959. 512 p.

8853. Nelson, James Poyntz. *The Chesapeake and Ohio Railway*. Richmond, Va., Lewis Printing Co., 1927. 193 p.

8854. _____. *Claudius Crozet; his story of the four tunnels in the Blue Ridge region of Virginia on the Chesapeake and Ohio Railway, constructed 1849-1858*. Richmond, Va., Mitchell & Hotchkiss, 1917. 13 p.

8855. Nelson, James R. *Railroad mergers and the economy of New England*. Boston, New England Economic Research Foundation, 1966. 236 p.

8856. Nelson, Larry D. *The feasibility of a fundamental innovation in intermodal transportation in the railroad industry*. 1982. 113 l. (Thesis, M.A., Massachusetts Institute of Technology, Alfred P. Sloan School of Management.)

8857. Nelson, Sarah Elizabeth. *Settling "the vexed question of social equality on railroad trains" : South Carolina's struggle over separate cars*. 1997. 27 l. (Thesis, M.A., University of Virginia.)

8858. Nelson, Randy, Walter R. Grande. *4449 album*. Portland, OR: Pacific Northwest Chapter, National Railway Historical Society, 1984. 24 p. (Southern Pacific)

8859. Nelson, Scott Reynolds. *Iron confederacies: Southern railways, Klan violence, and Reconstruction*. Chapel Hill, University of North Carolina Press, 1999. 257 p.

8860. _____. *Public fictions: the Southern Railway and the construction of the South, 1848-1885*. 1994. 232 l. (Thesis, Ph.D., University of North Carolina at Chapel Hill.)

8861. _____. *Steel drivin' man: John Henry, the untold story of an American legend*. New York, Oxford University Press, 2006. 214 p. (C&O)

8862. Nelson, Tom. *50 years of railroading in southern California, 1936-1986*

(Plus updates through 1996). San Marino, CA: Pacific Railroad Society, 2001. 204 p.

8863. *NEMA mining and industrial locomotive standards* / New York, National Electrical Manufacturers Association, 1938. 22 p. (*Publication, no. 38-48.)*

8864. Nemeth, Tom, Homer Hill. *The Gladstone Branch: affectionately known as the P & D (Passaic & Delaware.)* Bernardsville, NJ: Hill Press, 1978. 12 p. (Passaic and Delaware Extension Railroad)

8865. Neubauer, Eric A. *ACF Center Flow: CF 4600.* Monrovia, CA: Society of Freight Car Historians, 1994. 30 p.

8866. _____. *ACF Center Flow: CF 5701.* Monrovia, CA: Society of Freight Car Historians, 1995. 48 p.

8867. _____. *Carbon black cars.* S.l., Society of Freight Car Historians, 1990. 87 p. (*Freight cars journal monograph, 15.)*

8868. _____. *FMC boxcars since 1972.* S.l., Modern Transport Technical & Historical Society, 1985. 34 p.

8869. _____. *A history of the ACF Center Flow.* Monrovia, CA: Society of Freight Car Historians, 1987. 229 p.

8870. _____. *A history of the General American Airslide and other covered hopper cars.* Monrovia, CA: Society of Freight Car Historians, 1989. 91 p.

8871. _____. *The Lehigh and New England Railroad freight car diagram book.* Monrovia, CA: Society of Freight Car Historians, 1993. 56 p. (*Freight cars journal. Monograph, no. 18.)*

8872. _____. *Northampton and Bath freight cars.* Monrovia, CA: Society of Freight Car Historians, 1994. 26 p.

8873. _____. *Philadelphia & Reading freight cars: the 19th century.* Monrovia, CA: Society of Freight Car Historians, 1994. 94 p.

8874. _____, David G. Casdorph. *Southern modern freight car roster.* Monrovia, CA: Society of Freight Car Historians, 1989. 88 p.

8875. Nevada-California-Oregon Railway Company. [Tentative valuation of the property of the Nevada-California-Oregon Railway as of June 30, 1917]. Washington, DC: Interstate Commerce Commission, 1926. 55 l.

8876. Nevada County Narrow-Gauge Railroad Company. *By-laws, franchise, and list of officers.* Grass Valley, CA: C.H. Mitchell, Printer, 1874. 24 p.

8877. Nevada. Department of Highways. Planning Survey Division; Public Service

Commission. *Nevada state rail plan: executive summary.* Carson City, NV: Nevada Dept. of Highways, Planning Survey Division, 1978. 1 v.

8878. _____. _____. *Appendices 1982 update, Nevada state rail plan.* Carson City, NV: Nevada Department of Transportation, 1982. 70 l.

8879. _____. _____. *Final report, 1982 update, Nevada state rail plan.* Carson City, NV: Nevada Dept. of Transportation, 1980. 208 p.

8880. _____. _____. *1987 Nevada rail plan update.* Carson City, NV: Nevada Dept. of Transportation, 1987. 384 p.

8881. _____. _____. *1992 Nevada rail plan.* Carson City, NV: Nevada Dept. of Transportation, 1992. 198 p.

8882. _____. _____ *State of Nevada rail plan update.* Carson City, NV: Nevada Dept. of Transportation, 1980. 128 p.

8883. Nevada Northern Railway Company. [Tentative valuation of the property of Nevada Northern Railway Company as of June 30, 1917]. Washington, DC: Interstate Commerce Commission, 1923. 13 l.

8884. Nevada. Railroad Commission. *Annual reports, 1909-1918.* Carson City, NV: NSLA Preservation Microfilming and Research Resource Project, 1991. 1 microfilm reel 18 mm.

8885. Nevada State Museum. *Restoration feasibility investigation on nine selected passenger and freight cars, Virginia & Truckee Collection, Nevada State Museum /* Arcadia, CA: Short Line Enterprises, 1981. 306 p.

8886. Nevada State Railroad Museum. *Nevada State Railroad Museum equipment guidebook.* Carson City, Nev., Friends of the Nevada State Railroad Museum, 1999. 54 p.

8887. Nevel, Bonnie. *Closing the gaps: the potential for using abandoned railroad corridors to help complete the North Country National Scenic Trail.* Washington, D.C., Rails-to-Trails Conservancy, 1990. 54 p. (In cooperation with Midwest Region and Recreation Resources Assistance Division, National Park Service, United States Department of the Interior.)

8889. _____, Peter Harnik. *Railroads recycled: how local initiative and federal support launched the Rails-to-Trails movement 1965-1990.* Washington, D.C., Rails-to-Trails Conservancy, 1990. 100 p.

8890. Nevins, Deborah. *Grand Central Terminal: city within the city.* New York, Municipal Art Society of New York, 1982. 145 p.

8890a. *New applications of aluminum in the electric railway field.* Pittsburgh: Aluminum Company of America,1929. 29 p.

8891. *New Cascade tunnel number* / Seattle, Wash., Railway and Marine News, 1929. 66 p. (Offprint from *The Railway and marine news,* v. 26, no. 1, January 1929

8892. New England Association of Railway Superintendents. *Report of the trial of locomotive engines, made upon 1ˢᵗ and 2d October, 1851.* Boston, Mass., J.B. Yerrinton & Son, Printers, 1852. 19 p.

8893. New England Roadmasters' Association. *Proceedings of the ... annual convention of the New England Roadmasters' Association.* Ware, MA: New England Roadmasters' Association, 1882-1898. Annual. 16 v. (>*Eastern Maintenance of Way Association. Proceedings.*)

8894. *The new Flying Yankee.* Philadelphia, : Edward G. Budd Manufacturing Co., 1935. 12 p. Reprint: Railway Age, Feb. 1934.

8895. New Hampshire. Bureau of Railroads and Public Transportation. *New Hampshire state rail plan, 1991.* Concord, NH: New Hampshire Department of Transportation, Bureau of Railroads and Public Transportation, 1991. 1 v.

8896. _____. New Hampshire Department of Transportation. Bureau of Rail and Transit. *New Hampshire state rail plan, 2001.* Concord, NH: New Hampshire Department of Transportation, Bureau of Rail and Transit, 2001. 1 v.

8897. _____. Public Utilities Commission. *New Hampshire state rail plan: phase I-II.* Concord, The Commission, 1975. 2 v

8898. *The New Haven Railroad electric locomotive parade, 1888-1938.* New Haven? New Haven Railroad, 1938. 12 p.

8899. New Haven Railroad Historical and Technical Association. *Diesel locomotive, rail diesel car and gas electric car diagram book.* 2d ed. Montgomery, Ala., The New Haven Railroad Historical and Technical Association, 1978. 24 p.

8900. *New ideas for high-speed rail systems: an annual progress report of the High-Speed Rail IDEA Program.* Washington, DC: Transportation Research Board, National Research Council, 1990s-   . Annual. http://www4.trb.org/trb/dive.nsf/web/high-speed%5Frail%5idea

8901. New Jersey. Department of Transportation. Bureau of Project Location and Design Concepts. *Abandoned railroad rights-of-way in New Jersey: inventory and evaluation of potential usage for bicycle transportation.* Trenton, NJ: New Jersey Department of Transportation, Division of Project Development, Bureau of Project Location & Design Concepts, 1980. 104 p.

8902. *New Jersey & New York railroad service between New York City and Haverstraw.* Vineland, NJ: Railroadians of America, 1974. 1 v.

8903. New Jersey. Governor (1947-1954 : Driscoll). Port of New York Authority. Port Development Department. *Survey of the New Jersey waterfront of the port of New York : progress report to Governor Alfred E. Driscoll* / New York: Port of New York Authority, 1948. 1 v. (various foliations) ill., maps, plans

8904. New Mexico. Economic Development Commission. *Freight rate equalization and the economic development of New Mexico.* Santa Fe: New Mexico Economic Development Commission, 1951. 23 p.

8905. _____. State Planning Division. *New Mexico state railroad plan update 1980.* Santa Fe: The Division, 1980. 54 l.

8906. *New 1953 installations of diesel-electric locomotives.* New York, Railway Age, 1954. 7 p.

8907. *A new standard for railroad welding : conference proceedings : September 25-26, 1986, Chicago.* Miami: American Welding Society, 1986. 143 l.

8908. New York Air Brake Company. *Air brake instructions for electric locomotives.* New York, The New York Air Brake Company, 1929. 1 v.

8909. _____. *Automatic connector: Forsyth patent.* New York, The Company, 1900. 11 p.

8910. _____. *Catalog and price list.* Watertown, N.Y., Hungerford-Holbrook Company, 1910. 416 p.

8911. _____. *The New York Air Brake Company.* New York, The Company, 1940. 33 p. (Fiftieth anniversary)

8912. _____. The New York Air Brake Co. *Catalog.* 2d ed. New York, The Company, 1900. 102 p.

8913. *New York air brake, apparatus and its operation.* Scranton, Pa., International Textbook Co., 1926. 1 v.

8914. The *New York air brake system; a complete and strictly up-to-date treatise, containing, detailed descriptions and explanations of the various parts of the New York air brake* / Chicago, F.J. Drake & Company, 1911. 374 p.

8915. New York and Boston Railroad Company. *New York and Boston Railroad.* S.l., s.n., 1852. 14 p.

8916. _____. *Report upon the New York and Boston or Air Line Railroad and its connections.* Boston, J.S. Potter & Company, Printers, 1855. 22 p.

8917. New York and Erie Railroad Company. *Instructions for the running of trains, etc., on the New York and Erie Railroad : to go into effect on Monday, March 6, 1854.* New

York: Printed at the company's printing office, 1854. 47 p.

8918. _____. *Instructions for the running of trains, etc., on the New York and Erie Railroad, to go into effect on Saturday, August 1, 1857.* New York, Press of the New York and Erie Railroad Company, 1857. 107 p.

8918a. _____. *Instructions for the running of trains, etc.: to go into effect on Monday, march 31, 1851.* New York : Printed at the Office of Parker's Journal, 1851. 34 p.

8919. _____. *New-York and Erie Railroad Company: organization and general regulations, for working and conducting the business of the railroad & its branches, adopted by the Board of Directors, February 21, 1852.* New York: New-York and Erie Railroad printing office, 1852. 11 p.

8920. _____. *Ross Winans, against the New York and Erie Railroad Co : general statement of facts.* New York: Wm. C. Bryant, 1856. 33 p.

8921. New York and Long Branch Railroad Company. *Rules and instructions governing the use of automatic block and interlocking signals, New York and Long Branch Railroad* / Compiled by Rufus Blodgett. New York, M.B. Brown Press, 1906. 58 p. (Reprint: S.l., Railroadians of America, 1975. 58 p.)

8921a. New York and New England Railroad. *Rules and regulations ... regulating the running of trains and the use of signals* / Boston : Collins Press and Bindery, 1892. 146 p.

8921b. _____. [Rules for the movement of trains by telegraph.] Boston? s.n., 1883. 35 p.

8922. *New York and Washington Blue Line. Central Railroad of New Jersey; Philadelphia & Reading Railroad Co.; Baltimore and Ohio Railroad Co.* New York : Press of American Bank Note Co., 1892. 38 p.

8923. New York Car Wheel Works, Buffalo. *Car wheels and axles. "NYCO" special wheels.* Buffalo : New York Car Wheel Works, 1890. 24 p.

8924. New York Central and Hudson River Railroad Company. *Block signals on "America's Greatest Railroad."* New York, Passenger Department, NYC&HRRR, 1895. 61 p. (*Four track series, no. 17.*)

8925. _____. *Care of air brakes: instructions on the care of air-brakes for all classes of railroad men: as adopted by the American Railway Master Mechanics' and the Master Car Builders' Association.* East Orange, N.J., Engineering Literature Company, 1892. 39 p.

8926. _____. *Care of air-brakes; instructions on the care of air-brakes for all classes of railroad men, as adopted by the American Railway Master Mechanics' and the Master Car Builders' Association.* New York, NY: Locomotive Engineering, 1898. 39 p.

8927. _____. *Dimensions and classification of locomotives of the New York Central & Hudson River, Boston & Albany, Rutland, and New York & Ottawa Railroads.* New York? s.n., 1905. 349 p.

8928. _____. *Dimensions and classification of locomotives of the New York Central & Hudson River, Boston & Albany, Rutland and New York & Ottawa Railroads.* S.l., s.n., 1909. 369 p.

8929. _____. *Emergency directory.* S.l., s.n., 1907. 48 p. (Electrical Department)

8930. _____. *436 ½ miles in 425 ¾ minutes: all the fast runs of the world eclipsed.* Buffalo, N.Y., Matthews-Northrup Company, 1892. 26 p. (*Four track series, no. 14.*)

8931. _____. *General specifications.* New York : New York Central and Hudson River Railroad Co., 1902. 1 v. (unpaged)

8932. _____. *Grand Central Terminal Agreement dated July 24, 1907 [between] the New York Central and Hudson River Railroad Company, the New York, New Haven and Hartford Railroad Company, and New York and Harlem Railroad Company.* New York? 1907. 1 v. (various pagings)

8933. _____. *Illustrated catalogue of the "Four Track Series."* Rev. ed. New York : Passenger Department, NYC & HRRR, 1896. 30 p. (*Four Track series, no. 16.*)

8934. _____. *Improving crop yields by the use of dynamite.* S.l. New York Central and Hudson River Railroad Company, 1911. 107 p.

8935. _____. *The luxury of modern railway travel.* New York, NYC&HRRR, 1893. 32 p. (*Four track series, no. 1.*)

8936. _____. *N.Y.C. & H.R.R.R. and leased lines. Specifications. Grand Central Yard improvement, New York City.* New York' s.n., 1906. 44 p.

8937. _____. *The New York Central and Hudson River Railway classified business directory : between New York and Albany, for the years 1884-'85 with an appendix.* Newburgh, NY: L.H. Crum & Co., 1884. 177 p. Includes advertising. Includes index.

8938. _____. *An object lesson in transportation, from the World's Fair Chicago. Consisting of a part of the exhibits of the Wagner Palace Car Company, London & Northwestern Railways of England.* New York : American Bank Note Company, 1893. 12 p. (*Four Track series, no. 13.*)

8939. _____. *Organization of the Operating Department, effective March 1, 1908.* New York : Geo. F. Nesbitt & Col., 1908. 39 p.

8940. _____. *Pan-American Express: the new train between New York and Buffalo and Niagara Falls.* Buffalo, Matthews-Northrup, 1901. 32 p. (*Four-track series, no. 15.*)

8941. _____. [Progress photographs, New York District [1904-1905] New York, s.n., 1905. 5 l. 186 photographs. 20 x 35 cm. Location: Brown University.

8942. _____. [Proposal, contract, and specifications for electrical rolling stock] New York : The Company, 1903-1906. 220 p.

8943. _____. *The railroad and the dictionary.* New York, The R.R., 1893. 14 p. (*Four track series, no. 2.*)

8944. _____. *Rates of pay : for passenger and freight conductors, assistance conductors, train baggagemen, passenger trainmen, freight brakemen and flagmen, yard conductors and brakemen and arrangement for handling same.* Buffalo : G. Sutton, 1910. 30 p.

8945. _____. *Real rapid transit to ninety suburban towns; located in the commutation district within from 10 minutes to one hour's ride from Grand Central Station.* New York, New York Central & Hudson River Railroad Company, 1904. 48 p. (*Four-track series, no. 23.*)

8946. _____. *Rules and regulations for the guidance & instruction of employees. Grand Central Station and Harlem Line, January 1, 1885.* New York, The R.R., 1884. 46 p.

8947. _____. *Rules for the government of the Maintenance of Way Department in the maintenance of track, third rail and appliances for electric operation, superseding all existing orders or instructions inconsistent therewith.* New York : Evening Post Job Printing Co., 1908. 33 p.

8948. _____. *Rules governing the use of the block signal system of the Mohawk and Western divisions : to take effect December 15, 1903.* New York : Wynkoof Hallenbeck Crawford, 1903. 31 p.

8949. _____. *Rules of the Engineering Department-(maintenance of way and structures) April 1st, 1900. Rev. January 1st, 1903.* New York? s.n., 1903. 150 p.

8950. _____. *Rules of the Grand Central Station and Harlem Line for the government of the employes : superseding all existing orders or instructions inconsistent therewith. : To take effect January 1, 1904.* S.l., s.n., 1903. 179 p.

8951. _____. *Rules of the New York Central and Hudson River Railroad Company for the government of the Electrical Power Department in effect August 1st, 1907.* S.l., s.n., 1907. 40 p.

8952. _____. *Rules of the New York Central and Hudson River Railroad Company for the government of the Maintenance of Way Department, superseding all existing orders or instructions there-with, to take effect August 1st, 1906.* Paterson, NJ : The News printing Co, 1906. 177 p.

8953. _____. *Rules of the New York Central and Hudson River Railroad Company, for the government of the Operating Department. Effective January 19, 1908.* New York : The De Vinne Press, 1915. 138 p.

8954. _____. *Rules of the New York Central & Hudson River Railroad Company: for the government of the Operating Department, to take effect May 1, 1895.* New York, Wynkoop Hallenbeck Crawford, 1895. 120 p.

8955. _____. *Rules of the New York Central and Hudson River Railroad Company: governing the operation and use of interlocking, block and special signals.* S.l., s.n., 1912. 96 p.

8956. _____. *Signal rules governing the use of interlocking, controlled manual block and automatic block signal systems at Grand Central Terminal and on the electric division of the N.Y.C. & H.R.R.R.. Taking effect at 4:00 a.m., August 25, 1907.* New York: s.n., 1907. 73 p.

8957. _____. *Specifications covering electric locomotives for passenger service.* New York, s.n., 1905. 59 l.

8958. _____. [Specifications for sub-stations, third rail and transmission lines. Cables, plans, equipments, etc.] New York: The Company, 1906. 1 v. (various pagings) 30 plans.

8959. _____. *Specifications. New York Central & Hudson River Railroad Co. and Westinghouse Electric Manufacturing Co. Covering railway motors for suburban train service. Electric Traction System, New York District.* New York: 1905. 14 l.

8960. _____. *Specifications of New York Central & Hudson River Railroad Co. and Westinghouse Electric & Manufacturing Co. for multiple unit control equipments. Electric traction system, New York District.* New York: s.n., 1905. 24 f.

8961. _____. *Specifications of New York Central & Hudson River Railroad Co. and Westinghouse Electric & Manufacturing Co. for switchboards, wiring and appurtenances. Electric traction system, New York District.* New York: 1905. 54 l.

8961a. _____. [Standard blueprint drawings]. 1911-1917. 3 v. Location: Bowling Green State University, Bowling Green, Ohio,

8962. _____. *Standard plans.* S.l., s.n., 1904. 1 v.

8963. _____. *Standard plans for roadbed, masonry* / Prepared under the direction of William J. Wilgus, Vice-President. New York, 1906? 406 plates.

8964. _____. *Standard specifications and standard plans.* New York? s.n., 1902-1904. 2 v. (v. 1: Standard specifications, 204 p.; v. 2: Standard plans

8965. _____. *The terminal improvements…in the city of New York and vicinity* / New York, s.n., 1904. 14 p.

8966. _____. *Trials of freight-train brakes of the Westinghouse Air Brake Company and New York Air Brake Company at Karner, N.Y., September 8, 9 and 10, 1892 /* S.l., New York Central & Hudson River Railroad Co., 1893. 67 p.

8967. _____. *West Side tracks, City of New York.* New York, New York Central and Hudson River Railroad Company, 1907. 29 p.

8968. New York Central Lines Bridge Engineers Committee. *New York Central Lines : specifications for steel railroad bridges, 1917.* New York : Eilert Ptg. Co., 1926. 64 p.

8969. *New York Central Lines magazine.* New York : New York Central Lines, 1920-   .
Monthly. (< *New York Central magazine*)

8970. *New York Central magazine.* New York: New York Central Railroad, 1919-1920.
Monthly. 2 v. (> *New York Central Lines magazine.*)

8971. New York Central Railroad Company. *Agreement between the New York Central Railroad Company, The Pittsburgh and Lake Erie Railroad Company, Rutland Railroad Company, and the Pullman Company.* Chicago: Gunthrop-Warren Printing Co., 1936.
22 p.

8971a. _____. *Book of the Century: flagship of New York Central's great steel fleet* New York? New York Central System, 1948. 18 p.

8972. _____. *Book of the Century : the new 20ᵗʰ Century Limited, world premier 1948; new from diesel to lookout lounge.* New York : New York Central System, 1948. 18 p.

8973. _____. *A brief statement of the problem to be solved and the proposed method of solution under plans and profiles submitted to the Board of Estimate and Apportionment, city of New York, to the railroad company, April 7, 1916.* New York, 1917. 15 p.

8974. _____. *Dimensions and classification of freight car equipment of the New York Central System.* S.l., s.n., 1938. 1 v. Reprint: Omaha, NB: George R. Cockle and Associates; Lincoln, NB: Fate Graphics, Inc., 1974, 1944. 1 v.

8975. _____. *Dimensions and classification of freight car equipment of the New York Central System.* S.l., s.n., 1957. 1 v.

8976. _____. *Dimensions and classification of locomotives of the New York Central System.* S.l., s.n., 1946-1954. 2 v. v. 1- Diagrams and specifications for steam on the New York Central System. v. 2- Diagrams and specifications for diesel and electric on the New York Central system.

8977. _____. *The dining car of tomorrow : may we have your ideas?* New York : New York Central System, 1945. 20 p.

8978. _____. *The E.H. Harriman memorial medal : gold medal awarded to New York Central System in recognition of its outstanding safety record for the year 1937.* New York : New York Central Railroad Co?, 1938. 4 p.

8979. _____. *Florida Royal Palm, Chicago-Jacksonville : Big Four Route, Queen & Crescent Route, Southern Railway :) Chicago, Indianapolis, Cincinnati, Chattanooga, Atlanta, Macon, Jacksonville* / S.l., New York Central Lines, 1915. 22 columns (Two columns per page.)

8980. _____. *Grand Central Terminal: New York Central Lines: for the public service.* New York, New York Central Lines, 1912. 1 v.

8981. _____. *Grand Central Terminal, New York City : The New York Central System.* New York : New York Central System, 1947. 12 p.

8982. _____. *Grand Central Terminal: the new civic center of New York.* New York: [New York Central Lines] 1912. 22 p.

8983. _____. *Instructions for the preparation and maintenance of locomotive fires.* S.l., s.n., 1943. 23 p.

8984. _____. *The James Whitcomb Riley : del-luxe all coach streamliner, Cincinnati-Indianapolis-Lafayette-Kankakee-Chicago, New York Central System.* New York? New York Central System, 1941. 4 p.

8985. _____. *The locomotive booster; a study of dynamometer tests of K-11 class engine 3149 on the River Division, New York Central Railroad, equipped with the locomotive booster.* S.l., s.n., 190-? 7, 6 l.

8986. _____. *Mail carrying equipment.* New York? New York Central System?, 19--? 15 l.

8987. _____. *The Michigan industrial corridor; Detroit to Chicago area industrial sites.* Detroit, s.n., 1959. 1 v.

8988. _____. *The new Empire State Express: streamlined luxury for day travel.* New York, New York Central System, 1941. 12 p.

8989. _____. *"The New England States" : first all-room dreamliner between New England and the Midwest* / S.l., New York Central System, 1949. 16 p.

8990. _____. *The new 20th Century Limited.* New York, New York Central System. 1938. 16 p.

8991. *New York Central cars.* New York : Wayner Publications, 1972. 1 v. (unpaged)

8992. _____. *The New York Central Railroad Company before the Commission created by Chapter 720 of the Laws of 1917, entitled: "An Act creating a commission*

to investigate the surface railroad situation in the city of New York on the west side /
New York? 1918. 99 p. Responsibility: Ira Adelbert Place.

8993. [New York Central Railroad from Grand Central to the Bronx : construction photographs] New York? The Company? 1906. {88} leaves of plates. Location; Columbia University.

8994. _____. *New York Central Railroad wins Harriman Medal for the utmost progress in safety and accident prevention.* New York: New York Central Lines, 1915, 8 p.

8995. _____. *New York Central system rules for enginemen and firemen for the operation of intermittent inductive automatic train stop.* New York ? The Railroad, 1935. 10 p.

8996. _____. *New York Central System : war emergency train schedules.* New York : New York Central System, 1945. 48 p.

8997. _____. *Operating instructions.* New York, Office of the General Superintendent of Equipment, 1949. 1 v. (Operation of diesel-electric locomotives)

8998. _____. *Passenger equipment diagrams : New York Central System.* Medina, OH: Alvin F. Staufer, 2004. 111 p.

8999. _____. [Pictures of early locomotives of the New York Central system]. New York : New York Central Railroad Co., 1938. 16 plates 36 x 44 cm.

9000. _____. *Pittsburgh and Lake Erie Railroad Company.* New York : s.n., 1956. 149 p.

9001. _____ *The post-war railroad coach, as I would like it.* New York, New York Central Railroad, 1944. 37 p. (A customer preference survey questionnaire)

9002. _____. *A railroad's cost of living.* S.l., New York Central Lines, 1913. 33 p.

9003. _____. *Road of progress : the story of the New York Central System.* S.l., Printed by the publishers of Trains Magazine, 1945. 8 p.

9004. _____. *Rules and rates of pay for Engineers : effective September 1, 1946.* S.l., s.n., 1946. 68 p.

9005. _____. *Rules and rates of pay for enginemen, effective March 1, 1940.* Indianapolis, IN: The Company, 1940. 40 p. (New York Central Railroad Company; Cleveland, Cincinnati, Chicago, and St. Louis Railway Company; Peoria and Eastern Railway Company.)

9006. _____. *Rules for the government of the Operating Department* / New York : Wynkoop, Hallenbeck, Crawford Co., 1918. 155 p. Issued in accordance with the Standard Code of the American Railway Association, November 17, 1915.

9007. _____. *Rules for the government of the Transportation Department.* Cleveland: A.S. Gilman printing Co., 1910. 144 p.

9008. _____. *Rules governing the use of interlocking, block and train order signals.* Cleveland, OH: A.S. Gilman Printing Co., 1905. 69 p.

9009. _____. *Rules of the Operating Department, effective October 28, 1956.* S.l., New York Central System, 1956. 165 p.

9010. _____. *Rules for the operation and supervision of air brake, train air signal, and steam heat equipment: locomotive and cars, effective February 1, 1930.* S.l., s.n., 1930. 32 p.

9011. _____. *Scheduled merchandise cars.* New York : New York Central System, 1951 ed.

9012. _____ *The sleeping car of tomorrow—and how you can help plan it today.* New York, New York Central System, 1944. 22 p.

9013. _____. *Silver anniversary 20th Century Limited: 1902-June 15, 1927.* New York? New York Central Lines, 1927. 16 p.

9014. _____. *Survey of passenger preferences and attitudes concerning post-war design and services for coach travel.* New York : New York Central System, 1944. 80 l.

9015. _____. *West Side improvement plans; track and part treatment sheets* / New York? The Company, 1916. 44 p. Approved by the Board of Estimate and Apportionment of the City of New York.

9016. New York Central Railroad Company. New York Central and Hudson River Railroad Company. *Plans and profiles showing the things required to be shown on plans and profiles which the New York Central and Hudson River Railroad Company was directed by chapter 777 of the laws of 1911 to submit, in duplicate, on or before the first day of October, 1911 (and which were so submitted on the twenty-eighth day of September, 1911) to the Board of Estimate and Apportionment of the city of New York, as amended and modified in accordance with amendments and modifications which have been agreed to by said the New York Central Railroad Company and approved by the Board of Estimate and Apportionment of the city of New York./* N[ew] Y[ork] R.A. Welcke, Photo-Lith, 1916. 44 (i.e. 30) numb. l. of plates (6 folded) maps, plans. 28 x 61 cm. Leaves of plates in this work are only those related to "Track Plans" and "Park Treatment Plans;" the plates relating to "Land and Rights (nos. 4, 6, 10. 13, 18-21, 27, 30, 32, 35, 38, and 42) are not included. West Side improvement plans. At head of title: New York Central Railroad Company, successor, by consolidation, to the New York Central and Hudson River Railroad Company.

9017. *New York Central Terminal.* Buffalo, NY: School of Architecture and Planning, State University of New York at Buffalo, 1990. 42 p. (Projects, 2.) "A Studio in Historic

Preservation and Adaptive Reuse of the New York Central Terminal, Buffalo, New York."

9018. New York Chamber of Commerce. Committee on the Harbor and Shipping. *New York Central West Side plans.* New York : s.n., 1916. 7 p.

9019. New York, Chicago and St. Louis Railroad Company. *American railroad steam locomotives: Nickel Plate Road, 1934-1958.* Compiled by Wayne York. S.l., Fort Wayne Railroad Historical Society, Inc., n.d. 950 drawings. (Location: Bowling Green State University, Center for Archival Collections.)

9020. _____. *Nickel-Plate Road, Lake Erie and Western District: physical data and other information of interest.* Cleveland? OH : New York, Chicago & St. Louis Railroad Company, 1954. 34 p.

9020a. _____. *Nickel Plate Road, Nickel Plate District : physical data and other information of interest/* New York: New York, Chicago & St. Louis Railroad, 1954. 32 p.

9021. _____. *Nickel Plate Road, the New York, Chicago & St. Louis Railroad Company, Lake Erie & Western District: rates of pay and rules for engineers and firemen.* S.l., New York, Chicago & St. Louis Railroad Company, 1924. 31 p.

9022. New York City Economic Development Corporation. *Cross Harbor Freight Movement Project : draft environmental impact statement /* Washington, DC: U.S. Department of Transportation, Federal Highway Administration, Federal Railroad Administration, 2004. 2 v. (*FHWA-NY-EIS-04-01.*)

9023. _____. *Scope of work for the Cross Harbor Freight Movement Project: environmental impact statement.* New York, Cross Harbor Freight Movement Project, 2001. 37 p.

9024. New York General Agency. *A list of government and railroad lands open to pre-emption, or homestead, or to purchase along the lines of the Central Pacific, and the California and Oregon railroads.* New York: New York General Agency, 1886. 96 p.

9025. *The New York improvement and tunnel extension of the Pennsylvania Railroad.* Philadephia : s.n., 1910. 34 p.

9026. New York, Lake Erie, and Western Railroad Company. *Additional reply of the New York, Lake Erie & Western R.R. Co. to the proposed award of Albert Fink, commissioner, on the division of west-bound traffic from New York.* New York? s.n., 1879. 6 l.

9027. _____. *By-laws and organization for conduction the business of the New York, lake Erie and Western Railroad Company, as approved by the Board of Directors, September 25th, 1879.* New York : M.B. Brown, 1879. 33 p.

9028. _____. *Comparative fuel tests on New York, Lake Erie, and Western Railroad /*

Philadelphia : New York, Lake Erie, and Western Railroad Company, 1894. 8 p.
Printed by Martin B. Brown, 1886. 62 p.

9029. _____. *The Erie system : a statement of the organization and operations
of the corporations controlled by the Lake Erie & Western Railroad Company, 1886.*
New York: Printed by Martin B. Brown, 1886. 62 p.

9030. _____. *The past and present of a great railroad.* S.l., s.n., 1881. 17 p.

9031. _____. *Rules and regulations: defining the duties of officers and agents
in the Transportation Department, and regulating the running of trains and the use
of signals on the New York, Lake Erie and Western Railroad.* New York, The Railroad,
1883.140 p.

9032. _____. *To the engineers, conductors, firemen and trainmen of the lines
of the Company.* New York : New York, Lake Erie and Western Railroad Company,
1890. 28 p.

9033. New York, New Haven, and Hartford Railroad Company. *Agreement between
the National Organization Masters, Mates and Pilots of America and the New York, New
Haven and Hartford Railroad Company covering bridgemaster, bridge motormen
and bridgemen employed at the float bridges of the carrier in the New York harbor
district.* New Haven, 1937. 5 l

9034. _____. *Agreement between the New York, New Haven and Hartford Railroad
Company and National Organization of Masters, Mates and Pilots of America, covering
working conditions of captains, first and second deckhands and floatmen employed
on the tug boats, steam lighters and car floats of the railroad company in the New York
harbor district.* New haven, 1935. 5 l.

9035. _____. *Agreement between the New York, New Haven and Hartford Railroad
Company and the American Train Dispatchers' Association, governing working
conditions of train dispatchers, effective as of November 12, 1937.* New Haven, 1937.
5 l.

9036. _____. *Agreement between the New York, New Haven and Hartford Railroad
Company and the Brotherhood of Railroad Trainmen covering dining car stewards.*
New Haven, 1938. 8 l.

9037. _____. *Agreement between the New York, New Haven and Hartford Railroad
Company, debtor, and the brotherhood of Maintenance of Way Employees representing
shop and roundhouse laborers as designated /* New Haven : Whaples-Bullis Co., 1936.
30 p.

9038. _____. *Agreement between the New York, New Haven & Hartford Railroad
and the Yardmasters and Stationmasters Association, inc., of the New York, New Haven
and Hartford Railroad System, effective November 19th, 1937.* New Haven, 1937. 2 l.

9039. _____. *Agreement covering working conditions of engineers, firemen and oilers employed on the tug boats of the New York, New Haven and Hartford Railroad Company in the New Yrok*[!] *harbor district.* New Haven: 1935. 5 l.

9040. _____. *Arranged freight train service symbol book no. 79: revised to April 25, 1948, superseding all previous issues.* New Haven, The Railroad, 1948. 193 p.

9041. _____. *A brief history of the New York, New Haven & Hartford Railroad Company during the past twenty years.* Boston, Hornblower & Weeks, 1926. 19 p.

9042. _____. *Coordinating rail + auto for more efficient and more economical business travel.* Boston : New Haven Railroad, 1938. 4 p.

9043. _____. *Definitions and rules for the controlled manual block signal system and interlocking ... in effect July 1, 1907 /* New Haven? 1907. 23 p.

9044. _____. *Description of the Cedar Hills Yards and explanation of their operation.* New Haven: s.n., 1939. 7 l.

9045. _____. *The devastation and restoration of New England's vital life-line ... the New Haven R.R.* Boston, Mass., The New Haven R.R., 1939? 46 p.

9046. _____. *Diesel locomotive diagrams.* S.l., s.n., 1900s. 1 v. 24 x 14 cm.

9047. _____. *Electric locomotive diagrams.* S.l., s.n., 1900s. 1 v. 24 x 14 cm.

9048. _____. *Engineering rules and instructions, February 1, 1907.* Boston: New York, New Haven & Hartford Railroad Co., 1907. 48 p.

9049. _____. *Examination for train dispatchers, conductors, ticket collectors and enginemen /* New Haven: The Railroad, 1940s. 114 p.

9050. _____. *Freight car and work equipment diagrams.* S.l., s.n., 1900s. 1 v. 15 x 25 cm.

9051. _____. *General rules and regulations /* S.l., New York, New Haven, and Hartford Railroad Company, 1881. 16 p.

9052. _____. *General rules and regulations of the New York, New Haven & Hartford Railroad Co. taking effect October 1, 1872.* New Haven? s.n., 1872. 8 p.

9053. _____. *General rules and regulations of the New York, New Haven 7 Hartford Railroad Co.: taking effect October 1, 1874.* New York : Van Kleeck, Clark & Co., 1874. 10 p.

9054. _____. *Good firing.* New Haven Conn., New York, New Haven & Hartford; Central New England Railway, 1924. 118 p.

9055. _____ *In the District Court of the United States for the District of Connecticut : in proceedings for the reorganization of a railroad : in the matter of the New York, New Haven and Hartford Railroad Company, debtor, no. 16562.* S.l., s.n., 1947. 19 v.

9056. _____. *Instructions governing train load for engines and engine ratings ... no. 1, in effect December 15, 1905.* New Haven? 1905. 30 p.

9057. _____. *NH description of passenger equipment.* New Haven, Conn., New York, New Haven & Hartford R.R. Co., 1956 62 p.

9058. _____. *NH passenger car diagrams.* New Haven, New York, New Haven & Hartford Railroad Co., 1955. 1 v.

9058a. _____. [Locomotive register] 0.25 linear feet. Location: State University of New York, Special Collections and Archives, Albany, N.Y.

9059. _____. *Official commercial and industrial reference book: giving list of stations, etc., lists of dealers in staple commodities, etc. ... on the lines of New York, New Haven & Hartford Railroad.* Chicago: Lanward Pub. Co., 1896. 122, 4 p. Advertisements throughout.

9060. _____. *Passenger car diagrams.* S.l., s.n., 1900s. 1 v. 24 x 14 cm.

9061. _____. *Rates of pay and regulations affecting conductors, trainmen and yardmen* / New Haven: s.n., 1926. 71 p.

9062. _____. *Rates of pay and regulations for locomotive firemen and hostlers.* New York: 1955- . Periodical.

9063. _____. *Rules and instructions for the maintenance of way and structures. Effective September 1st, 1916.* New Haven, Conn., New York, New Haven, and Hartford Railroad Company, 1916. 1 v.

9064. _____. *Rules and rates of pay for telegraphers* / New Haven : Quinnipiack Press, Inc., 1927. 57 p. Agreement of the railroad companies with the Order of Railroad Telegraphers.

9065. _____. *Rules for the government of the Operating Department.* S.l., s.n., 1899. 123 p.

9066. _____. *Rules for the government of the Operating Department.* New Haven : The Railroad, 1914. 333 p.

9067. _____. *Rules for the government of the Operating Department.* New Haven, Conn., Press of the Wilson H. Lee Co., 1924. 280 p. Effective January 1, 1925.

9068. _____. *Rules for the government of the Operating Department .. [to] take effect January 1, 1943* / New Haven: s.n., 1943. 171 p.

9069. _____. *Rules for the government of the Operating Department.* S.l., s.n., 1956. 226 p.

9070. _____. *Rules for the maintenance, operation and inspection of air brakes* / New Haven : Wilson H. Lee Co., 1931. 91 p.

9071. _____. *Rules of the New York, New Haven and Hartford Railroad Company for the government of the Operating Department.* S.l., The Company, 1907. 175 p.

9072. _____. *Safety rules..* New York, 1943- . Periodical.

9073. _____. *Safety rules.* New Haven: The Railroad, 1942. 96 p.

9074. _____. *Schedule of instructions and rates of pay affecting locomotive engineers* / New Haven : 1931. 92 p.

9075. _____. *Schedules of instructions and rates of pay affecting locomotive engineers* … [Supplements, no. 1-] New Haven : 1937- (Grand International Brotherhood of Locomotive Engineers.)

9076. _____. *Schedules of rules governing working conditions and rates of pay affecting locomotive engineers.* New York: 1955- . Periodical

9077. _____. *The Shore Line Route: trains de luxe, New York and Boston: Bay State Limited, Knickerbocker Limited, Merchants Limited.* New York, Press of the Kalkhoff Company, 1915? 26 p.

9078. _____. *Special rules and regulations for conductors and engineers of freight trains: also governing the use of automatic electric signals and semaphore signals, February 18, 1883.* Buffalo? The Company? 1883. 17 p. New York and Harlem River Branch of New York Division.)

9079. _____. *Standard recipe book : New York, New Haven, and Hartford Railroad Company.* Boston : Ackermann Printing, 1900s. 1 v (unpaged)

9080. _____. *Summary of equipment.* New York, 1955- . Periodical.

9081. _____. *Traffic study.* Boston? 1936. 4 v. Prepared by the Traffic Department in collaboration with Loomis, Sayles and Company, Inc.

9082. *New York, New Haven & Hartford Railroad : efficient management is restoring earning power.* New York; Chicago: J.S. Bache & Co., 1926. 4 p.

9083. New York (N.Y.). *Draft form of deed to accompany proposed agreement submitted to the Board of Estimate and Apportionment.* New York, 1917. 176 p. New York Central Railroad Company.

9084. _____. Board for the Atlantic Avenue Improvement. *Terminal improvements of Long Island Railroad: including Atlantic Avenue improvements, Brooklyn, and tunnel under East River to New York City.* Brooklyn, N.Y., Brooklyn Daily Eagle Book Printing Department, 1898. 51 p.

9085. New York (N.Y.) Board of Estimate and Apportionment. *The City of New York and The New York Central Railroad Company: draft form of deed : to accompany proposed agreement submitted to the Board of Estimate and Apportionment.* New York: s.n., 1917. 176p.

9086. _____. _____. *Report in re-plan of New York Central R. R. for readjustment of line, north of 60th St., Oct 3d, 1912.* New York, s.n., 1912. 9 l.

9087. _____. _____. *The position of the New York Central Railroad Company with respect to the plans and profiles submitted to it by the Board of Estimate and Apportionment, April 7, 1916, under chapter 777 of the Laws of 1911, and the proposed contract and deed prepared by the corporation counsel.* New York, 1917. 38 p.

9088. _____. _____. Committee on Port and Terminal Facilities. *Report[s] ... upon the rail terminal facilities of the New York Central Railroad Company on the west sides of the Boroughs of Manhattan and the Bronx.* New York: The Board, 1916-1917. 3 v. in 1.

9089. _____. _____. Committee on Terminal Improvements. *Report of Committee on terminal improvements: board of Estimate and Apportionment upon organization of rail terminal facilities upon the West Side of Manhattan Island and the elimination of surface operation of by the New York Central Railroad Company upon the streets of the city* / New York : M.B. Brown Printing and Binding Co., 1913. 47 p.

9090. _____. Borough of Queens. *Discussion of the proposed West Side improvement contract* / New York, s.n., 1917. 19 p. Addressed to the Board of Estimate and Apportionment, city of New York, February 16, 1917 by Maurice E. Connolly, president of the borough of Queens.

9091. _____. Common Council. *Railroads and railroad grants in the City of New York.* New York, Published by the Clerk of the Board of Councilmen, C.T. McClenachan, 1860. 199-368 p.

9092. _____. Department of Bridges. *Agreement for operation of surface cars on Williamsburg Bridge, dated May 21, 1904.* Brooklyn : Eagle Press, 1904. 36 p. Brooklyn Heights Railroad Company; New York City Railway Company; the Coney Island and Brooklyn Railroad Company; Bridge Operating Company.

9092a. _____. _____. *Contracts with railroad companies: New York and Brooklyn Bridge and Williamsburg Bridge/* New York: Martin B. Brown Press, 1904. 111 p. 8 folded leaves.

9093. _____. Docks Department. *Report on the plans of the New York Central and Hudson River Railroad Company ... and their relation to a general system of freight terminals.* New York: Brown, 1911. 23, 6 p. Includes: "A Plan for the comprehensive organization and connection of the interstate terminals of the port of New York."

9094. _____. Law Department. *Opinion of the corporation counsel of the City of New York, dated May 28, 1909, in respect to the rights of the new York Central and Hudson River Railroad Company in the streets and avenues on the West side of the borough of Manhattan.* New York, 1909. 43 p.

9095. _____. Office of the Comptroller. *Statement of William A. Prendergast, comptroller of the city of New York, in regard to the proposed form of agreement covering the West Side improvement between the Board of Estimate and Apportionment and the New York Central Railroad Company. New York, January 16, 1917.* New York : M.B. Brown Printing and Binding, 1917. 16 p.

9096. _____. Port and Terminal Facilities Commission. *Report of Committee on Terminal improvements, Board of Estimate and Apportionment, upon organization of rail terminal facilities upon the West Side of Manhattan Island and the elimination of surface operation by the New York Central Railroad Company upon the streets of the city.* New York : M.B. Brown Printing & Biding Co., 1913. 47 p.

9097. _____. West Side Improvement Engineering Committee. *Plans for the removal of the tracks of the New York Central Railroad Company : from the public streets along the Hudson River waterfront and for related public improvements. Part no. 1. Plans.* New York : R.A. Welcke, 1927. 22 l. 28 x 61 cm.

9098. New York (N.Y.). Office of the Superintendent. Railway Mail Service. *The United States Railway Mail Service at the new post office and Pennsylvania Station, New York City.* New York : Office of Superintendent, Railway Mail Service, 1910. 11 p.

9099. New York, Ontario, and Western Railway Co. *Examination on Book of rules of the operating Department taking effect May 15, 1913.* New York? New York, Ontario, and Western Railway Co., 1913. 46 p.

9100. New York Produce Exchange. *Rules regulating the grain trade ... including the rate for grain, and the several grades established by the Committee on Grain.* 4 ed. New York, s.n., 1876. 24 p. Includes: Articles of agreement between the New York Produce Exchange and the New York Central & Hudson River Railroad, Erie Railway Company,, and Pennsylvania Railroad Company, "relating to the inspection, grading, consolidation and delivery of grain arriving by rail at the port of New York."

9101. New York Rail Insulation and Equipment Company. *The insulation of rails.* Newark, NJ: The Company, 1910? 9 p.

9102. New York Railroad Club. *Official proceedings of the New York Railroad Club.* Brooklyn, N.Y., The Club, 1888-191961. 71 v. (> *Marker lamp.*)

9103. _____. *Yearbook.* New York, The Club, 1900- Annual.

9104. *New York Railways: the Green Line.* Hicksville, N.Y., N.J. International, 1994. 64 p.

9105. New York (State). Board of Mediation and Arbitration. *Special report ... on New York Central and Hudson River Railroad strike.* Albany : 1891. 104 p.

9106. _____. Board of Railroad Commissioners. *Codification of the rules and regulations for running trains on the rail-roads of the state of New York; with modifications suggested by the Board of Rail-Road Commissioners, January, 1856.* Albany, N.Y., Parson and Co., Printers, 1856. 21 p. (*Circular. New York State. Board of Railroad Commissioners, no. 19.*)

9107. _____. _____*Drawings of maps, bridges, profiles, coal burning locomotives, chairs, brakes, splices, &c.: accompanying the report of the Board of Railroad Commissioners, for 1856.* S.l., s.n., 1857. 1 v. (Issued by the State Engineer and Surveyor's Office.)

9108. _____. _____. *General railroad laws of the state of New York; with amendments to and including the session of the legislature of 1905.* Albany, N.Y., Brandow Printing Company, 1906. 733 p.

9109. _____. Commission to Investigate the Surface Railroad Situation in the City of New York on the West Side. *Brief in support of legislation proposed by the Commission as directed by the legislature /* New York : 1918. 31 p.

9110. _____. *The New York Central Railroad Company before the Commission created by Chapter 720 of the Laws of 1917, entitled : "An act creating a Commission to Investigate the Surface Railroad Situation in the city of New York, on the West Side, as affected by the enactment of chapter seven hundred and seventy-seven of the laws of nineteen hundred and eleven, and making an appropriation therefore"/* S.l., 1918. 99 p.

9111. _____. _____. *Report of the Commission ... appointed under Chapter 720 of the laws of 1917 ... Transmitted to the Governor and Legislature on January 31, 1918.* New York: s.n., 1918. 84 p.

9112. _____. Department of Transportation. *Full Freight Access Program, New York City and Long Island.* Albany, NY: New York State Department of Transportation, 1984. 16 p. (Andrews & Clark, Inc., consulting engineers for the New York State Dept. of Transportation.)

9113. _____. Department of Transportation. Planning Division. *New York State Rail Plan: prepared in response to Title IV, Section 402, of the Regional Rail Reorganization Act of 1973 and the Rules and regulations of the Secretary of Transportation.* Albany, NY: New York State Department of Transportation, 1976. 250 p.

9114. _____. Department of Transportation. Policy and Programs Group. *Report on profitability of New York State branch lines.* Albany, N.Y.? New York State Dept. of Transportation, Policy & Programs Group, 1974. 93 p.

9115. _____. Legislature. Assembly. *Exhibits. New York Central & Hudson River Railroad Company and New York, Lake Erie & Western Railroad Company.* S.l., s.n., 1879. 643, 13 p.

9116. _____.._____. _____. Special Commission on Railroads 1879. *Proceedings of the Special Committee on Railroads, appointed under the resolution of the Assembly to investigate alleged abuses in the management of railroads chartered by the state of New York.* New York, NY: Weed, Parsons and Co., Printers, 1879. 3 v.

9117. _____. Legislature. Senate. Committee Appointed to Examine and Report the Causes of Railroad Accidents. *Report of the Committee appointed to examine and report the causes of railroad accidents, the means of preventing their recurence, &c.* S.l., s.n., 1853. 156 p. (*State of New York, Senate, no. 13.*)

9118. _____. _____. _____. Committee on Rail-Roads. *Testimony taken before the Senate Committee on Railroads, in relation to the process charged by the railroads of the State for riding in drawing-room cars and sleeping-cars, and the laws, if any, under which such cars are put upon the roads and such charges made.* Albany, NY? The Senate, 1870. 65 p. (In *Senate, 1870, no. 40.*)

9119. _____. _____. _____. Special Committee Appointed to Investigate the Subject of Railroad Accidents. *Railway accident investigation by a special committee of the New York Senate* [with report] Albany : 1882. 482 p.

9120. _____. _____. Office of Public Transportation, Rail Division. *West Side line connection.* Albany, NY: New York State Dept. of Transportation, Office of Public Transportation, Rail Division, 1983. 15 l.

9121. _____. Public Service Commission. 1st District. [A formal request to the Board of Estimate and Apportionment of the City of New York to terminate permits granted to the New York Central and Hudson River Railroad Company and to other companies and corporations and to various individuals for laying switches, sidings, spurs, etc. connecting with the mainline of the company's tracks on the west side of the city] New York : 1907. 8 p.

9122. _____. _____. _____. *In the matter of the Ottinger-Ellenbogen bill in relation to the "West Side improvement contract" in New York City. Memorandum of the Public Service Commission for the First District as to the bill prepared and recommended for dealing with the "West Side problem" in New York City.* Albany? 1917. 12p.

9123. _____. _____. _____.*Memorandum. West Side improvement—New York Central Railroad Company. Public Service Commission. First District.* Responsibility: Ralph R. Monroe. New York. New York? s.n., 1919. 19 p.

9124. _____. _____.*In the matter of Senate bill (int. no. 9; print no. 2067), in relation to the "west side trackage" situation and the proposed contract between the city of New York and the New York Central Railroad Company.* Albany? 1917. 66 p.

9125. _____. _____. [Report upon the value of lands and rights under the proposed agreement between the City of New York and the New York Central Railroad Company relative to the west side tracks] New York? 1917. 21 p.

9126. _____. Supreme Court. *In the matter of Riverside Park : appeal of the New York Central and Hudson River Railroad Company, papers on appeal; Strong & Shephard, attorneys for appellant; Richard O'Gorman, attorney for respondent.* New York : Evening Post Steam Presses, 1871. 37 p.

9127. _____. Transit Commission. *In the matter of the petition of the New York Central Railroad Company for an order ... determining the elimination of certain street crossings by its railroad at grade on the west side of Manhattan Island from the southerly terminus of said railroad at St. Johns Park to the Harlem Ship Canal, formerly Spuyten Duyvil Creek. Petition.* New York, 1924. 9 p.

9128. _____. _____. *In the matter of the petition of the New York Central Railroad Company for an order of the transit commission determining the elimination of certain street crossings by its railroad at grade on the West side of Manhattan Island, from the southerly terminus of said railroad at St. John's Park to the Harlem Ship Canal, formerly Spuyten Duyvil Creek. Case no. 2703. Opinion by Commissioner O'Ryan /* 1924. 23 p.

9129. New York Sabbath Committee. *Sunday railroad work.* New York: Sabbath Committee, 1869. 16 p.

9130. New York Transit Museum. *Subway style: 100 years of architecture and design in the New York subway.* Introduction by Joseph Giovannini; original photography by Andrew Garn. New York, Stewart, Tabori & Chang,, 2004. 252 p.

9131. *New York tunnel extension, the Pennsylvania Railroad; description of the work and facilities.* New York, American Society of Civil Engineers, 1910. 2 v. (*Transactions. American Society of Civil Engineers, v. LXVIII, LXIX, September, October, 1910.*)

9132. New York World's Fair. *Book of the pageant; railroads on parade, presented at the New York World's Fair, 1939, to do full tribute to the American railroad.* New York, Select Printing Company, 1939. 16 p. (Eastern Presidents' Conference)

9133. Newbern, R.H. *The tragedy—and the cost—of railroad trespassing.* Harrisburg, PA? Pennsylvania Industrial Welfare and Efficiency Conference, 1913. 4 p. At head of title: Pennsylvania Railroad System.

9134. *The Newbold electric car lighting system : coach equipped with Newbold electric car-lighting system.* Chicago : Adams & Westlake Co., 1917. 112 p.

9135. Newcomb, H.T. *Railway economics.* Philadelphia, Railway World Pub. Co.,1898. 152 p.

9136. _____. *The work of the Interstate Commerce Commission.* New York, Gibson Bros., 1905. 102 p. (Reprint: Arno Press,1981.)

9136a. Newport News Shipbuilding and Dry Dock Company. *Specifications for a bulk-oil steamship : for the Southern Pacific Co./* Newport News, VA: Newport News Shipbuilding and Dry Dock Co., 1915. 120 p. (Completed vessel named : Torres. Hull no. 202.)

9136b. _____. *Specifications for the construction of a steel freight steamship : for the Southern Pacific Company, Atlantic Steam Lines /* Newport News, VA: Newport news Shipbuilding and Dry Dock Co., 1909. 145 p. (Completed vessels to be named: El Mundo, El Sol, El Occidente. Hulls nos. 130-133.)

9136c. _____. *Specifications for the construction of a steel freight steamship : for the Southern Pacific Co., Atlantic Steamship Lines.* Newport News, VA: Newport News Shipbuilding and Dry Dock Co., 1915. 160 p. (Completed vessels named El Amirante and El Capitan. Hulls nos. 203-204.)

9137. Newell, John C., P.R. Griswold. *Narrow gauge east from Denver; the Colorado Eastern Railroad.* Boulder, CO: Pruett Publishing Company, 1982. 94 p.

9138. *Newsletter.* Mount Pleasant, MI: GTW Historical Society, 1990- -. Quarterly. Other title: GTWHS newsletter. (> *Semaphore.*)

9139. Newton, J.S. *Hydraulic transmissions for locomotives /* New York, American Society of Mechanical Engineers, 1953. 8, 11 p.

9140. Newton, Sidney. *Train time with the Tabor & Northern: "the slow train through Arkansas.* Newell, IA: Bireline Publishing Company, 1983. 102 p.

9141. Newnan, Douglas G. *An economic analysis of railway grade crossings on the California state highway system.* 1965. 207 l. (Thesis, Ph.D., Civil Engineering, Stanford University)

9142. Newman, Marc. *The railroad switching terminal at Maybrook, New York: gateway to the east.* Fleischmanns, NY: Purple Mountain Press, 2008. 85 p.

9143. Newman, W.A., C.F. Pascoe. *Tougher locomotive frames.* New York, International Nickel Company, 1930. 6 p.

9144. Blank entry.

9145. *Newsletter; official publication of the Illinois Central Historical Society.* Paxton, IL: Illinois Central Historical Society, 2000s-   . Quarterly. (< Illinois Central Railroad Historical Society. *Membership newsletter.)*

9146. Nexsen, Randolph H. *Branch line and switching transportation problems.* New York, s.n., 1929. 25 p.

9147. *The next station will be--an album of photographs of railroad depots in 1910.* Livingston, NJ: Railroadians of America,1973-1994. 13 v.

9148. *Next stop Westchester! People and the railroad.* Yonkers, NY: Hudson River Museum of Westchester, 1996. 28 p.

9149. *The Niagara Gorge Belt Line: a pictorial album.* Edited by Gordon J. Thompson. Niagara Falls, NY: Niagara Frontier Chapter, National Railway Historical Society, 2000. 67 p.

9150, Nice, David C. *Amtrak; the history and politics of a national railroad.* Boulder, CO: Lynne Rienner, 1998. 119 p.

9151. Nicholas, C.J., D. Fischer. *Moving agricultural products by double stack trains: an update* / Washington, DC: Office of Transportation, U.S. Department of Agriculture, 1989. 11 p.

9152. Nichols, Jim. *Norfolk and Western color guide to freight and passenger equipment.* Scotch Plains, NJ: Morning Sun Books, 2000. 127 p.

9153. _____. *Norfolk and Western in color.* Scotch Plains, NJ: Morning Sun Books,1997-

9154. Nichols, Joseph. *Condensed history of the construction of the Union Pacific Railway.* Omaha, Neb., Klopp, Bartlett, 1892. 192 p.

9155. Nicholls, Michael L. *Like pearls on a string: Illinois Central railroad town development, 1851-1870.* 1999. 174 p. (Thesis, Ph.D., University of North Carolina at Chapel Hill.)

9156. Nicholson, David M. *Santa Fe: how it governed its timepieces throughout the system.* Enid, OK: P.O. Box 1792 Enid 73702, 1984. 48 p.

9157. Nicholson, George T., H.E. Townsend. *The California Limited: the Santa Fe, 1902-1903.* Chicago? Atchison, Topeka, and Santa Fe Railroad Company, 1902. 32 p.

9158. Nicholson, George W. *Days of the iron horse.* Paso Robles, CA: s.n., 1981, c1976. 55 p. (Michigan Central Railroad Company)

9159. Nicholson, Loren. *Rails across the ranchos.* Fresno, CA: Valley Publishers, 1980. 197 p. (Reissued: San Luis Obispo, CA: California Heritage Pub. Associates, 1993. 197 p.)

9159a. *Nickel Plate comes to St. Louis.* St. Louis, MO: Terminal Railroad Association of St. Louis Historical and Technical Society, 2013. 175 p.

9160. Nickel Plate Road Historical and Technical Society. *The making of a merger: special 10th year commemorative issue.* Fort Waybe, IN: Nickel Plate Road Historical and Technical Society, 1964. 35 p. (*Nickel Plate Road Magazine, v. 8, no. 3.*)

9161. _____. *MIKES of the Nickel Plate Road.* Rutledge, TN: Tioga Publications, 1976. 112 p.

9162. *Nickel Plate Road Historical & Technical Society newsletter.* New Haven, IN: Nickel Plate Road Historical and Technical Society, 1900s- . Quarterly.

9163. Nickel Plate Road magazine. New York : Geffen, Dunn & Co., 1948- . Monthly.

9164. *Nickel Plate Road magazine.* Westlake, OH: Nickel Plate Road Historical and Technical Society, 1900s- . Quarterly.

9165. Nickens, Paul R., Kathleen Nickens. *Touring the West: with the Fred Harvey Co. & the Santa Fe Railway* / Atglen, PA: Schiffer Pub., 2009. 110 p.

9166.Nickle, Dyson Venn. *One hundred sources on East Texas history: a bibliography of East Texas.* 2007. 121 l. (Thesis, M.A., Stephen F. Austin State University)

9166a. Nicodemus, Frederick Bowman. *Investigation of a through plate girder railroad bridge.* 1909. 2, 36 l. (Thesis, B.S., University of Illinois.)

9167. Nicolls, G.A. *Conductor's rules.* Reading, Pa., Philadelphia & Reading Railroad Co., 1861. 18 [i.e. 19] p.

9168. Nicolls, William Jasper. *The railway builder: a handbook for estimating the probable cost of American railway construction and equipment.* Philadelphia, Pa., H.C. Baird & Company, 1878. 259 p.

9169. Niederauer, George F. *Locomotive 325 : the lives, times, and rebirth of an 1895 steam engine.* Durango : Durango Railroad Historical Society, 2010. 514 p.

9170. Niehoff, Walter H. *The reincarnation of the Switch Back Gravity Railroad : the story of the Switch Back and the Switch back operating model* / Vestal, NY: W.H. Niehoff, 1995. 110 p.

9171. Nielsen, Howard A., Jr. *From locomotives to strain gauges: the true story of a tortuous conversion from smokestack to high-technology industry.* New York, Vantage Press, 1985. 160 p. (Baldwin-Lima-Hamilton Corporation)

9172. Nielsen, Marvin. *Locomotives of the Upper Midwest: photo archive. Diesel power in the 1960s & 1970s.* Hudson, WI: Iconografix, 2004. 126 p.

9173. _____. *Trains of the Twin Ports: photo archive - Duluth-Superior in the 1950s.*

Hudson, WI: Iconografix, 1999. 126 p.

9174. _____. *Trains of the Upper Midwest: photo archive: steam and diesel in the 1950s & 1960s*. Hudson, WI: Iconografix, 2001. 126 p.

9175. Nielsen, Waldo. *Right-of-way: a guide to abandoned railroads in the United States*. Bend, OR: Maverick, 1992. 237 p.

9176. Niemann, Linda. *Boomer: railroad memoirs*. Berkeley, University of California Press, 1990. 252 p. (Reissue: Pittsburgh, PA: Cleis Press, 1992; Bloomington: Indiana University Press, 2011. 254 p.

9177. _____. *Gender roles in a cornfield meet: a study of women railroaders on the Southern Pacific*. Santa Cruz, CA: Kresge College, UCSC, Santa Cruz; Feminist Studies Focused Research Activity, University of California, Santa Cruz, 1991. 6 p.

9178. _____. *On the rails: a woman's journey*. Introduction by Leslie Marmom Silko. Pittsburgh, PA: Cleis Press, 1996. 249 p.

9179. _____. *Railroad voices*. Narratives by Linda Niemann; photographs by Lina Bertucci. Stanford, CA: Stanford University Press, 1998. 158 p.

9180. _____, Joel Jensen. *Railroad noir : the American West at the end of the twentieth century*. Bloomington : Indiana University Press, 2010. 151 p.

9181. Nighswonger, Doug. *Northern Pacific in color*. Scotch Plains, NJ: Morning Sun Books, 2002-

9182. _____, William F. Stauss. *Milwaukee Road color guide to freight and passenger equipment*. Scotch Plains, NJ: Morning Sun Books, 1999-

9183. Niles, Robert. *History of the California Door Co. and its logging railroads*. Rev. ed. S.l., Eldorado National Forest, Forest Service, U.S. Department of Agriculture, 1980. 41 l.

9184. Niles Car & Manufacturing Company. *Niles cars*. Caldwell, ID: Caxton Printers, 1982. 43 p.

9185. Nilson, Allan T., Raymond E. Johnson. *They built railway cars: the Pullman social experiment and the Swedish immigration*. Bowie, MD: Heritage Books, 2002. 127 p.

9186. Nimick, Reade B. *The Pittsburgh and Connellsville Railroad* / Princeton, NJ : The Author, 1950. 102 p.

9187. *The 1980 National Rail-Highway Crossing Safety Conference proceedings, June 17-19, 1980, Transportation Center, The University of Tennessee*/ Washington, DC: U.S. Department of Transportation, 1980. 112 p.

9188. *The 1981 Operation Lifesaver National Symposium, August 27-29, 1981, Chicago, Illinois;* sponsored by the Federal Railroad Administration, National Safety Council. Washington, DC: Federal Railroad Administration, 1982. 40 p.

9189. Nimke, R.W. *The Central New England Railway* / Westmoreland, NH: R.W. Nimke, 1995-1996. 3 v.

9190. _____. *The Rutland: arrivals and departures: train schedules, 1901-1961.* Walpole, NH: R.W. Nimke, 1990. 204 p.

9191. _____. *Rutland Railroad side track diagram: December 1, 1934; also shows locations of stations, freight houses, industries, turntables, siding capacities, etc.* Walpole, NH: The Author,1986. 24 l.

9192. _____, Stearns Jenkins. *The St. Johnsbury and Lake Champlain Railroad: plans.* Westmoreland, NH: R.W. Nimke, 1994. 42 p.

9193. *1955 survey of diesel-electric motive power in railway service; and new 1954 installations of diesel-electric motive* power. New York, Railway Age, 1955. 18 p.

9194. *1974 National Conference on Railroad-Highway Crossing Safety, August 19-22, 1974;* sponsored by U.S. Dept. of Transportation, held at U.S. Air Force Academy. Washington, DC: U.S. Dept. Of Transportation, 1974. 93 p.

9195. Nimmo, Joseph, Jr. *The Commerce Commission and its record*/ Washington, DC: s.n., 1905. 12 p.

9196. _____. *The commercial and political considerations involved in sympathetic railroad strikes.* Washington, DC: s.n., 1893. 9 p.

9197. _____. *The evolution of the American railroad system. An address by Joseph Nimmo, Jr. before the World's congress auxiliary of the World's Columbian exposition of 1893.Delivered at Chicago, Ill, June 22, 1893.* Washington, 1893. 42 p.

9197a. Noble, Joseph A. *From cab to caboose; fifty years of railroading.* Norman, University of Oklahoma Press, 1964. 205 p. (AT&SF)

9198. Noble, Mark. *Articulated locomotives of the Western Pacific.* San Marino, CA: Pacific Railway Journal, 1932. 21 p. (Reprint from Baldwin Locomotive magazine.) (Reissued with additional photographs: San Marino, CA: s.n., 1959. 21 p.)

9199. _____. *Men and motive power: a story of the Southern Pacific Company.* San Marino, CA: Southern California Chapter, Railway and Locomotive Historical Society, Pacific Railroad Society, 1955? 23 p.

9200. Nock, O.S. *Railways of the USA.* New York, Hastings House, 1979. 317 p.

9201. Noe, Kenneth W. *Southwest Virginia: the Virginia and Tennessee Railroad and the Union, 1816-1865.* 1990. 376 l. (Thesis, Ph.D., University of Illinois at Urbana-Champaign.)

9202. _____. *Southwest Virginia's railroad: modernization and the sectional crisis.* Urbana, University of Illinois Press, 1994. 221 p.

9203. Nolan, Edward W. *Exploring the Northern Pacific Railroad route: W. Milnor Robert's letters from the expedition of 1869* / 1971. 112 . (Thesis, M.A., University of Oregon.)

9203a. _____. *Northern Pacific views: the railroad photography of F. Jay Haynes, 1876-1905.* Helena, Montana Historical Society Press, 1983. 206 p.

9204. Nolan, J.J. *List of standard and tourist cars, with plan number, form number of diagrams, system of air conditioning, ownership and voltage of cars. No. 35, canceling no. 34.* Chicago? Pullman Co., 1950. 66 p.

9204a. Nollau, Louis Edward. [Railroad glass negative collection.] ca. 1909-1917. 2693 4x5 commercial dry glass negatives: rolling stock, railroads stations, water tanks, workshops, etc. of the Southern Railway system.

9205. Noonan, Edward J. *The railway passenger terminal situation at Chicago; report to the City Council Committee on Railway Terminals.* Chicago, Ill., City Council Committee on Railway Terminals, 1931. 38 p.

9206. Nooner, Thompson Alexander. *Industrial development as undertaken by the railroads.* 1951. 137 l. (Thesis, M.B.A. in Transportation and Public Utilities, Graduate School of Arts and Sciences, University of Pennsylvania)

9207. Nordhoff, Charles. *C.P.R.R. : the Central Pacific Railroad* / Silverthorne, CO: Vistabooks, 1996. 48 p.

9208. Norfolk and Western Historical Society. *Coal on the move: via the Virginian Railway, Norfolk, Virginia.* Roanoke, VA? Norfolk & Western Historical Society, 1995, 1957?. 1 v.

9209. _____. *Norfolk and Western Railway freight car diagrams.* Forest, VA: Norfolk and Western Historical Society, 1996, 1972. 30 l.

9210. *Norfolk and Western magazine.* Roanoke, Va., Norfolk and Western Railway Company, 1923-1982. 60 v. Monthly. Merged with: Ties (Washington, D.C.), to form: Norfolk Southern World.

9211. Norfolk and Western Railway Company. *Along the right of way. Route of the Pocohontas, the Powhatan Arrow.* Roanoke, Va., The Railway, 194-? 120 p.

9212. _____. *Are accidents really being reduced on the Norfolk & Western? This question, so frequently asked, finds its answer in this pamphlet, which presents a simple, graphic survey of what has been accomplished in the prevention of accident on the Norfolk & Western Railway since the inauguration of the safety movement.* Roanoke, VA: Norfolk and Western Railway Co., Office of Safety Commission, 1917. 6 p.

9213. _____. *A century of service; a presentation of the Norfolk and Western Railway.* S.l., s.n., 1938. 1 v.

9214. _____. *The Cincinnati Union Terminal : facts compiled by the Norfolk and Western Railway.* Cincinnati, OH: Cincinnati Museum Center, 2008, 1980s. 16 p.

9215. _____. *Coal.* Roanoke, Va., Norfolk and Western Railway, 1929. 24 p.

9216. _____. *Coal & coke.* Roanoke? Norfolk and Western Railway Company, Coal Traffic Department, 1963. 81 p.

9217. _____. *Coal and coke manual.* Roanoke, Va., Norfolk and Western Railway, 1965. 116 p.

9218. _____. *Coal and coke operations: coal car equipment.* Roanoke, Va., Norfolk and Western Railway, 1960. 74 p.

9219. _____. *Coal and the Norfolk and Western.* Roanoke, Va., Norfolk and Western Railway, 1927. 24 p.

9220. _____. *Coal car equipment/* S.l., Norfolk and Western Railway Compnay, 1937. 19 p.

9221. _____. *Coal car equipment: carrier of fuel satisfaction.* Forest Park, IL: Heimburger House, 1992. 20 p. (Originally published by the railway in1937.)

9222. _____. *The end of the line: the Pocahontas, the Wabash Cannon Ball.* S.l., Norfolk & Western, 197-? 12 p. ("Published …in connection with the last intercity passenger service to be operated by the N & W."

9223. _____. *Freight train classifications for yards and terminals.* Roanoke, VA., Superintendent, Transportation, 1947. a-e, 71 l.

9224. _____. *Industrial and shippers guide.* Roanoke, Va., Union Print and Manufacturing Company, 1916. 310 p. (Agricultural and Industrial Department)

9225. _____. *Industrial, shippers' and buyers' official guide/* New York? General Freight Department, 1905. 308 p.

9226. _____. *Instructions governing the use of automatic block and interlocking signals* / S.l., Norfolk and Western Railway Company, 1910. 55 p. (*Form S.E. 15.*)

9227. _____. *Instructions relating to the proper handling of air brakes and signals; also heating, lighting and ventilation of passenger equipment cars : for the use of trainmen and inspectors.* Roanoke, VA : Norfolk & Western Railway Co., Motive Power Department, 1912. 42 p. (*Form M.P. 229.*)

9228. _____. *Instructions relating to the proper heating, lighting and ventilating of passenger equipment cars : for the use of trainmen and inspectors.* Roanoke : Motive Power Department, 1924. 44 p. (*Form M.P. 229.*)

9229. _____. *List of coal and coke operations and briquetting plants on the Norfolk and Western Railway ... showing location, name of operator and post office address, mine numbers and names, billing districts selling agents and stations at which cars are weighed and waybilled.* Roanoke? 1900s- . Periodical.

9230. _____. *List of coal and coke operations on the Norfolk and Western Railway... /* Roanoke, VA: Norfolk and Western Railway Co., 1900s-? . Periodical.

9231. _____. *List of coal operations.* Roanoke, Va., Norfolk & Western Railway, 1972. 8 p.

9232. _____. *List of stations and sidings and other related information /* Roanoke, VA: Office Superintendent Car Service, 1966. A-1-59, 224, N1-58 p.

9233. _____. *List of stations and sidings showing station numbers and alphabetical index to stations and sidings /* Roanoke, VA: Office Superintendent Car Service, 1959. 113 p.

9234. _____. *Lynchburg's first railway.* S.l., s.n., 1936. 15 p.

9235. _____. *Modern coal-burning steam locomotives of the Norfolk and Western Railway Company.* Roanoke, VA: Norfolk & Western Railway Company, 1945. 10 p.

9236. _____. *Operating rules.* S.l., Norfolk and Western Railway Co., 1981. 110 p.

9237. _____. *Rates of pay and regulations for conductors, brakemen, baggagemen and yardmen : in effect Sept. 1, 1911 /* Roanoke, VA: Norfolk & Western Railway Co., 1911. 32 p.

9238. _____. *Rates of pay and regulations for conductors, brakemen, baggagemen and yardmen : in effect September 1, 1912.* Roanoke, VA: Norfolk and Western Railway Co., 1912. 34 p.

9239. _____. *Rates of pay and regulations for enginemen : in effect February 1st, 1906.* Roanoke, VA: Norfolk and Western Railway Co., 1906. 16 p.

9240. _____. *Rates of pay and regulations for firemen, in effect Sept. 1, 1911 /* Roanoke, VA: Norfolk & Western Railway Co., 1911. 27 p.

9241. _____. *Rates of pay and regulations for locomotive engineers : in effect February 1st, 1907.* Roanoke, VA: Norfolk and Western Railway Co., 1907. 16 p.

9241. _____. *Rates of pay and regulations for locomotive engineers : in effect February 1st, 1908.* Roanoke, VA: Norfolk and Western Railway Co., 1908. 17 p.

9242. _____. *Reference book of the Norfolk & Western Railroad Co.: outlining the present condition of progress in mining, manufacturers and agriculture and the undeveloped resources of those portions of the state of Virginia traversed by its lines.* Roanoke, VA: The Company, 1885. 94 p.

9243. _____. *Rules and regulations for the government of the Operating Department.* Roanoke, VA: Stone Printing & Manufacturing Company, 1917. 182 p.

9244. _____. *Rules and regulations for the government of the Operating Department.* S.l., The Company, 1930. 198 p.

9245. _____. *Rules of equipment operation and handling: for the government of train and engine service employees of the Operating Department.* Roanoke, VA: Norfolk and Western Railway Company, 1959. 27 p.

9246. _____. *Safety rules : for the government of employes in the Operating Department.* Roanoke, VA: Norfolk and Western Railway Company, 1940. 45 p.

9247. _____. *Statistical supplement to the Norfolk and Western annual report.* Roanoke, VA: Norfolk and Western Railway Company, 1900s- . Annual.

9248. _____. *The story of fuel satisfaction.* Roanoke, Va: Norfolk and Western Railway, 1933. 32 p. (Issued for: Century of Progress Exposition, Chicago, 1933.)

9249. _____. *To the men of the Norfolk & Western. Remember it is better to be careful than to be crippled.* Roanoke, VA: Norfolk & Western Railway Co., 1914. 4 p. (Office of the Safety Commission, Roanoke, Virginia, 1913.)

9250. *The Norfolk and Western Railway: a list of references.* Washington, D.C., Bureau of Railway Economics, Association of American Railroads, 1924. 52 l.

9251. *Norfolk & Western Railway standards drawings.* Edited by James F. Brewer and Thomas D. Dressler. Baltimore, MD: Norfolk & Western Historical Society, 1992. 110 l.

9252. *Norfolk & Western signal diagrams.* Lilburn, GA: Norfolk & Western Historical Society, 1999. 63 l.

9253. *Norfolk Southern locomotive directory.* Halifax, PA: Withers Publishing, 1998-

9254. Norfolk Southern Railroad Company. *Corporate history of the Norfolk Southern Railroad Company /* S.l., s.n., 1914. 47, 2 l.

9255. _____. *Rules and regulations governing employees of the Norfolk Southern R.R.*

Company. Norfolk, VA: Virginia Steam Print., 1889. 72 p.

9256. *Norfolk Southern world.* Washington, DC: Norfolk Southern Corporation, Public Relations and Advertising Department, 1982-   . Bimonthly. Formed by the union of: Norfolk and Western magazine, and: Ties.

9256a. Norman, Dave. *White River junctions: empires of flour, steel, and ambition /* Portland ME: F/64 Publications, 2012. 285 p.

9257. Norman, Roy A. *Collation of methods, formulae and data on practical locomotive design.* 1909. 74 l. (Thesis, M.E. Iowa State College.)

9258. Norris, Frank. *The octopus: a story of California.* New York, Doubleday, Page & Company, 1901. 652 p.

9259. Norris, Frank B. *Spatial diffusion of intermodal rail technologies.* 1994. 508 l. (Thesis, Ph.D., University of Washington.)

9260. Norris, George L. *Steel tires: cause of defects and failures.* Philadelphia, Pa., Standard Steel Works Co., 1907. 38 p.

9261. Norris, Henry Hutchinson. *Electric railways: a comprehensive treatise on modern electric railway equipment, including practical details of equipment, power house design, maintenance of way, and management.* Chicago, Ill., American School of Correspondence, 1913. 281 p.

9262. Norris, Septimus. *Norris's hand-book for locomotive engineers and machinists.* Philadelphia, Pa., H.C. Baird, 1852. 302 p.

9263. _____. *Septimus Norris' patent guide wheel truck for locomotives; patent dated April 24ᵗʰ, 1860.* Philadelphia, Pa., E. Ketterlinus, 1860. 8 p.

9264. _____, Grahame H. Hardy. *Norris's hand-book for locomotive engineers and machinists: comprising the proportions and calculations for constructing locomotives, manner of setting valves, tables of squares, cubes, areas, &c/* Philadelphia, Pa., Henry Carey Baird, Industrial Publisher, 1867. 302, 26 p.(Reprint: H.C. Baird, 1872. 302 p.; 1884, 302 p.)

9265. Norris, William, A. Mehaffey. *Locomotive steam engines of William Norris. Philadelphia, United States of America.* Philadelphia, s.n., 1838. 18, 2 p.

9266. _____. *William Norris of Philadelphia presents the following testimonials of the performances &c &c of his locomotives received since the publication of his circular of 1838/* Philadelphia, s.n., 1841. 22 p.

9267. *North American freight car market.* West Linn, OR: Rail Theory Forecasts, 2003- Quarterly.

9268. North Carolina. Department of Transportation. Office of the Assistant Secretary for Planning. *East-west rail passenger service in North Carolina: a preliminary analysis.* Raleigh, NC: Dept. of Transportation, Office of the Assistant Secretary for Planning, 1980. 19 l.

9269. _____. _____. Rail Division. *The railroads were our magic carpet: North Carolina tales about train travel.* Raleigh Rail Division, North Carolina Department of Transportation, 1995. 63 p.

9270. _____. _____. _____. *Southeast high-speed rail, Richmond, VA to Raleigh, NC: Tier III, draft environmental impact statement and draft section 4(F) evaluation: submitted pursuant to National Environmental Policy Act 42 U.S.C. 4332 (2) (C) /* Raleigh, NC: NCDOT, 2010. 3 v. (various foliations)

9271. _____. _____. _____. *Western North Carolina passenger rail study: summary report.* Raleigh, North Carolina Department of Transportation, Rail Division, 2001. 16 p.

9272. _____. Historic Sites Section. *Historic Spencer Shops.* Raleigh, North Carolina; Historic Sites Section, 1979. 34 p.

9273. *North Coast Hiawatha passenger rail study.* Washington, DC: Amtrak, 2009. 52 p. (Prepared for the United States Congress.)

9274. *North Dakota state rail plan.* Fargo, ND: Upper Great Plains Transportation Institute, North Dakota State University, 1978-1979. 2 v. (v. 1: Analysis of rail transportation; v. 2: Branch railroad line assessment.)

9275. North, Paul. *American steam locomotives.* Baltimore, MD: Bookman Pub., 1998. 192 p.

9275a. *The North Western.* Chicago : Chicago and North Western Railway Co., Monthly.

9276. *North Western Lines: official publication of the Chicago & North Western Historical Society.* Sheboygan, WI: The Society, 1974-   Quarterly.

9277. *The North Western newsliner.* Chicago: Chicago & North Western Railway, 1900s. Monthly.

9278. *North Western Railway magazine.* Chicago: Chicago and North Western Railway Co., 1923. Monthly 1 v. Vol. 1, no. 1 (Jan. 1923) - v. 1, no. 11 (Nov. 1923). (> *North Western Railway System magazine.*)

9279. *North Western Railway system magazine.* Chicago: Chicago and North Western Railway System, 1923-1925. Monthly. 3 v. (< *North Western Railway magazine.*)

9280. *The Northeast and Midwest rail crises: a bibliography of current literature.*, William R. Black and James F. Runke, compilers. Lexington, KY: Council of State

Governments, 1975. 43 p. (*RM 558.*)

9281. *Northeast Corridor Improvement project: electrification, New Haven CT to Boston, MA: final environmental impact report supplement.* Washington, DC: Federal Railroad Administration, Office of Railroad Development, 1995. 1 v. (various pagings) (*DOT-VNTSC-FRA-94-8.1.*)

9282. *Northeast Corridor Improvement Project: electrification, New Haven, CT to Boston, MA: final environmental impact statement/report: record of decision.* Washington, DC: Federal Railroad Administration, 1995. 40 p.

9283. *Northeast rail corridor: information on users, funding sources, and expenditures: report to Chairman, Subcommittee on Surface Transportation and Merchant Marine, Committee on Commerce, Science and Transportation, U.S. Senate/* Washington, DC: General Accounting Office, 1996. 45 p. (*GAO/RCED-96-144.*)

9284. *Northern Pacific railroad journal.* St. Paul: Northern Pacific Railroad Journal Co., 1883-1884. 1 v.

9284a. *The Northern Pacific Railroad's land grant and the future business of the road /* Philadelphia? Jay Cooke & Co., 1870. 1, 32 p.

9285. Northern Pacific Railway Company. *Cipher book.* Saint Paul, MN: Northern Pacific Railway Company, 1897. 230 p.

9286. _____. *Engineering rules and instructions, January 1, 1899. ... Construction and Engineering Departments.* St. Paul : Dispatch Job Printing Co., 1899. 127 p. (*Form 118- Revised.*)

9286a. _____. *Guide to the lands of the Northern Pacific Railroad in Minnesota.* New York: MacGowan and Slipper, printers, 1872. 32 p.

9286b. _____. [Mechanical Department. Records.] 274 cubic feet. Location: Minnesota Historical Society. Drawings and photographs, locomotives and rolling stock.

9287. _____. *The North Coast Limited.* St. Paul : Passenger Department, Northern Pacific Railway Company, 1906. 48 p.

9288. _____. *Northern Pacific Railroad.* S.l., Northern Pacific Railroad, 1884. 45 p.

9289. _____. *Northern Pacific Railway Company : some comparative statistics, years ending June 30, 1903 and June 30, 1913.* New York? Northern Pacific Railway Company, 1913. 8 p.

9290. _____. *The Northern Pacific railroad's land grant and the future business of the road.* Philadelphia? issued by Jay Cooke 7 Co, bankers, 1870. 28 p.

9291. _____. *The official directory and shippers' guide of the Northern Pacific Railway.*

St. Paul: Northern Pacific Railway Company, 1890s-1900s.

9291a. _____. *Official statement to the New York Stock Exchange, of the condition of the Northern Pacific Railroad Company, July 1ˢᵗ, 1879.* New York: Northern Pacific Railroad Co., 1879. 4 p.

9292. _____. *On the wings of the wind. Northern Pacific train service.* S.l., s.n., 1910. 32 p.

9293. _____. *Reports and statistics supplementary to the ... annual report of the Northern Pacific Railway Company.* St. Paul : The Company, 1890s-1900s. Annual.

9293a. _____. [Steam locomotive and locomotive tender records, 1897-1944]. 5 microfilm reels. Location: Minnesota Historical Society.

9294. _____. *The story of the monad; Northern Pacific railway standard trade-mark. Colors: red and black.* S.l., Northern Pacific Railway Co., 1933. 22 p.

9295. _____. *Train rules, automatic block signal rules, interlocking rules, general regulations.* St. Paul? Northern Pacific Railway, 1926. 129 p.

9295a. _____. *Transportation rules : Northern Pacific system of railroads : in effect Sept. 1, 1883.* St. Paul : Northern Pacific Railroad Company; Pioneer Press, 1883. 105, xi p.

9296. _____. *Who is responsible for the discontinuance of a passenger train?* St. Paul:

9296a. _____. Engineering Department. *Track and ballast* / St. Paul: Dispatch Job Printing Company, 1899. 21 p. (Form 140)

9296b. _____. Engineer's Office. *Engineering facts and reasons for locating the Northern Pacific Railroad upon the line selected west of the Rocky Mountains*/ S.l., s.n., 1877. 4 p.

9297. *Northern Pacific Railway Company papers: part I, 1864-1922: guide.* Frederick, MD: University Publications of America, 1985. 22 p.

9298. *Northern rails: a complete guide to the railroads of Maine, New Hampshire, Vermont.* Ron Johnson, editor. South Portland, ME: 470 Railroad Club, 1978. 32 p.

9299. Northwest Rail Improvement Committee. *The abandonment of electric operation by the Chicago, Milwaukee, St. Paul and Pacific Railroad Company: a report.* Everett, WA: The Committee, 1975. 1 v.

9300. North-west Railway Club. *Official proceedings of the North-West Railway Club.* St. Paul, North-West Railway Club, 1895-1906?. Monthly 14 v.

9301. Northwestern Pacific Railroad Company. *Northwestern Pacific headlight.* San

Francisco, Northwestern Pacific Railroad Co., 1920-1928. Monthly.. Other title:
Northwesterner, Apr.-May 1920. (*< Perfect safety.*)

9302. *The Northwesterner*. Larkspur, CA: Northwestern Pacific Railroad Historical
Society, 1987-   . Semiannual. Imprint varies.

9303. *The Northwestern railroader*. St. Paul, Northwestern Railroad Pub. Co., 1887-
1891. 9 v. Bimonthly. (Official publication of: Railway Station Agents' Association
of North America, Northwest Railroad Club, and Railway Employees' Club
of Minneapolis.) (> *Railway age* [Chicago]; *Railway age and northwestern railroader.*)

9304. Norton, Jerry D., Keith A. Klindworth. *Railcars for grain: future need
and availability*. Washington, DC: Office of Transportation, Department of Agriculture,
1989. 58 p.

9305. Norwood, John B. *John Norwood's American railroads*. Forest Park, IL:
Heimburger House, 1995. 192 p.

9306. _____. *Rio Grande narrow gauge*. River Forest, IL: Heimburger House, 1983.
312 p.

9307. _____. *Rio Grande memories*. Forest Park, IL: Heimburger House, 1991. 192 p.

9308. _____. *Rio Grande narrow gauge recollections*. River Forest, IL: Heimburger
House, 1986. 272 p.

9309. (Blank entry.)

9310. Norwood, Thomas M. *The Texas Pacific Railway: (a dependency of the great
Pennsylvania monopoly) contrasted with a real Southern Pacific R.R. along the 32d
parallel of latitude, having termini and connections in southern states: a letter
to the people of the South*. Washington, D.C.: s.n., 1878. 20 p.

9311. *Notes on the railroad terminals (both passenger and freight) in and near New York
City* / New York? s.n., 1905. 55 p. Prepared by a committee of railroad officers
for the guidance of delegates to the International Railway Congress in New York, May,
1905.

9312. Nowak, Ed., Karl R. Zimmermann. *Ed Nowak's New York Central*. Homewood,
IL: PTJ Pub., 1983. 151 p.

9313. *NRHS bulletin*. Philadelphia, PA: National Railway Historical Society, 2005-
Quarterly.

9314. Nuckles, Douglas B. *Baltimore & Ohio E-unit diesel passenger locomotives*.
Lynchburg, VA: TLC Pub., 1994. 78 p.

9315. _____. *Seaboard Coastline Railroad*. Lynchburg, VA: TLC Pub., 1995. 108 p.

9316. _____, Thomas W. Dixon. *Chesapeake & Ohio Greenbrier type 4-8-4 locomotives.* Clifton Forge, VA: Chesapeake & Ohio Historical Society, 1994. 62 p.

9317. _____, _____. *Diesel locomotives of CSXT & predecessors in color.* Lynchburg, VA: TLC Pub., 1993. 64 p.

CPSIA information can be obtained at www.ICGtesting.com
Printed in the USA
BVOW06s2350210415

397174BV00010B/98/P

9 781497 595187